History of Modern India
16th Century to Present

Compiled by
Bailee Skeen

Scribbles

Year of Publication 2018

ISBN : 9789352979196

Book Published by

Scribbles

(An Imprint of Alpha Editions)

email - alphaedis@gmail.com

Produced by: PediaPress GmbH
Limburg an der Lahn
Germany
http://pediapress.com/

The content within this book was generated collaboratively by volunteers. Please be advised that nothing found here has necessarily been reviewed by people with the expertise required to provide you with complete, accurate or reliable information. Some information in this book may be misleading or simply wrong. Alpha Editions and PediaPress does not guarantee the validity of the information found here. If you need specific advice (for example, medical, legal, financial, or risk management) please seek a professional who is licensed or knowledgeable in that area.

Sources, licenses and contributors of the articles and images are listed in the section entitled "References". Parts of the books may be licensed under the GNU Free Documentation License. A copy of this license is included in the section entitled "GNU Free Documentation License"

The views and characters expressed in the book are those of the contributors and his/her imagination and do not represent the views of the Publisher.

Contents

Articles 1

Early Modern 1
    Mughal Empire 1
    Sur Empire 29
    Bengal Subah 32
    Maratha Empire 54
    Company rule in India 90
    Kingdom of Mysore 140
    Sikh Empire 172

Modern Period 185
    Indian Rebellion of 1857 185
    British Raj 251
    Indian independence movement 326

Modern India 361
    History of the Republic of India 361

1947-50 395
    Dominion of India 395
    Constitution of India 401
    Political integration of India 416
    Indo-Pakistani War of 1947 446

1950s and 60s   471

    States Reorganisation Act, 1956 471

    India and the Non-Aligned Movement 478

    Indo-Pakistani War of 1965 482

    Sino-Indian War 510

1970s   545

    Bangladesh Liberation War 545

    Green Revolution in India 574

    Operation Flood 578

    Indo-Pakistani War of 1971 581

    The Emergency (India) 610

1980s   627

    Operation Blue Star 627

    Assassination of Indira Gandhi 648

    1984 anti-Sikh riots 653

    Bhopal disaster 671

    Indian intervention in the Sri Lankan Civil War 701

    Siachen conflict 706

1990s   721

    Assassination of Rajiv Gandhi 721

    Insurgency in Jammu and Kashmir 729

    Bombay riots 743

    Economic liberalisation in India 760

2000s   771

    2001 Indian Parliament attack 771

    2002 Gujarat riots 776

    2001–02 India–Pakistan standoff 798

    2008 Mumbai attacks 802

    Concerns and controversies over the 2010 Commonwealth Games . 826

    2G spectrum case 847

    2011 Indian anti-corruption movement 873

Appendix   887

    References 887

    Article Sources and Contributors 939

    Image Sources, Licenses and Contributors 944

Article Licenses   957

Index   959

Early Modern

Mughal Empire

<indicator name="pp-default"> 🔒 </indicator>

Mughal Empire	
(Persian) گورکانیان *Gūrkāniyān* مغلیہ سلطنت (Urdu) *Mugliyah Salṭanat*	
• 1526–1540 • 1555–1857	
The empire at its greatest extent, in the late 17th and early 18th centuries	
Capital	• Agra (1526–1540; 1555–1571; 1598–1648) • Fatehpur Sikri (1571–1585) • Lahore (May 1586–1598) • Shahjahanabad, Delhi (1648–1857)
Languages	• Persian (official and court language) • Arabic (for religious ceremonies) • Chagatai Turkic (only initially) • Urdu (Language of the elite, later made official) • Other South Asian languages
Religion	• Sunni Islam (1526–1857) • Din-i Ilahi (1582–1605)

Government	Absolute monarchy, unitary state with federal structure, centralized autarchy
Emperor[1]	
• 1526–1530	Babur (first)
• 1837–1857	Bahadur Shah II (last)
Historical era	Early modern
• First Battle of Panipat	21 April 1526
• Empire interrupted by Sur Empire	1540–1555
• Mughal–Maratha Wars	1681-1707
• Death of Aurangzeb	3 March 1707
• Siege of Delhi	21 September 1857
Area	
• 1690	4,000,000 km^2 (1,500,000 sq mi)
Population	
• 1700 est.	158,400,000
Currency	Rupee, dam

Preceded by	Succeeded by
Timurid Empire	Maratha Empire
Delhi Sultanate	Bengal Subah
Rajput states	Durrani Empire
Bengal Sultanate	Sikh Empire
Deccan sultanates	Company rule in India
	British Raj

The **Mughal Empire** (Persian: گورکانیان, translit. *Gūrkāniyān*; Urdu: مغلیہ سلطنت, translit. *Mughliyah Saltanat*) or **Mogul Empire** was an empire in the Indian subcontinent, founded in 1526. It was established and ruled by a Muslim dynasty with Turco-Mongol Chagatai roots from Central Asia, but with significant Indian Rajput and Persian ancestry through marriage alliances;[2] only the first two Mughal emperors were fully Central Asian, while successive emperors were of predominantly Rajput and Persian ancestry. The dynasty was Indo-Persian in culture, combining Persianate culture with local Indian cultural influences visible in its traits and customs.

The Mughal Empire at its peak extended over nearly all of the Indian subcontinent and parts of Afghanistan. It was the second largest empire to have existed in the Indian subcontinent, spanning approximately four million square kilometres at its zenith, after only the Maurya Empire, which spanned approximately five million square kilometres. The Mughal Empire ushered in a period of proto-industrialization, and around the 17th century, Mughal India became the world's largest economic power, accounting for 24.4% of world GDP,[3] and the world leader in manufacturing, producing 25% of global industrial output up until the 18th century. The Mughal Empire is considered "India's last golden age" and one of the three Islamic Gunpowder Empires (along with the Ottoman Empire and Safavid Persia).

The beginning of the empire is conventionally dated to the victory by its founder Babur over Ibrahim Lodi, the last ruler of the Delhi Sultanate, in the First Battle of Panipat (1526). The Mughal emperors had roots in the Turco-Mongol Timurid dynasty of Central Asia, claiming direct descent from both Genghis Khan (founder of the Mongol Empire, through his son Chagatai Khan) and Timur (Turco-Mongol conqueror who founded the Timurid Empire). During the reign of Humayun, the successor of Babur, the empire was briefly interrupted by the Sur Empire. The "classic period" of the Mughal Empire started in 1556 with the ascension of Akbar the Great to the throne. Under the rule of Akbar and his son Jahangir, the region enjoyed economic progress as well as religious harmony, and the monarchs were interested in local religious and cultural traditions. Akbar was a successful warrior who also forged alliances with several Hindu Rajput kingdoms. Some Rajput kingdoms continued to pose a significant threat to the Mughal dominance of northwestern India, but most of them were subdued by Akbar. All Mughal emperors were Muslims; Akbar, however, propounded a syncretic religion in the latter part of his life called Dīn-i Ilāhī, as recorded in historical books like *Ain-i-Akbari* and *Dabistān-i Mazāhib*.

The Mughal Empire did not try to intervene in the local societies during most of its existence, but rather balanced and pacified them through new administrative practices[4,5] and diverse and inclusive ruling elites,[6] leading to more systematic, centralised, and uniform rule.[7] Traditional and newly coherent social groups in northern and western India, such as the Marathas, the Rajputs, the Pashtuns, the Hindu Jats and the Sikhs, gained military and governing ambitions during Mughal rule, which, through collaboration or adversity, gave them both recognition and military experience.[8]

The reign of Shah Jahan, the fifth emperor, between 1628 and 1658, was the zenith of Mughal architecture. He erected several large monuments, the best known of which is the Taj Mahal at Agra, as well as the Moti Masjid, Agra, the Red Fort, the Badshahi Mosque, the Jama Masjid, Delhi, and the Lahore Fort. The Mughal Empire reached the zenith of its territorial expanse during the reign of Aurangzeb and also started its terminal decline in his reign due to Maratha military resurgence. During his lifetime, victories in the south expanded the Mughal Empire to its greatest extent, ruling over more than 150 million subjects, nearly one quarter of the world's population at the time, with a GDP of over $90 billion.Wikipedia:Please clarify

Internal dissatisfaction arose due to the weakness of the empire's administrative and economic systems, leading to its break-up and declarations of independence of its former provinces by the Nawab of Bengal, the Nawab of Awadh, the Nizam of Hyderabad and other small states. In 1739, the Mughals were crushingly defeated in the Battle of Karnal by the forces of Nader Shah, the founder of the Afsharid dynasty in Persia, and Delhi was sacked and looted, drastically accelerating their decline. By the mid-18th century, the Marathas had routed Mughal armies and won over several Mughal provinces from the Punjab to Bengal.. During the following century Mughal power had become severely limited, and the last emperor, Bahadur Shah II, had authority over only the city of Shahjahanabad. He issued a *firman* supporting the Indian Rebellion of 1857 and following the defeat was therefore tried by the British East India Company for treason, imprisoned and exiled to Rangoon. The last remnants of the empire were formally taken over by the British, and the Government of India Act 1858 let the British Crown formally assume direct control of India in the form of the new British Raj.

Name

Contemporaries referred to the empire founded by Babur as the Timurid empire, which reflected the heritage of his dynasty, and this was the term preferred by the Mughals themselves.

The Mughal designation for their own dynasty was **Gurkani** (Persian: گورکانیان, *Gūrkāniyān*, meaning "sons-in-law"). The use of Mughal derived from the Arabic and Persian corruption of Mongol, and it emphasised the Mongol origins of the Timurid dynasty. The term gained currency during the 19th century, but remains disputed by Indologists. Similar terms had been used to refer to the empire, including "Mogul" and "Moghul".[9] Nevertheless, Babur's ancestors were sharply distinguished from the classical Mongols insofar as they were oriented towards Persian rather than Turco-Mongol culture.

Another name for the empire was Hindustan, which was documented in the Ain-i-Akbari, and which has been described as the closest to an official name for the empire. In the west, the term "Mughal" was used for the emperor, and by extension, the empire as a whole.

Figure 1: *Babur, founder of the Mughal Empire*

History

Babur and Humayun (1526–1556)

The Mughal Empire was founded by Babur (reigned 1526–1530), a Central Asian ruler who was descended from the Turco-Mongol conqueror Timur (the founder of the Timurid Empire) on his father's side and from Chagatai, the second son of the Mongol ruler Genghis Khan, on his mother's side. Ousted from his ancestral domains in Central Asia, Babur turned to India to satisfy his ambitions. He established himself in Kabul and then pushed steadily southward into India from Afghanistan through the Khyber Pass. Babur's forces occupied much of northern India after his victory at Panipat in 1526. The preoccupation with wars and military campaigns, however, did not allow the new emperor to consolidate the gains he had made in India.

The instability of the empire became evident under his son, Humayun (reigned 1530–1556), who was driven out of India and into Persia by rebels. The Sur Empire (1540–1555), founded by Sher Shah Suri (reigned 1540–1545), briefly interrupted Mughal rule. Humayun's exile in Persia established diplomatic ties between the Safavid and Mughal Courts, and led to increasing Persian cultural influence in the Mughal Empire. The restoration of Mughal rule began after Humayun's triumphant return from Persia in 1555, but he died from a fatal accident shortly afterwards.

Akbar to Aurangzeb (1556–1707)

Akbar the Great (reigned 1556–1605) was born Jalal-ud-din Muhammad in the Rajput Umarkot Fort, to Humayun and his wife Hamida Banu Begum, a Persian princess. Akbar succeeded to the throne under a regent, Bairam Khan, who helped consolidate the Mughal Empire in India. Through warfare and diplomacy, Akbar was able to extend the empire in all directions and controlled almost the entire Indian subcontinent north of the Godavari River. He created a new class of nobility loyal to him from the military aristocracy of India's social groups, implemented a modern government, and supported cultural developments. At the same time, Akbar intensified trade with European trading companies. India developed a strong and stable economy, leading to commercial expansion and economic development. Akbar allowed free expression of religion, and attempted to resolve socio-political and cultural differences in his empire by establishing a new religion, Din-i-Ilahi, with strong characteristics of a ruler cult. He left his successors an internally stable state, which was in the midst of its golden age, but before long signs of political weakness would emerge.

Jahangir (born Salim, reigned 1605–1627) was born to Akbar and his wife Mariam-uz-Zamani, an Indian Rajput princess. Jahangir ruled the empire at its peak, but he was addicted to opium, neglected the affairs of the state, and came under the influence of rival court cliques. Shah Jahan (reigned 1628–1658) was born to Jahangir and his wife Jagat Gosaini, a Rajput princess. During the reign of Shah Jahan, the culture and splendour of the luxurious Mughal court reached its zenith as exemplified by the Taj Mahal. The maintenance of the court, at this time, began to cost more than the revenue.

Shah Jahan's eldest son, the liberal Dara Shikoh, became regent in 1658, as a result of his father's illness. However, a younger son, Aurangzeb (reigned 1658–1707), allied with the Islamic orthodoxy against his brother, who championed a syncretistic Hindu-Muslim culture, and ascended to the throne. Aurangzeb defeated Dara in 1659 and had him executed. Although Shah Jahan fully recovered from his illness, Aurangzeb declared him incompetent to rule and had him imprisoned. During Aurangzeb's reign, the empire gained political strength once more. Aurangzeb expanded the empire to include almost the whole of South Asia, but at his death in 1707, many parts of the empire were in open revolt. Aurangzeb is considered India's most controversial king, with some historians arguing his religious conservatism and intolerance undermined the stability of Mughal society, while other historians question this, noting that he built Hindu temples, employed significantly more Hindus in his imperial bureaucracy than his predecessors did, opposed bigotry against Hindus and Shia Muslims, and married Hindu Rajput princess Nawab Bai.

Figure 2: *Akbar holds a religious assembly of different faiths in the Ibadat Khana in Fatehpur Sikri.*

Decline (1707–1857)

Aurangzeb's son, Shah Alam, repealed the religious policies of his father, and attempted to reform the administration. However, after his death in 1712, the Mughal dynasty sank into chaos and violent feuds. In 1719 alone, four emperors successively ascended the throne.

During the reign of Muhammad Shah (reigned 1719–1748), the empire began to break up, and vast tracts of central India passed from Mughal to Maratha hands. The far-off Indian campaign of Nadir Shah, who had priorly reestablished Iranian suzerainty over most of West Asia, the Caucasus, and Central Asia, culminated with the Sack of Delhi and shattered the remnants of Mughal power and prestige. Many of the empire's elites now sought to control their own affairs, and broke away to form independent kingdoms. But, according to Sugata Bose and Ayesha Jalal, the Mughal Emperor continued to be the highest manifestation of sovereignty. Not only the Muslim gentry, but the Maratha, Hindu, and Sikh leaders took part in ceremonial acknowledgements of the emperor as the sovereign of India.

The Mughal Emperor Shah Alam II (1759–1806) made futile attempts to reverse the Mughal decline but ultimately had to seek the protection of the Emir of Afghanistan, Ahmed Shah Abdali, which led to the Third Battle of Panipat between the Maratha Empire and the Afghans led by Abdali in 1761. In 1771, the Marathas recaptured Delhi from Afghan control and in 1784 they officially became the protectors of the emperor in Delhi,[10] a state of affairs that continued further until after the Third Anglo-Maratha War. Thereafter, the British East India Company became the protectors of the Mughal dynasty in Delhi. The British East India Company took control of the former Mughal province of Bengal-Bihar in 1793 after it abolished local rule (Nizamat) that lasted until 1858, marking the beginning of British colonial era over the Indian Subcontinent. By 1857 a considerable part of former Mughal India was under the East India Company's control. After a crushing defeat in the war of 1857–1858 which he nominally led, the last Mughal, Bahadur Shah Zafar, was deposed by the British East India Company and exiled in 1858. Through the Government of India Act 1858 the British Crown assumed direct control of East India Company-held territories in India in the form of the new British Raj. In 1876 the British Queen Victoria assumed the title of Empress of India.

Causes of decline

Historians have offered numerous explanations for the rapid collapse of the Mughal Empire between 1707 and 1720, after a century of growth and prosperity. In fiscal terms the throne lost the revenues needed to pay its chief officers, the emirs (nobles) and their entourages. The emperor lost authority, as the widely scattered imperial officers lost confidence in the central authorities, and made their own deals with local men of influence. The imperial army, bogged down in long, futile wars against the more aggressive Marathas lost its fighting spirit. Finally came a series of violent political feuds over control of the throne. After the execution of emperor Farrukhsiyar in 1719, local Mughal successor states took power in region after region.

Contemporary chroniclers bewailed the decay they witnessed, a theme picked up by the first British historians who wanted to underscore the need for a British-led rejuvenation.

Modern views on the decline

Since the 1970s historians have taken multiple approaches to the decline, with little consensus on which factor was dominant. The psychological interpretations emphasise depravity in high places, excessive luxury, and increasingly narrow views that left the rulers unprepared for an external challenge. A Marxist school (led by Irfan Habib and based at Aligarh Muslim University) emphasises excessive exploitation of the peasantry by the rich, which stripped away the will and the means to support the regime. Karen Leonard has focused on the failure of the regime to work with Hindu bankers, whose financial support was increasingly needed; the bankers then helped the Maratha and the British. In a religious interpretation, some scholars argue that the Hindu powers revolted against the rule of a Muslim dynasty.[11] Finally, other scholars argue that the very prosperity of the Empire inspired the provinces to achieve a high degree of independence, thus weakening the imperial court.

Jeffrey G. Williamson has argued that the Indian economy went through deindustrialization in the latter half of the 18th century as an indirect outcome of the collapse of the Mughal Empire, with British rule later causing further deindustrialization. According to Williamson, the decline of the Mughal Empire led to a decline in agricultural productivity, which drove up food prices, then nominal wages, and then textile prices, which led to India losing a share of the world textile market to Britain even before it had superior factory technology. Indian textiles, however, still maintained a competitive advantage over British textiles up until the 19th century.

Administrative divisions

Subah (Urdu: صوبہ) was the term for a province in the Mughal Empire. The word is derived from Arabic. The governor of a *Subah* was known as a *subahdar* (sometimes also referred to as a *"Subah"*[12]), which later became *subedar* to refer to an officer in the Indian Army. The *subahs* were established by padshah (emperor) Akbar during his administrative reforms of 1572–1580; initially they numbered 12, but his conquests expanded the number of *subahs* to 15 by the end of his reign. *Subahs* were divided into *Sarkars*, or districts. *Sarkars* were further divided into *Parganas* or *Mahals*. His successors, most notably Aurangzeb, expanded the number of *subahs* further through their conquests. As the empire began to dissolve in the early 18th century, many *subahs* became effectively independent, or were conquered by the Marathas or the British.

The original twelve subahs created as a result of administrative reform by Akbar:

- Agra Subah
- Ajmer subah
- Awadh Subah
- Bengal Subah
- Bihar Subah
- Delhi Subah
- Gujarat Subah
- Kabul Subah
- Illahabad Subah
- Lahore Subah

Figure 3: *A silver rupee coin made during the reign of the Mughal Emperor Alamgir II.*

- Malwa Subah
- Multan Subah

Economy

The Indian economy was large and prosperous under the Mughal Empire.[13] During the Mughal era, the gross domestic product (GDP) of India in 1600 was estimated at about 22.4% of the world economy, the second largest in the world, behind only Ming China but larger than Europe. By 1700, the GDP of Mughal India had risen to 24.4% of the world economy, the largest in the world, larger than both Qing China and Western Europe.[14] Mughal India was the world leader in manufacturing, producing about 25% of the world's industrial output up until the 18th century.[15] India's GDP growth increased under the Mughal Empire, with India's GDP having a faster growth rate during the Mughal era than in the 1,500 years prior to the Mughal era. Mughal India's economy has been described as a form of proto-industrialization, like that of 18th-century Western Europe prior to the Industrial Revolution.

The Mughals were responsible for building an extensive road system, creating a uniform currency, and the unification of the country.[16] The empire had an extensive road network, which was vital to the economic infrastructure, built by a public works department set up by the Mughals which designed, constructed and maintained roads linking towns and cities across the empire, making trade easier to conduct.

Coinage

The Mughals adopted and standardized the rupee (*rupiya*, or silver) and dam (copper) currencies introduced by Sur Emperor Sher Shah Suri during his brief rule.[17] The currency was initially 48 dams to a single rupee in the beginning of Akbar's reign, before it later became 38 dams to a rupee in the 1580s, with the dam's value rising further in the 17th century as a result of new industrial uses for copper, such as in bronze cannons and brass utensils. The dam was initially the most common coin in Akbar's time, before being replaced by the rupee as the most common coin in succeeding reigns. The dam's value was later worth 30 to a rupee towards the end of Jahangir's reign, and then 16 to a rupee by the 1660s. The Mughals minted coins with high purity, never dropping below 96%, and without debasement until the 1720s.[18]

Despite India having its own stocks of gold and silver, the Mughals produced minimal gold of their own, but mostly minted coins from imported bullion, as a result of the empire's strong export-driven economy, with global demand for Indian agricultural and industrial products drawing a steady stream of precious metals into India. Around 80% of Mughal India's imports were bullion, mostly silver,[19] with major sources of imported bullion including the New World and Japan, which in turn imported large quantities of textiles and silk from the Bengal Subah province.

Labour

The Mughal Empire's workforce in the early 17th century consisted of about 64% in the primary sector (including agriculture) and 36% in the secondary and tertiary sectors, including over 11% in the secondary sector (manufacturing) and about 25% in the tertiary sector (service).[20] Mughal India's workforce had a higher percentage in the non-primary sector than Europe's workforce did at the time; agriculture accounted for 65–90% of Europe's workforce in 1700, and 65–75% in 1750, including 65% of England's workforce in 1750. In terms of contributions to the Mughal economy, in the late 16th century, the primary sector contributed 52.4%, the secondary sector 18.2% and the tertiary sector 29.4%; the secondary sector contributed a higher percentage than in early 20th-century British India, where the secondary sector only contributed 11.2% to the economy. In terms of urban-rural divide, 18% of Mughal India's labour force were urban and 82% were rural, contributing 52% and 48% to the economy, respectively.

Real wages and living standards in 18th-century Mughal Bengal and South India were higher than in Britain, which in turn had the highest living standards in Europe. According to economic historian Paul Bairoch, India as well as

China had a higher GNP per capita than Europe up until the late 18th century,[21] before Western European per-capita income pulled ahead after 1800. Mughal India also had a higher per-capita income in the late 16th century than British India did in the early 20th century. However, in a system where wealth was hoarded by elites, wages were depressed for manual labour, though no less than labour wages in Europe at the time. In Mughal India, there was a generally tolerant attitude towards manual labourers, with some religious cults in northern India proudly asserting a high status for manual labour. While slavery also existed, it was limited largely to household servants.[22]

Agriculture

Indian agricultural production increased under the Mughal Empire. A variety of crops were grown, including food crops such as wheat, rice, and barley, and non-food cash crops such as cotton, indigo and opium. By the mid-17th century, Indian cultivators begun to extensively grow two new crops from the Americas, maize and tobacco.

The Mughal administration emphasized agrarian reform, which began under the non-Mughal emperor Sher Shah Suri, the work of which Akbar adopted and furthered with more reforms. The civil administration was organized in a hierarchical manner on the basis of merit, with promotions based on performance.[23] The Mughal government funded the building of irrigation systems across the empire, which produced much higher crop yields and increased the net revenue base, leading to increased agricultural production.

A major Mughal reform introduced by Akbar was a new land revenue system called *zabt*. He replaced the tribute system, previously common in India and used by Tokugawa Japan at the time, with a monetary tax system based on a uniform currency.[24] The revenue system was biased in favour of higher value cash crops such as cotton, indigo, sugar cane, tree-crops, and opium, providing state incentives to grow cash crops, in addition to rising market demand. Under the *zabt* system, the Mughals also conducted extensive cadastral surveying to assess the area of land under plow cultivation, with the Mughal state encouraging greater land cultivation by offering tax-free periods to those who brought new land under cultivation.[25]

Mughal agriculture was advanced compared to Europe at the time, such as the common use of the seed drill among Indian peasants before its adoption in European agriculture. While the average peasant across the world was only skilled in growing very few crops, the average Indian peasant was skilled in growing a wide variety of food and non-food crops, increasing their productivity. Indian peasants were also quick to adapt to profitable new crops, such as maize and tobacco from the New World being rapidly adopted and widely cultivated across Mughal India between 1600 and 1650. Bengali peasants rapidly learned techniques of mulberry cultivation and sericulture, establishing Bengal Subah as a major silk-producing region of the world. Sugar mills appeared in India shortly before the Mughal era. Evidence for the use of a draw bar for sugar-milling appears at Delhi in 1540, but may also date back earlier, and was mainly used in the northern Indian subcontinent. Geared sugar rolling mills first appeared in Mughal India, using the principle of rollers as well as worm gearing, by the 17th century.[26]

According to evidence cited by the economic historians Immanuel Wallerstein, Irfan Habib, Percival Spear, and Ashok Desai, per-capita agricultural output and standards of consumption in 17th-century Mughal India were higher than in 17th-century Europe and early 20th-century British India. The increased agricultural productivity led to lower food prices. In turn, this benefited the Indian textile industry. Compared to Britain, the price of grain was about one-half in South India and one-third in Bengal, in terms of silver coinage. This resulted in lower silver coin prices for Indian textiles, giving them a price advantage in global markets.

Industrial manufacturing

Up until the 18th century, Mughal India was the most important center of manufacturing in international trade. Up until 1750, India produced about 25% of the world's industrial output. Manufactured goods and cash crops from the Mughal Empire were sold throughout the world. Key industries included textiles, shipbuilding, and steel. Processed products included cotton textiles, yarns, thread, silk, jute products, metalware, and foods such as sugar, oils and butter. The growth of manufacturing industries in the Indian subcontinent during the Mughal era in the 17th–18th centuries has been referred to as a form of proto-industrialization, similar to 18th-century Western Europe prior to the Industrial Revolution.

In early modern Europe, there was significant demand for products from Mughal India, particularly cotton textiles, as well as goods such as spices, peppers, indigo, silks, and saltpeter (for use in munitions). European fashion, for example, became increasingly dependent on Mughal Indian textiles and silks. From the late 17th century to the early 18th century, Mughal India accounted for 95% of British imports from Asia, and the Bengal Subah province alone accounted for 40% of Dutch imports from Asia.[27] In contrast, there was very little demand for European goods in Mughal India, which was largely self-sufficient, thus Europeans had very little to offer, except for some woolens, unprocessed metals and a few luxury items. The trade imbalance caused Europeans to export large quantities of gold and silver to Mughal India in order to pay for South Asian imports. Indian goods, especially those from Bengal, were also exported in large quantities to other Asian markets, such as Indonesia and Japan.

Figure 4: *A woman in Dhaka clad in fine Bengali muslin, 18th century.*

Textile industry

The largest manufacturing industry in the Mughal Empire was textile manufacturing, particularly cotton textile manufacturing, which included the production of piece goods, calicos, and muslins, available unbleached and in a variety of colours. The cotton textile industry was responsible for a large part of the empire's international trade. India had a 25% share of the global textile trade in the early 18th century.[28] Indian cotton textiles were the most important manufactured goods in world trade in the 18th century, consumed across the world from the Americas to Japan. By the early 18th century, Mughal Indian textiles were clothing people across the Indian subcontinent, Southeast Asia, Europe, the Americas, Africa, and the Middle East. The most important center of cotton production was the Bengal province, particularly around its capital city of Dhaka.[29]

Bengal accounted for more than 50% of textiles and around 80% of silks imported by the Dutch from Asia, Bengali silk and cotton textiles were exported in large quantities to Europe, Indonesia, and Japan,[30] and Bengali muslin textiles from Dhaka were sold in Central Asia, where they were known as "daka" textiles. Indian textiles dominated the Indian Ocean trade for centuries, were sold in the Atlantic Ocean trade, and had a 38% share of the West African trade in the early 18th century, while Indian calicos were a major force in Europe, and Indian textiles accounted for 20% of total English trade with Southern Europe in the early 18th century.

The worm gear roller cotton gin, which was invented in India during the early Delhi Sultanate era of the 13th–14th centuries, came into use in the Mughal Empire some time around the 16th century, and is still used in India through to the present day. Another innovation, the incorporation of the crank handle in the cotton gin, first appeared in India some time during the late Delhi Sultanate or the early Mughal Empire.[31] The production of cotton, which may have largely been spun in the villages and then taken to towns in the form of yarn to be woven into cloth textiles, was advanced by the diffusion of the spinning wheel across India shortly before the Mughal era, lowering the costs of yarn and helping to increase demand for cotton. The diffusion of the spinning wheel, and the incorporation of the worm gear and crank handle into the roller cotton gin, led to greatly expanded Indian cotton textile production during the Mughal era.[32]

It was reported that, with an Indian cotton gin, which is half machine and half tool, one man and one woman could clean 28 pounds of cotton per day. With a modified Forbes version, one man and a boy could produce 250 pounds per day. If oxen were used to power 16 of these machines, and a few people's labour was used to feed them, they could produce as much work as 750 people did formerly.[33]

Shipbuilding industry

Mughal India had a large shipbuilding industry, which was also largely centered in the Bengal province. In terms of shipbuilding tonnage during the 16th–18th centuries, the annual output of Bengal alone totaled around 2,232,500 tons, larger than the combined output of the Dutch (450,000–550,000 tons), the British (340,000 tons), and North America (23,061 tons).[34]

The Mughals maintained a small fleet for carrying pilgrims to Mecca, and imported Arabian horses in Surat. Debal in Sindh was mostly autonomous. The Mughals also maintained various river fleets of Dhows, which transported soldiers over rivers and fought rebels. Among its admirals were Yahya Saleh, Munnawar Khan, and Muhammad Saleh Kamboh. The Mughals also protected the Siddis of Janjira. Its sailors were renowned and often voyaged to China and the East African Swahili Coast, together with some Mughal subjects carrying out private-sector trade.

Indian shipbuilding, particularly in Bengal, was advanced compared to European shipbuilding at the time, with Indians selling ships to European firms. Ship-repairing, for example, was very advanced in Bengal, where European shippers visited to repair vessels. An important innovation in shipbuilding

Figure 5: *Ruins of the Great Caravanserai in Dhaka.*

was the introduction of a flushed deck design in Bengal rice ships, resulting in hulls that were stronger and less prone to leak than the structurally weak hulls of traditional European ships built with a stepped deck design. The British East India Company later duplicated the flushed deck and hull designs of Bengal rice ships in the 1760s, leading to significant improvements in seaworthiness and navigation for European ships during the Industrial Revolution.

Bengal Subah

The Bengal Subah province was especially prosperous from the time of its takeover by the Mughals in 1590 until the British East India Company seized control in 1757.[35] It was the Mughal Empire's wealthiest province, and the economic powerhouse of the Mughal Empire, generating 50% of the empire's GDP. Domestically, much of India depended on Bengali products such as rice, silks and cotton textiles. Overseas, Europeans depended on Bengali products such as cotton textiles, silks and opium; Bengal accounted for 40% of Dutch imports from Asia, for example, including more than 50% of textiles and around 80% of silks. From Bengal, saltpeter was also shipped to Europe, opium was sold in Indonesia, raw silk was exported to Japan and the Netherlands, and cotton and silk textiles were exported to Europe, Indonesia and Japan.

Bengal was described as the *Paradise of Nations* by Mughal emperors. The Mughals introduced agrarian reforms, including the modern Bengali calendar. The calendar played a vital role in developing and organising harvests, tax collection and Bengali culture in general, including the New Year and Autumn festivals. The province was a leading producer of grains, salt, pearls, fruits, liquors and wines, precious metals and ornaments. Its handloom industry flourished under royal warrants, making the region a hub of the worldwide muslin trade, which peaked in the 17th and 18th centuries. The provincial capital Dhaka became the commercial capital of the empire. The Mughals expanded cultivated land in the Bengal delta under the leadership of Sufis, which consolidated the foundation of Bengali Muslim society.[36]

After 150 years of rule by Mughal viceroys, Bengal gained semi-independence as a dominion under the Nawab of Bengal in 1717. The Nawabs permitted European companies to set up trading posts across the region, including firms from Britain, France, the Netherlands, Denmark, Portugal and Austria-Hungary. An Armenian community dominated banking and shipping in major cities and towns. The Europeans regarded Bengal as the richest place for trade. By the late 18th century, the British displaced the Mughal ruling class in Bengal.

Demographics

Population

India's population growth accelerated under the Mughal Empire, with an unprecedented economic and demographic upsurge which boosted the Indian population by 60% to 253% in 200 years during 1500–1700.[37] The Indian population had a faster growth during the Mughal era than at any known point in Indian history prior to the Mughal era. The increased population growth rate was stimulated by Mughal agrarian reforms that intensified agricultural production.[38] By the time of Aurangzeb's reign, there were a total of 455,698 villages in the Mughal Empire.

The following table gives population estimates for the Mughal Empire, compared to the total population of India, including the regions of modern Pakistan and Bangladesh, and compared to the world population:

Year	Mughal Empire population	Total Indian population	% of Indian population	World population	% of world population
1500	—	100,000,000	—	425,000,000	—
1600	115,000,000	130,000,000	89	579,000,000[39]	20
1700	158,400,000	160,000,000	99	679,000,000	23

Urbanization

Cities and towns boomed under the Mughal Empire, which had a relatively high degree of urbanization for its time, with 15% of its population living in urban centres.[40] This was higher than the percentage of the urban population in contemporary Europe at the time and higher than that of British India in the 19th century; the level of urbanization in Europe did not reach 15% until the 19th century.

Under Akbar's reign in 1600, the Mughal Empire's urban population was up to 17 million people, 15% of the empire's total population. This was larger the entire urban population in Europe at the time, and even a century later in 1700, the urban population of England, Scotland and Wales did not exceed 13% of its total population, while British India had an urban population that was under 13% of its total population in 1800 and 9.3% in 1881, a decline from the earlier Mughal era. By 1700, Mughal India had an urban population of 23 million people, larger than British India's urban population of 22.3 million in 1871.

The historian Nizamuddin Ahmad (1551–1621) reported that, under Akbar's reign, there were 120 large cities and 3200 townships. A number of cities in India had a population between a quarter-million and half-million people, with larger cities including Agra (in Agra Subah) with up to 800,000 people, Lahore (in Lahore Subah) with up to 700,000 people, Dhaka (in Bengal Subah) with over 1 million people,[41] and Delhi (in Delhi Subah) with over 600,000 people.[42]

Cities acted as markets for the sale of goods, and provided homes for a variety of merchants, traders, shopkeepers, artisans, moneylenders, weavers, craftspeople, officials, and religious figures. However, a number of cities were military and political centres, rather than manufacturing or commerce centres.[43]

Figure 6: *Built by Mughal emperor Shah Jahan for his beloved wife, the Taj Mahal is a world-renowned testament to Mughal architecture.*

Culture

Mughal influence can be seen in cultural contributions such as:

- Centralized, imperialistic government that brought together many smaller kingdoms
- Persian art and culture amalgamated with Indian art and culture
- Revival of old trade routes to Arab and Turkic lands
- The development of Mughlai cuisine
- The development of Urdu, and by extension Hindustani.
- Landscape and Mughal gardening
- Mughal Architecture evolved with the influence of Indian architecture, and in turn influenced the local architecture, most conspicuously in the palaces built by Rajputs and Sikh rulers.

The Mughals built Maktab schools in every province under their authority, where youth were taught the Quran and Islamic law such as the Fatawa-i-Alamgiri in their indigenous languages.

Art and architecture

The Mughals made a major contribution to the Indian subcontinent with development of their unique architecture. Many monuments were built during the

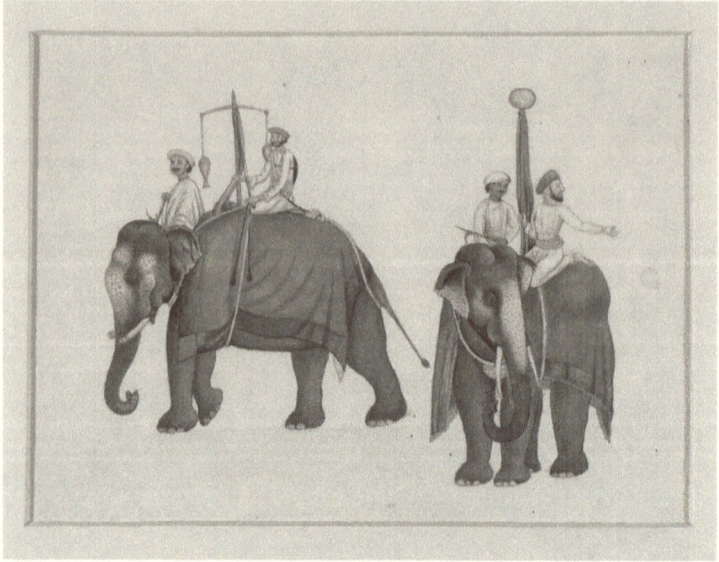

Figure 7: *Two elephants carrying the fish and sun insignia of Mughal sovereignty*

Mughal era by the Muslim emperors, especially Shah Jahan, including the Taj Mahal, a UNESCO World Heritage Site known to be one of the finer examples of Mughal architecture. Other World Heritage Sites include Humayun's Tomb, Fatehpur Sikri, the Red Fort, the Agra Fort, and the Lahore Fort.

The palaces, tombs, and forts built by the dynasty stand today in Agra, Aurangabad, Delhi, Dhaka, Fatehpur Sikri, Jaipur, Lahore, Kabul, Sheikhupura, and many other cities of India, Pakistan, Afghanistan, and Bangladesh. With few memories of Central Asia, Babur's descendants absorbed traits and customs of South Asia and became more or less naturalized.

Although the land the Mughals once ruled has separated into what is now India, Pakistan, Bangladesh, and Afghanistan, their influence can still be seen widely today. Tombs of the emperors are spread throughout India, Afghanistan, and Pakistan.

The Mughal artistic tradition was eclectic, borrowing from the European Renaissance as well as from Persian and Indian sources. Kumar concludes, "The Mughal painters borrowed individual motifs and certain naturalistic effects from Renaissance and Mannerist painting, but their structuring principle was derived from Indian and Persian traditions."[44]

Figure 8: *The phrase Zuban-i Urdū-yi Mu'allá ("Language of the exalted Urdu") written in Nasta'līq script.*

Language

Although Persian was the dominant and "official" language of the empire, the language of the elite was a Persianised form of Hindustani called Urdu. The language was written in a type of Perso-Arabic script known as Nastaliq, and with literary conventions and specialised vocabulary borrowed from Persian, Arabic and Turkic; the dialect was eventually given its own name of Urdu. Modern Hindi, which uses Sanskrit-based vocabulary along with Perso-Arabic loan words is mutually intelligible with Urdu.

Military

Gunpowder warfare

Mughal India was one of the three Islamic Gunpowder Empires, along with the Ottoman Empire and Safavid Persia. By the time he was invited by Lodi governor of Lahore, Daulat Khan, to support his rebellion against Lodi Sultan Ibrahim Khan, Babur was familiar with gunpowder firearms and field artillery, and a method for deploying them. Babur had employed Ottoman expert Ustad Ali Quli, who showed Babur the standard Ottoman formation—artillery and firearm-equipped infantry protected by wagons in the center and the mounted archers on both wings. Babur used this formation at the First Battle of Panipat in 1526, where the Afghan and Rajput forces loyal to the Delhi Sultanate,

Figure 9: *Mughal matchlock rifle, 16th century.*

Figure 10: *Mughal musketeer, 16th century.*

though superior in numbers but without the gunpowder weapons, were defeated. The decisive victory of the Timurid forces is one reason opponents rarely met Mughal princes in pitched battle over the course of the empire's history. In India, guns made of bronze were recovered from Calicut (1504) and Diu (1533).

Fathullah Shirazi (c. 1582), a Persian polymath and mechanical engineer who worked for Akbar, developed an early multi gun shot. As opposed to the polybolos and repeating crossbows used earlier in ancient Greece and China, respectively, Shirazi's rapid-firing gun had multiple gun barrels that fired hand cannons loaded with gunpowder. It may be considered a version of a volley gun.

By the 17th century, Indians were manufacturing a diverse variety of firearms; large guns in particular, became visible in Tanjore, Dacca, Bijapur and Murshidabad. Gujarāt supplied Europe saltpeter for use in gunpowder warfare during the 17th century,[45] and Mughal Bengal and Mālwa also participated in saltpeter production. The Dutch, French, Portuguese and English used Chāpra as a center of saltpeter refining.[46]

Rocketry and explosives

In the 16th century, Akbar was the first to initiate and use metal cylinder rockets known as *bans*, particularly against war elephants, during the Battle of Sanbal. In 1657, the Mughal Army used rockets during the Siege of Bidar. Prince Aurangzeb's forces discharged rockets and grenades while scaling the walls. Sidi Marjan was mortally wounded when a rocket struck his large gunpowder depot, and after twenty-seven days of hard fighting Bidar was captured by the victorious Mughals.

In *A History of Greek Fire and Gunpowder*, James Riddick Partington described Indian rockets and explosive mines:

> The Indian war rockets were formidable weapons before such rockets were used in Europe. They had bam-boo rods, a rocket-body lashed to the rod, and iron points. They were directed at the target and fired by lighting the fuse, but the trajectory was rather erratic. The use of mines and countermines with explosive charges of gunpowder is mentioned for the times of Akbar and Jahāngir.

Later, the Mysorean rockets were upgraded versions of Mughal rockets used during the Siege of Jinji by the progeny of the Nawab of Arcot. Hyder Ali's father Fatah Muhammad the constable at Budikote, commanded a corps consisting of 50 rocketmen (*Cushoon*) for the Nawab of Arcot. Hyder Ali realised the importance of rockets and introduced advanced versions of metal cylinder rockets. These rockets turned fortunes in favour of the Sultanate of

Mysore during the Second Anglo-Mysore War, particularly during the Battle of Pollilur. In turn, the Mysorean rockets were the basis for the Congreve rockets, which Britain deployed in the Napoleonic Wars against France and the War of 1812 against the United States.

Science

Astronomy

While there appears to have been little concern for theoretical astronomy, Mughal astronomers made advances in observational astronomy and produced nearly a hundred *Zij* treatises. Humayun built a personal observatory near Delhi; Jahangir and Shah Jahan were also intending to build observatories, but were unable to do so. The astronomical instruments and observational techniques used at the Mughal observatories were mainly derived from Islamic astronomy. In the 17th century, the Mughal Empire saw a synthesis between Islamic and Hindu astronomy, where Islamic observational instruments were combined with Hindu computational techniques.

During the decline of the Mughal Empire, the Hindu king Jai Singh II of Amber continued the work of Mughal astronomy. In the early 18th century, he built several large observatories called Yantra Mandirs, in order to rival Ulugh Beg's Samarkand observatory, and in order to improve on the earlier Hindu computations in the *Siddhantas* and Islamic observations in *Zij-i-Sultani*. The instruments he used were influenced by Islamic astronomy, while the computational techniques were derived from Hindu astronomy.

Chemistry

Sake Dean Mahomed had learned much of Mughal chemistry and understood the techniques used to produce various alkali and soaps to produce shampoo. He was also a notable writer who described the Mughal Emperor Shah Alam II and the cities of Allahabad and Delhi in rich detail and also made note of the glories of the Mughal Empire.

In Britain, Sake Dean Mahomed was appointed as shampooing surgeon to both Kings George IV and William IV.

Metallurgy

One of the most remarkable astronomical instruments invented in Mughal India is the seamless celestial globe. It was invented in Kashmir by Ali Kashmiri ibn Luqman in 998 AH (1589–90 CE), and twenty other such globes were later produced in Lahore and Kashmir during the Mughal Empire. Before they were rediscovered in the 1980s, it was believed by modern metallurgists to be technically impossible to produce metal globes without any seams.[47]

Further reading

<templatestyles src="Template:Refbegin/styles.css" />

- Alam, Muzaffar. *Crisis of Empire in Mughal North India: Awadh & the Punjab, 1707–48* (1988)
- Ali, M. Athar (1975), "The Passing of Empire: The Mughal Case", *Modern Asian Studies*, Cambridge University Press, **9** (3): 385–396, doi:10.1017/s0026749x00005825[48], JSTOR 311728[49], on the causes of its collapse
- Asher, C. B.; Talbot, C (1 January 2008), *India Before Europe* (1st ed.), Cambridge University Press, ISBN 978-0-521-51750-8
- Black, Jeremy. "The Mughals Strike Twice", *History Today* (April 2012) 62#4 pp 22–26. full text online
- Blake, Stephen P. (November 1979), "The Patrimonial-Bureaucratic Empire of the Mughals", *Journal of Asian Studies*, Association for Asian Studies, **39** (1): 77–94, JSTOR 2053505[50]
- Dale, Stephen F. *The Muslim Empires of the Ottomans, Safavids and Mughals* (Cambridge U.P. 2009)
- Dalrymple, William (2007). *The Last Mughal: The Fall of a Dynasty : Delhi, 1857*[51]. Random House Digital, Inc.
- Faruqui, Munis D. (2005), "The Forgotten Prince: Mirza Hakim and the Formation of the Mughal Empire in India", *Journal of the Economic and Social History of the Orient*, Brill, **48** (4): 487–523, doi:10.1163/1568520057749188133[52], JSTOR 25165118[53], on Akbar and his brother
- Gommans; Jos. *Mughal Warfare: Indian Frontiers and Highroads to Empire, 1500–1700* (Routledge, 2002) online edition[54]
- Gordon, S. *The New Cambridge History of India, II, 4: The Marathas 1600–1818* (Cambridge, 1993).
- Habib, Irfan. *Atlas of the Mughal Empire: Political and Economic Maps* (1982).
- Markovits, Claude, ed. (2004) [First published 1994 as *Histoire de l'Inde Moderne*]. *A History of Modern India, 1480–1950*[55] (2nd ed.). London: Anthem Press. ISBN 978-1-84331-004-4.
- Metcalf, B.; Metcalf, T. R. (9 October 2006), *A Concise History of Modern India*[56] (2nd ed.), Cambridge University Press, ISBN 978-0-521-68225-1
- Richards, John F. (1996). *The Mughal Empire*[57]. Cambridge University Press.
- Majumdar, Ramesh Chandra (1974). *The Mughul Empire*[58]. B.V. Bhavan.

- Richards, John F. *The Mughal Empire* (The New Cambridge History of India) (1996) excerpt and online search[59]
- Richards, J. F. (April 1981), "Mughal State Finance and the Pre-modern World Economy", *Comparative Studies in Society and History*, Cambridge University Press, **23** (2): 285–308, doi: 10.1017/s0010417500013311[60], JSTOR 178737[61]
- Robb, P. (2001), *A History of India*, London: Palgrave, ISBN 978-0-333-69129-8
- Srivastava, Ashirbadi Lal. *The Mughul Empire, 1526-1803* (1952) online.
- Stein, B. (16 June 1998), *A History of India*[62] (1st ed.), Oxford: Wiley-Blackwell, ISBN 978-0-631-20546-3
- Stein, B. (27 April 2010), Arnold, D., ed., *A History of India*[63] (2nd ed.), Oxford: Wiley-Blackwell, ISBN 978-1-4051-9509-6

Culture

- Berinstain, V. *Mughal India: Splendour of the Peacock Throne* (London, 1998).
- Busch, Allison. *Poetry of Kings: The Classical Hindi Literature of Mughal India* (2011) excerpt and text search[64]
- Diana Preston; Michael Preston (2007). *Taj Mahal: Passion and Genius at the Heart of the Moghul Empire*. Walker & Company. ISBN 0-8027-1673-3.
- Schimmel, Annemarie. *The Empire of the Great Mughals: History, Art and Culture* (Reaktion 2006)
- Welch, S.C.; et al. (1987). *The Emperors' album: images of Mughal India*[65]. New York: The Metropolitan Museum of Art. ISBN 0-87099-499-9.

Society and economy

- Chaudhuri, K. N. (1978), "Some Reflections on the Town and Country in Mughal India", *Modern Asian Studies*, Cambridge University Press, **12** (1): 77–96, doi: 10.1017/s0026749x00008155[66], JSTOR 311823[67]
- Habib, Irfan. *Atlas of the Mughal Empire: Political and Economic Maps* (1982).
- Habib, Irfan. *Agrarian System of Mughal India* (1963, revised edition 1999).
- Heesterman, J. C. (2004), "The Social Dynamics of the Mughal Empire: A Brief Introduction", *Journal of the Economic and Social History of the Orient*, Brill, **47** (3): 292–297, doi: 10.1163/1568520041974729[68], JSTOR 25165051[69]

- Khan, Iqtidar Alam (1976), "The Middle Classes in the Mughal Empire", *Social Scientist*, **5** (1): 28–49, JSTOR 3516601[70]
- Rothermund, Dietmar. *An Economic History of India: From Pre-Colonial Times to 1991* (1993)

Primary sources

- Bernier, Francois (1891). *Travels in the Mogul Empire, A.D. 1656–1668*[71]. Archibald Constable, London.
- Hiro, Dilip, ed, *Journal of Emperor Babur* (Penguin Classics 2007)
  - *The Baburnama: Memoirs of Babur, Prince and Emperor* ed. by W.M. Thackston Jr. (2002); this was the first autobiography in Islamic literature
- Jackson, A.V. et al., eds. *History of India* (1907) v.9. Historic accounts of India by foreign travellers, classic, oriental, and occidental, by A.V.W. Jackson online edition[72]
- Jouher (1832). *The Tezkereh al vakiat or Private Memoirs of the Moghul Emperor Humayun Written in the Persian language by Jouher A confidential domestic of His Majesty*[73]. Translated by Major Charles Stewart. John Murray, London.

Older histories

- Elliot, Sir H. M., Edited by Dowson, John. *The History of India, as Told by Its Own Historians. The Muhammadan Period*; published by London Trubner Company 1867–1877. (Online Copy at Packard Humanities Institute – Other Persian Texts in Translation; historical books: Author List and Title List)
- Adams, W. H. Davenport (1893). *Warriors of the Crescent*[74]. London: Hutchinson.
- Holden, Edward Singleton (1895). *The Mogul emperors of Hindustan, A.D. 1398- A.D. 1707*[75]. New York : C. Scribner's Sons.
- Malleson, G. B (1896). *Akbar and the rise of the Mughal empire*[76]. Oxford : Clarendon Press.
- Manucci, Niccolao; tr. from French by François Catrou (1826). *History of the Mogul dynasty in India, 1399–1657*[77]. London : J.M. Richardson.
- Lane-Poole, Stanley (1906). *History of India: From Reign of Akbar the Great to the Fall of Moghul Empire (Vol. 4)*[78]. London, Grolier society.
- Manucci, Niccolao; tr. by William Irvine (1907). *Storia do Mogor; or, Mogul India 1653–1708, Vol. 1*[79]. London, J. Murray.
- Manucci, Niccolao; tr. by William Irvine (1907). *Storia do Mogor; or, Mogul India 1653–1708, Vol. 2*[80]. London, J. Murray.

- Manucci, Niccolao; tr. by William Irvine (1907). *Storia do Mogor; or, Mogul India 1653–1708, Vol. 3*[81]. London, J. Murray.
- Owen, Sidney J (1912). *The Fall of the Mogul Empire*[82]. London, J. Murray.

External links

- Mughals and Swat[83]
- Mughal India[84] an interactive experience from the British Museum
- The Mughal Empire[85] from BBC
- Mughal Empire[86]
- The Great Mughals[87]
- Gardens of the Mughal Empire[88]
- *Indo-Iranian Socio-Cultural Relations at Past, Present and Future*, by M. Reza Pourjafar, Ali A. Taghvaee, in *Web Journal on Cultural Patrimony* (Fabio Maniscalco ed.)[89], vol. 1, January–June 2006
- Adrian Fletcher's Paradoxplace — PHOTOS — Great Mughal Emperors of India[90]
- A Mughal diamond on BBC[91]
- Some Mughal coins with brief history[92]
- The Mughal Empire[93], BBC Radio 4 discussion with Sanjay Subrahmanyam, Susan Stronge & Chandrika Kaul (*In Our Time*, Feb. 26, 2004)

Sur Empire

Sur Empire	
1532–1556	
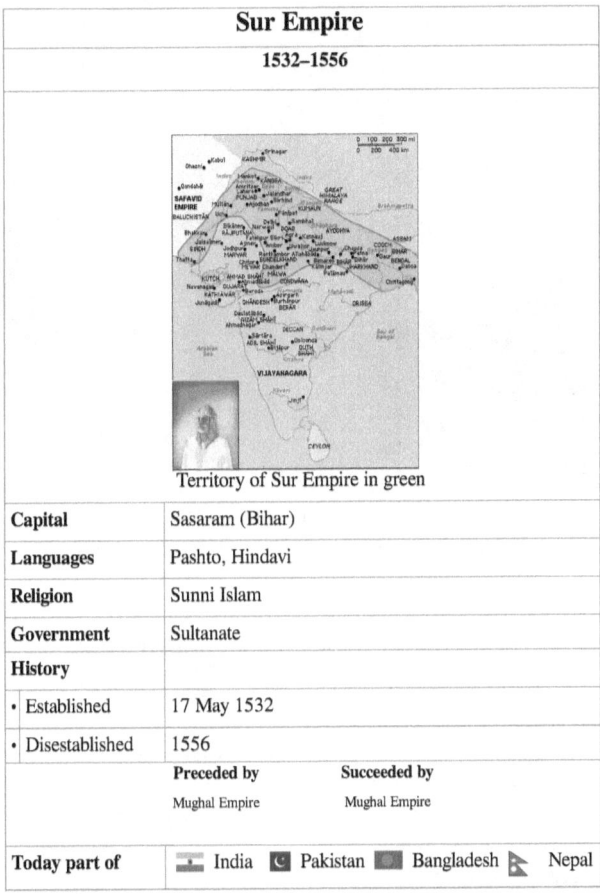 Territory of Sur Empire in green	
Capital	Sasaram (Bihar)
Languages	Pashto, Hindavi
Religion	Sunni Islam
Government	Sultanate
History	
• Established	17 May 1532
• Disestablished	1556
Preceded by	**Succeeded by**
Mughal Empire	Mughal Empire
Today part of	India Pakistan Bangladesh Nepal

The **Sur Empire** was an empire established by a Muslim dynasty of Pashtun origin who ruled a large territory in northern part of the Indian subcontinent for nearly 16 years, between 1540 and 1556, with Delhi serving as its capital.

History

The empire was founded by Sher Shah Suri, an ethnic Afghan of the tribal house of Sur, who supplanted the Mughal dynasty as rulers of North India during the reign of the relatively ineffectual second Mughal Humayun. Sher Shah defeated *badshah-i-Hind* ('Hindustani emperor') Humayun in the Battle of Chausa (26 June 1539) and again in the *Battle of Bilgram* (17 May 1540).

Figure 11: *The Rohtas Fort in northern Pakistan was built under Sher Shah Suri, and is now a UNESCO World Heritage Site.*

The Sur dynasty held control of nearly all the Mughal territories, from modern-day eastern Afghanistan in the west to Bengal in modern-day Bangladesh in the east.

During the almost 17-year rule of the Sur dynasty, until the return of the Mughals to the throne, the region of the South Asia witnessed much economic development and administrative reforms. A systematised relationship was created between the people and the ruler, minimising corruption and the oppression of the public.Wikipedia:Citation needed

Their rule came to an end by a defeat that led to restoration of the Mughal Empire.

> *It was at the time of this bounty of Sultán Bahlol [Lodi], that the grandfather of Sher Sháh, by name Ibráhím Khán Súr,* *[The Súr represent themselves as descendants of Muhammad Súr, one of the princes of the house of the Ghorian, who left his native country, and married a daughter of one of the Afghán chiefs of Roh.] with his son Hasan Khán, the father of Sher Sháh, came to Hindu-stán from Afghánistán, from a place which is called in the Afghán tongue "Shargarí," * but in the Multán tongue "Rohrí." It is a ridge, a spur of the Sulaimán Mountains, about six or seven kos in length, situated on the banks of the Gumal. They entered into the service of Muhabbat Khán Súr, Dáúd*

Sur Empire

Figure 12: *The 178 grams silver coin, Rupiya released by Sher Shah Suri, 1540–1545 CE, was the first Rupee*[94]

Sáhú-khail, to whom Sultán Bahlol had given in jágír the parganas of Hariána and Bahkála, etc., in the Panjáb, and they settled in the pargana of Bajwára.

—Abbas Khan Sarwani, 1580

List of Sur dynasty rulers

Name	Picture	Reign started	Reign ended
Sher Shah Suri		17 May 1532[95]	22 May 1545
Islam Shah Suri		26 May 1545[96]	22 November 1554
Firuz Shah Suri		1554[97]	
Muhammad Adil Shah		1554	1555[98]
Ibrahim Shah Suri		1555	1555
Sikandar Shah Suri		1555	22 June 1555
Adil Shah Suri		22 June 1555	1556

References

 Wikimedia Commons has media related to *Suri Empire*.

Bengal Subah

Subah of Bengal	
صوبه بنگال (Persian) বাংলার সুবাহ (Bengali)	
Subdivision of the Mughal Empire	
1576–1757	
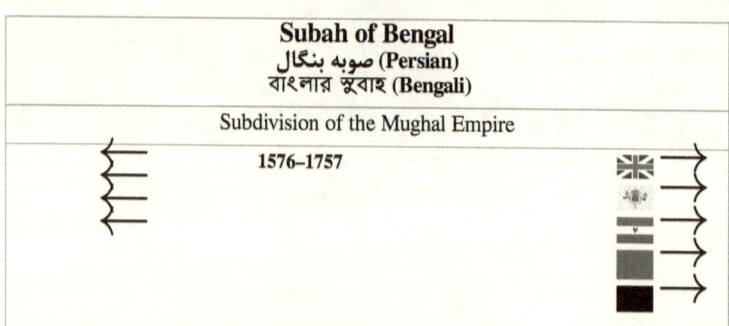 A German map from 1740 showing North India and Central Asia, including Mughal Bengal on the eastern flank	
Capital	<ul><li>Dhaka (1608–39 and 1660–1704)</li><li>Murshidabad (1704-1757)</li><li>Rajmahal (1595-96 and 1639-1660)</li><li>Tandah</li></ul>
Government	Viceregal
Historical era	Early modern period
• Battle of Raj Mahal	1576
• Nawabs of Bengal	1717
• Battle of Plassey	1757

Today part of	• Bangladesh
	• India

The **Bengal Subah** was a subdivision of the Mughal Empire encompassing modern Bangladesh and the Indian state of West Bengal between the 16th and 18th centuries. The state was established following the dissolution of the Bengal Sultanate, when the region was absorbed into one of the largest empires in the world. The Mughals played an important role in developing modern Bengali culture and society.

Bengal was the Mughal Empire's wealthiest province. It generated 50% of the empire's GDP and 12% of the world's GDP, globally dominant in industries such as textile manufacturing and shipbuilding, with the capital Dhaka having a population exceeding a million people. It was an exporter of silk and cotton textiles, steel, saltpeter, and agricultural and industrial produce. By the 18th century, Mughal Bengal emerged as a quasi-independent state, under the Nawabs of Bengal, before being conquered by the British East India Company at the Battle of Plassey in 1757, which directly contributed to the Industrial Revolution in Britain (such as textile manufacture during the Industrial Revolution), but led to deindustrialization and famine in Bengal.

History

Mughal Empire

The Mughal absorption of Bengal began during the reign of the first Mughal emperor Babur. In 1529, Babur defeated Sultan Nasiruddin Nasrat Shah of the Bengal Sultanate during the Battle of Ghaghra. Babur later annexed parts of Bengal. His son and successor Humayun occupied the Bengali capital Gaur, where he stayed for six months. Humayun was later forced to seek in refuge in Persia because of Sher Shah Suri's conquests. Sher Shah Suri briefly interrupted the reigns of the both the Mughals and Bengal Sultans.

After the defeat of expansionist Bengal Sultan Daud Khan Karrani at Rajmahal in 1576, Mughal padshah (emperor) Akbar the Great announced the creation of Bengal as one of the original twelve Subahs (top-level provinces), bordering Bihar and Orissa subahs, as well as Burma.

Bengal's physical features gave it such a fertile soil, and a favourable climate that it became a terminus of a continent-wide process of Turko-Mongol conquest and migration, informs Prof. Richard Eaton. The Mughal conquest of Bengal began with the decisive victory of Akbar's army over the independent Afghan ruler of the province Daud Karrani, at Tukaroi (near Danton, Midnapore district) on March 3, 1575. It took many years to overcome the resistance

Figure 13: *The Mughal absorption of Bengal progressed during the reigns of the first two emperors Babur and Humayun*

Figure 14: *Akbar developed the modern Bengali calendar*

Figure 15: *Dhaka, the capital of Bengal, was named Jahangir Nagar in honor of the fourth Mughal monarch Jahangir*

of ambitious and local chiefs. By a royal decree of November 24, 1586 Akbar introduced uniform subah administration throughout the empire. However, in Tapan Raychaudhuri's view the consolidation of Mughal power in Bengal and the pacification of the province really began in 1594.

Most prominent local chiefs or landlords being the 'Bara Bhuiyas' or Baro-Bhuyans (twelve bhuiyas). Many of the chiefs subjugated by the Mughals, some of the Bara Bhuiyas in particular, were Hindu or Pathan upstarts who grabbed territories during the transition from Afghan to Mughal rule, but a few such as the Rajas of Bishnupur, Susang, and Chandradwip; were older Hindu princes who had ruled independently from time immemorial. By the 17th century, the Mughals subdued opposition from the Baro-Bhuyans landlords, notably Isa Khan. Bengal was integrated into a powerful and prosperous empire; and shaped by imperial policies of pluralistic government. The Mughals built a new imperial metropolis in Dhaka from 1610, with well-developed fortifications, gardens, tombs, palaces and mosques. It served as the Mughal capital of Bengal for 75 years. The city was renamed in honour of Emperor Jahangir. Dhaka emerged as the commercial capital of the Mughal Empire, given that it was the centre for the empire's largest exports: cotton muslin textiles.

The Mughal conquest of Chittagong in 1666 defeated the (Burmese) Kingdom of Arakan and reestablished Bengali control of the port city, which was renamed as Islamabad. The Chittagong Hill Tracts frontier region was made a tributary state of Mughal Bengal and a treaty was signed with the Chakma Circle in 1713.[99]

Between 1576 and 1717, Bengal was ruled by a Mughal Subedar (imperial governor). Members of the imperial family were often appointed to the position. Viceroy Prince Shah Shuja was the son of Emperor Shah Jahan. During the struggle for succession with his brothers Prince Aurangazeb, Prince Dara Shikoh and Prince Murad Baksh, Prince Shuja proclaimed himself as the Mughal Emperor in Bengal. He was eventually defeated by the armies of Aurangazeb. Shuja fled to the Kingdom of Arakan, where he and his family were killed on the orders of the King at Mrauk U. Shaista Khan was an influential viceroy during the reign of Aurangazeb. He consolidated Mughal control of eastern Bengal. Prince Muhammad Azam Shah, who served as one of Bengal's viceroys, was installed on the Mughal throne for four months in 1707. Viceroy Ibrahim Khan II gave permits to English and French traders for commercial activities in Bengal. The last viceroy Prince Azim-us-Shan gave permits for the establishment of the British East India Company's Fort William in Calcutta, the French East India Company's Fort Orleans in Chandernagore and the Dutch East India Company's fort in Chinsura. During Azim-us-Shan's tenure, his prime minister Murshid Quli Khan emerged as a powerful figure in Bengal. Khan gained control of imperial finances. Azim-us-Shan was transferred to Bihar. In 1717, the Mughal Court upgraded the prime minister's position to the hereditary Nawab of Bengal. Khan founded a new capital in Murshidabad. His descendants formed the Nasiri dynasty. Alivardi Khan founded a new dynasty in 1740. The Nawabs ruled over a territory which included Bengal proper, Bihar and Orissa.

Nawabs of Bengal

The authority of the Mughal Court rapidly disintegrated in the 18th century, following the rise of the Maratha Empire in India and foreign invasions by Nader Shah of Persia and Ahmad Shah Abdali of Afghanistan. In Bengal, the system saw most wealth hoarded by the elites, with low wages for manual labour.

The Nawabs of Bengal entered into treaties with numerous European colonial powers, including joint-stock companies representing Britain, Austria, Denmark, France and the Netherlands.

Bengal Subah

Figure 16: *A sculpture of the Nawab's royal peacock barge, Los Angeles County Museum*

Maratha invasions

The resurgent Hindu Maratha Empire launched brutal raids against the prosperous Bengali state in the 18th century, which further added to the decline of the Nawabs of Bengal. A decade of ruthless Maratha invasions of Bengal from the 1740s to early 1750s forced the Nawab of Bengal to pay Rs. 1.2 million of tribute annually as the *Chauth* of Bengal and Bihar to the Marathas, and the Marathas agreed not to invade Bengal again.[100] The expeditions, led by Raghuji Bhonsle of Nagpur, also established the *De facto* Maratha control over Orissa, which was formally incorporated in the Maratha Dominion in 1752. The Nawab of Bengal also paid Rs. 3.2 million to the Marathas, towards the arrears of chauth for the preceding years. The chauth was paid annually by the Nawab of Bengal to the Marathas upto 1758, till the British occupation of Bengal.

During their occupation of Bihar and western Bengal up to the Hooghly River, the Maratha invaders, called "Bargi" in Bengali, perpetrated atrocities against the local population. The Marathas are estimated to have killed about 400,000 people. This devastated Bengal's economy, as many of the people killed in the Maratha raids included merchants, textile weavers, silk winders, and mulberry cultivators. The Cossimbazar factory reported in 1742, for example, that the Marathas burnt down many of the houses where silk piece goods were made, along with weavers' looms.

Figure 17: *British soldiers firing at Bengali forces underneath a mango orchard in Plassey (Palashi), 1757*

British colonization

By the late-18th century, the British East India Company emerged as the foremost military power in the region, defeating the French-allied Siraj-ud-Daulah at the Battle of Plassey in 1757, that was largely brought about by the betrayal of the Nawab's once trusted general Mir Jafar. The company gained administrative control over the Nawab's dominions, including Bengal, Bihar and Orissa. It gained the right to collect taxes on behalf of the Mughal Court after the Battle of Buxar in 1765. Bengal, Bihar and Orissa were made part of the Bengal Presidency and annexed into the British colonial empire in 1793. The Indian mutiny of 1857 formally ended the authority of the Mughal court, when the British Raj replaced Company rule in India.

Other European powers also carved out small colonies on the territory of Mughal Bengal, including the Dutch East India Company's Dutch Bengal settlements, the French colonial settlement in Chandernagore, the Danish colonial settlement in Serampore and the Habsburg Monarchy Ostend Company settlement in Bankipur.

Military campaigns

According to João de Barros, Bengal enjoyed military supremacy over Arakan and Tripura due to good artillery. Its forces possessed notable large cannons. It was also a major exporter of gunpowder and saltpeter to Europe.[101] The

Mughal Army built fortifications across the region, including Idrakpur Fort, Sonakanda Fort, Hajiganj Fort, Lalbagh Fort and Jangalbari Fort. The Mughals expelled Arakanese and Portuguese pirates from the northeastern coastline of the Bay of Bengal. Throughout the late medieval and early modern periods, Bengal was notable for its navy and shipbuilding. The following table covers a list of notable military engagements by Mughal Bengal:-

Conflict	Year(s)	Leader(s)	Enemy	Rival Leader(s)	Result
Battle of Tukaroi	1575	Akbar	Bengal Sultanate	Daud Khan Karrani	Mughal victory
Battle of Raj Mahal	1576	Khan Jahan I	Bengal Sultanate	Daud Khan Karrani	Mughal victory
Conquest of Bhati	1576–1611	• Khan Jahan I • Shahbaz Khan Kamboh • Man Singh	Baro-Bhuyan	• Isa Khan • Musa Khan	Mughal victory
Ahom-Mughal conflicts	1615–1682	• Qasim Khan Chishti • Mir Jumla • Ram Singh I	Ahom kingdom	Ahom kings	Assamese victory
Mughal-Arakan War	1665–66	Shaista Khan	Kingdom of Mrauk U	Thiri Thudhamma	Mughal victory
Battle of Plassey	1757	Siraj-ud-Daulah	British Empire	Robert Clive	British victory

Architecture

Mughal architecture proliferated Bengal in the 16th, 17th and 18th centuries, with the earliest example being the Kherua Mosque in Bogra (1582). They replaced the earlier sultanate-style of architecture. It was in Dhaka that the imperial style was most lavishly indulged in. Located on the banks of the Buriganga River, the old Mughal city was described as the Venice of the East. Its Lalbagh Fort was an elaborately designed complex of gardens, fountains, a mosque, a tomb, an audience hall (Diwan-i-Khas) and a walled enclosure with gates. The Great Caravanserai and Shaista Khan Caravanserai in Dhaka were centres of commercial activities. Other monuments in the city include the Dhanmondi Shahi Eidgah (1640), the Sat Gambuj Mosque (c. 1664–76), the Shahbaz Khan Mosque (1679) and the Khan Mohammad Mridha Mosque (1704). The city of Murshidabad also became a haven of Mughal architecture under the Nawabs of Bengal, with the Caravanserai Mosque (1723) being its most prominent monument.

In rural hinterlands, the indigenous Bengali Islamic style continued to flourish, blended with Mughal elements. One of the finest examples of this style is

Figure 18: *Bengali curved roofs were copied by Mughal architects in other parts of the empire, such as in the Naulakha Pavilion in Lahore*

Figure 19: *View of the hammam and audience hall in Lalbagh Fort*

Figure 20: *Nimtoli Deuri, named after the neem tree, is now a property of the Asiatic Society of Bangladesh*

the Atiya Mosque in Tangail (1609). Several masterpieces of terracotta Hindu temple architecture were also created during this period. Notable examples include the Kantajew Temple (1704) and the temples of Bishnupur (1600–1729).

Art

An authentic Bengali-Mughal art was reflected in the muslin fabric of Jamdani (meaning "flower" in Persian). The making of Jamdani was pioneered by Persian weavers. The art passed to the hands of Bengali Muslim weavers known as *juhulas*. The artisan industry was historically based around the city of Dhaka. The city had over 80,000 weavers. Jamdanis traditionally employ geometric designs in floral shapes. Its motifs are often similar to those in Iranian textile art (buta motif) and Western textile art (paisley). Dhaka's jamdanis enjoyed a loyal following and received imperial patronage from the Mughal court in Delhi and the Nawabs of Bengal.

A provincial Bengali style of Mughal painting flourished in Murshidabad during the 18th century. Scroll painting and ivory sculptures were also prevalent.

Figure 21: *A riverside mosque in Mughal Dhaka*

Demographics

Population

Bengal's population is estimated to be 30 million in 1769, after the British East India Company's conquest of Bengal at the Battle of Plassey in 1757 and prior to the resulting Great Bengal famine of 1770.[102] In comparison, the entire Indian population is estimated to be 190 million in 1750[103] (with Bengal accounting for 16% of its population), the Asian population is estimated at 502 million in 1750[104] (with Bengal accounting for 6% of its population), and the world population is estimated at 791 million in 1750 (with Bengal accounting for 3.8% of its population).

Prior to British rule, Bengal's capital city of Dhaka had a population exceeding a million people.

Religion

Bengal was an affluent province with a Bengali Muslim majority, along with a large Bengali Hindu minority.

Figure 22: *The Armenian church and cemetery in Dhaka*

Immigration

There was a significant influx of migrants from the Safavid Empire into Bengal during the Mughal period. Persian administrators and military commanders were enlisted by the Mughal government in Bengal. An Armenian community settled in Dhaka and was involved in the city's textile trade, paying a 3.5% tax.

Economy and trade

The Bengal Subah had the largest regional economy in the Mughal Empire. It was described as the *paradise of nations*. 50% of the gross domestic product (GDP) of the empire was generated in Bengal. The region exported grains, fine cotton muslin and silk, liquors and wines, salt, ornaments, fruits, metals and pearls. European companies set up numerous trading posts in Mughal Bengal during the 17th and 18th centuries. Dhaka was the largest city in Mughal Bengal and the commercial capital of the empire. Chittagong was the largest seaport, with maritime trade routes connecting the port city to Arakan, Ayuthya, Balasore, Aceh, Melaka, Johore, Bantam, Makassar, Ceylon, Bandar Abbas, Mecca, Jeddah, Basra, Aden, Masqat, Mocha and the Maldives.

Real wages and living standards in 18th-century Bengal were higher than in Britain, which in turn had the highest living standards in Europe.

Figure 23: *A Dutch trading post in Mughal Bengal, 1665*

Local Sufi leaders combined Islamic and Bengali cultural practices which developed Bengali Muslim society.

Agrarian reform

The Mughals launched a vast economic development project in the Bengal delta which transformed its demographic makeup. The government cleared vast swathes of forest in the fertile Bhati region to expand farmland. It encouraged settlers, including farmers and jagirdars, to populate the delta. It assigned Sufis as the chieftains of villages. Emperor Akbar re-adapted the modern Bengali calendar to improve harvests and tax collection. The region became the largest grain producer in the subcontinent.

Being so fertile and climatically favourable for agriculture, Bengal became one of the most important khalisa or crown lands and the most desired *jagirs*, as it was one of the highest revenue yielding subahs. For instance, in the year 1595-6 it is said to have yielded 25,69,94,043 dams in revenue.

We find meagre accounts of the Bengal revenue administration in Abul Fazl's *Ain-i-Akbari* and some in Mirza Nathan's *Baharistan-i-Ghaybi*. According to the *Ain*,

> 'The demands of each year are paid by installments in eight months, they (the ryots) themselves bringing mohurs and rupees to the appointed place for the receipt of revenue, as the division of grain between the government and the husbandman is not here customary. The harvests are always

Figure 24: *A 3D reconstruction of the Bara Katra in modern-day Dhaka*

abundant, measurement is not insisted upon, and the revenue demands are determined by estimate of the crop."

From the above extract we learn that the payment of the annual revenue demand was carried out in eight monthly instalments. However, Raychaudhuri points out that according to the *Baharistan*, there were two collections a year following the two harvests in autumn and spring. Secondly, it tells us that the payments were made in cash, and directly to the government. The last fact obviously refers to only *khalisa* lands. Finally, the most important fact that we come across is that the method of crop-estimation and not land measurement was current in Bengal. However, the other point that poses itself as pointed out by Sir Irfan Habib is that, since, in Bengal the authorities levied revenue not upon the peasants but upon the zamindars, it does not become immediately clear where in this passage Abul Fazl is speaking of the payment of revenue by the peasants to the zamindars and where of the payment by the zamindars to the state. The initial statements, as they contain an explicit reference to the peasants would seem to be referring to them only. It seems that the resort to measurement took place in Bengal largely when the old jama fixed on the zamindars was thought to be completely obsolete. A mid- eighteenth century manual *Risala-i-Zira'at* describes this as a recognised practice in Bengal. This may really be the meaning of Abul Fazl's rather vague statement that measurement was not objected to. It is possible that since such measurements were so rarely employed, and then with the use of local standards, no regular area statistics could be compiled on its basis. Abul Fazl's statement that the revenue demand was based on *nasaq* must then refer to the demand on the zamindars being retained at the same set of figures for long periods of years.

Bengali peasants were quick to adapt to profitable new crops between 1600 and 1650. Bengali peasants rapidly learned techniques of mulberry cultivation and sericulture, establishing Bengal Subah as a major silk-producing region of the world.[105]

The increased agricultural productivity led to lower food prices. In turn, this benefited the Indian textile industry. Compared to Britain, the price of grain was about one-half in South India and one-third in Bengal, in terms of silver coinage. This resulted in lower silver coin prices for Indian textiles, giving them a price advantage in global markets.

Industrial economy

The Mughal Empire had 25% of the world's GDP. Under the Mughals, Bengal Subah generated 50% of the empire's GDP, and thus had 12% of the world's GDP. Bengal was an affluent province that was globally dominant in industries such as textile manufacturing and shipbuilding.[106,107,108] Bengal's capital city of Dhaka was the empire's financial capital, with a population exceeding a million people, and with an estimated 80,000 skilled textile weavers. It was an exporter of silk and cotton textiles, steel, saltpeter, and agricultural and industrial produce. Bengal's industrial economy in the Mughal era has been described as a form of proto-industrialization.[109]

The plunder of Bengal directly contributed to the Industrial Revolution in Britain,[110] with the capital amassed from Bengal used to invest in British industries such as textile manufacture during the Industrial Revolution and greatly increase British wealth, while at the same time leading to deindustrialization and famines in Bengal.

Textile industry

Under Mughal rule, Bengal was a center of the worldwide muslin, silk and pearl trades.[111] During the Mughal era, the most important center of cotton production was Bengal, particularly around its capital city of Dhaka, leading to muslin being called "daka" in distant markets such as Central Asia.[112] Domestically, much of India depended on Bengali products such as rice, silks and cotton textiles. Overseas, Europeans depended on Bengali products such as cotton textiles, silks and opium; Bengal accounted for 40% of Dutch imports from Asia, for example, including more than 50% of textiles and around 80% of silks.[113] From Bengal, saltpeter was also shipped to Europe, opium was sold in Indonesia, raw silk was exported to Japan and the Netherlands, and cotton and silk textiles were exported to Europe, Indonesia and Japan.[114]

Bengal Subah

Figure 25: *A woman in Dhaka clad in fine Bengali muslin, 18th century*

Shipbuilding industry

Bengal had a large shipbuilding industry. In terms of shipbuilding tonnage during the 16th–18th centuries, the annual output of Bengal alone totaled around 2,232,500 tons, larger than the combined output of the Dutch (450,000–550,000 tons), the British (340,000 tons), and North America (23,061 tons).[115]

Bengali shipbuilding was advanced compared to European shipbuilding at the time. Ship-repairing, for example, was very advanced in Bengal, where European shippers visited to repair vessels. An important innovation in shipbuilding was the introduction of a flushed deck design in Bengal rice ships, resulting in hulls that were stronger and less prone to leak than the structurally weak hulls of traditional European ships built with a stepped deck design. The British East India Company later duplicated the flushed deck and hull designs of Bengal rice ships in the 1760s, leading to significant improvements in seaworthiness and navigation for European ships during the Industrial Revolution.

Figure 26: *A 16th century map of Bengal*

Administrative divisions

In the revenue settlement by Todar Mal in 1582, Bengal Subah was divided into 24 *sarkars* (districts), which included 19 *sarkars* of Bengal proper and 5 *sarkars* of Orissa. In 1607, during the reign of Jahangir Orissa became a separate *Subah*. These 19 *sarkars* were further divided into 682 *parganas*.[116] In 1658, subsequent to the revenue settlement by Shah Shuja, 15 new *sarkars* and 361 new *parganas* were added. In 1722, Murshid Quli Khan divided the whole Subah into 13 *chakalah*s, which were further divided into 1660 *parganas*.

Initially the capital of the *Subah* was Tanda. On 9 November 1595, the foundations of a new capital were laid at Rajmahal by Man Singh I who renamed it Akbarnagar. In 1610 the capital was shifted from Rajmahal to Dhaka and it was renamed Jahangirnagar. In 1639, Shah Shuja again shifted the capital to Rajmahal. In 1660, Muazzam Khan (Mir Jumla) again shifted the capital to Dhaka. In 1703, Murshid Quli Khan, then *diwan* (prime minister in charge of finance) of Bengal shifted his office from Dhaka to Maqsudabad and later renamed it Murshidabad.

The *sarkars* (districts) and the *parganas* (tehsils) of Bengal Subah were:

Sarkar	Pargana
Udamabar (Tanda)	52 parganas
Jannatabad (Lakhnauti)	66 parganas
Fathabad	31 parganas
Mahmudabad	88 parganas
Khalifatabad	35 parganas
Bakla	4 parganas
Purniyah	9 parganas
Tajpur	29 parganas
Ghoraghat	84 parganas
Pinjarah	21 parganas
Barbakabad	38 parganas
Bazuha	32 parganas
Sonargaon	52 parganas
Sylhet	8 parganas
Chittagong	7 parganas
Sharifabad	26 parganas
Sulaimanabad	31 parganas
Satgaon	53 parganas
Mandaran	16 parganas

Government

The state government was headed by a Viceroy (Subedar Nizam) appointed by the Mughal Emperor between 1576 and 1717. The Viceroy exercised tremendous authority, with his own cabinet and four prime ministers (Diwan). The three deputy viceroys for Bengal proper, Bihar and Orissa were known as the *Naib Nazims*. An extensive landed aristocracy was established by the Mughals in Bengal. The aristocracy was responsible for taxation and revenue collection. Land holders were bestowed with the title of Jagirdar. The Qadi title was reserved for the chief judge. Mansabdars were leaders of the Mughal Army, while faujdars were generals. The Mughals were credited for secular pluralism during the reign of Akbar, who promoted the religious doctrine of Din-i Ilahi. Later rulers promoted more conservative Islam.

In 1717, the Mughal government replaced Viceroy Azim-us-Shan due to conflicts with his influential deputy viceroy and prime minister Murshid Quli Khan. Growing regional autonomy caused the Mughal Court to establish a

Figure 27: *Man Singh I, the Rajput Viceroy of Mughal Bengal (1594–1606)*

hereditary principality in Bengal, with Khan being recognised in the official title of Nazim. He founded the Nasiri dynasty. In 1740, following the Battle of Giria, Alivardi Khan staged a coup and founded the short-lived Afsar dynasty. For all practical purposes, the Nazims acted as independent princes. European colonial powers referred to them as Nawabs or Nababs.

List of Viceroys

Personal Name	Reign
Munim Khan *Khan-i-Khanan* منعم خان، خان خانا	25 September 1574 – 23 October 1575
Hussain Quli Beg *Khan Jahan I* حسین قلی بیگ، خان ج اول	15 November 1575 – 19 December 1578
Muzaffar Khan Turbati مظفر خان تربتی	1579–1580
Mirza Aziz Koka *Khan-e-Azam* میرزا عزیز کوک،خان اعظم	1582–1583
Shahbaz Khan Kamboh ش باز خان کمبو	1583–1585

Sadiq Khan صادق خان	1585–1586
Wazir Khan Tajik وزیر خان	1586–1587
Sa'id Khan سعید خان	1587–1594
Raja Man Singh I راجہ مان سنگھ	4 June 1594 – 1606
Qutb-ud-din Khan Koka قطب الدین خان کوکہ	2 September 1606 – May 1607
Jahangir Quli Beg جہانگیر قلی بیگ	1607–1608
Sheikh Ala-ud-din Chisti *Islam Khan Chisti* اسلام خان چشتی	June 1608 – 1613
Qasim Khan Chishti قاسم خان چشتی	1613–1617
Ibrahim Khan Fateh Jang ابراہیم خان فتح جنگ	1617–1622
Mahabat Khan محابت خان	1622–1625
Mirza Amanullah *Khan Zaman II* میرزا أمان اللہ ، خان زمان ثانی	1625
Mukarram Khan مکرم خان	1625–1627
Fidai Khan فدای خان	1627–1628
Qasim Khan Juvayni *Qasim Manija* قاسم خان جوینی، قاسم مانیجہ	1628–1632
Mir Muhammad Baqir *Azam Khan* میر محمد باقر، اعظم خان	1632–1635
Mir Abdus Salam *Islam Khan Mashhadi* اسلام خان مشہدی	1635–1639
Sultan Shah Shuja شاہ شجاع	1639 -1660
Mir Jumla II میر جملہ	May 1660 – 30 March 1663
Mirza Abu Talib *Shaista Khan I* میرزا ابو طالب، شایستہ خان	March 1664 – 1676
Azam Khan Koka, *Fidai Khan II* اعظم خان کوکہ، فدای خان ثانی	1676–1677

Sultan Muhammad Azam Shah *Alijah* محمد اعظم شاہ عالی جاہ	1678- 1679
Mirza Abu Talib *Shaista Khan I* میرزا ابو طالب، شایستہ خان	1679–1688
Ibrahim Khan ibn Ali Mardan Khan ابراہیم خان ابن علی مردان خان	1688–1697
Sultan Azim-us-Shan عظیم الشان	1697–1712
Others appointed but did not show up from 1712 to 1717 and managed by Deputy Subahdar Murshid Quli Khan.	
Murshid Quli Khan مرشد قلی خان	1717–1727

List of Nawab Nazims

Portrait	Titular Name	Personal Name	Birth	Reign	Death
	Nasiri Dynasty					
	Jaafar Khan Bahadur Nasiri	Murshid Quli Khan	1665	1717– 1727	30 June 1727
	Ala-ud-Din Haidar Jang	Sarfaraz Khan Bahadur	?	1727-1727	29 April 1740
	Shuja ud-Daula	Shuja-ud-Din Muhammad Khan	Around 1670 (date not available)	July 1727 – 26 August 1739	26 August 1739
	Ala-ud-Din Haidar Jang	Sarfaraz Khan Bahadur	?	13 March 1739 – April 1740	29 April 1740
	Afsar Dynasty					
	Hashim ud-Daula	Muhammad Alivardi Khan Bahadur	Before 10 May 1671	29 April 1740 – 9 April 1756	9 April 1756
	Siraj ud-Daulah	Muhammad Siraj-ud-Daulah	1733	April 1756 – 2 June 1757	2 July 1757

Figure 28: *Shaista Khan, Viceroy (1664–1688)*

Figure 29: *Viceroy Muhammad Azam Shah (1678–1679), later the Mughal Emperor*

Figure 30: *Viceroy Azim-us-Shan (1697–1712), later the Mughal Emperor*

Maratha Empire

Maratha Empire

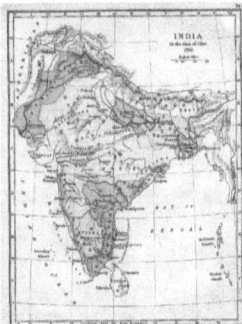

Territory under Maratha control in 1760 (yellow).

Capital		Raigad Fort Gingee Satara Pune
Languages		Marathi and Sanskrit[117]
Religion		Hinduism
Government		Absolute monarchy
Chhatrapati		
•	1645–1680	Shivaji (first)
•	1808–1818	Pratap Singh (last)
Peshwa		
•	1674–1689	Moropant Pingle (first)
•	1803–1818	Baji Rao II (last)
Legislature		Ashta Pradhan
History		
•	Deccan Wars	1674
•	Anglo-Maratha War	1818
Area		
		2,800,000 km^2 (1,100,000 sq mi)
Population		
•	1700 est.	Not known
Currency		Rupee, Paisa, Mohor, Shivrai, Hon
	Preceded by Mughal Empire Adil Shahi dynasty	**Succeeded by** Company rule in India

Today part of	<ul><li>India</li><li>Pakistan</li></ul>

Part of a series on the
History of India

- v
- t
- e[118]

The **Maratha Empire** or the **Maratha Confederacy** was an Indian power that dominated much of the Indian subcontinent in the 17th and 18th century. The empire formally existed from 1674 with the coronation of *Chhatrapati* Shivaji and ended in 1818 with the defeat of *Peshwa* Bajirao II. The Marathas are credited to a large extent for ending Mughal rule in India.[119,120,121] may consider 1645 as the founding of the empire because that was the year when the teenaged Shivaji captured a fort from Adilshahi sultanate.</ref>

The Marathas were a Marathi warrior group from the western Deccan Plateau (present day Maharashtra) that rose to prominence by establishing a Hindavi Swarajya (meaning "self-rule of Hindu/Indian people").[122] The Marathas became prominent in the 17th century under the leadership of Shivaji who revolted against the Adil Shahi dynasty and the Mughal Empire and carved out a kingdom with Raigad as his capital. Known for their mobility, the Marathas were able to consolidate their territory during the Mughal–Maratha Wars and later controlled a large part of the Indian subcontinent.

After the death of Aurangzeb in 1707, Chhattrapati Shahu, grandson of Shivaji, was released by the Mughals. Following a brief struggle with his aunt Tarabai, Shahu became the ruler and appointed Balaji Vishwanath and later, his descendants, as the peshwas or prime ministers of the empire.[123] Balaji and his descendants played a key role in the expansion of Maratha rule. The empire at its peak stretched from Tamil Nadu[124] in the south, to Peshawar (modern-day Khyber Pakhtunkhwa, Pakistan[125,126]</ref>) in the north, and Bengal Subah in the east. The Marathas even discussed abolishing the Mughal throne and placing Vishwasrao Peshwa on the Mughal imperial throne in Delhi.[127] In 1761, the Maratha Army lost the Third Battle of Panipat to Ahmad Shah Abdali of the Afghan Durrani Empire, which halted their imperial expansion into Afghanistan. Ten years after Panipat, the young Peshwa Madhavrao I's Maratha Resurrection reinstated Maratha authority over North India.

In a bid to effectively manage the large empire, Madhavrao I gave semi-autonomy to the strongest of the knights, which created a confederacy of Maratha states. They became known as the Gaekwads of Baroda, the Holkars of Indore and Malwa, the Scindias of Gwalior and Ujjain, the Bhonsales of Nagpur and the Puars of Dhar and Dewas. In 1775, the East India Company intervened in a Peshwa family succession struggle in Pune, which led to the First Anglo-Maratha War, resulting in a Maratha victory. The Marathas remained the pre-eminent power in India until their defeat in the Second and Third Anglo-Maratha Wars (1805-1818), which left the East India Company in control of most of India.

A large portion of the Maratha empire was coastline, which had been secured by the potent Maratha Navy under commanders such as Kanhoji Angre. He was very successful at keeping foreign naval ships, particularly of the Portuguese and British, at bay. Securing the coastal areas and building land-based fortifications were crucial aspects of the Maratha's defensive strategy and regional military history.

Nomenclature

The Maratha Empire is also referred to as the Maratha Confederacy. The historian Barbara Ramusack says that the former is a designation preferred by Indian nationalists, while the latter was that used by British historians. She notes, "neither term is fully accurate since one implies a substantial degree of centralisation and the other signifies some surrender of power to a central government and a longstanding core of political administrators. Maratha power was fragmented among several discrete fragments".Wikipedia:Citation needed

Figure 31: *A portrait of Chattrapati Shivaji*

Although at present, the word Maratha refers to a particular caste of warriors and peasants, in the past the word has been used to describe Marathi people, including Marathas themselves.

History

The empire had its head in the Chhatrapati as de jure, but the de facto governance was in the hands of the Peshwas.Wikipedia:Citation needed After the death of Chhatrapati Shahu and with the death of Madhavrao – I, various chiefs played the role of the de facto rulers in their own regions.

Shivaji and his descendants

Shivaji

Shivaji (1627–1680) was a Maratha aristocrat of the Bhosle clan who is considered to be the founder of the Maratha empire. Shivaji led a resistance to free the Marathi people from the Sultanate of Bijapur from 1645 and establish Hindavi Swarajya (self-rule of Hindu people). He created an independent Maratha kingdom with Raigad as its capital and successfully fought against the

Maratha Empire

Figure 32: *Sambhaji, eldest son of Chhatrapati Shivaji Maharaj*

Mughals to defend his kingdom. He was crowned as Chhatrapati (sovereign) of the new Maratha kingdom in 1674.

The state Shivaji founded was a Maratha kingdom comprised about 4.1% of the subcontinent, but spread over large tracts. At the time of his death it was dotted with about 300 forts, about 40,000 cavalry, 50,000 foot soldiers and naval establishments all over the west coast. Over time, the kingdom would increase in size and heterogeneity; by the time of his grandson, and later under the Peshwas in the early 18th century, it was a full-fledged empire.[128]

Sambhaji

Shivaji had two sons: Sambhaji and Rajaram. Sambhaji, the elder son, was very popular among the courtiers.Wikipedia:Citation needed In 1681, Sambhaji had himself crowned and resumed his father's expansionist policies. Sambhaji had earlier defeated the Portuguese and Chikka Deva Raya of Mysore. To nullify alliance between his rebel son, Akbar, and the Marathas, Aurangzeb himself headed south in 1681. With his entire imperial court, administration and an army of about 500,000 troops he proceeded to expand the Mughal empire, gaining territories such as the sultanates of Bijapur and Golconda. During the eight years that followed, Sambhaji led the Marathas, never losing a battle or a fort to Aurangzeb.Wikipedia:Citation needed

In early 1689, Sambhaji called his commanders for a strategic meeting at Sangameshwar to consider a final onslaught on the Mughal forces.Wikipedia:Citation needed In a meticulously planned operation, Ganoji and Aurangzeb's commander, Mukarrab Khan, attacked Sangameshwar when Sambhaji was accompanied by just a few men. Sambhaji was ambushed and captured by Mughal troops on February 01, 1689. He and his advisor, Kavi Kalash, were taken to Bahadurgad, where they were executed by the Mughals on 21 March 1689. Aurangzeb had Sambhaji executed on charges of atrocities committed by Maratha forces in the attack on Burhanpur that included plunder, killing, rape, and torture.

Rajaram and Tarabai

Upon Sambhaji's death, his half-brother Rajaram assumed the throne. The Mughal siege of Raigad continued, and he had to flee to Vishalgad and then to Gingee for safety. From there the Marathas raided Mughal territory, and many forts were recaptured by Maratha commanders such as Santaji Ghorpade, Dhanaji Jadhav, Parshuram Pant Pratinidhi, Shankaraji Narayan Sacheev and Melgiri Pandit. In 1697, Rajaram offered a truce but this was rejected by Aurangzeb. Rajaram died in 1700 at Sinhagad. His widow, Tarabai, assumed control in the name of her son, Ramaraja (Shivaji II). She led the Marathas against the Mughals, and by 1705 they had crossed the Narmada River and entered Malwa, then in Mughal possession.Wikipedia:Citation needed

Shahu

After Aurangzeb's death in 1707, Shahu, son of Sambhaji (and grandson of Shivaji), was released by Bahadur Shah I, the new Mughal emperor. His mother was kept as a hostage of the Mughals, however, in order to ensure that Shahu adhered to the release conditions. Upon release, Shahu immediately claimed the Maratha throne and challenged his aunt Tarabai and her son. This promptly turned the now-spluttering Mughal-Maratha war into a three-cornered affair. The states of Satara and Kolhapur came into being in 1707 because of the succession dispute over the Maratha kingship. Shahu appointed Balaji Vishwanath as Peshwa.[129] The Peshwa was instrumental in getting Shahu accepted as rightful heir of Shivaji and the Chhatrapati of the Marathas by The Mughals.[130] Balaji also got Shahu's mother, Yesubai, released from Mughal captivity in 1719.

During Shahu's reign, Raghoji Bhosale expanded the empire in the East, reaching present-day Bengal. Khanderao Dabhade and later his son, Trimbakrao, expanded in the West in Gujarat. Peshwa Bajirao and his three chiefs, Pawar (Dhar), Holkar (Indore), and Scindia (Gwalior), expanded in the North.

Figure 33: *Peshwa Balaji Vishwanath*

Peshwa era

Shaniwarwada palace fort in Pune, it was the seat of the Peshwa rulers of the Maratha Empire until 1818.

During this era, Peshwas belonging to the Bhat family controlled the Maratha Army and later became de facto rulers of the Maratha Empire. During their reign, the Maratha Empire dominated most of the Indian subcontinent.

Balaji Vishwanath

Shahu appointed Peshwa Balaji Vishwanath in 1713. From his time, the office of Peshwa became supreme while Shahuji became a figurehead.

Figure 34: *Peshwa Baji Rao I*

- His first major achievement was the conclusion of the *Treaty of Lonavala* in 1714 with Kanhoji Angre, the most powerful naval chief on the Western Coast. He later accepted Shahuji as Chhatrapati.
- In 1719, an army of Marathas marched to Delhi after defeating Sayyid Hussain Ali, the Mughal governor of Deccan, and deposed the Mughal emperor. The Mughal Emperors became puppets in the hands of their Maratha overlords from this point on.[131]

Baji Rao I

After Balaji Vishwanath's death in April 1720, his son, Baji Rao I, was appointed Peshwa by Shahu. Bajirao is credited with expanding the Maratha Empire tenfold from 3% to 30% of the modern Indian landscape during 1720–1740. He fought over 41 battles before his death in April 1740 and is reputed to have never lost one.[132]WP:NOTRS

- The Battle of Palkhed was a land battle that took place on February 28, 1728 at the village of Palkhed, near the city of Nashik, Maharashtra, India between Baji Rao I and the Qamar-ud-din Khan, Asaf Jah I of Hyderabad. The Marathas defeated the Nizam.The battle is considered an example of brilliant execution of military strategy.

Figure 35: *Peshwa Balaji Bajirao*

- In 1737, Marathas under Bajirao I raided the suburbs of Delhi in a blitzkrieg in the Battle of Delhi (1737).[133,134]
- The Nizam left Deccan to rescue Mughals from the invasion of Marathas, but was defeated decisively in the Battle of Bhopal.[135] The Marathas extracted a large tribute from the Mughals and signed a treaty which ceded Malwa to the Marathas.[136]
- The Battle of Vasai was fought between the Marathas and the Portuguese rulers of Vasai, a village lying on the northern shore of Vasai creek, 50 km north of Mumbai. The Marathas were led by Chimaji Appa, brother of Baji Rao. The Maratha victory in this war was a major achievement of Baji Rao's time in office.

Balaji Baji Rao

Baji Rao's son, Balaji Bajirao (Nanasaheb), was appointed as the next Peshwa by Shahuji despite opposition of other chiefs.

- In 1740, the Maratha forces, under Raghoji Bhosale, came down upon Arcot and defeated the Nawab of Arcot, Dost Ali, in the pass at Damalcherry. In the war that followed, Dost Ali, one of his sons Hasan Ali, and a number of other prominent persons lost their lives. This initial success at once enhanced Maratha prestige in the south. From Damalcherry, the Marathas proceeded to Arcot, which surrendered to

them without much resistance. Then, Raghuji invaded Trichinopoly in December 1740. Unable to resist, Chanda Saheb surrendered the fort to Raghuji on March 14, 1741. Chanda Saheb and his son were arrested and sent to Nagpur.[137]
- Rajputana also came under Maratha domination during this time.
- In June 1756 Luís Mascarenhas, Count of Alva(Conde de Alva), the Portuguese Viceroy was killed in action by Maratha Army in Goa.

Invasions in Bengal

After the successful campaign of Karnatak and the Trichinopolly, Raghuji returned from Karnatak. He undertook six expeditions into Bengal from 1741 to 1748.[138] Raghuji was able to annex Odisha to his kingdom permanently as he successfully exploited the chaotic conditions prevailing in Bengal after the death of its governor Murshid Quli Khan in 1727. Constantly harassed by the Bhonsles, Odisha, Bengal and parts of Bihar were economically ruined. Alivardi Khan, the Nawab of Bengal made peace with Raghuji in 1751 ceding Cuttack (Odisha) up to the river Subarnarekha, and agreeing to pay Rs.1.2 million annually as the Chauth for Bengal and Bihar.[139]

During their occupation of western Bengal, the Marathas perpetrated atrocities against the local population. The Maratha atrocities were recorded by both Bengali and European sources, which reported that the Marathas demanded payments, and tortured and killed anyone who couldn't pay. Dutch sources estimate a total of 400,000 people in Bengal were killed by the Marathas. According to Bengali sources, the atrocities led to much of the local population opposing the Marathas and developing support for the Nawabs.

Maratha's Afghan conquests

- Balaji Bajirao encouraged agriculture, protected the villagers and brought about a marked improvement in the state of the territory. Raghunath Rao, brother of Nanasaheb, pushed into the wake of the Afghan withdrawal after Ahmed Shah Abdali's plunder of Delhi in 1756. Delhi was captured by the Maratha army under Raghunath Rao in August 1757, defeating the Afghan garrison in the Battle of Delhi. This laid the foundation for the Maratha conquest of North-west India. In Lahore, as in Delhi, the Marathas were now major players. After the Battle of Attock, 1758, the Marathas captured Peshawar defeating the Afghan troops in the Battle of Peshawar on 8 May 1758.

Maratha invasion of Delhi and Rohilkhand

Just prior to the battle of Panipat in 1761, Marathas looted "Diwan-i-Khas" or *Hall of Private Audiences* in the Red Fort of Delhi, which was the place where the Mughal emperors used to receive courtiers and state guests, in one of their expeditions of Delhi.

> *'The Marathas who were hard pressed for money stripped the ceiling of Diwan-i-Khas of its silver and looted the shrines dedicated to Muslim saints".*

During the Maratha invasion of Rohilkhand in the 1750s

> *'The Marathas defeated the Rohillas, forced them to seek shelter in hills and ransacked their country in such a manner that the Rohillas dreaded the Marathas and hated them ever afterwards".*

Third battle of Panipat

In 1759, the Marathas under Sadashivrao Bhau (referred to as the Bhau or Bhao in sources) responded to the news of the Afghans' return to North India by sending a large army north. Bhau's force was bolstered by some Maratha forces under Holkar, Scindia, Gaikwad and Govind Pant Bundele. The combined army of over 100,000 regular troops re-captured the former Mughal capital, Delhi, from an Afghan garrison in August 1760.[140] Delhi had been reduced to ashes many times due to previous invasions, and there was an acute shortage of supplies in the Maratha camp. Bhau ordered the sacking of the already depopulated city.[141] He is said to have planned to place his nephew and the Peshwa's son, Vishwasrao, on the Mughal throne. By 1760, with defeat of the Nizam in the Deccan, Maratha power had reached its zenith with a territory of over 2,500,000 km² acres.[142]

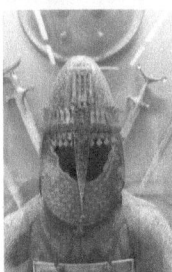

Signature Maratha helmet with curved back, front view

Signature Maratha helmet with curved back, side view

Maratha armour from Hermitage Museum, St. Petersburg, Russia

Ahmad Shah Durrani called on the Rohillas and the Nawab of Oudh to assist him in driving out the Marathas from Delhi.Wikipedia:Citation needed Huge armies of Muslim forces and Marathas collided with each other on January 14, 1761 in the Third Battle of Panipat. The Maratha Army lost the battle, which halted their imperial expansion. The Jats and Rajputs did not support the Marathas. Their withdrawal from the ensuing battle played a crucial role in its result.Wikipedia:Citation needed Historians have criticised the Maratha treatment of fellow Hindu groups. Kaushik Roy says "The treatment of Marathas with their co-religionist fellows – Jats and Rajputs was definitely unfair and ultimately they had to pay its price in Panipat where Muslim forces had united in the name of religion." The Marathas had antagonised the Jats and Rajputs by taxing them heavily, punishing them after defeating the Mughals and interfering in their internal affairs. The Marathas were abandoned by Raja Suraj Mal of Bharatpur and the Rajputs, who quit the Maratha alliance at Agra before the start of the great battle and withdrew their troops as Maratha general Sadashivrao Bhau did not heed the advice to leave soldier's families (women and children) and pilgrims at Agra and not take them to the battle field with the soldiers, rejected their co-operation. Their supply chains (earlier assured by Raja Suraj Mal and Rajputs) did not exist.Wikipedia:Citation needed

Peshwa Madhav Rao I

Peshwa Madhavrao I was the fourth Peshwa of the Maratha Empire. It was during his tenure that the Maratha Resurrection took place. He worked as a unifying force in the Maratha Empire and moved to the south to subdue Nizam and Mysore to assert Maratha power. He sent generals such as Bhonsle, Scindia and Holkar to the north, where they re-established Maratha authority by the early 1770s.Wikipedia:Citation needed

Prof G. S. Chhabra wrote:

Maratha Empire

Figure 36: *Peshwa Madhavrao I*

Young though he was, Madhav Rao had a cool and calculating head of a seasoned and experienced man. The diplomacy by which he could win over his uncle Raghoba when he had no strength to fight and the way he could crush his power when he had the means to do so later on proved in him a genius who knows when and how to act. The formidable power of the Nizam was crushed, Hyder Ali, who was a terror even to the British, was effectually humbled and before he died in 1772, the Marathas were almost there in the north where they had been before Panipat. What could not have the Marathas achieved if Madhav had continued living just for a few years more? Destiny was not in favour of the Marathas, the death of Madhav was a greater blow than their defeat of Panipat and from this blow they could never again recover.[143]

Madhav Rao died in 1772, at the age of 27. His death is considered to be a fatal blow to the Maratha Empire and from that time Maratha power started to move on a downward trajectory, less an empire than a confederacy.Wikipedia:Citation needed

Figure 37: *Mahadaji Shinde restored the Maratha domination of northern India*

Confederacy era

In a bid to effectively manage the large empire, Madhavrao Peshwa gave semi-autonomy to the strongest of the knights. After the death of Peshwa Madhavrao I, various chiefs and statesman became *de facto* rulers and regents for the infant Peshwa Madhavrao II.Wikipedia:Citation needed Thus, the semi-autonomous Maratha states came into being in far-flung regions of the empire:Wikipedia:Citation needed

- Peshwas of Pune
- Gaekwads of Baroda
- Holkars of Indore
- Scindias (aka Shindes) of Gwalior (Chambal region) and Ujjain (Malwa Region)
- Bhonsales of Nagpur (no blood relation with Shivaji's or Tarabai's family)
- Puars (or Pawars) of Dewas and Dhar
- Even in the original kingdom of Shivaji itself, many knights were given semi-autonomous charges of small districts, which led to princely states Sangli, Aundh, Bhor, Bawda, Phaltan, Miraj, etc. Pawars of Udgir were also part of confederacy.

Major events

- After the 1761 Battle of Panipat, Malhar Rao Holkar attacked the Rajputs and defeated them at the battle of Mangrol. This largely restored Maratha power in Rajasthan.[144]
- Under the leadership of Mahadji Shinde, the ruler of the state of Gwalior in central India, the Marathas defeated the Jats, the Rohilla Afghans and took Delhi which remained under Maratha control for the next three decades.[145] His forces conquered modern day Haryana Shinde was instrumental in resurrecting Maratha power after the débâcle of the Third Battle of Panipat, and in this he was assisted by Benoît de Boigne.
- In 1767 Madhavrao I crossed the Krishna River and defeated Hyder Ali in the battles of Sira and Madgiri. He also rescued the last queen of the Keladi Nayaka Kingdom, who had been kept in confinement by Hyder Ali in the fort of Madgiri.[146]
- In early 1771, ten years after the collapse of Maratha authority over North India following the Third Battle of Panipat, Mahadji recaptured Delhi and installed Shah Alam II as a puppet ruler on the Mughal throne.[147] receiving in return the title of deputy *Vakil-ul-Mutlak* or vice-regent of the Empire and that of *Vakil-ul-Mutlak* being at his request conferred on the Peshwa. The Mughals also gave him the title of *Amir-ul-Amara* (head of the amirs).
- After taking control of Delhi, the Marathas sent a large army in 1772 to punish Afghan Rohillas for their involvement in Panipat. Their army devastated Rohilkhand by looting and plundering as well as taking members of the royal family as captives.[147]
- After the growth in power of feudal lords like Malwa sardars, landlords of Bundelkhand and Rajput kingdoms of Rajasthan, they refused to pay tribute to Mahadji. So he sent his army conquer the states such as Bhopal, Datiya, Chanderi, Narwar, Salbai and Gohad. However, he launched an unsuccessful expedition against the Raja of Jaipur, but withdrew after the inconclusive Battle of Lalsot in 1787.[148]
- The Battle of Gajendragad was fought between the Marathas under the command of Tukojirao Holkar (the adopted son of Malharrao Holkar) and Tipu Sultan from March 1786 to March 1787 in which Tipu Sultan was defeated by the Marathas. By the victory in this battle, the border of the Maratha territory extended till Tungabhadra river.
- The strong fort of Gwalior was then in the hands of Chhatar Singh, the Jat ruler of Gohad. In 1783, Mahadji besieged the fort of Gwalior and conquered it. He delegated the administration of Gwalior to Khanderao Hari Bhalerao. After celebrating the conquest of Gwalior, Mahadji Shinde turned his attention to Delhi again.[149]

Figure 38: *Maratha king of Gwalior at his palace*

- In 1788, Mahadji's armies defeated Ismail Beg, a Mughal noble who resisted the Marathas.[150] The Rohilla chief Ghulam Kadir, Ismail Beg's ally, took over Delhi, capital of the Mughal dynasty and deposed and blinded the king Shah Alam II, placing a puppet on the Delhi throne. Mahadji intervened and killed him, taking possession of Delhi on October 02 restoring Shah Alam II to the throne and acting as his protector.
- Jaipur and Jodhpur, the two most powerful Rajput states, were still out of direct Maratha domination. So, Mahadji sent his general Benoît de Boigne to crush the forces of Jaipur and Jodhpur at the Battle of Patan.[151] Marwar was also captured on September 10, 1790.
- Another achievement of the Marathas was their victories over the Nizam of Hyderabad's armies including in the Battle of Kharda.[152,153]
- In 1788, Mahadji's armies defeated Ismail Beg, a Mughal noble who resisted the Marathas.[150] The Rohilla chief Ghulam Kadir, Ismail Beg's ally, took over Delhi, capital of the Mughal dynasty and deposed and blinded the king Shah Alam II, placing a puppet on the Delhi throne. Mahadji intervened and killed him, taking possession of Delhi on October 02 restoring Shah Alam II to the throne and acting as his protector.

Mysore war, Sringeri sacking, British alliance

The Marathas came into conflict with Tipu Sultan and his Kingdom of Mysore, leading to the Maratha–Mysore War in 1785. The war ended in 1787 with the Marathas being defeated by Tipu Sultan. In 1791–92, large areas of the Maratha Confederacy suffered massive population loss due to the Doji bara famine.

In 1791, irregulars like *lamaans* and pindari of Maratha army raided and looted the temple of Sringeri *Shankaracharya*, killing and wounding many people including Brahmins, plundering the monastery of all its valuable possessions, and desecrating the temple by displacing the image of goddess Sarada . The incumbent *Shankaracharya* petitioned Tipu Sultan for help. A bunch of about 30 letters written in Kannada, which were exchanged between Tipu Sultan's court and the Sringeri Shankaracharya were discovered in 1916 by the Director of Archaeology in Mysore. Tipu Sultan expressed his indignation and grief at the news of the raid:

> "People who have sinned against such a holy place are sure to suffer the consequences of their misdeeds at no distant date in this Kali age in accordance with the verse: "Hasadbhih kriyate karma rudadbhir-anubhuyate" (People do [evil] deeds smilingly but suffer the consequences crying)."[154]

Tipu Sultan immediately ordered the Asaf of Bednur to supply the Swami with 200 *rahati*s (*fanam*s) in cash and other gifts and articles. Tipu Sultan's interest in the Sringeri temple continued for many years, and he was still writing to the Swami in the 1790s.[155]

The Maratha Empire soon allied with the British East India Company (based in the Bengal Presidency) against Mysore in the Anglo-Mysore Wars. After the British had suffered defeat against Mysore in the first two Anglo-Mysore War, the Maratha cavalry assisted the British in the last two Anglo-Mysore Wars from 1790 onwards, eventually helping the British conquer Mysore in the Fourth Anglo-Mysore War in 1799. After the British conquest, however, the Marathas launched frequent raids in Mysore to plunder the region, which they justified as compensation for past losses to Tipu Sultan.

British intervention

In 1775, the British East India Company, from its base in Bombay, intervened in a succession struggle in Pune, on behalf of Raghunathrao (also called Raghobadada), who wanted to become Peshwa of the empire. Marathas forces under Tukojirao Holkar and Mahadaji Shinde defeated a British expeditionary force at the Battle of Wadgaon, but the heavy surrender terms, which included the return of annexed territory and a share of revenues, were disavowed by

Figure 39: *A mural depicting the British surrender during the First Anglo-Maratha War. The mural is a part of the Victory Memorial (Vijay Stambh) located at Vadgaon Maval (off NH-4, Malinagar, Vadgaon Maval, Pune)*

the British authorities at Bengal and fighting continued. What became known as the First Anglo-Maratha War ended in 1782 with a restoration of the pre-war status quo and the East India Company's abandonment of Raghunathrao's cause.[156]

In 1799, Yashwantrao Holkar was crowned King of Holkars, he captured Ujjain. He started campaigning towards the north to expand his empire in that region. Yashwant Rao rebelled against the policies of the Peshwa Baji Rao II. In May 1802, he marched towards Pune the seat of the Peshwa. This gave rise to the Battle of Poona in which the Peshwa was defeated. After the Battle of Poona, the flight of Peshwa left the government of Maratha state in the hands of Yashwantrao Holkar.[157] He appointed Amrutrao as the Peshwa and went to Indore on March 13, 1803. All except Gaikwad chief of Baroda, who had already accepted British protection by a separate treaty on July 26, 1802, supported the new regime. He made a treaty with the British. Also, Yashwant-Rao successfully resolved the disputes with Scindia and the Peshwa. He tried to unite the Maratha Confederacy but to no avail. In 1802, the British intervened in Baroda to support the heir to the throne against rival claimants and they signed a treaty with the new Maharaja recognising his independence from the Maratha Empire in return for his acknowledgement of British paramountcy.

Maratha Empire

Figure 40: *Peshwa Madhavrao II in his court in 1790, concluding a treaty with the British*

Before the Second Anglo-Maratha War (1803–1805), the Peshwa Baji Rao II signed a similar treaty. The defeat in Battle of Delhi, 1803 during Second Anglo-Maratha War resulted in the loss of the city of Delhi for the Marathas.[158]

The Second Anglo-Maratha War represents the military high-water mark of the Marathas who posed the last serious opposition to the formation of the British Raj. The real contest for India was never a single decisive battle for the subcontinent. Rather it turned on a complex social and political struggle for control of the South Asian military economy. The victory in 1803 hinged as much on finance, diplomacy, politics and intelligence as it did on battlefield manoeuvre and war itself.[159]

Ultimately, the Third Anglo-Maratha War (1817–1818) resulted in the loss of Maratha independence. It left the British in control of most of India. The Peshwa was exiled to Bithoor (Marat, near Kanpur, Uttar Pradesh) as a pensioner of the British. The Maratha heartland of Desh, including Pune, came under direct British rule, with the exception of the states of Kolhapur and Satara, which retained local Maratha rulers (descendants of Shivaji and Sambhaji II ruled over Kolhapur). The Maratha-ruled states of Gwalior, Indore, and Nagpur all lost territory and came under subordinate alliance with the British Raj as princely states that retained internal sovereignty under British paramountcy. Other small princely states of Maratha knights were retained under the British Raj as well.Wikipedia:Citation needed

Figure 41: *Battle of Assaye during the Second Anglo-Maratha War*

Figure 42: *Peshwa Baji Rao II signing of the Treaty of Bassein with the British*

Figure 43: *Maratha Court*

The Third Anglo-Maratha War was fought by Maratha war lords separately instead of forming a common front and they surrendered one by one. Shinde and the Pashtun Amir Khan were subdued by the use of diplomacy and pressure, which resulted in the Treaty of Gwalior[160] on November 05, 1817.Wikipedia:Citation needed All other Maratha chiefs like Holkars, Bhonsles and Peshwa gave up arms by 1818. British historian Percival Spear describes 1818 as a watershed year in the history of India, saying that by the year "the British dominion in India became the British dominion of India".

The war left the British, under the auspices of the British East India Company, in control of virtually all of present-day India south of the Sutlej River. The famed Nassak Diamond was acquired by the Company as part of the spoils of the war.[161] The British acquired large chunks of territory from the Maratha Empire and in effect put an end to their most dynamic opposition.[162] The terms of surrender Major-general John Malcolm offered to the Peshwa were controversial amongst the British for being too liberal: The Peshwa was offered a luxurious life near Kanpur and given a pension of about 80,000 pounds.Wikipedia:Citation needed

Administration

The Ashtapradhan (*The Council of Eight*) was a council of eight ministers that administered the Maratha empire. This system was formed by Shivaji. Ministerial designations were drawn from the Sanskrit language and comprised:Wikipedia:Citation needed

- *Pantpradhan* or *Peshwa* – Prime Minister, general administration of the Empire
- *Amatya* or *Mazumdar* – Finance Minister, managing accounts of the Empire[163]Wikipedia:Identifying reliable sources
- *Sachiv* – Secretary, preparing royal edicts
- *Mantri* – Interior Minister, managing internal affairs especially intelligence and espionage
- *Senapati* – Commander-in-Chief, managing the forces and defence of the Empire
- *Sumant* – Foreign Minister, to manage relationships with other sovereigns
- *Nyayadhyaksh* – Chief Justice, dispensing justice on civil and criminal matters
- *Panditrao* – High Priest, managing internal religious matters

With the notable exception of the priestly *Panditrao* and the judicial *Nyayadisha*, the other *pradhans* held full-time military commands and their deputies performed their civil duties in their stead. In the later era of the Maratha Empire, these deputies and their staff constituted the core of the Peshwa's bureaucracy.Wikipedia:Citation needed

The Peshwa was the titular equivalent of a modern Prime Minister. Shivaji created the Peshwa designation in order to more effectively delegate administrative duties during the growth of the Maratha Empire. Prior to 1749, Peshwas held office for 8–9 years and controlled the Maratha Army. They later became the *de facto* hereditary administrators of the Maratha Empire from 1749 till its end in 1818.Wikipedia:Citation needed

Under Peshwa administration and with the support of several key generals and diplomats (listed below), the Maratha Empire reached its zenith, ruling most of the Indian subcontinent. It was also under the Peshwas that the Maratha Empire came to its end through its formal annexation into the British Empire by the British East India Company in 1818.

The Marathas used a secular policy of administration and allowed complete freedom of religion.[164]Wikipedia:Citing sources#What information to include There were many notable Muslims in the military and administration of Marathas like Ibrahim Khan Gardi, Haider Ali Kohari, Daulat Khan, Siddi Ibrahim, and Jiva Mahal.Wikipedia:Citation needed

Figure 44: *Gold coins minted during Shivaji's era, 17th century*

Shivaji was an able administrator who established a government that included modern concepts such as cabinet, foreign policy and internal intelligence. He established an effective civil and military administration. He believed that there was a close bond between the state and the citizens. He is remembered as a just and welfare-minded king. Cosme da Guarda says of him that:[165]

> *Such was the good treatment Shivaji accorded to people and such was the honesty with which he observed the capitulations that none looked upon him without a feeling of love and confidence. By his people he was exceedingly loved. Both in matters of reward and punishment he was so impartial that while he lived he made no exception for any person; no merit was left unrewarded, no offence went unpunished; and this he did with so much care and attention that he specially charged his governors to inform him in writing of the conduct of his soldiers, mentioning in particular those who had distinguished themselves, and he would at once order their promotion, either in rank or in pay, according to their merit. He was naturally loved by all men of valor and good conduct.*

English traveller John Fryer found Shivaji's tax-collecting regime oppressive, describing it as poor people having land "imposed upon them at double the former Rates," and if they refused it, being "carried to Prison, there they are famished almost to death. While French physician Dellon reports that Shivaji was "looked upon as one of the most politic princes in those parts."

Maratha empire carried out a number of sea raids, such as plunders targeting Mughal pilgrim ships and European trading vessels. European traders described these attacks as piracy, but the Marathas viewed them as legitimate targets because they were trading with, and thus financially supporting, their Mughal and Bijapur enemies. After the representatives of various European powers signed agreements with Shivaji or his successors that the threat of plundering or raids against Europeans began to reduce.

Geography

The Maratha Empire, at its peak, ruled over a large area in the Indian subcontinent. Apart from capturing various regions, the Marathas maintained a large number of tributaries who were bounded by agreement to pay a certain amount of regular tax, known as Chauth. The empire defeated the Sultanate of Mysore under Hyder Ali and Tipu Sultan, Nawab of Oudh, Nawab of Bengal, Nizam of Hyderabad and Nawab of Arcot as well as the Polygar kingdoms of South India. They extracted *chauth* from the rulers in Delhi, Oudh, Bengal, Bihar, Odisha, Punjab, Hyderabad, Mysore, Uttar Pradesh and Rajputana.[166]

The Marathas were requested by Safdarjung, the Nawab of Oudh, in 1752 to help him defeat Afghani Rohilla. The Maratha force left Pune and defeated Afghan Rohilla in 1752, capturing the whole of Rohilkhand (present-day northwestern Uttar Pradesh). In 1752, Marathas entered into an agreement with the Mughal emperor, through his *wazir*, Safdarjung, Mughals gave Marathas the *chauth* of Punjab, Sindh and Doab in addition to the *subedari* of Ajmer and Agra. In 1758, Marathas started their north-west conquest and expanded their boundary till Afghanistan. They defeated Afghan forces of Ahmed Shah Abdali, in what is now Pakistan, including Pakistani Punjab Province and Khyber Pakhtunkhwa. The Afghans were numbered around 25,000–30,000 and were led by Timur Shah, the son of Ahmad Shah Durrani. The Marathas massacred and looted thousands of Afghan soldiers and captured Lahore, Multan, Dera Ghazi Khan, Attock, Peshawar in the Punjab region and Kashmir.

During the confederacy era, Mahadji Shinde resurrected the Maratha domination on much of North India, which was lost after the Third battle of Panipat including the cis-Sutlej states (south of Sutlej) like Kaithal, Patiala, Jind, Thanesar, Maler Kotla and Faridkot, Delhi and Uttar Pradesh were under the suzerainty of the Scindhias of the Maratha Empire, following the Second Anglo-Maratha War of 1803–1805, Marathas lost these territories to the British East India Company.

Legacy

During the 17th century through late 18th century, the Maratha emperors, prime ministers, and dominion/fiefdom chiefs contributed on military as well as non-military fronts such as building forts, naval facilities, development of towns, constructing and patronizing temples, among others. During the 19th

Figure 45: *A painted scroll depicting different types of ships of the Marathan Navy including some captured English ships*

and 20th centuries, when Maratha principalities ruled as a feudatory of the British, Maratha rulers built palaces, contributed towards fine arts, introduced social reforms, and developed civic amenities in their territories.

Military contributions

- Some historians have credited Maratha Navy for laying the foundation of Indian Navy and bringing significant changes in naval warfare. A series of sea forts and battleships were built in 17th century during the reign of Shivaji. It has been noted that vessels built in the dockyards of Konkan were mostly indigenous, constructed without foreign aid. Further, in 18th centuries, during the reign of Admiral Kanhoji Angre, a host of dockyard facilities were built along the entire western coastline of present-day Maharashtra. The Marathas fortified the entire coastline with sea fortresses with navigational facilities.

- Nearly all the hill forts, which dot the landscape of present-day western Maharashtra were built by the Marathas. The renovation of Gingee fortress in Tamil Nadu, has been particularly applauded.

Development of towns and civic amenities

- During the 18th century, the Peshwas of Pune brought significant changes to the town of Pune building dams, bridges, and an underground water supply system.
- During the 18th century, misrule and pursuance of oppressive policies by the Marathas have been noted in the town of Ahmedabad

Patronizing religion

- Queen Ahilyabai Holkar has been noted as a just ruler and an avid patron of religion. She has been credited for building and patronizing numerous temples in the town of Maheshwar in Madhya Pradesh. Its handloom industry is also said to have been flourished under the rule of Holkars.
- The Bhosales of Nagpur ruled present-day state of Odisha in the latter half of the 18th century, during which misrule, anarchy, and violence has been reported. However at the same time, it is to be noted that the Maratha rulers patronized religion and religious institutions which made Odisha a center of attraction.
- Several Ghats in Varanasi (in present-day Uttar Pradesh) were repaired and re-constructed during the Maratha rule of 18th century.
- The Maratha rulers of Tanjore are said to have constructed several temples in the town of Tanjore

Fine arts and palaces

- The Maratha rulers of Tanjore (present-day Tamil Nadu) were patrons of fine arts and their reign has been considered as the golden period of Tanjore history. Art and culture reached new heights during their rule. They also considered themselves as representatives of Cholas referring themselves as *Cholasimhasanathipathi*. They made significant contributions towards Sanskrit and Marathi literature, Bharatanatyam (dance form), and Carnatic music.
- Several majestic palaces were built by Maratha principalities which include the Shaniwar Wada (built by the Peshwas of Pune)

Military

The Maratha army was not homogenous, but employed soldiers of different backgrounds, both locals and foreign mercenaries, including large numbers of Arabs, Sikhs, Rajputs, Sindhis, Rohillas, Abyssinians, Pathans, Topiwalas and Europeans. The army of Nana Fadnavis, for example, included 5,000 Arabs.[167]

Afghan accounts

The Maratha army, especially its infantry, was praised by almost all the enemies of Maratha Empire, ranging from Duke of Wellington to Ahmad Shah AbdaliWikipedia:Citation needed. After the Third Battle of Panipat, Abdali was relieved as Maratha army in the initial stages were almost in the position of destroying the Afghan armies and their Indian Allies Nawab of Oudh and Rohillas. The grand wazir of Durrani Empire, Sardar Shah Wali Khan

Figure 46: *Maratha Gurabs ships attacking a British East India Company ship*

was shocked when Maratha commander-in-chief Sadashivrao Bhau launched a fierce assault on the centre of Afghan Army, over 3,000 Durrani soldiers were killed alongside Haji Atai Khan, one of the chief commander of Afghan army and nephew of wazir Shah Wali Khan. Such was the fierce assault of Maratha infantry in hand-to-hand combat that Afghan armies started to flee and the wazir in desperation and rage shouted, "Comrades Whither do you fly, our country is far off".[168] Post battle, Ahmad Shah Abdali in a letter to one Indian ruler claimed that Afghans were able to defeat the Marathas only because of the blessings of almighty and any other army would have been destroyed by the Maratha army on that particular day even though Maratha army was numerically inferior to Afghan army and its Indian allies.Wikipedia:Citing sources#What information to include Though Abdali won the battle, he also had heavy casualties on his side. So, he sought immediate peace with the Marathas. Abdali wrote in his letter to Peshwa on February 10, 1761:

> There is no reason to have animosity amongst us. Your son Vishwasrao and your brother Sadashivrao died in battle, was unfortunate. Bhau started the battle, so I had to fight back unwillingly. Yet I feel sorry for his death. Please continue your guardianship of Delhi as before, to that I have no opposition. Only let Punjab until Sutlaj remain with us. Reinstate Shah Alam on Delhi's throne as you did before and let there be peace and friendship between us, this is my ardent desire. Grant me that desire.[169]

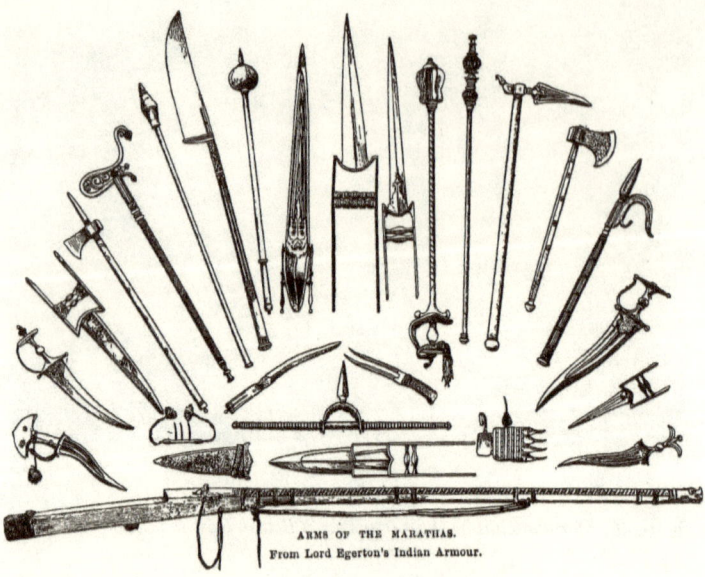

Figure 47: *Arms of Maratha*

European accounts

Similarly, the Duke of Wellington, after defeating the Marathas, noted that the Marathas, though poorly led by their Generals, had regular infantry and artillery that matched the level of that of the Europeans and warned other British officers from underestimating the Marathas on the battlefield. He cautioned one British general that: "You must never allow Maratha infantry to attack head on or in close hand to hand combat as in that your army will cover itself with utter disgrace". Even when Arthur Wellesley, 1st Duke of Wellington, became the Prime Minister of Britain, he held the Maratha infantry in utmost respect, claiming it to be one of the best in the world. However, at the same time he noted the poor leadership of Maratha Generals, who were often responsible for their defeats. Charles Metcalfe, one of the ablest of the British Officials in India and later acting Governor-General, wrote in 1806:

> India contains no more than two great powers, British and Mahratta, and every other state acknowledges the influence of one or the other. Every inch that we recede will be occupied by them.

Norman Gash says that the Maratha infantry was equal to that of British infantry. After the Third Anglo-Maratha war in 1818, Britain listed the Marathas as one of the Martial Races to serve in the British Indian Army.

Figure 48: *Sadashivrao Bhau (centre)*

The 19th century diplomat Sir Justin Sheil commented about the British East India Company copying the French Indian army in raising an army of Indians:

It is to the military genius of the French that we are indebted for the formation of the Indian army. Our warlike neighbours were the first to introduce into India the system of drilling native troops and converting them into a regularly disciplined force. Their example was copied by us, and the result is what we now behold.

The French carried to Persia the same military and administrative faculties, and established the origin of the present Persian regular army, as it is styled. When Napoleon the Great resolved to take Iran under his auspices, he dispatched several officers of superior intelligence to that country with the mission of General Gardanne in 1808. Those gentlemen commenced their operations in the provinces of Azerbaijan and Kermanshah, and it is said with considerable success.

—*Sir Justin Sheil (1803–1871).*[170]

Notable generals and administrators

Ramchandra Pant Amatya Bawdekar

Ramchandra Pant Amatya Bawdekar was a court administrator who rose from the ranks of a local Kulkarni to the ranks of Ashtapradhan under guidance and support of Shivaji. He was one of the prominent Peshwas from the time of Shivaji, prior to the rise of the later Peshwas who controlled the empire after Shahuji.[171]

When Rajaram fled to Jinji in 1689 leaving Maratha Empire, he gave a *Hukumat Panha* (King Status) to Pant before leaving. Ramchandra Pant managed the entire state under many challenges like influx of Mughals, betrayal from Vatandars (local satraps under the Maratha state) and social challenges like scarcity of food. With the help of Pantpratinidhi, Sachiv, he kept the economic condition of Maratha Empire in an appropriate state.

He received military help from the Maratha commanders – Santaji Ghorpade and Dhanaji Jadhav. On many occasions he himself participated in battles against Mughals.Wikipedia:Citation needed

In 1698, he stepped down from the post of *Hukumat Panha* when Rajaram offered this post to his wife, Tarabai. Tarabai gave an important position to Pant among senior administrators of Maratha State. He wrote Adnyapatra (मराठी: आज्ञापत्र) in which he has explained different techniques of war, maintenance of forts and administration etc. But owing to his loyalty to Tarabai against Shahuji (who was supported by more local satraps), he was sidelined after arrival of Shahuji in 1707.Wikipedia:Citation needed

Nana Phadnavis

Nana Phadnavis was an influential minister and statesman of the Maratha Empire during the Peshwa administration.After the assassination of Peshwa Narayanrao in 1773, Nana Phadnavis managed the affairs of the state with the help of a twelve-member regency council known as the Barbhai council and he remained the chief strategist of Maratha state till his death in 1800 AD.[172] Nana Phadnavis played a pivotal role in holding the Maratha Confederacy together in the midst of internal dissension and the growing power of British. Nana's administrative, diplomatic and financial skills brought prosperity to the Maratha Empire and his management of external affairs kept the Maratha Empire away from the thrust of the British East India Company.

Rulers, administrators and generals

Royal houses

- Shivaji (1630–1680)
- Sambhaji (1657–1689)
- Rajaram Chhatrapati (1670–1700)

Satara:

- Chhattrapati Shahu (r. 1708–1749) (alias Shivaji II, son of Chhatrapati Sambhaji)
- Ramaraja II (nominally, grandson of Chhatrapati Rajaram and Queen Tarabai) (r. 1749–1777)
- Shahu II (r. 1777–1808)
- Pratap Singh (r. 1808–1839) – signed a treaty with the East India company ceding part of sovereignty to the company

Kolhapur:

- Tarabai (1675–1761) (wife of Chhatrapati Rajaram) in the name of her son Shivaji II
- Shivaji II (1700–1714)
- Sambhaji II (1714 to 1760) – came to power by deposing his half brother Shivaji II
- Shivaji III (1760–1812) (adopted from the family of Khanwilkar)

Peshwas

- Moropant Trimbak Pingle (1657–1683)
- Nilakanth Moreshvar Pingale (1683-1689)
- Ramchandra Pant Amatya (1689-1708)
- Bahiroji Pingale (1708–1711)

Peshwas from Bhat family

From Balaji Vishwanath onwards, actual power gradually shifted to the Bhat family Peshwas based in Pune.

- Balaji Vishwanath (1713–1720)
- Bajirao (1720–1740)
- Balaji Bajirao (4 Jul. 1740-23 Jun. 1761) (b. 8 Dec. 1721, d. 23 Jun. 1761)
- Madhavrao Peshwa (1761–18 Nov.1772) (b. 16 Feb. 1745, d. 18 Nov. 1772)
- Narayanrao Bajirao (13 Dec. 1772–30 Aug.1773) (b. 10 Aug. 1755, d. 30 Aug. 1773)

- Raghunathrao (5 Dec. 1773–1774) (b. 18 Aug. 1734, d. 11 Dec. 1783)
- Sawai Madhava Rao II Narayan (1774–27 Oct. 1795) (b. 18 Apr. 1774, d. 27 Oct. 1795)
- Baji Rao II (6 Dec. 1796 – 3 Jun.1818) (d. 28 Jan. 1851)

Houses of Maratha Confederacy

- Holkars of Indore
- Scindias of Gwalior
- Gaikwads of Baroda
- Bhonsales of Nagpur
- Puars of Dewas and Dhar
- Patwardhans

Maps showing the Maratha Empire at different stages of history

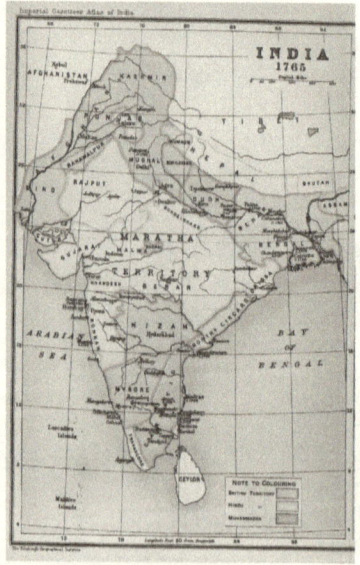

Figure 49: *Maratha Empire in 1765 (yellow)*

Figure 50: *Thanjavur Maratha palace*

Thanjavur Maratha Kingdom (Tamil Nadu)

The Thanjavur Marathas were the rulers of Thanjavur principality of Tamil Nadu between the 17th and 19th centuries. Their native language was Thanjavur Marathi. Venkoji, Shahaji's son and Shivaji's half brother, was the founder of the dynasty.[173]

List of rulers of Thanjavur Maratha dynasty :

- Venkoji
- Shahuji I of Thanjavur
- Serfoji I
- Tukkoji
- Pratapsingh of Thanjavur
- Thuljaji
- Serfoji II
- Shivaji II of Thanjavur

Bibliography

<templatestyles src="Template:Refbegin/styles.css" />

- Beck, Sanderson. *India & Southeast Asia to 1800* (2006) "Marathas and the English Company 1701–1818" online[174]. Retrieved Oct. 1, 2004.

- Gordon, Stewart. *Marathas, marauders, and state formation in eighteenth-century India* (Oxford University Press, 1994).
- Gordon, Stewart. "The Marathas," in *New Cambridge History of India*, vol II. ch 4, (Cambridge U Press, 1993).
- Kumar, Ravinder. *Western India in the nineteenth century* (Routledge, 2013).
- Laine, James W. *Shivaji: Hindu King in Islamic India* (New York, 2003).
- McEldowney, Philip F (1966), *Pindari Society and the Establishment of British Paramountcy in India*[175], Madison: University of Wisconsin, OCLC 53790277[176]
- Mehta, J. L (2005), *Advanced Study in the History of Modern India 1707–1813*[177], **II**, Sterling Publishers Pvt. Ltd, ISBN 978-1-932705-54-6
- Moon, Penderel. *The British Conquest and Dominion of India: Part One 1745-1857* (1989).
- Roy, Tirthankar. "Rethinking the origins of British India: state formation and military-fiscal undertakings in an eighteenth century world region." *Modern Asian Studies* 47.4 (2013): 1125+ online[178]
- Majumdar, R. C. (1991). The history and culture of the Indian people: V. 8. Bombay: Bharatiya Vidya Bhavan.
- Sardesai, Govind Sakharam. *New history of the Marathas, vol. I: Shivaji and his line, 1600–1707* (Phoenix publications, 1946).
- Sen, Sailendra Nath (1994), *Anglo-Maratha Relations, 1785–96*[179], Volume 2 of Anglo-Maratha Relations, Sailendra Nath Sen, Bombay: Popular Prakashan, ISBN 978-81-7154-789-0
- Sen, S.N. *History Modern India* (3rd ed. 2006) online[180]
- Seshan, Radhika. "The Maratha State: Some Preliminary Considerations." *Indian Historical Review* 41.1 (2014): 35–46. online[181]
- Wink, Andre. *Land and Sovereignty in India: Agrarian Society and Politics under the Eighteenth Century Maratha Swarajya*, (Cambridge UP, 1986).
- Bombay University – *Maratha History – Seminar Volume*
- Samant, S. D. – *Vedh Mahamanavacha*
- Kasar, D.B. – *Rigveda to Raigarh making of Shivaji the great*, Mumbai: Manudevi Prakashan (2005)
- Apte, B.K. (editor) – *Chhatrapati Shivaji: Coronation Tercentenary Commemoration Volume, Bombay: University of Bombay* (1974–75)
- Desai, Ranjeet – *Shivaji the Great, Janata Raja* (1968), Pune: Balwant Printers – English Translation of popular Marathi book.
- Pagdi, Setu Madhavrao – *Hindavi Swaraj Aani Moghul* (1984), Girgaon Book Depot, Marathi book
- Deshpande, S.R. – *Marathyanchi Manaswini*, Lalit Publications, Marathi book

- Bakshi, S.R; Ralhan, O.P. (2007), *Madhya Pradesh Through the Ages*[182], New Delhi: Sarup & Sons, ISBN 978-81-7625-806-7
- Black, Jeremy (2006), *A Military History of Britain: from 1775 to the Present*[183], Westport, Conn.: Greenwood Publishing Group, ISBN 978-0-275-99039-8
- Chhabra, G.S. (2005), *Advance Study in the History of Modern India*[184], Volume 1: 1707–1803, New Delhi: Lotus Press, ISBN 81-89093-06-1
- Government of Maharashtra (1961), *Land Acquisition Act*[185] (PDF), Bombay
- Kulkarni, Sumitra (1995), *The Satara Raj, 1818–1848: A Study in History, Administration, and Culture*[186], New Delhi: Mittal Publications, ISBN 978-81-7099-581-4
- McDonald, Ellen E. (1968), *The Modernizing of Communication: Vernacular Publishing in Nineteenth Century Maharashtra*, Berkeley: University of California Press, OCLC 483944794[187]
- Nadkarni, Dnyaneshwar (2000), *Husain: Riding The Lightning*[188], Bombay: Popular Prakashan, ISBN 81-7154-676-5
- Naravane, M.S (2006), *Battles of the Honourable East India Company: Making of the Raj*[189], New Delhi: APH Publishing, pp. 78–105, ISBN 978-81-313-0034-3
- Prakash, Om (2002), *Encyclopaedic History of Indian Freedom Movement*[190], New Delhi: Anmol Publications Pvt. Ltd., ISBN 978-81-261-0938-8
- Ramusack, Barbara N. (2004), *The Indian Princes and their States*[191], The New Cambridge History of India, Cambridge University Press, ISBN 978-1-139-44908-3
- Rathod, N. G. (1994), *The Great Maratha Mahadaji Scindia*[192]
- Rao, S. Venugopala (1977), *Power and Criminality: a Survey of Famous Crimes in Indian History*[193], Bombay: Allied Publishers, OCLC 4076888[194]
- Sarkar, Sumit; Pati, Biswamoy (2000), Biswamoy Pati, ed., *Issues in Modern Indian History: for Sumit Sarkar*[195], Mumbai: Popular Prakashan, ISBN 978-81-7154-658-9
- Schmidt, Karl J. (1995), *An Atlas and Survey of South Asian History*[196], Armonk, N.Y.: M.E. Sharpe, ISBN 978-1-56324-334-9
- United States Court of Customs and Patent Appeals (1930), *Court of Customs and Patent Appeals Reports*[197], **18**, Washington: Supreme Court of the United States, OCLC 2590161[198]
- Suryanath U. Kamath (2001). A Concise History of Karnataka from prehistoric times to the present, Jupiter books, MCC, Bangalore (Reprinted 2002), OCLC: 7796041.

Company rule in India

Company rule in India	
Joint-stock colony established by the East India Company and regulated by the British Parliament.	
1757–1858	
 Flag Coat of arms	
Motto *Auspicio Regis et Senatus Angliae* "By command of the King and Parliament of England"	
Capital	Calcutta (1757–1858)
Languages	English, and others
Government	Corporatocracy
Governor-General	
• 1774–75	Warren Hastings (first)
• 1857–58	Charles Canning (last)
History	
• Battle of Plassey	23 June 1757
• Treaty of Allahabad	16 August 1765
• Treaty of Seringapatam	18 March 1792
• Treaty of Bassein	31 December 1802
• Treaty of Yandabo	24 February 1826
• Treaty of Lahore	9 March 1846
• Treaty of Lahore	29 March 1849
• Government of India Act	2 August 1858

Company rule in India

Area		
•	1858	1,942,481 km² (749,996 sq mi)
Currency		Rupee

	Preceded by	Succeeded by	
	Maratha Empire		
	Mughal Empire	British Raj	
	Kingdom of Mysore	Straits Settlements	
	Sikh Empire		

Today part of	
	• Bahrain
	• Bangladesh
	• China
	• Christmas Island
	• Cocos (Keeling) Islands
	• India
	• Kuwait
	• Malaysia
	• Maldives
	• Myanmar
	• Nepal (Banke, Bardiya, Kailali and Kanchanpur)[199]
	• Oman
	• Pakistan
	• Qatar
	• Saudi Arabia (nominal)
	• Singapore
	• Somalia
	• Sri Lanka
	• United Arab Emirates
	• Yemen

Part of a series on the
History of India

- v
- t
- e[200]

Colonial India

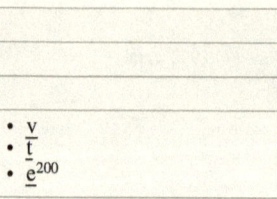

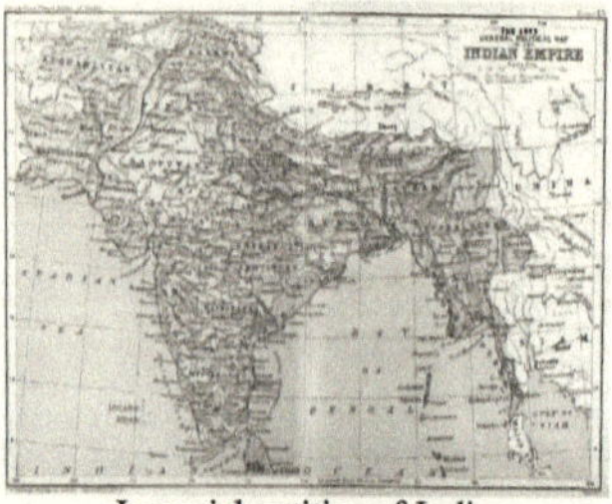

Imperial entities of India

Dutch India	1605–1825
Danish India	1620–1869
French India	1668–1954

Portuguese India (1505–1961)	
Casa da Índia	1434–1833
Portuguese East India Company	1628–1633

British India (1612–1947)	
East India Company	1612–1757
Company rule in India	1757–1858
British Raj	1858–1947
British rule in Burma	1824–1948
Princely states	1721–1949
Partition of India	1947

- v
- t
- e[201]

Company rule in India (sometimes, **Company Raj**,[202] "*raj*", lit. "rule" in Hindi[203]) refers to the rule or dominion of the British East India Company over parts of the Indian subcontinent. This is variously taken to have commenced in 1757, after the Battle of Plassey, when Mir Jafar, the new Nawab of Bengal enthroned by Robert Clive, became a puppet in the Company's hands;[204,205] in 1765, when the Company was granted the *diwani*, or the right to collect revenue, in Bengal and Bihar; or in 1773, when the Company established a capital in Calcutta, appointed its first Governor-General, Warren Hastings, and became directly involved in governance, By 1818, with the defeat of the Marathas, followed by the pensioning of the Peshwa and the annexation of his territories, British supremacy in India was complete.

The East India Company was a private company owned by stockholders and reporting to a board of directors in London. Originally formed as a monopoly on trade, it increasingly took on governmental powers with its own army and judiciary. It seldom turned a profit, as employees diverted funds into their own pockets. The British government had little control, and there was increasing anger at the corruption and irresponsibility of Company officials or "nabobs" who made vast fortunes in a few years. Pitt's India Act of 1784 gave the British government effective control of the private company for the first time. The new policies were designed for an elite civil service career that minimized temptations for corruption. Increasingly Company officials lived in separate compounds according to British standards. The Company's rule lasted until 1858, when, after the Indian rebellion of 1857, it was abolished. With the Government of India Act 1858, the British government assumed the task of directly administering India in the new British Raj.

Origins

The English East India Company ("the Company") was founded in 1600, as *The Company of Merchants of London Trading into the East Indies*. It gained a foothold in India with the establishment of a factory in Masulipatnam on the Eastern coast of India in 1611 and the grant of the rights to establish a factory in Surat in 1612 by the Mughal emperor Jahangir. In 1640, after receiving similar permission from the Vijayanagara ruler farther south, a second factory was established in Madras on the southeastern coast. Bombay island, not far from Surat, a former Portuguese outpost gifted to England as dowry in the marriage of Catherine of Braganza to Charles II, was leased by the Company in 1668. Two decades later, the Company established a presence on the eastern coast as well; far up that coast, in the Ganges river delta, a factory was set up in Calcutta. Since, during this time other *companies*—established by the Portuguese, Dutch, French, and Danish—were similarly expanding in the region, the English Company's unremarkable beginnings on coastal India offered no clues to what would become a lengthy presence on the Indian subcontinent.

The Company's victory under Robert Clive in the 1757 Battle of Plassey and another victory in the 1764 Battle of Buxar (in Bihar), consolidated the Company's power, and forced emperor Shah Alam II to appoint it the *diwan*, or revenue collector, of Bengal, Bihar, and Orissa. The Company thus became the de facto ruler of large areas of the lower Gangetic plain by 1773. It also proceeded by degrees to expand its dominions around Bombay and Madras. The Anglo-Mysore Wars (1766–99) and the Anglo-Maratha Wars (1772–1818) left it in control of large areas of India south of the Sutlej River. With the defeat of the Marathas, no native power represented a threat for the Company any longer.

The expansion of the Company's power chiefly took two forms. The first of these was the outright annexation of Indian states and subsequent direct governance of the underlying regions, which collectively came to comprise British India. The annexed regions included the North-Western Provinces (comprising Rohilkhand, Gorakhpur, and the Doab) (1801), Delhi (1803), Assam (Ahom Kingdom 1828), and Sindh (1843). Punjab, North-West Frontier Province, and Kashmir, were annexed after the Anglo-Sikh Wars in 1849–56 (Period of tenure of Marquess of Dalhousie Governor General); however, Kashmir was immediately sold under the Treaty of Amritsar (1850) to the Dogra Dynasty of Jammu, and thereby became a princely state. In 1854 Berar was annexed, and the state of Oudh two years later.

The second form of asserting power involved treaties in which Indian rulers acknowledged the Company's hegemony in return for limited internal autonomy. Since the Company operated under financial constraints, it had to set up *political* underpinnings for its rule. The most important such support came from the *subsidiary alliances* with Indian princes during the first 75 years of Company rule. In the early 19th century, the territories of these princes accounted for two-thirds of India. When an Indian ruler, who was able to secure his territory, wanted to enter such an alliance, the Company welcomed it as an economical method of indirect rule, which did not involve the economic costs of direct administration or the political costs of gaining the support of alien subjects.

In return, the Company undertook the "defense of these subordinate allies and treated them with traditional respect and marks of honor." Subsidiary alliances created the princely states, of the Hindu maharajas and the Muslim nawabs. Prominent among the princely states were: Cochin (1791), Jaipur (1794), Travancore (1795), Hyderabad (1798), Mysore (1799), Cis-Sutlej Hill States (1815), Central India Agency (1819), Cutch and Gujarat Gaikwad territories (1819), Rajputana (1818), and Bahawalpur (1833).

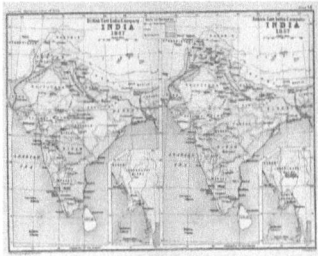

Expansion

The area encompassed by modern India was significantly fractured following the decline of the Mughal Empire in the first half of the 18th century[206]

Chronology

- 1757: 24 Parganas of the Sundarbans annexed to Clive after the Battle of Plassey.
- 1760: Northern Circars annexed.
- 1765: Nawabs of Bengal and Murshidabad (and Bihar) annexed after the Battle of Buxar.
- 1773: Raja of Banares annexed.
- 1775: Nawab of Ghazipur annexed.
- 1795: Asaf Jah II the Nizam of Hyderabad was defeated at the Battle of Kharda,[207] after the Maratha-Mysore War.
- 1799: Fall of Mysore after Siege of Seringapatam (1799); Nawab of Kadapa and Nawab of Kurnool annexed.
- 1801: Nawab of the Carnatic (of Arcot and Nellore), Nawab of Junagarh, and Rohilkhand of Lower Doab annexed.
- 1803: Rohilkhand of Upper Doab annexed; nonresistance from the Emperor; Nawab of Bhawalpur accepts borders with British India.

India in 1765 and 1805 showing East India Company Territories in pink.

India in 1837 and 1857 showing East India Company (pink) and other territories

The Governors-General

(The Governors-General (locum tenens) are not included in this table unless a major event occurred during their tenure.)

Governor-General	Period of Tenure	Events
Warren Hastings	20 October 1773 – 1 February 1785	Bengal famine of 1770 (1769–73) Rohilla War (1773–74) First Anglo-Maratha War (1777–83) *Chalisa* famine (1783–84) Second Anglo-Mysore War (1780–1784)
Charles Cornwallis	12 September 1786 – 28 October 1793	Cornwallis Code (1793) Permanent Settlement Cochin become semi-protected States under British (1791) Third Anglo-Mysore War (1789–92) *Doji bara* famine (1791–92)
John Shore	28 October 1793 – March 1798	East India Company Army re-organised and down-sized. First Pazhassi Revolt in Malabar(1793–97) Jaipur (1794) & Travancore (1795) come under British protection. Andaman Islands occupied (1796) Company took control of coastal region Ceylon from Dutch (1796).
Richard Wellesley	18 May 1798 – 30 July 1805	Nizam of Hyderabad becomes first State to sign Subsidiary alliance introduced by Wellesley (1798). Fourth Anglo-Mysore War (1798–99) Second Pazhassi Revolt in Malabar(1800–1805) Nawab of Oudh cedes Gorakhpur and Rohilkhand divisions; Allahabad, Fatehpur, Cawnpore, Etawah, Mainpuri, Etah districts; part of Mirzapur; and *terai* of Kumaun (*Ceded Provinces*, 1801) Treaty of Bassein signed by Peshwa Baji Rao II accepting Subsidiary Alliance Battle of Delhi (1803). Second Anglo-Maratha War (1803–05) Remainder of Doab, Delhi and Agra division, parts of Bundelkhand annexed from Maratha Empire (1805). Ceded and Conquered Provinces established (1805)
Charles Cornwallis (second term)	30 July 1805 – 5 October 1805	Financial strain in East India Company after costly campaigns. Cornwallis reappointed to bring peace, but dies in Ghazipur.
George Hilario Barlow (locum tenens)	10 October 1805 – 31 July 1807	Vellore Mutiny (10 July 1806)
Lord Minto	31 July 1807 – 4 October 1813	Invasion of Java Occupation of Mauritius

Company rule in India

Marquess of Hastings	4 October 1813 – 9 January 1823	Anglo-Nepal War of 1814 Annexation of Kumaon, Garhwal, and east Sikkim. Cis-Sutlej states (1815). Third Anglo-Maratha War (1817–18) States of Rajputana accept British suzerainty (1817). Singapore was founded (1818). Cutch accepts British suzerainty (1818). Gaikwads of Baroda accept British suzerainty (1819). Central India Agency (1819).
Lord Amherst	1 August 1823 – 13 March 1828	First Anglo–Burmese War (1823–26) Annexation of Assam, Manipur, Arakan, and Tenasserim from Burma
William Bentinck	4 July 1828 – 20 March 1835	Bengal Sati Regulation, 1829 Thuggee and Dacoity Suppression Acts, 1836–48 Mysore State goes under British administration (1831–81) Bahawalpur accepts British Suzerainty (1833) Coorg annexed (1834).
Lord Auckland	4 March 1836 – 28 February 1842	North-Western Provinces established (1836) Post Offices were established (1837) Agra famine of 1837–38 Aden is captured by Company (1839) First Anglo-Afghan War (1839–1842) Massacre of Elphinstone's army (1842).
Lord Ellenborough	28 February 1842 – June 1844	First Anglo-Afghan War (1839–42) Annexation of Sindh (1843) Indian Slavery Act, 1843
Henry Hardinge	23 July 1844 – 12 January 1848	First Anglo-Sikh War (1845–46) Sikhs cede Jullundur Doab, Hazara, and Kashmir to the British under Treaty of Lahore (1846) Sale of Kashmir to Gulab Singh of Jammu under Treaty of Amritsar (1846).
Marquess of Dalhousie	12 January 1848 – 28 February 1856	Second Anglo-Sikh War (1848–1849) Annexation of Punjab and North-West Frontier Province (1849–56) Construction begins on Indian Railways (1850) Caste Disabilities Removal Act, 1850 First telegraph line laid in India (1851) Second Anglo-Burmese War (1852–53) Annexation of Lower Burma Ganges Canal opened (1854) Annexation of Satara (1848), Jaipur and Sambalpur (1849), Nagpur and Jhansi (1854) under Doctrine of Lapse. Annexation of Berar (1853) and Awadh (1856). Postage Stamps for India were introduced. (1854). Public Telegram services starts operation (1855).
Charles Canning	28 February 1856 – 1 November 1858	Hindu Widows Remarriage Act (25 July 1856) First Indian universities founded (January–September 1857) Indian Rebellion of 1857 (10 May 1857 – 20 June 1858) largely in North-Western Provinces and Oudh Liquidation of the English East India Company under Government of India Act 1858

Regulation of Company rule

A view of Calcutta from Fort William, 1807.

Government House, Fort St. George, Madras, the headquarters of the Madras Presidency.

Warren Hastings, the first Governor-General of Fort William (Bengal) who oversaw the Company's territories in India.

The trial of Warren Hastings in the Court of Westminster Hall, 1789.

Until Clive's victory at Plassey, the East India Company territories in India, which consisted largely of the presidency towns of Calcutta, Madras, and Bombay, were governed by the mostly autonomous—and sporadically unmanageable—*town councils*, all composed of merchants. The councils barely had enough powers for the effective management of their local affairs, and the ensuing lack of oversight of the overall Company operations in India led to some grave abuses by Company officers or their allies. Clive's victory, and the

Company rule in India

Figure 51: *Robert Clive*

award of the *diwani* of the rich region of Bengal, brought India into the public spotlight in Britain. The Company's money management practices came to be questioned, especially as it began to post net losses even as some Company servants, the "Nabobs," returned to Britain with large fortunes, which—according to rumours then current—were acquired unscrupulously.[208] By 1772, the Company needed British government loans to stay afloat, and there was fear in London that the Company's corrupt practices could soon seep into British business and public life. The rights and duties of the British government with regards the Company's new territories came also to be examined. The British parliament then held several inquiries and in 1773, during the premiership of Lord North, enacted the *Regulating Act*, which established regulations, its long title stated, "for the better Management of the Affairs of the *East India Company*, as well in *India* as in *Europe*"

Although Lord North himself wanted the Company's territories to be taken over by the British state, he faced determined political opposition from many quarters, including some in the City of London and the British parliament. The result was a compromise in which the Regulating Act—although implying the ultimate sovereignty of the British Crown over these new territories—asserted that the Company could act as a sovereign power on behalf of the Crown. It could do this while concurrently being subject to oversight and regulation by the British government and parliament. The Court of Directors of the Company were required under the Act to submit all communications regarding civil, military, and revenue matters in India for scrutiny by the British government. For the governance of the Indian territories, the act asserted the supremacy of the Presidency of Fort William (Bengal) over those of Fort St. George (Madras) and Bombay. It also nominated a Governor-General (Warren Hastings) and four councillors for administering the Bengal Presidency (and for overseeing the Company's operations in India). "The subordinate Presidencies were forbidden to wage war or make treaties without the previous consent of the Governor-General of Bengal in Council,[209] except in case of imminent necessity. The Governors of these Presidencies were directed in general terms to obey the orders of the Governor-General-in-Council, and to transmit to him intelligence of all important matters." However, the imprecise wording of the Act, left it open to be variously interpreted; consequently, the administration in India continued to be hobbled by disunity between the provincial governors, between members of the Council, and between the Governor-General himself and his Council. The *Regulating Act* also attempted to address the prevalent corruption in India: Company servants were henceforth forbidden to engage in private trade in India or to receive "presents" from Indian nationals.

William Pitt's India Act of 1784 established a Board of Control in England both to supervise the East India Company's affairs and to prevent the Company's shareholders from interfering in the governance of India. The Board of Control consisted of six members, which included one Secretary of State from the British cabinet, as well as the Chancellor of the Exchequer. Around this time, there was also extensive debate in the British Parliament on the issue of landed rights in Bengal, with a consensus developing in support of the view advocated by Philip Francis, a member of the Bengal council and political adversary of Warren Hastings, that all lands in Bengal should be considered the "estate and inheritance of native land-holders and families ..."[210]

Mindful of the reports of abuse and corruption in Bengal by Company servants, the India Act itself noted numerous complaints that "'divers Rajahs, Zemindars, Polygars, Talookdars, and landholders'" had been unjustly deprived of 'their lands, jurisdictions, rights, and privileges'." At the same time the Company's directors were now leaning towards Francis's view that the land-tax in Bengal should be made fixed and permanent, setting the stage for the Permanent Settlement (see section Revenue settlements under the Company below).

The India Act also created in each of the three presidencies a number of administrative and military posts, which included: a Governor and three Councilors, one of which was the Commander in Chief of the Presidency army. Although the supervisory powers of the Governor-General-in-Council in Bengal (over Madras and Bombay) were extended—as they were again in the Charter Act of 1793—the subordinate presidencies continued to exercise some autonomy until both the extension of British possessions into becoming contiguous and the advent of faster communications in the next century.

Still, the new Governor-General appointed in 1786, Lord Cornwallis, not only had more power than Hastings, but also had the support of a powerful British cabinet minister, Henry Dundas, who, as Secretary of State for the Home Office, was in charge of the overall India policy. From 1784 onwards, the British government had the final word on all major appointments in India; a candidate's suitability for a senior position was often decided by the strength of his political connections rather than that of his administrative ability. Although this practice resulted in many Governor-General nominees being chosen from Britain's conservative landed gentry, there were some liberals as well, such as Lord William Bentinck and Lord Dalhousie.

British political opinion was also shaped by the attempted Impeachment of Warren Hastings; the trial, whose proceedings began in 1788, ended with Hastings' acquittal, in 1795. Although the effort was chiefly coordinated by Edmund Burke, it also drew support from within the British government. Burke accused Hastings not only of corruption, but—appealing to universal standards of justice—also of acting solely upon his own discretion, without concern for law, and of wilfully causing distress to others in India. Hastings' defenders countered that his actions were consistent with Indian customs and traditions. Although Burke's speeches at the trial drew applause and focused attention on India, Hastings was eventually acquitted, due in part to the revival of nationalism in Britain in the wake of the French Revolution. Nonetheless, Burke's effort had the effect of creating a sense of responsibility in British public life for the Company's dominion in India.

Soon rumblings appeared amongst merchants in London that the monopoly granted to the East India Company in 1600, intended to facilitate its competition against Dutch and French in a distant region, was no longer needed. In response, in the Charter Act of 1813, the British Parliament renewed the Company's charter but terminated its monopoly except with regard to tea and trade with China, opening India both to private investment and missionaries. With increased British power in India, supervision of Indian affairs by the British Crown and Parliament increased as well. By the 1820s British nationals could transact business or engage in missionary work under the protection of the

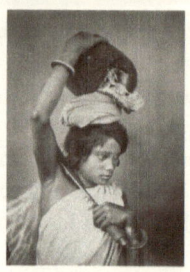

Crown in the three presidencies. Finally, under the terms of The Saint Helena Act 1833, the British Parliament revoked the Company's monopoly in the China trade and made it an agent for the administration of British India. The Governor-General of Bengal was redesignated as the Governor-General of India. The Governor-General and his executive council were given exclusive legislative powers for the whole of British India. Since the British territories in north India had now extended up to Delhi, the Act also sanctioned the creation of a Presidency of Agra. With the annexation of Oudh in 1856, this territory was extended and eventually became the United Provinces of Agra and Oudh. In addition, in 1854, a Lieutenant-Governor was appointed for the region of Bengal, Bihar and Odisha, leaving the Governor-General to concentrate on the governance of India as a whole.

Revenue collection

A riverside scene in rural east Bengal (present-day Bangladesh), 1860.

A Kochh Mandai woman of east Bengal (now Bangladesh) with an agricultural knife and a freshly harvested jackfruit. (1860)

Paddy fields in the Madras Presidency, ca. 1880. Two-thirds of the presidency fell under the *Ryotwari* system.

An East India Company half anna coin.

In the remnant of the Mughal Empire revenue system existing in pre-1765 Bengal, zamindars, or "land holders," collected revenue on behalf of the Mughal

Company rule in India

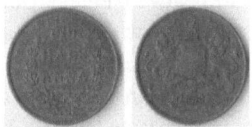

emperor, whose representative, or *diwan* supervised their activities. In this system, the assortment of rights associated with land were not possessed by a "land owner," but rather shared by the several parties with stake in the land, including the peasant cultivator, the *zamindar*, and the state. The *zamindar* served as an intermediary who procured economic rent from the cultivator, and after withholding a percentage for his own expenses, made available the rest, as revenue to the state. Under the Mughal system, the land itself belonged to the state and not to the *zamindar*, who could transfer only his right to collect rent. On being awarded the *diwani* or overlordship of Bengal following the Battle of Buxar in 1764, the East India Company found itself short of trained administrators, especially those familiar with local custom and law; tax collection was consequently farmed out. This uncertain foray into land taxation by the Company, may have gravely worsened the impact of a famine that struck Bengal in 1769-70, in which between seven and ten million people—or between a quarter and third of the presidency's population—may have died. However, the company provided little relief either through reduced taxation or by relief efforts, and the economic and cultural impact of the famine was felt decades later, even becoming, a century later, the subject of Bankim Chandra Chatterjee's novel *Anandamath*.

In 1772, under Warren Hastings, the East India Company took over revenue collection directly in the Bengal Presidency (then Bengal and Bihar), establishing a Board of Revenue with offices in Calcutta and Patna, and moving the pre-existing Mughal revenue records from Murshidabad to Calcutta. In 1773, after Oudh ceded the tributary state of Benaras, the revenue collection system was extended to the territory with a Company Resident in charge. The following year—with a view to preventing corruption—Company *district collectors*, who were then responsible for revenue collection for an entire district, were replaced with provincial councils at Patna, Murshidabad, and Calcutta, and with

Indian collectors working within each district. The title, "collector," reflected "the centrality of land revenue collection to government in India: it was the government's primary function and it moulded the institutions and patterns of administration."

The Company inherited a revenue collection system from the Mughals in which the heaviest proportion of the tax burden fell on the cultivators, with one-third of the production reserved for imperial entitlement; this pre-colonial system became the Company revenue policy's baseline. However, there was vast variation across India in the methods by which the revenues were collected; with this complication in mind, a Committee of Circuit toured the districts of expanded Bengal Presidency in order to make a five-year settlement, consisting of five-yearly inspections and temporary tax farming. In their overall approach to revenue policy, Company officials were guided by two goals: first, preserving as much as possible the balance of rights and obligations that were traditionally claimed by the farmers who cultivated the land and the various intermediaries who collected tax on the state's behalf and who reserved a cut for themselves; and second, identifying those sectors of the rural economy that would maximise both revenue and security. Although their first revenue settlement turned out to be essentially the same as the more informal pre-existing Mughal one, the Company had created a foundation for the growth of both information and bureaucracy.

In 1793, the new Governor-General, Lord Cornwallis, promulgated the permanent settlement of land revenues in the presidency, the first socio-economic regulation in colonial India. By the terms of the settlement Rajas and Taluqdars were recognised as Zamindars and they were asked to collect the rent from the peasants and pay revenue to the Company. It was named *permanent* because it fixed the land tax in perpetuity in return for landed property rights for zamindars; it simultaneously defined the nature of land ownership in the presidency, and gave individuals and families separate property rights in occupied land. Since the revenue was fixed in perpetuity, it was fixed at a high level, which in Bengal amounted to £3 million at 1789-90 prices. According to the Permanent Settlement if the Zamindars failed to pay the revenue on time, the Zmaindari right would be taken from them. According to one estimate, this was 20% higher than the revenue demand before 1757. Over the next century, partly as a result of land surveys, court rulings, and property sales, the change was given practical dimension. An influence on the development of this revenue policy were the economic theories then current, which regarded agriculture as the engine of economic development, and consequently stressed the fixing of revenue demands in order to encourage growth. The expectation behind the permanent settlement was that knowledge of a fixed government demand would encourage the zamindars to increase both their average outcrop and the

Figure 52: *Charles Cornwallis, he was the Governor-General of India when Permanent Settlement was introduced.*

land under cultivation, since they would be able to retain the profits from the increased output; in addition, it was envisaged that land itself would become a marketable form of property that could be purchased, sold, or mortgaged. A feature of this economic rationale was the additional expectation that the zamindars, recognising their own best interest, would not make unreasonable demands on the peasantry.

However, these expectations were not realised in practice, and in many regions of Bengal, the peasants bore the brunt of the increased demand, there being little protection for their traditional rights in the new legislation. Forced labour of the peasants by the zamindars became more prevalent as cash crops were cultivated to meet the Company revenue demands. Although commercialised cultivation was not new to the region, it had now penetrated deeper into village society and made it more vulnerable to market forces. The zamindars themselves were often unable to meet the increased demands that the Company had placed on them; consequently, many defaulted, and by one estimate, up to one-third of their lands were auctioned during the first three decades following the permanent settlement. The new owners were often Brahmin and Kayastha employees of the Company who had a good grasp of the new system, and, in many cases, some had prospered under it.

Figure 53: *Thomas Munro, Governor of Madras*

Since the zamindars were never able to undertake costly improvements to the land envisaged under the Permanent Settlement, some of which required the removal of the existing farmers, they soon became rentiers who lived off the rent from their tenant farmers. In many areas, especially northern Bengal, they had to increasingly share the revenue with intermediate tenure holders, called *jotedars*, who supervised farming in the villages. Consequently, unlike the contemporaneous Enclosure movement in Britain, agriculture in Bengal remained the province of the subsistence farming of innumerable small paddy fields.

The zamindari system was one of two principal revenue settlements undertaken by the Company in India. In southern India, Thomas Munro, who would later become Governor of Madras, promoted the *ryotwari* system or the Munro system, in which the government settled land-revenue directly with the peasant farmers, or *ryots*. It was first tried in small scale by Captain Alexander Read in the areas that were taken over from the wars with Tipu Sultan. Subsequently, developed by Thomas Munro, this system was gradually extended all over South India. This was, in part, a consequence of the turmoil of the Anglo-Mysore Wars, which had prevented the emergence of a class of large landowners; in addition, Munro and others felt that *ryotwari* was closer to traditional practice in the region and ideologically more progressive, allowing the benefits of Company rule to reach the lowest levels of rural society. At the heart of the *ryotwari* system was a particular theory of economic rent—and based on David Ricardo's Law of Rent—promoted by utilitarian James Mill who formulated the Indian revenue policy between 1819 and 1830. "He believed that the government was the ultimate lord of the soil and should not renounce its right to 'rent', *i.e.* the profit left over on richer soil when wages and other working expenses had been settled." Another keystone of the new system of temporary settlements was the classification of agricultural fields according to soil type and produce, with average rent rates fixed for the period of the settlement. According to Mill, taxation of land rent would promote efficient agriculture and simultaneously prevent the emergence of a "parasitic landlord class." Mill advocated *ryotwari* settlements which consisted of government measurement and assessment of each plot (valid for 20 or 30 years) and subsequent taxation which was dependent on the fertility of the soil. The taxed amount was nine-tenths of the "rent" in the early 19th century and gradually fell afterwards. However, in spite of the appeal of the *ryotwari* system's abstract principles, class hierarchies in southern Indian villages had not entirely disappeared—for example village headmen continued to hold sway—and peasant cultivators sometimes came to experience revenue demands they could not meet. In the 1850s, a scandal erupted when it was discovered that some Indian revenue agents of the Company were using torture to meet the Company's revenue demands.

Land revenue settlements constituted a major administrative activity of the various governments in India under Company rule. In all areas other than the Bengal Presidency, land settlement work involved a continually repetitive process of surveying and measuring plots, assessing their quality, and recording landed rights, and constituted a large proportion of the work of Indian Civil Service officers working for the government. After the Company lost its trading rights, it became the single most important source of government revenue, roughly half of overall revenue in the middle of the 19th century; even so, between the years 1814 and 1859, the government of India ran debts in 33 years. With expanded dominion, even during non-deficit years, there was just enough money to pay the salaries of a threadbare administration, a skeleton police force, and the army.

Army and civil service

A Royal Artillery encampment at Arcot, Madras Presidency, 1804.

East India Company *Sepoys* (Indian infantrymen) in red coats outside Tipu Sultan's former summer palace in Bangalore, 1804

Military Orphan School for private soldiers of the East India Company, Howrah, Bengal Presidency, 1794.

A new "writer" in the East India Company Civil Service arrives in Calcutta. A palanquin transport awaits him.

In 1772, when Hastings became the first Governor-General one of his first undertakings was the rapid expansion of the Presidency's army. Since the available soldiers, or *Sepoys*, from Bengal—many of whom had fought against the British in the Battle of Plassey – were now suspect in British eyes, Hastings recruited farther west from the "major breeding ground of India's infantry in eastern Awadh and the lands around Banaras including Bihar. The high caste rural Hindu Rajputs and Brahmins of this region (known as *Purbiyas* (Hindi, lit. "easterners") had been recruited by Mughal Empire armies for two hundred years; the East India Company continued this practice for the next 75 years, with these soldiers comprising up to eighty per cent of the Bengal army. However, in order to avoid any friction within the ranks, the Company also took pains to adapt its military practices to their religious requirements. Consequently, these soldiers dined in separate facilities; in addition, overseas service, considered polluting to their caste, was not required of them, and the army soon came to recognise Hindu festivals officially. "This encouragement

of high caste ritual status, however, left the government vulnerable to protest, even mutiny, whenever the sepoys detected infringement of their prerogatives."

East India Company armies after the Re-organisation of 1796			
British troops	Indian troops		
	Bengal Presidency	Madras Presidency	Bombay Presidency
	24,000	24,000	9,000
13,000	Total Indian troops: 57,000		
Grand total, British and Indian troops: 70,000			

The Bengal Army was used in military campaigns in other parts of India and abroad: to provide crucial support to a weak Madras army in the Third Anglo-Mysore War in 1791, and also in Java and Ceylon. In contrast to the soldiers in the armies of Indian rulers, the Bengal sepoys not only received high pay, but also received it reliably, thanks in great measure to the Company's access to the vast land-revenue reserves of Bengal. Soon, bolstered both by the new musket technology and naval support, the Bengal army came to be widely regarded. The well-disciplined sepoys attired in red-coats and their British officers began to arouse "a kind of awe in their adversaries. In Maharashtra and in Java, the sepoys were regarded as the embodiment of demonic forces, sometimes of antique warrior heroes. Indian rulers adopted red serge jackets for their own forces and retainers as if to capture their magical qualities."

In 1796, under pressure from the Company's Board of Directors in London, the Indian troops were re-organised and reduced during the tenure of John Shore as Governor-General. However, the closing years of the 18th century saw, with Wellesley's campaigns, a new increase in the army strength. Thus in 1806, at the time of the Vellore Mutiny, the combined strength of the three presidencies' armies stood at 154,500, making them one of the largest standing armies in the world.

East India Company armies on the eve of the Vellore Mutiny of 1806			
Presidencies	British troops	Indian troops	Total
Bengal	7,000	57,000	64,000
Madras	11,000	53,000	64,000
Bombay	6,500	20,000	26,500
Total	24,500	130,000	154,500

As the East India Company expanded its territories, it added irregular "local corps," which were not as well trained as the army. In 1846, after the Second Anglo-Sikh War, a frontier brigade was raised in the Cis-Sutlej Hill States mainly for police work; in addition, in 1849, the "Punjab Irregular Force" was added on the frontier. Two years later, this force consisted of "3 light field batteries, 5 regiments of cavalry, and 5 of infantry." The following year, "a garrison company was added, ... a sixth infantry regiment (formed from the Sind Camel Corps) in 1853, and one mountain battery in 1856." Similarly, a local force was raised after the annexation of Nagpur in 1854, and the "Oudh Irregular Force" was added after Oudh was annexed in 1856. Earlier, as a result of the treaty of 1800, the Nizam of Hyderabad had begun to maintain a contingent force of 9,000 horse and 6,000-foot which was commanded by Company officers; in 1853, after a new treaty was negotiated, this force was assigned to Berar and stopped being a part of the Nizam's army.

Company rule in India

Presi-dencies	British troops				Indian troops				
	Cav-alry	Ar-tillery	In-fantry	Total	Cav-alry	Ar-tillery	Sappers & Miners	In-fantry	Total
Bengal	1,366	3,063	17,003	21,432	19,288	4,734	1,497	112,052	137,571
Madras	639	2,128	5,941	8,708	3,202	2,407	1,270	42,373	49,252
Bombay	681	1,578	7,101	9,360	8,433	1,997	637	33,861	44,928
Local forces & contingents					6,796	2,118		23,640	32,554
" " (unclas-sified)									7,756
Military police									38,977
Total	2,686	6,769	30,045	39,500	37,719	11,256	3,404	211,926	311,038
Grand Total, British and Indian troops									350,538

East India Company armies on the eve of the Indian rebellion of 1857

In the Indian rebellion of 1857 almost the entire Bengal army, both regular and irregular, revolted. It has been suggested that after the annexation of Oudh by the East India Company in 1856, many sepoys were disquieted both from losing their perquisites, as landed gentry, in the Oudh courts and from the anticipation of any increased land-revenue payments that the annexation might augur. With British victories in wars or with annexation, as the extent of British jurisdiction expanded, the soldiers were now not only expected to serve in less familiar regions (such as in Burma in the Anglo-Burmese Wars in 1856), but also make do without the "foreign service," remuneration that had previously been their due, and this caused resentment in the ranks. The Bombay and Madras armies, and the Hyderabad contingent, however, remained loyal. The Punjab Irregular Force not only didn't revolt, it played an active role in suppressing the mutiny. The rebellion led to a complete re-organisation of the Indian army in 1858 in the new British Raj.

Civil service

The reforms initiated after 1784 were designed to create an elite civil service where very talented young Britons would spend their entire careers. Advanced training was promoted especially at the Haileybury and Imperial Service College (until 1853). Haileybury emphasised the Anglican religion and morality and trained students in the classical Indian languages. Many students held to Whiggish, evangelical, and Utilitarian convictions of their duty to represent

their nation and to modernise India. At most there were about 600 of these men who managed the Raj's customs service, taxes, justice system, and its general administration.[211,212] The Company's original policy was one of "Orientalism", that is of adjusting to the way of life and customs of the Indian people and not trying to reform them. That changed after 1813, as the forces of reform in the home country, especially evangelical religion, Whiggish political outlook, and Utilitarian philosophy worked together to make the Company an agent of Anglicization and modernisation. Christian missionaries became active, but made few converts. The Raj set out to outlaw sati (widow-burning) and thuggee (ritual banditry) and upgrade the status of women. Schools would be established in which they would teach the English language. The 1830s and 1840s, however, were not times of prosperity: After its heavy spending on the military, the Company had little money to engage in large-scale public works projects or modernisation programs.

Trade

Photograph of East India Company factory in Painam, Sonargaon, Bangladesh, a major producer of the celebrated Dhaka muslins.

"Mellor Mill" in Marple, Greater Manchester, England, was constructed in 1790-93 for manufacturing muslim cloth.

Opium *Godown* (Storehouse) in Patna, Bihar (c. 1814). Patna was the centre of the Company opium industry.

Indigo dye factory in Bengal. Bengal was the world's largest producer of natural indigo in the 19th century.

After gaining the right to collect revenue in Bengal in 1765, the Company largely ceased importing gold and silver, which it had hitherto used to pay for goods shipped back to Britain.

Export of Bullion to India, by EIC (1708-1810)

Years	Bullion (£)	Average per Annum
1708/9-1733/4	12,189,147	420,315
1734/5-1759/60	15,239,115	586,119
1760/1-1765/6	842,381	140,396
1766/7-1771/2	968,289	161,381
1772/3-1775/6	72,911	18,227
1776/7-1784/5	156,106	17,345
1785/6-1792/3	4,476,207	559,525
1793/4-1809/10	8,988,165	528,715

In addition, as under Mughal Empire rule, land revenue collected in the Bengal Presidency helped finance the Company's wars in other parts of India. Consequently, in the period 1760–1800, Bengal's money supply was greatly diminished; furthermore, the closing of some local mints and close supervision of the rest, the fixing of exchange rates, and the standardisation of coinage, paradoxically, added to the economic downturn. During the period, 1780–1860, India changed from being an exporter of processed goods for which it received payment in bullion, to being an exporter of raw materials and a buyer of manufactured goods. More specifically, in the 1750s, mostly fine cotton and silk was exported from India to markets in Europe, Asia, and Africa; by the second quarter of the 19th century, raw materials, which chiefly consisted of raw cotton, opium, and indigo, accounted for most of India's exports. Also, from the late 18th century British cotton mill industry began to lobby the government to both tax Indian imports and allow them access to markets in India. Starting in the 1830s, British textiles began to appear in—and soon to inundate—the Indian markets, with the value of the textile imports growing from £5.2 million 1850 to £18.4 million in 1896. The American Civil War too would have a major impact on India's cotton economy: with the outbreak of the war, American cotton was no longer available to British manufacturers; consequently, demand for Indian cotton soared, and the prices soon quadrupled. This led many farmers in India to switch to cultivating cotton as a quick cash crop; however, with the end of the war in 1865, the demand plummeted again, creating another downturn in the agricultural economy.

At this time, the East India Company's trade with China began to grow as well. In the early 19th century demand for Chinese tea had greatly increased in Britain; since the money supply in India was restricted and the Company was indisposed to shipping bullion from Britain, it decided upon opium, which had a large underground market in China and which was grown in many parts of India, as the most profitable form of payment. However, since the Chinese authorities had banned the importation and consumption of opium, the Company engaged them in the First Opium War, and at its conclusion, under the Treaty of Nanjing, gained access to five Chinese ports, Guangzhou, Xiamen, Fuzhou, Shanghai, and Ningbo; in addition, Hong Kong was ceded to the British Crown. Towards the end of the second quarter of the 19th century, opium export constituted 40% of India's exports.

Another major, though erratic, export item was indigo dye, which was extracted from natural indigo, and which came to be grown in Bengal and northern Bihar. In late 17th and early 18th century Europe, blue clothing was favoured as a fashion, and blue uniforms were common in the military; consequently, the demand for the dye was high. In 1788, the East India Company offered advances to ten British planters to grow indigo; however, since the

Company rule in India

new (landed) property rights defined in the Permanent Settlement, didn't allow them, as Europeans, to buy agricultural land, they had to in turn offer cash advances to local peasants, and sometimes coerce them, to grow the crop. The European demand for the dye, however, proved to be unstable, and both creditors and cultivators bore the risk of the market crashes in 1827 and 1847. The peasant discontent in Bengal eventually led to the *Indigo rebellion* in 1859-60 and to the end of indigo production there. In Bihar, however, indigo production continued well into the 20th century; the centre of indigo production there, Champaran district, became the staging ground, in 1917, for Mohandas Karamchand Gandhi's first experiment in non-violent resistance against the British Raj.

Justice system

The house of Sir Thomas Strange, who in 1800 became the first Chief Justice of the Fort of St. George (Madras) and wrote *Elements of Hindu Law* (1825).

An 1833 Lithograph of the *Sadr Diwāni Adālat*, the Chief Civil Court for Indians, on Chowringhee Road, Calcutta.

Coloured engraving of the judges and officers of Hindu (top row) and Muslim (bottom row) law in the Recorder Court in Bombay, 1805.

The Court-House Building on Apollo Street, Bombay (third building on left, just beyond the domed Ice House) shown in 1850.

Until the British gained control of Bengal in the mid-18th century, the system of justice there was presided over by the Nawab of Bengal himself, who, as the chief law officer, *Nawāb Nāzim*, attended to cases qualifying for capital punishment in his headquarters, Murshidabad. His deputy, the *Naib Nāzim*, attended to the slightly less important cases. The ordinary lawsuits belonged to the jurisdiction of a hierarchy of court officials consisting of *faujdārs*, *muhtasils*, and *kotwāls*. In the rural areas, or the *Mofussil*, the *zamindars*—the rural overlords with the hereditary right to collect rent from peasant farmers—also had the power to administer justice. This they did with little routine oversight, being required to report only their judgments in capital punishment cases to the *Nawāb*.

By the mid-18th century, the British too had completed a century and a half in India, and had a burgeoning presence in the three *presidency* towns of Madras, Bombay, and Calcutta. During this time the successive Royal Charters had gradually given the East India Company more power to administer justice in these towns. In the charter granted by Charles II in 1683, the Company was given the power to establish "courts of judicature" in locations of its choice, each court consisting of a lawyer and two merchants. This right was renewed in the subsequent charters granted by James II and William III in 1686 and 1698 respectively. In 1726, however, the Court of Directors of the Company felt that more customary justice was necessary for European residents in the presidency towns, and petitioned the King to establish *Mayor's Courts*. The petition was approved and Mayor's courts, each consisting of a Mayor and nine aldermen, and each having the jurisdiction in lawsuits *between* Europeans, were created in Fort William (Calcutta), Madras, and Bombay. Judgments handed down by a Mayor's Court could be disputed with an appeal to the respective Presidency government and, when the amount disputed was greater than Rs. 4,000, with a further appeal to the King-in-Council. In 1753, the Mayor's courts were renewed under a revised letters patent; in addition, Courts of Requests for lawsuits involving amounts less than Rs. 20 were introduced. Both types of courts were regulated by the Court of Directors of the East India Company.

After its victory in the Battle of Buxar, the Company obtained in 1765 the *Diwāni* of Bengal, the right not only to collect revenue, but also to administer civil justice in Bengal. The administration of criminal justice, the *Nizāmat* or *Faujdāri*, however, remained with the *Nawāb*, and for criminal cases the prevailing Islamic law remained in place. However, the Company's new duties associated with the *Diwāni* were leased out to the Indian officials who had formerly performed them. This makeshift arrangement continued—with much accompanying disarray—until 1771, when the Court of Directors of the Company decided to obtain for the Company the jurisdiction of both criminal and civil cases.

Soon afterwards Warren Hastings arrived in Calcutta as the first Governor-General of the Company's Indian dominions and resolved to overhaul the Company's organisation and in particular its judicial affairs. In the interior, or *Mofussil*, *diwāni adālats*, or a civil courts of first instance, were constituted in each district; these courts were presided over by European *Zilā* judges employed by the Company, who were assisted in the interpretation of customary Indian law by Hindu *pandits* and Muslim *qazis*. For small claims, however, Registrars and Indian commissioners, known as *Sadr Amīns* and *Munsifs*, were appointed. These in their turn were supervised by provincial civil courts of appeal constituted for such purpose, each consisting of four British judges. All these were under the authority of the *Sadr Diwāni Adālat*, or the Chief Civil Court of Appeals, consisting of the Governor of the Presidency and his Council, assisted by Indian officers.

Similarly for criminal cases, Mofussil *nizāmat adālats*, or Provincial courts of criminal judicature, were created in the interior; these again consisted of Indian court officers (*pandits* and *qazis*), who were supervised by officials of the Company. Also constituted were Courts of circuit with appellate jurisdiction in criminal cases, which were usually presided over by the judges of the civil appellate courts. All these too were under a *Sadr Nizāmat Adālat* or a Chief Court of Criminal Appeal.

Around this time the business affairs of the East India Company began to draw increased scrutiny in the House of Commons. After receiving a report by a committee, which condemned the Mayor's Courts, the Crown issued a charter for a new judicial system in the Bengal Presidency. The British Parliament consequently enacted the *Regulating Act of 1773* under which the King-in-Council created a Supreme Court in the *Presidency town*, *i.e.* Fort William. The tribunal consisted of one Chief Justice and three puisne judges; all four judges were to be chosen from barristers. The Supreme Court supplanted the

Figure 54: *The family of Chief Justice Sir Elijah Impey in Calcutta, 1783*

Mayor's Court; however, it left the Court of Requests in place. Under the charter, the Supreme Court, moreover, had the authority to exercise all types of jurisdiction in the region of Bengal, Bihar, and Odisha, with the only caveat that in situations where the disputed amount was in excess of Rs. 4,000, their judgment could be appealed to the Privy Council. Both the Act and the charter said nothing about the relation between the judiciary (Supreme Court) and the executive branch (Governor-General); equally, they were silent on the *Adālats* (both *Diwāni* and *Nizāmat*) created by Warren Hastings just the year before. In the new Supreme Court, the civil and criminal cases alike were interpreted and prosecuted accorded to English law; in the *Sadr Adālats*, however, the judges and law-officers had no knowledge of English law, and were required only, by the Governor-General's order, "to proceed according to equity, justice, and good conscience, unless Hindu or Muhammadan law was in point, or some Regulation expressly applied."

There was a good likelihood, therefore, that the Supreme Court and the *Sadr Adālats* would act in opposition to each other and, predictably, many disputes resulted. Hastings' premature attempt to appoint the Chief Justice, Sir Elijah Impey, an old schoolmate from Winchester, to the bench of the *Sadr Diwāni Adālat*, only complicated the situation further. The appointment had to be annulled in 1781 by a parliamentary intervention with the enactment of the Declaration Act. The Act exempted the Executive Branch from the jurisdiction

Company rule in India

of the Supreme Court. It recognised the independent existence of the *Sadr Adālats* and all subsidiary courts of the Company. Furthermore, it headed off future legal turf wars by prohibiting the Supreme Court any jurisdiction in matters of revenue (*Diwāni*) or Regulations of the Government enacted by the British Parliament. This state of affairs continued until 1797, when a new Act extended the jurisdiction of the Supreme Court to the province of Benares (which had since been added to the Company's dominions) and "all places for the time being included in Bengal." With the constituting of the Ceded and Conquered Provinces in 1805, the jurisdiction would extend as far west as Delhi.

In the other two presidencies, Madras and Bombay, a similar course of legal changes unfolded; there, however, the Mayor's Courts were first strengthened to Recorder's Courts by adding a legal president to the bench. The Supreme Courts in Madras and Bombay were finally established in 1801 and 1823, respectively. Madras Presidency was also unusual in being the first to rely on village headmen and *panchāyats* for cases involving small claims. This judicial system in the three presidencies was to survive the Company's rule, the next major change coming only in 1861.

Education

A coloured-in photograph (1851) of Hindu College, Calcutta, which had been founded in 1817 by a committee headed by Raja Ram Mohun Roy. In 1855, the Government of the Bengal Presidency renamed it *Presidency College* and opened it to all students.

An engraving (1844) of a youth, who according to the engraver, Emily Eden, was "a favourite and successful young student at the Hindu College in Calcutta, where scholars acquire a very perfect knowledge of English, and have a familiarity with the best English writers ..."

An 1844 engraving of Grant Medical College (left) and Sir Jamsetjee Jeejeebhoy Hospital (right background) in Bombay made by G. R. Sargeant the year before the medical college was formally opened.

An 1855 photograph of the same two institutions. In 1857, Grant Medical College became one of three institutions affiliated with the newly established University of Bombay. The college was funded partly by the Jeejeebhoy family and partly by the East India Company.

Education of Indians had become a topic of interest among East India Company officials from the outset of the Company's rule in Bengal. In the last two decades of the 18th century and the first decade of the nineteenth, Company officials pursued a policy of conciliation towards the native culture of its new dominion, especially in relation to education policy. During the 19th century, the Indian literacy rates were rumoured to be less than half of post independence levels which were 18.33% in 1951. The policy was pursued in the aid of three goals: "to sponsor Indians in their own culture, to advance knowledge of India, and to employ that knowledge in government."

The first goal was supported by some administrators, such as Warren Hastings, who envisaged the Company as the successor of a great Empire, and saw the support of vernacular learning as only befitting that role. In 1781, Hastings founded the *Madrasa 'Aliya*, an institution in Calcutta for the study of Arabic and Persian languages, and Islamic Law. A few decades later a related perspective appeared among the governed population, one that was expressed by the conservative Bengali reformer *Radhakanta Deb* as the "duty of the Rulers of Countries to preserve and Customs and the religions of their subjects."

The second goal was motivated by the concerns among some Company officials about being seen as foreign rulers. They argued that the Company should try to win over its subjects by outdoing the region's previous rulers in the support of indigenous learning. Guided by this belief, the Benares Sanskrit College was founded in Varanasi in 1791 during the administration of Lord Cornwallis. The promotion of knowledge of Asia had attracted scholars as well to the Company's service. Earlier, in 1784, the Asiatick Society had been founded in Calcutta by William Jones, a puisne judge in the newly established Supreme Court of Bengal. Soon, Jones was to advance his famous thesis on the common origin of Indo-European languages.

The third related goal grew out of the philosophy then current among some Company officials that they would themselves become better administrators if they were better versed in the languages and cultures of India. It led in 1800 to the founding of the College of Fort William, in Calcutta by Lord Wellesley, the then Governor-General. The College was later to play an important role both in the development of modern Indian languages and in the Bengal Renaissance. Advocates of these related goals were termed, "Orientalists." The Orientalist group was led by Horace Hayman Wilson. Many leading Company officials, such as Thomas Munro and Montstuart Elphinstone, were influenced by the Orientalist ethos and felt that the Company's government in India should be responsive to Indian expectations. The Orientalist ethos would prevail in education policy well into the 1820s, and was reflected in the founding of the Poona Sanskrit College in Pune in 1821 and the Calcutta Sanskrit College in 1824.

The Orientalists were, however, soon opposed by advocates of an approach that has been termed *Anglicist*. The Anglicists supported instruction in the English language in order to impart to Indians what they considered modern Western knowledge. Prominent among them were evangelicals who, after 1813—when the Company's territories were opened to Christian missionaries—were interested in spreading Christian belief; they also believed in using theology to promote liberal social reform, such as the abolition of slavery. Among them was Charles Grant, the Chairman of the East India Company. Grant supported state-sponsored education in India 20 years before a similar system was set up in Britain. Among Grant's close evangelical friends were William Wilberforce, a prominent abolitionist and member of the British Parliament, and Sir John Shore, the Governor-General of India from 1793 to 1797. During this period, many Scottish Presbyterian missionaries also supported the British rulers in their efforts to spread English education and established many reputed colleges like Scottish Church College (1830), Wilson

College (1832), Madras Christian College (1837), and Elphinstone College (1856).

However, the Anglicists also included utilitarians, led by James Mill, who had begun to play an important role in fashioning Company policy. The utilitarians believed in the moral worth of an education that aided the good of society and promoted instruction in *useful knowledge*. Such *useful* instruction to Indians had the added consequence of making them more suitable for the Company's burgeoning bureaucracy. By the early 1830s, the Anglicists had the upper hand in devising education policy in India. Many utilitarian ideas were employed in Thomas Babbington Macaulay's *Minute on Indian Education* of 1835. The *Minute*, which later aroused great controversy, was to influence education policy in India well into the next century.

Since English was increasingly being employed as the language of instruction, Persian was abolished as the official language of the Company's administration and courts by 1837. However, bilingual educations was proving to be popular as well, and some institutions such as the Poona Sanskrit College commenced teaching both Sanskrit and English. Charles Grant's son, Sir Robert Grant, who in 1834 was appointed Governor of the Bombay Presidency, played an influential role in the planning of the first medical college in Bombay, which after his unexpected death was named Grant Medical College when it was established in 1845. During 1852–1853 some citizens of Bombay sent petitions to the British Parliament in support of both establishing and adequately funding university education in India. The petitions resulted in the *Education Dispatch* of July 1854 sent by Sir Charles Wood, the President of the Board of Control of the East India Company, the chief official on Indian affairs in the British government, to Lord Dalhousie, the then Governor-General of India. The dispatch outlined a broad plan of state-sponsored education for India, which included:

1. Establishing a Department of Public Instruction in each presidency or province of British India.
2. Establishing universities modelled on the University of London (as primarily examining institutions for students studying in affiliated colleges) in each of the *Presidency towns* (*i.e.* Madras, Bombay, and Calcutta)
3. Establishing teachers-training schools for all levels of instruction
4. Maintaining existing Government colleges and high-schools and increasing their number when necessary.
5. Vastly increasing vernacular schools for elementary education in villages.
6. Introducing a system of grants-in-aid for private schools.

The Department of Public Instruction was in place by 1855. In January 1857, the University of Calcutta was established, followed by the University of Bombay in June, 1857, and the University of Madras in September 1857. The

University of Bombay, for example, consisted of three affiliated institutions: the Elphinstone Institution, the Grant Medical College, and the Poona Sanskrit College. The Company's administration also founded high-schools *en masse* in the different provinces and presidencies, and the policy was continued during Crown rule which commenced in 1858. By 1861, 230,000 students were attending public educational institutions in the four provinces (the three Presidencies and North-Western Provinces), of whom 200,000 were in primary schools. Over 5,000 primary schools and 142 secondary schools had been established in these provinces. Earlier, during the Indian rebellion of 1857, some civilian leaders, such as Khan Bhadur Khan of Bareilly, had stressed the threat posed to the populace's religions by the new education programmes begun by the Company; however, historical statistics have shown that this was not generally the case. For example, in Etawah district in the then North-Western Provinces (present-day Uttar Pradesh), where during the period 1855–57, nearly 200 primary, middle-, and high-schools had been opened by the Company and tax levied on the population, relative calm prevailed and the schools remained open during the rebellion.

Social reform

In the first half of the 19th century, the British legislated reforms against what they considered were iniquitous Indian practices. In most cases, the legislation alone was unable to change Indian society sufficiently for it to absorb both the ideal and the ethic underpinning the reform. For example, upper-caste Hindu society had long looked askance at the remarriage of widows in order to protect both what it considered was family honour and family property. Even adolescent widows were expected to live a life of austerity and denial. The Hindu Widows' Remarriage Act, 1856, enacted in the waning years of Company rule, provided legal safeguards against loss of certain forms of inheritance for a remarrying Hindu widow, though not of the inheritance due her from her deceased husband. However, very few widows actually remarried. Some Indian reformers, such as Raja Ram Mohan Roy, Ishwar Chandra Vidyasagar, even offered money to men who would take widows as brides, but these men often deserted their new wives.

Post and telegraph

Lithograph of the General Post Office on Chowringhee Street, Calcutta, 1833, four years before the India-wide postal service was established under the Indian Postal Act of 1837.

Two four anna stamps issued in 1854. Stamps were issued for the first time for all of British India in 1854. The lowest denomination was ½ anna blue, followed by 1 anna

red, and 4 annas blue and red. The stamps were printed from lithographic stones at the Surveyor-General's Office in Calcutta.

A semaphore "telegraph" signalling tower in Silwar (Bihar), 13 February 1823, thirty years before electric telegraphy was rapidly introduced into India by the East India Company.

Postal services

Before 1837, the East India Company's dominions in India had no universal public postal service, one that was shared by all regions. Although courier services did exist, connecting the more important towns with their respective seats of provincial government (*i.e.* the *Presidency towns* of Fort William (Calcutta), Fort St. George (Madras), and Bombay), private individuals were, upon payment, only sparingly allowed their use. That situation changed in 1837, when, by Act XVII of that year, a public post, run by the Company's Government, was established in the Company's territory in India. Post offices were established in the principal towns and postmasters appointed. The postmasters of the Presidency towns oversaw a few provincial post offices in addition to being responsible for the main postal services between the provinces. By contrast, the District collectors (originally, collectors of land-tax) directed the District post offices, including their local postal services. Postal services required payment in cash, to be made in advance, with the amount charged usually varying with weight and distance. For example, the charge of sending

a letter from Calcutta to Bombay was one rupee; however, that from Calcutta to Agra was 12 annas (or three-quarter of a rupee) for each tola (three-eighths of an ounce).[213]

After the recommendations of the commission appointed in 1850 to evaluate the Indian postal system were received, Act XVII of 1837 was superseded by the Indian Postal Act of 1854. Under its provisions, the entire postal department was headed by a *Director-General*, and the duties of a *Postmaster-General* were set apart from those of a Presidency Postmaster; the former administered the postal system of the larger provinces (such as the Bombay Presidency or the North-Western Provinces), whereas the latter attended to the less important Provinces (such as Ajmer-Merwara and the major Political Agencies such as Rajputana). Postage stamps were introduced at this time and the postal rates fixed by weight, dependent no longer also on the distance travelled in the delivery. The lowest inland letter rate was half anna for 1/4 tola, followed by one anna for 1/2 tola, and 2 annas for a tola, a great reduction from the rates of 17 years before. The Indian Post Office delivered letters, newspapers, postcards, book packets, and parcels. These deliveries grew steadily in number; by 1861 (three years after the end of Company rule), a total of 889 post offices had been opened, and almost 43 million letters and over four and a half million newspapers were being delivered annually.

Telegraphy

Before the advent of electric telegraphy, the word "telegraph" had been used for semaphore signalling. During the period 1820–30, the East India Company's Government in India seriously considered constructing signalling towers ("telegraph" towers), each a hundred feet high and separated from the next by eight miles, along the entire distance from Calcutta to Bombay. Although such towers were built in Bengal and Bihar, the India-wide semaphore network never took off. By mid-century, electric telegraphy had become viable, and hand signalling obsolete.

Dr. W. B. O'Shaughnessy, a Professor of Chemistry in the Calcutta Medical College, received permission in 1851 to conduct a trial run for a telegraph service from Calcutta to Diamond Harbour along the river Hooghly. Four telegraph offices, mainly for shipping-related business, were also opened along the river that year. The telegraph receiver used in the trial was a galvanoscope of Dr. O'Shaughnessy's design and manufactured in India. When the experiment was deemed to be a success a year later, the Governor-General of India, Lord Dalhousie, sought permission from the Court of Directors of the Company for the construction of telegraph lines from "Calcutta to Agra, Agra to Bombay, Agra to Peshawar, and Bombay to Madras, extending in all over 3,050 miles and including forty-one offices." The permission was soon granted; by February 1855 all the proposed telegraph lines had been constructed and were being used to send paid messages. Dr. O'Shaughnessy's instrument was used all over India until early 1857, when it was supplanted by the Morse instrument. By 1857, the telegraph network had expanded to 4,555 miles of lines and sixty two offices, and had reached as far as the hill station of Ootacamund in the Nilgiri Hills and the port of Calicut on the southwest coast of India. During the Indian rebellion of 1857, more than seven hundred miles of telegraph lines were destroyed by the rebel forces, mainly in the North-Western Provinces. The East India Company was nevertheless able to use the remaining intact lines to warn many outposts of impending disturbances. The political value of the new technology was, thus, driven home to the Company, and, in the following year, not only were the destroyed lines rebuilt, but the network was expanded further by 2,000 miles.

O'Shaughnessy's experimental set-up of 1851–52 consisted of both overhead and underground lines; the latter included underwater ones that crossed two rivers, the Hooghly and the Haldi. The overhead line was constructed by welding uninsulated iron rods, 13½ feet long and 3/8 inch wide, end to end. These lines, which weighed 1,250 pounds per mile, were held aloft by fifteen-foot lengths of bamboo, planted into the ground at equal intervals—200 to the mile—and covered with a layer each of coal tar and pitch for insulation. The underwater cables had been manufactured in England and consisted of copper wire covered with gutta-percha. Furthermore, in order to protect the cables from dragging ship anchors, the cables were attached to the links of a $^7/_8$-inch-thick (22 mm) chain cable. An underwater cable of length 2,070 yards was laid across the Hooghly river at Diamond Harbour, and another, 1,400 yards long, was laid across the Haldi at Kedgeree.

Work on the long lines from Calcutta to Peshawar (through Agra), Agra to Bombay, and Bombay to Madras began in 1853. The conducting material chosen for these lines was now lighter, and the support stronger. The wood used for the support consisted of teak, sal, fir, ironwood, or blackwood (*Terminalia elata*), and was either fashioned into whole posts, or used in attachments to iron *screw-piles* or masonry columns. Some sections had uniformly strong support; one such was the 322-mile Bombay-Madras line, which was supported by granite obelisks sixteen feet high. Other sections had less secure support, consisting, in some cases, of sections of toddy palm, insulated with pieces of sal wood fastened to their tops. Some of the conducting wires or rods were insulated, the insulating material being either manufactured in India or England; other stretches of wire remained uninsulated. By 1856, iron tubes had begun to be employed to provide support, and would see increased use in the second half of the 19th century all over India.

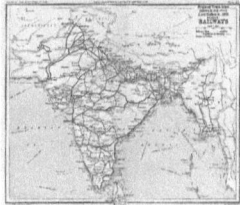

The first Telegraph Act for India was Parliament's Act XXXIV of 1854. When the public telegramme service was first set up in 1855, the charge was fixed at one rupee for every sixteen words (including the address) for every 400 miles of transmission. The charges were doubled for telegrammes sent between 6PM and 6AM. These rates would remain fixed until 1882. In the year 1860–61, two years after the end of Company rule, India had 11,093 miles of telegraph lines and 145 telegraph offices. That year telegrammes totalling Rs. 500,000 in value were sent by the public, the working expense of the *Indian Telegraph Department* was Rs. 1.4 million, and the capital expenditure until the end of the year totalled Rs. 6.5 million.

Railways

Photograph (1855) of the Dapoorie Viaduct, Bombay. The viaduct, shown with a train steaming across it, was completed in 1853 and linked Bombay Island with Thane on the mainland.

The trunk lines proposed by the Governor-General of India, Lord Dalhousie in his *Railway minute of 1853* (shown in red on a 1908 railway map of India).

The first locomotive, shown on the right and christened "multum in parvo" (barely visible on the wheel casing), which was used by the East Indian Railway Company in 1854 on its 23-mile line from Howrah to Pandua.

Photograph (1855) showing the construction of the Bhor Ghat incline bridge, Bombay; the incline was conceived by George Clark, the Chief Engineer in the East India Company's Government of Bombay.

The first inter-city railway service in England, the Stockton-Darlington railway, had been established in 1825;[214] in the following decade other intercity railways were rapidly constructed between cities in England. In 1845, the Court of Directors of the East India Company, forwarded to the Governor-General of India, Lord Dalhousie, a number of applications they had received from private contractors in England for the construction of a wide-ranging railway network in India, and requested a feasibility report. They added that, in their view, the enterprise would be profitable only if large sums of money could be raised for the construction. The Court was concerned that in addition to the usual difficulties encountered in the construction of this new form of transportation, India might present some unique problems, among which they counted floods, tropical storms in coastal areas, damage by "insects and luxuriant tropical vegetation," and the difficulty of finding qualified technicians at a reasonable cost. It was suggested, therefore, that three experimental lines be constructed and their performance evaluated.

Contracts were awarded in 1849 to the East Indian Railway Company to construct a 120-mile railway from Howrah-Calcutta to Raniganj; to the Great Indian Peninsular Railway Company for a service from Bombay to Kalyan, thirty miles away; and to the *Madras Railway Company* for a line from Madras city to Arkonam, a distance of some thirty nine miles. Although construction began first, in 1849, on the East Indian Railways line, with an outlay of £1 million, it was the first-leg of the Bombay-Kalyan line—a 21-mile stretch from Bombay to Thane—that, in 1853, was the first to be completed (see picture below).

The feasibility of a train network in India was comprehensively discussed by Lord Dalhousie in his *Railway minute of 1853*. The Governor-General vigorously advocated the quick and widespread introduction of railways in India, pointing to their political, social, and economic advantages. He recommended

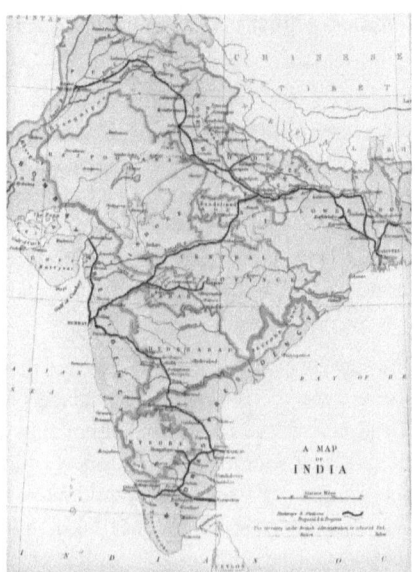

Figure 55: *Map of the completed and planned railway lines in India in 1871, thirteen years after the end of Company rule.*

that a network of *trunk lines* be first constructed connecting the inland regions of each presidency with its chief port as well as each presidency with several others. His recommended trunk lines included the following ones: (i) from Calcutta, in the Bengal Presidency, on the eastern coast to Lahore in the north-western region of the Punjab, annexed just three years before; (ii) from Agra in north-central India (in, what was still being called North-Western Provinces) to Bombay city on the western coast; (iii) from Bombay to Madras city on the southeastern coast; and (iv) from Madras to the southwestern Malabar coast (see map above). The proposal was soon accepted by the Court of Directors.

During this time work had been proceeding on the experimental lines as well. The first leg of the East Indian Railway line, a broad gauge railway, from Howrah to Pandua, was opened in 1854 (see picture of locomotive below), and the entire line up to Raniganj would become functional by the time of the Indian rebellion of 1857. The Great Indian Peninsular Railway was permitted to extend its experimental line to Poona. This extension required planning for the steep rise in the *Bor Ghat* valley in the Western Ghats, a section 15¾ miles long with an ascent of 1,831 feet. Construction began in 1856 and was completed in 1863, and, in the end, the line required a total of twenty five tunnels and fifteen miles of gradients (inclines) of 1 in 50 or steeper, the most extreme being the *Bor Ghat Incline*, a distance of 1¾ miles at a gradient of 1 in 37 (see picture above).

Each of the three companies (and later five others that were given contracts in 1859) was joint stock company domiciled in England with its financial capital raised in pound sterling. Each company was guaranteed a 5 per cent return on its capital outlay and, in addition, a share of half the profits. Although the *Government of India* had no capital expenditure other than the provision of the underlying land free of charge, it had the onus of continuing to provide the 5 percent return in the event of net loss, and soon all anticipation of profits would fall by the wayside as the outlays would mount.

The technology of railway construction was still new and there was no railway engineering expertise in India; consequently, all engineers had to be brought in from England. These engineers were unfamiliar not only with the language and culture of India, but also with the physical aspect of the land itself and its concomitant engineering requirements. Moreover, never before had such a large and complex construction project been undertaken in India, and no pool of semi-skilled labour was already organised to aid the engineers. The work, therefore, proceeded in fits and starts—many practical trials followed by a final construction that was undertaken with great caution and care—producing an outcome that was later criticised as being "built to a standard which was far in excess of the needs to the time." The Government of India's administrators, moreover, made up in their attention to the fine details of expenditure and management what they lacked in professional expertise. The resulting delays soon led to the appointment of a Committee of the House of Commons in 1857–58 to investigate the matter. However, by the time the Committee concluded that all parties needed to honour the spirit rather than the letter of the contracts, Company rule in India had ended.

Although, railway construction had barely begun in the last years of this rule, its foundations had been laid, and it would proceed apace for much of the next half century. By the turn of the 20th century, India would have over 28,000 miles of railways connecting most interior regions to the ports of Karachi, Bombay, Madras, Calcutta, Chittagong, and Rangoon, and together they would constitute the fourth-largest railway network in the world.[215]

Canals

Watercolor (1863) titled, "The Ganges Canal, Roorkee, Saharanpur District (U.P.)." The canal was the brainchild of Sir Proby Cautley; construction began in 1840, and the canal was opened by Governor-General Lord Dalhousie in April 1854

Photograph (2008) of an East India Company-era (1854) bridge on the Ganges Canal near Roorkee, Uttar Pradesh, India.

Photograph (1860) of the head works of the Ganges Canal in Haridwar taken by Samuel Bourne

Photograph (2008) of the head works of the Ganges Canal in Haridwar, viewed from the opposite side.

The first irrigation works undertaken during East India Company's rule were begun in 1817. Consisting chiefly of extensions or reinforcements of previous Indian works, these projects were limited to the plains north of Delhi and to the river deltas of the Madras Presidency. A small dam in the Kaveri river delta, built some 1,500 years before, and known as the *Grand Anicut*, was one such indigenous work in South India. In 1835–36, Sir Arthur Cotton successfully reinforced the dam, and his success prompted more irrigation projects on the river. A little farther north, on the Tungabhadra river, the 16th century Vijayanagara ruler, Krishna Deva Raya, had constructed several weirs; these too would be extended under British administration.

In plains above Delhi, the mid-14th century Sultan of Delhi, Firoz Shah Tughlaq, had constructed the 150-mile long *Western Jamna Canal*. Taking off from the right bank of the Jamna river early in its course, the canal irrigated the Sultan's territories in the Hissar region of Eastern Punjab. By the mid-16th century, however, the fine sediment carried by the Himalayan river had gradually choked the canal. Desilted and reopened several decades later by Akbar

the Great, the *Western Jamna Canal* was itself tapped by Akbar's grandson Shah Jahan, and some of its water was diverted to Delhi. During this time another canal was cut off the river. The 129-mile *Eastern Jamna Canal* or *Doab Canal*, which took off from the *left* bank of the Jamna, also high in its course, presented a qualitatively different difficulty. Since it was cut through steeply sloped land, its flow became difficult to control, and it was never to function efficiently. With the decline of Mughal Empire power in the 18th century, both canals fell into disrepair and closed. The Western Jamna Canal was repaired by British army engineers and it reopened in 1820. The *Doab Canal* was reopened in 1830; its considerable renovation involved raising the embankment by an average height of 9 ft. for some 40 miles.

Farther west in the Punjab region, the 130-mile long *Hasli Canal*, had been constructed by previous rulers. Taking off from the Ravi river and supplying water to the cities of Lahore and Amritsar, this left-bank canal was extended by the British in the *Bari Doab Canal* works during 1850–57. The Punjab region, moreover, had much rudimentary irrigation by "inundation canals." Consisting of open cuts on the side of a river and involving no regulation, the inundation canals had been used in both the Punjab and Sindh for many centuries. The energetic administrations of the Sikh and Pathan governors of Mughal West Punjab had ensured that many such canals in Multan, Dera Ghazi Khan, and Muzaffargarh were still working efficiently at the time of the British annexation of the Punjab in 1849-1856 (Period of tenure of Marquess of Dalhousie Governor General).

The first new British work—with no Indian antecedents—was the Ganges Canal built between 1842 and 1854. Contemplated first by Col. John Russell Colvin in 1836, it did not at first elicit much enthusiasm from its eventual architect Sir Proby Thomas Cautley, who balked at idea of cutting a canal through extensive low-lying land in order to reach the drier upland destination. However, after the Agra famine of 1837–38, during which the East India Company's administration spent Rs. 2,300,000 on famine relief, the idea of a canal became more attractive to the Company's budget-conscious Court of

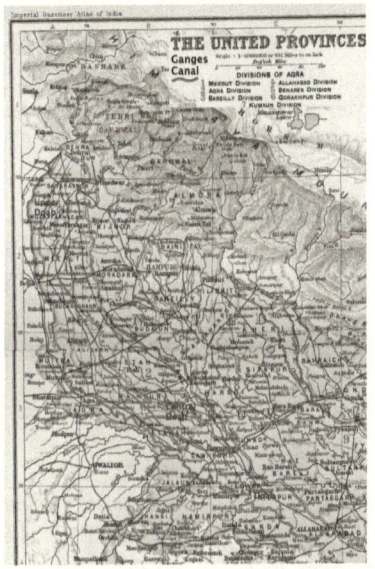

Figure 56: *The Ganges Canal highlighted in red stretching between its headworks off the Ganges river in Hardwar and its confluence with the Jumna river below Cawnpore (now Kanpur).*

Directors. In 1839, the Governor General of India, Lord Auckland, with the Court's assent, granted funds to Cautley for a full survey of the swath of land that underlay and fringed the projected course of the canal. The Court of Directors, moreover, considerably enlarged the scope of the projected canal, which, in consequence of the severity and geographical extent of the famine, they now deemed to be the entire Doab region.

The enthusiasm, however, proved to be short lived. Auckland's successor as Governor General, Lord Ellenborough, appeared less receptive to large-scale public works, and for the duration of his tenure, withheld major funds for the project. Only in 1844, when a new Governor-General, Lord Hardinge, was appointed, did official enthusiasm and funds return to the Ganges canal project. Although the intervening impasse, had seemingly affected Cautely's health and required him to return to Britain in 1845 for recuperation, his European sojourn gave him an opportunity to study contemporary hydraulic works in Great Britain and Italy. By the time of his return to India even more supportive men were at the helm, both in the North-Western Provinces, with James Thomason as Lt. Governor, and in British India with Lord Dalhousie as Governor-General. Canal construction, under Cautley's supervision, now went into full swing. A 350-mile long canal, with another 300 miles of branch lines, eventually stretched between the headworks in Hardwar and—after splitting into two branches at Nanau near Aligarh—the confluence with the Ganges at Cawnpore (now Kanpur) and with the Jumna (now Yamuna) mainstem at Etawah. The Ganges Canal, which required a total capital outlay of £2.15 million, was officially opened in 1854 by Lord Dalhousie. According to historian Ian Stone:

> It was the largest canal ever attempted in the world, five times greater in its length than all the main irrigation lines of Lombardy and Egypt put together, and longer by a third than even the largest USA navigation canal, the Pennsylvania Canal.

References

General histories

- Bandyopādhyāya, Śekhara (2004), *From Plassey to partition: a history of modern India*[216], Delhi: Orient Blackswan, ISBN 978-81-250-2596-2
- Bayly, Christopher Alan. *Indian society and the making of the British Empire* (1988.)
- Bayly, C.A. *The Raj: India and the British 1600-1947* (1990)
- Bose, Sugata; Jalal, Ayesha (2004), *Modern South Asia: History, Culture, Political economy: second edition*[217], Routledge, ISBN 978-1-134-39715-0
- Brown, Judith Margaret (1994), *Modern India: the origins of an Asian democracy*[218], Oxford University Press, ISBN 978-0-19-873112-2
- Judd, Denis (2010), *The lion and the tiger: the rise and fall of the British Raj, 1600-1947*[219], Oxford University Press, ISBN 978-0-19-280579-9
- Kulke, Hermann; Rothermund, Dietmar (2004), *A history of India*[220], Routledge, ISBN 978-0-415-32920-0
- Lawson, Philip. *The East India Company: A History* (Routledge, 1993) excerpt and text search[221]
- Ludden, David (2002), *India and South Asia: a short history*[222], Oneworld, ISBN 978-1-85168-237-9
- Markovits, Claude (2004), *A history of modern India, 1480-1950*[223], Anthem Press, ISBN 978-1-84331-152-2, retrieved 5 November 2011
- Metcalf, Barbara Daly; Metcalf, Thomas R. (2006), *A concise history of modern India*[224], Cambridge University Press, ISBN 978-0-521-86362-9
- Peers, Douglas M. (2006), *India under colonial rule: 1700-1885*[225], Pearson Education, ISBN 978-0-582-31738-3
- Moon, Penderel. *The British conquest and dominion of India* (2 vol. India Research Press, 1989)

- Riddick, John F. *The history of British India: a chronology* (2006) excerpt and text search[226], covers 1599–1947
- Riddick, John F. *Who Was Who in British India* (1998), covers 1599–1947
- Robb, Peter (2011), *A History of India*[227], Palgrave Macmillan, ISBN 978-0-230-34549-2
- Spear, Percival (1990) [First published 1965], *A History of India*[228], Volume 2, Penguin Books, ISBN 978-0-14-013836-8
- Stein, Burton; Arnold, David (2010), *A History of India*[229], John Wiley and Sons, ISBN 978-1-4051-9509-6
- Wolpert, Stanley (2008), *A new history of India*[230], Oxford University Press, ISBN 978-0-19-533756-3

Monographs and collections

- Ambirajan, S. (2007) [1978], *Classical Political Economy and British Policy in India*[231], Cambridge University Press, ISBN 978-0-521-05282-5, retrieved 20 February 2012
- Anderson, Clare (2007), *The Indian Uprising of 1857-8: prisons, prisoners, and rebellion*[232], Anthem Press, ISBN 978-1-84331-295-6, retrieved 5 November 2011
- Bayly, C. A. (1989), *Indian Society and the Making of the British Empire*[233], Cambridge University Press, ISBN 978-0-521-38650-0, retrieved 5 November 2011
- Bayly, C. A. (2000), *Empire and Information: Intelligence Gathering and Social Communication in India, 1780–1870 (Cambridge Studies in Indian History and Society)*, Cambridge and London: Cambridge University Press. Pp. 426, ISBN 0-521-66360-1
- Chakrabarti, D.K. 2003. The Archaeology of European Expansion in India, Gujarat, c. 16th–18th Centuries (2003) Delhi: Aryan Books International
- Chaudhuri, Kirti N. *The Trading World of Asia and the English East India Company: 1660-1760* (Cambridge University Press, 1978)
- Bose, Sumit (1993), *Peasant Labour and Colonial Capital: Rural Bengal since 1770 (New Cambridge History of India)*, Cambridge and London: Cambridge University Press..
- Chandavarkar, Rajnarayan (1998), *Imperial Power and Popular Politics: Class, Resistance and the State in India, 1850–1950*, (Cambridge Studies in Indian History & Society). Cambridge and London: Cambridge University Press. Pp. 400, ISBN 0-521-59692-0.
- Erikson, Emily. *Between Monopoly and Free Trade: The English East India Company, 1600-1757* (Princeton University Press, 2014)

- Farnie, D. A. (1979), *The English Cotton Industry and the World Market, 1815–1896*, Oxford, UK: Oxford University Press. Pp. 414, ISBN 0-19-822478-8
- Gilmour, David. *The Ruling Caste: Imperial Lives in the Victorian Raj* (New York: Farrar, Straus and Giroux, 2005).
- Guha, R. (1995), *A Rule of Property for Bengal: An Essay on the Idea of the Permanent Settlement*, Durham, NC: Duke University Press, ISBN 0-521-59692-0.
- Hossain, Hameeda. *The Company weavers of Bengal: the East India Company and the organization of textile production in Bengal, 1750-1813* (Oxford University Press, 1988)
- Marshall, P. J. (1987), *Bengal: The British Bridgehead, Eastern India, 1740–1828*, Cambridge and London: Cambridge University Press
- Marshall, P. J. (2007), *The Making and Unmaking of Empires: Britain, India, and America c.1750–1783*, Oxford and New York: Oxford University Press. Pp. 400, ISBN 0-19-922666-0
- Metcalf, Thomas R. (1991), *The Aftermath of Revolt: India, 1857–1870*, Riverdale Co. Pub. Pp. 352, ISBN 81-85054-99-1
- Metcalf, Thomas R. (1997), *Ideologies of the Raj*, Cambridge and London: Cambridge University Press, Pp. 256, ISBN 0-521-58937-1
- Misra, Maria (1999), *Business, Race, and Politics in British India, c.1850–1860*, Delhi: Oxford University Press. Pp. 264, ISBN 0-19-820711-5
- Porter, Andrew, ed. (2001), *Oxford History of the British Empire: Nineteenth Century*[234], Oxford and New York: Oxford University Press. Pp. 800, ISBN 0-19-924678-5
- Roy, Tirthankar (2011), *Economic History of India, 1857-1947*[235], Oxford University Press, ISBN 978-0-19-807417-5, retrieved 19 February 2012
- Stokes, Eric; Bayly (ed.), C.A. (1986), *The Peasant Armed: The Indian Revolt of 1857*, Oxford: Clarendon Press, p. 280, ISBN 0-19-821570-3.
- Stone, Ian (2002), *Canal Irrigation in British India: Perspectives on Technological Change in a Peasant Economy (Cambridge South Asian Studies)*, Cambridge and London: Cambridge University Press. Pp. 392, ISBN 0-521-52663-9
- Tomlinson, B. R. (1993), *The Economy of Modern India, 1860–1970 (The New Cambridge History of India, III.3)*, Cambridge and London: Cambridge University Press..
- Travers, Robert (2007), *Ideology and Empire in Eighteenth Century India: The British in Bengal (Cambridge Studies in Indian History and Society)*, Cambridge and London: Cambridge University Press. Pp. 292, ISBN 0-521-05003-0

Articles in journals or collections

- Banthia, Jayant; Dyson, Tim (December 1999), "Smallpox in Nineteenth-Century India", *Population and Development Review*, Population Council, **25** (4): 649–689, doi: 10.2307/172481[236], JSTOR 172481[237]
- Broadberry, Stephen; Gupta, Bishnupriya (2009), "Lancashire, India, and shifting competitive advantage in cotton textiles, 1700–1850: the neglected role of factor prices", *Economic History Review*, **62** (2): 279–305, doi: 10.1111/j.1468-0289.2008.00438.x[238]
- Caldwell, John C. (December 1998), "Malthus and the Less Developed World: The Pivotal Role of India", *Population and Development Review*, Population Council, **24** (4): 675–696, doi: 10.2307/2808021[239], JSTOR 2808021[240]
- Clingingsmith, David; Williamson, Jeffrey G. (2008), "Deindustrialization in 18th and 19th century India: Mughal decline, climate shocks and British industrial ascent", *Explorations in Economic History*, **45** (3): 209–234, doi: 10.1016/j.eeh.2007.11.002[241]
- Drayton, Richard (2001), "Science, Medicine, and the British Empire", in Winks, Robin, *Oxford History of the British Empire: Historiography*, Oxford and New York: Oxford University Press, pp. 264–276, ISBN 0-19-924680-7
- Frykenberg, Robert E. (2001), "India to 1858", in Winks, Robin, *Oxford History of the British Empire: Historiography*, Oxford and New York: Oxford University Press, pp. 194–213, ISBN 0-19-924680-7
- Harnetty, Peter (July 1991), "'Deindustrialization' Revisited: The Handloom Weavers of the Central Provinces of India, c. 1800-1947", *Modern Asian Studies*, Cambridge University Press, **25** (3): 455–510, doi: 10.1017/S0026749X00013901[242], JSTOR 312614[243]
- Heuman, Gad (2001), "Slavery, the Slave Trade, and Abolition", in Winks, Robin, *Oxford History of the British Empire: Historiography*, Oxford and New York: Oxford University Press, pp. 315–326, ISBN 0-19-924680-7
- Klein, Ira (1988), "Plague, Policy and Popular Unrest in British India", *Modern Asian Studies*, Cambridge University Press, **22** (4): 723–755, doi: 10.2307/312523[244], JSTOR 312523[245]
- Klein, Ira (July 2000), "Materialism, Mutiny and Modernisation in British India", *Modern Asian Studies*, Cambridge University Press, **34** (3): 545–580, JSTOR 313141[246]
- Kubicek, Robert (2001), "British Expansion, Empire, and Technological Change", in Porter, Andrew, *Oxford History of the British Empire: The Nineteenth Century*, Oxford and New York: Oxford University Press, pp. 247–269, ISBN 0-19-924678-5

- Raj, Kapil (2000), "Colonial Encounters and the Forging of New Knowledge and National Identities: Great Britain and India, 1760–1850", *Osiris, 2nd Series*, The University of Chicago Press, **15** (Nature and Empire: Science and the Colonial Enterprise): 119–134, doi: 10.1086/649322[247], JSTOR 301944[248]
- Ray, Rajat Kanta (July 1995), "Asian Capital in the Age of European Domination: The Rise of the Bazaar, 1800–1914", *Modern Asian Studies*, Cambridge University Press, **29** (3): 449–554, doi: 10.1017/S0026749X00013986[249], JSTOR 312868[250]
- Roy, Tirthankar (Summer 2002), "Economic History and Modern India: Redefining the Link", *The Journal of Economic Perspectives*, American Economic Association, **16** (3): 109–130, doi: 10.1257/089533002760278749[251], JSTOR 3216953[252]
- Tomlinson, B. R. (2001), "Economics and Empire: The Periphery and the Imperial Economy", in Porter, Andrew, *Oxford History of the British Empire: The Nineteenth Century*, Oxford and New York: Oxford University Press, pp. 53–74, ISBN 0-19-924678-5
- Washbrook, D. A. (2001), "India, 1818–1860: The Two Faces of Colonialism", in Porter, Andrew, *Oxford History of the British Empire: The Nineteenth Century*, Oxford and New York: Oxford University Press, pp. 395–421, ISBN 0-19-924678-5
- Wylie, Diana (2001), "Disease, Diet, and Gender: Late Twentieth Century Perspectives on Empire", in Winks, Robin, *Oxford History of the British Empire: Historiography*, Oxford and New York: Oxford University Press, pp. 277–289, ISBN 0-19-924680-7

Classic histories and gazetteers

- Allan, J., and Sir T. Wolseley Haig. *The Cambridge shorter history of India* (edited by Henry Dodwell. 1934) pp 399–589
- Imperial Gazetteer of India vol. IV (1908), *The Indian Empire, Administrative*, Published under the authority of His Majesty's Secretary of State for India in Council, Oxford at the Clarendon Press. Pp. xxx, 1 map, 552.
- Majumdar, R. C.; Raychaudhuri, H. C.; Datta, Kalikinkar (1950), *An Advanced History of India*, London: Macmillan and Company Limited. 2nd edition. Pp. xiii, 1122, 7 maps, 5 coloured maps.
- Wilson, Horace H (1845), *The History of British India from 1805 to 1835*[253], London: James Madden and Co., OCLC 63943320[254]
- Smith, Vincent A. (1921), *India in the British Period: Being Part III of the Oxford History of India*, Oxford: At the Clarendon Press. 2nd edition. Pp. xxiv, 316 (469-784)
- Thompson, Edward, and G. T. Garratt. *Rise and fulfilment of British rule in India* (Macmillan and Company, 1934.) 699pp; from 1599 to 1933

- Unknown (1829), *Historical and Ecclesiastical Sketches of Bengal; From the Earliest Settlement, Until the Virtual Conquest of that Country by the English, in 1757*[255]
- Bruce, John (1810), *Annals of the Honorable East-India Company: from their establishment by the charter of queen Elizabeth, 1600 to the Union of the London and the English East India Companies 1707-8, Vol-I*[256]
- Bruce, John (1810), *Annals of the Honorable East-India Company: from their establishment by the charter of queen Elizabeth, 1600 to the Union of the London and the English East India Companies 1707-8, Vol-II*[257]
- Marshman, John Clark (1867), *The History of India From the Earliest Period to the Close of Lord Dalhousie's Administration - 1867, Vol-I*[258]
- ⓔ This article incorporates public domain material from the Library of Congress Country Studies website http://lcweb2.loc.gov/frd/cs/[259].
- India[260] from Congress
- Pakistan[261] from Congress

Kingdom of Mysore

Kingdom of Mysore Princely State of Mysore	
Kingdom (Subordinate to Vijayanagara Empire until 1565) Princely state under the suzerainty of the British Crown from 1799	
1399–1948	
Flag  Coat of arms	
Anthem *Kayou Sri Gowri*	
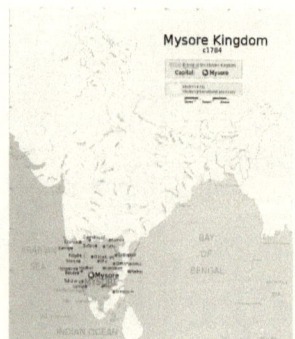 Kingdom of Mysore, 1784 AD (at its greatest extent)	
Capital	Mysore, Srirangapatna
Languages	Kannada
Religion	Hinduism, Islam
Government	Monarchy until 1799, Principality thereafter
Maharaja	
•	1399–1423 (first)	Yaduraya Wodeyar
•	1940–50 (last)	Jayachamaraja Wodeyar
History	
•	Established	1399

Kingdom of Mysore

	Earliest records	1551
	Disestablished	1948
	Preceded by	**Succeeded by**
	Vijayanagara Empire	Mysore State
Today part of		Republic of India

The **Kingdom of Mysore** was a kingdom in southern India, traditionally believed to have been founded in 1399 in the vicinity of the modern city of Mysore. The kingdom, which was ruled by the Wodeyar family, initially served as a vassal state of the Vijayanagara Empire. With the decline of the Vijayanagara Empire (c. 1565), the kingdom became independent. The 17th century saw a steady expansion of its territory and during the rule of Narasaraja Wodeyar I and Chikka Devaraja Wodeyar, the kingdom annexed large expanses of what is now southern Karnataka and parts of Tamil Nadu to become a powerful state in the southern Deccan.

The kingdom reached the height of its economic and military power and dominion in the latter half of the 18th century under the de facto ruler Haider Ali and his son Tipu Sultan. During this time, it came into conflict with the Marathas, the Nizam of Hyderabad, the Kingdom of Travancore and the British, which culminated in the four Anglo-Mysore Wars. Success in the first Anglo-Mysore war and a stalemate in the second was followed by defeat in the third and fourth. Following Tipu's death in the fourth war of 1799, large parts of his kingdom were annexed by the British, which signalled the end of a period of Mysorean hegemony over southern Deccan. The British restored the Wodeyars to their throne by way of a subsidiary alliance and the diminished Mysore was transformed into a princely state. The Wodeyars continued to rule the state until Indian independence in 1947, when Mysore acceded to the Union of India.

Even as a princely state, Mysore came to be counted among the more developed and urbanized regions of India. This period (1799–1947) also saw Mysore emerge as one of the important centres of art and culture in India. The Mysore kings were not only accomplished exponents of the fine arts and men of letters, they were enthusiastic patrons as well, and their legacies continue to influence music and art even today.

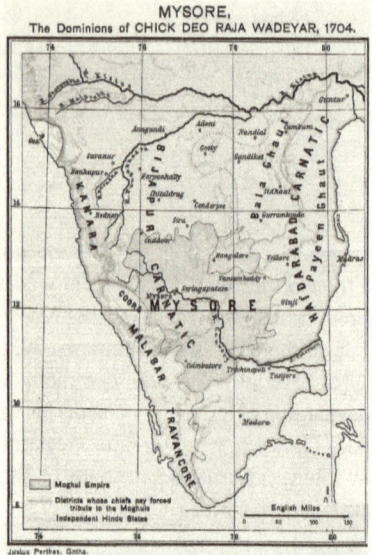

Figure 57: *Kingdom of Mysore (1704) during the rule of King Chikka Devaraja Wodeyar*

History

Early history

Sources for the history of the kingdom include numerous extant lithic and copper plate inscriptions, records from the Mysore palace and contemporary literary sources in Kannada, Persian and other languages.[262,263,264] According to traditional accounts, the kingdom originated as a small state based in the modern city of Mysore and was founded by two brothers, Yaduraya (also known as Vijaya) and Krishnaraya. Their origins are mired in legend and are still a matter of debate; while some historians posit a northern origin at Dwarka,[265,266] others locate it in Karnataka.[267,268] Yaduraya is said to have married Chikkadevarasi, the local princess and assumed the feudal title "Wodeyar" (*lit*, "Lord"), which the ensuing dynasty retained.[269] The first unambiguous mention of the Wodeyar family is in 16th century Kannada literature from the reign of the Vijayanagara king Achyuta Deva Raya (1529–1542); the earliest available inscription, issued by the Wodeyars themselves, dates to the rule of the petty chief Timmaraja II in 1551.[270]

Autonomy: advances and reversals

The kings who followed ruled as vassals of the Vijayanagara empire until the decline of the latter in 1565. By this time, the kingdom had expanded to thirty-three villages protected by a force of 300 soldiers. King Timmaraja II conquered some surrounding chiefdoms,[271] and King *Bola* Chamaraja IV (*lit*, "Bald"), the first ruler of any political significance among them, withheld tribute to the nominal Vijayanagara monarch Aravidu Ramaraya.[272] After the death of Aravidu Aliya Rama Raya, the Wodeyars began to assert themselves further and King Raja Wodeyar I wrested control of Srirangapatna from the Vijayanagara governor (*Mahamandaleshvara*) Aravidu Tirumalla – a development which elicited, if only *ex post facto*, the tacit approval of Venkatapati Raya, the incumbent king of the diminished Vijayanagar empire ruling from Chandragiri.[273] Raja Wodeyar I's reign also saw territorial expansion with the annexation of Channapatna to the north from Jaggadeva Raya[274] – a development which made Mysore a regional political factor to reckon with.[275]

Consequently, by 1612–13, the Wodeyars exercised a great deal of autonomy and even though they acknowledged the nominal overlordship of the Aravidu dynasty, tributes and transfers of revenue to Chandragiri stopped. This was in marked contrast to other major chiefs *Nayaks* of Tamil country who continued to pay off Chandragiri emperors well into the 1630s. Chamaraja VI and Kanthirava Narasaraja I attempted to expand further northward but were thwarted by the Bijapur Sultanate and its Maratha subordinates, though the Bijapur armies under Ranadullah Khan were effectively repelled in their 1638 siege of Srirangapatna.[276,277] Expansionist ambitions then turned southward into Tamil country where Narasaraja Wodeyar acquired Satyamangalam (in modern northern Coimbatore district) while his successor Dodda Devaraja Wodeyar expanded further to capture western Tamil regions of Erode and Dharmapuri, after successfully repulsing the chiefs of Madurai. The invasion of the Keladi Nayakas of Malnad was also dealt with successfully. This period was followed by one of complex geo-political changes, when in the 1670s, the Marathas and the Mughals pressed into the Deccan.

Chikka Devaraja (r. 1672–1704), the most notable of Mysore's early kings, who ruled during much of this period, managed to not only survive the exigencies but further expanded territory. He achieved this by forging strategic alliances with the Marathas and the Mughals.[278,279] The kingdom soon grew to include Salem and Bangalore to the east, Hassan to the west, Chikkamagaluru and Tumkur to the north and the rest of Coimbatore to the south.[280] Despite this expansion, the kingdom, which now accounted for a fair share of land in the southern Indian heartland, extending from the Western Ghats to the western boundaries of the Coromandel plain, remained landlocked without direct coastal access. Chikka Devaraja's attempts to remedy this brought Mysore into conflict with the *Nayaka* chiefs of Ikkeri and the kings (*Rajas*) of Kodagu (modern Coorg); who between them controlled the Kanara coast (coastal areas of modern Karnataka) and the intervening hill region respectively.[281] The conflict brought mixed results with Mysore annexing Periyapatna but suffering a reversal at Palupare.[282]

Nevertheless, from around 1704, when the kingdom passed on to "Muteking" (*Mukarasu*) Kanthirava Narasaraja II, the survival and expansion of the kingdom was achieved by playing a delicate game of alliance, negotiation, subordination on occasion, and annexation of territory in all directions. According to historians Sanjay Subrahmanyam and Sethu Madhava Rao, Mysore was now formally a tributary of the Mughal empire. Mughul records claim a regular tribute (*peshkash*) was paid by Mysore. However, historian Suryanath U. Kamath feels the Mughals may have considered Mysore an ally, a situation brought about by Mughal–Maratha competition for supremacy in southern India.[283] By the 1720s, with the Mughal empire in decline, further complications arose with the Mughal residents at both Arcot and Sira claiming tribute. The years that followed saw Krishnaraja Wodeyar I tread cautiously on the matter while keeping the Kodagu chiefs and the Marathas at bay. He was followed by Chamaraja Wodeyar VII during whose reign power fell into the hands of prime minister (*Dalwai* or *Dalavoy*) Nanjarajiah (or Nanjaraja) and chief minister (*Sarvadhikari*) Devarajiah (or Devaraja), the influential brothers from Kalale town near Nanjangud who would rule for the next three decades with the Wodeyars relegated to being the titular heads.[284,285] The latter part of the rule of Krishnaraja II saw the Deccan Sultanates being eclipsed by the Mughals and in the confusion that ensued, Haider Ali, a captain in the army, rose to prominence. His victory against the Marathas at Bangalore in 1758, resulting in the annexation of their territory, made him an iconic figure. In honour of his achievements, the king gave him the title "Nawab Haider Ali Khan Bahadur".

Under Haider Ali and Tipu Sultan

Though illiterate, Haider Ali has earned an important place in the history of Karnataka for his fighting skills and administrative acumen.[286,287] The rise of Haidar came at a time of important political developments in the sub-continent. While the European powers were busy transforming themselves from trading companies to political powers, the Nizam as the *subedar* of the Mughals pursued his ambitions in the Deccan, and the Marathas, following their defeat at Panipat, sought safe havens in the south. The period also saw the French vie with the British for control of the Carnatic – a contest in which the British would eventually prevail as British commander Sir Eyre Coote decisively defeated the French under the Comte de Lally at the Battle of Wandiwash in 1760, a watershed in Indian history as it cemented British supremacy in South

Kingdom of Mysore

Figure 58: *Admiral Suffren meeting with ally Hyder Ali in 1783. J.B. Morret engraving, 1789*

Figure 59: *The flag of the Sultanate of Mysore at the entrance into the fort of Bangalore*

Figure 60: *A portrait of Tipu Sultan, made during the Third Anglo-Mysore War*

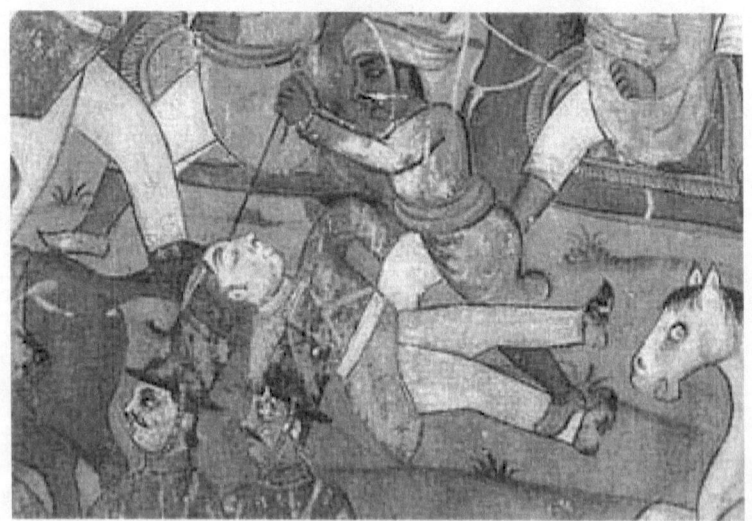

Figure 61: *Mural of the famous Battle of Pollilur in Tipu Sultan's summer palace in Srirangapatna*

Figure 62: *Lord Cornwallis hastily retreats after his unsuccessful Siege of Srirangapatna (1792).*

Asia.[288] Though the Wodeyars remained the nominal heads of Mysore during this period, real power lay in the hands of Haider Ali and his son Tipu.[289]

By 1761, the Maratha menace had diminished and by 1763, Haider Ali had captured the Keladi kingdom, defeated the rulers of Bilgi, Bednur and Gutti, invaded the Malabar in the south and conquered the Zamorin's capital Calicut with ease in 1766 and extended the Mysore kingdom up to Dharwad and Bellary in the north.[290,291] Mysore was now a major political power in the subcontinent and Haider's meteoric rise from relative obscurity and his defiance formed one of the last remaining challenges to complete British hegemony over the Indian subcontinent – a challenge which would take them more than three decades to overcome.[292]

In a bid to stem Haidar's rise, the British formed an alliance with the Marathas and the Nizam of Golconda, culminating in the First Anglo-Mysore War in 1767. Despite numerical superiority Haider Ali suffered defeats at the battles of Chengham and Tiruvannamalai. The British ignored his overtures for peace until Haider Ali had strategically moved his armies to within five miles of Madras (modern Chennai) and was able to successfully sue for peace.[293] In 1770, when the Maratha armies of Madhavrao Peshwa invaded Mysore (three wars were fought between 1764 and 1772 by Madhavrao against Haider, in which Haider lost), Haider expected British support as per the 1769 treaty but they betrayed him by staying out of the conflict. The British betrayal and Haider's subsequent defeat reinforced Haider's deep distrust of the British—a sentiment that would be shared by his son and one which would inform Anglo-Mysore rivalries of the next three decades. In 1777, Haider Ali recovered the previously lost territories of Coorg and Malabar from the Marathas. Haider Ali's army advanced towards the Marathas and fought them at the Battle of Saunshi and came out victorious during the same year.

By 1779, Haider Ali had captured parts of modern Tamil Nadu and Kerala in the south, extending the Kingdom's area to about 80,000 mi² (205,000 km²). In 1780, he befriended the French and made peace with the Marathas and the Nizam.[294] However, Haider Ali was betrayed by the Marathas and the Nizam, who made treaties with the British as well. In July 1779 Haider Ali headed an army of 80,000, mostly cavalry, descending through the passes of the Ghats amid burning villages, before laying siege to British forts in northern Arcot starting the Second Anglo-Mysore War. Haider Ali had some initial successes against the British notably at Pollilur, the worst defeat the British suffered in India until Chillianwala, and Arcot, until the arrival of Sir Eyre Coote, when the fortunes of the British began to change.[295] On 1 June 1781 Sir Eyre Coote struck the first heavy blow against Haider Ali in the decisive Battle of Porto Novo. The battle was won by Sir Eyre Coote against odds of five to one, and is regarded as one of the greatest feats of the British in India. It was followed up by another hard-fought battle at Pollilur (the scene of an earlier triumph of Haider Ali over a British force) on 27 August, in which the British won another success, and by the rout of the Mysore troops at Sholinghur a month later. Haider Ali died on 7 December 1782, even as fighting continued with the British. He was succeeded by his son Tipu Sultan who continued hostilities against the British by recapturing Baidanur and Mangalore.[296]

By 1783 neither the British nor Mysore were able to obtain a clear overall victory. The French withdrew their support of Mysore following the peace settlement in Europe.[297] Undaunted, Tipu, popularly known as the "Tiger of Mysore", continued the war against the British but lost some regions in modern coastal Karnataka to them. The Maratha-Mysore War occurred between 1785 and 1787 and consisted of a series of conflicts between the Sultanate of Mysore and the Maratha Empire. Following Tipu Sultan's victory against the Marathas at the Siege of Bahadur Benda, a peace agreement was signed between the two kingdoms with mutual gains and losses. Similarly, the treaty of Mangalore was signed in 1784 bringing hostilities with the British to a temporary and uneasy halt and restored the others' lands to the status quo ante bellum.[298] The treaty is an important document in the history of India, because it was the last occasion when an Indian power dictated terms to the British, who were made to play the role of humble supplicants for peace. A start of fresh hostilities between the British and French in Europe would have been sufficient reason for Tipu to abrogate his treaty and further his ambition of striking at the British.[299] His attempts to lure the Nizam, the Marathas, the French and the King of Turkey failed to bring direct military aid.

Tipu's successful attacks in 1790 on the Kingdom of Travancore, a British ally, was an effective victory for him, however it resulted in greater hostilities with the British which resulted in the Third Anglo-Mysore War. In the beginning, the British made gains, taking the Coimbatore district, but Tipu's counterattack reversed many of these gains. By 1792, with aid from the Marathas who attacked from the north-west and the Nizam who moved in from the northeast, the British under Lord Cornwallis successfully besieged Srirangapatna, resulting in Tipu's defeat and the Treaty of Srirangapatna. Half of Mysore was distributed among the allies, and two of his sons were held to ransom.[300] A humiliated but indomitable Tipu went about re-building his economic and military power. He attempted to covertly win over support from Revolutionary France, the Amir of Afghanistan, the Ottoman Empire and Arabia. However, these attempts to involve the French soon became known to the British, who were at the time fighting the French in Egypt, were backed by the Marathas and the Nizam. In 1799, Tipu died defending Srirangapatna in the Fourth Anglo-Mysore War, heralding the end of the Kingdom's independence.[301] Modern Indian historians consider Tipu Sultan an inveterate enemy of the British, an able administrator and an innovator.[302]

Princely state

Following Tipu's fall, a part of the kingdom of Mysore was annexed and divided between the Madras Presidency and the Nizam. The remaining territory was transformed into a Princely State; the five-year-old scion of the Wodeyar family, Krishnaraja III, was installed on the throne with chief minister (*Diwan*) Purnaiah, who had earlier served under Tipu, handling the reins as regent and Lt. Col. Barry Close taking charge as the British Resident. The British then took control of Mysore's foreign policy and also exacted an annual tribute and a subsidy for maintaining a standing British army at Mysore.[303,304,305] As Diwan, Purnaiah distinguished himself with his progressive and innovative administration until he retired from service in 1811 (and died shortly thereafter) following the 16th birthday of the boy king.[306,307]

The years that followed witnessed cordial relations between Mysore and the British until things began to sour in the 1820s. Even though the Governor of Madras, Thomas Munro, determined after a personal investigation in 1825 that there was no substance to the allegations of financial impropriety made by A. H. Cole, the incumbent Resident of Mysore, the Nagar rebellion (a civil

Figure 63: *"Palace of the Maharajah of Mysore, India," from the Illustrated London News, 1881 (with modern hand coloring)*

Figure 64: *Mysore Palace built between 1897 and 1912*

insurrection) which broke out towards the end of the decade changed things considerably. In 1831, close on the heels of the insurrection and citing maladministration, the British took direct control of the princely state.[308,309] For the next fifty years, Mysore passed under the rule of successive British Commissioners; Sir Mark Cubbon, renowned for his statesmanship, served from 1834 until 1861 and put into place an efficient and successful administrative system which left Mysore a well-developed state.[310]

In 1876–77, however, towards the end of the period of direct British rule, Mysore was struck by a devastating famine with estimated mortality figures ranging between 700,000 and 1,100,000, or nearly a fifth of the population.[311] Shortly thereafter, Maharaja Chamaraja X, educated in the British system, took over the rule of Mysore in 1881, following the success of a lobby set up by the Wodeyar dynasty that was in favour of rendition. Accordingly, a resident British officer was appointed at the Mysore court and a Diwan to handle the Maharaja's administration.[312] From then onwards, until Indian independence in 1947, Mysore remained a Princely State within the British Indian Empire, with the Wodeyars continuing their rule.

After the demise of Maharaja Chamaraja X, Krishnaraja IV, still a boy of eleven, ascended the throne in 1895. His mother Maharani Kemparajammanniyavaru ruled as regent until Krishnaraja took over the reins on 8 February 1902.[313] Under his rule, with Sir M. Vishweshwariah as his Diwan, the Maharaja set about transforming Mysore into a progressive and modern state, particularly in industry, education, agriculture and art. Such were the strides that Mysore made that Mahatma Gandhi called the Maharaja a "saintly king" (*Rajarishi*).[314] Paul Brunton, the British philosopher and orientalist, John Gunther, the American author, and British statesman Lord Samuel praised the ruler's efforts. Much of the pioneering work in educational infrastructure that took place during this period would serve Karnataka invaluably in the coming decades. The Maharaja was an accomplished musician, and like his predecessors, avidly patronised the development of the fine arts.[315] He was followed by his nephew Jayachamaraja whose rule came to an end when he signed the instrument of accession and Mysore joined the Indian Union on 9 August 1947.[316]

Administration

Mysore Kings (1399–present)	
Feudatory Monarchy (As vassals of Vijayanagara Empire) (1399–1553)	
Yaduraya Wodeyar	(1399–1423)
Chamaraja Wodeyar I	(1423–1459)
Timmaraja Wodeyar I	(1459–1478)
Chamaraja Wodeyar II	(1478–1513)
Chamaraja Wodeyar III	(1513–1553)
Absolute Monarchy (Independent Wodeyar Kings) (1553–1761)	
Timmaraja Wodeyar II	(1553–1572)
Chamaraja Wodeyar IV	(1572–1576)
Chamaraja Wodeyar V	(1576–1578)
Raja Wodeyar I	(1578–1617)
Chamaraja Wodeyar VI	(1617–1637)
Raja Wodeyar II	(1637–1638)
Narasaraja Wodeyar I	(1638–1659)
Dodda Devaraja Wodeyar	(1659–1673)
Chikka Devaraja Wodeyar	(1673–1704)
Narasaraja Wodeyar II	(1704–1714)
Krishnaraja Wodeyar I	(1714–1732)
Chamaraja Wodeyar VII	(1732–1734)
Krishnaraja Wodeyar II	(1734–1761)
Puppet Monarchy (Under Haider Ali and Tipu Sultan) (1761–1799)	
Krishnaraja Wodeyar II	(1761–1766)
Nanjaraja Wodeyar	(1766–1770)
Chamaraja Wodeyar VIII	(1770–1776)
Chamaraja Wodeyar IX	(1776–1796)
Puppet Monarchy (Under British Rule) (1799–1831)	
Krishnaraja Wodeyar III	(1799–1831)

Titular Monarchy (Monarchy abolished) (1831–1881)	
Krishnaraja Wodeyar III	(1831–1868)
Chamaraja Wodeyar X	(1868–1881)
Absolute Monarchy Monarchy restored (As allies of the British Crown) (1881–1947)	
Chamaraja Wodeyar X	(1881–1894)
Krishnaraja Wodeyar IV	(1894–1940)
Jayachamaraja Wodeyar	(1940–1947)
Constitutional Monarchy (In Dominion of India) (1947–1950)	
Jayachamaraja Wodeyar	(1947–1950)
Titular Monarchy (Monarchy abolished) (1950–present)	
Jayachamaraja Wodeyar	(1950–1974)
Srikanta Wodeyar	(1974–2013)
Yaduveera Chamaraja Wadiyar	(2015–present)

There are no records relating to the administration of the Mysore territory during the Vijayanagara Empire's reign (1399–1565). Signs of a well-organised and independent administration appear from the time of Raja Wodeyar I who is believed to have been sympathetic towards peasants (*raiyats*) who were exempted from any increases in taxation during his time. The first sign that the kingdom had established itself in the area was the issuing of gold coins (*Kanthirayi phanam*) resembling those of the erstwhile Vijayanagara Empire during Narasaraja Wodeyar's rule.[317]

The rule of Chikka Devaraja saw several reforms were effected. Internal administration was remodeled to suit the kingdom's growing needs and became more efficient. A postal system came into being. Far reaching financial reforms were also introduced. A number of petty taxes were imposed in place of direct taxes, as a result of which the peasants were compelled to pay more by way of land tax.[318] The king is said to have taken a personal interest in the regular collection of revenues the treasury burgeoned to 90,000,000 *Pagoda* (a unit of currency) – earning him the epithet "Nine crore Narayana" (*Navakoti Narayana*). In 1700, he sent an embassy to Aurangazeb's court who bestowed upon him the title *Jug Deo Raja* and awarded permission to sit on the ivory throne. Following this, he founded the district offices (*Attara Kacheri*), the central secretariat comprising eighteen departments, and his administration was modeled on Mughal lines.[319]

During Haider Ali's rule, the kingdom was divided into five provinces (*Asofis*) of unequal size, comprising 171 taluks (*Paraganas*) in total.[320] When Tipu Sultan became the *de facto* ruler, the kingdom, which encompassed 160,000 km² (61,776 sq mi) (62,000 mi²), was divided into 37 provinces and a total of 124 taluks (*Amil*). Each province had a governor (*Asof*), and one deputy governor. Each taluk had a headman called *Amildar* and a group of villages were in charge of a *Patel*. The central administration comprised six departments headed by ministers, each aided by an advisory council of up to four members.[321]

When the princely state came under direct British rule in 1831, early commissioners Lushington, Briggs and Morrison were followed by Mark Cubbon, who took charge in 1834.[322] He made Bangalore the capital and divided the princely state into four divisions, each under a British superintendent. The state was further divided into 120 taluks with 85 taluk courts, with all lower level administration in the Kannada language. The office of the commissioner had eight departments; revenue, post, police, cavalry, public works, medical, animal husbandry, judiciary and education. The judiciary was hierarchical with the commissioners' court at the apex, followed by the *Huzur Adalat*, four superintending courts and eight *Sadar Munsiff* courts at the lowest level.[323] Lewin Bowring became the chief commissioner in 1862 and held the position until 1870. During his tenure, the property "Registration Act", the "Indian Penal code" and "Code of Criminal Procedure" came into effect and the judiciary was separated from the executive branch of the administration. The state was divided into eight districts – Bangalore, Chitraldroog, Hassan, Kadur, Kolar, Mysore, Shimoga, and Tumkur.[324]

After rendition, C. V. Rungacharlu, was made the Diwan. Under him, the first Representative Assembly of British India, with 144 members, was formed in 1881.[325] He was followed by K. Seshadri Iyer in 1883 during whose tenure gold mining at the Kolar Gold Fields began, the Shivanasamudra hydroelectric project was initiated in 1899 (the first such major attempt in India) and electricity and drinking water (the latter through pipes) was supplied to Bangalore.[326] Seshadri Iyer was followed by P. N. Krishnamurti, who founded The Secretariat Manual to maintain records and the Co-operative Department in 1905, V. P. Madhava Rao who focussed on conservation of forests and T. Ananda Rao, who finalised the Kannambadi Dam project.[327]

Sir M. Visvesvaraya, popularly known as the "Maker of Modern Mysore", holds a key place in the history of Karnataka.[328] An engineer by education, he became the Diwan in 1909.[329] Under his tenure, membership of the Mysore Legislative Assembly was increased from 18 to 24, and it was given the power to discuss the state budget. The Mysore Economic Conference was expanded into three committees; industry and commerce, education, and agriculture, with publications in English and Kannada.[330] Important projects commissioned during his time included the construction of the Kannambadi Dam, the founding of the Mysore Iron Works at Bhadravathi, founding of the Mysore University in 1916, the University Visvesvaraya College of Engineering in Bangalore, establishment of the Mysore state railway department and numerous industries in Mysore. In 1955, he was awarded the Bharat Ratna, India's highest civilian honor.[331]

Sir Mirza Ismail took office as Diwan in 1926 and built on the foundation laid by his predecessor. Amongst his contributions were the expansion of the Bhadravathi Iron Works, the founding of a cement and paper factory in Bhadravathi and the launch of Hindustan Aeronautics Limited. A man with a penchant for gardens, he founded the Brindavan Gardens (Krishnaraja Sagar) and built the Kaveri River high-level canal to irrigate 120,000 acres (490 km^2) in modern Mandya district.[332]

In 1939 Mandya District was carved out of Mysore District, bringing the number of districts in the state to nine.

Economy

The vast majority of the people lived in villages and agriculture was their main occupation. The economy of the kingdom was based on agriculture. Grains, pulses, vegetables and flowers were cultivated. Commercial crops included sugarcane and cotton. The agrarian population consisted of landlords (*vokkaliga, zamindar, heggadde*) who tilled the land by employing a number of landless labourers, usually paying them in grain. Minor cultivators were also willing to hire themselves out as labourers if the need arose.[333] It was due to the availability of these landless labourers that kings and landlords were able to execute major projects such as palaces, temples, mosques, anicuts (dams) and tanks.[334] Because land was abundant and the population relatively sparse, no rent was charged on land ownership. Instead, landowners paid tax for cultivation, which amounted to up to one-half of all harvested produce.

Under Hyder Ali and Tipu Sultan

The Kingdom of Mysore reached a peak in economic power under Hyder Ali and Tipu Sultan, in the post-Mughal era of the mid-late 18th century. They embarked on an ambitious program of economic development, aiming to increase the wealth and revenue of Mysore. Under their reign, Mysore overtook the Bengal Subah as India's dominant economic power, with productive agriculture and textile manufacturing.

Tipu Sultan is credited to have founded state trading depots in various locations of his kingdom. In addition, he founded depots in foreign locations such as Karachi, Jeddah and Muscat, where Mysore products were sold.[335] During Tipu's rule French technology was used for the first time in carpentry and smithy, Chinese technology was used for sugar production, and technology from Bengal helped improve the sericulture industry.[336] State factories were established in Kanakapura and Taramandelpeth for producing cannons and gunpowder respectively. The state held the monopoly in the production of essentials such as sugar, salt, iron, pepper, cardamom, betel nut, tobacco and sandalwood, as well as the extraction of incense oil from sandalwood and the mining of silver, gold and precious stones. Sandalwood was exported to China and the Persian Gulf countries and sericulture was developed in twenty-one centers within the kingdom.[337]

The Mysore silk industry was first initiated during the rule of Tipu Sultan. Later the industry was hit by a global depression and competition from imported silk and rayon. In the second half of the 20th century, it however revived and the Mysore State became the top multivoltine silk producer in India.

Under Tipu Sultan, Mysore enjoyed one of the world's highest real wages and living standards in the late 18th century, higher than Britain, which in turn had the highest living standards in Europe. Mysore's average per-capita income was five times higher than subsistence level, i.e. five times higher than $400 (1990 international dollars), or $2,000 per capita. In comparison, the highest national per-capita incomes in 1820 were $1,838 for the Netherlands and $1,706 for Britain.[338]

British rule

This system changed under the British, when tax payments were made in cash, and were used for the maintenance of the army, police and other civil and public establishments. A portion of the tax was transferred to England as the "Indian tribute".[339] Unhappy with the loss of their traditional revenue system and the problems they faced, peasants rose in rebellion in many parts of south India.[340] After 1800, the Cornwallis land reforms came into effect. Reade, Munro, Graham and Thackeray were some administrators who improved the economic conditions of the masses.[341] However, the homespun textile industry suffered during British rule, with the exception of the producers of the finest cloth and the coarse cloth which was popular with the rural masses. This was due to the manufacturing mills of Manchester, Liverpool and Scotland being more than a match for the traditional handweaving industry, especially in spinning and weaving.[342,343]

The economic revolution in England and the tariff policies of the British also caused massive de-industrialization in other sectors throughout India and

Figure 65: *Temple pond constructed by King Chikka Devaraja Wodeyar at Shravanabelagola, an important Jain temple town*

Mysore. For example, the gunny bag weaving business had been a monopoly of the Goniga people, which they lost when the British began ruling the area. The import of a chemical substitute for saltpetre (potassium nitrate) affected the Uppar community, the traditional makers of saltpetre for use in gunpowder. The import of kerosene affected the Ganiga community which supplied oils. Foreign enamel and crockery industries affected the native pottery business, and mill-made blankets replaced the country-made blankets called *kambli*.[344] This economic fallout led to the formation of community-based social welfare organisations to help those within the community to cope better with their new economic situation, including youth hostels for students seeking education and shelter.[345] However, the British economic policies created a class structure consisting of a newly established middle class comprising various blue and white-collared occupational groups, including agents, brokers, lawyers, teachers, civil servants and physicians. Due to a more flexible caste hierarchy, the middle class contained a heterogeneous mix of people from different castes.[346]

Culture

Religion

The early kings of the Wodeyar dynasty worshipped the Hindu god Shiva. The later kings, starting from the 17th century, took to Vaishnavism, the worship of

Figure 66: *Shweta Varahaswamy temple (1673–1704) in the Mysore Palace grounds*

the Hindu god Vishnu.[347] According to musicologist Meera Rajaram Pranesh, King Raja Wodeyar I was a devotee of the god Vishnu, King Dodda Devaraja was honoured with the title "Protector of Brahmins" (*Deva Brahmana Paripalaka*) for his support to Brahmins, and Maharaja Krishnaraja III was devoted to the goddess Chamundeshwari (a form of Hindu goddess Durga).[348] Wilks ("History of Mysore", 1800) wrote about a *Jangama* (Veerashaiva saint-devotee of Shiva) uprising, related to excessive taxation, which was put down firmly by Chikka Devaraja. Historian D.R. Nagaraj claims that four hundred *Jangamas* were murdered in the process but clarifies that Veerashiava literature itself is silent about the issue.[349] Historian Suryanath Kamath claims King Chikka Devaraja was a Srivaishnava (follower of Sri Vaishnavism, a sect of Vaishnavism) but was not anti-Veerashaiva.[350] Historian Aiyangar concurs that some of the kings including the celebrated Narasaraja I and Chikka Devaraja were Vaishnavas, but suggests this may not have been the case with all Wodeyar rulers.[351] The rise of the modern day Mysore city as a centre of south Indian culture has been traced from the period of their sovereignty.[352] Raja Wodeyar I initiated the celebration of the Dasara festival in Mysore, a proud tradition of the erstwhile Vijayanagara royal family.[353,354]

Jainism, though in decline during the late medieval period, also enjoyed the patronage of the Mysore kings, who made munificent endowments to the Jain monastic order at the town of Shravanabelagola.[355,356] Records indicate that some Wodeyar kings not only presided over the *Mahamastakabhisheka* ceremony, an important Jain religious event at Shravanabelagola, but also personally offered prayers (*puja*) during the years 1659, 1677, 1800, 1825, 1910, 1925, 1940, and 1953.[357]

The contact between South India and Islam goes back to the 7th century, when trade between Hindu kingdoms and Islamic caliphates thrived. These Muslim traders settled on the Malabar Coast and married local Hindu women, and their descendants came to be known as *Mappillas*.[358] By the 14th century, Muslims had become a significant minority in the south, though the advent of Portuguese missionaries checked their growth. Haider Ali, though a devout Muslim, did not allow his faith to interfere with the administration of the predominantly Hindu kingdom. Historians are, however, divided on the intentions of Haider Ali's son, Tipu Sultan. It has been claimed that Tipu raised Hindus to prominent positions in his administration, made generous grants to Hindu temples and brahmins, and generally respected other faiths, and that any religious conversions that Tipu undertook were as punishment to those who rebelled against his authority.[359] However, this has been countered by other historians who claim that Tipu Sultan treated the non-Muslims of Mysore far better than those of the Malabar, Raichur and Kodagu regions. They opine that Tipu was responsible for mass conversions of Christians and Hindus in these regions, either by force or by offering them tax incentives and revenue benefits to convert.[360,361]

Society

Prior to the 18th century, the society of the kingdom followed age-old and deeply established norms of social interaction between people. Accounts by contemporaneous travellers indicate the widespread practice of the Hindu caste system and of animal sacrifices during the nine-day celebrations (called *Mahanavami*).[362] Later, fundamental changes occurred due to the struggle between native and foreign powers. Though wars between the Hindu kingdoms and the Sultanates continued, the battles between native rulers (including Muslims) and the newly arrived British took centre stage. The spread of English education, the introduction of the printing press and the criticism of the prevailing social system by Christian missionaries helped make the society more open and flexible. The rise of modern nationalism throughout India also affected Mysore.[363]

With the advent of British power, English education gained prominence in addition to traditional education in local languages. These changes were orchestrated by Lord Elphinstone, the governor of the Madras Presidency. His plan became the constitution of the central collegiate institution or University Board

Figure 67: *The Crawford Hall on Mysore University campus houses the university offices.*

in 1841.[364] Accordingly, a high school department of the university was established. For imparting education in the interior regions, schools were raised in principal towns which eventually were elevated to college level, with each college becoming central to many local schools (*zilla* schools).[365] The earliest English-medium schools appeared in 1833 in Mysore and spread across the region. In 1858, the department of education was founded in Mysore and by 1881, there were an estimated 2,087 English-medium schools in the state of Mysore. Higher education became available with the formation of Bangalore Central College in Bangalore (1870), Maharaja's College (1879), Maharani's College (1901) and the Mysore University (1916) in Mysore and the St. Agnes College in Mangalore (1921).[366]

Social reforms aimed at removing practices such as sati and social discrimination based upon untouchability, as well as demands for the emancipation of the lower classes, swept across India and influenced Mysore territory.[367] In 1894, the kingdom passed laws to abolish the marriage of girls below the age of eight. Remarriage of widowed women and marriage of destitute women was encouraged, and in 1923, some women were granted the permission to exercise their franchise in elections.[368] There were, however, uprisings against British authority in the Mysore territory, notably the Kodagu uprising in 1835 (after the British dethroned the local ruler Chikkaviraraja) and the Kanara uprising of 1837.[369] The era of printing heralded by Christian missionaries, no-

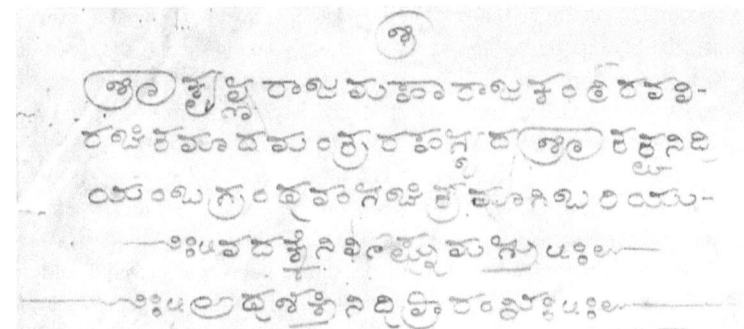

Figure 68: *Opening page of the musical treatise Sritattvanidhi proclaiming Krishnaraja Wodeyar III as the author*

tably Hermann Mögling, resulted in the founding of printing presses across the kingdom. The publication of ancient and contemporary Kannada books (such as the *Pampa Bharata* and the *Jaimini Bharata*), a Kannada-language Bible, a bilingual dictionary and a Kannada newspaper called *Kannada Samachara* began in the early 19th century.[370] Aluru Venkata Rao published a consolidated Kannada history glorifying the achievements of Kannadigas in his book *Karnataka Gatha Vaibhava*.[371]

Classical English and Sanskrit drama,[372] and native Yakshagana musical theater influenced the Kannada stage and produced famous dramatists like Gubbi Veeranna.[373] The public began to enjoy Carnatic music through its broadcast via public address systems set up on the palace grounds.[374] Mysore paintings, which were inspired by the Bengal Renaissance, were created by artists such as Sundarayya, Ala Singarayya, and B. Venkatappa.[375]

Literature

The era of the Kingdom of Mysore is considered a golden age in the development of Kannada literature. Not only was the Mysore court adorned by famous Brahmin and Veerashaiva writers and composers,[376] the kings themselves were accomplished in the fine arts and made important contributions.[377,378] While conventional literature in philosophy and religion remained popular, writings in new genres such as chronicle, biography, history, encyclopedia, novel, drama, and musical treatise became popular.[379] A native form of folk literature with dramatic representation called Yakshagana gained popularity.[380,381] A remarkable development of the later period was the influence of English literature and classical Sanskrit literature on Kannada.[382]

Govinda Vaidya, a native of Srirangapatna, wrote *Kanthirava Narasaraja Vijaya*, a eulogy of his patron King Narasaraja I. Written in *sangatya* metre (a composition meant to be rendered to the accompaniment of a musical instrument), the book describes the king's court, popular music and the types of musical compositions of the age in twenty-six chapters.[383,384] King Chikka Devaraja was the earliest composer of the dynasty.[385] To him is ascribed the famous treatise on music called *Geetha Gopala*. Though inspired by Jayadeva's Sanskrit writing *Geetha Govinda*, it had an originality of its own and was written in *saptapadi* metre.[386] Contemporary poets who left their mark on the entire Kannada-speaking region include the brahmin poet Lakshmisa and the itinerant Veerashaiva poet Sarvajna. Female poets also played a role in literary developments, with Cheluvambe (the queen of Krishnaraja Wodeyar I), Helavanakatte Giriyamma, Sri Rangamma (1685) and Sanchi Honnamma (*Hadibadeya Dharma*, late 17th century) writing notable works.[387,388]

A polyglot, King Narasaraja II authored fourteen Yakshaganas in various languages, though all are written in Kannada script.[389] Maharaja Krishnaraja III was a prolific writer in Kannada for which he earned the honorific *Abhinava Bhoja* (a comparison to the medieval King Bhoja).[390] Over forty writings are attributed to him, of which the musical treatise *Sri Tatwanidhi* and a poetical romance called *Saugandika Parinaya* written in two versions, a *sangatya* and a drama, are most well known.[391] Under the patronage of the Maharaja, Kannada literature began its slow and gradual change towards modernity. Kempu Narayana's *Mudramanjusha* ("The Seal Casket", 1823) is the earliest work that has touches of modern prose.[392] However, the turning point came with the historically important *Adbhuta Ramayana* (1895) and *Ramaswamedham* (1898) by Muddanna, whom the Kannada scholar Narasimha Murthy considers "a Janus like figure" of modern Kannada literature. Muddanna has deftly handled an ancient epic from an entirely modern viewpoint.[393]

Basavappa Shastry, a native of Mysore and a luminary in the court of Maharaja Krishnaraja III and Maharaja Chamaraja X, is known as the "Father of Kannada theatre" (*Kannada Nataka Pitamaha*).[394] He authored dramas in Kannada and translated William Shakespeare's "Othello" to *Shurasena Charite*. His well-known translations from Sanskrit to Kannada are many and include *Kalidasa* and *Abhignyana Shakuntala*.[395]

Music

Under Maharaja Krishnaraja III and his successors – Chamaraja X, Krishnaraja IV and the last ruler, Jayachamaraja, the Mysore court came to be the largest and most renowned patron of music.[396] While the Tanjore and Travancore courts also extended great patronage and emphasised preservation of the art, the unique combination of royal patronage of individual musicians, founding of music schools to kindle public interest and a patronage of European music publishers and producers set Mysore apart.[397] Maharaja Krishnaraja III,

Figure 69: *Legendary Vainikas – Veene Subbanna and Veene Sheshanna (photographed in 1902)*

himself a musician and musicologist of merit, composed a number of *javalis* (light lyrics) and devotional songs in Kannada under the title *Anubhava pancharatna*. His compositions bear the nom de plume (*mudra*) "Chamundi" or "'Chamundeshwari'", in honour of the Wodeyar family deity.[398] His successor Chamaraja X founded the Oriental Library in 1891 to house music books and also commissioned phonograph recordings of several musicians for the palace library.

Under Krishnaraja IV, art received further patronage. A distinct school of music which gave importance to *raga* and *bhava* evolved.[399,400] The Royal School of Music founded at the palace helped institutionalise teaching of the art. Carnatic compositions were printed and the European staff notation came to be employed by royal musicians. Western music was also encouraged – Margaret Cousins' piano concerto with the Palace Orchestra marked the celebrations of Beethoven's centenary in Bangalore. Maharaja Jayachamaraja, also a renowned composer of Carnatic *kritis* (a musical composition), sponsored a series of recordings of Russian composer Nikolas Medtner and others. The court ensured that Carnatic music also kept up with the times. Gramophone recordings of the palace band were made and sold commercially.[401] Attention was paid to "technology of the concert". Lavish sums were spent on acquiring various instruments including the unconventional horn violin, theremin and calliaphone, a mechanical music player.[402]

The Mysore court was home to several renowned experts (*vidwan*) of the time. Veena Sheshanna, a court musician during the rule of Maharaja Chamaraja X,[403] is considered one of the greatest exponents of the veena.[404] His achievements in classical music won Mysore a premier place in the art of instrumental Carnatic music and he was given the honorific *Vainika Shikhamani* by Maharaja Krishnaraja Wodeyar IV.[405] Mysore Vasudevacharya was a noted musician and composer in Sanskrit and Telugu from Mysore.[406] He holds the unique distinction of being patronised by four generations of Mysore kings and rulers and for being court musician to three of them.[407,408] H.L. Muthiah Bhagavatar was another musician-composer who adorned the Mysore court.[409] Considered one of the most important composers of the post-Tyagaraja period,[410] he is credited with about 400 compositions in Sanskrit, Kannada, Telugu and Tamil under the pen name "Harikesha". Among violinists, T. Chowdiah emerged as one of the most accomplished exponents of the time. He is known to have mastered the seven-stringed violin.[411] Chowdiah was appointed court musician by Maharaja Krishnaraja Wodeyar IV in 1939 and received such titles as "Sangeeta Ratna" and "Sangeeta Kalanidhi". He is credited with compositions in Kannada, Telugu and Sanskrit under the pen name "Trimakuta".[412]

Architecture

The architectural style of courtly and royal structures in the kingdom underwent profound changes during British rule – a mingling of European traditions with native elements. The Hindu temples in the kingdom were built in typical South Indian Dravidian style – a modest version of the Vijayanagara building idiom.[413] When in power, Tipu Sultan constructed a palace and a mosque in Srirangapatna, his capital. However, it is the city of Mysore that is best known for its royal palaces, earning it the nickname "City of Palaces". The city's main palace, the Mysore Palace, is also known as the Amba Vilas Palace. The original complex was destroyed by fire and a new palace was commissioned by the Queen-Regent and designed by the English architect Henry Irwin in 1897.[414] The overall design is a combination of Hindu, Islamic, Indo-Saracenic and Moorish styles, which for the first time in India, used cast iron columns and roof frames. The striking feature of the exterior is the granite columns that support cusped arches on the portico, a tall tower whose finial is a gilded dome with an umbrella (*chattri*) on it, and groups of other domes around it.[415] The interior is richly decorated with marbled walls and a teakwood ceiling on which are sculptures of Hindu deities. The Durbar hall leads to an inner private hall through silver doors. This opulent room has floor panels that are inlaid with semi-precious stones, and a stained glass roof supported centrally by columns and arches. The marriage hall (*Kalyana mantapa*) in the palace complex is noted for its stained glass octagonal dome with peacock motifs.[416]

The Lalitha Mahal Palace was built in 1921 by E.W. Fritchley under the commission of Maharaja Krishnaraja IV. The architectural style is called "Renaissance" and exhibits concepts from English manor houses and Italian palazzos.[417] The central dome is believed to be modelled on St. Paul's Cathedral in London. Other important features are the Italian marble staircase, the polished wooden flooring in the banquet and dance halls, and the Belgian cut glass lamps. The Jaganmohan Palace was commissioned in 1861 and was completed in 1910. The three-storeyed building with attractive domes, finials and cupolas was the venue of many a royal celebration. It is now called the Chamarajendra Art Gallery and houses a rich collection of artifacts.[418]

The Mysore University campus, also called "Manasa Gangotri", is home to several architecturally interesting buildings. Some of them are in European style and were completed in the late 19th century. They include the Jayalakshmi Vilas mansion, the Crawford Hall, the Oriental Research Institute (built between 1887 and 1891) with its Ionic and Corinthian columns, and the district offices (*Athara Kutchery*, 1887). The Athara Kutchery, which initially served as the office of the British commissioner, has an octagonal dome and a finial that adds to its beauty.[419] The maharaja's summer palace, built in 1880, is called the Lokaranjan Mahal, and initially served as a school for royalty. The Rajendra Vilas Palace, built in the Indo-British style atop the Chamundi Hill, was commissioned in 1922 and completed in 1938 by Maharaja Krishnaraja IV. Other royal mansions built by the Mysore rulers were the Chittaranjan Mahal in Mysore and the Bangalore Palace in Bangalore, a structure built on the lines of England's Windsor Castle.[420] The Central Food Technical Research Institute (Cheluvamba Mansion), built in baroque European renaissance style, was once the residence of princess Cheluvambaamani Avaru, a sister of Maharaja Krishnaraja IV. Its extensive pilaster work and mosaic flooring are noteworthy.[421]

Most famous among the many temples built by the Wodeyars is the Chamundeshwari Temple atop the Chamundi Hill. The earliest structure here was consecrated in the 12th century and was later patronised by the Mysore rulers. Maharaja Krishnaraja III added a Dravidian-style gopuram in 1827. The temple has silver-plated doors with images of deities. Other images include those of the Hindu god Ganesha and of Maharaja Krishnaraja III with his three queens.[422] Surrounding the main palace in Mysore and inside the fort are a group of temples, built in various periods. The Prasanna Krishnaswamy Temple (1829), the Lakshmiramana Swamy Temple whose earliest structures date to 1499, the Trinesvara Swamy Temple (late 16th century), the Shweta

Varaha Swamy Temple built by Purnaiah with a touch of Hoysala style of architecture, the Prasanna Venkataramana Swami Temple (1836) notable for 12 murals of the Wodeyar rulers.[423] Well-known temples outside Mysore city are the yali ("mythical beast") pillared Venkataramana temple built in the late 17th century in the Bangalore fort, and the Ranganatha temple in Srirangapatna.[424]

Tipu Sultan built a wooden colonnaded palace called the Dariya Daulat Palace (*lit*, "garden of the wealth of the sea") in Srirangapatna in 1784. Built in the Indo-Saracenic style, the palace is known for its intricate woodwork consisting of ornamental arches, striped columns and floral designs, and paintings. The west wall of the palace is covered with murals depicting Tipu Sultan's victory over Colonel Baillie's army at Pollilur, near Kanchipuram in 1780. One mural shows Tipu enjoying the fragrance of a bouquet of flowers while the battle is in progress. In that painting, the French soldiers' moustaches distinguish them from the cleanshaven British soldiers.[425,426] Also in Srirangapatna is the Gumbaz mausoleum, built by Tipu Sultan in 1784. It houses the graves of Tipu and Haider Ali. The granite base is capped with a dome built of brick and pilaster.[427]

Figure 70: *Mysore Palace*

Figure 71: *The Gopura (tower) of the Chamundeshwari Temple on the Chamundi Hills. The temple is dedicated to Mysore's patron deity.*

Figure 72: *The Jaganmohan Palace at Mysore – now an art gallery which is home to some of Raja Ravi Varma's masterpieces*

Figure 73: *Tipu Sultan's tomb at Srirangapatna*

Figure 74: *Lalitha Mahal at Mysore, now a five-star hotel, plays host to visiting dignitaries and VIPs.*

Military technology

The first iron-cased and metal-cylinder rocket artillery were developed by Tipu Sultan and his father Hyder Ali, in the 1780s. He successfully used these metal-cylinder rockets against the larger forces of the British East India Company during the Anglo-Mysore Wars. The Mysore rockets of this period were much more advanced than what the British had seen, chiefly because of the use of iron tubes for holding the propellant; this enabled higher thrust and longer range for the missile (up to 2 km (1 mi) range). After Tipu's eventual defeat in the Fourth Anglo-Mysore War and the capture of the Mysore iron rockets, they were influential in British rocket development, inspiring the Congreve rocket, which was soon put into use in the Napoleonic Wars.[428]

According to Stephen Oliver Fought and John F. Guilmartin, Jr. in *Encyclopædia Britannica* (2008):

> Hyder Ali, prince of Mysore, developed war rockets with an important change: the use of metal cylinders to contain the combustion powder. Although the hammered soft iron he used was crude, the bursting strength of the container of black powder was much higher than the earlier paper construction. Thus a greater internal pressure was possible, with a resultant greater thrust of the propulsive jet. The rocket body was lashed with leather thongs to a long bamboo stick. Range was perhaps up to three-quarters of a mile (more than a kilometre). Although individually these rockets were not accurate, dispersion error became less important when large numbers were fired rapidly in mass attacks. They were particularly effective against cavalry and were hurled into the air, after lighting, or skimmed along the hard dry ground. Tipu Sultan, continued to develop and expand the use of rocket weapons, reportedly increasing the number of rocket troops from 1,200 to a corps of 5,000. In battles at Seringapatam in 1792 and 1799 these rockets were used with considerable effect against the British.'[429]

References

<templatestyles src="Template:Refbegin/styles.css" />

- Abram, David; Edwards, Nick; Ford, Mike; Sen, Devdan; Wooldridge, Beth (2003). *South India*. Rough Guides. ISBN 1-84353-103-8.
- Aiyangar, Krishnaswami S. (1911). *Ancient India: Collected Essays on the Literary and Political History of Southern India*. New Delhi: (Facsimile Reprint 2004) Asian Educational Services. ISBN 81-206-1850-5.
- Bakshi, Shiri Ram (1996). *Gandhi and the Congress*. New Delhi: Sarup and Sons. ISBN 81-85431-65-5.

- Bradnock, Robert (2000) [2000]. *South India Handbook – The Travel Guide*. Footprint Travel Guide. ISBN 1-900949-81-4.
- Chopra, P. N.; Ravindran, T. K.; Subrahmanian, N. (2003). *History of South India (Ancient, Medieval and Modern) Part III*. New Delhi: Sultan Chand and Sons. ISBN 81-219-0153-7.
- Indian Science Congress Association (various authors), Presidential Address, vol 1: 1914–1947 (2003). *The Shaping of Indian Science*. Orient Blackswan. ISBN 81-7371-432-0.
- Kamath, Suryanath U. (2001) [1980]. *A concise history of Karnataka : from pre-historic times to the present*. Bangalore: Jupiter books. LCCN 80905179[430]. OCLC 7796041[431].
- Manchanda, Bindu (2006) [2006]. *Forts & Palaces of India: Sentinels of History*. Roli Books Private Limited. ISBN 81-7436-381-5.
- Michell, George. "Temple Architecture: The Kannada and Telugu zones". *The New Cambridge History of India: Architecture and Art of Southern India*. Cambridge University Press. ISBN 0-521-44110-2.
- Mukherjee, Sujit (1999) [1999]. *A Dictionary of Indian Literature*. Orient Blackswan. ISBN 81-250-1453-5.
- Murthy, K. Narasimha (1992). "Modern Kannada Literature". In George K.M. *Modern Indian Literature:An Anthology – Vol 1*. Sahitya Akademi. ISBN 81-7201-324-8.
- Nagaraj, D.R. (2003) [2003]. "Critical Tensions in the History of Kannada Literary Culture". In Sheldon I. Pollock. *Literary Cultures in History: Reconstructions from South Asia*. Berkeley and London: University of California Press. ISBN 0-520-22821-9.
- Narasimhacharya, R (1988) [1934]. *History of Kannada Literature*. New Delhi: Asian Educational Services. ISBN 81-206-0303-6.
- Pranesh, Meera Rajaram (2003) [2003]. *Musical Composers during Wodeyar Dynasty (1638–1947 A.D.)*. Bangalore: Vee Emm.
- Raman, Afried (1994). *Bangalore – Mysore: A Disha Guide*. Bangalore: Orient Blackswan. ISBN 0-86311-431-8.
- Rice, E. P. (1921). *Kannada Literature*. New Delhi: (Facsimile Reprint 1982) Asian Educational Services. ISBN 81-206-0063-0.
- Rice, B.L. (2001) [1897]. *Mysore Gazetteer Compiled for Government-vol 1*. New Delhi, Madras: Asian Educational Services. ISBN 81-206-0977-8.
- Sastri, Nilakanta K.A. (2005) [1955]. *A history of South India from prehistoric times to the fall of Vijayanagar*. New Delhi: Indian Branch, Oxford University Press. ISBN 0-19-560686-8.
- Singh, Nagendra Kr (2001). *Encyclopaedia of Jainism*. Anmol Publications. ISBN 81-261-0691-3.
- Stein, Burton (1987). *Vijayanagara (The New Cambridge History of*

India). Cambridge and New York: Cambridge University Press. Pp. 156. ISBN 0-521-26693-9.
- Subrahmanyam, Sanjay (2001). "Warfare and State Finance in Wodeyar Mysore". In Subrahmanyam, Sanjay. *Penumbral Visions.* Ann Arbor: University of Michigan Press. pp. 161–193. ISBN 978-0-472-11216-6.
- Subramaniyan, V.K. (2006) [2006]. *101 Mystics of India.* Abhinav Publications. ISBN 81-7017-471-6.
- Various (1988) [1988]. *Encyclopaedia of Indian literature – vol 2.* Sahitya Akademi. ISBN 81-260-1194-7.
- Venkata Ramanappa, M. N. (1975) [1975]. *Outlines of South Indian history : with special reference to Karnataka.* Delhi : Vikas Pub. House ; London (38 Kennington La., SE11 4LS) : [Distributed by] Independent Pub. Co.,. ISBN 0-7069-0378-1.
- Weidman, Amanda J (2006) [2006]. *Singing the Classical, Voicing the Modern.* Duke University Press. ISBN 0-8223-3620-0.

Further reading

- Yazdani, Kaveh. *India, Modernity and the Great Divergence: Mysore and Gujarat (17th to 19th C.)* (Leiden: Brill), 2017. xxxi + 669 pp. online review[432]

Further reading

<templatestyles src="Template:Refbegin/styles.css" />

- "India"[433]. *Life.* Time, Inc.: 94–103 12 May 1941.

<indicator name="featured-star"> ☆ </indicator>

Coordinates: 12.30°N 76.65°E[434]

Sikh Empire

Sikh Empire	
Sarkar-i-Khalsa امپراطوری سیک ਸਿੱਖ ਖਾਲਸਾ ਰਾਜ	
1799–1849	
Flag	
Anthem Deg Tegh Fateh	
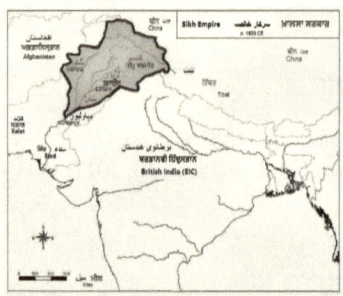 Maharaja Ranjit Singh's Sikh Empire at its peak in c. 1839	
Capital	Lahore
Languages	• Persian (court) • Punjabi • Dogri • Kashmiri • Pashto
Religion	Sikhism
Government	Federal monarchy
Maharaja	
• 1801–1839	Ranjit Singh
• 1839	Kharak Singh
• 1839–1840	Nau Nihal Singh
• 1840–1841	Chand Kaur
• 1841–1843	Sher Singh
• 1843–1849	Duleep Singh
Wazir	

•	1799–1818	Jamadar Khushal Singh
•	1818–1843	Dhian Singh Dogra
•	1843–1844	Hira Singh Dogra
•	1844–1845	Jawahar Singh Aulakh
•	31 January 1846 – 9 March 1846	Gulab Singh[435]
Historical era		Early modern period
•	Capture of Lahore by Ranjit Singh	7 July 1799
•	End of Second Anglo-Sikh War	29 March 1849
Area		491,463 km² (189,755 sq mi)
Population		
•	est.	35,000,000
Density		71/km² (184/sq mi)
Currency		Nanak Shahi Rupee

Preceded by	Succeeded by
Sikh Confederacy	Punjab Province (British India)
Durrani Empire	Jammu_and_Kashmir_(princely_state)
Maratha Empire	

Today part of	• China • India • Pakistan

Part of a series on the
History of India

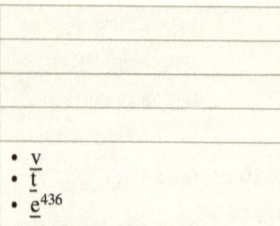

The **Sikh Empire** (also **Sikh Khalsa Raj**, **Sarkar-i-Khalsa** or **Pañjab (Punjab) Empire**) was a major power in the Indian subcontinent, formed under the leadership of Maharaja Ranjit Singh, who established a secular empire based in the Punjab. The empire existed from 1799, when Ranjit Singh captured Lahore, to 1849 and was forged on the foundations of the Khalsa from a collection of autonomous Sikh misls.[437] At its peak in the 19th century, the Empire extended from the Khyber Pass in the west to western Tibet in the east, and from Mithankot in the south to Kashmir in the north. The religious demography of the Sikh Empire was Muslim (74%), Sikh (3%), Hindu (23%). The population was 3.5 million.[438] It was the last major region of the Indian subcontinent to be annexed by the British.

The foundations of the Sikh Empire can be traced to as early as 1707, the year of Aurangzeb's death and the start of the downfall of the Mughal Empire. With the Mughals significantly weakened, the Sikh army, known as the Dal Khalsa, a rearrangement of the Khalsa inaugurated by Guru Gobind Singh, led expeditions against them and the Afghans in the west. This led to a growth of the army which split into different confederacies or semi-independent *misls*. Each of these component armies controlled different areas and cities. However, in the period from 1762 to 1799, Sikh commanders of the misls appeared to be coming into their own as independent warlords.

The formation of the empire began with the capture of Lahore, by Ranjit Singh, from its Afghan ruler, Zaman Shah Durrani, and the subsequent and progressive expulsion of Afghans from the Punjab, by defeating them in the Afghan-Sikh Wars, and the unification of the separate Sikh misls. Ranjit Singh was proclaimed as Maharaja of the Punjab on 12 April 1801 (to coincide with Vaisakhi), creating a unified political state. Sahib Singh Bedi, a descendant of Guru Nanak, conducted the coronation.[439] Ranjit Singh rose to power in a very short period, from a leader of a single misl to finally becoming the Maharaja of Punjab. He began to modernise his army, using the latest training as well as weapons and artillery. After the death of Ranjit Singh, the empire was weakened by internal divisions and political mismanagement. Finally, by 1849 the state was dissolved after the defeat in the Anglo-Sikh wars.

The Sikh Empire was divided into four provinces: Lahore, in Punjab, which became the Sikh capital, Multan, also in Punjab, Peshawar and Kashmir from 1799 to 1849.

History

Background

The Sikh religion began around the time of the conquest of Northern India by Babur, the founder of the Mughal Empire. His conquering grandson, Akbar the Great, supported religious freedom and after visiting the langar of Guru Amar Das got a favourable impression of Sikhism. As a result of his visit he donated land to the langar and the Mughals did not have any conflict with Sikh gurus until his death in 1605. His successor Jahangir, however, saw the Sikhs as a political threat. He ordered Guru Arjun Dev, who had been arrested for supporting the rebellious Khusrau Mirza, to change the passage about Islam in the Adi Granth. When the Guru refused, Jahangir ordered him to be put to death by torture. Guru Arjan Dev's martyrdom led to the sixth Guru, Guru Hargobind, declaring Sikh sovereignty in the creation of the Akal Takht and the establishment of a fort to defend Amritsar. Jahangir attempted to assert authority over the Sikhs by jailing Guru Hargobind at Gwalior, but released him after a number of years when he no longer felt threatened. The Sikh community did not have any further issues with the Mughal empire until the death of Jahangir in 1627. The succeeding son of Jahangir, Shah Jahan, took offence at Guru Hargobind's "sovereignty" and after a series of assaults on Amritsar forced the Sikhs to retreat to the Sivalik Hills.

The next guru, Guru Har Rai, maintained the guruship in these hills by defeating local attempts to seize Sikh land and playing a neutral role in the power struggle between two of the sons of Shah Jahan, Aurangzeb and Dara Shikoh, for control of the Mughal Empire. The ninth Guru, Guru Tegh Bahadur, moved the Sikh community to Anandpur and travelled extensively to visit and preach in defiance of Aurangzeb, who attempted to install Ram Rai as new guru. Guru Tegh Bahadur aided Kashmiri Pandits in avoiding conversion to Islam and was arrested by Aurangzeb. When offered a choice between conversion to Islam and death, he chose to die rather than compromise his principles and was executed.

Guru Gobind Singh assumed the guruship in 1675 and to avoid battles with Sivalik Hill rajas moved the guruship to Paunta. There he built a large fort to protect the city and garrisoned an army to protect it. The growing power of the Sikh community alarmed the Sivalik Hill rajas who attempted to attack the city but Guru Gobind Singh's forces routed them at the Battle of Bhangani. He moved on to Anandpur and established the Khalsa, a collective army of baptised Sikhs, on 30 March 1699. The establishment of the Khalsa united the Sikh community against various Mughal-backed claimants to the guruship. In 1701, a combined army of the Sivalik Hill rajas and the Mughals under Wazir Khan attacked Anandpur. The Khalsa retreated but regrouped to defeat the Mughals at the Battle of Muktsar. In 1707, Guru Gobind Singh accepted an invitation by Aurangzeb's successor Bahadur Shah I to meet him. The meeting took place at Agra on 23 July 1707.

In August 1708 Guru Gobind Singh visited Nanded, the seat of Mughal Telangana Subah. There he met a Bairāgī recluse, Madho Das, and converted him to Sikhism, giving him a new name, Banda Singh.

Banda Singh Bahadur (1670–1716; also known as *Lachman Das*, *Lachman Dev* and *Madho Das*) met Guru Gobind Singh at Nanded and adopted the Sikh religion. A short time before his death, Guru Gobind Singh ordered him to reconquer Punjab region and gave him a letter that commanded all Sikhs to join him. After two years of gaining supporters, Banda Singh Bahadur initiated an agrarian uprising by breaking up the large estates of Zamindar families and distributing the land to the poor peasants who farmed the land. Banda Singh Bahadur started his rebellion with the defeat of Mughal armies at Samana and Sadhaura and the rebellion culminated in the defeat of Sirhind. During the rebellion, Banda Singh Bahadur made a point of destroying the cities in which Mughals had been cruel to the supporters of Guru Gobind Singh. He executed Wazir Khan in revenge for the deaths of Guru Gobind Singh's sons and Pir Budhu Shah after the Sikh victory at Sirhind. He ruled the territory between the Sutlej river and the Yamuna river, established a capital in the Himalayas at Lohgarh and struck coinage in the names of Guru Nanak and Guru Gobind Singh. In 1716, his army was defeated by the Mughals after he attempted to defend his fort at Gurdas Nangal. He was captured along with 700 of his men and sent to Delhi, where they were all tortured and executed after refusing to convert to Islam.

Formation of the Sikh Empire
Start

Maharaja Ranjit Singh

Maharaja Ranjit Singh in 1830 CE.[440]

Maharaja Ranjit Singh's throne, c. 1820–1830 CE.

Ranjit Singh holding court in 1838 CE.

The Samadhi of Ranjit Singh is located in Lahore, Pakistan, adjacent to the iconic Badshahi Mosque.

The formal start of the Sikh Empire began with the merger of these "Misls" by the time of coronation of Ranjit Singh in 1801, creating a unified political state. All the Misl leaders, who were affiliated with the army, were the nobility with usually long and prestigious family backgrounds in Sikh history. The main geographical footprint of the empire was from the Punjab region to Khyber Pass in the west, to Kashmir in the north, Sindh in the south, and Tibet in the east. The religious demography of the Sikh Empire was Muslim (74%), Sikh (3%), Hindu (23%). The population was 3.5 million, according to Amarinder Singh's The Last Sunset: The Rise and Fall of the Lahore Durbar. In 1799 Ranjit Singh moved the capital to Lahore from Gujranwala, where it had been established in 1763 by his grandfather, Charat Singh.

End of the Sikh Empire

After Ranjit Singh's death in 1839, the empire was severely weakened by internal divisions and political mismanagement. This opportunity was used by the British East India Company to launch the Anglo-Sikh Wars.

The Battle of Ferozeshah in 1845 marked many turning points, the British encountered the Punjab Army, opening with a gun-duel in which the Sikhs "had the better of the British artillery". As the British made advances, Europeans in their army were especially targeted, as the Sikhs believed if the army "became demoralised, the backbone of the enemy's position would be broken".[441] The fighting continued throughout the night. The British position "grew graver as the night wore on", and "suffered terrible casualties with every single member of the Governor General's staff either killed or wounded".[442] Nevertheless, the British army took and held Ferozeshah. British General Sir James Hope Grant recorded: "Truly the night was one of gloom and forbidding and perhaps never in the annals of warfare has a British Army on such a large scale been nearer to a defeat which would have involved annihilation."

The reasons for the withdrawal of the Sikhs from Ferozeshah are contentious. Some believe that it was treachery of the non-Sikh high command of their own army which led to them marching away from a British force in a precarious and battered state. Others believe that a tactical withdrawal was the best policy.[443]

The Sikh empire was finally dissolved at the end of the Second Anglo-Sikh War in 1849 into separate princely states and the British province of Punjab. Eventually, a Lieutenant Governorship was formed in Lahore as a direct representative of the British Crown.

Geography

The Punjab was a region straddling India and the Afghan Durrani Empire. The following modern-day political divisions made up the historical Sikh Empire:

- Punjab till Multan in south
  - parts of Panjab (Punjab), Pakistan, with the capital Lahaur (Lahore)
  - Parts of Punjab, India
  - Parts of Himachal Pradesh, India
  - Jammu Division, Jammu and Kashmir, India and Pakistan.
- Kashmir, conquered 5 July 1819 - 15 March 1846, India/Pakistan/China[444,445]
  - Gilgit, Gilgit–Baltistan, Pakistan. (Occupied from 1842 to 1846)
  - Ladakh, India
- Khyber Pass, Afghanistan/Pakistan[446]
  - Peshawar, Pakistan[447] (taken in 1818, retaken in 1834)

Sikh Empire

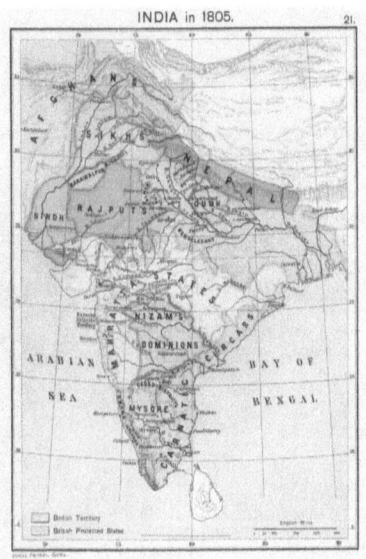

Figure 75: *Indian subcontinent in 1805 CE.*

- Khyber Pakhtunkhwa and the Federally Administered Tribal Areas, Pakistan (documented from Hazara (taken in 1818, again in 1836) to Bannu)[448]

Jamrud District (Khyber Agency, Pakistan) was the westernmost limit of the Sikh Empire. The westward expansion was stopped in the Battle of Jamrud, in which the Afghans managed to kill the prominent Sikh general Hari Singh Nalwa in an offensive, though the Sikhs successfully held their position at their Jamrud fort. Ranjit Singh sent his General Sirdar Bahadur Gulab Singh Powind thereafter as reinforcement and he crushed the Pashtun rebellion harshly.[449] In 1838, Ranjit Singh with his troops marched into Kabul to take part in the victory parade along with the British after restoring Shah Shoja to the Afghan throne at Kabul.[450]

Religious policy

Religious policy

Maharaja Ranjit Singh rebuilt Harmandir Sahib in marble and copper in 1809, overlaid the sanctum with gold foil in 1830. This has led to the name the Golden Temple.[451]

In 1835, Maharaja Ranjit Singh donated 1 tonne of gold for plating the Kashi Vishwanath Temple's dome.

The Sikh Empire was idiosyncratic in that it allowed men from religions other than their own to rise to commanding positions of authority.[452]

A ban on cow slaughter, which can be related to Hindu sentiments, was universally imposed in the Sarkar Khalsaji.[453,454] Ranjit Singh also donated huge amounts of gold for the construction of Hindu temples not only in his state, but also in the areas which were under the control of the Marathas, with whom Sikhs had a cordial relation.

The Sikhs attempted not to offend the prejudices of Muslims, noted Baron von Hügel, the Austrian botanist and explorer,[455] yet the Sikhs were described as harsh. In this regard, Masson's explanation is perhaps the most pertinent: "Though compared to the Afghans, the Sikhs were mild and exerted a protecting influence, yet no advantages could compensate to their Mohammedan subjects, the idea of subjection to infidels, and the prohibition to slay kine, and to repeat the *azan*, or 'summons to prayer'."[456]

Timeline

- 1699 - Formation of the Khalsa by Guru Gobind Singh.
- 1710–1716, Banda Singh defeats the Mughals and declares Khalsa rule.
- 1716–1738, turbulence, no real ruler; Mughals take back the control for two decades but Sikhs engage in guerrilla warfare
- 1733–1735, the Khalsa accepts, only to reject, the confederal status given by Mughals.
- 1748–1757, Afghan invasion of Ahmad Shah Durrani
- 1757-1761, Maratha rule with help of Sikhs
- 1761-1767, Recapture of Punjab region by Afghan in Third Battle of Panipat

Sikh Empire

Figure 76: *The Battle of Sobraon in 1846. Contemporary picture*

- 1763–1774, Charat Singh Sukerchakia, Misldar of Sukerchakia misl, establishes himself in Gujranwala.
- 1764–1783, Baba Baghel Singh, Misldar of Karor Singhia Misl, imposes taxes on the Mughals.
- 1783- Sikh Occupation of Delhi and Red Fort
- 1773, Ahmad Shah Durrani dies and his son Timur Shah launches several invasions into Punjab.
- 1774–1790, Maha Singh becomes Misldar of the Sukerchakia misl.
- 1790–1801, Ranjit Singh becomes Misldar of the Sukerchakia misl.
- 1799, formation of the Sikh Khalsa Army
- 12 April 1801 (coronation) – 27 June 1839, reign of Maharaja Ranjit Singh.
- 1st June 1813, Ranjit Singh is given the Kohinoor Diamond.
- 13 July 1813, Battle of Attock, the Sikh Empire's first significant victory over the Durrani Empire.
- March – 2 June 1818, Battle of Multan, the 2nd battle in the Afghan–Sikh wars.
- 3 July 1819, Battle of Shopian

- 14 March 1823, Battle of Nowshera
- 30 April 1837, Battle of Jamrud
- 27 June 1839 – 5 November 1840, reign of Maharaja Kharak Singh
- 5 November 1840 – 18 January 1841, Chand Kaur is briefly Regent.
- 18 January 1841 – 15 September 1843, reign of Maharaja Sher Singh.
- May 1841 – August 1842, Sino-Sikh war
- 15 September 1843 – 31 March 1849, reign of Maharaja Duleep Singh.
- 1845–1846, First Anglo-Sikh War.

Figure 77: *The charge of the British 16th Lancers at Aliwal on 28 January 1846, during the Anglo-Sikh war*

- 1848–1849, Second Anglo-Sikh War.

Preceded by **Durrani Empire**	**Sikh Empire** 1799–1849	Succeeded by **British East India Company**

References

Sources

- Heath, Ian (2005), *The Sikh Army 1799-1849*, Osprey Publishing (UK), ISBN 1-84176-777-8
- Kalsi, Sewa Singh (2005), *Sikhism*, Religions of the World, Chelsea House Publications, ISBN 978-0-7910-8098-6
- Markovits, Claude (2004), *A history of modern India, 1480-1950*, London, England: Anthem Press, ISBN 978-1-84331-152-2
- Jestice, Phyllis G. (2004), *Holy people of the world: a cross-cultural encyclopedia, Volume 3*[457], ABC-CLIO, ISBN 978-1-57607-355-1
- Johar, Surinder Singh (1975), *Guru Tegh Bahadur*[458], University of Wisconsin–Madison Center for South Asian Studies, ISBN 81-7017-030-3
- Singh, Pritam (2008), *Federalism, Nationalism and Development: India and the Punjab Economy*[459], Routledge, pp. 25–26, ISBN 978-0-415-45666-1
- Nesbitt, Eleanor (2005), *Sikhism: A Very Short Introduction*, Oxford University Press, USA, p. 61, ISBN 978-0-19-280601-7

Further reading

- *Volume 2: Evolution of Sikh Confederacies (1708–1769)*, By Hari Ram Gupta. (Munshiram Manoharlal Publishers. Date: 1999, ISBN 81-215-0540-2, 383 pages, illustrated).
- *The Sikh Army (1799–1849) (Men-at-arms)*, By Ian Heath. (Date: 2005, ISBN 1-84176-777-8).
- *The Heritage of the Sikhs By Harbans Singh*. (Date: 1994, ISBN 81-7304-064-8).
- *Sikh Domination of the Mughal Empire*. (Date: 2000, Second Edition. ISBN 81-215-0213-6).
- *The Sikh Commonwealth or Rise and Fall of Sikh Misls*. (Date: 2001, revised edition. ISBN 81-215-0165-2).
- *Maharaja Ranjit Singh, Lord of the Five Rivers*, By Jean-Marie Lafont. (Oxford University Press. Date: 2002, ISBN 0-19-566111-7).
- *History of Panjab*, By Dr L. M. Joshi and Dr Fauja Singh.

External links

 Wikimedia Commons has media related to *Sikh Empire*.

- Article on Coins of the Sikh Empire[460]
- Sikh Confederacy[461]
- Confederacy of Punjab[462]
- Sikh Kingdom of Ranjit Singh[463]
- Battle of Jamrud[464]

Modern Period

Indian Rebellion of 1857

Indian Rebellion of 1857	
 A 1912 map showing the centres of the rebellion	
Date	10 May 1857 – 1 November 1858 (1 year and 6 months)
Location	India
Result	British victory • Suppression of revolt • Formal end of the Mughal empire • End of Company rule in India • Transfer of rule to the British Crown
Territorial changes	British Indian Empire created out of former East India Company territory (some land returned to native rulers, other land confiscated by the British crown)
Belligerents	

• Sepoy Mutineers • Gwalior Factions • Forces of Rani Laxmi bai, the deposed ruler of Jhansi • Forces of Nana Sahib Peshwa • Followers of Birjis Qadra • Oudh • Followers of Babu Kunwar Singh • Followers of Drig Narayan Singh • Forces of Ballabgarh king Nahar Singh • Followers of Rewari Chief Rao Tularam • Forces of Shahmal Tomar	• British Empire • Kingdom of Nepal • TibetWikipedia:Citation needed • East India Company • 21 Princely States: • Ajaigarh • Alwar • Bharathpur • Bhopal • Bijawar • Bikaner • Bundi • Hyderabad • Jaipur • Jaora • Jodhpur • Kapurthala • Jammu and Kashmir • Kendujhar • Nabha • Patiala • Rampur • Rewa • Sirmur • Sirohi • Udaipur • Mysore • Travancore
Commanders and leaders	
• Bakht Khan † • Bahadur Shah II • Mirza Mughal • Nana Sahib • Tatya Tope • Rani Lakshmibai † • Begum Hazrat Mahal • Birjis Qadr • Babu Kunwar Singh (d. April 1858)	• Lord Canning • George Anson (d. May 1857) • Patrick Grant • Colin Campbell (From August 1857) • John Nicholson † • Jung Bahadur Rana[465]
Casualties and losses	
at least 100,000[466] Wikipedia:Verifiability-nearly 806,000 and possibly more, both in the rebellion and in famines and epidemics of disease in its wake, by comparison of sketchy pre-existing population estimates with Indian Census of 1871.[467]	

Indian Rebellion of 1857

Part of a series on the
History of India

- v
- t
- e[468]

The **Indian Rebellion of 1857** was a major uprising in India between 1857–58 against the rule of the British East India Company, which functioned as a sovereign power on behalf of the British Crown. The event is known by many names, including the Sepoy Mutiny, the Indian Mutiny, the Great Rebellion, the Revolt of 1857, the Indian Insurrection, and India's First War of Independence.[469]

The rebellion began on 10 May 1857 in the form of a mutiny of sepoys of the Company's army in the garrison town of Meerut, 40 miles northeast of Delhi (now Old Delhi). It then erupted into other mutinies and civilian rebellions chiefly in the upper Gangetic plain and central India,[470,471] though incidents of revolt also occurred farther north and east.[472] The rebellion posed a considerable threat to British power in that region,[473] and was contained only with the rebels' defeat in Gwalior on 20 June 1858.[474] On 1 November 1858, the British granted amnesty to all rebels not involved in murder, though they did not declare the hostilities formally to have ended until 8 July 1859.

The Indian rebellion was fed by resentment that had emerged from British rule, including invasive British-style social reforms, harsh land taxes, summary treatment of some rich landowners and princes,[475,476] and broader scepticism about the improvements brought about by British rule.[477] Many Indians did rise against the British, but many others fought *for* the British, and the majority remained seemingly compliant to British rule.[478,479] Violence, which sometimes betrayed exceptional cruelty, was inflicted on both sides; on British officers and civilians (including women and children) by the rebels, and on the rebels and their supporters (sometimes including entire villages) by British reprisals. The cities of Delhi and Lucknow were laid waste in the fighting and during the British retaliation.[480]

After the outbreak of the mutiny in Meerut, the rebels very quickly reached Delhi, whose 81-year-old Mughal ruler, Bahadur Shah Zafar, was declared by the rebels as the Emperor of Hindustan. Soon, the rebels also captured large tracts of the North-Western Provinces and Awadh (Oudh). The East India Company's response came rapidly as well. With help from reinforcements, Kanpur was retaken by mid-July 1857 and Delhi by the end of September. Even so, it then took the remainder of 1857 and the better part of 1858 for the rebellion to be suppressed in Jhansi, Lucknow, and especially the Awadh countryside. Other regions of Company controlled India—the Bengal Presidency, the Bombay Presidency and the Madras Presidency—remained largely calm.[481] In the Punjab, the Sikhs crucially helped the British by providing both soldiers and support.[482] The large princely states, Hyderabad, Mysore, Travancore, and Kashmir, as well as the smaller ones of Rajputana, did not join the rebellion, serving the British, in the Governor-General Lord Canning's words, as "breakwaters in a storm."

In some regions, most notably in Awadh, the rebellion took on the attributes of a patriotic revolt against European presence and power. However, the rebel leaders proclaimed no articles of faith that presaged a new political system.[483] Even so, the rebellion proved to be an important watershed in Indian and British Empire history.[484] It led to the dissolution of the East India Company, and forced the British to reorganize the army, the financial system, and the administration in India, through the passage of the Government of India Act 1858. India was thereafter administered directly by the British government in the new British Raj. On 1 November 1858, Queen Victoria issued a proclamation to Indians, which while lacking the authority of a constitutional provision,[485] promised rights similar to those of other British subjects.[486,487] In the following decades, when admission to these rights was not always forthcoming, Indians were to pointedly refer to the Queen's proclamation in growing avowals of a new nationalism.[488,489]

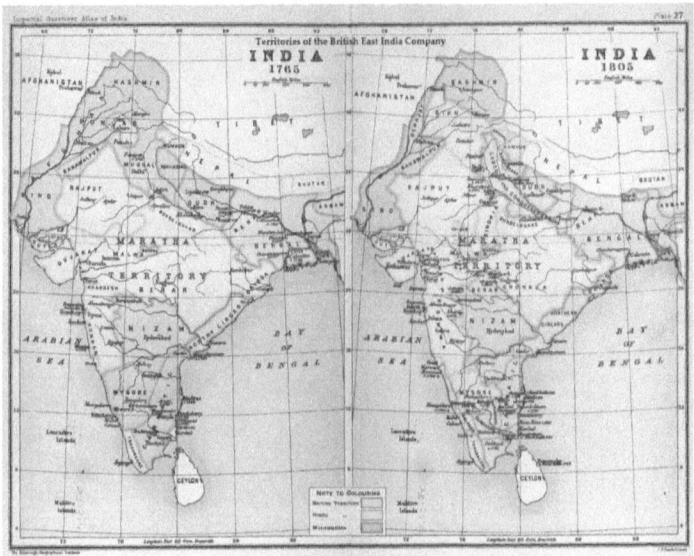

Figure 78: *India in 1765 and 1805, showing East India Company-governed territories in pink*

East India Company's expansion in India

Although the British East India Company had established a presence in India as far back as 1612, and earlier administered the factory areas established for trading purposes, its victory in the Battle of Plassey in 1757 marked the beginning of its firm foothold in eastern India. The victory was consolidated in 1764 at the Battle of Buxar, when the East India Company army defeated Mughal Emperor Shah Alam II. After his defeat, the emperor granted the Company the right to the "collection of Revenue" in the provinces of Bengal (modern day Bengal, Bihar, and Odisha), known as "Diwani" to the Company. The Company soon expanded its territories around its bases in Bombay and Madras; later, the Anglo-Mysore Wars (1766–1799) and the Anglo-Maratha Wars (1772–1818) led to control of even more of India.

In 1806, the Vellore Mutiny was sparked by new uniform regulations that created resentment amongst both Hindu and Muslim sepoys.

After the turn of the 19th century, Governor-General Wellesley began what became two decades of accelerated expansion of Company territories. This was achieved either by subsidiary alliances between the Company and local rulers or by direct military annexation. The subsidiary alliances created the princely states of the Hindu maharajas and the Muslim nawabs. Punjab, North-West

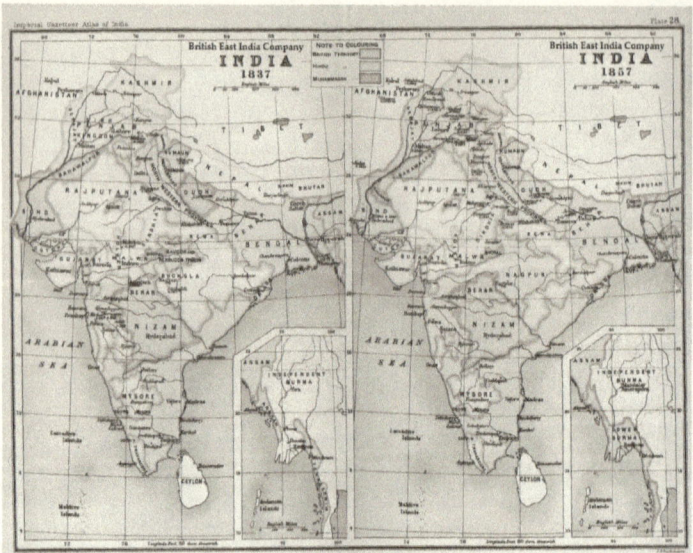

Figure 79: *India in 1837 and 1857, showing East India Company-governed territories in pink*

Frontier Province, and Kashmir were annexed after the Second Anglo-Sikh War in 1849; however, Kashmir was immediately sold under the 1846 Treaty of Amritsar to the Dogra Dynasty of Jammu and thereby became a princely state. The border dispute between Nepal and British India, which sharpened after 1801, had caused the Anglo-Nepalese War of 1814–16 and brought the defeated Gurkhas under British influence. In 1854, Berar was annexed, and the state of Oudh was added two years later. For practical purposes, the Company was the government of much of India.

Causes of the rebellion

The Indian Rebellion of 1857 occurred as the result of an accumulation of factors over time, rather than any single event.

The *sepoys* were Indian soldiers who were recruited into the Company's army. Just before the rebellion, there were over 300,000 sepoys in the army, compared to about 50,000 British. The forces were divided into three presidency armies: Bombay, Madras, and Bengal. The Bengal Army recruited higher castes, such as Rajputs and Bhumihar, mostly from the Awadh and Bihar regions, and even restricted the enlistment of lower castes in 1855. In contrast, the Madras Army and Bombay Army were "more localized, caste-neutral

Figure 80: *Two sepoy officers; a private sepoy, 1820s*

armies" that "did not prefer high-caste men."[490] The domination of higher castes in the Bengal Army has been blamed in part for initial mutinies that led to the rebellion.

In 1772, when Warren Hastings was appointed India's first Governor-General, one of his first undertakings was the rapid expansion of the Company's army. Since the sepoys from Bengal – many of whom had fought against the Company in the Battles of Plassey and Buxar – were now suspect in British eyes, Hastings recruited farther west from the high-caste rural Rajputs and Bhumihar of Awadh and Bihar, a practice that continued for the next 75 years. However, in order to forestall any social friction, the Company also took action to adapt its military practices to the requirements of their religious rituals. Consequently, these soldiers dined in separate facilities; in addition, overseas service, considered polluting to their caste, was not required of them, and the army soon came officially to recognise Hindu festivals. "This encouragement of high caste ritual status, however, left the government vulnerable to protest, even mutiny, whenever the sepoys detected infringement of their prerogatives." Stokes argues that "The British scrupulously avoided interference with the social structure of the village community which remained largely intact."

After the annexation of Oudh (Awadh) by the East India Company in 1856, many sepoys were disquieted both from losing their perquisites, as landed gentry, in the Oudh courts, and from the anticipation of any increased land-revenue payments that the annexation might bring about. Other historians have stressed that by 1857, some Indian soldiers, interpreting the presence of missionaries as a sign of official intent, were convinced that the Company was masterminding mass conversions of Hindus and Muslims to Christianity. Although earlier in the 1830s, evangelicals such as William Carey and William Wilberforce had successfully clamoured for the passage of social reform, such as the abolition of *sati* and allowing the remarriage of Hindu widows, there is little evidence that the sepoys' allegiance was affected by this.

However, changes in the terms of their professional service may have created resentment. As the extent of the East India Company's jurisdiction expanded with victories in wars or annexation, the soldiers were now expected not only to serve in less familiar regions, such as in Burma, but also to make do without the "foreign service" remuneration that had previously been their due.

A major cause of resentment that arose ten months prior to the outbreak of the rebellion was the General Service Enlistment Act of 25 July 1856. As noted above, men of the Bengal Army had been exempted from overseas service. Specifically, they were enlisted only for service in territories to which they could march. Governor-General Lord Dalhousie saw this as an anomaly, since all sepoys of the Madras and Bombay Armies and the six "General Service" battalions of the Bengal Army had accepted an obligation to serve overseas if required. As a result, the burden of providing contingents for active service in Burma, readily accessible only by sea, and China had fallen disproportionately on the two smaller Presidency Armies. As signed into effect by Lord Canning, Dalhousie's successor as Governor-General, the act required only new recruits to the Bengal Army to accept a commitment for general service. However, serving high-caste sepoys were fearful that it would be eventually extended to them, as well as preventing sons following fathers into an army with a strong tradition of family service.[491]

There were also grievances over the issue of promotions, based on seniority. This, as well as the increasing number of European officers in the battalions,[492] made promotion slow, and many Indian officers did not reach commissioned rank until they were too old to be effective.[493]

The Enfield Rifle

The final spark was provided by the ammunition for the new Enfield P-53 rifle. These rifles, which fired Minié balls, had a tighter fit than the earlier muskets, and used paper cartridges that came pre-greased. To load the rifle, sepoys had to bite the cartridge open to release the powder.[494] The grease used on these cartridges was rumoured to include tallow derived from beef, which would be offensive to Hindus,[495] and pork, which would be offensive to Muslims. At least one Company official pointed out the difficulties this may cause:

> unless it be proven that the grease employed in these cartridges is not of a nature to offend or interfere with the prejudices of caste, it will be expedient not to issue them for test to Native corps.[496]

However, in August 1856, greased cartridge production was initiated at Fort William, Calcutta, following a British design. The grease used included tallow supplied by the Indian firm of Gangadarh Banerji & Co. By January, rumours were abroad that the Enfield cartridges were greased with animal fat.

Company officers became aware of the rumours through reports of an altercation between a high-caste sepoy and a low-caste labourer at Dum Dum. The labourer had taunted the sepoy that by biting the cartridge, he had himself lost caste, although at this time such cartridges had been issued only at Meerut and not at Dum Dum. There had been rumours that the British sought to destroy the religions of the Indian people, and forcing the native soldiers to break their sacred code would have certainly added to this rumour, as it apparently did. The Company was quick to reverse the effects of this policy in hopes that the unrest would be quelled.[497]

On 27 January, Colonel Richard Birch, the Military Secretary, ordered that all cartridges issued from depots were to be free from grease, and that sepoys could grease them themselves using whatever mixture "they may prefer". A modification was also made to the drill for loading so that the cartridge was torn with the hands and not bitten. This however, merely caused many sepoys to be convinced that the rumours were true and that their fears were justified. Additional rumours started that the paper in the new cartridges, which was glazed and stiffer than the previously used paper, was impregnated with grease. In February, a court of inquiry was held at Barrackpore to get to the bottom of these rumours. Native soldiers called as witnesses complained of the paper "being stiff and like cloth in the mode of tearing", said that when the paper was burned it smelled of grease, and announced that the suspicion that the paper itself contained grease could not be removed from their minds.[498]

Civilian disquiet

The civilian rebellion was more multifarious. The rebels consisted of three groups: the feudal nobility, rural landlords called *taluqdars*, and the peasants. The nobility, many of whom had lost titles and domains under the Doctrine of Lapse, which refused to recognise the adopted children of princes as legal heirs, felt that the Company had interfered with a traditional system of inheritance. Rebel leaders such as Nana Sahib and the Rani of Jhansi belonged to this group; the latter, for example, was prepared to accept East India Company supremacy if her adopted son was recognised as her late husband's heir.[499] In other areas of central India, such as Indore and Saugar, where such loss of privilege had not occurred, the princes remained loyal to the Company, even in areas where the sepoys had rebelled. The second group, the *taluqdars*, had lost half their landed estates to peasant farmers as a result of the land reforms that came in the wake of annexation of Oudh. As the rebellion gained ground, the *taluqdars* quickly reoccupied the lands they had lost, and paradoxically, in part because of ties of kinship and feudal loyalty, did not experience significant opposition from the peasant farmers, many of whom joined the rebellion, to the great dismay of the British. It has also been suggested that heavy land-revenue assessment in some areas by the British resulted in many landowning families either losing their land or going into great debt to money lenders, and providing ultimately a reason to rebel; money lenders, in addition to the Company, were particular objects of the rebels' animosity.[500] The civilian rebellion was also highly uneven in its geographic distribution, even in areas of north-central India that were no longer under British control. For example, the relatively prosperous Muzaffarnagar district, a beneficiary of a Company irrigation scheme, and next door to Meerut, where the upheaval began, stayed relatively calm throughout.

Figure 81: *Charles Canning, the Governor-General of India during the rebellion.*

Figure 82: *Lord Dalhousie, the Governor-General of India from 1848 to 1856, who devised the Doctrine of Lapse.*

Figure 83: *Lakshmibai, the Rani of Maratha-ruled Jhansi, one of the principal leaders of the rebellion who earlier had lost her kingdom as a result of the Doctrine of Lapse.*

Figure 84: *Bahadur Shah Zafar the last Mughal Emperor, crowned Emperor of India, by the Indian troops, he was deposed by the British, and died in exile in Burma*

"Utilitarian and evangelical-inspired social reform",[501] including the abolition of sati and the legalisation of widow remarriage were considered by many—especially the British themselves—to have caused suspicion that Indian religious traditions were being "interfered with", with the ultimate aim of conversion. Recent historians, including Chris Bayly, have preferred to frame this as a "clash of knowledges", with proclamations from religious authorities before the revolt and testimony after it including on such issues as the "insults to women", the rise of "low persons under British tutelage", the "pollution" caused by Western medicine and the persecuting and ignoring of traditional astrological authorities. European-run schools were also a problem: according to recorded testimonies, anger had spread because of stories that mathematics was replacing religious instruction, stories were chosen that would "bring contempt" upon Indian religions, and because girl children were exposed to "moral danger" by education.

The justice system was considered to be inherently unfair to the Indians. The official Blue Books, *East India (Torture) 1855–1857*, laid before the House of Commons during the sessions of 1856 and 1857, revealed that Company officers were allowed an extended series of appeals if convicted or accused of brutality or crimes against Indians.

The economic policies of the East India Company were also resented by many Indians.[502]

The Bengal Army

Each of the three "Presidencies" into which the East India Company divided India for administrative purposes maintained their own armies. Of these, the Army of the Bengal Presidency was the largest. Unlike the other two, it recruited heavily from among high-caste Hindus and comparatively wealthy Muslims. The Muslims formed a larger percentage of the 18 irregular cavalry units within the Bengal army, whilst Hindus were mainly to be found in the 84 regular infantry and cavalry regiments. The sepoys were therefore affected to a large degree by the concerns of the landholding and traditional members of Indian society. In the early years of Company rule, it tolerated and even encouraged the caste privileges and customs within the Bengal Army, which recruited its regular soldiers almost exclusively amongst the landowning Brahmins and Rajputs of the Bihar and Awadh regions. These soldiers were known as Purbiyas. By the time these customs and privileges came to be threatened by modernising regimes in Calcutta from the 1840s onwards, the sepoys had become accustomed to very high ritual status and were extremely sensitive to suggestions that their caste might be polluted.[503]

The sepoys also gradually became dissatisfied with various other aspects of army life. Their pay was relatively low and after Awadh and the Punjab were annexed, the soldiers no longer received extra pay (*batta* or *bhatta*) for service there, because they were no longer considered "foreign missions". The junior European officers became increasingly estranged from their soldiers, in many cases treating them as their racial inferiors. In 1856, a new Enlistment Act was introduced by the Company, which in theory made every unit in the Bengal Army liable to service overseas. Although it was intended to apply only to new recruits, the serving sepoys feared that the Act might be applied retroactively to them as well. A high-caste Hindu who travelled in the cramped conditions of a wooden troop ship could not cook his own food on his own fire, and accordingly risked losing caste through ritual pollution.

Onset of the Rebellion

Several months of increasing tensions coupled with various incidents preceded the actual rebellion. On 26 February 1857 the 19th Bengal Native Infantry (BNI) regiment became concerned that new cartridges they had been issued were wrapped in paper greased with cow and pig fat, which had to be opened by mouth thus affecting their religious sensibilities. Their Colonel confronted them supported by artillery and cavalry on the parade ground, but after some negotiation withdrew the artillery, and cancelled the next morning's parade.[504]

Figure 85: *Indian mutiny map showing position of troops on 1 May 1857*

Mangal Pandey

On 29 March 1857 at the Barrackpore parade ground, near Calcutta, 29-year-old Mangal Pandey of the 34th BNI, angered by the recent actions of the East India Company, declared that he would rebel against his commanders. Informed about Pandey's behaviour Sergeant-Major James Hewson went to investigate, only to have Pandey shoot at him. Hewson raised the alarm. When his adjutant Lt. Henry Baugh came out to investigate the unrest, Pandey opened fire but hit Baugh's horse instead.[505]

General John Hearsey came out to the parade ground to investigate, and claimed later that Mangal Pandey was in some kind of "religious frenzy". He ordered the Indian commander of the quarter guard Jemadar Ishwari Prasad to arrest Mangal Pandey, but the Jemadar refused. The quarter guard and other sepoys present, with the single exception of a soldier called Shaikh Paltu, drew back from restraining or arresting Mangal Pandey. Shaikh Paltu restrained Pandey from continuing his attack.[506]

After failing to incite his comrades into an open and active rebellion, Mangal Pandey tried to take his own life, by placing his musket to his chest and pulling the trigger with his toe. He managed only to wound himself. Court-martialled on 6 April, he was hanged two days later.

The Jemadar Ishwari Prasad was sentenced to death and hanged on 22 April. The regiment was disbanded and stripped of its uniforms because it was felt that it harboured ill-feelings towards its superiors, particularly after this incident. Shaikh Paltu was promoted to the rank of havildar in the Bengal Army, but was murdered shortly before the 34th BNI dispersed.

Sepoys in other regiments thought these punishments were harsh. The demonstration of disgrace during the formal disbanding helped foment the rebellion in view of some historians. Disgruntled ex-sepoys returned home to Awadh with a desire for revenge.

Unrest during April 1857

During April, there was unrest and fires at Agra, Allahabad and Ambala. At Ambala in particular, which was a large military cantonment where several units had been collected for their annual musketry practice, it was clear to General Anson, Commander-in-Chief of the Bengal Army, that some sort of rebellion over the cartridges was imminent. Despite the objections of the civilian Governor-General's staff, he agreed to postpone the musketry practice and allow a new drill by which the soldiers tore the cartridges with their fingers rather than their teeth. However, he issued no general orders making this standard practice throughout the Bengal Army and, rather than remain at Ambala to defuse or overawe potential trouble, he then proceeded to Simla, the cool "hill station" where many high officials spent the summer.

Although there was no open revolt at Ambala, there was widespread arson during late April. Barrack buildings (especially those belonging to soldiers who had used the Enfield cartridges) and European officers' bungalows were set on fire.

Meerut

At Meerut, a large military cantonment, 2,357 Indian sepoys and 2,038 British soldiers were stationed along with 12 British-manned guns. The station held one of the largest concentrations of British troops in India and this was later to be cited as evidence that the original rising was a spontaneous outbreak rather than a pre-planned plot.

Although the state of unrest within the Bengal Army was well known, on 24 April Lieutenant Colonel George Carmichael-Smyth, the unsympathetic commanding officer of the 3rd Bengal Light Cavalry, ordered 90 of his men to parade and perform firing drills. All except five of the men on parade refused to accept their cartridges. On 9 May, the remaining 85 men were court martialled, and most were sentenced to 10 years' imprisonment with hard labour. Eleven comparatively young soldiers were given five years' imprisonment. The entire garrison was paraded and watched as the condemned men were stripped of their uniforms and placed in shackles. As they were marched off to jail, the condemned soldiers berated their comrades for failing to support them.

The next day was Sunday. Some Indian soldiers warned off-duty junior European officers that plans were afoot to release the imprisoned soldiers by force,

Figure 86: *"The Sepoy revolt at Meerut," from the Illustrated London News, 1857*

Figure 87: *An 1858 photograph by Felice Beato of a mosque in Meerut where some of the rebel soldiers may have prayed*

but the senior officers to whom this was reported took no action. There was also unrest in the city of Meerut itself, with angry protests in the bazaar and some buildings being set on fire. In the evening, most European officers were preparing to attend church, while many of the European soldiers were off duty and had gone into canteens or into the bazaar in Meerut. The Indian troops, led by the 3rd Cavalry, broke into revolt. European junior officers who attempted to quell the first outbreaks were killed by the rebels. European officers' and civilians' quarters were attacked, and four civilian men, eight women and eight children were killed. Crowds in the bazaar attacked off-duty soldiers there. About 50 Indian civilians, some of them officers' servants who tried to defend or conceal their employers, were killed by the sepoys. While the action of the sepoys in freeing their 85 imprisoned comrades appears to have been spontaneous, some civilian rioting in the city was reportedly encouraged by kotwal (local police commander) Dhan Singh Gurjar

Some sepoys (especially from the 11th Bengal Native Infantry) escorted trusted British officers and women and children to safety before joining the revolt.[507] Some officers and their families escaped to Rampur, where they found refuge with the Nawab.

The British historian Philip Mason notes that it was inevitable that most of the sepoys and sowars from Meerut should have made for Delhi on the night of 10 May. It was a strong walled city located only forty miles away, it was the ancient capital and present seat of the nominal Mughal Emperor and finally there were no British troops in garrison there in contrast to Meerut. No effort was made to pursue them.

Delhi

Early on 11 May, the first parties of the 3rd Cavalry reached Delhi. From beneath the windows of the King's apartments in the palace, they called on him to acknowledge and lead them. Bahadur Shah did nothing at this point, apparently treating the sepoys as ordinary petitioners, but others in the palace were quick to join the revolt. During the day, the revolt spread. European officials and dependents, Indian Christians and shop keepers within the city were killed, some by sepoys and others by crowds of rioters.[508]

There were three battalion-sized regiments of Bengal Native Infantry stationed in or near the city. Some detachments quickly joined the rebellion, while others held back but also refused to obey orders to take action against the rebels. In the afternoon, a violent explosion in the city was heard for several miles. Fearing that the arsenal, which contained large stocks of arms and ammunition, would fall intact into rebel hands, the nine British Ordnance officers there had opened fire on the sepoys, including the men of their own guard. When resistance

Figure 88: *Massacre of officers by insurgent cavalry at Delhi*

Figure 89: *The Flagstaff Tower, Delhi, where the European survivors of the rebellion gathered on 11 May 1857; photographed by Felice Beato*

appeared hopeless, they blew up the arsenal. Six of the nine officers survived, but the blast killed many in the streets and nearby houses and other buildings. The news of these events finally tipped the sepoys stationed around Delhi into open rebellion. The sepoys were later able to salvage at least some arms from the arsenal, and a magazine two miles (3 km) outside Delhi, containing up to 3,000 barrels of gunpowder, was captured without resistance.

Many fugitive European officers and civilians had congregated at the Flagstaff Tower on the ridge north of Delhi, where telegraph operators were sending news of the events to other British stations. When it became clear that the help expected from Meerut was not coming, they made their way in carriages to Karnal. Those who became separated from the main body or who could not reach the Flagstaff Tower also set out for Karnal on foot. Some were helped by villagers on the way; others were killed.

The next day, Bahadur Shah held his first formal court for many years. It was attended by many excited sepoys. The King was alarmed by the turn events had taken, but eventually accepted the sepoys' allegiance and agreed to give his countenance to the rebellion. On 16 May, up to 50 Europeans who had been held prisoner in the palace or had been discovered hiding in the city were killed by some of the King's servants under a peepul tree in a courtyard outside the palace.[509]

Supporters and opposition

The news of the events at Delhi spread rapidly, provoking uprisings among sepoys and disturbances in many districts. In many cases, it was the behaviour of British military and civilian authorities themselves which precipitated disorder. Learning of the fall of Delhi by telegraph, many Company administrators hastened to remove themselves, their families and servants to places of safety. At Agra, 160 miles (260 km) from Delhi, no less than 6,000 assorted non-combatants converged on the Fort.

The military authorities also reacted in disjointed manner. Some officers trusted their sepoys, but others tried to disarm them to forestall potential uprisings. At Benares and Allahabad, the disarmings were bungled, also leading to local revolts.[510]

Most Muslims did not share the rebels' dislike of the British administration and their ulema could not agree on whether to declare a jihad. There were Islamic scholars such as Maulana Muhammad Qasim Nanautavi and Maulana Rashid Ahmad Gangohi who took up arms against the colonial rule. But a large number of Muslims, among them ulema from both the Sunni and Shia sects, sided with the British. Various Ahl-i-Hadith scholars and colleagues of

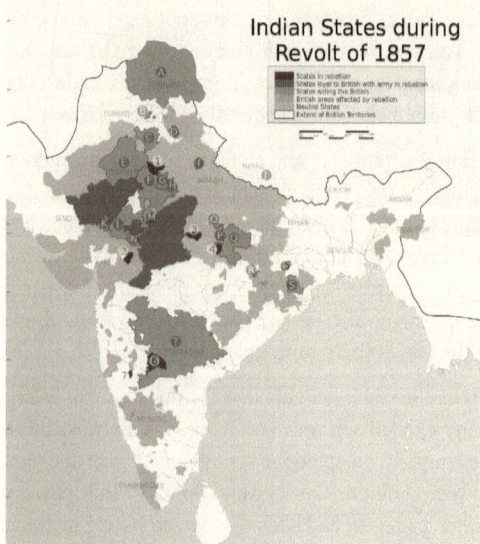

Figure 90: *States during the rebellion*

Figure 91: *Troops of the Native Allies by George Francklin Atkinson, 1859.*

Figure 92: *Sikh Troops Dividing the Spoil Taken from Mutineers, circa 1860*

Nanautavi rejected the jihad. The most influential member of Ahl-i-Hadith ulema in Delhi, Maulana Sayyid Nazir Husain Dehlvi, resisted pressure from the mutineers to call for a jihad and instead declared in favour of British rule, viewing the Muslim-British relationship as a legal contract which could not be broken unless their religious rights were breached.

Although most of the mutinous sepoys in Delhi were Hindus, a significant proportion of the insurgents were Muslims. The proportion of *ghazis* grew to be about a quarter of the local fighting force by the end of the siege and included a regiment of suicide *ghazis* from Gwalior who had vowed never to eat again and to fight until they met certain death at the hands of British troops.

The Sikhs and Pathans of the Punjab and North-West Frontier Province supported the British and helped in the recapture of Delhi.[511] Historian John Harris has asserted that the Sikhs wanted to avenge the annexation of the Sikh Empire eight years earlier by the Company with the help of *Purbiyas* ('Easterners'), Biharis and those from the United Provinces of Agra and Oudh who had formed part of the East India Company's armies in the First and Second Anglo-Sikh Wars. He has also suggested that Sikhs felt insulted by the attitude of sepoys who, in their view, had beaten the Khalsa only with British help; they resented and despised them far more than they did the British.

The Sikhs feared reinstatement of Mughal rule in northern India because they had been persecuted heavily in the past by the Mughal dynasty.

Sikh support for the British resulted from grievances surrounding sepoys' perceived conduct during and after the Anglo-Sikh Wars. Firstly, many Sikhs resented that Hindustanis/Purbiyas in service of the Sikh state had been foremost in urging the wars, which lost them their independence. Sikh soldiers also recalled that the bloodiest battles of the war, Chillianwala and Ferozeshah, were won by British troops, and they believed that the Hindustani sepoys had refused to meet them in battle. These feelings were compounded when Hindustani sepoys were assigned a very visible role as garrison troops in Punjab and awarded profit-making civil posts in Punjab.

In 1857, the Bengal Army had 86,000 men, of which 12,000 were European, 16,000 Sikh and 1,500 Gurkha. There were 311,000 native soldiers in India altogether, 40,160 European soldiers and 5,362 officers. Fifty-four of the Bengal Army's 74 regular Native Infantry Regiments mutinied, but some were immediately destroyed or broke up, with their sepoys drifting away to their homes. A number of the remaining 20 regiments were disarmed or disbanded to prevent or forestall mutiny. In total, only twelve of the original Bengal Native Infantry regiments survived to pass into the new Indian Army.[512] All ten of the Bengal Light Cavalry regiments mutinied.

The Bengal Army also contained 29 irregular cavalry and 42 irregular infantry regiments. Of these, a substantial contingent from the recently annexed state of Awadh mutinied *en masse*. Another large contingent from Gwalior also mutinied, even though that state's ruler supported the British. The remainder of the irregular units were raised from a wide variety of sources and were less affected by the concerns of mainstream Indian society. Some irregular units actively supported the Company: three Gurkha and five of six Sikh infantry units, and the six infantry and six cavalry units of the recently raised Punjab Irregular Force.[513]

On 1 April 1858, the number of Indian soldiers in the Bengal army loyal to the Company was 80,053.[514,515] However large numbers were hastily raised in the Punjab and North-West Frontier after the outbreak of the Rebellion. The Bombay army had three mutinies in its 29 regiments, whilst the Madras army had none at all, although elements of one of its 52 regiments refused to volunteer for service in Bengal. Nonetheless, most of southern India remained passive, with only intermittent outbreaks of violence. Many parts of the region were ruled by the Nizams or the Mysore royalty, and were thus not directly under British rule.

Figure 93: *Fugitive British officers and their families attacked by mutineers.*

The Revolt

Initial stages

Bahadur Shah Zafar was proclaimed the Emperor of the whole of India. Most contemporary and modern accounts suggest that he was coerced by the sepoys and his courtiers to sign the proclamation against his will.[516] In spite of the significant loss of power that the Mughal dynasty had suffered in the preceding centuries, their name still carried great prestige across northern India. Civilians, nobility and other dignitaries took an oath of allegiance. The emperor issued coins in his name, one of the oldest ways of asserting imperial status. The adhesion of the Mughal emperor, however, turned the Sikhs of the Punjab away from the rebellion, as they did not want to return to Islamic rule, having fought many wars against the Mughal rulers. The province of Bengal was largely quiet throughout the entire period. The British, who had long ceased to take the authority of the Mughal Emperor seriously, were astonished at how the ordinary people responded to Zafar's call for war.

Initially, the Indian rebels were able to push back Company forces, and captured several important towns in Haryana, Bihar, the Central Provinces and the United Provinces. When European troops were reinforced and began to counterattack, the mutineers were especially handicapped by their lack of centralized command and control. Although the rebels produced some natural leaders

Figure 94: *An etching of Nynee Tal (today Nainital) and accompanying story in the Illustrated London News, August 15, 1857, describing how the resort town in the Himalayas served as a refuge for British families escaping from the rebellion of 1857 in Delhi and Meerut.*

such as Bakht Khan, whom the Emperor later nominated as commander-in-chief after his son Mirza Mughal proved ineffectual, for the most part they were forced to look for leadership to rajahs and princes. Some of these were to prove dedicated leaders, but others were self-interested or inept.

In the countryside around Meerut, a general Gurjar uprising posed the largest threat to the British. In Parikshitgarh near Meerut, Gurjars declared Choudhari Kadam Singh (Kuddum Singh) their leader, and expelled Company police. Kadam Singh Gurjar led a large force, estimates varying from 2,000 to 10,000. Bulandshahr and Bijnor also came under the control of Gurjars under Walidad Khan and Maho Singh respectively. Contemporary sources report that nearly all the Gurjar villages between Meerut and Delhi participated in the revolt, in some cases with support from Jullundur, and it was not until late July that, with the help of local Jats, the British managed to regain control of the area.

The Imperial Gazetteer of India states that throughout the Indian Rebellion of 1857, Gurjars and Ranghars (Muslim rajpoots) proved the "most irreconcilable enemies" of the British in the Bulandshahr area.

Figure 95: *Attack of the mutineers on the Redan Battery at Lucknow, 30 July 1857*

Mufti Nizamuddin, a renowned scholar of Lahore, issued a Fatwa against the British forces and called upon the local population to support the forces of Rao Tula Ram. Casualties were high at the subsequent engagement at Narnaul (Nasibpur). After the defeat of Rao Tula Ram on 16 November 1857, Mufti Nizamuddin was arrested, and his brother Mufti Yaqinuddin and brother-in-law Abdur Rahman (alias Nabi Baksh) were arrested in Tijara. They were taken to Delhi and hanged. Having lost the fight at Nasibpur, Rao Tula Ram and Pran Sukh Yadav requested arms from Russia, which had just been engaged against Britain in the Crimean War.

Delhi

The British were slow to strike back at first. It took time for troops stationed in Britain to make their way to India by sea, although some regiments moved overland through Persia from the Crimean War, and some regiments already *en route* for China were diverted to India.

It took time to organise the European troops already in India into field forces, but eventually two columns left Meerut and Simla. They proceeded slowly towards Delhi and fought, killed, and hanged numerous Indians along the way. Two months after the first outbreak of rebellion at Meerut, the two forces met near Karnal. The combined force including two Gurkha units serving in the Bengal Army under contract from the Kingdom of Nepal, fought the main army of the rebels at Badli-ke-Serai and drove them back to Delhi.

Figure 96: *Assault of Delhi and capture of the Cashmere Gate, 14 September 1857*

The Company established a base on the Delhi ridge to the north of the city and the Siege of Delhi began. The siege lasted roughly from 1 July to 21 September. However, the encirclement was hardly complete, and for much of the siege the Company forces were outnumbered and it often seemed that it was the Company forces and not Delhi that were under siege, as the rebels could easily receive resources and reinforcements. For several weeks, it seemed likely that disease, exhaustion and continuous sorties by rebels from Delhi would force the Company forces to withdraw, but the outbreaks of rebellion in the Punjab were forestalled or suppressed, allowing the Punjab Movable Column of British, Sikh and Pakhtun soldiers under John Nicholson to reinforce the besiegers on the Ridge on 14 August.[517,518] On 30 August the rebels offered terms, which were refused.[519]

Figure 97: *The Jantar Mantar observatory in Delhi in 1858, damaged in the fighting*

Figure 98: *Mortar damage to Kashmiri Gate, Delhi, 1858*

Figure 99: *Hindu Rao's house in Delhi, now a hospital, was extensively damaged in the fighting*

Figure 100: *Bank of Delhi was attacked by mortar and gunfire*

Figure 101: *Capture of Bahadur Shah Zafar and his sons by William Hodson at Humayun's tomb on 20 September 1857*

An eagerly awaited heavy siege train joined the besieging force, and from 7 September, the siege guns battered breaches in the walls and silenced the rebels' artillery.:478 An attempt to storm the city through the breaches and the Kashmiri Gate was launched on 14 September.:480 The attackers gained a foothold within the city but suffered heavy casualties, including John Nicholson. The British commander wished to withdraw, but was persuaded to hold on by his junior officers. After a week of street fighting, the British reached the Red Fort. Bahadur Shah Zafar had already fled to Humayun's tomb. The British had retaken the city.

The troops of the besieging force proceeded to loot and pillage the city. A large number of the citizens were killed in retaliation for the Europeans and Indian civilians that had been slaughtered by the rebels. During the street fighting, artillery was set up city's main mosque, neighbourhoods within range were bombarded; the homes of the Muslim nobility that contained innumerable cultural, artistic, literary and monetary riches destroyed.

The British soon arrested Bahadur Shah, and the next day the British agent William Hodson had his sons Mirza Mughal, Mirza Khazir Sultan, and grandson Mirza Abu Bakr shot under his own authority at the Khooni Darwaza (the bloody gate) near Delhi Gate. On hearing the news Zafar reacted with shocked silence while his wife Zinat Mahal was content as she believed her son was now Zafar's heir. Shortly after the fall of Delhi, the victorious attackers organised

Figure 102: *Tatya Tope's Soldiery*

a column that relieved another besieged Company force in Agra, and then pressed on to Cawnpore, which had also recently been retaken. This gave the Company forces a continuous, although still tenuous, line of communication from the east to west of India.

Cawnpore (Kanpur)

In June, sepoys under General Wheeler in Cawnpore (now Kanpur) rebelled and besieged the European entrenchment. Wheeler was not only a veteran and respected soldier but also married to a high-caste Indian lady. He had relied on his own prestige, and his cordial relations with the Nana Sahib to thwart rebellion, and took comparatively few measures to prepare fortifications and lay in supplies and ammunition.

The besieged endured three weeks of the Siege of Cawnpore with little water or food, suffering continuous casualties to men, women and children. On 25 June Nana Sahib made an offer of safe passage to Allahabad. With barely three days' food rations remaining, the British agreed provided they could keep their small arms and that the evacuation should take place in daylight on the morning of the 27th (the Nana Sahib wanted the evacuation to take place on the night of the 26th). Early in the morning of 27 June, the European party left their entrenchment and made their way to the river where boats provided by the

Figure 103: *A memorial erected (circa 1860) by the British after the Mutiny at the Bibighar Well. After India's Independence the statue was moved to the All Souls Memorial Church, Cawnpore. Albumen silver print by Samuel Bourne, 1860*

Nana Sahib were waiting to take them to Allahabad.[520] Several sepoys who had stayed loyal to the Company were removed by the mutineers and killed, either because of their loyalty or because "they had become Christian." A few injured British officers trailing the column were also apparently hacked to death by angry sepoys. After the European party had largely arrived at the dock, which was surrounded by sepoys positioned on both banks of the Ganges,[521] with clear lines of fire, firing broke out and the boats were abandoned by their crew, and caught or were set[522] on fire using pieces of red hot charcoal. The British party tried to push the boats off but all except three remained stuck. One boat with over a dozen wounded men initially escaped, but later grounded, was caught by mutineers and pushed back down the river towards the carnage at Cawnpore. Towards the end rebel cavalry rode into the water to finish off any survivors. After the firing ceased the survivors were rounded up and the men shot. By the time the massacre was over, most of the male members of the party were dead while the surviving women and children were removed and held hostage to be later killed in the Bibighar massacre.[523] Only four men eventually escaped alive from Cawnpore on one of the boats: two private soldiers, a lieutenant, and Captain Mowbray Thomson, who wrote a first-hand account of his experiences entitled *The Story of Cawnpore* (London, 1859).

During his trial, Tatya Tope denied the existence of any such plan and described the incident in the following terms: the Europeans had already boarded the boats and Tatya Tope raised his right hand to signal their departure. That very moment someone from the crowd blew a loud bugle, which created disorder and in the ongoing bewilderment, the boatmen jumped off the boats. The rebels started shooting indiscriminately. Nana Sahib, who was staying in Savada Kothi (Bungalow) nearby, was informed about what was happening and immediately came to stop it.[524] Some British histories allow that it might well have been the result of accident or error; someone accidentally or maliciously fired a shot, the panic-stricken British opened fire, and it became impossible to stop the massacre.[525]

The surviving women and children were taken to the Nana Sahib and then confined first to the Savada Kothi and then to the home of the local magistrate's clerk (the Bibighar) where they were joined by refugees from Fatehgarh. Overall five men and two hundred and six women and children were confined in The Bibigarh for about two weeks. In one week 25 were brought out dead, from dysentery and cholera. Meanwhile, a Company relief force that had advanced from Allahabad defeated the Indians and by 15 July it was clear that the Nana Sahib would not be able to hold Cawnpore and a decision was made by the Nana Sahib and other leading rebels that the hostages must be killed. After the sepoys refused to carry out this order, two Muslim butchers, two Hindu peasants and one of Nana's bodyguards went into The Bibigarh. Armed with knives and hatchets they murdered the women and children. After the massacre the walls were covered in bloody hand prints, and the floor littered with fragments of human limbs. The dead and the dying were thrown down a nearby well. When the 50-foot (15 m) deep well was filled with remains to within 6 feet (1.8 m) of the top,[526] the remainder were thrown into the Ganges.[527]

Historians have given many reasons for this act of cruelty. With Company forces approaching Cawnpore and some believing that they would not advance if there were no hostages to save, their murders were ordered. Or perhaps it was to ensure that no information was leaked after the fall of Cawnpore. Other historians have suggested that the killings were an attempt to undermine Nana Sahib's relationship with the British.[528] Perhaps it was due to fear, the fear of being recognised by some of the prisoners for having taken part in the earlier firings.

Figure 104: *Photograph entitled, "The Hospital in General Wheeler's entrenchment, Cawnpore." (1858) The hospital was the site of the first major loss of European lives in Cawnpore*

Figure 105: *1858 picture of Sati Chaura Ghat on the banks of the Ganges River, where on 27 June 1857 many British men lost their lives and the surviving women and children were taken prisoner by the rebels.*

Figure 106: *Bibigarh house where European women and children were killed and the well where their bodies were found, 1858.*

Figure 107: *The Bibighar Well site where a memorial had been built. Samuel Bourne, 1860.*

Figure 108: *A contemporary image of the massacre at the Satichaura Ghat*

The killing of the women and children hardened British attitudes against the sepoys. The British public was aghast and the anti-Imperial and pro-Indian proponents lost all their support. Cawnpore became a war cry for the British and their allies for the rest of the conflict. Nana Sahib disappeared near the end of the Rebellion and it is not known what happened to him.

Other British accounts[529,530,531] state that indiscriminate punitive measures were taken in early June, two weeks before the murders at the Bibighar (but after those at both Meerut and Delhi), specifically by Lieutenant Colonel James George Smith Neill of the Madras Fusiliers, commanding at Allahabad while moving towards Cawnpore. At the nearby town of Fatehpur, a mob had attacked and murdered the local European population. On this pretext, Neill ordered all villages beside the Grand Trunk Road to be burned and their inhabitants to be killed by hanging. Neill's methods were "ruthless and horrible"[532] and far from intimidating the population, may well have induced previously undecided sepoys and communities to revolt.

Neill was killed in action at Lucknow on 26 September and was never called to account for his punitive measures, though contemporary British sources lionised him and his "gallant blue caps".[533] When the British retook Cawnpore, the soldiers took their sepoy prisoners to the Bibighar and forced them to lick the bloodstains from the walls and floor. They then hanged or "blew from the cannon", the traditional Mughal punishment for mutiny, the majority of the sepoy prisoners. Although some claimed the sepoys took no actual part in the

Figure 109: *The interior of the Secundra Bagh, several months after its storming during the second relief of Lucknow. Albumen silver print by Felice Beato, 1858*

killings themselves, they did not act to stop it and this was acknowledged by Captain Thompson after the British departed Cawnpore for a second time.

Lucknow

Very soon after the events at Meerut, rebellion erupted in the state of Awadh (also known as Oudh, in modern-day Uttar Pradesh), which had been annexed barely a year before. The British Commissioner resident at Lucknow, Sir Henry Lawrence, had enough time to fortify his position inside the Residency compound. The Company forces numbered some 1700 men, including loyal sepoys. The rebels' assaults were unsuccessful, and so they began a barrage of artillery and musket fire into the compound. Lawrence was one of the first casualties. The rebels tried to breach the walls with explosives and bypass them via underground tunnels that led to underground close combat.:[486] After 90 days of siege, defended by John Eardley Inglis, numbers of Company forces were reduced to 300 loyal sepoys, 350 British soldiers and 550 non-combatants.

On 25 September, a relief column under the command of Sir Henry Havelock and accompanied by Sir James Outram (who in theory was his superior) fought its way from Cawnpore to Lucknow in a brief campaign, in which the numerically small column defeated rebel forces in a series of increasingly large battles. This became known as 'The First Relief of Lucknow', as this force was not strong enough to break the siege or extricate themselves, and so was forced to join the garrison. In October another, larger, army under the new Commander-in-Chief, Sir Colin Campbell, was finally able to relieve the garrison and on 18 November, they evacuated the defended enclave within the city, the women and children leaving first. They then conducted an orderly withdrawal, firstly to Alambagh 4 miles (6.4 km) north where a force of 4,000 were left to construct a fort, then to Cawnpore, where they defeated an attempt by Tatya Tope to recapture the city in the Second Battle of Cawnpore.

In March 1858, Campbell once again advanced on Lucknow with a large army, meeting up with the force at Alambagh, this time seeking to suppress the rebellion in Awadh. He was aided by a large Nepalese contingent advancing from the north under Jang Bahadur. Campbell's advance was slow and methodical, with a force under General Outram crossing the river on cask bridges on 4 March to enable them to fire artillery in flank, the forces drove the large but disorganised rebel army from Lucknow with the final fighting shooting on 21 March,:[491] there were few casualties to his own troops. This nevertheless allowed large numbers of the rebels to disperse into Awadh, and Campbell was forced to spend the summer and autumn dealing with scattered pockets of resistance while losing men to heat, disease and guerrilla actions.

Jhansi

Jhansi was a Maratha-ruled princely state in Bundelkhand. When the Raja of Jhansi died without a biological male heir in 1853, it was annexed to the British Raj by the Governor-General of India under the doctrine of lapse. His widow, Rani Lakshmi Bai, the Rani of Jhansi protested against the denial of rights of their adopted son. When war broke out, Jhansi quickly became a centre of the rebellion. A small group of Company officials and their families took refuge in Jhansi Fort, and the Rani negotiated their evacuation. However, when they left the fort they were massacred by the rebels over whom the Rani had no control; the Europeans suspected the Rani of complicity, despite her repeated denials.

By the end of June 1857, the Company had lost control of much of Bundelkhand and eastern Rajasthan. The Bengal Army units in the area, having rebelled, marched to take part in the battles for Delhi and Cawnpore. The many princely states that made up this area began warring amongst themselves. In September and October 1857, the Rani led the successful defence of Jhansi against the invading armies of the neighbouring rajas of Datia and Orchha.

On 3 February, Sir Hugh Rose broke the 3-month siege of Saugor. Thousands of local villagers welcomed him as a liberator, freeing them from rebel occupation.[534]

Figure 110: *Jhansi Fort, which was taken over by rebel forces, and subsequently defended against British recapture by the Rani of Jhansi*

In March 1858, the Central India Field Force, led by Sir Hugh Rose, advanced on and laid siege to Jhansi. The Company forces captured the city, but the Rani fled in disguise.

After being driven from Jhansi and Kalpi, on 1 June 1858 Rani Lakshmi Bai and a group of Maratha rebels captured the fortress city of Gwalior from the Scindia rulers, who were British allies. This might have reinvigorated the rebellion but the Central India Field Force very quickly advanced against the city. The Rani died on 17 June, the second day of the Battle of Gwalior, probably killed by a carbine shot from the 8th King's Royal Irish Hussars according to the account of three independent Indian representatives. The Company forces recaptured Gwalior within the next three days. In descriptions of the scene of her last battle, she was compared to Joan of Arc by some commentators.[535]

Indore

Colonel Henry Marion Durand, the then-Company resident at Indore, had brushed away any possibility of uprising in Indore. However, on 1 July, sepoys in Holkar's army revolted and opened fire on the cavalry pickets of the Bhopal Contingent (a locally raised force with British officers). When Colonel Travers rode forward to charge, the Bhopal Cavalry refused to follow. The Bhopal Infantry also refused orders and instead levelled their guns at European sergeants and officers. Since all possibility of mounting an effective deterrent was lost,

Figure 111: *Execution of mutineers at Peshawar*

Durand decided to gather up all the European residents and escape, although 39 European residents of Indore were killed.

Other regions

Punjab

What was then referred to by the British as the Punjab was a very large administrative division, centered on Lahore. It included not only the present-day Indian and Pakistani Punjabi regions but also the North West Frontier districts bordering Afghanistan

Much of the region had been the Sikh Empire, ruled by Ranjit Singh until his death in 1839. The kingdom had then fallen into disorder, with court factions and the Khalsa (the Sikh army) contending for power at the Lahore Durbar (court). After two Anglo-Sikh Wars, the entire region was annexed by the East India Company in 1849. In 1857, the region still contained the highest numbers of both European and Indian troops.

The inhabitants of the Punjab were not as sympathetic to the sepoys as they were elsewhere in India, which limited many of the outbreaks in the Punjab to disjointed uprisings by regiments of sepoys isolated from each other. In some garrisons, notably Ferozepore, indecision on the part of the senior European officers allowed the sepoys to rebel, but the sepoys then left the area, mostly

Figure 112: *Marble Lectern in memory of 35 British soldiers in Jhelum*

heading for Delhi. At the most important garrison, that of Peshawar close to the Afghan frontier, many comparatively junior officers ignored their nominal commander, General Reed, and took decisive action. They intercepted the sepoys' mail, thus preventing their coordinating an uprising, and formed a force known as the "Punjab Movable Column" to move rapidly to suppress any revolts as they occurred. When it became clear from the intercepted correspondence that some of the sepoys at Peshawar were on the point of open revolt, the four most disaffected Bengal Native regiments were disarmed by the two British infantry regiments in the cantonment, backed by artillery, on 22 May. This decisive act induced many local chieftains to side with the British.[536]

Jhelum in Punjab saw a mutiny of native troops against the British. Here 35 British soldiers of Her Majesty's 24th Regiment of Foot (South Wales Borderers) were killed by mutineers on 7 July 1857. Among the dead was Captain Francis Spring, the eldest son of Colonel William Spring. To commemorate this event St. John's Church Jhelum was built and the names of those 35 British soldiers are carved on a marble lectern present in that church.

The final large-scale military uprising in the Punjab took place on 9 July, when most of a brigade of sepoys at Sialkot rebelled and began to move to Delhi. They were intercepted by John Nicholson with an equal British force as they tried to cross the Ravi River. After fighting steadily but unsuccessfully for

Figure 113: *Lieutenant William Alexander Kerr, 24th Bombay Native Infantry, near Kolapore, July 1857*

several hours, the sepoys tried to fall back across the river but became trapped on an island. Three days later, Nicholson annihilated the 1,100 trapped sepoys in the Battle of Trimmu Ghat.[537]

The British had been recruiting irregular units from Sikh and Pakhtun communities even before the first unrest among the Bengal units, and the numbers of these were greatly increased during the Rebellion, 34,000 fresh levies eventually being raised.[538]

At one stage, faced with the need to send troops to reinforce the besiegers of Delhi, the Commissioner of the Punjab (Sir John Lawrence) suggested handing the coveted prize of Peshawar to Dost Mohammed Khan of Afghanistan in return for a pledge of friendship. The British Agents in Peshawar and the adjacent districts were horrified. Referring to the massacre of a retreating British army in 1842, Herbert Edwardes wrote, "Dost Mahomed would not be a mortal Afghan ... if he did not assume our day to be gone in India and follow after us as an enemy. Europeans cannot retreat – Kabul would come again."[539] In the event Lord Canning insisted on Peshawar being held, and Dost Mohammed, whose relations with Britain had been equivocal for over 20 years, remained neutral.

In September 1858 Rae Ahmed Nawaz Khan Kharal, head of the Khurrul tribe, led an insurrection in the Neeli Bar district, between the Sutlej, Ravi and Chenab rivers. The rebels held the jungles of Gogaira and had some initial successes against the British forces in the area, besieging Major Crawford Chamberlain at Chichawatni. A squadron of Punjabi cavalry sent by Sir John Lawrence raised the siege. Ahmed Khan was killed but the insurgents found a new leader in Mahr Bahawal Fatyana, who maintained the uprising for three months until Government forces penetrated the jungle and scattered the rebel tribesmen.[540]

Bihar

Kunwar Singh, the 80-year-old Rajput Zamindar of Jagdispur, whose estate was in the process of being sequestrated by the Revenue Board, instigated and assumed the leadership of revolt in Bihar.

On 25 July, mutiny erupted in the garrisons of Dinapur. Mutinying sepoys from the 7th, 8th and 40th regiments of Bengal Native Infantry quickly moved towards the city of Arrah and were joined by Kunwar Singh and his men. Mr. Boyle, a British railway engineer in Arrah, had already prepared an outbuilding on his property for defence against such attacks.[541] As the rebels approached Arrah, all European residents took refuge at Mr. Boyle's house. A siege soon ensued – eighteen civilians and 50 loyal sepoys from the Bengal Military Police Battalion under the command of Herwald Wake, the local magistrate, defended the house against artillery and musketry fire from an estimated 2000 to 3000 mutineers and rebels.

On 29 July 400 men were sent out from Dinapore to relieve Arrah, but this force was ambushed by the rebels around a mile away from the siege house, severely defeated, and driven back. On 30 July, Major Vincent Eyre, who was going up the river with his troops and guns, reached Buxar and heard about the siege. He immediately disembarked his guns and troops (the 5th Fusiliers) and started marching towards Arrah, disregarding direct orders not to do so. On 2 August, some 6 miles (9.7 km) short of Arrah, the Major was ambushed by the mutineers and rebels. After an intense fight, the 5th Fusiliers charged and stormed the rebel positions successfully. On 3 August, Major Eyre and his men reached the siege house and successfully ended the siege.

After receiving reinforcements Major Eyre pursued Kunwar Singh to his palace in Jagdispur, however Singh had left by the time Eyre's forces arrived. Eyre then proceeded to destroy the palace and the homes of Singh's brothers.

Bengal and Tripura

In September 1857, sepoys took control of the treasury in Chittagong. The treasury remained under rebel control for several days. Further mutinies on 18 November saw the 2nd, 3rd and 4th companies of the 34th Bengal Infantry Regiment storming the Chittagong Jail and releasing all prisoners. The mutineers were eventually suppressed by the Gurkha regiments. The mutiny also spread to Dacca, the former Mughal capital of Bengal. Residents in the city's Lalbagh area were kept awake at night by the rebellion. Sepoys joined hands with the common populace in Jalpaiguri to take control of the city's cantonment. In January 1858, many sepoys received shelter from the royal family of the princely state of Hill Tippera.

The interior areas of Bengal proper were already experiencing growing resistance to Company rule due to the Muslim Faraizi movement.

Gujarat

In central and north Gujarat, the rebellion was sustained by land owner Jagirdars, Talukdars and Thakors with the support of armed communities of Bhil, Koli, Pathans and Arabs, unlike the mutiny by sepoys in north India. Their main opposition of British was due to Inam commission. The Bet Dwarka island, along with Okhamandal region of Kathiawar peninsula which was under Gaekwad of Baroda State, saw a revolt by the Vaghers in January 1858 who, by July 1859, controlled that region. In October 1859, a joint offensive by British, Gaekwad and other princely states troops ousted the rebels and recaptured the region.

British Empire

The authorities in British colonies with an Indian population, sepoy or civilian, took measures to secure themselves against copycat uprisings. In the Straits Settlements, and Trinidad the annual Hosay processions were banned,[542] riots broke out in penal settlements in Burma, and the Settlements, in Penang the loss of a musket provoked a near riot,[543] and security was boosted especially in locations with an Indian convict population.[544]

Figure 114: *"The Relief of Lucknow" by Thomas Jones Barker*

Aftermath

Death toll and atrocities

Both combatant sides committed atrocities against civilians.[545]

In Oudh alone, 150,000 Indians were estimated to have been killed during the war, with 100,000 of them being civilians. The general population in places such as such as Delhi, Allahabad, Kanpur and Lucknow was massacred after being recaptured by British forces.

Another notable atrocity was carried out by General Neill who massacred thousands of Indian mutineers and Indian civilians suspected of supporting the rebellion.

The rebels' murder of women, children and wounded British soldiers at Cawnpore, and the subsequent printing of the events in the British papers, left many British soldiers outraged and seeking revenge. As well as hanging mutineers, the British had some "blown from cannon," (an old Mughal punishment adopted many years before in India), in which sentenced rebels were tied over the mouths of cannons and blown to pieces when the cannons were fired.[546] A particular act of cruelty on behalf of the British troops at Cawnpore included forcing many Muslim or Hindu rebels to eat pork or beef, as well as licking buildings freshly stained with blood of the dead before subsequent public hangings.

Most of the British press, outraged by the stories of rape and the killings of civilians and wounded British soldiers, did not advocate clemency of any kind.

Figure 115: *British soldiers looting Qaisar Bagh, Lucknow, after its recapture (steel engraving, late 1850s)*

Governor General Canning ordered moderation in dealing with native sensibilities and earned the scornful sobriquet "Clemency Canning" from the press[547] and later parts of the British public.

In terms of sheer numbers, the casualties were much higher on the Indian side. A letter published after the fall of Delhi in the *Bombay Telegraph* and reproduced in the British press testified to the scale of the Indian casualties:

> .... All the city's people found within the walls of the city of Delhi when our troops entered were bayoneted on the spot, and the number was considerable, as you may suppose, when I tell you that in some houses forty and fifty people were hiding. These were not mutineers but residents of the city, who trusted to our well-known mild rule for pardon. I am glad to say they were disappointed.

From the end of 1857, the British had begun to gain ground again. Lucknow was retaken in March 1858. On 8 July 1858, a peace treaty was signed and the rebellion ended. The last rebels were defeated in Gwalior on 20 June 1858. By 1859, rebel leaders Bakht Khan and Nana Sahib had either been slain or had fled.

Edward Vibart, a 19-year-old officer whose parents, younger brothers, and two of his sisters had died in the Cawnpore massacre,[548] recorded his experience:

Figure 116: *Blowing from a gun, 8 September 1857*

The orders went out to shoot every soul.... It was literally murder... I have seen many bloody and awful sights lately but such a one as I witnessed yesterday I pray I never see again. The women were all spared but their screams on seeing their husbands and sons butchered, were most painful... Heaven knows I feel no pity, but when some old grey bearded man is brought and shot before your very eyes, hard must be that man's heart I think who can look on with indifference...

Some British troops adopted a policy of "no prisoners". One officer, Thomas Lowe, remembered how on one occasion his unit had taken 76 prisoners – they were just too tired to carry on killing and needed a rest, he recalled. Later, after a quick trial, the prisoners were lined up with a British soldier standing a couple of yards in front of them. On the order "fire", they were all simultaneously shot, "swept... from their earthly existence".

The aftermath of the rebellion has been the focus of new work using Indian sources and population studies. In *The Last Mughal*, historian William Dalrymple examines the effects on the Muslim population of Delhi after the city was retaken by the British and finds that intellectual and economic control of the city shifted from Muslim to Hindu hands because the British, at that time, saw an Islamic hand behind the mutiny.

Figure 117: *Justice, a print by Sir John Tenniel in a September 1857 issue of Punch*

Reaction in Britain

The scale of the punishments handed out by the British "Army of Retribution" were considered largely appropriate and justified in a Britain shocked by embellished reports of atrocities carried out against British and European civilians by the rebels. Accounts of the time frequently reach the "hyperbolic register", according to Christopher Herbert, especially in the often-repeated claim that the "Red Year" of 1857 marked "a terrible break" in British experience. Such was the atmosphere – a national "mood of retribution and despair" that led to "almost universal approval" of the measures taken to pacify the revolt.

Incidents of rape allegedly committed by Indian rebels against European women and girls appalled the British public. These atrocities were often used to justify the British reaction to the rebellion. British newspapers printed various eyewitness accounts of the rape of English women and girls. One such account was published by *The Times*, regarding an incident where 48 English girls as young as 10 had been raped by Indian rebels in Delhi. Karl Marx criticized this story as false propaganda, and pointed out that the story was written by a clergyman in Bangalore, far from the events of the rebellion, with no evidence to support his allegation. Individual incidents captured the public's interest and were heavily reported by the press. One such incident was that of

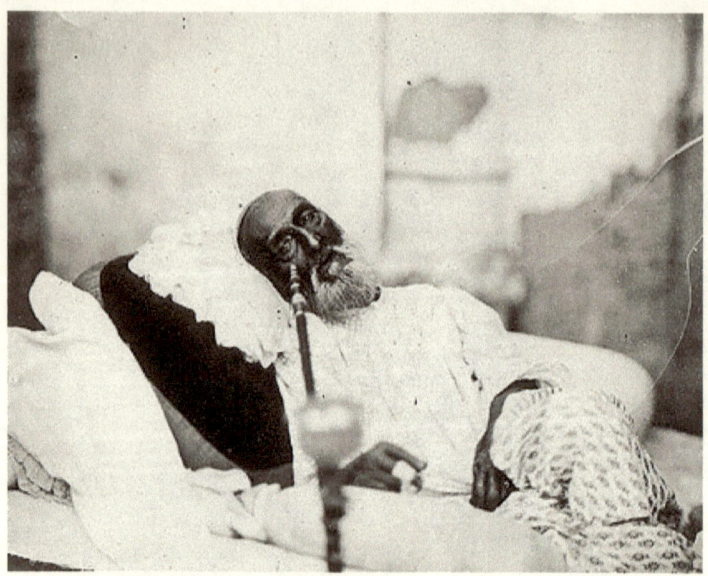

Figure 118: *Bahadur Shah Zafar (the last Mughal emperor) in Delhi, awaiting trial by the British for his role in the Uprising. Photograph by Robert Tytler and Charles Shepherd, May 1858*

General Wheeler's daughter Margaret being forced to live as her captor's concubine, though this was reported to the Victorian public as Margaret killing her rapist then herself. Another version of the story suggested that Margaret had been killed after her abductor had argued with his wife over her.[549]

During the aftermath of the rebellion, a series of exhaustive investigations were carried out by British police and intelligence officials into reports that British women prisoners had been "dishonored" at the Bibighar and elsewhere. One such detailed enquiry was at the direction of Lord Canning. The consensus was that there was no convincing evidence of such crimes having been committed, although numbers of European women and children had been killed outright.

The term 'Sepoy' or 'Sepoyism' became a derogatory term for nationalists, especially in Ireland.

Reorganisation

Bahadur Shah was tried for treason by a military commission assembled at Delhi, and exiled to Rangoon where he died in 1862, bringing the Mughal dynasty to an end. In 1877 Queen Victoria took the title of Empress of India on the advice of Prime Minister, Benjamin Disraeli.

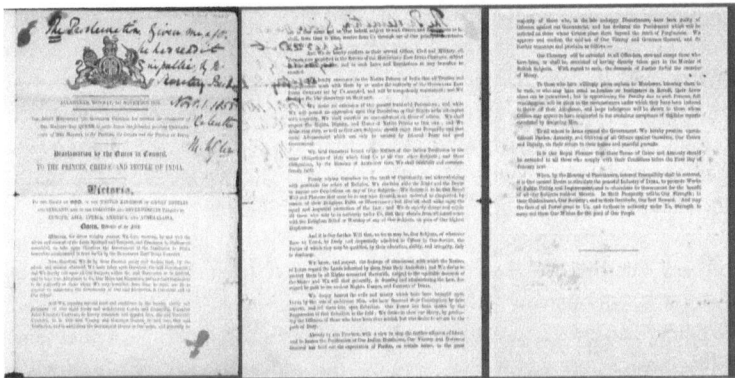

Figure 119: *The proclamation to the "Princes, Chiefs, and People of India," issued by Queen Victoria on November 1, 1858. "We hold ourselves bound to the natives of our Indian territories by the same obligation of duty which bind us to all our other subjects." (p. 2)*

The rebellion saw the end of the East India Company's rule in India. In August, by the Government of India Act 1858, the company was formally dissolved and its ruling powers over India were transferred to the British Crown. A new British government department, the India Office, was created to handle the governance of India, and its head, the Secretary of State for India, was entrusted with formulating Indian policy. The Governor-General of India gained a new title, Viceroy of India, and implemented the policies devised by the India Office. Some former East India Company territories, such as the Straits Settlements, became colonies in their own right. The British colonial administration embarked on a program of reform, trying to integrate Indian higher castes and rulers into the government and abolishing attempts at Westernization. The Viceroy stopped land grabs, decreed religious tolerance and admitted Indians into civil service, albeit mainly as subordinates.

Essentially the old East India Company bureaucracy remained, though there was a major shift in attitudes. In looking for the causes of the Rebellion the authorities alighted on two things: religion and the economy. On religion it was felt that there had been too much interference with indigenous traditions, both Hindu and Muslim. On the economy it was now believed that the previous attempts by the Company to introduce free market competition had undermined traditional power structures and bonds of loyalty placing the peasantry at the mercy of merchants and money-lenders. In consequence the new British Raj was constructed in part around a conservative agenda, based on a preservation of tradition and hierarchy.

On a political level it was also felt that the previous lack of consultation between rulers and ruled had been another significant factor in contributing to the uprising. In consequence, Indians were drawn into government at a local level. Though this was on a limited scale a crucial precedent had been set, with the creation of a new 'white collar' Indian elite, further stimulated by the opening of universities at Calcutta, Bombay and Madras, a result of the Indian Universities Act. So, alongside the values of traditional and ancient India, a new professional middle class was starting to arise, in no way bound by the values of the past. Their ambition can only have been stimulated by Queen Victoria's Proclamation of November 1858, in which it is expressly stated, "We hold ourselves bound to the natives of our Indian territories by the same obligations of duty which bind us to our other subjects...it is our further will that... our subjects of whatever race or creed, be freely and impartially admitted to offices in our service, the duties of which they may be qualified by their education, ability and integrity, duly to discharge."

Acting on these sentiments, Lord Ripon, viceroy from 1880 to 1885, extended the powers of local self-government and sought to remove racial practices in the law courts by the Ilbert Bill. But a policy at once liberal and progressive at one turn was reactionary and backward at the next, creating new elites and confirming old attitudes. The Ilbert Bill had the effect only of causing a white mutiny and the end of the prospect of perfect equality before the law. In 1886 measures were adopted to restrict Indian entry into the civil service.

Military reorganisation

The Bengal army dominated the Indian army before 1857 and a direct result after the rebellion was the scaling back of the size of the Bengali contingent in the army.[550] The Brahmin presence in the Bengal Army was reduced because of their perceived primary role as mutineers. The British looked for increased recruitment in the Punjab for the Bengal army as a result of the apparent discontent that resulted in the Sepoy conflict.

The rebellion transformed both the native and European armies of British India. Of the 74 regular Bengal Native Infantry regiments in existence at the beginning of 1857, only twelve escaped mutiny or disbandment.[551] All ten of the Bengal Light Cavalry regiments were lost. The old Bengal Army had accordingly almost completely vanished from the order of battle. These troops were replaced by new units recruited from castes hitherto under-utilised by the British and from the minority so-called "Martial Races", such as the Sikhs and the Gurkhas.

The inefficiencies of the old organisation, which had estranged sepoys from their British officers, were addressed, and the post-1857 units were mainly

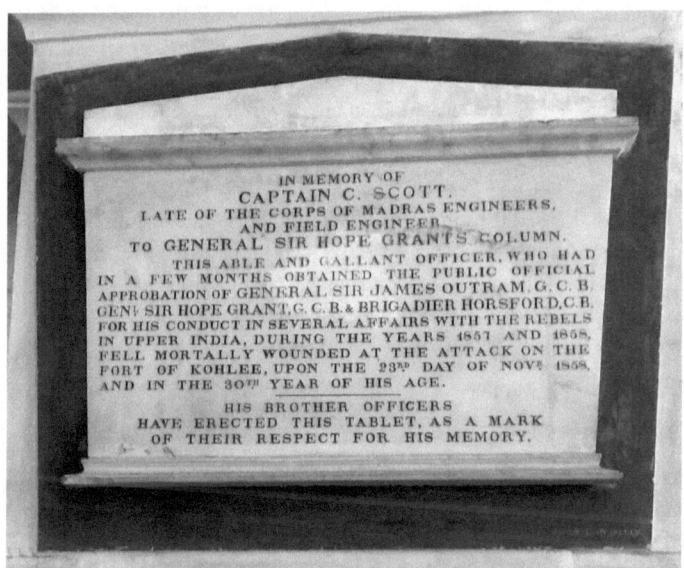

Figure 120: *Captain C Scott of the Gen. Sir. Hope Grant's Column, Madras Regiment, who fell on the attack of Fort of Kohlee, 1858. Memorial at the St. Mary's Church, Madras*

Figure 121: *Memorial inside the York Minster*

organised on the "irregular" system. From 1797 until the rebellion of 1857, each regular Bengal Native Infantry regiment had had 22 or 23 British officers,[552] who held every position of authority down to the second-in-command of each company. In irregular units there were fewer European officers, but they associated themselves far more closely with their soldiers, while more responsibility was given to the Indian officers.

The British increased the ratio of British to Indian soldiers within India. From 1861 Indian artillery was replaced by British units, except for a few mountain batteries.[553] The post-rebellion changes formed the basis of the military organisation of British India until the early 20th century.

Awards

Victoria Cross

Medals were awarded to members of the British Armed Forces and the British Indian Army during the rebellion. The 182 recipients of the Victoria Cross are listed here.

Indian Mutiny Medal

290,000 Indian Mutiny Medals were awarded. Clasps were awarded for the siege of Delhi and the siege and relief of Lucknow.[554]

Indian Order of Merit

A military and civilian decoration of British India, the Indian Order of Merit was first introduced by the East India Company in 1837, and was taken over by the Crown in 1858, following the Indian Mutiny of 1857. The Indian Order of Merit was the only gallantry medal available to Native soldiers between 1837 and 1907.

Nomenclature

There is no universally agreed name for the events of this period.

In India and Pakistan it has been termed as the "War of Independence of 1857" or "First War of Indian Independence"[555] but it is not uncommon to use terms such as the "Revolt of 1857". The classification of the Rebellion being "First War of Independence" is not without its critics in India.[556,557] The use of the term "Indian Mutiny" is considered by some Indian politicians as belittling the importance of what happened and therefore reflecting an imperialistic attitude. Others dispute this interpretation.

In the UK and parts of the Commonwealth it is commonly called the "Indian Mutiny", but terms such as "Great Indian Mutiny", the "Sepoy Mutiny", the

Figure 122: *The Mutiny Memorial in Delhi, a monument to those killed on the British side during the fighting*

"Sepoy Rebellion", the "Sepoy War", the "Great Mutiny", the "Rebellion of 1857", "the Uprising", the "Mahomedan Rebellion", and the "Revolt of 1857" have also been used.[558] "The Indian Insurrection" was a name used in the press of the UK and British colonies at the time.[559]

Historiography

Adas (1971) examines the historiography with emphasis on the four major approaches: the Indian nationalist view; the Marxist analysis; the view of the Rebellion as a traditionalist rebellion; and intensive studies of local uprisings.[560] Many of the key primary and secondary sources appear in Biswamoy Pati, ed. *1857 Rebellion*.[561,562]

Thomas Metcalf has stressed the importance of the work by Cambridge professor Eric Stokes (1924–1981), especially Stokes' *The Peasant and the Raj: Studies in Agrarian Society and Peasant Rebellion in Colonial India* (1978). Metcalf says Stokes undermines the assumption that 1857 was a response to general causes emanating from entire classes of people. Instead, Stokes argues that 1) those Indians who suffered the greatest relative deprivation rebelled and that 2) the decisive factor in precipitating a revolt was the presence of prosperous magnates who supported British rule. Stokes also explores issues of

Figure 123: *Vasily Vereshchagin. Suppression of the Indian Revolt by the English (1884).*

economic development, the nature of privileged landholding, the role of moneylenders, the usefulness of classical rent theory, and, especially, the notion of the "rich peasant."[563]

To Professor Kim Wagner, who has the most recent survey of the historiography, modern Indian historiography is yet to move beyond responding to the "prejudice" of colonial accounts. Wagner sees no reason why atrocities committed by Indians should be understated or inflated merely because these things "offend our post-colonial sensibilities."

Wagner also stresses the importance of William Dalrymple's *The Last Mughal: The Fall of a Dynasty, Delhi 1857*. Dalrymple was assisted by Mahmood Farooqui, who translated key Urdu and Shikastah sources and published a selection in *Besieged: Voices from Delhi 1857*.[564] Dalrymple emphasized the role of religion, and explored in detail the internal divisions and politico-religious discord amongst the rebels. He did not discover much in the way of proto-nationalism or any of the roots of modern India in the rebellion.[565,566] Sabbaq Ahmed has looked at the ways in which ideologies of royalism, militarism, and Jihad influenced the behaviour of contending Muslim factions.[567]

Almost from the moment the first sepoys mutinied in Meerut, the nature and the scope of the Indian Rebellion of 1857 has been contested and argued over. Speaking in the House of Commons in July 1857, Benjamin Disraeli labelled it a 'national revolt' while Lord Palmerston, the Prime Minister, tried to downplay the scope and the significance of the event as a 'mere military mutiny'.[568] Reflecting this debate, an early historian of the rebellion, Charles Ball, used the word mutiny in his title, but labelled it a 'struggle for liberty and independence

Figure 124: *The hanging of two participants in the Indian Rebellion, Sepoys of the 31st Native Infantry. Albumen silver print by Felice Beato, 1857*

as a people' in the text.[569] Historians remain divided on whether the rebellion can properly be considered a war of Indian independence or not,[570] although it is popularly considered to be one in India. Arguments against include:

- A united India did not exist at that time in political, cultural, or ethnic terms;
- The rebellion was put down with the help of other Indian soldiers drawn from the Madras Army, the Bombay Army and the Sikh regiments; 80% of the East India Company forces were Indian;[571]
- Many of the local rulers fought amongst themselves rather than uniting against the British;
- Many rebel Sepoy regiments disbanded and went home rather than fight;
- Not all of the rebels accepted the return of the Mughals;
- The King of Delhi had no real control over the mutineers;[572]
- The revolt was largely limited to north and central India. Whilst risings occurred elsewhere they had little impact because of their limited nature;
- A number of revolts occurred in areas not under British rule, and against native rulers, often as a result of local internal politics;
- The revolt was fractured along religious, ethnic and regional lines.[573]

A second school of thought while acknowledging the validity of the above-mentioned arguments opines that this rebellion may indeed be called a war of India's independence. The reasons advanced are:

- Even though the rebellion had various causes, most of the rebel sepoys who were able to do so, made their way to Delhi to revive the old Mughal empire that signified national unity for even the Hindus amongst them;
- There was a widespread popular revolt in many areas such as Awadh, Bundelkhand and Rohilkhand. The rebellion was therefore more than just a military rebellion, and it spanned more than one region;
- The sepoys did not seek to revive small kingdoms in their regions, instead they repeatedly proclaimed a "country-wide rule" of the Mughals and vowed to drive out the British from "India", as they knew it then. (The sepoys ignored local princes and proclaimed in cities they took over: *Khalq Khuda Ki, Mulk Badshah Ka, Hukm Subahdar Sipahi Bahadur Ka* – "the people belong to God, the country to the Emperor and authority to the Sepoy Commandant"). The objective of driving out "foreigners" from not only one's own area but from their conception of the entirety of "India", signifies a nationalist sentiment;
- The mutineers, although some were recruited from outside Oudah, displayed a common purpose.[574]

150th anniversary

The Government of India celebrated the year 2007 as the 150th anniversary of "India's First War of Independence". Several books written by Indian authors were released in the anniversary year including Amresh Mishra's "War of Civilizations", a controversial history of the Rebellion of 1857, and "Recalcitrance" by Anurag Kumar, one of the few novels written in English by an Indian based on the events of 1857.

In 2007, a group of retired British soldiers and civilians, some of them descendants of British soldiers who died in the conflict, attempted to visit the site of the Siege of Lucknow. However, fears of violence by Indian demonstrators, supported by the Hindu nationalist Bharatiya Janata Party, prevented the British visitors from visiting the site. Despite the protests, Sir Mark Havelock was able to make his way past police to visit the grave of his ancestor, General Henry Havelock.

Figure 125: *Henry Nelson O'Neil's 1857 painting Eastward Ho! depicting British soldiers say farewell to their loved ones as they embark on a deployment to India.*

In popular culture

Films

- *Bengal Brigade* – A 1954 film: at the outbreak of the Indian Mutiny. A British officer, Captain Claybourne (Hudson), is cashiered from his regiment over a charge of disobeying orders, but finds that his duty to his men is far from over
- *Shatranj Ke Khilari* – A 1977 Indian film directed by Satyajit Ray, chronicling the events just before the onset of the Revolt of 1857. The focus is on the British annexation of Oudh, and the detachment of the nobility from the political sphere in 19th-century India.
- *Junoon (1978 film)* – Directed by Shyam Benegal, it is a critically acclaimed film about the love affair between a Pathan feudal chief and a British girl sheltered by his family during the revolt.
- *Mangal Pandey: The Rising* (2005) – Ketan Mehta's Hindi film chronicles the life of Mangal Pandey.
- *The Charge of the Light Brigade* (1936) features a sequence inspired by the massacre at Cawnpore.
- *Indiana Jones and the Temple of Doom* – During the dinner scene at the fictional Pankot Palace, Indiana Jones mentions that Captain Blumburtt

was telling him about the role which the palace played in "the mutiny" and Chattar Lal complains, "It seems the British never forget the Mutiny of 1857".

- *The Last Cartridge, an Incident of the Sepoy Rebellion in India* (1908) – A fictionalized account of a British fort besieged during the Rebellion.

Theatre

- *1857: Ek Safarnama* – A play by Javed Siddiqui, set during the Rebellion of 1857 and staged at Purana Qila, Delhi.

Literature

- Malcolm X's autobiography *The Autobiography of Malcolm X* details his first encounters with atrocities in the non-European world and his reaction to the rebellion and massacres in 1857.
- John Masters's novel *Nightrunners of Bengal*, first published by Michael Joseph in 1951 and dedicated to the Sepoy of India, is a fictionalised account of the Rebellion as seen through the eyes of a British Captain in the Bengal Native Infantry who was based in Bhowani, itself a fictionalised version of the town of Jhansi. Captain Savage and his turbulent relationship with the Rani of Kishanpur form an analogous interrelationship of the Indian people and the British and sepoy regiments at that time.
- J. G. Farrell's 1973 novel *The Siege of Krishnapur* details the siege of the fictional Indian town of Krishnapur during the Rebellion.
- George MacDonald Fraser's 1975 novel *Flashman in the Great Game* deals with the events leading up to and during the Rebellion.
- Two of Sir Arthur Conan Doyle's Sherlock Holmes stories, *The Sign of the Four* and "The Adventure of the Crooked Man," feature events that took place during the Rebellion.
- Michael Crichton's 1975 novel *The Great Train Robbery* mentions the Rebellion and briefly details the events of the Siege of Cawnpore, as the Rebellion was happening in tandem with the trial of Edward Pierce.
- The majority of M. M. Kaye's novel *Shadow of the Moon* is set between 1856–58, and the Rebellion is shown to greatly affect the lives of the main characters, who were inhabitants of the Residency at Lunjore (a fictional town in north India). The early chapters of her novel *The Far Pavilions* take place during the Rebellion, which leads to the protagonist, a child of British ancestry, being raised as a Hindu.
- Indian writer Ruskin Bond's fictional novella *A Flight of Pigeons* is set around the Indian Rebellion of 1857. It is from this story that the film *Junoon* was later adapted in 1978 by Shyam Benegal.

- The 1880 novel *The Steam House* by Jules Verne takes place in the aftermath of the Indian Rebellion of 1857.
- Jules Verne's famous character Captain Nemo, originally an Indian prince, fought on the side of the rebels during the rebellion (as stated in Verne's later novel The Mysterious Island).
- E. M. Forster's 1924 novel *A Passage to India* alludes several times to the Mutiny.
- Flora Annie Steel's novel *On the Face of the Waters* (1896) describes incidents of the Mutiny.
- The plot of H. Beam Piper's science fiction novel Uller Uprising is based on the events of the Indian Rebellion of 1857.
- *Rujub, the juggler* and *In Times of Peril: A tale of India* by G.A. Henty are each based on the Indian Rebellion of 1857

References

Text-books and academic monographs

<templatestyles src="Template:Refbegin/styles.css" />

- Alavi, Seema (1996), *The Sepoys and the Company: Tradition and Transition 1770–1830*, Oxford University Press, p. 340, ISBN 0-19-563484-5.
- Anderson, Clare (2007), *Indian Uprising of 1857–8: Prisons, Prisoners and Rebellion*, New York: Anthem Press, p. 217, ISBN 978-1-84331-249-9.
- Bandyopadhyay, Sekhara (2004), *From Plassey to Partition: A History of Modern India*, New Delhi: Orient Longman, p. 523, ISBN 81-250-2596-0.
- Bayly, Christopher Alan (1988), *Indian Society and the Making of the British Empire*, Cambridge University Press, p. 230, ISBN 0-521-25092-7.
- Bayly, Christopher Alan (2000), *Empire and Information: Intelligence Gathering and Social Communication in India, c 1780–1870*, Cambridge University Press, p. 412, ISBN 0-521-57085-9.
- Bose, Sugata; Jalal, Ayesha (2004), *Modern South Asia: History, Culture, Political Economy* (2nd ed.), London: Routledge, p. 253, ISBN 0-415-30787-2.
- Brown, Judith M. (1994), *Modern India: The Origins of an Asian Democracy*[575] (2nd ed.), Oxford University Press, p. 480, ISBN 0-19-873113-2.
- Greenwood, Adrian (2015), *Victoria's Scottish Lion: The Life of Colin Campbell, Lord Clyde*[576], UK: History Press, p. 496, ISBN 0-75095-685-2.

- Harris, John (2001), *The Indian Mutiny*, Ware: Wordsworth Editions, p. 205, ISBN 1-84022-232-8.
- Hibbert, Christopher (1980), *The Great Mutiny: India 1857*, London: Allen Lane, p. 472, ISBN 0-14-004752-2.
- Jain, Meenakshi (2010), *Parallel Pathways: Essays On Hindu-Muslim Relations (1707-1857)*, Delhi: Konark, ISBN 978-8122007831.
- Judd, Denis (2004), *The Lion and the Tiger: The Rise and Fall of the British Raj, 1600–1947*, Oxford University Press, xiii, 280, ISBN 0-19-280358-1.
- Keene, Henry George (1883), *Fifty-Seven. Some account of the administration of Indian Districts during the revolt of the Bengal Army*, London: W.H. Allen, p. 145.
- Kulke, Hermann; Rothermund, Dietmar (2004), *A History of India* (4th ed.), London: Routledge, xii, 448, ISBN 0-415-32920-5.
- Leasor, James (1956), *The Red Fort*[577], London: W. Lawrie, p. 377, ISBN 0-02-034200-4.
- Ludden, David (2002), *India And South Asia: A Short History*, Oxford: Oneworld, xii, 306, ISBN 1-85168-237-6.
- Majumdar, R.C.; Raychaudhuri, H.C.; Datta, Kalikinkar (1967), *An Advanced History of India* (3rd ed.), London: Macmillan, p. 1126.
- Markovits, Claude, ed. (2004), *A History of Modern India 1480–1950*, London: Anthem, p. 607, ISBN 1-84331-152-6.
- Marshall, P. J. (2007), *The Making and Unmaking of Empires: Britain, India, and America c.1750–1783*, Oxford and New York: Oxford University Press. Pp. 400, ISBN 0-19-922666-0
- Metcalf, Barbara D.; Metcalf, Thomas R. (2006), *A Concise History of Modern India* (2nd ed.), Cambridge University Press, p. 337, ISBN 0-521-68225-8.
- Metcalf, Thomas R. (1990), *The Aftermath of Revolt: India, 1857–1870*, New Delhi: Manohar, p. 352, ISBN 81-85054-99-1.
- Metcalf, Thomas R. (1997), *Ideologies of the Raj*, Cambridge University Press, p. 256, ISBN 0-521-58937-1.
- Mukherjee, Rudrangshu (2002), *Awadh in Revolt 1857–1858: A Study of Popular Resistance* (2nd ed.), London: Anthem, ISBN 1-84331-075-9.
- Palmer, Julian A.B. (1966), *The Mutiny Outbreak at Meerut in 1857*, Cambridge University Press, p. 175, ISBN 0-521-05901-1.
- Peers, Douglas M. (2013), *India Under Colonial Rule: 1700–1885*[578], Routledge, ISBN 978-1-317-88286-2
- Ray, Rajat Kanta (2002), *The Felt Community: Commonality and Mentality before the Emergence of Indian Nationalism*, Oxford University Press, p. 596, ISBN 0-19-565863-9.

- Robb, Peter (2002), *A History of India*, Basingstoke: Palgrave, p. 344, ISBN 0-333-69129-6.
- Roy, Tapti (1994), *The politics of a popular uprising: Bundelkhand 1857*, Delhi: Oxford University Press, p. 291, ISBN 0-19-563612-0.
- Spear, Percival (1990) [First published 1965], *A History of India*, Volume 2, New Delhi and London: Penguin Books, ISBN 978-0-14-013836-8.
- Stanley, Peter (1998), *White Mutiny: British Military Culture in India, 1825–1875*, London: Hurst, p. 314, ISBN 1-85065-330-5.
- Stein, Burton (2001), *A History of India*, New Delhi: Oxford University Press, p. 432, ISBN 0-19-565446-3.
- Stokes, Eric (1980), *The Peasant and the Raj: Studies in Agrarian Society and Peasant Rebellion in Colonial India*, Cambridge University Press, p. 316, ISBN 0-521-29770-2.
- Stokes, Eric; Bayly, C.A. (1986), *The Peasant Armed: The Indian Revolt of 1857*, Oxford: Clarendon, p. 280, ISBN 0-19-821570-3.
- Taylor, P.J.O. (1997), *What really happened during the mutiny: a day-by-day account of the major events of 1857–1859 in India*, Delhi: Oxford University Press, p. 323, ISBN 0-19-564182-5.
- Wolpert, Stanley (2004), *A New History of India* (7th ed.), Oxford University Press, p. 530, ISBN 0-19-516678-7.

Articles in journals and collections

- Alam Khan, Iqtidar (May–June 2013), "The Wahabis in the 1857 Revolt: A Brief Reappraisal of Their Role", *Social Scientist*, **41** (5/6): 15–23, JSTOR 23611115[579]
- Alavi, Seema (February 1993), "The Company Army and Rural Society: The Invalid Thanah 1780–1830", *Modern Asian Studies*, Cambridge University Press, **27** (1): 147–178, doi: 10.1017/S0026749X00016097[580], JSTOR 312880[581]
- Baker, David (1991), "Colonial Beginnings and the Indian Response: The Revolt of 1857–58 in Madhya Pradesh", *Modern Asian Studies*, **25** (3): 511–543, doi: 10.1017/S0026749X00013913[582], JSTOR 312615[583]
- Blunt, Alison (July 2000), "Embodying war: British women and domestic defilement in the Indian "Mutiny", 1857–8", *Journal of Historical Geography*, **26** (3): 403–428, doi: 10.1006/jhge.2000.0236[584]
- English, Barbara (February 1994), "The Kanpur Massacres in India in the Revolt of 1857", *Past & Present*, Oxford University Press, **142**: 169–178, doi: 10.1093/past/142.1.169[585], JSTOR 651200[586]
- Hasan, Farhat; Roy, Tapti (1998), "Review of Tapti Roy, The Politics of a Popular Uprising, OUP, 1994", *Social Scientist*, **26** (1): 148–151, doi: 10.2307/3517586[587]

- Klein, Ira (July 2000), "Materialism, Mutiny and Modernization in British India", *Modern Asian Studies*, Cambridge University Press, **34** (3): 545–580, JSTOR 313141[588]
- Lahiri, Nayanjot (June 2003), "Commemorating and Remembering 1857: The Revolt in Delhi and Its Afterlife", *World Archaeology*, Taylor & Francis, **35** (1): 35–60, doi: 10.1080/0043824032000078072[589], JSTOR 3560211[590]
- Mukherjee, Rudrangshu (August 1990), "'Satan Let Loose upon Earth': The Kanpur Massacres in India in the Revolt of 1857", *Past & Present*, Oxford University Press, **128**: 92–116, doi: 10.1093/past/128.1.92[591], JSTOR 651010[592]
- Mukherjee, Rudrangshu (February 1994), "The Kanpur Massacres in India in the Revolt of 1857: Reply", *Past & Present*, Oxford University Press, **142**: 178–189, doi: 10.1093/past/142.1.178[593], JSTOR 651201[594]
- Nanda, Krishan (September 1965), *The Western Political Quarterly*, **18** (3), University of Utah on behalf of the Western Political Science Association, pp. 700–701.
- Roy, Tapti (February 1993), "Visions of the Rebels: A Study of 1857 in Bundelkhand", *Modern Asian Studies*, Cambridge University Press, **27** (1): 205–228 (Special Issue: How Social, Political and Cultural Information Is Collected, Defined, Used and Analyzed), doi: 10.1017/S0026749X00016115[595], JSTOR 312882[596]
- Stokes, Eric (December 1969), "Rural Revolt in the Great Rebellion of 1857 in India: A Study of the Saharanpur and Muzaffarnagar Districts", *The Historical Journal*, Cambridge University Press, **12** (4): 606–627, doi: 10.1017/s0018246x00010554[597], JSTOR 2638016[598]
- Washbrook, D. A. (2001), "India, 1818–1860: The Two Faces of Colonialism", in Porter, Andrew, *Oxford History of the British Empire: The Nineteenth Century*, Oxford and New York: Oxford University Press, pp. 395–421, ISBN 0-19-924678-5
- Hakim Syed Zillur Rahman (2008), "1857 ki Jung-e Azadi main Khandan ka hissa", *Hayat Karam Husain* (2nd ed.), Aligarh/India: Ibn Sina Academy of Medieval Medicine and Sciences, pp. 253–258, OCLC 852404214[599]

Historiography and memory

- Bates, Crispin, ed. *Mutiny at the Margins: New Perspectives on the Indian Uprising of 1857* (5 vol. SAGE Publications India, 2013–14). online guide[600]; With illustrations, maps, selected text and more.
- Chakravarty, Gautam. *The Indian Mutiny and the British Imagination* (Cambridge University Press, 2005).

- Deshpande, Prachi. "The Making of an Indian Nationalist Archive: Lakshmibai, Jhansi, and 1857." *journal of Asian studies* **67**#3 (2008): 855–879.
- Erll, Astrid. "Re-writing as re-visioning: Modes of representing the 'Indian Mutiny'in British novels, 1857 to 2000." *European Journal of English Studies* 10.2 (2006): 163–185. online[601]
- Frykenberg, Robert E. (2001), "India to 1858", in Winks, Robin, *Oxford History of the British Empire: Historiography*, Oxford and New York: Oxford University Press, pp. 194–213, ISBN 0-19-924680-7
- Pati, Biswamoy (12–18 May 2007). "Historians and Historiography: Situating 1857". *Economic and Political Weekly.* **42** (19): 1686–1691. JSTOR 4419570[602].
- Perusek, Darshan (Spring 1992). "Subaltern Consciousness and the Historiography of the Indian Rebellion of 1857". *NOVEL: A Forum on Fiction.* Duke University Press. **25** (3): 286–301. doi: 10.2307/1345889[603]. JSTOR 1345889[604].
- Wagner, Kim A. (October 2011). "The Marginal Mutiny: The New Historiography of the Indian Uprising of 1857". *History Compass.* **9** (10): 760–766. doi: 10.1111/j.1478-0542.2011.00799.x[605].

Other histories

- Dalrymple, William (2006), *The Last Mughal*, Viking Penguin, ISBN 0-670-99925-3
- David, Saul (2003), *The Indian Mutiny: 1857*, London: Penguin Books, Pp. 528, ISBN 0-14-100554-8
- David, Saul (2007), *Victoria's Wars*, London: Penguin Books, ISBN 978-0-141-00555-3
- Mishra, Amaresh. 2007. *War of Civilisations: The Long Revolution (India AD 1857, 2 Vols.)*, ISBN 978-81-291-1282-8
- Ward, Andrew. *Our Bones Are Scattered*. New York: Holt & Co., 1996.

First person accounts and classic histories

- Parag Tope , "Tatya Tope's Operation Red Lotus" , Publisher: Rupa Publications India
- Anderson, Clare. The Indian Uprising of 1857–8: Prisons, Prisoners, and Rebellion. London, 2007.
- Barter, Captain Richard *The Siege of Delhi. Mutiny memories of an old officer*, London, The Folio Society, 1984.
- Campbell, Sir Colin. *Narrative of the Indian Revolt*. London: George Vickers, 1858.
- Collier, Richard. *The Great Indian Mutiny*. New York: Dutton, 1964.

- Forrest, George W. *A History of the Indian Mutiny*, William Blackwood and Sons, London, 1904. (4 vols)
- Fitchett, W.H., B.A., LL.D., *A Tale of the Great Mutiny*, Smith, Elder & Co., London, 1911.
- Inglis, Julia Selina, Lady, 1833–1904, *The Siege of Lucknow: a Diary*[606], London: James R. Osgood, McIlvaine & Co., 1892. Online at A Celebration of Women Writers.[607]
- Innes, Lt. General McLeod: *The Sepoy Revolt*, A.D. Innes & Co., London, 1897.
- Kaye, John William. *A History of the Sepoy War In India* (3 vols). London: W.H. Allen & Co., 1878.
- Kaye, Sir John & Malleson, G.B.: *The Indian Mutiny of 1857*, Rupa & Co., Delhi, (1st edition 1890) reprint 2005.
- Khan, Syed Ahmed (1859), Asbab-e Baghawat-e Hind, Translated as *The Causes of the Indian Revolt*, Allahabad, 1873
- Malleson, Colonel G.B. *The Indian Mutiny of 1857*. New York: Scribner & Sons, 1891.
- Marx, Karl & Freidrich Engels. *The First Indian War of Independence 1857–1859*. Moscow: Foreign Languages Publishing House, 1959.
- Pandey, Sita Ram, *From Sepoy to Subedar, Being the Life and Adventures of Subedar Sita Ram, a Native Officer of the Bengal Native Army, Written and Related by Himself*, trans. Lt. Col. Norgate, (Lahore: Bengal Staff Corps, 1873), ed. James Lunt, (Delhi: Vikas Publications, 1970).
- Raikes, Charles: *Notes on the Revolt in the North-Western Provinces of India*, Longman, London, 1858.
- Roberts, Field Marshal Lord, *Forty-one Years in India*, Richard Bentley, London, 1897
- *Forty-one years in India* at Project Gutenberg
- Russell, William Howard, *My Diary in India in the years 1858-9*, Routledge, London, 1860, (2 vols.)
- Sen, Surendra Nath, *Eighteen fifty-seven*, (with a foreword by Maulana Abul Kalam Azad), Indian Ministry of Information & Broadcasting, Delhi, 1957.
- Thomson, Mowbray (Capt.), *The Story of Cawnpore*, Richard Bentley, London, 1859.
- Trevelyan, Sir George Otto, *Cawnpore*, Indus, Delhi, (first edition 1865), reprint 2002.
- Wilberforce, Reginald G, *An Unrecorded Chapter of the Indian Mutiny, Being the Personal Reminiscences of Reginald G. WIlberforce, Late 52nd Infantry, Compiled from a Diary and Letters Written on the Spot* London: John Murray 1884, facsimile reprint: Gurgaon: The Academic Press, 1976.

Tertiary sources

- "Indian Mutiny." Encyclopædia Britannica Online. Online. https://www.britannica.com/event/Indian-Mutiny. 23 March 1998.
- " Lee-Enfield Rifle[608]." Encyclopædia Britannica Online. 23 March 1998.

Fictional and narrative literature

- Conan Doyle, Arthur. *The Sign of the Four*, featuring Sherlock Holmes, originally appearing in *Lippincott's Monthly Magazine* 1890.
- Farrell, J.G. *The Siege of Krishnapur*. New York: Carroll & Graf, 1985 (orig. 1973; Booker Prize winner).
- Fenn, Clive Robert. *For the Old Flag: A Tale of the Mutiny*. London: Sampson Low, 1899.
- Fraser, George MacDonald. *Flashman in the Great Game*. London: Barrie & Jenkins, 1975.
- Grant, James. *First Love and Last Love: A Tale of the Mutiny*. New York: G. Routledge & Sons, 1869.
- Kaye, Mary Margaret. *Shadow of the Moon*. New York: St. Martin's Press, 1979.
- Kilworth, Garry Douglas. *Brothers of the Blade*: Constable & Robinson, 2004.
- Leasor, James. *Follow the Drum*[609]. London: Heinemann, 1972, reissued James Leasor Ltd, 2011.
- Masters, John. *Nightrunners of Bengal*. New York: Viking Press, 1951.
- Raikes, William Stephen. *12 Years of a Soldier's Life In India*. Boston: Ticknor and Fields, 1860.
- Julian Rathbone, *The Mutiny*.
- Rossetti, Christina Georgina. "In the Round Tower at Jhansi, 8 June 1857." *Goblin Market and Other Poems*. 1862.
- Anurag Kumar. *Recalcitrance: a novel based on events of 1857–58 in Lucknow*. Lucknow: AIP Books, Lucknow 2008.
- Stuart, V.A. The Alexander Sheridan Series: # 2: 1964. *The Sepoy Mutiny*; # 3: 1974. *Massacre at Cawnpore*; # 4: 1974. *The Cannons of Lucknow*; 1975. # 5: *The Heroic Garrison*. Reprinted 2003 by McBooks Press. (Note: # 1 – *Victors & Lords* deals with the Crimean War.)
- Valerie Fitzgerald "Zemindar": 1981 Bodley Head. historic novel.
- Frédéric Cathala, *1857*, KDP, 2017, historical novel.

External links

 Wikimedia Commons has media related to *Indian Rebellion of 1857*.

Library resources about
Indian Rebellion of 1857

- Online books[610]
- Resources in your library[611]
- Resources in other libraries[612]

- Detailed Map: The revolt of 1857–1859, Historical Atlas of South Asia, Digital South Asia Library, hosted by the University of Chicago[613]
- Development of Situation-January to July 1857 – Maj (Retd) AGHA HUMAYUN AMIN from WASHINGTON DC defencejounal.com[614]
- The Indian Mutiny BritishEmpire.co.uk[615]
- Karl Marx, *New York Tribune*, 1853–1858, The Revolt in India marxists.org[616]

Preceded by **Second Anglo-Sikh War**	Indo-British conflicts	Succeeded by **Hindu German Conspiracy**

British Raj

• India	
	Imperial political structure comprising (a) British India (a quasi-federation of presidencies and provinces directly governed by the British Crown through the Viceroy and Governor-General of India); (b) Princely states, governed by Indian rulers, under the suzerainty of the British Crown exercised through the Viceroy and Governor-General of India[617]
	1858–1947
	 Flag Star of India
	Anthem "God Save the King/Queen"
	 The British Indian Empire in 1936
Capital	• 1858–1911 Calcutta • 1911–1947 New Delhi
Languages	• English • Urdu • Hindi (official, Urdu from 1857. Hindi added from 1900)Wikipedia:Citation needed South Asian languages
Government	Colony
Monarch of the United Kingdom and Emperor/Empress[a]	
• 1858–1901	Victoria
• 1901–1910	Edward VII

•	1910–1936	George V
•	1936	Edward VIII
•	1936–1947	George VI
Viceroy and Governor-General[c]		
•	1858–1862	(first) Charles Canning
•	1947	(last) Louis Mountbatten
Secretary of State		
•	1858–1859	(first) Edward Stanley
•	1947	(last) William Hare
Legislature		Imperial Legislative Council
History		
•	Battle of Plassey and Indian Rebellion	23 June 1757 and 10 May 1857
•	Government of India Act	2 August 1858
•	Indian Independence Act	18 July 1947
•	Partition of India	15 August 1947
Currency		Indian rupee

Preceded by	Succeeded by
	Interim Government of India
	Dominion of India
Company rule in India	Dominion of Pakistan
Mughal Empire	Kingdom of Jammu and Kashmir
Emirate of Afghanistan	British rule in Burma
Azad Hind	Trucial States
	Colony of Aden
	Straits Settlements

Today part of	Bangladesh India Myanmar Pakistan United Arab Emirates Yemen
a.	Title existed 1876–1948
c.	Full title was "Viceroy and Governor-General of India"

British Raj

Part of a series on the
History of India

- v
- t
- e[618]

The **British Raj** (/rɑːdʒ/; from *rāj*, literally, "rule" in Hindustani)[619] was the rule by the British Crown in the Indian subcontinent between 1858 and 1947.[620,621,622,623] The rule is also called **Crown rule in India**,[624] or **direct rule in India**.[625] The region under British control was commonly called **British India** or simply **India** in contemporaneous usage, and included areas directly administered by the United Kingdom, which were collectively called British India, and those ruled by indigenous rulers, but under British tutelage or paramountcy, and called the princely states. The *de facto* political amalgamation was also called the **Indian Empire** and after 1876 issued passports under that name.[626,627] As India, it was a founding member of the League of Nations, a participating nation in the Summer Olympics in 1900, 1920, 1928, 1932, and 1936, and a founding member of the United Nations in San Francisco in 1945.[628]

This system of governance was instituted on 28 June 1858, when, after the Indian Rebellion of 1857, the rule of the British East India Company was transferred to the Crown in the person of Queen Victoria (who, in 1876, was proclaimed Empress of India). It lasted until 1947, when Britain's Indian Empire was partitioned into two sovereign dominion states: the Dominion of India

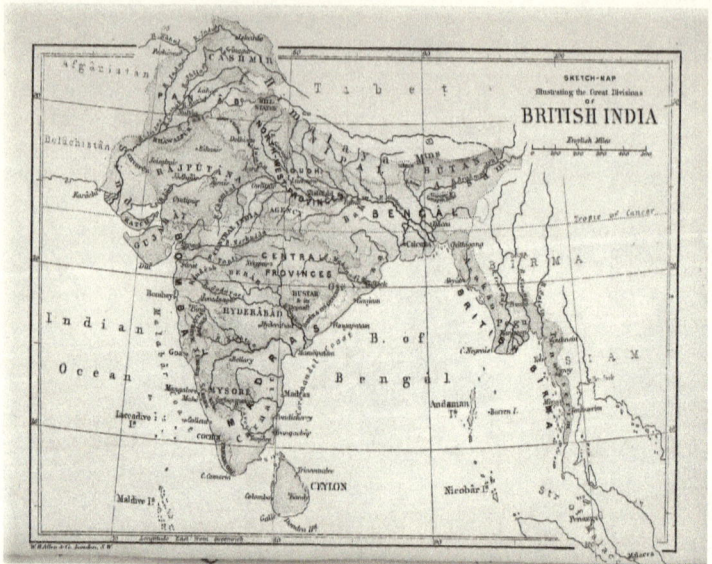

Figure 126: *British India in 1880*

(later the Republic of India) and the Dominion of Pakistan (later the Islamic Republic of Pakistan, the eastern part of which, still later, became the People's Republic of Bangladesh). At the inception of the Raj in 1858, Lower Burma was already a part of British India; Upper Burma was added in 1886, and the resulting union, Burma, was administered as an autonomous province until 1937, when it became a separate British colony, gaining its own independence in 1948.

Geographical extent

The British Raj extended over almost all present-day India, Pakistan, and Bangladesh, except for small holdings by other European nations such as Goa and Pondicherry. This area is very diverse, containing the Himalayan mountains, fertile floodplains, the Indo-Gangetic Plain, a long coastline, tropical dry forests, arid uplands, and the Thar desert. In addition, at various times, it included Aden (from 1858 to 1937),[629] Lower Burma (from 1858 to 1937), Upper Burma (from 1886 to 1937), British Somaliland (briefly from 1884 to 1898), and Singapore (briefly from 1858 to 1867). Burma was separated from India and directly administered by the British Crown from 1937 until its independence in 1948. The Trucial States of the Persian Gulf and the states under the Persian Gulf Residency were theoretically princely states as well as Presidencies and provinces of British India until 1947 and used the rupee as their unit of currency.

Among other countries in the region, Ceylon (now Sri Lanka) was ceded to Britain in 1802 under the Treaty of Amiens. Ceylon was part of Madras Presidency between 1793 and 1798.[630] The kingdoms of Nepal and Bhutan, having fought wars with the British, subsequently signed treaties with them and were recognised by the British as independent states.[631,632] The Kingdom of Sikkim was established as a princely state after the Anglo-Sikkimese Treaty of 1861; however, the issue of sovereignty was left undefined.[633] The Maldive Islands were a British protectorate from 1887 to 1965, but not part of British India.

British India and the Princely States

India during the British Raj was made up of two types of territory: *British India* and the *Native States* (or *Princely States*). In its Interpretation Act 1889, the British Parliament adopted the following definitions in Section 18:

(4.) The expression "British India" shall mean all territories and places within Her Majesty's dominions which are for the time being governed by Her Majesty through the Governor-General of India or through any governor or other officer subordinates to the Governor-General of India.
(5.) The expression "India" shall mean British India together with any territories of any native prince or chief under the suzerainty of Her Majesty exercised through the Governor-General of India, or through any governor or other officer subordinates to the Governor-General of India.

In general, the term "British India" had been used (and is still used) to refer also to the regions under the rule of the British East India Company in India from 1600 to 1858.[634] The term has also been used to refer to the "British in India".[635]

The terms "Indian Empire" and "Empire of India" (like the term "British Empire") were not used in legislation. The monarch was known as Empress or Emperor of India and the term was often used in Queen Victoria's Queen's Speeches and Prorogation Speeches. The passports issued by the British Indian government had the words "Indian Empire" on the cover and "Empire of India" on the inside.[636] In addition, an order of knighthood, the Most Eminent Order of the Indian Empire, was set up in 1878.

Suzerainty over 175 princely states, some of the largest and most important, was exercised (in the name of the British Crown) by the central government of British India under the Viceroy; the remaining approximately 500 states were dependents of the provincial governments of British India under a Governor,

Lieutenant-Governor, or Chief Commissioner (as the case might have been). A clear distinction between "dominion" and "suzerainty" was supplied by the jurisdiction of the courts of law: the law of British India rested upon the laws passed by the British Parliament and the legislative powers those laws vested in the various governments of British India, both central and local; in contrast, the courts of the Princely States existed under the authority of the respective rulers of those states.

Major provinces

Colonial India

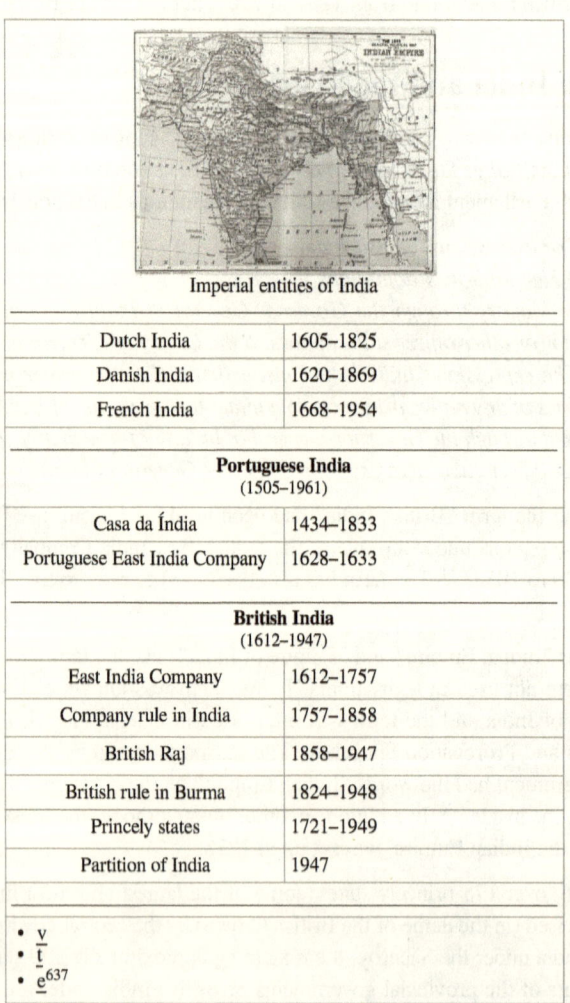

Imperial entities of India

Dutch India	1605–1825
Danish India	1620–1869
French India	1668–1954

Portuguese India (1505–1961)	
Casa da Índia	1434–1833
Portuguese East India Company	1628–1633

British India (1612–1947)	
East India Company	1612–1757
Company rule in India	1757–1858
British Raj	1858–1947
British rule in Burma	1824–1948
Princely states	1721–1949
Partition of India	1947

- v
- t
- e[637]

At the turn of the 20th century, British India consisted of eight provinces that were administered either by a Governor or a Lieutenant-Governor.

Province of British India (and present day territories)	Total area in km² (sq mi)	Population in 1901 (in millions)	Chief administrative officer
Assam (Assam, Arunachal Pradesh, Meghalaya, Mizoram, Nagaland)	130,000 (50,000)	6	Chief Commissioner
Bengal (Bangladesh, West Bengal, Bihar, Jharkhand and Odisha)	390,000 (150,000)	75	Lieutenant-Governor
Bombay (Sindh and parts of Maharashtra, Gujarat and Karnataka)	320,000 (120,000)	19	Governor-in-Council
Burma (Myanmar)	440,000 (170,000)	9	Lieutenant-Governor
Central Provinces and Berar (Madhya Pradesh and parts of Maharashtra, Chhattisgarh and Odisha)	270,000 (100,000)	13	Chief Commissioner
Madras (Andhra Pradesh, Tamil Nadu and parts of Kerala, Karnataka, Odisha and Telangana)	370,000 (140,000)	38	Governor-in-Council
Punjab (Punjab Province, Islamabad Capital Territory, Punjab, Haryana, Himachal Pradesh, Chandigarh and the National Capital Territory of Delhi)	250,000 (97,000)	20	Lieutenant-Governor
United Provinces (Uttar Pradesh and Uttarakhand)	280,000 (110,000)	48	Lieutenant-Governor

I+ Areas and populations (excluding the dependent Native States) c. 1907

During the partition of Bengal (1905–1913), the new provinces of Assam and East Bengal were created as a Lieutenant-Governorship. In 1911, *East Bengal* was reunited with Bengal, and the new provinces in the east became: Assam, Bengal, Bihar and Orissa.

Minor provinces

In addition, there were a few minor provinces that were administered by a Chief Commissioner:

Minor province of British India (and present day territories)	Total area in km² (sq mi)	Population in 1901 (in thousands)	Chief administrative officer
Ajmer-Merwara (parts of Rajasthan)	7,000 (2,700)	477	*ex officio* Chief Commissioner
Andaman and Nicobar Islands (Andaman and Nicobar Islands)	78,000 (30,000)	25	Chief Commissioner
British Baluchistan (Balochistan)	120,000 (46,000)	308	*ex officio* Chief Commissioner
Coorg (Kodagu district)	4,100 (1,600)	181	*ex officio* Chief Commissioner
North West Frontier Province (Khyber Pakhtunkhwa)	41,000 (16,000)	2,125	Chief Commissioner

Princely states

A Princely State, also called a Native State or an Indian State, was a British vassal state in India with an indigenous nominal Indian ruler, subject to a subsidiary alliance. There were 565 princely states when India and Pakistan became independent from Britain in August 1947. The princely states did not form a part of British India (i.e. the presidencies and provinces), as they were not directly under British rule. The larger ones had treaties with Britain that specified which rights the princes had; in the smaller ones the princes had few rights. Within the princely states external affairs, defence and most communications were under British control. The British also exercised a general influence over the states' internal politics, in part through the granting or withholding of recognition of individual rulers. Although there were nearly 600 princely states, the great majority were very small and contracted out the business of government to the British. Some two hundred of the states had an area of less than 25 square kilometres (10 square miles).

The states were grouped into Agencies and Residencies.

British Raj

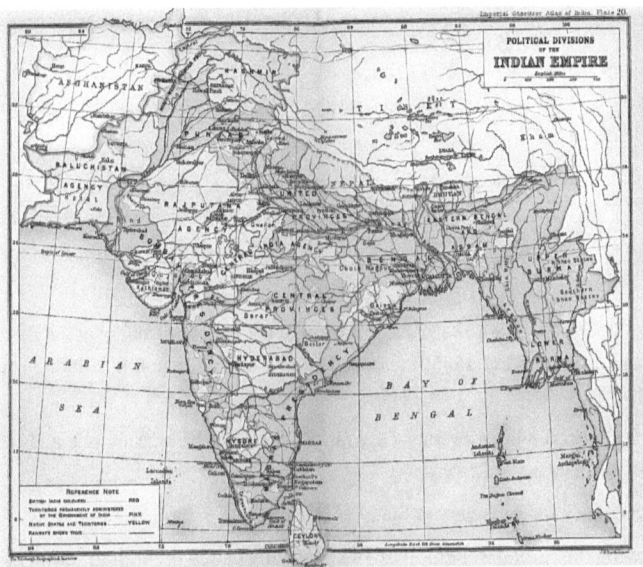

Figure 127: *1909 Map of the British Indian Empire, showing British India in two shades of pink and the princely states in yellow.*

Organization

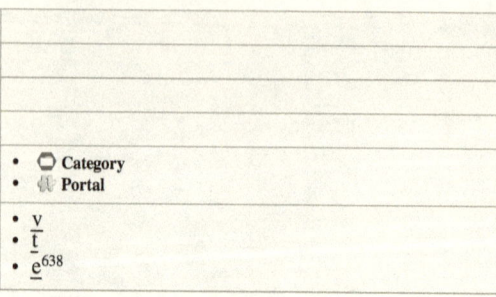

Sir Charles Wood (1800–1885) was President of the Board of Control of the East India Company from 1852 to 1855; he shaped British education policy in India, and was Secretary of State for India 1859–66.

Lord Canning, the last Governor-General of India under Company rule and the first Viceroy of India under Crown rule.

Lord Salisbury was Secretary of State for India 1874–78.

Following the Indian Rebellion of 1857 (usually called the Indian Mutiny by the British), the Government of India Act 1858 made changes in the governance of India at three levels:

1. in the imperial government in London,
2. in the central government in Calcutta, and
3. in the provincial governments in the presidencies (and later in the provinces).[639]

In London, it provided for a cabinet-level Secretary of State for India and a fifteen-member Council of India, whose members were required, as one prerequisite of membership, to have spent at least ten years in India and to have done so no more than ten years before.[640] Although the Secretary of State formulated the policy instructions to be communicated to India, he was required in most instances to consult the Council, but especially so in matters relating to spending of Indian revenues. The Act envisaged a system of "double government" in which the Council ideally served both as a check on excesses in imperial policy making and as a body of up-to-date expertise on India. However, the Secretary of State also had special emergency powers that allowed him to make unilateral decisions, and, in reality, the Council's expertise was sometimes outdated. From 1858 until 1947, twenty seven individuals served as Secretary of State for India and directed the India Office; these included: Sir Charles Wood (1859–1866), Marquess of Salisbury (1874–1878; later Prime Minister of Britain), John Morley (1905–1910; initiator of the Minto-Morley Reforms), E. S. Montagu (1917–1922; an architect of the Montagu-Chelmsford reforms), and Frederick Pethick-Lawrence (1945–1947; head of the 1946 Cabinet Mission to India). The size of the advisory Council was reduced over the next

half-century, but its powers remained unchanged. In 1907, for the first time, two Indians were appointed to the Council.[641] They were K.G. Gupta and Syed Hussain Bilgrami.

In Calcutta, the Governor-General remained head of the Government of India and now was more commonly called the Viceroy on account of his secondary role as the Crown's representative to the nominally sovereign princely states; he was, however, now responsible to the Secretary of State in London and through him to Parliament. A system of "double government" had already been in place during the Company's rule in India from the time of Pitt's India Act of 1784. The Governor-General in the capital, Calcutta, and the Governor in a subordinate presidency (Madras or Bombay) was each required to consult his advisory council; executive orders in Calcutta, for example, were issued

in the name of "Governor-General-in-Council" (*i.e.* the Governor-General with the advice of the Council). The Company's system of "double government" had its critics, since, from the time of the system's inception, there had been intermittent feuding between the Governor-General and his Council; still, the Act of 1858 made no major changes in governance. However, in the years immediately thereafter, which were also the years of post-rebellion reconstruction, Viceroy Lord Canning found the collective decision making of the Council to be too time-consuming for the pressing tasks ahead, so he requested the "portfolio system" of an Executive Council in which the business of each government department (the "portfolio") was assigned to and became the responsibility of a single council member. Routine departmental decisions were made exclusively by the member, but important decisions required the consent of the Governor-General and, in the absence of such consent, required discussion by the entire Executive Council. This innovation in Indian governance was promulgated in the Indian Councils Act 1861.

If the Government of India needed to enact new laws, the Councils Act allowed for a Legislative Council—an expansion of the Executive Council by up to twelve additional members, each appointed to a two-year term—with half the members consisting of British officials of the government (termed *official*) and allowed to vote, and the other half, comprising Indians and domiciled Britons in India (termed *non-official*) and serving only in an advisory capacity. All laws enacted by Legislative Councils in India, whether by the Imperial Legislative Council in Calcutta or by the provincial ones in Madras and Bombay, required the final assent of the Secretary of State in London; this prompted Sir Charles Wood, the second Secretary of State, to describe the Government of India as "a despotism controlled from home". Moreover, although the appointment of Indians to the Legislative Council was a response to calls after the 1857 rebellion, most notably by Sayyid Ahmad Khan, for more consultation with Indians, the Indians so appointed were from the landed aristocracy, often chosen for their loyalty, and far from representative. Even so, the "... tiny advances in the practice of representative government were intended to provide safety valves for the expression of public opinion, which had been so badly misjudged before the rebellion". Indian affairs now also came to be more closely examined in the British Parliament and more widely discussed in the British press.

With the promulgation of the Government of India Act 1935, the Council of India was abolished with effect from 1 April 1937 and a modified system of government enacted. The Secretary of State for India represented the Government of India in the UK. He was assisted by a body of advisers numbering from 8–12 individuals, at least half of whom were required to have held office in India for a minimum of 10 years, and had not relinquished office earlier than two years prior to their appointment as advisers to the Secretary of State.[642]

The Viceroy and Governor-General of India, a Crown appointee, typically held office for five years though there was no fixed tenure, and received an annual salary of Rs. 250,800 p.a. (£18,810 p.a.).[643] He headed the Viceroy's Executive Council, each member of which had responsibility for a department of the central administration. From 1 April 1937, the position of Governor-General in Council, which the Viceroy and Governor-General concurrently held in the capacity of representing the Crown in relations with the Indian princely states, was replaced by the designation of "HM Representative for the Exercise of the Functions of the Crown in its Relations with the Indian States," or the "Crown Representative." The Executive Council was greatly expanded during the Second World War, and in 1947 comprised 14 Members (Secretaries), each of whom earned a salary of Rs. 66,000 p.a. (£4950 p.a.). The portfolios in 1946–1947 were:

- External Affairs and Commonwealth Relations
- Home and Information and Broadcasting
- Food and transportation
- Transport and Railways
- Labour
- Industries and Supplies,
- Works, Mines and Power
- Education
- Defence
- Finance
- Commerce
- Communications
- Health
- Law

Until 1946, the Viceroy held the portfolio for External Affairs and Commonwealth Relations, as well as heading the Political Department in his capacity as the Crown Representative. Each department was headed by a Secretary excepting the Railway Department, which was headed by a Chief Commissioner of Railways under a Secretary.[644]

The Viceroy and Governor-General was also the head of the bicameral Indian Legislature, consisting of an upper house (the Council of State) and a lower house (the Legislative Assembly). The Viceroy was the head of the Council of State, while the Legislative Assembly, which was first opened in 1921, was headed by an elected President (appointed by the Viceroy from 1921–1925). The Council of State consisted of 58 members (32 elected, 26 nominated), while the Legislative Assembly comprised 141 members (26 nominated officials, 13 others nominated and 102 elected). The Council of State existed in five-year periods and the Legislative Assembly for three-year periods, though either could be dissolved earlier or later by the Viceroy. The Indian Legislature was empowered to make laws for all persons resident in British India including all British subjects resident in India, and for all British Indian subjects residing outside India. With the assent of the King-Emperor and after copies of a proposed enactment had been submitted to both houses of the British Parliament, the Viceroy could overrule the legislature and directly enact any measures in the perceived interests of British India or its residents if the need arose.[645]

Effective from 1 April 1936, the Government of India Act created the new provinces of Sind (separated from the Bombay Presidency) and Orissa (separated from the Province of Bihar and Orissa). Burma and Aden became separate Crown Colonies under the Act from 1 April 1937, thereby ceasing to be part of the Indian Empire. From 1937 onwards, British India was divided into 17 administrations: the three Presidencies of Madras, Bombay and Bengal, and the 14 provinces of the United Provinces, Punjab, Bihar, the Central Provinces and Berar, Assam, the North-West Frontier Province (NWFP), Orissa, Sind, British Baluchistan, Delhi, Ajmer-Merwara, Coorg, the Andaman and Nicobar Islands and Panth Piploda. The Presidencies and the first eight provinces were each under a Governor, while the latter six provinces were each under a Chief Commissioner. The Viceroy directly governed the Chief Commissioner provinces through each respective Chief Commissioner, while the Presidencies and the provinces under Governors were allowed greater autonomy under the Government of India Act.[646,647] Each Presidency or province headed by a Governor had either a provincial bicameral legislature (in the Presidencies, the United Provinces, Bihar and Assam) or a unicameral legislature (in the Punjab, Central Provinces and Berar, NWFP, Orissa and Sind). The Governor of each presidency or province represented the Crown in his capacity, and was assisted by a ministers appointed from the members of each provincial legislature. Each provincial legislature had a life of five years, barring any special circumstances such as wartime conditions. All bills passed by the provincial legislature were either signed or rejected by the Governor, who could also issue proclamations or promulgate ordinances while the legislature was in recess, as the need arose.

Each province or presidency comprised a number of divisions, each headed by a Commissioner and subdivided into districts, which were the basic administrative units and each headed by a Collector and Magistrate or Deputy Commissioner; in 1947, British India comprised 230 districts.

Timeline of major events, legislation, public works

The reigning British monarchs during the period of the British Raj, 1858–1947, in silver one rupee coins.

Two silver one rupee coins used in India during the British Raj, showing Victoria, Queen, 1862 (left) and Victoria, Empress, 1886 (right)

Silver one rupee coins showing Edward VII, King-Emperor, 1903 (left) and 1908 (right)

Silver one rupee coins used in India during the British Raj, showing George V, King-Emperor, 1913 (left) and 1919 (right)

One rupee coins showing George VI, King-Emperor, 1940 (left) and just before India's independence in 1947 (right).[648]

Period	Major Events, Legislation, Public Works	Presiding Viceroy
1 November 1858 – 21 March 1862	1858 reorganisation of British Indian Army (contemporaneously and hereafter Indian Army) Construction begins (1860): University of Bombay, University of Madras, and University of Calcutta Indian Penal Code passed into law in 1860. Upper Doab famine of 1860–1861 Indian Councils Act 1861 Establishment of Archaeological Survey of India in 1861 James Wilson, financial member of Council of India reorganises customs, imposes income tax, creates paper currency. Indian Police Act of 1861, creation of Imperial Police later known as Indian Police Service.	The Viscount Canning
21 March 1862–20 November 1863	Vicerory dies prematurely in Dharamsala	The Earl of Elgin
12 January 1864 – 12 January 1869	Anglo-Bhutan Duar War (1864–1865) Orissa famine of 1866 Rajputana famine of 1869 Creation of Department of Irrigation. Creation of Imperial Forestry Service in 1867 (now Indian Forest Service). "Nicobar Islands annexed and incorporated into India 1869"	Sir John Lawrence, Bt
12 January 1869 – 8 February 1872	Creation of Department of Agriculture (now Ministry of Agriculture) Major extension of railways, roads, and canals Indian Councils Act of 1870 Creation of Andaman and Nicobar Islands as a Chief Commissionership (1872). Assassination of Lord Mayo in the Andamans.	The Earl of Mayo
3 May 1872 – 12 April 1876	Mortalities in Bihar famine of 1873–74 prevented by importation of rice from Burma. Gaikwad of Baroda dethroned for misgovernment; dominions continued to a child ruler. Indian Councils Act of 1874 Visit of the Prince of Wales, future Edward VII in 1875–76.	The Lord Northbrook

12 April 1876 – 8 June 1880	Baluchistan established as a Chief Commissionership Queen Victoria (in absentia) proclaimed Empress of India at Delhi Durbar of 1877. Great Famine of 1876–78: 5.25 million dead; reduced relief offered at expense of Rs. 80 million. Creation of Famine Commission of 1878–80 under Sir Richard Strachey. Indian Forest Act of 1878 Second Anglo-Afghan War.	The Lord Lytton
8 June 1880 – 13 December 1884	End of Second Anglo-Afghan War. Repeal of Vernacular Press Act of 1878. Compromise on the Ilbert Bill. Local Government Acts extend self-government from towns to country. University of Punjab established in Lahore in 1882 Famine Code promulgated in 1883 by the Government of India. Creation of the Education Commission. Creation of indigenous schools, especially for Muslims. Repeal of import duties on cotton and of most tariffs. Railway extension.	The Marquess of Ripon
13 December 1884 – 10 December 1888	Passage of Bengal Tenancy Bill Third Anglo-Burmese War. Joint Anglo-Russian Boundary Commission appointed for the Afghan frontier. Russian attack on Afghans at Panjdeh (1885). The Great Game in full play. Report of Public Services Commission of 1886–87, creation of Imperial Civil Service (later Indian Civil Service (ICS), and today Indian Administrative Service) University of Allahabad established in 1887 Queen Victoria's Jubilee, 1887.	The Earl of Dufferin[649]
10 December 1888 – 11 October 1894	Strengthening of NW Frontier defence. Creation of Imperial Service Troops consisting of regiments contributed by the princely states. Gilgit Agency leased in 1899 British Parliament passes Indian Councils Act 1892, opening the Imperial Legislative Council to Indians. Revolution in princely state of Manipur and subsequent reinstatement of ruler. High point of The Great Game. Establishment of the Durand Line between British India and Afghanistan, Railways, roads, and irrigation works begun in Burma. Border between Burma and Siam finalised in 1893. Fall of the Rupee, resulting from the steady depreciation of silver currency worldwide (1873–93). Indian Prisons Act of 1894	The Marquess of Lansdowne
11 October 1894 – 6 January 1899	Reorganisation of Indian Army (from Presidency System to the four Commands). Pamir agreement Russia, 1895 The Chitral Campaign (1895), the Tirah Campaign (1896–97) Indian famine of 1896–97 beginning in Bundelkhand. Bubonic plague in Bombay (1896), Bubonic plague in Calcutta (1898); riots in wake of plague prevention measures. Establishment of Provincial Legislative Councils in Burma and Punjab; the former a new Lieutenant Governorship.	The Earl of Elgin

Date	Events	Viceroy
6 January 1899 – 18 November 1905	Creation of the North West Frontier Province under a Chief Commissioner (1901). Indian famine of 1899–1900. Return of the bubonic plague, 1 million deaths Financial Reform Act of 1899; Gold Reserve Fund created for India. Punjab Land Alienation Act Inauguration of Department (now Ministry) of Commerce and Industry. Death of Queen Victoria (1901); dedication of the Victoria Memorial Hall, Calcutta as a national gallery of Indian antiquities, art, and history. Coronation Durbar in Delhi (1903); Edward VII (in absentia) proclaimed Emperor of India. Francis Younghusband's British expedition to Tibet (1903–04) North-Western Provinces (previously Ceded and Conquered Provinces) and Oudh renamed United Provinces in 1904 Reorganisation of Indian Universities Act (1904). Systemisation of preservation and restoration of ancient monuments by Archaeological Survey of India with Indian Ancient Monument Preservation Act. Inauguration of agricultural banking with Cooperative Credit Societies Act of 1904 Partition of Bengal; new province of East Bengal and Assam under a Lieutenant-Governor. Census of 1901 gives the total population at 294 million, including 62 million in the princely states and 232 million in British India. About 170,000 are Europeans. 15 million men and 1 million women are literate. Of those school-aged, 25% of the boys and 3% of the girls attend. There are 207 million Hindus, and 63x million Muslims, along with 9 million Buddhists (in Burma), 3 million Christians, 2 million Sikhs, 1 million Jains, and 8.4 million who practise animism.[651]	The Lord Curzon of Kedleston[650]
18 November 1905 – 23 November 1910	Creation of the Railway Board Anglo-Russian Convention of 1907 Indian Councils Act 1909 (also Minto-Morley Reforms) Appointment of Indian Factories Commission in 1909. Establishment of Department of Education in 1910 (now Ministry of Education)	The Earl of Minto
23 November 1910 – 4 April 1916	Visit of King George V and Queen Mary in 1911: commemoration as Emperor and Empress of India at last Delhi Durbar King George V announces creation of new city of New Delhi to replace Calcutta as capital of India. Indian High Courts Act of 1911 Indian Factories Act of 1911 Construction of New Delhi, 1912–1929 World War I, Indian Army in: Western Front, Belgium, 1914; German East Africa (Battle of Tanga, 1914); Mesopotamian Campaign (Battle of Ctesiphon, 1915; Siege of Kut, 1915–16); Battle of Galliopoli, 1915–16 Passage of Defence of India Act 1915	The Lord Hardinge of Penshurst
4 April 1916 – 2 April 1921	Indian Army in: Mesopotamian Campaign (Fall of Baghdad, 1917); Sinai and Palestine Campaign (Battle of Megiddo, 1918) Passage of Rowlatt Act, 1919 Government of India Act 1919 (also Montagu-Chelmsford Reforms) Jallianwala Bagh Massacre, 1919 Third Anglo-Afghan War, 1919 University of Rangoon established in 1920.	The Lord Chelmsford
2 April 1921 – 3 April 1926	University of Delhi established in 1922. Indian Workers Compensation Act of 1923	The Earl of Reading

3 April 1926 – 18 April 1931	Indian Trade Unions Act of 1926, Indian Forest Act, 1927 Appointment of Royal Commission of Indian Labour, 1929 Indian Constitutional Round Table Conferences, London, 1930–32, Gandhi-Irwin Pact, 1931.	The Lord Irwin
18 April 1931 – 18 April 1936	New Delhi inaugurated as capital of India, 1931. Indian Workmen's Compensation Act of 1933 Indian Factories Act of 1934 Royal Indian Air Force created in 1932. Indian Military Academy established in 1932. Government of India Act 1935 Creation of Reserve Bank of India	The Earl of Willingdon
18 April 1936 – 1 October 1943	Indian Payment of Wages Act of 1936 Burma administered independently after 1937 with creation of new cabinet position Secretary of State for India and Burma, and with the Burma Office separated off from the India Office Indian Provincial Elections of 1937 Cripps' mission to India, 1942. Indian Army in Mediterranean, Middle East and African theatres of World War II (North African campaign): (Operation Compass, Operation Crusader, First Battle of El Alamein, Second Battle of El Alamein. East African campaign, 1940, Anglo-Iraqi War, 1941, Syria-Lebanon campaign, 1941, Anglo-Soviet invasion of Iran, 1941) Indian Army in Battle of Hong Kong, Battle of Malaya, Battle of Singapore Burma Campaign of World War II begins in 1942.	The Marquess of Linlithgow
1 October 1943 – 21 February 1947	Indian Army becomes, at 2.5 million men, the largest all-volunteer force in history. World War II: Burma Campaign, 1943–45 (Battle of Kohima, Battle of Imphal) Bengal famine of 1943 Indian Army in Italian campaign (Battle of Monte Cassino) British Labour Party wins UK General Election of 1945 with Clement Attlee as prime minister. 1946 Cabinet Mission to India Indian Elections of 1946.	The Viscount Wavell
21 February 1947 – 15 August 1947	Indian Independence Act 1947 of the British Parliament enacted on 18 July 1947. Radcliffe Award, August 1947 Partition of India India Office and position of Secretary of State for India abolished; ministerial responsibility within the United Kingdom for British relations with India and Pakistan is transferred to the Commonwealth Relations Office.	The Viscount Mountbatten of Burma

1858–1914

Aftermath of the Rebellion of 1857: Indian critiques, British response

Figure 128: *Lakshmibai, The Rani of Jhansi, one of the principal leaders of the Indian Rebellion of 1857, who earlier had lost her kingdom as a result of Lord Dalhousie's Doctrine of Lapse.*

Figure 129: *Sir Syed Ahmed Khan founder of the Muhammedan Anglo-Oriental College, later the Aligarh Muslim University, wrote one of the early critiques, The Causes of the Indian Mutiny.*

Figure 130: *An 1887 souvenir portrait of Queen Victoria as Empress of India, 30 years after the war.*

Although the rebellion had shaken the British enterprise in India, it had not derailed it. After the war, the British became more circumspect. Much thought was devoted to the causes of the rebellion, and from it three main lessons were drawn. At a more practical level, it was felt that there needed to be more communication and camaraderie between the British and Indians—not just between British army officers and their Indian staff but in civilian life as well. The Indian army was completely reorganised: units composed of the Muslims and Brahmins of the United Provinces of Agra and Oudh, who had formed the core of the rebellion, were disbanded. New regiments, like the Sikhs and Baluchis, composed of Indians who, in British estimation, had demonstrated steadfastness, were formed. From then on, the Indian army was to remain unchanged in its organisation until 1947.[652] The 1861 Census had revealed that the English population in India was 125,945. Of these only about 41,862 were civilians as compared with about 84,083 European officers and men of the Army. In 1880, the standing Indian Army consisted of 66,000 British soldiers, 130,000 Natives, and 350,000 soldiers in the princely armies.[653]

It was also felt that both the princes and the large land-holders, by not joining the rebellion, had proved to be, in Lord Canning's words, "breakwaters in a storm". They too were rewarded in the new British Raj by being officially recognised in the treaties each state now signed with the Crown.Wikipedia:Verifiability At the same time, it was felt that the peasants,

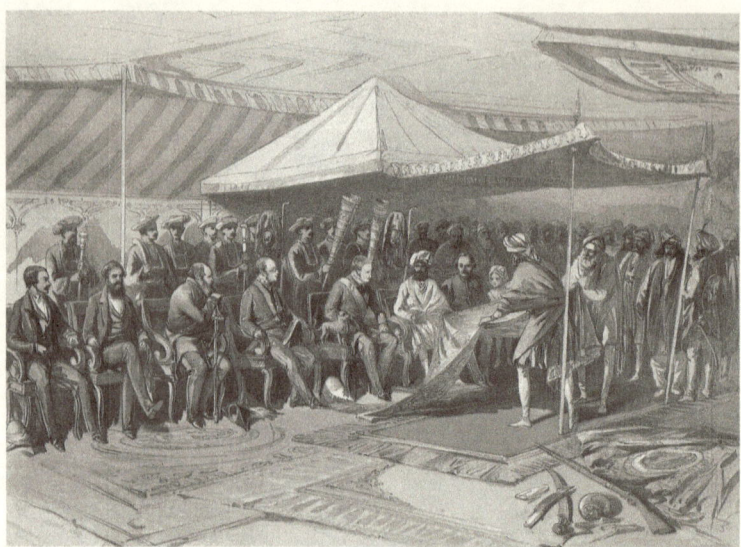

Figure 131: *Viceroy Lord Canning meets Maharaja Ranbir Singh of Jammu & Kashmir, 9 March 1860.*

for whose benefit the large land-reforms of the United Provinces had been undertaken, had shown disloyalty, by, in many cases, fighting for their former landlords against the British. Consequently, no more land reforms were implemented for the next 90 years: Bengal and Bihar were to remain the realms of large land holdings (unlike the Punjab and Uttar Pradesh).

Lastly, the British felt disenchanted with Indian reaction to social change. Until the rebellion, they had enthusiastically pushed through social reform, like the ban on *sati* by Lord William Bentinck. It was now felt that traditions and customs in India were too strong and too rigid to be changed easily; consequently, no more British social interventions were made, especially in matters dealing with religion, even when the British felt very strongly about the issue (as in the instance of the remarriage of Hindu child widows). This was exemplified further in Queen Victoria's Proclamation released immediately after the rebellion. The proclamation stated that 'We disclaim alike our Right and Desire to impose Our Convictions on any of Our Subjects';[654] demonstrating official British commitment to abstaining from social intervention in India.

Demographic history

The population of the territory that became the British Raj was 100 million by 1600 and remained nearly stationary until the 19th century. The population of the Raj reached 255 million according to the first census taken in 1881 of India.[655,656]

Studies of India's population since 1881 have focused on such topics as total population, birth and death rates, growth rates, geographic distribution, literacy, the rural and urban divide, cities of a million, and the three cities with populations over eight million: Delhi, Greater Bombay, and Calcutta.

Mortality rates fell in 1920–45 era, primarily due to biological immunisation. Other factors included rising incomes and better living conditions, improved better nutrition, a safer and cleaner environment, and better official health policies and medical care.

Severe overcrowding in the cities caused major public health problems, as noted in an official report from 1938:[657]

> In the urban and industrial areas ... cramped sites, the high values of land and the necessity for the worker to live in the vicinity of his work ... all tend to intensify congestion and overcrowding. In the busiest centres houses are built close together, eave touching eave, and frequently back to back .... Space is so valuable that, in place of streets and roads, winding lanes provide the only approach to the houses. Neglect of sanitation is often evidenced by heaps of rotting garbage and pools of sewage, whilst the absence of latrines enhance the general pollution of air and soil.

Legal modernisation

Singha argues that after 1857 the colonial government strengthened and expanded its infrastructure via the court system, legal procedures, and statutes. New legislation merged the Crown and the old East India Company courts and introduced a new penal code as well as new codes of civil and criminal procedure, based largely on English law. In the 1860s–1880s the Raj set up compulsory registration of births, deaths, and marriages, as well as adoptions, property deeds, and wills. The goal was to create a stable, usable public record and verifiable identities. However, there was opposition from both Muslim and Hindu elements who complained that the new procedures for census-taking and registration threatened to uncover female privacy. Purdah rules prohibited women from saying their husband's name or having their photograph taken. An all-India census was conducted between 1868 and 1871, often using total numbers of females in a household rather than individual names. Select groups which the Raj reformers wanted to monitor statistically included those reputed to practice female infanticide, prostitutes, lepers, and eunuchs.[658]

Figure 132: *Elephant Carriage of the Maharaja of Rewa, Delhi Durbar of 1903.*

Murshid argues that women were in some ways more restricted by the modernisation of the laws. They remained tied to the strictures of their religion, caste, and customs, but now with an overlay of British Victorian attitudes. Their inheritance rights to own and manage property were curtailed; the new English laws were somewhat harsher. Court rulings restricted the rights of second wives and their children regarding inheritance. A woman had to belong to either a father or a husband to have any rights.[659]

Civilising mission

Thomas Babington Macaulay (1800–1859) presented his Whiggish interpretation of English history as an upward progression always leading to more liberty and more progress. Macaulay simultaneously was a leading reformer involved in transforming the educational system of India. He would base it on the English language so that India could join the mother country in a steady upward progress. Macaulay took Burke's emphasis on moral rule and implemented it in actual school reforms, giving the British Empire a profound moral mission to civilise the natives.

Yale professor Karuna Mantena has argued that the civilising mission did not last long, for she says that benevolent reformers were the losers in key debates,

Figure 133: *University of Lucknow founded by the British in 1867 in India*

such as those following the 1857 rebellion in India, and the scandal of Governor Edward Eyre's brutal repression of the Morant Bay rebellion in Jamaica in 1865. The rhetoric continued but it became an alibi for British misrule and racism. No longer was it believed that the natives could truly make progress, instead they had to be ruled by heavy hand, with democratic opportunities postponed indefinitely. As a result:

> The central tenets of liberal imperialism were challenged as various forms of rebellion, resistance and instability in the colonies precipitated a broad-ranging reassessment....the equation of 'good government' with the reform of native society, which was at the core of the discourse of liberal empire, would be subject to mounting skepticism.[660]

English historian Peter Cain, has challenged Mantena, arguing that the imperialists truly believed that British rule would bring to the subjects the benefits of 'ordered liberty', thereby Britain could fulfil its moral duty and achieve its own greatness. Much of the debate took place in Britain itself, and the imperialists worked hard to convince the general population that the civilising mission was well under-way. This campaign served to strengthen imperial support at home, and thus, says Cain, to bolster the moral authority of the gentlemanly elites who ran the Empire.

Figure 134: *The University of Calcutta, established 1857, is one of the three oldest modern state universities in India.*

Education

The British made widespread education in English a high priority. During the time of the East India Company, Thomas Babington Macaulay had made schooling taught in English a priority for the Raj in his famous minute of February 1835 and succeeded in implementing ideas previously put forward by Lord William Bentinck (the governor general between 1828 and 1835). Bentinck favoured the replacement of Persian by English as the official language, the use of English as the medium of instruction, and the training of English-speaking Indians as teachers. He was inspired by utilitarian ideas and called for "useful learning." However, Bentinck's proposals were rejected by London officials.[661] Under Macaulay, thousands of elementary and secondary schools were opened; they typically had an all-male student body.

Missionaries opened their own schools that taught Christianity and the three Rs. Bellenoit argues that as civil servants became more isolated and resorted to scientific racism, missionary schools became more engaged with Indians, grew increasingly sympathetic to Indian culture, and adamantly opposed scientific racism.[662]

Universities in Calcutta, Bombay, and Madras were established in 1857, just before the Rebellion. By 1890 some 60,000 Indians had matriculated, chiefly in the liberal arts or law. About a third entered public administration, and another third became lawyers. The result was a very well educated professional state bureaucracy. By 1887 of 21,000 mid-level civil service appointments,

Figure 135: *St. Paul's Cathedral was built in 1847 and served as the chair of the Bishop of Calcutta, who served as the metropolitan of the Church of India, Burma and Ceylon.*

45% were held by Hindus, 7% by Muslims, 19% by Eurasians (European father and Indian mother), and 29% by Europeans. Of the 1000 top-level positions, almost all were held by Britons, typically with an Oxbridge degree.[663] The government, often working with local philanthropists, opened 186 universities and colleges of higher education by 1911; they enrolled 36,000 students (over 90% men). By 1939 the number of institutions had doubled and enrolment reached 145,000. The curriculum followed classical British standards of the sort set by Oxford and Cambridge and stressed English literature and European history. Nevertheless, by the 1920s the student bodies had become hotbeds of Indian nationalism.[664]

Missions

As the Anglican Church was the established church of England, "it had an impact on India with the arrival of the British". Citing the Great Commission, Joseph White, a Laudian Professor of Arabic at the University of Oxford, "preached before the university in 1784 on the duty of promoting the universal and progressive message of Christianity 'among our Mahometan and Gentoo Subjects in India'." In 1889, the Prime Minister of Great Britain, Robert

Gascoyne-Cecil, 3rd Marquess of Salisbury expressed similar sentiments, stating that "It is not only our duty but is in our interest to promote the diffusion of Christianity as far as possible throughout the length and breadth of India."

The growth of the British Indian Army led to the arrival of many Anglican chaplains in India. Following the arrival of the Church of England's Church Mission Society in 1814, the Diocese of Calcutta of the Church of India, Burma and Ceylon (CIBC) was erected, with its St. Paul's Cathedral being built in 1847. By 1930, the Church of India, Burma and Ceylon had fourteen dioceses across the Indian Empire.

Missionaries from other Christian denominations came to British India as well; Lutheran missionaries, for example, arrived in Calcutta in 1836 and by "the year 1880 there were over 31,200 Lutheran Christians spread out in 1,052 villages". Methodists began arriving in India in 1783 and established missions with a focus on "education, health ministry, and evangelism". In the 1790s, Christians from the London Missionary Society and Baptist Missionary Society, began doing missionary work in the Indian Empire. In Neyoor, the London Missionary Society Hospital "pioneered improvements in the public health system for the treatment of diseases even before organized attempts were made by the colonial Madras Presidency, reducing the death rate substantially".

After 1857, the establishment of schools and hospitals by British Christian missionaries became the "a pivotal feature of missionary work and the principal vehicles for conversion". Christ Church College (1866) and St. Stephen's College (1881) are two examples of prominent church-affiliated educational institutions founded during the British Raj. Within educational institutions established during the British Raj, Christian texts, especially the Bible, were a part of the curricula. During the British Raj, Christian missionaries developed writing systems for Indian languages that previously did not have one. Christian missionaries in India also worked to increase literacy and also engaged in social activism, such as fighting against prostitution, championing the right of widowed women to remarry, and trying to stop early marriages for women. Among British women, zenana missions became a popular method to win converts to Christianity.

Figure 136: *One Mohur depicting Queen Victoria (1862)*

Economic history

Economic trends

The Indian economy grew at about 1% per year from 1880 to 1920, and the population also grew at 1%.[665] All three sectors of the economy – agriculture, manufacturing, and services – accelerated in the postcolonial India. In agriculture a "green revolution" took place in the 1970s. The most important difference between colonial and postcolonial India was the utilization of land surplus with productivity-led growth by using high-yielding variety seeds, chemical fertilizers and more intensive application of water. All these three inputs were subsidized by the state. The result was, on average, no long-term change in per capita income levels, though cost of living had grown higher. Agriculture was still dominant, with most peasants at the subsistence level. Extensive irrigation systems were built, providing an impetus for switching to cash crops for export and for raw materials for Indian industry, especially jute, cotton, sugarcane, coffee and tea.[666] India's global share of GDP fell drastically from above 20% to less than 5% in the colonial period. Historians have been bitterly divided on issues of economic history, with the Nationalist school (following Nehru) arguing that India was poorer at the end of British rule than at the beginning and that impoverishment occurred because of the British.

Much of the economic activity in British India was for the benefit of the British economy and was carried out relentlessly through repressive British imperial policies and with negative repercussions for the Indian population. This is reified in India's large exports of wheat to Britain: despite a major famine that claimed between 6 and 10 million lives in the late 1870s, these exports remained unchecked. A colonial government committed to laissez-faire economics refused to interfere with these exports or provide any relief, declaring it "a mistake to spend so much money to save a lot of black fellows."

Industry

The entrepreneur Jamsetji Tata (1839–1904) began his industrial career in 1877 with the Central India Spinning, Weaving, and Manufacturing Company in Bombay. While other Indian mills produced cheap coarse yarn (and later cloth) using local short-staple cotton and cheap machinery imported from Britain, Tata did much better by importing expensive longer-stapled cotton from Egypt and buying more complex ring-spindle machinery from the United States to spin finer yarn that could compete with imports from Britain.[667]

In the 1890s, he launched plans to move into heavy industry using Indian funding. The Raj did not provide capital, but, aware of Britain's declining position against the US and Germany in the steel industry, it wanted steel mills in India. It promised to purchase any surplus steel Tata could not otherwise sell.[668] The Tata Iron and Steel Company (TISCO), now headed by his son Dorabji Tata (1859–1932), opened its plant at Jamshedpur in Bihar in 1908. It used American technology, not British,[669] and became the leading iron and steel producer in India, with 120,000 employees in 1945. TISCO became India's proud symbol of technical skill, managerial competence, entrepreneurial flair, and high pay for industrial workers.[670] The Tata family, like most of India's big businessmen, were Indian nationalists but did not trust the Congress because it seemed too aggressively hostile to the Raj, too socialist, and too supportive of trade unions.[671]

Railways

British India built a modern railway system in the late nineteenth century which was the fourth largest in the world. The railways at first were privately owned and operated. It was run by British administrators, engineers and craftsmen. At first, only the unskilled workers were Indians.

The East India Company (and later the colonial government) encouraged new railway companies backed by private investors under a scheme that would provide land and guarantee an annual return of up to five percent during the initial years of operation. The companies were to build and operate the lines under a 99-year lease, with the government having the option to buy them earlier.

Two new railway companies, Great Indian Peninsular Railway (GIPR) and East Indian Railway (EIR) began in 1853–54 to construct and operate lines near Bombay and Calcutta. The first passenger railway line in North India between Allahabad and Kanpur opened in 1859.

Figure 137: *Extent of Great Indian Peninsular Railway network in 1870. The GIPR was one of the largest rail companies at that time.*

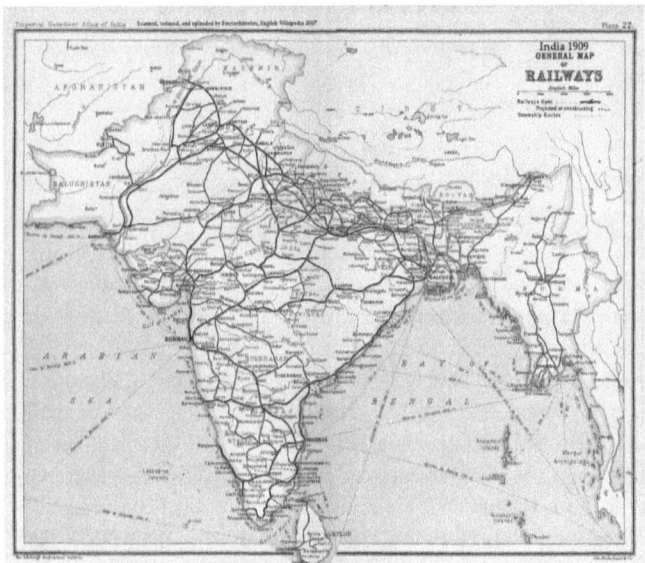

Figure 138: *The railway network of India in 1909, when it was the fourth largest railway network in the world.*

Figure 139: *"The most magnificent railway station in the world." says the caption of the stereographic tourist picture of Victoria Terminus, Bombay, which was completed in 1888.*

In 1854, Governor-General Lord Dalhousie formulated a plan to construct a network of trunk lines connecting the principal regions of India. Encouraged by the government guarantees, investment flowed in and a series of new rail companies were established, leading to rapid expansion of the rail system in India. Soon several large princely states built their own rail systems and the network spread to the regions that became the modern-day states of Assam, Rajasthan and Andhra Pradesh. The route mileage of this network increased from 1,349 kilometres (838 mi) in 1860 to 25,495 kilometres (15,842 mi) in 1880, mostly radiating inland from the three major port cities of Bombay, Madras, and Calcutta.

Most of the railway construction was done by Indian companies supervised by British engineers. The system was heavily built, using a wide gauge, sturdy tracks and strong bridges. By 1900 India had a full range of rail services with diverse ownership and management, operating on broad, metre and narrow gauge networks. In 1900, the government took over the GIPR network, while the company continued to manage it. During the First World War, the railways were used to transport troops and grains to the ports of Bombay and Karachi en route to Britain, Mesopotamia, and East Africa. With shipments of equipment and parts from Britain curtailed, maintenance became much more difficult; critical workers entered the army; workshops were converted to making artillery; some locomotives and cars were shipped to the Middle East. The railways could barely keep up with the increased demand.[672] By the end of the war, the railways had deteriorated for lack of maintenance and were not profitable. In 1923, both GIPR and EIR were nationalised.

Headrick shows that until the 1930s, both the Raj lines and the private companies hired only European supervisors, civil engineers, and even operating personnel, such as locomotive engineers. The government's Stores Policy required that bids on railway contracts be made to the India Office in London, shutting out most Indian firms. The railway companies purchased most of their hardware and parts in Britain. There were railway maintenance workshops in India, but they were rarely allowed to manufacture or repair locomotives. TISCO steel could not obtain orders for rails until the war emergency.[673]

The Second World War severely crippled the railways as rolling stock was diverted to the Middle East, and the railway workshops were converted into munitions workshops. After independence in 1947, forty-two separate railway systems, including thirty-two lines owned by the former Indian princely states, were amalgamated to form a single nationalised unit named the *Indian Railways*.

India provides an example of the British Empire pouring its money and expertise into a very well built system designed for military reasons (after the Mutiny of 1857), with the hope that it would stimulate industry. The system was overbuilt and too expensive for the small amount of freight traffic it carried. Christensen (1996), who looked at colonial purpose, local needs, capital, service, and private-versus-public interests, concluded that making the railways a creature of the state hindered success because railway expenses had to go through the same time-consuming and political budgeting process as did all other state expenses. Railway costs could therefore not be tailored to the timely needs of the railways or their passengers.[674]

Irrigation

The British Raj invested heavily in infrastructure, including canals and irrigation systems in addition to railways, telegraphy, roads and ports.[675,676,677] The Ganges Canal reached 350 miles from Haridwar to Kanpur, and supplied thousands of miles of distribution canals. By 1900 the Raj had the largest irrigation system in the world. One success story was Assam, a jungle in 1840 that by 1900 had 4,000,000 acres under cultivation, especially in tea plantations. In all, the amount of irrigated land multiplied by a factor of eight. Historian David Gilmour says:

> By the 1870s the peasantry in the districts irrigated by the Ganges Canal were visibly better fed, housed and dressed than before; by the end of the century the new network of canals in the Punjab at producing even more prosperous peasantry there.

Figure 140: *The Queen's Own Madras Sappers and Miners, 1896*

Policies

In the second half of the 19th century, both the direct administration of India by the British Crown and the technological change ushered in by the industrial revolution had the effect of closely intertwining the economies of India and Great Britain. In fact many of the major changes in transport and communications (that are typically associated with Crown Rule of India) had already begun before the Mutiny. Since Dalhousie had embraced the technological revolution underway in Britain, India too saw rapid development of all those technologies. Railways, roads, canals, and bridges were rapidly built in India and telegraph links equally rapidly established in order that raw materials, such as cotton, from India's hinterland could be transported more efficiently to ports, such as Bombay, for subsequent export to England.[678] Likewise, finished goods from England, were transported back, just as efficiently, for sale in the burgeoning Indian markets. Massive railway projects were begun in earnest and government railway jobs and pensions attracted a large number of upper caste Hindus into the civil service for the first time. The Indian Civil Service was prestigious and paid well, but it remained politically neutral.[679] Imports of British cotton covered 55% of the Indian market by 1875.[680] Industrial production as it developed in European factories was unknown until the 1850s when the first cotton mills were opened in Bombay, posing a challenge to the cottage-based home production system based on family labour.[681]

Taxes in India decreased during the colonial period for most of India's population; with the land tax revenue claiming 15% of India's national income during Mogul times compared with 1% at the end of the colonial period. The percentage of national income for the village economy increased from 44% during Mogul times to 54% by the end of colonial period. India's per capita GDP decreased from $550Wikipedia:Please clarify in 1700 to $520 by 1857, although it later increased to $618, by 1947.[682]

Economic impact

— Jawaharlal Nehru, on the economic effects of the British rule, in his book *The Discovery of India*

Historians continue to debate whether the long-term impact of British rule was to accelerate the economic development of India, or to distort and retard it. In 1780, the conservative British politician Edmund Burke raised the issue of India's position: he vehemently attacked the East India Company, claiming that Warren Hastings and other top officials had ruined the Indian economy and society. Indian historian Rajat Kanta Ray (1998) continues this line of attack, saying the new economy brought by the British in the 18th century was a form of "plunder" and a catastrophe for the traditional economy of the Mughal Empire. Ray accuses the British of depleting the food and money stocks and of imposing high taxes that helped cause the terrible Bengal famine of 1770, which killed a third of the people of Bengal.[683]

P. J. Marshall shows that recent scholarship has reinterpreted the view that the prosperity of the formerly benign Mughal rule gave way to poverty and anarchy. He argues the British takeover did not make any sharp break with the past, which largely delegated control to regional Mughal rulers and sustained a generally prosperous economy for the rest of the 18th century. Marshall notes the British went into partnership with Indian bankers and raised revenue through local tax administrators and kept the old Mughal rates of taxation.

Many historians agree that the East India Company inherited an onerous taxation system that took one-third of the produce of Indian cultivators. Instead of the Indian nationalist account of the British as alien aggressors, seizing power by brute force and impoverishing all of India, Marshall presents the interpretation (supported by many scholars in India and the West) that the British were not in full control but instead were players in what was primarily an Indian play and in which their rise to power depended upon excellent co-operation with Indian elites. Marshall admits that much of his interpretation is still highly controversial among many historians.[684]

Famines, epidemics, public health
Major famines in India during British rule

Famine	Years	Deaths[685]
Great Bengal Famine	1769–1770	10[686]
Chalisa famine	1783–1784	11[687]
Doji bara famine	1789–1795	11[688]
Agra famine of 1837–38	1837–1838	0.8[689]
Eastern Rajputana	1860–1861	2[689]
Orissa famine of 1866	1865–1867	1[690]
Rajputana famine of 1869	1868–1870	1.5[691]
Bihar famine of 1873–74	1873–1874	0
Great Famine of 1876–78	1876–1878	10.3[692]
Odisha, Bihar	1888–1889	0.15[693]
Indian famine of 1896–97	1896–1897	5[689]
Indian famine of 1899–1900	1899–1900	1[689]
Bombay Presidency	1905–1906	0.23[694]
Bengal famine of 1943	1943–1944	1.5[694]
Total (1765–1947)[695,696,697]	1769–1944	55.48

According to economist Angus Maddison, "The British contributed to public health by introducing smallpox vaccination, establishing Western medicine and training modern doctors, by killing rats, and establishing quarantine procedures. As a result, the death rate fell and the population of India grew more than two-and-a-half times between 1757 and 1947."

> *Population growth worsened the plight of the peasantry. As a result of peace and improved sanitation and health, the Indian population rose from perhaps 100 million in 1700 to 300 million by 1920. While encouraging agricultural productivity, the British also provided economic incentives to have more children to help in the fields. Although a similar population increase occurred in Europe at the same time, the growing numbers could be absorbed by industrialisation or emigration to the Americas and Australia. India enjoyed neither an industrial revolution nor an increase in food growing. Moreover, Indian landlords had a stake in the cash crop system and discouraged innovation. As a result, population numbers far outstripped the amount of available food and land, creating dire poverty and widespread hunger.*
>
> —*Craig A. Lockard, Societies, Networks, and Transitions*

Figure 141: *Child who starved to death during the Bengal famine of 1943*

During the British Raj, India experienced some of the worst famines ever recorded, including the Great Famine of 1876–1878, in which 6.1 million to 10.3 million people died[698] and the Indian famine of 1899–1900, in which 1.25 to 10 million people died.[699] Recent research, including work by Mike Davis and Amartya Sen,[700] argue that famines in India were made more severe by British policies in India. An El Niño event caused the Indian famine of 1876–1878.[701]

Having been criticised for the badly bungled relief-effort during the Orissa famine of 1866, British authorities began to discuss famine policy soon afterwards, and in early 1868 Sir William Muir, Lieutenant-Governor of the North Western Provinces, issued a famous order stating that:

> ... every District officer would be held personally responsible that no deaths occurred from starvation which could have been avoided by any exertion or arrangement on his part or that of his subordinates.

The first cholera pandemic began in Bengal, then spread across India by 1820. Ten thousand British troops and countless Indians died during this pandemic. Estimated deaths in India between 1817 and 1860 exceeded 15 million. Another 23 million died between 1865 and 1917.[702] The Third Pandemic of plague started in China in the middle of the 19th century, spreading disease to all inhabited continents and killing 10 million people in India alone.[703] Waldemar Haffkine, who mainly worked in India, became the first microbiologist to develop and deploy vaccines against cholera and bubonic plague. In 1925 the Plague Laboratory in Bombay was renamed the Haffkine Institute.

Fevers ranked as one of the leading causes of death in India in the 19th century.[704] Britain's Sir Ronald Ross, working in the Presidency General Hospital in Calcutta, finally proved in 1898 that mosquitoes transmit malaria, while on assignment in the Deccan at Secunderabad, where the Centre for Tropical and Communicable Diseases is now named in his honour.

In 1881 there were around 120,000 leprosy patients. The central government passed the Lepers Act of 1898, which provided legal provision for forcible confinement of leprosy sufferers in India.[705] Under the direction of Mountstuart Elphinstone a program was launched to propagate smallpox vaccination. Mass vaccination in India resulted in a major decline in smallpox mortality by the end of the 19th century. In 1849 nearly 13% of all Calcutta deaths were due to smallpox. Between 1868 and 1907, there were approximately 4.7 million deaths from smallpox.[706]

Sir Robert Grant directed his attention to establishing a systematic institution in Bombay for imparting medical knowledge to the natives. In 1860, Grant Medical College became one of the four recognised colleges for teaching courses leading to degrees (alongside Elphinstone College, Deccan College and Government Law College, Mumbai).

1860s–1890s: New middle class, Indian National Congress

By 1880, a new middle class had arisen in India and spread thinly across the country. Moreover, there was a growing solidarity among its members, created by the "joint stimuli of encouragement and irritation." The encouragement felt by this class came from its success in education and its ability to avail itself of the benefits of that education such as employment in the Indian Civil Service. It came too from Queen Victoria's proclamation of 1858 in which she had declared, "We hold ourselves bound to the natives of our Indian territories by the same obligation of duty which bind us to all our other subjects." Indians were especially encouraged when Canada was granted dominion status in 1867 and established an autonomous democratic constitution. Lastly, the encouragement came from the work of contemporaneous Oriental scholars like Monier Monier-Williams and Max Müller, who in their works had been presenting ancient India as a great civilisation. Irritation, on the other hand, came not just from incidents of racial discrimination at the hands of the British in

India, but also from governmental actions like the use of Indian troops in imperial campaigns (e.g. in the Second Anglo-Afghan War) and the attempts to control the vernacular press (e.g. in the *Vernacular Press Act of 1878*).[707]

It was, however, Viceroy Lord Ripon's partial reversal of the Ilbert Bill (1883), a legislative measure that had proposed putting Indian judges in the Bengal Presidency on equal footing with British ones, that transformed the discontent into political action. On 28 December 1885, professionals and intellectuals from this middle-class—many educated at the new British-founded universities in Bombay, Calcutta, and Madras, and familiar with the ideas of British political philosophers, especially the utilitarians assembled in Bombay. The seventy men founded the Indian National Congress; Womesh Chandra Bonerjee was elected the first president. The membership comprised a westernised elite, and no effort was made at this time to broaden the base.

During its first twenty years, the Congress primarily debated British policy toward India; however, its debates created a new Indian outlook that held Great Britain responsible for draining India of its wealth. Britain did this, the nationalists claimed, by unfair trade, by the restraint on indigenous Indian industry, and by the use of Indian taxes to pay the high salaries of the British civil servants in India.

1870s–1907: Social reformers, moderates vs. extremists

Thomas Baring served as Viceroy of India 1872–1876. Baring's major accomplishments came as an energetic reformer who was dedicated to upgrading the quality of government in the British Raj. He began large scale famine relief, reduced taxes, and overcame bureaucratic obstacles in an effort to reduce both starvation and widespread social unrest. Although appointed by a Liberal government, his policies were much the same as Viceroys appointed by Conservative governments.[708]

Gopal Krishna Gokhale, a constitutional social reformer and moderate nationalist, was elected president of the Indian National Congress in 1905.

Congress "extremist" Bal Gangadhar Tilak speaking in 1907 as the party split into the Moderates and the Extremists. Seated at the table is Aurobindo Ghosh and to his right (in the chair) is Lala Lajpat Rai, both allies of Tilak.

Social reform was in the air by the 1880s. For example, Pandita Ramabai, poet, Sanskrit scholar, and a champion of the emancipation of Indian women, took up the cause of widow remarriage, especially of Brahamin widows, later converted to Christianity.[709] By 1900 reform movements had taken root within the Indian National Congress. Congress member Gopal Krishna Gokhale founded the Servants of India Society, which lobbied for legislative reform (for example, for a law to permit the remarriage of Hindu child widows), and whose members took vows of poverty, and worked among the untouchable community.[710]

By 1905, a deep gulf opened between the moderates, led by Gokhale, who downplayed public agitation, and the new "extremists" who not only advocated agitation, but also regarded the pursuit of social reform as a distraction from nationalism. Prominent among the extremists was Bal Gangadhar Tilak, who attempted to mobilise Indians by appealing to an explicitly Hindu political identity, displayed, for example, in the annual public Ganapati festivals that he inaugurated in western India.[711]

Partition of Bengal (1905–1911)

Bal Gangadhar Tilak was the first leader of the Indian Independence Movement and known as Father of Indian Unrest and Maker of Modern India

Viceroy Curzon (1899–1905). He promoted many reforms but his partitioning of Bengal into Muslim and Hindu provinces outraged the people.

Sir Khawaja Salimullah, an influential Bengali aristocrat and British ally, who strongly favoured the creation of Eastern Bengal and Assam

Surendranath Banerjee, a Congress moderate, who led the opposition to the partition of Bengal with the *Swadeshi* movement to buy Indian-made cloth.

Cover of a 1909 issue of the Tamil magazine *Vijaya* showing "Mother India" with her diverse progeny and the rallying cry "Vande Mataram".

The Viceroy Lord Curzon (1899–1905) was unusually energetic in pursuit of efficiency and reform.[712] His agenda included the creation of the North-West

Frontier Province; small changes in the Civil Service; speeding up the operations of the secretariat; setting up a gold standard to ensure a stable currency; creation of a Railway Board; irrigation reform; reduction of peasant debts; lowering the cost of telegrams; archaeological research and the preservation of antiquities; improvements in the universities; police reforms; upgrading the roles of the Native States; a new Commerce and Industry Department; promotion of industry; revised land revenue policies; lowering taxes; setting up agricultural banks; creating an Agricultural Department; sponsoring agricultural research; establishing an Imperial Library; creating an Imperial Cadet Corps; new famine codes; and, indeed, reducing the smoke nuisance in Calcutta.[713]

Trouble emerged for Curzon when he divided the largest administrative subdivision in British India, the Bengal Province, into the Muslim-majority province of Eastern Bengal and Assam and the Hindu-majority province of West Bengal (present-day Indian states of West Bengal, Bihar, and Odisha). Curzon's act, the Partition of Bengal—which some considered administratively felicitous, communally charged, sowed the seeds of division among Indians in Bengal and, which had been contemplated by various colonial administrations since the time of Lord William Bentinck, but never acted upon—was to transform nationalist politics as nothing else before it. The Hindu elite of Bengal, among them many who owned land in East Bengal that was leased out to Muslim peasants, protested fervidly.[714]

Following the Partition of Bengal, which was a strategy set out by Lord Curzon to weaken the nationalist movement, Tilak encouraged the Swadeshi movement and the Boycott movement.[715] The movement consisted of the boycott of foreign goods and also the social boycott of any Indian who used foreign goods. The Swadeshi movement consisted of the usage of natively produced goods. Once foreign goods were boycotted, there was a gap which had to be filled by the production of those goods in India itself. Bal Gangadhar Tilak said that the Swadeshi and Boycott movements are two sides of the same coin. The large Bengali Hindu middle-class (the *Bhadralok*), upset at the prospect of Bengalis being outnumbered in the new Bengal province by Biharis and

Oriyas, felt that Curzon's act was punishment for their political assertiveness. The pervasive protests against Curzon's decision took the form predominantly of the *Swadeshi* ("buy Indian") campaign led by two-time Congress president, Surendranath Banerjee, and involved boycott of British goods.[716]

The rallying cry for both types of protest was the slogan *Bande Mataram* ("Hail to the Mother"), which invoked a mother goddess, who stood variously for Bengal, India, and the Hindu goddess Kali. Sri Aurobindo never went beyond the law when he edited the *Bande Mataram* magazine; it preached independence but within the bounds of peace as far as possible. Its goal was Passive Resistance.[717] The unrest spread from Calcutta to the surrounding regions of Bengal when students returned home to their villages and towns. Some joined local political youth clubs emerging in Bengal at the time, some engaged in robberies to fund arms, and even attempted to take the lives of Raj officials. However, the conspiracies generally failed in the face of intense police work. The *Swadeshi* boycott movement cut imports of British textiles by 25%. The *swadeshi* cloth, although more expensive and somewhat less comfortable than its Lancashire competitor, was worn as a mark of national pride by people all over India.[718]

1906–1909: Muslim League, Minto-Morley reforms

1909 Prevailing Religions, Map of British India, 1909, showing the prevailing majority religions based on the Census of 1901.

Hakim Ajmal Khan, a founder of the Muslim League, became the president of the Indian National Congress in 1921.

Lord Minto, the Conservative viceroy met with the Muslim delegation in June 1906. The Minto-Morley Reforms of 1909 called for separate Muslim electorates.

The Hindu protests against the partition of Bengal led the Muslim elite in India to organise in 1906 the All India Muslim League. The League favoured the partition of Bengal, since it gave them a Muslim majority in the eastern half. In 1905, when Tilak and Lajpat Rai attempted to rise to leadership positions in the Congress, and the Congress itself rallied around symbolism of Kali, Muslim fears increased. The Muslim elite, including Dacca Nawab and Khwaja Salimullah, expected that a new province with a Muslim majority would directly benefit Muslims aspiring to political power.[719]

The first steps were taken toward self-government in British India in the late 19th century with the appointment of Indian counsellors to advise the British viceroy and the establishment of provincial councils with Indian members; the British subsequently widened participation in legislative councils with the Indian Councils Act of 1892. Municipal Corporations and District Boards were created for local administration; they included elected Indian members.

The Indian Councils Act 1909, known as the Morley-Minto Reforms (John Morley was the secretary of state for India, and Minto was viceroy) – gave Indians limited roles in the central and provincial legislatures. Upper class Indians, rich landowners and businessmen were favoured. The Muslim community was made a separate electorate and granted double representation. The goals were quite conservative but they did advance the elective principle.

The partition of Bengal was rescinded in 1911 and announced at the Delhi Durbar at which King George V came in person and was crowned Emperor of India. He announced the capital would be moved from Calcutta to Delhi, a Muslim stronghold. Morley was especially vigilant in crushing revolutionary groups.

1914–1947

1914–1918: First World War, Lucknow Pact

Indian medical orderlies attending to wounded soldiers with the *Mesopotamian Expeditionary Force* in Mesopotamia during World War I.

Sepoy Khudadad Khan, the first Indian to be awarded the Victoria Cross, the British Empire's highest war-time medal for gallantry. Khan, from Chakwal District, Punjab (present-day Pakistan) was fighting on the Western Front in 1914.

Mohandas Karamchand Gandhi (seated in carriage, on the right, eyes downcast, with black flat-top hat) receives a big welcome in Karachi in 1916 after his return to India from South Africa.

Muhammad Ali Jinnah, seated, third from the left, was a supporter of the Lucknow Pact, which, in 1916, ended the three-way rift between the Extremists, the Moderates and the League.

The First World War would prove to be a watershed in the imperial relationship between Britain and India. Shortly prior to the outbreak of war, the Government of India had indicated that they could furnish two divisions plus a cavalry brigade, with a further division in case of emergency. Some 1.4 million Indian and British soldiers of the British Indian Army took part in the war, primarily in Iraq and the Middle East. Their participation had a wider cultural fallout as news spread how bravely soldiers fought and died alongside British soldiers, as well as soldiers from dominions like Canada and Australia. India's international profile rose during the 1920s, as it became a founding member of the League of Nations in 1920 and participated, under the name, "Les Indes Anglaises" (British India), in the 1920 Summer Olympics in Antwerp. Back in India, especially among the leaders of the Indian National Congress, the war led to calls for greater self-government for Indians.

After the 1906 split between the moderates and the extremists, organised political activity by the Congress had remained fragmented until 1914, when Bal Gangadhar Tilak was released from prison and began to sound out other Congress leaders about possible re-unification. That, however, had to wait until the demise of Tilak's principal moderate opponents, Gopal Krishna Gokhale and Pherozeshah Mehta, in 1915, whereupon an agreement was reached for Tilak's ousted group to re-enter the Congress. In the 1916 Lucknow session of the Congress, Tilak's supporters were able to push through a more radical resolution which asked for the British to declare that it was their, "aim and intention ... to confer self-government on India at an early date." Soon, other such rumblings began to appear in public pronouncements: in 1917, in the Imperial Legislative Council, Madan Mohan Malaviya spoke of the expectations the war had generated in India, "I venture to say that the war has put the clock ... fifty years forward ... (The) reforms after the war will have to be such, ... as will satisfy the aspirations of her (India's) people to take their legitimate part in the administration of their own country."

The 1916 Lucknow Session of the Congress was also the venue of an unanticipated mutual effort by the Congress and the Muslim League, the occasion for which was provided by the wartime partnership between Germany and Turkey. Since the Turkish Sultan, or *Khalifah*, had also sporadically claimed guardianship of the Islamic holy sites of Mecca, Medina, and Jerusalem, and since the British and their allies were now in conflict with Turkey, doubts began to increase among some Indian Muslims about the "religious neutrality" of the British, doubts that had already surfaced as a result of the reunification of Bengal in 1911, a decision that was seen as ill-disposed to Muslims. In the Lucknow Pact, the League joined the Congress in the proposal for greater self-government that was campaigned for by Tilak and his supporters; in return, the Congress accepted separate electorates for Muslims in the provincial legislatures as well as the Imperial Legislative Council. In 1916, the Muslim League had anywhere between 500 and 800 members and did not yet have its wider following among Indian Muslims of later years; in the League itself, the pact did not have unanimous backing, having largely been negotiated by a group of "Young Party" Muslims from the United Provinces (UP), most prominently, two brothers Mohammad and Shaukat Ali, who had embraced the Pan-Islamic cause; however, it did have the support of a young lawyer from Bombay, Muhammad Ali Jinnah, who was later to rise to leadership roles in both the League and the Indian independence movement. In later years, as the full ramifications of the pact unfolded, it was seen as benefiting the Muslim minority *élites* of provinces like UP and Bihar more than the Muslim majorities of Punjab and Bengal, nonetheless, at the time, the "Lucknow Pact", was an important milestone in nationalistic agitation and was seen so by the British.

During 1916, two Home Rule Leagues were founded within the Indian National Congress by Tilak and Annie Besant, respectively, to promote Home Rule among Indians, and also to elevate the stature of the founders within the Congress itself. Mrs. Besant, for her part, was also keen to demonstrate the superiority of this new form of organised agitation, which had achieved some success in the Irish home rule movement, to the political violence that had intermittently plagued the subcontinent during the years 1907–1914. The two Leagues focused their attention on complementary geographical regions: Tilak's in western India, in the southern Bombay presidency, and Mrs. Besant's in the rest of the country, but especially in the Madras Presidency and in regions like Sind and Gujarat that had hitherto been considered politically dormant by the Congress. Both leagues rapidly acquired new members – approximately thirty thousand each in a little over a year – and began to publish inexpensive newspapers. Their propaganda also turned to posters, pamphlets, and political-religious songs, and later to mass meetings, which not only attracted greater numbers than in earlier Congress sessions, but also entirely new social groups such as non-Brahmins, traders, farmers, students, and lower-level government workers. Although they did not achieve the magnitude or character of a nationwide mass movement, the Home Rule leagues both deepened and widened organised political agitation for self-rule in India. The British authorities reacted by imposing restrictions on the Leagues, including shutting out students from meetings and banning the two leaders from travelling to certain provinces.

The year 1915 also saw the return of Mohandas Karamchand Gandhi to India. Already known in India as a result of his civil liberties protests on behalf of the Indians in South Africa, Gandhi followed the advice of his mentor Gopal Krishna Gokhale and chose not to make any public pronouncements during the first year of his return, but instead spent the year travelling, observing the country first-hand, and writing. Earlier, during his South Africa sojourn, Gandhi, a lawyer by profession, had represented an Indian community, which, although small, was sufficiently diverse to be a microcosm of India itself. In tackling the challenge of holding this community together and simultaneously confronting the colonial authority, he had created a technique of non-violent resistance, which he labelled *Satyagraha* (or, Striving for Truth). For Gandhi, *Satyagraha* was different from "passive resistance", by then a familiar technique of social protest, which he regarded as a practical strategy adopted by the weak in the face of superior force; *Satyagraha*, on the other hand, was for him the "last resort of those strong enough in their commitment to truth to undergo suffering in its cause." Ahimsa or "non-violence", which formed the underpinning of *Satyagraha*, came to represent the twin pillar, with Truth, of Gandhi's unorthodox religious outlook on life. During the years 1907–1914, Gandhi tested the technique of *Satyagraha* in a number of protests on behalf of the Indian community in South Africa against the unjust racial laws.

Also, during his time in South Africa, in his essay, *Hind Swaraj*, (1909), Gandhi formulated his vision of *Swaraj*, or "self-rule" for India based on three vital ingredients: solidarity between Indians of different faiths, but most of all between Hindus and Muslims; the removal of untouchability from Indian society; and the exercise of *swadeshi* – the boycott of manufactured foreign goods and the revival of Indian cottage industry. The first two, he felt, were essential for India to be an egalitarian and tolerant society, one befitting the principles of Truth and *Ahimsa*, while the last, by making Indians more self-reliant, would break the cycle of dependence that was not only perpetrating the direction and tenor of the British rule in India, but also the British commitment to it. At least until 1920, the British presence itself, was not a stumbling block in Gandhi's conception of *swaraj*; rather, it was the inability of Indians to create a modern society.

1917–1919: *Satyagraha*, Montagu-Chelmsford reforms, Jallianwalla Bagh

Gandhi made his political debut in India in 1917 in Champaran district in Bihar, near the Nepal border, where he was invited by a group of disgruntled tenant farmers who, for many years, had been forced into planting indigo (for dyes) on a portion of their land and then selling it at below-market prices to

Figure 142: *Gandhi at the time of the Kheda Satyagraha, 1918*

Figure 143: *Edwin Montagu, left, the Secretary of State for India, whose report, led to the Government of India Act 1919, also known as the Montford Reforms or the Montagu-Chelmsford Reforms*

Figure 144: *Headlines about the Rowlatt Bills (1919) from a nationalist newspaper in India. Although all non-official Indians on the Legislative Council voted against the Rowlatt Bills, the government was able to force their passage by using its majority.*

the British planters who had leased them the land. Upon his arrival in the district, Gandhi was joined by other agitators, including a young Congress leader, Rajendra Prasad, from Bihar, who would become a loyal supporter of Gandhi and go on to play a prominent role in the Indian independence movement. When Gandhi was ordered to leave by the local British authorities, he refused on moral grounds, setting up his refusal as a form of individual Satyagraha. Soon, under pressure from the Viceroy in Delhi who was anxious to maintain domestic peace during wartime, the provincial government rescinded Gandhi's expulsion order, and later agreed to an official enquiry into the case. Although the British planters eventually gave in, they were not won over to the farmers' cause, and thereby did not produce the optimal outcome of a Satyagraha that Gandhi had hoped for; similarly, the farmers themselves, although pleased at the resolution, responded less than enthusiastically to the concurrent projects of rural empowerment and education that Gandhi had inaugurated in keeping with his ideal of *swaraj*. The following year Gandhi launched two more Satyagrahas – both in his native Gujarat – one in the rural Kaira district where land-owning farmers were protesting increased land-revenue and the other in the city of Ahmedabad, where workers in an Indian-owned textile mill were

Figure 145: *The Jallianwalla Bagh in 1919, a few months after the massacre which had occurred on 13 April*

distressed about their low wages. The satyagraha in Ahmedabad took the form of Gandhi fasting and supporting the workers in a strike, which eventually led to a settlement. In Kaira, in contrast, although the farmers' cause received publicity from Gandhi's presence, the satyagraha itself, which consisted of the farmers' collective decision to withhold payment, was not immediately successful, as the British authorities refused to back down. The agitation in Kaira gained for Gandhi another lifelong lieutenant in Sardar Vallabhbhai Patel, who had organised the farmers, and who too would go on to play a leadership role in the Indian independence movement.[720] Champaran, Kaira, and Ahmedabad were important milestones in the history of Gandhi's new methods of social protest in India.

In 1916, in the face of new strength demonstrated by the nationalists with the signing of the Lucknow Pact and the founding of the Home Rule leagues, and the realisation, after the disaster in the Mesopotamian campaign, that the war would likely last longer, the new Viceroy, Lord Chelmsford, cautioned that the Government of India needed to be more responsive to Indian opinion. Towards the end of the year, after discussions with the government in London, he suggested that the British demonstrate their good faith – in light of the Indian war role – through a number of public actions, including awards of titles and honours to princes, granting of commissions in the army to Indians, and removal of the much-reviled cotton excise duty, but, most importantly, an announcement of Britain's future plans for India and an indication of some concrete steps. After more discussion, in August 1917, the new Liberal Secretary of State for India, Edwin Montagu, announced the British aim of "increasing association of Indians in every branch of the administration, and the gradual development of self-governing institutions, with a view to the progressive realisation of responsible government in India as an integral part of the British Empire." Although the plan envisioned limited self-government at first only in the provinces – with India emphatically within the British Empire – it represented the first British proposal for any form of representative government in a non-white colony.

Earlier, at the onset of World War I, the reassignment of most of the British army in India to Europe and Mesopotamia, had led the previous Viceroy, Lord Harding, to worry about the "risks involved in denuding India of troops." Revolutionary violence had already been a concern in British India; consequently, in 1915, to strengthen its powers during what it saw was a time of increased vulnerability, the Government of India passed the Defence of India Act, which allowed it to intern politically dangerous dissidents without due process, and added to the power it already had – under the 1910 Press Act – both to imprison journalists without trial and to censor the press. It was under the Defence of India act that the Ali brothers were imprisoned in 1916, and Annie Besant, a European woman, and ordinarily more problematic to imprison, was arrested in 1917. Now, as constitutional reform began to be discussed in earnest, the British began to consider how new moderate Indians could be brought into the fold of constitutional politics and, simultaneously, how the hand of established constitutionalists could be strengthened. However, since the Government of India wanted to ensure against any sabotage of the reform process by extremists, and since its reform plan was devised during a time when extremist violence had ebbed as a result of increased governmental control, it also began to consider how some of its wartime powers could be extended into peacetime.

Consequently, in 1917, even as Edwin Montagu, announced the new constitutional reforms, a committee chaired by a British judge, Mr. S. A. T. Rowlatt, was tasked with investigating "revolutionary conspiracies", with the unstated goal of extending the government's wartime powers. The Rowlatt committee presented its report in July 1918 and identified three regions of conspiratorial insurgency: Bengal, the Bombay presidency, and the Punjab. To combat subversive acts in these regions, the committee recommended that the government use emergency powers akin to its wartime authority, which included the ability to try cases of sedition by a panel of three judges and without juries, exaction of securities from suspects, governmental overseeing of residences of suspects, and the power for provincial governments to arrest and detain suspects in short-term detention facilities and without trial.

With the end of World War I, there was also a change in the economic climate. By the end of 1919, 1.5 million Indians had served in the armed services in either combatant or non-combatant roles, and India had provided £146 million in revenue for the war. The increased taxes coupled with disruptions in both domestic and international trade had the effect of approximately doubling the index of overall prices in India between 1914 and 1920. Returning war veterans, especially in the Punjab, created a growing unemployment crisis, and post-war inflation led to food riots in Bombay, Madras, and Bengal provinces, a situation that was made only worse by the failure of the 1918–19 monsoon and by profiteering and speculation. The global influenza epidemic and the Bolshevik Revolution of 1917 added to the general jitters; the former among the population already experiencing economic woes, and the latter among government officials, fearing a similar revolution in India.

To combat what it saw as a coming crisis, the government now drafted the Rowlatt committee's recommendations into two Rowlatt Bills. Although the bills were authorised for legislative consideration by Edwin Montagu, they were done so unwillingly, with the accompanying declaration, "I loathe the suggestion at first sight of preserving the Defence of India Act in peacetime to such an extent as Rowlatt and his friends think necessary." In the ensuing discussion and vote in the Imperial Legislative Council, all Indian members voiced opposition to the bills. The Government of India was, nevertheless, able to use of its "official majority" to ensure passage of the bills early in 1919. However, what it passed, in deference to the Indian opposition, was a lesser version of the first bill, which now allowed extrajudicial powers, but for a period of exactly three years and for the prosecution solely of "anarchical and revolutionary movements", dropping entirely the second bill involving modification the Indian Penal Code. Even so, when it was passed, the new Rowlatt Act aroused widespread indignation throughout India, and brought Gandhi to the forefront of the nationalist movement.

Meanwhile, Montagu and Chelmsford themselves finally presented their report in July 1918 after a long fact-finding trip through India the previous winter. After more discussion by the government and parliament in Britain, and another tour by the Franchise and Functions Committee for the purpose of identifying who among the Indian population could vote in future elections, the Government of India Act 1919 (also known as the Montagu-Chelmsford Reforms) was passed in December 1919. The new Act enlarged both the provincial and Imperial legislative councils and repealed the Government of India's recourse to the "official majority" in unfavourable votes. Although departments like defence, foreign affairs, criminal law, communications, and income-tax were retained by the Viceroy and the central government in New Delhi, other departments like public health, education, land-revenue, local self-government were transferred to the provinces. The provinces themselves were now to be administered under a new dyarchical system, whereby some areas like education, agriculture, infrastructure development, and local self-government became the preserve of Indian ministers and legislatures, and ultimately the Indian electorates, while others like irrigation, land-revenue, police, prisons, and control of media remained within the purview of the British governor and his executive council. The new Act also made it easier for Indians to be admitted into the civil service and the army officer corps.

A greater number of Indians were now enfranchised, although, for voting at the national level, they constituted only 10% of the total adult male population, many of whom were still illiterate. In the provincial legislatures, the British continued to exercise some control by setting aside seats for special interests they considered cooperative or useful. In particular, rural candidates, generally sympathetic to British rule and less confrontational, were assigned more seats than their urban counterparts. Seats were also reserved for non-Brahmins, landowners, businessmen, and college graduates. The principal of "communal representation", an integral part of the Minto-Morley Reforms, and more recently of the Congress-Muslim League Lucknow Pact, was reaffirmed, with seats being reserved for Muslims, Sikhs, Indian Christians, Anglo-Indians, and domiciled Europeans, in both provincial and Imperial legislative councils. The Montagu-Chelmsford reforms offered Indians the most significant opportunity yet for exercising legislative power, especially at the provincial level; however, that opportunity was also restricted by the still limited number of eligible voters, by the small budgets available to provincial legislatures, and by the presence of rural and special interest seats that were seen as instruments of British control. Its scope was unsatisfactory to the Indian political leadership, famously expressed by Annie Beasant as something "unworthy of England to offer and India to accept".Template:Harvard citation documentation#Wikilink to citation does not work

The Jallianwala Bagh massacre or "Amritsar massacre", took place in the Jallianwala Bagh public garden in the predominantly Sikh northern city of Amritsar. After days of unrest Brigadier-General Reginald E.H. Dyer forbade public meetings and on Sunday 13 April 1919 fifty British Indian Army soldiers commanded by Dyer began shooting at an unarmed gathering of thousands of men, women, and children without warning. Casualty estimates vary widely, with the Government of India reporting 379 dead, with 1,100 wounded.[721] The Indian National Congress estimated three times the number of dead. Dyer was removed from duty but he became a celebrated hero in Britain among people with connections to the Raj.[722] Historians consider the episode was a decisive step towards the end of British rule in India.[723]

1920s: Non-cooperation, *Khilafat*, Simon Commission, Jinnah's fourteen points

Mahatma Gandhi with Dr. Annie Besant *en route* to a meeting in Madras in September 1921. Earlier, in Madurai, on 21 September 1921, Gandhi had adopted the loin-cloth for the first time as a symbol of his identification with India's poor.

An early 1920s poster advertising a Congress non-co-operation "Public Meeting" and a "Bonfire of Foreign Clothes" in Bombay, and expressing support for the "Karachi Khilafat Conference."

Hindus and Muslims, displaying the flags of both the Indian National Congress and the Muslim League, collecting clothes to be later burnt as a part of the non-co-operation movement initiated by Gandhi.

Photograph of the staff and students of the National College, Lahore, founded in 1921 by Lala Lajpat Rai for students preparing for the non-co-operation movement. Standing, fourth from the right, is future revolutionary Bhagat Singh.

In 1920, after the British government refused to back down, Gandhi began his campaign of non-cooperation, prompting many Indians to return British awards and honours, to resign from civil service, and to again boycott British goods. In addition, Gandhi reorganised the Congress, transforming it into a mass movement and opening its membership to even the poorest Indians. Although Gandhi halted the non-cooperation movement in 1922 after the violent incident at Chauri Chaura, the movement revived again, in the mid-1920s.

The visit, in 1928, of the British Simon Commission, charged with instituting constitutional reform in India, resulted in widespread protests throughout the country. Earlier, in 1925, non-violent protests of the Congress had resumed too, this time in Gujarat, and led by Patel, who organised farmers to refuse payment of increased land taxes; the success of this protest, the Bardoli Satyagraha, brought Gandhi back into the fold of active politics.

1929–1937: Round Table conferences, Government of India Act

Allama Muhammad Iqbal, fifth from left, arriving at the 1930 session of the All India Muslim League, where he delivered his presidential address outlining his plan for a homeland for the Muslims of British India.

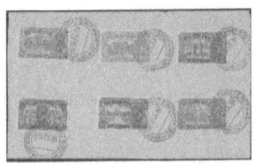

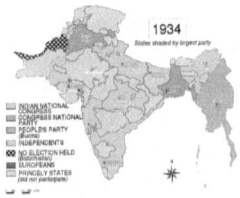

British PM Ramsay MacDonald to the right of Gandhi at the 2nd Round Table Conference. Foreground, fourth from left, is B. R. Ambedkar representing the "Depressed Classes."

A second-day cancellation of the series "Inauguration of New Delhi," 27 February 1931, commemorating the new city designed by Sir Edwin Lutyens and Sir Herbert Baker.

The Indian general election, 1934 was the first general election that the INC participated in. The party won a majority of the general seats.

A first-day cover issued on 1 April 1937 commemorating the separation of Burma from the British Indian Empire.

At its annual session in Lahore, the Indian National Congress, under the presidency of Jawaharlal Nehru, issued a demand for *Purna Swaraj* (Hindustani language: "complete independence"), or Purna Swarajya. The declaration was drafted by the Congress Working Committee, which included Gandhi, Nehru, Patel, and Chakravarthi Rajagopalachari. Gandhi subsequently led an expanded movement of civil disobedience, culminating in 1930 with the Salt Satyagraha, in which thousands of Indians defied the tax on salt, by marching to the sea and making their own salt by evaporating seawater. Although, many, including Gandhi, were arrested, the British government eventually gave in,

and in 1931 Gandhi travelled to London to negotiate new reform at the Round Table Conferences.

In local terms, British control rested on the Indian Civil Service, but it faced growing difficulties. Fewer and fewer young men in Britain were interested in joining, and the continuing distrust of Indians resulted in a declining base in terms of quality and quantity. By 1945 Indians were numerically dominant in the ICS and at issue was loyal divided between the Empire and independence.[724] The finances of the Raj depended on land taxes, and these became problematic in the 1930s. Epstein argues that after 1919 it became harder and harder to collect the land revenue. The Raj's suppression of civil disobedience after 1934 temporarily increased the power of the revenue agents but after 1937 they were forced by the new Congress-controlled provincial governments to hand back confiscated land. Again the outbreak of war strengthened them, in the face of the Quit India movement the revenue collectors had to rely on military force and by 1946–47 direct British control was rapidly disappearing in much of the countryside.[725]

In 1935, after the Round Table Conferences, Parliament passed the Government of India Act 1935, which authorised the establishment of independent legislative assemblies in all provinces of British India, the creation of a central government incorporating both the British provinces and the princely states, and the protection of Muslim minorities. The future Constitution of independent India was based on this act. However, it divided the electorate into 19 religious and social categories, e.g., Muslims, Sikhs, Indian Christians, Depressed Classes, Landholders, Commerce and Industry, Europeans, Anglo-Indians, etc., each of which was given separate representation in the Provincial Legislative Assemblies. A voter could cast a vote only for candidates in his own category.

The 1935 Act provided for more autonomy for Indian provinces, with the goal of cooling off nationalist sentiment. The act provided for a national parliament and an executive branch under the purview of the British government, but the rulers of the princely states managed to block its implementation. These states remained under the full control of their hereditary rulers, with no popular government. To prepare for elections Congress built up its grass roots membership from 473,000 in 1935 to 4.5 million in 1939.[726]

In the 1937 elections Congress won victories in seven of the eleven provinces of British India. Congress governments, with wide powers, were formed in these provinces. The widespread voter support for the Indian National Congress surprised Raj officials, who previously had seen the Congress as a small elitist body.[727]

1938–1941: World War II, Muslim League's Lahore Resolution

Mahatma Gandhi and Rajendra Prasad (left) on their way to meet the viceroy Lord Linlithgow (13 October 1939) after the outbreak of World War II.

A. K. Fazlul Huq, known as the *Sher-e-Bangla* or *Tiger of Bengal*, was the first elected Premier of Bengal, leader of the K. P. P. and an important ally of the All India Muslim League

Chaudhari Khaliquzzaman (left) seconding the 1940 Lahore Resolution of the Muslim League with Jinnah (right) presiding, and Liaquat Ali Khan (centre)

Newly arrived Indian troops on the quayside in Singapore, November 1941

Indian Army troops in action during Operation *Crusader* in Western Desert Campaign in North Africa in November/December 1941.

While the Muslim League was a small elite group in 1927 with only 1300 members, it grew rapidly once it became an organisation that reached out to the

masses, reaching 500,000 members in Bengal in 1944, 200,000 in Punjab, and hundreds of thousands elsewhere. Jinnah now was well positioned to negotiate with the British from a position of power.[728] With the outbreak of World War II in 1939, the viceroy, Lord Linlithgow, declared war on India's behalf without consulting Indian leaders, leading the Congress provincial ministries to resign in protest. The Muslim League, in contrast, supported Britain in the war effort and maintained its control of the government in three major provinces, Bengal, Sind and the Punjab.

Jinnah repeatedly warned that Muslims would be unfairly treated in an independent India dominated by the Congress. On 24 March 1940 in Lahore, the League passed the "Lahore Resolution", demanding that, "the areas in which the Muslims are numerically in majority as in the North-Western and Eastern zones of India should be grouped to constitute independent states in which the constituent units shall be autonomous and sovereign." Although there were other important national Muslim politicians such as Congress leader Ab'ul Kalam Azad, and influential regional Muslim politicians such as A. K. Fazlul Huq of the leftist Krishak Praja Party in Bengal, Sikander Hyat Khan of the landlord-dominated Punjab Unionist Party, and Abd al-Ghaffar Khan of the pro-Congress Khudai Khidmatgar (popularly, "red shirts") in the North West Frontier Province, the British, over the next six years, were to increasingly see the League as the main representative of Muslim India.

The Congress was secular and strongly opposed to having any religious state. It insisted there was a natural unity to India, and repeatedly blamed the British for "divide and rule" tactics based on prompting Muslims to think of themselves as alien from Hindus.Wikipedia:Citation needed Jinnah rejected the notion of a united India, and emphasised that religious communities were more basic than an artificial nationalism. He proclaimed the Two-Nation Theory, stating at Lahore on 23 March 1940:

> [*Islam and Hinduism*] *are not religions in the strict sense of the word, but are, in fact, different and distinct social orders and it is a dream that the Hindus and Muslims can ever evolve a common nationality* ... *The Hindu and Muslim belong to two different religions, philosophies, social customs and literature* [*sic*]. *They neither intermarry nor interdine together and indeed they belong to two different civilizations which are based mainly on conflicting ideas and conceptions. Their aspects on life and of life are different* ... *To yoke together two such nations under a single state, one as a numerical minority and the other as a majority must lead to growing discontent and final destruction of any fabric that may be so built up for the government of such a state.*

While the regular Indian army in 1939 included about 220,000 native troops, it expanded tenfold during the war,[729] and small naval and air force units were created. Over two million Indians volunteered for military service in the British Army. They played a major role in numerous campaigns, especially in the Middle East and North Africa. Casualties were moderate (in terms of the world war), with 24,000 killed; 64,000 wounded; 12,000 missing (probably dead), and 60,000 captured at Singapore in 1942.[730]

London paid most of the cost of the Indian Army, which had the effect of erasing India's national debt; it ended the war with a surplus of £1,300 million. In addition, heavy British spending on munitions produced in India (such as uniforms, rifles, machine-guns, field artillery, and ammunition) led to a rapid expansion of industrial output, such as textiles (up 16%), steel (up 18%), and chemicals (up 30%). Small warships were built, and an aircraft factory opened in Bangalore. The railway system, with 700,000 employees, was taxed to the limit as demand for transportation soared.[731]

1942–1945: Cripps mission, Quit India Resolution, INA

The British government sent the Cripps' mission in 1942 to secure Indian nationalists' co-operation in the war effort in exchange for a promise of independence as soon as the war ended. Top officials in Britain, most notably Prime Minister Winston Churchill, did not support the Cripps Mission and negotiations with the Congress soon broke down.[732]

Congress launched the "Quit India" movement in July 1942 demanding the immediate withdrawal of the British from India or face nationwide civil disobedience. On 8 August the Raj arrested all national, provincial and local

Figure 146: *Subhas Chandra Bose (second from left) with Heinrich Himmler (right), 1942.*

Figure 147: *The series of stamps, "Victory," issued by the Government of India to commemorate the allied victory in World War II.*

Congress leaders, holding tens of thousands of them until 1945. The country erupted in violent demonstrations led by students and later by peasant political groups, especially in Eastern United Provinces, Bihar, and western Bengal. The large wartime British Army presence crushed the movement in a little more than six weeks; nonetheless, a portion of the movement formed for a time an underground provisional government on the border with Nepal. In other parts of India, the movement was less spontaneous and the protest less intensive, however it lasted sporadically into the summer of 1943. It did not slow down the British war effort or recruiting for the army.

Earlier, Subhas Chandra Bose, who had been a leader of the younger, radical, wing of the Indian National Congress in the late 1920s and 1930s, had risen to become Congress President from 1938 to 1939.[733] However, he was ousted from the Congress in 1939 following differences with the high command,[734] and subsequently placed under house arrest by the British before escaping from India in early 1941.[735] He turned to Nazi Germany and Imperial Japan for help in gaining India's independence by force.[736] With Japanese support, he organised the Indian National Army, composed largely of Indian soldiers of the British Indian army who had been captured by the Japanese in the Battle of Singapore. As the war turned against them, the Japanese came to support a number of puppet and provisional governments in the captured regions, including those in Burma, the Philippines and Vietnam, and in addition, the Provisional Government of Azad Hind, presided by Bose.[736]

Bose's effort, however, was short lived. In mid-1944 the British army first halted and then reversed the Japanese U-Go offensive, beginning the successful part of the Burma Campaign. Bose's Indian National Army largely disintegrated during the subsequent fighting in Burma, with its remaining elements surrendering with the recapture of Singapore in September 1945. Bose died in August from third degree burns received after attempting to escape in an overloaded Japanese plane which crashed in Taiwan,[737] which many Indians believe did not happen.[738,739] Although Bose was unsuccessful, he roused patriotic feelings in India.[740]

1946: Elections, Cabinet mission, Direct Action Day

In January 1946, a number of mutinies broke out in the armed services, starting with that of RAF servicemen frustrated with their slow repatriation to Britain. The mutinies came to a head with mutiny of the Royal Indian Navy in Bombay in February 1946, followed by others in Calcutta, Madras, and Karachi. Although the mutinies were rapidly suppressed, they had the effect of spurring the new Labour government in Britain to action, and leading to the Cabinet Mission to India led by the Secretary of State for India, Lord Pethick Lawrence, and including Sir Stafford Cripps, who had visited four years before.

Figure 148: *Members of the 1946 Cabinet Mission to India meeting Muhammad Ali Jinnah. Far left is Lord Pethick Lawrence; far right is Sir Stafford Cripps.*

Also in early 1946, new elections were called in India. Earlier, at the end of the war in 1945, the colonial government had announced the public trial of three senior officers of Bose's defeated Indian National Army who stood accused of treason. Now as the trials began, the Congress leadership, although ambivalent towards the INA, chose to defend the accused officers. The subsequent convictions of the officers, the public outcry against the convictions, and the eventual remission of the sentences, created positive propaganda for the Congress, which only helped in the party's subsequent electoral victories in eight of the eleven provinces. The negotiations between the Congress and the Muslim League, however, stumbled over the issue of the partition. Jinnah proclaimed 16 August 1946, Direct Action Day, with the stated goal of highlighting, peacefully, the demand for a Muslim homeland in British India. The following day Hindu-Muslim riots broke out in Calcutta and quickly spread throughout British India. Although the Government of India and the Congress were both shaken by the course of events, in September, a Congress-led interim government was installed, with Jawaharlal Nehru as united India's prime minister.

British Raj

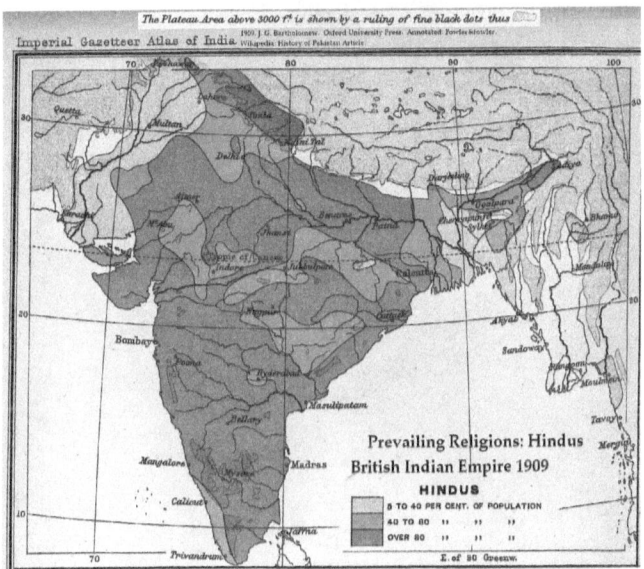

Figure 149: *Percentage of Hindus by district. Map of British Indian Empire, 1909.*

1947: Planning for partition

Later that year, the Labour government in Britain, its exchequer exhausted by the recently concluded World War II, and conscious that it had neither the mandate at home, the international support, nor the reliability of native forces for continuing to control an increasingly restless British India,

> By the end of 1945, he and the Commander-in-Chief of India, General Auckinleck were advising that there was a real threat in 1946 of large-scale anti-British disorder amounting to even a well-organised rising aiming to expel the British by paralysing the administration.

...it was clear to Attlee that everything depended on the spirit and reliability of the Indian Army:

> "Provided that they do their duty, armed insurrection in India would not be an insoluble problem. If, however, the Indian Army was to go the other way, the picture would be very different ...

Thus, Wavell concluded, if the army and the police "failed" Britain would be forced to go. In theory, it might be possible to revive and reinvigorate the services, and rule for another fifteen to twenty years, but:

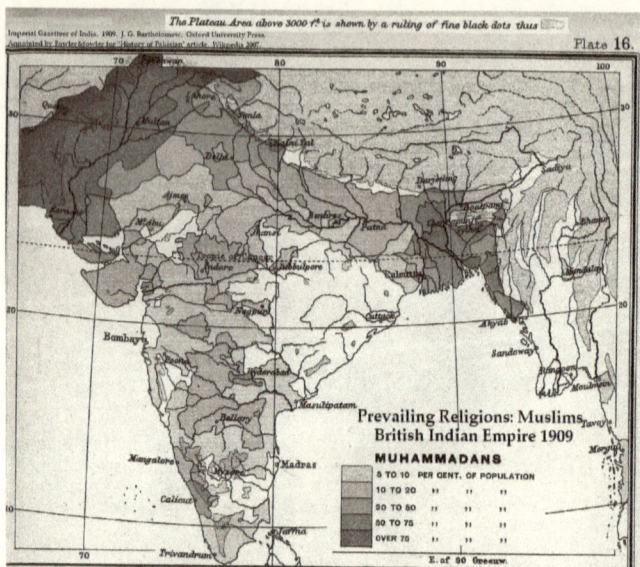

Figure 150: *Percentage of Muslims by district. Map of British Indian Empire, 1909.*

It is a fallacy to suppose that the solution lies in trying to maintain status quo. We have no longer the resources, nor the necessary prestige or confidence in ourselves.[741] decided to end British rule of India, and in early 1947 Britain announced its intention of transferring power no later than June 1948.

As independence approached, the violence between Hindus and Muslims in the provinces of Punjab and Bengal continued unabated. With the British army unprepared for the potential for increased violence, the new viceroy, Louis Mountbatten, advanced the date for the transfer of power, allowing less than six months for a mutually agreed plan for independence. In June 1947, the nationalist leaders, including Sardar Patel, Nehru and Abul Kalam Azad on behalf of the Congress, Jinnah representing the Muslim League, B. R. Ambedkar representing the Untouchable community, and Master Tara Singh representing the Sikhs, agreed to a partition of the country along religious lines in stark opposition to Gandhi's views. The predominantly Hindu and Sikh areas were assigned to the new nation of India and predominantly Muslim areas to the new nation of Pakistan; the plan included a partition of the Muslim-majority provinces of Punjab and Bengal.

1947: Violence, partition, independence

On 15 August 1947, the new Dominion of Pakistan (later Islamic Republic of Pakistan), with Muhammad Ali Jinnah as the Governor-General; and the Union of India, (later Republic of India) with Jawaharlal Nehru as the prime minister, and the viceroy, Louis Mountbatten, staying on as its first Governor General came into being; with official ceremonies taking place in Karachi on 14 August and New Delhi on 15 August. This was done so that Mountbatten could attend both ceremonies.[742]

The great majority of Indians remained in place with independence, but in border areas millions of people (Muslim, Sikh, and Hindu) relocated across the newly drawn borders. In Punjab, where the new border lines divided the Sikh regions in half, there was much bloodshed; in Bengal and Bihar, where Gandhi's presence assuaged communal tempers, the violence was more limited. In all, somewhere between 250,000 and 500,000 people on both sides of the new borders, among both the refugee and resident populations of the three faiths, died in the violence.[743] Other estimates of the number of deaths are as high as 1,500,000.[744]

Ideological impact

At independence and after the independence of India, India has maintained such central British institutions as parliamentary government, one-person, one-vote and the rule of law through nonpartisan courts. It retained as well the institutional arrangements of the Raj such as district administration, universities and stock exchanges. One major change was the rejection of its former separate princely states. Metcalf shows that over the course of two centuries, British intellectuals and Indian specialists made the highest priority bringing peace, unity and good government to India. They offered many competing methods to reach the goal. For example, Cornwallis recommended turning Bengali Zamindar into the sort of English landlords that controlled local affairs in England. Munro proposed to deal directly with the peasants. Sir William Jones and the Orientalists promoted Sanskrit, while Macaulay promoted the English language.[745] Zinkin argues that in the long-run, what matters most about the legacy of the Raj is the British political ideologies which the Indians took over after 1947, especially the belief in unity, democracy, the rule of law and a certain equality beyond caste and creed. Zinkin sees this not just in the Congress party but also among Hindu Nationalists in the Bharatiya Janata Party, which specifically emphasises Hindu traditions.[746,747]

Bibliography

Surveys

<templatestyles src="Template:Refbegin/styles.css" />

- Allan, J., T. Wolseley Haig, H. H. Dodwell. *The Cambridge Shorter History of India* (1934) 996 pp. online[748]; at Google[749]
- Bandhu, Deep Chand. *History of Indian National Congress* (2003) 405pp
- Bandyopadhyay, Sekhar (2004), *From Plassey to Partition: A History of Modern India*, New Delhi and London: Orient Longmans. Pp. xx, 548., ISBN 978-81-250-2596-2.
- Bayly, C. A. (1990), *Indian Society and the Making of the British Empire (The New Cambridge History of India)*, Cambridge and London: Cambridge University Press. Pp. 248, ISBN 978-0-521-38650-0.
- Brown, Judith M. (1994), *Modern India: The Origins of an Asian Democracy*, Oxford University Press. Pp. xiii, 474, ISBN 978-0-19-873113-9.
- Bose, Sugata; Jalal, Ayesha (2003), *Modern South Asia: History, Culture, Political Economy*, Routledge, ISBN 978-0-415-30787-1
- Copland, Ian (2001), *India 1885–1947: The Unmaking of an Empire (Seminar Studies in History Series)*, Harlow and London: Pearson Longmans. Pp. 160, ISBN 978-0-582-38173-5
- Coupland, Reginald. *India: A Re-Statement* (Oxford University Press, 1945), evaluation of the Raj, emphasising government. online edition[750]
- Dodwell H. H., ed. *The Cambridge History of India. Volume 6: The Indian Empire 1858–1918. With Chapters on the Development of Administration 1818–1858* (1932) 660 pp. online edition[751]; also published as vol 5 of the *Cambridge History of the British Empire*
- Herbertson, A.J. and O.J.R. Howarth. eds. *The Oxford Survey Of The British Empire* (6 vol 1914) online vol 2 on Asia[752] pp. 1–328 on India
- James, Lawrence. *Raj: The Making and Unmaking of British India* (2000)
- Judd, Denis (2004), *The Lion and the Tiger: The Rise and Fall of the British Raj, 1600–1947*, Oxford and New York: Oxford University Press. Pp. xiii, 280, ISBN 978-0-19-280358-0.
- Kumar, Dharma, and Meghnad Desai, eds. *The Cambridge Economic History of India, Volume 2: c. 1757–2003* (2010), 1114pp; articles by scholars ISBN 978-81-250-2731-7
- Louis, William Roger, and Judith M. Brown, eds. *The Oxford History of the British Empire* (5 vol 1999–2001), with numerous articles on the Raj
- Ludden, David. *India And South Asia: A Short History* (2002)
- Majumdar, Ramesh Chandra; Raychaudhuri, Hemchandra; Datta, Kalikinkar (1950), *An advanced history of India*

- Majumdar, R. C. ed. (1970). British paramountcy and Indian renaissance. (The history and culture of the Indian people) Bombay: Bharatiya Vidya Bhavan.
- Mansingh, Surjit *The A to Z of India* (2010), a concise historical encyclopaedia
- Marshall, P. J. (2001), *The Cambridge Illustrated History of the British Empire, 400 pp.*, Cambridge and London: Cambridge University Press., ISBN 978-0-521-00254-7.
- Markovits, Claude, ed. (2005), *A History of Modern India 1480–1950 (Anthem South Asian Studies)*, Anthem Press. Pp. 607, ISBN 978-1-84331-152-2.
- Metcalf, Barbara (2006), *A Concise History of Modern India (Cambridge Concise Histories)*, Cambridge and New York: Cambridge University Press. Pp. xxxiii, 372, ISBN 978-0-521-68225-1
- Moon, Penderel. *The British Conquest and Dominion of India* (2 vol. 1989) 1235pp; the fullest scholarly history of political and military events from a British top-down perspective;
- Panikkar, K. M. (1953). Asia and Western dominance, 1498-1945, by K.M. Panikkar. London: G. Allen and Unwin.
- Peers, Douglas M. (2006), *India under Colonial Rule 1700–1885*, Harlow and London: Pearson Longmans. Pp. xvi, 163, ISBN 0-582-31738-X.
- Riddick, John F. *The history of British India: a chronology* (2006) excerpt and text search[753], covers 1599–1947
- Riddick, John F. *Who Was Who in British India* (1998), covers 1599–1947
- Sarkar, Sumit. *Modern India, 1885–1947* (2002)
- Smith, Vincent A. (1958) *The Oxford History of India* (3rd ed.) the Raj section was written by Percival Spear
- Somervell, D.C. *The Reign of King George V,* (1936) covers Raj 1910–35 pp. 80–84, 282–91, 455–64 online free[754]
- Spear, Percival (1990) [First published 1965], *A History of India, Volume 2*[755], New Delhi and London: Penguin Books. Pp. 298, ISBN 978-0-14-013836-8.
- Stein, Burton (2001), *A History of India*, New Delhi and Oxford: Oxford University Press. Pp. xiv, 432, ISBN 978-0-19-565446-2.
- Thompson, Edward, and G.T. Garratt. *Rise and Fulfilment of British Rule in India* (1934) 690 pages; scholarly survey, 1599–1933 excerpt and text search[756]
- Wolpert, Stanley (2003), *A New History of India*, Oxford and New York: Oxford University Press. Pp. 544, ISBN 978-0-19-516678-1.
- Wolpert, Stanley, ed. *Encyclopedia of India* (4 vol. 2005) comprehensive coverage by scholars

Specialised topics

<templatestyles src="Template:Refbegin/styles.css" />

- Baker, David (1993), *Colonialism in an Indian Hinterland: The Central Provinces, 1820–1920*, Delhi: Oxford University Press. Pp. xiii, 374, ISBN 978-0-19-563049-7
- Bayly, C. A. (2000), *Empire and Information: Intelligence Gathering and Social Communication in India, 1780–1870 (Cambridge Studies in Indian History and Society)*, Cambridge and London: Cambridge University Press. Pp. 426, ISBN 978-0-521-66360-1
- Bayly, Christopher; Harper, Timothy (2007), *Forgotten Wars: Freedom and Revolution in Southeast Asia*[757], Harvard University Press, ISBN 978-0-674-02153-2, retrieved 21 September 2013
- Bayly, Christopher; Harper, Timothy (2005), *Forgotten Armies: The Fall of British Asia, 1941–1945*[758], Harvard University Press, ISBN 978-0-674-01748-1, retrieved 22 September 2013
- Brown, Judith M. *Gandhi: Prisoner of Hope* (1991), scholarly biography
- Brown, Judith M.; Louis, Wm. Roger, eds. (2001), *Oxford History of the British Empire: The Twentieth Century*, Oxford University Press. pp. 800, ISBN 978-0-19-924679-3
- Buckland, C.E. *Dictionary of Indian Biography* (1906) 495 pp. full text[759]
- Carrington, Michael. Officers, Gentlemen, and Murderers: Lord Curzon's campaign against "collisions" between Indians and Europeans, 1899–1905, Modern Asian Studies / Volume 47 / Issue 03 / May 2013, pp. 780–819.
- Chandavarkar, Rajnarayan (1998), *Imperial Power and Popular Politics: Class, Resistance and the State in India, 1850–1950*, (Cambridge Studies in Indian History & Society). Cambridge University Press. Pp. 400, ISBN 978-0-521-59692-3.
- Chatterji, Joya (1993), *Bengal Divided: Hindu Communalism and Partition, 1932–1947*, Cambridge University Press. Pp. 323, ISBN 978-0-521-52328-8.
- Copland, Ian (2002), *Princes of India in the Endgame of Empire, 1917–1947*, (Cambridge Studies in Indian History & Society). Cambridge University Press. Pp. 316, ISBN 978-0-521-89436-4.
- Manmath Nath Das (1964). *India under Morley and Minto: politics behind revolution, repression and reforms*[760]. G. Allen and Unwin.
- Dewey, Clive. *Anglo-Indian Attitudes: The Mind of the Indian Civil Service* (2003)
- Ewing, Ann. "Administering India: The Indian Civil Service", *History Today*, June 1982, 32#6 pp. 43–48, covers 1858–1947

- Gilmartin, David. 1988. *Empire and Islam: Punjab and the Making of Pakistan*. University of California Press. 258 pages. ISBN 978-0-520-06249-8.
- Gilmour, David. *The Ruling Caste: Imperial Lives in the Victorian Raj* (2007) Excerpt and text search[761]
- Gilmour, David. *Curzon: Imperial Statesman* (2006) excerpt and text search[762]
- Gopal, Sarvepalli (1 January 1976). *Jawaharlal Nehru: A Biography*[763]. Harvard U. Press. ISBN 978-0-674-47310-2. Retrieved 21 February 2012.
- Sarvepalli Gopal (1953). *The viceroyalty of Lord Ripon, 1880–1884*[764]. Oxford U. Press. Retrieved 21 February 2012.
- Gould, William (2004), *Hindu Nationalism and the Language of Politics in Late Colonial India*, Cambridge U. Press. Pp. 320.
- Gopal, Sarvepalli. *British Policy in India 1858–1905* (2008)
- Gopal, Sarvepalli. *Viceroyalty of Lord Irwin 1926–1931* (1957)
- Jalal, Ayesha (1993), *The Sole Spokesman: Jinnah, the Muslim League and the Demand for Pakistan*, Cambridge U. Press, 334 pages.
- Kaminsky, Arnold P. *The India Office, 1880–1910* (1986) excerpt and text search[765], focus on officials in London
- Khan, Yasmin. *India At War: The Subcontinent and the Second World War* (2015), wide-ranging scholarly survey excerpt[766]; also published as Khan, Yasmin. *The Raj At War: A People's History Of India's Second World War* (2015) a major, comprehensive scholarly study
- Khan, Yasmin (2007), *The Great Partition: The Making of India and Pakistan*, Yale U. Press, 250 pages, ISBN 978-0-300-12078-3
- Klein, Ira (July 2000), "Materialism, Mutiny and Modernization in British India", *Modern Asian Studies*, Cambridge University Press, **34** (3): 545–80, JSTOR 313141[767]
- Kumar, Deepak. *Science and the Raj: A Study of British India* (2006)
- Low, D. A. (2002), *Britain and Indian Nationalism: The Imprint of Ambiguity 1929–1942*, Cambridge University Press. Pp. 374, ISBN 978-0-521-89261-2.
- Lipsett, Chaldwell. *Lord Curzon in India 1898–1903* (1903) excerpt and text search[768] 128pp
- MacMillan, Margaret. *Women of the Raj: The Mothers, Wives, and Daughters of the British Empire in India* (2007)
- Metcalf, Thomas R. (1991), *The Aftermath of Revolt: India, 1857–1870*, Riverdale Co. Pub. Pp. 352, ISBN 978-81-85054-99-5
- Metcalf, Thomas R. (1997), *Ideologies of the Raj*[769], Cambridge University Press, Pp. 256, ISBN 978-0-521-58937-6

- Moore, Robin J. "Imperial India, 1858–1914", in Porter, ed. *Oxford History of the British Empire: The Nineteenth Century*, (2001a), pp. 422–46
- Moore, Robin J. "India in the 1940s", in Robin Winks, ed. *Oxford History of the British Empire: Historiography*, (2001b), pp. 231–42
- Porter, Andrew, ed. (2001), *Oxford History of the British Empire: Nineteenth Century*, Oxford University Press. Pp. 800, ISBN 978-0-19-924678-6
- Masood Ashraf Raja. *Constructing Pakistan: Foundational Texts and the Rise of Muslim National Identity*, 1857–1947, Oxford 2010, ISBN 978-0-19-547811-2
- Ramusack, Barbara (2004), *The Indian Princes and their States (The New Cambridge History of India)*, Cambridge University Press. Pp. 324, ISBN 978-0-521-03989-5
- Moore, Robin J. "India in the 1940s", in Robin Winks, ed. *Oxford History of the British Empire: Historiography* (2001), pp. 231–42
- Raghavan, Srinath. *India's War: World War II and the Making of Modern South Asia* (2016). wide-ranging scholarly survey excerpt[770]
- Read, Anthony, and David Fisher; *The Proudest Day: India's Long Road to Independence* (W. W. Norton, 1999) online edition[771]; detailed scholarly history of 1940–47
- Riddick, John F. *The History of British India: A Chronology* (2006) excerpt[753]
- Riddick, John F. *Who Was Who in British India* (1998); 5000 entries excerpt[772]
- Shaikh, Farzana (1989), *Community and Consensus in Islam: Muslim Representation in Colonial India, 1860—1947*, Cambridge University Press. Pp. 272., ISBN 978-0-521-36328-0.
- Talbot, Ian; Singh, Gurharpal, eds. (1999), *Region and Partition: Bengal, Punjab and the Partition of the Subcontinent*, Oxford University Press. Pp. 420, ISBN 978-0-19-579051-1.
- Thatcher, Mary. *Respected Memsahibs: an Anthology* (Hardinge Simpole, 2008)
- Tinker, Hugh (1968), *"India in the First World War and after"* Journal of Contemporary History, *Vol. 3, No. 4, 1918–19: From War to Peace. (Oct. 1968), pp. 89–107*, ISSN 0022-0094[773].
- Voigt, Johannes. *India in The Second World War* (1988)
- Wainwright, A. Martin (1993), *Inheritance of Empire: Britain, India, and the Balance of Power in Asia, 1938–55*, Praeger Publishers. Pp. xvi, 256, ISBN 978-0-275-94733-0.
- Wolpert, Stanley A. *Jinnah of Pakistan* (2005)
- Wolpert, Stanley (2007), "India: British Imperial Power 1858–1947 (Indian nationalism and the British response, 1885–1920; Prelude to

Independence, 1920–1947)"[774], *Encyclopædia Britannica*.
- Wolpert, Stanley A. *Tilak and Gokhale: revolution and reform in the making of modern India* (1962) full text online[775]

Economic history

<templatestyles src="Template:Refbegin/styles.css" />

- Anstey, Vera. *The economic development of India* (4th ed. 1952), 677pp; thorough scholarly coverage; focus on 20th century down to 1939
- Chaudhary, Latika, et al. eds. *A New Economic History of Colonial India* (2015)
- Derbyshire, I. D. (1987), "Economic Change and the Railways in North India, 1860–1914", *Population Studies*, Cambridge University Press, **21** (3): 521–45, doi: 10.1017/s0026749x00009197[776], JSTOR 312641[777]
- Dutt, Romesh C. *The Economic History of India under early British Rule*, first published 1902, 2001 edition by Routledge, ISBN 978-0-415-24493-0
- Kumar, Dharma, ed. *Cambridge Economic History of India: Vol. 2, 1757–2003* (2nd ed. 2005); 1150pp; comprehensive coverage by international scholars
- Lockwood, David. *The Indian Bourgeoisie: A Political History of the Indian Capitalist Class in the Early Twentieth Century* (I.B. Tauris, 2012) 315 pages; focus on Indian entrepreneurs who benefited from the Raj, but ultimately sided with the Indian National Congress.
- Roy, Tirthankar (Summer 2002), "Economic History and Modern India: Redefining the Link", *The Journal of Economic Perspectives*, American Economic Association, **16** (3): 109–30, doi: 10.1257/089533002760278749[778], JSTOR 3216953[779]
- Sarkar, J. (2013, reprint). Economics of British India ... Third edition. Enlarged and partly rewritten. Calcutta: M.C. Sarkar & Sons.
- Simmons, Colin (1985), "'De-Industrialization', Industrialization and the Indian Economy, c. 1850–1947", *Modern Asian Studies*, Cambridge University Press, **19** (3): 593–622, doi: 10.1017/s0026749x00007745[780], JSTOR 312453[781]
- Tirthankar, Roy. "Financing the Raj: the City of London and colonial India 1858–1940." *Business History* 56#6 (2014): 1024–1026.
- Tomlinson, B. R. *The Economy of Modern India, 1860–1970* (The New Cambridge History of India) (1996) excerpt and text search[782]
- Tomlinson, B. H. "India and the British Empire, 1880–1935", *Indian Economic and Social History Review*, (Oct 1975), 12#4 pp. 337–380

Historiography and memory

- Andrews, C.F. (2017). *India and the Simon Report*[783]. Routledge reprint of 1930 first edition. p. 11. ISBN 9781315444987.
- Durant, Will (2011, reprint). The case for India. New York, N.Y: Simon and Schuster.
- Ellis, Catriona (2009). "Education for All: Reassessing the Historiography of Education in Colonial India". *History Compass*. **7** (2): 363–75. doi: 10.1111/j.1478-0542.2008.00564.x[784].
- Gilmartin, David (2015). "The Historiography of India's Partition: Between Civilization and Modernity". *The Journal of Asian Studies*. **74** (1): 23–41. doi: 10.1017/s0021911814001685[785].
- Major, Andrea (2011). "Tall tales and true: India, historiography and British imperial imaginings". *Contemporary South Asia*. **19** (3): 331–32. doi: 10.1080/09584935.2011.594257[786].
- Mantena, Rama Sundari. *The Origins of Modern Historiography in India: Antiquarianism and Philology* (2012)
- Moor-Gilbert, Bart. *Writing India, 1757–1990: The Literature of British India* (1996) on fiction written in English
- Mukherjee, Soumyen. "Origins of Indian Nationalism: Some Questions on the Historiography of Modern India." *Sydney Studies in Society and Culture* 13 (2014). online[787]
- Parkash, Jai. "Major trends of historiography of revolutionary movement in India-Phase II." (PhD dissertation, Maharshi Dayanand University, 2013). online[788]
- Philips, Cyril H. ed. *Historians of India, Pakistan and Ceylon* (1961), reviews the older scholarship
- Stern, Philip J (2009). "History and Historiography of the English East India Company: Past, Present, and Future". *History Compass*. **7** (4): 1146–80. doi: 10.1111/j.1478-0542.2009.00617.x[789].
- Whitehead, Clive. "The historiography of British imperial education policy, Part I: India." *History of Education* 34#3 (2005): 315–329.
- Winks, Robin, ed. *Historiography* (1999) vol. 5 in William Roger Louis, eds. *The Oxford History of the British Empire*, chapters 11–15, online[790]
- Winks, Robin W. *The Historiography of the British Empire-Commonwealth: Trends, Interpretations and Resources* (1966); this book is by a different set of authors from the previous 1999 entry online[791]
- Young, Richard Fox, ed., *Indian Christian Historiography from Below, from Above, and in Between India and the Indianness of Christianity: Essays on Understanding—Historical, Theological, and Bibliographical—in Honor of Robert Eric Frykenberg* (2009)

Further reading

Wikiquote has quotations related to: *British Raj*

Wikimedia Commons has media related to *British Raj*.

Wikivoyage has a travel guide for *British Raj*.

- Simon Report (1930) vol 1[792], wide-ranging survey of conditions
- Keith, Arthur Berriedale (1912). *Responsible government in the dominions*[793]. The Clarendon press., major primary source

Year books and statistical records

- *Indian Year-book for 1862: A review of social, intellectual, and religious progress in India and Ceylon* (1863), ed. by John Murdoch online edition[794] 1861 edition[795]
- *The Year-book of the Imperial Institute of the United Kingdom, the colonies and India: a statistical record of the resources and trade of the colonial and Indian possessions of the British Empire*[796] (2nd. ed.), India, 1893, pp. 375–462 – via Google Books
- *The Imperial Gazetteer of India* (26 vol, 1908–31), highly detailed description of all of India in 1901. online edition[797]
- *Statistical abstract relating to British India, from 1895–96 to 1904–05* (London, 1906) full text online[798],
- *The Cyclopedia of India: biographical, historical, administrative, commercial*[799] (1908) business history, biographies, illustrations
- *The Indian year book: 1914* (1914) snippets[800]
- *The Indian Annual Register: A digest of public affairs of India regarding the nation's activities in the matters, political, economic, industrial, educational, etc. during the period 1919–1947* online[801]
  - 1930 edition[801]
  - 1921 edition[802]
  - 1919–1947 editions[803]

Indian independence movement

Colonial India

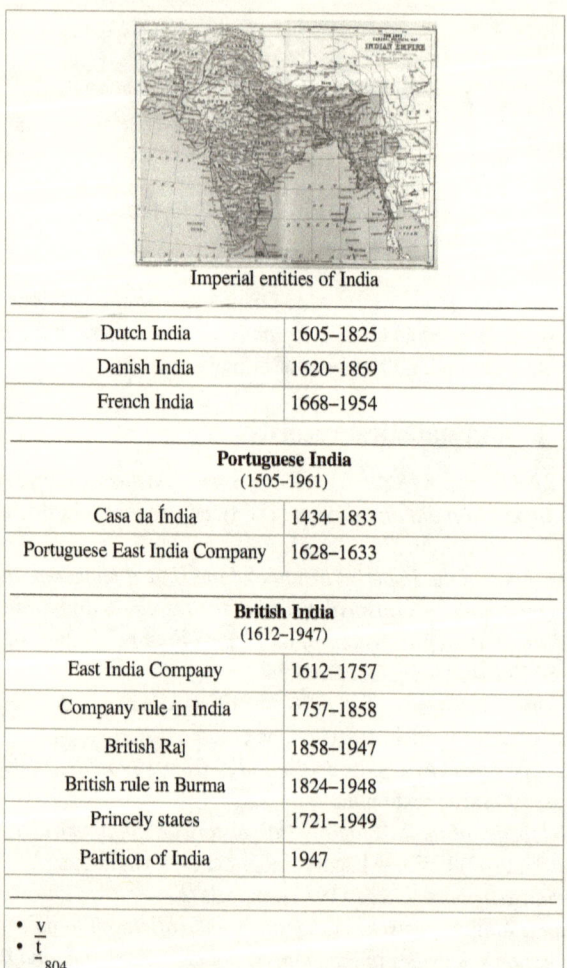

Imperial entities of India

Dutch India	1605–1825
Danish India	1620–1869
French India	1668–1954
Portuguese India (1505–1961)	
Casa da Índia	1434–1833
Portuguese East India Company	1628–1633
British India (1612–1947)	
East India Company	1612–1757
Company rule in India	1757–1858
British Raj	1858–1947
British rule in Burma	1824–1948
Princely states	1721–1949
Partition of India	1947

- v
- t
- e^{804}

Indian independence movement

Part of a series on
Revolution

Politics portal
- v
- t
- e⁸⁰⁵

The **Indian independence movement** it was a series of protests that consists in ending the oppression of the British Empire in India and that the country lived in independence, encompassed activities and ideas aiming to end the East India Company rule (1757–1857) and the British Indian Empire (1857–1947) in the Indian subcontinent. The movement spanned a total of 90 years (1857–1947).

The first organised militant movements were in Bengal, but they later took movement in the newly formed Indian National Congress with prominent moderate leaders seeking only their basic right to appear for Indian Civil Service (British India) examinations, as well as more rights, economic in nature, for the people of the soil. The early part of the 20th century saw a more radical approach towards political self-rule proposed by leaders such as the Lal, Bal, Pal and Aurobindo Ghosh, V. O. Chidambaram Pillai. The last stages of the self-rule struggle from the 1920s onwards saw Congress adopt Mohandas Karamchand Gandhi's policy of nonviolence and civil disobedience, and several other campaigns. Nationalists like Subhash Chandra Bose, Bhagat Singh, Bagha Jatin preached armed revolution to achieve self-rule. Poets and writers such as Subramania Bharati, Rabindranath Tagore, Muhammad Iqbal, Josh Malihabadi, Mohammad Ali Jouhar, Bankim Chandra Chattopadhyay and Kazi Nazrul Islam used literature, poetry and speech as a tool for political awareness. Feminists such as Sarojini Naidu and Begum Rokeya promoted the emancipation of Indian women and their participation in national politics. B. R. Ambedkar championed the cause of the disadvantaged sections of Indian society within the larger self-rule movement. The period of the Second World War saw the peak of the campaigns by the Quit India Movement led by Congress, and the Indian National Army movement led by Subhas Chandra Bose.

The Indian self-rule movement was a mass-based movement that encompassed various sections of society. It also underwent a process of constant ideological evolution. Although the basic ideology of the movement was anti-colonial, it was supported by a vision of independent capitalist economic development coupled with a secular, democratic, republican, and civil-libertarian political structure. After the 1930s, the movement took on a strong socialist orientation, owing to the influence of Bhagat Singh's demand of Purn Swaraj (Complete Self-Rule). The work of these various movements led ultimately to the Indian Independence Act 1947, which ended the suzerainty in India and the creation of Pakistan. India remained a Dominion of the Crown until 26 January 1950, when the *Constitution of India* came into force, establishing the Republic of India; Pakistan was a dominion until 1956, when it adopted its first republican constitution. In 1971, East Pakistan declared independence as the People's Republic of Bangladesh.

Background (1757–1883)

Early British colonialism in India

European traders first reached Indian shores with the arrival of the Portuguese explorer Vasco da Gama in 1498 at the port of Calicut, in search of the lucrative spice trade. Just over a century later, the Dutch and English established trading outposts on the subcontinent, with the first English trading post set up at Surat in 1613. Over the course of the seventeenth and early eighteenth centuries, the British[806] defeated the Portuguese and Dutch militarily, but remained in conflict with the French, who had by then sought to establish themselves in the subcontinent. The decline of the Mughal Empire in the first half of the eighteenth century provided the British with the opportunity to establish a firm foothold in Indian politics. After the Battle of Plassey in 1757, during which the East India Company's Indian Army under Robert Clive defeated Siraj ud-Daulah, the Nawab of Bengal, the Company established itself as a major player in Indian affairs, and soon afterwards gained administrative rights over the regions of Bengal, Bihar and Midnapur part of Orissa, following the Battle of Buxar in 1764. After the defeat of Tipu Sultan, most of South India came either under the Company's direct rule, or under its indirect political control as part a princely state in a subsidiary alliance. The Company subsequently gained control of regions ruled by the Maratha Empire, after defeating them in

Indian independence movement

Figure 151: *Robert Clive with Mir Jafar after the Battle of Plassey*

Figure 152: *After the defeat of Tipu Sultan, most of South India was now either under the company's direct rule, or under its indirect political control*

a series of wars. The Punjab was annexed in 1849, after the defeat of the Sikh armies in the First (1845–1846) and Second (1848–49) Anglo-Sikh Wars.

English was made the medium of instruction in India's schools in 1835, and many Indians increasingly disliked British rule. The English tried to impose the Western standards of education and culture on Indian masses, believing in the 18th century racist notion of the superiority of Western culture and enlightenment.

Early rebellion

Puli Thevar was one of the opponents of the British rule in India. He was in conflict with the Nawab of Arcot who was supported by the British. His prominent exploits were his confrontations with Marudhanayagam, who later rebelled against the British in the late 1750s and early 1760s. Nelkatumseval the present Tirunelveli Dist of Tamil Nadu state of India was the headquarters of Puli Thevan.

Syed Mir Nisar Ali Titumir; 27 January 1782 – 19 November 1831) was an Islamic preacher who led a peasant uprising against the Hindu zamindars, British India during the 19th century. Along with his followers, he built a bamboo fort (Bansher Kella in Bengali) in Narkelberia Village, which passed into Bengali folk legend. After the storming of the fort by British soldiers, Titumir died of his wounds on 19 November 1831.[807]

The toughest resistance the Company experienced was offered by Mysore. The Anglo–Mysore Wars were a series of wars fought in over the last three decades of the 18th century between the Kingdom of Mysore on the one hand, and the British East India Company (represented chiefly by the Madras Presidency), and Maratha Confederacyand the Nizam of Hyderabad on the other. Hyder Ali and his successor Tipu Sultan fought a war on four fronts with the British attacking from the west, south and east, while the Marathas and the Nizam's forces attacked from the north. The fourth war resulted in the overthrow of the house of Hyder Ali and Tipu (who was killed in the final war, in 1799), and the dismantlement of Mysore to the benefit of the East India Company, which won and took control of much of India.

Kerala Varma Pazhassi Raja was one of the earliest freedom fighters in India. He was the prince regent of the princely state of Kottiyur or Cotiote in North Malabar, near Kannur, India between 1774 and 1805. He fought a guerrilla war with tribal people from Wynad supporting him. He was caught by the British and his fort was razed to the ground.

Rani Velu Nachiyar (1730–1796), was a queen of Indian Sivaganga from 1760 to 1790. She was the first queen to fight against the British in India. Rani Nachiyar was trained in war match weapons usage, martial arts like Valari,

Silambam (fighting using stick), horse riding and archery. She was a scholar in many languages and she had proficiency with languages like French, English and Urdu. When her husband, Muthuvaduganathaperiya Udaiyathevar, was killed by British soldiers and the son of the Nawab of Arcot, she was drawn into battle. She formed an army and sought an alliance with Gopala Nayaker and Hyder Ali with the aim of attacking the British, whom she did successfully fight in 1780. When Rani Velu Nachiyar found the place where the British stored their ammunition, she arranged a suicide attack: a faithful follower, Kuyili, doused herself in oil, set herself alight and walked into the storehouse. Rani Velu Nachiyar formed a woman's army named "udaiyaal" in honour of her adopted daughter, Udaiyaal, who died detonating a British arsenal. Rani Nachiyar was one of the few rulers who regained her kingdom, and ruled it for ten more years.

Veerapandiya Kattabomman was an eighteenth-century Polygar and chieftain from Panchalankurichi in Tamil Nadu, India who waged a war against the East India Company. He was captured by the British and hanged in 1799 CE. Kattabomman refused to accept the sovereignty of East India Company, and fought against them. Dheeran Chinnamalai was a Kongu chieftain and Palayakkarar from Tamil Nadu who fought against the East India Company. After Kattabomman and Tipu Sultan's deaths, Chinnamalai sought the help of Marathas and Maruthu Pandiyar to attack the British at Coimbatore in 1800. British forces managed to stop the armies of the allies and hence Chinnamalai was forced to attack Coimbatore on his own. His army was defeated and he escaped from the British forces. Chinnamalai engaged in guerrilla warfare and defeated the British in battles at Cauvery in 1801, Odanilai in 1802 and Arachalur in 1804.

In September 1804, the King of Khordha, Kalinga was deprived of the traditional rights of Jagannath Temple which was a serious shock to the King and the people of Odisha. Consequently, in October 1804 a group of armed Paiks attacked the British at Pipili. This event alarmed the British force. Jayee Rajguru, the chief of Army of Kalinga requested all the kings of the state to join hands for a common cause against the British. Rajguru was killed on 6 December 1806. After Rajguru's death, Bakshi Jagabandhu commanded an armed rebellion against the East India Company's rule in Odisha which is known as Paik Rebellion.

The rebellion of 1857

The Indian rebellion of 1857 was a large-scale rebellion in the northern and central India against the British East India Company's rule. It was suppressed and the British government took control of the company. The conditions of

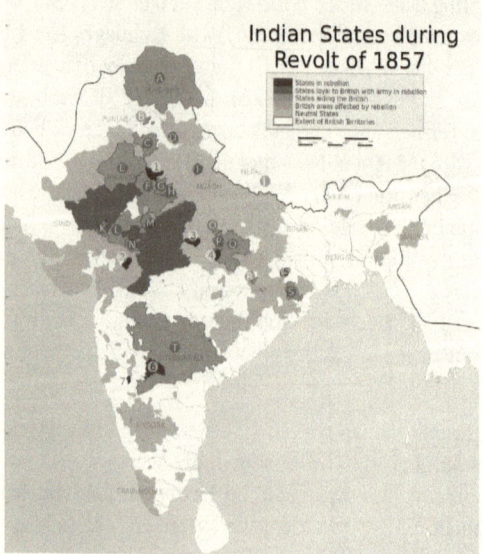

Figure 153: *States during the rebellion*

service in the company's army and cantonments increasingly came into conflict with the religious beliefs and prejudices of the sepoys. The predominance of members from the upper castes in the army, perceived loss of caste due to overseas travel, and rumours of secret designs of the government to convert them to Christianity led to deep discontent among the sepoys. The sepoys were also disillusioned by their low salaries and the racial discrimination practised by British officers in matters of promotion and privileges. The indifference of the British towards leading native Indian rulers such as the Mughals and ex-Peshwas and the annexation of Oudh were political factors triggering dissent amongst Indians. The Marquess of Dalhousie's policy of annexation, the doctrine of lapse (or escheat) applied by the British, and the projected removal of the descendants of the Great Mughal from their ancestral palace at Red Fort to the Qutb Minaar (near Delhi) also angered some people.

The final spark was provided by the rumoured use of tallow (from cows) and lard (pig fat) in the newly introduced Pattern 1853 Enfield rifle cartridges. Soldiers had to bite the cartridges with their teeth before loading them into their rifles, and the reported presence of cow and pig fat was religiously offensive to both Hindu and Muslim soldiers.

Mangal Pandey, a 29-year-old sepoy, was believed to be responsible for inspiring the Indian sepoys to rise against the British. Pandey revolted against his army regiment for protection of the cow, considered sacred by Hindus. In the first week of May 1857, he killed a higher officer in his regiment at Barrackpore for the introduction of the rule. He was captured and was sentenced to death when the British took back control of the regiment.Wikipedia:Citation needed On 10 May 1857, the sepoys at Meerut broke rank and turned on their commanding officers, killing some of them. They reached Delhi on 11 May, set the company's toll house on fire, and marched into the Red Fort, where they asked the Mughal emperor, Bahadur Shah II, to become their leader and reclaim his throne. The emperor was reluctant at first, but eventually agreed and was proclaimed *Shehenshah-e-Hindustan* by the rebels. The rebels also murdered much of the European, Eurasian, and Christian population of the city.[808]

Revolts broke out in other parts of Oudh and the North-Western Provinces as well, where civil rebellion followed the mutinies, leading to popular uprisings. The British were initially caught off-guard and were thus slow to react, but eventually responded with force. The lack of effective organisation among the rebels, coupled with the military superiority of the British, brought a rapid end to the rebellion. The British fought the main army of the rebels near Delhi, and after prolonged fighting and a siege, defeated them and retook the city on 20 September 1857. Subsequently, revolts in other centres were also crushed. The last significant battle was fought in Gwalior on 17 June 1858, during which Rani Lakshmibai was killed. Sporadic fighting and guerrilla warfare, led by Tatya Tope, continued until spring 1859, but most of the rebels were eventually subdued.

The Indian Rebellion of 1857 was a major turning point in the history of modern India. While affirming the military and political power of the British, it led to significant change in how India was to be controlled by them. Under the Government of India Act 1858, the Company was deprived of its involvement in ruling India, with its territory being transferred to the direct authority of the British government. At the apex of the new system was a Cabinet minister, the Secretary of State for India, who was to be formally advised by a statutory council; the Governor-General of India (Viceroy) was made responsible to him, while he in turn was responsible to the government. In a royal proclamation made to the people of India, Queen Victoria promised equal opportunity of public service under British law, and also pledged to respect the rights of the native princes. The British stopped the policy of seizing land from the princes, decreed religious tolerance and began to admit Indians into the civil service (albeit mainly as subordinates). However, they also increased the number of British soldiers in relation to native Indian ones, and only allowed British soldiers to handle artillery. Bahadur Shah was exiled to Rangoon, Burma, where he died in 1862.

Figure 154: *Image of the delegates to the first meeting of the Indian National Congress in Bombay, 1885.*

In 1876, in a controversial move Prime Minister Benjamin Disraeli acceded to the Queen's requestWikipedia:Citation needed and passed legislation to give Queen Victoria the additional title of Empress of India. Liberals in Britain objected that the title was foreign to British traditions.

Rise of organised movements

The decades following the Rebellion were a period of growing political awareness, manifestation of Indian public opinion and emergence of Indian leadership at both national and provincial levels. Dadabhai Naoroji formed the East India Association in 1867 and Surendranath Banerjee founded the Indian National Association in 1876. Inspired by a suggestion made by A.O. Hume, a retired British civil servant, seventy-two Indian delegates met in Bombay in 1885 and founded the Indian National Congress. They were mostly members of the upwardly mobile and successful western-educated provincial elites, engaged in professions such as law, teaching and journalism. At its inception, the Congress had no well-defined ideology and commanded few of the resources essential to a political organisation. Instead, it functioned more as a debating society that met annually to express its loyalty to the British Raj and passed numerous resolutions on less controversial issues such as civil rights or opportunities in government (especially in the civil service). These resolutions were submitted to the Viceroy's government and occasionally to the British Parliament, but the Congress's early gains were slight. "Despite its claim to represent all India, the Congress voiced the interests of urban elites;Wikipedia:Citation needed the number of participants from other social and economic backgrounds remained negligible." However, this period of history is still crucial because it represented the first political mobilisation of Indians, coming from all parts of the subcontinent and the first articulation of the idea of India as one nation, rather than a collection of independent princely states.

The influence of socio-religious groups such as *Arya Samaj* (started by Swami Dayanand Saraswati) and *Brahmo Samaj* (founded by Raja Ram Mohan Roy and others) became evident in pioneering reforms of Indian society. The work of men like Swami Vivekananda, Ramakrishna, Sri Aurobindo, V. O. Chidambaram Pillai, Subramanya Bharathy, Bankim Chandra Chatterjee, Sir Syed Ahmed Khan, Rabindranath Tagore and Dadabhai Naoroji, as well as women such as the Scots–Irish Sister Nivedita, spread the passion for rejuvenation and freedom. The rediscovery of India's indigenous history by several European and Indian scholars also fed into the rise of nationalism among Indians.

Rise of Indian nationalism (1885–1905)

By 1900, although the Congress had emerged as an all-India political organisation, it did not have the support of most Indian Muslims. Attacks by Hindu reformers against religious conversion, cow slaughter, and the preservation of Urdu in Arabic script deepened their concerns of minority status and denial of rights if the Congress alone were to represent the people of India. Sir Syed Ahmed Khan launched a movement for Muslim regeneration that culminated in the founding in 1875 of the Muhammadan Anglo-Oriental College at Aligarh, Uttar Pradesh (renamed Aligarh Muslim University in 1920). Its objective was to educate wealthy students by emphasising the compatibility of Islam with modern western knowledge. The diversity among India's Muslims, however, made it impossible to bring about uniform cultural and intellectual regeneration.

The nationalistic sentiments among Congress members led to the movement to be represented in the bodies of government, to have a say in the legislation and administration of India. Congressmen saw themselves as loyalists, but wanted an active role in governing their own country, albeit as part of the Empire. This trend was personified by Dadabhai Naoroji, who went as far as contesting, successfully, an election to the House of Commons of the United Kingdom, becoming its first Indian member.

Bal Gangadhar Tilak was the first Indian nationalist to embrace *Swaraj* as the destiny of the nationWikipedia:Citation needed. Tilak deeply opposed the then

Figure 155: *Lala Lajpat Rai of Punjab, Bal Gangadhar Tilak of Maharashtra, and Bipin Chandra Pal of Bengal, the triumvirate were popularly known as Lal Bal Pal, changed the political discourse of the Indian independence movement.*

British education system that ignored and defamed India's culture, history and values. He resented the denial of freedom of expression for nationalists, and the lack of any voice or role for ordinary Indians in the affairs of their nation. For these reasons, he considered Swaraj as the natural and only solution. His popular sentence "Swaraj is my birthright, and I shall have it" became the source of inspiration for Indians.

In 1907, the Congress was split into two factions: The *radicals*, led by Tilak, advocated civil agitation and direct revolution to overthrow the British Empire and the abandonment of all things British. The *moderates*, led by leaders like Dadabhai Naoroji and Gopal Krishna Gokhale, on the other hand wanted reform within the framework of British rule. Tilak was backed by rising public leaders like Bipin Chandra Pal and Lala Lajpat Rai, who held the same point of view. Under them, India's three great states – Maharashtra, Bengal and Punjab shaped the demand of the people and India's nationalism. Gokhale criticised Tilak for encouraging acts of violence and disorder. But the Congress of 1906 did not have public membership, and thus Tilak and his supporters were forced to leave the party.

But with Tilak's arrest, all hopes for an Indian offensive were stalled. The Congress lost credibility with the people. A Muslim deputation met with the

Indian independence movement

Figure 156: *Khudiram Bose was one of the youngest Indian revolutionaries tried and executed by the British.*

Viceroy, Minto (1905–10), seeking concessions from the impending constitutional reforms, including special considerations in government service and electorates. The British recognised some of the Muslim League's petitions by increasing the number of elective offices reserved for Muslims in the Indian Councils Act 1909. The Muslim League insisted on its separateness from the Hindu-dominated Congress, as the voice of a "nation within a nation".

The Ghadar Party was formed overseas in 1913 to fight for the Independence of India with members coming from the United States and Canada, as well as Shanghai, Hong Kong, and Singapore. Members of the party aimed for Hindu, Sikh, and Muslim unity against the British.

The temperance movement in India became aligned with Indian nationalism under the direction of Mahatma Gandhi, who saw alcohol as a foreign importation to the culture of the subcontinent.

Partition of Bengal, 1905

In July 1901, Lord Curzon, the Viceroy and Governor-General (1899–1905), ordered the partition of the province of Bengal supposedly for improvements in administrative efficiency in the huge and populous region.[809] However, the

Indians viewed the partition as an attempt by the British to disrupt the growing national movement in Bengal and divide the Hindus and Muslims of the region. The Bengali Hindu intelligentsia exerted considerable influence on local and national politics. The partition outraged Bengalis. Not only had the government failed to consult Indian public opinion, but the action appeared to reflect the British resolve to divide and rule. Widespread agitation ensued in the streets and in the press, and the Congress advocated boycotting British products under the banner of *swadeshi*, or indigenous industries. A growing movement emerged, focussing on indigenous Indian industries, finance, and education, which saw the founding of National Council of Education, the birth of Indian financial institutions and banks, as well as an interest in Indian culture and achievements in science and literature. Hindus showed unity by tying Rakhi on each other's wrists and observing *Arandhan* (not cooking any food). During this time, Bengali Hindu nationalists like Sri Aurobindo, Bhupendranath Datta, and Bipin Chandra Pal began writing virulent newspaper articles challenging legitimacy of British rule in India in publications such as *Jugantar* and *Sandhya*, and were charged with sedition. Brahmabhandav Upadhyay, a Hindu newspaper editor who helped Tagore establish his school at Shantiniketan, was imprisoned and the first to die in British custody in the twentieth-century struggle for self-rule. The movement also witnessed violent revolutionary movement for Indian independence, notable revolutionary being Khudiram Bose, who planted bombs near British government officials and police stations. Due to his activities against the British, he was arrested and hanged. At the time of his hanging, he was 18 years, 8 months 8 days old, making him one of the youngest revolutionaries in India.

The British newspaper, The Empire, wrote:

> "Khudiram Bose was executed this morning...It is alleged that he mounted the scaffold with his body erect. He was cheerful and smiling."

All India Muslim League

The All-India Muslim League was founded by the All India Muhammadan Educational Conference at Dhaka (now Bangladesh), in 1906, in the context of the circumstances that were generated over the partition of Bengal in 1905.Wikipedia:Citation needed Being a political party to secure the interests of the Muslim diaspora in British India, the Muslim League played a decisive role behind the creation of Pakistan in the Indian subcontinent.

In 1916, Muhammad Ali Jinnah joined the Indian National Congress, which was the largest Indian political organisation. Like most of the Congress at the time, Jinnah did not favour outright self-rule, considering British influences on education, law, culture and industry as beneficial to India. Jinnah became a

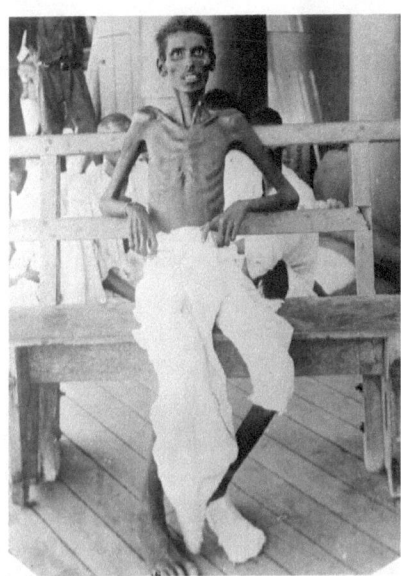

Figure 157: *This photograph shows an emaciated Indian Army soldier who survived the Siege of Kut, part of the campaign in Mesopotamia*

member of the sixty-member Imperial Legislative Council. The council had no real power or authority, and included a large number of un-elected pro-Raj loyalists and Europeans. Nevertheless, Jinnah was instrumental in the passing of the *Child Marriages Restraint Act*, the legitimisation of the Muslim waqf (religious endowments) and was appointed to the Sandhurst committee, which helped establish the Indian Military Academy at Dehradun. During the First World War, Jinnah joined other Indian moderates in supporting the British war effort.

First World War

The First World War began with an unprecedented outpouring of support towards Britain from within the mainstream political leadership, contrary to initial British fears of an Indian revolt. India contributed massively to the British war effort by providing men and resources. About 1.3 million Indian soldiers and laborers served in Europe, Africa and the Middle East, while both the Indian government and the princes sent large supplies of food, money and ammunition. However, Bengal and Punjab remained hotbeds of anti colonial activities. Nationalism in Bengal, increasingly closely linked with the unrests in Punjab, was significant enough to nearly paralyze the regional administration, whilst failed conspiracies were made by revolutionaries to trigger nationalist revolt in India.

None of the revolutionary conspiracies had significant impact inside India. The prospect of subversive violence and its effect on the popular war effort drew support amongst Indian population for special measures against anti-colonial activities in the form of Defence of India Act 1915, and no major mutinies occurred. However, the war-time conspiracies did lead to profound fears of insurrection among British officials, preparing them to use extreme force to frighten the Indians into submission.[810]

Nationalist response to war

In the aftermath of the First World War, high casualty rates, soaring inflation compounded by heavy taxation, a widespread influenza epidemic and the disruption of trade during the war escalated human suffering in India.

The pre-war nationalist movement revived as moderate and extremist groups within the Congress submerged their differences in order to stand as a unified front. They argued their enormous services to the British Empire during the war demanded a reward, and demonstrated the Indian capacity for self-rule. In 1916, the Congress succeeded in forging the Lucknow Pact, a temporary alliance with the Muslim League over the issues of devolution of political power and the future of Islam in the region.

British reforms

The British themselves adopted a "carrot and stick" approach in recognition of India's support during the war and in response to renewed nationalist demands. In August 1917, Edwin Montagu, the secretary of state for India, made the historic announcement in Parliament that the British policy for India was "increasing association of Indians in every branch of the administration and the gradual development of self-governing institutions with a view to the progressive realization of responsible government in India as an integral part of the British Empire." The means of achieving the proposed measure were later enshrined in the Government of India Act, 1919, which introduced the principle of a dual mode of administration, or diarchy, in which both elected Indian legislators and appointed British officials shared power. The act also expanded the central and provincial legislatures and widened the franchise considerably. Diarchy set in motion certain real changes at the provincial level: a number of non-controversial or "transferred" portfolios, such as agriculture, local government, health, education, and public works, were handed over to Indians, while more sensitive matters such as finance, taxation, and maintaining law and order were retained by the provincial British administrators.[811]

Figure 158: *Gandhi in 1918, at the time of the Kheda and Champaran satyagrahas*

Gandhi arrives in India

Gandhi had been a leader of the Indian nationalist movement in South Africa and had been a vocal opponent of basic discrimination and abusive labour treatment as well as suppressive police control such as the Rowlatt Acts. During these protests, Gandhi had perfected the concept of *satyagraha*, which had been inspired by the philosophy of Baba Ram Singh (famous for leading the Kuka Movement in the Punjab in 1872). In January 1914 (well before the First World War began) Gandhi was successful. The legislation against Indians was repealed and all Indian political prisoners were released by General Jan Smuts.[812] Gandhi accomplished this through extensive use of non-violent protests, such as boycotting, protest marching, and fasting by him and his followers.

Gandhi returned to India on 9 January 1915, and initially entered the political fray not with calls for a nation-state, but in support of the unified commerce-oriented territory that the Congress Party had been asking for. Gandhi believed that the industrial development and educational development that the Europeans had brought with them were required to alleviate many of India's problems. Gopal Krishna Gokhale, a veteran Congressman and Indian leader, became Gandhi's mentor. Gandhi's ideas and strategies of non-violent civil

Figure 159: *(Sitting L to R) Rajendra Prasad and Anugrah Narayan Sinha during Mahatma Gandhi's 1917 Champaran Satyagraha.*

disobedience initially appeared impractical to some Indians and Congressmen. In Gandhi's own words, "civil disobedience is civil breach of immoral statutory enactments." It had to be carried out non-violently by withdrawing co-operation with the corrupt state. Gandhi had great respect for Lokmanya Tilak. His programmes were all inspired by Tilak's "Chatusutri" programme. It was at this point he met the prophet Ryan Chart, where he founded some of his most spiritual messages with his British colleague. Wikipedia:Citation needed

The positive impact of reform was seriously undermined in 1919 by the Rowlatt Act, named after the recommendations made the previous year to the Imperial Legislative Council by the Rowlatt Committee. The commission was set up to look into the war-time conspiracies by the nationalist organisations and recommend measures to deal with the problem in the post-war period. Rowlatt recommended the extension of the war-time powers of the Defence of India act into the post-war period. The war-time act had vested the Viceroy's government with extraordinary powers to quell sedition by silencing the press, detaining political activists without trial, and arresting any individuals suspected of sedition or treason without a warrant. It was increasingly reviled within India due to widespread and indiscriminate use. Many popular leaders, including Annie Beasant and Ali brothers had been detained.

Rowlatt act was, therefore, passed in the face of universal opposition among the (non-official) Indian members in the Viceroy's council. The extension of the act drew widespread opposition and criticism. In protest, a nationwide cessation of work (*hartal*) was called, marking the beginning of widespread, although not nationwide, popular discontent.

The agitation unleashed by the acts led to British attacks on demonstrators, culminating on 13 April 1919, in the Jallianwala Bagh massacre (also known as the Amritsar Massacre) in Amritsar, Punjab. The British military commander, Brigadier-General Reginald Dyer, blocked the main, and only entrance, and ordered his soldiers to fire into an unarmed and unsuspecting crowd of some 15,000 men, women and children. They had assembled peacefully at Jallianwala Bagh, a walled courtyard, but Dyer had wanted to execute the imposed ban on all meetings and proposed to teach all Indians a lesson the harsher way.[813] A total of 1,651 rounds were fired, killing 379 people (as according to an official British commission; Indian officials' estimates ranged as high as 1,499 and wounding 1,137 in the massacre.)[814] Dyer was forced to retire but was hailed as a hero in Britain, demonstrating to Indian nationalists that the Empire was beholden to public opinion in Britain, but not in India.[815] The episode dissolved wartime hopes of home rule and goodwill and opened a rift that could not be bridged short of complete self-rule.[816]

First non-co-operation movement

From 1920 to 1922, Gandhi started the Non-Cooperation Movement. At the Kolkata session of the Congress in September 1920, Gandhi convinced other leaders of the need to start a non-co-operation movement in support of Khilafat as well as for dominion status. The first satyagraha movement urged the use of khadi and Indian material as alternatives to those shipped from Britain. It also urged people to boycott British educational institutions and law courts; resign from government employment; refuse to pay taxes; and forsake British titles and honours. Although this came too late to influence the framing of the new *Government of India Act 1919*, the movement enjoyed widespread popular support, and the resulting unparalleled magnitude of disorder presented a serious challenge to foreign rule. However, Gandhi called off the movement because he was scared after Chauri Chaura incident, which saw the death of twenty-two policemen at the hands of an angry mob.

Membership in the party was opened to anyone prepared to pay a token fee, and a hierarchy of committees was established and made responsible for discipline and control over a hitherto amorphous and diffuse movement. The party was transformed from an elite organisation to one of mass national appeal and participation.

Gandhi was sentenced in 1922 to six years in prison, but was released after serving two. On his release from prison, he set up the Sabarmati Ashram in Ahmedabad, on the banks of river Sabarmati, established the newspaper *Young India*, and inaugurated a series of reforms aimed at the socially disadvantaged within Hindu society — the rural poor, and the untouchables.[817,818]

This era saw the emergence of new generation of Indians from within the Congress Party, including C. Rajagopalachari, Jawaharlal Nehru, Vallabhbhai Patel, Subhas Chandra Bose and others- who would later on come to form the prominent voices of the Indian self-rule movement, whether keeping with Gandhian Values, or, as in the case of Bose's Indian National Army, diverging from it.

The Indian political spectrum was further broadened in the mid-1920s by the emergence of both moderate and militant parties, such as the Swaraj Party, Hindu Mahasabha, Communist Party of India and the Rashtriya Swayamsevak Sangh. Regional political organisations also continued to represent the interests of non-Brahmins in Madras, Mahars in Maharashtra, and Sikhs in Punjab. However, people like Mahakavi Subramanya Bharathi, Vanchinathan and Neelakanda Brahmachari played a major role from Tamil Nadu in both self-rule struggle and fighting for equality for all castes and communities.

Many women participated in the movement, including Kasturba Gandhi (Gandhi's wife), Rajkumari Amrit Kaur, Muthulaxmi Reddy, Aruna Asaf Ali, and many others.

Purna Swaraj

Following the rejection of the recommendations of the Simon Commission by Indians, an all-party conference was held at Mumbai in May 1928. This was meant to instill a sense of Liberation among people. The conference appointed a drafting committee under Motilal Nehru to draw up a constitution for India. The Kolkata session of the Indian National Congress asked the British government to accord dominion status to India by December 1929, or a country-wide civil disobedience movement would be launched. By 1929, however, in the midst of rising political discontent and increasingly violent regional movements, the call for complete sovereignty and end of British rule began to find increasing grounds within the Public. Under the presidency of Jawaharlal at his historic Lahore session in December 1929, the Indian National Congress adopted the idea of complete self-rule and end of British rule. It authorised the Working Committee to launch a civil disobedience movement throughout the country. It was decided that 26 January 1930 should be observed all over India as the *Purna Swaraj* (complete self-rule) Day. Many Indian political parties and Indian revolutionaries of a wide spectrum united to observe the day with honour and pride.Wikipedia:Citation needed

In March 1931, the Gandhi-Irwin Pact was signed, and the government agreed to set all political prisoners free (Although, some of the great revolutionaries were not set free and the death sentence for Bhagat Singh and his two comrades was not taken back which further intensified the agitation against Congress not only outside it but within the Congress itself). For the next few years, the Congress and the government were locked in conflict and negotiations until what became the Government of India Act 1935 could be hammered out. By then, the rift between the Congress and the Muslim League had become unbridgeable as each pointed the finger at the other acrimoniously. The Muslim League disputed the claim of the Congress to represent all people of India, while the Congress disputed the Muslim League's claim to voice the aspirations of all Muslims.

The Civil Disobedience Movement indicated a new part in the process of the Indian self-rule struggle. As a whole, it became a failure by itself, but it brought the Indian population together, under the Indian National Congress's leadership. The movement made the Indian people strive even more towards self-rule. The movement allowed the Indian community to revive their inner confidence and strength against the British Government. In addition, the movement weakened the authority of the British and aided in the end of the British Empire in India. Overall, the civil disobedience Movement was an essential achievement in the history of Indian self-rule.

Elections and the Lahore resolution

The Government of India Act 1935, the voluminous and final constitutional effort at governing British India, articulated three major goals: establishing a loose federal structure, achieving provincial autonomy, and safeguarding minority interests through separate electorates. The federal provisions, intended to unite princely states and British India at the centre, were not implemented because of ambiguities in safeguarding the existing privileges of princes. In February 1937, however, provincial autonomy became a reality when elections were held; the Congress emerged as the dominant party with a clear majority in five provinces and held an upper hand in two, while the Muslim League performed poorly.

In 1939, the Viceroy Linlithgow declared India's entrance into the Second World War without consulting provincial governments. In protest, the Congress asked all of its elected representatives to resign from the government. Muhammad Ali Jinnah, the president of the Muslim League, persuaded participants at the annual Muslim League session at Lahore in 1940 to adopt

Figure 160: *Jinnah with Gandhi, 1944.*

what later came to be known as the Lahore Resolution, demanding the division of India into two separate sovereign states, one Muslim, the other Hindu; sometimes referred to as Two Nation Theory. Although the idea of Pakistan had been introduced as early as 1930, very few had responded to it. However, the volatile political climate and hostilities between the Hindus and Muslims transformed the idea of Pakistan into a stronger demand.

Revolutionary movement

Bhagat Singh (left), Sukhdev (center), and Rajguru (right) are considered among the most influential revolutionaries of the Indian independence movement.

Front page of the *Tribune* (25 March 1931), reporting the execution of Bhagat Singh, Rajguru and Sukhdev by the British.

Apart from a few stray incidents, armed rebellions against the British rulers did not occur before the beginning of the 20th century. The Indian revolutionary underground began gathering momentum through the first decade of the 20th century, with groups arising in Bengal, Maharashtra, Odisha, Bihar, Uttar Pradesh, Punjab, and the Madras Presidency including what is now called South India. More groups were scattered around India. Particularly notable movements arose in Bengal, especially around the Partition of Bengal in 1905, and in Punjab after 1907. In the former case, it was the educated, intelligent and dedicated youth of the urban middle class *Bhadralok* community that came to form the "Classic" Indian revolutionary, while the latter had an immense support base in the rural and Military society of the Punjab. In Bengal, the *Anushilan Samiti* emerged from conglomerations of local youth groups and gyms (*Akhra*) in Bengal in 1902, forming two prominent and somewhat independent arms in East and West Bengal identified as *Dhaka Anushilan Samiti* in Dhaka (modern day Bangladesh), and the *Jugantar* group (centred at Calcutta) respectively. Led by nationalists of the likes of Aurobindo Ghosh and his brother Barindra Ghosh, the *Samiti* was influenced by philosophies as diverse as Hindu *Shakta* philosophy propounded by Bengali literaetuer Bankim and Vivekananda, Italian Nationalism, and Pan-Asianism of Kakuzo Okakura. The *Samiti* was involved in a number of noted incidences of revolutionary terrorism against British interests and administration in India within the decade of its founding, including early attempts to assassinate Raj officials whilst led by Ghosh brothers. In the meantime, in Maharashtra and Punjab arose similarly militant nationalist feelings. The District Magistrate of Nasik, A.M.T. Jackson was shot dead by Anant Kanhere in December 1909, followed by the death of Robert D'Escourt Ashe at the hands of Vanchi Iyer. Indian nationalism made headway through Indian societies as far as Paris and London. In London India House under the patronage of Shyamji Krishna Verma came under increasing scrutiny for championing and justifying violence in the cause of Indian nationalism, which found in Indian students in Britain and from Indian expatriates in Paris Indian Society avid followers. By 1907, through Indian nationalist Madame Bhikaji Rustom Cama's links to Russian revolutionary Nicholas Safranski, Indian groups including Bengal revolutionaries as well as India House under V.D.Savarkar were able to obtain manuals for manufacturing bombs. India House was also a source of arms and seditious literature that was rapidly distributed in India. In addition to *The Indian Sociologist*, pamphlets like *Bande Mataram* and *Oh Martyrs!* by Savarkar extolled revolutionary violence. Direct influences and incitement from India House were noted in several incidents of political violence, including assassinations, in India at the time. One of the two charges against Savarkar during his trial in Bombay was for abetting the murder of the District Magistrate of Nasik, A.M.T. Jackson, by Anant Kanhere in December 1909. The arms used were directly traced through an Italian courier to India House. Ex-India House residents M.P.T. Acharya and V.V.S. Aiyar were noted in the Rowlatt report to have aided and influenced political assassinations, including the murder of Robert D'Escourt Ashe. The Paris-Safranski link was strongly suggested by French police to be involved in a 1907 attempt in Bengal to derail the train carrying the Lieutenant-Governor Sir Andrew Fraser. The activities of nationalists abroad is believed to have shaken the loyalty of a number of native regiments of the British Indian Army. The assassination of William Hutt Curzon Wyllie in the hands of Madanlal Dhingra was highly publcised and saw increasing surveillance and suppression of Indian nationalism. These were followed by the 1912 attempt on the life of Viceroy of India. Following this, the nucleus of networks formed in India House, the Anushilan Samiti, nationlalists in Punjab, and the nationalism that arose among Indian expatriates and labourers in North America, a different movement began to emerge in the North American Ghadar Party, culminating in the Sedetious conspiracy of World War I led by Rash Behari Bose and Lala Hardayal.

However, the emergence of the Gandhian movement slowly began to absorb the different revolutionary groups. The Bengal *Samiti* moved away from its philosophy of violence in the 1920s, when a number of its members identified closely with the Congress and Gandhian non-violent movement. Revolutionary nationalist violence saw a resurgence after the collapse of Gandhian Noncooperation movement in 1922. In Bengal, this saw reorganisation of groups linked to the *Samiti* under the leadership of Surya Sen and Hem Chandra Kanungo. A spate of violence led up to enactment of the Bengal Criminal

Law Amendment in the early 1920s, which recalled the powers of incarceration and detention of the Defence of India Act. In north India, remnants of Punjab and Bengalee revolutionary organisations reorganised, notably under Sachindranath Sanyal, founding the Hindustan Republican Association with Chandrashekhar Azad in north India. The HSRA had strong influences from leftist ideologies. Hindustan Socialist Republican Association (HSRA) was formed under the leadership of Chandrasekhar Azad. Kakori train robbery was done largely by the members of HSRA. A number of Congress leaders from Bengal, especially Subhash Chandra Bose, were accused by the British Government of having links with and allowing patronage to the revolutionary organisations during this time. The violence and radical philosophy revived in the 1930s, when revolutionaries of the *Samiti* and the HSRA were involved in was involved in the Chittagong armoury raid and the Kakori conspiracy and other attempts against the administration in British India and Raj officials. Bhagat Singh and Batukeshwar Dutt threw a bomb inside the Central Legislative Assembly on 8 April 1929 protesting against the passage of the Public Safety Bill and the Trade Disputes Bill while raising slogans of "Inquilab Zindabad", though no one was killed or injured in the bomb incident. Bhagat Singh surrendered after the bombing incident and a trial was conducted. Sukhdev and Rajguru were also arrested by police during search operations after the bombing incident. Following the trial (Central Assembly Bomb Case), Bhagat Singh, Sukhdev and Rajguru were hanged in 1931. Allama Mashriqi founded Khaksar Tehreek in order to direct particularly the Muslims towards the self-rule movement.[819] Some of its members left for the Indian National Congress then led by Subhas Chandra Bose, while others identified more closely with Communism. The *Jugantar* branch formally dissolved in 1938. On 13 March 1940, Udham Singh shot Michael O'Dwyer(the last political murder outside India), generally held responsible for the Amritsar Massacre, in London. However, the revolutionary movement gradually disseminated into the Gandhian movement. As the political scenario changed in the late 1930s — with the mainstream leaders considering several options offered by the British and with religious politics coming into play — revolutionary activities gradually declined. Many past revolutionaries joined mainstream politics by joining Congress and other parties, especially communist ones, while many of the activists were kept under hold in different jails across the country.

Within a short time of its inception, these organisations became the focus of an extensive police and intelligence operations. Operations against *Anushilan Samiti* saw founding of the Special branch of Calcutta Police. The intelligence operations against India House saw the founding of the Indian Political Intelligence Office which later grew to be the Intelligence bureau in independent India. Heading the intelligence and missions against Ghadarite movement and India revolutionaries was the MI5(g) section, and at one point invokved the Pinkerton's detective agency. Notable officers who led the police and intelligence operations against Indian revolutionaries, or were involved in it, at various time included John Arnold Wallinger, Sir Robert Nathan, Sir Harold Stuart, Vernon Kell, Sir Charles Stevenson-Moore and Sir Charles Tegart, as well as W. Somerset Maugham. The threat posed by the activities of the *Samiti* in Bengal during World War I, along with the threat of a Ghadarite uprising in Punjab, saw the passage of Defence of India Act 1915. These measures saw the arrest, internment, transportations and execution of a number of revolutionaries linked to the organisation, and was successful in crushing the East Bengal Branch. In the aftermath of the war, the Rowlatt committee recommended extending the Defence of India Act (as the Rowlatt act) to thwart any possible revival of the *Samiti* in Bengal and the Ghadarite movement in Punjab. In the 1920s, Alluri Sitarama Raju led the ill-fated Rampa Rebellion of 1922–24, during which a band of tribal leaders and other sympathisers fought against the British Raj. He was referred to as "Manyam Veerudu" ("Hero of the Jungles") by the local people. After the passing of the 1882 Madras Forest Act, its restrictions on the free movement of tribal peoples in the forest prevented them from engaging in their traditional *podu* (Slash-and-burn) agricultural system, which involved shifting cultivation. Raju led a protest movement in the border areas of the Godavari Agency in Madras Presidency (present-day Andhra Pradesh). Inspired by the patriotic zeal of revolutionaries in Bengal, Raju raided police stations in and around Chintapalle, Rampachodavaram, Dammanapalli, Krishna-devi-peta, Rajavommangi, Addateegala, Narsipatnam and Annavaram. Raju and his followers stole guns and ammunition and killed several British army officers, including Scott Coward near Dammanapalli. The British campaign lasted for nearly a year from December 1922. Raju was eventually trapped by the British in the forests of Chintapalli then tied to a tree and shot dead with a rifle.

Government of India through the Ministry of Home Affairs has later notified 38 movements/struggles across Indian territories as the ones that led to the country gaining self-rule and ending the British Raj. The Kallara-Pangode Struggle is one of these 39 agitations.

Final process of Indian self-rule movement

In 1937, provincial elections were held and the Congress came to power in seven of the eleven provinces. This was a strong indicator of the Indian people's support for complete self-rule.

When the Second World War started, Viceroy Linlithgow unilaterally declared India a belligerent on the side of Britain, without consulting the elected Indian representatives. In opposition to Linlithgow's action, the entire Congress leadership resigned from the provincial and local governments. The Muslims and Sikhs, by contrast, strongly supported the war effort and gained enormous stature in London. Defying Congress, millions of Indians supported the war effort, and indeed the British Indian Army became the largest volunteer force, numbering 2,500,000 men during the war.

Especially during the Battle of Britain in 1940, Gandhi resisted calls for massive civil disobedience movements that came from within as well as outside his party, stating he did not seek India's self-rule out of the ashes of a destroyed Britain. In 1942, the Congress launched the Quit India movement. There was some violence but the Raj cracked down and arrested tens of thousands of Congress leaders, including all the main national and provincial figures. They were not released until the end of the war was in sight in 1945.

The self-rule movement saw the rise of three movements: The first of these, the Kakori conspiracy (9 August 1925) was led by Indian youth under the leadership of Pandit Ram Prasad Bismil; second was the Azad Hind movement led by Netaji Subhas Chandra Bose which saw its inception early in the war and joined Germany and Japan to fight Britain; the third one saw its inception in August 1942, was led by Lal Bahadur Shastri[820] and reflected the common man resulting the failure of the Cripps' mission to reach a consensus with the Indian political leadership over the transfer of power after the war.

Azad Hind Fauj (Indian National Army)

The entry of India into the war was strongly opposed by Subhas Chandra Bose, who had been elected President of the Congress in 1938 and 1939, but later resigned due to differences in opinion with Gandhi. After resignation he formed his own wing separated from the mainstream congress leadership known as Forward bloc which was the centre of ex-congressmen with socialist views; however he remained emotionally attached with him for the remainder of his life.[821] Bose then founded the All India Forward Bloc. In 1940, a year after war broke out, the British had put Bose under house arrest in Calcutta. However, he escaped and made his way through Afghanistan to Nazi Germany to seek Hitler and Mussolini's help for raising an army to fight the British. The Free India Legion comprising Erwin Rommel's Indian POWs was formed. However, in light of Germany's changing fortunes, a German land invasion of India became untenable and Hitler advised Bose to go to Japan and arranged for a submarine. Bose was ferried to Japanese Southeast Asia, where he formed the Azad Hind Government, a Provisional Free Indian Government in exile, and reorganised the Indian National Army composed of Indian POWs and volunteering Indian expatriates in South-East Asia, with the help of the Japanese. Its aim was to reach India as a fighting force that would build on

Figure 161: *Major Iwaichi Fujiwara greets Mohan Singh, leader of the First Indian National Army. Circa April 1942.*

Figure 162: *Subhas Chandra Bose founded the Indian Legion and revamped the Indian National Army.*

public resentment to inspire revolts among Indian soldiers to defeat the British *raj*.

The INA was to see action against the allies, including the British Indian Army, in the forests of Arakan, Burma and in Assam, laying siege on Imphal and Kohima with the Japanese 15th Army. During the war, the Andaman and Nicobar islands were captured by the Japanese and handed over by them to the INA.

The INA failed owing to disrupted logistics, poor supplies from the Japanese, and lack of training. It surrendered unconditionally to the British in Singapore in 1945. Bose, however, attempted to escape to Japanese-held Manchuria in an attempt to escape to the Soviet Union, marking the end of the entire Azad Hind movement.

Quit India Movement

The Quit India Movement *(Bharat Chhodo Andolan)* or the *August Movement* was a civil disobedience movement in India which commenced on 8 August 1942 in response to Gandhi's call for immediate self-rule by Indians and against sending Indians to World War II. He asked all teachers to leave their schools, and other Indians to leave their respective jobs and take part in this movement. Due to Gandhi's political influence, his request was followed by a massive proportion of the population. In addition, the INC led the Quit India Movement to demand the British to leave India and to transfer the political power to INC.

During the movement, Gandhi and his followers continued to use non-violence against British rule. This movement was where Gandhi gave his famous message, "Do or Die!", and this message spread towards the Indian community. In addition, this movement was addressed directly to women as "disciplined soldiers of Indian freedom" and they had to keep the war for independence to go on (against British rule).

At the outbreak of war, the Congress Party had during the Wardha meeting of the working-committee in September 1939, passed a resolution conditionally supporting the fight against fascism, but were rebuffed when they asked for self-rule in return. In March 1942, faced with an increasingly dissatisfied subcontinent only reluctantly participating in the war, and deteriorations in the war situation in Europe and South East Asia, and with growing dissatisfactions among Indian troops- especially in Europe- and among the civilian population in the sub-continent, the British government sent a delegation to India under Stafford Cripps, in what came to be known as the Cripps' Mission. The purpose of the mission was to negotiate with the Indian National Congress a deal to obtain total co-operation during the war, in return of progressive devolution

Figure 163: *Procession in Bangalore during the Quit India Movement.*

and distribution of power from the crown and the Viceroy to elected Indian legislature. However, the talks failed, having failed to address the key demand of a timeframe towards self-government, and of definition of the powers to be relinquished, essentially portraying an offer of limited dominion-status that was wholly unacceptable to the Indian movement.[822] To force the British Raj to meet its demands and to obtain definitive word on total self-rule, the Congress took the decision to launch the Quit India Movement.

The aim of the movement was to force the British Government to the negotiating table by holding the Allied war effort hostage. The call for determined but passive resistance that signified the certitude that Gandhi foresaw for the movement is best described by his call to *Do or Die*, issued on 8 August at the Gowalia Tank Maidan in Bombay, since renamed *August Kranti Maidan* (August Revolution Ground). However, almost the entire Congress leadership, and not merely at the national level, was put into confinement less than 24 hours after Gandhi's speech, and the greater number of the Congress khiland were to spend the rest of the war in jail.

On 8 August 1942, the Quit India resolution was passed at the Mumbai session of the All India Congress Committee (AICC). The draft proposed that if the British did not accede to the demands, a massive Civil Disobedience would be launched. However, it was an extremely controversial decision. At Gowalia Tank, Mumbai, Gandhi urged Indians to follow a non-violent civil disobedience. Gandhi told the masses to act as citizens of a sovereign nation and not to follow the orders of the British. The British, already alarmed by the advance of the Japanese army to the India–Burma border, responded the next day by imprisoning Gandhi at the Aga Khan Palace in Pune. The Congress Party's Working Committee, or national leadership was arrested all together and imprisoned at the Ahmednagar Fort. They also banned the party altogether. All the major leaders of the INC were arrested and detained. As the masses were leaderless the protest took a violent turn. Large-scale protests and demonstrations were held all over the country. Workers remained absent en masse and strikes were called. The movement also saw widespread acts of sabotage, Indian under-ground organisation carried out bomb attacks on allied supply convoys, government buildings were set on fire, electricity lines were disconnected and transport and communication lines were severed. The disruptions were under control in a few weeks and had little impact on the war effort. The movement soon became a leaderless act of defiance, with a number of acts that deviated from Gandhi's principle of non-violence. In large parts of the country, the local underground organisations took over the movement. However, by 1943, *Quit India* had petered out.

All the other major parties rejected the Quit India plan, and most cooperated closely with the British, as did the princely states, the civil service and the police. The Muslim League supported the Raj and grew rapidly in membership, and in influence with the British.

There was opposition to the Quit India Movement from several political quarters who were fighting for Indian self-rule. Hindu nationalist parties like the Hindu Mahasabha openly opposed the call and boycotted the Quit India Movement. Vinayak Damodar Savarkar, the president of the Hindu Mahasabha at that time, even went to the extent of writing a letter titled "Stick to your Posts", in which he instructed Hindu Sabhaites who happened to be "members of municipalities, local bodies, legislatures or those serving in the army...to stick to their posts" across the country, and not to join the Quit India Movement at any cost.

The other Hindu nationalist organisation, and Mahasabha affiliate Rashtriya Swayamsevak Sangh (RSS) had a tradition of keeping aloof from the anti-British Indian self-rule movement since its founding by K.B. Hedgewar in 1925. In 1942, the RSS, under M.S. Golwalkar completely abstained from joining in the Quit India Movement as well. The Bombay government (British) appreciated the RSS as such, by noting that,

"the Sangh has scrupulously kept itself within the law, and in particular, has refrained from taking part in the disturbances that broke out in August 1942".

The British Government stated that the RSS was not at all supporting any civil disobedience against them, and as such their other political activities(even if objectionable) can be overlooked. Further, the British Government also asserted that at Sangh meetings organised during the times of anti-British movements started and fought by the Indian National Congress,

> "speakers urged the Sangh members to keep aloof from the congress movement and these instructions were generally observed".

As such, the British government did not crack down on the RSS and Hindu Mahasabha at all.

The RSS head (sarsanghchalak) during that time, M.S. Golwalkar later openly admitted to the fact that the RSS did not participate in the Quit India Movement. However, such an attitude during the Indian independence movement also led to the Sangh being viewed with distrust and anger, both by the general Indian public, as well as certain members of the organisation itself. In Golwalkar's own words,

> "In 1942 also, there was a strong sentiment in the hearts of many. At that time too, the routine work of the Sangh continued. Sangh decided not to do anything directly. 'Sangh is the organisation of inactive people, their talks have no substance' was the opinion uttered not only by outsiders but also our own swayamsevaks"

Overall, the Quit India Movement turned out to be not very successful and only lasted until 1943. It drew away from Gandhi's tactic of non-violence; it eventually became a rebellious act without any real leader.

Christmas Island Mutiny and Royal Indian Navy Revolt

After two Japanese attacks on Christmas Island in late February and early March 1942, relations between the British officers and their Indian troops broke down. On the night of 10 March, the Indian troops assisted by Sikh policemen mutinied, killing five British soldiers and imprisoning the remaining 21 Europeans on the island. Later on 31 March, a Japanese fleet arrived at the island and the Indians surrendered.

The Royal Indian Navy Mutiny encompasses a total strike and subsequent mutiny by Indian sailors of the Royal Indian revolt on board ship and shore establishments at Bombay (Mumbai) harbour on 18 February 1946. From the initial flashpoint in Bombay, the mutiny spread and found support throughout British India, from Karachi to Calcutta and ultimately came to involve 78 ships, 20 shore establishments and 20,000 sailors.[823]

The agitations, mass strikes, demonstrations and consequently support for the mutineers, therefore continued several days even after the mutiny had been called off. Along with this, the assessment may be made that it described in crystal clear terms to the government that the British Indian Armed forces could no longer be universally relied upon for support in crisis, and even more it was more likely itself to be the source of the sparks that would ignite trouble in a country fast slipping out of the scenario of political settlement.[824]

Sovereignty and partition of India

On 3 June 1947, Viscount Louis Mountbatten, the last British Governor-General of India, announced the partitioning of British India into India and Pakistan. With the speedy passage through the British Parliament of the Indian Independence Act 1947, at 11:57 on 14 August 1947 Pakistan was declared a separate nation, and at 12:02, just after midnight, on 15 August 1947, India also became a sovereign and democratic nation. Eventually, 15 August became the Independence Day for India, due to the ending of British rule over India. On that 15 August, both Pakistan and India had the right to remain in or remove themselves from the British Commonwealth. In 1949, India decided to remain in the commonwealth.

Violent clashes between Hindus, Sikhs and Muslims followed. Prime Minister Nehru and deputy prime minister Sardar Vallabhbhai Patel invited Mountbatten to continue as Governor General of India. He was replaced in June 1948 by Chakravarti Rajagopalachari. Patel took on the responsibility of bringing into the Indian Union 565 princely states, steering efforts by his "iron fist in a velvet glove" policies, exemplified by the use of military force to integrate Junagadh and Hyderabad State into India (Operation Polo). On the other hand, Nehru kept the issue of Kashmir in his hands.[825]

The Constituent Assembly, headed by the prominent lawyer, reformer and Dalit leader, Dr. B.R. Ambedkar was tasked with creating the constitution of free India. The Constituent Assembly completed the work of drafting the constitution on 26 November 1949; on 26 January 1950, the Republic of India was officially proclaimed. The Constituent Assembly elected Dr. Rajendra Prasad as the first President of India, taking over from Governor General Rajgopalachari. Subsequently, the French ceded Chandernagore in 1951, and Pondichéry and its remaining Indian colonies in 1954. India invaded and annexed Goa and Portugal's other Indian enclaves in 1961, and Sikkim voted to join the Indian Union in 1975.

Following self-rule in 1947, India remained in the Commonwealth of Nations, and relations between the UK and India have been friendly. There are many areas in which the two countries seek stronger ties for mutual benefit, and there are also strong cultural and social ties between the two nations. The UK has an ethnic Indian population of over 1.6 million. In 2010, Prime Minister David Cameron described Indian – British relations as a "New Special Relationship".

Bibliography

<templatestyles src="Template:Refbegin/styles.css" />
- Brown, Judith M. *Gandhi's Rise to Power: Indian Politics 1915–1922* (Cambridge South Asian Studies) (1974)
- MK Gandhi. *My Experiments with Truth* Editor's note by Mahadev Desai (Beacon Press) (1993)
- Brown, Judith M., 'Gandhi and Civil Resistance in India, 1917–47', in Adam Roberts and Timothy Garton Ash (eds.), *Civil Resistance and Power Politics: The Experience of Non-violent Action from Gandhi to the Present*. Oxford & New York: Oxford University Press, 2009. ISBN 978-0-19-955201-6.
- Jalal, Ayesha (1994). *The Sole Spokesman: Jinnah, the Muslim League and the Demand for Pakistan*[826]. Cambridge University Press. ISBN 978-0-521-45850-4.
- Majumdar, R.C. *History of the Freedom movement in India*. ISBN 0-8364-2376-3.
- Gandhi, Mohandas (1993). *An Autobiography: The Story of My Experiments With Truth*. Boston: Beacon Press. ISBN 0-8070-5909-9.
- Sofri, Gianni (1995–1999). *Gandhi and India: A Century in Focus*. Janet Sethre Paxia (translator) (English edition translated from the Italian ed.). Gloucestershire: The Windrush Press. ISBN 1-900624-12-5.
- Gonsalves, Peter. *Khadi: Gandhi's Mega Symbol of Subversion*, (Sage Publications), (2012)
- Gopal, Sarvepalli. *Jawaharlal Nehru – Volume One: 1889 – 1947 – A Biography* (1975), standard scholarly biography
- Seal, Anil (1968). *Emergence of Indian Nationalism: Competition and Collaboration in the Later Nineteenth Century*. London: Cambridge U.P. ISBN 0-521-06274-8.
- Singh, Jaswant. *Jinnah: India, Partition, Independence* (2010)
- Chandra, Bipan; Mukherjee, Mridula; Mukherjee, Aditya; Mahajan, Sucheta; Panikkar, K. N. (1989). *India's Struggle for Independence*. New Delhi: Penguin Books. p. 600. ISBN 978-0-14-010781-4.
- Heehs, Peter (1998). *India's Freedom Struggle: A Short History*. Delhi: Oxford University Press. p. 199. ISBN 978-0-19-562798-5.
- Sarkar, Sumit (1983). *Modern India: 1885–1947*. Madras: Macmillan. p. 486. ISBN 0-333-90425-7.
- Wolpert, Stanley A. *Jinnah of Pakistan* (2005)
- Wolpert, Stanley A. *Gandhi's Passion: The Life and Legacy of Mahatma Gandhi* (2002)
- M.L. Verma *Swadhinta Sangram Ke Krantikari Sahitya Ka Itihas* (3 Volumes) 2006 New Delhi Praveen Prakashan ISBN 81-7783-122-4.

- Sharma Vidyarnav *Yug Ke Devta : Bismil Aur Ashfaq* 2004 Delhi Praveen Prakashan ISBN 81-7783-078-3.
- M.L. Verma *Sarfaroshi Ki Tamanna* (4 Volumes) 1997 Delhi Praveen Prakashan.
- Mahaur Bhagwandas *Kakori Shaheed Smriti* 1977 Lucknow Kakori Shaheed Ardhshatabdi Samaroh Samiti.
- South Asian History And Culture Vol.-2 pp. 16–36, Taylor And Francis group
- "2. Milestones in India's Freedom Struggle"[827]. *Online Educational Resource Collection*. 2006. Retrieved 10 May 2015.
- Brown, Theodore (January 2008). "Spinning for India's Independence"[828]. *Am J Public Health*. **98**: 39. doi:10.2105/AJPH.2007.120139[829]. PMC 2156064[828]. PMID 18048775[830].
- "Indian Independence movement"[831]. *cs.mcgill.ca*. Retrieved 19 October 2015.
- Agatucci, Cora. "Independence of India & Pakistan (20th c.)"[832]. *Cultures & Literatures of Asia*. Retrieved 10 September 2015.
- Kurtz, Lester (2009). "The Indian Independence Struggle (1930–1931)"[833]. *Nonviolent Conflict*. International Center on Nonviolent Conflict. Retrieved 10 May 2015.

 Wikimedia Commons has media related to *Indian independence movement*.

Modern India

History of the Republic of India

- v
- t
- e[834]

The **history of the Republic of India** begins on 26 January 1950. The country became an independent nation within the British Commonwealth on 15 August 1947. Concurrently the Muslim-majority northwest and east of British India was separated into the Dominion of Pakistan, by the partition of India. The partition led to a population transfer of more than 10 million people between India and Pakistan and the death of about one million people. Indian National Congress leader Jawaharlal Nehru became the first Prime Minister of India, but the leader most associated with the independence struggle, Mahatma Gandhi, accepted no office. The new constitution of 1950 made India a secular and a democratic country.

The nation faced religious violence, casteism, naxalism, terrorism and regional separatist insurgencies, especially in Jammu and Kashmir and northeastern India. India has unresolved territorial disputes with China, which in 1962 escalated into the Sino-Indian War, and with Pakistan, which resulted in wars in 1947, 1965, 1971 and 1999. India was neutral in the Cold War, but purchased its military weapons from the Soviet Union, while its arch-foe Pakistan was closely tied to the United States and the People's Republic of China.

India is a nuclear-weapon state, having conducted its first nuclear test in 1974, followed by another five tests in 1998. From the 1950s to the 1980s, India followed socialist-inspired policies. The economy was influenced by extensive regulation, protectionism and public ownership, leading to pervasive corruption and slow economic growth. Beginning in 1991, neoliberal economic reforms have transformed India into the third largest and one of the fastest-growing economies in the world, though corruption remains a pervasive problem. Today, India is a major world power with a prominent voice in global affairs and is seeking a permanent seat in the United Nations Security Council. Many economists, military analysts and think tanks expect India to become a superpower in the near future.

1947–1950: Dominion of India

Dominion of India

The first Cabinet of independent India: (L to R sitting) B.R. Ambedkar, Rafi Ahmed Kidwai, Sardar Baldev Singh, Maulana Abul Kalam Azad, Jawaharlal Nehru, Rajendra Prasad, Sardar Patel, John Mathai, Jagjivan Ram, Amrit Kaur and Syama Prasad Mukherjee. (L to R standing) Khurshed Lal, R.R. Diwakar, Mohanlal Saksena, N. Gopalaswami Ayyangar, N.V. Gadgil, K. C. Neogy, Jairamdas Daulatram, K. Santhanam, Satya Narayan Sinha and B. V. Keskar.

A group photo of people accused in Gandhi's murder case. *Standing*: Shankar Kistaiya, Gopal Godse, Madanlal Pahwa, Digambar Badge (Approver). *Sitting*: Narayan Apte, Vinayak D. Savarkar, Nathuram Godse, Vishnu Karkare.

Independent India's first years were marked with turbulent events – a massive exchange of population with Pakistan, the Indo-Pakistani War of 1947 and the integration of over 500 princely states to form a united nation. Credit for the political integration of India is largely attributed to Vallabhbhai Patel (deputy Prime Minister of India at the time),[835] who post-independence and before the death of Mahatma Gandhi teamed up with Jawaharlal Nehru and the Mahatma to ensure that the constitution of independent India would be secular.[836]

Partition of India

" "
I find no parallel in history for a body of converts and their descendants claiming to be a nation apart from the parent stock.

— Mahatma Gandhi, opposing the division of India on the basis of religion in 1944.

An estimated 3.5 million[837,838,839,840] Hindus and Sikhs living in West Punjab, North-West Frontier Province, Baluchistan, East Bengal and Sind migrated to India in fear of domination and suppression in Muslim Pakistan. Communal violence killed an estimated one million Hindus, Muslims and Sikhs, and gravely destabilised both dominions along their Punjab and Bengal boundaries, and the cities of Calcutta, Delhi and Lahore. The violence was stopped by early September owing to the co-operative efforts of both Indian and Pakistani leaders, and especially due to the efforts of Mohandas Gandhi, the leader of the Indian freedom struggle, who undertook a *fast-unto-death* in Calcutta and later in Delhi to calm people and emphasise peace despite the threat to his life. Both governments constructed large relief camps for incoming and leaving refugees, and the Indian Army was mobilised to provide humanitarian assistance on a massive scale.

The assassination of Mohandas Gandhi on 30 January 1948 was carried out by Nathuram Vinayak Godse, a Hindu nationalist, who held him responsible for partition and charged that Mohandas Gandhi was appeasing Muslims. More than one million people flooded the streets of Delhi to follow the procession to cremation grounds and pay their last respects.

In 1949, India recorded almost 1 million Hindu refugees into West Bengal and other states from East Pakistan, owing to communal violence, intimidation and repression from Muslim authorities. The plight of the refugees outraged Hindus and Indian nationalists, and the refugee population drained the resources of Indian states, who were unable to absorb them. While not ruling out war, Prime Minister Nehru and Sardar Patel invited Liaquat Ali Khan for talks in Delhi. Although many Indians termed this appeasement, Nehru signed a pact with Liaquat Ali Khan that pledged both nations to the protection of minorities and creation of minority commissions. Although opposed to the principle, Patel decided to back this pact for the sake of peace, and played a critical role in garnering support from West Bengal and across India, and enforcing the provisions of the pact. Khan and Nehru also signed a trade agreement, and committed to resolving bilateral disputes through peaceful means. Steadily, hundreds of thousands of Hindus returned to East Pakistan, but the thaw in relations did not last long, primarily owing to the Kashmir dispute.

Integration of princely states

Sardar Vallabhbhai Patel as Minister for Home and States Affairs had the responsibility of welding the British Indian provinces and the princely states into a united India.

General El Edroos (at right) offers his surrender of the Hyderabad State Forces to Major General (later General and Army Chief) Joyanto Nath Chaudhuri at Secunderabad.

Queen Kanchan Prabha Devi of the Kingdom of Tripura signed the instrument of accession to India. She played a pivotal role in rehabilitating refugees and victims of the violence associated with the Partition of India in the state of Tripura.

Sheikh Mohammed Abdullah (right), chosen to head the emergency interim government in Kashmir after Maharaja Hari Singh signed Kashmir's Instrument of Accession to India.

British India consisted of 17 provinces and 562 princely states. The provinces were given to India or Pakistan, in some cases in particular — Punjab and Bengal — after being partitioned. The princes of the princely states, however, were given the right to either remain independent or join either dominion. Thus India's leaders were faced with the prospect of inheriting a fragmented nation with independent provinces and kingdoms dispersed across the mainland. Under the leadership of Sardar Vallabhbhai Patel, the new Government of India employed political negotiations backed with the option (and, on several occasions, the use) of military action to ensure the primacy of the central government and of the Constitution then being drafted. Sardar Patel and V. P. Menon convinced the rulers of princely states contiguous to India to accede to India. Many rights and privileges of the rulers of the princely states, especially their personal estates and privy purses, were guaranteed to convince them to accede. Some of them were made Rajpramukh (governor) and Uprajpramukh (deputy governor) of the merged states. Many small princely states were merged to form viable administrative states such as Saurashra, PEPSU, Vindhya Pradesh and Madhya Bharat. Some princely states such as Tripura and Manipur acceded later in 1949.

There were three states that proved more difficult to integrate than others:

1. Junagadh (Hindu majority state with a Muslim nawab) – a December 1947 plebiscite resulted in a 99% vote to merge with India, annulling the controversial accession to Pakistan, which was made by the Nawab against the wishes of the people of the state who were overwhelmingly Hindu and despite Junagadh not being contiguous with Pakistan.
2. Hyderabad (Hindu majority state with a Muslim nizam)– Patel ordered the Indian army to depose the government of the Nizam, code named Operation Polo, after the failure of negotiations, which was done between 13–17 September 1948. It was incorporated as a state of India the next year.
3. The area of Kashmir (Muslim majority state with a Hindu king) in the far north of the subcontinent quickly became a source of controversy that erupted into the First Indo-Pakistani War which lasted from 1947 to 1949. Eventually a United Nations-overseen ceasefire was agreed that left India in control of two-thirds of the contested region. Jawaharlal Nehru initially agreed to Mountbatten's proposal that a plebiscite be held in the entire state as soon as hostilities ceased, and a UN-sponsored cease-fire was agreed to by both parties on 1 Jan. 1949. No statewide plebiscite was held, however, for in 1954, after Pakistan began to receive arms from the United States, Nehru withdrew his support. The Indian Constitution came into force in Kashmir on 26 January 1950 with special clauses for the state.

Figure 164: *Indian soldiers during the Indo-Pakistani War of 1947.*

Constitution

The Constituent Assembly adopted the Constitution of India, drafted by a committee headed by Dr. B. R. Ambedkar, on 26 November 1949. India became a sovereign democratic republic after its constitution came into effect on 26 January 1950. Dr. Rajendra Prasad became the first President of India. The three words 'socialist', 'secular' and 'integrity' were added later with the 42nd Constitution Amendment 1976.

Indo-Pakistani War of 1947–1948

The Indo-Pakistani War of 1947–1948 was fought between India and Pakistan over the princely state of Kashmir and Jammu from 1947 to 1948. It was the first of four Indo-Pakistan Wars fought between the two newly independent nations. Pakistan precipitated the war a few weeks after independence by launching tribal *lashkar* (militia) from Waziristan,[841] in an effort to secure Kashmir, the future of which hung in the balance. The inconclusive result of the war still affects the geopolitics of both countries.

Figure 165: *Jawaharlal Nehru, the first Prime Minister of India. He oversaw India's transition from a colony to a republic, while nurturing a plural, multi-party system. In foreign policy, he took a leading role in the Non-Aligned Movement while projecting India as a regional hegemon in South Asia.*

1950s and 1960s

India held its first national elections under the Constitution in 1952, where a turnout of over 60% was recorded. The National Congress Party won an overwhelming majority, and Jawaharlal Nehru began a second term as Prime Minister. President Prasad was also elected to a second term by the electoral college of the first Parliament of India.

Nehru administration (1952–1964)

Prime Minister Nehru led the Congress to major election victories in 1957 and 1962. The Parliament passed extensive reforms that increased the legal rights of women in Hindu society, and further legislated against caste discrimination and untouchability.[842] Nehru advocated a strong initiative to enroll India's children to complete primary education, and thousands of schools, colleges and institutions of advanced learning, such as the Indian Institutes of Technology, were founded across the nation.[843] Nehru advocated a socialist model for the economy of India — Five-Year Plans were shaped by the Soviet model

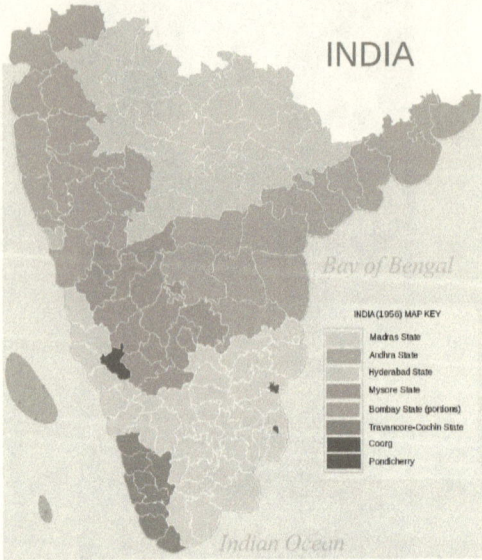

Figure 166: *South Indian states prior to the States Reorganisation Act.*

based on centralised and integrated national economic programs[844] — no taxation for Indian farmers, minimum wage and benefits for blue-collar workers, and the nationalisation of heavy industries such as steel, aviation, shipping, electricity and mining. Village common lands were seized, and an extensive public works and industrialisation campaign resulted in the construction of major dams, irrigation canals, roads, thermal and hydroelectric power stations and many more.[842]

States reorganisation

Potti Sreeramulu's *fast-unto-death*, and consequent death for the demand of an Andhra State in 1953 sparked a major re-shaping of the Indian Union. Nehru appointed the States Re-organisation Commission, upon whose recommendations the States Reorganisation Act was passed in 1956. Old states were dissolved and new states created on the lines of shared linguistic and ethnic demographics. The separation of Kerala and the Telugu-speaking regions of Madras State enabled the creation of an exclusively Tamil-speaking state of Tamil Nadu. On 1 May 1960, the states of Maharashtra and Gujarat were created out of the bilingual Bombay State, and on 1 November 1966, the larger Punjab state was divided into the smaller, Punjabi-speaking Punjab and Haryanvi-speaking Haryana states.

Foreign policy and military conflicts

Military conflicts

Nehru's foreign policy was the inspiration of the Non-Aligned Movement, of which India was a co-founder. Nehru maintained friendly relations with both the United States and the Soviet Union, and encouraged the People's Republic of China to join the global community of nations. In 1956, when the Suez Canal Company was seized by the Egyptian government, an international conference voted 18-4 to take action against Egypt. India was one of the four backers of Egypt, along with Indonesia, Sri Lanka, and the USSR. India had opposed the partition of Palestine and the 1956 invasion of the Sinai by Israel, the United Kingdom and France, but did not oppose the Chinese direct control over Tibet, and the suppression of a pro-democracy movement in Hungary by the Soviet Union. Although Nehru disavowed nuclear ambitions for India, Canada and France aided India in the development of nuclear power stations for electricity. India also negotiated an agreement in 1960 with Pakistan on the just use of the waters of seven rivers shared by the countries. Nehru had visited Pakistan in 1953, but owing to political turmoil in Pakistan, no headway was made on the Kashmir dispute.

1. India has fought a total of four wars/military conflicts with its rival nation Pakistan, two in this period. In the Indo-Pakistani War of 1947, fought over the disputed territory of Kashmir, Pakistan captured one-third of Kashmir (which India claims as its territory), and India reclaimed three-fifths (which Pakistan claims as its territory). In the Indo-Pakistani War of 1965, India attacked Pakistan on all fronts after attempts by Pakistani troops to infiltrate Indian-controlled Kashmir.
2. In 1961, after continual petitions for a peaceful handover, India invaded and annexed the Portuguese colony of Goa on the west coast of India.
3. In 1962 China and India engaged in the brief Sino-Indian War over the border in the Himalayas. The war was a complete rout for the Indians and led to a refocusing on arms build-up and an improvement in relations with the United States. China withdrew from disputed territory in what is to China South Tibet, and to India part of the North-East Frontier Agency that it crossed during the war. Unrelated to that war, India disputes China's sovereignty over the smaller Aksai Chin territory that it controls on the western part of the Sino-Indian border.

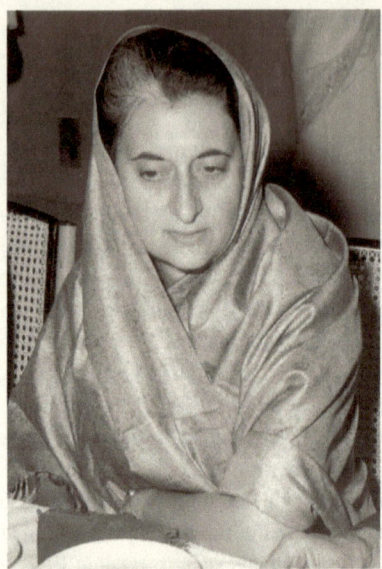

Figure 167: *Nehru's daughter Indira Gandhi served as prime minister for three consecutive terms (1966–77) and a fourth term (1980–84).*

Post-Nehru India

Jawaharlal Nehru died on 27 May 1964. Lal Bahadur Shastri succeeded him as Prime Minister. In 1965 in the Second Kashmir War India and Pakistan again went to war over Kashmir, but without any definitive outcome or alteration of the Kashmir boundary. The Tashkent Agreement was signed under the mediation of the Soviet government, but Shastri died on the night after the signing ceremony. A leadership election resulted in the elevation of Indira Gandhi, Nehru's daughter who had been serving as Minister for Information and Broadcasting, as the third Prime Minister. She defeated right-wing leader Morarji Desai. The Congress Party won a reduced majority in the 1967 elections owing to widespread disenchantment over rising prices of commodities, unemployment, economic stagnation and a food crisis. Indira Gandhi had started on a rocky note after agreeing to a devaluation of the rupee, which created much hardship for Indian businesses and consumers, and the import of wheat from the United States fell through due to political disputes.

Morarji Desai entered Gandhi's government as Deputy Prime Minister and Finance Minister, and with senior Congress politicians attempted to constrain Gandhi's authority. But following the counsel of her political advisor P. N.

Figure 168: *Indian aircraft carrier INS Vikrant launches an Alize aircraft during the Indo-Pakistan War of 1971.*

Haksar, Gandhi resuscitated her popular appeal by a major shift towards socialist policies. She successfully ended the Privy Purse guarantee for former Indian royalty, and waged a major offensive against party hierarchy over the nationalisation of India's banks. Although resisted by Desai and India's business community, the policy was popular with the masses. When Congress politicians attempted to oust Gandhi by suspending her Congress membership, Gandhi was empowered with a large exodus of Members of Parliament to her own Congress (R). The bastion of the Indian freedom struggle, the Indian National Congress, had split in 1969. Gandhi continued to govern with a slim majority.

1970s

In 1971, Indira Gandhi and her Congress (R) were returned to power with a massively increased majority. The nationalisation of banks was carried out, and many other socialist economic and industrial policies enacted. India intervened in the Bangladesh War of Independence, a civil war taking place in Pakistan's Bengali half, after millions of refugees had fled the persecution of the Pakistani army. The clash resulted in the independence of East Pakistan, which became known as Bangladesh, and Prime Minister Indira Gandhi's elevation to immense popularity. Relations with the United States grew strained,

Figure 169: *Rumtek Monastery in Sikkim. Sikkim became the 22nd state of the Indian Union.*

and India signed a 20-year treaty of friendship with the Soviet Union - breaking explicitly for the first time from non-alignment. In 1974, India tested its first nuclear weapon in the desert of Rajasthan, near Pokhran.

Annexation of Sikkim

In 1973, anti-royalist riots took place in the Kingdom of Sikkim. In 1975, the Prime Minister of Sikkim appealed to the Indian Parliament for Sikkim to become a state of India. In April of that year, the Indian Army took over the city of Gangtok and disarmed the Chogyal's palace guards. Thereafter, a referendum was held in which 97.5 per cent of voters supported abolishing the monarchy, effectively approving union with India.

India is said to have stationed 20,000–40,000 troops in a country of only 200,000 during the referendum. On 16 May 1975, Sikkim became the 22nd state of the Indian Union, and the monarchy was abolished. To enable the incorporation of the new state, the Indian Parliament amended the Indian Constitution. First, the 35th Amendment laid down a set of conditions that made Sikkim an "Associate State", a special designation not used by any other state. A month later, the 36th Amendment repealed the 35th Amendment, and made Sikkim a full state, adding its name to the First Schedule of the Constitution.

Formation of Northeastern states

In the Northeast India, the state of Assam was divided into several states beginning in 1970 within the borders of what was then Assam. In 1963, the Naga Hills district became the 16th state of India under the name of Nagaland. Part of Tuensang was added to Nagaland. In 1970, in response to the demands of the Khasi, Jaintia and Garo people of the Meghalaya Plateau, the districts embracing the Khasi Hills, Jaintia Hills, and Garo Hills were formed into an autonomous state within Assam; in 1972 this became a separate state under the name of Meghalaya. In 1972, Arunachal Pradesh (the North East Frontier Agency) and Mizoram (from the Mizo Hills in the south) were separated from Assam as union territories; both became states in 1986.

Green revolution and Operation Flood

The state of Punjab led India's Green Revolution and earned the distinction of being the country's bread basket.[845]

Amul Dairy Plant at Anand, Gujarat, was a highly successful co-operative started during Operation Flood in the 1970s.

India's population passed the 500 million mark in the early 1970s, but its long-standing food crisis was resolved with greatly improved agricultural productivity due to the Green Revolution. The government sponsored modern agricultural implements, new varieties of generic seeds, and increased financial assistance to farmers that increased the yield of food crops such as wheat, rice and corn, as well as commercial crops like cotton, tea, tobacco and coffee. Increased agricultural productivity expanded across the states of the Indo-Gangetic Plain and the Punjab.

Under Operation Flood, the government encouraged the production of milk, which increased greatly, and improved rearing of livestock across India. This enabled India to become self-sufficient in feeding its own population, ending two decades of food imports.

Figure 170: *The Indo-Pakistani War of 1971 concluded with Lieutenant-General A. A. K. Niazi, the commander of Pakistan Eastern Command, signing the instrument of surrender in Dhaka on 16 Dec 1971, in the presence of India's Lt. Gen. Jagjit Singh Aurora. Standing immediately behind from left to right: Indian Navy Vice Admiral Krishnan, Indian Air Force Air Marshal Dewan, Indian Army Lt Gen Sagat Singh, Maj Gen JFR Jacob (with Flt Lt Krishnamurthy peering over his shoulder). Veteran newscaster Surojit Sen of All India Radio is seen holding a microphone on the right.*

Indo-Pakistan War of 1971

The Indo-Pakistani War of 1971 was the third in four wars fought between the two nations. In this war, fought over the issue of self rule in East Pakistan, India decisively defeated Pakistan, resulting in the creation of Bangladesh.

Indian Emergency

Economic and social problems, as well as allegations of corruption, caused increasing political unrest across India, culminating in the Bihar Movement. In 1974, the Allahabad High Court found Indira Gandhi guilty of misusing government machinery for election purposes. Opposition parties conducted nationwide strikes and protests demanding her immediate resignation. Various political parties united under Jaya Prakash Narayan to resist what he termed Gandhi's dictatorship. Leading strikes across India that paralysed its economy and administration, Narayan even called for the Army to oust Gandhi. In 1975, Gandhi advised President Fakhruddin Ali Ahmed to declare a state of emergency under the constitution, which allowed the central government to assume sweeping powers to defend law and order in the nation. Explaining the breakdown of law and order and threat to national security as her primary reasons, Gandhi suspended many civil liberties and postponed elections at national and state levels. Non-Congress governments in Indian states were dismissed, and nearly 1,000 opposition political leaders and activists were imprisoned and a programme of compulsory birth control introduced.[846] Strikes and public protests were outlawed in all forms.

India's economy benefited from an end to paralysing strikes and political disorder. India announced a 20-point programme which enhanced agricultural and industrial production, increasing national growth, productivity and job growth. But many organs of government and many Congress politicians were accused of corruption and authoritarian conduct. Police officers were accused of arresting and torturing innocent people. Indira's son and political advisor, Sanjay Gandhi, was accused of committing gross excesses - Sanjay was blamed for the Health Ministry carrying out forced vasectomies of men and sterilisation of women as a part of the initiative to control population growth, and for the demolition of slums in Delhi near the Turkmen Gate, which left thousands of people dead and many more displaced.

Janata interlude

Indira Gandhi's Congress Party called for general elections in 1977, only to suffer a humiliating electoral defeat at the hands of the Janata Party, an amalgamation of opposition parties.[847] Morarji Desai became the first non-Congress Prime Minister of India. The Desai administration established tribunals to investigate Emergency-era abuses, and Indira and Sanjay Gandhi were arrested after a report from the Shah Commission.[848]

But in 1979, the coalition crumbled and Charan Singh formed an interim government. The Janata party had become intensely unpopular due to its internecine warfare, and a perceived lack of leadership on solving India's serious economic and social problems.

1980s

Indira Gandhi and her Congress Party splinter group, the Indian National Congress or simply "Congress", were swept back into power with a large majority in January 1980.

Figure 171: *Morarji Desai, the first non-Congress Prime Minister of India, signing the "New Delhi" declaration during a visit by US President Jimmy Carter.*

Figure 172: *Akal Takht and Harmandir Sahib (Golden Temple), was repaired by the Indian Government after Operation Blue Star.*

But the rise of an insurgency in Punjab would jeopardise India's security. In Assam, there were many incidents of communal violence between native villagers and refugees from Bangladesh, as well as settlers from other parts of India. When Indian forces, undertaking Operation Blue Star, raided the hideout of self-rule pressing Khalistan militants in the Golden Temple — Sikhs' most holy shrine — in Amritsar, the inadvertent deaths of civilians and damage to the temple building inflamed tensions in the Sikh community across India. The Government used intensive police operations to crush militant operations, but it resulted in many claims of abuse of civil liberties. Northeast India was paralysed owing to the ULFA's clash with Government forces.

On 31 October 1984, the Prime Minister's own Sikh bodyguards assassinated her, and 1984 anti-Sikh riots erupted in Delhi and parts of Punjab, causing the deaths of thousands of Sikhs along with terrible pillage, arson and rape. Senior members of the Congress Party have been implicated in stirring the violence against Sikhs. Government investigation has failed to date to discover the causes and punish the perpetrators, but public opinion blamed Congress leaders for directing attacks on Sikhs in Delhi.

Rajiv Gandhi administration

The Congress party chose Rajiv Gandhi, Indira's older son, as the next Prime Minister. Rajiv had been elected to Parliament only in 1982, and at 40, was the youngest national political leader and Prime Minister ever. But his youth and inexperience were an asset in the eyes of citizens tired of the inefficacy and corruption of career politicians, and looking for newer policies and a fresh start to resolve the country's long-standing problems. The Parliament was dissolved, and Rajiv led the Congress party to its largest majority in history (over 415 seats out of 545 possible), reaping a sympathy vote over his mother's assassination.

Rajiv Gandhi initiated a series of reforms - the Licence Raj was loosened, and government restrictions on foreign currency, travel, foreign investment and imports decreased considerably. This allowed private businesses to use resources and produce commercial goods without government bureaucracy interfering, and the influx of foreign investment increased India's national reserves. As Prime Minister, Rajiv broke from his mother's precedent to improve relations with the United States, which increased economic aid and scientific co-operation. Rajiv's encouragement of science and technology resulted in a major expansion of the telecommunications industry and India's space programme, and gave birth to the software industry and information technology sector.

Figure 173: *Victims of Bhopal disaster march demanding the extradition of American Warren Anderson from the United States.*

In December 1984, gas leaked out at the Union Carbide pesticides plant in the central Indian city of Bhopal. Thousands were killed immediately, while many more subsequently died or were left disabled.

India in 1987 brokered an agreement between the Government of Sri Lanka and agreed to deploy troops for peacekeeping operation in Sri Lanka's ethnic conflict led by the LTTE. Rajiv sent Indian troops to enforce the agreement and disarm the Tamil rebels, but the Indian Peace Keeping Force, as it was known, became entangled in outbreaks of violence - ultimately ending up fighting the Tamil rebels itself, and becoming a target of attack from Sri Lankan nationalists. V. P. Singh withdrew the IPKF in 1990, but thousands of Indian soldiers had died. Rajiv's departure from Socialist policies did not sit well with the masses, who did not benefit from the innovations. Unemployment was a serious problem, and India's burgeoning population added ever-increasing needs for diminishing resources.

Rajiv Gandhi's image as an honest politician (he was nicknamed "Mr. Clean" by the press) was shattered when the Bofors scandal broke, revealing that senior government officials had taken bribes over defence contracts by a Swedish guns producer.

Janata Dal

General elections in 1989 gave Rajiv's Congress a plurality, a far cry from the majority which propelled him to power.

Power came instead to his former finance and defence minister, VP Singh of Janata Dal. Singh had been moved from the Finance ministry to the Defence ministry after he unearthed some scandals which made the Congress leadership uncomfortable. Singh then unearthed the Bofors scandal, and was sacked from the party and office. Becoming a popular crusader for reform and clean government, Singh led the Janata Dal coalition to a majority. He was supported by BJP and the leftist parties from outside. Becoming Prime Minister, Singh made an important visit to the Golden Temple shrine, to heal the wounds of the past. He started to implement the controversial Mandal Commission report, to increase the quota in reservation for low-caste Hindus. The BJP protested these implementations and took its support back, following which he resigned. Chandra Shekhar split to form the Janata Dal (Socialist), supported by Rajiv's Congress. This new government also collapsed in a matter of months, when Congress withdrew its support.

1990s

The then-Chief Minister of Jammu and Kashmir Farooq Abdullah (son of former Chief Minister Sheikh Abdullah) announced an alliance with the ruling Congress party for the elections of 1987. But, the elections were allegedly rigged in favour of him. This led to the rise of the armed Muslim insurgency in Jammu and Kashmir composed, in part, of those who unfairly lost elections. Pakistan supplied these groups with logistical support, arms, recruits and training.

Islamist militants in Kashmir tortured and killed local Kashmiri Pandits, who were Hindu, forcing them to leave Kashmir in large numbers. Around 90% of the Kashmiri Pandits left Kashmir during the 1990s, resulting in the ethnic cleansing of Kashmiri Hindus.

On 21 May 1991, while former Prime Minister Rajiv Gandhi campaigned in Tamil Nadu on behalf of Congress (Indira), a Liberation Tigers of Tamil Eelam (LTTE) female suicide bomber assassinated him and many others, setting off the bomb in her belt by leaning forward while garlanding him. In the elections, Congress (Indira) won 244 parliamentary seats and put together a coalition, returning to power under the leadership of P.V. Narasimha Rao. This Congress-led government, which served a full five-year term, initiated a gradual process of economic liberalisation and reform, which has opened the Indian economy to global trade and investment. India's domestic politics also took new shape,

Figure 174: *The stone mosaic that stands at the exact location where Rajiv Gandhi was assassinated in Sriperumbudur.*

as traditional alignments by caste, creed, and ethnicity gave way to a plethora of small, regionally-based political parties.

But India was rocked by communal violence (see Bombay riots) between Hindus and Muslims that killed over 10,000 people, following the Babri Mosque demolition by Hindu extremists in the course of the Ram Janmabhoomi dispute in Ayodhya in 1992. The final months of the Rao-led government in the spring of 1996 suffered the effects of several major political corruption scandals, which contributed to the worst electoral performance by the Congress Party in its history as the Hindu nationalist Bharatiya Janata Party emerged as the largest single party.

Economic reforms

P. V. Narasimha Rao

Manmohan Singh

Economic liberalisation in India was initiated in 1991 by Prime Minister P. V. Narasimha Rao and his then-Finance Minister Dr. Manmohan Singh. Rao was often referred to as *Chanakya* for his ability to steer tough economic and political legislation through the parliament at a time when he headed a minority government.[849]

Under the policies initiated by late Prime Minister P. V. Narasimha Rao and his then-Finance Minister Dr. Manmohan Singh, India's economy expanded rapidly. The economic reforms were a reaction to an impending balance of payment crisis. The Rao administration initiated the privatisation of large, inefficient, and loss-inducing government corporations. The UF government had attempted a progressive budget that encouraged reforms, but the 1997 Asian financial crisis and political instability created economic stagnation. The Vajpayee administration continued with privatisation, reduction of taxes, a sound fiscal policy aimed at reducing deficits and debts, and increased initiatives for public works. Cities like Bangalore, Hyderabad, Pune, and Ahmedabad have risen in prominence and economic importance, becoming centres of rising industries and destinations for foreign investment and firms. Strategies like forming Special Economic Zones - tax amenities, good communications infrastructure, low regulation - to encourage industries has paid off in many parts of the country.

A rising generation of well-educated and skilled professionals in scientific sectors of industry began propelling the Indian economy, as the information technology industry took hold across India with the proliferation of computers. The new technologies increased the efficiency of activity in almost every type of industry, which also benefitted from the availability of skilled labor. Foreign investment and outsourcing of jobs to India's labor markets further enhanced India's economic growth. A large middle class has arisen across India, which has increased the demand, and thus production of a wide array of consumer goods. Unemployment is steadily declining, and poverty has fallen to approximately 22%. Gross Domestic Product growth increased to beyond 7%. While serious challenges remain, India is enjoying a period of economic expansion that has propelled it to the forefront of the world economy, and has correspondingly increased its influence in political and diplomatic terms.[850]

Figure 175: *Nuclear capable Agni-II ballistic missile. Since May 1998, India declared itself to be a full-fledged nuclear state.*

Era of coalitions

The Bharatiya Janata Party (BJP) emerged from the May 1996 national elections as the single-largest party in the Lok Sabha but without enough strength to prove a majority on the floor of that Parliament. Under Prime Minister Atal Bihari Vajpayee, the BJP coalition lasted in power 13 days. With all political parties wishing to avoid another round of elections, a 14-party coalition led by the Janata Dal emerged to form a government known as the United Front. A United Front government under former Chief Minister of Karnataka H.D. Deve Gowda lasted less than a year. The leader of the Congress Party withdrew support in March 1997. Inder Kumar Gujral replaced Deve Gowda as the consensus choice for Prime Minister of a 16-party United Front coalition.

In November 1997, the Congress Party again withdrew support for the United Front. New elections in February 1998 brought the BJP the largest number of seats in Parliament (182), but this fell far short of a majority. On 20 March 1998, the President inaugurated a BJP-led coalition government, with Vajpayee again serving as Prime Minister. On 11 and 13 May 1998, this government conducted a series of five underground nuclear weapons tests, known collectively as Pokhran-II — which caused Pakistan to conduct its own tests that same year.[851] India's nuclear tests prompted President of the United States Bill Clinton and Japan to impose economic sanctions on India pursuant to the

Figure 176: *Indian Army soldiers after winning a battle during the Kargil War.*

1994 Nuclear Proliferation Prevention Act and led to widespread international condemnation.

In the early months of 1999, Prime Minister Vajpayee made a historic bus trip to Pakistan and met with Pakistan's Prime Minister Nawaz Sharif, signing the bilateral Lahore peace declaration.

In April 1999, the coalition government led by the Bharatiya Janata Party (BJP) fell apart, leading to fresh elections in September. In May and June 1999, India discovered an elaborate campaign of terrorist infiltration that resulted in the Kargil War in Kashmir, derailing a promising peace process that had begun only three months earlier when Prime Minister Vajpayee visited Pakistan, inaugurating the Delhi-Lahore bus service. Indian forces killed Pakistan-backed infiltrators and reclaimed important border posts in high-altitude warfare.

Soaring on popularity earned following the successful conclusion of the Kargil conflict, the National Democratic Alliance - a new coalition led by the BJP - gained a majority to form a government with Vajpayee as Prime Minister in October 1999. The end of the millennium was devastating to India, as a cyclone hit Orissa, killing at least 10,000.

Figure 177: *Atal Bihari Vajpayee became the first non-Congress Prime Minister to complete a full term. His tenure saw rapid growth of infrastructure, improved diplomatic relationship with the United States, economic reforms, nuclear tests, several foreign policy and military victories.*

2000s

Under Bharatiya Janata Party

In 2000 May, India's population exceeded 1 billion. President of the United States Bill Clinton made a groundbreaking visit to India to improve ties between the two nations. In January, massive earthquakes hit Gujarat state, killing at least 30,000.

Prime Minister Vajpayee met with Pakistan's President Pervez Musharraf in the first summit between Pakistan and India in more than two years in the middle of 2001. But the meeting failed without a breakthrough or even a joint statement because of differences over Kashmir region.

Three new states — Chhattisgarh, Jharkhand and Uttarakhand (originally Uttaranchal) — were formed in November 2000.

The National Democratic Alliance government's credibility was adversely affected by a number of political scandals (such as allegations that the Defence Minister George Fernandes took bribes) as well as reports of intelligence failures that led to the Kargil incursions going undetected, and the apparent failure

Figure 178: *Section of Golden Quadrilateral highway. The project was launched in 2001 by NDA government led by Prime Minister Atal Bihari Vajpayee.*

of his talks with the Pakistani President. Following the 11 September attacks, the United States lifted sanctions which it had imposed against India and Pakistan in 1998. The move was seen as a reward for their support for the War on Terror. The tensions of an imminent war between India and Pakistan again rose by the heavy Indian firing on Pakistani military posts along the Line of Control and the subsequent deadly Indian Parliament attack and the 2001–02 India–Pakistan standoff.

In 2002, 59 Hindu pilgrims returning from Ayodhya were killed in a train fire in Godhra, Gujarat. This sparked off the 2002 Gujarat violence, leading to the deaths of 790 Muslims and 254 Hindus and with 223 people reported missing.

Throughout 2003, India's speedy economic progress, political stability and a rejuvenated peace initiative with Pakistan increased the government's popularity. India and Pakistan agreed to resume direct air links and to allow overflights, and a groundbreaking meeting was held between the Indian government and moderate Kashmir separatists. The Golden Quadrilateral project aimed to link India's corners with a network of modern highways.

Congress rule returns

In January 2004 Prime Minister Vajpayee recommended early dissolution of the Lok Sabha and general elections. The Congress Party-led alliance won a surprise victory in elections held in May 2004. Manmohan Singh became the Prime Minister, after the Congress President Sonia Gandhi (born Antonia Edvige Albina Maino), the widow of former Prime Minister Rajiv Gandhi, declined to take the office, in order to defuse the controversy about whether her foreign birth should be considered a disqualification for the Prime Minister's post. The Congress formed a coalition called the United Progressive Alliance with Socialist and regional parties, and enjoyed the outside support of India's Communist parties. Manmohan Singh became the first Sikh and non-Hindu to hold India's most powerful office. Singh continued economic liberalisation, although the need for support from Indian Socialists and Communists forestalled further privatisation for some time.[852]

By the end of 2004, India began to withdraw some of its troops from Kashmir. By the middle of the next year, the Srinagar–Muzaffarabad Bus service was inaugurated, the first in 60 years to operate between Indian-administered and Pakistani-administered Kashmirs. However, in May 2006, suspected Islamic extremist militants killed 35 Hindus in the worst attacks in Indian-administered Kashmir for several months.

The 2004 Indian Ocean earthquake and tsunami devastated Indian coastlines and islands, killing an estimated 18,000 and displacing around 650,000. The tsunami was caused by a powerful undersea earthquake off the Indonesian coast. Natural disasters such as the Mumbai floods (killing more than 1,000) and Kashmir earthquake (killing 79,000) hit the subcontinent in the next year. In February 2006, the United Progressive Alliance government launched India's largest-ever rural jobs scheme, aimed at lifting around 60 million families out of poverty.

The United States and India signed a major nuclear co-operation agreement during a visit by United States President George W. Bush in March 2006. According to the nuclear deal, the United States was to give India access to civilian nuclear technology while India agreed to greater scrutiny for its nuclear programme. Later United States approved a controversial law allowing India to buy their nuclear reactors and fuel for the first time in 30 years. In July 2008, the United Progressive Alliance survived a vote of confidence brought after left-wing parties withdrew their support over the nuclear deal. After the vote, several left-wing and regional parties formed a new alliance to oppose the government, saying it had been tainted by corruption. Within three months, following approval by the U.S. Congress, George W. Bush signed into law a nuclear deal with India, which ended a three-decade ban on American nuclear trade with Delhi.

Figure 179: *U.S. President George W. Bush and India's Prime Minister Manmohan Singh exchange handshakes in New Delhi on 2 March 2006 vis-à-vis the India–United States Civil Nuclear Agreement.*

In 2007 India got its first female President as Pratibha Patil was sworn in. Long associated with the Nehru–Gandhi family, Pratibha Patil was a low-profile governor of the state of Rajasthan before emerging as the favoured presidential candidate of Sonia Gandhi.[853] In February, the infamous Samjhauta Express bombings took place, killing Pakistani civilians in Panipat, Haryana. As of 2011, nobody had been charged for the crime, though it has been linked to Abhinav Bharat, a shadowy Hindu fundamentalist group headed by a former Indian army officer.[854] In 2008 October, India successfully launched its first mission to the Moon, the unmanned lunar probe called *Chandrayaan-1*. In the previous year, India had launched its first commercial space rocket, carrying an Italian satellite. In July 2009, the Delhi High Court decriminalised consensual homosexual sex, declaring the British Raj-era law, Section 377 of the Indian Penal Code, as unconstitutional.

In November 2008, Mumbai attacks took place. India blamed militants from Pakistan for the attacks and announced a "pause" in the ongoing peace process. In the Indian general election in 2009, the United Progressive Alliance won a convincing and resounding 262 seats, with Congress alone winning 206 seats. However, the Congress-led government faced many allegations of corruption. Inflation rose to an all-time high, and the ever-increasing prices of food commodities caused widespread agitation.

Figure 180: *A view of the Taj Mahal Palace Hotel with smoke during the 2008 Mumbai attack.*

21st-century India is facing the Naxalite-Maoist rebels, in the words of Prime Minister Manmohan Singh, India's "greatest internal security challenge",[855] and other terrorist tensions (such as Islamist terrorist campaigns in and out of Jammu & Kashmir and terrorism in India's Northeast).[856] Terrorism has increased in India, with bomb blasts in leading cities like Mumbai, New Delhi, Jaipur, Bangalore, and Hyderabad. In the new millennium, India improved relations with many countries and foreign unions including the United States, the European Union, Israel, and the People's Republic of China. The economy of India has grown at a very rapid pace. India is now being looked at as a potential superpower.

2010s

The concerns and controversies over the 2010 Commonwealth Games rocked the country in 2010, raising questions about the credibility of the government followed by the 2G spectrum case and Adarsh Housing Society scam. In mid-2011, Anna Hazare, a prominent social activist, staged a 12-day hunger strike in Delhi in protest at state corruption, after government proposals to tighten up anti-graft legislation fell short of his demands.

Figure 181: *The 2010 Commonwealth Games opening ceremony in Jawaharlal Nehru Stadium is one of the largest international multi-sport event to be staged in Delhi and India.*

Despite all this, India showed great promise with a higher growth rate in gross domestic product. In January 2011, India assumed a nonpermanent seat in the United Nations Security Council for the 2011-12 term. In 2004, India had launched an application for a permanent seat on the UN Security Council, along with Brazil, Germany and Japan. In March, India overtook China to become the world's largest importer of arms.

The Telangana movement reached its peak in 2011-12, leading to formation of India's 29th state, Telangana, in June 2014.

The 2012 Delhi gang rape case and subsequent protest by civil society resulted in changes in the laws related to rape and offences against women. In April 2013, the Saradha Group financial scandal was unearthed, caused by the collapse of a Ponzi scheme run by Saradha Group, a consortium of over 200 private companies in Eastern India, causing an estimated loss of INR 200–300 billion (US$4–6 billion) to over 1.7 million depositors. In December 2013, the Supreme Court of India overturned the Delhi High Court ruling on Sec 377, criminalising homosexual sex between consenting adults once again in the country.

In August 2010, cloudbursts and the ensuing flooding in the Ladakh region of North India resulted in the deaths of around 255 people, while affecting 9,000 people directly. In June 2013, a multi-day cloudburst in Uttarakhand and other north Indian states caused devastating floods and landslides, with

Figure 182: *2010 Ladakh floods damaged 71 towns and villages, including the main town in the area, Leh, and nearby town of Thiksey, where Thikse Monastery is located.*[857]

more than 5,700 people "presumed dead." In September 2014, floods in the state of Jammu and Kashmir, following heavy rains due to monsoon season, killed around 277 people and brought extensive damage to property. A further 280 people died in the neighbouring Pakistani regions, particularly in Pakistani Punjab.

In August - September 2013, clashes between Hindus and Muslims in Muzaffarnagar, Uttar Pradesh, resulted in at least 62 deaths, injured 93, and left more than 50,000 displaced.

In November 2013, India launched its first interplanetary mission, the Mars Orbiter Mission, popularly known as *Mangalyaan*, to Mars and, was successful, so ISRO on 24 September 2014, became the fourth space agency to reach Mars, after the Soviet space program, NASA, and the European Space Agency. ISRO also became the first space agency and India the first country to reach Mars on its maiden attempt.

2014 – Return of Bharatiya Janata Party (BJP) Government

The Hindutva movement advocating Hindu nationalism originated in the 1920s and has remained a strong political force in India. The major party of the religious right, Bharatiya Janata Party (BJP), since its foundation in 1980

Figure 183: *Artist's rendering of the Mars Orbiter Mission spacecraft.*

Figure 184: *Prime Minister Modi at the launch of the Make in India programme.*

won elections, and after a defeat in 2004 remained one of the leading forces against the coalition government of the Congress Party. The 16th national general election, held in early 2014, saw a dramatic victory of the BJP; it gained an absolute majority and formed a government under the premiership of Narendra Modi, a BJP leader and till then the Chief Minister of Gujarat. The Modi government's sweeping mandate and popularity helped the BJP win several State Assembly elections in India. The Modi government implemented several initiatives and campaigns to increase manufacturing and infrastructure — notably — Make in India, Digital India and Swachh Bharat Abhiyan.

Further reading

- Bipan Chandra, Mridula Mukherjee and Aditya Mukherjee. "India Since Independence"
- Bates, Crispin, and Subho Basu. *The Politics of Modern India since Independence* (Routledge/Edinburgh South Asian Studies Series) (2011)
- Brass, Paul R. *The Politics of India since Independence* (1980)
- Dalmia, Vasudha and Rashmi Sadana (editors) (2012). *The Cambridge Companion to Modern Indian Culture*[858]. Cambridge University Press.
- Dixit, Jyotindra Nath (2004). *Makers of India's foreign policy: Raja Ram Mohun Roy to Yashwant Sinha*[859]. HarperCollins.
- Frank, Katherine (2002). *Indira: The Life of Indira Nehru Gandhi*[860]. Houghton Mifflin. ISBN 9780395730973.
- Ghosh, Anjali (2009). *India's Foreign Policy*[861]. Pearson Education India. ISBN 9788131710258.
- Gopal, Sarvepalli. *Jawaharlal Nehru: A Biography, Volume Two, 1947-1956* (1979); *Jawaharlal Nehru: A Biography: 1956-64 Vol 3* (1985)
- Guha, Ramachandra (2011). *India After Gandhi: The History of the World's Largest Democracy*[862]. Pan Macmillan. ISBN 9780330540209. excerpt and text search[863]
- Guha, Ramachandra. *Makers of Modern India* (2011) excerpt and text search[864]
- Jain, B. M. (2009). *Global Power: India's Foreign Policy, 1947-2006*[865]. Lexington Books. ISBN 9780739121450.
- Kapila, Uma (2009). *Indian Economy Since Independence*[866]. Academic Foundation. p. 854. ISBN 9788171887088.
- McCartney, Matthew. *India – The Political Economy of Growth, Stagnation and the State, 1951-2007* (2009); *Political Economy, Growth and Liberalisation in India, 1991-2008* (2009) excerpt and text search[867]
- Mansingh, Surjit. *The A to Z of India* (The A to Z Guide Series) (2010)
- Nilekani, Nandan; and Thomas L. Friedman (2010). *Imagining India: The Idea of a Renewed Nation*[868]. Penguin. ISBN 9781101024546.
- Panagariya, Arvind (2010). *India: The Emerging Giant*[869]. Oxford University Press. ISBN 9780198042990.
- Tomlinson, B.R. *The Economy of Modern India 1860–1970* (1996) excerpt and text search[870]
- Zachariah, Benjamin. *Nehru* (Routledge Historical Biographies) (2004) excerpt and text search[871]

Primary sources

- Appadorai A., ed. *Select Documents on India's Foreign Policy and Relations* (Delhi: Oxford University Press, 1982)

External links

- [872] BBC India profile

1947-50

Dominion of India

India	
1947–1950	
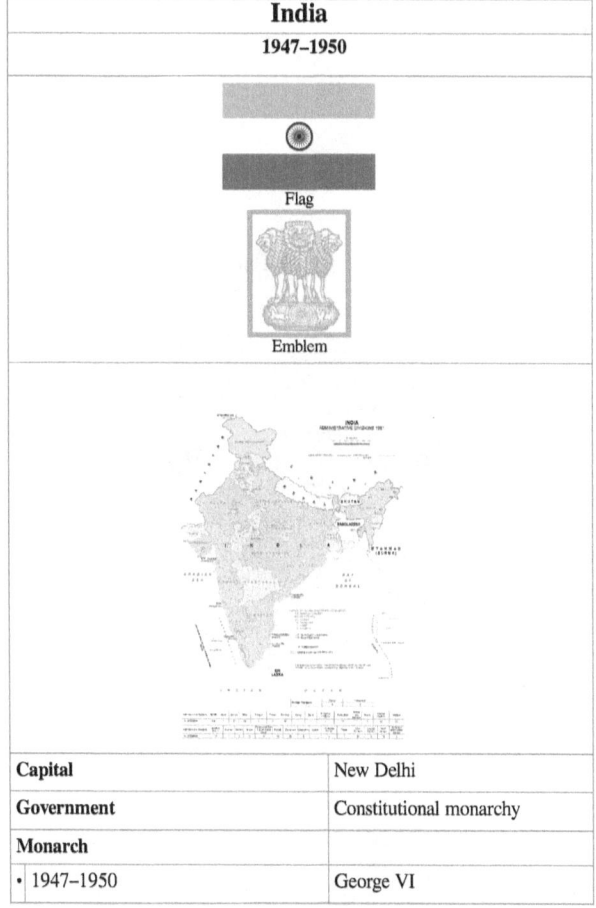	
Flag / Emblem	
Capital	New Delhi
Government	Constitutional monarchy
Monarch	
• 1947–1950	George VI

Governor-General	
• 1947–1948	Louis Mountbatten
• 1948–1950	Chakravarthy Rajagopalachari
Prime Minister	
• 1947–1950	Jawaharlal Nehru
Legislature	Constituent Assembly
History	
• Indian Independence Act	15 August 1947
• Indo-Pakistani War	22 October 1947
• Republican constitution adopted	26 January 1950
Area	
• 1950	3,287,263 km² (1,269,219 sq mi)
Currency	Indian rupee
Preceded by	**Succeeded by**
British Raj Interim Government of India	Republic of India

Part of **a series** on the
History of India

Between gaining independence from the United Kingdom on 15 August 1947 and the proclamation of a republic on 26 January 1950, **India** was an independent dominion in the British Commonwealth of Nations with King George VI as its head of state. Although the country shared its head of state with the United Kingdom, it was a fully sovereign independent state. It was created by the Indian Independence Act 1947 and was transformed into the Republic of India by the promulgation of the Constitution of India in 1950.

The king was represented by the Governor-General of India. However, the governor-general was not designated *viceroy*, as had been customary under the British Raj. The office of Viceroy was abolished on Indian independence. Two governors-general held office in India between independence and its transformation into a republic: Lord Mountbatten of Burma (1947–48) and Chakravarti Rajagopalachari (1948–50). Jawaharlal Nehru was Prime Minister of India throughout this period.

History

Partition of India

The Partition of British India on 15 August 1947[874] led to the creation of two sovereign states, both dominions: Pakistan (which later split into the Islamic Republic of Pakistan and the People's Republic of Bangladesh in 1971) and India (later the Republic of India).

Since the 1920s the Indian independence movement had been demanding *Pūrṇa Swarāj* (complete self-rule) for the Indian nation and the establishment of the Dominion of India and the Dominion of Pakistan was a major victory for the Swarajis. Nevertheless, the Partition was controversial among the people, and resulted in significant political instability and displacement.

Aftermath

Most of the 552 princely states within Indian territory acceded to the Dominion of India due to the work of the civil servant V. P. Menon. The Hindu-majority Junagadh State located in modern-day Gujarat attempted to accede to Pakistan under the Muslim Nawab Muhammad Mahabat Khanji III. It was annexed militarily by the Indian government. Similarly, the State of Hyderabad sought to remain independent and was also annexed by India in 1948.

Conflict with Pakistan

The newly created states of Pakistan and India both joined the Commonwealth, a platform for cooperation between the countries that had been part of the British Empire. Nevertheless, they soon found themselves at war beginning in October 1947, over the contested princely state of Jammu and Kashmir. Pakistani militants entered the state, alarming Maharaja Hari Singh who appealed to India for military intervention, in exchange for the signing of the Instrument of Accession and annexation into India. The region is contested to this day and two other Indo-Pakistan wars occurred as part of the Kashmir conflict.

Hostilities and Mahatma Gandhi's attempt to reconcile the two nations via a fast led to his assassination in 1948 by Nathuram Godse, further increasing tensions between the two new states.

The Dominion of India began working towards a constitution based on liberal democracy immediately after independence.

Republic of India

The Constituent Assembly adopted the Constitution of India, drafted by a committee headed by B. R. Ambedkar, on 26 November 1949. India became a federal, democratic republic after its constitution came into effect on 26 January 1950, henceforth celebrated as Republic Day. The governmental structure was similar to that of the United Kingdom but within a federal system. Rajendra Prasad became the first President of India.

Government

Monarchy

The sovereign and head of state of the dominion of India was a hereditary monarch, George VI, who was also the sovereign of the United Kingdom and the other dominions in the British Commonwealth of Nations. His constitutional roles were mostly carried out by the Governor-General of India. The royal succession was governed by the Act of Settlement 1701.

The monarchy was abolished on 26 January 1950, when India became a republic within the Commonwealth, the first Commonwealth country to do so.

List of monarchs

The King in relation to independent India held the following official style and titles:

- 15 August 1947 to 22 June 1948: *His Majesty George the Sixth, by the Grace of God, of Great Britain, Ireland and the British Dominions beyond the Seas King, Defender of the Faith, Emperor of India*[875]
- 22 June 1948 to 26 January 1950: *His Majesty George the Sixth, by the Grace of God, of Great Britain, Ireland and the British Dominions beyond the Seas King, Defender of the Faith*[876]

Portrait	Name	Birth	Death	Monarch From	Monarch Until	Relationship with Predecessor(s)
House of Windsor							
	King George VI	14 December 1895	6 February 1952	15 August 1947	26 January 1950	Son of George V, Emperor of India

List of Governors-General

Name (birth–death)	Picture	Took office	Left office	Appointer
Governors-General India, 1947–1950				
The Viscount Mountbatten of Burma[877] (1900–1979)		15 August 1947	21 June 1948	George VI
Chakravarti Rajagopalachari (1878–1972)		21 June 1948	26 January 1950	

Figure 185: *Standard of the Governor-General (1947–1950)*

List of Prime Ministers

№	Name (birth–death); constituency	Portrait	Party (*Alliance*)	Term of office		Elections (Lok Sabha)	Council of Ministers	Appointed by
1	Jawaharlal Nehru (1889–1964) MP for Phulpur		Indian National Congress	15 August 1947	26 January 1950	—	Nehru I	Lord Mountbatten

References

 Wikimedia Commons has media related to *Partition of India*.

Constitution of India

<indicator name="pp-default"> 🔒 </indicator>

Constitution of India	
 The original text[878] of the preamble	
Original title	भारतीय संविधान *(IAST:* Bhāratīya Saṃvidhāna)[879]
Jurisdiction	Whole of India
Ratified	November 26, 1949
Date effective	January 26, 1950
System	Constitutional parliamentary socialist secular republic
Branches	3 (Executive, legislature and judiciary)
Chambers	2 (Rajya Sabha and Lok Sabha)
Executive	Prime minister-led cabinet responsible to the lower house of the parliament
Judiciary	Supreme court, high courts and district courts
Federalism	Unitary (Quasi-federal)
Electoral college	Yes, for presidential and vice-presidential elections
Entrenchments	2
Amendments	101
Last amended	1 July 2017 (101st)

Location	Parliament House, New Delhi, India
Author(s)	B. R. Ambedkar and the drafting committee of the Constituent Assembly of India
Signatories	284 members of the Constituent Assembly
Supersedes	Government of India Act 1935 Indian Independence Act 1947

Part of a series on
Constitution of India

सत्यमेव जयते

Preamble

- v
- t
- e^{880}

The **Constitution of India** (IAST: *Bhāratīya Saṃvidhāna*) is the supreme law of India. The document lays down the framework demarcating fundamental political code, institutes the structure, procedures, powers and duties of government institutions and sets out fundamental rights, directive principles and the duties of citizens. It is the longest written constitution of any sovereign country in the world. B. R. Ambedkar, the chairman of the drafting committee, is widely considered to be its chief architect.

It imparts constitutional supremacy and not parliamentary supremacy, as it is not created by the parliament, but by a constituent assembly, and adopted by its people with a declaration in its preamble. The parliament cannot override the constitution.

It was adopted by the Constituent Assembly of India on 26 November 1949, and came into effect on 26 January 1950. With its adoption, it replaced the Government of India Act, 1935 as the country's fundamental governing document, and the Dominion of India became the modern and contemporary Republic of India. To ensure constitutional autochthony, the framers of the constitution repealed the prior Acts of the UK parliament via Article 395 of the

Figure 186: *Babasaheb Ambedkar, chairman of the drafting committee, presenting the final draft of the Indian constitution to Constituent Assembly president Rajendra Prasad on 25 November 1949*

constitution. India celebrates its coming into force on 26 January each year as Republic Day.

The constitution declares India a sovereign, socialist, secular, democratic republic, assuring its citizens of justice, equality, and liberty, and endeavours to promote fraternity among them.

Background

The major portion of the Indian subcontinent was under British rule from 1857 to 1947. The Constitution of India repealed the Indian Independence Act 1947 and Government of India Act, 1935 when it came into effect on 26 January 1950; India also ceased to be a dominion of the British Crown and became a sovereign democratic republic after the constitution's commencement. The date of 26 January was chosen to commemorate the anniversary Purna Swaraj of 1930.Wikipedia:Citation needed

Articles 5, 6, 7, 8, 9, 60, 324, 366, 367, 379, 380, 388, 391, 392, 393 and 394 of the constitution came into force on 26 November 1949 and the remaining articles on 26 January 1950.

Figure 187: *A meeting of the Constituent Assembly of India, 1950 CE*

Previous legislation used as sources

It is drawn from many sources. Keeping in mind the needs and conditions of India its framers borrowed different features freely from previous legislation *viz.* Government of India Act 1858, Indian Councils Act 1861, Indian Councils Act 1892, Indian Councils Act 1909, Government of India Act 1919, Government of India Act 1935 and the Indian Independence Act 1947. The last legislation which led to the creation of the two independent nations of India and Pakistan provided for the division of the erstwhile Constituent Assembly into two, with each new assembly having sovereign powers transferred to it, to enable each to draft and enact a new constitution, for the separate states.

Constituent assembly

The constitution was drafted by the Constituent Assembly, which was elected by elected members of the provincial assemblies. The 389-member — which was reduced to 299 after the partition of India — Constituent Assembly took almost three years to complete its task of drafting the constitution for an independent India, during which, it held eleven sessions over 165 days. Of these, 114 days were spent on the consideration of the draft constitution.Wikipedia:Citation needed

Membership and structure

B.R. Ambedkar, Sanjay Phakey, Jawaharlal Nehru, C. Rajagopalachari, Rajendra Prasad, Vallabhbhai Patel, Kanaiyalal Maneklal Munshi, Ganesh Vasudev Mavalankar, Sandipkumar Patel, Abul Kalam Azad, Shyama Prasad Mukherjee, Nalini Ranjan Ghosh, and Balwantrai Mehta were some key figures in the assembly. There were more than 30 members of the scheduled classes. Frank Anthony was the representative of the Anglo-Indian community, the Parsis were represented by H. P. Modi. A vice president of the assembly, Harendra Coomar Mookerjee was made the chairman of the minorities committee, a Christian, Mookerjee also represented non-Anglo-Indian Christians. Ari Bahadur Gurung was the Gorkha community's representative. Noted jurists like Alladi Krishnaswamy Iyer, Benegal Narsing Rau and K. M. Munshi, Ganesh Mavlankar were members of the assembly. Prominent women members of the assembly included Sarojini Naidu, Hansa Mehta, Durgabai Deshmukh, Amrit Kaur and Vijaya Lakshmi Pandit.

The first temporary, two-day president of the Constituent Assembly was Sachchidananda Sinha. Later, Rajendra Prasad was elected president of the Constituent Assembly. The members of the assembly met for the first time on 9 December 1946.

Drafting

Benegal Narsing Rau, a civil servant who later became the first Indian judge in the International Court of Justice and also served as the United Nations Security Council's president, was appointed as the constitutional adviser to the Constituent Assembly in formulating the Indian constitution in 1946. He was responsible for the general structure of the constitution and prepared its initial draft in February 1948.

On 14 August 1947 meeting of the Assembly, it was proposed that committees be formed. In all, the work of the assembly was overseen by five committees, the drafting committee, the committee on fundamental rights, the union powers committee, the minorities committee and union constitution committee.Wikipedia:Citation needed

Rau's draft was then considered, debated and amended by the drafting committee, appointed on 29 August 1947 with B. R. Ambedkar as its chairman, it had seven other members and was assisted by the constitutional advisor. The drafting committee's members were United Provinces chief minister Govind Ballabh Pant; former Bombay Presidency home minister Kanaiyalal Maneklal Munshi; former Madras State advocate general Alladi Krishnaswamy Iyer; former Jammu and Kashmir prime minister, N Gopalaswami Ayyangar; former Indian advocate general B. L. Mitter; former Assam prime minister and Muslim League politician Muhammed Saadulah; and D. P. Khaitan.Wikipedia:Citation needed Later, B. L. Mitter resigned and was replaced by Madhav Rao, a former legal adviser of the Maharaja of Baroda.Wikipedia:Citation needed On D. P. Khaitan's death, Congress politician and a member of the Madras Legislative Assembly, T. T. Krishnamachari was included in the drafting committee.Wikipedia:Citation needed A revised draft constitution was prepared by the committee and submitted to the assembly on 4 November 1947.

While deliberating upon the revised draft constitution, the assembly moved, discussed and disposed of as many as 2,473 amendments out of a total of 7,635 tabled. Before adopting the constitution, the Constituent Assembly held eleven sessions over 165 days. On 26 November 1949, the process was completed and the Constituent Assembly adopted the constitution. 284 members signed the document and the process of constitution making was complete. This day is celebrated as National Law Day,[881] or, Constitution Day.[882]

The assembly's final session convened on 24 January 1950 in which each member of the assembly signed two copies of the document, one each in Hindi and English. The original Constitution of India is hand-written and illustrated-calligraphed, with each page being beautified and decorated by artists from Shantiniketan including Beohar Rammanohar Sinha and Nandalal Bose. The illustrations on the cover and pages represent styles from the different civilisations of the subcontinent, ranging from the prehistoric Indus Valley Civilisation to the present.Wikipedia:Citation needed The calligraphy in the book was done by Prem Behari Narain Raizada. It was published in Dehradun and photolithographed at the offices of Survey of India. The entire exercise to produce the original took nearly five years. Two days later, on 26 January 1950, the Constitution of India became the law of all the states and union territories of India. Rs. 6.3 crore (63 million) was the official estimate of expenditure on constituent assembly. The constitution has undergone many amendments since its enactment.

The original 1950 Constitution of India is preserved in helium-filled cases in the Parliament House, New Delhi. There are two original versions of the constitution — one in Hindi and the other in English. The original constitution can be viewed here[883].

Influence of other constitutions

UK constitution
- Parliamentary form of government.
- The idea of single citizenship.
- The idea of the rule of law.
- The institution of speaker and its role.
- Lawmaking procedure.
- The procedure established by law.

United States Constitution
- United States Bill of Rights.
- The federal structure of government.
- Electoral College.
- Independence of the judiciary and separation of powers among the three branches of the government.
- Judicial review.
- President as supreme commander of armed forces.
- Equal protection under the law.

Irish constitution
- Directive principles of state policy.

Australian constitution
- Freedom of trade and commerce within the country and between the states.
- Power of the national legislature to make laws for implementing treaties, even on matters outside normal federal jurisdiction.
- Concurrent List.
- Terminology for the Preamble.

French constitution
- Ideals of liberty, equality and fraternity.

Canadian constitution
- A quasi-federal form of government — a federal system with a strong central government.
- Distribution of powers between the central government and state governments.
- Residual powers retained by the central government.Wikipedia:Identifying reliable sources

USSR constitution
- Fundamental Duties under article 51-A.
- A mandated Planning Commission to oversee the development of the economy.

Other constitutions
- The emergency provision under article 356 from the Weimar Constitution (Germany).
- Amendment of the constitution from South Africa.
- The due procedure of the law from Japan.

Structure

The Indian constitution is the world's longest for a sovereign nation.[884] At its commencement, it had 395 articles in 22 parts and 8 schedules. It is made up of approximately 145,000 words, making it the second longest active constitution — after the Constitution of Alabama — in the world.

In its current form, it has a preamble, 448 articles,[885] which are grouped into 25 parts,[886]; it also has 12 schedules,[887] and 5 appendices, and has been amended 101 times, the latest of which came into force on 1 July 2017.

Parts

The individual articles of the constitution are grouped together into the following parts:

Figure 188: *Jawaharlal Nehru signing the constitution*

- **Preamble**
  with the words "socialist" and "secular" added to it in 1976 by the 42nd constitutional amendment.
- **Part I**[888] – Union and its Territory
- **Part II**[889] – Citizenship.
- **Part III** – Fundamental Rights
- **Part IV**[890] – Directive Principles of State Policy
- **Part IVA** – Fundamental Duties
- **Part V**[891] – The Union
- **Part VI**[892] – The States
- **Part VII**[893] – States in the B part of the First schedule *(repealed)*
- **Part VIII**[894] – The Union Territories
- **Part IX**[895] – The Panchayats
- **Part IXA**[896] – The Municipalities
- **Part IXB** – The Co-operative Societies.[897]
- **Part X** – The scheduled and Tribal Areas
- **Part XI** – Relations between the Union and the States
- **Part XII** – Finance, Property, Contracts and Suits
- **Part XIII** – Trade and Commerce within the territory of India
- **Part XIV** – Services Under the Union, the States
- **Part XIVA** – Tribunals
- **Part XV** – Elections
- **Part XVI** – Special Provisions Relating to certain Classes
- **Part XVII** – Languages
- **Part XVIII** – Emergency Provisions
- **Part XIX** – Miscellaneous
- **Part XX** – Amendment of the Constitution
- **Part XXI** – Temporary, Transitional and Special Provisions
- **Part XXII** – Short title, date of commencement, Authoritative text in Hindi and Repeals.

Schedules

Schedules are lists in the constitution that categorise and tabulate bureaucratic activity and policy of the Government.

- **First Schedule** (Articles 1 and 4) – This lists the states and territories of India, lists any changes to their borders and the laws used to make that change.
- **Second Schedule** (Articles 59(3), 65(3), 75(6), 97, 125, 148(3), 158(3), 164(5), 186 and 221) – This lists the salaries of officials holding public office, judges, and the Comptroller and Auditor General of India.
- **Third Schedule** (Articles 75(4), 99, 124(6), 148(2), 164(3), 188 and 219) – Forms of oaths – This lists the oaths of offices for elected officials and judges.
- **Fourth Schedule** (Articles 4(1) and 80(2)) – This details the allocation of seats in the *Rajya Sabha* (the upper house of Parliament) per state or union territory.
- **Fifth Schedule** (Article 244(1)) – This provides for the administration and control of Scheduled Area[898] and Scheduled Tribes[899] (areas and tribes needing special protection due to disadvantageous conditions).
- **Sixth Schedule** (Articles 244(2) and 275(1)) – Provisions made for the administration of tribal areas in Assam, Meghalaya, Tripura, and Mizoram.
- **Seventh Schedule** (Article 246) — The union (central government), state, and concurrent lists of responsibilities.
- **Eighth Schedule** (Articles 344(1) and 351)—The official languages.
- **Ninth Schedule** (Article 31-B) – Validation of certain Acts and Regulations.[900]
- **Tenth Schedule** (Articles 102(2) and 191(2)) – "Anti-defection" provisions for members of the parliament and members of state legislatures.
- **Eleventh Schedule** (Article 243-G) —*Panchayat Raj* (rural local government),
- **Twelfth Schedule** (Article 243-W) — Municipalities (urban local government).

Appendices

- **Appendix I** – The Constitution (Application to Jammu and Kashmir) Order, 1954.
- **Appendix II** – Re-statement, with reference to the present text of the Constitution, of the exceptions and modifications subject to which the Constitution applies to the State of Jammu and Kashmir.
- **Appendix III** – Extracts from the Constitution (Forty-fourth Amendment) Act, 1978.

- **Appendix IV** – The Constitution (Eighty-sixth Amendment) Act, 2002.
- **Appendix V** – The Constitution (Eighty-eighth Amendment) Act, 2003.

The constitution and the government

Branches of the government – the legislature, the executive and the judiciary get their power from the constitution and are bound by it. With the aid of the constitution, India is governed by a parliamentary system of government with the executive directly accountable to the legislature. It states that there shall be a President of India who shall be the head of the executive, under Articles 52 and 53. The President's duty is to preserve, protect and defend the constitution and the law under Article 60 of the Indian constitution. Article 74 provides that there shall be a prime minister as the head of the Council of Ministers which would serve binding aid and advise the president in performing his constitutional duty. The union cabinet is collectively responsible to the House of the People per Article 75(3).

The Constitution of India is considered to be federal in nature but unitary in spirit. The common features of a federation such as codified constitution, supremacy of constitution, rigidity of constitution, three-tier governmental structure (centre, state, local), division of powers, bicameralism and independent judiciary as well as unitary features like single constitution, single citizenship, integrated judiciary, flexible constitution, a strong centre, appointment of state governors by the centre, All India Services (IAS, IFS and IPS), emergency provisions etc. can be seen in Indian constitution. This unique combination makes it quasi-federal in form.

Each state and union territory of India has its own government. Analogous to president and prime minister, each has a governor or — in case of union territories — a lieutenant governor and a chief minister. Article 356 permits the president to dismiss a state government and assume direct authority when a situation has arisen in which the state government cannot be carried on in accordance with the provisions of the constitution. This power, known as President's rule, was abused earlier as state governments came to be dismissed on the flimsiest of grounds, and more due to the political discomfiture of the party in power at the centre. Post – *S. R. Bommai v. Union of India* judgment, such a course of action has been rendered rather difficult, as the courts have asserted their right to review it. Consequently, very few state governments have been disbanded since.

The 73rd and 74th amendments acts also introduced the system of panchayati raj in rural areas and nagar palikas in urban areas. Also, Article 370 of the constitution gives special status to the state of Jammu and Kashmir.

The constitution and the legislature

Amendment

The process of addition, variation or repeal of any part of the constitution by the parliament under its constituent powers, is called amendment of the constitution. The procedure is laid out in Article 368. An amendment bill must be passed by each House of the Parliament by a majority of the total membership of that House when at least two-thirds members are present and voted. In addition to this, certain amendments which pertain to the federal nature of the constitution must be ratified by a majority of state legislatures. Unlike the ordinary bills under legislative powers of parliament as per Article 245 (with exception to money bills), there is no provision for a joint sitting of the two houses of the parliament (Lok Sabha and Rajya Sabha) to pass a constitutional amendment bill. During a parliamentary recess, the president can not promulgate ordinances under his legislative powers per Article 123, Chapter III which needs a constitutional amendment. Deemed amendments to the constitution which can be passed under the legislative powers of parliament are no more valid after the addition of Article 368(1) by Twenty-fourth Amendment of the Constitution of India.

As of July 2018[901], there have been 124 amendment bills presented in the parliament, out of which 101 have been passed to become Amendment Acts.[902] Despite the supermajority requirement for amendments to pass, the Constitution of India is the most frequently amended national governing document in the world. The constitution is so specific in spelling out government powers that many of these amendments address issues dealt with by ordinary statute in other democracies. As a result, the document is amended roughly twice a year, and three times every two years.Wikipedia:Citation needed

In 2000, the National Commission to Review the Working of the Constitution was set up to look into updating the constitution.[903] The Government of India establishes term based law commissions to recommend law reforms for maximising justice in society and for promoting good governance under the rule of law.

Limitations of the legislature

The supreme court has ruled in *Kesavananda Bharati v. State of Kerala* case that an amendment cannot destroy what it seeks to modify, which means, while amending anything in the constitution, it cannot tinker with the "basic structure" or its framework, which is immutable. Such an amendment will be declared invalid even though no part of the constitution is explicitly prevented from being amended, nor does the *basic structure* doctrine protect any single provision of the constitution. Yet, this "doctrine of basic features" lays down that, the constitution when "read as a whole", that what comes to be understood as its basic features cannot be abridged, deleted or abrogated. What these "basic features" are, have not been defined exhaustively anywhere, and whether a particular provision of the Constitution of India is a "basic feature" is decided as and when an issue is raised before a court in an instant case.

The judgment in the *Kesavananda Bharati v. State of Kerala* case laid down the following as the basic structure of the Constitution of India:

1. The supremacy of the constitution.
2. A republican and democratic form of the Government.
3. The secular character of the constitution.
4. Maintenance of separation of powers.
5. The federal character of the constitution.

This implies that the parliament, while amending the constitution, can only amend it to the extent so as to not destroy any of the aforesaid characters. The supreme court — or a high court — may declare the amendment null and void if this is violated, by performing a judicial review. This is typical of parliamentary governments, where the judiciary has to exercise an effective check on the exercise of the powers of the parliament, which in many respects is supreme.

In the *Golak Nath v. State of Punjab* case of 1967, the supreme court ruled that the State of Punjab could not restrict any of the fundamental rights protected by the basic structure doctrine. The extent of land ownership and practice of profession, in this case, were held to be a fundamental right. The ruling of the *Golak Nath v. State of Punjab* case was eventually overturned with the ratification of the 24th Amendment in 1971.

The constitution and the judiciary

The judiciary interprets the constitution as its final arbiter. It is its duty as mandated by the constitution, to be its watchdog, by calling for scrutiny any act of the legislature or the executive, who otherwise, are free to enact or implement these, from overstepping bounds set for them by the constitution. It acts like a guardian in protecting the fundamental rights of the people, as enshrined in the constitution, from infringement by any organ of the state. It also balances the conflicting exercise of power between the centre and a state or among states, as assigned to them by the constitution.

While pronouncing decisions under its constitutional mandate, it is expected to remain unaffected by pulls and pressures exerted by other branches of the state, citizens or interest groups. And crucially, independence of the judiciary has been held to be a basic feature of the constitution, and which being inalienable, has come to mean – that which cannot be taken away from it by any act or amendment by the legislature or the executive.

Judicial review

Judicial review is adopted in the Constitution of India from judicial review in the United States. In the Indian constitution, Judicial review is dealt with under Article 13. Judicial review refers that the constitution is the supreme power of the nation and all laws are under its supremacy. Article 13 states that:

1. All pre-constitutional laws, if in part or completely in conflict with the constitution, shall have all conflicting provisions deemed ineffective until an amendment to the constitution ends the conflict. In such a situation the provision of that law will again come into force if it is compatible with the constitution as amended. This is called the *Doctrine of Eclipse*.
2. In a similar manner, laws made after the adoption of the constitution by the Constituent Assembly must be compatible with the constitution, otherwise, the laws and amendments will be deemed to be void *ab initio*.
3. In such situations, the supreme court or a state high court interprets the laws to decide if they are in conformity with the constitution. If such an interpretation is not possible because of inconsistency, and where a separation is possible, the provision that is inconsistent with the constitution is considered to be void. In addition to article 13, articles 32, 226 and 227 provide a constitutional basis for judicial review in India.[904]

Due to the adoption of the thirty-eighth amendment, the Indian supreme court was not allowed to preside over any laws adopted during a state of emergency that infringes upon fundamental rights under article 32 i.e. right to constitutional remedies. Later with the Forty-second Amendment of the Constitution of India, article 31 C was widened and article 368(4) and 368(5) were added, which stated that any law passed by the parliament can't be challenged in the court on any ground. The supreme court in the *Minerva Mills v. Union of India* case said that judicial review is one of the basic characters of the constitution and therefore can't be taken away quashing articles 368(4), 368(5) and 31 C.

The constitution – a living document

"The Indian constitution is first and foremost a social document, and is aided by its Parts III & IV (Fundamental Rights & Directive Principles of State Policy, respectively) acting together, as its chief instruments and its conscience, in realising the goals set by it for all the people."[905]

The constitution's provisions have consciously been worded in generalities, though not in vague terms, instead of making them rigid and static with a fixed meaning or content as in an ordinary statute, so that they may be interpreted by coming generations of citizens with the onward march of time, to apply to new and ever-changing and demanding situations, making the constitution a living and an organic document. Fourth Chief Justice of the United States, John Marshall said that it is the nature of a constitution that its "great outlines should be marked, its important objects designated, and the minor ingredients which compose those objects be deduced from the nature of the objects themselves, ..." It is a document "intended to endure for ages to come", and therefore, it has to be interpreted not merely on the basis of the intention and understanding of its framers but on the experience of its working effectively, in the existing social and political context.

For instance, "right to life" as guaranteed under Article 21,[906] has by interpretation been expanded to progressively mean a whole lot of human rights, including — but not necessarily limited to — the right to speedy trial;; the right to water; the right to livelihood; the right to health; and the right to education.

In the conclusion of his book, *Making of India's Constitution*, Justice H.R. Khanna — a retired judge of the Supreme Court of India — writes:

> "If the Indian constitution is our heritage bequeathed to us by our founding fathers, no less are we, the people of India, the trustees and custodians of the values which pulsate within its provisions! A constitution is not a parchment of paper, it is a way of life and has to be lived up to. Eternal vigilance is the price of liberty and in the final analysis, its only keepers are the people."
>
> —Khanna, Hans Raj (2008). *Making of India's constitution*[907] *(2nd ed.)*. Lucknow: Eastern Book Co (published 1 January 2008). ISBN 978-81-7012-108-4. OCLC 294942170[908].

Notes

Bibliography

- Khanna, Justice H.R (2015). *Making of India's Constitution* (2nd Edition 2008, (Reprinted 2015) ed.). Eastern Book Company. ISBN 978-81-7012-188-6.
- Austin, Granville (1999). *The Indian Constitution: Cornerstone of a Nation* (2nd ed.). Oxford University Press. ISBN 978-01-9564-959-8.
- Austin, Granville (2003). *Working a Democratic Constitution: A History of the Indian Experience* (2nd ed.). Oxford University Press. ISBN 978-01-9565-610-7.

- Baruah, Aparajita (2007). *Preamble of the Constitution of India : An Insight & Comparison*. Eastern Book Co. ISBN 978-81-7629-996-1.
- Basu, Durga Das (1965). *Commentary on the constitution of India : (being a comparative treatise on the universal principles of justice and constitutional government with special reference to the organic instrument of India)*. **1-2**. S. C. Sarkar & Sons (Private) Ltd.
- Basu, Durga Das (1984). *Introduction to the Constitution of India* (10th ed.). South Asia Books. ISBN 0-8364-1097-1.
- Basu, Durga Das (1981). *Shorter Constitution of India*. Prentice-Hall of India. ISBN 978-0-87692-200-2.
- Das, Hari Hara (2002). *Political System of India*. Anmol Publications. ISBN 81-7488-690-7.
- Dash, Shreeram Chandra (1968). *The Constitution of India; a Comparative Study*. Chaitanya Pub. House.
- Dhamija, Dr. Ashok (2007). *Need to Amend a Constitution and Doctrine of Basic Features*. Wadhwa and Company. ISBN 9788180382536.
- Ghosh, Pratap Kumar (1966). *The Constitution of India: How it Has Been Framed*. World Press.
- Jayapalan, N. (1998). *Constitutional History of India*. Atlantic Publishers & Distributors. ISBN 81-7156-761-4.
- Khanna, Hans Raj (1981). *Making of India's Constitution*. Eastern Book Co. ISBN 978-81-7012-108-4.
- Rahulrai, Durga Das (1984). *Introduction to the Constitution of India* (10th ed.). South Asia Books. ISBN 0-8364-1097-1.
- Pylee, M.V. (1997). *India's Constitution*. S. Chand & Co. ISBN 81-219-0403-X.
- Pylee, M.V. (2004). *Constitutional Government in India*. S. Chand & Co. ISBN 81-219-2203-8.
- Sen, Sarbani (2007). *The Constitution of India: Popular Sovereignty and Democratic Transformations*. Oxford University Press. ISBN 978-0-19-568649-4.
- Sharma, Dinesh; Singh, Jaya; Maganathan, R.; et al. (2002). *Indian Constitution at Work*. Political Science, Class XI. NCERT.
- "The Constituent Assembly Debates (Proceedings):(9th December,1946 to 24 January 1950)"[909]. The Parliament of India Archive. Retrieved 22 February 2008.

External links

- Original as published in the Gazette of India[910]
- Original Unamended version of the Constitution of India[883]
- Ministry of Law and Justice of India – The Constitution of India Page[911]

- Constitution of India as of 29 July 2008[912]
- Constitutional predilections[913]
- "Constitution of India"[914]. *Commonwealth Legal Information Institute.* – online copy

Political integration of India

At the time of Indian independence in 1947, India was divided into two sets of territories, one under direct British rule, and the other under the suzerainty of the British Crown, with control over their internal affairs remaining in the hands of their hereditary rulers. In addition, there were several colonial enclaves controlled by France and Portugal. The political integration of these territories into India was a declared objective of the Indian National Congress, and the Government of India pursued this over the next decade. Through a combination of factors, Sardar Vallabhbhai Patel and V. P. Menon convinced most of the rulers of the various princely states to accede to India. Having secured their accession, they then proceeded, in a step-by-step process, to secure and extend the central government's authority over these states and transform their administrations until, by 1956, there was little difference between the territories that had been part of British India and those that had been princely states. Simultaneously, the Government of India, through a combination of diplomatic and military means, acquired *de facto* and *de jure* control over the remaining colonial enclaves, which too were integrated into India.

Although this process successfully integrated the vast majority of the princely states into India, it was not as successful for a few, notably the former princely states of Jammu and Kashmir, Tripura and Manipur, where active secessionist movements exist.

Princely states in India

The early history of British expansion in India was characterised by the co-existence of two approaches towards the existing princely states. The first was a policy of annexation, where the British sought to forcibly absorb the Indian princely states into the provinces which constituted their Empire in India. The second was a policy of indirect rule, where the British assumed suzerainty and paramountcy over princely states, but conceded to them sovereignty and varying degrees of internal self-government. During the early part of the 19th century, the policy of the British tended towards annexation, but the Indian Rebellion of 1857 forced a change in this approach, by demonstrating both the difficulty of absorbing and subduing annexed states, and the usefulness of princely

Political integration of India 417

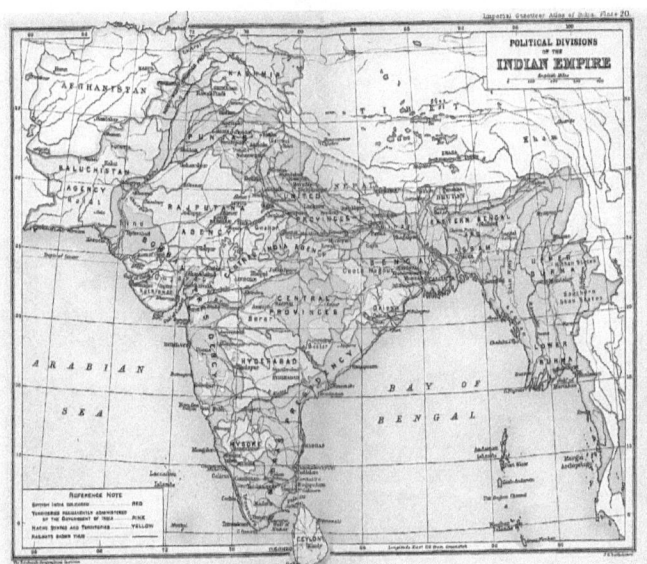

Figure 189: *British India and the princely states in 1909*

states as a source of support. In 1858, the policy of annexation was formally renounced, and British relations with the remaining princely states thereafter were based on subsidiary alliances, whereby the British exercised paramountcy over all princely states, with the British crown as ultimate suzerain, but at the same time respected and protected them as allies, taking control of their external relations. The exact relations between the British and each princely state were regulated by individual treaties and varied widely, with some states having complete internal self-government, others being subject to significant control in their internal affairs, and some rulers being in effect little more than the owners of landed estates, with little autonomy.

During the 20th century, the British made several attempts to integrate the princely states more closely with British India, in 1921 creating the Chamber of Princes as a consultative and advisory body, and in 1936 transferring the responsibility for the supervision of smaller states from the provinces to the centre and creating direct relations between the Government of India and the larger princely states, superseding political agents. A more ambitious aim was a scheme of federation contained in the Government of India Act 1935, which envisaged the princely states and British India being united under a federal government. This scheme came close to success, but was abandoned in 1939 as a result of the outbreak of the Second World War. As a result, in the 1940s the relationship between the princely states and the crown remained regulated

Figure 190: *The Saurashtra and Kathiawar regions of Gujarat were home to over two hundred princely states, many with non-contiguous territories, as this map of Baroda shows.*

by the principle of paramountcy and by the various treaties between the British crown and the states.

Neither paramountcy nor the subsidiary alliances could continue after Indian independence. The British took the view that because they had been established directly between the British crown and the princely states, they could not be transferred to the newly independent dominions of India and Pakistan. At the same time, the alliances imposed obligations on Britain that it was not prepared to continue to carry out, such as the obligation to maintain troops in India for the defence of the princely states. The British government therefore decided that paramountcy, together with all treaties between them and the princely states, would come to an end upon the British departure from India.

Reasons for integration

The termination of paramountcy meant that all rights flowing from the states' relationship with the British crown would return to them, leaving them free to negotiate relationships with the new states of India and Pakistan "on a basis of complete freedom". Early British plans for the transfer of power, such as the offer produced by the Cripps Mission, recognised the possibility that some princely states might choose to stand out of independent India. This was unacceptable to the Indian National Congress, which regarded the independence of princely states as a denial of the course of Indian history, and consequently regarded this scheme as a "Balkanisation" of India. The Congress had traditionally been less active in the princely states because of their limited resources which restricted their ability to organise there and their focus on the goal of independence from the British, and because Congress leaders, in particular Mohandas Gandhi, were sympathetic to the more progressive princes as examples of the capacity of Indians to rule themselves. This changed in the 1930s as a result of the federation scheme contained in the Government of India Act 1935 and the rise of socialist Congress leaders such as Jayaprakash Narayan, and the Congress began to actively engage with popular political and labour activity in the princely states. By 1939, the Congress's formal stance was that the states must enter independent India, on the same terms and with the same autonomy as the provinces of British India, and with their people granted responsible government. As a result, it attempted to insist on the incorporation of the princely states into India in its negotiations with the British, but the British took the view that this was not in their power to grant.

A few British leaders, particularly Lord Mountbatten, the last British viceroy of India, were also uncomfortable with breaking links between independent India and the princely states. The development of trade, commerce and communications during the 19th and 20th centuries had bound the princely states to the British India through a complex network of interests. Agreements relating to railways, customs, irrigation, use of ports, and other similar agreements would get terminated, posing a serious threat to the economic life of the subcontinent. Mountbatten was also persuaded by the argument of Indian officials such as V. P. Menon that the integration of the princely states into independent India would, to some extent, assuage the wounds of partition. The result was that Mountbatten personally favoured and worked towards the accession of princely states to India following the transfer of power, as proposed by the Congress. However, Sardar Patel looked back on events at a press conference in January 1948, declaring "As you are all aware, on the lapse of Paramountcy every Indian State became a separate independent entity."

Accepting integration

The princes' position

The rulers of the princely states were not uniformly enthusiastic about integrating their domains into independent India. Some, such as the rulers of Bikaner and Jawhar, were motivated to join India out of ideological and patriotic considerations, but others insisted that they had the right to join either India or Pakistan, to remain independent, or form a union of their own. Bhopal, Travancore and Hyderabad announced that they did not intend to join either dominion. Hyderabad went as far as to appoint trade representatives in European countries and commencing negotiations with the Portuguese to lease or buy Goa to give it access to the sea, and Travancore pointed to the strategic importance to western countries of its thorium reserves while asking for recognition. Some states proposed a subcontinent-wide confederation of princely states, as a third entity in addition to India and Pakistan. Bhopal attempted to build an alliance between the princely states and the Muslim League to counter the pressure being put on rulers by the Congress.

A number of factors contributed to the collapse of this initial resistance and to nearly all non-Muslim majority princely states agreeing to accede to India. An important factor was the lack of unity among the princes. The smaller states did not trust the larger states to protect their interests, and many Hindu rulers did not trust Muslim princes, in particular Hamidullah Khan, the Nawab of Bhopal and a leading proponent of independence, whom they viewed as an agent for Pakistan. Others, believing integration to be inevitable, sought to build bridges with the Congress, hoping thereby to gain a say in shaping the final settlement. The resultant inability to present a united front or agree on a common position significantly reduced their bargaining power in negotiations with the Congress. The decision by the Muslim League to stay out of the Constituent Assembly was also fatal to the princes' plan to build an alliance with it to counter the Congress, and attempts to boycott the Constituent Assembly altogether failed on 28 April 1947, when the states of Baroda, Bikaner, Cochin, Gwalior, Jaipur, Jodhpur, Patiala and Rewa took their seats in the Assembly.

Many princes were also pressured by popular sentiment favouring integration with India, which meant their plans for independence had little support from their subjects. The Maharaja of Travancore, for example, definitively abandoned his plans for independence after the attempted assassination of his dewan, Sir C. P. Ramaswami Iyer. In a few states, the chief ministers or dewans played a significant role in convincing the princes to accede to India. The key factors that led the states to accept integration into India were, however, the efforts of Lord Mountbatten, Sardar Vallabhbhai Patel and V. P. Menon. The latter two were respectively the political and administrative heads of the States Department, which was in charge of relations with the princely states.

Figure 191: *Lord Louis Mountbatten played an important role in convincing reluctant monarchs to accede to the Indian Union.*

Mountbatten's role

Mountbatten believed that securing the states' accession to India was crucial to reaching a negotiated settlement with the Congress for the transfer of power. As a relative of the British King, he was trusted by most of the princes and was a personal friend of many, especially the Nawab of Bhopal, Hamidullah Khan. The princes also believed that he would be in a position to ensure that independent India adhered to any terms that might be agreed upon, because Prime Minister Jawaharlal Nehru and Patel had asked him to become the first Governor General of the Dominion of India.

Mountbatten used his influence with the princes to push them towards accession. He declared that the British Government would not grant dominion status to any of the princely states, nor would it accept them into the British Commonwealth, which meant that the states would sever all connections with the British crown unless they joined either India or Pakistan. He pointed out that the Indian subcontinent was one economic entity, and that the states would suffer most if the link were broken. He also pointed to the difficulties that princes would face maintaining order in the face of threats such as the rise of communal violence and communist movements.

Mountbatten stressed that he would act as the trustee of the princes' commitment, as he would be serving as India's head of state well into 1948. He engaged in a personal dialogue with reluctant princes, such as the Nawab of Bhopal, who he asked through a confidential letter to sign the Instrument of Accession making Bhopal part of India, which Mountbatten would keep locked up in his safe. It would be handed to the States Department on 15 August only if the Nawab did not change his mind before then, which he was free to do. The Nawab agreed, and did not renege over the deal.

At the time, several princes complained that they were being betrayed by Britain, who they regarded as an ally, and Sir Conrad Corfield resigned his position as head of the Political Department in protest at Mountbatten's policies. Mountbatten's policies were also criticised by the opposition Conservative Party. Winston Churchill compared the language used by the Indian government with that used by Adolf Hitler before the invasion of Austria. Modern historians such as Lumby and Moore, however, take the view that Mountbatten played a crucial role in ensuring that the princely states agreed to accede to India.

Pressure and diplomacy

By far the most significant factor that led to the princes' decision to accede to India was the policy of the Congress and, in particular, of Patel and Menon. The Congress' stated position was that the princely states were not sovereign entities, and as such could not opt to be independent notwithstanding the end of paramountcy. The princely states must therefore accede to either India or Pakistan. In July 1946, Nehru pointedly observed that no princely state could prevail militarily against the army of independent India. In January 1947, he said that independent India would not accept the divine right of kings, and in May 1947, he declared that any princely state which refused to join the Constituent Assembly would be treated as an enemy state. Other Congress leaders, such as C. Rajagopalachari, argued that as paramountcy "came into being as a fact and not by agreement", it would necessarily pass to the government of independent India, as the successor of the British.

Patel and Menon, who were charged with the actual job of negotiating with the princes, took a more conciliatory approach than Nehru. The official policy statement of the Government of India made by Patel on 5 July 1947 made no threats. Instead, it emphasised the unity of India and the common interests of the princes and independent India, reassured them about the Congress' intentions, and invited them to join independent India "to make laws sitting together as friends than to make treaties as aliens". He reiterated that the States Department would not attempt to establish a relationship of domination over

Figure 192: *Vallabhbhai Patel as Minister for Home and States Affairs had the responsibility of welding the British Indian, provinces and the princely states into a united India.*

the princely states. Unlike the Political Department of the British Government, it would not be an instrument of paramountcy, but a medium whereby business could be conducted between the states and India as equals.

Instruments of accession

Patel and Menon backed up their diplomatic efforts by producing treaties that were designed to be attractive to rulers of princely states. Two key documents were produced. The first was the Standstill Agreement, which confirmed the continuance of the pre-existing agreements and administrative practices. The second was the Instrument of Accession, by which the ruler of the princely state in question agreed to the accession of his kingdom to independent India, granting the latter control over specified subject matters. The nature of the subject matters varied depending on the acceding state. The states which had internal autonomy under the British signed an Instrument of Accession which only ceded three subjects to the government of India—defence, external affairs, and communications, each defined in accordance with List 1 to Schedule VII of the Government of India Act 1935. Rulers of states which were in effect estates or talukas, where substantial administrative powers were exercised by the Crown, signed a different Instrument of Accession, which vested all residuary powers and jurisdiction in the Government of India. Rulers of states which had an intermediate status signed a third type of Instrument, which preserved the degree of power they had under the British.

The Instruments of Accession implemented a number of other safeguards. Clause 7 provided that the princes would not be bound to the Indian constitution as and when it was drafted. Clause 8 guaranteed their autonomy in all areas that were not ceded to the Government of India. This was supplemented by a number of promises. Rulers who agreed to accede would receive guarantees that their extra-territorial rights, such as immunity from prosecution in Indian courts and exemption from customs duty, would be protected, that they would be allowed to democratise slowly, that none of the eighteen major states would be forced to merge, and that they would remain eligible for British honours and decorations. In discussions, Lord Mountbatten reinforced the statements of Patel and Menon by emphasising that the documents gave the princes all the "practical independence" they needed. Mountbatten, Patel and Menon also sought to give princes the impression that if they did not accept the terms put to them then, they might subsequently need to accede on substantially less favourable terms. The Standstill Agreement was also used as a negotiating tool, as the States Department categorically ruled out signing a Standstill Agreement with princely states that did not sign an Instrument of Accession.

Accession process

The limited scope of the Instruments of Accession and the promise of a wide-ranging autonomy and the other guarantees they offered, gave sufficient comfort to many rulers, who saw this as the best deal they could strike given the lack of support from the British, and popular internal pressures. Between May 1947 and the transfer of power on 15 August 1947, the vast majority of states signed Instruments of Accession. A few, however, held out. Some simply delayed signing the Instrument of Accession. Piploda, a small state in central India, did not accede until March 1948. The biggest problems, however, arose with a few border states, such as Jodhpur, which tried to negotiate better deals with Pakistan, with Junagadh, which actually did accede to Pakistan, and with Hyderabad and Kashmir, which declared that they intended to remain independent.

Border states

The ruler of Jodhpur, Hanwant Singh, was antipathetic to the Congress, and did not see much future in India for him or the lifestyle he wished to lead. Along with the ruler of Jaisalmer, he entered into negotiations with Muhammad Ali Jinnah, who was the designated head of state for Pakistan. Jinnah was keen to attract some of the larger border states, hoping thereby to attract other Rajput states to Pakistan and compensate for the loss of half of Bengal and Punjab. He offered to permit Jodhpur and Jaisalmer to accede to Pakistan on any terms they chose, giving their rulers blank sheets of paper and asking them to write down their terms, which he would sign. Jaisalmer refused, arguing that it would be difficult for him to side with Muslims against Hindus in the event of communal problems. Hanwant Singh came close to signing. However, the atmosphere in Jodhpur was in general hostile to accession to Pakistan. Mountbatten also pointed out that the accession of a predominantly Hindu state to Pakistan would violate the principle of the two-nation theory on which Partition was based, and was likely to cause communal violence in the State. Hanwant Singh was persuaded by these arguments, and somewhat reluctantly agreed to accede to India.

Junagadh

Although the states were in theory free to choose whether they wished to accede to India or Pakistan, Mountbatten had pointed out that "geographic compulsions" meant that most of them must choose India. In effect, he took the position that only the states that shared a border with Pakistan could choose to accede to it.

The Nawab of Junagadh, a princely state located on the south-western end of Gujarat and having no common border with Pakistan, chose to accede to Pakistan ignoring Mountbatten's views, arguing that it could be reached from Pakistan by sea. The rulers of two states that were subject to the suzerainty of Junagadh—Mangrol and Babariawad—reacted to this by declaring their independence from Junagadh and acceding to India. In response, the Nawab of Junagadh militarily occupied the states. The rulers of neighbouring states reacted angrily, sending their troops to the Junagadh frontier and appealed to the Government of India for assistance. A group of Junagadhi people, led by Samaldas Gandhi, formed a government-in-exile, the *Aarzi Hukumat* ("temporary government").

India believed that if Junagadh was permitted to go to Pakistan, the communal tension already simmering in Gujarat would worsen, and refused to accept the accession. The government pointed out that the state was 80% Hindu, and called for a plebiscite to decide the question of accession. Simultaneously,

Figure 193: *Shown in green is the Kashmiri region under Pakistani control. The dark-brown region represents Indian-administered Jammu and Kashmir while the Aksai Chin is under Chinese administration.*

they cut off supplies of fuel and coal to Junagadh, severed air and postal links, sent troops to the frontier, and reoccupied the principalities of Mangrol and Babariawad that had acceded to India. Pakistan agreed to discuss a plebiscite, subject to the withdrawal of Indian troops, a condition India rejected. On 26 October, the Nawab and his family fled to Pakistan following clashes with Indian troops. On 7 November, Junagadh's court, facing collapse, invited the Government of India to take over the State's administration. The Government of India agreed. A plebiscite was conducted in February 1948, which went almost unanimously in favour of accession to India.

Jammu and Kashmir

At the time of the transfer of power, the state of Jammu and Kashmir (widely called "Kashmir") was ruled by Maharaja Hari Singh, a Hindu, although the state itself had a Muslim majority. Hari Singh was equally hesitant about acceding to either India or Pakistan, as either would have provoked adverse reactions in parts of his kingdom. He signed a Standstill Agreement with Pakistan and proposed one with India as well, but announced that Kashmir intended to remain independent. However, his rule was opposed by Sheikh Abdullah, the popular leader of Kashmir's largest political party, the National Conference, who demanded his abdication.

Pakistan, attempting to force the issue of Kashmir's accession, cut off supplies and transport links. The chaos in Punjab resulting from Partition had also severed transport links with India, meaning that Kashmir's only links with the two dominions was by air. Rumours about atrocities against the Muslim population of Poonch by the Maharajah's forces caused the outbreak of civil unrest. Shortly thereafter, Pathan tribesmen from the North-West Frontier Province of Pakistan crossed the border and entered Kashmir. The invaders made rapid progress towards Srinagar. The Maharaja of Kashmir wrote to India, asking for military assistance. India required the signing of an Instrument of Accession and setting up an interim government headed by Sheikh Abdullah in return. The Maharaja complied, but Nehru declared that it would have to be confirmed by a plebiscite, although there was no legal requirement to seek such confirmation.

Indian troops secured Jammu, Srinagar and the valley itself during the First Kashmir War, but the intense fighting flagged with the onset of winter, which made much of the state impassable. Prime Minister Nehru, recognising the degree of international attention brought to bear on the dispute, declared a ceasefire and sought UN arbitration, arguing that India would otherwise have to invade Pakistan itself, in view of its failure to stop the tribal incursions. The plebiscite was never held, and on 26 January 1950, the Constitution of India came into force in Kashmir, but with special provisions made for the state. India did not, however, secure administrative control over all of Kashmir. The northern and western portions of Kashmir came under Pakistan's control in 1947, and are today Pakistan-administered Kashmir. In the 1962 Sino-Indian War, China occupied Aksai Chin, the north-eastern region bordering Ladakh, which it continues to control and administer.

Hyderabad

Hyderabad was a landlocked state that stretched over 82,000 square miles (over 212,000 square kilometres) in southeastern India. While 87% of its 17 million people were Hindu, its ruler Nizam Osman Ali Khan was a Muslim, and its politics were dominated by a Muslim elite. The Muslim nobility and the Ittehad-ul-Muslimeen, a powerful pro-Nizam Muslim party, insisted Hyderabad remain independent and stand on an equal footing to India and Pakistan. Accordingly, the Nizam in June 1947 issued a *firman* announcing that on the transfer of power, his state would be resuming independence. The Government of India rejected the firman, terming it a "legalistic claim of doubtful validity". It argued that the strategic location of Hyderabad, which lay astride the main lines of communication between northern and southern India, meant

Figure 194: *Hyderabad state in 1909. Its former territories are today incorporated in the Indian states of Telangana, Karnataka and Maharashtra.*

it could easily be used by "foreign interests" to threaten India, and that in consequence, the issue involved national-security concerns. It also pointed out that the state's people, history and location made it unquestionably Indian, and that its own "common interests" therefore mandated its integration into India.

The Nizam was prepared to enter into a limited treaty with India, which gave Hyderabad safeguards not provided for in the standard Instrument of Accession, such as a provision guaranteeing Hyderabad's neutrality in the event of a conflict between India and Pakistan. India rejected this proposal, arguing that other states would demand similar concessions. A temporary Standstill Agreement was signed as a stopgap measure, even though Hyderabad had not yet agreed to accede to India. By December 1947, however, India was accusing Hyderabad of repeatedly violating the Agreement, while the Nizam alleged that India was blockading his state, a charge India denied.

The Nizam was also beset by the Telangana Rebellion, led by communists, which started in 1946 as a peasant revolt against feudal elements; and one which the Nizam was not able to subjugate. The situation deteriorated further in 1948. The Razakars ("volunteers"), a militia affiliated to the Ittehad-ul-Muslimeen and set up under the influence of Muslim radical Qasim Razvi, assumed the role of supporting the Muslim ruling class against upsurges by the Hindu populace, and began intensifying its activities and was accused of attempting to intimidate villages. The Hyderabad State Congress Party, affiliated to the Indian National Congress, launched a political agitation. Matters were made worse by communist groups, which had originally supported the Congress but now switched sides and began attacking Congress groups. Attempts by Mountbatten to find a negotiated solution failed and, in August, the Nizam, claiming that he feared an imminent invasion, attempted to approach the UN Security Council and the International Court of Justice. Patel now insisted that if Hyderabad was allowed to continue its independence, the prestige of the Government would be tarnished and then neither Hindus nor Muslims would feel secure in its realm.

On 13 September 1948, the Indian Army was sent into Hyderabad under Operation Polo on the grounds that the law and order situation there threatened the peace of South India. The troops met little resistance by the Razakars and between 13 and 18 September took complete control of the state. The operation led to massive communal violence with estimates of deaths ranging from the official one of 27,000-40,000 to scholarly ones of 200,000 or more. The Nizam was retained as the head of state in the same manner as the other princes who acceded to India. He thereupon disavowed the complaints that had been made to the UN and, despite vehement protests from Pakistan and strong criticism from other countries, the Security Council did not deal further with the question, and Hyderabad was absorbed into India.

Completing integration

The Instruments of Accession were limited, transferring control of only three matters to India, and would by themselves have produced a rather loose federation, with significant differences in administration and governance across the various states. Full political integration, in contrast, would require a process whereby the political actors in the various states were "persuaded to shift their loyalties, expectations, and political activities towards a new center", namely, the Republic of India. This was not an easy task. While some princely states such as Mysore had legislative systems of governance that were based on a broad franchise and not significantly different from those of British India, in others, political decision-making took place in small, limited aristocratic circles and governance was, as a result, at best paternalistic and at worst the result of courtly intrigue. Having secured the accession of the princely states, the Government of India between 1948 and 1950 turned to the task of welding the states and the former British provinces into one polity under a single republican constitution.

Figure 195: *Central Provinces and Berar, which form part of modern Chhattisgarh, Madhya Pradesh and Maharashtra*

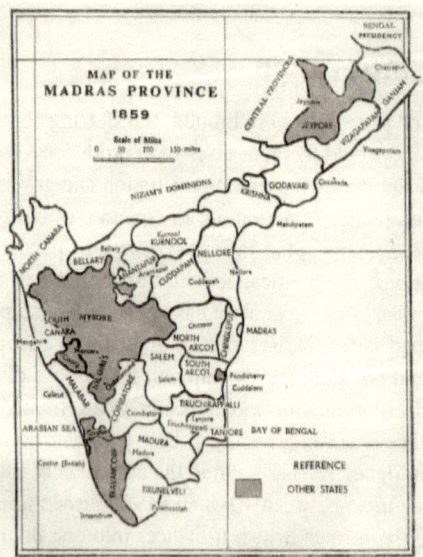

Figure 196: *The British-ruled Madras Province and adjacent princely states*

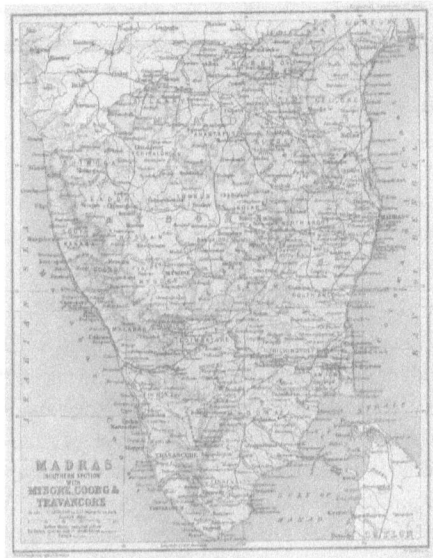

Figure 197: *The Madras Presidency was divided and merged with neighbouring princely states to produce Kerala, Tamil Nadu, Karnataka and Andhra Pradesh.*

Fast-track integration

The first step in this process, carried out between 1947 and 1949, was to merge the smaller states that were not seen by the Government of India to be viable administrative units either into neighbouring provinces, or with other princely states to create a "princely union". This policy was contentious, since it involved the dissolution of the very states whose existence India had only recently guaranteed in the Instruments of Accession. Patel and Menon emphasised that without integration, the economies of states would collapse, and anarchy would arise if the princes were unable to provide democracy and govern properly. They pointed out that many of the smaller states were very small and lacked resources to sustain their economies and support their growing populations. Many also imposed tax rules and other restrictions that impeded free trade, and which had to be dismantled in a united India.

Given that merger involved the breach of guarantees personally given by Mountbatten, initially Patel and Nehru intended to wait until after his term as Governor-General ended. An adivasi uprising in Orissa in late 1947, however, forced their hand. In December 1947, princes from the Eastern India Agency and Chhattisgarh Agency were summoned to an all-night meeting with Menon, where they were persuaded to sign Merger Agreements integrating their states into Orissa, the Central Provinces and Bihar with effect from 1 January 1948. Later that year, 66 states in Gujarat and the Deccan were merged into Bombay, including the large states of Kolhapur and Baroda. Other small states were merged into Madras, East Punjab, West Bengal, the United Provinces and Assam. Not all states that signed Merger Agreements were integrated into provinces, however. Thirty states of the former Punjab Hill States Agency which lay near the international border and had signed Merger Agreements were integrated into Himachal Pradesh, a distinct entity which was administered directly by the centre as a Chief Commissioner's Province, for reasons of security.

The Merger Agreements required rulers to cede "full and exclusive jurisdiction and powers for and in relation to governance" of their state to the Dominion of India. In return for their agreement to entirely cede their states, it gave princes a large number of guarantees. Princes would receive an annual payment from the Indian government in the form of a privy purse as compensation for the surrender of their powers and the dissolution of their states. While state property would be taken over, their private property would be protected, as would all personal privileges, dignities and titles. Succession was also guaranteed according to custom. In addition, the provincial administration was obliged to take on the staff of the princely states with guarantees of equal pay and treatment.

Although the Merger Agreements were principally intended for smaller, non-viable states, they were also applied to a few larger states. Kutch in western India, and Tripura and Manipur in Northeast India, all of which lay along international borders, were also asked to sign Merger Agreements, despite being larger states, following which they became Chief Commissioners' Provinces. Bhopal, whose ruler was proud of the efficiency of his administration and feared that it would lose its identity if merged with the Maratha states that were its neighbours, also became a directly administered Chief Commissioner's Province, as did Bilaspur, much of which was likely to be flooded on completion of the Bhakra dam.

Four-step integration

Merger

The bulk of the larger states, and some groups of small states, were integrated through a different, four-step process. The first step in this process was to convince groups of large states to combine to form a "princely union" through the execution by their rulers of Covenants of Merger. Under the Covenants of Merger, all rulers lost their ruling powers, save one who became the Rajpramukh of the new union. The other rulers were associated with two bodies—the council of rulers, whose members were the rulers of salute states, and a presidium, one or more of whose members were elected by the rulers of non-salute states, with the rest elected by the council. The Rajpramukh and his deputy *Uprajpramukh* were chosen by the council from among the members of the presidium. The Covenants made provision for the creation of a constituent assembly for the new union which would be charged with framing its constitution. In return for agreeing to the extinction of their states as discrete entities, the rulers were given a privy purse and guarantees similar to those provided under the Merger Agreements.

Through this process, Patel obtained the unification of 222 states in the Kathiawar peninsula of his native Gujarat into the princely union of Saurashtra in January 1948, with six more states joining the union the following year. Madhya Bharat emerged on 28 May 1948 from a union of Gwalior, Indore and eighteen smaller states. In Punjab, the Patiala and East Punjab States Union was formed on 15 July 1948 from Patiala, Kapurthala, Jind, Nabha, Faridkot, Malerkotla, Nalargarh, and Kalsia. The United State of Rajasthan was formed as the result of a series of mergers, the last of which was completed on 15 May 1949. Travancore and Cochin were merged in the middle of 1949 to form the princely union of Travancore-Cochin. The only princely states which signed neither Covenants of Merger nor Merger Agreements were Kashmir, Mysore and Hyderabad.

Democratisation

Merging the administrative machineries of each state and integrating them into one political and administrative entity was not easy, particularly as many of the merged states had a history of rivalry. In the former Central India Agency, whose princely states had initially been merged into a princely union called Vindhya Pradesh, the rivalry between two groups of states became so bad that the Government of India persuaded the rulers to sign a Merger Agreement abrogating the old Covenants of Merger, and took direct control of the state as a Chief Commissioner's State. As such, the mergers did not meet the expectations of the Government of India or the States Department. In December 1947, Menon suggested requiring the rulers of states to take "practical steps towards the establishment of popular government". The States Department accepted his suggestion, and implemented it through a special covenant signed by the rajpramukhs of the merged princely unions, binding them to act as constitutional monarchs. This meant that their powers were *de facto* no different from those of the Governors of the former British provinces, thus giving the people of their territories the same measure of responsible government as the people of the rest of India.

The result of this process has been described as being, in effect, an assertion of paramountcy by the Government of India over the states in a more pervasive

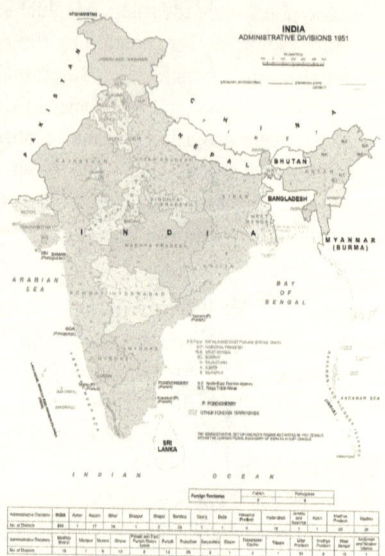

Figure 198: *States of India in 1951*

form. While this contradicted the British statement that paramountcy would lapse on the transfer of power, the Congress position had always been that independent India would inherit the position of being the paramount power.

Centralisation and constitutionalisation

Democratisation still left open one important distinction between the former princely states and the former British provinces, namely, that since the princely states had signed limited Instruments of Accession covering only three subjects, they were insulated from government policies in other areas. The Congress viewed this as hampering its ability to frame policies that brought about social justice and national development. Consequently, they sought to secure to the central government the same degree of powers over the former princely states as it had over the former British provinces. In May 1948, at the initiative of V. P. Menon, a meeting was held in Delhi between the Rajpramukhs of the princely unions and the States Department, at the end of which the Rajpramukhs signed new Instruments of Accession which gave the Government of India the power to pass laws in respect of all matters that fell within the seventh schedule of the Government of India Act 1935. Subsequently, each of the princely unions, as well as Mysore and Hyderabad, agreed to adopt the Constitution of India as the constitution of that state, thus ensuring that they were placed in exactly the same legal position vis-à-vis the central government as the former British provinces. The only exception was Kashmir, whose relationship with India continued to be governed by the original Instrument of Accession, and the constitution produced by the state's Constituent Assembly.

Effective from 1950, the Constitution of India classified the constituent units of India into three classes—Part A, B, and C states. The former British provinces, together with the princely states that had been merged into them, were the Part A states. The princely unions, plus Mysore and Hyderabad, were the Part B states. The former Chief Commissioners' Provinces and other centrally administered areas, except the Andaman and Nicobar Islands, were the Part C states. The only practical difference between the Part A states and the Part B states was that the constitutional heads of the Part B states were the Rajpramukhs appointed under the terms of the Covenants of Merger, rather than Governors appointed by the central government. In addition, Constitution gave the central government a significant range of powers over the former princely states, providing amongst other things that "their governance shall be under the general control of, and comply with such particular directions, if any, as may from time to time be given by, the President". Apart from that, the form of government in both was identical.

Reorganisation

The distinction between Part A and Part B states was only intended to last for a brief, transitional period. In 1956, the States Reorganisation Act reorganised the former British provinces and princely states on the basis of language. Simultaneously, the Seventh Amendment to the Constitution removed the distinction between Part A and Part B states, both of which were now treated only as "states", with Part C states being renamed "union territories". The Rajpramukhs lost their authority, and were replaced as the constitutional heads of state by Governors, who were appointed by the central government. These changes finally brought the princely order to an end. In both legal and practical terms, the territories that had been part of the princely states were now fully integrated into India and did not differ in any way from those that had been part of British India. The personal privileges of the princes—the privy purse, the exemption from customs duty, and customary dignities—survived, only to be abolished in 1971.

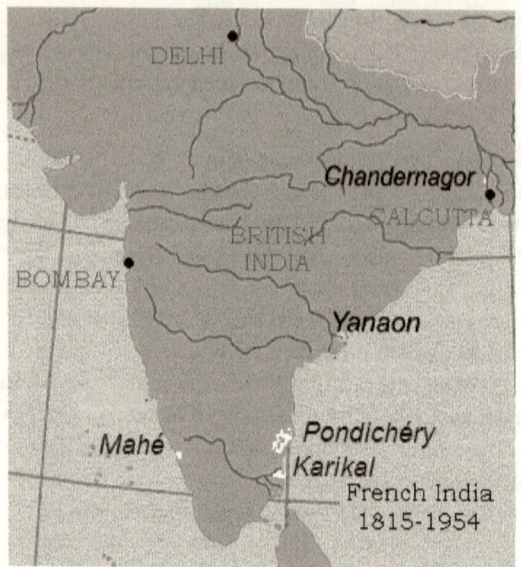

Figure 199: *The French enclaves in 1947*

Post-integration issues

The princes

Although the progressive integration of the princely states into India was largely peaceful, not all princes were happy with the outcome. Many had expected the Instruments of Accession to be permanent, and were unhappy about losing the autonomy and the guaranteed continued existence of their states they had expected to gain. Some felt uneasy about the disappearance of states that generations of their family had controlled, while others were unhappy about the disappearance of administrative structures they had worked hard to build up and which they believed to be efficient. The majority, however, despite the "strain and tension" of adapting to life as private citizens, were content to retire on the generous pension provided by the privy purse. Several took advantage of their eligibility to hold public offices under the central government. The Maharaja of Bhavnagar, Col. Krishna Kumarasingh Bhavasingh Gohil, for example, became the Governor of Madras State, and several others were appointed to diplomatic posts overseas.

Colonial enclaves

The integration of the princely states raised the question of the future of the remaining colonial enclaves in India. At independence, the regions of

Pondicherry, Karaikal, Yanam, Mahe and Chandernagore were still colonies of France, and Daman and Diu, Dadra and Nagar Haveli and Goa remained colonies of Portugal. An agreement between France and India in 1948 provided for an election in France's remaining Indian possessions to choose their political future. A plebiscite held in Chandernagore on 19 June 1949 resulted in a vote of 7,463 to 114 in favour of being integrated with India. It was ceded to India on a *de facto* basis on 14 August 1949 and *de jure* on 2 May 1950. In the other enclaves, however, the pro-French camp, led by Edouard Goubert, used the administrative machinery to suppress the pro-merger groups. Popular discontent rose, and in 1954 demonstrations in Yanam and Mahe resulted in pro-merger groups assuming power. A referendum in Pondicherry and Karaikal in October 1954 resulted in a vote in favour of merger, and on 1 November 1954, de facto control over all four enclaves was transferred to the Republic of India. A treaty of cession was signed in May 1956, and following ratification by the French National Assembly in May 1962, *de jure* control of the enclaves was also transferred.

Portugal, in contrast, resisted diplomatic solutions. It viewed its continued possession of its Indian enclaves as a matter of national pride and, in 1951, it amended its constitution to convert its possessions in India into Portuguese provinces. In July 1954, an uprising in Dadra and Nagar Haveli threw off Portuguese rule. The Portuguese attempted to send forces from Daman to reoccupy the enclaves, but were prevented from doing so by Indian troops. Portugal initiated proceedings before the International Court of Justice to compel India to allow its troops access to the enclave, but the Court rejected its complaint in 1960, holding that India was within its rights in denying Portugal military access. In 1961, the Constitution of India was amended to incorporate Dadra and Nagar Haveli into India as a Union Territory.

Goa, Daman and Diu remained an outstanding issue. On 15 August 1955, five thousand non-violent demonstrators marched against the Portuguese at the border, and were met with gunfire, killing 22. In December 1960, the United Nations General Assembly rejected Portugal's contention that its overseas possessions were provinces, and formally listed them as "non-self-governing territories". Although Nehru continued to favour a negotiated solution, the Portuguese suppression of a revolt in Angola in 1961 radicalised Indian public opinion, and increased the pressure on the Government of India to take military action. African leaders, too, put pressure on Nehru to take action in Goa, which they argued would save Africa from further horrors. On 18 December 1961, following the collapse of an American attempt to find a negotiated solution, the Indian Army entered Portuguese India and defeated the Portuguese garrisons there. The Portuguese took the matter to the Security Council but a resolution calling on India to withdraw its troops immediately was defeated

Figure 200: *The former princely state of Sikkim, located at a strategically important point on the border between India and China, was integrated into India in 1975 as its 22nd state.*

by the USSR's veto. Portugal surrendered on 19 December. This take-over ended the last of the European colonies in India. Goa was incorporated into India as a centrally administered union territory and, in 1987, became a state.

Sikkim

Three princely states bordering India—Nepal, Bhutan and Sikkim—were not integrated into the Republic of India in the period between 1947 and 1950. Nepal had been recognised by the British and the Government of India as being *de jure* independent. Bhutan had in the British period been considered a protectorate outside the international frontier of India. The Government of India entered into a treaty with Bhutan in 1949 continuing this arrangement, and providing that Bhutan would abide by the advice of the Government of India in the conduct of its external affairs.

Historically, Sikkim was a British dependency, with a status similar to that of the other princely states, and was therefore considered to be within the frontiers of India in the colonial period. On independence, however, the Chogyal of Sikkim resisted full integration into India. Given the region's strategic importance to India, the Government of India signed first a Standstill Agreement and then in 1950 a full treaty with the Chogyal of Sikkim which in effect made it a protectorate which was no longer part of India. India had responsibility for defence, external affairs and communications, and ultimate responsibility for law and order, but Sikkim was otherwise given full internal autonomy. In the late 1960s and early 1970s, the Chogyal Palden Thondup Namgyal, supported by the minority Bhutia and Lepcha upper classes, attempted to negotiate greater powers, particularly over external affairs, to give Sikkim more of an international personality. These policies were opposed by Kazi Lhendup Dorji and the Sikkim State Congress, who represented the ethnic Nepali middle classes and took a more pro-Indian view.

In April 1973, anti-Chogyal agitation broke out and protestors demanded popular elections. The Sikkim police were unable to control the demonstrations, and Dorji asked India to exercise its responsibility for law and order and intervene. India facilitated negotiations between the Chogyal and Dorji, and produced an agreement, which envisaged the reduction of the Chogyal to the role of a constitutional monarch and the holding of elections based on a new ethnic power-sharing formula. The Chogyal's opponents won an overwhelming victory, and a new Constitution was drafted providing for Sikkim to be associated with the Republic of India. On 10 April 1975, the Sikkim Assembly passed a resolution calling for the state to be fully integrated into India. This resolution was endorsed by 97 percent of the vote in a referendum held on 14 April 1975, following which the Indian Parliament amended the constitution to admit Sikkim into India as its 22nd state.

Secessionism and sub-nationalism

While the majority of princely states absorbed into India have been fully integrated, a few outstanding issues remain. The most prominent of these is in relation to Kashmir, where a violent secessionist insurgency has been raging since the late 1980s.

Some academics suggest that the insurgency in Kashmir is at least partly a result of the manner in which it was integrated into India. Kashmir, uniquely amongst princely states, was not required to sign either a Merger Agreement or a revised Instrument of Accession giving India control over a larger number of issues than the three originally provided for. Instead, the power to make laws relating to Kashmir was granted to the Government of India by Article 5 of the Constitution of Jammu and Kashmir and was, under Article 370 of the Constitution of India, somewhat more restricted than in relation to other states. Widmalm argues that during the 1980s, a number of Kashmiri youth began to feel that the Indian government was increasingly interfering in the politics of Jammu and Kashmir. The elections of 1987 caused them to lose faith in the political process and begin the violent insurgency which is still ongoing. Similarly, Ganguly suggests that the policies of the Indian government towards Kashmir meant that the state, unlike other parts of India, never developed the solid political institutions associated with a modern multi-ethnic democracy. As a result, the growing dissatisfaction with the *status quo* felt by an increasingly politically aware youth was expressed through non-political channels which Pakistan, seeking to weaken India's hold over Kashmir, transformed into an active insurgency.

Separatist movements also exist in two other former princely states located in Northeast India—Tripura and Manipur. These separatist movements are generally treated by scholars as being part of the broader problem of insurgencies in North-east India, rather being a result of specific problems in integrating the princely states into India, as the Kashmir problem is and, in particular, to reflect the failure of the Government of India to adequately address the aspirations of tribal groups in the Northeast, or to tackle the tensions arising from the immigration of people from other parts of India to the north-eastern areas.[915]

The integration of former princely states with other provinces to form new states has also given rise to some issues. The Telangana region, comprising the Telugu-speaking districts of the former Hyderabad State, were in many ways different from the Telugu-speaking areas of British India with which they were merged. In recognition of these differences, the States Reorganisation Commission originally recommended that Telangana be created as a separate state, rather than as part of a broader Telugu-speaking entity. This recommendation was rejected by the Government of India, and Telangana was merged into Andhra Pradesh. The result was the emergence in the 1960s of a movement demanding a separate Telangana state. The demand has been accepted by the Union Government, leading to formation of Telangana as the 29th state of India in June 2014. A similar movement, although less strong, exists in the Vidarbha region of Maharashtra, which consists of the former Nagpur state and the Berar region of the former Hyderabad state.

Critical perspectives on the process of integration

The integration process repeatedly brought Indian and Pakistani leaders into conflict. During negotiations, Jinnah, representing the Muslim League, strongly supported the right of the princely states to remain independent, joining neither India nor Pakistan, an attitude which was diametrically opposed to the stance taken by Nehru and the Congress and which was reflected in Pakistan's support of Hyderabad's bid to stay independent. Post-partition, the Government of Pakistan accused India of hypocrisy on the ground that there was little difference between the accession of the ruler of Junagadh to Pakistan—which India refused to recognise—and the accession of the Maharajah of Kashmir to India, and for several years refused to recognise the legality of India's incorporation of Junagadh, treating it as *de jure* Pakistani territory.

Different theories have been proposed to explain the designs of Indian and Pakistani leaders in this period. Rajmohan Gandhi postulates that an ideal deal working in the mind of Patel was that if Muhammad Ali Jinnah let India have Junagadh and Hyderabad, Patel would not object to Kashmir acceding to Pakistan. In his book *Patel: A Life*, Gandhi asserts that Jinnah sought to engage the questions of Junagadh and Hyderabad in the same battle. It is suggested that he wanted India to ask for a plebiscite in Junagadh and Hyderabad, knowing thus that the principle then would have to be applied to Kashmir, where the Muslim-majority would, he believed, vote for Pakistan. A speech by Patel at the Bahauddin College in Junagadh following the latter's take-over, where he said that "we would agree to Kashmir if they agreed to Hyderabad", suggests that he may have been amenable to this idea. Although Patel's opinions were not India's policy, nor were they shared by Nehru, both leaders were angered at Jinnah's courting the princes of Jodhpur, Bhopal and Indore, leading them to take a harder stance on a possible deal with Pakistan.

Modern historians have also re-examined the role of the States Department and Lord Mountbatten during the accession process. Ian Copland argues that the Congress leaders did not intend the settlement contained in the Instruments of Accession to be permanent even when they were signed, and at all times privately contemplated a complete integration of the sort that ensued between 1948 and 1950. He points out that the mergers and cession of powers to the Government of India between 1948 and 1950 contravened the terms of the Instruments of Accession, and were incompatible with the express assurances of internal autonomy and preservation of the princely states which Mountbatten had given the princes. Menon in his memoirs stated that the changes to the initial terms of accession were in every instance freely consented to by the princes with no element of coercion. Copland disagrees, on the basis that foreign diplomats at the time believed that the princes had been given no choice but to sign, and that a few princes expressed their unhappiness with the arrangements. He also criticises Mountbatten's role, saying that while he stayed within the letter of the law, he was at least under a moral obligation to do something for the princes when it became apparent that the Government of India was going to alter the terms on which accession took place, and that he should never have lent his support to the bargain given that it could not be guaranteed after independence. Both Copland and Ramusack argue that, in the ultimate analysis, one of the reasons why the princes consented to the demise of their states was that they felt abandoned by the British, and saw themselves as having little other option. Older historians such as Lumby, in contrast, take the view that the princely states could not have survived as independent entities after the transfer of power, and that their demise was inevitable. They therefore view successful integration of all princely states into India as a triumph for the Government of India and Lord Mountbatten, and as a tribute to the sagacity of the majority of princes, who jointly achieved in a few months what the Empire had attempted, unsuccessfully, to do for over a century—unite all of India under one rule.

Also see

- Praja Mandal

References

- Ashton, S.R. (1982), *British Policy towards the Indian States, 1905–1938*, London Studies on South Asia no. 2, London: Curzon Press, ISBN 0-7007-0146-X
- Bhargava, R. P. (1991), *The Chamber of Princes*, India: Northern Book Centre, ISBN 978-8172110055
- Brown, Judith M. (1984), "The Mountbatten Viceroyalty. Announcement and Reception of the 3 June Plan, 31 May-7 July 1947", *The English Historical Review*, **99** (392): 667–668
- Copland, Ian (1987), "Congress Paternalism: The "High Command" and the Struggle for Freedom in Princely India"", in Masselos, Jim, *Struggling and Ruling: The Indian National Congress 1885–1985*, New Delhi: Sterling Publishers, pp. 121–140, ISBN 81-207-0691-9
- Copland, Ian (1993), "Lord Mountbatten and the Integration of the Indian States: A Reappraisal", *The Journal of Imperial and Commonwealth History*, **21** (2): 385–408, doi: 10.1080/03086539308582896[916]
- Copland, Ian (1997), *The Princes of India in the Endgame of Empire, 1917–1947*, Cambridge, England: Cambridge University Press, ISBN 0-521-57179-0
- Eagleton, Clyde (1950), "The Case of Hyderabad Before the Security Council", *The American Journal of International Law*, American Society of International Law, **44** (2): 277–302, doi: 10.2307/2193757[917], JSTOR 2193757[918]
- Fifield, Russell H. (1950), "The Future of French India", *Far Eastern Review*, **19** (6): 62–64, doi: 10.1525/as.1950.19.6.01p0582b[919]
- Fifield, Russell H. (1952), "New States in the Indian Realm", *The American Journal of International Law*, American Society of International Law, **46** (3): 450–463, doi: 10.2307/2194500[920], JSTOR 2194500[921]

- Fisher, Margaret W. (1962), "Goa in Wider Perspective", *Asian Survey*, **2** (2): 3–10, doi: 10.1525/as.1962.2.2.01p1537e[922]
- Fisher, Michael H. (1984), "Indirect Rule in the British Empire: The Foundations of the Residency System in India (1764–1858)", *Modern Asian Studies*, **18** (3): 393–428, doi: 10.1017/S0026749X00009033[923]
- Furber, Holden (1951), "The Unification of India, 1947–1951", *Pacific Affairs*, Pacific Affairs, University of British Columbia, **24** (4): 352–371, doi: 10.2307/2753451[924], JSTOR 2753451[925]
- Gandhi, Rajmohan (1991), *Patel: A Life*, Ahmedabad: Navajivan Publishing House
- Ganguly, Sumit (1996), "Explaining the Kashmir Insurgency: Political Mobilization and Institutional Decay", *International Security*, The MIT Press, **21** (2): 76–107, doi: 10.2307/2539071[926], JSTOR 2539071[927]
- Gledhill, Alan (1957), "Constitutional and Legislative Development in the Indian Republic", *Bulletin of the School of Oriental and African Studies, University of London*, **20** (1–3): 267–278, doi: 10.1017/S0041977X00061838[928]
- Gray, Hugh (1971), "The Demand for a Separate Telangana State in India", *Asian Survey*, **11** (5): 463–474, doi: 10.1525/as.1971.11.5.01p0113d[929]
- Guha, Amalendu (1984), "Nationalism: Pan-Indian and Regional in a Historical Perspective", *Social Scientist*, Social Scientist, **12** (2): 42–65, doi: 10.2307/3517093[930], JSTOR 3517093[931]
- Gupta, Ranjan (1975), "Sikkim: The Merger with India", *Asian Survey*, **15** (9): 786–798, doi: 10.1525/as.1975.15.9.01p0110k[932]
- Hardgrave, Robert L. (1983), "The Northeast, the Punjab, and the Regionalization of Indian Politics", *Asian Survey*, **23** (11): 1171–1181, doi: 10.1525/as.1983.23.11.01p0095g[933]
- Karan, Pradyumna P. (1960), "A Free Access to Colonial Enclaves", *Annals of the Association of American Geographers*, **50** (2): 188–190, doi: 10.1111/j.1467-8306.1960.tb00345.x[934]
- Keith, Arthur Berriedale (1969), *A Constitutional History of India, 1600–1935* (2nd ed.), London: Methuen
- Lee-Warner, Sir William (1910), *The Native States of India* (2nd ed.), London: Macmillan
- Lumby, E.W.R. (1954), *The Transfer of Power in India, 1945–1947*, London: George Allen and Unwin
- McLeod, John (1999), *Sovereignty, Power, Control: Politics in the State of Western India, 1916–1947*, Leiden: Brill, ISBN 90-04-11343-6
- Menon, V.P. (1956), *The Story of the Integration of the Indian States*, New York: Macmillan
- Mitra, Subrata Kumar (2006), *The Puzzle of India's Governance: Culture,*

Context and Comparative Theory, London: Routledge, ISBN 0-415-34861-7
- Moore, R.J. (1983), *Escape from Empire: The Attlee Government and the Indian Problem*, Oxford: Clarendon Press, ISBN 0-19-822688-8
- Morris-Jones, W.H. (1983), "Thirty-Six Years Later: The Mixed Legacies of Mountbatten's Transfer of Power", *International Affairs*, **59** (4): 621–628, doi: 10.2307/2619473[935]
- Mosley, Leonard (1961), *The last days of the British Raj*, London: Weidenfeld & Nicolson
- Note (1975), "Current Legal Developments: Sikkim, Constituent Unit of India", *International and Comparative Law Quarterly*, **24** (4): 884, doi: 10.1093/iclqaj/24.4.884[936]
- Phadnis, Urmila (1968), *Towards the Integration of the Indian States, 1919–1947*, London: Asia Publishing House
- Phadnis, Urmila (1969), "Gandhi and Indian States: A Probe in Strategy", in Biswas, S.C., *Gandhi: Theory and Practice, Social Impact and Contemporary Relevance*, Transactions of the Indian Institute of Advanced Study Vol. 2, Shimla: Indian Institute of Advanced Study, pp. 360–374
- Potter, Pitman B. (1950), "The Principal Legal and Political Problems Involved in the Kashmir Case", *The American Journal of International Law*, American Society of International Law, **44** (2): 361–363, doi: 10.2307/2193764[937], JSTOR 2193764[938]
- Ramusack, Barbara N. (1978), *The Princes of India in the Twilight of Empire: Dissolution of a patron-client system, 1914–1939*, Colombus, Ohio: Ohio State University Press, ISBN 0-8142-0272-1
- Ramusack, Barbara N. (1988), "Congress and the People's Movement in Princely India: Ambivalence in Strategy and Organisation", in Sisson, Richard; Wolpert, Stanley, *Congress and Indian Nationalism*, Berkeley: University of California Press, pp. 377–403, ISBN 0-520-06041-5
- Ramusack, Barbara N. (2004), *The Indian Princes and Their States*, The New Cambridge History of India III.6, Cambridge, England: Cambridge University Press, ISBN 0-521-26727-7
- Rangaswami, Vanaja (1981), *The Story of Integration: A New Interpretation in the Context of the Democratic Movements in the Princely States of Mysore, Travancore and Cochin 1900–1947*, New Delhi: Manohar
- Roberts, Neal A. (1972), "The Supreme Court in a Developing Society: Progressive or Reactionary Force? A Study of the Privy Purse Case in India", *The American Journal of Comparative Law*, American Society of Comparative Law, **20** (1): 79–110, doi: 10.2307/839489[939], JSTOR 839489[940]
- Security Council (1957), "Security Council: India-Pakistan Question", *International Organization*, **11** (2): 368–372, doi:

10.1017/S0020818300023808[941]
- Singh, B.P. (1987), "North-East India: Demography, Culture and Identity Crisis", *Modern Asian Studies*, **21** (2): 257–282, doi: 10.1017/S0026749X00013809[942]
- Spate, O.H.K. (1948), "The Partition of India and the Prospects of Pakistan", *Geographical Review*, American Geographical Society, **38** (1): 5–29, doi: 10.2307/210736[943], JSTOR 210736[944]
- Talbot, Phillips (1949), "Kashmir and Hyderabad", *World Politics*, Cambridge University Press, **1** (3): 321–332, doi: 10.2307/2009033[945], JSTOR 2009033[946]
- Vincent, Rose (1990), *The French in India: From Diamond Traders to Sanskrit Scholars*, Bombay: Popular Prakashan, translated by Latika Padgaonkar
- Wainwright, A. M. (1994), *Inheritance of Empire: Britain, India and the Balance of Power in Asia, 1938–55*, Westport: Praeger, ISBN 0-275-94733-5
- Widmalm, Sten (1997), "The Rise and Fall of Democracy in Jammu and Kashmir", *Asian Survey*, **37** (11): 1005–1030, doi: 10.1525/as.1997.37.11.01p02937[947]
- Wright, Quincy (1962), "The Goa Incident", *The American Journal of International Law*, American Society of International Law, **56** (3): 617–632, doi: 10.2307/2196501[948], JSTOR 2196501[949]
- Wood, John (1984), "British versus Princely Legacies and the Political Integration of Gujarat", *The Journal of Asian Studies*, **44** (1): 65–99, doi: 10.2307/2056747[950], JSTOR 2056747[951]
- Wood, John; Moon, Penderel; Blake, David M.; Ashton, Stephen R. (1985), "Dividing the Jewel: Mountbatten and the Transfer of Power to India and Pakistan", *Pacific Affairs*, Pacific Affairs, University of British Columbia, **58** (4): 653–662, doi: 10.2307/2758474[952], JSTOR 2758474[953]
- Puchalapalli, Sundarayya (March 1973), "Telangana People's Armed Struggle, 1946-1951. Part Two: First Phase and Its Lessons"[954], *Social Scientist*, Social Scientist, **1** (8): 18–42, doi: 10.2307/3516214[955], JSTOR 3516214[956], archived from the original[957] on 3 February 2014
- Metcalf, Barbara D.; Metcalf, Thomas R. (2006). *A Concise History of India*[958] (2nd ed.). Cambridge University Press. ISBN 978-0521682251.
- Thomson, Mike (September 24, 2013). "Hyderabad 1948: India's hidden massacre"[959]. *BBC*. Retrieved September 24, 2013.
- Noorani, A.G. (Mar 3–16, 2001). "Of a massacre untold"[960]. *Frontline*. **18** (05). Retrieved 8 September 2014.

<indicator name="featured-star"> ⭐ </indicator>

Indo-Pakistani War of 1947

Indo-Pakistani War of 1947–1948
۱۹۴۸-بھارت پاکستان جنگ ۱۹۴۷
भारत-पाकिस्तान युद्ध १९४७-१९४८

Part of the Indo-Pakistani wars and conflicts

Indian soldiers during the 1947–1948 war.

Date	22 October 1947 – 5 January 1949 (1 year, 2 months and 2 weeks)
Location	Kashmir
Result	Ceasefire agreement • Princely state of Jammu and Kashmir acceded to India • UN Ceasefire Line of 1949 (later becomes Line of Control after the Simla Agreement of 1972)
Territorial changes	Pakistan controls roughly a third of Kashmir (Azad Kashmir and Gilgit–Baltistan), whereas India controls the rest (Kashmir valley, Jammu and Ladakh).

Belligerents

Dominion of India • Jammu and Kashmir	Dominion of Pakistan • Azad Kashmir irregular forces • Muslim League National Guard[961] • Pashtun tribal militias • Kurram Militia[962] • Frontier Scouts[962] • Swat Army[962] • Furqan Force • Gilgit Scouts

Commanders and leaders

Indo-Pakistani War of 1947

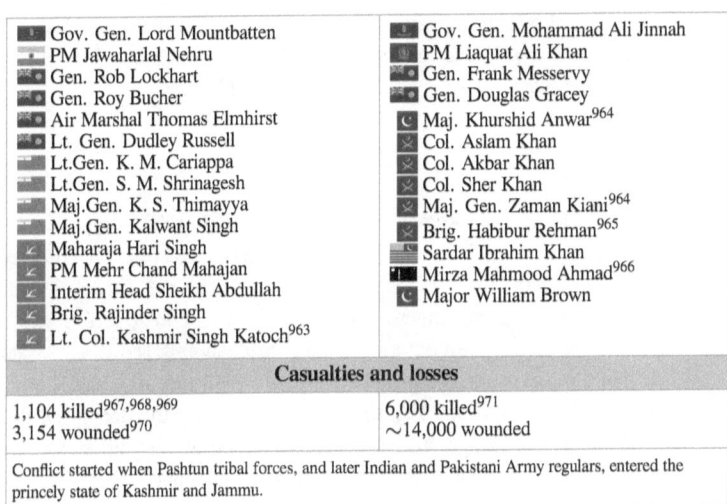

■ Gov. Gen. Lord Mountbatten ■ PM Jawaharlal Nehru ■ Gen. Rob Lockhart ■ Gen. Roy Bucher ■ Air Marshal Thomas Elmhirst ■ Lt. Gen. Dudley Russell ■ Lt.Gen. K. M. Cariappa ■ Lt.Gen. S. M. Shrinagesh ■ Maj.Gen. K. S. Thimayya ■ Maj.Gen. Kalwant Singh ■ Maharaja Hari Singh ■ PM Mehr Chand Mahajan ■ Interim Head Sheikh Abdullah ■ Brig. Rajinder Singh ■ Lt. Col. Kashmir Singh Katoch[963]	■ Gov. Gen. Mohammad Ali Jinnah ■ PM Liaquat Ali Khan ■ Gen. Frank Messervy ■ Gen. Douglas Gracey ■ Maj. Khurshid Anwar[964] ■ Col. Aslam Khan ■ Col. Akbar Khan ■ Col. Sher Khan ■ Maj. Gen. Zaman Kiani[964] ■ Brig. Habibur Rehman[965] ■ Sardar Ibrahim Khan ■ Mirza Mahmood Ahmad[966] ■ Major William Brown
Casualties and losses	
1,104 killed[967],[968],[969] 3,154 wounded[970]	6,000 killed[971] ~14,000 wounded

Conflict started when Pashtun tribal forces, and later Indian and Pakistani Army regulars, entered the princely state of Kashmir and Jammu.

The **Indo-Pakistani War of 1947–1948**, sometimes known as the **First Kashmir War**, was fought between India and Pakistan over the princely state of Kashmir and Jammu from 1947 to 1948. It was the first of four Indo-Pakistan Wars fought between the two newly independent nations. Pakistan precipitated the war a few weeks after independence by launching tribal *lashkar* (militia) from Waziristan,[972] in an effort to secure Kashmir, the future of which hung in the balance. The inconclusive result of the war still affects the geopolitics of both countries.

The Maharaja faced an uprising by his Muslim subjects in Poonch, and lost control of the western districts of his kingdom. On 22 October 1947, Pakistan's Pashtun tribal militias crossed the border of the state. These local tribal militias and irregular Pakistani forces moved to take Srinagar, but on reaching Baramulla, they took to plunder and stalled. Hari Singh made a plea to India for assistance, and help was offered, but it was subject to his signing an Instrument of Accession to India.

The war was initially fought by the Jammu and Kashmir State Forces[973] and by tribal militias from the Frontier Tribal Areas adjoining the North-West Frontier Province.[974] Following the accession of the state to India on 26 October 1947, Indian troops were air-lifted to Srinagar, the state capital. The British commanding officers initially refused the entry of Pakistani troops into the conflict, citing the accession of the state to India. However, later in 1948, they relented and the Pakistani armies entered the war after this. The fronts solidified gradually along what came to be known as the Line of Control. A formal cease-fire was declared at 23:59 on the night of 31 December 1948 and became effective on the night of 1 January 1949.[975] The result of the war was inconclusive. However, most neutral assessments agree that India was the victor of the war as it was able to successfully defend about two-thirds of the Kashmir including Kashmir valley, Jammu and Ladakh.

Background

Prior to 1815, the area now known as "Jammu and Kashmir" comprised 22 small independent states (16 Hindu and six Muslim) carved out of territories controlled by the Amir (King) of Afghanistan, combined with those of local small rulers. These were collectively referred to as the "Punjab Hill States". These small states, ruled by Rajput kings, were variously independent, vassals of the Mughal Empire since the time of Emperor Akbar or sometimes controlled from Kangra state in the Himachal area. Following the decline of the Mughals, turbulence in Kangra and invasions of Gorkhas, the hill states fell successively under the control of the Sikhs under Ranjit Singh.:536

The First Anglo-Sikh War (1845–46) was fought between the Sikh Empire, which asserted sovereignty over Kashmir, and the East India Company. In the Treaty of Lahore of 1846, the Sikhs were made to surrender the valuable region (the Jullundur Doab) between the Beas River and the Sutlej River and required to pay an indemnity of 1.2 million rupees. Because they could not readily raise this sum, the East India Company allowed the Dogra ruler Gulab Singh to acquire Kashmir from the Sikh kingdom in exchange for making a payment of 750,000 rupees to the Company. Gulab Singh became the first Maharaja of the newly formed princely state of Jammu and Kashmir,[976] founding a dynasty, that was to rule the state, the second-largest principality during the British Raj, until India gained its independence in 1947.

Partition of India

The years 1946–1947 saw the rise of All-India Muslim League and Muslim nationalism, demanding a separate state for India's Muslims. The demand took a violent turn on the Direct Action Day (16 August 1946) and inter-communal violence between Hindus and Muslims became endemic. Consequently, a decision was taken on 3 June 1947 to divide British India into two separate states, the Dominion of Pakistan comprising the Muslim majority areas and the Union of India comprising the rest. The two provinces Punjab and Bengal with large Muslim-majority areas were to be divided between the two dominions. An estimated 11 million people eventually migrated between the two parts of Punjab, and possibly 1 million perished in the inter-communal violence. Jammu and Kashmir, being adjacent to the Punjab province, was directly affected by the happenings in Punjab.

Indo-Pakistani War of 1947

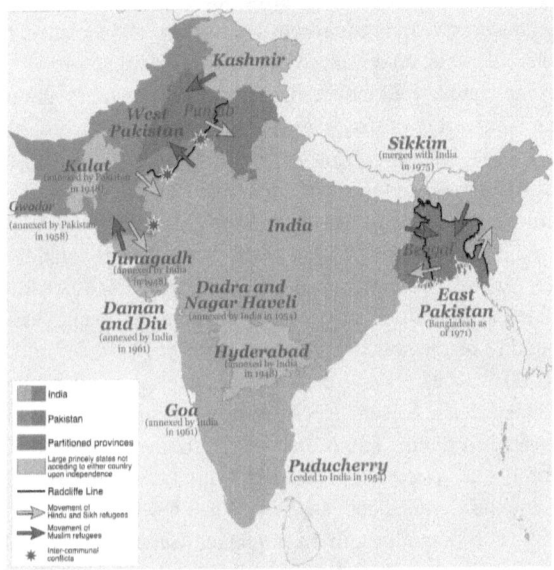

Figure 201: *Partition of India and the movement of refugees*

Figure 202: *Field Marshal Claude Auchinleck, Supreme Commander of Indian and Pakistani armed forces*

The original target date for the transfer of power to the new dominions was June 1948. However, fearing the rise of inter-communal violence, the British Viceroy Lord Mountbatten advanced the date to 15 August 1947. This gave only 6 weeks to complete all the arrangements for partition.[977] Mountbatten's original plan was to stay on the joint Governor General for both the dominions till June 1948. However, this was not accepted by the Pakistani leader Mohammad Ali Jinnah. In the event, Mountbatten stayed on as the Governor General of India, whereas Pakistan chose Jinnah as its Governor General.[978] It was envisaged that the nationalisation of the armed forces could not be completed by 15 August.[979] Pakistan had only four lieutenant colonels,[980] two of whom were involved in the Kashmir conflict: Akbar Khan and Sher Khan.[981] At the beginning of the war, India had about 500 British officers and Pakistan over 1000.[982]</ref> Hence British officers stayed on after the transfer of power. The service chiefs were appointed by the Dominion governments and were responsible to them. The overall administrative control, but not operational control, was vested with Field Marshal Claude Auchinleck, who was titled the 'Supreme Commander', answerable to a newly formed Joint Defence Council of the two dominions. India appointed General Rob Lockhart as its Army chief and Pakistan appointed General Frank Messervy.[983]

The presence of the British commanding officers on both sides made the Indo-Pakistani War of 1947 a strange war. The two commanding officers were in daily telephone contact and adopted mutually defensive positions. The attitude was that "you can hit them so hard but not too hard, otherwise there will be all kinds of repercussions."[984] Both Lockhart and Messervy were replaced in the course of war, and their successors Roy Bucher and Douglas Gracey tried to exercise restraint on their respective governments. Roy Bucher was apparently successful in doing so in India, but Gracey yielded and let British officers be used in operational roles on the side of Pakistan. One British officer even died in action.[985]

Developments in Jammu and Kashmir (August–October 1947)

With the independence of the Dominions, the British Paramountcy over the princely states came to an end. The rulers of the states were advised to join one of the two dominions by executing an Instrument of Accession. Maharaja Hari Singh of Jammu and Kashmir, along with his prime minister Ram Chandra Kak, decided not to accede to either dominion. The reasons cited were that the Muslim majority population of the State would not be comfortable with joining India, and that the Hindu and Sikh minorities would become vulnerable if the state joined Pakistan.[986]

Figure 203: *Maharaja Hari Singh of Jammu and Kashmir*

In 1947, the princely state of Jammu and Kashmir had a wide range of ethnic and religious communities. The Kashmir province consisting of the Kashmir Valley and the Muzaffarabad district had a majority Muslim population (over 90%). The Jammu province, consisting of 5 districts, had a roughly equal division of Hindus and Muslims in the eastern districts (Udhampur, Jammu and Reasi) and Muslim majority in the western districts (Mirpur and Poonch). The mountainous Ladakh district (*wazarat*) in the east had a significant Buddhist presence with a Muslim majority in Baltistan. The Gilgit Agency in the north was overwhelmingly Muslim and was directly governed by the British under an agreement with the Maharaja. Shortly before the transfer of power, the British returned the Gilgit Agency to the Maharaja, who appointed a Dogra governor for the district and a British commander for the local forces.

The predominant political movement in the Kashmir Valley, the National Conference led by Sheikh Abdullah, believed in secular politics. It was allied with the Indian National Congress and was believed to favour joining India. On the other hand, the Muslims of the Jammu province supported the Muslim Conference, which was allied to the All-India Muslim League and favoured joining Pakistan. The Hindus of the Jammu province favoured an outright merger with India. In the midst of all the diverging views, the Maharaja's decision to remain independent was apparently a judicious one.[987]

Figure 204: *Sheikh Abdullah, Leader of the National Conference*

Operation Gulmarg plan

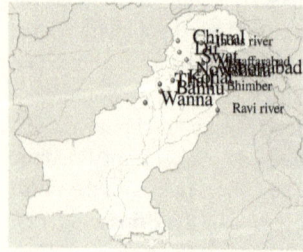

File:Pakistan location map.svg

Operation Gulmarg locations

According to Indian military sources, the Pakistani Army prepared a plan called **Operation Gulmarg** and put it into action as early as 20 August, a few days after Pakistan's independence. The plan got accidentally revealed to an Indian officer, Major O. S. Kalkat serving with the Bannu Brigade.[988]</ref> According to the plan, 20 *lashkars* (tribal militias), each consisting of 1000 Pashtun tribesmen, were to be recruited from among various Pashtun tribes, and armed at the brigade headquarters at Bannu, Wanna, Peshawar, Kohat, Thall and Nowshera by the first week of September. They were expected to reach the launching point of Abbottabad on 18 October, and cross into Jammu and Kashmir on 22 October. Ten lashkars were expected to attack the Kashmir Valley through Muzaffarabad and another ten lashkars were expected to join the rebels in Poonch, Bhimber and Rawalakot with a view to advance to Jammu. Detailed arrangements for the military leadership and armaments were described in the plan.[989]

The regimental records show that, by the last week of August, the Prince Albert Victor's Own Cavalry (PAVO Cavalry) regiment was briefed about the invasion plan. Colonel Sher Khan, the Director of Military Intelligence, was in charge of the briefing, along with Colonels Akbar Khan and Khanzadah. The Cavalry regiment was tasked with procuring arms and ammunition for the 'freedom fighters' and establishing three wings of the insurgent forces: the South Wing commanded by General Kiani, a Central Wing based at Rawalpinidi and a North Wing based at Abbottabad. By 1 October, the Cavalry regiment completed the task of arming the insurgent forces. "Throughout the war there was no shortage of small arms, ammunitions, or explosives at any time." The regiment was also told to be on stand by for induction into fighting at an appropriate time.[990,991]

Scholars have noted considerable movement of Pashtun tribes during September–October. By 13 September, armed Pashtuns drifted into Lahore and Rawalpindi. The Deputy Commissioner of Dera Ismail Khan noted a scheme to send tribesmen from Malakand to Sialkot, in lorries provided by the Pakistan Government. Preparations for attacking Kashmir were also noted in the princely states of Swat, Dir, and Chitral. Scholar Robin James Moore states there is "little doubt" that Pashtuns were involved in border raids all along the Punjab border from the Indus to the Ravi.[992]

Pakistani sources deny the existence of any plan called Operation Gulmarg. However, Shuja Nawaz does list 22 Pashtun tribes involved in the invasion of Kashmir on 22 October.[993]

Rebellion in Poonch

Sometime in August 1947, the first signs of trouble broke out in Poonch, about which diverging views have been received. Poonch was originally an internal *jagir* (autonomous principality), governed by an alternative family line of Maharaja Hari Singh. The taxation is said to have been heavy. The Muslims of Poonch had long campaigned for the principality to be absorbed into the Punjab province of British India. In 1938, a notable disturbance occurred for religious reasons, but a settlement was reached.[994] During the Second World War, over 60,000 men from Poonch and Mirpur districts enrolled in the British Indian Army. After the war, they were discharged with arms, which is said to have alarmed the Maharaja.[995] In June, Poonchis launched a 'No Tax' campaign. In July, the Maharaja ordered that all the soldiers in the region be disarmed.[996]</ref> The absence of employment prospects coupled with high taxation drove the Poonchis to rebellion.[995] The "gathering head of steam", states scholar Srinath Raghavan, was utilised by the local Muslim Conference led by Sardar Muhammad Ibrahim Khan (Sardar Ibrahim) to further their campaign for accession to Pakistan.[997]

According to state government sources, the rebellious militias gathered in the Naoshera-Islamabad area, attacking the state troops and their supply trucks. A battalion of state troops was dispatched, which cleared the roads and dispersed the militias. By September, order was reestablished.[998] The Muslim Conference sources, on the other hand, narrate that hundreds of people were killed in Bagh during flag hoisting around 15 August and that the Maharaja unleased a 'reign of terror' on 24 August. Local Muslims also told Richard Symonds, a British Quaker social worker, that the army fired on crowds, and burnt houses and villages indiscriminately.[999] According to the Assistant British High Commissioner in Pakistan, H. S. Stephenson, "the Poonch affair... was greatly exaggerated".[998]

Pakistan's preparations, Maharaja's manoeuvring

Scholar Prem Shankar Jha states that the Maharaja had decided, as early as April 1947, that he would accede to India if it was not possible to stay independent.:[115] The rebellion in Poonch possibly unnerved the Maharaja. Accordingly, on 11 August, he dismissed his pro-Pakistan Prime Minister, Ram Chandra Kak, and appointed retired Major Janak Singh in his place. On 25 August, he sent an invitation to Justice Mehr Chand Mahajan of the Punjab High Court to come as the Prime Minister.[1000] On the same day, the Muslim Conference wrote to the Pakistani Prime Minister Liaquat Ali Khan warning him that "if, God forbid, the Pakistan Government or the Muslim League do not act, Kashmir might be lost to them".[1001] This set the ball rolling in Pakistan.

Liaquat Ali Khan sent a Punjab politician Mian Iftikharuddin to explore the possibility of organising a revolt in Kashmir.[1002] Meanwhile, Pakistan cut off essential supplies to the state, such as petrol, sugar and salt. It also stopped trade in timber and other products, and suspended train services to Jammu.[1003,1004] Iftikharuddin returned in mid-September to report that the National Conference held strong in the Kashmir Valley and ruled out the possibility of a revolt.

Meanwhile, Sardar Ibrahim had escaped to West Punjab, along with dozens of rebels, and established a base in Murree. From there, the rebels attempted to

Figure 205: *Liaquat Ali Khan, Prime Minister of Pakistan*

Figure 206: *Murree, overlooking Kashmir*

Figure 207: *Jawaharlal Nehru, Prime Minister of India*

acquire arms and ammunition for the rebellion and smuggle them into Kashmir. Colonel Akbar Khan, one of a handful of high-ranking officers in the Pakistani Army,[1005]</ref> with a keen interest in Kashmir, arrived in Murree, and got enmeshed in these efforts. He arranged 4,000 rifles for the rebellion by diverting them from the Army stores. He also wrote out a draft plan titled *Armed Revolt inside Kashmir* and gave it to Mian Iftikharuddin to be passed on to the Pakistan's Prime Minister.[1006,1007,964]

On 12 September, the Prime Minister held a meeting with Mian Iftikharuddin, Colonel Akbar Khan and another Punjab politician Sardar Shaukat Hayat Khan. Hayat Khan had a separate plan, involving the Muslim League National Guard and the militant Pashtun tribes from the Frontier regions. The Prime Minister approved both the plans, and despatched Khurshid Anwar, the head of the Muslim League National Guard, to mobilise the Frontier tribes.[1007,964]

The Maharaja was increasingly driven to the wall with the rebellion in the western districts and the Pakistani blockade. He managed to persuade Justice Mahajan to accept the post of Prime Minister (but not to arrive for another month, for procedural reasons). He sent word to the Indian leaders through Mahajan that he was willing to accede to India but needed more time to implement political reforms. Jawaharlal Nehru, Prime Minister of India, hoping to generate popular support against Pakistan and to secure Kashmir's accession to India before Pakistan could invade, realised that the popular leader Sheikh Abdullah would need to be brought to the forefront. In May 1946 Sheikh Abdullah launched the Quit Kashmir agitation against the Maharajah and was arrested and sentenced to three years imprisonment, and as Nehru urged for his release, he was released on 29 September.

Nehru, foreseeing a number of disputes over princely states, formulated a policy that states

> "*wherever there is a dispute in regard to any territory, the matter should be decided by a referendum or plebiscite of the people concerned. We shall accept the result of this referendum whatever it may be.*"[1008,1009]

The policy was communicated to Liaquat Ali Khan on 1 October at a meeting of the Joint Defence Council. Khan's eyes are said to have "sparkled" at the proposal. However, he made no response.[1008,1009]

The historian Rakesh Ankit explains this promise of plebiscite as having been made in the context of Nehru's confidence in the pro-India position and popularity of Sheikh Abdullah.

Operations in Poonch and Mirpur

Armed rebellion started in the Poonch district at the beginning of October 1947. The fighting elements consisted of "bands of deserters from the State Army, serving soldiers of the Pakistan Army on leave, ex-servicemen, and other volunteers who had risen spontaneously."[965] The first clash is said to have occurred at Thorar (near Rawalakot) on 3–4 October 1947.[1010] The rebels quickly gained control of almost the entire Poonch district. The State Forces garrison at Poonch came under heavy siege.

In the Mirpur district, the border posts at Saligram and Owen Pattan on the Jhelum river were captured by rebels around 8 October. Sehnsa and Throchi were abandoned by State Forces after attack.[1011,1012]

Radio communications between the fighting units were operated by the Pakistan Army.[1013] Even though the Indian Navy intercepted the communications, lacking intelligence in Jammu and Kashmir, it was unable to determine immediately where the fighting was taking place.

Accession of Kashmir

Following the Muslim revolution in the Poonch and Mirpur area[1014] and Pakistani backed:18 Pashtun tribal intervention from the Khyber Pakhtunkhwa aimed at supporting the revolution,[1015,1016] the Maharaja asked for Indian military assistance. Mountbatten urged him to accede to India temporarily to complete the legal formalities, although Mountbatten's insistence on accession before assistance has been questioned. The Maharaja complied, and the Government of India recognised the accession of the princely state to India. However, Nehru, according to his biographer Sarvepalli Gopal, did not give any importance to Mountbatten's insistence that there be a temporary accession. Neither did Sardar Patel. Indian troops were sent to the state to defend it. The Jammu & Kashmir National Conference volunteers aided the Indian Army in its campaign to drive out the Pathan invaders.

Pakistan refused to recognise the accession of Kashmir to India, claiming that it was obtained by "fraud and violence."[1017] Governor General Mohammad Ali Jinnah ordered its Army Chief General Douglas Gracey to move Pakistani troops to Kashmir at once. However, the Indian and Pakistani forces were still under a joint command, and Field Marshal Auchinleck prevailed upon him to withdraw the order. With its accession to India, Kashmir became legally Indian territory, and the British officers could not a play any role in an inter-Dominion war.[1018] The Pakistan army made available arms, ammunition and supplies to the rebel forces who were dubbed the 'Azad Army'. Pakistani army officers 'conveniently' on leave and the former officers of the Indian National Army were recruited to command the forces. In May 1948, the Pakistani army officially entered the conflict, in theory to defend the Pakistan borders, but it made plans to push towards Jammu and cut the lines of communications of the Indian forces in the Mehndar Valley.[1019] In Gilgit, the force of Gilgit Scouts under the command of a British officer Major William Brown mutinied and overthrew the governor Ghansara Singh. Brown prevailed on the forces to declare accession to Pakistan.[1020] They are also believed to have received assistance from the Chitral Scouts and the Chitral State Bodyguard's of the state of Chitral, one of the princely states of Pakistan, which had acceded to Pakistan on 6 October 1947.[1021]

India claimed that the accession had the people's support through the support of the National Conference, the most popular organisation in the state. Historians have questioned the representativeness of the National Conference and the clarity of its leaderships' goals. They observe that while many Kashmiris supported Sheikh Abdullah and the National Conference at the state level, they also supported Jinnah and the Muslim League at the all-India level.

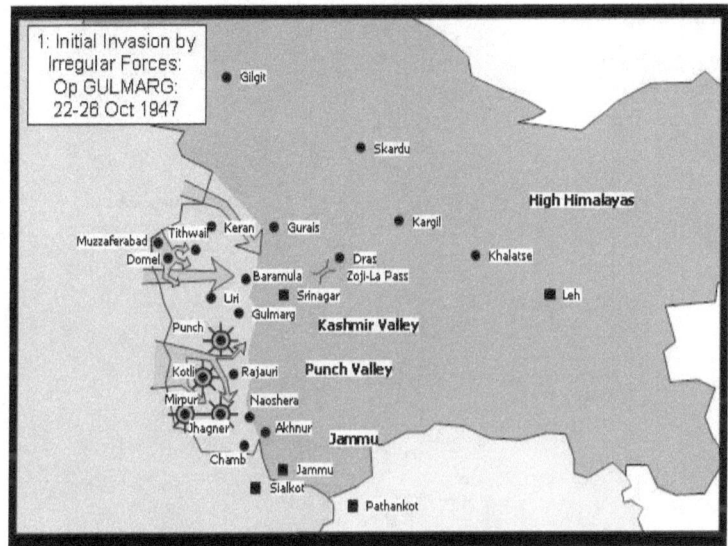

Figure 208: *State defence of the Kashmir Valley 22 October 1947 – 26 October 1947*

Stages of the war

Initial invasion

The first clash occurred at Thorar on 3–4 October 1947. On 22 October another attack was launched in the Muzaffarabad sector. The state forces stationed in the border regions around Muzaffarabad and Domel were quickly defeated by tribal forces (some Muslim state forces mutinied and joined them) and the way to the capital was open. Among the raiders, there were many active Pakistani Army soldiers disguised as tribals. They were also provided logistical help by the Pakistan Army. Rather than advancing toward Srinagar before state forces could regroup or be reinforced, the invading forces remained in the captured cities in the border region engaging in looting and other crimes against their inhabitants.[1022] In the Poonch valley, the state forces retreated into towns where they were besieged.[1023]

Indian operation in the Kashmir Valley

After the accession, India airlifted troops and equipment to Srinagar under the command of Lt. col. Dewan Ranjit Rai, where they reinforced the princely state forces, established a defence perimeter and defeated the tribal forces on the outskirts of the city. Initial defense operations included the notable defense

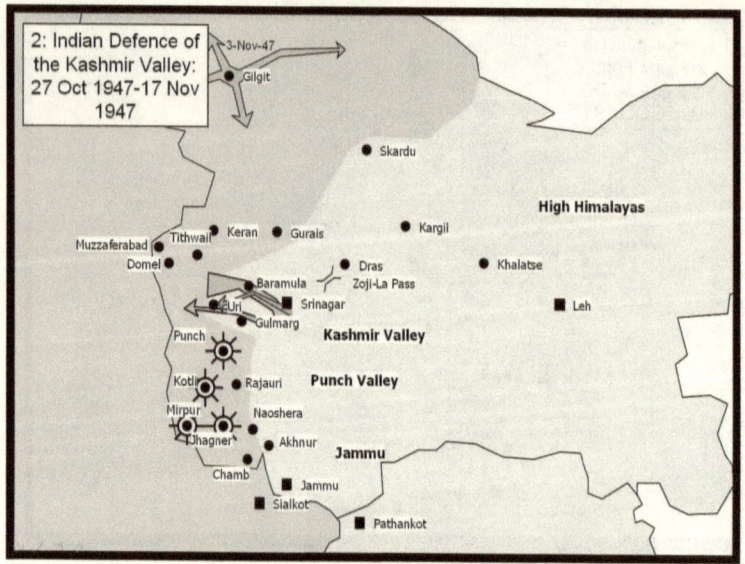

Figure 209: *Indian defence of the Kashmir Valley 27 October 1947 – 17 November 1947*

of Badgam holding both the capital and airfield overnight against extreme odds. The successful defence included an outflanking manoeuvre by Indian armoured cars during the Battle of Shalateng. The defeated tribal forces were pursued as far as Baramulla and Uri and these towns, too, were recaptured.

In the Poonch valley, tribal forces continued to besiege state forces.

In Gilgit, the state paramilitary forces, called the Gilgit Scouts, joined the invading tribal forces, who thereby obtained control of this northern region of the state. The tribal forces were also joined by troops from Chitral, whose ruler, Muzaffar ul-Mulk the Mehtar of Chitral, had acceded to Pakistan.

Attempted link-up at Poonch and fall of Mirpur

Indian forces ceased pursuit of tribal forces after recapturing Uri and Baramula, and sent a relief column southwards, in an attempt to relieve Poonch. Although the relief column eventually reached Poonch, the siege could not be lifted. A second relief column reached Kotli, and evacuated the garrisons of that town and others but were forced to abandon it being too weak to defend it. Meanwhile, Mirpur was captured by the tribal forces on 25 November 1947. Hindu women were reportedly abducted by tribal forces and taken into Pakistan. They were sold in the brothels of Rawalpindi. Around 400

Indo-Pakistani War of 1947

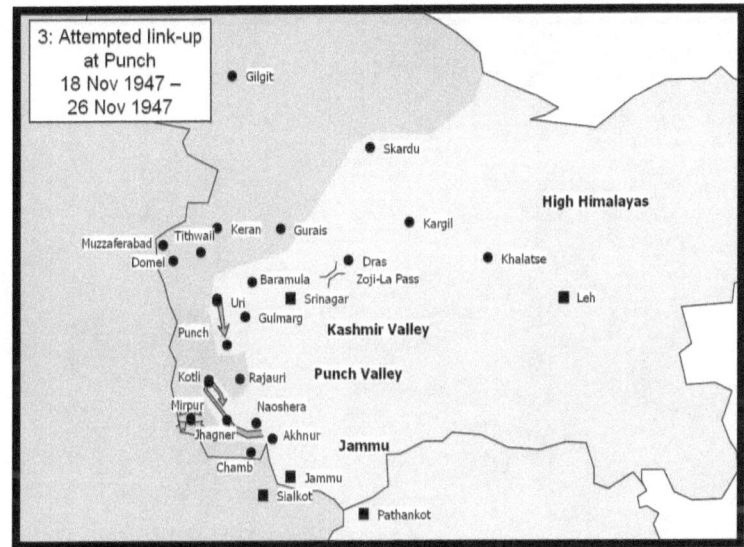

Figure 210: *Attempted link-up at Poonch 18 November 1947 – 26 November 1947*

women jumped into wells in Mirpur committing suicide to escape from being abducted.

Fall of Jhanger and attacks on Naoshera and Uri

The tribal forces attacked and captured Jhanger. They then attacked Naoshera unsuccessfully, and made a series of unsuccessful attacks on Uri. In the south a minor Indian attack secured Chamb. By this stage of the war the front line began to stabilise as more Indian troops became available.Wikipedia:Citation needed

Operation Vijay: counterattack to Jhanger

The Indian forces launched a counterattack in the south recapturing Jhanger and Rajauri. In the Kashmir Valley the tribal forces continued attacking the Uri garrison. In the north Skardu was brought under siege by the Gilgit scouts.

Indian spring offensive

The Indians held onto Jhanger against numerous counterattacks, who were increasingly supported by regular Pakistani Forces. In the Kashmir Valley the Indians attacked, recapturing Tithwail. The Gilgit scouts made good progress in the High Himalayas sector, infiltrating troops to bring Leh

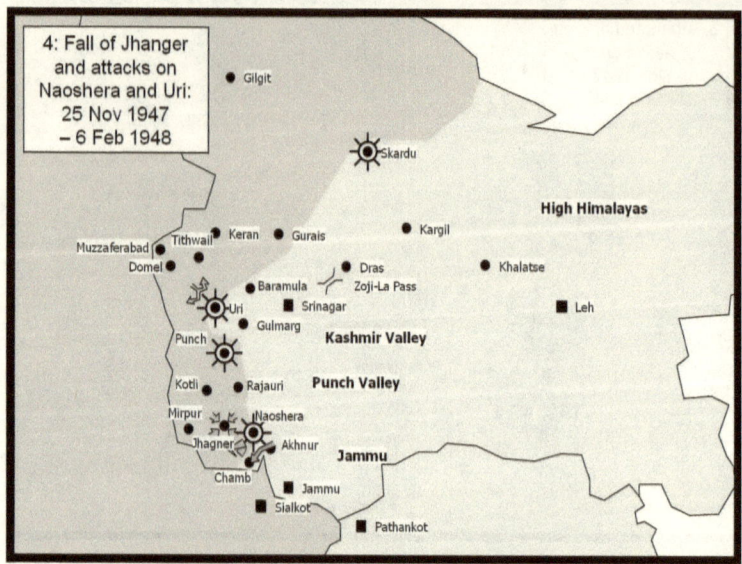

Figure 211: *Fall of Jhanger and attacks on Naoshera and Uri 25 November 1947 – 6 February 1948*

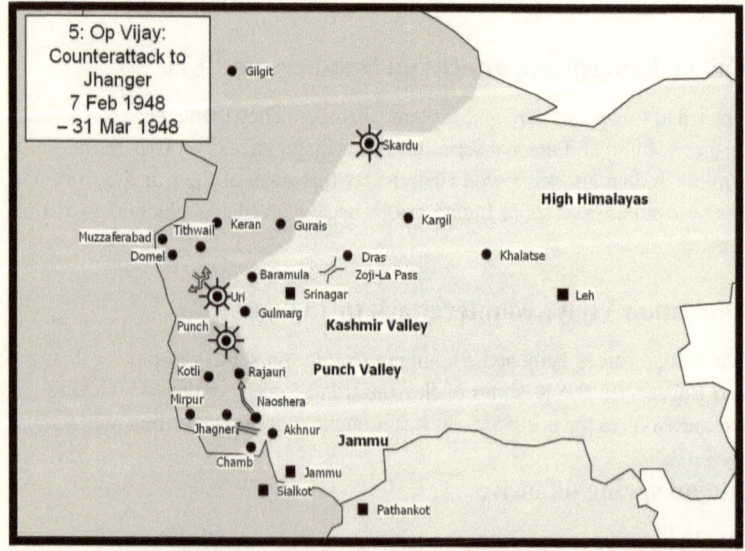

Figure 212: *Operation Vijay: counterattack to Jhanger 7 February 1948 – 1 May 1948*

Indo-Pakistani War of 1947

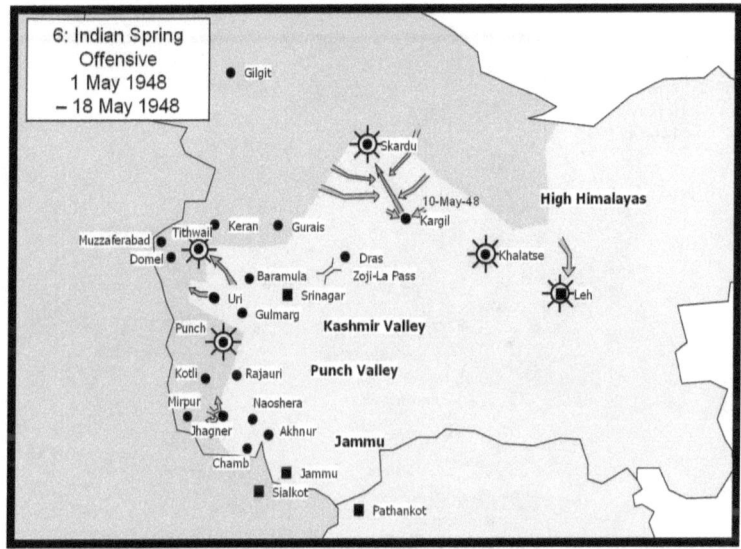

Figure 213: *Indian Spring Offensive 1 May 1948 – 19 May 1948*

under siege, capturing Kargil and defeating a relief column heading for Skardu.Wikipedia:Citation needed

Operations Gulab and Eraze

The Indians continued to attack in the Kashmir Valley sector driving north to capture Keran and Gurais (Operation Eraze).:308–324 They also repelled a counterattack aimed at Tithwal. In the Jammu region, the forces besieged in Poonch broke out and temporarily linked up with the outside world again. The Kashmir State army was able to defend Skardu from the Gilgit Scouts impeding their advance down the Indus valley towards Leh. In August the Chitral Scouts and Chitral Bodyguard under Mata ul-Mulk besieged Skardu and with the help of artillery were able to take Skardu. This freed the Gilgit Scouts to push further into Ladakh.

Operation Bison

During this time the front began to settle down. The siege of Poonch continued. An unsuccessful attack was launched by 77 Parachute Brigade (Brig Atal) to capture Zoji La pass. Operation Duck, the earlier epithet for this assault, was renamed as Operation Bison by Cariappa. M5 Stuart light tanks of 7 Cavalry were moved in dismantled conditions through Srinagar and winched across bridges while two field companies of the Madras Sappers converted the

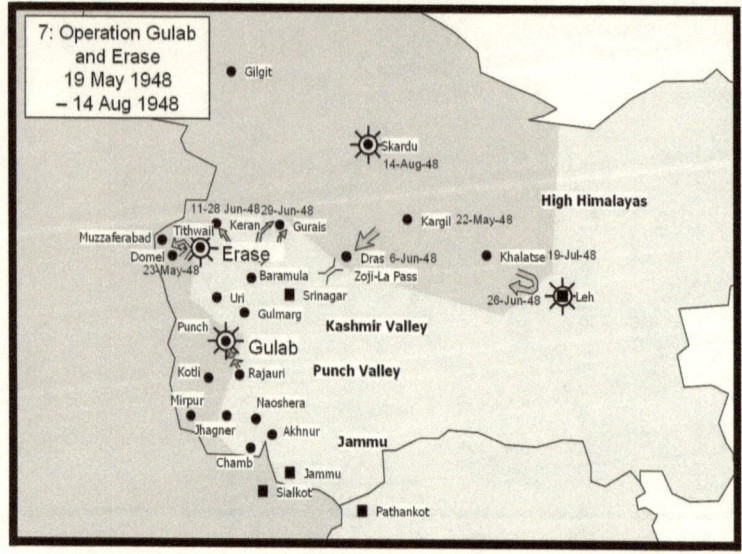

Figure 214: *Indian Spring Offensive 19 May 1948 – 14 August 1948*

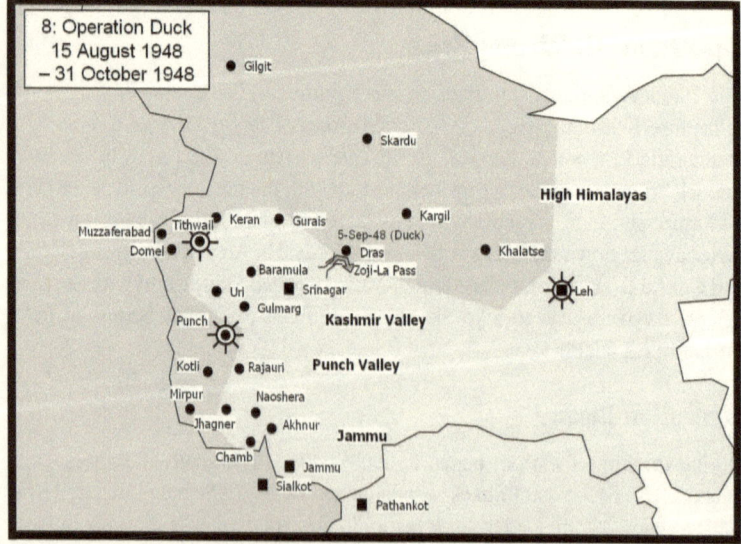

Figure 215: *Operation Duck 15 August 1948 – 1 November 1948*

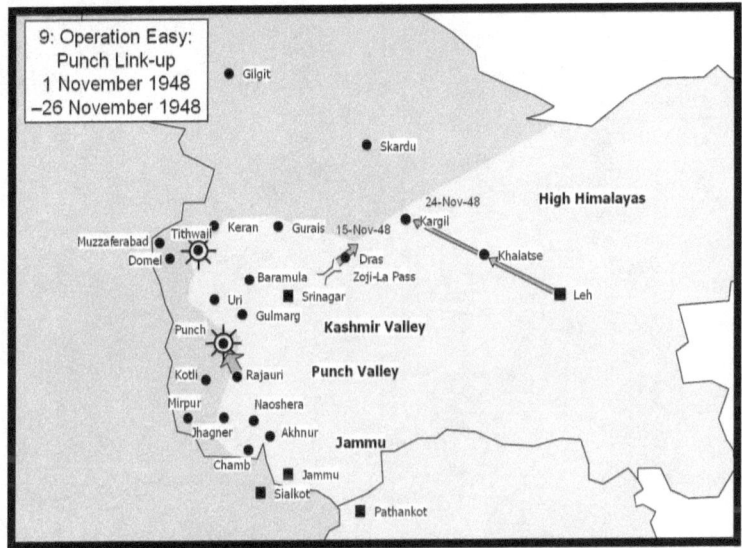

Figure 216: *Operation Easy. Poonch link-up 1 November 1948 – 26 November 1948*

mule track across Zoji La into a jeep track. The surprise attack on 1 November by the brigade with armour supported by two regiments of 25 pounders and a regiment of 3.7-inch guns, forced the pass and pushed the tribal and Pakistani forces back to Matayan and later Dras. The brigade linked up on 24 November at Kargil with Indian troops advancing from Leh while their opponents eventually withdrew northwards toward Skardu.:[103-127] The Pakistani attacked the Skardu on 10 February 1948 which was repulsed by the Indian soldiers. Thereafter, the Skardu Garrison was subjected to continuous attacks by the Pakistan Army for the next three months and each time, their attack was repulsed by the Colonel Sher Jung Thapa and his men. Thapa held the Skardu with hardly 250 men for whole six long months without any reinforcement and replenishment. On 14 August Indian General Sher Jung Thapa had to surrender Skardu to the Pakistani Army. and raiders after a year long siege.

Operation Easy; Poonch link-up

The Indians now started to get the upper hand in all sectors. Poonch was finally relieved after a siege of over a year. The Gilgit forces in the High Himalayas, who had previously made good progress, were finally defeated. The Indians pursued as far as Kargil before being forced to halt due to supply problems. The

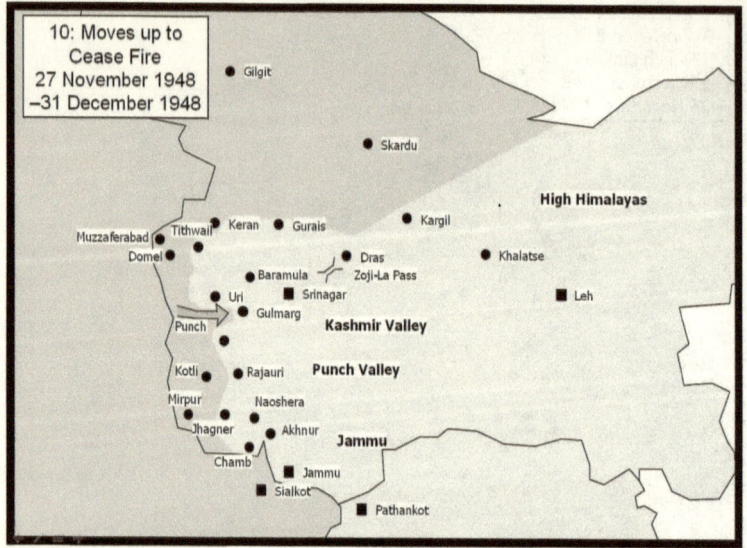

Figure 217: *Moves up to cease-fire. 27 November 1948 – 31 December 1948*

Zoji La pass was forced by using tanks (which had not been thought possible at that altitude) and Dras was recaptured.Wikipedia:Citation needed

Moves up to cease-fire

After protracted negotiations a cease-fire was agreed to by both countries, which came into effect. The terms of the cease-fire as laid out in a United Nations resolution of 13 August 1948, were adopted by the UN on 5 January 1949. This required Pakistan to withdraw its forces, both regular and irregular, while allowing India to maintain minimum strength of its forces in the state to preserve law and order. On compliance of these conditions a plebiscite was to be held to determine the future of the territory. Indian losses were 1,104 killed and 3,154 wounded, whereas Pakistani losses were 6,000 killed and 14,000 wounded. India gained control of the two-thirds Kashmir whereas, Pakistan gained roughly one-third of Kashmir. Most neutral assessments agree that India was the victor of the war as it was able to successfully defend about two thirds of Kashmir including Kashmir valley, Jammu and Ladakh.

Military awards

Battle honours

After the war, a total of number of 11 battle honours and one theatre honour were awarded to units of the Indian Army, the notable amongst which are:

- Jammu and Kashmir 1947–48 (theatre honour)
- Gurais
- Kargil
- Naoshera
- Punch
- Rajouri
- Srinagar
- Tithwal
- Zoji La

Gallantry awards

For bravery, a number of soldiers and officers were awarded the highest gallantry award of their respective countries. Following is a list of the recipients of the Indian award Param Vir Chakra, and the Pakistani award Nishan-E-Haider:

India

- Major Som Nath Sharma (Posthumous)
- Lance Naik Karam Singh
- Second Lieutenant Rama Raghoba Rane
- Naik Jadu Nath Singh
- Company Havildar Major Piru Singh Shekhawat

Pakistan

- Captain Muhammad Sarwar

Bibliography

- Ankit, Rakesh (May 2010). "Henry Scott: The forgotten soldier of Kashmir"[1024]. *Epilogue*. **4** (5): 44–49.
- Ankit, Rakesh (August 2010), "The Problem of Poonch"[1025], *Epilogue*, **4** (8): 8–49
- Ankit, Rakesh (November 2010), "October 1947"[1026], *Epilogue*, **4** (11): 9–
- Ankit, Rakesh (2016), *The Kashmir Conflict: From Empire to the Cold War, 1945–66*[1027], Routledge, ISBN 978-1-317-22525-6
  - Ankit, Rakesh (2014), *Kashmir, 1945–66: From Empire to the Cold War*[1028], University of Southampton
- Bajwa, Kuldip Singh (2003), *Jammu and Kashmir War, 1947–1948: Political and Military Perspective*[1029], Har-Anand Publications, ISBN 978-81-241-0923-6

- Bangash, Yaqoob Khan (2010), "Three Forgotten Accessions: Gilgit, Hunza and Nagar", *The Journal of Imperial and Commonwealth History*, **38** (1): 117–143, doi: 10.1080/03086530903538269[1030], (Subscription required (help))
- Barua, Pradeep (2003), *Gentlemen of the Raj: The Indian Army Officer Corps, 1817-1949*[1031], Greenwood Publishing Group, pp. 133–, ISBN 978-0-275-97999-7
- Bhattacharya, Brigadier Samir (2013), *NOTHING BUT!: Book Three: What Price Freedom*[1032], Partridge Publishing, pp. 42–, ISBN 978-1-4828-1625-9
- Cheema, Brig Amar (2015), *The Crimson Chinar: The Kashmir Conflict: A Politico Military Perspective*[1033], Lancer Publishers, pp. 51–, ISBN 978-81-7062-301-4
- Dasgupta, C. (2014) [first published 2002], *War and Diplomacy in Kashmir, 1947–48*[1034], SAGE Publications, ISBN 978-81-321-1795-7
- Effendi, Col. M. Y. (2007), *Punjab Cavalry: Evolution, Role, Organisation and Tactical Doctrine 11 Cavalry, Frontier Force, 1849-1971*[1035], Karachi: Oxford University Press, ISBN 978-0-19-547203-5
- Guha, Ramachandra (2008), *India after Gandhi: The History of the World's Largest Democracy*[1036], Pan Macmillian, ISBN 0330396110
- Hajari, Nisid (2015), *Midnight's Furies: The Deadly Legacy of India's Partition*[1037], Houghton Mifflin Harcourt, pp. 185–, ISBN 978-0-547-66924-3
- Hiro, Dilip (2015), *The Longest August: The Unflinching Rivalry Between India and Pakistan*[1038], Nation Books, ISBN 978-1-56858-503-1
- Jamal, Arif (2009), *Shadow War: The Untold Story of Jihad in Kashmir*[1039], Melville House, ISBN 978-1-933633-59-6
- Joshi, Manoj (2008), *Kashmir, 1947-1965: A Story Retold*[1040], India Research Press, ISBN 978-81-87943-52-5
- Hodson, H. V. (1969), *The Great Divide: Britain, India, Pakistan*[1041], London: Hutchinson
- Korbel, Josef (1966) [first published 1954], *Danger in Kashmir*[1042] (second ed.), Princeton University Press
- Mahajan, Mehr Chand (1963), *Looking Back: The Autobiography of Mehr Chand Mahajan, Former Chief Justice of India*[1043], Asia Publishing House
- Moore, Robin James (1987), *Making the new Commonwealth*[1044], Clarendon Press, ISBN 978-0-19-820112-0
- Palit, D. K. (1972), *Jammu and Kashmir Arms: History of the J & K Rifles*[1045], Palit & Dutt
- Prasad, Sri Nandan; Pal, Dharm (1987), *Operations in Jammu & Kashmir, 1947-48*[1046], History Division, Ministry of Defence, Government of

India
- Raghavan, Srinath (2010), *War and Peace in Modern India*[1047], Palgrave Macmillan, pp. 101–, ISBN 978-1-137-00737-7
- Nawaz, Shuja (May 2008), "The First Kashmir War Revisited", *India Review*, 7 (2): 115–154, doi: 10.1080/14736480802055455[1048], (Subscription required (help))
- Sarila, Narendra Singh (2007), *The Shadow of the Great Game: The Untold Story of India's Partition*[1049], Constable, ISBN 978-1-84529-588-2
- Schofield, Victoria (2003) [First published in 2000], *Kashmir in Conflict*, London and New York: I. B. Taurus & Co, ISBN 1860648983
- Snedden, Christopher (2013) [first published as *The Untold Story of the People of Azad Kashmir*, 2012], *Kashmir: The Unwritten History*[1050], HarperCollins India, ISBN 9350298988
- Zaheer, Hasan (1998), *The Times and Trial of the Rawalpindi Conspiracy, 1951: The First Coup Attempt in Pakistan*[1051], Oxford University Press, ISBN 978-0-19-577892-2

Further reading

Major sources

- Ministry of Defence, Government of India. *Operations in Jammu and Kashmir 1947–1948*. (1987). Thomson Press (India) Limited, New Delhi. This is the Indian Official History.
- Lamb, Alastair. *Kashmir: A Disputed Legacy, 1846–1990*. (1991). Roxford Books. ISBN 0-907129-06-4.
- Praval, K.C. *The Indian Army After Independence*. (1993). Lancer International, ISBN 1-897829-45-0
- Sen, Maj Gen L.P. *Slender Was The Thread: The Kashmir confrontation 1947–1948*. (1969). Orient Longmans Ltd, New Delhi.
- Vas, Lt Gen. E. A. *Without Baggage: A personal account of the Jammu and Kashmir Operations 1947–1949*. (1987). Natraj Publishers Dehradun. ISBN 81-85019-09-6.

Other sources

- Cohen, Lt Col Maurice. *Thunder over Kashmir*. (1955). Orient Longman Ltd. Hyderabad
- Hinds, Brig Gen SR. *Battle of Zoji La*. (1962). Military Digest, New Delhi.
- Sandhu, Maj Gen Gurcharan. *The Indian Armour: History Of The Indian Armoured Corps 1941–1971*. (1987). Vision Books Private Limited, New Delhi, ISBN 81-7094-004-4.

- Singh, Maj K Brahma. *History of Jammu and Kashmir Rifles (1820–1956).* (1990). Lancer International New Delhi, ISBN 81-7062-091-0.
- Ayub, Muhammad (2005). An army, Its Role and Rule: A History of the Pakistan Army from Independence to Kargil, 1947–1999. RoseDog Books. ISBN 9780805995947.

External links

- Partition and Indo Pak War of 1947-48[1052], Indian Army, archived 5 April 2011.

1950s and 60s

States Reorganisation Act, 1956

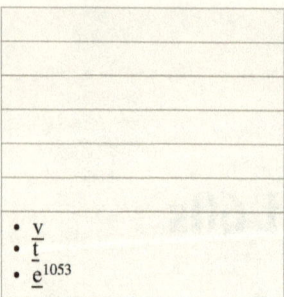

The **States Reorganisation Act, 1956** was a major reform of the boundaries of India's states and territories, organising them along linguistic lines.

Although additional changes to India's state boundaries have been made since 1956, the States Reorganisation Act of 1956 remains the single most extensive change in state boundaries since the independence of India in 1947.

The Act came into effect at the same time as the **Constitution (Seventh Amendment) Act, 1956**, which (among other things) restructured the constitutional framework for India's existing states and the requirements to pass the States Reorganisation Act, 1956 under the provisions of Part I of the Constitution of India, Articles 3 & 4.

Political integration after independence and the Constitution of 1950

The British Indian Empire, which included present-day India, Pakistan and Bangladesh, was divided into two types of territories: the Provinces of British India, which were governed directly by British officials responsible to the Governor-General of India; and the Indian States, under the rule of local hereditary rulers who recognised British suzerainty in return for local autonomy, in most cases as established by treaty. As a result of the reforms of the early 20th century, most of the British provinces had directly elected legislatures as well as governors, although some of the smaller provinces were governed by a chief commissioner appointed by the Governor-General. Major reforms put forward by the British in the 1930s also recognised the principle of federalism, which was carried forward into the governance of independent India.

On 15 August 1947, British India was granted independence as the separate dominions of India and Pakistan. The British dissolved their treaty relations with more than five hundred princely states, who were encouraged to accede to either India or Pakistan, while under no compulsion to do so. Most of the states acceded to India, and a few to Pakistan. Bhutan, Hyderabad and Kashmir

Figure 218: *Administrative divisions of India in 1951*

opted for independence, although the armed intervention of India conquered Hyderabad and brought it into the Indian Union.

Between 1947 and about 1950, the territories of the princely states were politically integrated into the Indian Union. Most were merged into existing provinces; others were organised into new provinces, such as Rajputana, Himachal Pradesh, Madhya Bharat, and Vindhya Pradesh, made up of multiple princely states; a few, including Mysore, Hyderabad, Bhopal, and Bilaspur, became separate provinces. The Government of India Act 1935 remained the constitutional law of India pending adoption of a new Constitution.

The new Constitution of India, which came into force on 26 January 1950, made India a sovereign democratic republic. The new republic was also declared to be a "Union of States". The constitution of 1950 distinguished between three main types of states and a class of territories:

- Part A states, which were the former governors' provinces of British India, were ruled by a governor appointed by the president and an elected state legislature. The nine Part A states were Assam, Bihar, Bombay, Madhya Pradesh (formerly Central Provinces and Berar), Madras, Orissa, Punjab (formerly East Punjab), Uttar Pradesh (formerly the United Provinces), and West Bengal.

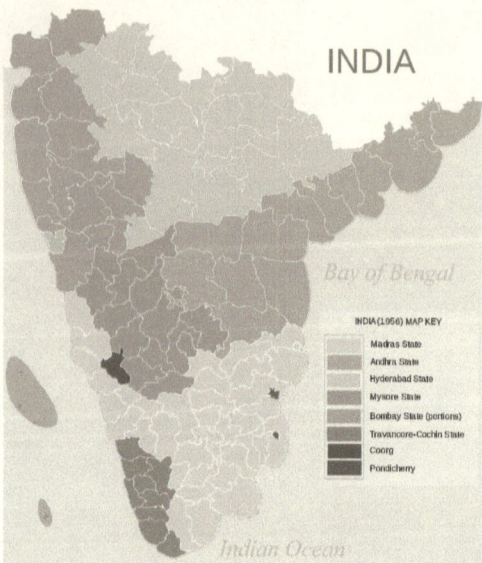

Figure 219: *South Indian states prior to the States Reorganisation Act*

- Part B states, which were former princely states or groups of princely states, governed by a rajpramukh, who was usually the ruler of a constituent state, and an elected legislature. The rajpramukh was appointed by the President of India. The eight Part B states were Hyderabad, Jammu and Kashmir, Madhya Bharat, Mysore, Patiala and East Punjab States Union (PEPSU), Rajasthan, Saurashtra, and Travancore-Cochin.
- Part C states included both the former chief commissioners' provinces and some princely states, and each was governed by a chief commissioner appointed by the President of India. The ten Part C states were Ajmer, Bhopal, Bilaspur, Coorg, Delhi, Himachal Pradesh, Cutch, Manipur, Tripura, and Vindhya Pradesh.
- The sole Part D territory was the Andaman and Nicobar Islands, which were administered by a lieutenant governor appointed by the central government.

Movement for linguistic states

The demand for states to be organised on a linguistic basis was developed even before India achieved independence from British rule. A first-of-its-kind linguistic movement started in 1895, in what is now Odisha. The movement gained momentum in later years with the demand for a separate Orissa

Province to be formed by bifurcating the existing Bihar and Orissa Province. Due to the efforts of Madhusudan Das, the Father of Oriya nationalism, the movement eventually achieved its objective in 1936, when Orissa Province became the first Indian state (pre-independence) to be organised on the basis of common languages.

The post-independence period saw the ascent of political movements for the creation of new states developed on linguistic lines. The movement to create a Telugu-speaking state out of the northern portion of Madras State gathered strength in the years after independence, and in 1953, the sixteen northern Telugu-speaking districts of Madras State became the new State of Andhra.

During the 1950–1956 period, other small changes were made to state boundaries: the small state of Bilaspur was merged with Himachal Pradesh on 1 July 1954; and Chandernagore, a former enclave of French India, was incorporated into West Bengal in 1955. However, post-independence, the first state to be created on a linguistic basis was Andhra in 1953, created out of the Telugu-speaking northern parts of Madras State.

States Reorganisation Commission

The States Reorganisation Commission was preceded by the Linguistic Provinces Commission (aka Dhar Commission), which was set up in June 1948. Prime Minister Jawaharlal Nehru appointed the States Reorganisation Commission in December 1953, with the remit to reorganise the Indian states. The new commission was headed by the retired Chief Justice of the Supreme Court, Fazal Ali; its other two members were H. N. Kunzru and K. M. Panikkar. The efforts of the commission were overseen by Govind Ballabh Pant, who served as the Home Minister from December 1954.

The States Reorganisation Commission submitted a report on September 30, 1955, with recommendations for the reorganisation of India's states, which was then debated by the Indian parliament. Subsequently, bills were passed to make changes to the constitution and to administer the reorganisation of the states.

not only thus

Related changes by other legislation

The States Reorganisation Act was enacted on 31 August 1956. Before it came into effect on 1 November, an important amendment was made to the Constitution of India. Under the Seventh Amendment, the existing distinction among Part A, Part B, Part C, and Part D states was abolished. The distinction

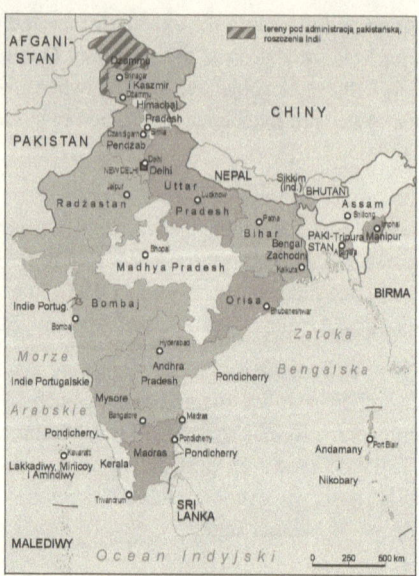

Figure 220: *Indian states after the States Reorganisation Act*

between Part A and Part B states was removed, becoming known simply as "states". A new type of entity, the Union Territory, replaced the classification as a Part C or Part D state.

A further Act also came into effect on 1 November, transferring certain territories from Bihar to West Bengal.[1054]

Effect of the changes

The following list sets out the states and union territories of India as reorganised on 1 November 1956:

States

1. Andhra Pradesh: formed by the merger of Andhra State (1953-56) with the Telugu-speaking areas of Hyderabad State (1948–56).
2. Assam: No change of boundary in 1956.
3. Bihar: reduced slightly by the transfer of minor territories to West Bengal.
4. Bombay State: the state was enlarged by the addition of Saurashtra State and Kutch State, the Marathi-speaking districts of Nagpur Division of Madhya Pradesh and Marathwada region of Hyderabad State. The southernmost districts of the Bombay Presidency were transferred to Mysore State.

5. Jammu and Kashmir: No change of boundary in 1956.
6. Kerala: formed by the merger of Travancore-Cochin state with the Malabar district and Kasaragod taluk of South Canara district of the Madras Presidency. The southern part of Travancore-Cochin, Kanyakumari district was transferred to Madras State.
7. Madhya Pradesh: Madhya Bharat, Vindhya Pradesh, and Bhopal State were merged into Madhya Pradesh; the Marathi-speaking districts of Nagpur Division were transferred to Bombay State.
8. Madras State: Malabar District was transferred to the new state of Kerala, and a new union territory, Laccadive, Minicoy and Amindivi Islands, was created. The southern part of Travancore-Cochin, Kanyakumari district was added to the state.
9. Mysore State: enlarged by the addition of Coorg State and the Kannada speaking districts from western Madras Presidency, southern Bombay Presidency and western Hyderabad State.
10. Orissa: No change of boundary in 1956.
11. Punjab: enlarged by addition of the Patiala and East Punjab States Union.
12. Rajasthan: enlarged by the addition of Ajmer state and parts of Bombay and Madhya Bharat states.
13. Uttar Pradesh: No change of boundary in 1956.
14. West Bengal: enlarged by addition of minor territory previously forming part of Bihar.

Union territories

1. Andaman and Nicobar Islands
2. Delhi
3. Manipur
4. Tripura
5. Himachal Pradesh
6. Laccadive, Minicoy & Amindivi Islands

External links

- Text of the Act[1055]

India and the Non-Aligned Movement

India played an important role in the multilateral movements of colonies and newly independent countries that wanted into the **Non-Aligned Movement**. India's policy was neither negative nor positive.

Origin of Non alignment movement

Nonalignment had its origins in India's colonial experience and the nonviolent Indian independence struggle, which left India determined to be the master of its fate in an international system dominated politically by Cold War alliances and economically by Western capitalism and Soviet communism. In the words of Rejaul Karim Laskar, a scholar of India's foreign policy and ideologue of the Congress party which was the ruling party of India for the most part of the Cold War years, the Non-Aligned movement was the "formula" devised by Nehru and other leaders of the newly independent countries of the third world to "guard" their independence "in face of complex international situation demanding allegiance to either of the two warring superpowers". The principles of nonalignment, as articulated by Nehru and his successors, were preservation of India's freedom of action internationally through refusal to align India with any bloc or alliance, particularly those led by the United States or the Soviet Union; nonviolence and international cooperation as a means of settling international disputes. Nonalignment was a consistent feature of Indian foreign policy by the late 1940s and enjoyed strong, almost unquestioning support among the Indian elite.

The term "Non-Alignment" was coined by V K Menon in his speech at UN in 1953 which was later used by Indian Prime Minister Jawaharlal Nehru during his speech in 1954 in Colombo, Sri Lanka. In this speech, Nehru described the five pillars to be used as a guide for Sino-Indian relations, which were first put forth by Chinese Premier Zhou Enlai Called Panchsheel (five restraints), these principles would later serve as the basis of the Non-Aligned Movement. Jawaharlal Nehru was the architect of the Non-Alignment Movement. The five principles were:

1. *Mutual respect for each other's territorial integrity and sovereignty*
2. *Mutual non-aggression*
3. *Mutual non-interference in domestic affairs*
4. *Equality and mutual benefit*
5. *Peaceful co-existence*

Jawaharlal Nehru's concept of nonalignment brought India considerable international prestige among newly independent states that shared India's concerns about the military confrontation between the superpowers and the influence of the former colonial powers. New Delhi used nonalignment to establish a significant role for itself as a leader of the newly independent world in such multilateral organisations as the United Nations (UN) and the Nonaligned Movement. The signing of the Treaty of Peace, Friendship, and Cooperation between India and the Soviet Union in 1971 and India's involvement in the internal affairs of its smaller neighbours in the 1970s and 1980s tarnished New Delhi's image as a nonaligned nation and led some observers to note that in practice, nonalignment applied only to India's relations with countries outside South Asia.

Early developments

The movement had its origins in the 1947 Asian Relations Meeting in New Delhi and the 1955 Asian-African Conference in Bandung, Indonesia. India also participated in the 1961 Belgrade Conference that officially established the Nonaligned Movement, but Jawaharlal Nehru's declining prestige limited his influence. In the 1960s and 1970s, New Delhi concentrated on internal problems and bilateral relations, yet retained membership in an increasingly factionalised and radicalised movement. During the contentious 1979 Havana summit, India worked with moderate nations to reject Cuban president Fidel Castro's proposition that "socialism" (that is, the Soviet Union) was the "natural ally" of nonalignment.

In 1980s

Under Indira Gandhi in the early 1980s, India attempted to reassert its prominent role in the Nonaligned Movement by focusing on the relationship between disarmament and economic development. By appealing to the economic grievances of developing countries, Indira Gandhi and her successors exercised a moderating influence on the Nonaligned Movement, diverting it from some of the Cold War issues that marred the controversial 1979 Havana meeting. Although hosting the 1983 summit at Delhi boosted Indian prestige within the movement, its close relations with the Soviet Union and its pro-Soviet positions on Afghanistan and Cambodia limited its influence.

The end of the Cold War left the Nonaligned Movement without its original raison d'être, and its membership became deeply divided over international disputes, strategy, and organisation. During the 1992 Jakarta summit, India took a middle position between countries favoring confrontation with developed nations on international economic issues, such as Malaysia, and those that favored a more cooperative approach, such as Indonesia. Although New Delhi played a minor role compared with Kuala Lumpur and Jakarta on most issues facing the summit, India formulated the Nonaligned Movement position opposing developed countries' linkage of foreign aid to human rights criteria.

Consequences

The early 1990s demise of the bipolar world system, which had existed since the end of World War II, shook the underpinnings of India's foreign policy. The Cold War system of alliances had been rendered meaningless by the collapse of the East European communist states, the dissolution of the Warsaw Pact, and the demise of the Soviet Union. In the early 1990s, most colonies had become independent, and apartheid in South Africa was being dismantled, diminishing the value of anticolonialism and making it impossible for antiracism to serve as a rallying point for international political action (India and South Africa restored full diplomatic relations in 1993 after a thirty nine year lapse). The Panchsheel (Panch Shila), peaceful resolution of international disputes, and international cooperation to spur economic development which was being enhanced by domestic economic reforms were broad objectives in a changing world. Thus, the 1990s saw India redefining nonalignment and the view of India's place in the world.

India also is a founding member of the Group of fifteen, a group of developing nations established at the ninth Nonaligned Movement summit in Belgrade in 1989 to facilitate dialogue with the industrialised countries. India played host to the fourth Group of Fifteen summit in March 1994. At the summit, Prime Minister Narsimha Rao and other leaders expressed concern over new trade barriers being raised by the industrialised countries despite the conclusion of a new world trade agreement.

In the twenty-first century, India continues to practice the policy of non-alignment which allows it to maintain national sovereignty while still receiving economic and military assistance when needed. Non-alignment has propelled India to achieve one of their main strategic objectives: non-dependence. In recent years India has used this policy to its advantage in order to strengthen external partnerships and seek out material needs when necessary, while still ensuring that India as a country is able to pursue its own foreign policy goals. Although technically non-aligned India received the assistance it needed when it could – like in the late 1940s, in 1963 following the defect against the PRC and later in the twenty first century when it entered into a major nuclear agreement with both the US and the NSG (Chaudhuri 257). More recently though India has been able to openly exercise non-alignment in its decisions to side with major world powers on international diplomatic issues of the time. During the Korean crisis, India adjusted and amended its approach when it was considered vital to do so. Most importantly, however, Indian leaders were able to say no – as was the case in 2003 when India considered sending troops to Iraq – when it did not suit its security objective (Chaudhuri 257).

India continues to practice a policy of non-alignment in an attempt to maintain sovereignty and oppose imperialism. Since its inception, the movement attempted to create an independent path in world politics that would not result in lesser states becoming pawns in the struggles between major world powers. Today, India has a working security relationship with the United States. Over the course of history, these two countries have inherently forged a deeper sense for each other's motivations and aspirations while never establishing a formal alliance. India continues to serve as an example of a country that is overcoming the continuum gap and advancing its policies to better fit an emerging world power. India's non-alignment policy has made the free development of the individual as well as the economic and social progress of society and of nations its central focus in its strategic objectives. This strategy combines the goals of peace and economic development within the country with the emancipation of peoples from all forms of subordination and exploitation. As a result, India's non-alignment stance functions as a benchmark for positive development of international relations on a global scale.

References

- "Library of Congress: Federal Research Division Country Profile: India, September 1995"[1056]. *Library of Congress Country Studies (All works are released in Public domain)*. Retrieved 2007-11-06.

- Chaudhuri, Rudra. *Forged in Crisis: India and the United States since 1947.* Oxford University Press, 2014.

External links

- India reasserts firm commitment to NAM[1057]
- https://www.foreignaffairs.com/articles/asia/1992-03-01/india-after-nonalignment
- International Institute for Non-Aligned Movement[1058]

Ⓢ This article incorporates public domain material from the Library of Congress Country Studies website http://lcweb2.loc.gov/frd/cs/[1059].

Indo-Pakistani War of 1965

<indicator name="pp-default"> 🔒 </indicator>

Indo–Pakistani War of 1965
Part of the Indo–Pakistani wars and conflicts

Geopolitical map of Kashmir provided by the United States CIA, ca. 2004

Date	August – 23 September 1965

Location	**Western Front**
	• Indo-Pakistani border
	    • Line of Control, Working Boundary, Radcliffe Line, Sir Creek, and Zero-Point
	    • Arabian sea
	Eastern Front
	• India-East Pakistan border

Result	Indian victory • United Nations mandated ceasefire. • No permanent territorial changes (see Tashkent Declaration).

Belligerents	
India	Pakistan
Commanders and leaders	

Indo-Pakistani War of 1965

S. Radhakrishnan (President of India)	Ayub Khan (President of Pakistan)
Lal Bahadur Shastri (Prime Minister of India)	Gen Musa Khan Hazara (Cdr-in-Chief, Army)
Gen J.N. Chaudhuri (Chief of the Army Staff)	Lt.Gen Bakhtiar Rana (Commander, I Corps)
Lt Gen Harbaksh Singh (GOC-in-C, Western Command)	Lt.Gen Attiqur Rahman (Commander, IV Corps)
Lt Gen P.O. Dunn (GOC, I Corps)	MGen A.H. Malik (GOC, 12th Infantry Division)
Lt Gen Joginder Dhillon (GOC, XI Corps)	MGen Yahya Khan (GOC, 7th Infantry Division)
Lt Gen Kashmir Singh Katoch (GOC, XV Corps)	AM Nur Khan (Cdr-in-Chief, Air Force)
AM Arjan Singh (Chief of the Air Staff)	VAdm A.R. Khan (Cdr-in-Chief, Navy)
Adm Bhaskar Soman (Chief of the Naval Staff)	RAdm S.M. Ahsan ((Cdr. Eastern Naval Command)
	Cdre S.M. Anwar (OTC, 25th Destroyer Sqn)
Strength	
700,000 Infantry **700+ aircraft**[1060] **720 Tanks** • 186 Centurions • 346 Shermans • 90 AMX • 90 PT-76 **628 Artillery** • 66x 3.7"How • 450x 25pdr • 96x 5.5" • 16x 7.2"	**260,000 Infantry** **280 aircraft**[1060] **756 Tanks** • 352 Pattons • 308 Shermans • 96 Chaffees **552 Artillery** • 72x105mm How • 234X25pdr • 126x155mm How • 48x8" How • 72x3.7" How • POK Lt Btys
Casualties and losses	
Neutral claims • 3,000 men • 150–190 tanks • 60–75 aircraft • 540 km² (210mi²) of territory lost (primarily in Rann of Kutch)[1061] **Indian claims** • 35[1062]–59 aircraft lost In addition, Indian sources claim that there were 13 IAF aircraft lost in accidents, and 3 Indian civilian aircraft shot down.[1063] • 322 km² territory lost **Pakistani claims** • 8,200 men killed or captured • 110[1064]–113 aircraft destroyed • 500 tanks captured or destroyed • 2602,[1065] 2575 km² territory gained 1600 square miles territory gained according to Husain Haqqani	**Neutral claims** • 3,800 men • 200-300 Tanks • 20 aircraft • Over 1,840 km² (710 mi²) of territory lost (primarily in Sialkot, Lahore, and Kashmir sectors)[1061] **Pakistani claims** • 19 aircraft lost **Indian claims** • 5259 men killed or captured • 43[1066]–73 aircraft destroyed • 471 tanks destroyed • 3,900 km² territory gained

The **Indo-Pakistani War of 1965** was a culmination of skirmishes that took place between April 1965 and September 1965 between Pakistan and India.

The conflict began following Pakistan's Operation Gibraltar, which was designed to infiltrate forces into Jammu and Kashmir to precipitate an insurgency against Indian rule. India retaliated by launching a full-scale military attack on West Pakistan. The seventeen-day war caused thousands of casualties on both sides and witnessed the largest engagement of armored vehicles and the largest tank battle since World War II.[1067,1068] Hostilities between the two countries ended after a United Nations-mandated ceasefire was declared following diplomatic intervention by the Soviet Union and the United States, and the subsequent issuance of the Tashkent Declaration. Much of the war was fought by the countries' land forces in Kashmir and along the border between India and Pakistan. This war saw the largest amassing of troops in Kashmir since the Partition of British India in 1947, a number that was overshadowed only during the 2001–2002 military standoff between India and Pakistan. Most of the battles were fought by opposing infantry and armoured units, with substantial backing from air forces, and naval operations. Many details of this war, like those of other Indo-Pakistani Wars, remain unclear.

India had the upper hand over Pakistan when the ceasefire was declared.[1069,1070,1071,1072,1073,1074] Although the two countries fought to a standoff, the conflict is seen as a strategic and political defeat for Pakistan,[1075,1076,1077,1078] as it had neither succeeded in fomenting insurrection in Kashmir[1079] nor had it been able to gain meaningful support at an international level.[1080]

Internationally, the war was viewed in the context of the greater Cold War, and resulted in a significant geopolitical shift in the subcontinent. Before the war, the United States and the United Kingdom had been major material allies of both India and Pakistan, as their primary suppliers of military hardware and foreign developmental aid. During and after the conflict, both India and Pakistan felt betrayed by the perceived lack of support by the western powers for their respective positions; those feelings of betrayal were increased with the imposition of an American and British embargo on military aid to the opposing sides. As a consequence, India and Pakistan openly developed closer relationships with the Soviet Union and China, respectively. The perceived negative stance of the western powers during the conflict, and during the 1971 war, has continued to affect relations between the West and the subcontinent. In spite of improved relations with the U.S. and Britain since the end of the Cold War, the conflict generated a deep distrust of both countries within the subcontinent which to an extent lingers to this day.[1081,1082,1083]

```
(36)                          POL 27 INDIA-PAK

INCOMING TELEGRAM Department of State

43                        CONFIDENTIAL
Action
NEA    RCXP-ICJHK RUEHCR RUEHDT RUFHDN RUQVKR
       DE RUSBAE 646 2881455
       ZNY CCCCC
Info   R 151445Z
       FM AMEMBASSY NEWDELHI
SS     TO RUEHCR/SECSTATE WASHDC 1883         1 2 1 6 9
G      INFO RUQVKR/AMEMBASSY KARACHI 423
SP     RUFHDN/AMEMBASSY LONDON 330             1965 OCT 15 AM 11 35
SAH    RUEHDT/USUN NEWYORK 272
L      RUCJHK/CINCMEAFSA FOR POLAD
H      STATE GRNC
EUR    BT
FE     C O N F I D E N T I A L OCTOBER 15
IO     NEW YORK TIMES CORRESPONDENT LUKAS RETURNED FROM THREE DAY
P      VISIT KASHMIR OCT 14. LUKAS SAID KASHMIR HOME MIN D.P. DHAR
CU     TOLD HIM THAT HE ESTIMATED ONLY ABOUT 30 INFILTRATORS LEFT IN
USIA   KASHMIR VALLEY AND ABOUT 300 IN THE REST OF J&K STATE. ON RETURN
NSC    TO DELHI LUKAS CHECKED WITH DEFENCE MINISTRY'S SPOKESMAN FOR
INR    CONFIRMATION DHAR'S FIGURES. AFTER AN INTERVAL SPOKESMAN CALLED BACK
CIA    SAID MOD ESTIMATED ABOUT 500-600 INFILTRATORS LEFT IN J&K
       STATE AND THAT PROBABLY DHAR'S FIGURES ON THE VALLEY WERE
       "ABOUT RIGHT".
```

Figure 221: *A declassified US State Department letter that confirms the existence of hundreds of "infiltrators" in the Indian-administered part of the disputed Kashmir region. Dated during the events running up to the 1965 war.*

Pre-war escalation

Since the Partition of British India in 1947, Pakistan and India remained in contention over several issues. Although the Kashmir conflict was the predominant issue dividing the nations, other border disputes existed, most notably over the Rann of Kutch, a barren region in the Indian state of Gujarat. The issue first arose in 1956 which ended with India regaining control over the disputed area. Pakistani patrols began patrolling in territory controlled by India in January 1965, which was followed by attacks by both countries on each other's posts on 8 April 1965. Initially involving border police from both nations, the disputed area soon witnessed intermittent skirmishes between the countries' armed forces. In June 1965, British Prime Minister Harold Wilson successfully persuaded both countries to end hostilities and set up a tribunal to resolve the dispute. The verdict, which came later in 1968, saw Pakistan awarded 350 square miles (910 km^2) of the Rann of Kutch, as against its original claim of 3,500 square miles (9,100 km^2).[1084]

After its success in the Rann of Kutch, Pakistan, under the leadership of General Ayub Khan, believed the Indian Army would be unable to defend itself against a quick military campaign in the disputed territory of Kashmir as the

Indian military had suffered a loss to China in 1962 in the Sino-Indian War. Pakistan believed that the population of Kashmir was generally discontented with Indian rule and that a resistance movement could be ignited by a few infiltrating saboteurs. Pakistan attempted to ignite the resistance movement by means of a covert infiltration, codenamed Operation Gibraltar.[1085] The Pakistani infiltrators were soon discovered, however, their presence reported by local Kashmiris, and the operation ended unsuccessfully.

The war

On 5 August 1965 between 26,000 and 33,000 Pakistani soldiers crossed the Line of Control dressed as Kashmiri locals headed for various areas within Kashmir. Indian forces, tipped off by the local populace, crossed the cease fire line on 15 August.

Initially, the Indian Army met with considerable success, capturing three important mountain positions after a prolonged artillery barrage. By the end of August, however, both sides had relative progress; Pakistan had made progress in areas such as Tithwal, Uri and Poonch and India had captured the Haji Pir pass, 8 km into Pakistan-Administered Kashmir.[1086]

On 1 September 1965, Pakistan launched a counterattack, called Operation Grand Slam, with the objective to capture the vital town of Akhnoor in Jammu, which would sever communications and cut off supply routes to Indian troops. Ayub Khan calculated that "Hindu morale would not stand more than a couple of hard blows at the right time and place" although by this time Operation Gibraltar had failed and India had captured the Haji Pir Pass. At 3:30 hours, on 1 September 1965, the entire Chhamb area came under massive artillery bombardment. Pakistan had launched operation Grand Slam and India's Army Headquarter was taken by surprise. Attacking with an overwhelming ratio of troops and technically superior tanks, Pakistan made gains against Indian forces, who were caught unprepared and suffered heavy losses. India responded by calling in its air force to blunt the Pakistani attack. The next day, Pakistan retaliated, its air force attacked Indian forces and air bases in both Kashmir and Punjab. India's decision to open up the theatre of attack into Pakistani Punjab forced the Pakistani army to relocate troops engaged in the operation to defend Punjab. Operation Grand Slam therefore failed, as the Pakistan Army was unable to capture Akhnoor; it became one of the turning points in the war when India decided to relieve pressure on its troops in Kashmir by attacking Pakistan further south. In the valley, another area of strategic importance was Kargil. Kargil town was in Indian hands but Pakistan occupied high ground overlooking Kargil and Srinagar-Leh road. However, after

Figure 222: *Indian Army's officers of 4 Sikh Regiment had captured a Police Station in Lahore, Pakistan*

the launch of a massive anti-infiltration operation by the Indian army, the Pakistani infiltrators were forced out of that area in the month of August.

India crossed the International Border on the Western front on 6 September[1087] On 6 September, the 15th Infantry Division of the Indian Army, under World War II veteran Major General Prasad, battled a massive counterattack by Pakistan near the west bank of the Icchogil Canal (BRB Canal), which was a *de facto* border of India and Pakistan. The General's entourage itself was ambushed and he was forced to flee his vehicle. A second, this time successful, attempt to cross the Ichhogil Canal was made over the bridge in the village of Barki, just east of Lahore. These developments brought the Indian Army within the range of Lahore International Airport. As a result, the United States requested a temporary ceasefire to allow it to evacuate its citizens in Lahore. However, the Pakistani counterattack took Khem Karan from Indian forces which tried to divert the attention of Pakistanis from Khem Karan by an attack on Bedian and the adjacent villages.

The thrust against Lahore consisted of the 1st Infantry Division supported by the three tank regiments of the 2nd Independent Armoured Brigade; they quickly advanced across the border, reaching the Ichhogil (BRB) Canal by 6 September. The Pakistani Army held the bridges over the canal or blew up those it could not hold, effectively stalling any further advance by the Indians

Figure 223: *General Musa Khan, C-in-C of Pakistani Armed Forces at Captured Khem Karan Railway Station, India. Gen. Abdul Hamid Khan and Brig. Sahib Dad Khan are on his right and left.*

on Lahore. One unit of the Indian Jat Regiment, 3 Jat, had also crossed the Icchogil canal and captured[1088] the town of Batapore (Jallo Mur to Pakistan) on the west side of the canal. The same day, a counter offensive consisting of an armoured division and infantry division supported by Pakistan Air Force Sabres forced the Indian 15th Division to withdraw to its starting point. Although 3 Jat suffered minimal casualties, the bulk of the damage being taken by ammunition and stores vehicles, the higher commanders had no information of 3 Jat's capture of Batapore and misleading information led to the command to withdraw from Batapore and Dograi to Ghosal-Dial. This move brought extreme disappointment[1089] to Lt-Col Desmond Hayde, CO of 3 Jat. Dograi was eventually recaptured by 3 Jat on 21 September, for the second time but after a much harder battle due to Pakistani reinforcements.

On 8 September 1965, a company of 5 Maratha Light Infantry was sent to reinforce a Rajasthan Armed Constabulary (RAC) post at Munabao – a strategic hamlet about 250 kilometres from Jodhpur. Their brief was simple. To hold the post and to keep Pakistan's infantry battalions from overrunning the post at bay. But at Maratha Hill (in Munabao) – as the post has now been christened – the Indian company could barely manage to thwart the intense attack for 24 hours. A company of 3 Guards with 954 heavy mortar battery ordered to reinforce the RAC post at Munabao could never reach. The Pakistani Air Force had strafed the entire area, and also hit a railway train coming from Barmer with reinforcements near Gadra road railway station. On 10 September, Munabao fell into Pakistani hands, and efforts to capture the strategic point did not succeed.[1090]

On the days following 9 September, both nations' premiere formations were routed in unequal battles. India's 1st Armoured Division, labeled the "pride of the Indian Army", launched an offensive towards Sialkot. The Division divided itself into two prongs, was forced back by the Pakistani 6th Armoured Division at Chawinda and was forced to withdraw after suffering heavy losses of nearly 100 tanks.

The Pakistanis followed up their success by launching Operation Windup, which forced the Indians back farther. Similarly, Pakistan's pride, the 1st Armoured Division, pushed an offensive towards Khem Karan, with the intent to capture Amritsar (a major city in Punjab, India) and the bridge on River Beas to Jalandhar.

The Pakistani 1st Armoured Division never made it past Khem Karan, however, and by the end of 10 September lay disintegrated by the defences of the Indian 4th Mountain Division at what is now known as the Battle of *Asal Uttar* (lit. meaning – "Real Answer", or more appropriate English equivalent – "Fitting Response"). The area became known as 'Patton Nagar' (Patton Town), because of the large number of US-made Pakistani Patton tanks. Approximately 97 Pakistani tanks were destroyed or abandoned, with only 32 Indian tanks destroyed or damaged. The Pakistani 1st Armoured Division less 5th Armoured Brigade was next sent to Sialkot sector behind Pakistani 6th Armoured Division where it didn't see action as 6th Armoured Division was already in process of routing Indian 1st Armoured Division which was superior to it in strength.

The hostilities in the Rajasthan sector commenced on September the 8th. Initially Pakistan Desert Force and the Hur militia (followers of Pir Pagaro) was placed in a defensive role, a role for which they were well suited as it turned out. The Hurs were familiar with the terrain and the local area and possessed many essential desert survival skills which their opponents and their comrades in the Pakistan Army did not. Fighting as mainly light infantry, the Hur inflicted many casualties on the Indian forces as they entered Sindh. The Hurs were also employed as skirmishers, harassing the Indians LOC, a task they often undertook on camels. As the battle wore on the Hurs and the Desert Force were increasingly used to attack and capture Indian villages inside Rajasthan.[1091]

The war was heading for a stalemate, with both nations holding territory of the other. The Indian army suffered 3,000 battlefield deaths, while Pakistan suffered 3,800. The Indian army was in possession of 758.9 miles² (1,920 km²) of Pakistani territory and the Pakistan army held 210 mile² (550 km²) of Indian territory. The territory occupied by India was mainly in the fertile Sialkot, Lahore and Kashmir sectors,[1092] while Pakistani land gains were primarily south in deserts opposite to Sindh and in Chumb sector near Kashmir in north.[1093] Pakistan claims that it held 1600 square miles of Indian territory, while lost 450 square miles of its own territory.[1094]

Aerial warfare

The war saw aircraft of the Indian Air Force (IAF) and the Pakistan Air Force (PAF) engaging in combat for the first time since independence. Though the two forces had previously faced off in the First Kashmir War during the late 1940s, that engagement was very limited in scale compared to the 1965 conflict.

The IAF was flying large numbers of Hawker Hunters, Indian-manufactured Folland Gnats, de Havilland Vampires, EE Canberra bombers and a squadron of MiG-21s. The PAF's fighter force comprised 102 F-86F Sabres and 12 F-104 Starfighters, along with 24 B-57 Canberra bombers. During the conflict, the PAF claimed it was out-numbered by around 5:1.[1095]

The PAF's aircraft were largely of American origin, whereas the IAF flew an assortment of British and Soviet aeroplanes. It has been widely reported that the PAF's American aircraft were superior to those of the IAF.

The F-86 was vulnerable to the diminutive Folland Gnat, nicknamed "Sabre Slayer."[1096] The Gnat is credited by many independent and Indian sources as having shot down seven Pakistani Canadair Sabres[1097] in the 1965 war.[1098,1099] while two Gnats were downed by PAF fighters. The PAF's F-104 Starfighter of the PAF was the fastest fighter operating in the subcontinent at that time and was often referred to as "the pride of the PAF". However, according to Sajjad Haider, the F-104 did not deserve this reputation. Being "a high level interceptor designed to neutralise Soviet strategic bombers in altitudes above 40,000 feet," rather than engage in dogfights with agile fighters at low altitudes, it was "unsuited to the tactical environment of the region."[1100] In combat the Starfighter was not as effective as the IAF's far more agile, albeit much slower, Folland Gnat fighter. Yet it zoomed into an ongoing dogfight between Sabres and Gnats, at supersonic speed, successfully broke off the fight and caused the Gnats to egress. An IAF Gnat, piloted by Squadron Leader Brij Pal Singh Sikand, landed at an abandoned Pakistani airstrip at Pasrur and was captured by the Pakistan Army. The pilot claimed that most of his equipment failed

Figure 224: *Captured Indian Folland Gnat on display at the PAF Museum Karachi.*

and even if he could get some chance on that, the Starfighters snuffed it.[1101] This Gnat is displayed as a war trophy in the Pakistan Air Force Museum, Karachi. Sqn Ldr Saad Hatmi who flew the captured aircraft to Sargodha, and later tested and evaluated its flight performance, was of view that Gnat was no "Sabre Slayer" when it came to dog fighting. The Pakistan Air Force had fought well in countering the much large Indian Air Force and supported the ground forces.

The two countries have made contradictory claims of combat losses during the war and few neutral sources have verified the claims of either country. The PAF claimed it shot down 104 IAF planes and lost 19 of its own, while the IAF claimed it shot down 73 PAF planes and lost 59. According to PAF, It flew 86 F-86 Sabres, 10 F-104 Starfighters and 20 B-57 Canberras in a parade soon after the war was over. Thus disproving the IAF's claim of downing 73 PAF fighters, which at the time constituted nearly the entire Pakistani front-line fighter force.[1102]

Indian sources have pointed out that, despite PAF claims of losing only a squadron of combat craft, Pakistan sought to acquire additional aircraft from Indonesia, Iraq, Iran, Turkey and China within 10 days of the beginning war.Wikipedia:Citation needed

Figure 225: *Sqn Ldr. Muhammad Mahmood Alam, Pakistani Ace in a Day, shot down 9 Indian Jets with 5 Hawker Hunters downed in just one minute.*

The two air forces were rather equal in the conflict, because much of the Indian air force remained farther east to guard against the possibility of China entering the war.[1103] According to the independent sources, the PAF lost some 20 aircraft while the Indians lost 60–75. Pakistan ended the war having depleted 17 percent of its front line strength, while India's losses amounted to less than 10 percent.Wikipedia:Citation needed Moreover, the loss rate had begun to even out, and it has been estimated that another three week's fighting would have seen the Pakistani losses rising to 33 percent and India's losses totalling 15 percent.Wikipedia:Citation needed Air superiority was not achieved, and were unable to prevent IAF fighter bombers and reconnaissance Canberras from flying daylight missions over Pakistan. Thus 1965 was a stalemate in terms of the air war with neither side able to achieve complete air superiority. However, according to Kenneth Werrell, the Pakistan Air Force "did well in the conflict and probably had the edge". When hostilities broke out, the Pakistan Air Force with around 100 F-86s faced an enemy with five times as many combat aircraft; the Indians were also equipped with comparatively modern aircraft inventory. Despite this, Werrell credits the PAF as having the advantage of a "decade's experience with the Sabre" and pilots with long flight hours experience. One Pakistani fighter pilot, MM Alam, was credited with the record of downing five Indian aircraft in less than a minute, becoming the first known flying ace since the Korean War. However, his claims were never confirmed by the PAF and is disputed by Indian sources[1104,1105] and some PAF officials.[1106,1107]

Figure 226: *1965 Indo-Pak War Destroyed Sherman Tank*

Tank battles

The 1965 war witnessed some of the largest tank battles since World War II. At the beginning of the war, the Pakistani Army had both a numerical advantage in tanks, as well as better equipment overall.[1108] Pakistani armour was largely American-made; it consisted mainly of Patton M-47 and M-48 tanks, but also included many M4 Sherman tanks, some M24 Chaffee light tanks and M36 Jackson tank destroyers, equipped with 90 mm guns.[1109] The bulk of India's tank fleet were older M4 Sherman tanks; some were up-gunned with the French high velocity CN 75 50 guns and could hold their own, whilst some older models were still equipped with the inferior 75 mm M3 L/40 gun. Besides the M4 tanks, India fielded the British-made Centurion Tank Mk 7, with the 105 mm Royal Ordnance L7 gun, and the AMX-13, PT-76, and M3 Stuart light tanks. Pakistan fielded a greater number and more modern artillery; its guns out-ranged those of the Indian artillery, according to Pakistan's Major General T.H. Malik.[1110]

At the outbreak of war in 1965, Pakistan had about 15 armoured cavalry regiments, each with about 45 tanks in three squadrons. Besides the Pattons, there were about 200 M4 Shermans re-armed with 76 mm guns, 150 M24 Chaffee light tank and a few independent squadrons of M36B1 tank destroyers. Most of these regiments served in Pakistan's two armoured divisions, the 1st and 6th Armoured divisions – the latter being in the process of formation.

The Indian Army of the time possessed 17 cavalry regiments, and in the 1950s had begun modernizing them by the acquisition of 164 AMX-13 light tanks

Figure 227: *Destroyed Sherman Tank*

and 188 Centurions. The remainder of the cavalry units were equipped with M4 Shermans and a small number of M3A3 Stuart light tanks. India had only a single armoured division, the 1st 'Black Elephant' Armoured Division, which consisted of the 17th Horse (The Poona Horse), also called 'Fakhr-i-Hind' ('Pride of India'), the 4th Horse (Hodson's Horse), the 16th Cavalry, the 7th Light Cavalry, the 2nd Lancers, the 18th Cavalry and the 62nd Cavalry, the two first named being equipped with Centurions. There was also the 2nd Independent Armoured Brigade, one of whose three regiments, the 3rd Cavalry, was also equipped with Centurions.

Despite the qualitative and numerical superiority of Pakistani armour, Pakistan was outfought on the battlefield by India, which made progress into the Lahore-Sialkot sector, whilst halting Pakistan's counteroffensive on Amritsar; they were sometimes employed in a faulty manner, such as charging prepared defences during the defeat of Pakistan's 1st Armoured Division at Asal Uttar.

After India breached the Madhupur canal on 11 September, the Khem Karan counter-offensive was halted, affecting Pakistan's strategy substantially. Although India's tank formations experienced some results, India's attack at the Battle of Chawinda, led by its 1st Armoured Division and supporting units, was brought to halt by the newly raised 6th Armoured Division (ex-100th independent brigade group) in the Chawinda sector. Pakistan claimed that Indians lost 120 tanks at Chawinda. compared to 44 of its ownBut later, Indian official sources confirmed India lost only 29 tanks at Chawinda. Neither the Indian nor Pakistani Army showed any great facility in the use of armoured formations in offensive operations, whether the Pakistani 1st Armoured Division at Asal Uttar or the Indian 1st Armoured Division at Chawinda. In contrast, both proved adept with smaller forces in a defensive role such as India's 2nd Armoured Brigade at Asal Uttar and Pakistan's 25th Cavalry at Chawinda.

The Centurion battle tank, with its 105 mm gun and heavy armour, performed better than the overly complexWikipedia:Verifiability Pattons.

Naval hostilities

Naval operations did not play a prominent role in the war of 1965. On 7 September, a flotilla of the Pakistan Navy under the command of Commodore S.M. Anwar, carried out a bombardment of the Indian Navy's radar station coastal down of Dwarka, which was 200 miles (320 km) south of the Pakistani port of Karachi. Operation Dwarka, as it is known, is a significant naval operation of the 1965 war[1111,1112] contested as a nuisance raid by some.[1113,1114] The attack on Dwarka led to questions being asked in India's parliament and subsequent post-war modernization and expansion of the Indian Navy, with an increase in budget from Rs. 35 crores to Rs. 115 crores.[1115]

According to some Pakistani sources, one submarine, PNS Ghazi, kept the Indian Navy's aircraft carrier INS Vikrant besieged in Bombay throughout the war. Indian sources claim that it was not their intention to get into a naval conflict with Pakistan, and wished to restrict the war to a land-based conflict.[1116] Moreover, they note that the Vikrant was in dry dock in the process of refitting. Some Pakistani defence writers have also discounted claims that the Indian Navy was bottled up in Bombay by a single submarine, instead stating that 75% of the Indian Navy was under maintenance in harbour.[1117]

Covert operations

The Pakistan Army launched a number of covert operations to infiltrate and sabotage Indian airbases. On 7 September 1965, the Special Services Group (SSG) commandos were parachuted into enemy territory. According to Chief of Army Staff General Muhammad Musa, about 135 commandos were airdropped at three Indian airfields (Halwara, Pathankot and Adampur). The daring attempt proved to be an "unmitigated disaster". Only 22 commandos returned to Pakistan as planned, 93 were taken prisoner (including one of the Commanders of the operations, Major Khalid Butt), and 20 were killed in encounters with the army, police or civilians.Wikipedia:Citation needed The reason for the failure of the commando mission is attributed to the failure to provide maps, proper briefings and adequate planning or preparation.[1118]

Despite failing to sabotage the airfields, Pakistan sources claim that the commando mission affected some planned Indian operations. As the Indian 14th Infantry Division was diverted to hunt for paratroopers, the Pakistan Air Force found the road filled with transport, and destroyed many vehicles.[1119]

India responded to the covert activity by announcing rewards for captured Pakistani spies or paratroopers.[1120] Meanwhile, in Pakistan, rumors spread that India had retaliated with its own covert operations, sending commandos deep into Pakistan territory, but these rumors were later determined to be unfounded.[1121]

Assessment of losses

India and Pakistan make widely divergent claims about the damage they inflicted on each other and the amount of damage suffered by them. The following summarizes each nation's claims.

	Indian claims	Pakistani claims	Independent Sources
Casualties	• Army: 169 commissioned officers (1 brigadier, 9 lieutenant-colonels, 30 majors, 39 captains, 11 lieutenants, 79 second lieutenants), 80 junior commissioned officers (JCO), 1820 other ranks • Air force: 19 officers, 21 other ranks	–	3,000 Indian soldiers, 3,800 Pakistani soldiers
Combat flying effort	4,073+ combat sorties	2,279 combat sorties	
Aircraft lost	59 IAF (official), 43 PAF. In addition, Indian sources claim that there were 13 IAF aircraft lost in accidents, and 3 Indian civilian aircraft shot down.	19 PAF, 104 IAF	20 PAF, 60–75 IAF; Pakistan claims India rejected neutral arbitration.[1122]
Aerial victories	17 + 3 (post war)	30	–
Tanks destroyed	128 Indian tanks, 152 Pakistani tanks captured, 150 Pakistani tanks destroyed. Officially 471 Pakistani tanks destroyed and 38 captured	165 Pakistan tanksWikipedia:Accuracy dispute#Disputed statementWikipedia:Citation needed	
Land area won	1,500 sq mi (3,900 km^2) of Pakistani territory	250 sq mi (650 km^2) of Indian territory	India held 1,840 km^2 (710 sq mi) of Pakistani territory and Pakistan held 210 sq mi (540 km^2) of Indian territory

Indo-Pakistani War of 1965   497

Neutral assessments

There have been several neutral assessments of the losses incurred by both India and Pakistan during the war. Most of these assessments agree that India had the upper hand over Pakistan when ceasefire was declared. Some of the neutral assessments are mentioned below —

- According to the Library of Congress Country Studies conducted by the Federal Research Division of the United States –

  The war was militarily inconclusive; each side held prisoners and some territory belonging to the other. Losses were relatively heavy—on the Pakistani side, twenty aircraft, 200 tanks, and 3,800 troops. Pakistan's army had been able to withstand Indian pressure, but a continuation of the fighting would only have led to further losses and ultimate defeat for Pakistan. Most Pakistanis, schooled in the belief of their own martial prowess, refused to accept the possibility of their country's military defeat by "Hindu India" and were, instead, quick to blame their failure to attain their military aims on what they considered to be the ineptitude of Ayub Khan and his government.

- Former *New York Times* reporter Arif Jamal wrote in his book *Shadow War*[1061] —

  This time, India's victory was nearly total: India accepted cease-fire only after it had occupied 740 square miles, though Pakistan had made marginal gains of 210 square miles of territory. Despite the obvious strength of the Indian wins, both countries claim to have been victorious.

- Devin T. Hagerty wrote in his book *"South Asia in world politics"* –

  The invading Indian forces outfought their Pakistani counterparts and halted their attack on the outskirts of Lahore, Pakistan's second-largest city. By the time United Nations intervened on September 22, Pakistan had suffered a clear defeat.

- In his book *"National identity and geopolitical visions"*, Gertjan Dijkink writes –

  The superior Indian forces, however, won a decisive victory and the army could have even marched on into Pakistani territory had external pressure not forced both combatants to cease their war efforts.

- An excerpt from Stanley Wolpert's *India*,[1123] summarizing the Indo-Pakistani War of 1965,

In three weeks the second Indo-Pak War ended in what appeared to be a draw when the embargo placed by Washington on U.S. ammunition and replacements for both armies forced cessation of conflict before either side won a clear victory. India, however, was in a position to inflict grave damage to, if not capture, Pakistan's capital of the Punjab when the cease-fire was called, and controlled Kashmir's strategic Uri-Poonch bulge, much to Ayub's chagrin.

- In his book titled *The greater game: India's race with destiny and China*, David Van Praagh wrote –

India won the war. It held on to the Vale of Kashmir, the prize Pakistan vainly sought. It gained 1,840 km^2 (710 sq mi) of Pakistani territory: 640 km^2 (250 sq mi) in Azad Kashmir, Pakistan's portion of the state; 460 km^2 (180 sq mi) of the Sailkot sector; 380 km^2 (150 sq mi) far to the south of Sindh; and most critical, 360 km^2 (140 sq mi) on the Lahore front. Pakistan took 540 km^2 (210 sq mi) of Indian territory: 490 km^2 (190 sq mi) in the Chhamb sector and 50 km^2 (19 sq mi) around Khem Karan.

- Dennis Kux's *"India and the United States estranged democracies"* also provides a summary of the war,[1124]

Although both sides lost heavily in men and material, and neither gained a decisive military advantage, India had the better of the war. New Delhi achieved its basic goal of thwarting Pakistan's attempt to seize Kashmir by force. Pakistan gained nothing from a conflict which it had instigated.

- *"A region in turmoil: South Asian conflicts since 1947"* by Robert Johnson mentions –

India's strategic aims were modest – it aimed to deny Pakistani Army victory, although it ended up in possession of 720 square miles (1,900 km^2) of Pakistani territory for the loss of just 220 square miles (570 km^2) of its own.

- An excerpt from William M. Carpenter and David G. Wiencek's *"Asian security handbook: terrorism and the new security environment"* –

A brief but furious 1965 war with India began with a covert Pakistani thrust across the Kashmiri cease-fire line and ended up with the city of Lahore threatened with encirclement by Indian Army. Another UN-sponsored cease-fire left borders unchanged, but Pakistan's vulnerability had again been exposed.

- English historian John Keay's *"India: A History"* provides a summary of the 1965 war –

The 1965 Indo-Pak war lasted barely a month. Pakistan made gains in the Rajasthan desert but its main push against India's Jammu-Srinagar road link was repulsed and Indian tanks advanced to within a sight of Lahore. Both sides claimed victory but India had most to celebrate.

- Uk Heo and Shale Asher Horowitz write in their book "*Conflict in Asia: Korea, China-Taiwan, and India-Pakistan*" –

Again India appeared, logistically at least, to be in a superior position but neither side was able to mobilize enough strength to gain a decisive victory.

- According to the Office of the Historian within the U.S Department of State:[1125]

Conflict resumed again in early 1965, when Pakistani and Indian forces clashed over disputed territory along the border between the two nations. Hostilities intensified that August when the Pakistani army attempted to take Kashmir by force. The attempt to seize the state was unsuccessful, and the second India-Pakistan War reached a stalemate.

Ceasefire

The United States and the Soviet Union used significant diplomatic tools to prevent any further escalation in the conflict between the two South Asian nations. The Soviet Union, led by Premier Alexei Kosygin, hosted ceasefire negotiations in Tashkent (now in Uzbekistan), where Indian Prime Minister Lal Bahadur Shastri and Pakistani President Ayub Khan signed the Tashkent Agreement, agreeing to withdraw to pre-August lines no later than 25 February 1966.

With declining stockpiles of ammunition, Pakistani leaders feared the war tilting in India's favor. Therefore, they quickly accepted the ceasefire in Tashkent. Despite strong opposition from Indian military leaders, India bowed to growing international diplomatic pressure and accepted the ceasefire. On 22 September, the United Nations Security Council unanimously passed a resolution that called for an unconditional ceasefire from both nations. The war ended the following day.

India's Prime Minister, Shastri, suffered a fatal heart attack soon after the declaration of the ceasefire. As a consequence, the public outcry in India against the ceasefire declaration transformed into a wave of sympathy for the ruling Indian National Congress. The ceasefire was criticised by many Pakistanis who, relying on fabricated official reports and the controlled Pakistani press, believed that the leadership had surrendered military gains. The protests led to student riots.[1126] Pakistan State's reports had suggested that their military was performing admirably in the war – which they incorrectly blamed as being initiated by India – and thus the Tashkent Declaration was seen as having forfeited the gains.[1127] Some recent books written by Pakistani authors, including one by ex-ISI chief titled "The Myth of 1965 Victory",[1128] reportedly exposed Pakistani fabrications about the war, but all copies of the book were bought by Pakistan Army to prevent circulation because the topic was "too sensitive".[1129,1130]

India and Pakistan accused each other of ceasefire violations; India charged Pakistan with 585 violations in 34 days, while Pakistan countered with accusations of 450 incidents by India.[1131] In addition to the expected exchange of small arms and artillery fire, India reported that Pakistan utilized the ceasefire to capture the Indian village of Chananwalla in the Fazilka sector. This village was recaptured by Indian troops on 25 December. On 10 October, a B-57 Canberra on loan to the PAF was damaged by 3 SA-2 missiles fired from the IAF base at Ambala.[1132] A Pakistani Army Auster AOP was shot down on 16 December, killing one Pakistani army captain; on 2 February 1967, an AOP was shot down by IAF Hunters.

The ceasefire remained in effect until the start of the Indo-Pakistani War of 1971.

Intelligence failures

Strategic miscalculations by both India and Pakistan ensured that the war ended in a stalemate —

Indian miscalculations

Indian military intelligence gave no warning of the impending Pakistan invasion. The Indian Army failed to recognize the presence of heavy Pakistani artillery and armaments in Chumb and suffered significant losses as a result.

The " Official War History - 1965[1133]", drafted by the Ministry of Defence of India in 1992, was a long suppressed document that revealed other miscalculations. According to the document, on 22 September when the Security Council was pressing for a ceasefire, the Indian Prime Minister asked commanding Gen. Chaudhuri if India could possibly win the war, were he to delay accepting the ceasefire. The general replied that most of India's frontline ammunition had been used up and the Indian Army had suffered considerable tank losses. It was determined later that only 14% of India's frontline ammunition had been fired and India held twice the number of tanks as Pakistan. By this time, the Pakistani Army had used close to 80% of its ammunition.

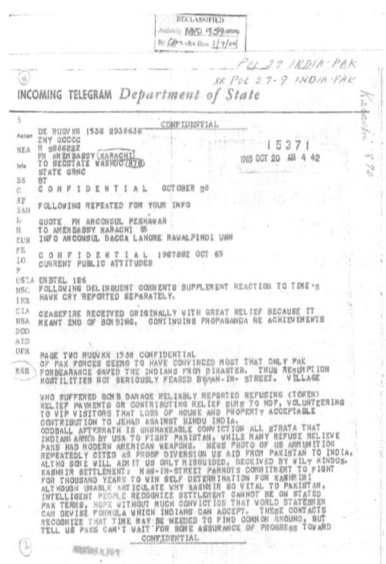

Figure 228: *Telegram from the Embassy of the United States in Karachi: "Continuing propaganda regarding achievements of Pak forces seems to have convinced most that only Pak forbearance saved the Indians from disaster."*

Air Chief Marshal (retd) P.C. Lal, who was the Vice Chief of Air Staff during the conflict, points to the lack of coordination between the IAF and the Indian army. Neither side revealed its battle plans to the other. The battle plans drafted by the Ministry of Defence and General Chaudhari, did not specify a role for the Indian Air Force in the order of battle. This attitude of Gen. Chaudhari was referred to by ACM Lal as the "Supremo Syndrome", a patronizing attitude sometimes held by the Indian army towards the other branches of the Indian Military.

Pakistani miscalculations

The Pakistani Army's failures started with the supposition that a generally discontented Kashmiri people, given the opportunity provided by the Pakistani advance, would revolt against their Indian rulers, bringing about a swift and decisive surrender of Kashmir. The Kashmiri people, however, did not revolt. Instead, the Indian Army was provided with enough information to learn of Operation Gibraltar and the fact that the Army was battling not insurgents, as they had initially supposed, but Pakistani Army regulars.

The Pakistani Army also failed to recognize that the Indian policy makers would order an attack on the southern sector in order to open a second front.

Pakistan was forced to dedicate troops to the southern sector to protect Sialkot and Lahore instead using them to support penetrating into Kashmir.

"Operation Grand Slam", which was launched by Pakistan to capture Akhnoor, a town north-east of Jammu and a key region for communications between Kashmir and the rest of India, was also a failure. Many Pakistani commentators criticised the Ayub Khan administration for being indecisive during Operation Grand Slam. These critics claim that the operation failed because Ayub Khan knew the importance of Akhnur to India (having called it India's "jugular vein") and did not want to capture it and drive the two nations into an all-out war. Despite progress being made in Akhnur, General Ayub Khan relieved the commanding Major General Akhtar Hussain Malik and replaced him with Gen. Yahya Khan. A 24-hour lull ensued the replacement, which allowed the Indian army to regroup in Akhnur and successfully oppose a lackluster attack headed by General Yahya Khan. "The enemy came to our rescue", asserted the Indian Chief of Staff of the Western Command. Later, Akhtar Hussain Malik criticised Ayub Khan for planning Operation Gibraltar, which was doomed to fail, and for relieving him of his command at a crucial moment in the war. Malik threatened to expose the truth about the war and the army's failure, but later dropped the idea for fear of being banned.[1134]

Some authors have noted that Pakistan might have been emboldened by a war game – conducted in March 1965, at the Institute of Defence Analysis, USA. The exercise concluded that, in the event of a war with India, Pakistan would win.[1135,1136] Other authors like Stephen Philip Cohen, have consistently commented that the Pakistan Army had "acquired an exaggerated view of the weakness of both India and the Indian military ... the 1965 war was a shock".[1137]

Pakistani Air Marshal and Commander-in-Chief of PAF during the war, Nur Khan, later said that the Pakistan Army, and not India, should be blamed for starting the war.[1138,1139] However propaganda in Pakistan about the war continued; the war was not rationally analysed in Pakistan,[1140,1141] with most of the blame being heaped on the leadership and little importance given to intelligence failures that persisted until the debacle of the Indo-Pakistani War of 1971.

Involvement of other nations

The United States and the United Kingdom had been the principal suppliers of military matériel to India and Pakistan since 1947. Both India and Pakistan were Commonwealth republics. While India had pursued a policy of nominal non-alignment, Pakistan was a member of both CENTO and SEATO and a purported ally of the West in its struggle against Communism. Well before the conflict began, however, Britain and the United States had suspected Pakistan of joining both alliances out of opportunism to acquire advanced weapons for a war against India. They had therefore limited their military aid to Pakistan to maintain the existing balance of power in the subcontinent.[1142] In 1959, however, Pakistan and the United States had signed an Agreement of Cooperation in 1959 under which the United States agreed to take "appropriate action, including the use of armed forces" in order to assist the Government of Pakistan at its request. By 1965, American and British analysts had recognised the two international groupings, CENTO and SEATO, and Pakistan's continued alliance with the West as being largely meaningless.

Following the start of the 1965 war, both the United States and Britain took the view that the conflict was largely Pakistan's fault, and suspended all arms shipments to both India and Pakistan. While the United States maintained a neutral stance, the British Prime Minister, Harold Wilson, condemned India for aggression after its army advanced towards Lahore; his statement was met with a furious rebuttal from India.

Internationally, the level of support which Pakistan received was limited at best. Iran and Turkey issued a joint communiqué on 10 September which placed the blame on India, backed the United Nations' appeal for a cease-fire and offered to deploy troops for a UN peacekeeping mission in Kashmir. Pakistan received support from Indonesia, Iran, Turkey, and Saudi Arabia in the form of six naval vessels, jet fuel, guns and ammunition and financial support, respectively.[1143]

Since before the war, the People's Republic of China had been a major military associate of Pakistan and a military opponent of India, with whom it had fought a brief war in 1962. China had also become a foreign patron for Pakistan and had given Pakistan $60 million in development assistance in 1965.[1144] During the war, China openly supported the Pakistani position. It took advantage of the conflict to issue a strongly worded ultimatum to India condemning its "aggression" in Tibet and hinting at nuclear retaliation by China (China had exploded its first nuclear device the previous year). Despite strong fears of Chinese intervention on the side of Pakistan, the Chinese government ultimately exercised restraint. This was partly due to the logistical difficulties of a direct Chinese military intervention against India and India's improved military strength after its defeat by China in 1962. China had also received strong warnings by the American and Soviet governments against expanding the scope of the conflict by intervening. In the face of this pressure, China backed down, extending the deadline for India to respond to its ultimatum and warning India against attacking East Pakistan. Ultimately, Pakistan rejected Chinese offers of military aid, recognising that accepting it would only result in further alienating Pakistan internationally. International opinion considered

China's actions to be dangerously reckless and aggressive, and it was soundly rebuked in the world press for its unnecessarily provocative stance during the conflict.

India's participation in the Non-Aligned Movement yielded little support from its members. Support given by Indonesia to Pakistan was seen as a major Indian diplomatic failure, as Indonesia had been among the founding members of the Non-Aligned Movement along with India.Wikipedia:Citation needed Despite its close relations with India, the Soviet Union was more neutral than other nations during the war, inviting both nations to peace talks under its aegis in Tashkent.[1145]Wikipedia:Verifiability

Aftermath

India

Despite the declaration of a ceasefire, India was perceived as the victor due to its success in halting the Pakistan-backed insurgency in Kashmir. In its October 1965 issue, the TIME magazine quoted a Western official assessing the consequences of the war[1146] —

> Now it's apparent to everybody that India is going to emerge as an Asian power in its own right.

In light of the failures of the Sino-Indian War, the outcome of the 1965 war was viewed as a "politico-strategic" victory in India. The Indian premier, Lal Bahadur Shastri, was hailed as a national hero in India.[1147]

While the overall performance of the Indian military was praised, military leaders were criticised for their failure to effectively deploy India's superior armed forces so as to achieve a decisive victory over Pakistan.[1148] In his book "War in the modern world since 1815", noted war historian Jeremy Black said that though Pakistan "lost heavily" during the 1965 war, India's hasty decision to call for negotiations prevented further considerable damage to the Pakistan Armed Forces. He elaborates —

> India's chief of army staff urged negotiations on the ground that they were running out ammunition and their number of tanks had become seriously depleted. In fact, the army had used less than 15% of its ammunition compared to Pakistan, which had consumed closer to 80 percent and India had double the number of serviceable tanks.

In 2015, Marshal of the Indian Air Force Arjan Singh, the last surviving armed force commander of the conflict, gave his assessment that the war ended in a stalemate, but only due to international pressure for a ceasefire, and that India would have achieved a decisive victory had hostilities continued for a few days more:

> For political reasons, Pakistan claims victory in the 1965 war. In my opinion, the war ended in a kind of stalemate. We were in a position of strength. Had the war continued for a few more days, we would have gained a decisive victory. I advised then prime minister Lal Bahadur Shastri not to agree for ceasefire. But I think he was under pressure from the United Nations and some countries.

As a consequence, India focussed on enhancing communication and coordination within and among the tri-services of the Indian Armed Forces. Partly as a result of the inefficient information gathering preceding the war, India established the Research and Analysis Wing for external espionage and intelligence. Major improvements were also made in command and control to address various shortcomings and the positive impact of these changes was clearly visible during the Indo-Pakistani War of 1971 when India achieved a decisive victory over Pakistan within two weeks.

China's repeated threats to intervene in the conflict in support of Pakistan increased pressure on the government to take an immediate decision to develop nuclear weapons. Despite repeated assurances, the United States did little to prevent extensive use of American arms by Pakistani forces during the conflict, thus irking India.[1149] At the same time, the United States and United Kingdom refused to supply India with sophisticated weaponry which further strained the relations between the West and India. These developments led to a significant change in India's foreign policy – India, which had previously championed the cause of non-alignment, distanced itself further from Western powers and developed close relations with the Soviet Union. By the end of the 1960s, the Soviet Union emerged as the biggest supplier of military hardware to India. From 1967 to 1977, 81% of India's arms imports were from the Soviet Union. After the 1965 war, the arms race between India and Pakistan became even more asymmetric and India was outdistancing Pakistan by far.

Pakistan

At the conclusion of the war, many Pakistanis considered the performance of their military to be positive. 6 September is celebrated as Defence Day in Pakistan, in commemoration of the successful defence of Lahore against the Indian army. The performance of the Pakistani Air Force, in particular, was praised.

However, the Pakistani government was accused by foreign analysts of spreading disinformation among its citizens regarding the actual consequences of the war.[1150] In his book *"Mainsprings of Indian and Pakistani foreign policies"*, S.M. Burke writes —

> *After the Indo-Pakistani war of 1965 the balance of military power had decisively shifted in favor of India. Pakistan had found it difficult to replace the heavy equipment lost during that conflict while her adversary, despite her economic and political problems, had been determinedly building up her strength.*

Most observers agree that the myth of a mobile, hard hitting Pakistan Army was badly dented in the war, as critical breakthroughs were not made.[1151] Several Pakistani writers criticised the military's ill-founded belief that their "martial race" of soldiers could defeat "Hindu India" in the war.[1152,1153] Rasul Bux Rais, a Pakistani political analyst wrote –

> *The 1965 war with India proved that Pakistan could neither break the formidable Indian defences in a blitzkrieg fashion nor could she sustain an all-out conflict for long.*

The Pakistan airforce on the other hand gained a lot of credibility and reliability among Pakistan military and international war writers for successful defence of lahore and other important areas of Pakistan and heavy retaliation to India on the next day. The alertness of the airforce was also related to the fact that some pilots were scrambled 6 times in less than an hour on indication of Indian air raids. The Pakistan airforce along with the army is celebrated on Defence day and Airforce day in commemoration of this in Pakistan (6 and 7 September respectively).[1154]

Moreover, Pakistan had lost more ground than it had gained during the war and, more importantly, failed to achieve its goal of capturing Kashmir; this result has been viewed by many impartial observers as a defeat for Pakistan.

Many senior Pakistani officials and military experts later criticised the faulty planning of Operation Gibraltar, which ultimately led to the war. The Tashkent declaration was also criticised in Pakistan, though few citizens realised the gravity of the situation that existed at the end of the war. Political leaders were also criticised. Following the advice of Zulfikar Ali Bhutto, Pakistan's foreign minister, Ayub Khan had raised very high expectations among the people of Pakistan about the superiority – if not invincibility – of its armed forces,[1155] but Pakistan's inability to attain its military aims during the war created a political liability for Ayub. The defeat of its Kashmiri ambitions in the war led to the army's invincibility being challenged by an increasingly vocal opposition.[1156]

One of the farthest reaching consequences of the war was the wide-scale economic slowdown in Pakistan.[1157,1158] The war ended the impressive economic growth Pakistan had experienced since the early 1960s. Between 1964 and 1966, Pakistan's defence spending rose from 4.82% to 9.86% of GDP, putting a tremendous strain on Pakistan's economy. By 1970-71, defence spending comprised a whopping 55.66% of government expenditure. According to veterans of the war, the war greatly cost Pakistan economically, politically, and militarily. Nuclear theorist Feroze Khan maintained that the 1965 war was a last conventional attempt to snatch Kashmir by military force, and Pakistan's own position in the international community, especially with the United States, began to deteriorate from the point the war started, while on the other hand, the alliance with China saw improvements. Chairman joint chiefs General Tariq Majid claims in his memoirs that Chou En-Lai had longed advised the government in the classic style of Sun Tzu: "to go slow, not to push India hard; and avoid a fight over Kashmir, 'for at least, 20-30 years, until you have developed your economy and consolidated your national power'." General Majid maintained in *Eating Grass* that the "sane, philosophical and political critical thinking" was missing in Pakistan, and that the country had lost extensive human resources by fighting the war.

Pakistan was surprised by the lack of support from the United States, an ally with whom the country had signed an Agreement of Cooperation. The US turned neutral in the war when it cut off military supplies to Pakistan (and India); an action that the Pakistanis took as a sign of betrayal.[1159] After the war, Pakistan would increasingly look towards China as a major source of military hardware and political support.

Another negative consequence of the war was growing resentment against the Pakistani government in East Pakistan (present day Bangladesh), particularly for West Pakistan's obsession with Kashmir.[1160] Bengali leaders accused the central government of not providing adequate security for East Pakistan during the conflict, even though large sums of money were taken from the east to finance the war for Kashmir.[1161] In fact, despite some Pakistan Air Force attacks being launched from bases in East Pakistan during the war, India did not retaliate in that sector,[1162] although East Pakistan was defended only by an understrengthed infantry division (14th Division), sixteen planes and no tanks.[1163] Sheikh Mujibur Rahman was critical of the disparity in military resources deployed in East and West Pakistan, calling for greater autonomy for East Pakistan, an action that ultimately led to the Bangladesh Liberation War and another war between India and Pakistan in 1971.

Military awards

Battle honours

After the war, a total of 16 battle honours and 3 theatre honours were awarded to units of the Indian Army, the notable amongst which are:

- Jammu and Kashmir 1965 (theatre honour)
- Punjab 1965 (theatre honour)
- Rajasthan 1965 (theatre honour)
- Assal Uttar
- Burki
- Dograi
- Hajipir
- Hussainiwala
- Kalidhar
- OP Hill
- Phillora

Gallantry awards

For bravery, the following soldiers were awarded the highest gallantry award of their respective countries, the Indian award Param Vir Chakra and the Pakistani award Nishan-e-Haider:

India

- Company Quarter Master Havildar Abdul Hamid (Posthumous)
- Lieutenant-Colonel Ardeshir Burzorji Tarapore (Posthumous)

Pakistan

- Major Raja Aziz Bhatti Shaheed (Posthumous)

Bibliography

<templatestyles src="Template:Refbegin/styles.css" />

- *First & Further reflections on the second Kashmir War* (South Asia series) – 2 books by Louis Dupree.
- Asghar Khan, Mohammed (1979). *The first round: Indo-Pakistan War, 1965*[1164]. Islamic Information Services. ISBN 0-906041-11-2.
- Ayub, Muhammad (2005). *An army, its role and rule: a history of the Pakistan Army from Independence to Kargil, 1967–1999*[1165]. RoseDog Books. ISBN 0-8059-9594-3.
- Berindranath, Dewan (1966). *The war with Pakistan: A pictorial narration of the fifty days which rocked the sub-continent*[1166]. Asia Press.

- Bisht, Rachna (15 August 2015), *1965: Stories from the Second Indo-Pakistan War*, Penguin UK, p. 60, ISBN 978-93-5214-129-6
- Brines, Russell (1968). *The Indo-Pakistan Conflict*[1167]. Pall Mall P. ISBN 0-269-16232-1.
- Faruquii, Ahmad (2003). *Rethinking the national security of Pakistan: the price of strategic myopia*[1168]. Ashgate Publishing. ISBN 0-7546-1497-2.
- Fricker, John (1979). *Battle for Pakistan: the air war of 1965*[1169]. Ian Allan. ISBN 0-7110-0929-5.
- Gupta, Hari Ram (1967). *India-Pakistan war, 1965*[1170]. **1** (1 ed.). Hariyana Prakashan. ASIN B0006FFBK8[1171].
- Haqqani, Hussain (2005). *Pakistan: Between Mosque and Military*[1172]. United Book Press. ISBN 0-87003-214-3. ISBN 0-87003-223-2.
- Higgins, David R. (20 January 2016), *M48 Patton vs Centurion: Indo-Pakistan War 1965*, Osprey Publishing, p. 103, ISBN 978-1-4728-1094-6
- Ismail Siddiqui, Muhammad (1983). *Die to live: A selection of short stories based on the 1965 Indo-Pakistan war*[1173] (1 ed.). Wajidalis. ASIN B0006EL2OI[1174].
- Jamal, Arif (2009), *Shadow War: The Untold Story of Jihad in Kashmir*[1175], Melville House, ISBN 978-1-933633-59-6
- McGarr, Paul (2013). *The Cold War in South Asia: Britain, the United States and the Indian Subcontinent, 1945–1965*. Cambridge University Press. ISBN 978-1-139-02207-1.
- Mohan, Jagan; Chopra, Samir (2005) [2005]. *The India Pakistan Air War of 1965*[1176] (1 ed.). Manohar Publishers. ISBN 81-7304-641-7.
- Paul, T. V. (10 March 1994), *Asymmetric Conflicts: War Initiation by Weaker Powers*, Cambridge University Press, ISBN 978-0-521-46621-9
- Praval, Maj K C (2009). *Indian Army after Independence*[1177]. Lancer InterConsult, Inc. ISBN 1-935501-10-0.
- Singh, Bhupinder (1982). *1965 war, role of tanks in India-Pakistan war*[1178]. B.C. Publishers. ASIN B0000CQ9GQ[1179].
- Singh, Lt. Gen. Harbaksh (1991). *War despatches: Indo-Pak Conflict, 1965*[1180]. Lancer InterConsult, Inc. ISBN 81-7062-117-8.

Sources and external links

- IAF Combat Kills – 1965 war[1181],(Center for Indian Military History)
- Mohammed Muhammad Musa (1983). *My Version: India-Pakistan War 1965*. Wajidalis.
- United States Library of Congress Country Studies – India[1182]
- Official History of the Indian Armed Forces in the 1965 War with Pakistan[1183]

- GlobalSecurity.org Indo-Pakistan War 1965[1184]
- Pakistan Columnist AH Amin analyses the war.[1185]
- Grand Slam – A Battle of lost Opportunities, Maj (Retd) Agha Humayun Amin[1186] – very detailed roll of events and analysis
- The India-Pakistan War, 1965: 40 Years On[1187] – From Rediff.com
- Lessons of the 1965 War from Daily Times (Pakistan)[1188]
- Spirit of '65 & the parallels with today – Ayaz Amir[1189]

Sino-Indian War

Sino-Indian War	
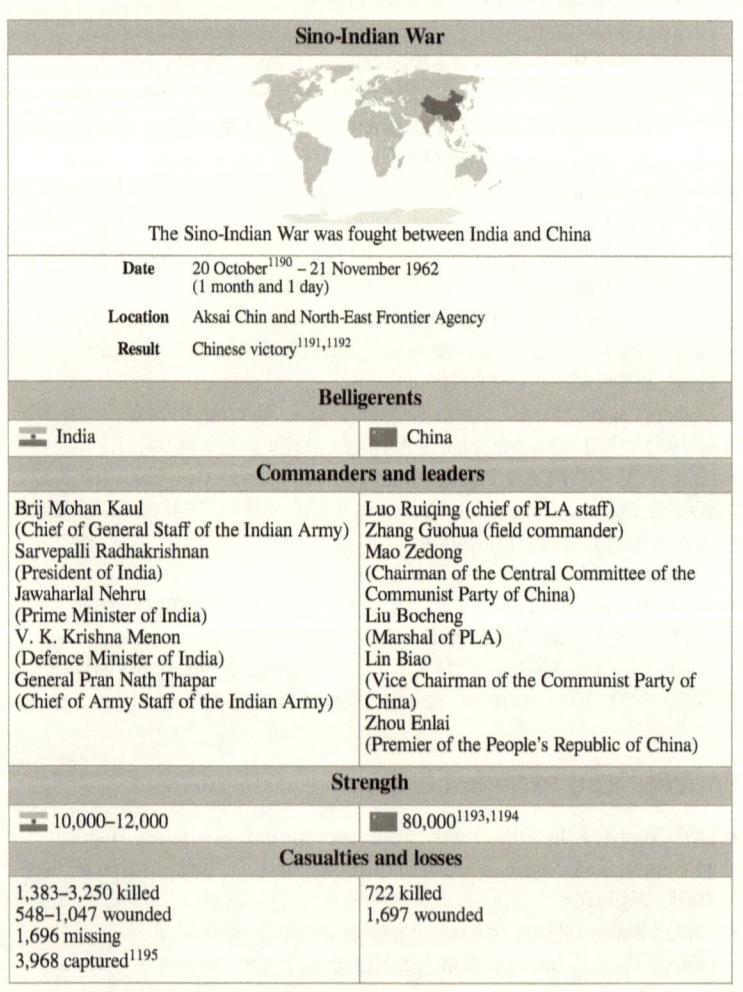	
The Sino-Indian War was fought between India and China	
Date	20 October[1190] – 21 November 1962 (1 month and 1 day)
Location	Aksai Chin and North-East Frontier Agency
Result	Chinese victory[1191,1192]
Belligerents	
India	China
Commanders and leaders	
Brij Mohan Kaul (Chief of General Staff of the Indian Army) Sarvepalli Radhakrishnan (President of India) Jawaharlal Nehru (Prime Minister of India) V. K. Krishna Menon (Defence Minister of India) General Pran Nath Thapar (Chief of Army Staff of the Indian Army)	Luo Ruiqing (chief of PLA staff) Zhang Guohua (field commander) Mao Zedong (Chairman of the Central Committee of the Communist Party of China) Liu Bocheng (Marshal of PLA) Lin Biao (Vice Chairman of the Communist Party of China) Zhou Enlai (Premier of the People's Republic of China)
Strength	
10,000–12,000	80,000[1193,1194]
Casualties and losses	
1,383–3,250 killed 548–1,047 wounded 1,696 missing 3,968 captured[1195]	722 killed 1,697 wounded

The **Sino-Indian War** (Hindi: भारत-चीन युद्ध Bhārat-Chīn Yuddh), also known as the **Sino-Indian Border Conflict** (simplified Chinese: 中印边境战争 ; traditional Chinese: 中印 邊境 戰爭 ; pinyin: *Zhōng-Yìn Biānjìng Zhànzhēng*), was a war between China and India that occurred in 1962. A disputed Himalayan border was the main pretext for war, but other issues played a role. There had been a series of violent border incidents after the 1959 Tibetan uprising, when India had granted asylum to the Dalai Lama. India initiated a Forward Policy in which it placed outposts along the border, including several north of the McMahon Line, the eastern portion of a Line of Actual Control proclaimed by Chinese Premier Zhou Enlai in 1959.

Unable to reach political accommodation on disputed territory along the 3,225-kilometre-long Himalayan border, the Chinese launched simultaneous offensives in Ladakh and across the McMahon Line on 20 October 1962, coinciding with the Cuban Missile Crisis. Chinese troops advanced over Indian forces in both theatres, capturing Rezang La in Chushul in the western theatre, as well as Tawang in the eastern theatre. The war ended when China declared a cease-fire on 20 November 1962, and simultaneously announced its withdrawal to its claimed 'line of actual control'.

Much of the battle took place in harsh mountain conditions, entailing large-scale combat at altitudes of over 4,000 metres (14,000 feet). The Sino-Indian War was also noted for the non-deployment of the navy or air force by either the Chinese or Indian side.

The buildup and offensive from China occurred concurrently with the 13-day Cuban Missile Crisis (16–28 October 1962) that saw both the United States and the Soviet Union confronting each other, and India did not receive assistance from either of these world powers until the Cuban Missile Crisis was resolved.

Location

China and India shared a long border, sectioned into three stretches by Nepal, Sikkim (then an Indian protectorate), and Bhutan, which follows the Himalayas between Burma and what was then West Pakistan. A number of disputed regions lie along this border. At its western end is the Aksai Chin region, an area the size of Switzerland, that sits between the Chinese autonomous region of Xinjiang and Tibet (which China declared as an autonomous region in 1965). The eastern border, between Burma and Bhutan, comprises the present Indian state of Arunachal Pradesh (formerly the North East Frontier Agency). Both of these regions were overrun by China in the 1962 conflict.

Most combat took place at high altitudes. The Aksai Chin region is a desert of salt flats around 5,000 metres above sea level, and Arunachal Pradesh is

Figure 229: *Pre-Simla British map published in 1909 shows the so-called "Outer Line" as India's northern boundary*

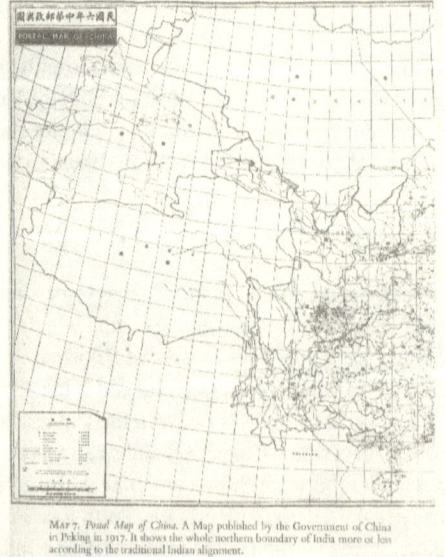

Figure 230: *Postal Map of China published by the Government of China in 1917*

Figure 231: *Traditional borders of Jammu and Kashmir (CIA map). The northern boundary is along the Karakash valley. Aksai Chin is the shaded region in the east.*

mountainous with a number of peaks exceeding 7,000 metres. The Chinese Army had possession of one of the highest ridges in the regions. The high altitude and freezing conditions also cause logistical and welfare difficulties; in past similar conflicts (such as the Italian Campaign of World War I) harsh conditions have caused more casualties than have enemy action. The Sino-Indian War was no different, with many troops on both sides dying in the freezing cold.

Background

The cause of the war was a dispute over the sovereignty of the widely separated Aksai Chin and Arunachal Pradesh border regions. Aksai Chin, claimed by India to belong to Kashmir and by China to be part of Xinjiang, contains an important road link that connects the Chinese regions of Tibet and Xinjiang. China's construction of this road was one of the triggers of the conflict.

Aksai Chin

The western portion of the Sino-Indian boundary originated in 1834, with the conquest of Ladakh by the armies of Raja Gulab Singh (Dogra) under the

Figure 232: *1873 map of trade routes between Ladakh and Chinese Turkestan. The international border between the British Indian Empire (including the Kashmir region) and Chinese Turkestan is shown in two-toned purple and pink.*

suzerainty of the Sikh Empire. Following an unsuccessful campaign into Tibet, Gulab Singh and the Tibetans signed a treaty in 1842 agreeing to stick to the "old, established frontiers", which were left unspecified.[1196,1197] The British defeat of the Sikhs in 1846 resulted in the transfer of the Jammu and Kashmir region including Ladakh to the British, who then installed Gulab Singh as the Maharaja under their suzerainty. British commissioners contacted Chinese officials to negotiate the border, who did not show any interest.[1198] The British boundary commissioners fixed the southern end of the boundary at Pangong Lake, but regarded the area north of it till the Karakoram Pass as *terra incognita*.[1199]

The Maharaja of Kashmir and his officials were keenly aware of the trade routes from Ladakh. Starting from Leh, there were two main routes into Central Asia: one passed through the Karakoram Pass to Shahidulla at the foot of the Kunlun Mountains and went on to Yarkand through the Kilian and Sanju passes; the other went east via the Chang Chenmo Valley, passed the Lingzi Tang Plains in the Aksai Chin region, and followed the course of the Karakash River to join the first route at Shahidulla.[1200] The Maharaja regarded Shahidulla as his northern outpost, in effect treating the Kunlun mountains as the boundary of his domains. His British suzerains were sceptical of such an

Sino-Indian War 515

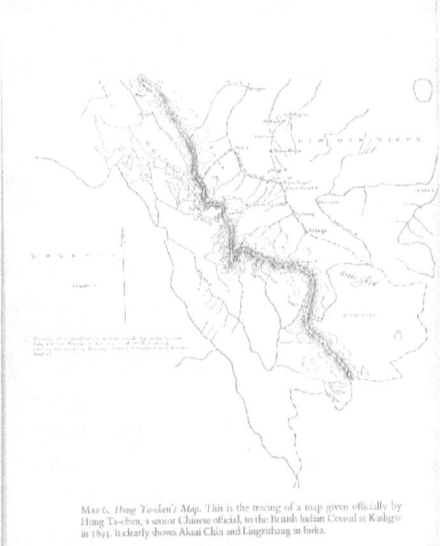

Figure 233: *The map given by Hung Ta-chen to the British consul at Kashgar in 1893. The boundary, marked with a thin dot-dashed line, matches the 1873 British map.*

extended boundary because Shahidulla was 79 miles away from the Karakoram pass and the intervening area was uninhabited. Nevertheless, the Maharaja was allowed to treat Shahidulla as his outpost for more than 20 years.[1201,1202,1203]

Chinese Turkestan regarded the high mountains of the Kunlun range with the Kilian and Sanju passes as its southern boundary. Thus the Maharaja's claim was uncontested.[1204,1205] After the 1862 Dungan Revolt, which saw the expulsion of the Chinese from Turkestan, the Maharaja of Kashmir constructed a small fort at Shahidulla in 1864. The fort was most likely supplied from Khotan, whose ruler was now independent and on friendly terms with Kashmir. When the Khotanese ruler was deposed by the Kashgaria strongman Yakub Beg, the Maharaja was forced to abandon his post in 1867. It was then occupied by Yakub Beg's forces until the end of the Dungan Revolt.[1206] In the intervening period, W. H. Johnson of Survey of India was commissioned to survey the Aksai Chin region. While in the course of his work, he was "invited" by the Khotanese ruler to visit his capital. After returning, Johnson declared that Khotan's border was at Brinjga, in the Kunlun mountains, and the entire the Karakash Valley was within the territory of Kashmir. The boundary of Kashmir that he drew, stretching from Shahidullah to the eastern edge of Chang Chenmo Valley along the Kunlun mountains, is referred to as the "Johnson Line" (or "Ardagh-Johnson Line").[1207,1208]</ref>

After the Chinese reconquered Turkestan in 1878, renaming it Xinjiang, they again reverted to their traditional boundary. By now, the Russian Empire was entrenched in Central Asia, and the British were anxious to avoid a common border with the Russians. After creating the Wakhan corridor as the buffer in the northwest of Kashmir, they wanted the Chinese to fill out the "no man's land" between the Karakoram and Kunlun ranges. Under British (and possibly Russian) encouragement, the Chinese occupied the area up to the Yarkand River valley (called Raskam), including Shahidulla, by 1890.[1209] They also erected a boundary pillar at the Karakoram pass by about 1892. These efforts appear half-hearted. A map provided by Hung Ta-chen, a senior Chinese official at St. Petersburgh, in 1893 showed the boundary of Xinjiang up to Raskam. In the east, it was similar to the Johnson line, placing Aksai Chin in Kashmir territory.[1210]

By 1892, the British settled on the policy that their preferred boundary for Kashmir was the "Indus watershed", i.e., the water-parting from which waters flow into the Indus river system on one side and into the Tarim basin on the other. In the north, this water-parting was along the Karakoram range. In the east, it was more complicated because the Chip Chap River, Galwan River and the Chang Chenmo River flow into the Indus whereas the Karakash River flows into the Tarim basin.[1211] A boundary alignment along this water-parting was defined by the Viceroy Lord Elgin and communicated to London. The British government in due course proposed it to China via its envoy Sir Claude MacDonald in 1899. This boundary, which came to be called the Macartney–MacDonald Line, ceded to China the Aksai Chin plains in the northeast, and the Trans-Karakoram Tract in the north. In return, the British wanted China to cede its 'shadowy suzerainty' on Hunza.[1212,1213]</ref>

In 1911 the Xinhai Revolution resulted in power shifts in China, and by the end of World War I, the British officially used the Johnson Line. They took no steps to establish outposts or assert control on the ground. According to Neville Maxwell, the British had used as many as 11 different boundary lines in the region, as their claims shifted with the political situation. From 1917 to 1933, the "Postal Atlas of China", published by the Government of China in Peking had shown the boundary in Aksai Chin as per the Johnson line, which runs along the Kunlun mountains.[1214] The "Peking University Atlas", published in 1925, also put the Aksai Chin in India.[1215] Upon independence in 1947, the government of India used the Johnson Line as the basis for its official boundary in the west, which included the Aksai Chin. On 1 July 1954, India's first Prime Minister Jawaharlal Nehru definitively stated the Indian position, claiming that

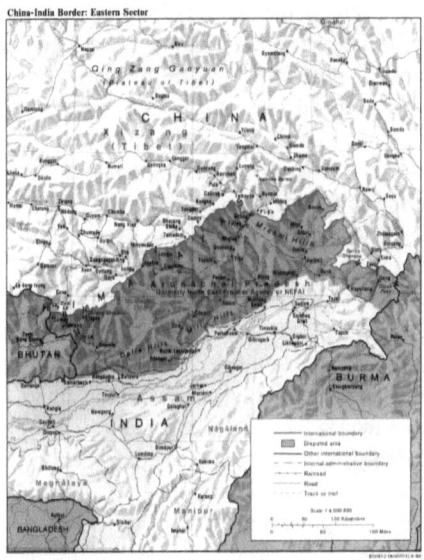

Figure 234: *The McMahon Line is the red line marking the northern boundary of the disputed area.*

Aksai Chin had been part of the Indian Ladakh region for centuries, and that the border (as defined by the Johnson Line) was non-negotiable. According to George N. Patterson, when the Indian government finally produced a report detailing the alleged proof of India's claims to the disputed area, "the quality of the Indian evidence was very poor, including some very dubious sources indeed".[1216:275]

In 1956–57, China constructed a road through Aksai Chin, connecting Xinjiang and Tibet, which ran south of the Johnson Line in many places. Aksai Chin was easily accessible to the Chinese, but access from India, which meant negotiating the Karakoram mountains, was much more difficult. The road came on Chinese maps published in 1958.

The McMahon Line

In 1826, British India gained a common border with China after the British wrested control of Manipur and Assam from the Burmese, following the First Anglo-Burmese War of 1824–1826. In 1847, Major J. Jenkins, agent for the North East Frontier, reported that the Tawang was part of Tibet. In 1872, four monastic officials from Tibet arrived in Tawang and supervised a boundary settlement with Major R. Graham, NEFA official, which included the Tawang

Tract as part of Tibet. Thus, in the last half of the 19th century, it was clear that the British treated the Tawang Tract as part of Tibet. This boundary was confirmed in a 1 June 1912 note from the British General Staff in India, stating that the "present boundary (demarcated) is south of Tawang, running westwards along the foothills from near Ugalguri to the southern Bhutanese border." A 1908 map of The Province of Eastern Bengal and Assam prepared for the Foreign Department of the Government of India, showed the international boundary from Bhutan continuing to the Baroi River, following the Himalayas foothill alignment. In 1913, representatives of Great Britain, China and Tibet attended a conference in Simla regarding the borders between Tibet, China and British India. Whilst all three representatives initialed the agreement, Beijing later objected to the proposed boundary between the regions of Outer Tibet and Inner Tibet, and did not ratify it. The details of the Indo-Tibetan boundary was not revealed to China at the time. The foreign secretary of the British Indian government, Henry McMahon, who had drawn up the proposal, decided to bypass the Chinese (although instructed not to by his superiors) and settle the border bilaterally by negotiating directly with Tibet. According to later Indian claims, this border was intended to run through the highest ridges of the Himalayas, as the areas south of the Himalayas were traditionally Indian. The McMahon Line lay south of the boundary India claims. India's government held the view that the Himalayas were the ancient boundaries of the Indian subcontinent, and thus should be the modern boundaries of India, while it is the position of the Chinese government that the disputed area in the Himalayas have been geographically and culturally part of Tibet since ancient times.[1217]

Months after the Simla agreement, China set up boundary markers south of the McMahon Line. T. O'Callaghan, an official in the Eastern Sector of the North East Frontier, relocated all these markers to a location slightly south of the McMahon Line, and then visited Rima to confirm with Tibetan officials that there was no Chinese influence in the area. The British-run Government of India initially rejected the Simla Agreement as incompatible with the Anglo-Russian Convention of 1907, which stipulated that neither party was to negotiate with Tibet "except through the intermediary of the Chinese government".[1218] The British and Russians cancelled the 1907 agreement by joint consent in 1921.[1219] It was not until the late 1930s that the British started to use the McMahon Line on official maps of the region.

China took the position that the Tibetan government should not have been allowed to make such a treaty, rejecting Tibet's claims of independent rule. For its part, Tibet did not object to any section of the McMahon Line excepting the demarcation of the trading town of Tawang, which the Line placed under British-Indian jurisdiction. Up until World War II, Tibetan officials were allowed to administer Tawang with complete authority. Due to the increased threat of Japanese and Chinese expansion during this period, British Indian troops secured the town as part of the defence of India's eastern border.

In the 1950s, India began patrolling the region. It found that, at multiple locations, the highest ridges actually fell north of the McMahon Line. Given India's historic position that the original intent of the line was to separate the two nations by the highest mountains in the world, in these locations India extended its forward posts northward to the ridges, regarding this move as compliant with the original border proposal, although the Simla Convention did not explicitly state this intention.

Events leading up to war

Tibet and the border dispute

The 1940s saw huge change in South Asia with the Partition of India in 1947 (resulting in the establishment of the two new states of India and Pakistan), and the establishment of the People's Republic of China (PRC) after the Chinese Civil War in 1949. One of the most basic policies for the new Indian government was that of maintaining cordial relations with China, reviving its ancient friendly ties. India was among the first nations to grant diplomatic recognition to the newly created PRC.

At the time, Chinese officials issued no condemnation of Nehru's claims or made any opposition to Nehru's open declarations of control over Aksai Chin. In 1956, Chinese Premier Zhou Enlai stated that he had no claims over Indian-controlled territory. He later argued that Aksai Chin was already under Chinese jurisdiction and that the McCartney-MacDonald Line was the line China could accept. Zhou later argued that as the boundary was undemarcated and had never been defined by treaty between any Chinese or Indian government, the Indian government could not unilaterally define Aksai Chin's borders.

In 1950, the Chinese People's Liberation Army took control of Tibet, which all Chinese governments regarded as still part of China. Later the Chinese extended their influence by building a road in 1956–67 and placing border posts in Aksai Chin. India found out after the road was completed, protested against these moves and decided to look for a diplomatic solution to ensure a stable Sino-Indian border. To resolve any doubts about the Indian position, Prime Minister Jawaharlal Nehru declared in parliament that India regarded the McMahon Line as its official border. The Chinese expressed no concern at this statement, and in 1951 and 1952, the government of China asserted that there were no frontier issues to be taken up with India.

In 1954, Prime Minister Nehru wrote a memo calling for India's borders to be clearly defined and demarcated; in line with previous Indian philosophy,

Indian maps showed a border that, in some places, lay north of the McMahon Line.[1220] Chinese Premier Zhou Enlai, in November 1956, again repeated Chinese assurances that the People's Republic had no claims on Indian territory, although official Chinese maps showed 120,000 square kilometres (46,000 sq mi) of territory claimed by India as Chinese. CIA documents created at the time revealed that Nehru had ignored Burmese premier Ba Swe when he warned Nehru to be cautious when dealing with Zhou.[1221] They also allege that Zhou purposefully told Nehru that there were no border issues with India.

In 1954, China and India negotiated the Five Principles of Peaceful Coexistence, by which the two nations agreed to abide in settling their disputes. India presented a frontier map which was accepted by China, and the slogan *Hindi-Chini bhai-bhai* (Indians and Chinese are brothers) was popular then. Nehru in 1958 had privately told G. Parthasarathi, the Indian envoy to China not to trust the Chinese at all and send all communications directly to him, bypassing the Defence Minister VK Krishna Menon since his communist background clouded his thinking about China. According to Georgia Tech scholar John W Garver, Nehru's policy on Tibet was to create a strong Sino-Indian partnership which would be catalysed through agreement and compromise on Tibet. Garver believes that Nehru's previous actions had given him confidence that China would be ready to form an "Asian Axis" with India.

This apparent progress in relations suffered a major setback when, in 1959, Nehru accommodated the Tibetan religious leader at the time, the 14th Dalai Lama, who fled Lhasa after a failed Tibetan uprising against Chinese rule. The Chairman of the Chinese Communist Party, Mao Zedong, was enraged and asked the Xinhua News Agency to produce reports on Indian expansionists operating in Tibet.Wikipedia:Citation needed

Border incidents continued through this period. In August 1959, the People's Liberation Army took an Indian prisoner at Longju, which had an ambiguous position in the McMahon Line, and two months later in Aksai Chin, a clash led to the death of nine Indian frontier policemen.

On 2 October, Soviet Premier Nikita Khrushchev defended Nehru in a meeting with Mao. This action reinforced China's impression that the Soviet Union, the United States and India all had expansionist designs on China. The People's Liberation Army went so far as to prepare a self-defence counterattack plan. Negotiations were restarted between the nations, but no progress was made.[1222]

As a consequence of their non-recognition of the McMahon Line, China's maps showed both the North East Frontier Area (NEFA) and Aksai Chin to be Chinese territory. In 1960, Zhou Enlai unofficially suggested that India drop its claims to Aksai Chin in return for a Chinese withdrawal of claims over NEFA. Adhering to his stated position, Nehru believed that China did not have a legitimate claim over either of these territories, and thus was not ready to concede them. This adamant stance was perceived in China as Indian opposition to Chinese rule in Tibet. Nehru declined to conduct any negotiations on the boundary until Chinese troops withdrew from Aksai Chin, a position supported by the international community. India produced numerous reports on the negotiations, and translated Chinese reports into English to help inform the international debate.Wikipedia:Citation needed China believed that India was simply securing its claim lines in order to continue its "grand plans in Tibet". India's stance that China withdraw from Aksai Chin caused continual deterioration of the diplomatic situation to the point that internal forces were pressuring Nehru to take a military stance against China.

1960 meetings to resolve the boundary question

In 1960, based on an agreement between Nehru and Zhou Enlai, officials from India and China held discussions in order to settle the boundary dispute.[1223] China and India disagreed on the major watershed that defined the boundary in the western sector.[1224] The Chinese statements with respect to their border claims often misrepresented the cited sources.[1225]

The Forward Policy

At the beginning of 1961, Nehru appointed General B. M. Kaul as army Chief of General Staff, but he refused to increase military spending and prepare for a possible war.Wikipedia:Verifiability According to James Barnard Calvin of the U.S. Navy, in 1959, India started sending Indian troops and border patrols into disputed areas. This program created both border skirmishes and deteriorating relations between India and China. The aim of this policy was to create outposts behind advancing Chinese troops to interdict their supplies, forcing them north of the disputed line.[1226] There were eventually 60 such outposts, including 43 north of the McMahon Line, to which India claimed sovereignty. China viewed this as further confirmation of Indian expansionist plans directed towards Tibet. According to the Indian official history, implementation of the Forward Policy was intended to provide evidence of Indian occupation in the previously unoccupied region through which Chinese troops had been advancing. Kaul was confident, through contact with Indian Intelligence and CIA information, that China would not react with force. Indeed, at first the PLA simply withdrew, but eventually Chinese forces began to counter-encircle the Indian positions which clearly encroached into the north of McMahon Line. This led to a tit-for-tat Indian reaction, with each force attempting to outmanoeuver the other. Despite the escalating nature of the dispute, the two forces withheld from engaging each other directly.

Chinese attention was diverted for a time by the military activity of the Nationalists on Taiwan, but on 23 June the U.S. assured China that a Nationalist invasion would not be permitted.[1227] China's heavy artillery facing Taiwan could then be moved to Tibet. It took China six to eight months to gather the resources needed for the war, according to Anil Athale, author of the official Indian history. The Chinese sent a large quantity of non-military supplies to Tibet through the Indian port of Calcutta.

Early incidents

Various border conflicts and "military incidents" between India and China flared up throughout the summer and autumn of 1962. In May, the Indian Air Force was told not to plan for close air support, although it was assessed as being a feasible way to counter the unfavourable ratio of Chinese to Indian troops. In June, a skirmish caused the deaths of dozens of Chinese troops. The Indian Intelligence Bureau received information about a Chinese buildup along the border which could be a precursor to war.

During June–July 1962, Indian military planners began advocating "probing actions" against the Chinese, and accordingly, moved mountain troops forward to cut off Chinese supply lines. According to Patterson, the Indian motives were threefold:

1. Test Chinese resolve and intentions regarding India.
2. Test whether India would enjoy Soviet backing in the event of a Sino-Indian war.
3. Create sympathy for India within the U.S., with whom relations had deteriorated after the Indian annexation of Goa.:[279]

On 10 July 1962, 350 Chinese troops surrounded an Indian post in Chushul (north of the McMahon Line) but withdrew after a heated argument via loudspeaker. On 22 July, the Forward Policy was extended to allow Indian troops to push back Chinese troops already established in disputed territory.[1228] Whereas Indian troops were previously ordered to fire only in self-defence, all post commanders were now given discretion to open fire upon Chinese forces if threatened. In August, the Chinese military improved its combat readiness along the McMahon Line and began stockpiling ammunition, weapons and fuel.

Given his foreknowledge of the coming Cuban Missile Crisis, Mao Zedong was able to persuade Nikita Khrushchev to reverse the Russian policy of backing India, at least temporarily. In mid-October, the Communist organ *Pravda* encouraged peace between India and China. When the Cuban Missile Crisis ended and Mao's rhetoric changed, Russia reversed course.

Confrontation at Thag La

In June 1962, Indian forces established an outpost at Dhola, on the southern slopes of the Thag La Ridge. Dhola lay north of the McMahon Line but south of the ridges along which India interpreted the McMahon Line to run.[1229] In August, China issued diplomatic protests and began occupying positions at the top of Thag La. On 8 September, a 60-strong PLA unit descended to the south side of the ridge and occupied positions that dominated one of the Indian posts at Dhola. Fire was not exchanged, but Nehru said to the media that the Indian Army had instructions to "free our territory" and the troops had been given discretion to use force. On 11 September, it was decided that "all forward posts and patrols were given permission to fire on any armed Chinese who entered Indian territory".

The operation to occupy Thag La was flawed in that Nehru's directives were unclear and it got underway very slowly because of this. In addition to this, each man had to carry 35 kilograms (77 lb) over the long trek and this severely slowed down the reaction. By the time the Indian battalion reached the point of conflict, Chinese units controlled both banks of the Namka Chu River. On 20 September, Chinese troops threw grenades at Indian troops and a firefight developed, triggering a long series of skirmishes for the rest of September.

Some Indian troops, including Brigadier Dalvi who commanded the forces at Thag La, were also concerned that the territory they were fighting for was not strictly territory that "we should have been convinced was ours". According to Neville Maxwell, even members of the Indian defence ministry were categorically concerned with the validity of the fighting in Thag La.

On 4 October, Kaul assigned some troops to secure regions south of the Thag La Ridge. Kaul decided to first secure Yumtso La, a strategically important position, before re-entering the lost Dhola post. Kaul had then realised that the attack would be desperate and the Indian government tried to stop an escalation into all-out war. Indian troops marching to Thag La had suffered in the previously unexperienced conditions; two Gurkha soldiers died of pulmonary edema.

On 10 October, an Indian Punjabi patrol of 50 troops to Yumtso La were met by an emplaced Chinese position of some 1,000 soldiers. Indian troops were in no position for battle, as Yumtso La was 16,000 feet (4,900 m) above sea level and Kaul did not plan on having artillery support for the troops. The Chinese troops opened fire on the Indians under their belief that they were north of the McMahon Line. The Indians were surrounded by Chinese positions which used mortar fire. They managed to hold off the first Chinese assault, inflicting heavy casualties.

At this point, the Indian troops were in a position to push the Chinese back with mortar and machine gun fire. Brigadier Dalvi opted not to fire, as it would mean decimating the Rajput who were still in the area of the Chinese regrouping. They helplessly watched the Chinese ready themselves for a second assault. In the second Chinese assault, the Indians began their retreat, realising the situation was hopeless. The Indian patrol suffered 25 casualties, and the Chinese 33. The Chinese troops held their fire as the Indians retreated, and then buried the Indian dead with military honours, as witnessed by the retreating soldiers. This was the first occurrence of heavy fighting in the war.

This attack had grave implications for India and Nehru tried to solve the issue, but by 18 October, it was clear that the Chinese were preparing for an attack on India, with massive troop buildups on the border. A long line of mules and porters had also been observed supporting the buildup and reinforcement of positions south of the Thag La Ridge.

Chinese and Indian preparations

Motives

Two of the major factors leading up to China's eventual conflicts with Indian troops were India's stance on the disputed borders and perceived Indian subversion in Tibet. There was "a perceived need to punish and end perceived Indian efforts to undermine Chinese control of Tibet, Indian efforts which were perceived as having the objective of restoring the pre-1949 status quo ante of Tibet". The other was "a perceived need to punish and end perceived Indian aggression against Chinese territory along the border". John W. Garver argues that the first perception was incorrect based on the state of the Indian military and polity in the 1960s. It was, nevertheless a major reason for China's going to war. He argues the Chinese perception of Indian aggression to be "substantially accurate".

The CIA's declassified POLO documents reveal contemporary American analysis of Chinese motives during the war. According to this document, "Chinese apparently were motivated to attack by one primary consideration — their determination to retain the ground on which PLA forces stood in 1962 and to punish the Indians for trying to take that ground". In general terms, they tried to show the Indians once and for all that China would not acquiesce in a military "reoccupation" policy. Secondary reasons for the attack were to damage Nehru's prestige by exposing Indian weakness and to expose as traitorous Khrushchev's policy of supporting Nehru against a Communist country.

Another factor which might have affected China's decision for war with India was a perceived need to stop a Soviet-U.S.-India encirclement and isolation of China. India's relations with the Soviet Union and United States were both strong at this time, but the Soviets (and Americans) were preoccupied by the Cuban Missile Crisis and would not interfere with the Sino-Indian War. P. B. Sinha suggests that China waited until October to attack because the timing of the war was exactly in parallel with American actions so as to avoid any chance of American or Soviet involvement. Although American buildup of forces around Cuba occurred on the same day as the first major clash at Dhola, and China's buildup between 10 and 20 October appeared to coincide exactly with the United States establishment of a blockade against Cuba which began 20 October, the Chinese probably prepared for this before they could anticipate what would happen in Cuba. Another explanation is that the confrontation in the Taiwan Strait had eased by then.

Garver argues that the Chinese correctly assessed Indian border policies, particularly the Forward Policy, as attempts for incremental seizure of Chinese-controlled territory. On Tibet, Garver argues that one of the major factors leading to China's decision for war with India was a common tendency of humans "to attribute others behavior to interior motivations, while attributing their own behavior to situational factors". Studies from China published in the 1990s confirmed that the root cause for China going to war with India was the perceived Indian aggression in Tibet, with the forward policy simply catalysing the Chinese reaction.

Neville Maxwell and Allen Whiting argue that the Chinese leadership believed they were defending territory that was legitimately Chinese, and which was already under de facto Chinese occupation prior to Indian advances, and regarded the Forward Policy as an Indian attempt at creeping annexation. Mao Zedong himself compared the Forward Policy to a strategic advance in Chinese chess:

> Their [India's] continually pushing forward is like crossing the Chu Han boundary. What should we do? We can also set out a few pawns, on our side of the river. If they don't then cross over, that's great. If they do cross, we'll eat them up [chess metaphor meaning to take the opponent's pieces]. Of course, we cannot blindly eat them. Lack of forbearance in small matters upsets great plans. We must pay attention to the situation.

India claims that the motive for the Forward Policy was to cut off the supply routes for Chinese troops posted in NEFA and Aksai Chin. According to the official Indian history, the forward policy was continued because of its initial success, as it claimed that Chinese troops withdrew when they encountered areas already occupied by Indian troops. It also claimed that the Forward Policy was having success in cutting out supply lines of Chinese troops who had advanced South of the McMahon Line, though there was no evidence of such advance before the 1962 war. The Forward Policy rested on the assumption that Chinese forces "were not likely to use force against any of our posts, even if they were in a position to do so". No serious re-appraisal of this policy took place even when Chinese forces ceased withdrawing. Nehru's confidence was probably justified given the difficulty for China to supply the area over the high altitude terrain over 5000 km from the more populated areas of China.

The Chinese leadership initially held a sympathetic view towards India as the latter had been ruled by British colonial masters for centuries. Nehru's forward policy convinced PRC leadership that the independent Indian leadership was a reincarnation of British imperialism. Mao Zedong stated: "Rather than being constantly accused of aggression, it's better to show the world what really happens when China indeed moves its muscles."

Chinese policy toward India, therefore, operated on two contradictory assumptions in the first half of 1961. On the one hand, the Chinese leaders continued to entertain a hope, although a shrinking one, that some opening for talks would appear. On the other hand, they read Indian statements and actions as clear signs that Nehru wanted to talk only about a Chinese withdrawal. Regarding the hope, they were willing to negotiate and tried to prod Nehru into a similar attitude. Regarding Indian intentions, they began to act politically and to build a rationale based on the assumption that Nehru already had become a lackey of imperialism; for this reason he opposed border talks.

Krishna Menon is reported to have said that when he arrived in Geneva on 6 June 1961 for an international conference in Laos, Chinese officials in Chen Yi's delegation indicated that Chen might be interested in discussing the border dispute with him. At several private meetings with Menon, Chen avoided any discussion of the dispute and Menon surmised that the Chinese wanted him to broach the matter first. He did not, as he was under instructions from Nehru to avoid taking the initiative, leaving the Chinese with the impression that Nehru was unwilling to show any flexibility.

In September, the Chinese took a step toward criticising Nehru openly in their commentary. After citing Indonesian and Burmese press criticism of Nehru by name, the Chinese critiqued his moderate remarks on colonialism (People's Daily Editorial, 9 September): "Somebody at the Non-Aligned Nations Conference advanced the argument that the era of classical colonialism is gone and dead...contrary to facts." This was a distortion of Nehru's remarks but appeared close enough to be credible. On the same day, Chen Yi referred to Nehru by implication at the Bulgarian embassy reception: "Those who attempted to deny history, ignore reality, and distort the truth and who attempted to divert the Conference from its important object have failed to gain support and were isolated." On 10 September, they dropped all circumlocutions and criticised him by name in a China Youth article and NCNA report—the first time in almost two years that they had commented extensively on the Prime Minister.

By early 1962, the Chinese leadership began to believe that India's intentions were to launch a massive attack against Chinese troops, and that the Indian leadership wanted a war. In 1961, the Indian army had been sent into Goa, a small region without any other international borders apart from the Indian one, after Portugal refused to surrender the exclave colony to the Indian Union. Although this action met little to no international protest or opposition, China saw it as an example of India's expansionist nature, especially in light of heated rhetoric from Indian politicians. India's Home Minister declared, "If the Chinese will not vacate the areas occupied by it, India will have to repeat what it did in Goa. India will certainly drive out the Chinese forces", while another member of the Indian Congress Party pronounced, "India will take steps to end [Chinese] aggression on Indian soil just as it ended Portuguese aggression in Goa". By mid-1962, it was apparent to the Chinese leadership that negotiations had failed to make any progress, and the Forward Policy was increasingly perceived as a grave threat as Delhi increasingly sent probes deeper into border areas and cut off Chinese supply lines. Foreign Minister Marshal Chen Yi commented at one high-level meeting, "Nehru's forward policy is a knife. He wants to put it in our heart. We cannot close our eyes and await death." The Chinese leadership believed that their restraint on the issue was being perceived by India as weakness, leading to continued provocations, and that a major counterblow was needed to stop perceived Indian aggression.

Xu Yan, prominent Chinese military historian and professor at the PLA's National Defense University, gives an account of the Chinese leadership's decision to go to war. By late September 1962, the Chinese leadership had begun to reconsider their policy of "armed coexistence", which had failed to address their concerns with the forward policy and Tibet, and consider a large, decisive strike. On 22 September 1962, the *People's Daily* published an article which claimed that "the Chinese people were burning with 'great indignation' over the Indian actions on the border and that New Delhi could not 'now say that warning was not served in advance'."[1230]

Military planning

The Indian side was confident war would not be triggered and made little preparations. India had only two divisions of troops in the region of the conflict. In August 1962, Brigadier D. K. Palit claimed that a war with China in the near future could be ruled out. Even in September 1962, when Indian troops were ordered to "expel the Chinese" from Thag La, Maj. General J. S. Dhillon expressed the opinion that "experience in Ladakh had shown that a few rounds fired at the Chinese would cause them to run away." Because of this, the Indian army was completely unprepared when the attack at Yumtso La occurred.

Recently declassified CIA documents which were compiled at the time reveal that India's estimates of Chinese capabilities made them neglect their military in favour of economic growth.[1231] It is claimed that if a more military-minded man had been in place instead of Nehru, India would have been more likely to have been ready for the threat of a counter-attack from China.

On 6 October 1962, the Chinese leadership convened. Lin Biao reported that PLA intelligence units had determined that Indian units might assault Chinese positions at Thag La on 10 October (Operation Leghorn). The Chinese leadership and the Central Military Council decided upon war to launch a large-scale attack to punish perceived military aggression from India. In Beijing, a larger meeting of Chinese military was convened in order to plan for the coming conflict.

Mao and the Chinese leadership issued a directive laying out the objectives for the war. A main assault would be launched in the eastern sector, which would be coordinated with a smaller assault in the western sector. All Indian troops within China's claimed territories in the eastern sector would be expelled, and the war would be ended with a unilateral Chinese ceasefire and withdrawal, followed by a return to the negotiating table. India led the Non-Aligned Movement, Nehru enjoyed international prestige, and China, with a larger military, would be portrayed as an aggressor. He said that a well-fought war "will guarantee at least thirty years of peace" with India, and determined the benefits to offset the costs.

China also reportedly bought significant amount of Indian rupee currency notes from Hong Kong, supposedly to distribute amongst its soldiers in preparation for the war.

On 8 October, additional veteran and elite divisions were ordered to prepare to move into Tibet from the Chengdu and Lanzhou military regions.

On 12 October, Nehru declared that he had ordered the Indian army to "clear Indian territory in the NEFA of Chinese invaders" and personally met with Kaul, issuing instructions to him.

On 14 October, an editorial on *People's Daily* issued China's final warning to India: "So it seems that Mr. Nehru has made up his mind to attack the Chinese frontier guards on an even bigger scale. ... It is high time to shout to Mr. Nehru that the heroic Chinese troops, with the glorious tradition of resisting foreign aggression, can never be cleared by anyone from their own territory ... If there are still some maniacs who are reckless enough to ignore our well-intentioned advice and insist on having another try, well, let them do so. History will pronounce its inexorable verdict ... At this critical moment ... we still want to appeal once more to Mr. Nehru: better rein in at the edge of the precipice and do not use the lives of Indian troops as stakes in your gamble."

Marshal Liu Bocheng headed a group to determine the strategy for the war. He concluded that the opposing Indian troops were among India's best, and to achieve victory would require deploying crack troops and relying on force concentration to achieve decisive victory. On 16 October, this war plan was approved, and on the 18th, the final approval was given by the Politburo for a "self-defensive counter-attack", scheduled for 20 October.

Chinese offensive

On 20 October 1962, the Chinese People's Liberation Army launched two attacks, 1000 kilometres apart. In the western theatre, the PLA sought to expel Indian forces from the Chip Chap valley in Aksai Chin while in the eastern theatre, the PLA sought to capture both banks of the Namka Chu river. Some skirmishes also took place at the Nathula Pass, which is in the Indian state of Sikkim (an Indian protectorate at that time). Gurkha rifles travelling north were targeted by Chinese artillery fire. After four days of fierce fighting, the three regiments of Chinese troops succeeded in securing a substantial portion of the disputed territory.

Eastern theatre

Chinese troops launched an attack on the southern banks of the Namka Chu River on 20 October. The Indian forces were undermanned, with only an understrength battalion to support them, while the Chinese troops had three regiments positioned on the north side of the river. The Indians expected Chinese forces to cross via one of five bridges over the river and defended those crossings. The PLA bypassed the defenders by crossing the shallow October river instead. They formed up into battalions on the Indian-held south side of the river under cover of darkness, with each battalion assigned against a separate group of Rajputs.

At 5:14 am, Chinese mortar fire began attacking the Indian positions. Simultaneously, the Chinese cut the Indian telephone lines, preventing the defenders from making contact with their headquarters. At about 6:30 am, the Chinese infantry launched a surprise attack from the rear and forced the Indians to leave their trenches.

The Chinese overwhelmed the Indian troops in a series of flanking manoeuvres south of the McMahon Line and prompted their withdrawal from Namka Chu. Fearful of continued losses, Indian troops retreated into Bhutan. Chinese forces respected the border and did not pursue. Chinese forces now held all of the territory that was under dispute at the time of the Thag La confrontation, but they continued to advance into the rest of NEFA.

On 22 October, at 12:15 am, PLA mortars fired on Walong, on the McMahon line. Flares launched by Indian troops the next day revealed numerous Chinese milling around the valley. The Indians tried to use their mortars against the Chinese but the PLA responded by lighting a bush fire, causing confusion among the Indians. Some 400 Chinese troops attacked the Indian position. The initial Chinese assault was halted by accurate Indian mortar fire. The Chinese were then reinforced and launched a second assault. The Indians managed to hold them back for four hours, but the Chinese used weight of numbers to break through. Most Indian forces were withdrawn to established positions in Walong, while a company supported by mortars and medium machine guns remained to cover the retreat.

On the morning 23 October, the Indian Army discovered a Chinese force gathered in a cramped pass and opened fire with mortars and machine guns, leading to heavy fighting. About 200 Chinese soldiers were killed and wounded in this action.Wikipedia:Citation needed Nine Indian soldiers were also killed. The fighting continued well into the afternoon, until the company was ordered to withdraw. Meanwhile, the 4th Sikhs made contact with the Chinese and subjected them to withering mortar and machine gun fire as the Chinese set off a brush fire and attempted to sneak forward.Wikipedia:Citation needed

Elsewhere, Chinese troops launched a three-pronged attack on Tawang, which the Indians evacuated without any resistance.

Over the following days, there were clashes between Indian and Chinese patrols at Walong as the Chinese rushed in reinforcements. On 25 October, the Chinese made a probe, which was met with resistance from the 4th Sikhs. The following day, a patrol from the 4th Sikhs was encircled, and after being unable to break the encirclement, an Indian unit was able to flank the Chinese, allowing the Sikhs to break free.

Western theatre

On the Aksai Chin front, China already controlled most of the disputed territory. Chinese forces quickly swept the region of any remaining Indian troops.[1232] Late on 19 October, Chinese troops launched a number of attacks throughout the western theatre. By 22 October, all posts north of Chushul had been cleared.

On 20 October, the Chinese easily took the Chip Chap Valley, Galwan Valley, and Pangong Lake. Many outposts and garrisons along the Western front were unable to defend against the surrounding Chinese troops. Most Indian troops positioned in these posts offered resistance but were either killed or taken prisoner. Indian support for these outposts was not forthcoming, as evidenced by the Galwan post, which had been surrounded by enemy forces in August, but

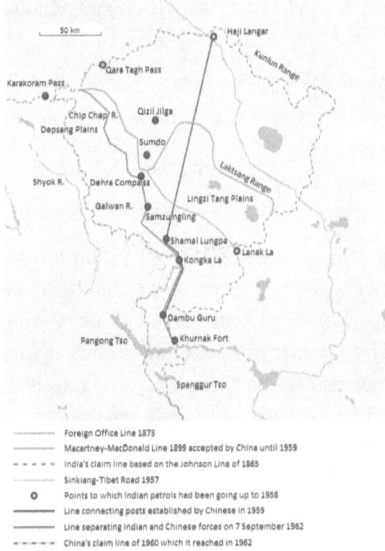

Figure 235: *The map shows the Indian and Chinese claims of the border in the Aksai Chin region, the Macartney-MacDonald line, the Foreign Office Line, as well as the progress of Chinese forces as they occupied areas during the Sino-Indian War.*

no attempt made to relieve the besieged garrison. Following the 20 October attack, nothing was heard from Galwan.

On 24 October, Indian forces fought hard to hold the Rezang La Ridge, in order to prevent a nearby airstrip from falling to the Chinese.[1233]

After realising the magnitude of the attack, the Indian Western Command withdrew many of the isolated outposts to the south-east. Daulet Beg Oldi was also evacuated, but it was south of the Chinese claim line and was not approached by Chinese forces. Indian troops were withdrawn in order to consolidate and regroup in the event that China probed south of their claim line.

Lull in the fighting

By 24 October, the PLA had entered territory previously administered by India to give the PRC a diplomatically strong position over India. The majority of Chinese forces had advanced sixteen kilometres south of the control line prior to the conflict. Four days of fighting were followed by a three-week lull. Zhou ordered the troops to stop advancing as he attempted to negotiate with Nehru. The Indian forces had retreated into more heavily fortified positions around Se

La and Bomdi La which would be difficult to assault. Zhou sent Nehru a letter, proposing

1. A negotiated settlement of the boundary
2. That both sides disengage and withdraw twenty kilometres from present lines of actual control
3. A Chinese withdrawal north in NEFA
4. That China and India not cross lines of present control in Aksai Chin.

Nehru's 27 October reply expressed interest in the restoration of peace and friendly relations and suggested a return to the "boundary prior to 8 September 1962". He was categorically concerned about a mutual twenty kilometre withdrawal after "40 or 60 kilometres of blatant military aggression". He wanted the creation of a larger immediate buffer zone and thus resist the possibility of a repeat offensive. Zhou's 4 November reply repeated his 1959 offer to return to the McMahon Line in NEFA and the Chinese traditionally claimed MacDonald Line in Aksai Chin. Facing Chinese forces maintaining themselves on Indian soil and trying to avoid political pressure, the Indian parliament announced a national emergency and passed a resolution which stated their intent to "drive out the aggressors from the sacred soil of India". The United States and the United Kingdom supported India's response. The Soviet Union was preoccupied with the Cuban Missile Crisis and did not offer the support it had provided in previous years. With the backing of other great powers, a 14 November letter by Nehru to Zhou once again rejected his proposal.

Neither side declared war, used their air force, or fully broke off diplomatic relations, but the conflict is commonly referred to as a war. This war coincided with the Cuban Missile Crisis and was viewed by the western nations at the time as another act of aggression by the Communist bloc. According to Calvin, the Chinese side evidently wanted a diplomatic resolution and discontinuation of the conflict.

Continuation of war

After Zhou received Nehru's letter (rejecting Zhou's proposal), the fighting resumed on the eastern theatre on 14 November (Nehru's birthday), with an Indian attack on Walong, claimed by China, launched from the defensive position of Se La and inflicting heavy casualties on the Chinese. The Chinese resumed military activity on Aksai Chin and NEFA hours after the Walong battle.

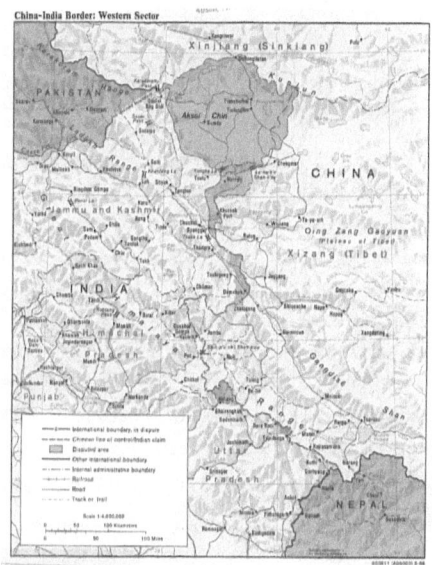

Figure 236: *The disputed areas in the western sector.*

Eastern theatre

In the eastern theatre, the PLA attacked Indian forces near Se La and Bomdi La on 17 November. These positions were defended by the Indian 4th Infantry Division. Instead of attacking by road as expected, PLA forces approached via a mountain trail, and their attack cut off a main road and isolated 10,000 Indian troops.

Se La occupied high ground, and rather than assault this commanding position, the Chinese captured Thembang, which was a supply route to Se La.

Western theatre

On the western theatre, PLA forces launched a heavy infantry attack on 18 November near Chushul. Their attack started at 4:35 am, despite a mist surrounding most of the areas in the region. At 5:45 the Chinese troops advanced to attack two platoons of Indian troops at Gurung Hill.

The Indians did not know what was happening, as communications were dead. As a patrol was sent, China attacked with greater numbers. Indian artillery could not hold off the superior Chinese forces. By 9:00 am, Chinese forces attacked Gurung Hill directly and Indian commanders withdrew from the area and also from the connecting Spangur Gap.

The Chinese had been simultaneously attacking Rezang La which was held by 123 Indian troops. At 5:05 am, Chinese troops launched their attack audaciously. Chinese medium machine gun fire pierced through the Indian tactical defences.

At 6:55 am the sun rose and the Chinese attack on the 8th platoon began in waves. Fighting continued for the next hour, until the Chinese signaled that they had destroyed the 7th platoon. Indians tried to use light machine guns on the medium machine guns from the Chinese but after 10 minutes the battle was over. Logistical inadequacy once again hurt the Indian troops.[1234] The Chinese gave the Indian troops a respectful military funeral. The battles also saw the death of Major Shaitan Singh of the Kumaon Regiment, who had been instrumental in the first battle of Rezang La. The Indian troops were forced to withdraw to high mountain positions. Indian sources believed that their troops were just coming to grips with the mountain combat and finally called for more troops. The Chinese declared a ceasefire, ending the bloodshed.

Indian forces suffered heavy casualties, with dead Indian troops' bodies being found in the ice, frozen with weapons in hand. The Chinese forces also suffered heavy casualties, especially at Rezang La. This signalled the end of the war in Aksai Chin as China had reached their claim line – many Indian troops were ordered to withdraw from the area. China claimed that the Indian troops wanted to fight on until the bitter end. The war ended with their withdrawal, so as to limit the amount of casualties.

The PLA penetrated close to the outskirts of Tezpur, Assam, a major frontier town nearly fifty kilometres from the Assam-North-East Frontier Agency border. The local government ordered the evacuation of the civilians in Tezpur to the south of the Brahmaputra River, all prisons were thrown open, and government officials who stayed behind destroyed Tezpur's currency reserves in anticipation of a Chinese advance.

Ceasefire

China had reached its claim lines so the PLA did not advance farther, and on 19 November, it declared a unilateral cease-fire. Zhou Enlai declared a unilateral ceasefire to start on midnight, 21 November. Zhou's ceasefire declaration stated,

> Beginning from 21 November 1962, the Chinese frontier guards will cease fire along the entire Sino-Indian border. Beginning from 1 December 1962, the Chinese frontier guards will withdraw to positions 20 kilometres behind the line of actual control which existed between China and India on 7 November 1959. In the eastern sector, although the Chinese

frontier guards have so far been fighting on Chinese territory north of the traditional customary line, they are prepared to withdraw from their present positions to the north of the illegal McMahon Line, and to withdraw twenty kilometres back from that line. In the middle and western sectors, the Chinese frontier guards will withdraw twenty kilometres from the line of actual control.

Zhou had first given the ceasefire announcement to Indian chargé d'affaires on 19 November (before India's request for United States air support), but New Delhi did not receive it until 24 hours later. The aircraft carrier was ordered back after the ceasefire, and thus, American intervention on India's side in the war was avoided. Retreating Indian troops, who hadn't come into contact with anyone knowing of the ceasefire, and Chinese troops in NEFA and Aksai Chin, were involved in some minor battles, but for the most part, the ceasefire signalled an end to the fighting. The United States Air Force flew in supplies to India in November 1962, but neither side wished to continue hostilities.

Toward the end of the war India increased its support for Tibetan refugees and revolutionaries, some of them having settled in India, as they were fighting the same common enemy in the region. The Nehru administration ordered the raising of an elite Indian-trained "Tibetan Armed Force" composed of Tibetan refugees.

World opinion

The Chinese military action has been viewed by the United States as part of the PRC's policy of making use of aggressive wars to settle its border disputes and to distract both its own population and international opinion from its internal issues.[1235] According to James Calvin from the United States Marine Corps, western nations at the time viewed China as an aggressor during the China–India border war, and the war was part of a monolithic communist objective for a world dictatorship of the proletariat. This was further triggered by Mao Zedong's views that: "The way to world conquest lies through Havana, Accra, and Calcutta". Calvin believes that Chinese actions show a "pattern of conservative aims and limited objectives, rather than expansionism" and blames this particular conflict on India's provocations towards China. Calvin also expresses that China, in the past, has been adamant to gain control over regions to which it has a "traditional claim", which triggered the dispute over NEFA and Aksai Chin and indeed Tibet. Calvin's assumption, based on the history of the Cold War and the Domino Effect, assumed that China might ultimately try to regain control of everything that it considers as "traditionally Chinese" which in its view includes the entirety of South East Asia.

The Kennedy administration was disturbed by what they considered "blatant Chinese communist aggression against India". In a May 1963 National Security Council meeting, contingency planning on the part of the United States in the event of another Chinese attack on India was discussed. Defense Secretary Robert McNamara and General Maxwell Taylor advised the president to use nuclear weapons should the Americans intervene in such a situation. McNamara stated "Before any substantial commitment to defend India against China is given, we should recognise that in order to carry out that commitment against any substantial Chinese attack, we would have to use nuclear weapons. Any large Chinese Communist attack on any part of that area would require the use of nuclear weapons by the U.S., and this is to be preferred over the introduction of large numbers of U.S. soldiers." After hearing this and listening to two other advisers, Kennedy stated "We should defend India, and therefore we will defend India." It remains unclear if his aides were trying to dissuade the President of considering any measure with regard to India by immediately raising the stakes to an unacceptable level, nor is it clear if Kennedy was thinking of conventional or nuclear means when he gave his reply. By 1964 China had developed its own nuclear weapon which would have likely caused any American nuclear policy in defense of India to be reviewed. The Johnson Administration considered and then rejected giving nuclear weapons technology to the Indians. India developed its own nuclear weapon by 1974, within 10 years of the Chinese.

The United States was unequivocal in its recognition of the Indian boundary claims in the eastern sector, while not supporting the claims of either side in the western sector. Britain, on the other hand, agreed with the Indian position completely, with the foreign secretary stating, 'we have taken the view of the government of India on the present frontiers and the disputed territories belong to India.'

The non-aligned nations remained mostly uninvolved, and only the United Arab RepublicWikipedia:Please clarify openly supported India.[1236] Of the non-aligned nations, six, Egypt, Burma, Cambodia, Sri Lanka, Ghana and Indonesia, met in Colombo on 10 December 1962. The proposals stipulated a Chinese withdrawal of 20 km from the customary lines without any reciprocal withdrawal on India's behalf. The failure of these six nations to unequivocally condemn China deeply disappointed India.

In 1972, Chinese Premier Zhou explained the Chinese point of view to President Nixon of the US. As for the causes of the war, Zhou asserted that China did not try to expel Indian troops from south of the McMahon line and that three open warning telegrams were sent to Nehru before the war. Indian patrols south of the McMahon line were expelled and suffered casualties in the Chinese attack. Zhou also told Nixon that Chairman Mao ordered the troops to return to show good faith. The Indian government maintains that the Chinese military could not advance further south due to logistical problems and the cut-off of resource supplies.

While Western nations did not view Chinese actions favourably because of fear of the Chinese and competitiveness, Pakistan, which had had a turbulent relationship with India ever since the Indian partition, improved its relations with China after the war. Prior to the war, Pakistan also shared a disputed boundary with China, and had proposed to India that the two countries adopt a common defence against "northern" enemies (i.e. China), which was rejected by India. China and Pakistan took steps to peacefully negotiate their shared boundaries, beginning on 13 October 1962, and concluding in December of that year. Pakistan also expressed fear that the huge amounts of western military aid directed to India would allow it to threaten Pakistan's security in future conflicts. Mohammed Ali, External Affairs Minister of Pakistan, declared that massive Western aid to India in the Sino-Indian dispute would be considered an unfriendly act towards Pakistan. As a result, Pakistan made efforts to improve its relations with China. The following year, China and Pakistan peacefully settled disputes on their shared border, and negotiated the China-Pakistan Border Treaty in 1963, as well as trade, commercial, and barter treaties. On 2 March 1963, Pakistan conceded its northern claim line in Pakistani-controlled Kashmir to China in favor of a more southerly boundary along the Karakoram Range. The border treaty largely set the border along the MacCartney-Macdonald Line. India's military failure against China would embolden Pakistan to initiate the Second Kashmir War with India. It effectively ended in a stalemate as Calvin states that the Sino-Indian War had caused the previously passive government to take a stand on actively modernising India's military. China offered diplomatic support to Pakistan in this war but did not offer military support. In January 1966, China condemned the Tashkent Agreement between India and Pakistan as a Soviet-US plot in the region. In the Indo-Pakistani War of 1971, Pakistan expected China to provide military support, but it was left alone as India successfully helped the rebels in East Pakistan to found the new nation-state of Bangladesh.[1237]

Involvement of other nations

During the conflict, Nehru wrote two desperate letters to U.S. President John F. Kennedy, requesting 12 squadrons of fighter jets and a modern radar system. These jets were seen as necessary to beef up Indian air strength so that air-to-air combat could be initiated safely from the Indian perspective (bombing troops was seen as unwise for fear of Chinese retaliatory action). Nehru also asked that these aircraft be manned by American pilots until Indian airmen were trained to replace them. These requests were rejected by the Kennedy

Administration (which was involved in the Cuban Missile Crisis during most of the Sino-Indian War). The U.S. nonetheless provided non-combat assistance to Indian forces and planned to send the carrier USS *Kitty Hawk* to the Bay of Bengal to support India in case of an air war.[1238]

Some reports suggest a contradictory response from the U.S. According to former Indian diplomat G. Parthasarathy, "only after we got nothing from the US did arms supplies from the Soviet Union to India commence." In 1962, President of Pakistan Ayub Khan made clear to India that Indian troops could safely be transferred from the Pakistan frontier to the Himalayas.

Aftermath

China

According to the China's official military history, the war achieved China's policy objectives of securing borders in its western sector, as China retained de facto control of the Aksai Chin. After the war, India abandoned the Forward Policy, and the de facto borders stabilised along the Line of Actual Control.

According to James Calvin of Marine Corps Command and Staff College, even though China won a military victory it lost in terms of its international image. China's first nuclear weapon test in October 1964 and its support of Pakistan in the 1965 India Pakistan War tended to confirm the American view of communist world objectives, including Chinese influence over Pakistan.

Lora Saalman opined in a study of Chinese military publications, that while the war led to much blame, debates and ultimately acted as causation of military modernisation of India but the war is now treated as basic reportage of facts with relatively diminished interest by Chinese analysts.

India

The aftermath of the war saw sweeping changes in the Indian military to prepare it for similar conflicts in the future, and placed pressure on Indian prime minister Jawaharlal Nehru, who was seen as responsible for failing to anticipate the Chinese attack on India. Indians reacted with a surge in patriotism and memorials were erected for many of the Indian troops who died in the war. Arguably, the main lesson India learned from the war was the need to strengthen its own defences and a shift from Nehru's foreign policy with China based on his stated concept of "brotherhood". Because of India's inability to anticipate Chinese aggression, Prime Minister Nehru faced harsh criticism from government officials, for having promoted pacifist relations with China. Indian President Radhakrishnan said that Nehru's government was naive and negligent about preparations, and Nehru admitted his failings. According to

Figure 237: *U.S. Ambassador to India John Kenneth Galbraith and Prime Minister Nehru conferring at the time of the conflict. This photograph was taken by the United States Information Service (USIS) and sent to President John F. Kennedy with a letter from Galbraith dated 9 November 1962.*

Inder Malhotra, a former editor of *The Times of India* and a commentator for *The Indian Express*, Indian politicians invested more effort in removing Defence Minister Krishna Menon than in actually waging war. Krishna Menon's favoritism weakened the Indian Army, and national morale dimmed. The public saw the war as a political and military debacle. Under American advice (by American envoy John Kenneth Galbraith who made and ran American policy on the war as all other top policy makers in the US were absorbed in coincident Cuban Missile Crisis) Indians refrained, not according to the best choices available, from using the Indian air force to beat back the Chinese advances. The CIA later revealed that at that time the Chinese had neither the fuel nor runways long enough for using their air force effectively in Tibet. Indians in general became highly sceptical of China and its military. Many Indians view the war as a betrayal of India's attempts at establishing a long-standing peace with China and started to question the once popular "Hindi-Chini bhai-bhai" (meaning "Indians and Chinese are brothers"). The war also put an end to Nehru's earlier hopes that India and China would form a strong Asian Axis to counteract the increasing influence of the Cold War bloc superpowers.

The unpreparedness of the army was blamed on Defence Minister Menon, who resigned his government post to allow for someone who might modernise India's military further. India's policy of weaponisation via indigenous sources and self-sufficiency was thus cemented. Sensing a weakened army, Pakistan, a close ally of China, began a policy of provocation against India by infiltrating Jammu and Kashmir and ultimately triggering the Second Kashmir War with India in 1965 and Indo-Pakistani war of 1971. The Attack of 1965 was successfully stopped and ceasefire was negotiated under international pressure. In the Indo-Pakistani war of 1971 India won a clear victory, resulting in liberation of Bangladesh (formerly East-Pakistan).

As a result of the war, the Indian government commissioned an investigation, resulting in the classified Henderson Brooks–Bhagat Report on the causes of the war and the reasons for failure. India's performance in high-altitude combat in 1962 led to an overhaul of the Indian Army in terms of doctrine, training, organisation and equipment. Neville Maxwell claimed that the Indian role in international affairs after the border war was also greatly reduced after the war and India's standing in the non-aligned movement suffered. The Indian government has attempted to keep the Hendersen-Brooks-Bhagat Report secret for decades, although portions of it have recently been leaked by Neville Maxwell.

According to James Calvin, an analyst from the U.S. Navy, India gained many benefits from the 1962 conflict. This war united the country as never before. India got 32,000 square miles (8.3 million hectares, 83,000 km^2) of disputed territory even if it felt that NEFA was hers all along. The new Indian republic had avoided international alignments; by asking for help during the war, India demonstrated its willingness to accept military aid from several sectors. And, finally, India recognised the serious weaknesses in its army. It would more than double its military manpower in the next two years and it would work hard to resolve the military's training and logistic problems to later become the second-largest army in the world. India's efforts to improve its military posture significantly enhanced its army's capabilities and preparedness. This played a role in subsequent wars against Pakistan.

Internment and deportation of Chinese Indians

Soon after the end of the war, the Indian government passed the Defence of India Act in December 1962, permitting the "apprehension and detention in custody of any person [suspected] of being of hostile origin." The broad language of the act allowed for the arrest of any person simply for having a Chinese surname, Chinese ancestry or a Chinese spouse. The Indian government incarcerated thousands of Chinese-Indians in an internment camp in Deoli, Rajasthan, where they were held for years without trial. The last internees were not released until 1967. Thousands more Chinese-Indians were forcibly deported or coerced to leave India. Nearly all internees had their properties sold off or looted. Even after their release, the Chinese Indians faced many restrictions in their freedom. They could not travel freely until the mid-1990s.

Later conflicts

India also reported some military conflicts with China after the 1962 war. In late 1967, there were two incidents in which both countries exchanged fire in Sikkim. The first one was dubbed the "Nathu La incident", and the other being "Chola incident" in which advancing Chinese forces were forced to withdraw from Sikkim, then a protectorate of India and later a state of India after annexation in 1975. In the 1987 Sino-Indian skirmish, both sides showed military restraint and it was a bloodless conflict.

Diplomatic process

In 1993 and 1996, the two sides signed the Sino-Indian Bilateral Peace and Tranquility Accords, agreements to maintain peace and tranquility along the Line of Actual Control (LoAC). Ten meetings of a Sino-Indian Joint Working Group (SIJWG) and five of an expert group have taken place to determine where the LoAC lies, but little progress has occurred.

On 20 November 2006 Indian politicians from Arunachal Pradesh expressed their concern over Chinese military modernization and appealed to parliament to take a harder stance on the PRC following a military buildup on the border similar to that in 1962. Additionally, China's military aid to Pakistan as well is a matter of concern to the Indian public, as the two sides have engaged in various wars.

On 6 July 2006, the historic Silk Road passing through this territory via the Nathu La pass was reopened. Both sides have agreed to resolve the issues by peaceful means.

In October 2011, it was stated that India and China will formulate a border mechanism to handle different perceptions as to the LAC and resume the bilateral army exercises between Indian and Chinese army from early 2012.

In popular culture

- Vidyadhar Shastri wrote a Sanskrit poem *Himadri Mahtyam* to exhort Indians to defend the Himalaya
- Australian author Jon Cleary wrote a novel set during the conflict, *The Pulse of Danger* (1966).
- A Hindi film, *Haqeeqat* (1964), and a Tamil film, *Ratha Thilagam* (1963), were based on events of the Sino-Indian war.

- On 27 June 1963, against the backdrop of the Sino-Indian War, Lata Mangeshkar sang the patriotic song "*Ae Mere Watan Ke Logon*" (literally, "Oh, the People of My Country") in the presence of Jawaharlal Nehru, Prime Minister of India. The song, composed by C. Ramchandra and written by Pradeep, is said to have brought the Prime Minister to tears.
- The 2017 Hindi film *Tubelight* is set during the Sino-Indian war.

Bibliography

- Das Gupta, Amit R.; Lüthi, Lorenz M., eds. (2016), *The Sino-Indian War of 1962: New perspectives*[1239], Taylor & Francis, ISBN 978-1-315-38892-2
  - Lüthi, Lorenz M. (2016), "India's Relations with China, 1945–1974"[1240], *Ibid*, pp. 29–47
  - Chaowu, Dai (2016), "From 'Hindi-Chini Bhai-Bhai' to 'international class struggle' against Nehru: China's India policy and the frontier dispute, 1950–62"[1241], *Ibid*, pp. 68–84
- Fisher, Margaret W.; Rose, Leo E.; Huttenback, Robert A. (1963), *Himalayan Battleground: Sino-Indian Rivalry in Ladakh*[1242], Praeger – via Questia, (Subscription required (help))
- Maxwell, Neville (1970), *India's China War*[1243], Pantheon Books, ISBN 978-0-394-47051-1
- Mehra, Parshotham (1991), ""John Lall, Aksai Chin and Sino-Indian Conflict" (Book review)", *China Report*, **27** (2): 147–154, doi:10.1177/000944559102700206[1244]
- Mehra, Parshotam (1992), *An "agreed" frontier: Ladakh and India's northernmost borders, 1846-1947*[1245], Oxford University Press
- Noorani, A.G. (2010), *India–China Boundary Problem 1846–1947: History and Diplomacy*[1246], Oxford University Press India, doi: 10.1093/acprof:oso/9780198070689.001.0001[1247], ISBN 978-0-19-908839-3
- Palit, D. K. (1991), *War in High Himalaya: The Indian Army in Crisis, 1962*[1248], C. Hurst & Co. Publishers, ISBN 978-1-85065-103-1
- Snedden, Christopher (2015), *Understanding Kashmir and Kashmiris*[1249], Oxford University Press, ISBN 978-1-84904-342-7
- Van Eekelen, Willem Frederik (2013), *Indian Foreign Policy and the Border Dispute with China*[1250], Springer, ISBN 978-94-017-6555-8
- Warikoo, K., ed. (2009), *Himalayan Frontiers of India: Historical, Geo-Political and Strategic Perspectives*[1251], Routledge, ISBN 978-1-134-03294-5
  - Karim, Afsir (2009), "Strategic dimensions of the trans-Himalayan frontiers"[1252], *Ibid*, pp. 56–66

- Warikoo, K. (2009), "India's gateway to Central Asia: trans-Himalayan trade and cultural movements through Kashmir and Ladakh, 1846–1947"[1253], *Ibid*, pp. 1–13
- Woodman, Dorothy (1970) [first published in 1969 by Barrie & Rockliff, The Cresset Press], *Himalayan Frontiers: A Political Review of British, Chinese, Indian, and Russian Rivalries*[1254], Praeger

Further reading

- Garver, John W. (2011), *Protracted Contest: Sino-Indian Rivalry in the Twentieth Century*[1255], University of Washington Press, ISBN 978-0-295-80120-9
- *David Malone*, The Border War of 1962 // Does the Elephant Dance?: Contemporary Indian Foreign Policy - Oxford University Press, 2011 - 425 p. - ISBN 9780199552023
- Himalayan Blunder by Brigadier John Dalvi. Natraj Publishers
- Lamb, Alastair (1964). *The China-India Border: The Origins of the Disputed Boundaries*. L. Oxford University Press.
- Gunnar Myrdal. *Asian Drama; An Inquiry into the Poverty of Nations*. New York: Random House, 1968
- *History of the Conflict with China*, 1962. P.B. Sinha, A.A. Athale, with S.N. Prasad, chief editor, History Division, Ministry of Defence, Government of India, 1992. — Official Indian history of the Sino-Indian War.
- Allen S. Whiting. *The Chinese Calculus of Deterrence: India and Indochina*.
- *The Sino-Indian Boundary Question* [Enlarged Edition], Foreign Languages Press, Peking, 1962
- *The History of Counterattack Action on Sino-Indian Border*(中印边境自卫反击作战史）, Military science publishing house, Beijing.

External links

- Sino-Indian War (1962)[1256]
- Remembering a War: The 1962 India-China Conflict[1257] — Rediff.com.
- Neville Maxwell: Henderson Brooks Report[1258]
- 1962 Sino-Indian War, *Hindustan Times*[1259]
- Why India lost the 1962 border war? – Tejas Patel[1260]
- War in the Himalayas: 1962 Indo-Sino Conflict[1261] (includes official war history) from History Division, Ministry of Defence, Government of India
- Critical Asian Studies Article: Sino Indian War 1962[1262]

- India, China to speed up border dispute talks: 2005 Xinhuanet[1263]
- The Rediff Special/Claude Arpi[1264]
- 1962 War and Its Implications fr Sino-India Relations[1265]
- Historical maps of the Sino-Indian border[1266] (in Chinese)
- Conflict in Kashmir: Selected Internet Resources by the Library, University of California, Berkeley, US[1267]; University of California, Berkeley Library Bibliographies and Web-Bibliographies list
- Frontier India India-China Section[1268]
- China, India, and the fruits of Nehru's folly[1269] by Venkatesan Vembu, *Daily News & Analysis*, 6 June 2007

1970s

Bangladesh Liberation War

<indicator name="pp-default"> 🔒 </indicator>

	Bangladesh Liberation War
	মুক্তিযুদ্ধ Muktijuddho
	Part of the Cold War
	 Clockwise from top left; Martyred Intellectuals Memorial, Bangladesh Forces howitzer, Surrender of Pakistan to Indian and Bangladesh forces,[1270] the PNS Ghazi.
Date	26 March 1971 – 16 December 1971
Location	East Pakistan (In modern times, Bangladesh) India-East Pakistan border, the Bay of Bengal, the Pasha enclave, parts of East India.
Result	• Decisive Indo-Bangladeshi victory • Collapse of the Eastern Command of Pakistan in Eastern Front • Establishment of the sovereignty of Bangladesh
Territorial changes	Independence of East Pakistan from Pakistan as a sovereign Peoples' Republic of Bangladesh
	Belligerents

Provisional Government of Bangladesh • Mukti Bahini	Pakistan • Govt. of East Pakistan
India • Indian Armed Forces (3–16 December 1971)	• Pakistan Armed Forces • Paramilitary forces: • Jamaat-e-Islami • Nagorik Shanti Committee • Razakars • Al-Badr • Al-Shams
Commanders and leaders	
Sheikh Mujibur Rahman (President of Provisional Government of Bangladesh) Tajuddin Ahmad (Prime Minister of Provisional Government of Bangladesh) M. A. G. Osmani (Cdr-in-C, Bangladesh Forces) Maj. K.M. Shafiullah (Commander, S Force) Maj. Ziaur Rahman (Commander, Z Force) Maj. Khaled Mosharraf (Commander, K Force) V. V. Giri (President of India) Indira Gandhi (Prime Minister of India) Swaran Singh (External Minister of India) Gen Sam Manekshaw (Chief of Army Staff) Lt.Gen J.S. Arora (GOC-in-C, Eastern Command) Lt.Gen Sagat Singh (GOC-in-C, IV Corps) Maj.Gen Inderjit Singh Gill (Dir., Military Operations) Maj.Gen Om Malhotra (COS, IV Corps) Maj.Gen Farj R. Jacob (COS, Eastern Command) Maj.Gen Shabeg Singh (GOC, Garhwal Rifles/Training MB) V.Adm Nilakanta Krishnan (FOC-in-C, Eastern Naval Command) AM Hari Chand Dewan (AOC-in-C, Eastern Air Command) K. Sankaran Nair (Deputy Director, R&AW)	Abdul Motaleb Malik (Governor of East Pakistan) Ghulam Azam (Chair, Nagorik Shanti Committee) Motiur Rahman Nizami (Emir of Jamaat-e-Islami) Abdul Quader Molla (Leader, Al-Badr) Abul Kalam Azad (Leader, Razakar) Fazlul Qadir Chaudhry (Leader, Al-Shams) Yahya Khan (President of Pakistan) Nurul Amin (Prime Minister of Pakistan) Gen. A.H. Khan (Chief of Staff, Army GHQ) Lt.Gen A.A.K. Niazi (POW) (Commander, Eastern Command) MGen Rao Farman Ali (POW) (Mil.Adv., Govt. EPk) MGen Khadim Hussain (POW) (GOC, 14th Infantry Division) RAdm Moh'd Shariff (POW) (Cdr, Eastern Naval Command) Capt. Ahmad Zamir (POW) (CO, Pakistan Marines East) Cdr Zafar Muhammad † (CO, PNS Ghazi) Air Cdre Inamul Haque (POW) (AOC, Eastern Air Command) Air Cdre Mitty Masud (AOC, Eastern Air Cmnd. (1969–71))
Units involved	
175,000[1271] 250,000	~365,000 regular troops (~97,000+ in East Pakistan) ~25,000 militiamen[1272]
Casualties and losses	

~30,000 killed 1,426–1,525 killed[1273] 3,611–4,061 wounded[1273]	~8,000 killed ~10,000 wounded 90,000—93,000 captured (including 79,676 troops and 10,324—12,192 local militiamen)[1274]
Civilian death: Estimates range between 300,000 and 3 million.	

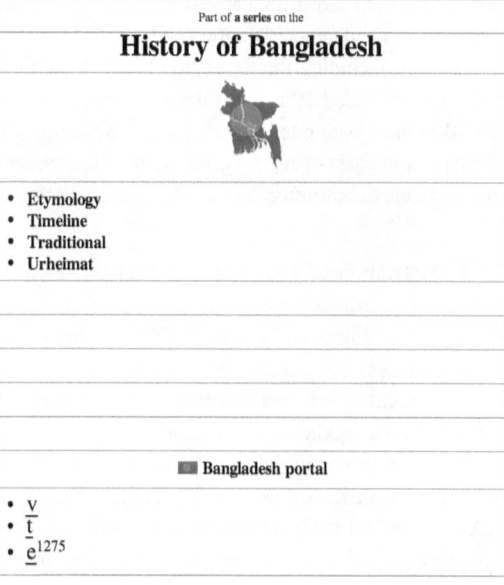

Part of **a series** on the
History of Bangladesh

- Etymology
- Timeline
- Traditional
- Urheimat

■ Bangladesh portal

- v
- t
- e[1275]

The **Bangladesh Liberation War**[1276]

> This war is also called the Civil War in Pakistan

</ref> (Bengali: মুক্তিযুদ্ধ *Muktijuddho*), also known as the **Bangladesh War of Independence**, or simply the **Liberation War** in Bangladesh, was a revolution and armed conflict sparked by the rise of the Bengali nationalist and self-determination movement in what was then East Pakistan during the 1971 Bangladesh genocide. It resulted in the independence of the People's Republic of Bangladesh. The war began after the Pakistani military junta based in West Pakistan launched Operation Searchlight against the people of East Pakistan on the night of 25 March 1971. It pursued the systematic elimination of nationalist Bengali civilians, students, intelligentsia, religious minorities and armed personnel. The junta annulled the results of the 1970 elections and arrested Prime minister-designate Sheikh Mujibur Rahman. The war ended on 16 December 1971 after West Pakistan surrendered.

Rural and urban areas across East Pakistan saw extensive military operations and air strikes to suppress the tide of civil disobedience that formed following the 1970 election stalemate. The Pakistan Army, which had the backing of Islamists, created radical religious militias – the Razakars, Al-Badr and Al-Shams – to assist it during raids on the local populace.[1277,1278] Urdu-speaking Biharis in Bangladesh (ethnic minority) were also in support of Pakistani military. Members of the Pakistani military and supporting militias engaged in mass murder, deportation and genocidal rape. The capital Dhaka was the scene of numerous massacres, including the Operation Searchlight and Dhaka University massacre. An estimated 10 million Bengali refugees fled to neighboring India, while 30 million were internally displaced. Sectarian violence broke out between Bengalis and Urdu-speaking immigrants. An academic consensus prevails that the atrocities committed by the Pakistani military were a genocide.

The Bangladeshi Declaration of Independence was proclaimed from Chittagong by members of the Mukti Bahini – the national liberation army formed by Bengali military, paramilitary and civilians. The East Bengal Regiment and the East Pakistan Rifles played a crucial role in the resistance. Led by General M. A. G. Osmani and eleven sector commanders, the Bangladesh Forces waged a mass guerrilla war against the Pakistani military. They liberated numerous towns and cities in the initial months of the conflict. The Pakistan Army regained momentum in the monsoon. Bengali guerrillas carried out widespread sabotage, including Operation Jackpot against the Pakistan Navy. The nascent Bangladesh Air Force flew sorties against Pakistani military bases. By November, the Bangladesh forces restricted the Pakistani military to its barracks during the night. They secured control of most parts of the countryside.

The Provisional Government of Bangladesh was formed on 17 April 1971 in Mujibnagar and moved to Calcutta as a government in exile. Bengali members of the Pakistani civil, military and diplomatic corps defected to the Bangladeshi provisional government. Thousands of Bengali families were interned in West Pakistan, from where many escaped to Afghanistan. Bengali cultural activists operated the clandestine Free Bengal Radio Station. The plight of millions of war-ravaged Bengali civilians caused worldwide outrage and alarm. The Indian state led by Indira Gandhi provided substantial diplomatic, economic and military support to Bangladeshi nationalists. British, Indian and American musicians organised the world's first benefit concert in New York City to support the Bangladeshi people. Senator Ted Kennedy in the United States led a congressional campaign for an end to Pakistani military persecution; while US diplomats in East Pakistan strongly dissented with the Nixon administration's close ties to the Pakistani military dictator Yahya Khan.

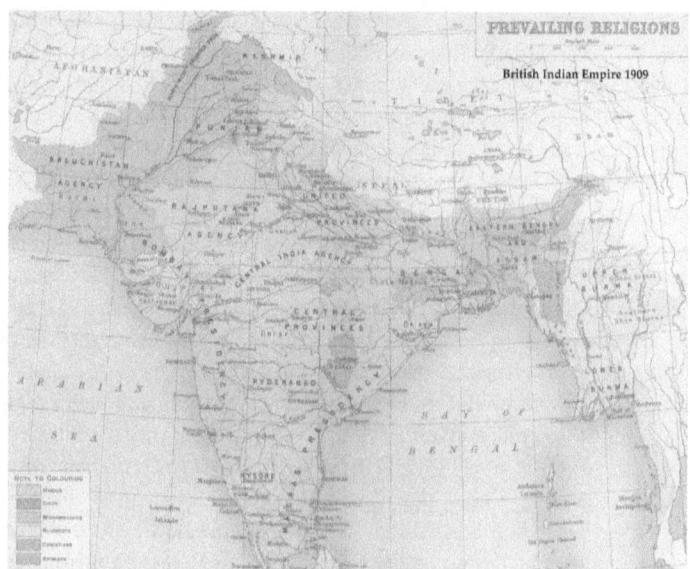

Figure 238: *Map of the British Raj in 1909 showing Muslim majority areas in green, including modern-day Bangladesh on the east and Pakistan on the west.*

India joined the war on 3 December 1971, after Pakistan launched preemptive air strikes on North India. The subsequent Indo-Pakistani War witnessed engagements on two war fronts. With air supremacy achieved in the eastern theatre and the rapid advance of the Allied Forces of Bangladesh and India, Pakistan surrendered in Dacca on 16 December 1971.

The war changed the geopolitical landscape of South Asia, with the emergence of Bangladesh as the seventh-most populous country in the world. Due to complex regional alliances, the war was a major episode in Cold War tensions involving the United States, the Soviet Union and the People's Republic of China. The majority of member states in the United Nations recognised Bangladesh as a sovereign nation in 1972.

Background

Prior to the Partition of British India, the Lahore Resolution initially envisaged separate Muslim-majority states in the eastern and northwestern zones of British India. A proposal for an independent United Bengal was mooted by Prime Minister Huseyn Shaheed Suhrawardy in 1946, but was opposed by the colonial authorities. The East Pakistan Renaissance Society advocated the creation of a sovereign state in eastern British India. Eventually, political negotiations led, in August 1947, to the official birth of two states, Pakistan and India, giving presumably permanent homes for Muslims and Hindus respectively following the departure of the British. The Dominion of Pakistan comprised two geographically and culturally separate areas to the east and the west with India in between. The western zone was popularly (and for a period, also officially) termed West Pakistan and the eastern zone (modern-day Bangladesh) was initially termed East Bengal and later, East Pakistan. Although the population of the two zones was close to equal, political power was concentrated in West Pakistan and it was widely perceived that East Pakistan was being exploited economically, leading to many grievances. Administration of two discontinuous territories was also seen as a challenge. On 25 March 1971, after an election won by an East Pakistani political party (the Awami League) was ignored by the ruling (West Pakistani) establishment, rising political discontent and cultural nationalism in East Pakistan was met by brutal suppressive force from the ruling elite of the West Pakistan establishment, in what came to be termed Operation Searchlight. The violent crackdown by the Pakistan Army led to Awami League leader Sheikh Mujibur Rahman declaring East Pakistan's independence as the state of Bangladesh on 26 March 1971. Most Bengalis threw their support behind this move although Islamists and Biharis opposed this and sided with the Pakistan Army instead. Pakistani President Agha Muhammad Yahya Khan ordered the Pakistani military to restore the Pakistani government's authority, beginning the civil war. The war led to a sea of refugees (estimated at the time to be about 10 million) flooding into the eastern provinces of India.[1279] Facing a mounting humanitarian and economic crisis, India started actively aiding and organising the Bangladeshi resistance army known as the Mukti Bahini.

Language controversy

In 1948, Governor-General Muhammad Ali Jinnah declared that "Urdu, and only Urdu" would be the federal language of Pakistan. However, Urdu was historically prevalent only in the north, central, and western region of the subcontinent; whereas in East Bengal, the native language was Bengali, one of the two most easterly branches of the Indo-European languages. The Bengali-speaking people of Pakistan constituted over 30% of the country's population. The government stand was widely viewed as an attempt to suppress the culture of the eastern wing. The people of East Bengal demanded that their language be given federal status alongside Urdu and English. The Language Movement began in 1948, as civil society protested the removal of the Bengali script from currency and stamps, which were in place since the British Raj. The movement reached its climax in 1952, when on 21 February, the police fired on protesting students and civilians, causing several deaths. The day is revered in

Figure 239: *Language movement memorial*

Bangladesh as the Language Movement Day. Later, in memory of the deaths in 1952, UNESCO declared 21 February as International Mother Language Day in November 1999.

Disparities

Although East Pakistan had a larger population, West Pakistan dominated the divided country politically and received more money from the common budget.

Year	Spending on West Pakistan (in millions of Pakistani rupees)	Spending on East Pakistan (in millions of Pakistani rupees)	Amount spent on East as percentage of West
1950–55	11,290	5,240	46.4
1955–60	16,550	5,240	31.7
1960–65	33,550	14,040	41.8
1965–70	51,950	21,410	41.2
Total	113,340	45,930	40.5

Source: Reports of the Advisory Panels for the Fourth Five Year Plan 1970–75, Vol. I, published by the planning commission of Pakistan.

Bengalis were under-represented in the Pakistan military. Officers of Bengali origin in the different wings of the armed forces made up just 5% of overall force by 1965; of these, only a few were in command positions, with the majority in technical or administrative posts. West Pakistanis believed that Bengalis were not "martially inclined" unlike Pashtuns and Punjabis; the "Martial races" notion was dismissed as ridiculous and humiliating by Bengalis. Moreover, despite huge defence spending, East Pakistan received none of the benefits, such as contracts, purchasing and military support jobs. The Indo-Pakistani War of 1965 over Kashmir also highlighted the sense of military insecurity among Bengalis, as only an under-strength infantry division and 15 combat aircraft without tank support were in East Pakistan to thwart any Indian retaliations during the conflict.[1280]

Religious and cultural differences

The only common bond between the two Pakistani wings was religion. But there were differences even in religious practices. Bengali Muslims tended to be less conservative in religious zeal, and had come to accept their Hindu minority and neighbours despite some communal clashes. Many Bengali Muslims strongly objected to the Islamist paradigm imposed by the Pakistani state. Most members of West Pakistan's ruling elite also belonged to a liberal society, yet understood a common faith as the mobilising factor behind Pakistan's creation and the subsuming of Pakistan's multiple identities into one.

Cultural and linguistic differences between the two wings outweighed any religious unity. The Bengalis were very proud of their culture and language which, with its Eastern Nagari script and Pali vocabulary, was unacceptable to the West Pakistani elite, who considered it to smack of Hindu culture.

The Bangladeshi liberation struggle against Pakistan was led by secular leaders. With this reality and the feeling of Islamic solidarity in the background, Islamists in East Pakistan viewed Bengali nationalism as unacceptable and instead sided with the Pakistani Army's efforts to crush the Bengali independence movement. Secularists hailed the Bangladeshi victory as the triumph of secular Bengali nationalism over religion-centred Pakistani nationalism.

Most of the politically-active ulama of East Pakistan either remained neutral or sided with the Pakistani state, since they perceived the break-up of Pakistan as a loss for Islam.

Political differences

Although East Pakistan accounted for a slight majority of the country's population, political power remained in the hands of West Pakistanis. Since a straightforward system of representation based on population would have concentrated political power in East Pakistan, the West Pakistani establishment came up with the "One Unit" scheme, where all of West Pakistan was considered one province. This was solely to counterbalance the East wing's votes.

After the assassination of Liaquat Ali Khan, Pakistan's first prime minister, in 1951, political power began to devolve to the new President of Pakistan, which replaced the office of Governor General when Pakistan became a republic, and, eventually, the military. The nominal elected chief executive, the Prime Minister, was frequently sacked by the establishment, acting through the President.

The East Pakistanis observed that the West Pakistani establishment would swiftly depose any East Pakistanis elected Prime Minister of Pakistan, such as Khawaja Nazimuddin, Mohammad Ali Bogra, or Huseyn Shaheed Suhrawardy. Their suspicions were further aggravated by the military dictatorships of Ayub Khan (27 October 1958 – 25 March 1969) and Yahya Khan (25 March 1969 – 20 December 1971), both West Pakistanis. The situation reached a climax in 1970, when the Bangladesh Awami League, the largest East Pakistani political party, led by Sheikh Mujibur Rahman, won a landslide victory in the national elections. The party won 167 of the 169 seats allotted to East Pakistan, and thus a majority of the 313 seats in the National Assembly. This gave the Awami League the constitutional right to form a government. However, Zulfikar Ali Bhutto (a former Foreign Minister), the leader of the Pakistan Peoples Party, refused to allow Rahman to become the Prime Minister of Pakistan. Instead, he proposed the idea of having two Prime Ministers, one for each wing. The proposal elicited outrage in the east wing, already chafing under the other constitutional innovation, the "One Unit scheme". Bhutto also refused to accept Rahman's Six Points. On 3 March 1971, the two leaders of the two wings along with the President General Yahya Khan met in Dacca to decide the fate of the country. After their discussions yielded no satisfactory results, Sheikh Mujibur Rahman called for a nationwide strike. Bhutto feared a civil war, therefore, he sent his trusted companion, Mubashir Hassan. A message was conveyed, and Rahman decided to meet Bhutto. Upon his arrival, Rahman met with Bhutto and both agreed to form a coalition government with Rahman as Premier and Bhutto as President. However, the military was unaware of these developments, and Bhutto increased his pressure on Rahman to reach a decision.

On 7 March 1971, Sheikh Mujibur Rahman (soon to be the prime minister) delivered a speech at the Racecourse Ground (now called the Suhrawardy

Udyan). In this speech he mentioned a further four-point condition to consider at the National Assembly Meeting on 25 March:

- The immediate lifting of martial law.
- Immediate withdrawal of all military personnel to their barracks.
- An inquiry into the loss of life.
- Immediate transfer of power to the elected representative of the people before the assembly meeting 25 March.

He urged his people to turn every house into a fort of resistance. He closed his speech saying, "Our struggle is for our freedom. Our struggle is for our independence." This speech is considered the main event that inspired the nation to fight for its independence. General Tikka Khan was flown into Dacca to become Governor of East Bengal. East-Pakistani judges, including Justice Siddique, refused to swear him in.

Between 10 and 13 March, Pakistan International Airlines cancelled all their international routes to urgently fly "government passengers" to Dacca. These "government passengers" were almost all Pakistani soldiers in civilian dress. MV *Swat*, a ship of the Pakistan Navy carrying ammunition and soldiers, was harboured in Chittagong Port, but the Bengali workers and sailors at the port refused to unload the ship. A unit of East Pakistan Rifles refused to obey commands to fire on the Bengali demonstrators, beginning a mutiny among the Bengali soldiers.

Response to the 1970 cyclone

The 1970 Bhola cyclone made landfall on the East Pakistan coastline during the evening of 12 November, around the same time as a local high tide, killing an estimated 300,000 to 500,000 people. Though the exact death toll is not known, it is considered the deadliest tropical cyclone on record. A week after the landfall, President Khan conceded that his government had made "slips" and "mistakes" in its handling of the relief efforts due to a lack of understanding of the magnitude of the disaster.

A statement released by eleven political leaders in East Pakistan ten days after the cyclone hit charged the government with "gross neglect, callous and utter indifference". They also accused the president of playing down the magnitude of the problem in news coverage. On 19 November, students held a march in Dacca protesting the slowness of the government's response. Abdul Hamid Khan Bhashani addressed a rally of 50,000 people on 24 November, where he accused the president of inefficiency and demanded his resignation.

As the conflict between East and West Pakistan developed in March, the Dacca offices of the two government organisations directly involved in relief efforts were closed for at least two weeks, first by a general strike and then by a ban on

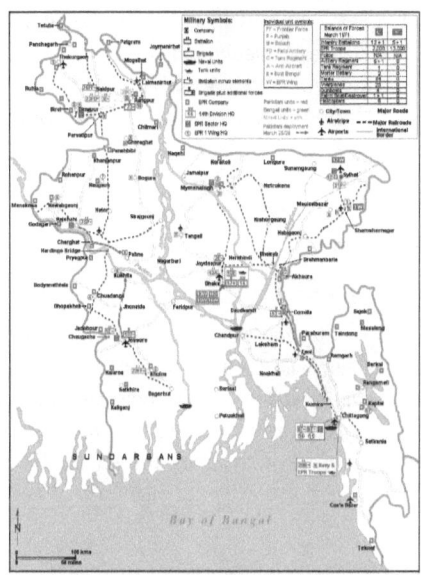

Figure 240: *Location of Bengali and Pakistani military units during Operation Searchlight, March 1971*

government work in East Pakistan by the Awami League. With this increase in tension, foreign personnel were evacuated over fears of violence. Relief work continued in the field, but long-term planning was curtailed. This conflict widened into the Bangladesh Liberation War in December and concluded with the creation of Bangladesh. This was one of the first times that a natural event helped trigger a civil war.

Operation Searchlight

A planned military pacification carried out by the Pakistan Army – codenamed *Operation Searchlight* – started on 25 March 1971 to curb the Bengali independence movement by taking control of the major cities on 26 March, and then eliminating all opposition, political or military,[1281] within one month. The Pakistani state claimed to justify starting Operation Searchlight on the basis of anti-Bihari violence by Bengalis in early March.

Before the beginning of the operation, all foreign journalists were systematically deported from East Pakistan.

The main phase of Operation Searchlight ended with the fall of the last major town in Bengali hands in mid-May. The operation also began the 1971 Bangladesh genocide. These systematic killings served only to enrage the

Bengalis, which ultimately resulted in the secession of East Pakistan later in the same year. Bangladeshi media and reference books in English have published casualty figures which vary greatly, from 5,000–35,000 in Dacca, and 200,000–3,000,000 for Bangladesh as a whole, although independent researchers, including the British Medical Journal, have put forward the figure ranging from between 125,000 and 505,000. American political scientist Rudolph Rummel puts total deaths at 1.5 million. The atrocities have been referred to as acts of genocide.

According to the *Asia Times*,

> *At a meeting of the military top brass, Yahya Khan declared: "Kill 3 million of them and the rest will eat out of our hands." Accordingly, on the night of 25 March, the Pakistani Army launched Operation Searchlight to "crush" Bengali resistance in which Bengali members of military services were disarmed and killed, students and the intelligentsia systematically liquidated and able-bodied Bengali males just picked up and gunned down.*

Although the violence focused on the provincial capital, Dacca, it also affected all parts of East Pakistan. Residential halls of the University of Dacca were particularly targeted. The only Hindu residential hall – Jagannath Hall – was destroyed by the Pakistani armed forces, and an estimated 600 to 700 of its residents were murdered. The Pakistani army denied any cold blooded killings at the university, though the Hamoodur Rahman Commission in Pakistan concluded that overwhelming force was used at the university. This fact, and the massacre at Jagannath Hall and nearby student dormitories of Dacca University, are corroborated by a videotape secretly filmed by Professor Nurul Ula of the East Pakistan University of Engineering and Technology, whose residence was directly opposite the student dormitories.

The scale of the atrocities was first made clear in the West when Anthony Mascarenhas, a Pakistani journalist who had been sent to the province by the military authorities to write a story favourable to Pakistan's actions, instead fled to the United Kingdom and, on 13 June 1971, published an article in *The Sunday Times* describing the systematic killings by the military. The BBC wrote: "There is little doubt that Mascarenhas' reportage played its part in ending the war. It helped turn world opinion against Pakistan and encouraged India to play a decisive role", with Indian Prime Minister Indira Gandhi herself stating that Mascarenhas' article has led her "to prepare the ground for India's armed intervention".

Hindu areas suffered particularly heavy blows. By midnight, Dacca was burning, especially the Hindu-dominated eastern part of the city. *Time* magazine reported on 2 August 1971, "The Hindus, who account for three-fourths of

Figure 241: *Following the Pakistan Army's brutal Operation Searchlight on 25 March 1971, Sheikh Mujibur Rahman declared the Independence of Bangladesh and called for nationwide resistance on 26 March midnight which led the Bangladesh Liberation War to officially start within hours.*

the refugees and a majority of the dead, have borne the brunt of the Pakistani military hatred."

Sheikh Mujibur Rahman was arrested by the Pakistani Army. Yahya Khan appointed Brigadier (later General) Rahimuddin Khan to preside over a special tribunal prosecuting Rahman with multiple charges. The tribunal's sentence was never made public, but Yahya caused the verdict to be held in abeyance in any case. Other Awami League leaders were arrested as well, while a few fled Dacca to avoid arrest. The Awami League was banned by General Yahya Khan.

Declaration of independence

The violence unleashed by the Pakistani forces on 25 March 1971 proved the last straw to the efforts to negotiate a settlement. Following these outrages, Sheikh Mujibur Rahman signed an official declaration that read:

> *Today Bangladesh is a sovereign and independent country. On Thursday night, West Pakistani armed forces suddenly attacked the police barracks at Razarbagh and the EPR headquarters at Pilkhana in Dacca. Many*

innocent and unarmed have been killed in Dhaka city and other places of Bangladesh. Violent clashes between E.P.R. and Police on the one hand and the armed forces of Pakistan on the other, are going on. The Bengalis are fighting the enemy with great courage for an independent Bangladesh. May Allah aid us in our fight for freedom. Joy Bangla [May Bangladesh be victorious].

Sheikh Mujib also called upon the people to resist the occupation forces through a radio message. Rahman was arrested on the night of 25–26 March 1971 at about 1:30 am (as per Radio Pakistan's news on 29 March 1971).

A telegram containing the text of Sheikh Mujibur Rahman's declaration reached some students in Chittagong. The message was translated to Bengali by Dr. Manjula Anwar. The students failed to secure permission from higher authorities to broadcast the message from the nearby Agrabad Station of Pakistan Broadcasting Corporation. However, the message was read several times by the independent Swadhin Bangla Betar Kendro Radio established by some rebel Bangali Radio workers in Kalurghat. Major Ziaur Rahman was requested to provide security of the station and he also read the Declaration on 27 March 1971. Major Ziaur Rahman broadcast announcement of the declaration of independence on behalf of Sheikh Mujibur Rahman.

This is Swadhin Bangla Betar Kendra. I, Major Ziaur Rahman, at the direction of Bangobondhu Mujibur Rahman, hereby declare that Independent People's Republic of Bangladesh has been established. At his direction, I have taken the command as the temporary Head of the Republic. In the name of Sheikh Mujibur Rahman, I call upon all Bengalees to rise against the attack by the West Pakistani Army. We shall fight to the last to free our motherland. Victory is, by the Grace of Allah, ours. Joy Bangla.

The Kalurghat Radio Station's transmission capability was limited, but the message was picked up by a Japanese ship in the Bay of Bengal. It was then re-transmitted by Radio Australia and later by the British Broadcasting Corporation.

M. A. Hannan, an Awami League leader from Chittagong, is said to have made the first announcement of the declaration of independence over the radio on 26 March 1971.

26 March 1971 is considered the official Independence Day of Bangladesh, and the name Bangladesh was in effect henceforth. In July 1971, Indian Prime Minister Indira Gandhi openly referred to the former East Pakistan as Bangladesh.[1282] Some Pakistani and Indian officials continued to use the name "East Pakistan" until 16 December 1971.

Liberation war

March–June

At first, resistance was spontaneous and disorganised, and was not expected to be prolonged.[1283] However, when the Pakistani Army cracked down upon the population, resistance grew. The Mukti Bahini became increasingly active. The Pakistani military sought to quell them, but increasing numbers of Bengali soldiers defected to this underground "Bangladesh army". These Bengali units slowly merged into the Mukti Bahini and bolstered their weaponry with supplies from India. Pakistan responded by airlifting in two infantry divisions and reorganising their forces. They also raised paramilitary forces of Razakars, Al-Badrs and Al-Shams (who were mostly members of the Muslim League and other Islamist groups), as well as other Bengalis who opposed independence, and Bihari Muslims who had settled during the time of partition.

On 17 April 1971, a provisional government was formed in Meherpur District in western Bangladesh bordering India with Sheikh Mujibur Rahman, who was in prison in Pakistan, as President, Syed Nazrul Islam as Acting President, Tajuddin Ahmad as Prime Minister, and General Muhammad Ataul Ghani Osmani as Commander-in-Chief, Bangladesh Forces. As fighting grew between the occupation army and the Bengali Mukti Bahini, an estimated 10 million Bengalis sought refuge in the Indian states of Assam and West Bengal.

June–September

Bangladesh forces command was set up on 11 July, with Col. M. A. G. Osmani as commander-in-chief (C-in-C) with the status of Cabinet Minister, Lt. Col., Abdur Rabb as chief of Staff (COS), Group Captain A K Khandker as Deputy Chief of Staff (DCOS) and Major A R Chowdhury as Assistant Chief of Staff (ACOS).

General Osmani had differences of opinion with the Indian leadership regarding the role of the Mukti Bahini in the conflict. Indian leadership initially envisioned Bengali forces to be trained into a small elite guerrilla force of 8,000 members, led by the surviving East Bengal Regiment soldiers operating in small cells around Bangladesh to facilitate the eventual Indian intervention,[1284] but with the Bangladesh government in exile, General Osmani favoured a different strategy:[1285,1286]

- Bengali conventional forces would occupy lodgment areas inside Bangladesh and then the Bangladesh government would request international diplomatic recognition and intervention. Initially Mymensingh was picked for this operation, but Gen. Osmani later settled on Sylhet.

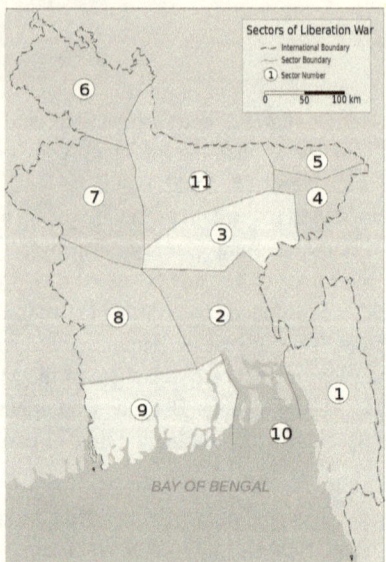

Figure 242: *The eleven sectors during the Bangladesh Liberation War.*

Figure 243: *Advertisement for former Beatle George Harrison's "Bangla Desh" single, released in July 1971 to raise international awareness and funds for the millions of Bangladeshi refugees.*

- Sending the maximum number to guerrillas inside Bangladesh as soon as possible with the following objectives:[1287,1288]
  - Increasing Pakistani casualties through raids and ambush.
  - Cripple economic activity by hitting power stations, railway lines, storage depots and communication networks.
  - Destroy Pakistan army mobility by blowing up bridges/culverts, fuel depots, trains and river crafts.
  - The strategic objective was to make the Pakistanis spread their forces inside the province, so attacks could be made on isolated Pakistani detachments.

Bangladesh was divided into eleven sectors in July,[1289] each with a commander chosen from defected officers of the Pakistani army who joined the Mukti Bahini to conduct guerrilla operations and train fighters. Most of their training camps were situated near the border area and were operated with assistance from India. The 10th Sector was directly placed under the Commander in Chief (C-in-C) General M. A. G. Osmani and included the Naval Commandos and C-in-C's special force. Three brigades (11 Battalions) were raised for conventional warfare; a large guerrilla force (estimated at 100,000) was trained.[1290]

Three brigades (eight infantry battalions and three artillery batteries) were put into action between July and September.[1291] During June and July, Mukti Bahini had regrouped across the border with Indian aid through Operation Jackpot and began sending 2000–5000 guerrillas across the border,[1292] the so-called Monsoon Offensive, which for various reasons (lack of proper training, supply shortage, lack of a proper support network inside Bangladesh) failed to achieve its objectives.[1293,1294,1295] Bengali regular forces also attacked BOPs in Mymensingh, Comilla and Sylhet, but the results were mixed. Pakistani authorities concluded that they had successfully contained the Monsoon Offensive, which proved a near-accurate observation.[1296,1297]

Guerrilla operations, which slackened during the training phase, picked up after August. Economic and military targets in Dacca were attacked. The major success story was Operation Jackpot, in which naval commandos mined and blew up berthed ships in Chittagong, Mongla, Narayanganj and Chandpur on 15 August 1971.

October–December

Major battles

- Battle of Boyra
- Battle of Garibpur

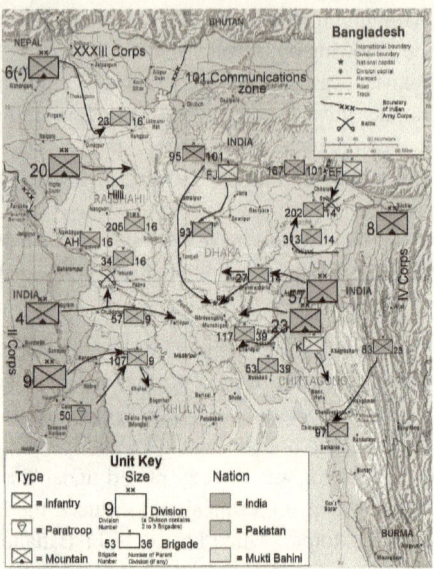

Figure 244: *Illustration showing military units and troop movements during the war.*

- Battle of Dhalai
- Battle of Hilli
- Battle of Kushtia

Bangladeshi conventional forces attacked border outposts. Kamalpur, Belonia and the Battle of Boyra are a few examples. 90 out of 370 BOPs fell to Bengali forces. Guerrilla attacks intensified, as did Pakistani and Razakar reprisals on civilian populations. Pakistani forces were reinforced by eight battalions from West Pakistan. The Bangladeshi independence fighters even managed to temporarily capture airstrips at Lalmonirhat and Shalutikar. Both of these were used for flying in supplies and arms from India. Pakistan sent another five battalions from West Pakistan as reinforcements.

Indian involvement

All unprejudiced persons objectively surveying the grim events in Bangladesh since March 25 have recognised the revolt of 75 million people, a people who were forced to the conclusion that neither their life, nor

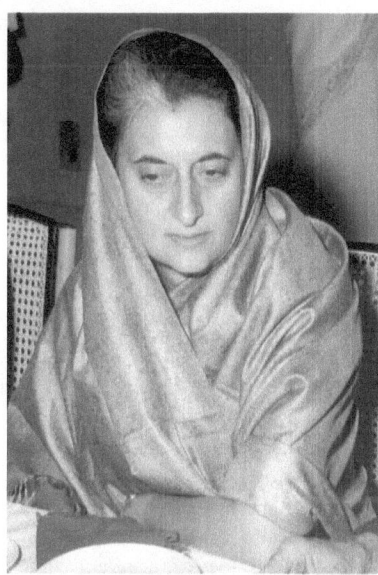

Figure 245: *Indira Gandhi*

their liberty, to say nothing of the possibility of the pursuit of happiness, was available to them.

—*Indira Gandhi, Letter to Richard Nixon, 15 December 1971*

Indian Prime Minister Indira Gandhi had concluded that instead of taking in millions of refugees, India would be economically better to go to war against Pakistan. As early as 28 April 1971, the Indian Cabinet had asked General Manekshaw (Chairman of the Chiefs of Staff Committee) to "Go into East Pakistan". Hostile relations in the past between India and Pakistan added to India's decision to intervene in Pakistan's civil war. Resultantly, the Indian government decided to support the creation of a separate state for ethnic Bengalis by supporting the Mukti Bahini. RAW helped to organise, train and arm these insurgents. Consequently, the Mukti Bahini succeeded in harassing Pakistani military in East Pakistan, thus creating conditions conducive for a full-scale Indian military intervention in early December.

The Pakistan Air Force (PAF) launched a pre-emptive strike on Indian Air Force bases on 3 December 1971. The attack was modelled on the Israeli Air Force's Operation Focus during the Six-Day War, and intended to neutralise the Indian Air Force planes on the ground. The strike was seen by India as an open act of unprovoked aggression, which marked the official start of the Indo-Pakistani War. As a response to the attack, both India and Pakistan formally acknowledged the "existence of a state of war between the two countries" even though neither government had formally issued a declaration of war.

Three Indian corps were involved in the liberation of East Pakistan. They were supported by nearly three brigades of Mukti Bahini fighting alongside them, and many more who were fighting irregularly. That was far superior to the Pakistani army of three divisions. The Indians quickly overran the country, selectively engaging or bypassing heavily defended strongholds. Pakistani forces were unable to effectively counter the Indian attack, as they had been deployed in small units around the border to counter the guerrilla attacks by the Mukti Bahini.[1298] Unable to defend Dacca, the Pakistanis surrendered on 16 December 1971.

Air and naval war

The Indian Air Force carried out several sorties against Pakistan, and within a week, IAF aircraft dominated the skies of East Pakistan. It achieved near-total air supremacy by the end of the first week, as the entire Pakistani air contingent in the east, PAF No.14 Squadron, was grounded because of Indian and Bangladesh airstrikes at Tejgaon, Kurmitolla, Lal Munir Hat and Shamsher Nagar. Sea Hawks from the carrier INS *Vikrant* also struck Chittagong, Barisal and Cox's Bazar, destroying the eastern wing of the Pakistan Navy and effectively blockading the East Pakistan ports, thereby cutting off any escape routes for the stranded Pakistani soldiers. The nascent Bangladesh Navy (comprising officers and sailors who defected from the Pakistani Navy) aided the Indians in the marine warfare, carrying out attacks, most notably Operation Jackpot.

Surrender and aftermath

On 16 December 1971, Lt. Gen Amir Abdullah Khan Niazi, CO of Pakistan Army forces located in East Pakistan signed the Instrument of Surrender. At the time of surrender only a few countries had provided diplomatic recognition to the new nation. Over 93,000 Pakistani troops surrendered to the Indian forces & Bangladesh Liberation forces, making it the largest surrender since World War II, although the Pakistani Army had fought gallantly according to Indian Army Chief Sam Manekshaw. Bangladesh sought admission in the UN with most voting in its favour, but China vetoed this as Pakistan was its key ally. The United States, also a key ally of Pakistan, was one of the last nations to accord Bangladesh recognition.[1299] To ensure a smooth transition, in 1972 the Simla Agreement was signed between India and Pakistan. The treaty ensured that Pakistan recognised the independence of Bangladesh in exchange

Figure 246: *Signing of Pakistani Instrument of Surrender by Pakistan's Lt.Gen. A. A. K. Niazi in the presence of Indian military officers in Dhaka on 16 Dec' 1971.*

for the return of the Pakistani PoWs. India treated all the PoWs in strict accordance with the Geneva Convention, rule 1925. It released more than 93,000 Pakistani PoWs in five months. Further, as a gesture of goodwill, nearly 200 soldiers who were sought for war crimes by Bengalis were also pardoned by India. The accord also gave back 13,000 km^2 (5,019 sq mi) of land that Indian troops had seized in West Pakistan during the war, though India retained a few strategic areas; most notably Kargil (which would in turn again be the focal point for a war between the two nations in 1999). This was done as a measure of promoting "lasting peace" and was acknowledged by many observers as a sign of maturity by India. However, some in India felt that the treaty had been too lenient to Bhutto, who had pleaded for leniency, arguing that the fragile democracy in Pakistan would crumble if the accord was perceived as being overly harsh by Pakistanis.

Reaction in West Pakistan to the war

Reaction to the defeat and dismemberment of half the nation was a shocking loss to top military and civilians alike. Few had expected that they would lose the formal war in under a fortnight, and there was also unsettlement over what was perceived as a meek surrender of the army in East Pakistan. Yahya

Figure 247: *Memorial for freedom fighters*

Khan's dictatorship collapsed and gave way to Bhutto, who took the opportunity to rise to power. General Niazi, who surrendered along with 93,000 troops, was viewed with suspicion and contempt upon his return to Pakistan. He was shunned and branded a traitor. The war also exposed the shortcomings of Pakistan's declared strategic doctrine that the "defence of East Pakistan lay in West Pakistan".

Atrocities

During the war there were widespread killings and other atrocities – including the displacement of civilians in Bangladesh (East Pakistan at the time) and widespread violations of human rights began with the start of Operation Searchlight on 25 March 1971. Members of the Pakistani military and supporting Islamist militias from Jamaat e Islami killed an estimated 300,000 to 3,000,000 people and raped between 200,000 and 400,000 Bangladeshi women in a systematic campaign of genocidal rape.[1300,1301,1302] Some Islamic clerics issued fatwas (a ruling on a point of Islamic law) in support of raping Bengali women, especially Hindu women, as they considered the conflict a holy war. During the war, a fatwa in Pakistan declared that the Bengali freedom fighters were Hindus and that their women could be taken as "the booty of war".

A large section of the intellectual community of Bangladesh were murdered, mostly by the Al-Shams and Al-Badr forces,[1303] at the instruction of the Pakistani Army. Just two days before the surrender, on 14 December 1971, Pakistan Army and Razakar militia (local collaborators) picked up at least 100 physicians, professors, writers and engineers in Dacca, and murdered them, leaving the dead bodies in a mass grave.

Many mass graves have been discovered in Bangladesh. The first night of war on Bengalis, which is documented in telegrams from the American Consulate in Dacca to the United States State Department, saw indiscriminate killings of students of Dacca University and other civilians. Numerous women were tortured, raped and killed during the war; the exact numbers are not known and are a subject of debate. The widespread rape of Bangladeshi women led to birth of thousands of war babies. The Pakistan Army also kept numerous Bengali women as sex-slaves inside the Dacca Cantonment. Most of the girls were captured from Dacca University and private homes. There was significant sectarian violence not only perpetrated and encouraged by the Pakistani army,[1304] but also by Bengali nationalists against non-Bengali minorities, especially Biharis. In June 1971, Bihari representatives stated that 500,000 Biharis were killed by Bengalis. R.J. Rummel gives a prudent estimate of 150,000 killed.

On 16 December 2002, the George Washington University's National Security Archive published a collection of declassified documents, consisting mostly of communications between US embassy officials and United States Information Service centres in Dacca and India, and officials in Washington, D.C. These documents show that US officials working in diplomatic institutions within Bangladesh used the terms "selective genocide"[1305] and "genocide" (see The Blood Telegram) for information on events they had knowledge of at the time. *Genocide* is the term that is still used to describe the event in almost every major publication and newspaper in Bangladesh, although in Pakistan, the accusations against Pakistani forces continue to be disputed.

Foreign reaction

Following Sheikh Mujibur Rahman's declaration of independence in March 1971, a worldwide campaign was undertaken by the Provisional Government of Bangladesh to drum up political support for the independence of East Pakistan as well as humanitarian support for the Bengali people.

Indian Prime Minister Indira Gandhi provided extensive diplomatic and political support to the Bangladesh movement. She toured many countries in a bid to create awareness of the Pakistani atrocities against Bengalis. This effort was to prove vital later during the war, in framing the world's context of the

Figure 248: *French minister Andre Malraux vowed to fight alongside the Mukti Bahini in the Liberation War.*

war and to justify military action by India. Also, following Pakistan's defeat, it ensured prompt recognition of the newly independent state of Bangladesh.

United Nations

Though the United Nations condemned the human rights violations during and following Operation Searchlight, it failed to defuse the situation politically before the start of the war.

Following India's entry into the war, Pakistan, fearing certain defeat, made urgent appeals to the United Nations to intervene and force India to agree to a ceasefire. The UN Security Council assembled on 4 December 1971 to discuss the hostilities in South Asia. After lengthy discussions on 7 December, the United States made a resolution for "immediate cease-fire and withdrawal of troops". While supported by the majority, the USSR vetoed the resolution twice. In light of the Pakistani atrocities against Bengalis, the United Kingdom and France abstained on the resolution.

On 12 December, with Pakistan facing imminent defeat, the United States requested that the Security Council be reconvened. Pakistan's Deputy Prime Minister and Foreign Minister, Zulfikar Ali Bhutto, was rushed to New York City to make the case for a resolution on the cease fire. The council continued

Figure 249: *Senator Ted Kennedy led US congressional support for Bangladeshi independence*

deliberations for four days. By the time proposals were finalised, Pakistan's forces in the East had surrendered and the war had ended, making the measures merely academic. Bhutto, frustrated by the failure of the resolution and the inaction of the United Nations, ripped up his speech and left the council.

Most UN member nations were quick to recognise Bangladesh within months of its independence.

Bhutan

As the Bangladesh Liberation War approached the defeat of the Pakistan Army, the Himalayan kingdom of Bhutan became the first state in the world to recognise the newly independent country on 6 December 1971. Sheikh Mujibur Rahman, the first President of Bangladesh visited Bhutan to attend the coronation of Jigme Singye Wangchuck, the fourth King of Bhutan in June 1974.

US and USSR

The US government stood by its old ally Pakistan both politically and materially. US President Richard Nixon and his National Security Advisor Henry Kissinger feared Soviet expansion into South and Southeast Asia. Pakistan

Figure 250: *The Nixon administration was widely criticised for its close ties with the military junta led by General Yahya Khan. American diplomats in East Pakistan expressed profound dissent in the Blood Telegram.*

was a close ally of the People's Republic of China, with whom Nixon had been negotiating a *rapprochement* and which he intended to visit in February 1972. Nixon feared that an Indian invasion of West Pakistan would mean total Soviet domination of the region, and that it would seriously undermine the global position of the United States and the regional position of America's new tacit ally, China. To demonstrate to China the *bona fides* of the United States as an ally, and in direct violation of the US Congress-imposed sanctions on Pakistan, Nixon sent military supplies to Pakistan and routed them through Jordan and Iran,[1306] while also encouraging China to increase its arms supplies to Pakistan. The Nixon administration also ignored reports it received of the genocidal activities of the Pakistani Army in East Pakistan, most notably the Blood telegram.

Nixon denied getting involved in the situation, saying that it was an internal matter of Pakistan, but when Pakistan's defeat seemed certain, Nixon sent the aircraft carrier USS *Enterprise* to the Bay of Bengal, a move deemed by the Indians as a nuclear threat. *Enterprise* arrived on station on 11 December 1971. On 6 and 13 December, the Soviet Navy dispatched two groups of ships, armed with nuclear missiles, from Vladivostok; they trailed US Task Force 74 in the Indian Ocean from 18 December until 7 January 1972.

The Soviet Union supported Bangladesh and Indian armies, as well as the Mukti Bahini during the war, recognising that the independence of Bangladesh would weaken the position of its rivals – the United States and China. It gave assurances to India that if a confrontation with the United States or China developed, the USSR would take countermeasures. This was enshrined in the Indo-Soviet friendship treaty signed in August 1971. The Soviets also sent a nuclear submarine to ward off the threat posed by USS *Enterprise* in the Indian Ocean.

At the end of the war, the Warsaw Pact countries were among the first to recognise Bangladesh. The Soviet Union accorded recognition to Bangladesh on 25 January 1972. The United States delayed recognition for some months, before according it on 8 April 1972.

China

As a long-standing ally of Pakistan, the People's Republic of China reacted with alarm to the evolving situation in East Pakistan and the prospect of India invading West Pakistan and Pakistani-controlled Kashmir. Believing that just such an Indian attack was imminent, Nixon encouraged China to mobilise its armed forces along its border with India to discourage it. The Chinese did not, however, respond to this encouragement, because unlike the 1962 Sino-Indian War when India was caught entirely unaware, this time the Indian Army was prepared and had deployed eight mountain divisions to the Sino-Indian border to guard against such an eventuality. China instead threw its weight behind demands for an immediate ceasefire.

When Bangladesh applied for membership to the United Nations in 1972, China vetoed their application because two United Nations resolutions regarding the repatriation of Pakistani prisoners of war and civilians had not yet been implemented. China was also among the last countries to recognise independent Bangladesh, refusing to do so until 31 August 1975.

Footnotes

Notes

Citations

References

Ⓒ This article incorporates public domain material from the Library of Congress Country Studies website http://lcweb2.loc.gov/frd/cs/[1307].

Further reading

<templatestyles src="Template:Refbegin/styles.css" />

- Ayoob, Mohammed and Subrahmanyam, K., *The Liberation War*, S. Chand and Co. pvt Ltd. New Delhi, 1972.
- Ayub, Muhammad (2005). An Army, its Role and Rule: A History of the Pakistan Army from Independence to Kargil 1947–1999. Pittsburgh: RoseDog Books. ISBN 0-8059-9594-3.
- Bass, Gary J. *The Blood Telegram: Nixon, Kissinger, and a Forgotten Genocide*. Vintage, 2014. ISBN 0307744620
- Bhargava, G.S., *Crush India or Pakistan's Death Wish*, ISSD, New Delhi, 1972.
- Bhattacharyya, S. K., *Genocide in East Pakistan/Bangladesh: A Horror Story*, A. Ghosh Publishers, 1988.
- Blood, A. K. (2005). The cruel birth of Bangladesh: Memoirs of an American diplomat. Dhaka: University Press.
- Brownmiller, Susan: *Against Our Will: Men, Women, and Rape*, Ballantine Books, 1993.
- Choudhury, G. W. (April 1972). "Bangladesh: Why It Happened". *International Affairs*. Royal Institute of International Affairs. **48** (2): 242–249. doi: 10.2307/2613440[1308]. ISSN 0020-5850[1309]. JSTOR 2613440[1310].
- Choudhury, G. W. (1994) [First published 1974]. *The Last Days of United Pakistan*. Dhaka: University Press. ISBN 978-984-05-1242-3.
- Govt. of Bangladesh, *Documents of the war of Independence*, Vol 01-16, Ministry of Information.
- Hitchens, Christopher, *The Trials of Henry Kissinger*, Verso (2001). ISBN 1-85984-631-9
- Kanjilal, Kalidas, *The Perishing Humanity*, Sahitya Loke, Calcutta, 1976
- Johnson, Rob, 'A Region in Turmoil' (New York and London, 2005)
- Malik, Amita, *The Year of the Vulture*, Orient Longmans, New Delhi, 1972.
- Matinuddin, General Kamal, *Tragedy of Errors: East Pakistan Crisis, 1968–1971*, Wajidalis, Lahore, Pakistan, 1994.
- Mookherjee, Nayanika, *A Lot of History: Sexual Violence, Public Memories and the Bangladesh Liberation War of 1971*, D. Phil thesis in Social Anthropology, SOAS, University of London, 2002.
- National Security Archive, The Tilt: the U.S. and the South Asian Crisis of 1971[1311]
- Quereshi, Major General Hakeem Arshad, *The 1971 Indo-Pak War, A Soldiers Narrative*, Oxford University Press, 2002.
- Raghavan, Srinath, *1971: A Global History of the Creation of Bangladesh*, Harvard Univ. Press, 2013.

- Rummel, R.J., *Death By Government*, Transaction Publishers, 1997.
- Salik, Siddiq, *Witness to Surrender*, Oxford University Press, Karachi, Pakistan, 1977.
- Sisson, Richard & Rose, Leo, *War and secession: Pakistan, India, and the creation of Bangladesh*, University of California Press (Berkeley), 1990.
- Stephen, Pierre, and Payne, Robert, *Massacre*, Macmillan, New York, (1973). ISBN 0-02-595240-4
- Totten, Samuel et al., eds., *Century of Genocide: Eyewitness Accounts and Critical Views*, Garland Reference Library, 1997
- US Department of State Office of the Historian, *Foreign Relations of the United States, 1969–1976, Volume XI, South Asia Crisis, 1971*[1312]
- Zaheer, Hasan: *The separation of East Pakistan: The rise and realisation of Bengali Muslim nationalism*, Oxford University Press, 1994.
- Raja, Dewan Mohammad Tasawwar (2010). *O GENERAL MY GENERAL (Life and Works of General M. A. G. Osmani)*. The Osmani Memorial Trust, Dacca, Bangladesh. ISBN 978-984-8866-18-4.

External links

 Wikimedia Commons has media related to *Bangladesh Liberation War*.

- Rare video documentary[1313] on YouTube
- Dateline Bangladesh: Documentary by Gita Mehta[1314] on YouTube
- The Liberation war of Bangladesh[1315]
- 1971 Bangladesh Genocide Archive[1316]
- Freedom In the Air[1317]
- Video, audio footage, news reports, pictures and resources from Muktomona[1318]
- Eyewitness Accounts: Genocide in Bangladesh[1319]
- The women of 1971. Tales of abuse and rape by the Pakistan Army[1320]
- 1971 Massacre in Bangladesh and the Fallacy in the Hamoodur Rahman Commission Report, Dr. M.A. Hasan[1321]
- Women of Pakistan Apologize for War Crimes, 1996[1322]
- Study finds no cases of rape by Pakistan Army in 1971[1323]
- Sheikh Mujib wanted a confederation: US papers, by Anwar Iqbal, Dawn, 7 July 2005[1324]
- Page containing copies of the surrender documents[1325]
- Bangladesh Liberation War Picture Gallery[1326]

Graphic images, viewer discretion advised

- Rashid Askari:Liberation War facts[1327]
- 1971 War: How Russia sank Nixon's gunboat diplomacy[1328]
- PM reiterated her vow to declare March 25 as Genocide Day[1329]
- Call for international recognition and observance of genocide day[1330]
- Genocide Day: As it was in March 1971[1331]
- The case for UN recognition of Bangladesh genocide[1332]
- Bangladesh war: The article that changed history By Mark Dummett[1333]

Green Revolution in India

The **Green Revolution in India** refers to a period of time when agriculture in India changed to an industrial system due to the adoption of modern methods and technology such as high yielding variety (HYV) seeds, tractors, irrigation facilities, pesticides, fertilizers etc. Green revolution was started by Norman Borlaug. The key leadership role played by the Indian agricultural scientist M.S.Swaminathan together with many others including GS Kalkat, M.S.Swaminathan earned him the popularly used title 'Father of Green Revolution of India'. The Green Revolution allowed developing countries, like India, to try to overcome poor agricultural productivity. Within India, this started in the early 1960s and led to an increase in food grain production, especially in Punjab, Haryana and Uttar Pradesh(especially Western UP) during the early phase. The main development was higher-yielding varieties of wheat, for developing rust resistant strains of wheat.

Practices

Wheat

The main development was higher-yielding varieties of wheat, for developing rust resistant strains of wheat. The introduction of high-yielding varieties(HYV) of seeds and the increased quality of fertilizers and irrigation technique led to the increase in production to make the country self-sufficient in food grains, thus improving agriculture in India. The methods adopted included the use of high-yielding varieties (HYVs) of seeds with modern farming methods.

The production of wheat has produced the best results in fueling self-sufficiency of India. Along with high-yielding seeds and irrigation facilities, the enthusiasm of farmers mobilised the idea of agricultural revolution. Due to the rise in use of chemical pesticides and fertilizers, there was a negative effect on the soil and the land (e.g., land degradation).

Green Revolution in India

Figure 251: *The state of Punjab led India's Green Revolution and earned the distinction of being the country's bread basket.*[1334]

Other practices

- Irrigation infrastructure
- Use of pesticides
  - Use of insecticides
  - Use of herbicides
- Consolidation of holdings
- Land reforms
- Improved rural infrastructure
- Supply of agricultural credit
- Use of chemical or synthetic fertilizers
- Use of sprinklers or drip irrigation systems
- Use of advanced machinery
- Use of vector quantity

Problems that were addressed

Frequent famines

Famines in India were very frequent during the period 1940s to 1970s. Due to faulty distribution of food, and because farmers did not receive the true value for their labour, the majority of the population did not get enough food.[1335] Malnutrition and starvation was a huge problem.Wikipedia:Citation needed

Lack of finance

Marginal farmers found it very difficult to get finance and credit at economical rates from the government and banks and hence, fell as easy prey to the money lenders. They took loans from zamindars, who charged high rates of interests and also exploited the farmers later on to work in their fields to repay the loans (farm labourers).Wikipedia:Citation needed Proper financing was not given during the Green Revolution period, which created a lot of problems and sufferings to the farmers of India. Government also helped those under loans.

Lack of self-sufficiency

Due to traditional agricultural practices, low productivity, and a growing population, often food grains were imported — draining scarce foreign reserves. It was thought that with the increased production due to the Green Revolution, the government could maintain buffer stock and India could achieve self-sufficiency and self-reliability.Wikipedia:Citation needed

Agriculture was basically for subsistence and, therefore, less agricultural product was offered for sale in the market. Hence, the need was felt to encourage the farmers to increase their production and offer a greater portion of their products for sale in the market. The new methods in agriculture increased the yield of rice and wheat, which reduced India's dependence on food imports.

Criticisms

Indian Economic Sovereignty

Criticism of the effects of the green revolution include the cost for many small farmers using HYV seeds, with their associated demands of increased irrigation systems and pesticides. A case study is found in India, where farmers are buying Monsanto BT cotton seeds—sold on the idea that these seeds produced 'natural insecticides'. In reality, they need to still pay for expensive pesticides and irrigation systems, which might lead to increased borrowing to finance the change from traditional seed varieties. Many farmers have difficulty in paying for the expensive technologies, especially if they have a bad harvest.

Indian environmentalist Vandana Shiva writes that this is the "second Green Revolution". The first Green Revolution, she suggests, was mostly publicly funded (by the Indian Government). This new Green Revolution, she says, is driven by private (and foreign) interest – notably MNCs like Monsanto. Ultimately, this is leading to foreign ownership over most of India's farmland.[1336]

Environmental Damage

Excessive and inappropriate use of fertilizers and pesticides has polluted waterway, killed beneficial insects and wild life. It has caused over-use of soil and rapidly depleted its nutrients. The rampant irrigation practices have led to eventually soil degradation. Groundwater practices have fallen dramatically. Further, heavy dependence on few major crops has led to loss of biodiversity of farmers. These problems were aggravated due to absence of training to use modern technology and vast illiteracy leading to excessive use of chemicals.[1337]

Increased Regional disparities

Green revolution spread only in irrigated and high-potential rain fed areas. The villages or regions without the access of sufficient water were left out that widened the regional disparities between adopters and non-adopters. Since, the HYV seeds technically can be applied only in land with assured water supply and availability of other inputs like chemicals, fertilizers etc. The application of the new technology in the dry-land areas is simply ruled out.

The states like Punjab, Haryana, Western UP etc. having good irrigation and other infrastructure facilities were able to derive the benefits of green revolution and achieve faster economic development while other states have recorded slow growth in agriculture production.

Restrictive Crop Coverage

The new agriculture strategy involving use of HYV seeds was initially limited to wheat, maize and bajra. The other major crop i.e. rice responded much later. The progress of developing and application of HYV seeds in other crops especially commercial crops like oilseeds, jute etc. has been very slow. In fact, in certain period a decline in the output of commercial crops is witnessed because of diversion of area under commercial crop to food crop production. The basic factor for non-spread of green revolution to many crops was that in the early 1960s the severe shortage in food grains existed and imports were resorted to overcome the shortage. Government initiated green revolution to increase food grain productivity and non-food grain crops were not covered. The substantial rise in one or two food grain crop cannot make big difference in the total agricultural production. Thus new technology contributed insignificantly in raising the overall agricultural production due to limited crop coverage. So it is important that the revolutionary efforts should be made in all major crops.

Operation Flood

Operation Flood, launched in 1970, was a project of India's National Dairy Development Board (NDDB), which was the world's biggest dairy development program. It transformed India from a milk-deficient nation into the world's largest milk producer, surpassing the USA in 1998, with about 17 percent of global output in 2010–11. In 30 years it doubled milk available per person, and made dairy farming India's largest self-sustainable rural employment generator. It was launched to help farmers direct their own development, placing control of the resources they create in their own hands. All this was achieved not merely by mass production, but by production by the masses.

The *Anand pattern experiment at Amul*, a single, cooperative dairy, was the engine behind the success of the program. Verghese Kurien, the chairman and founder of Amul, was named the chairman of NDDB by the then Prime Minister of India Lal Bahadur Shastri. Kurien gave the necessary thrust using his professional management skills to the program, and is recognized as its architect.

Introduction

Operation Flood is the program behind "the white revolution." It created a national milk grid linking producers throughout India with consumers in over 700 towns and cities, reducing seasonal and regional price variations while ensuring that the producer gets a major share of the price consumers pay, by cutting out middlemen. The bedrock of Operation Flood has been village milk producers' co-operatives, which procure milk and provide inputs and services, making modern management and technology available to members. Operation Flood's objectives included:

- Increase milk production ("a flood of milk")
- Augment rural incomes
- Fair prices for consumers

Figure 252: *Amul Dairy Plant at Anand, Gujarat, was a highly successful co-operative started during Operation Flood in the 1970s.*

Program implementation

Operation Flood was implemented in three phases.

Phase I

Phase I (1970–1980) was financed by the sale of skimmed milk powder and butter oil donated by the European Union (then the European Economic Community) through the World Food Program. NDDB planned the program and negotiated the details of EEC assistance. During this phase, Operation Flood linked 18 of India's premier milksheds with consumers in India's major metropolitan cities: Delhi, Mumbai, Kolkata and Chennai, establishing mother dairies in four metros. Operation Flood – It was originally meant to be completed in 1975, actually spanned the period of about nine years from 1970–79, at a total cost of Rs.116 crores.:[44] At the start of Operation Flood-I in 1970 certain aims were kept in view for the implementation of the programs: Improving the organized dairy sector in the metropolitan cities Mumbai (then Bombay), Kolkata (then Calcutta), Chennai (then Madras) and Delhi through marketing, increasing producers' share of the milk market, and speeding up development of dairy animals in rural areas to increase both production and procurement.

Phase II

Operation Flood Phase II (1981–1985) increased the milk-sheds from 18 to 136; urban markets expanded the outlets for milk to 290. By the end of 1985, a self-sustaining system of 43,000 village cooperatives with 4,250,000 milk producers were covered. Domestic milk powder production increased from

22,000 tons in the pre-project year to 140,000 tons by 1989, all of the increase coming from dairies set up under Operation Flood. In this way EEC gifts and the World Bank loan helped promote self-reliance. Direct marketing of milk by producers' cooperatives increased by several million liters a day.

Phase III

Phase III (1985–1996) enabled dairy cooperatives to expand and strengthen the infrastructure required to procure and market increasing volumes of milk. Veterinary first-aid health care services, feed and artificial insemination services for cooperative members were extended, along with intensified member education. Operation Flood's Phase III consolidated India's dairy cooperative movement, adding 30,000 new dairy cooperatives to the 43,000 existing societies organized during Phase II. Milk-sheds peaked at 173 in 1988-89 with the numbers of women members and Women's Dairy Cooperative Societies increasing significantly. Phase III increased emphasis on research and development in animal health and animal nutrition. Innovations like vaccine for Theileriosis, bypassing protein feed and urea-molasses mineral blocks, all contributed to the enhanced productivity of milk producing animals.

Features

There were some distinctive features behind the success of 'Operation Flood':

- Adopting new methods in case of cattle in animal husbandry through white revolution
- Changing the composition of feed ingredients in different proportions
- Fixing of different producer costs on a sliding scale of India

Criticisms

Critics of the project argue that the emphasis on imported breeds of cattle has resulted in the decimation of Indian breeds; while foreign breeds give higher yields, they require more feed and are not suited to Indian conditions.

External links

- Operation Flood on NDDB[1338]

Indo-Pakistani War of 1971

<indicator name="pp-default"> 🔒 </indicator>

Indo-Pakistani War of 1971
Part of the Indo-Pakistani wars and conflicts and Bangladesh Liberation War

Lieutenant-General A. A. K. Niazi, the commander of Pakistan Eastern Command, signing the instrument of surrender in Dhaka on 16 Dec 1971, in the presence of India's Lt. Gen. Jagjit Singh Aurora. Standing immediately behind from Left to Right: Indian Navy Vice Admiral Krishnan, Indian Air Force Air Marshal Dewan, Indian Army Lt Gen Sagat Singh, Maj Gen JFR Jacob (with Flt Lt Krishnamurthy peering over his shoulder). Veteran newscaster, Surojit Sen of All India Radio, is seen holding a microphone on the right.

Date	3–16 December 1971 (13 days)

Location	Eastern Front:
	• India–East Pakistan border
	  • Bay of Bengal
	  • Pasha enclaves
	Western Front:
	• India–Pakistan border
	  • Line of Control
	  • Arabian Sea

Result	Decisive Indian victory. **Eastern front:** Surrender of East Pakistan military command. **Western front:** Unilateral Ceasefire.
Territorial changes	Eastern Front: • Independence of East Pakistan as Bangladesh Western Front: • Indian forces captured around 5,795 square miles (15,010 km^2) land in the West but returned it in the Simla Agreement as a gesture of goodwill.

Belligerents	
🇮🇳 India	☪ Pakistan
🏴 Provisional Government of Bangladesh	East Pakistan

| Commanders and leaders ||

V. V. Giri (President of India)	Yahya Khan (President of Pakistan)
Indira Gandhi (Prime Minister of India)	Nurul Amin (Prime Minister of Pakistan)
Swaran Singh (External Minister of India)	Gen. A.H. Khan (Chief of Staff, Army GHQ)
Jagjivan Ram (Defence Minister of India)	Lt.Gen A.A.K. Niazi ⚑ (Commander, Eastern Command)
Gen Sam Manekshaw (Chief of Army Staff)	Lt.Gen Gul Hassan Khan (Chief of General Staff)
Lt.Gen J.S. Arora (GOC-in-C, Eastern Command)	Lt.Gen Abdul Ali Malik (Commander, I Corps)
Lt.Gen G.G. Bewoor (GOC-in-C, Southern Command)	Lt.Gen Tikka Khan (Commander, II Corps)
Lt.Gen K. P. Candeth (GOC-in-C, Western Command)	Lt.Gen Sher Khan (Commander, IV Corps)
Lt.Gen Manohar Lal (GOC-in-C, Northern Command)	MGen Iftikhar Janjua † (GOC, 23rd Infantry Division)
Lt.Gen Premindra Bhagat (GOC-in-C, Central Command)	MGen Khadim Hussain (GOC, 14th Infantry Division)
Lt.Gen Sagat Singh (GOC-in-C, IV Corps)	VAdm Muzaffar Hassan (Cdr-in-Chief, Navy)
Lt.Gen T. N. Raina (GOC-in-C, II Corps)	RAdm Rashid Ahmed (COS, Navy NHQ)
Lt.Gen Sartaj Singh (GOC-in-C, XV Corps)	RAdm Moh'd Shariff ⚑ (Cdr, Eastern Naval Command)
Lt.Gen Karan Singh (GOC-in-C, I Corps)	RAdm M.A.K. Lodhi (Cdr, Western Naval Command)
Lt.Gen Depinder Singh (GOC-in-C, XII Corps)	RAdm Leslie Norman (Commander, Pakistan Marines)
MajGen Farj R. Jacob (COS, Eastern Command)	AM Abdul Rahim Khan (Cdr-in-Chief, Air Force)
MajGen Om Malhotra (COS, IV Corps)	AVM P.D. Callaghan (Chief Ins, Pakistan Air Force)
MajGen Inderjit Singh Gill (Dir, Military Operations)	Air Cdre Inamul Haq ⚑ (Cdr Eastern Air Command)
Adm S. M. Nanda (Chief of Naval Staff)	Gp.Capt. Z.A. Khan ⚑ (COS, Air AHQ Dhaka)
VAdm S. N. Kohli (Cdr. Western Naval Command)	Abdul Motaleb Malik ⚑ (Governor of East Pakistan)
ACM Pratap C. Lal (Chief of Air Staff)	
Rameshwar Kao (Director of RAW)	
Tajuddin Ahmad (PM Provisional Government)	
Col. M.A.G. Osmani (Commander, Mukti Bahini)	
Strength	
Indian Armed Forces: 500,000 Mukti Bahini: 175,000 Total: **675,000**	Pakistan Armed Forces: **365,000**
Casualties and losses	

2,500–3,843 killed.[1339] • 1 Naval aircraft • Damage to western Indian airfields. **Pakistani claims** • 130 IAF Aircraft **Indian claims** • 45 IAF Aircraft **Neutral claims** • 45 IAF Aircraft	9,000 killed 25,000 wounded[1340] 97,368 captured 2 Destroyers 1 Minesweeper 1 Submarine 3 Patrol vessels 7 Gunboats • Pakistani main port Karachi facilities damaged/-fuel tanks destroyed • Pakistani airfields damaged and cratered **Pakistani claims** • 42 PAF Aircraft **Indian claims** • 94 PAF Aircraft **Neutral claims** • 75 PAF Aircraft

The **Indo-Pakistani War of 1971** was a military confrontation between India and Pakistan that occurred during the liberation war in East Pakistan from 3 December 1971 to the fall of Dacca (Dhaka) on 16 December 1971. The war began with preemptive aerial strikes on 11 Indian air stations, that led to the commencement of hostilities with Pakistan and Indian entry into the war of independence in East Pakistan on the side of Bengali nationalist forces. Lasting just 13 days, it is one of the shortest wars in history.

During the war, Indian and Pakistani militaries simultaneously clashed on the eastern and western fronts; the war ended after the Eastern Command of the Pakistan military signed the Instrument of Surrender on 16 December 1971 in Dhaka, marking the formation of East Pakistan as the new nation of Bangladesh. Officially, East Pakistan had earlier called for its secession from the unity of Pakistan on 26 March 1971. Approximately 90,000 to 93,000 Pakistani servicemen were taken prisoner by the Indian Army, which included 79,676 to 81,000 uniformed personnel of the Pakistan Armed Forces, including some Bengali soldiers who had remained loyal to Pakistan. The remaining 10,324 to 12,500 prisoners were civilians, either family members of the military personnel or collaborators (razakars).[1341] It is estimated that between 300,000 and 3,000,000 civilians were killed in Bangladesh.[1342,1343] As a result of the conflict, a further eight to ten million people fled the country to seek refuge in India.[1344]

During the 1971 Bangladesh war for independence, members of the Pakistani military and supporting Islamist militias called the Razakars raped between 200,000 and 400,000 Bangladeshi women and girls in a systematic campaign of genocidal rape.[1345,1346,1347]

Background

The Indo-Pakistani conflict was sparked by the armed liberation struggle in East Pakistan between the dominant Bengalis and the multi-ethnic West Pakistanis over the right to govern and the constitution.:24 The political tensions between East Bengal and West Pakistan had its origin in the creation of Pakistan as a result of the partition of India by the United Kingdom in 1947; the popular language movement in 1950; mass riots in East Bengal in 1964; and the mass protests in 1969. These led to the resignation of President Ayub Khan, who invited army chief General Yahya Khan to take over the central government.:xxx The geographical distance between the eastern and western wings of Pakistan was vast; East Pakistan lay over 1,000 miles (1,600 km) away, which greatly hampered any attempt to integrate the Bengali and the Pakistani cultures.:13–14Wikipedia:Verifiability#Self-published sources:xxi

To overcome the Bengali domination and prevent formation of the central government in Islamabad, the controversial One Unit program established the two wings of East and West Pakistan. West Pakistanis' opposition to these efforts made it difficult to effectively govern both wings.:xxx In 1969, President Yahya Khan announced the first general elections and disestablished the status of West Pakistan as a single province in 1970, in order to restore it to its original heterogeneous status comprising four provinces, as defined at the time of establishment of Pakistan in 1947. In addition, there were also religious and racial tensions between Bengalis and the multi-ethnic West Pakistanis, as Bengalis looked different from the dominant West Pakistanis.:24–25

The general elections, held in 1970, resulted in East Pakistan's Awami League gaining 167 out of 169 seats for the East Pakistan Legislative Assembly, and a near-absolute majority in the 313-seat National Assembly, while the vote in West Pakistan was mostly won by the socialist Pakistan Peoples Party.:686–687 The Awami League leader Sheikh Mujibur Rahman stressed his political position by presenting his Six Points and endorsing the Bengalis' right to govern.:xxx The League's election success caused many West Pakistanis to fear that it would allow the Bengalis to draft the constitution based on the six-points and liberalism.:xlv

To resolve the crisis, the Ahsan–Yaqub Mission was formed to provide recommendations, and its findings were met with favourable reviews from the Awami League, the Pakistan Peoples Party, and the Pakistan Muslim League as well as from President Yahya Khan.:109–110

However, the mission was not supported by the elements in the National Security Council and was subsequently vetoed.:110 Zulfikar Ali Bhutto, the chairman of Pakistan Peoples Party, endorsed the veto and subsequently refused to yield the premiership of Pakistan to Sheikh Mujibur Rahman. The Awami

Indo-Pakistani War of 1971

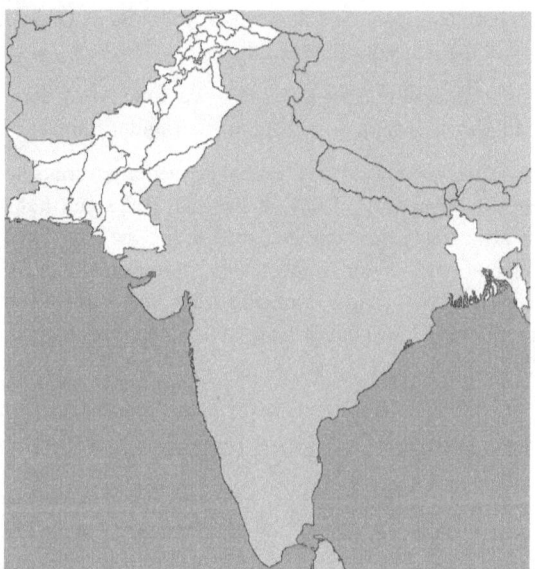

Figure 253: *Maps shows Pakistan and East Pakistan. Distance between East and Pakistan laid 1,000 miles (1,600 km) of Indian territory.*

League called for general strikes in the country.[110] President Yahya Khan postponed the inauguration of the National Assembly, causing a shattering disillusionment to the Awami League and their supporters throughout East Pakistan. In reaction, Sheikh Mujibur Rahman called for general strikes that eventually shutdown the government, and dissidents in the East began targeting the ethnic Bihari community, which had supported West Pakistan.

In early March 1971, approximately 300 Biharis were slaughtered in riots by Bengali mobs in Chittagong alone. The Government of Pakistan used the "Bihari massacre" to justify its deployment of the military in East Pakistan on 25 March, when it initiated its military crackdown. President Yahya Khan called on the military - which was overwhelmingly led by West Pakistanis - to suppress dissent in the East, after accepting the resignation of Lieutenant-General Yaqub Ali Khan, the chief of staff of the East-Pakistani military.[1348]

Mass arrests of dissidents began and, after several days of strikes and non-cooperation, the Pakistani military, led by Lieutenant-General Tikka Khan, cracked down on Dhaka on the night of 25 March 1971. The government outlawed the Awami League, which forced many of its members and sympathisers into refuge in Eastern India. Mujib was arrested on the night of 25/26 March 1971 at about 1:30 am (as per Radio Pakistan's news on 29 March 1971) and taken to West Pakistan. Operation Searchlight, followed by Operation Barisal, attempted to kill the intellectual elite of the east.

On 26 March 1971, Major Ziaur Rahman of Pakistan Army declared the independence of Bangladesh on behalf of Sheikh Mujibur Rahman.[1349,1350]

In April, the exiled Awami League leaders formed a government-in-exile in Baidyanathtala of Meherpur. The East Pakistan Rifles and Bengali officers in Pakistan's army, navy, and marines, defected to the rebellion after taking refuge in different parts of India. The Bangladesh Force, namely the Mukti Bahini, consisting of Niyomito Bahini (Regular Force) and Oniyomito Bahini (Guerilla Force), was formed under the retired colonel Mohammad Ataul Gani Osmani.[1351]

India's involvement in Bangladesh Liberation War

After the resignations of Admiral S.M. Ahsan and Lieutenant-General Yaqub Ali Khan, the media correspondents began airing reports of the Pakistani military's widespread genocide against their Bengali citizens, particularly aimed at the minority Bengali Hindu population,[1352] which led to approximately 10 million people seeking refuge in the neighbouring states of Eastern India. The Indian government opened the East Pakistan–India border to allow the Bengali refugees to find safe shelter; the governments of West Bengal, Bihar, Assam, Meghalaya and Tripura established refugee camps along the border.:[23–24] The resulting flood of impoverished East Pakistani refugees strained India's already overburdened economy.

The Indian government repeatedly appealed to the international community for assistance, but failed to elicit any response, despite the External Affairs minister Swaran Singh meeting foreign ministers of other countries. Prime Minister Indira Gandhi on 27 March 1971 expressed full support of her government for the independence struggle of the people of East Pakistan, and concluded that instead of taking in millions of refugees, it was economical to go to war against Pakistan. On 28 April 1971, the Gandhi cabinet had ordered the Chief of the Army Staff General Sam Manekshaw to "Go into East Pakistan". Defected East Pakistan military officers and the elements of Indian Research and Analysis Wing (RAW) immediately started using the Indian refugee camps for recruitment and training of Mukti Bahini guerrillas that were to be trained against Pakistan. In 1971, a strong wave of Indian-supported Bangladeshi nationalism emerged in the East. Violence and the systematic targeted killings of unarmed multi-ethic Pakistanis living in the East started.:[164] Vehicle bombings on government secretariats became a normal narrative in news reports, and high-profile assassinations of Bengali politicians loyal to Pakistan became common in the East.:[164] According to Jussi Hanhimäki, Finnish historian of terrorism, the Bengali terrorism in the East is a somewhat "forgotten episode of annals of terrorism.":164 The Hamoodur Rahman Commission endorsed the claims of Bengali terrorism when it critically penned that the ill-treatment of families of multi-ethnic Pakistanis led to the Pakistani military soldiers reacting violently to restore the writ of the government.

The news media's mood in Pakistan had also turned increasingly jingoistic and militaristic against East Pakistan and India when the Pakistani news media reported the complexity of the situation in the East, though the reactions from Pakistan's news media pundits were mixed. By the end of September 1971, a propaganda campaign, possibly orchestrated by elements within the Government of Pakistan, resulted in stickers endorsing *Crush India* becoming a standard feature on the rear windows of vehicles in Rawalpindi, Islamabad and Lahore; this soon spread to the rest of West Pakistan. By October, other stickers proclaimed *Hang the Traitor* in an apparent reference to Sheikh Mujibur Rahman. By the first week of December, the conservative print media outlets in the country had published *jihad* related materials to boost the recruitment in the military.

India's official engagement with Pakistan

Objective

By the end of April 1971, Prime Minister Indira Gandhi had asked the Indian Army chief General Sam Manekshaw if he was ready to go to war with Pakistan.[1353] According to Manekshaw's own personal account, he refused, citing the onset of monsoon season in East Pakistan and also the fact that the army tanks were being being refitted. He offered his resignation, which Gandhi declined. He then said he could guarantee victory if she would allow him to prepare for the conflict on his terms, and set a date for it; Gandhi accepted his conditions.[1354] In reality, Gandhi was well aware of the difficulties of a hasty military action, but she needed to get the military's views to satisfy her hawkish colleagues and the public opinion, which were critical of India's restraint.

By November 1971, and Indian-Pakistani war seemed inevitable. The Soviet Union reportedly warned Pakistan against the war, which they termed as "suicidal course for Pakistan's unity.":part-3 Despite this warning, in November 1971, thousands of people led by conservative Pakistani politicians marched in Lahore and across Pakistan, calling for Pakistan to *Crush India*. India responded by starting a massive buildup of the Indian Army on the western borders; the army waited until December, when the drier ground in the East would have made for easier operations and the Himalayan passes would have been

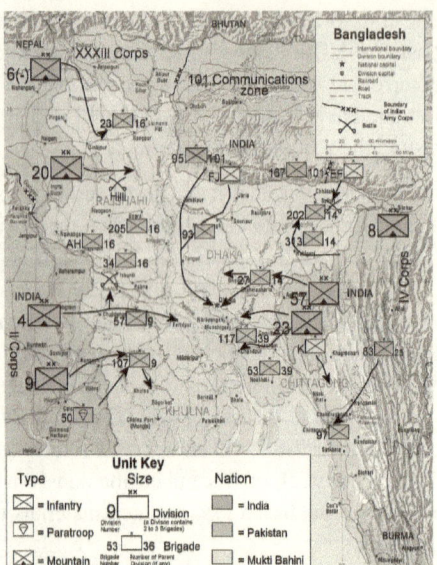

Figure 254: *Illustration showing military units and troop movements during operations in the Eastern sector of the war.*

closed by snow, preventing any Chinese intervention.:174–175 On 23 November, President Yahya Khan declared a state of emergency in all of Pakistan and told his people to prepare for war.

On the evening of 3 December, at about 5:40 pm, the Pakistan Air Force (PAF) launched surprise pre-emptive strikes on eleven airfields in north-western India, including Agra, which was 300 miles (480 km) from the border.:82–83 At the time of this attack, the Taj Mahal had been camouflaged with a forest of twigs and leaves and draped with burlap, because its marble glowed like a white beacon in the moonlight.

These preemptive strikes, known as Operation Chengiz Khan, were inspired by the success of Israeli Operation Focus in the Arab–Israeli Six-Day War. Unlike the Israeli attack on Arab airbases in 1967, which involved a large number of Israeli planes, Pakistan flew no more than 50 planes to India.:821355

In an address to the nation on radio that same evening, Prime Minister Gandhi held that the air strikes were a declaration of war against India and the Indian Air Force (IAF) responded with initial air strikes that very night. These expanded to massive retaliatory air strikes the next morning.

This air action marked the official start of the Indo-Pakistani War of 1971; Prime Minister Gandhi ordered the immediate mobilisation of troops and

Figure 255: *Pakistan's PNS Ghazi sank off the fairway buoy of Visakhapatnam near the eastern coast of India, making it the first submarine casualty in the waters around the Indian subcontinent.*

launched a full-scale invasion of Pakistan.:333 This involved Indian forces in massive coordinated air, sea and land assaults on Pakistan from all fronts.:333 The main Indian objective on the Eastern front was to capture Dacca, and on the Western front was to prevent Pakistan from entering Indian soil. There was no Indian intention of conducting any major offensive into Pakistan to dismember it into different states.

Naval hostilities

Unlike the 1965 war, the Navy NHQ staffers and commanders of the Pakistan Navy knew very well that the Navy was ill-prepared for the naval conflict with India.:65 The Pakistan Navy was in no condition of fighting an offensive war in deep sea against the Indian Navy, and neither was it in a condition to mount serious defence against Indian Navy's seaborne encroachment.:75–76

In the western theatre of the war, the Indian Navy's Western Naval Command under Vice Admiral S.N. Kohli, successfully launched a surprise attack on Karachi port on the night of 4/5 December 1971 under the codename *Trident*. The naval attack involving the Soviet-built Osa missile boats sank the Pakistan Navy's destroyer PNS *Khyber* and minesweeper PNS *Muhafiz* while

PNS *Shah Jahan* was also badly damaged. Pakistani naval sources reported that about 720 Pakistani sailors were killed or wounded, and Pakistan lost reserve fuel and many commercial ships, thus crippling the Pakistan Navy's further involvement in the conflict.:85–87 In retaliation, the Pakistan Navy submarines, *Hangor*, *Mangro*, and *Shushuk*, began their operations to seek out the major Indian warships.:86–95[1356] On 9 December 1971, *Hangor* reportedly sank INS *Khukri*, inflicting 194 Indian casualties, and this attack was the first submarine kill since World War II.:229

The sinking of INS *Khukri* was followed by another Indian attack on Karachi port on the night of 8/9 December 1971 under the codename *Python*. A squadron of Indian Navy's Osa missile boats approached the Karachi port and launched a series of Soviet-acquired Styx missiles, that resulted in further destruction of reserve fuel tanks and the sinking of three Pakistani merchant ships, as well as foreign ships docked in Karachi. The Pakistan Air Force did not attack the Indian Navy ships, and confusion remained the next day when the civilian pilots of Pakistan International, acting as reconnaissance war pilots, misidentified PNS *Zulfiqar* and the air force attacked its own warship, inflicting major damages and killing several officers on board.

In the eastern theatre of the war, the Indian Eastern Naval Command, under Vice Admiral Nilakanta Krishnan, completely isolated East Pakistan by a naval blockade in the Bay of Bengal, trapping the Eastern Pakistan Navy and eight foreign merchant ships in their ports.:82–83 From 4 December onwards, the aircraft carrier INS *Vikrant* was deployed, and its Sea Hawk fighter-bombers attacked many coastal towns in East Pakistan, including Chittagong and Cox's Bazar. Pakistan countered the threat by sending the submarine PNS *Ghazi*, which sank en route under mysterious circumstances off Visakhapatnam's coast.[1357]

Due to high number of defections, the Navy relied on deploying the Pakistan Marines - led by Rear Admiral Leslie Mungavin - where they had to conduct riverine operations against the Indian Army, but they too suffered major losses, mainly due to their lack of understanding of expeditionary warfare and the wet terrain of East Pakistan.

The damage inflicted on the Pakistan Navy stood at 7 gunboats, 1 minesweeper, 1 submarine, 2 destroyers, 3 patrol crafts belonging to the coast guard, 18 cargo, supply and communication vessels; and large-scale damage inflicted on the naval base and docks in the coastal town of Karachi. Three merchant navy ships – *Anwar Baksh*, *Pasni* and *Madhumathi* – and ten smaller vessels were captured. Around 1900 personnel were lost, while 1413 servicemen were captured by Indian forces in Dacca. According to one Pakistani scholar, Tariq Ali, Pakistan lost half its navy in the war.

Figure 256: *Indian aircraft carrier INS Vikrant launches an Alize aircraft*

Air operations

After the sneak attack, the PAF adopted a defensive stance in response to the Indian retaliation. As the war progressed, the IAF continued to battle the PAF over conflict zones, but the number of sorties flown by the PAF decreased day–by–day.[1358,1359] The IAF flew 4,000 sorties while the PAF offered little in retaliation, partly because of the paucity of non-Bengali technical personnel.

This lack of retaliation has also been attributed to the deliberate decision of the PAF's Air AHQ to cut its losses, as it had already incurred huge losses in the conflict in the liberation war in the East. The PAF avoided making contacts with the Indian Navy after the latter raided the port of Karachi twice, but the PAF did retaliate by bombing Okha harbour, destroying the fuel tanks used by the boats that had attacked.

In the East, No. 14 Squadron Tail Choppers under Squadron Leader PQ Mehdi, who was taken as POW, was destroyed, putting the Dhaka air defence out of commission and resulting in Indian air superiority in the East.

At the end of the war, PAF pilots made successful daring escapes from East Pakistan to neighbouring Burma; many PAF personnel had already left the East for Burma on their own before Dacca was overrun by the Indian military in December 1971.

Indian attacks on Pakistan

As Indian Army tightened its grip in the East Pakistan, the Indian Air Force continued with its attacks against Pakistan as the campaign developed into a series of daylight anti-airfield, anti-radar, and close-support attacks by fighter jets, with night attacks against airfields and strategic targets by B-57s and C-130s of Pakistan and Canberras and An-12s of India.:[107–108]

The PAF deployed the F-6s mainly on defensive combat air patrol missions over their own bases, but without the preferential air superiority, it was unable to conduct effective offensive operations.:[107–108] The IAF's raids damaged one USAF and one UN aircraft in Dacca, while the RCAF's DHC-4 Caribou was also destroyed in Islamabad, along with the USAF's Beech U-8 owned by the US military's liaison chief Brigadier-General Chuck Yeager.:[107] Sporadic raids by the IAF continued against PAF forward air bases in Pakistan until the end of the war, and interdiction and close-support operations were maintained.:[107]

One of the most successful air raids by India into West Pakistan happened on 8 December 1971, when Indian Hunter aircraft from the Pathankot-based 20 Squadron, attacked the Pakistani base in Murid and destroyed 5 F-86 aircraft on the ground. This was confirmed by Pakistan's military historian, Air Commodore M Kaiser Tufail, in his book 'In The Ring and On Its Feet - Pakistan Air Force in the 1971 Indo-Pak War'.

The PAF played a more limited role in the operations and were reinforced by F-104s from Jordan, Mirages from an unidentified Middle Eastern ally (whose identity remains unknown), and by F-86s from Saudi Arabia.:[107] Their arrival helped camouflage the extent of PAF losses, and the Libyan F-5s were reportedly deployed to Sargodha AFB, perhaps as a potential training unit to prepare Pakistani pilots for an influx of more F-5s from Saudi Arabia.:[112] The IAF was able to conduct a wide range of missions – troop support; air combat; deep penetration strikes; para-dropping behind enemy lines; feints to draw enemy fighters away from the actual target; bombing and reconnaissance.:[107] The PAF, which was solely focused on air combat, was blown out of the subcontinent's skies within the first week of the war.:[107] Those PAF aircraft that survived took refuge at Iranian air bases or in concrete bunkers, refusing to offer a fight.[1360]

India flew 1,978 sorties in the East and about 4,000 in Pakistan, while the PAF flew about 30 and 2,840 at the respective fronts.:[107] More than 80 percent of IAF sorties were close-support and interdiction and about 45 IAF aircraft were lost.

Pakistan lost 75 aircraft, not including any F-6s, Mirage IIIs, or the six Jordanian F-104s which failed to return to their donors. The imbalance in air losses was explained by the IAF's considerably higher sortie rate and its emphasis on ground-attack missions.

Ground operations

Before the start of the war, the Indian Army was well organised on both fronts and enjoyed significant numerical superiority over the Pakistan Army.:596 The Indian Army's extraordinary war performance at both fronts brought up the prestige, confidence, and dignity that it had lost during the war with China in 1962.

When the conflict started, the war immediately took a decisive turn in favour of India and their Bengali rebel allies militarily and diplomatically.:596 On both fronts, Pakistan launched several ground offensives, but the Indian Army held its ground and initiated well-coordinated ground operations on both fronts.:596 Major ground attacks were concentrated on the western border by the Pakistan Army, together with the Pakistan Marines in the south border, but the Indian Army was successful in penetrating into Pakistani soil. It eventually made some quick and initial gains, including the capture of around 5,795 square miles (15,010 km^2) of Pakistani territory; this land gained by India in Azad Kashmir, Punjab and Sindh sectors was later ceded in the Simla Agreement of 1972, as a gesture of goodwill. Casualties inflicted to Pakistan Army's I Corps and II Corps were very high, and many soldiers perished due to lack of operational planning and lack of coordination within the army's formations against Indian Army's Southern and Western Commands.:82–93 By the time the war came to end, Pakistan Army soldiers and marines were highly demoralized - both emotionally and psychologically - on the western front and had no will to put up a defensive fight against the approaching Indian Army soldiers.:1–2:26–27Wikipedia:Verifiability#Self-published sources

The War Enquiry Commission later exposed the fact that for the Pakistan Army, the arms and training of soldiers and officers were needed at every level, and every level of command.

On 23 November 1971, the Indian Army conventionally penetrated to the eastern fronts and crossed East Pakistan's borders to join their Bengali nationalist allies.:156 Contrary to the 1965 war, which had emphasised set-piece battles and slow advances, this time the strategy adopted was a swift, three-pronged assault of nine infantry divisions with attached armoured units and close air support that rapidly converged on Dacca, the capital of East Pakistan.:156 Lieutenant General Jagjit Singh Aurora, the GOC-in-C of the Indian Army's Eastern Command, led the full Indian thrust into East Pakistan. As the Indian Eastern Command attacked the Pakistan Eastern Command, the Indian Air Force rapidly destroyed the small air contingent in East Pakistan and put the Dacca airfield out of commission.:156 In the meantime, the Indian Navy effectively blockaded East Pakistan.:156

The Indian campaign's "*blitzkrieg*" techniques exploited weaknesses in the Pakistani positions and bypassed opposition; this resulted in a swift victory.[1361:802] Faced with insurmountable losses, the Pakistani military capitulated in less than a fortnight and psychological panic spread in the Eastern Command's military leadership.[:802] Subsequently, the Indian Army encircled Dacca and issued an ultimatum to surrender in "30-minutes" time window on 16 December 1971. Upon hearing the ultimatum, the Pakistan Eastern Command, led by its commander Lieutenant-General A.A.K. Niazi, surrendered without offering any resistance. On 16 December 1971, Pakistan ultimately called for unilateral ceasefire and surrendered its combined military to the Indian Army– hence ending the Indo-Pakistani war of 1971.

On the ground, Pakistan suffered the most, with 8,000 killed and 25,000 wounded, while India only had 3,000 dead and 12,000 wounded.[1340] The loss of armoured vehicles was similarly imbalanced and this finally represented a major defeat for Pakistan.

Surrender of Pakistan Eastern Command in East Pakistan

Officially, the Instrument of Surrender of Pakistan Eastern Command stationed in East Pakistan, was signed between the Lieutenant General Jagjit Singh Aurora, the GOC-in-C of Indian Eastern Command and Lieutenant-General A.A.K. Niazi, the Commander of the Pakistan Eastern Command, at the Ramna Race Course in Dacca at 16:31Hrs IST on 16 December 1971.[:156–157]Wikipedia:Verifiability#Self-published sources As the surrender was accepted silently by Lieutenant-General Aurora, the surrounding crowds on the race course started shouting anti-Pakistan slogans, and there were reports of abuses aimed at the surrendering commanders of Pakistani military.[:157]Wikipedia:Verifiability#Self-published sourcesWikipedia:Verifiability#Self-published sources

Hostilities officially ended at 14:30 GMT on 17 December, after the fall of Dacca on 15 December, and India claimed large gains of territory in Pakistan (although pre-war boundaries were recognised after the war). The war confirmed the independence of Bangladesh.[:107]

Following the surrender, the Indian Army took approximately 90,000 Pakistani servicemen and their Bengali supporters as POWs, making it the largest surrender since World War II.[:157]Wikipedia:Verifiability#Self-published sources Initial counts recorded that approximately 79,676 war prisoners were uniformed personnel, and the overwhelming majority of the war prisoners were officers - most of them were from the Army and Navy, while relatively small numbers were from the Air Force and Marines; others in larger number were serving in the paramilitary.

The remaining prisoners were civilians who were either family members of the military personnel or collaborators (razakars). The Hamoodur Rahman Commission and the POW Investigation Commission reports instituted by Pakistan lists the Pakistani POWs as given in the table below. Apart from soldiers, it was estimated that 15,000 Bengali civilians were also made prisoners of war.

Inter-Service Branch	Number of captured Pakistani POWs	Officer Commanding
Pakistan Army	54,154	Lieutenant-General Amir Abdullah Khan Niazi
Pakistan Navy/Pakistan Marines	1,381	Rear-Admiral Mohammad Shariff
Pakistan Air Force	833	Air Commodore Inamul Haq
Paramilitary/East Pakistan Rifles/Police	22,000	Major-General Rao Farman Ali
Civil government personnel	12,000	Governor Abdul Motaleb Malik
Total:	90,368	~

Foreign reaction and involvement

United States and Soviet Union

The Soviet Union sympathised with the East Pakistanis, and supported the Indian Army and Mukti Bahini's incursion against Pakistan during the war, in a broader view of recognising that the succession of East Pakistan as Independent Bangladesh would weaken the position of its rivals— the United States and China. The Soviet Union gave assurances to India that if a confrontation with the United States or China developed, it would take counter-measures. This assurance was enshrined in the Indo-Soviet Treaty of Friendship and Cooperation signed in August 1971.

However, the Indo-Soviet treaty did not mean a total commitment to every Indian position, even though the Soviet Union had accepted the Indian position during the conflict, according to author Robert Jackson.:72–73 The Soviet Union continued its sympathetic gesture to Pakistan until mid-October 1971, when it stressed Pakistan to come up with a political settlement and affirmed its continuation of industrial aid to Pakistan.:73 By November 1971, the Soviet ambassador to Pakistan Alexei Rodionov directed a secretive message (*Rodionov message*) that ultimately warned Pakistan that "it will be embarking on a suicidal course if it escalates tensions in the subcontinent.:part-3

The United States stood with Pakistan by supporting it morally, politically, economically and materially when U.S. President Richard Nixon and his Secretary of State Henry Kissinger refused to use rhetoric in a hopeless attempt to

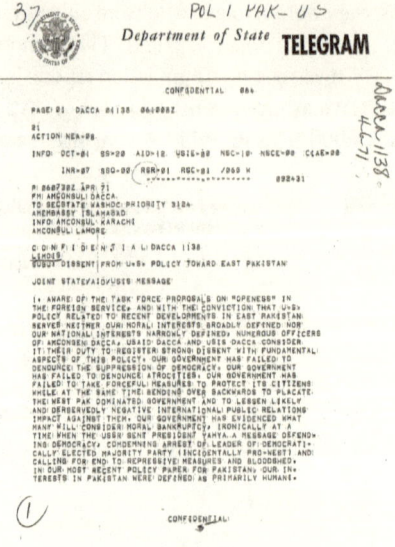

Figure 257: *The Blood Telegram*

intervene in a large civil war. The U.S. establishment perceived to the impression that they needed Pakistan to help stop Soviet influence in South Asia in an informal alliance with India.:281 During the Cold War, Pakistan was a close formal ally of the United States and also had close relations with the People's Republic of China, with whom Nixon had been negotiating a *rapprochement* and where he intended to visit in February 1972.[1362] Nixon feared that an Indian invasion of Pakistan would mean total Soviet domination of the region, and that it would seriously undermine the global position of the United States and the regional position of America's new tactical ally, China.:281–282 Nixon encouraged Jordan and Iran to send military supplies to Pakistan, while also encouraging China to increase its arms supplies to Pakistan, but all supplies were very limited.:61 The Nixon administration also ignored reports it received of the "genocidal" activities of the Pakistani military in East Pakistan, most notably the Blood telegram, and this prompted widespread criticism and condemnation - both by the United States Congress and in the international press.

Then U.S. Ambassador to the United Nations, George Bush, Sr, introduced a resolution in the UN Security Council calling for a cease-fire and the withdrawal of armed forces by India and Pakistan.:73 However, it was vetoed by the Soviet Union, and the following days witnessed the use of great pressure on the Soviets from the Nixon-Kissinger duo to get India to withdraw, but to no avail.

When Pakistan's defeat in the eastern sector seemed certain, Nixon deployed Task Force 74 - led by the aircraft carrier USS *Enterprise* - into the Bay of Bengal. *Enterprise* and its escort ships arrived on station on 11 December 1971.:xxxx According to a Russian documentary, the United Kingdom also deployed a carrier battle group led by the aircraft carrier HMS *Eagle* to the Bay,WP:NOTRS on her final deployment.

On 6 and 13 December, the Soviet Navy dispatched two groups of cruisers and destroyers from Vladivostok; they trailed US Task Force 74 into the Indian Ocean from 18 December 1971 until 7 January 1972. The Soviets also had a nuclear submarine to help ward off the threat posed by the USS *Enterprise* task force in the Indian Ocean.

As the war progressed, it became apparent to the United States that India was going to invade and disintegrate Pakistan in a matter of weeks, therefore President Nixon spoke with the USSR Secretary General Leonid Brezhnev on a hotline on 10 December, where Nixon reportedly urged Brezhnev to restrain India as he quoted: "in the strongest possible terms to restrain India with which ... you [Brezhnev] have great influence and for whose actions you must share responsibility."

After the war, the United States accepted the new balance of power and recognised India as a dominant player in South Asia; the US immediately engaged in strengthening bilateral relations between the two countries in the successive years.:69 The Soviet Union, while being sympathetic to Pakistan's loss, decided to engage with Pakistan after sending an invitation through Rodionov to Z A Bhutto, who paid a state visit to the Soviet Union in 1972 to strengthen bilateral relations that continued over the years.:16

China and Iran

During the course of the war, China harshly criticised India for its involvement in the East Pakistan crises, and accused India of having imperialistic designs in South Asia.:19 Before the war started, Chinese leaders and officials had long been philosophically advising the Pakistan government to make peaceful political settlements with the East Pakistani leaders, as China feared that India was secretly supporting, infiltrating, and arming the Bengali rebels against the East Pakistani government.:61:285 China was also critical of the Government of East Pakistan, led by its Governor Lieutenant-General Tikka Khan - which used ruthless measures to deal with the Bengali opposition - and did not endorse the Pakistani position on that issue.:285

When the war started, China reproached India for its direct involvement and infiltration in East Pakistan.:285 It disagreed with Pakistani President Yahya Khan's consideration of military options, and criticised East Pakistan Awami League politicians' ties with India.:285 China reacted with great alarm when the prospects of Indian invasion of Pakistan and integration of Pakistan-administered Kashmir into their side of Kashmir, became imminent. US President Nixon encouraged China to mobilise its armed forces along its border with India to discourage the Indian assault, but the Chinese did not respond to this encouragement since the Indian Army's Northern Command was well prepared to guard the Line of Actual Control, and was already engaging and making advances against the Pakistan Army's X Corps in the Line of Control.:xxxiiiWikipedia:Verifiability#Self-published sources

China did not welcome the break-up of Pakistan's unity by the East Pakistani politicians, and effectively vetoed the membership of Bangladesh when it applied to the United Nations in 1972. China objected to admitting Bangladesh on the grounds that two UN resolutions concerning Bangladesh, requiring the repatriation of Pakistani POWs and civilians, had not yet been implemented. Furthermore, China was also among the last countries to recognise the independence of Bangladesh, refusing to do so until 31 August 1975.:226–227 To this date, its relations with Bangladesh are determined by the Pakistan factor.:69

During the course of the conflict, Iran also stood with Pakistan politically and diplomatically.:78–79 It was concerned with the imminent break-up of Pakistan which, it feared, would have caused the state to fractionalise into small pieces, ultimately resulting in Iran's encirclement by rivals. After the war, however, Iran began cementing ties with India based on mutual security cooperation.:79Wikipedia:Verifiability At the beginning of the conflict, Iran had helped Pakistan by sheltering PAF's fighter jets and providing it with free fuel to take part in the conflict, in an attempt to keep Pakistan's regional integrity united.:80Wikipedia:Verifiability When Pakistan called for unilateral ceasefire and the surrender was announced, the Shah of Iran hastily responded by preparing the Iranian military to come up with contingency plans to forcefully invade Pakistan and annex its Balochistan province into its side of Balochistan, by any means necessary, before anybody else did it.:79Wikipedia:Verifiability

Aftermath

India

The war stripped Pakistan of more than half of its population, and with nearly one-third of its army in captivity, clearly established India's military and political dominance of the subcontinent. India successfully led a diplomatic campaign to isolate Pakistan and skillfully manipulate Pakistan's supporting countries to limit the extent of support to Pakistan.:596 In addition, Prime Minister Indira Gandhi's state visit to United Kingdom and France further helped break ice with the United States, and blocked any pro-Pakistan resolution in the United Nations.:596 There was also a meeting between Prime Minister Gandhi and President Nixon in November 1971,Wikipedia:Please clarify where she rejected the US advice against intervening in the conflict.:596

The victory also defined India's much broader role in foreign politics, as many countries in the world had come to realise - including the United States - that the balance of power had shifted to India as a major player in the region.:80:57 In the wake of changing geopolitical realities, India sought to establish closer relations with regional countries such as Iran, which was a traditional ally of Pakistan.:57 The United States itself accepted a new balance of power, and when India conducted a surprise nuclear test in 1974, the US notified India that it had no "interest in actions designed to achieve new balance of power.":69

In spite of the magnitude of the victory, India was surprisingly restrained in its reaction. Mostly, Indian leaders seemed pleased by the relative ease with which they had accomplished their goals—the establishment of Bangladesh and the prospect of an early return to their homeland of the 10 million Bengali refugees who were the cause of the war. In announcing the Pakistani surrender, Prime Minister Indira Gandhi declared in the Indian Parliament:

> *Dacca is now the free capital of a free country. We hail the people of Bangladesh in their hour of triumph. All nations who value the human spirit will recognise it as a significant milestone in man's quest for liberty.*

Colonel John Gill of National Defense University, US, remarks that, while India achieved a military victory, it was not able to reap the political fruits it might have hoped for in Bangladesh. After a brief 'honeymoon' phase between India and Bangladesh, their relationship began to sour. India's relations with Bangladesh have remained frequently problematic and tense. Whilst India enjoys excellent relations with Bangladesh during Awami League tenures, relations deteriorate when the Bangladesh Nationalist Party is in power. A 2014 Pew Research Center opinion poll in Bangladesh found that India was perceived as the greatest threat to Bangladesh. This was the top choice (27%) of Bangladeshis. However, 70% of Bangladeshis held a positive view of India: while 50% of Bangladeshis held a positive view of Pakistan.

Pakistan

For Pakistan, the war was a complete and humiliating defeat, a psychological setback that came from a defeat at the hands of rival India. Pakistan lost half its population and a significant portion of its economy, and suffered setbacks to its geopolitical role in South Asia. In the post-war era, Pakistan struggled to absorb the lessons learned from the military interventions in the democratic system and the impact of the Pakistani military's failure was grave and long-lasting.

From the geopolitical point of view, the war ended in the breaking-up of the unity of Pakistan from being the largest Muslim country in the world to its politico-economic and military collapse that resulted from a direct foreign intervention in 1971.:50Wikipedia:Verifiability#Self-published sources:47:1[1363] The Pakistani policy-making institutions further feared that the historicity of the Two-nation theory had been disproved by the war, that Muslim nationalism had proved insufficient to keep Bengalis a part of Pakistan.

The Pakistani people were not mentally prepared to accept the magnitude of this kind of defeat, as the state electronic media had been projecting imaginary victories; however, the privately-owned electronic news media coverage in East Pakistan had reported the complexity of the situation. When the cease-fire that came from the surrender of East Pakistan was finally announced, the people could not come to terms with the magnitude of defeat; spontaneous demonstrations and massive protests erupted on the streets of major metropolitan cities in Pakistan. According to Pakistani historians, the trauma was extremely severe, and the cost of the war for Pakistan in monetary terms and in human resources was very high.:xxx[1364] Demoralized and finding unable to control the situation, the Yahya administration fell when President Yahya Khan turned over his presidency to Zulfiqar Ali Bhutto, who was sworn in on 20 December 1971 as President with the control of the military.

The loss of East Pakistan shattered the prestige of the Pakistani military. Pakistan lost half its navy, a quarter of its air force, and a third of its army. The war also exposed the shortcomings of Pakistan's declared strategic doctrine that the "defence of East Pakistan lay in West Pakistan". Hussain Haqqani, in his book *Pakistan: Between Mosque and Military* notes,

> Moreover, the army had failed to fulfill its promises of fighting to the last man. The eastern command had laid down arms after losing only 1,300 men in battle. In West Pakistan 1,200 military deaths had accompanied lackluster military performance.[1365]

In his book *The 1971 Indo-Pak War: A Soldier's Narrative*, Pakistan Army's Major General Hakeem Arshad Qureshi, a veteran of this conflict, noted:

We must accept the fact that, as a people, we had also contributed to the bifurcation of our own country. It was not a Niazi, or a Yahya, even a Mujib, or a Bhutto, or their key assistants, who alone were the cause of our break-up, but a corrupted system and a flawed social order that our own apathy had allowed to remain in place for years. At the most critical moment in our history we failed to check the limitless ambitions of individuals with dubious antecedents and to thwart their selfish and irresponsible behaviour. It was our collective 'conduct' that had provided the enemy an opportunity to dismember us.

The Indian Army Chief in 1971, Field Marshal Sam Manekshaw, had the highest respect for the fighting capability of the Pakistan Army, and he did not accept the theory that they did not fight the war with enough vigour and zeal. In a BBC interview, he said:

The Pakistan Army in East Pakistan fought very gallantly. But they had no chance. They were a thousand miles away from their base. I had eight or nine months to make my preparations. I had got a superiority of almost 15 to 1....[1366]

However, independent defence sources stated that the Indian superiority was less than 2 to 1.[1367] The United States Air Force's Brigadier-General Chuck Yeager, the World War II veteran and US flying ace who witnessed the war in 1971, is of the view that Pakistan did not lose the war, as India did not annex it.

After the war, the Pakistan Army's generals in the East held each other responsible for the atrocities committed, but most of the burden was laid on Lieutenant-General Tikka Khan, who earned notoriety from his actions as governor of the East; he was called the "Butcher of Bengal" because of the widespread atrocities committed within the areas of his responsibility. Unlike his contemporary Yaqub who was a pacifist and knew well of the limits of force, Tikka was a "soldier known for his eager use of force" to settle his differences.[100]

Confessing at the hearings of the War Enquiry Commission, Lieutenant-General A.A.K. Niazi reportedly commented on Tikka's actions and noted: "On the night between 25/26 March 1971, [General] Tikka struck. Peaceful night was turned into a time of wailing, crying and burning. [General] Tikka let loose everything at his disposal as if raiding an enemy, not dealing with his own misguided and misled people. The military action was a display of stark cruelty more merciless than the massacres at Bukhara and Baghdad by Chengiz Khan and Halaku Khan... [General] Tikka... resorted to the killing of civilians and a scorched earth policy. His orders to his troops were: "I want the land, not the people...""."Wikipedia:Verifiability#Self-published sources:[295]

Major-General Rao Farman reportedly had written in his table diary: "Green land of East Pakistan will be painted red. It was painted red by Bengali blood." However, Farman forcefully denied writing that comment, and laid all responsibility on Tikka, while testifying at the War Enquiry Commission in 1974.

Major reforms were carried out by successive governments in Pakistan after the war in the light of many insightful recommendations made in the Hamoodur Rahman Commission's Report.:254 To address the economic disparity, the NFC system was established to equally distribute the taxation revenue among the four provinces, the large-scale nationalization of industries and nationwide census were carried out in 1972. The Constitution was promulgated in 1973 that reflected this equal balance and a compromise between Islamism and Humanism, and provided guaranteed equal human rights to all. The military was heavily reconstructed and heavily reorganised, with President Bhutto appointing chiefs of staff in each inter-service, contrary to C-in-Cs, and making instruction on human rights compulsory in the military syllabus in each branch of inter-services.:62–100 Major investments were directed towards modernising the navy.:100 The military's chain of command was centralized in JS HQ led by an appointed Chairman joint chiefs committee to coordinate the combined and well-integrated military efforts to safeguard the nation's defence and unity.:62–63 In addition, Pakistan sought to have a diversified foreign policy, as Pakistani geostrategists had been shocked that both China and the United States provided limited support to Pakistan during the course of the war, with the US displaying an inability to supply weapons that Pakistan needed the most.:xxxiii

On January 20, 1972, Pakistan under Bhutto launched the clandestine development of nuclear weapons in a view of "never to allow another foreign invasion of Pakistan.":133–135 This crash program reached parity in 1977 when the first weapon design was successfully achieved.

Bangladesh

As a result of the war, East Pakistan disintegrated and became an independent country, Bangladesh, as the world's fourth most populous Muslim state on 16 December 1971.:xxxv Pakistan itself secured the release of Sheikh Mujibur Rahman from the Headquarter Prison and allowed him to return to Dacca. On 19 January 1972, Mujib was inaugurated as the first President of Bangladesh, later becoming the Prime Minister of Bangladesh in 1974.:xxxv

On the brink of defeat in around 14 December 1971, the media reports indicated that the Pakistan Army soldiers, the local East Pakistan Police they controlled, *razakars* and the *Shanti Committee* carried out systematic killings of professionals such as physicians, teachers, and other intellectuals, as part of a pogrom against the Bengali Hindu minorities who constituted the majority of urban educated intellectuals.

Young men, especially students, who were seen as possible rebels and recruiters were also targeted by the stationed military, but the extent of casualties in East Pakistan is not known, and the issue is itself controversial and contradictory among the authors who wrote books on the pogrom; the Pakistani government itself denied the charges of its involvement in 2015.:511–512 R.J. Rummel cites estimates ranging from one to three million people killed.[1344] Other estimates place the death toll lower, at 300,000. Bangladesh government figures state that Pakistani forces aided by collaborators killed three million people, raped 200,000 women and displaced millions of others.

According to the authors Kenton Worcester, Sally Bermanzohn, and Mark Ungar, Bengalis themselves killed about 150,000 non-Bengalis living in the East.[111] There had been reports of Bengali insurgents indiscriminately killing non-Bengalis throughout the East; however, neither side provided substantial proofs for their claims and both Bangladeshi and Pakistani figures contradict each other over this issue.:108:133 Bihari representatives in June 1971 claimed a higher figure of 500,000 killed by Bengalis.

In 2010, the Awami League's government decided to set up a tribunal to prosecute the people involved in alleged war crimes and those who collaborated with Pakistan. According to the government, the defendants would be charged with crimes against humanity, genocide, murder, rape and arson.

According to John H. Gill, there was widespread polarisation between pro-Pakistan Bengalis and pro-liberation Bengalis during the war, and those internal battles are still playing out in the domestic politics of modern-day Bangladesh. To this day, the issue of committed atrocities and pogroms is an influential factor in the foreign relations between Pakistan and Bangladesh.

Impact

Pakistan: War Enquiry Commission and War prisoners

In the aftermath of the war, the Pakistani Government constituted the War Enquiry Commission, to be headed by Chief Justice Hamoodur Rahman, who was an ethnic Bengali, and composed of the senior justices of the Supreme Court of Pakistan. The War Enquiry Commission was mandated with carrying out thorough investigations into the intelligence, strategic, political and military failures that causes the defeat in the war.:44Wikipedia:Verifiability#Self-published sources

The War Commission also looked into Pakistan's political and military involvement in the history of East Pakistan that encompasses

1947–71.:⁴⁴Wikipedia:Verifiability#Self-published sources The First War Report was submitted in July 1972, but it was very critically opined and penned on political misconducts of politicians and the military interference in national politics.:22–197 Written in moral and philosophical perspective, the First Report was lengthy and provided accounts that were unpalatable to be released to the public. Initially, there were 12 copies that were all destroyed, except for the one that was kept and marked as "Top Secret" to prevent the backlash effects on the demoralised military.:127 In 1976, the Supplementary Report was submitted, which was the comprehensive report compiled together with the First Report; this report was also marked as classified.

In 2000, the excerpts of the Supplementary Report were leaked to a political correspondent of Pakistan's *Dawn*, which the *Dawn* published together with *India Today*. The First Report is still marked as classified, while the Supplementary Report's excerpts were suppressed by the news correspondents.:288–289 The War Report's supplementary section was published by the Pakistan Government, but it did not officially hand over the report to Bangladesh despite its requests.)

The War Report exposed many military failures, from the strategic to the tactical–intelligence levels, while it confirmed the looting, rapes and the unnecessary killings by the Pakistan military and their local agents. It laid the blame squarely on Pakistan Army generals, accusing them of debauchery, smuggling, war crimes and neglect of duty. The War Commission had recommended public trial of Pakistan Army generals on the charges that they had been responsible for the situation in the first place and that they had succumbed without a fight, but no actions were ever taken against those responsible, except the dismissal of chiefs of the Pakistan Army, Pakistan Air Force, Pakistan Navy, and decommissioning of the Pakistan Marines.

The War Commission, however, rejected the charge that 200,000 Bengali girls were raped by the Pakistan Army, remarking, "It is clear that the figures mentioned by the Dacca authorities are altogether fantastic and fanciful," and cited the evidence of a British abortion team that had carried out the termination of "only a hundred or more pregnancies".[1368] The Commission also claimed that "approximately 26,000 persons (were) killed during the action by the Pakistan military"[1369] Bina D'Costa states that the War Commission was aware of the military's brutality in East Pakistan, but "chose to downplay the scale of the atrocities committed."

The second commission was known as Indo-Pakistani War of 1971 Prisoners of War Investigation, conducted solely by the Pakistani government, that was to determine the numbers of Pakistani military personnel who surrendered, including the number of civilian POWs. The official number of the surrendered military personnel was soon released by the Government of Pakistan after the war was over.

India: Indo-Pakistani Summits

On 2 July 1972, the Indo-Pakistani summit was held in Simla, Himachal Pradesh, India where the Simla Agreement was reached and signed between President Zulfikar Ali Bhutto and Prime Minister Indira Gandhi. The treaty provided insurance to Bangladesh that Pakistan recognised Bangladesh's sovereignty, in exchange for the return of the Pakistani POWs. In mere five months, India systematically released more than 90,000 war prisoners, with Lieutenant-General A.A.K. Niazi being the last war prisoner to be handed over to Pakistan.

The treaty also gave back more than 13,000 km^2 of land that the Indian Army had seized in Pakistan during the war, though India retained a few strategic areas, including Turtuk, Dhothang, Tyakshi (earlier called Tiaqsi) and Chalunka of Chorbat Valley, which was more than 804 km^2. The Indian hardliners, however, felt that the treaty had been too lenient to President Bhutto, who had pleaded for leniency, arguing that the fragile stability in Pakistan would crumble if the accord was perceived as being overly harsh by Pakistanis and that he would be accused of losing Kashmir in addition to the loss of East Pakistan. As a result, Prime Minister Gandhi was criticised by a section in India for believing Bhutto's "sweet talk and false vows", while the other section claimed the agreement to be successful, for not letting it to fall into "Versailles Syndrome" trap.

In 1973, India and Pakistan reached another compromise when both countries signed a trilateral agreement with Bangladesh that actually brought the war prisoners, non-Bengali and Pakistan-loyal Bengali bureaucrats and civilian servants to Pakistan. The Delhi Agreement witnessed the largest mass population transfer since the Partition of India in 1947.

Bangladesh: International Crimes Tribunal

In 2009, the issue of establishing the International Crimes Tribunal began to take public support. The tribunal was formally established in 2010 to investigate and prosecute suspects for the genocide committed in 1971 by the Pakistan Army and their local collaborators, *Razakars*, *Al-Badr* and *Al-Shams* during the Bangladesh Liberation War.[1370:169]

Long-term consequences

- Steve Coll, in his book *Ghost Wars*, argues that the Pakistan military's experience with India, including Pervez Musharraf's experience in 1971, influenced the Pakistani government to support jihadist groups in Afghanistan even after the Soviets left, because the jihadists were a tool to use against India, including bogging down the Indian Army in Kashmir.[1371,1372]
- After the war, Zulfikar Ali Bhutto authorised the highly secretive and clandestine atomic bomb programme, as part of its new deterrence policy, to defend itself and never to allow another armed invasion from India.Wikipedia:Citation needed Many Pakistani scientists, working abroad at the IAEA and European and American nuclear programmes, immediately returned to what remained of Pakistan and participated in making Pakistan a nuclear power.Wikipedia:Citation needed
- Writing about the war in *Foreign Affairs* magazine, Zulfikar Ali Bhutto stated "There is no parallel in contemporary history to the cataclysm which engulfed Pakistan in 1971. A tragic civil war, which rent asunder the people of the two parts of Pakistan, was seized by India as an opportunity for armed intervention. The country was dismembered, its economy shattered and the nation's self-confidence totally undermined." This statement of Bhutto has given rise to the myth of betrayal prevalent in modern Pakistan. This view was contradicted by the post-War Hamoodur Rahman Commission, ordered by Bhutto himself, which in its 1974 report indicted generals of the Pakistan Army for creating conditions which led to the eventual loss of East Pakistan and for inept handling of military operations in the East.

Military awards

Battle honours

After the war, 41 battle honours and 4 theatre honours were awarded to units of the Indian Army; notable among them are:

- East Pakistan 1971 (theatre honour)
- Sindh 1971 (theatre honour)
- Jammu and Kashmir 1971 (theatre honour)
- Punjab 1971 (theatre honour)
- Basantar River
- Bogra
- Chachro
- Chhamb
- Defence of Punch
- Dera Baba Nanak
- Gadra City
- Harar Kalan
- Hilli
- Longewala
- Parbat Ali
- Poongli Bridge
- Shehjra
- Shingo River Valley
- Sylhet

Gallantry awards

For bravery, a number of soldiers and officers on both sides were awarded the highest gallantry award of their respective countries. Following is a list of the recipients of the Indian award Param Vir Chakra, Bangladeshi award Bir Sreshtho and the Pakistani award Nishan-E-Haider:

India

Recipients of the Param Vir Chakra:

- Lance Naik Albert Ekka (Posthumously)
- Flying Officer Nirmal Jit Singh Sekhon (Posthumously)
- Major Hoshiar Singh
- Second Lieutenant Arun Khetarpal (Posthumously)

Bangladesh

Recipients of the Bir Sreshtho:

- Captain Mohiuddin Jahangir (Posthumously)
- Lance Naik Munshi Abdur Rouf (Posthumously)
- Sepoy Hamidur Rahman (Posthumously)
- Sepoy Mostafa Kamal (Posthumously)
- ERA Mohammad Ruhul Amin (Posthumously)
- Flight Lieutenant Matiur Rahman (Posthumously)
- Lance Naik Nur Mohammad Sheikh (Posthumously)

Pakistan

Recipients of the Nishan-E-Haider:

- Major Muhammad Akram (Posthumously)
- Pilot Officer Rashid Minhas (Posthumously)
- Major Shabbir Sharif (Posthumously)
- Sarwar Muhammad Hussain (Posthumously)
- Lance Naik Muhammad Mahfuz (Posthumously)

Civilian awards

On 25 July 2011, Bangladesh Swadhinata Sammanona, the Bangladesh Freedom Honour, was posthumously conferred on former Indian Prime Minister Indira Gandhi.

On 28 March 2012, President of Bangladesh Zillur Rahman and the Prime Minister Sheikh Hasina conferred Bangladesh Liberation War Honour and Friends of Liberation War Honour to 75 individuals, six organisations, Mitra Bahini and the people of India at a special ceremony at the Bangabandhu International Conference Centre, Dhaka. This included eight heads of states: former Nepalese President Ram Baran Yadav, the third King of Bhutan Jigme Dorji Wangchuck, former Soviet Presidents Leonid Ilyich Brezhnev and Nikolai Viktorovich Podgorny, former Soviet Prime Minister Alexei Nikolaevich Kosygin, former Yugoslav President Marshal Josip Broz Tito, former UK Prime Minister Sir Edward Richard George Heath and former Nepalese Prime Minister Bishweshwar Prasad Koirala. The organisations include the BBC, Akashbani (All India Radio), International Committee of the Red Cross, United Nations High Commissioner for Refugees, Oxfam and Kolkata University Shahayak Samiti.

The list of foreign friends of Bangladesh has since been extended to 568 people. It includes 257 Indians, 88 Americans, 41 Pakistanis, 39 Britons, 9 Russians, 18 Nepalese, 16 French and 18 Japanese.

Dramatization

Films

- *Border*, a 1997 Bollywood war film directed by J.P.Dutta. This movie is an adaptation from real life events that happened at the Battle of Longewala fought in Rajasthan (Western Theatre) during the 1971 Indo-Pak war. *Border*[1373] on IMDb
- *Hindustan Ki Kasam*, a 1973 Bollywood war film directed by Chetan Anand. The aircraft in the film are all authentic aircraft used in the 1971 war against Pakistan. These include MiG-21s, Gnats, Hunters and Su-7s. Some of these aircraft were also flown by war veterans such as Samar Bikram Shah (2 kills) and Manbir Singh. *Hindustan Ki Kasam*[1374] on IMDb
- *Aakraman*, 1975 Bollywood film set during this war featuring a romantic love triangle.
- *1971 – Prisoners of War*, a 2007 Bollywood war film directed by Sagar Brothers. Set against the backdrop of a prisoners' camp in Pakistan, follows six Indian prisoners awaiting release after their capture in the 1971 India-Pakistan war.

- *The Ghazi Attack*, a 2017 war film directed by Sankalp Reddy. Based on the sinking of PNS Ghazi during the war.
- *1971: Beyond Borders*, a 2017 Indian war drama film written and directed by Major Ravi

Short Films

- *Mukti - Birth of a Nation*, a 2017 short film directed by Manu Chobe depicts the negotiations between Jacob and Niazi over the Instrument of Surrender.[1375]

Miniseries/Dramas

- *PNS Ghazi*, an Urdu (Pakistani) drama based on sinking of PNS Ghazi, ISPR

Further reading

- Cilano, Cara, ed. (2010). *Pakistaniaat: Special issue on 1971 War*.
- Hanhimäki, Jussi M. (2004). *The Flawed Architect: Henry Kissinger and American Foreign Policy*[1376]. Oxford University Press. ISBN 978-0-19-517221-8.
- Haqqani, Hussain (2005). *Pakistan: Between Mosque and Military*[1377]. United Book Press. ISBN 978-0-87003-214-1.
- Niazi, General A. A. K. (1999). *Betrayal of East Pakistan*[1378]. Oxford University Press. ISBN 978-0-19-579275-1.
- Palit, D K (1972). *The Lightning Campaign: The Indo-Pakistan War 1971*[1379]. Compton Press Ltd. ISBN 978-0-900193-10-1.
- Raghavan, Srinath (2013). *1971 – A global History of Creation of Bangladesh*[1380] (PDF). Harvard University Press. ISBN 978-0-674-72864-6.
- Raja, Dewan Mohammad Tasawwar (2010). *O General My General (Life and Works of General M A G Osmany)*. The Osmany Memorial Trust, Dhaka, Bangladesh. ISBN 978-984-8866-18-4.
- Saigal, J R (2000). *Pakistan Splits: The Birth of Bangladesh*[1381]. Manas Publications. ISBN 9788170491248.

External links

- Video of General Niazi Surrendering[1382]
- A complete coverage of the war from the Indian perspective[1383]
- An Atlas of the 1971 India – Pakistan War: The Creation of Bangladesh by John H. Gill[1384]

- Actual conversation from the then US President Nixon and Henry Kissinger during the 1971 War[1385] – US Department of State's Official archive.
- Indian Army: Major Operations[1386]
- Pakistan: Partition and Military Succession USA Archives[1387]
- Pakistan intensifies air raid on India BBC[1388]
- A day by day account of the war as seen in a virtual newspaper.[1389]
- The Tilt: The U.S. and the South Asian Crisis of 1971.[1390]
- *16 December 1971: any lessons learned?* By Ayaz Amir[1391] – Pakistan's Dawn
- India-Pakistan 1971 War as covered by TIME[1392]
- Indian Air Force Combat Kills in the 1971 war (unofficial), Centre for Indian Military History[1393]
- Op Cactus Lilly: 19 Infantry Division in 1971, a personal recall by Lt Col Balwant Singh Sahore[1394]
- All for a bottle of Scotch, a personal recall of Major (later Major General) C K Karumbaya, SM, the battle for Magura[1395]
- "The Rediff Interview/Lt Gen A A Khan Niazi"[1396]. Rediff. 2 February 2004.

The Emergency (India)

In India, "**the Emergency**" refers to a 21-month period from 1975 to 1977 when Prime Minister Indira Gandhi had a state of emergency declared across the country. Officially issued by President Fakhruddin Ali Ahmed under Article 352 of the Constitution because of the prevailing "internal disturbance", the Emergency was in effect from 25 June 1975 until its withdrawal on 21 March 1977. The order bestowed upon the Prime Minister the authority to rule by decree, allowing elections to be suspended and civil liberties to be curbed. For much of the Emergency, most of Gandhi's political opponents were imprisoned and the press was censored. Several other human rights violations were reported from the time, including a forced mass-sterilization campaign spearheaded by Sanjay Gandhi, the Prime Minister's son. The Emergency is one of the most controversial periods of independent India's history.

The final decision to impose an emergency was proposed by Indira Gandhi, agreed upon by the president of India, and thereafter ratified by the cabinet and the parliament (from July to August 1975), based on the rationale that there were imminent internal and external threats to the Indian state.

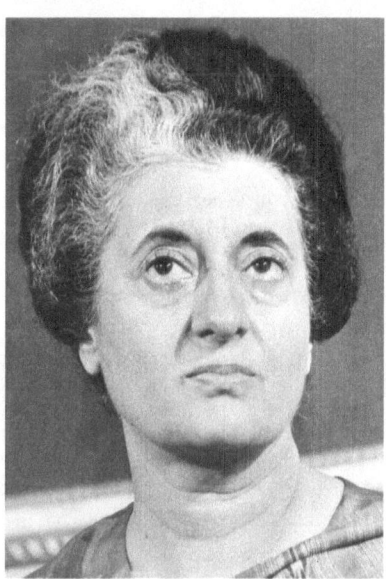

Figure 258: *Prime Minister Indira Gandhi, who had President of India Fakhruddin Ali Ahmed proclaim a state of national emergency on 25 June 1975*

Prelude

Rise of Indira Gandhi

—Congress president D. K. Barooah, c. 1974[1397]

Between 1967 and 1971, Prime Minister Indira Gandhi came to obtain near-absolute control over the government and the Indian National Congress party, as well as a huge majority in Parliament. The first was achieved by concentrating the central government's power within the Prime Minister's Secretariat, rather than the Cabinet, whose elected members she saw as a threat and distrusted. For this she relied on her principal secretary, P. N. Haksar, a central figure in Indira's inner circle of advisors. Further, Haksar promoted the idea of a "committed bureaucracy" that required hitherto-impartial government officials to be "committed" to the ideology of the ruling party of the day.

Within the Congress, Indira ruthlessly outmanoeuvred her rivals, forcing the party to split in 1969—into the Congress (O) (comprising the old-guard known as the "Syndicate") and her Congress (R). A majority of the All-India Congress Committee and Congress MPs sided with the prime minister. Indira's party was of a different breed from the Congress of old, which had been a robust institution with traditions of internal democracy. In the Congress (R), on the other hand, members quickly realised that their progress within the ranks depended solely on their loyalty to Indira Gandhi and her family, and ostentatious displays of sycophancy became routine. In the coming years, Indira's influence was such that she could install hand-picked loyalists as chief ministers of states, rather than their being elected by the Congress legislative party.

Indira's ascent was backed by her charismatic appeal among the masses that was aided by her government's near-radical leftward turns. These included the July 1969 nationalisation of several major banks and the September 1970 abolition of the privy purse; these changes were often done suddenly, via ordinance, to the shock of her opponents. Subsequently, unlike the Syndicate and other opponents, Indira was seen as "standing for socialism in economics and secularism in matters of religion, as being pro-poor and for the development of the nation as a whole."[1398] The prime minister was especially adored by the disadvantaged sections—the poor, Dalits, women and minorities.Wikipedia:Citation needed For them, she was their *Indira Amma*, a personification of Mother India.Wikipedia:Citation needed

In the 1971 general elections, the people rallied behind Indira's populist slogan of *Garibi Hatao!* (get rid of poverty!) to award her a huge majority (352 seats out of 518). "By the margin of its victory," historian Ramachandra Guha later wrote, Congress (R) came to be known as the real Congress, "requiring no qualifying suffix." In December 1971, under her proactive war leadership, India routed arch-enemy Pakistan in a war that led to the independence of Bangladesh, formerly East Pakistan. Awarded the Bharat Ratna the next month, she was at her greatest peak; for her biographer Inder Malhotra, "*The Economist*'s description of her as the 'Empress of India' seemed apt." Even opposition leaders, who routinely accused her of being a dictator and of fostering a personality cult, referred to her as *Durga*, a Hindu goddess.[1399]

Increasing government control of the judiciary

In 1967's *Golaknath* case, the Supreme Court said that the Constitution could not be amended by Parliament if the changes affect basic issues such as fundamental rights. To nullify this judgement, Parliament dominated by the Indira Gandhi Congress, passed the 24th Amendment in 1971. Similarly, after the government lost a Supreme Court case for withdrawing the privy purse given to erstwhile princes, Parliament passed the 26th Amendment. This gave constitutional validity to the government's abolition of the privy purse and nullified the Supreme Court's order.

This judiciary–executive battle would continue in the landmark *Kesavananda Bharati* case, where the 24th Amendment was called into question. With a wafer-thin majority of 7 to 6, the bench of the Supreme Court restricted Parliament's amendment power by stating it could not be used to alter the "basic structure" of the Constitution. Subsequently, Prime Minister Gandhi made A. N. Ray—the senior most judge amongst those in the minority in *Kesavananda Bharati*—Chief Justice of India. Ray superseded three judges more senior to him—J. M. Shelat, K.S. Hegde and Grover—all members of the majority in *Kesavananda Bharati*. Indira Gandhi's tendency to control the judiciary met with severe criticism, both from the press and political opponents such as Jayaprakash Narayan ("JP").

Political and civic unrest

During 1973–75, political unrest against the Indira Gandhi government increased across the country. (This led some Congress party leaders to demand a move towards a presidential system, with a more powerful directly elected executive.) The most significant of the initial such movement was the Nav Nirman movement in Gujarat, between December 1973 and March 1974. Student unrest against the state's education minister ultimately forced the central government to dissolve the state legislature, leading to the resignation of the chief minister, Chimanbhai Patel, and the imposition of President's rule. After the re-elections in June 1975, Gandhi's party was defeated by the Janata alliance, formed by parties opposed to the ruling Congress party. Meanwhile there were assassination attempts on public leaders as well as the assassination of the railway minister L.N.Mishra by a bomb. All of these indicated a growing law and order problem in the entire country, which Mrs. Gandhi's advisors warned her of for months.

In March–April 1974, a student agitation by the Bihar Chatra Sangharsh Samiti received the support of Gandhian socialist Jayaprakash Narayan, referred to as *JP*, against the Bihar government. In April 1974, in Patna, JP called for "total revolution," asking students, peasants, and labour unions to non-violently transform Indian society. He also demanded the dissolution of the state government, but this was not accepted by Centre. A month later, the railway-employees union, the largest union in the country, went on a nationwide railways strike. This strike was brutally suppressed by the Indira Gandhi government, which arrested thousands of employees and drove their families out of their quarters.

Raj Narain verdict

Raj Narain, who had been defeated in the 1971 parliamentary election by Indira Gandhi, lodged cases of election fraud and use of state machinery for election purposes against her in the Allahabad High Court. Shanti Bhushan fought the case for Narain. Indira Gandhi was also cross-examined in the High Court which was the first such instance for an Indian Prime Minister.

On 12 June 1975, Justice Jagmohanlal Sinha of the Allahabad High Court found the prime minister guilty on the charge of misuse of government machinery for her election campaign. The court declared her election null and void and unseated her from her seat in the Lok Sabha. The court also banned her from contesting any election for an additional six years. Serious charges such as bribing voters and election malpractices were dropped and she was held responsible for misusing government machinery, and found guilty on charges such as using the state police to build a dais, availing herself of the services of a government officer, Yashpal Kapoor, during the elections before he had resigned from his position, and use of electricity from the state electricity department.

Because the court unseated her on comparatively frivolous charges, while she was acquitted on more serious charges, *The Times* described it as "firing the Prime Minister for a traffic ticket".Wikipedia:Citation needed Her supporters organized mass pro-Indira demonstrations in the streets of Delhi close to the Prime Minister's residence. The persistent efforts of Narain were praised worldwide as it took over four years for Justice Sinha to pass judgement against the prime minister.Wikipedia:Citation needed

Indira Gandhi challenged the High Court's decision in the Supreme Court. Justice V. R. Krishna Iyer, on 24 June 1975, upheld the High Court judgement and ordered all privileges Gandhi received as an MP be stopped, and that she be debarred from voting. However, she was allowed to continue as Prime Minister pending the resolution of her appeal. JP Narayan and Morarji Desai called for daily anti-government protests. The next day, JP organised a large rally in Delhi, where he said that a police officer must reject the orders of government if the order is immoral and unethical as this was Mahatma Gandhi's motto during the freedom struggle. Such a statement was taken as a sign of inciting rebellion in the country. Later that day, Indira Gandhi requested a compliant President Fakhruddin Ali Ahmed to issue a proclamation of a state of emergency. Within three hours, the electricity to all major newspapers was cut and the political opposition arrested. The proposal was sent without discussion with the Union Cabinet, who only learnt of it and ratified it the next morning.

Proclamation of the Emergency

The Government cited threats to national security, as a war with Pakistan had recently been concluded. Due to the war and additional challenges of drought and the 1973 oil crisis, the economy was in poor condition. The Government claimed that the strikes and protests had paralysed the government and hurt the economy of the country greatly. In the face of massive political opposition, desertion and disorder across the country and the party, Gandhi stuck to the advice of a few loyalists and her younger son Sanjay Gandhi, whose own power had grown considerably over the last few years to become an "extra-constitutional authority". Siddhartha Shankar Ray, the Chief Minister of West Bengal, proposed to the prime minister to impose an "internal emergency". He drafted a letter for the President to issue the proclamation on the basis of information Indira had received that "there is an imminent danger to the security of India being threatened by internal disturbances". He showed how democratic freedom could be suspended while remaining within the ambit of the Constitution.[1400]

After a quick question regarding a procedural matter, President Fakhruddin Ali Ahmed declared a state of internal emergency upon the prime minister's advice on the night of 25 June 1975, just a few minutes before the clock struck midnight.

As the constitution requires, Mrs. Gandhi advised and President Ahmed approved the continuation of Emergency over every six-month period until her decision to hold elections in 1977.

Administration

Indira Gandhi devised a '20-point' economic programme to increase agricultural and industrial production, improve public services and fight poverty and illiteracy, through "the discipline of the graveyard".[1401] In addition to the official twenty points, Sanjay Gandhi declared his own five-point programme promoting literacy, family planning, tree planting, the eradication of casteism and the abolition of dowry. Later during the Emergency, the two projects merged into a twenty-five point programme.

Arrests

Invoking article 352 of the Indian Constitution, Gandhi granted herself extraordinary powers and launched a massive crackdown on civil liberties and political opposition. The Government used police forces across the country to place thousands of protestors and strike leaders under preventive detention. Vijayaraje Scindia, Jayaprakash Narayan, Raj Narain, Morarji Desai, Charan Singh, Jivatram Kripalani, Atal Bihari Vajpayee, Lal Krishna Advani, Arun Jaitley, Satyendra Narayan Sinha, Gayatri Devi, the dowager queen of Jaipur and other protest leaders were immediately arrested. Organisations like the Rashtriya Swayamsevak Sangh (RSS) and Jamaat-e-Islami along with some political parties were banned. Numerous Communist leaders were arrested along with many others involved with their party. Congress leaders who dissented the Emergency declaration and amendment to the constitution such as Mohan Dharia and Chandra Shekhar resigned their government and party positions and were arrested and placed under detention,[1402]

In Tamil Nadu, the M. Karunanidhi government was dissolved and the leaders of the DMK were incarcerated. In particular, Karunanidhi's son M. K. Stalin, was arrested under the Maintenance of Internal Security Act. At least nine High Courts pronounced that even after the declaration of an emergency, a person could challenge his detention. The Supreme Court, now under the Indira Gandhi-appointed Chief Justice A. N. Ray, overruled all of them, upholding the state's plea for power to detain a person without the necessity of informing him of the grounds for his arrest, or to suspend his personal liberties, or to deprive him of his right to life, in an absolute manner (the *habeas corpus* case').[1403,1404] Many political workers who were not arrested in the first wave, went 'underground' continuing organising protests.[1405]

Laws, human rights and elections

Elections for the Parliament and state governments were postponed. Gandhi and her parliamentary majorities could rewrite the nation's laws, since her Congress party had the required mandate to do so – a two-thirds majority in the Parliament. And when she felt the existing laws were 'too slow', she got the President to issue 'Ordinances' – a law-making power in times of urgency, invoked sparingly – completely bypassing the Parliament, allowing her to rule by decree. Also, she had little trouble amending the Constitution that exonerated her from any culpability in her election-fraud case, imposing President's Rule in Gujarat and Tamil Nadu, where anti-Indira parties ruled (state legislatures were thereby dissolved and suspended indefinitely), and jailing thousands of opponents. The 42nd Amendment, which brought about extensive changes to the letter and spirit of the Constitution, is one of the lasting legacies of the Emergency. In the conclusion of his *Making of India's Constitution*, Justice Khanna writes:

> *If the Indian constitution is our heritage bequeathed to us by our founding fathers, no less are we, the people of India, the trustees and custodians of the values which pulsate within its provisions! A constitution is not a parchment of paper, it is a way of life and has to be lived up to. Eternal vigilance is the price of liberty and in the final analysis, its only keepers are the people. Imbecility of men, history teaches us, always invites the impudence of power."*

A fallout of the Emergency era was the Supreme Court laid down that, although the Constitution is amenable to amendments (as abused by Indira Gandhi), changes that tinker with its *basic structure*[1406] cannot be made by the Parliament. (see *Kesavananda Bharati v. State of Kerala*)[1407]

In the *Rajan* case, P. Rajan of the Regional Engineering College, Calicut, was arrested by the police in Kerala on 1 March 1976,[1408] tortured in custody until he died and then his body was disposed of and was never recovered. The facts of this incident came out owing to a habeas corpus suit filed in the Kerala High Court.[1409,1410]

Forced sterilization

In September 1976, Sanjay Gandhi initiated a widespread compulsory sterilization programme to limit population growth. The exact extent of Sanjay Gandhi's role in the implementation of the programme is disputed, with some writers holding Gandhi directly responsible for his authoritarianism, and other writers blaming the officials who implemented the programme rather than Gandhi himself. Rukhsana Sultana was a socialite known for being one of Sanjay Gandhi's close associates and she gained a lot of notoriety in leading Sanjay Gandhi's sterilisation campaign in Muslim areas of old Delhi. The campaign primarily involved getting males to undergo vasectomy. Quotas were set up that enthusiastic supporters and government officials worked hard to achieve. There were allegations of coercion of unwilling candidates too.[1411] In 1976–1977, the programme led to 8.3 million sterilisations, most of them forced, up from 2.7 million the previous year. The bad publicity led every government since 1977 to stress that family planning is entirely voluntary.[1412]

- Kartar, a cobbler, was taken to a Block Development Officer (BDO) by six policemen, where he was asked how many children he had. He was forcefully taken for sterilisation in a jeep. En route, the police forced a man on the bicycle into the jeep because he was not sterilised. Kartar had an infection and pain because of the procedure and could not work for months.
- Shahu Ghalake, a peasant from Barsi in Maharashtra, was taken for sterilization. After mentioning that he was already sterilised, he was beaten. A sterilisation procedure was undertaken on him for a second time.
- Hawa Singh, a young widower, from Pipli was taken from the bus against his will and sterilised. The infection took his life.
- Harijan, a 70-year-old with no teeth and bad eyesight, was sterilized forcefully.
- Uttawar, a village 80 kilometres south of Delhi, woke up to the police loudspeakers at 03:00. Police gathered 400 men at the bus stop. In the process of finding more villagers, police broke into homes and looted. Total of 800 forced sterilisations were done.

- In Muzaffarnagar, Uttar Pradesh, on 18 October 1976, police picked up 17 people, nine Hindu and eight Muslims out of which two were over 75 and two under 18. Hundreds of Hindus and Muslims surrounded the police station demanding to free captives. The police refused to release them and used tear gas shells. Crowd retaliated by throwing stones and to control the situation, the police fired on the crowd. 30 people died as a result.

Criticism against the Government

Criticism and accusations of the Emergency-era may be grouped as:
- Detention of people by police without charge or notification of families
- Abuse and torture of detainees and political prisoners
- Use of public and private media institutions, like the national television network Doordarshan, for government propaganda
- During the Emergency, Sanjay Gandhi asked the popular singer Kishore Kumar to sing for a Congress party rally in Bombay, but he refused. As a result, Information and broadcasting minister Vidya Charan Shukla put an unofficial ban on playing Kishore Kumar songs on state broadcasters All India Radio and Doordarshan from 4 May 1976 till the end of Emergency.
- Forced sterilization.
- Destruction of the slum and low-income housing in the Turkmen Gate and Jama Masjid area of old Delhi.
- Large-scale and illegal enactment of laws (including modifications to the Constitution).

The Emergency years were the biggest challenge to India's commitment to democracy, which proved vulnerable to the manipulation of powerful leaders and hegemonic Parliamentary majorities.

Resistance movements

The role of RSS

Rashtriya Swayamsevak Sangh, which was seen close to opposition leaders, and with its large organisational base was seen as having the potential of organising protests against the Government, was also banned.[1413] Police clamped down on the organisation and thousands of its workers were imprisoned.[1414] The RSS defied the ban and thousands participated in Satyagraha (peaceful protests) against the ban and against the curtailment of fundamental rights. Later, when there was no letup, the volunteers of the RSS formed underground movements for the restoration of democracy. Literature that was censored in the media was clandestinely published and distributed on a large scale and funds were collected for the movement. Networks were established between leaders of different political parties in the jail and outside for the co-ordination of the movement.[1415]

The Economist described the movement as "the only non-left revolutionary force in the world". It said that the movement was "dominated by tens of thousands of RSS cadres, though more and more young recruits are coming". Talking about its objectives it said "its platform at the moment has only one plank: to bring democracy back to India".[1416]

The claims of RSS leaders have been contested by political scientist Professor DL Sheth saying that these organisations have never borne the brunt Indira's oppressive regime. The RSS projects itself as the champion of anti-Emergency struggle but it was in fact, it's only lifeline.[1417] In a 2000 Hindu daily article, Dr. Subrahmanian Swamy, had alleged that several Sangh leaders were hobnobbing with Indira. He added that the Sangh, at the instance of Vajpayee, even went farther to sign a peace accord with Indira Gandhi.[1418]

Sikh opposition

Shortly after the declaration of the Emergency, the Sikh leadership convened meetings in Amritsar where they resolved to oppose the "fascist tendency of the Congress".[1419] The first mass protest in the country, known as the "Campaign to Save Democracy" was organised by the Akali Dal and launched in Amritsar, 9 July. A statement to the press recalled the historic Sikh struggle for freedom under the Mughals, then under the British, and voiced concern that what had been fought for and achieved was being lost. The police were out in force for the demonstration and arrested the protestors, including the Shiromani Akali Dal and Shiromani Gurdwara Prabandhak Committee (SGPC) leaders.

> "The question before us is not whether Indira Gandhi should continue to be prime minister or not. The point is whether democracy in this country is to survive or not."[1420]

According to Amnesty International, 140,000 people had been arrested without trial during the twenty months of Gandhi's Emergency. Jasjit Singh Grewal estimates that 40,000 of them came from India's two percent Sikh minority.[1421]

Elections of 1977

On 18 January 1977, Gandhi called fresh elections for March and released all political prisoners though the Emergency officially ended on 23 March 1977. The opposition Janata movement's campaign warned Indians that the elections might be their last chance to choose between "democracy and dictatorship."

In the Lok Sabha elections, held in March, Mrs. Gandhi and Sanjay both lost their Lok Sabha seats, as did all the Congress Candidates in Northern states such as Bihar and Uttar Pradesh. Many Congress Party loyalists deserted Mrs. Gandhi. The Congress was reduced to just 153 seats, 92 of which were from four of the southern states. The Janata Party's 298 seats and its allies' 47 seats (of a total 542) gave it a massive majority. Morarji Desai became the first non-Congress Prime Minister of India.

Voters in the electorally largest state of Uttar Pradesh, historically a Congress stronghold, turned against Gandhi and her party failed to win a single seat in the state. Dhanagare says the structural reasons behind the discontent against the Government included the emergence of a strong and united opposition, disunity and weariness inside Congress, an effective underground opposition, and the ineffectiveness of Gandhi's control of the mass media, which had lost much credibility. The structural factors allowed voters to express their grievances, notably their resentment of the emergency and its authoritarian and repressive policies. One grievance often mentioned as the 'nasbandi' (vasectomy) campaign in rural areas. The middle classes also emphasised the curbing of freedom throughout the state and India.[1422] Meanwhile, Congress hit an all-time low in West Bengal because of the poor discipline and factionalism among Congress activists as well as the numerous defections that weakened the party.[1423] Opponents emphasised the issues of corruption in Congress and appealed to a deep desire by the voters for fresh leadership.[1424]

The tribunal

The efforts of the Janata administration to get government officials and Congress politicians tried for Emergency-era abuses and crimes were largely unsuccessful due to a disorganised, over-complex and politically motivated process of litigation. The Thirty-eighth Amendment of the Constitution of India, put in place shortly after the outset of the Emergency and which among other things prohibited judicial reviews of states of emergencies and actions taken during them, also likely played a role in this lack of success. Although special tribunals were organised and scores of senior Congress Party and government officials arrested and charged, including Mrs. Gandhi and Sanjay Gandhi, police were unable to submit sufficient evidence for most cases, and only a few low-level officials were convicted of any abuses.

The people lost interest in the hearings owing to their continuous fumbling and complex nature, and the economic and social needs of the country grew more important to them.Wikipedia:Citation needed

Legacy

The Emergency lasted 21 months, and its legacy remains intensely controversial. A few days after the Emergency was imposed, the Bombay edition of *The Times of India* carried an obituary that read

> Democracy, beloved husband of Truth, loving father of Liberty, brother of Faith, Hope and Justice, expired on June 26.[1425]

A few days later censorship was imposed on newspapers. The Delhi edition of the *Indian Express* on 28 June, carried a blank editorial, while the *Financial Express* reproduced in large type Rabindranath Tagore's poem "Where the mind is without fear".

However, the Emergency also received support from several sections. It was endorsed by social reformer Vinoba Bhave (who called it *Anushasan parva*, a time for discipline), industrialist J. R. D. Tata, writer Khushwant Singh, and Indira Gandhi's close friend and Orissa Chief Minister Nandini Satpathy. However, Tata and Satpathy later regretted that they spoke in favour of the Emergency.[1426,1427] Others have argued that Gandhi's Twenty Point Programme increased agricultural production, manufacturing activity, exports and foreign reserves.Wikipedia:Citation needed Communal Hindu–Muslim riots, which had resurfaced in the 1960s and 1970s, also reduced in intensity.Wikipedia:Citation needed

In the book *JP Movement and the Emergency*, historian Bipan Chandra wrote, "Sanjay Gandhi and his cronies like Bansi Lal, Minister of Defence at the time, were keen on postponing elections and prolonging the emergency by several years ... In October–November 1976, an effort was made to change the basic civil libertarian structure of the Indian Constitution through the 42nd amendment to it. ... The most important changes were designed to strengthen the executive at the cost of the judiciary, and thus disturb the carefully crafted system of Constitutional checks and balance between the three organs of the government."

In culture

Literature

- Writer Rahi Masoom Raza criticised the Emergency through his novel *Qatra bi Aarzoo*.[1428]
- Shashi Tharoor portrays the Emergency allegorically in his *The Great Indian Novel*(1989), describing it as "The Siege". He also authored a satirical play on the Emergency, *Twenty-Two Months in the Life of a Dog*, that was published in his *The Five-Dollar Smile and Other Stories*.
- *A Fine Balance* and *Such a Long Journey* by Rohinton Mistry take place during the Emergency and highlight many of the abuses that occurred during that period, largely through the lens of India's small but culturally influential Parsi minority.
- Booker Prize-winner *Midnight's Children* by Salman Rushdie, has the protagonist, Saleem Sinai, in India during the Emergency. His home in a low income area, called the "magician's ghetto", is destroyed as part of the national beautification program. He is forcibly sterilised as part of the vasectomy program. The principal antagonist of the book is "the Widow" (a likeness that Indira Gandhi successfully sued Rushdie for). There was one line in the book that repeated an old Indian rumour that Indira Gandhi's son didn't like his mother because he suspected her of causing the death of his father. As this was a rumour; there was no substantiation to be found.[1429]
- *India: A Wounded Civilization*, a book by V S Naipaul is also oriented around Emergency.
- *The Plunge* An English novel by Sanjeev Tare is their own story told by four youths studying at Kalidas College in Nagpur. They tell the reader what they went through during those politically turbulent times.
- The Malayalam novel *Delhi Gadhakal* (*Tales from Delhi*) by M. Mukundan highlights many abuses that occurred during the Emergency including forced sterilization of men and the destruction of houses and shops owned by Muslims in Turkmen Gate.
- *Brutus, You!*, a book by Chanakya Sen is based on internal politics of Jawaharlal Nehru University, Delhi during the period of Emergency.
- *Vasansi Jirnani*, a play by Torit Mitra is inspired by Ariel Dorfman's *Death and the Maiden* and effects of emergency.
- The Tamil novel *Marukkozhunthu Mangai* (*Girl with Fragrant Chinese Mugwort*) by Ra. Su. Nallaperumal which is based on the history of Pallavas & People's rising in Kanchi during 725 A.D explains how the widow Queen and the Princess kill the freedom of the people. Most of the incidents described in the novel resemble the emergency period. Even

the name of the characters in the novel are similar to Mrs Gandhi and her family.
- The Malayalam autobiographical diary by political activist R.C. Unnithan penned while the author was imprisoned as a political prisoner during emergency under MISA for sixteen months at Poojappura state prison in Thiruvananthapuram, Kerala, gives a personal account of his travails during the dark days of Indian democracy.
- The Tamil Novel *Karisal"* (*Black Soil*) by Ponneelan deals with the Social political changes during the period
- The Tamil Novel *Ashwamedam* by Ramachandra Vaidhanath deals with the political movements during the period
- In 2001's *Life of Pi*, Pi's father decides to sell the zoo and move his family to Canada, around the same time of the Emergency.

Film

- Gulzar's *Aandhi* (1975) was banned, because the film was supposedly based on Indira Gandhi.
- Amrit Nahata's film *Kissa Kursi Ka* (1977) a bold spoof on the Emergency, where Shabana Azmi plays 'Janata' (the public) a mute, dumb protagonist, was subsequently banned and reportedly, all its prints were burned by Sanjay Gandhi and his associates at his Maruti factory in Gurgaon.[1430]
- Yamagola a 1977 Telugu film (Hindi re-make Lok Parlok) spoofs the emergency issues.
- I. S. Johar's 1978 Bollywood Film Nasbandi is a sarcasm on the sterilization drive of the Government of India, where each one of the characters is trying to find sterilization cases. The film was banned after its release due to its portrayal of the Indira Gandhi government.
- Although Satyajit Ray's 1980 film *Hirak Rajar Deshe* was a children's comedy, it was a satire on the Emergency.
- The 1985 Malayalam film *Yathra* directed by Balu Mahendra has the human rights violations by the police during *the Emergency* as its main plotline.
- 1988 Malayalam film *Piravi* is about a father searching for his son Rajan, who had been arrested by the police (and allegedly killed in custody).
- The 2005 Hindi film *Hazaaron Khwaishein Aisi* is set against the backdrop of the Emergency. The film, directed by Sudhir Mishra, also tries to portray the growth of the Naxalite movement during the Emergency era. The movie tells the story of three youngsters in the 1970s, when India was undergoing massive social and political changes.
- The 2012 Marathi film *Shala* discusses the issues related to the Emergency.

- The critically acclaimed 2012 film adaptation, *Life of Pi*, uses the Emergency as the backdrop of which Pi's father decides to sell the zoo and move his family to Canada.
- *Midnight's Children*, a 2012 adaptation of Rushdie's novel, created widespread controversy due to the negative portrayal of Indira Gandhi and other leaders. The film was not shown at the International Film Festival of India and was banned from further screening at the International Film Festival of Kerala where it was premièred in India.
- *Indu Sarkar*, 2017 Hindi political thriller film about the emergency, directed by Madhur Bhandarkar.

Sources

- Atul Kohli. *Democracy and Discontent: India's Growing Crisis of Governability*. Cambridge University Press. 1991. ISBN 0-521-39161-X.
- Atul Kohli (ed.). *The Success of India's Democracy*. Cambridge University Press. 2001 [2004]. ISBN 81-7596-107-4.
- Ayesha Jalal. *Democracy and Authoritarianism in South Asia: a Comparative and Historical Perspective*. Cambridge University Press. 1995 [1996]. ISBN 81-85618-75-5
- B. G. Verghese. *Warrior of the Fourth Estate: Ramnath Goenka of the Express*. Viking, Penguin India. 2005. ISBN 978-0-67005-842-6.
- Bipan Chandra et al. *India Since Independence*. Penguin India. 2008 [2011 digital edition]. e-ISBN 978-81-8475-053-9.
- Durga Das Basu. *Introduction to the Constitution of India*. LexisNexis Butterworths. 1960 [20th edition, 2011 reprint]. ISBN 978-81-8038-559-9.
- Inder Malhotra. *Indira Gandhi: A Personal and Political Biography*. Hodder and Stoughton. 1989. ISBN 0-340-40540-6.
- Mary C. Carras. *Indira Gandhi: In the Crucible of Leadership*. Jaico Publishing House. 1979 [1980].
- Partha Chatterjee. *Lineages of Political Society*. Permanent Black. 2011. ISBN 81-7824-317-2.
- Partha Chatterjee. *Empire and Nation: Essential Writings, 1985–2005*. Permanent Black. 2010. ISBN 81-7824-267-2.
- Ramachandra Guha. *India After Gandhi: The History of the World's Largest Democracy*. HarperCollins. 2008. ISBN 978-0-330-50554-3.
- S. S. Gill. *The Dynasty: A Political Biography of the Premier Ruling Family of Modern India*. HarperCollins. 1996. ISBN 81-7223-245-4.
- Subhash C. Kashyap. *Indian Constitution: Conflicts and Controversies*. Vitasta Publishing. 2010. ISBN 978-81-89766-41-2.

- T. V. Sathyamurthy. *State and Nation in the Context of Social Change.* Oxford University Press. 1994. ISBN 0-19-563136-6.

Further reading

- Aaron S. Klieman. "Indira's India: Democracy and Crisis Government", *Political Science Quarterly* (1981) 96#2 pp. 241–259 in JSTOR[1431]
- Advani, L. K. (2002). A prisoner's scrap-book. New Delhi: Ocean Books.
- Kuldip Nayar. *The Judgement: Inside Story of the Emergency in India.* 1977. Vikas Publishing House. ISBN 0-7069-0557-1.
- P. N. Dhar. *Indira Gandhi, the "Emergency", and Indian Democracy* (2000), 424pp
- Malkani, K. R. (1978). The midnight knock. New Delhi: Vikas Pub. House.
- Ramashray Roy and D. L. Sheth. "The 1977 Lok Sabha Election Outcome: The Salience of Changing Voter Alignments Since 1969," *Political Science Review* (1978), Vol. 17 Issue 3/4, pp. 51–63
- Shourie, Arun (1984). Mrs Gandhi's second reign. New Delhi: Vikas.
- Shourie, Arun (1978). Symptoms of fascism. New Delhi: Vikas.
- Sahasrabuddhe, P. G., & Vājapeyī, M. (1991). The people versus emergency: A saga of struggle. New Delhi: Suruchi Prakashan.

External links

- Telegram 8557 from the United States Embassy in India to the Department of State, 27 June 1975[1432]
- A. Z. Huq Democratic Norms, Human Rights and States of Emergency: Lessons from the Experience of Four Countries[1433]
- "Memories of a Father," a book by Eachara Varier, father of a student killed in police custody during the emergency[1434]

1980s

Operation Blue Star

Operation Blue Star	
	Akal Takht being repaired by the Indian Government after the attack. It was later pulled down and rebuilt by the Sikh community.
Date	1–8 June 1984
Location	Harmandir Sahib in Amritsar, Punjab, India
Result	• Jarnail Singh Bhindranwale killed. • Akal Takht and various other buildings heavily damaged. • Sikh militants cleared out of Harmandir Sahib complex. • Assassination of Prime Minister Indira Gandhi in October. • 1984 anti-Sikh riots
	**Belligerents**
India • Indian Army • Central Reserve Police Force • Border Security Force • Punjab Police **Supported by:** Special Air Service (alleged advisory role)	Sikh militants 1435,1436,1437
	**Commanders and leaders**
Major General Kuldip Singh Brar Lt Gen Ranjit Singh Dyal Lt Gen Krishnaswamy Sundarji	Jarnail Singh Bhindranwale † Amrik Singh † Shabeg Singh †
	**Strength**
10,000 armed troops. of 9th Division, 175 Parachute Regiment and Artillery units 700 jawans of CRPF 4th Battalion and BSF 7th Battalion 150 Jawans of Punjab Armed Police and officers from Harmandir Police Station.Wikipedia:Citation needed	200 Sikh militants
	**Casualties and losses**
83 dead	150 combatants killed

493 militants and civilian casualties (official).

Operation Blue Star was an Indian military operation carried out between 1 and 8 June 1984, ordered by Prime Minister Indira Gandhi to remove militant religious leader Jarnail Singh Bhindranwale and his armed followers from the buildings of the Harmandir Sahib complex in Amritsar, Punjab. In July 1983, the Sikh political party Akali Dal's President Harcharan Singh Longowal had invited Bhindranwale to take up residence in Golden Temple Complex to evade arrest.[1438] Bhindranwale later on made the sacred temple complex an armoury and headquarter. In the violent events leading up to the Operation Blue Star since the inception of Akali Dharm Yudh Morcha, the militants had killed 165 Hindus and Nirankaris, even 39 Sikhs opposed to Bhindranwale were killed. The total number of deaths was 410 in violent incidents and riots while 1,180 people were injured.

The operation had two components — Operation Metal, confined to the Harmandir Sahib complex, and Operation Shop, which raided the Punjabi countryside to capture other suspects.[1439] Following it, Operation Woodrose was launched in the Punjab countryside against the baptized Sikhs. The operation was carried out by Indian Army troops.[1440] Casualty figures for the Army were 83 dead and 249 injured. According to the official estimate presented by the Indian government, 1592 were apprehended and there were 493 combined militant and civilian casualties. High civilian casualties were attributed to militants using pilgrims trapped inside the temple as human shields.

The military action led to an uproar amongst Sikhs worldwide, and many Sikhs had interpreted the military action as an assault on Sikh religion. Many Sikh soldiers in the Army deserted their units, several Sikhs resigned from armed and civil administrative office and several returned awards and honours they had received from the Indian government.

Four months after the operation, on 31 October 1984, Indira Gandhi was assassinated in vengeance by her two Sikh bodyguards, Satwant Singh and Beant Singh. Public outcry over Gandhi's death led to the killings of more than 3,000 Sikhs in the ensuing 1984 anti-Sikh riots.

Golden Temple

The militants were able to claim a safe haven in the most sacred place for the Sikhs due to the whole or part support received by them from the key sikh religious leaders and institutions such as the SGPC, AISSF and Jathedar (head) of the Akal Takht. The support was either voluntary or forced by using violence or threat of violence. Several religious leaders who spoke against the occupation of Akal Takht were murdered by followers of Bhindranwale.

Figure 259: *Golden temple with Akal Takhat on the Right*

The Golden temple complex afforded the militants based inside a facade of fighting a "*holy war*". It also provided the militants access to new potential recruits from among the visitors. Several multi storied buildings were located around the Parikrama (walkway) around the reservoir of the temple that provided rooms and offices that were taken over by the militants. The temple complex also provided logistical advantage to the militants with easy access to food, water and communication lines. Further the sanctity of the Golden temple provided protection from arrests by the security forces who preferred not to enter the Temple premises so as not to hurt the religious sentiments of the Sikhs.

Jarnail Singh Bhindranwale in Harmandir Sahib

On 13 April 1978, the day to celebrate the birth of Khalsa, a peaceful Sant Nirankari convention was organized in Amritsar, with permission from the Akali state government. The practices of "Sant Nirankaris" sect of Nirankaris was considered as heretics by the orthodox sikhism expounded by Bhindranwale. Bhindranwale declared that he would not allow this convention and would *go there and cut them to pieces*. A procession of few hundred Sikhs led by Bhindranwale and Fauja Singh of the Akhand Kirtani Jatha left the Golden Temple, heading towards the Nirankari Convention. Fauja attempted to behead Nirankari chief Gurbachan Singh but was shot dead by his bodyguard, while Bhindranwale escaped. In the ensuing violence, several people were killed: two of Bhindranwale's followers, eleven members of the Akhand Kirtani Jatha and three Nirankaris. Bhindranwale's followers began keeping firearms and fortified the Gurdwara that served as the headquarter of religious center Damdami Taksal.

On 24 April 1980, The Nirankari head, Gurbachan was murdered. Bhindranwale took residence in Harmandir Sahib when he was accused of the assassination of Nirankari Gurbachan Singh.[1441] Police could not pursue him inside the Golden temple premises for fear of hurting the religious setiments of the Sikh community.

On 9 September 1981, Lala Jagat Narain, the founder editor of the newspaper Punjab Kesari, was murdered. He was viewed as a supporter of the Nirankari sect and had written several editorials that had condemned the acts of Bhindranwale. Bhindranwale declared that the killers of Gurbachan and Lala deserved to be rewarded. Police again suspected Bhindranwale in the editor's murder and issued a warrant for his arrest. On 20 September 1981, after absconding for several days, Bhindranwale surrendered to the police. His followers in order to obtain his release initiated a month long campaign of violence. They attacked Hindus, derailed trains, and even hijacked an Air India Plane He was released on 20 October after Home Minister of India declared lack of evidence.

Bhindranwale had risen to prominence in the Sikh political circle with his policy of getting the Anandpur Resolution passed, failing which he wanted to declare a separate country of Khalistan as a homeland for Sikhs.[1442] Indira Gandhi, the leader of the Akali Dal's rival Congress, considered the Anandpur Sahib Resolution as a secessionist document. The Government was of the view that passing of the resolution would have allowed India to be divided, making a Khalistan.

Bhindranwale was reportedly backed by Pakistan's ISI on his radical separatist stand, plans and operations. Bhindranwale had started the efforts for his demand in 1982, and by mid-1983 had managed to gain support for his plan to divide India. ISI reportedly supported and helped him in spreading militancy in the Indian Punjab state. The arms and ammunition used by his group were provided by ISI.

Guru Nanak Niwas

In July 1982, the then President of Shiromani Akali Dal, Harchand Singh Longowal invited Bhindranwale to take up residence at the Golden Temple complex to escape arrest. He called Bhindranwale "our stave to beat the government."[1443] On 19 July 1982, Bhindranwale anticipating his imminent arrest took shelter with approximately 200 armed followers, in the Guru Nanak Niwas (Guest house), in the precincts of the Golden Temple. Bhindranwale had made Golden Temple complex his headquarters. From here he met and was interviewed by international television crews.

On 23 April 1983, the Punjab Police Deputy Inspector General A. S. Atwal was shot dead as he left the Harmandir Sahib compound by a gunman from Bhindranwale's group. The following day, after the murder, Longowal claimed the involvement of Bhindranwale in the murder.[1444] Reportedly, militants responsible for bombings and murders were taking shelter in some gurdwaras in Punjab. Punjab assembly noted that the murder in the temple premises confirmed the charges that the extremists were being sheltered and given active support in religious places and the Guru Nanak Niwas. While Bhindranwale was openly supporting such elements. However, the Congress-led government declared that it could not enter the gurdwaras for the fear of hurting Sikh sentiments. After the murder of six Hindu bus passengers in October 1983, President's rule was imposed in Punjab.

Occupation of Akal Takht

During the debate in the Parliament of India members of both the houses demanded the arrest of Bhindranwale. Sensing a prospect of his arrest from the hostel premises, he convinced the SGPC president Tohra to set up his headquarter in Akal Takht (Shrine representing the temporal power of God) in the Golden temple. The temple high priest protested this move as a sacrilege since no Guru or leader ever resided in Akal Takht that too on the floor above Granth Sahib but Tohra agreed to Bhindranwale's demand to prevent his arrest. On 15 December 1983, Bhindranwale was asked to move out of Guru Nanak Niwas house by members of the Babbar Khalsa who acted with Longowal's support. Babbar Khalsa had also the support of the Congress party. Longowal by now feared for his own safety. Tohra then convinced the high priest to allow Bhindranwale to reside in the first floor of Akal Takht as he had nowhere to go to avoid arrest. Bhindranwale had assumed sacredness of the shrine will provide him immunity from arrest Bhindranwale claimed that he had to move to Akal Takht as Morcha dictator Longowal was negotiating with the government for his arrest. By December 1983, Bhindranwale and his followers had made the Golden Temple complex an armoury and headquarter for extremist activities.[1445]

Figure 260: *Bhindranwale and his followers occupied Akal Takht in December 1983*

Few leaders raised their voice against Bhindranwale in the Golden Temple and other Gurudwaras across the state. Among the prominent ones was Giani Partap Singh, an eighty year old spiritual leaders and a former Jathedar of the Akal Takht, Partap had openly criticized Bhindranwale for stocking arms and ammunition in the Akal Takht. Bhindranwale's occupation of the Akal Takht was called an act of sacrilege. Partap was shot dead at his home in Tahli Chowk. Other dissenters were also killed. They included Harbans Singh Manchanda, the Delhi Sikh Gurudwara Management Committee president, Niranjan Singh, the Granthi of Gurudwara Toot Sahib, Granthi Jarnail Singh of Valtoha and Granthi Surat Singh of Majauli. All those who spoke against Bhindranwale were perceived as his enemies who in turn were branded as enemies of the Sikh faith. Bhindranwale's group were killing the Sikhs who had been speaking against Bhindranwale and the idea of Khalistan. The Sikh religious leadership had heard and understood the message being spread and they had already succumbed to their fear.

Negotiations

In January 1984, India's secret service Research & Analysis Wing (RAW) prepared a covert plan codenamed Operation Sundown involving special forces to abduct Bhindranwale from the Golden Temple complex. A RAW unit was formed to rehearse Operation Sundown in the Sarsawa Air Force Base in Uttar Pradesh. But the operation never materialized due to Indira Gandhi's rejection. It would have caused numerous casualties as collateral damage, the Golden Temple being one of the most visited sites in Punjab. It would have also hurt the religious sentiments of the Sikhs. Other options such as negotiations were opted for instead.

The government sent a team led by Narasimha Rao to try to convince Bhindranwale to back out but he was adamant. The negotiations failed and the law and order situation in Punjab continued to deteriorate. Indira Gandhi tried to persuade the Akalis to support her in the arrest of Bhindranwale peacefully. These talks ended up being futile. During the days before the assault, government representatives met with Bhindranwale in a last ditch effort to negotiate a truce. Bhindranwale warned of a backlash by the Sikh community in the event of an armed assault on the Golden Temple.[1446] On 26 May, Tohra informed the government that he had failed to convince Bhindranwale for a peaceful resolution of the crisis and that Bhindranwale was no longer under anyone's control. Faced with imminent Army action and with the foremost Sikh political organisation, Shiromani Akali Dal (headed by Harchand Singh Longowal), abandoning him, Bhindranwale declared "This bird is alone. There are many hunters after it". In his final interview to Subhash Kirpekar, Bhindranwale stated that *Sikhs can neither live in India nor with India.*

Indira Gandhi then gave her permission to initiate Operation Blue Star on the recommendation of Army Chief Arun Shridhar Vaidya. She was apparently led to believe and had assumed that Operation Blue Star would not involve any civilian casualties. The assumption was that when confronted Bhindranwale would surrender to the Army.

Preparations

Fortification of Golden Temple

The violence rose to its peak in the months before Operation Bluestar and the Golden Temple was allegedly being defiled with weapons. An arsenal had been created within the Akal Takht over a period of several months. Trucks engaged for kar seva (religious service) and bringing in supplies for the daily langar were smuggling in guns and ammunition. The police never attempted to check these vehicles entering the Golden Temple, reportedly on instructions from superiors. During a random check one such truck was stopped and a large number of sten guns and ammunition were found. Later on after the operation Blue Star it was found that the militants had set up a 'grenade manufacturing' facility, and a workshop for the fabrication of sten-guns inside the Temple Complex.

Harmandir Sahib compound and some of the surrounding houses were fortified under the guidance of Major General Shabeg Singh who had joined Bhindranwale's group after dismissal from Army. During their occupation of Akal Takht, Bhindranwale's group had initated fortifying the building which had allegedly disfigured the Akal Takht. *The Statesman* reported that light machine guns and semi-automatic rifles were known to have been brought into the compound,[1447] and strategically placed to defend an armed assault on the complex.The modern weapons found inside the temple complex later indicated that foreign elements were involved. The heavier weapons were found with the Pakistan or Chinese markings on them.

Holes were smashed through the marble walls of Akal takht to create gun positions. Walls were broken to allow entry points from the basements in the Takht and from the rooms around the Parikrama, to the tiled courtyards. Secured machine gun 'nests' were made. Each of these 'positions' were protected by sandbags and newly made brick walls. The windows and arches of Akal Takht were blocked with bricks and sand bags. Sandbags were placed on the turrets. The entire Akal Takht had been converted into a large reinforced pillbox with weapons pointing all the directions. Every strategically significant building of the temple complex, apart from the Harmandir Sahib located at its very centre had been fortified in a similar manner and allegedly defaced. The fortifications also included seventeen private houses in the residential area near the Temple. All the high rise buildings and towers near the temple complex were occupied. The militants manning these vantage points were in wireless contact with Shabeg Singh in Akal Takht. Under the military leadership of the cashiered Major General Shabeg Singh, ex-Army veterans and deserters had provided weapons training to Bhindranwale's men in the Temple Complex. Young Sikhs were occupying firing positions in the shrine and the buildings on all sides of Akal Takht.

The militants in the complex were anticipating an attack by the government troops. The defences in the complex were created with a purpose of holding out long enough to provoke an uprising among Sikhs in the villages so that they march enmasse towards the Golden temple in support of the militants. Sufficient food that would have lasted a month was stocked in the complex.

During this period police and the security forces stationed around the Temple Complex were allowed only beyond a sanitised area of more than 200 yards. This was to avoid the 'desecration' of the temple by their presence. The security forces were prevented by the politicians to take actions in enforcing the law. Even self defence from the terrorists was made difficult. On February 14, 1984, a police post near the entrance of the Temple was attacked by a group of militants. Six fully armed policemen were 'captured' and taken inside. After twenty four hours the police responded and sent in a senior police officer for negotiation. He asked Bhindranwale in the Akal Takht to release his men and return their weapons. Bhindranwale agreed only to return the corpse of one of the policemen who had been killed. Later the remaining five policemen who were still alive were also released, but their weapons, including three sten guns, and a wireless set, were not returned.

The fortifications of the temple denied Army the possibility of commando operation. The buildings were close by and had labyrinthine passages all under the control of the militants. Militants in the temple premises had access to Langars food supplies and water from the Sarovar (temple pond). Militants were well stocked with weapons and ammunitions. Any siege under these circumstances would have been long and difficult. The option of laying over a long siege was ruled out by the Army due to the risk of emotionally aroused villagers marching to the temple and clashing with the Army. The negotiated settlement had already been rejected by Bhindranwale and the only option left to the government was to raid the temple.

Rise in militant incidents

On 12th May 1984, Ramesh Chander, Son of Lala Jagat Narain and editor of media house Hind Samachar group was also murdered by the militants of Bhindranwale. In addition, seven editors and seven news hawkers and newsagents were also killed in a planned attack on the freedom of media house to cripple it financially. Punjab Police had to provide protection to the entire distribution staff and scenes of armed policemen escorting news hawkers on their morning rounds became common.

Bhindranwale used vituperative language in his speeches against the Hindus. In order to solve the Hindu-Sikh problem Bhindranwale exhorted every Sikh to kill thirty-two Hindus. Bhindranwale had injuncted young Sikhs to buy motorcycles and weapons to attack enemies of Sikhs, and many young Sikhs followed this. The terror had spread to all of the countryside. The numbers of violent incidents were increasing every month. It was nine in September 1983, in October it increased to thirty six and in May 1984 there were more than fifty violent incidents. These incidents included bank robberies, attack on police, arson at railway stations, bombings, indiscriminate shootings and killing of Hindu bus passengers forcibly taken out of the bus. In the twenty two months since the launching of the Akali Dharm Yudh Morcha till June 1984, Bhindranwale's militants had already killed 165 Hindus and Nirankaris per the official figures. Militants had also killed 39 Sikhs due to their opposition to Bhindranwale. The total number of deaths was 410 in violent incidents and riots while 1,180 people were injured.

By April 1984, it appeared as if Bhindranwale would be successful in driving away the Hindus from Punjab to Haryana and other states due to the terror of violent attacks and riots. There were intelligence reports of interception of messages from Bhindranwale and Shabeg Singh to their followers in the state asking them to start a fierce movement of mass killings of Hindus on 5 June. According to Amarjit Kaur, Bhindranwale wanted to start a civil war between the Hindus and Sikhs. Meanwhile, the killing rate had been rising all over the state, with sometimes more than a dozen killings in a day. On 2 June in the last 24 hours before the announcement of the operation 23 people were killed.

In June 1984, the Army was called out to help the civil administration in Punjab in response to a request from the Punjab Governor, B. D. Pande, *"in view of the escalating violence by terrorists in Punjab."* On 2 June Operation Bluestar had been initated to flush out the militants from the Golden Temple.

Khalistan

Certain radical groups had already started the movement to drive out Hindus from certain areas to make way for Sikhs coming in from other states. Due to the increased incidents of religious violence, exchange of population had already started in Punjab. The Sikhs from other states were moving into Punjab and the Punjabi Hindus were moving to neighbouring states in increasing numbers. New Khalistani currency was being printed and distributed. By May 1984, the declaration of Independence of Khalistan was imminent. Pakistan had been supporting the militants with arms and money. Once Khalistan would have got declared, there was the risk of Pakistan recognizing the new country and sending Pakistani Army into Indian Punjab to guarantee its security.

Operation

Operation Blue Star was launched to remove Jarnail Singh Bhindranwale and his followers who had sought cover in the Amritsar Harmandir Sahib Complex.

On 3 June, a 36-hour curfew was imposed on the state of Punjab with all methods of communication and public travel suspended. The electricity supply was also interrupted, creating a total blackout and cutting off the state from the rest of the world. Complete media censorship was enforced.

The Army stormed Harmandir Sahib on the night of 5 June under the command of Kuldip Singh Brar. The forces had full control of Harmandir Sahib

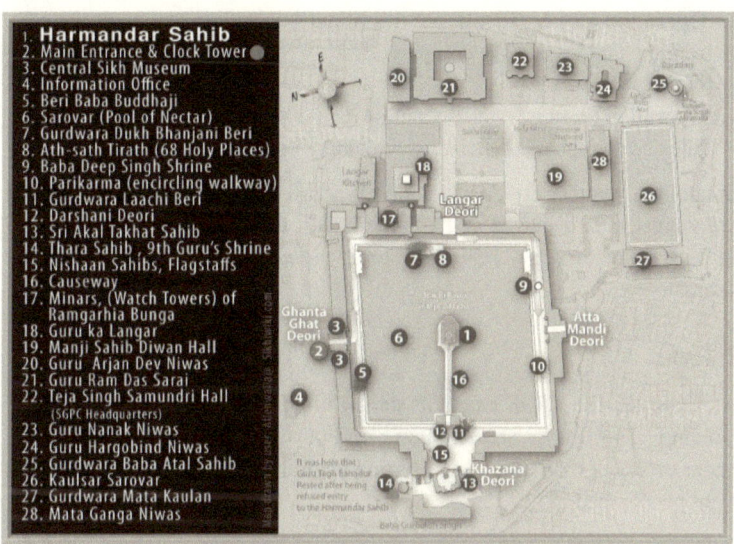

Figure 261: *Map of the Harmandir Sahib Complex*

by the morning of 7 June. There were casualties among the Army, civilians, and militants. Sikh leaders Bhindranwale and Shabeg Singh were killed in the operation.

Generals

The armed Sikhs within the Harmandir Sahib were led by Bhindranwale, former Maj. Gen. Shabeg Singh and Amrik Singh the President of the All India Sikh Students Federation from Damdami Taksal.

General Arun Shridhar Vaidya as the Chief of the Indian army. General Vaidya, assisted by Lt. Gen. Sundarji as Vice-Chief, planned and coordinated Operation Blue Star. From the Indian Army Lt. Gen. Kuldip Singh Brar had command of the action, operating under General Krishnaswamy Sundarji. Brar was in charge of an infantry division at Meerut. On 31 May Lt. General K S Brar had been summoned from Meerut and asked to lead the operation to remove the terrorists from the temple. Brar was a Jat Sikh, same caste as Bhindranwale and had his ancestral village a few miles from Bhindranwale's village. Brar was also acquainted with Shabeg Singh as his student at the Indian Military Academy at Dehradun. Both of them had worked together in the Bangladesh operations.

The Army operation was further subdivided along two subcategories:

1. **Operation Metal** : To take out the militants including Bhindranwale from the Golden Temple complex. Brar's 9 Infantry Division was deputed for this.
2. **Operation Shop** : To raid extremist hide-outs throughout the Punjab state and to mop up the terrorist remaining in the countryside.

In addition, another critical Operation Woodrose was done, under which the army units were deployed in the border areas, replacing the pickets routinely held by the paramilitary BSF. The border pickets held by at least a company strength.

1 June

At 12:40 hrs the CRPF and BSF started firing at "Guru Ram Das Langar" building. The Border Security Force and the Central Reserve Police Force, under orders of the Army, started firing upon the Complex, in which at least eight people died.[1448]

2 June

The Army had already sealed the international border from Kashmir to Ganga Nagar, Rajasthan. At least seven divisions of Army were deployed in villages of Punjab. Army began taking control of the city of Amritsar from the paramilitary. A young Sikh officer posing as a pilgrim was sent to the temple for scouting. He spent an hour in the complex noting the defence preparations in the complex. Plans were made to clear the vantage points outside the complex which were occupied by the miltants, before the assault. Patrols were also sent to study these locations.

By nightfall media and the press were gagged and rail, road and air services in Punjab were suspended. Foreigners' and NRIs' entry was also banned. General Gauri Shankar was appointed as the Security Advisor to the Governor of Punjab. The water and electricity supply was cut off.

3 June

In the morning the curfew was relaxed to allow the Sikh pilgrims to go inside the temple to celebrate Sikhism's fifth guru Arjan's martyrdom day who died in the early 17th century. Around 200 young Sikhs were allowed to escape from the temple premises during this period. Most of whom were criminals and left wing extremists (naxalites). In the night the curfew was ore-imposed with the Army and para-military patrolling all of Punjab. The Army sealed off all routes of ingress and exit around the temple complex.

Figure 262: *Akal takhat amritsar*

4 June

On 4 and 5 June announcements were broadcast over loudspeakers and the pilgrims inside were asked to leave the temple. The Army started bombarding the historic Ramgarhia Bunga, the water tank, and other fortified positions. The Army used Ordnance QF 25 pounder and destroyed the outer defences laid by Shabeg Singh. The Army then placed tanks and APCs on the road separating the Guru Nanak Niwas building.[1449]

The Army helicopters spotted the massive movements, and General K. Sunderji sent tanks and APCs to meet them.[1450]

The artillery and small arms firing stopped for a while, and Gurcharan Singh Tohra, former head of SGPC was sent to negotiate with Bhindranwale for his surrender. He was, however, unsuccessful and the firing resumed.

5 June

In the morning, shelling started on the building inside the Harmandir Sahib complex.[1451] The 9th division launched a frontal attack on the Akal Takht, although it was unable to secure the building. The Golden temple complex had honey combed tunnel structures. The Army was kept under withering machine gun fire from the manholes of the tunnels. The militants would pop out of the manholes and fire machineguns and then disappear back into the tunnels.

19:00 hrs

The BSF and CRPF attacked Hotel Temple View and Brahm Boota Akhara respectively on the southwest fringes of the complex. By 22:00 hours both the structures were under their control.[1452] The Army simultaneously attacked various other gurdwaras. Sources mention either 42 or 74 locations.

22:00–07:30 hrs

Late in the evening, the generals decided to launch a simultaneous attack from three sides. 10 Guards, 1 Para Commandos and Special Frontier Force (SFF) would attack from the main entrance of the complex, and 26 Madras and 9 Kumaon battalions from the hostel complex side entrance from the south. The objective of the 10 Guards was to secure the northern wing of the Temple complex and draw attention away from SFF who were to secure the western wing of the complex and 1 Para Commandos who were to gain a foothold in Akal Takht and in Harmandir Sahab, with the help of divers. 26 Madras was tasked with securing the southern and the eastern complexes, and the 9 Kumaon regiment with SGPC building and Guru Ramdas Serai. 12 Bihar was charged with providing a cordon and fire support to the other regiments by neutralising enemy positions under their observance.[1453]

An initial attempt by the commandos to gain a foothold at Darshani Deori failed as they came under devastating fire, after which several further attempts were made with varying degrees of success. Eventually, other teams managed to reach Darshani Deori, a building north of the Nishan Sahib, and started to fire at the Akal Takth and a red building towards its left, so that the SFF troops could get closer to the Darshani Deori and fire gas canisters at Akal Takth. The canisters bounced off the building and affected the troops instead.

Meanwhile, 26 Madras and 9 Garhwal Rifles (reserve troops) had come under heavy fire from the Langar rooftop, Guru Ramdas Serai and the buildings in the vicinity. Moreover, they took a lot of time in forcing open the heavy Southern Gate, which had to be shot open with tank fire. This delay caused a lot of casualties among the Indian troops fighting inside the complex. Three tanks and an APC had entered the complex.

Crawling was impossible as Shabeg Singh had placed light machine guns nine or ten inches above the ground. The attempt caused many casualties among the Indian troops. A third attempt to gain the Pool was made by a squad of 200 commandos from both the. On the southern side, the Madras and Garhwal battalions were not able to make it to the pavement around the pool because they were engaged by positions on the southern side.

Figure 263: *The Army used seven Vijayanta Tanks during the operation*

Despite the mounting casualties, General Sunderji ordered a fourth assault by the commandos. This time, the Madras battalion was reinforced with two more companies of the 7th Garhwal Rifles under the command of General Kuldip Singh Brar. However, the Madras and Garhwal troops under Brigadier A. K. Dewan once again failed to move towards the parikarma (the pavement around the pool).

Brigadier Dewan reported heavy casualties and requested more reinforcements. General Brar sent two companies of 15 Kumaon Regiment. This resulted in yet more heavy casualties, forcing Brigadier Dewan to request tank support. As one APC inched closer to the Akal Takth it was hit with an anti-tank RPG, which immediately immobilized it. Brar also requested tank support. The tanks received the clearance to fire their main guns (105 mm high-explosive squash head shells) only at around 7:30 a.m.

6 June

Vijayanta tanks shelled the Akal Takht. It suffered some damage but the structure was still standing. The Commanders in charge of the operation were shocked by this discovery that Militants in Akal Takhts had two Chinese made Rocket-propelled grenade launchers with armour piercing capabilities.

7 June

The Army entered the Akal Takht. Dead bodies of Bhindranwale, Shabeg Singh and Amrik Singh were discovered in the building. The Army gained effective control of the Harmandir Sahib complex.Wikipedia:Citation needed

8–10 June

The Army fought about four Sikhs holed up in basement of a tower. A colonel of the commandos was shot dead by an LMG burst while trying to force his way into the basement. By the afternoon of 10 June, the operation was over.Wikipedia:Citation needed

Casualties

The Indian Army placed total casualties at:

- Sikh militants and civilians: 493 dead
- Military: 83 killed (4 officers, 79 soldiers) and 236 wounded.

Unofficial casualty figures were higher. Bhindranwale and large number of his militants were killed. There were high civilian casualties as well, since militants used pilgrims trapped inside the temple as human shields. The pilgrims were not allowed by the militants to escape from the temple premises in spite of relaxation in the curfew hours by the security forces. The militants hoped the presence of thousands of pilgrims inside the temple premises would prevent action by the army.

Aftermath

President Zail Singh visited the temple premises after the operation, while making the round, he was shot at by a sniper from one of the buildings that the Army had not yet cleared. The bullet hit the arm of an Army Colonel accompanying the president. The operation also led to the assassination of Prime Minister Indira Gandhi on 31 October 1984 by two of her Sikh bodyguards as an act of vengeance, triggering the 1984 anti-Sikh riots. The widespread killing of Sikhs, principally in the national capital Delhi but also in other major cities in North India, led to major divisions between the Sikh community and the Indian Government. The Army withdrew from Harmandir Sahib later in 1984 under pressure from Sikh demands.[1454] The 1985 bombing of Air India Flight 182 is thought to have been a revenge action.

General Arun Shridhar Vaidya, the Chief of Army Staff at the time of Operation Blue Star, was assassinated in 1986 in Pune by two Sikhs, Harjinder Singh

Jinda and Sukhdev Singh Sukha. Both were sentenced to death, and hanged on 7 October 1992.

In March 1986, Sikh militants again occupied and continued to use the temple compound which necessitated another police action known as Operation Black Thunder on 1 May 1986, Indian paramilitary police entered the temple and arrested 200 militants that had occupied Harmandir Sahib for more than three months. On 2 May 1986 the paramilitary police undertook a 12-hour operation to take control of Harmandir Sahib at Amritsar from several hundred militants, but almost all the major radical leaders managed to escape.[1455] In June 1990, the Indian government ordered the area surrounding the temple to be vacated by local residents in order to prevent militants activity around the temple.[1456]

Mutinies by Sikh soldiers

In the aftermath of the Operation Blue Star, cases of mutinies by Sikh soldiers, mostly raw recruits, were reported from different places. On 7 June, six hundred soldiers of the 9th Battalion of the Sikh Regiment, almost the entire other ranks' strength, mutinied in Sri Ganganagar. While some managed to escape to Pakistan, most were rounded up by men of Rajputana Rifles. The largest mutiny took place in Sikh Regimental Centre at Ramgarh in Bihar where recruits for the Sikh Regiment are trained. There, 1461 soldiers - 1050 of them raw recruits, stormed the armoury, killing one officer and injuring two before they set out for Amritsar. The leaders of the mutiny divided the troops into two groups just outside of Banaras to avoid a rumoured roadblock. One half was engaged by Army artillery at Shakteshgarh railway station; those who managed to escape were rounded up by 21st Mechanised Infantry Regiment. The other half engaged with the artillery and troops of 20th Infantry Brigade, during which 35 soldiers (both sides) were killed. There were five more smaller mutinies in different parts of India. In total 55 mutineers were killed and 2,606 were captured alive.

The captured mutineers were court-martialed, despite efforts by various groups including retired Sikh officers to get them reinstated. In August 1985, 900 of the 2,606 mutineers were rehabilitated by the Central government as part of the Rajiv-Longowal accord.

Long Term Result

The long-term result of the operation are

1. The "ISI-backed" secessionist Khalistan movement was defeated.
2. Unity of India was maintained successfully
3. Indian state of Punjab was made free of militancy and
4. Operation ensured that the Golden Temple remains free from violence, guns and ammunition.

Criticisms

The operation is criticised on several grounds including: the government's choice of timing for the attack, the heavy casualties, the loss of property, and allegations of human rights violations.

Timing

Operation Blue Star was planned on a Sikh religious day — the martyrdom day of Guru Arjan Dev, the founder of the Harmandir Sahib. Sikhs from all over the world visit the temple on this day. Many Sikhs view the timing and attack by the Army as an attempt to inflict maximum casualties on Sikhs and demoralise them, and the government is in turn blamed for the inflated number of civilian casualties by choosing to attack on that day. Additionally, Longowal had announced a statewide civil disobedience movement that would launch on 3 June 1984. Participants planned to block the flow of grain out of Punjab and refuse to pay land revenue, water and electricity bills.[1457,1458]

The Government justified the timing stating that the mission to arrest Bhindranwale anymore could not be delayed any more as he was going to be more aggressive in his approach towards killings of Hindus. Bhindranwale was about to launch a fierce movement planned to murder Hindus in all the villages across Punjab. Plans included killings of All congress (I) MPs and MLAs on 5th June. According to Amarjit Kaur, Bhindranwale wanted to start a civil war between the Hindus and Sikhs. Before the Operation Blue Star started, there was already a rise in the killings of Hindus and 23 people were killed in the final 24 hours before the announcement of the operation. The spate in killings confirmed the doubts of the government which then decided that the operation had to be initiated soon.

When asked about why the Army entered the temple premises just after Guru Arjan Dev's martyrdom day (when the number of devotees is much higher), General Brar said that it was just a coincidence and Army had only three to four days to complete the operation. Based on the intelligence sources Bhindranwale was planning to declare Khalistan an independent country any moment with support from Pakistan. Khalistani currency had already been distributed. This declaration would have increased chances of Punjab Police and security personnel siding with Bhindranwale. The Army waited for the surrender of militants on the night of June 5 but the surrender did not happen. The operation had to be completed before dawn. Otherwise, exaggerated messages of Army besieging the temple would have attracted mobs from nearby villages to the temple premises. The Army could not have fired upon these civilians. More importantly, Pakistan would have come in the picture, declaring its support for Khalistan. He described the operation as traumatic and painful, but necessary.

Media blackout

Before the attack by the Army, a media blackout was imposed in Punjab. *The Times* reporter Michael Hamlyn reported that journalists were picked up from their hotels at 5 a.m. in a military bus, taken to the adjoining border of the state of Haryana and "were abandoned there." The main towns in Punjab were put under curfew, transportation was banned, a news blackout was imposed, and Punjab was "cut off from the outside world." A group of journalists who later tried to drive into Punjab were stopped at the road block at Punjab border and were threatened with being shot if they proceeded. Indian nationals who worked with the foreign media also were banned from the area. The press criticized these actions by government as an "obvious attempt to attack the temple without the eyes of the foreign press on them." The media blackout throughout Punjab resulted in spread of rumours. The only available source of information during the period was All India Radio and Doordarshan channel.[1459]

Human rights

Sikh militants

The militants used pilgrims trapped inside the temple as human shields, to prevent the attack by the army. The civilians were prevented from leaving the complex during the ease in curfew. This led to large number of civilian deaths.

On 6th of June, a group of some 350 persons, including Longowal and Tohra surrendered to the Army near the Guru Nanak Niwas. To prevent their surrender to the security forces the terrorists opened fire and hurled grenades on the group. 70 people were killed in this firing, including 30 women and 5 children. Gurcharan Singh Secretary of the Akali Dal and a prominent member of the Longowal faction was also killed.

Two Junior Commissioned Officers of the Army were captured by the terrorists during the fight and were subjected to tortures and then murdered. The terrorists skinned one of them alive and then strapped explosives on to his body and then blew him up while he was thrown from the upper floor of the Akal Takht.

On June 8, 1984, an unarmed army doctor who had entered a basement to treat some civilian casualties was abducted by the militants and was hacked to death.

Indian army

Brahma Chellaney, the Associated Press's South Asia correspondent, was the only foreign reporter who managed to stay on in Amritsar despite the media blackout. His dispatches, filed by telex, provided the first non-governmental news reports on the bloody operation in Amritsar. His first dispatch, front-paged by *The New York Times, The Times of London* and *The Guardian*, reported a death toll about twice of what authorities had admitted. According to the dispatch, about 780 militants and civilians and 400 troops had perished in fierce gunbattles. Chellaney reported that about "eight to 10" men suspected Sikh militants had been shot with their hands tied. In that dispatch, Mr. Chellaney interviewed a doctor who said he was picked up by the Army and forced to conduct postmortems despite the fact he had never done any postmortem examination before. In reaction to the dispatch, the Indian government charged Chellaney with violating Punjab press censorship, two counts of fanning sectarian hatred and trouble, and later with sedition, calling his report baseless and disputing his casualty figures. The Supreme Court of India ordered Chellaney to cooperate with Amritsar police, who interrogated him concerning his report and sources. Chellaney declined to reveal his source, citing journalistic ethics and the constitutional guarantee of freedom of the press. In September 1985 charges against Chellaney were dropped. The Associated Press stood by the accuracy of the reports and figures, which were "supported by Indian and other press accounts".

Similar accusations of highhandedness by the Army and allegations of human rights violations by security forces in Operation Blue Star and subsequent military operations in Punjab have been levelled by Justice V. M. Tarkunde,[1460] Mary Anne Weaver, human rights lawyer Ram Narayan Kumar,[1461] and anthropologists Cynthia Mahmood and Joyce Pettigrew.[1462,1463]

The Indian Army responded to this criticism by stating that they "answered the call of duty as disciplined, loyal and dedicated members of the Armed Forces of India. . . our loyalties are to the nation, the armed forces to which we belong, the uniforms we wear and to the troops we command".:[156]

Strategy

Army's strategy was criticised by comparing it with the blockade approach taken by KPS Gill five years later in Operation Black Thunder—when Sikh militants had again taken over the temple complex—was highly successful, Operation Blue Star could have been averted by using similar blockade tactics. The Army responded by stating that "no comparison is possible between the two situations", as "there was no cult figure like Bhindranwale to idolise, and no professional military general like Shahbeg Singh to provide military leadership" and "the confidence of militants having been shattered by Operation Blue Star." Furthermore, it is pointed out that the separatists in the temple were armed with machine guns, anti tank missiles and Chinese made armour piercing rocket launchers, and that they strongly resisted the Army's attempts to dislodge them from the shrine, appearing to have planned for a long standoff, having arranged for water to be supplied from wells within the temple compound and had stocked food provisions that could have lasted months.:[153-154]

Honours to the soldiers

The soldiers and generals involved in the Operation were presented with gallantry awards, honours, decoration strips and promotions by the Indian president Zail Singh, a Sikh, in a ceremony conducted on 10 July 1985. The act was criticized by authors and activists such as Harjinder Singh Dilgeer, who accused the troops of human rights violations during the operation.[1464]

Alleged British involvement

The United Kingdom's Thatcher government was reportedly aware of the Indian government's intention to storm the temple, and had provided an SAS officer to advise the Indian authorities. This and other assistance was reportedly intended to safeguard the UK's arms sales to India. Relevant UK government records have been censored.

Published accounts

Documentaries

Operation Blue Star and the assassination of Indira Gandhi (2013) is a TV documentary which premièred on ABP News Channel series, Pradhanmantri. This documentary directed by Puneet Sharma and narrated by Shekhar Kapur showed the circumstances preceeding the Operation Blue Star and the events that occurred during it including the aftermath.

Further reading

- Harjinder Singh Dilgeer (2012). *Sikh History in 10 volumes*. Sikh University Press. ISBN 2-930247-47-9.: presents comprehensive details of the invasion of Indian Army (causes and events). Vols 7 to 10 also give precious information.
- K. S. Brar (1993). *Operation Blue Star: the true story*. UBS Publishers' Distributors. ISBN 978-81-85944-29-6.: presents the version of the Indian Army general Kuldip Singh Brar, who led the operation.

- Kirapal Singh and Anurag Singh, ed. (1999). *Giani Kirpal Singh's eyewitness account of Operation Blue Star*. B. Chattar Singh Jiwan Singh. ISBN 978-81-7601-318-5.: presents the version of Giani Kirpal Singh, the Jathedar of the Akal Takht.
- Johncy Itty (1985). *Operation Bluestar: the political ramifications*.
- Man Singh Deora (1992). *Aftermath of Operation Bluestar*. Anmol Publications. ISBN 978-81-7041-645-6.
- Kuldip Nayar; Khushwant Singh (1984). *Tragedy of Punjab: Operation Bluestar & after*. Vision Books.
- Satyapal Dang; Ravi M. Bakaya (1 January 2000). *Terrorism in Punjab*. Gyan Books. ISBN 978-81-212-0659-4.

External links

- Operation Blue Star Gallery[1465] (Archive[1466])
- Operation Blue Star Photos[1467]

Assassination of Indira Gandhi

Indira Gandhi, the 3rd Prime Minister of India, was assassinated at 9:20 a.m. on 31 October 1984, at her Safdarjung Road, New Delhi residence. She was killed by two of her bodyguards, Satwant Singh and Beant Singh, in the aftermath of Operation Blue Star, the Indian Army's June 1984 assault on the Golden Temple in Amritsar which left the Sikh temple heavily damaged.

Post Operation Blue Star

Operation Blue Star had wider impact on politics in India as many Sikh youth joined the Khalistan Movement. Pakistan's ISI and orthodox Sikh groups actively supported and abetted the secessionist movement. Indira Gandhi was unpopular among the sikhs due to her role in allowing Operation Blue Star which had destroyed and damaged portions of the Akal Takht with massive casualties of Sikh pilgrims. The Sikh sensibilities were also offended at the alleged entry of the army personnel with boots in the temple complex and the alleged destruction of Sikh scriptures, manuscripts in the temple library that was burnt in the firing during the course of operation. Such claims and other rumours led to an atmosphere of mistrust with the government and later ended in a conspiracy to assassinate Indira Gandhi within four months of conclusion of Operation Blue Star.

Assassination of Indira Gandhi

Figure 264: *Memorial at the place of assassination, Safdarjung Road, New Delhi*

The threat perception to Indira Gandhi's life was increased after the operation. Accordingly Sikhs were removed from her personal bodyguard by the Intelligence Bureau due to the fear of assassination. However, Gandhi was of the opinion that this would reinforce her anti-Sikh image among the public and arm her political opponents. She forced the Special Protection Group to reinstate her Sikh bodyguards including Beant Singh who was reported to be her personal favourite.

Assassination

At about 9:20 a.m. on 31 October 1984, Indira Gandhi was on her way to be interviewed by British actor Peter Ustinov, who was filming a documentary for Irish television. She was walking through the garden of the Prime Minister's Residence at No. 1, Safdarjung Road in New Delhi towards the neighboring 1 Akbar Road office.

As she passed a wicket gate guarded by Satwant Singh and Beant Singh, the two opened fire. Sub-inspector Beant Singh fired three rounds into her abdomen from his .38 revolver. Satwant Singh then fired 30 rounds from his Sterling submachine gun into her after she had fallen to the ground. After the shooting, both threw their weapons down and Beant Singh said "I have done what I had to do. You do what you want to do." In the next six minutes Tarsem Singh

Figure 265: *The spot where Indira Gandhi was shot down is marked by a glass opening in the crystal pathway at the Indira Gandhi Memorial.*

Jamwal and Ram Saran, soldiers in the Indo-Tibetan Border Police, captured and killed Beant Singh in a separate room. Satwant Singh was arrested by Gandhi's other bodyguards along with an accomplice trying to escape, and was seriously wounded in the attack initiated by Beant Singh. Satwant Singh was hanged in 1989 with accomplice Kehar Singh.[1468]

Salma Sultan gave the first news of the assassination of Indira Gandhi on Doordarshan's evening news on 31 October 1984, more than 10 hours after she was shot. It is alleged that R. K. Dhawan, Mrs. Gandhi's secretary, overruled intelligence and security officials who had ordered the removal of Sikh policemen, including her eventual assassins, as a security threat.

Beant Singh was one of Gandhi's favorite guards, whom she had known for ten years. The other assassin, Satwant Singh, was 22 years old when the assassination occurred and had been assigned to Gandhi's guard just five months before the assassination.

Figure 266: *Indira Gandhi's blood-stained saree and her belongings at the time of her assassination, preserved at the Indira Gandhi Memorial Museum in New Delhi.*

Death

Indira Gandhi was brought at 9:30 a.m. to the All India Institutes of Medical Sciences in New Delhi, where doctors operated on her. She was declared dead at 2:20 p.m. The postmortem examination was conducted by a team of doctors headed by Tirath Das Dogra. He stated that as many as 30 bullets struck Gandhi, from two sources, a Sterling and a revolver. The assailants had fired 33 bullets at her, of which 30 had hit; 23 had passed through her body while seven were trapped inside. Dogra extricated bullets to establish the identity of the weapons and to correlate each weapon with the bullets recovered by ballistic examination. The bullets were matched with respective weapons at CFSL Delhi. Subsequently, Dogra appeared in the court of Shri Mahesh Chandra as an expert witness (PW-5). The cross-examination was conducted by Pran Nath Lekhi, the defence counsel. Her body was brought in a gun carriage through Delhi roads on the morning of 1 November to Teen Murti Bhavan where her father stayed, and where she lay in state. She was cremated on 3 November, nearWikipedia:Citation needed Raj Ghat, a memorial to Mahatma Gandhi, at an area named *Shakti Sthal*. Her elder (and the then surviving) son and successor, Rajiv Gandhi, lit the pyre.

Aftermath

Over the next four days, thousands of Sikhs were killed in retaliatory violence.

The Justice Thakkar Commission of Inquiry set up to probe Indira Gandhi's assassination recommended a separate probe for the conspiracy angle behind the assassination. The Thakkar Report stated that the "needle of suspicion"Wikipedia:Citation needed pointed at R. K. Dhawan for complicity in the conspiracy.

Satwant Singh and alleged conspirator Kehar Singh were sentenced to death. Both were executed on 6 January 1989.

A Punjabi movie titled *Kaum De Heere* (translation: People's Diamonds) highlighting the role/lives of two guards that assassinated Gandhi was set to be released on 22 August 2014, but was banned by the Indian government.

External links

- Indira Gandhi Memorial[1469] Indira Gandhi assassination books in Tamil in two volumes by Mrs. Z.Y. Himsagar and S. Padmavathi, M.A., M.L., Notion press.com, CHENNAI, 2016 edition, ISBN 9789352065967 ISBN 9789352065974
- Explore the Virtual Memorial of Indira Gandhi[1470]

1984 anti-Sikh riots

1984 anti-Sikh riots	
Sikh man surrounded and beaten by a mob	
Location	Punjab, Delhi
Date	31 October – 3 November 1984
Target	Sikhs
Attack type	Massacre, mass murder, forced conversion, arson, abduction, rape, acid throwing
Deaths	(official) 2,800 (unofficial) 8,000
Perpetrators	Congress Party members
Motive	Avenging the assassination of Indira Gandhi

The **1984 anti-Sikh riots**, also known as the **1984 Sikh Massacre**, was a series of organised pogroms against Sikhs in India by anti-Sikh mobs (notably Congress Party members and temporarily released convicts) in response to the assassination of Indira Gandhi by her Sikh bodyguards. Official Indian government reports numbered about 2,800 killed across India, including 2,100 in Delhi. Independent sources estimate the number of deaths at about 8,000, including at least 3,000 in Delhi. The Central Bureau of Investigation, the main Indian investigative agency, believes that the violence was organised with support from the Delhi police and some central-government officials. Rajiv Gandhi, who was sworn in as prime minister after his mother's death, said when asked about the riots: "When a big tree falls, the earth shakes".

Sporadic violence continued as the result of an armed Sikh separatist movement which sought independence. In June 1984, during Operation Blue Star, Indira Gandhi ordered the Indian Army to attack the Golden Temple and eliminate any insurgents; it had been occupied by Sikh separatists, who were reportedlyWikipedia:Avoid weasel words stockpiling weapons. Later operations by Indian paramilitary forces were conducted to clear the separatists from the state of Punjab.

The violence in Delhi was triggered by the assassination of Prime Minister Indira Gandhi on 31 October 1984 by two of her Sikh bodyguards who responded to her authorisation of the military operation. One of the assassins was fatally shot by Gandhi's other bodyguards while the other was shot, hospitalized, convicted of Gandhi's murder and then executed. The Indian government reported 2,700 deaths in the ensuing chaos. In the aftermath of the riots, the government reported that 20,000 had fled the city; the People's Union for Civil Liberties reported "at least" 1,000 displaced persons. The most-affected regions were the Sikh neighbourhoods of Delhi. Human rights organisations and newspapers across India believed that the massacre was organised.[1471] The collusion of political officials in the violence and judicial failure to penalise the perpetrators alienated Sikhs and increased support for the Khalistan movement. The Akal Takht, Sikhism's governing body, considers the killings genocide.

In 2011, Human Rights Watch reported that the Government of India had "yet to prosecute those responsible for the mass killings". According to the 2011 WikiLeaks cable leaks, the United States was convinced of Indian National Congress complicity in the riots and called it "opportunism" and "hatred" by the Congress government of Sikhs. Although the U.S. has not identified the riots as genocide, it acknowledged that "grave human rights violations" occurred. In 2011, a new group of mass graves was discovered in Haryana and Human Rights Watch reported that "widespread anti-Sikh attacks in Haryana were part of broader revenge attacks" in India.

Background

In 1972 Punjab state elections, Congress won and Akali Dal was defeated. In 1973 Akali Dal put forward the Anandpur Sahib Resolution resolution to demand more autonomy to Punjab. It demanded that power be generally devoluted from the Central to state governments. The Congress government considered the resolution a secessionist document and rejected it. Bhindranwale then joined the Akali Dal to launch the Dharam Yudh Morcha in 1982, to implement Anandpur Sahib resolution. Bhindranwale had risen to prominence in the Sikh political circle with his policy of getting the Anandpur Resolution passed, failing which he wanted to declare a separate country of Khalistan as a homeland for Sikhs.[1472] Others demanded an autonomous state in India, based on the Anandpur Sahib Resolution. Many Sikhs condemned the militants' actions.

Bhindranwale symbolized the revivalist, extremist and terrorist movement in the 1980s in Punjab. He is credited with the launching the Sikh Militancy in Punjab. Under Bhindranwale, the number of people initiating into the Khalsa increased. He also increased the level of rhetoric on the perceived "assault" on Sikh values from the Hindu community. Bhindranwale and his followers started carrying firearms at all times. In 1983, to escape arrest, he along with his militant cadre occupied and fortified the sikh shrine Akal Takht.

By 1983, the situation in Punjab was volatile. In October, Sikh militants stopped a bus and shot six passengers. On the same day, another group killed two officials on a train.[174] The Congress-led central government dismissed the Punjab state government (led by their party), invoking the president's rule.

During the five months before Operation Blue Star, from 1 January to 3 June 1984, 298 people were killed in violent incidents across Punjab. In the five days preceding the operation, 48 people were killed by violence.:[175] In the violent events leading up to the Operation Blue Star since the inception of Akali Dharm Yudh Morcha, the militants had killed 165 Hindus and Nirankaris, even 39 Sikhs opposed to Bhindranwale were killed. The total number of deaths was 410 in violent incidents and riots while 1,180 people were injured.

On 1 June Operation Blue Star was launched to remove him and the armed militants from the Golden Temple complex. On 6 June Bhindranwale died in the operation. Casualty figures for the Army were 83 dead and 249 injured. According to the official estimate presented by the Indian government, 1592 were apprehended and there were 493 combined militant and civilian casualties. High civilian casualties were attributed to militants using pilgrims trapped inside the temple as human shields.

The operation carried out in the temple caused outrage among the Sikhs and increased the support for Khalistan Movement. Four months after the operation, on 31 October 1984, Indira Gandhi was assassinated in vengeance by her two Sikh bodyguards, Satwant Singh and Beant Singh. Public outcry over Gandhi's death led to the killings of Sikhs in the ensuing 1984 anti-Sikh riots.

Violence

After the assassination of Indira Gandhi on 31 October 1984 by two of her Sikh bodyguards, anti-Sikh riots erupted the following day. They continued in some areas for several days, killing more than 3,000 Sikhs in New Delhi and an estimated 8,000 or more in 40 cities across India by the anti-Sikh mobs. Sultanpuri, Mangolpuri, Trilokpuri, and other Trans-Yamuna areas of Delhi were the worst affected. Perpetrators carried iron rods, knives, clubs, and combustible material (including kerosene and petrol). They entered Sikh neighbourhoods, killing Sikhs indiscriminately and destroying shops and houses. Armed mobs stopped buses and trains in and near Delhi, pulling off Sikh passengers for lynching; some were burnt alive. Others were dragged from their homes and hacked to death, and Sikh women were reportedly gang-raped and Sikhs also had acid thrown on them.[1473]

> *Such wide-scale violence cannot take place without police help. Delhi Police, whose paramount duty was to upkeep law and order situation and protect innocent lives, gave full help to rioters who were in fact working under able guidance of sycophant leaders like Jagdish Tytler and H K L Bhagat. It is a known fact that many jails, sub-jails and lock-ups were opened for three days and prisoners, for the most part hardened criminals, were provided fullest provisions, means and instruction to "teach the*

Sikhs a lesson". But it will be wrong to say that Delhi Police did nothing, for it took full and keen action against Sikhs who tried to defend themselves. The Sikhs who opened fire to save their lives and property had to spend months dragging heels in courts after-wards.

—*Jagmohan Singh Khurmi, The Tribune Wikipedia:Citing sources#What information to include*

The riots are identified as pogroms,[1474] massacres[1475,1476] or genocide.

Meetings and weapons distribution

On 31 October, a crowd around the All India Institute of Medical Sciences began shouting vengeance slogans such as "Blood for blood!" and became an unruly mob. At 17:20, President Zail Singh arrived at the hospital and the mob stoned his car. It began assaulting Sikhs, stopping cars and buses to pull Sikhs out and burn them. The violence on 31 October, restricted to the area around the AIIMS, resulted in many Sikh deaths. Residents of other parts of Delhi reported that their neighbourhoods were peaceful.

During the night of 31 October and the morning of 1 November, Congress Party leaders met with local supporters to distribute money and weapons. Congress MP Sajjan Kumar and trade-union leader Lalit Maken handed out ▯100 notes and bottles of liquor to the assailants. On the morning of 1 November, Sajjan Kumar was observed holding rallies in the Delhi neighbourhoods of Palam Colony (from 06:30 to 07:00), Kiran Gardens (08:00 to 08:30), and Sultanpuri (about 08:30 to 09:00). In Kiran Gardens at 8:00 am, Kumar was observed distributing iron rods from a parked truck to a group of 120 people and ordering them to "attack Sikhs, kill them, and loot and burn their properties". During the morning he led a mob along the Palam railway road to Mangolpuri, where the crowd chanted: "Kill the Sardars" and "Indira Gandhi is our mother and these people have killed her". In Sultanpuri, Moti Singh (a Sikh Congress Party member for 20 years) heard Kumar make the following speech:

> *Whoever kills the sons of the snakes, I will reward them. Whoever kills Roshan Singh and Bagh Singh will get 5,000 rupees each and 1,000 rupees each for killing any other Sikhs. You can collect these prizes on November 3 from my personal assistant Jai Chand Jamadar.*[1477] </ref>

The Central Bureau of Investigation told the court that during the riot, Kumar said that "not a single Sikh should survive". The bureau accused Delhi police of keeping its "eyes closed" during the riot, which was planned.

In the Shakarpur neighbourhood, Congress Party leader Shyam Tyagi's home was used as a meeting place for an undetermined number of people. Minister of Information and Broadcasting H. K. L. Bhagat gave money to Boop Tyagi (Tyagi's brother), saying: "Keep these two thousand rupees for liquor and do as I have told you ... You need not worry at all. I will look after everything."

During the night of 31 October, Balwan Khokhar (a local Congress Party leader who was implicated in the massacre) held a meeting at Pandit Harkesh's ration shop in Palam. Congress Party supporter Shankar Lal Sharma held a meeting, where he assembled a mob which swore to kill Sikhs, in his shop at 08:30 on 1 November.

Kerosene, the primary mob weapon, was supplied by a group of Congress Party leaders who owned filling stations. In Sultanpuri, Congress Party A-4 block president Brahmanand Gupta distributed oil while Sajjan Kumar "instructed the crowd to kill Sikhs, and to loot and burn their properties" (as he had done at other meetings throughout New Delhi). Similar meetings were held at locations such as Cooperative Colony in Bokaro, where local Congress president and gas-station owner P. K. Tripathi distributed kerosene to mobs. Aseem Shrivastava, a graduate student at the Delhi School of Economics, described the mobs' organised nature in an affidavit submitted to the Misra Commission:

> *The attack on Sikhs and their property in our locality appeared to be an extremely organized affair ... There were also some young men on motorcycles, who were instructing the mobs and supplying them with kerosene oil from time to time. On more than a few occasions we saw auto-rickshaw arriving with several tins of kerosene oil and other inflammable material, such as jute sacks.*

A senior official at the Ministry of Home Affairs told journalist Ivan Fera that an arson investigation of several businesses burned in the riots had found an unnamed combustible chemical "whose provision required large-scale coordination". Eyewitness reports confirmed the use of a combustible chemical in addition to kerosene. The Delhi Sikh Gurdwara Management Committee later cited 70 affidavits noting the use of a highly-flammable chemical in its written reports to the Misra Commission.

Congress Party voter-list use

On 31 October, Congress Party officials provided assailants with voter lists, school registration forms, and ration lists. The lists were used to find Sikh homes and business, an otherwise-impossible task because they were in unmarked, diverse neighbourhoods. During the night of 31 October, before the massacres began, assailants used the lists to mark Sikh houses with an "S". Because most mob members were illiterate, Congress Party officials provided help reading the lists and leading the mobs to Sikh homes and businesses in other neighbourhoods. With the lists, the mobs could pinpoint the location of Sikhs they otherwise would have missed.

Sikh men not at home were easily identified by their turbans and beards, and Sikh women were identified by their dress. In some cases, the mobs returned to locations where they knew Sikhs were hiding because of the lists. Amar Singh escaped the initial attack on his house by having a Hindu neighbour drag him into the neighbour's house and announce that he was dead. A group of 18 assailants later came looking for his body; when his neighbour said that his body had been taken away, an assailant showed him a list and said: "Look, Amar Singh's name has not been struck off from the list, so his body has not been taken away."

Timeline

31 October

- 09:20: Indira Gandhi is shot by two of her Sikh security guards at her residence, and is rushed to the All India Institute of Medical Sciences (AIIMS).
- 10:50: Gandhi dies.
- 11:00: All India Radio reports that the guards who shot Gandhi were Sikhs.
- 16:00: Rajiv Gandhi returns from West Bengal to the AIIMS, where isolated attacks occur.
- 17:30: The motorcade of President Zail Singh, returning from a foreign visit, is stoned as it approaches the AIIMS.

Evening and night

- Organized, equipped gangs fan out from the AIIMS.
- Violence towards Sikhs and destruction of Sikh property spreads.
- Rajiv Gandhi is sworn in as Prime Minister.
- Senior advocate and BJP leader Ram Jethmalani meets Home Minister P. V. Narasimha Rao and urges him to take immediate steps to protect Sikhs from further attacks.
- Delhi lieutenant governor P. G. Gavai and police commissioner S. C. Tandon visit affected areas.

1 November

- The first Sikh is killed in East Delhi.
- 09:00: Armed mobs take over the streets in Delhi. Gurdwaras are among the first targets. The worst-affected areas are low-income neighbourhoods such as Trilokpuri, Shahdara, Geeta, Mongolpuri, Sultanpuri and Palam Colony. Areas with prompt police intervention, such as Farsh Bazar and Karol Bagh, see few killings and little major violence.

2 November

A curfew is announced in Delhi, but is not enforced. Although the army is deployed throughout the city, the police did not co-operate with soldiers (who are forbidden to fire without the consent of senior police officers and executive magistrates).

3 November

By late evening, army and local police units work together to subdue the violence. After law-enforcement intervention, violence is comparatively mild and sporadic. In Delhi, the bodies of riot victims are brought to the All India Institute of Medical Sciences and the Civil Hospital mortuary in Delhi.

Aftermath

The Delhi High Court, delivering its verdict on a riot-related case in 2009, said:[1478]

> Though we boast of being the world's largest democracy and the Delhi being its national capital, the sheer mention of the incidents of 1984 anti-Sikh riots in general and the role played by Delhi Police and state machinery in particular makes our heads hang in shame in the eyes of the world polity.

The government allegedly destroyed evidence and shielded the guilty. *Asian Age*, an Indian daily newspaper, ran a front-page story calling the government actions "the mother of all cover-ups."

From 31 October 1984 to 10 November 1984 the People's Union for Democratic Rights and the People's Union for Civil Liberties conducted an inquiry into the riots, interviewing victims, police officers, neighbours of the victims, army personnel and political leaders. In their joint report, "Who Are The Guilty", the groups concluded:

> *The attacks on members of the Sikh Community in Delhi and its suburbs during the period, far from being a spontaneous expression of "madness"*

and of popular "grief and anger" at Mrs. Gandhi's assassination as made out to be by the authorities, were the outcome of a well organised plan marked by acts of both deliberate commissions and omissions by important politicians of the Congress (I) at the top and by authorities in the administration.

According to eyewitness accounts obtained by *Time* magazine, Delhi police looked on as "rioters murdered and raped, having gotten access to voter records that allowed them to mark Sikh homes with large Xs, and large mobs being bused in to large Sikh settlements". *Time* reported that the riots led to only minor arrests, with no major politicians or police officers convicted. The magazine quoted Ensaaf, an Indian human-rights organisation, as saying that the government attempted to destroy evidence of its involvement by refusing to record First Information Reports.

A 1991 Human Rights Watch report on violence between Sikh separatists and the Government of India traced part of the problem to government response to the violence:

Despite numerous credible eye-witness accounts that identified many of those involved in the violence, including police and politicians, in the months following the killings, the government sought no prosecutions or indictments of any persons, including officials, accused in any case of murder, rape or arson.

The violence was allegedly led (and often perpetrated) by Indian National Congress activists and sympathizers. The Congress-led government was widely criticised for doing little at the time and possibly conspiring in the riots, since voter lists were used to identify Sikh families.

A few days after the massacre, many surviving Sikh youths in Delhi had joined or created Sikh militant groups. This led to more violence in the Punjab, including the assassination of several senior Congress Party members. The Khalistan Commando Force and Khalistan Liberation Force claimed responsibility for the retaliation, and an underground network was established.

On 31 July 1985, Harjinder Singh Jinda, Sukhdev Singh Sukha and Ranjit Singh Gill of the Khalistan Commando Force assassinated Congress Party leader and MP Lalit Maken in retaliation for the riots. The 31-page report, "Who Are The Guilty?", listed 227 people who led the mobs; Maken was third on the list.

Harjinder Singh Jinda and Sukhdev Singh Sukha assassinated Congress Party leader Arjan Dass because of his involvement in the riots. Dass' name appeared in affidavits submitted by Sikh victims to the Nanavati Commission, headed by retired Supreme Court of India judge G. T. Nanavati.[1479]

Convictions

In Delhi, 442 rioters were convicted. Forty-nine were sentenced to the life imprisonment, and another three to more than 10 years' imprisonment. Six Delhi police officers were sanctioned for negligence during the riots. In April 2013, the Supreme Court of India dismissed the appeal of three people who had challenged their life sentences. That month, the Karkardooma district court in Delhi convicted five people – Balwan Khokkar (former councillor), Mahender Yadav (former MLA), Kishan Khokkar, Girdhari Lal and Captain Bhagmal – for inciting a mob against Sikhs in Delhi Cantonment. The court acquitted Congress leader Sajjan Kumar, which led to protests.

Investigations

Ten commissions or committees have been formed to investigate the riots. The most recent, headed by Justice G. T. Nanavati, submitted its 185-page report to Home Minister Shivraj Patil on 9 February 2005; the report was tabled in Parliament on 8 August of that year. The commissions below are listed in chronological order. Many of the accused were acquitted or never formally charged.

Marwah Commission

The Marwah Commission was appointed in November 1984. Ved Marwah, Additional Commissioner of Police, was tasked with enquiring into the role of the police during the riots. Many of the accused Delhi Police officers were tried in the Delhi High Court. As Marwah was completing his inquiry in mid-1985, he was abruptly directed by the Home Ministry not to proceed further. The Marwah Commission records were appropriated by the government, and most (except for Marwah's handwritten notes) were later given to the Misra Commission.

Misra Commission

The Misra Commission was appointed in May 1985; Justice Rangnath Misra was a judge on the Supreme Court of India. Misra submitted his report in August 1986, and the report was made public in February 1987. In his report, he said that it was not part of his terms of reference to identify any individual and recommended the formation of three committees.

The commission and its report was criticised as biased by the People's Union for Civil Liberties and Human Rights Watch. According to a Human Rights Watch report on the commission:

> *It recommended no criminal prosecution of any individual, and it cleared all high-level officials of directing the pogroms. In its findings, the commission did acknowledge that many of the victims testifying before it had received threats from local police. While the commission noted that there had been "widespread lapses" on the part of the police, it concluded that "the allegations before the commission about the conduct of the police are more of indifference and negligence during the riots than of any wrongful overt act."*

The People's Union for Civil Liberties criticised the Misra Commission for concealing information on the accused while disclosing the names and addresses of victims.

Kapur Mittal Committee

The Kapur Mittal Committee was appointed in February 1987 at the recommendation of the Misra Commission to enquire into the role of the police; the Marwah Commission had almost completed a police inquiry in 1985 when the government asked that committee not to continue. This committee consisted of Justice Dalip Kapur and Kusum Mittal, retired Secretary of Uttar Pradesh. It submitted its report in 1990, and 72 police officers were cited for conspiracy or gross negligence. Although the committee recommended the dismissal of 30 of the 72 officers, none have been punished.

Jain Banerjee Committee

The Jain Banerjee Committee was recommended by the Misra Commission for the registration of cases. The committee consisted of former Delhi High Court judge M. L. Jain and retired Inspector General of Police A. K. Banerjee.

In its report, the Misra Commission stated that many cases (particularly those involving political leaders or police officers) had not been registered. Although the Jain Banerjee Committee recommended the registration of cases against Sajjan Kumar in August 1987, no case was registered.

In November 1987, press reports criticised the government for not registering cases despite the committee's recommendation. The following month, Brahmanand Gupta (accused with Sajjan Kumar) filed a writ petition in the Delhi High Court and obtained a stay of proceedings against the committee which was not opposed by the government. The Citizen's Justice Committee filed an application to vacate the stay. The writ petition was decided in August 1989 and the high court abolished the committee. An appeal was filed by the Citizen's Justice Committee in the Supreme Court of India.

Potti Rosha Committee

The Potti Rosha Committee was appointed in March 1990 by the V. P. Singh government as a successor to the Jain Banerjee Committee. In August 1990, the committee issued recommendations for filing cases based on affidavits submitted by victims of the violence; there was one against Sajjan Kumar. When a CBI team went to Kumar's home to file the charges, his supporters held and threatened them if they persisted in pursuing Kumar. When the committee's term expired in September 1990, Potti and Rosha decided to end their inquiry.

Jain Aggarwal Committee

The Jain Aggarwal Committee was appointed in December 1990 as a successor to the Potti Rosha Committee. It consisted of Justice J. D. Jain and retired Uttar Pradesh director general of police D. K. Aggarwal. The committee recommended the registration of cases against H. K. L. Bhagat, Sajjan Kumar, Dharamdas Shastri and Jagdish Tytler.

It suggested establishing two or three special investigating teams in the Delhi Police under a deputy commissioner of police, supervised by an additional commissioner of police answerable to the CID, and a review of the work-load of the three special courts set up to deal with the riot cases. The appointment of special prosecutors to deal the cases was also discussed. The committee was wound up in August 1993, but the cases it recommended were not registered by the police.

Ahuja Committee

The Ahuja Committee was the third committee recommended by the Misra Commission to determine the total number of deaths in Delhi. According to the committee, which submitted its report in August 1987, 2,733 Sikhs were killed in the city.

Dhillon Committee

The Dhillon Committee, headed by Gurdial Singh Dhillon, was appointed in 1985 to recommend measures for the rehabilitation of victims. The committee submitted its report by the end of the year.Wikipedia:Vagueness One major recommendation was that businesses with insurance coverage whose claims were denied should receive compensation as directed by the government. Although the committee recommended ordering the (nationalised) insurance companies to pay the claims, the government did not accept its recommendation and the claims were not paid.

Narula Committee

The Narula Committee was appointed in December 1993 by the Madan Lal Khurana-led BJP government in Delhi. One recommendation of the committee was to convince the central government to impose sanctions.

Khurana took up the matter with the central government, which in the middle of 1994, the Central Government decided that the matter did not fall within its purview and sent the case to the lieutenant governor of Delhi. It took two years for the P. V. Narasimha Rao government to decide that it did not fall within its purview.

The Narasimha Rao Government further delayed the case. The committee submitted its report in January 1994, recommending the registration of cases against H. K. L. Bhagat and Sajjan Kumar. Despite the central-government delay, the CBI filed the charge sheet in December 1994.

The Nanavati Commission

The Nanavati Commission was established in 2000 after some dissatisfaction was expressed with previous reports. The Nanavati Commission was appointed by a unanimous resolution passed in the Rajya Sabha. This commission was headed by Justice G.T. Nanavati, retired Judge of the Supreme Court of India. The commission submitted its report in February 2004. The commission reported that recorded accounts from victims and witnesses "indicate that local Congress leaders and workers had either incited or helped the mobs in attacking the Sikhs". Its report also found evidence against Jagdish Tytler "to the effect that very probably he had a hand in organising attacks on Sikhs". It also recommended that Sajjan Kumar's involvement in the rioting required a closer look. The commission's report also cleared Rajiv Gandhi and other high ranking Congress (I) party members of any involvement in organising riots against Sikhs. It did find, however, that the Delhi Police fired about 392 rounds of bullets, arrested approximately 372 persons, and "remained passive and did not provide protection to the people" throughout the rioting.

Role of Jagdish Tytler

The Central Bureau of Investigation closed all cases against Jagdish Tytler in November 2007 for his alleged criminal conspiracy to engineer riots against Sikhs in the aftermath of Indira Gandhi's assassination. The bureau submitted a report to the Delhi court that no evidence or witness was found to corroborate allegations that Tytler led murderous mobs during 1984. It was alleged in court that Tytler – then an MP – complained to his supporters about the relatively- "small" number of Sikhs killed in his constituency (Delhi Sadar), which he thought had undermined his position in the Congress Party.

Figure 267: *Tytler in 2010*

In December 2007 a witness, Dushyant Singh (then living in California), appeared on several private television news channels in India saying that he was never contacted by the CBI. The opposition Bharatiya Janata Party (BJP) demanded an explanation in Parliament from Minister of State for Personnel Suresh Pachouri, who was in charge of the CBI. Pachouri, who was present, refused to make a statement. Additional Chief Metropolitan Magistrate of the Delhi Court Sanjeev Jain, who had dismissed the case against Tytler after the CBI submitted a misleading report, ordered the CBI to reopen cases against Tytler related to the riots on 18 December 2007.

In December 2008 a two-member CBI team went to New York to record statements from Jasbir Singh and Surinder Singh, two eyewitnesses. The witnesses said that they saw Tytler lead a mob during the riot, but did not want to return to India because they feared for their safety. They blamed the CBI for not conducting a fair trial, accusing the bureau of protecting Tytler.

In March 2009, the CBI cleared Tytler amidst protests from Sikhs and the opposition parties. On 7 April, Sikh *Dainik Jagran* reporter Jarnail Singh threw his shoe at Home Minister P. Chidambaram to protest the clearing of Tytler and Sajjan Kumar. Because of the upcoming Lok Sabha elections, Chidambaram did not press charges.[1480]

Figure 268: *Kamal Nath in 2008*

Two days later, over 500 protesters from Sikh organisations throughout India gathered outside the court which was scheduled to hear the CBI's plea to close the case against Tytler. Later in the day, Tytler announced that he was withdrawing from the Lok Sabha elections to avoid embarrassing his party. This forced the Congress Party to cut the Tytler and Sajjan Kumar Lok Sabha tickets.

On 10 April 2013, the Delhi court ordered the CBI to reopen the 1984 case against Tytler. The court ordered the bureau to investigate the killing of three people in the riot case, of which Tytler had been cleared.

New York civil case

Sikhs for Justice, a U.S.-based NGO, filed a civil suit in the United States District Court for the Southern District of New York on 14 March 2011 accusing the Indian government of complicity in the riots. The court issued a summons to the Congress Party and Kamal Nath, who was accused by the Nanavati commission of encouraging rioters. The complaint against Nath was dismissed in March 2012 by Judge Robert W. Sweet, who ruled that the court lacked jurisdiction in the case.[1481] The 22-page order granted Nath's motion to dismiss the claim, with Sweet noting that Sikhs for Justice failed to "serve the summons and its complaints to Nath in an appropriate and desired manner."[1482] On 3 September 2013, a federal court in New York issued a summons to Sonia

Gandhi for her alleged role in protecting participants in the riots. A U.S. court dismissed the lawsuit against Gandhi on 11 July 2014.

Cobrapost operation

According to an April 2014 *Cobrapost* sting operation, the government muzzled the Delhi Police during the riots. Messages were broadcast directing the police not to act against rioters, and the fire brigade would not go to areas where cases of arson were reported.

California State Assembly

On 16 April 2015, Assembly Concurrent Resolution 34 (ACR 34) was passed by the California State Assembly. Co-authored by Sacramento-area assembly members Jim Cooper, Kevin McCarty, Jim Gallagher and Ken Cooley, the resolution reads: "Government and law enforcement officials organized, participated in, and failed to intervene to prevent the killings." The assembly called the killings a "genocide", since they "resulted in the intentional destruction of many Sikh families, communities, homes, and businesses."

Representing the official position of the citizens of California, the resolution remembers the victims and those who fought it: "Many Sikh lives were saved from the massacre by compassionate Indians of all religious backgrounds who put their own lives at risk by providing shelter to their Sikh friends and neighbors." The assembly welcomed Sikhs from northern California, including representatives of Sikh temples in Stockton, Yuba City, Roseville, Sacramento and Fremont. Assembly member Jim Cooper said, "Although we cannot change the horror of the events of 1984, as an assembly member representing families of genocide victims, I felt it was important that we tell the truth about those events and honor the thousands of victims. Sikhs around the world should know that, here in California, we will always stand against intolerance and will not forget the tragedy of 1984."

The American Sikh Political Action Committee (PAC) wrote and sponsored the resolution to memorialise the atrocities committed by the Indian government and to honour the victims. The PAC has been increasingly active in California politics with fundraising, education and legislative campaigns. "This resolution is the first time that any nation or government has officially declared that the government of India was responsible for the slaughter of its own Sikh citizens across the country in November 1984", said attorney and American Sikh PAC board member Amar Shergill. "Indian officials and police officers led the way in the rape, torture and murder of thousands of Sikhs just a few miles from the prime minister's residence. Even today, Christians, Muslims, Dalits and Sikhs are at risk. The time has come for the Indian government to admit its culpability and make a commitment to protect all of India's minority communities."

Ontario Legislature

In April 2017, the Ontario Legislature passed a motion condemning the anti-Sikh riots as "genocide". The Indian government lobbied against the motion and condemned it upon its adoption.

Special Investigation Team (Supreme Court)

In January 2018, the Supreme Court of India decided to form a three-member Special Investigation Team (SIT) of its own to probe 186 cases related to 1984 anti-Sikh riots that were not further investigated by Union Government formed SIT. This SIT would consists of a former High court judge, a former IPS officer whose rank is not less than or equivalent to Inspector General and a serving IPS Officer.

Impact and legacy

A victim whose husband was burnt alive during the riots

On 12 August 2005, Manmohan Singh apologised in the Lok Sabha for the riots. The riots are cited as a reason to support the creation of a Sikh homeland in India, often called Khalistan.

Many Indians of different religions made significant efforts to hide and help Sikh families during the rioting.[1483] The Sikh Jathedar declared the events following the death of Indira Gandhi a Sikh "genocide", replacing "anti-Sikh riots" widely used by the Indian government, the media and writers, on 15 July 2010. The decision came soon after a similar motion was raised in the Canadian Parliament by a Sikh MP.Wikipedia:Citation needed Although several political parties and governments have promised compensation for the families of riot victims, compensation has not yet been paid.

In popular culture

The Delhi riots have been the subject of several films and novels:

- The 2005 English film *Amu*, by Shonali Bose and starring Konkona Sen Sharma and Brinda Karat, is based on Shonali Bose's novel of the same name. The film tells the story of a girl, orphaned during the riots, who reconciles with her adoption years later. Although it won the National Film Award for Best Feature Film in English, it was censored in India but was released on DVD without the cuts.

- The 2004 Hindi film *Kaya Taran (Chrysalis)*, directed by Shashi Kumar and starring Seema Biswas, is based on the Malayalam short story "When Big Tree Falls" by N.S. Madhavan. The film revolves around a Sikh woman and her young son, who took shelter in a Meerut nunnery during the riots.
- The 2003 Bollywood film *Hawayein*, a project of Babbu Maan and Ammtoje Mann, is based on the aftermath of Indira Gandhi's assassination, the 1984 riots and the subsequent victimisation of the Punjabi people.
- Mamoni Raisom Goswami's Assamese novel, *Tej Aru Dhulire Dhusarita Prishtha (Pages Stained with Blood)*, focuses on the riots.
- Khushwant Singh and Kuldip Nayar's book, *Tragedy of Punjab: Operation Bluestar & After*, focuses on the events surrounding the riots.
- Jarnail Singh's non-fiction book, *I Accuse*, describes incidents which occurred during the riots.
- Uma Chakravarthi and Nandita Hakser's book, *The Delhi Riots: Three Days in the Life of a Nation*, has interviews with victims of the Delhi riots.
- H. S. Phoolka and human-rights activist and journalist Manoj Mitta wrote the first account of the riots, *When a Tree Shook Delhi*.
- The 2014 Punjabi film, *Punjab 1984* with Diljit Dosanjh, is based on the aftermath of Indira Gandhi's assassination, the riots and the subsequent victimisation of the Punjabi people.
- The 2016 Bollywood film, *31st October* with Vir Das, is based on the riots.
- The 2016 Punjabi film, *Dharam Yudh Morcha*, is based on the riots.

Further reading

<templatestyles src="Template:Refbegin/styles.css" />

- Pav Singh. *1984 India's Guilty Secret.* (Rupa & Kashi House 2017).
- Amiya Rao; Aurobindo Ghose; N. D. Pancholi (1985). *Truth about Delhi violence: report to the nation*[1484]. India: Citizens for Democracy. Retrieved 30 July 2010.
- Jaskaran Kaur; Barbara Crossette (2006). *Twenty years of impunity: the November 1984 pogroms of Sikhs in India*[1485] (PDF) (2nd ed.). Portland, OR: Ensaaf. ISBN 978-0-9787073-0-9. Retrieved 4 November 2010.
- Cynthia Keppley Mahmood. *Fighting for Faith and Nation: Dialogues With Sikh Militants.* University of Pennsylvania Press, ISBN 978-0-8122-1592-2.
- Cynthia Keppley Mahmood. *A Sea Of Orange: Writings on the Sikhs and India.* Xlibris Corporation, ISBN 978-1-4010-2857-2Wikipedia:Verifiability#Self-published sources

- Ram Narayan Kumar et al. *Reduced to Ashes: The Insurgency and Human Rights in Punjab.*[1486] South Asia Forum for Human Rights, 2003. Archived from the Report original[1487] on 12 July 2003.
- Joyce Pettigrew. *The Sikhs of the Punjab: Unheard Voices of State and Guerrilla Violence.* Zed Books Ltd., 1995.
- Anurag Singh. *Giani Kirpal Singh's Eye-Witness Account of Operation Bluestar.* 1999.
- Patwant Singh. *The Sikhs.* New York: Knopf, 2000.
- Harnik Deol. *Religion and Nationalism in India: The Case of the Punjab.* London: Routledge, 2000
- Mark Tully. *Amritsar: Mrs Gandhi's Last Battle.* ISBN 978-0-224-02328-3.
- Ranbir Singh Sandhu. *Struggle for Justice: Speeches and Conversations of Sant Jarnail Singh Bhindranwale.* Ohio: SERF, 1999.
- Iqbal Singh. *Punjab Under Siege: A Critical Analysis.* New York: Allen, McMillan and Enderson, 1986.
- Paul Brass. *Language, Religion and Politics in North India.* Cambridge: Cambridge University Press, 1974.
- PUCL report "Who Are The Guilty. *Link to report.*[1488]
- Manoj Mitta & H.S. Phoolka. *When a Tree Shook Delhi* (Roli Books, 2007), ISBN 978-81-7436-598-9.
- Jarnail Singh, 'I Accuse...' (Penguin Books India, 2009), ISBN 978-0-670-08394-7
- Jyoti Grewal, 'Betrayed by the state: the anti-Sikh pogrom of 1984' (Penguin Books India, 2007), ISBN 978-0-14-306303-2

External links

- 1984 Anti-Sikh Riots Homepage[1489] at *Times of India*
- 1984 riots case records[1490], Government of Delhi
- Misra Commission Report[1491]
- Ahooja Committee Report[1492]
- Who Are The Guilty?[1493]
- In pictures: Massacre of the Sikhs[1494]

Bhopal disaster

<indicator name="pp-default"> 🔒 </indicator>
Bhopal disaster

Memorial by Dutch artist Ruth Kupferschmidt for those killed and disabled by the 1984 toxic gas release

Date	2 December 1984 – 3 December 1984
Location	Bhopal, Madhya Pradesh, India
Coordinates	23°16′51″N 77°24′38″E[1495] Coordinates: 23°16′51″N 77°24′38″E[1495]
Also known as	Bhopal gas tragedy
Cause	Methyl Isocyanate leak from Union Carbide India Limited plant
Deaths	At least 3,787; over 16,000 claimed
Non-fatal injuries	At least 558,125

The **Bhopal disaster**, also referred to as the **Bhopal gas tragedy**, was a gas leak incident on the night of 2–3 December 1984 at the Union Carbide India Limited (UCIL) pesticide plant in Bhopal, Madhya Pradesh, India. It was considered as of 2010 to be the world's worst industrial disaster.

Over 500,000 people were exposed to methyl isocyanate (MIC) gas. The highly toxic substance made its way into and around the shanty towns located near the plant.

Estimates vary on the death toll. The official immediate death toll was 2,259. The government of Madhya Pradesh confirmed a total of 3,787 deaths related to the gas release. A government affidavit in 2006 stated that the leak caused 558,125 injuries, including 38,478 temporary partial injuries and approximately 3,900 severely and permanently disabling injuries. Others estimate that 8,000 died within two weeks, and another 8,000 or more have since died from gas-related diseases.

The cause of the disaster remains under debate. The Indian government and local activists argue that slack management and deferred maintenance created a situation where routine pipe maintenance caused a backflow of water into a MIC tank, triggering the disaster. Union Carbide Corporation (UCC) argues water entered the tank through an act of sabotage.

The owner of the factory, UCIL, was majority owned by UCC, with Indian Government-controlled banks and the Indian public holding a 49.1 percent stake. In 1989, UCC paid $470 million ($907 million in 2014 dollars) to settle litigation stemming from the disaster. In 1994, UCC sold its stake in UCIL to Eveready Industries India Limited (EIIL), which subsequently merged with McLeod Russel (India) Ltd. Eveready ended clean-up on the site in 1998, when it terminated its 99-year lease and turned over control of the site to the state government of Madhya Pradesh. Dow Chemical Company purchased UCC in 2001, seventeen years after the disaster.

Civil and criminal cases were filed in the District Court of Bhopal, India, involving UCC and Warren Anderson, UCC CEO at the time of the disaster. In June 2010, seven former employees, including the former UCIL chairman, were convicted in Bhopal of causing death by negligence and sentenced to two years imprisonment and a fine of about $2,000 each, the maximum punishment allowed by Indian law. An eighth former employee was also convicted, but perished before the judgement was passed. Anderson similarly passed away on 29 September 2014.

The pre-event phase

The UCIL factory was built in 1969 to produce the pesticide Sevin (UCC's brand name for carbaryl) using methyl isocyanate (MIC) as an intermediate. An MIC production plant was added to the UCIL site in 1979.[1496] The chemical process employed in the Bhopal plant had methylamine reacting with phosgene to form MIC, which was then reacted with 1-naphthol to form the final product, carbaryl. Another manufacturer, Bayer, also used this MIC-intermediate process at the chemical plant once owned by UCC at Institute, West Virginia, in the United States.[1497]

After the Bhopal plant was built, other manufacturers (including Bayer) produced carbaryl without MIC, though at a greater manufacturing cost. This "route" differed from the MIC-free routes used elsewhere, in which the same raw materials were combined in a different manufacturing order, with phosgene first reacting with naphthol to form a chloroformate ester, which was then reacted with methylamine. In the early 1980s, the demand for pesticides had fallen, but production continued, leading to build-up of stores of unused MIC where that method was used.

Earlier leaks

In 1976, two local trade unions complained of pollution within the plant. In 1981, a worker was accidentally splashed with phosgene as he was carrying out a maintenance job of the plant's pipes. In a panic, he removed his gas mask and inhaled a large amount of toxic phosgene gas, leading to his death just 72 hours later.

In January 1982, a phosgene leak exposed 24 workers, all of whom were admitted to a hospital. None of the workers had been ordered to wear protective masks. One month later, in February 1982, an MIC leak affected 18 workers. In August 1982, a chemical engineer came into contact with liquid MIC, resulting in burns over 30 percent of his body. Later that same year, in October 1982, there was another MIC leak. In attempting to stop the leak, the MIC supervisor suffered severe chemical burns and two other workers were severely exposed to the gases. During 1983 and 1984, there were leaks of MIC, chlorine, monomethylamine, phosgene, and carbon tetrachloride, sometimes in combination.

The leakage and its subsequent effects

Liquid MIC storage

The Bhopal UCIL facility housed three underground 68,000 liters liquid MIC storage tanks: E610, E611, and E619. In the months leading up to the December leak, liquid MIC production was in progress and being used to fill these tanks. UCC safety regulations specified that no one tank should be filled more than 50% (here, 30 tons) with liquid MIC. Each tank was pressurized with inert nitrogen gas. This pressurization allowed liquid MIC to be pumped out of each tank as needed, and also kept impurities out of the tanks.

In late October 1984, tank E610 lost the ability to effectively contain most of its nitrogen gas pressure. It meant that the liquid MIC contained within could not be pumped out. At the time of this failure, tank E610 contained 42 tons of liquid MIC. Shortly after this failure, MIC production was halted at the Bhopal facility, and parts of the plant were shut down for maintenance. Maintenance included the shutdown of the plant's flare tower so that a corroded pipe could be repaired. With the flare tower still out of service, production of carbaryl was resumed in late November, using MIC stored in the two tanks still in service. An attempt to re-establish pressure in tank E610 on 1 December failed, so the 42 tons of liquid MIC contained within still could not be pumped out of it.

Figure 269: *Tank 610 in 2010. During decontamination of the plant, tank 610 was removed from its foundation and left aside.*

The release

In early December 1984, most of the plant's MIC related safety systems were malfunctioning and many valves and lines were in poor condition. In addition, several vent gas scrubbers had been out of service as well as the steam boiler, intended to clean the pipes. During the late evening hours of 2 December 1984, water was believed to have entered a side pipe and into Tank E610 whilst trying to unclog it, which contained 42 tons of MIC that had been there since late October. The introduction of water into the tank subsequently resulted in a runaway exothermic reaction, which was accelerated by contaminants, high ambient temperatures and various other factors, such as the presence of iron from corroding non-stainless steel pipelines. The pressure in tank E610, although initially normal at 10:30 p.m., had increased by a factor of five to 10 psi (34.5 to 69 kPa) by 11 p.m. Two different senior refinery employees assumed the reading was instrumentation malfunction. By 11:30 p.m., workers in the MIC area were feeling the effects of minor exposure to MIC gas, and began to look for a leak. One was found by 11:45 p.m., and reported to the MIC supervisor on duty at the time. The decision was made to address the problem after a 12:15 a.m. tea break, and in the meantime, employees were instructed to continue looking for leaks. The incident was discussed by MIC area employees during the break.

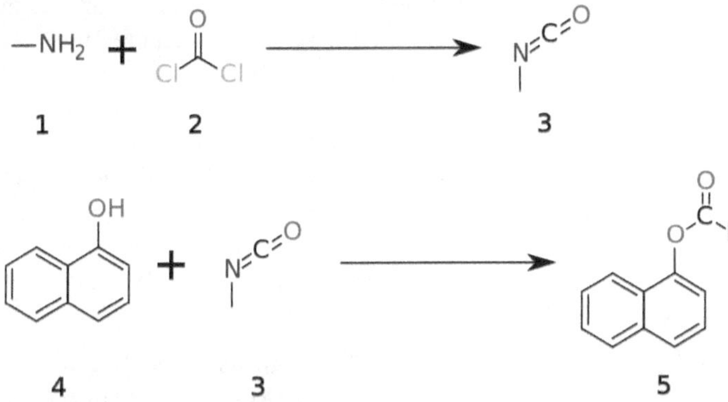

Figure 270: *Methylamine (1) reacts with phosgene (2) producing methyl isocyanate (3) which reacts with 1-naphthol (4) to yield carbaryl (5)*

In the five minutes after the tea break ended at 12:40 a.m., the reaction in tank E610 reached a critical state at an alarming speed. Temperatures in the tank were off the scale, maxed out beyond 25 °C (77 °F), and the pressure in the tank was indicated at 40 psi (275.8 kPa). One employee witnessed a concrete slab above tank E610 crack as the emergency relief valve burst open, and pressure in the tank continued to increase to 55 psi (379.2 kPa) even after atmospheric venting of toxic MIC gas had begun. Direct atmospheric venting should have been prevented or at least partially mitigated by at least three safety devices which were malfunctioning, not in use, insufficiently sized or otherwise rendered inoperable:

- A refrigeration system meant to cool tanks containing liquid MIC, shut down in January 1982, and whose freon had been removed in June 1984. Since the MIC storage system assumed refrigeration, its high temperature alarm, set to sound at 11 °C (52 °F) had long since been disconnected, and tank storage temperatures ranged between 15 °C (59 °F) and 40 °C (104 °F)
- A flare tower, to burn the MIC gas as it escaped, which had had a connecting pipe removed for maintenance, and was improperly sized to neutralise a leak of the size produced by tank E610
- A vent gas scrubber, which had been deactivated at the time and was in 'standby' mode, and similarly had insufficient caustic soda and power to safely stop a leak of the magnitude produced

About 30 metric tons of MIC escaped from the tank into the atmosphere in 45 to 60 minutes. This would increase to 40 metric tons within two hours time. The gases were blown in a southeasterly direction over Bhopal.

A UCIL employee triggered the plant's alarm system at 12:50 a.m. as the concentration of gas in and around the plant became difficult to tolerate. Activation of the system triggered two siren alarms: one that sounded inside the UCIL plant, and a second directed outward to the public and the city of Bhopal. The two siren systems had been decoupled from one another in 1982, so that it was possible to leave the factory warning siren on while turning off the public one, and this is exactly what was done: the public siren briefly sounded at 12:50 a.m. and was quickly turned off, as per company procedure meant to avoid alarming the public around the factory over tiny leaks. Workers, meanwhile, evacuated the UCIL plant, travelling upwind.

Bhopal's superintendent of police was informed by telephone, by a town inspector, that residents of the neighbourhood of Chola (about 2 km from the plant) were fleeing a gas leak at approximately 1 a.m. Calls to the UCIL plant by police between 1:25 and 2:10 a.m. gave assurances twice that "everything is OK", and on the last attempt made, "we don't know what has happened, sir". With the lack of timely information exchange between UCIL and Bhopal authorities, the city's Hamidia Hospital was first told that the gas leak was suspected to be ammonia, then phosgene. Finally, they received an updated report that it was "MIC" (rather than "methyl isocyanate"), about which hospital staff had never heard of, had no antidote for, and received no immediate information about.

The MIC gas leak emanating from tank E610 petered out at approximately 2:00 a.m. Fifteen minutes later, the plant's public siren was sounded for an extended period of time, after first having been quickly silenced an hour and a half earlier. Some minutes after the public siren sounded, a UCIL employee walked to a police control room to both inform them of the leak (their first acknowledgement that one had occurred at all), and that "the leak had been plugged." Most city residents who were exposed to the MIC gas were first made aware of the leak by exposure to the gas itself, or by opening their doors to investigate commotion, rather than having been instructed to shelter in place, or to evacuate before the arrival of the gas in the first place.

Acute effects

The initial effects of exposure were coughing, severe eye irritation and a feeling of suffocation, burning in the respiratory tract, blepharospasm, breathlessness, stomach pains and vomiting. People awakened by these symptoms fled away from the plant. Those who ran inhaled more than those who had a vehicle to ride. Owing to their height, children and other people of shorter stature inhaled higher concentrations, as methyl isocyanate gas is approximately twice as dense as air and hence in an open environment has a tendency to fall toward the ground.

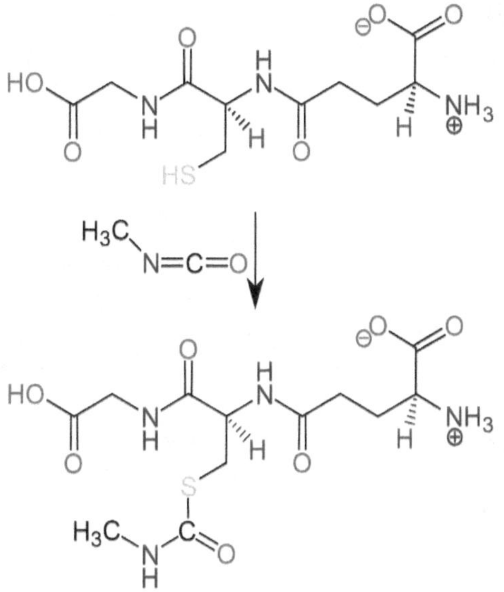

Figure 271: *Reversible reaction of glutathione (top) with methyl isocyanate (MIC, middle) allows the MIC to be transported into the body*

Thousands of people had died by the following morning.

Primary causes of deaths were choking, reflexogenic circulatory collapse and pulmonary oedema. Findings during autopsies revealed changes not only in the lungs but also cerebral oedema, tubular necrosis of the kidneys, fatty degeneration of the liver and necrotising enteritis.[1498] The stillbirth rate increased by up to 300% and neonatal mortality rate by around 200%.

Gas cloud composition

Apart from MIC, based on laboratory simulation conditions, the gas cloud most likely also contained chloroform, dichloromethane, hydrogen chloride, methyl amine, dimethylamine, trimethylamine and carbon dioxide, that was either present in the tank or was produced in the storage tank when MIC, chloroform and water reacted. The gas cloud, composed mainly of materials denser than air, stayed close to the ground and spread in the southeasterly direction affecting the nearby communities. The chemical reactions may have produced a liquid or solid aerosol. Laboratory investigations by CSIR and UCC scientists failed to demonstrate the presence of hydrogen cyanide.

Immediate aftermath

In the immediate aftermath, the plant was closed to outsiders (including UCC) by the Indian government, which subsequently failed to make data public, contributing to the confusion. The initial investigation was conducted entirely by the Council of Scientific and Industrial Research (CSIR) and the Central Bureau of Investigation. The UCC chairman and CEO Warren Anderson, together with a technical team, immediately traveled to India. Upon arrival Anderson was placed under house arrest and urged by the Indian government to leave the country within 24 hours. Union Carbide organized a team of international medical experts, as well as supplies and equipment, to work with the local Bhopal medical community, and the UCC technical team began assessing the cause of the gas leak.

The health care system immediately became overloaded. In the severely affected areas, nearly 70 percent were under-qualified doctors. Medical staff were unprepared for the thousands of casualties. Doctors and hospitals were not aware of proper treatment methods for MIC gas inhalation.:[6]

There were mass funerals and cremations. Photographer Pablo Bartholemew, on commission with press agency Rapho, took an iconic color photograph of a burial on December 4, *Bhopal gas disaster girl*. Another photographer present, Raghu Rai, took a black and white photo. The photographers did not ask for the identity of the father or child as she was buried, and no relative has since confirmed it. As such, the identity of the girl remains unknown. Both photos became symbolic of the suffering of victims of the Bhopal disaster, and Bartholomew's went on to win the 1984 World Press Photo of the Year.

Within a few days, trees in the vicinity became barren and bloated animal carcasses had to be disposed of. 170,000 people were treated at hospitals and temporary dispensaries, and 2,000 buffalo, goats, and other animals were collected and buried. Supplies, including food, became scarce owing to suppliers' safety fears. Fishing was prohibited causing further supply shortages.

Lacking any safe alternative, on 16 December, tanks 611 and 619 were emptied of the remaining MIC by reactivating the plant and continuing the manufacture of pesticide. Despite safety precautions such as having water carrying helicopters continually overflying the plant, this led to a second mass evacuation from Bhopal. The Government of India passed the "Bhopal Gas Leak Disaster Act" that gave the government rights to represent all victims, whether or not in India. Complaints of lack of information or misinformation were widespread. An Indian government spokesman said, "Carbide is more interested in getting information from us than in helping our relief work".

Figure 272: *Victims of Bhopal disaster march in September 2006 demanding the extradition of American Warren Anderson from the United States.*

Formal statements were issued that air, water, vegetation and foodstuffs were safe, but warned not to consume fish. The number of children exposed to the gases was at least 200,000. Within weeks, the State Government established a number of hospitals, clinics and mobile units in the gas-affected area to treat the victims.

Subsequent legal action

Legal proceedings involving UCC, the United States and Indian governments, local Bhopal authorities, and the disaster victims started immediately after the catastrophe. The Indian Government passed the Bhopal Gas Leak Act in March 1985, allowing the Government of India to act as the legal representative for victims of the disaster, leading to the beginning of legal proceedings. Initial lawsuits were generated in the United States federal court system. On April 17, 1985, Federal District court judge John F. Keenan (overseeing one lawsuit) suggested that "'fundamental human decency' required Union Carbide to provide between $5 million and $10 million to immediately help the injured" and suggested the money could be quickly distributed through the International Red Cross. UCC, on the notion that doing so did not constitute an admission of liability and the figure could be credited toward any future settlement or judgement, offered a $5 million relief fund two days later. The Indian government turned down the offer.

In March 1986 UCC proposed a settlement figure, endorsed by plaintiffs' U.S. attorneys, of $350 million that would, according to the company, "generate a fund for Bhopal victims of between $500–600 million over 20 years". In May, litigation was transferred from the United States to Indian courts by a U.S. District Court ruling. Following an appeal of this decision, the U.S. Court of Appeals affirmed the transfer, judging, in January 1987, that UCIL was a "separate entity, owned, managed and operated exclusively by Indian citizens in India".

The Government of India refused the offer from Union Carbide and claimed US$3.3 billion. The Indian Supreme Court told both sides to come to an agreement and "start with a clean slate" in November 1988. Eventually, in an out-of-court settlement reached in February 1989, Union Carbide agreed to pay US$470 million for damages caused in the Bhopal disaster. The amount was immediately paid.

Throughout 1990, the Indian Supreme Court heard appeals against the settlement. In October 1991, the Supreme Court upheld the original $470 million, dismissing any other outstanding petitions that challenged the original decision. The Court ordered the Indian government "to purchase, out of settlement fund, a group medical insurance policy to cover 100,000 persons who may later develop symptoms" and cover any shortfall in the settlement fund. It also requested UCC and its subsidiary UCIL "voluntarily" fund a hospital in Bhopal, at an estimated $17 million, to specifically treat victims of the Bhopal disaster. The company agreed to this.

Post-settlement activity

In 1991, the local Bhopal authorities charged Anderson, who had retired in 1986, with manslaughter, a crime that carries a maximum penalty of 10 years in prison. He was declared a fugitive from justice by the Chief Judicial Magistrate of Bhopal on 1 February 1992 for failing to appear at the court hearings in a culpable homicide case in which he was named the chief defendant. Orders were passed to the Government of India to press for an extradition from the United States. The U.S. Supreme Court refused to hear an appeal of the decision of the lower federal courts in October 1993, meaning that victims of the Bhopal disaster could not seek damages in a U.S. court.

In 2004, the Indian Supreme Court ordered the Indian government to release any remaining settlement funds to victims. And in September 2006, the Welfare Commission for Bhopal Gas Victims announced that all original compensation claims and revised petitions had been "cleared". The Second Circuit

Court of Appeals in New York City upheld the dismissal of remaining claims in the case of *Bano v. Union Carbide Corporation* in 2006. This move blocked plaintiffs' motions for class certification and claims for property damages and remediation. In the view of UCC, "the ruling reaffirms UCC's long-held positions and finally puts to rest—both procedurally and substantively—the issues raised in the class action complaint first filed against Union Carbide in 1999 by Haseena Bi and several organisations representing the residents of Bhopal".

In June 2010, seven former employees of UCIL, all Indian nationals and many in their 70s, were convicted of causing death by negligence: Keshub Mahindra, former non-executive chairman of Union Carbide India Limited; V. P. Gokhale, managing director; Kishore Kamdar, vice-president; J. Mukund, works manager; S. P. Chowdhury, production manager; K. V. Shetty, plant superintendent; and S. I. Qureshi, production assistant. They were each sentenced to two years imprisonment and fined Rs.100,000 (US$2,124). All were released on bail shortly after the verdict.

US Federal class action litigation, *Sahu v. Union Carbide and Warren Anderson*, had been filed in 1999 under the U.S. Alien Torts Claims Act (ATCA), which provides for civil remedies for "crimes against humanity." It sought damages for personal injury, medical monitoring and injunctive relief in the form of clean-up of the drinking water supplies for residential areas near the Bhopal plant. The lawsuit was dismissed in 2012 and subsequent appeal denied. Anderson died in 2014.

Long-term effects

In 2018, The Atlantic called it the "world's worst industrial disaster."

Long-term health effects

Some data about the health effects are still not available. The Indian Council of Medical Research (ICMR) was forbidden to publish health effect data until 1994.

A total of 36 wards were marked by the authorities as being "gas affected," affecting a population of 520,000. Of these, 200,000 were below 15 years of age, and 3,000 were pregnant women. The official immediate death toll was 2,259, and in 1991, 3,928 deaths had been officially certified. Ingrid Eckerman estimated 8,000 died within two weeks.

The government of Madhya Pradesh confirmed a total of 3,787 deaths related to the gas release.

Later, the affected area was expanded to include 700,000 citizens. A government affidavit in 2006 stated the leak caused 558,125 injuries including 38,478 temporary partial injuries and approximately 3,900 severely and permanently disabling injuries.

A cohort of 80,021 exposed people was registered, along with a control group, a cohort of 15,931 people from areas not exposed to MIC. Nearly every year since 1986, they have answered the same questionnaire. It shows overmortality and overmorbidity in the exposed group. Bias and confounding factors cannot be excluded from the study. Because of migration and other factors, 75% of the cohort is lost, as the ones who moved out are not followed.

A number of clinical studies are performed. The quality varies, but the different reports support each other. Studied and reported long term health effects are:

- Eyes: Chronic conjunctivitis, scars on cornea, corneal opacities, early cataracts
- Respiratory tracts: Obstructive and/or restrictive disease, pulmonary fibrosis, aggravation of TB and chronic bronchitis
- Neurological system: Impairment of memory, finer motor skills, numbness etc.
- Psychological problems: Post traumatic stress disorder (PTSD)
- Children's health: Peri- and neonatal death rates increased. Failure to grow, intellectual impairment, etc.

Missing or insufficient fields for research are female reproduction, chromosomal aberrations, cancer, immune deficiency, neurological sequelae, post traumatic stress disorder (PTSD) and children born after the disaster. Late cases that might never be highlighted are respiratory insufficiency, cardiac insufficiency (cor pulmonale), cancer and tuberculosis.

A 2014 report in *Mother Jones* quotes a "spokesperson for the Bhopal Medical Appeal, which runs free health clinics for survivors" as saying "An estimated 120,000 to 150,000 survivors still struggle with serious medical conditions including nerve damage, growth problems, gynecological disorders, respiratory issues, birth defects, and elevated rates of cancer and tuberculosis."

Health care

The Government of India had focused primarily on increasing the hospital-based services for gas victims thus hospitals had been built after the disaster. When UCC wanted to sell its shares in UCIL, it was directed by the Supreme Court to finance a 500-bed hospital for the medical care of the survivors. Thus, Bhopal Memorial Hospital and Research Centre (BMHRC) was inaugurated in 1998 and was obliged to give free care for survivors for eight years. BMHRC was a 350-bedded super speciality hospital where heart surgery and hemodialysis were done. There was a dearth of gynaecology, obstetrics and paediatrics.

Eight mini-units (outreach health centres) were started and free health care for gas victims were to be offered until 2006. The management had also faced problems with strikes, and the quality of the health care being disputed. Sambhavna Trust is a charitable trust, registered in 1995, that gives modern as well as ayurvedic treatments to gas victims, free of charge.

Environmental rehabilitation

When the factory was closed in 1986, pipes, drums and tanks were sold. The MIC and the Sevin plants are still there, as are storages of different residues. Isolation material is falling down and spreading. The area around the plant was used as a dumping area for hazardous chemicals. In 1982 tubewells in the vicinity of the UCIL factory had to be abandoned and tests in 1989 performed by UCC's laboratory revealed that soil and water samples collected from near the factory and inside the plant were toxic to fish. Several other studies had also shown polluted soil and groundwater in the area. Reported polluting compounds include 1-naphthol, naphthalene, Sevin, tarry residue, mercury, toxic organochlorines, volatile organochlorine compounds, chromium, copper, nickel, lead, hexachloroethane, hexachlorobutadiene, and the pesticide HCH.

In order to provide safe drinking water to the population around the UCIL factory, Government of Madhya Pradesh presented a scheme for improvement of water supply. In December 2008, the Madhya Pradesh High Court decided that the toxic waste should be incinerated at Ankleshwar in Gujarat, which was met by protests from activists all over India. On 8 June 2012, the Centre for incineration of toxic Bhopal waste agreed to pay ₪250 million (US$3.6 million) to dispose of UCIL chemical plants waste in Germany. On 9 August 2012, Supreme court directed the Union and Madhya Pradesh Governments to take immediate steps for disposal of toxic waste lying around and inside the factory within six months.

A U.S. court rejected the lawsuit blaming UCC for causing soil and water pollution around the site of the plant and ruled that responsibility for remedial measures or related claims rested with the State Government and not with UCC. In 2005, the state government invited various Indian architects to enter their "concept for development of a memorial complex for Bhopal gas tragedy victims at the site of Union Carbide". In 2011, a conference was held on the site, with participants from European universities which was aimed for the same.

Occupational and habitation rehabilitation

33 of the 50 planned work-sheds for gas victims started. All except one was closed down by 1992. 1986, the MP government invested in the Special Industrial Area Bhopal. 152 of the planned 200 work sheds were built and in 2000, 16 were partially functioning. It was estimated that 50,000 persons need alternative jobs, and that less than 100 gas victims had found regular employment under the government's scheme. The government also planned 2,486 flats in two- and four-story buildings in what is called the "widow's colony" outside Bhopal. The water did not reach the upper floors and it was not possible to keep cattle which were their primary occupation. Infrastructure like buses, schools, etc. were missing for at least a decade.

Economic rehabilitation

Immediate relieves were decided two days after the tragedy. Relief measures commenced in 1985 when food was distributed for a short period along with ration cards. Madhya Pradesh government's finance department allocated ₹874 million (US$13 million) for victim relief in July 1985. Widow pension of ₹200 (US$2.90)/per month (later ₹750 (US$11)) were provided. The government also decided to pay ₹1,500 (US$22) to families with monthly income ₹500 (US$7.30) or less. As a result of the interim relief, more children were able to attend school, more money was spent on treatment and food, and housing also eventually improved. From 1990 interim relief of ₹200 (US$2.90) was paid to everyone in the family who was born before the disaster.

The final compensation, including interim relief for personal injury was for the majority ₹25,000 (US$360). For death claim, the average sum paid out was ₹62,000 (US$900). Each claimant were to be categorised by a doctor. In court, the claimants were expected to prove "beyond reasonable doubt" that death or injury in each case was attributable to exposure. In 1992, 44 percent of the claimants still had to be medically examined.

By the end of October 2003, according to the Bhopal Gas Tragedy Relief and Rehabilitation Department, compensation had been awarded to 554,895 people for injuries received and 15,310 survivors of those killed. The average amount to families of the dead was $2,200.

In 2007, 1,029,517 cases were registered and decided. Number of awarded cases were 574,304 and number of rejected cases 455,213. Total compensation awarded was ₹15,465 million (US$230 million). On 24 June 2010, the Union Cabinet of the Government of India approved a ₹12,650 million (US$180 million) aid package which would be funded by Indian taxpayers through the government.

Other impacts

In 1985, Henry Waxman, a California Democrat, called for a U.S. government inquiry into the Bhopal disaster, which resulted in U.S. legislation regarding the accidental release of toxic chemicals in the United States.

Causes of the disaster: overview

There are two main lines of argument involving the disaster. The "Corporate Negligence" point of view argues that the disaster was caused by a potent combination of under-maintained and decaying facilities, a weak attitude towards safety, and an undertrained workforce, culminating in worker actions that inadvertently enabled water to penetrate the MIC tanks in the absence of properly working safeguards.

The "Worker Sabotage" point of view argues that it was not physically possible for the water to enter the tank without concerted human effort, and that extensive testimony and engineering analysis leads to a conclusion that water entered the tank when a rogue individual employee hooked a water hose directly to an empty valve on the side of the tank. This point of view further argues that the Indian government took extensive actions to hide this possibility in order to attach blame to UCC.

Theories differ as to how the water entered the tank. At the time, workers were cleaning out a clogged pipe with water about 400 feet from the tank. They claimed that they were not told to isolate the tank with a pipe slip-blind plate. The operators assumed that owing to bad maintenance and leaking valves, it was possible for the water to leak into the tank.

This water entry route could not be reproduced despite strenuous efforts by motivated parties. UCC claims that a "disgruntled worker" deliberately connecting a hose to a pressure gauge connection was the real cause.

Early the next morning, a UCIL manager asked the instrument engineer to replace the gauge. UCIL's investigation team found no evidence of the necessary connection; the investigation was totally controlled by the government, denying UCC investigators access to the tank or interviews with the operators.

Causes of the disaster: The "corporate negligence" argument

This point of view argues that management (and to some extent, local government) underinvested in safety, which allowed for a dangerous working environment to develop. Factors cited include the filling of the MIC tanks beyond recommended levels, poor maintenance after the plant ceased MIC production at the end of 1984, allowing several safety systems to be inoperable due to poor maintenance, and switching off safety systems to save money— including the MIC tank refrigeration system which could have mitigated the disaster severity, and non-existent catastrophe management plans. Other factors identified by government inquiries included undersized safety devices and the dependence on manual operations. Specific plant management deficiencies that were identified include the lack of skilled operators, reduction of safety management, insufficient maintenance, and inadequate emergency action plans.

Underinvestment

Underinvestment is cited as contributing to an environment. Attempts to reduce expenses affected the factory's employees and their conditions. Kurzman argues that "cuts ... meant less stringent quality control and thus looser safety rules. A pipe leaked? Don't replace it, employees said they were told ... MIC workers needed more training? They could do with less. Promotions were halted, seriously affecting employee morale and driving some of the most skilled ... elsewhere".[1499] Workers were forced to use English manuals, even though only a few had a grasp of the language.[1500]

Subsequent research highlights a gradual deterioration of safety practices in regard to the MIC, which had become less relevant to plant operations. By 1984, only six of the original twelve operators were still working with MIC and the number of supervisory personnel had also been halved. No maintenance supervisor was placed on the night shift and instrument readings were taken every two hours, rather than the previous and required one-hour readings. Workers made complaints about the cuts through their union but were ignored. One employee was fired after going on a 15-day hunger strike. 70% of the plant's employees were fined before the disaster for refusing to deviate from the proper safety regulations under pressure from the management.

In addition, some observers, such as those writing in the Trade Environmental Database (TED) Case Studies as part of the Mandala Project from American University, have pointed to "serious communication problems and management gaps between Union Carbide and its Indian operation", characterised by "the parent companies [sic] hands-off approach to its overseas operation" and "cross-cultural barriers".[1501]

Adequacy of equipment and safety regulations

The factory was not well equipped to handle the gas created by the sudden addition of water to the MIC tank. The MIC tank alarms had not been working for four years and there was only one manual back-up system, compared to a four-stage system used in the United States. The flare tower and several vent gas scrubbers had been out of service for five months before the disaster. Only one gas scrubber was operating: it could not treat such a large amount of MIC with sodium hydroxide (caustic soda), which would have brought the concentration down to a safe level. The flare tower could only handle a quarter of the gas that leaked in 1984, and moreover it was out of order at the time of the incident.[1502] To reduce energy costs, the refrigeration system was idle. The MIC was kept at 20 degrees Celsius, not the 4.5 degrees advised by the manual. Even the steam boiler, intended to clean the pipes, was non-operational for unknown reasons. Slip-blind plates that would have prevented water from pipes being cleaned from leaking into the MIC tanks, had the valves been faulty, were not installed and their installation had been omitted from the cleaning checklist. As MIC is water-soluble, deluge guns were in place to contain escaping gases from the stack. The water pressure was too weak for the guns to spray high enough to reach the gas which would have reduced the concentration of escaping gas significantly.[1503] In addition to it, carbon steel valves were used at the factory, even though they were known to corrode when exposed to acid.

According to the operators, the MIC tank pressure gauge had been malfunctioning for roughly a week. Other tanks were used, rather than repairing the gauge. The build-up in temperature and pressure is believed to have affected the magnitude of the gas release. UCC admitted in their own investigation report that most of the safety systems were not functioning on the night of 3 December 1984. The design of the MIC plant, following government guidelines, was "Indianized" by UCIL engineers to maximise the use of indigenous materials and products. Mumbai-based Humphreys and Glasgow Consultants Pvt. Ltd., were the main consultants, Larsen & Toubro fabricated the MIC storage tanks, and Taylor of India Ltd. provided the instrumentation.[1504] In 1998, during civil action suits in India, it emerged that the plant was not prepared for problems. No action plans had been established to cope with incidents of this magnitude. This included not informing local authorities of the quantities or dangers of chemicals used and manufactured at Bhopal.

Safety audits

Safety audits were done every year in the US and European UCC plants, but only every two years in other parts of the world. Before a "Business Confidential" safety audit by UCC in May 1982, the senior officials of the corporation were well aware of "a total of 61 hazards, 30 of them major and 11 minor in the dangerous phosgene/methyl isocyanate units" in Bhopal. In the audit 1982, it was indicated that worker performance was below standards. Ten major concerns were listed. UCIL prepared an action plan, but UCC never sent a follow-up team to Bhopal. Many of the items in the 1982 report were temporarily fixed, but by 1984, conditions had again deteriorated. In September 1984, an internal UCC report on the West Virginia plant in the USA revealed a number of defects and malfunctions. It warned that "a runaway reaction could occur in the MIC unit storage tanks, and that the planned response would not be timely or effective enough to prevent catastrophic failure of the tanks". This report was never forwarded to the Bhopal plant, although the main design was the same.

Causes of the disaster: the "disgruntled employee sabotage" case

Now owned by Dow Chemical Company, Union Carbide maintains a website dedicated to the tragedy and claims that the incident was the result of sabotage, stating that sufficient safety systems were in place and operative to prevent the intrusion of water.

The impossibility of the "negligence" argument

According to the "Corporate Negligence" argument, workers had been cleaning out pipes with water nearby. This water was diverted due to a combination of improper maintenance, leaking and clogging, and eventually ended up in the MIC storage tank. Indian scientists also suggested that additional water might have been introduced as a "back-flow" from a defectively designed vent-gas scrubber. None of these theoretical routes of entry were ever successfully demonstrated during tests by the Central Bureau of Investigators (CBI) and UCIL engineers.[1505]

A Union Carbide commissioned analysis conducted by Arthur D. Little claims that the Negligence argument was impossible for several tangible reasons:

1. The pipes being used by the nearby workers were only 1/2 inch in diameter and were physically incapable of producing enough hydraulic pressure to raise water the more than 10 feet that would have been necessary to enable the water to "backflow" into the MIC tank.
2. A key intermediate valve would have had to be open for the Negligence argument to apply. This valve was "tagged" closed, meaning that it had been inspected and found to be closed. While it is possible for open valves to clog over time, the only way a closed valve allows penetration is if there is leakage, and 1985 tests carried out by the government of India found this valve to be non-leaking.

3. In order for water to have reached the MIC tank from the pipe-cleaning area, it would have had to flow through a significant network of pipes ranging from 6 to 8 inches in diameter, before rising ten feet and flowing into the MIC tank. Had this occurred, most of the water that was in those pipes at the time the tank had its critical reaction would have remained in those pipes, as there was no drain for them. Investigation by the Indian government in 1985 revealed that the pipes were bone dry.

The argument for sabotage

The Union Carbide commissioned Arthur D. Little report concludes that it is likely that a single employee secretly and deliberately introduced a large amount of water into the MIC tank by removing a meter and connecting a water hose directly to the tank through the metering port.

UCC claims the plant staff falsified numerous records to distance themselves from the incident and absolve themselves of blame, and that the Indian Government impeded its investigation and declined to prosecute the employee responsible, presumably because that would weaken its allegations of negligence by Union Carbide.

The evidence in favor of this point of view includes:

1. A key witness (the "tea boy") testified that when he entered the control room at 12:15 am, prior to the disaster, the "atmosphere was tense and quiet".
2. Another key witness (the "instrument supervisor") testified that when he arrived at the scene immediately following the incident, he noticed that the local pressure indicator on the critical Tank 610 was missing, and that he had found a hose lying next to the empty manhead created by the missing pressure indicator, and that the hose had had water running out of it.
3. This testimony was corroborated by other witnesses.
4. Graphological analysis revealed major attempts to alter logfiles and destroy log evidence.
5. Other logfiles show that the control team had attempted to purge 1 ton of material out of Tank 610 immediately prior to the disaster. An attempt was then made to cover up this transfer via log alteration. Water is heavier than MIC, and the transfer line is attached to the bottom of the tank. The Arthur D. Little report concludes from this that the transfer was an effort to transfer water out of Tank 610 that had been discovered there.
6. A third key witness (the "off-duty employee of another unit") stated that "he had been told by a close friend of one of the MIC operators that water had entered through a tube that had been connected to the tank." This had

been discovered by the other MIC operators (so the story was recounted) who then tried to open and close valves to prevent the release.
7. A fourth key witness (the "operator from a different unit") stated that after the release, two MIC operators had told him that water had entered the tank through a pressure gauge.

The Little report argues that this evidence demonstrates that the following chronology took place:

- At 10:20pm, the tank was at normal pressure, indicating the absence of water.
- At 10:45pm, a shift change took place, after which the MIC storage area "would be completely deserted".
- During this period, a "disgruntled operator entered the storage area and hooked up one of the readily available rubber water hoses to Tank 610, with the intention of contaminating and spoiling the tank's contents."
- Water began to flow, beginning the chemical reaction that caused the disaster.
- After midnight, control room operators saw the pressure rising and realized there was a problem with Tank 610. They discovered the water connection, and decided to transfer one ton of the contents out to try and remove the water.
- The disaster then occurred, a major release of poisonous gas.
- The cover-up activities discovered during the investigation then took place.
- After over 30 years, S.P. Choudhary, former MIC Production Manager, broke the silence and told the truth about the disaster that it was not an accident but the result of a sabotage that claimed thousands of lives, a former official of the Union Carbide India Limited (UCIL) told the district and sessions court.

The theory of design defect was floated by the central government in its endeavour to do justice to the victims of the tragedy. Everyone else who was part of investigations into the case "just toed the line of the central government.... The government and the CBI suppressed the actual truth and saved the real perpetrators of the crime, the counsel, Anirban Roy told the court."

In November 2017, appearing for two accused S P Chaudhary and J Mukund, their advocate Anirban Roy told the district court on Monday that disgruntled plant operator M L Verma was behind the sabotage because he was unhappy with his seniors. Roy argued that the theory about defects in the plant causing the mishap was imaginary. He said truth had always been suppressed and it's for the CBI to bring it out. The counsel argued that there were discrepancies in the statements given by persons who were operating the plant at that time but the central agency chose not to investigate the case properly because it always wanted to prove that it was a mishap, and not sabotage. He alleged that Verma was unhappy with Chaudhary and Mukund.[1506]

Additional Union Carbide actions

The corporation denied the claim that the valves on the tank were malfunctioning, and claimed that the documented evidence gathered after the incident showed that the valve close to the plant's water-washing operation was closed and was leak-tight. Furthermore, process safety systems had prevented water from entering the tank by accident. Carbide states that the safety concerns identified in 1982 were all allayed before 1984 and had nothing to do with the incident.

The company admitted that the safety systems in place would not have been able to prevent a chemical reaction of that magnitude from causing a leak. According to Carbide, "in designing the plant's safety systems, a chemical reaction of this magnitude was not factored in" because "the tank's gas storage system was designed to automatically prevent such a large amount of water from being inadvertently introduced into the system" and "process safety systems—in place and operational—would have prevented water from entering the tank by accident". Instead, they claim that "employee sabotage—not faulty design or operation—was the cause of the tragedy".

Tactical response

The company stresses the immediate action taken after the disaster and its continued commitment to helping the victims. On 4 December, the day following the leak, Union Carbide sent material aid and several international medical experts to assist the medical facilities in Bhopal.

Financial response

The primary financial restitution paid by UCC was negotiated in 1989, when the Indian Supreme Court approved a settlement of US$470 million (₹1,055 crore (equivalent to ₹80 billion or US$1.2 billion in 2017)). This amount was immediately paid by UCC to the Indian government. The company states that the restitution paid "was $120 million more than plaintiffs' lawyers had told U.S. courts was fair" and that the Indian Supreme Court stated in its opinion that "compensation levels under the settlement were far greater than would normally be payable under Indian law."

In the immediate aftermath of the disaster, Union Carbide states on its website that it put $2 million into the Indian prime minister's immediate disaster relief fund on 11 December 1984. The corporation established the Employees' Bhopal Relief Fund in February 1985, which raised more than $5 million for immediate relief. According to Union Carbide, in August 1987, they made an additional $4.6 million in humanitarian interim relief available.

Union Carbide stated that it also undertook several steps to provide continuing aid to the victims of the Bhopal disaster. The sale of its 50.9 percent interest in UCIL in April 1992 and establishment of a charitable trust to contribute to the building of a local hospital. The sale was finalised in November 1994. The hospital was begun in October 1995 and was opened in 2001. The company provided a fund with around $90 million from sale of its UCIL stock. In 1991, the trust had amounted approximately $100 million. The hospital catered for the treatment of heart, lung and eye problems. UCC also provided a $2.2 million grant to Arizona State University to establish a vocational-technical center in Bhopal, which was opened, but was later closed by the state government. They also donated $5 million to the Indian Red Cross after the disaster. They also developed a Responsible Care system with other members of the chemical industry as a response to the Bhopal crisis, which was designed to help prevent such an event in the future.

Charges against UCC and UCIL employees

UCC chairman and CEO Warren Anderson was arrested and released on bail by the Madhya Pradesh Police in Bhopal on 7 December 1984. Anderson was taken to UCC's house after which he was released six hours later on $2,100 bail and flown out on a government plane. These actions were allegedly taken under the direction of then chief secretary of the state, who was possibly instructed from chief minister's office, who himself flew out of Bhopal immediately. Later in 1987, the Indian government summoned Anderson, eight other executives and two company affiliates with homicide charges to appear in Indian court. In response, Union Carbide said the company is not under Indian jurisdiction.

From 2014, Dow is a named respondent in a number of ongoing cases arising from Union Carbide's business in Bhopal.

Ongoing contamination

Chemicals abandoned at the plant continue to leak and pollute the groundwater. Whether the chemicals pose a health hazard is disputed. Contamination at the site and surrounding area was not caused by the gas leakage. The area around the plant was used as a dumping ground for hazardous chemicals and by 1982 water wells in the vicinity of the UCIL factory had to be abandoned. UCC states that "after the incident, UCIL began clean-up work at the site under the direction of Indian central and state government authorities", which was continued after 1994 by the successor to UCIL. The successor, Eveready Industries India, Limited (EIIL), ended cleanup on the site in 1998, when it

Figure 273: *Deteriorating section of the MIC plant, decades after the gas leak.*

terminated its 99-year lease and turned over control of the site to the state government of Madhya Pradesh.

UCC's laboratory tests in 1989 revealed that soil and water samples collected from near the factory were toxic to fish. Twenty-one areas inside the plant were reported to be highly polluted. In 1991 the municipal authorities declared that water from over 100 wells was hazardous for health if used for drinking. In 1994 it was reported that 21% of the factory premises were seriously contaminated with chemicals.[1507,1508] Beginning in 1999, studies made by Greenpeace and others from soil, groundwater, well water and vegetables from the residential areas around UCIL and from the UCIL factory area show contamination with a range of toxic heavy metals and chemical compounds. Substances found, according to the reports, are naphthol, naphthalene, Sevin, tarry residues, alpha naphthol, mercury, organochlorines, chromium, copper, nickel, lead, hexachlorethane, hexachlorobutadiene, pesticide HCH (BHC), volatile organic compounds and halo-organics.[1509,1510] Many of these contaminants were also found in breast milk of women living near the area. Soil tests were conducted by Greenpeace in 1999. One sample (IT9012) from "sediment collected from drain under former Sevin plant" showed mercury levels to be at "20,000 and 6 million times" higher than expected levels. Organochlorine compounds at elevated levels were also present in groundwater collected from (sample IT9040) a 4.4 meter depth "bore-hole within the former UCIL site". This sample was obtained from a source posted with a warning sign which read

"Water unfit for consumption".[1511] Chemicals that have been linked to various forms of cancer were also discovered, as well as trichloroethylene, known to impair fetal development, at 50 times above safety limits specified by the U.S. Environmental Protection Agency (EPA). In 2002, an inquiry by Fact-Finding Mission on Bhopal found a number of toxins, including mercury, lead, 1,3,5 trichlorobenzene, dichloromethane and chloroform, in nursing women's breast milk.

A 2004 BBC Radio 5 broadcast reported the site is contaminated with toxic chemicals including benzene hexachloride and mercury, held in open containers or loose on the ground. A drinking water sample from a well near the site had levels of contamination 500 times higher than the maximum limits recommended by the World Health Organization. In 2009, the Centre for Science and Environment, a Delhi-based pollution monitoring lab, released test results showing pesticide groundwater contamination up to three kilometres from the factory. Also in 2009, the BBC took a water sample from a frequently used hand pump, located just north of the plant. The sample, tested in UK, was found to contain 1,000 times the World Health Organization's recommended maximum amount of carbon tetrachloride, a carcinogenic toxin.

In 2010, a British photojournalist who ventured into the abandoned Union Carbide factory to investigate allegations of abandoned, leaking toxins, was hospitalized in Bhopal for a week after he was exposed to the chemicals. Doctors at the Sambhavna Clinic treated him with oxygen, painkillers and anti-inflammatories following a severe respiratory reaction to toxic dust inside the factory.

In October 2011, the Institute of Environmental Management and Assessment published an article and video by two British environmental scientists, showing the current state of the plant, landfill and solar evaporation ponds and calling for renewed international efforts to provide the necessary skills to clean up the site and contaminated groundwater.

In popular culture

In 1999, a Hindi film dealing with the tragedy, *Bhopal Express*, was released. The film stars Kay Kay Menon and Naseeruddin Shah.

Amulya Malladi's 2002 novel *A Breath of Fresh Air* relates the story of a mother and son who develop health issues as a result of exposure to gas at Bhopal. The book is based on Malladi's recollections of Bhopal during the incident.

Indra Sinha released *Animal's People* in 2007. The novel tells the story of a boy who is born with a spinal condition due to effects of the gas. The book was shortlisted for the Man Booker Prize.

In 2014, to coincide with the 30th anniversary of the disaster, historical-drama *Bhopal: A Prayer for Rain* was released, starring Martin Sheen as Union Carbide CEO Warren Anderson, Kal Penn, and Mischa Barton. The film earned global praise and *LA Times* critic Martin Tsai said the film was "ambitious and shattering" and that "Although the real-life events took place three decades ago, the cautionary tale could not be more relevant."

Arundhati Roy's 2017 novel *The Ministry of Utmost Happiness* which deals with many contemporary political issues in India also features several characters dealing with the aftermath of the gas leak still.

Activism

Since 1984, individual activists have played a role in the aftermath of the tragedy. The best-known is Satinath Sarangi (Sathyu), a metallurgic engineer who arrived at Bhopal the day after the leakage. He founded several activist groups, as well as Sambhavna Trust, the clinic for gas affected patients, where he is the manager. Other activists include Rashida Bee and Champa Devi Shukla, who received the Goldman Prize in 2004, Abdul Jabbar and Rachna Dhingra.

Local activism

Soon after the accident, representatives from different activist groups arrived. The activists worked on organising the gas victims, which led to violent repression from the police and the government.

Numerous actions have been performed: demonstrations, sit-ins, hunger strikes, marches combined with pamphlets, books, and articles. Every anniversary, actions are performed. Often these include marches around Old Bhopal, ending with burning an effigy of Warren Anderson.

International activism

Cooperation with international NGOs including Pesticide Action Network UK[1512] and Greenpeace[1513] started soon after the tragedy. One of the earliest reports is the Trade Union report from ILO 1985.

In 1992, a session of the Permanent Peoples' Tribunal on Industrial Hazards and Human Rights took place in Bhopal, and in 1996, the "Charter on Industrial Hazards and Human Rights"[1514] was adopted.

In 1994, the International Medical Commission on Bhopal (IMCB) met in Bhopal. Their work contributed to long term health effects being officially recognised.

Important international actions have been the tour to Europe and United States in 2003, the marches to Delhi in 2006 and 2008, all including hunger strikes, and the Bhopal Europe Bus Tour in 2009.

Activist organisations

At least 14 different NGOs were immediately engaged. The first disaster reports were published by activist organisations, Eklavya and the Delhi Science Forum.

Around ten local organisations, engaged on long term, have been identified. Two of the most active organisations are the women's organisations—Bhopal Gas Peedit Mahila-Stationery Karmachari Sangh and Bhopal Gas Peedit Mahila Udyog Sangthan.

More than 15 national organisations have been engaged along with a number of international organisations.

Some of the most important organisations are:

- International Campaign for Justice in Bhopal (ICJB), coordinates international activities.
- Bhopal Medical Appeal, collects funds for the Sambhavna Trust.
- Sambhavna Trust or Bhopal People's Health and Documentation Clinic. Provides medical care for gas affected patients and those living in water-contaminated area.
- Chingari Trust, provides medical care for children being born in Bhopal with malformations and brain damages.
- Students for Bhopal, based in USA.
- International Medical Commission on Bhopal, provided medical information 1994–2000.

Settlement fund hoax

On 3 December 2004, the twentieth anniversary of the disaster, a man falsely claiming to be a Dow representative named Jude Finisterra was interviewed on BBC World News. He claimed that the company had agreed to clean up the site and compensate those harmed in the incident, by liquidating Union Carbide for US$12 billion. Dow quickly issued a statement saying that they had no employee by that name—that he was an impostor, not affiliated with Dow, and that his claims were a hoax. The BBC later broadcast a correction and an apology.

Jude Finisterra was actually Andy Bichlbaum, a member of the activist prankster group The Yes Men. In 2002, The Yes Men issued a fake press release explaining why Dow refused to take responsibility for the disaster and started up a website, at "DowEthics.com", designed to look like the real Dow website, but containing hoax information.

Monitoring of Bhopal activists

The release of an email cache related to intelligence research organisation Stratfor was leaked by WikiLeaks on 27 February 2012. It revealed that Dow Chemical had engaged Stratfor to spy on the public and personal lives of activists involved in the Bhopal disaster, including the Yes Men. E-mails to Dow representatives from hired security analysts list the YouTube videos liked, Twitter and Facebook posts made and the public appearances of these activists. Journalists, film-makers and authors who were investigating Bhopal and covering the issue of ongoing contamination, such as Jack Laurenson and Max Carlson, were also placed under surveillance. Stratfor released a statement condemning the revelation by Wikileaks while neither confirming nor denying the accuracy of the reports, and would only state that it had acted within the bounds of the law. Dow Chemical also refrained to comment on the matter.

Ingrid Eckerman, a member of the International Medical Commission on Bhopal, has been denied a visa to visit India.

References

- Broughton E (10 May 2005). "The Bhopal disaster and its aftermath: a review"[1515]. *Environmental Health*. **4** (1): 6 pages. doi: 10.1186/1476-069X-4-6[1516]. PMC 1142333[1517] ∂. PMID 15882472[1518].
- *Carbon monoxide, Phosgene and Methyl isocyanate. Unit Safety Procedures Manual*. Union Carbide India Limited, Agricultural Products Division: Bhopal (1978)
- Cassels, J (1993). *The Uncertain Promise of Law: Lessons From Bhopal*. University of Toronto Press.
- Chouhan TR, et al. (2004) [1994]. *Bhopal: the Inside Story — Carbide Workers Speak Out on the World's Worst Industrial Disaster*. US and India: The Apex Press and Other India Press. ISBN 1-891843-30-3 and ISBN 81-85569-65-7. Main author Chouhan was an operator at the plant. Contains many technical details.
- Chouhan TR (2005). "The Unfolding of Bhopal Disaster"[1519]. *Journal of Loss Prevention in the process industry*. **18** (4–6): 205–208. doi: 10.1016/j.jlp.2005.07.025[1520].

- Dhara VR, Gassert TH (September 2005). "The Bhopal gas tragedy: Evidence for cyanide poisoning not convincing"[1521] (PDF). *Current Science*. **89** (6): 923–5. Archived from the original[1522] (PDF) on 30 October 2008.
- D'Silva T (2006). *The Black Box of Bhopal: A Closer Look at the World's Deadliest Industrial Disaster*[1523]. Victoria, B.C.: Trafford. ISBN 1-4120-8412-1. Review[1524] Written by a retired former employee of UCC who was a member of the investigation committee. Includes several original documents including correspondence between UCIL and the Ministries of the Government of India.
- Eckerman I (2001). *Chemical Industry and Public Health—Bhopal as an example*[1525] (PDF). Essay for MPH. A short overview, 57 pages, 82 references.
- Eckerman I (2005). *The Bhopal Saga—Causes and Consequences of the World's Largest Industrial Disaster*[1526]. India: Universities Press. ISBN 81-7371-515-7. Preview Google books[1527] All known facts 1960s – 2003, systematised and analysed. 283 pages, over 200 references.
- Eckerman I (2006). "The Bhopal Disaster 1984 – working conditions and the role of the trade unions"[1528] (PDF). *Asian Pacific Newsletter on occupational health and safety*. **13** (2). Archived from the original[1529] (PDF) on 16 July 2011.
- Eckerman I (2011). "Bhopal Gas Catastrophy 1984: Causes and consequences". In Nriagu JO. *Encyclopedia of Environmental Health*. **1**. Burlington: Elsevier. pp. 302–316. doi: 10.1016/B978-0-444-52272-6.00359-7[1530]. ISBN 978-0-444-52272-6.
- Eckerman I (2013). "Bhopal Gas Catastrophe 1984: Causes and Consequences"[1531]. *Reference Module in Earth Systems and Environmental Sciences*. Elsevier. ISBN 978-0-12-409548-9.
- Gassert TH, Dhara VR (September 2005). "Debate on cyanide poisoning in Bhopal victims"[1521] (PDF). *Current Science*. **89** (6). Archived from the original[1522] (PDF) on 30 October 2008.
- Hanna B, Morehouse W, Sarangi S (2005). *The Bhopal Reader. Remembering Twenty Years of the World's Worst Industrial Disaster*[1532]. US: The Apex Press. ISBN 1-891843-32-X USA, ISBN 81-85569-70-3 India. Reprinting and annotating landmark writing from across the years.
- Johnson S, Sahu R, Jadon N, Duca C (2009). *Contamination of soil and water inside and outside the Union Carbide India Limited, Bhopal*. New Delhi: Centre for Science and Environment. In Down to Earth
- Kalelkar AS, Little AD (1998). *Investigation of Large-magnitude incidents: Bhopal as a Case Study*[1533] (PDF). Archived from the original[1534] (PDF) on 30 October 2008. London: The Institution of Chemical Engineers Conference on Preventing Major Chemical Accidents

- Kovel J (2002). *The Enemy of Nature: The End of Capitalism or the End of the World?*[1535]. London: Zed Books. ISBN 978-1-55266-255-7.
- Kulling P, Lorin H (1987). *The Toxic Gas Disaster in Bhopal December 2–3, 1984*. Stockholm: National Defence Research Institute. [In Swedish]
- Kurzman, D. (1987). *A Killing Wind: Inside Union Carbide and the Bhopal Catastrophe*. New York: McGraw-Hill.
- Labunska I, Stephenson A, Brigden K, Stringer R, Santillo D, Johnston PA (1999). *The Bhopal Legacy. Toxic contaminants at the former Union Carbide factory site, Bhopal, India: 15 years after the Bhopal accident*[1536] (PDF). Archived from the original[1537] (PDF) on 30 October 2008.Greenpeace Research Laboratories, Department of Biological Sciences, University of Exeter, Exeter UK
- Lepowski W (19 December 1994). "Ten Years Later: Bhopal". *Chemical and Engineering News*.
- *Methyl Isocyanate. Union Carbide F-41443A – 7/76*. New York: Union Carbide Corporation. 1976.
- *Operating Manual Part II. Methyl Isocyanate Unit*. Union Carbide India Limited, Agricultural Products Division (1979).
- Ranjan N, Sarangi S, Padmanabhan VT, Holleran S, Ramakrishnan R, Varma DR (2003). "Methyl Isocyanate Exposure and Growth Patterns of Adolescents in Bhopal Methyl Isocyanate Exposure and Growth Patterns of Adolescents in Bhopal". *JAMA*. **290** (14): 1856–7. doi: 10.1001/jama.290.14.1856[1538]. PMID 14532313[1539].
- Sriramachari S (2004). "The Bhopal gas tragedy: An environmental disaster"[1540] (PDF). *Current Science*. **86**: 905–920. Archived from the original[1541] (PDF) on 30 October 2008.
- Stringer R, Labunska I, Brigden K, Santillo D (2003). *Chemical Stockpiles at Union Carbide India Limited in Bhopal: An investigation (Technical Note 12/2002)*[1542] (PDF). Greenpeace Research Laboratories.
- Shrishti (2002). *Toxic present—toxic future. A report on Human and Environmental Chemical Contamination around the Bhopal disaster site*. Delhi: The Other Media.
- Varadarajan S, et al. (1985). *Report on Scientific Studies on the Factors Related to Bhopal Toxic Gas Leakage*. New Delhi: Indian Council of Scientific and Industrial Research. https://bhopalgasdisaster.files.wordpress.com/2014/12/csir-report-on-scientific-studies-december-1985.pdf>
- Weir D (1987). *The Bhopal Syndrome: Pesticides, Environment and Health*. San Francisco: Sierra Club Books. ISBN 0-87156-718-0.
- Lapierre D, Moro J (2009). *Five Past Midnight in Bhopal: The Epic Story of the World's Deadliest Industrial Disaster*[1543]. Hachette Digital, Inc. ISBN 9780446561242.
- "Review 'Bhopal: A Prayer for Rain' an effective cautionary tale"[1544].

- See also http://www.pressreader.com/india/hindustan-times-st-indore/20160721/281603829819042

Union Carbide Corporation

- Methyl Isocyanate. Union Carbide F-41443A – 7/76. Union Carbide Corporation, New York (1976)
- Carbon monoxide, Phosgene and Methyl isocyanate. Unit Safety Procedures Manual. Union Carbide India Limited, Agricultural Products Division: Bhopal (1978)
- Operating Manual Part II. Methyl Isocyanate Unit. Union Carbide India Limited, Agricultural Products Division (1979).
- Bhopal Methyl Isocyanate Incident. Investigation Team Report. Union Carbide Corporation, Danbury, CT (1985).
- Presence of Toxic Ingredients in Soil/Water Samples Inside Plant Premises. Union Carbide Corporation, US (1989).

External links

Wikimedia Commons has media related to *Bhopal disaster*.

- International Campaign for Justice in Bhopal[1545]
- Bhopal Medical Appeal[1546]
- Bhopal Gas Tragedy Relief & Rehabilitation Department[1547] at the Government of Madhya Pradesh
- Bhopal Information Center[1548], Union Carbide
- India Environmental Portal[1549] Updated news on Bhopal Gas Disaster
- Bhopal:Anatomy of a Crisis[1550] Paul Shrivastava, Paul Chapman Publishing, 1987, ISBN 1-85396-192-2

Indian intervention in the Sri Lankan Civil War

Indian Intervention in the Sri Lankan Civil War	
Part of the Sri Lankan civil war	
Date	29 July 1987 – 24 March 1990 (2 years, 7 months, 3 weeks and 3 days)
Location	Sri Lanka
Result	Withdrawal of the IPKF from Sri Lanka, Civil war continues. No result.
Belligerents	
Indian Peace Keeping Force Sri Lanka	Liberation Tigers of Tamil Eelam (LTTE)
Commanders and leaders	
R. Venkataraman Rajiv Gandhi V P Singh Maj.Gen. Harkirat Singh Maj.Gen. Ashok K. Mehta	Velupillai Prabhakaran
Casualties and losses	
IPKF: 1,138 killed, 2762 Wounded	

The **Indian intervention in the Sri Lankan Civil War** was the deployment of the Indian Peace Keeping Force in Sri Lanka intended to perform a peacekeeping role. The deployment followed the Indo-Sri Lankan Accord between India and Sri Lanka of 1987 which was intended to end the Sri Lankan Civil War between militant Sri Lankan Tamil nationalists, principally the Liberation Tigers of Tamil Eelam (LTTE), and the Sri Lankan military.

The original intention was the Indian Peace Keeping Force would not be involved in large scale military operations. However, after a few months, the Indian Peace Keeping Force engaged the Liberation Tigers of Tamil Eelam in a series of battles. During the two years in which it was deployed, the IPKF fought numerous battles against the LTTE. The IPKF began withdrawing in 1989, and completed the withdrawal in 1990.

Background

According to Rejaul Karim Laskar, a scholar of Indian foreign policy, Indian intervention in Sri Lankan civil war became inevitable as that civil war threatened India's "unity, national interest and territorial integrity." According to Laskar, this threat came in two ways: On the one hand external powers could take advantage of the situation to establish their base in Sri Lanka thus posing a threat to India, and on the other, the LTTE's dream of a sovereign Tamil Eelam comprising all the Tamil inhibited areas (of Sri Lanka and India) posed a threat to India's territorial integrity.

The LTTE and other Tamil militant groups developed strong relationships with political parties in South India, such as Pure Tamil Movement (led by Perunchithiranar), Dravidar Kazhagam (led by K. Veeramani), Kamaraj Congress (led by Nedumaran) during the late 1970s. These Tamil parties firmly backed the militants' cause of creating a separate Tamil Eelam within Sri Lanka. Thereafter, LTTE developed relations with M. G. Ramachandran and M. Karunanidhi, who served as Chief Minister of Tamil Nadu, succeeding one another.

Although Sri Lanka was a key member of Non-Aligned Movement in its initial stages, the Government of Sri Lanka's policies became pro-western as J. R. Jayewardene was elected prime minister with his landslide victory in 1977 parliamentary election. Subsequently, he introduced a new constitution and Open economy to Sri Lanka. Sri Lanka is the first South-Asian country to adopt Liberal open economy.

Moreover, President J. R. Jayawardene did not enjoy the same warm relationship with Indian Prime Minister Indira Gandhi that he had enjoyed with her father, Prime Minister Jawaharlal Nehru. Thus, with the outbreak of Black July ethnic riots, the Indian government decided to support the insurgent groups operating in Northern Sri Lanka.Wikipedia:Citation needed From mid 1983, on the instructions of Indira Gandhi, RAW began funding, arming and training several Tamil insurgent groups.

Operation Poomalai

India became more actively involved in the late 1980s, and on June 5, 1987, the Indian Air Force airdropped food parcels to Jaffna while it was under siege by Sri Lankan forces. At a time when the Sri Lankan government stated they were close to defeating the LTTE, India dropped 25 tons of food and medicine by parachute into areas held by the LTTE in a direct move of support toward the rebels. Further Sri Lanka government accused this ridiculous action that not only food and medicine but weapons also supplied to the LTTE. Negotiations were held, and the Indo-Sri Lanka Peace Accord was signed on July 29, 1987, by Indian Prime Minister Rajiv Gandhi and Sri Lankan President Jayewardene. Under this accord, the Sri Lankan Government made a number of concessions to Tamil demands, including a devolution of power to the provinces, a merger—subject to later referendum—of the Northern and the Eastern provinces into the single province, and official status for the Tamil language (this was enacted as the 13th Amendment to the Constitution of Sri

Lanka). India agreed to establish order in the North and East through a force dubbed the Indian Peace Keeping Force (IPKF), and to cease assisting Tamil insurgents. Militant groups including the LTTE, although initially reluctant, agreed to surrender their arms to the IPKF, which initially oversaw a cease-fire and a modest disarmament of the militant groups.

The signing of the Indo-Lanka Accord, so soon after JR Jayawardene's declaration that he would fight the Indians to the last bullet, led to unrest in south. The arrival of the IPKF to take over control of most areas in the North of the country enabled the Sri Lanka government to shift its forces to the south (in Indian aircraft) to quell the protests. This led to an uprising by the Janatha Vimukthi Peramuna in the south, which was put down bloodily over the next two years.

Conflict with the LTTE

While most Tamil militant groups laid down their weapons and agreed to seek a peaceful solution to the conflict, the LTTE refused to disarm its fighters. Keen to ensure the success of the accord, the IPKF then tried to demobilize the LTTE by force and ended up in full-scale conflict with them. The three-year-long conflict was also marked by the IPKF being accused of committing various abuses of human rights by many human rights groups as well as some within the Indian media. The IPKF also soon met stiff opposition from the Tamils.[1551,1552]

Operation Pawan

Operation Pawan was the codename assigned to the operations by the Indian Peace Keeping Force to take control of Jaffna from the LTTE in late 1987 to enforce the disarmament of the LTTE as a part of the Indo-Sri Lankan Accord. In brutal fighting that took about three weeks, the IPKF wrested control of the Jaffna Peninsula from LTTE rule, something that the Sri Lankan army had then tried and failed to achieve for several years. Supported by Indian Army tanks, helicopter gunships and heavy artillery, the IPKF routed the LTTE. The IPKF lost around 214 soldiers in this operation.[1553]

The Jaffna University Helidrop

The Jaffna University Helidrop was the first of the operations launched by the Indian Peace Keeping Forces (IPKF) aimed at disarming the Tamil Tigers (LTTE) by force and securing the town of Jaffna, Sri Lanka, in the opening stages of Operation Pawan during the active Indian mediation in the Sri Lankan Civil War. Mounted on the midnight of 12 October 1987, the operation was planned as a fast heliborne assault involving Mi-8s of the No.109

HU, the 10th Para Commandos and a contingent of the 13th Sikh LI. The aim of the operation was to capture the LTTE leadership at Jaffna University building which served as the Tactical Headquarters of the LTTE, which was expected to shorten Operation Pawan, the battle for Jaffna. However, the operation ended disastrously, failing to capture its objectives -owing to intelligence and planning failures. The helidropped force suffered significant casualties, with nearly the entire Sikh LI detachment of twenty nine troops falling to a man, along with six Paracommandos falling in battle.

End of Indian involvement

Nationalist sentiment led many Sinhalese to oppose the continued Indian presence in Sri Lanka. These led to the Sri Lankan government's call for India to quit the island, and they allegedly entered into a secret deal with the LTTE that culminated in a ceasefire. But the LTTE and IPKF continued to have frequent hostilities. In April 1989, the Ranasinghe Premadasa government ordered the Sri Lanka Army to clandestinely hand over arms consignments to the LTTE to fight the IPKF and its proxy Tamil National Army (TNA).[1554] Although casualties among the IPKF mounted, and calls for the withdrawal of the IPKF from both sides of the Sri Lankan conflict grew, Rajiv Gandhi refused to remove the IPKF from Sri Lanka. However, following his defeat in Indian parliamentary elections in December 1989, the new prime Minister V. P. Singh ordered the withdrawal of the IPKF, and their last ship left Sri Lanka on 24 March 1990. The 32-month presence of the IPKF in Sri Lanka resulted in the deaths of 1200 Indian soldiers and over 5000 Sri Lankans. The cost for the Indian government was estimated at over ▯10.3 billion.

Rajiv Gandhi's assassination

Support for the LTTE in India dropped considerably in 1991, after the assassination of ex-Prime Minister Rajiv Gandhi by a female suicide bomber named Thenmozhi Rajaratnam. The Indian press has subsequently reported that Prabhakaran decided to eliminate Gandhi as he considered the ex-Prime Minister to be against the Tamil liberation struggle and feared that he might reinduct the IPKF, which Prabhakaran termed the "satanic force", if he won the 1991 Indian general election. In 1998 a court in India presided over by Special Judge V. Navaneetham found the LTTE and its leader Velupillai Prabhakaran responsible for the assassination. In a 2006 interview, LTTE ideologue Anton Balasingham stated regret over the assassination, although he stopped short of outright acceptance of responsibility for it. India remained an outside observer of the conflict, after the assassination.

Further reading

- Gunaratna, Rohan. (1997). *International & Regional Security Implications of the Sri Lankan Tamil Insurgency*, AABC for International Studies. ISBN 955-95060-0-5
- Gunaratna, Rohan. (1998). *Sri Lanka's Ethnic Crisis and National Security*, Colombo: South Asian Network on Conflict Research. ISBN 955-8093-00-9
- Gunaratna, Rohan. (October 1, 1987). *War and Peace in Sri Lanka: With a Post-Accord Report From Jaffna*, Sri Lanka: Institute of Fundamental Studies. ISBN 955-8093-00-9

 Wikimedia Commons has media related to *Sri Lankan Civil War*.

Siachen conflict

Siachen conflict

Part of the Indo-Pakistani wars and conflicts and the Kashmir conflict

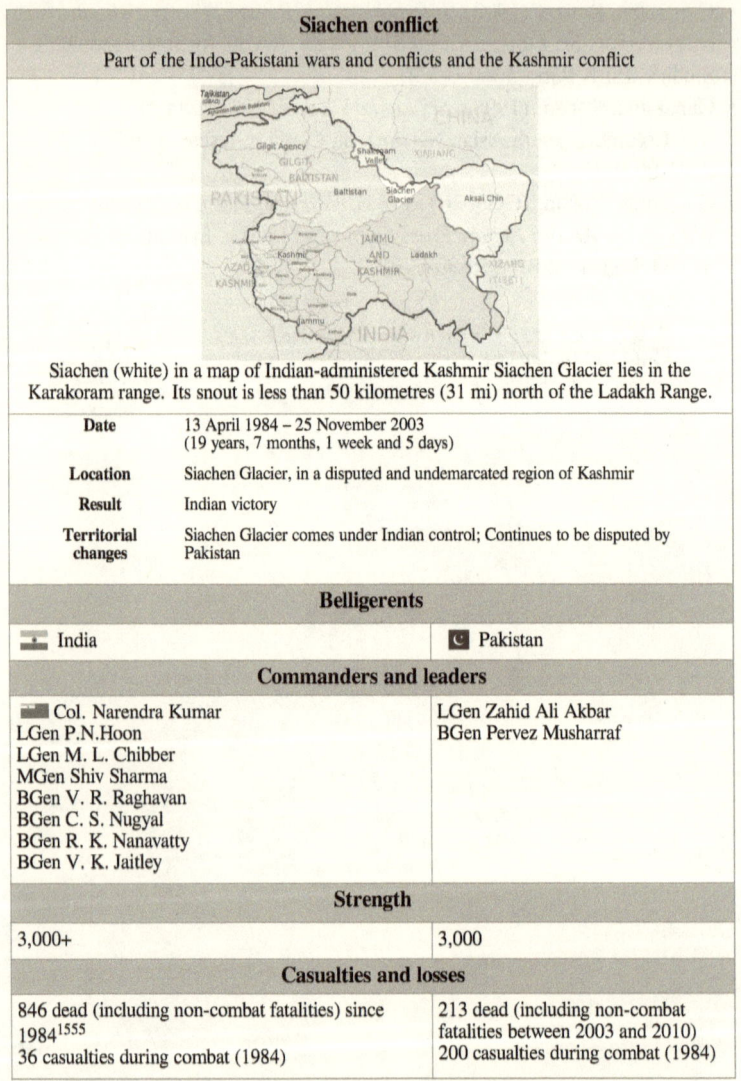

Siachen (white) in a map of Indian-administered Kashmir Siachen Glacier lies in the Karakoram range. Its snout is less than 50 kilometres (31 mi) north of the Ladakh Range.

Date	13 April 1984 – 25 November 2003 (19 years, 7 months, 1 week and 5 days)
Location	Siachen Glacier, in a disputed and undemarcated region of Kashmir
Result	Indian victory
Territorial changes	Siachen Glacier comes under Indian control; Continues to be disputed by Pakistan

Belligerents

India	Pakistan

Commanders and leaders

Col. Narendra Kumar LGen P.N.Hoon LGen M. L. Chibber MGen Shiv Sharma BGen V. R. Raghavan BGen C. S. Nugyal BGen R. K. Nanavatty BGen V. K. Jaitley	LGen Zahid Ali Akbar BGen Pervez Musharraf

Strength

3,000+	3,000

Casualties and losses

846 dead (including non-combat fatalities) since 1984[1555] 36 casualties during combat (1984)	213 dead (including non-combat fatalities between 2003 and 2010) 200 casualties during combat (1984)

The **Siachen conflict**, sometimes referred to as the **Siachen War**, was a military conflict between India and Pakistan over the disputed Siachen Glacier region in Kashmir. A cease-fire went into effect in 2003. The contended area is nearly 1,000 square miles (2,600 km^2) of territory.[1556] The conflict began in 1984 with India's successful Operation *Meghdoot* during which it gained control over all of the Siachen Glacier (unoccupied and undemarcated area).

Figure 274: *UN map of Siachen*

India has established control over all of the 70-kilometre-long (43 mi) Siachen Glacier and all of its tributary glaciers, as well as all the main passes and heights of the Saltoro Ridge immediately west of the glacier, including Sia La, Bilafond La, and Gyong La. Pakistan controls the glacial valleys immediately west of the Saltoro Ridge. According to *TIME* magazine, India gained more than 1,000 square miles (3,000 km^2) of territory because of its military operations in Siachen.

Causes

The Siachen Glacier is the highest battleground on earth,[1557,1558] where India and Pakistan have fought intermittently since 13 April 1984. Both countries maintain permanent military presence in the region at a height of over 6,000 metres (20,000 ft). More than 2000 people have died in this inhospitable terrain, mostly due to weather extremes and the natural hazards of mountain warfare.Wikipedia:Citation needed

The conflict in Siachen stems from the incompletely demarcated territory on the map beyond the map coordinate known as NJ9842 (35.008371°N 77.008805°E[1559]). The 1949 Karachi Agreement and 1972 Simla Agreement did not clearly mention who controlled the glacier, merely stating that the Cease

Fire Line (CFL) terminated at NJ9842. UN officials presumed there would be no dispute between India and Pakistan over such a cold and barren region.[1560]

Paragraph B 2 (d) of Karachi Agreement

Following the UN-mediated ceasefire in the 1949, the line between India and Pakistan was demarcated up to point NJ9842 at the foot of the Siachen Glacier. The largely inaccessible terrain beyond this point was not demarcated, but delimited as **thence north to the glaciers** in paragraph B 2 (d) of the Karachi Agreement.

Paragraph B 2 (d) of 1949 Karachi Agreement states:

> *(d) From Dalunang eastwards the cease-fire line will follow the general line point 15495, Ishman, Manus, Gangam, Gunderman, Point 13620, Funkar (Point 17628), Marmak, Natsara, Shangruti (Point 1,531), Chorbat La (Point 16700), Chalunka (on the Shyok River), Khor,* **thence north to the glaciers***. This portion of the cease-fire line shall be demarcated in detail on the basis of the factual position as of 27 July 1949, by the local commanders assisted by United Nations military observers.*

Later, following the Indo-Pakistani War of 1971, and the Simla Agreement in July 1972, the ceasefire line was converted into the "Line of Control" extending from the *"Chhamb sector on the international border [to] the Turtok-Partapur sector in the north."* The detailed description of its northern end stated that from Chimbatia in the Turtok sector *"the line of control runs north-eastwards to Thang (inclusive to India), thence eastwards joining the glaciers."* This vague formulation further sowed the seed for the bitter dispute to follow. The general description of CFL given in Section 1 of Karachi Agreement is further explained at Page 38 where it states:

> *"thence northwards along the boundary line going through Point 18402 up to NJ-9842"*

The U.N. document number S/1430/Add.2. is the second addendum to the 1949 Karachi Agreement, and shows the CFL marked on the Map of the State of Jammu and Kashmir as per the explanation of CFL in paragraph 'B' 2 (d) of the Karachi Agreement.

U.N. map of ceasefire line

Title of U.N. document number S/1430/Add.2 which illustrates the CFL as per the Karachi Agreement reads:

> *Map of the State of Jammu and Kashmir showing the Cease Fire Line as Agreed Upon in the Karachi Agreement, Ratified by the Governments of India and Pakistan on 29 and 30 July Respectively. (See Annex 26 to the third Interim Report of the United Nation Commission for India and Pakistan)*

 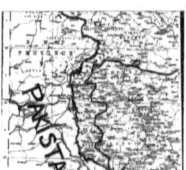 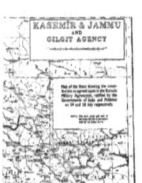 

Figure 275: *Page-1 of U.N. Map Number S/1430/Add. 2 to Karachi Agreement 1949*

Figure 276: *Page-2 of U.N. Map Number S/1430/Add.2 showing the CFL*

Figure 277: *Page-3 U.N. Map Number S/1430/Add. 2 showing the CFL up to Point NJ 9842*

Figure 278: *Present Map of Indian Jammu and Kashmir state including entire Siachen glacier*

A U.N. map showing CFL alignment superimposed on a satellite image depicts the CFL terminating at NJ9842. The extension of this line "thence north to the glaciers" never appeared on any authoritative map associated with either the 1948 or 1972 agreements, just in the text.

Oropolitics

In 1949, a Cease-Fire Line Agreement (CFL) was signed and ratified by India, Pakistan and the UN Military Observer Group that delineated entire CFL. In 1956–58, a scientific team led by the Geological Survey of India recorded its findings publicly including information about the Siachen and other glaciers.

After Pakistan ceded Shaksgam Valley to China in a boundary agreement in 1963, Pakistan started giving approval to western expeditions to the east of mountain K2.[1561] In 1957 Pakistan permitted a British expedition under Eric Shipton to approach the Siachen glacier through the Bilafond La, and recce Saltoro Kangri.[1562] Five years later a Japanese-Pakistani expedition put two Japanese and a Pakistani Army climber on top of Saltoro Kangri.[1563] These were early moves in this particular game of oropolitics.

In the 1970s and early 1980s several mountaineering expeditions applied to Pakistan to climb high peaks in the Siachen area due in part to US Defense Mapping Agency and most other maps and atlases showing it on the Pakistani side of the line. Pakistan granted a number of permits. This in turn reinforced the Pakistani claim on the area, as these expeditions arrived on the glacier with a permit obtained from the Government of Pakistan. Teram Kangri I (7,465 m or 24,491 ft) and Teram Kangri II (7,406 m or 24,298 ft) were climbed in 1975 by a Japanese expedition led by H. Katayama, which approached through Pakistan via the Bilafond La.[1564]

In 1978 a German Siachen-Kondus Expedition under the leadership of Jaroslav Poncar (further members Volker Stallbohm and Wolfgang Kohl, liaison officer major Asad Raza) entered Siachen via Bilafond La and established the base camp on the confuence of Siachen and Teram Shehr. The documentary "Expedition to the longest glacier" was shown on the 3rd channel of WDR (German TV) in 1979.

The Indian government and military took notice, and protested the cartography. Prior to 1984 neither India nor Pakistan had any permanent presence in the area. Having become aware of the US military maps and the permit incidents, Colonel Narendra Kumar, then commanding officer of the Indian Army's High Altitude Warfare School, mounted an Army expedition to the Siachen area as a counter-exercise. In 1978 this expedition climbed Teram Kangri II, claiming it as a first ascent in a typical 'oropolitical' riposte. Unusually for the normally secretive Indian Army, the news and photographs of this expedition were published in The Illustrated Weekly of India, a widely circulated popular magazine.

The first public acknowledgment of the maneuvers and the developing conflict situation in the Siachen was an abbreviated article titled "High Politics in the Karakoram" by Joydeep Sircar in *The Telegraph* newspaper of Calcutta in 1982. The full text was re-printed as "Oropolitics" in the Alpine Journal, London, in 1984.[1565]

Historic maps of Siachen Glacier

Maps from Pakistan, the United Nations and other global atlases depicted the CFL correctly till around 1967–72. The United States Defense Mapping Agency (now National Geospatial-Intelligence Agency) began in about 1967 to show international boundary on their Tactical Pilotage Charts as proceeding from NJ9842 east-northeast to the Karakoram Pass at 5,534 m (18,136 ft) on the China border.Wikipedia:Citation needed

US, Pakistani and Indian maps in the 1970s and 1980s were consistently showing a dotted line from NJ9842 (the northernmost demarcated point of the India-Pakistan cease-fire line, also known as the *Line of Control*) to the Karakoram Pass, which India believed to be a cartographic error.Wikipedia:Citation needed

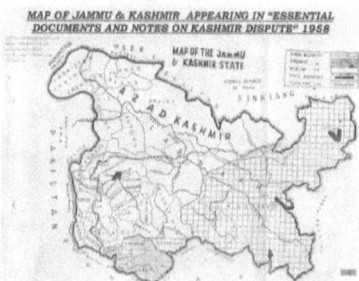

Figure 279: *Map showing Siachen Glacier as part of Pakistan*

Military expeditions

In 1977, an Indian colonel named Narendra Kumar, offended by international expeditions venturing onto the glacier from the Pakistani side, persuaded his superiors to allow him to lead a 70-man team of climbers and porters to the glacier. They returned in or around 1981, climbed several peaks and walked the length of Siachen.

Major combat operations

At army headquarters in Rawalpindi, the discovery of repeated Indian military expeditions to the glacier drove Pakistani generals to the idea of securing Siachen before India did. In the haste to pull together operational resources, Pakistan planners made a tactical error, according to a now retired Pakistani army colonel. "They ordered Arctic-weather gear from a London outfitters who also supplied the Indians," says the colonel. "Once the Indians got wind of it, they ordered 300 outfits—twice as many as we had—and rushed their men up to Siachen". The acquisition of key supplies needed for operations in glaciated zones marked the start of major combat operations on the glacier.

April 1984 Operation Meghdoot: Indian Army under the leadership of Lt. Gen. Manohar Lal Chibber, Maj. Gen. Shiv Sharma, and Lt. Gen. P. N. Hoon learned of the plan by Pakistan Army to seize Sia La, and Bilafond La, on the glacier. Indian Army launched an operation to preempt the seizure of the passes by the Pakistan Army. Men of the Ladakh Scouts and Kumaon Regiment occupy Bilafond La on 13 April and Sia La on 17 April 1984 with the help of the Indian Air Force. Pakistan Army in turn learned of the presence of Ladakh Scouts on the passes during a helicopter recon mission. In

Figure 280: *A memorial at the headquarters of the Dogra Regiment of the Indian Army in remembrance of members of the regiment who died or served in the Siachen Conflict.*

response to these developments Pakistan Army initiated an operation using troops from the Special Services Group and Northern Light Infantry to displace the three hundred or so Indian troops on the key passes. This operation led by the Pakistan Army led to the first armed clash on the glacier on 25 April 1984.

June – July 1987: Operation Rajiv: Over the next three years, with Indian troops positioned at the critical passes, Pakistan Army attempted to seize heights overlooking the passes. One of the biggest successes achieved by Pakistan in this period was the seizure of a feature overlooking Bilafond La. This feature was named "Qaid Post" and for three years it dominated Indian positions on the glacier. Pakistani Army held Qaid post overlooked Bilafond La area and offered and excellent vantage point to view Indian Army activities. On 25 June 1987 Indian Army under the leadership of Brig. Gen. Chandan Nugyal, Major Varinder Singh, Lt. Rajiv Pande and Naib Subedar Bana Singh launched a successful strike on Qaid Post and captured it from Pakistani forces. For his role in the assault, Subedar Bana Singh was awarded the Param Vir Chakra – India's highest gallantry award. The post was renamed Bana Post in his honour.

September 1987: Operation Vajrashakti/Op Qaidat: The Pakistan Army under Brig. Gen. Pervez Musharraf (later President of Pakistan) launched Operation Qaidat to retake Qaid peak. For this purpose units from Pakistan Army SSG (1st and 3rd battalions) assembled a major task force at the newly constructed Khaplu garrison.[1566] Having detected Pakistani movements ahead of Operation Qaidat, the Indian Army initiated Op Vajrashakti to secure the now renamed Bana Post from Pakistani attack.[1567]

March – May 1989: In March 1989 Operation Ibex by Indian Army attempted to seize the Pakistani post overlooking the Chumik Glacier. The operation was unsuccessful at dislodging Pakistani troops from their positions. Indian Army under Brig. R. K. Nanavatty launched an artillery attack on Kauser Base, the Pakistani logistical node in Chumik and successfully destroyed it. The destruction of Kauser Base induced Pakistani troops to vacate Chumik posts concluding Operation Ibex.[1568]

28 July – 3 August 1992: Indian Army launched Operation Trishul Shakti to protect the Bahadur post in Chulung when it was attacked by a large Pakistani assault team. On 1 August 1992, Pakistani helicopters were attacked by an Indian Igla missile and Brig. Masood Navid Anwari (PA 10117) then Force Commander Northern Areas and other accompanying troops were killed. This led to a loss of momentum on the Pakistani side and the assault stalled.

May 1995: Battle of Tyakshi Post: Pakistan Army NLI units attacked Tyakshi post at the very southern edge of the Saltoro defense line. The attack was repulsed by Indian troops.[1569]

June 1999: Indian Army under Brig. P. C. Katoch, Col. Konsam Himalaya Singh seized control of pt 5770 (Naveed Top/Cheema Top/Bilal Top) in southern edge of the Saltoro defense line from Pakistan troops.[1570]

Ground situation

In his memoirs, former Pakistani president General Pervez Musharraf states that Pakistan lost almost 900 square miles (2,300 km^2) of territory that it claimed.[1571] *TIME* states that the Indian advance captured nearly 1,000 square miles (2,600 km^2) of territory claimed by Pakistan.

Further attempts to reclaim positions were launched by Pakistan in 1990, 1995, 1996 and even in early 1999, just prior to the Lahore Summit.Wikipedia:Citation needed

The Indian army controls all of the 76 kilometres (47 mi) long Siachen Glacier and all of its tributary glaciers, as well as all the main passes and heights of the Saltoro Ridge[1572] immediately west of the glacier, including Sia La, Bilafond La, and Gyong La—thus holding onto the tactical advantage of high

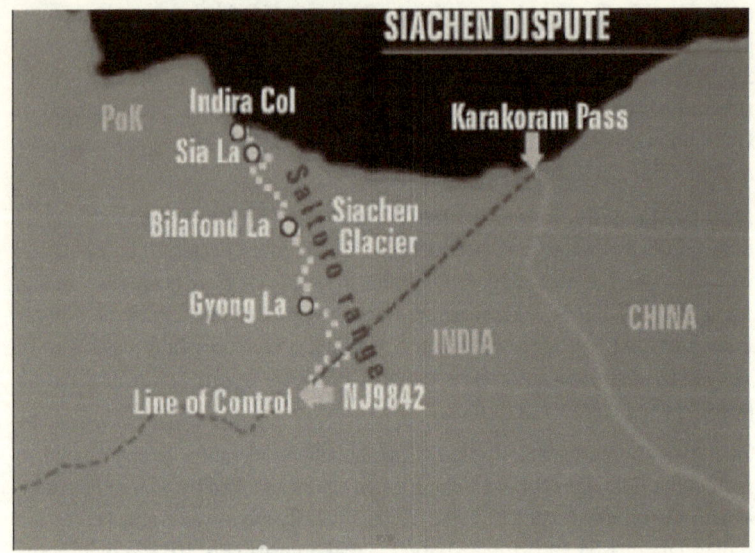

Figure 281: *Actual Ground Position Line shown with yellow-colored dotted line*

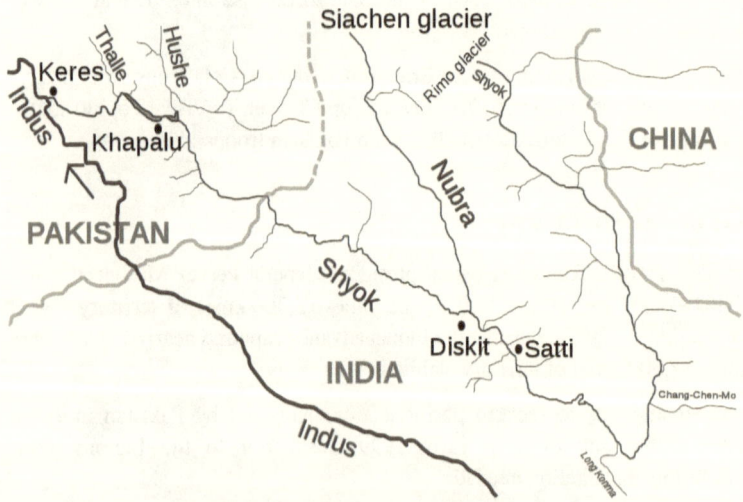

Figure 282: *Red dotted line is AGPL, right of which is Siachen Glacier controlled by Indian army.*

ground. Indians have been able to hold on to the tactical advantage of the high ground... Most of India's many outposts are west of the Siachen Glacier along the Saltoro Range. In an academic study with detailed maps and satellite images, co-authored by brigadiers from both the Pakistani and Indian military, pages 16 and 27: "Since 1984, the Indian army has been in physical possession of most of the heights on the Saltoro Range west of the Siachen Glacier, while the Pakistan army has held posts at lower elevations of western slopes of the spurs emanating from the Saltoro ridgeline. The Indian army has secured its position on the ridgeline."Wikipedia:Inline citation#When you must use inline citations

The line between where Indian and Pakistani troops are presently holding onto their respective posts is being increasingly referred to as the Actual Ground Position Line (AGPL).[1573,1574]

Views

Siachen is seen as a major military setback by the Pakistani Army.[1575,1576] Pakistani generals perceives the Siachen glacier as their land that had been stolen by Indians. When India occupied the Saltoro Ridge in April 1984, Benazir Bhutto publicly taunted the Pakistan Army as "fit only to fight its own citizens".[1577] When, in June 1987, the Indian Army captured the 21,153 foot high "Quaid Post" and renamed it to "Bana Top", in honour of Naib Subedar Bana Singh, Bhutto once again publicly taunted the Pakistani generals, telling them to wear bangles if they cannot fight on the Siachen.[1577,1578]

American observers say that the military conflict between India and Pakistan over the Siachen Glacier "made no military or political sense". An article in the Minneapolis Star Tribune stated: "Their combat over a barren, uninhabited world of questionable value is a forbidding symbol of their lingering, irreconcilability." Stephen P. Cohen compared the conflict to "a struggle between two bald men over a comb. Siachen is a symbol of the worst aspects of their relationship."

In the book *Asymmetric Warfare in South Asia: The Causes and Consequences of the Kargil Conflict*, Khan, Lavoy and Clary wrote:

> The Pakistan army sees India's 1984 occupation of the Siachen Glacier as a major scar, outweighed only by Dhaka's fall in 1971. The event underscored the dilution of the Simla Agreement and became a domestic issue as political parties, led by Benazir Bhutto's Peoples Party, blamed an incompetent military government under Zia ul-Haq for failing to defend Pakistani-held territory — while Zia downplayed the significance of the loss.[1579]

General Ved Prakash Malik, in his book *Kargil from Surprise to Victory*, wrote:

> Siachen is considered a military setback by the Pakistan Army. That the Indians dominate the area from the Saltoro Ridge and Pakistani troops are nowhere near the Siachen Glacier is a fact never mentioned in public. The perceived humiliation at Siachen manifests itself in many ways. It is synonymous with Indian perfidy and a violation of the Shimla Agreement... In Pakistan, Siachen is a subject that hurts, just like a thorn in its flesh; it is also a psychological drain on the Pakistani Army. Pervez Musharraf had himself once commanded the Special Services Group (SSG) troops in this area and made several futile attempts to capture Indian posts.[1575]

Severe conditions

A cease-fire went into effect in 2003. Even before then, every year more soldiers were killed because of severe weather than enemy firing. The two sides by 2003 had lost an estimated 2,000 personnel primarily due to frostbite, avalanches and other complications. Together, the nations have about 150 manned outposts along the glacier, with some 3,000 troops each. Official figures for maintaining these outposts are put at ~$300 and ~$200 million for India and Pakistan respectively. India built the world's highest helipad on the glacier at Point Sonam, 21,000 feet (6,400 m) above the sea level, to supply its troops. The problems of reinforcing or evacuating the high-altitude ridgeline have led to India's development of the Dhruv Mk III helicopter, powered by the Shakti engine, which was flight-tested to lift and land personnel and stores from the Sonam post, the highest permanently manned post in the world. India also installed the world's highest telephone booth on the glacier.

According to some estimates, 97% of the casualties in Siachen have been due to weather and altitude, rather than actual fighting. In 2012, an avalanche hit Pakistan's Gayari military base, killing 129 soldiers and 11 civilians.

Kargil War

One of the factors behind the Kargil War in 1999 when Pakistan sent infiltrators to occupy vacated Indian posts across the Line of Control was their belief that India would be forced to withdraw from Siachen in exchange of a Pakistani withdrawal from Kargil. After the Kargil War, India decided to maintain its military outposts on the glacier, wary of further Pakistani incursions into Kashmir if they vacate from the Siachen Glacier posts.

Visits

On 12 June 2005, Prime Minister Manmohan Singh became the first Indian Prime Minister to visit the area, calling for a peaceful resolution of the problem. In 2007, the President of India, Abdul Kalam became the first head of state to visit the area. Indian Prime Minister Narendra Modi visited Siachen on 23 October 2014 to celebrate Diwali with the troops and boost their morale.

The Chief of Staff of the US Army, General George Casey on 17 October 2008 visited the Siachen Glacier along with Indian Army Chief, General Deepak Kapoor. The US General visited for the purpose of "developing concepts and medical aspects of fighting in severe cold conditions and high altitude".

Since September 2007, India has welcomed mountaineering and trekking expeditions to the forbidding glacial heights. The expeditions have been meant to show the international audience that Indian troops hold "almost all dominating heights" on the important Saltoro Ridge west of Siachen Glacier, and to show that Pakistani troops are nowhere near the 43.5-mile (70 km) Siachen Glacier.[1580]

Artistic depiction

The Siachen glacier and its conflict was depicted in a 48-page comic book, *Siachen: The cold war*, released in August 2012. Later its sequel, *Battlefield Siachen*, was released in January 2013.

List of post-ceasefire avalanches and landslides
2010–2011

On 11 February 2010, an avalanche struck an Indian army post in the Southern Glacier, killing one soldier. A base camp was also struck, that killed two Ladakh scouts. The same day, a single avalanche hit a Pakistani military camp in Bevan sector, killing 8 soldiers.

In 2011, 24 Indian soldiers died on the Siachen glacier from the climate and accidents. On 22 July, two Indian officers burned to death when a fire caught on their shelter.

2012–2014

In the early morning of 7 April 2012, an avalanche hit a Pakistani military headquarters in the Gayari Sector, burying 129 soldiers of the 6th Northern Light Infantry battalion and 11 civilian contractors. In the aftermath of the disaster, Pakistan's army chief General Ashfaq Parvez Kayani suggested India and Pakistan should withdraw all troops from the contested glacier.

On 29 May, two Pakistani soldiers were killed in a landslide in the Chorbat Sector.

On 12 December, an avalanche killed 6 Indian soldiers in the Sub Sector Hanif in Turtuk area, when troops of the 1st Assam regiment were moving between posts. In 2012, a total of 12 Indian soldiers died of hostile weather conditions.

In 2013, 10 Indian soldiers died due to weather conditions.

2015

On 14 November 2015, an Indian captain from the Third Ladakh scouts died in an avalanche in the Southern Glacier while 15 others were rescued.

2016

On 4 January 2016, four Indian soldiers of the Ladakh Scouts, were killed in an avalanche on the Southern Glacier while on patrol duty in Nobra Valley.

On the morning of 3 February 2016, ten Indian soldiers including one Junior commissioned officer of the 6th Madras battalion were buried under the snow when a massive avalanche struck their post in the Northern Glacier at a height of 19,600 feet, on the Actual Ground Position Line. Pakistani officials offered their help in search and rescue operations 30 hours after the incident, although it was declined by Indian military authorities. During the rescue operations, the Indian army found Lance Naik Hanumanthappa alive, though in a critical condition, after being buried under 25 feet snow for 6 days. He was taken to Army Research and Referral Hospital in Delhi. His condition became critical later on due to multiple organ failure and lack of oxygen to brain and he died 11 February 2016.

On 27 February, a civilian porter working with the Indian army in the Northern Glacier, fell to his death in a 130-foot crevasse.

On 17 March, two Indian soldiers from the Chennai-21 regiment were killed, and bodies recovered in 12-feet deep ice.

On 25 March, two Indian jawans died after they were buried in an avalanche in the Turtuk sector while on patrol.

On 1 April, Indian General Dalbir Singh and General D. S. Hooda of the Northern Command visited the Siachen glacier in order to boost morale after 17 of its soldiers died in 2016.

References

Bibliography

<templatestyles src="Template:Refbegin/styles.css" />

- Lavoy, Peter R., ed. (2009). *Asymmetric Warfare in South Asia: The Causes and Consequences of the Kargil Conflict*. Cambridge University Press. ISBN 9781139482820.
- Malik, V. P. (2006). *Kargil from Surprise to Victory*. HarperCollins Publishers India. ISBN 9788172236359.
  - Gokhale, Nitin A (2015). *Beyond NJ 9842: The SIACHEN Saga*. Bloomsbury Publishing. ISBN 9789384052263.

Further reading

- Bearak, Barry (23 May 1999). "THE COLDEST WAR; Frozen in Fury on the Roof of the World"[1581]. *The New York Times*.
- *Siachen: Conflict Without End* by V.R. Raghavan
- Myra MacDonald (2008) *Heights of Madness: One Woman's Journey in Pursuit of a Secret War*, Rupa, New Delhi ISBN 81-291-1292-2. The first full account of the Siachen war to be told from the Indian and Pakistani sides.
- Baghel, Ravi; Nusser, Marcus (17 June 2015). "Securing the heights; The vertical dimension of the Siachen conflict between India and Pakistan in the Eastern Karakoram"[1582]. *Political Geography*. Elsevier. **48**: 31–32. doi: 10.1016/j.polgeo.2015.05.001[1583]. Retrieved 23 September 2016.
- Wirsing, Robert. *Pakistan's security under Zia, 1977–1988: the policy imperatives of a peripheral Asian state*. Palgrave Macmillan, 1991. ISBN 978-0-312-06067-1.

External links

- The Coldest War[1584]
- Time report[1585]
- Siachen: The stalemate continues[1586]
- Siachen Glacier – Highest Battlefield Of The World[1587]
- "The vertical dimension of the Siachen conflict"[1582]. *Political Geography*. **48**: 24–36. doi: 10.1016/j.polgeo.2015.05.001[1583].

1990s

Assassination of Rajiv Gandhi

The **assassination of Rajiv Gandhi**, former Prime Minister of India, occurred as a result of a suicide bombing in Sriperumbudur, near Chennai, in Tamil Nadu, India on Tuesday, 21 May 1991.[1588] At least 14 others were also killed. It was carried out by Thenmozhi Rajaratnam, also known as Dhanu, member of the Liberation Tigers of Tamil Eelam (LTTE), a militant organization from Sri Lanka; at the time India had just ended its involvement, through the Indian Peace Keeping Force, in the Sri Lankan Civil War. Subsequent accusations of conspiracy have been addressed by two commissions of inquiry and have brought down at least one national government.

Assassination

Rajiv Gandhi was campaigning for the upcoming elections in southern states of India. On 21 May, after successfully campaigning in Visakhapatnam, his next stop was Sriperumbudur, Tamil Nadu. About two hours after arriving in Madras (now Chennai), Rajiv Gandhi was driven by motorcade in a white Ambassador car to Sriperumbudur, stopping along the way at a few other election campaigning venues.[1589] When he reached a campaign rally in Sriperumbudur, he got out of his car and began to walk towards the dais where he would deliver a speech. Along the way, he was garlanded by many well-wishers, Congress party workers and school children. At 22:21 the assassin, Dhanu, approached and greeted him. She then bent down to touch his feet and detonated an RDX explosive-laden belt tucked below her dress. Gandhi, his assassin and 14 others were killed in the explosion that followed. The assassination was caught on film by a local photographer, whose camera and film was found at the site though the photographer also died in the blast.

Figure 283: *Remains of clothing worn by Rajiv Gandhi during his assassination*

Figure 284: *The stone mosaic that stands at the location where Rajiv Gandhi was assassinated in Sriperumbudur*

Figure 285: *Known as the "Path of Light", this was the path that Rajiv took before being assassinated*

Figure 286: *Seven pillars, each featuring a human value surrounds the site of the blast, at the Rajiv Gandhi Memorial in Sriperumbudur.*

Security lapses

The Supreme Court held that LTTE's decision of eliminating Rajiv was prompted by his interview to Sunday magazine (August 21–28, 1990), where he said he would send the IPKF to disarm LTTE if he came back to power again. Rajiv also defended the signing of the Indo-Sri Lanka accord in the same interview. The LTTE decision to kill him was perhaps aimed at preventing him from coming to power again. Thereafter, the Justice J S Verma Commission was formed to look into the security lapses that led to the killing.

The final report, submitted in June 1992, concluded that the security arrangements for the former PM were adequate but that the local Congress party leaders disrupted and broke these arrangements.

The Narasimha Rao government initially rejected *Verma's* findings but later accepted it under pressure. However, no action was taken on the recommendations of the Commission.

Despite no action, the findings throw up vital questions that have been consistently raised by political analysts. Sources have indicated that Rajiv was time and again informed that there was a threat to his life and that he should not travel to Tamil Nadu. In fact, the then governor of Tamil Nadu Bhism Narayan Singh, broke his official protocol and twice warned Rajiv about the threat to his life if he visited the state.

Dr Subramanian Swamy said in his book, *Sri Lanka in Crisis: India's Options (2007)*, that an LTTE delegation had met Rajiv Gandhi on March 5, 1991. Another delegation met him around March 14, 1991 at New Delhi.

Journalist Ram Bahadur Rai wrote that:

> *The message conveyed to Rajiv Gandhi by both these delegations was that there was no threat to his life and that he can travel to Tamil Nadu without fearing for his life. I did a series of articles after his assassination that pointed out how, after these meetings, Rajiv became complacent about his security and broke security rules in more than 40 rallies.*

Funeral

Following his assassination, Rajiv Gandhi's mutilated body was airlifted to New Delhi. From the Indira Gandhi International Airport, which was named after his mother, his body was sent to the All India Institute of Medical Sciences in New Delhi for post-mortem, reconstruction and embalming.

A state funeral was held for Rajiv Gandhi on 24 May 1991. His funeral was telecast live nationally and internationally, and was attended by dignitaries from over 60 countries. He was cremated on the banks of the river Yamuna, near the cremation spot of his mother, brother and grandfather. Today, the site where he was cremated is known as *Veer Bhumi*.

Investigation

Immediately after the assassination, the Chandrasekhar government handed the investigation over to CBI on May 22, 1991. The agency created a Special Investigation Team (SIT) under D. R. Karthikeyan[1590] to determine who was responsible for the assassination. The SIT probe confirmed the role of LTTE in the assassination, which was upheld by the Supreme Court of India.

The interim report of Justice Milap Chand Jain, looking into the conspiracy angle to the assassination, indicted the DMK for colluding with the LTTE. The report concluded that DMK provided sanctuary to the LTTE, which made it easy for the rebels to assassinate Rajiv Gandhi.

The Commission report stated that the year 1989 signified "the perpetuation of the general political trend of indulging the Tamil militants on Indian soil and tolerance of their wide-ranging criminal and anti-national activities." The report also alleged that LTTE leaders in Jaffna were in possession of sensitive coded messages exchanged between the Union government and the state government of DMK. "There is evidence to show that, during this period, some of the most vital wireless messages were passed between the LTTE operatives based in Tamil Nadu and Jaffna. These messages, which were decoded later, are directly related to the assassination of Rajiv Gandhi," the report stated. The Congress subsequently brought down the United Front (UF) government of I K Gujral after the report was leaked in November 1998. The party also demanded the removal of DMK from the UF government, arguing that it had played a key role in the death of Rajiv Gandhi.

Perpetrator

The assassination was carried out by Thenmozhi Rajaratnam, also known as Dhanu. She belonged to and was a member of the Liberation Tigers of Tamil Eelam (Tamil Tigers).

Supreme Court judgment

As per the Supreme Court of India judgment, by Judge K. T. Thomas, the killing was carried out due to personal animosity of the LTTE chief Prabhakaran towards Rajiv Gandhi. Additionally, the Rajiv Gandhi administration had antagonised other Tamil militant organisations like PLOTE for reversing the military coup in Maldives back in 1988.[1591]

The judgement further cites the death of Thileepan in a hunger strike and the suicide by 12 LTTE cadres in a vessel in October 1987. The judgment while convicting the accused, four of them to death and others to various jail terms, states that absolutely no evidence existed that any one of the conspirators ever desired the death of any Indian other than Rajiv Gandhi, though several people were killed. Judge Wadhwa further states there is nothing on record to show that the intention to kill Rajiv Gandhi was to overawe the Government. Hence it was held that it was not a terrorist act under TADA (Act). Judge Thomas further states that conspiracy was hatched in stages commencing from 1987 and that it spanned several years. The Special Investigation team of India's premier special investigation agency CBI was not able to pinpoint when the decision to kill Rajiv Gandhi was taken.

Trial

The trial was conducted under the Terrorist and Disruptive Activities Act (TADA). On January 28, 1998, the designated TADA court in Chennai gave death sentences to all the 26 accused. This created a storm in India. Legal experts were stunned. Human rights groups protested as the trial did not meet the standards of a free trial.[1592] The trial was held behind closed doors, in camera courts, and the identity of witnesses was not disclosed. Ms A. Athirai, an accused, was only 17 years old when she was arrested.

Under TADA an accused can appeal only to the Supreme Court. Appeal to the High Court is not allowed as in normal law. Confessions given by the accused to the Superintendent of Police are taken as evidence against the accused under TADA. Under TADA the accused could be convicted on the basis of evidence that would have been insufficient for conviction by an ordinary court under normal Indian law. In the Rajiv Gandhi case, confessions by the accused formed a major part of the evidence in the judgement against them which they later claimed was taken under duress.

On appeal to the Supreme Court, only four of the accused were sentenced to death and the others to various jail terms. S Nalini Sriharan is the lone surviving member of the five-member squad behind the assassination of Rajiv Gandhi and is serving life imprisonment. Arrested on June 14, 1991, she was sentenced to death, along with the other 25 accused. However, the court confirmed that the death sentence was given to only four of the convicts, including Nalini, on May 11, 1999. Nalini, who was a close friend of an LTTE operative known as V Sriharan alias Murugan, another convict in the case who had been sentenced to death, later gave birth to a girl, Harithra Murugan in prison. Upon the intervention of Rajiv Gandhi's widow and Congress president Sonia Gandhi, who petitioned for clemency for the sake of Nalini's daughter in 2000, the death sentence was commuted to life imprisonment. Nalini was treated as a class 'A' convict from September 10, 1999 till the privilege was withdrawn in May 2010 after a mobile phone was allegedly recovered from her cell during a surprise check. She "regrets" the killing of the former Prime Minister and claims that the real conspirators have not been booked yet. The President of India rejected the clemency pleas of Murugan and two others on death row, T Suthendraraja alias Santhan and A G Perarivalan alias Arivu in August 2011. The execution of the three convicts was scheduled for September 9, 2011. However, the Madras High Court intervened and stayed their execution for eight weeks based on their petitions. Nalini was shifted back to Vellore prison from Puzhal prison amidst tight security on September 7, 2011. In 2010, Nalini had moved the Madras High Court seeking release as she had served more than 20 years in prison. She argued that even life convicts were released after 14 years. However, the state government rejected her request. Murugan, Santhan and Perarivalan, the three convicts condemned to death, claimed that they were not ordinary criminals but political prisoners.

Controversies

In a report published on 30 October 2012 in DNA[1593], K Ragothaman, former chief investigator of the CBI, talks about his new book *Conspiracy to Kill Rajiv Gandhi: From the CBI Files*[1594] and tells the reporter that while the CBI had started a preliminary inquiry in which MK Narayanan, former West Bengal Governor and former Intelligence Bureau director, was named a suspect in hiding evidence, the case was buried by the CBI SIT Chief, D.R. Karthikeyan.

Jain Commission and other reports

In the Jain report, various people and agencies are named as suspected of having been involved in the murder of Rajiv Gandhi. Among them, the cleric Chandraswami was suspected of involvement, including financing the assassination.[1595] One of the accused, Ranganath, said Chandraswami was the godfather who financed the killing. Sikh Militants were also suspected.[1596,1597] The interim report of the Jain Commission created a storm when it accused Muthu and the Tamils of a role in the assassination, leading to Congress withdrawing its support for the I. K. Gujral government and fresh elections in 1998. Also other strong LTTE sympathizers Vaiko with MDMK and Thol. Thirumavalavan with VCK have supported Congress under Sonia Gandhi in the past. However it is worth noting that Vaiko left the UPA alliance before the 2009 election, partly due to the Sri Lankan issue. In the 2001 Norway peace talks, Prabhakaran told the press that the assassination of Rajiv Gandhi was a sorrowful event. In 2006, LTTE spokesman Anton Balasingham told the Indian television channel NDTV that the killing was a "great tragedy, a monumental historical tragedy which we deeply regret."[1598]

Memorial and popular culture

- The Rajiv Gandhi Memorial as built on the site and is one of the major tourist attractions in the small industrial town.
- *Assassination Of Rajiv Gandhi: Unanswered Questions And Unasked Queries* by Subramanian Swamy
- *Conspiracy to kill Rajiv Gandhi - From CBI files* by Central Bureau of Investigation officer and chief investigating officer of the assassination case.
- *Beyond the Tigers: Tracking Rajiv Gandhi's Assassination* by Rajeev Sharma.
- *Bypass: Flaws in the Forensic Investigation of Rajiv Gandhi Murder"* Feature Film, The first open source feature film from India.

Films

- *Kuttrapathirikai*, *Mission 90 Days*, *The Terrorist*, *Cyanide* and *Madras Cafe* are films based on the assassination.
- 2013 film Madras Cafe depicts a RAW agent's mission to save Rajiv Gandhi.

External links

- Harithra Murugan, daughter of Nalini Sriharan and Murugan interview[1599]

Coordinates: 12.9602°N 79.9452°E[1600]

Insurgency in Jammu and Kashmir

<indicator name="pp-default"> 🔒 </indicator>

Insurgency in Jammu and Kashmir
Part of the Kashmir conflict
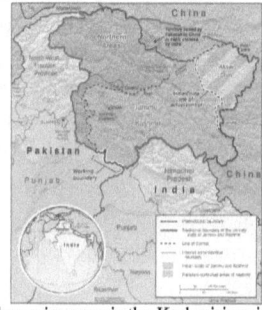
Kashmir : Shown in green is the Kashmiri region under Pakistani control. The dark-brown region represents Indian-controlled Jammu and Kashmir while the Aksai Chin is under Chinese control.

Date	13 July 1989–present
Location	Jammu and Kashmir
Result	Conflict ongoing

Belligerents	
India • Indian Army • Indian Air Force • Central Reserve Police Force • Border Security Force • Jammu and Kashmir Police • Sashastra Seema Bal	Harkat-ul-Jihad al-Islami Lashkar-e-Taiba Jaish-e-Mohammed Hizbul Mujahideen Harkat-ul-Mujahideen Al-Badr Jammu Kashmir Liberation Front ISIL-KP *Supported by:* Pakistan Taliban al-Qaeda

Commanders and leaders	
General Bipin Rawat Lt Gen Devraj Anbu Air Chief Marshal Birender Singh Dhanoa R R Bhatnagar	Hafiz Saeed Maulana Azhar Ilyas Kashmiri † Sayeed Salahudeen Fazlur Rehman Khalil Farooq Kashmiri Arfeen Bhai Amanullah Khan Bakht Zameen Dawood Ahmed Sofi †

Strength

30,000[1601] – 600,000 Army 65,000 CRPF	3,500 to 5,000 (2006 est.) ≈150 (2014 est.) ≈200 (2017 est.)
Casualties and losses	
5,462 security forces killed	>21,000 militants killed 3,000 captured ≈4,500 surrendered
20,228–100,000 civilians killed	

The **insurgency in Jammu and Kashmir** or the **Kashmiri Insurgency** (also known as **Kashmir Intifada**) is a conflict between various Kashmiri separatists and the Government of India. There are some groups that support the complete independence of Kashmir, while others seek Kashmir's accession to Pakistan.[1602] The conflict in Jammu and Kashmir has strong Islamist elements among the insurgents, with many of the "ultras" identifying with Jihadist movements and supported by such.

The roots of the conflict between the Kashmiri insurgents and the Indian government are tied to a dispute over local autonomy.[1603] Democratic development was limited in Kashmir until the late 1970s and by 1988 many of the democratic reforms provided by the Indian government had been reversed and non-violent channels for expressing discontent were limited and caused a dramatic increase in support for insurgents advocating violent secession from India. In 1987, a disputed State election created a catalyst for the insurgency when it resulted in some of the state's legislative assembly members forming armed insurgent groups. In July 1988, a series of demonstrations, strikes and attacks on the Indian government began the **Kashmir Insurgency**, which during the 1990s escalated into the most important internal security issue in India.

Thousands of people have died[1604] during fighting between insurgents and the government as well as thousands of civilians who have died as a result of being targeted by the various armed groups.[1605]

The Inter-Services Intelligence of Pakistan has been accused by India of supporting and training mujahideen. to fight in Jammu and Kashmir. In 2015, former President of Pakistan Pervez Musharraf admitted that Pakistan had supported and trained insurgent groups in the 1990s. According to official figures released in Jammu and Kashmir assembly, there were 3,400 disappearance cases and the conflict has left more than 47,000 people dead which also includes 7,000 police personnel as of July 2009.

However, the number of insurgency-related deaths in the state have fallen sharply since the start of a slow-moving peace process between India and Pakistan. Some rights groups claim a higher figure of 100,000 deaths since 1989.

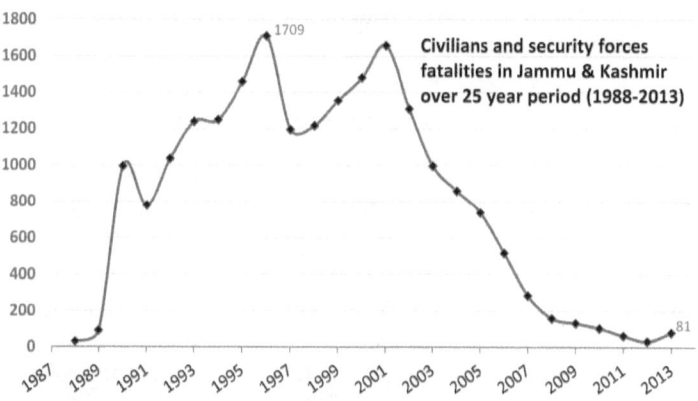

Figure 287: *The trend in total yearly civilian and security forces fatalities from insurgency-related violence over 25 years from 1988 to 2013.*[1606]

History of the insurgency

1947–1987

After independence from colonial rule India and Pakistan fought a war over the princely state of Kashmir. At the end of the war India controlled the most valuable parts of Kashmir. While there were sporadic periods of violence there was no organised insurgency movement.

During this period legislative elections in Jammu and Kashmir were first held in 1951 and Sheikh Abdullah's secular party stood unopposed. He was an instrumental member in the accession of the state to India.

However Sheikh Abdullah would fall in and out of favour with the central government and would often be dismissed only to be re-appointed later on. This was a time of political instability & power struggle in Jammu and Kashmir and it went through several periods of President's rule by the Federal Government.

1987–2004

After Sheikh Abdullah's death, his son Farooq Abdullah took over as Chief Minister of Jammu and Kashmir. Farooq Abdullah eventually fell out of favour with the Central Government and the Prime Minister of India, Indira Gandhi had him dismissed.Wikipedia:Citation needed A year later, Abdullah announced an alliance with the ruling Congress party for the elections of 1987. The elections were allegedly rigged in favour of Abdullah.

This led to the rise of an armed insurgency movement composed, in part, of those who unfairly lost elections. Pakistan supplied these groups with logistical support, arms, recruits and training.

In the second half of 1989 the alleged assassinations of the Indian spies and political collaborators by JKLF (Jammu and Kashmir Liberation Front) was intensified. Over six months more than a hundred officials were killed to paralyse government's administrative and intelligence apparatus. The daughter of then interior affairs minister, Mufti Mohammad Sayeed was kidnapped in December and four terrorists had to be released for her release. This event led to mass celebrations all over the valley. Farooq Abdullah resigned in January after the appointment of Jagmohan Malhotra as the Governor of Jammu and Kashmir. Subsequently, J&K was placed under governor rule under Article 356, Disturbed Areas Act of Indian constitution.

Under JKLF's leadership on January 21-23 large scale protests were organised in valley. As a response to this largely explosive situation paramilitary units of BSF and CRPF were called. These units were used by the government to combat Maoist insurgency and the North-Eastern insurgency. The challenge to them in this situation was not posed by armed insurgents but by the stone pelters. Their inexperience caused at least 50 casualties in Gawkadal massacre. In this incident the underground militant movement was transformed into a mass struggle. To curb the situation AFSPA (Armed Forces Special Powers Act) was imposed on Kashmir in September 1990 to suppress the insurgency by giving armed forces the powers to kill and arrest without warrant to maintain public order. During this time the dominant tactic involved killing of a prominent figure in a public gathering to push forces into action and the public prevented them from capturing these insurgents. This sprouting of sympathisers in Kashmir led to the hard-line approach of Indian army.

With JKLF at forefront large number of militant groups like Allah Tigers, People's League and Hizb-i-Islamia sprung up. Weapons were smuggled on a large scale from Pakistan. In Kashmir JKLF operated under the leadership of Ashfaq Majid Wani, Yasin Bhat, Hamid Shiekh and Javed Mir. To counter this growing pro-Pakistani sentiment in Kashmir, Indian media associated it exclusively with Pakistan.

JKLF used distinctly Islamic themes to mobilise crowds and justify their use of violence. They sought to establish an Islamic democratic state where the rights of minorities would be protected according to Quran and Sunna and economy would be organised on the principles of Islamic socialism.

The Indian army has conducted various operations to control and eliminate insurgency in the region such as Operation Sarp Vinash, in which a multi-battalion offensive was launched against terrorists from groups like Lashkar-e-Taiba, Harkat-ul-Jihad-e-Islami, al-Badr and Jaish-e-Mohammad who had been constructing shelters in the Pir Panjal region of Jammu and Kashmir over several years. The subsequent operations led to the death of over 60 terrorists and uncovered the largest network of militant hideouts in the history of insurgency in Jammu and Kashmir covering 100 square kilometers.

2004-11

Beginning in 2004 Pakistan began to end its support for insurgents in Kashmir. This happened because terrorist groups linked to Kashmir twice tried to assassinate Pakistani President General Pervez Musharraf. His successor, Asif Ali Zardari has continued the policy, calling insurgents in Kashmir "terrorists". Although it is unclear if Pakistan's intelligence agency, the Inter-Services Intelligence, thought to be the agency aiding and controlling the insurgency is following Pakistan's commitment to end support for the insurgency in Kashmir.

Despite the change in the nature of the insurgency from a phenomenon supported by external forces to a primarily domestic-driven movement the Indian government has continued to send large numbers of troops to the Indian border.

There have been widespread protests against the Indian army presence in Kashmir.

Once the most formidable face of Kashmir militancy, Hizbul Mujahideen is slowly fading away as its remaining commanders and cadres are being taken out on a regular interval by security forces. Some minor incidents of grenade throwing and sniper firing at security forces notwithstanding, the situation is under control and more or less peaceful. A record number of tourists including Amarnath pilgrims visited Kashmir during 2012. On 3 August 2012, a top Lashkar-e-Taiba militant commander, Abu Hanzulah involved in various attacks on civilians and security forces was killed in an encounter with security forces in a village in Kupwara district of north Kashmir.

2012-present

According to an Indian Army data – quoted by Reuters – at least 70 young Kashmiris joined the insurgency in the 2014, army records showed, with most joining the banned group Lashkar-e-Taiba, which was accused of carrying out attacks on the Indian city of Mumbai in 2008. Two of the new recruits have doctorates and eight were post graduates, the army data showed. According to BBC, that despite a Pakistani ban on militant activity in Kashmir in 2006, its fighters continue to attempt infiltration into Indian-administered Kashmir. These attempts were curtailed however when people living along the Line of Control which divides Indian and Pakistani Kashmir started to hold public protests against their activities.

Reasons for the insurgency

Rigging of 1987 Assembly elections

Following the rise of Islamisation in the Kashmir valley, during the 1987 state elections, various Islamic anti-establishment groups including Jamaat-e-Islami Kashmir were organised under a single banner named Muslim United Front (MUF), that is largely current Hurriyat. MUF's election manifesto stressed the need for a solution to all outstanding issues according to Simla Agreement, work for Islamic unity and against political interference from the centre. Their slogan was wanting the law of the Quran in the Assembly. But the MUF won only four seats, even though it had polled 31% votes in the election. However, the elections were widely believed to be rigged, changing the course of politics in the state. The insurgency was sparked by the apparent rigging of state elections in 1987.

ISI's role

The Pakistani Inter-Services Intelligence has allegedly encouraged and aided the Kashmir independence movement through an insurgency due to its dispute on the legitimacy of Indian rule in Kashmir, with the insurgency as an easy way to keep Indian troops distracted and cause international condemnation of India.

Former Pakistan President General Pervez Musharraf in Oct 2014 said during TV interview, "We have source (in Kashmir) besides the (Pakistan) army...People in Kashmir are fighting against (India). We just need to incite them."

The Federal Bureau of Investigation (FBI), in their first ever open acknowledgement in 2011 in US Court, said that the Inter-Services Intelligence (ISI) sponsors terrorism in Kashmir and it oversees terrorist separatist groups in Kashmir.

Mujahideen influence

After the invasion of Afghanistan by the Soviet Union, Mujahideen fighters, with the aid of Pakistan, slowly infiltrated Kashmir with the goal of spreading a radical Islamist ideology.

Religion

Jammu and Kashmir is the only Muslim majority state in Hindu-majority India. Indian-American journalist Asra Nomani states that while India itself is a secular state, Muslims are politically, culturally and economically marginalised when compared to Hindus in India as a whole. The government's decision to transfer 99 acres of forest land in near Amarnath in the Kashmir valley to a Hindu organisation (for setting up temporary shelters and facilities for Hindu pilgrims) solidified this feeling and led to one of the largest protest rallies in Jammu and Kashmir.

Human rights abuses

After insurgency started in Kashmir valley because of above reasons in the late 1980s, Indian troops entered in Kashmir valley to control the insurgency. Some analysts have suggested that the number of Indian troops in Jammu and Kashmir is close to 600,000 although estimates vary and the Indian government refuses to release official figures. The troops have been accused and held accountable for several humanitarian abuses and have engaged in mass extrajudicial killings, torture, rape and sexual abuse.

Indian security forces have been implicated in many reports for enforced disappearances of thousands of Kashmiris whereas the security forces deny having their information and/or custody. This is often in association with torture or extrajudicial killing. Human right activists estimate the number of disappeared to be over eight thousand, last seen in government detention. The disappeared are believed to be dumped in thousands of mass graves across Kashmir.[1607] A State Human Rights Commission inquiry in 2011, has confirmed there are thousands of bullet-ridden bodies buried in unmarked graves in Jammu and Kashmir. Of the 2730 bodies uncovered in 4 of the 14 districts, 574 bodies were identified as missing locals in contrast to the Indian governments insistence that all the graves belong to foreign militants.

Military forces in Jammu and Kashmir operate under impunity and emergency powers granted to them by the central government. These powers allow the military to curtail civil liberties, creating further support for the insurgency.

The insurgents have also abused human rights, engaging in what some have called an ethnic cleansing by exterminating Kashmiri Pandits from the valley of Kashmir. The government's inability to protect the people from both its own troops and the insurgency has further eroded support for the government.

Amnesty International accused security forces of exploiting the Armed Forces Special Powers Act (AFSPA) that enables them to "hold prisoners without trial". The group argues that the law, which allows security to detain individuals for as many as two years "without presenting charges, violating prisoners' human rights". The Army sources maintain that "any move to revoke AFSPA in Jammu and Kashmir would be detrimental to the security of the Valley and would provide a boost to the terrorists."

Former Indian Army Chief General V. K. Singh rejected the accusations that the action was not taken in the cases of human rights violations by Army personnel. On 24 October 2010, he has said that 104 Army personnel had been punished in Jammu and Kashmir in this regard, including 39 officers. He also said that 95% of the allegations of human rights abuses against Indian Army were proved to be false, of which he remarked, had apparently been made with the "ulterior motive of maligning the armed forces". However, according to Human Rights Watch, the military courts in India, in general, were proved to be incompetent to deal with cases of serious human rights abuses and were responsible in covering up evidence and protecting the involved officers. Amnesty International in its report in 2015, titled *"Denied"-Failures in Accountability in Jammu and Kashmir*, says, "...with respect to investigations, an inquiry that is conducted by the same authority accused of the crime raises serious questions about the independence and impartiality of those proceedings", adding that according to the international law, an independent authority that is not involved in the alleged violations has to investigate such crimes.

These human rights violations are said to have contributed to the rise of resistance in Kashmir.

Other reasons

Psychological

Psychologist Waheeda Khan, explaining the rebellious nature of the Kashmiris, says that because of the tense situations in the valley from the 1990s, the generation gap between parents and young generations has increased. Young generations tend to blame their parents for failing to do anything about the political situation. So they start experimenting with their own aggressive ways to show their curbed feelings and would go against any authority. A prominent psychiatrist of the valley, Margoob, described that children/teenagers are much more vulnerable to passionate actions and reactions, since the young minds are yet to completely develop psychological mechanisms. When they assume that they are "pushed against the wall", they get controlled by the emotions without bothering about the consequences. Also young people easily identify themselves with the "group" rather than with their individual identities. It leads to psychological distress which causes antisocial behaviour and aggressive attitude. Often, this situation gets worsened by the availability of weapons and people becoming familiar to violence after having exposed to conflict for so long. Waheeda Khan remarks, the major concern is that generations of children who are experiencing long-term violence in their lives, may reach adulthood perceiving that violence is a fair means of solving ethinic, religious, or political differences.[1608]

Economic

High unemployment and lack of economic opportunities in Kashmir are also said to have intensified the struggle.

Stone pelting

Since the 2008 protests and 2010 unrest, the turmoil has taken a new dimension when people, particularly youngsters of the Kashmir valley have started pelting stones on security forces to express their aggression and protest for the loss of freedom. In turn they get attacked by the armed personnel with pellets, rubber bullets, sling shots and tear gas shells. This leads to eye-injuries and several other kind of injuries to many people. Security forces also face injuries, and sometimes get beaten up during these events. According to Waheeda Khan, most of the 'stone-pelters' are school and college going students. Large number of these people get arrested during these events for allegedly resorting to stone pelting, after which some of them are also tortured. According to political activist Mannan Bukhari, Kashmiris made stone, an easily accessible and defenseless weapon, their weapon of choice for protest.

Kashmiri senior journalist Parvaiz Bukhari remarked:

> *The summer of 2010 witnessed a convulsion in the world's most militarized zone, the Indian-controlled part of Kashmir, an unprecedented and deadly civil unrest that is beginning to change a few things on the ground. [...] Little known and relatively anonymous resistance activists emerged, organizing an unarmed agitation more fierce than the armed rebellion against Indian rule two decades earlier. And apparently aware of the post 9/11 world, young Kashmiris, children of the conflict, made stones and rocks a weapon of choice against government armed forces, side-stepping the tag of a terrorist movement linked with Pakistan. The unrest represents a conscious transition to an unarmed mass movement, one that poses a moral challenge to New Delhi's military domination over the region.*

Human rights violations by militants

Further information: Human rights abuses by insurgents and Rape by militants

Islamic separatist militants are accused of violence against the Kashmir populace. They continue serious human rights violations: summary executions, rape, and torture. In the effort to curb support for pro-independence militants, Indian security forces have resorted to arbitrary arrest and collective punishments of entire neighbourhoods, tactics which have only led to further disaffection from India. The militants have kidnapped and killed civil servants and suspected informers. *Human Rights Watch* alleged that thousands of civilian Kashmiri Hindus have been killed over the past 10 years by Islamic militants organisations or Muslim mobs. The militants committed war rape during the 1980s. Tens of thousands of Kashmiri Pandits have emigrated as a result of the violence. Estimates of the displaced varies from 170,000 to 700,000. Thousands of Kasmiri Pandits had to move to Jammu because of militancy.[1609]

Notable terrorist attacks in J&K

- July and August 1989 – 3 CRPF personnel and politician Mohd. Yusuf Halwai of NC/F were killed.
- 1989 kidnapping of Rubaiya Sayeed daughter of the then Home Minister of India Mufti Sayeed.
- 1995 kidnapping of western tourists in Jammu and Kashmir – Six foreign trekkers from Anantnag district were kidnapped by Al Faran. One was beheaded later, one escaped, and the other four remain missing, presumably killed.
- 1997 Sangrampora massacre – On 22 March 1997, seven Kashmiri Pandits were killed in Sangrampora village in the Budgam district.
- Wandhama massacre – In January 1998, 24 Kashmiri Pandits living in the village of Wandhama were massacred by Pakistani militants. According to the testimony of one of the survivors, the militants dressed themselves as officers of the Indian Army, entered their houses and then started firing blindly. The incident was significant because it coincided with former US president Bill Clinton's visit to India and New Delhi used the massacre to present a case against the alleged Pakistan-supported terrorism in Kashmir.
- 1998 Prankote massacre – 26 Hindu villagers of Udhampur district were killed by militants.
- 1998 Champanari massacre – 25 Hindu villagers killed on 19 June 1998 by Islamic militants.

- 2000 Amarnath pilgrimage massacre – 30 Hindu pilgrims massacred by militants.
- Chittisinghpura massacre – 36 Sikhs massacred by LET militants.
- 2001 terrorist attack on Jammu and Kashmir legislative assembly – On 1 October 2001, a bombing at the Legislative Assembly in Srinagar killed 38.
- 2002 Raghunath temple attacks – First attack occurred on 30 March 2002 when two suicide bombers attacked the temple. Eleven persons including three security forces personnel were killed and 20 were injured. In second attack, the fidayeen suicide squad attacked the temple second time on 24 November 2002 when two suicide bombers stormed the temple and killed fourteen devotees and injured 45 others.
- 2002 Qasim Nagar massacre – On 13 July 2002, armed militants believed to be a part of the Lashkar-e-Toiba threw hand grenades at the Qasim Nagar market in Srinagar and then fired on civilians standing nearby killing 27 and injuring many more.
- 2003 Nadimarg Massacre – 24 Hindus killed in Nadimarg, Kashmir on 23 March 2003 by Lashkar-e-Taiba militants.
- 20 July 2005 Srinagar Bombing – A car bomb exploded near an armoured Indian Army vehicle in the famous Church Lane area in Srinagar killing 4 Indian Army personnel, one civilian and the suicide bomber. Militant group Hizbul Mujahideen, claimed responsibility for the attack.
- Budshah Chowk attack – A militant attack on 29 July 2005 at Srinigar's city centre, Budshah Chowk, killed 2 and left more than 17 people injured. Most of those injured were media journalists.
- Assassination of Ghulam Nabi Lone – On 18 October 2005, suspected Kashmiri militants killed Jammu and Kashmir's then education minister Ghulam Nabi Lone. Militant group called Al Mansurin claimed responsibility for the attack. Abdul Ghani Lone, a prominent All Party Hurriyat Conference leader, was assassinated by unidentified gunmen during a memorial rally in Srinagar. The assassination resulted in wide-scale demonstrations against the Indian forces for failing to provide enough security cover for Lone.
- 2006 Doda massacre – On 3 May 2006, militants massacred 35 Hindus in Doda and Udhampur districts in Jammu and Kashmir.
- On 12 June 2006, one person was killed and 31 were wounded when terrorists hurled three grenades on Vaishnodevi shrine-bound buses at the general bus stand.
- 2014 Kashmir Valley attacks – There were four attacks on 5 December 2014 on army, police and civilians resulted in 21 deaths and several injured. Their motive was to disrupt the ongoing assembly elections.

- 2016 Uri attack – Four armed terrorists sneaked into an army camp and lobbed grenades onto tents causing massive fire culminating in the death of 19 military personnel.
- 2018 Sunjuwan attack - On 10 February 2018, Jaish-e-Mohammad terrorists attacked Sunjuwan Army Camp in Jammu and Kashmir. 6 Indian army soldiers, 4 terrorists, 1 civilian died and 11 were injured.

Tactics

India

Over time the Indian government has increasingly relied on military presence to control the insurgency. The military has committed human rights violations. The government would often dissolve assemblies, arrest elected politicians and impose president's rule. The government also rigged elections in 1987. In recent times there have been signs that the government is taking local elections more seriously. The government has also funneled development aid to Kashmir and Kashmir has now become the biggest per capita receiver of Federal aid.

Pakistan

The Pakistani central government originally supported, trained and armed the insurgency in Kashmir, sometimes known as "ultras" (extremists), however after groups linked to the Kashmiri insurgency twice attempted to assassinate president Pervez Musharraf, Musharraf decided to end support for such groups. His successor, Asif Ali Zardari has continued the policy, calling insurgents in Kashmir "terrorists".

But the Pakistani Inter-Services Intelligence hasn't followed the lead of the government and has continued its support for insurgent groups in Kashmir although Pakistani support for the insurgency has certainly waned.

Insurgents

Since around 2000 the 'insurgency' has become far less violent and has instead taken on the form of protests and marches. Certain groups have also chosen to lay down their arms and look for a peaceful resolution to the conflict.

Groups

The different insurgent groups have different aims in Kashmir. Some want complete independence from both India and Pakistan, others want unification with Pakistan and still others just want greater autonomy from the Indian government.

A 2010 survey found that 43% in J&K and 44% in AJK would favour complete independence from both India and Pakistan, with support for the independence movement unevenly distributed across the region.

Identity

Over the last two years, the militant group, Lashkar-e-Toiba has split into two factions: *Al Mansurin* and *Al Nasirin*. Another new group reported to have emerged is the "Save Kashmir Movement". Harkat-ul-Mujahideen (formerly known as Harkat-ul-Ansar) and Lashkar-e-Toiba are believed to be operating from Muzaffarabad, Azad Kashmir and Muridke, Pakistan respectively. Wikipedia:Citation needed

Other less well known groups are the Freedom Force and Farzandan-e-Milat. A smaller group, Al-Badr, has been active in Kashmir for many years and is still believed to be functioning. All Parties Hurriyat Conference, an organisation that uses moderate means to press for the rights of the Kashmiris, is often considered as the *mediator* between New Delhi and insurgent groups. Wikipedia:Citation needed

Al-Qaeda

It is unclear if Al Qaeda has a presence in Jammu and Kashmir. Donald Rumsfeld suggested that they were active and in 2002 the SAS hunted for Osama bin Laden in Jammu and Kashmir. Al Qaeda claims that it has established a base in Jammu and Kashmir. However, there has been no evidence for any of these assertions. The Indian army also claims that there is no evidence of Al Qaeda presence in Jammu and Kashmir. Al Qaeda has established bases in Pakistani administered Kashmir and some, including Robert Gates have suggested that they have helped to plan attacks in India.

Casualties

According to Sumantra Bose in his book, *Kashmir: Roots of Conflict, Paths to Peace*, around 40000 (Indian estimates) to 80000 (Hurriyat estimates) civilians, separatist guerilla fighters and Indian security personnel died from the time period of 1989 to 2002 in both Kashmir Valley and Jammu. More than 4600 security personnel, 13500 civilians and 15937 militants including 3000 from outside Jammu and Kashmir (mostly Pakistanis and some Afghans) were killed in this fourteen-year period. Also in this period, 55,538 incidents of violence were recorded. Indian forces engaged in counter insurgency operations captured around 40,000 firearms, 150,000 explosive devices, and over 6 million rounds of assorted ammunition. Jammu and Kashmir Coalition of Civil Society posits a figure of 70,000 deaths, most of them civilians killed by Indian forces.

References

Bibliography

- Khan, Waheeda (2015), "Conflict in Kashmir: Psychosocial Consequences on Children", in Sibnath Deb, *Child Safety, Welfare and Wellbeing: Issues and Challenges*[1610], Springer, pp. 83–93, ISBN 978-81-322-2425-9

Bombay riots

1992-93 Bombay Riots	
Date	6 December 1992 – 26 January 1993
Location	Mumbai, India
Caused by	Demolition of Babri Mosque
Casualties	
Death(s)	900 (575 Muslims, 275 Hindus, 50 others)

Part of a series on
Violence against Hindus in independent India
Issues
<ul><li>Religious persecution</li><li>Freedom of religion</li><li>Religious violence</li></ul>
Incidents
<ul><li>1947 Jammu massacres</li><li>Mandai massacre</li><li>1991 Punjab killings</li><li>Bombay riots</li><li>1998 Chamba massacre</li><li>1998 Wandhama massacre</li><li>1998 Chapnari massacre</li><li>1998 Prankote massacre</li><li>Bagber massacre</li><li>Operation Roukhala</li><li>2000 Amarnath pilgrimage massacre</li><li>2001 Kishtwar massacre</li><li>2002 Qasim Nagar massacre</li><li>Akshardham Temple attack</li><li>Godhra train burning</li><li>2002 Raghunath temple attacks</li><li>2003 Nadimarg massacre</li><li>2006 Doda massacre</li></ul>
<ul><li>v</li><li>t</li><li>e[1611]</li></ul>

Part of a series on
Violence against Muslims in India
Incidents
• 1969 Gujarat riots • 1980 Moradabad riots • 1983 Nellie massacre • 1987 Hashimpura massacre • 1985 Gujarat riots • 1989 Bhagalpur violence • 1992 Bombay riots • 2002 Gujarat riots • 2006 Malegaon bombings • 2014 Assam Violence
Related topics
• Freedom of religion • Violence against Muslims
• v • t • e[1612]

The **Bombay riots** usually refers to the riots in Mumbai, in December 1992 and January 1993, in which around 900 people died. The riots were mainly due to escalations of hostilities after large scale protests (which were initially peaceful, but eventually turned violent) by Muslims in reaction to the 1992 Babri Masjid Demolition by Hindu Karsevaks in Ayodhya.

An investigative commission was formed under Justice B.N. Srikrishna, but the recommendations of the Inquiry were not enacted.

Many scholars stated that the riots were pre-planned, and that the Hindu rioters were granted access to information about the locations of Muslim homes and businesses through sources that were not public.[1613] The violence was widely reported as having been orchestrated by the Shiv Sena, a Hindu-nationalist political party in Maharashtra. A high-ranking member of the special branch later stated that the police were fully aware of the Shiv Sena's capabilities to commit acts of violence, and that they had incited hate against the minority communities. Historian Barbara Metcalf has stated that the riots were anti-Muslim pogrom.

The riots were followed by the retaliatory 12 March 1993 Bombay Bombings.[1614]

History

The riots started as a result of communal tension prevailing in the city after the Babri Mosque demolition on 6 December 1992. The Shrikrishna Commission identified **two phases** to the riots. *The first* was mainly a Muslim backlash as a result of the Babri Masjid demolition in the week immediately succeeding 6 December 1992 led by political leaders representing Hindutva in the city of Ayodhya. *The second phase* was a Hindu backlash occurring as a result of the killings of Hindu Mathadi Kamgar (workers) by Muslim fanatics in Dongri (an area of South Bombay), stabbing of Hindus in Muslim majority areas and burning of six Hindus, including a physically handicapped girl in Radhabai Chawl. This phase occurred in January 1993, with most incidents reported between 6 and 20 January.

The Report asserted that the communal passions of the Hindus were aroused to fever pitch by the inciting writings in print media, particularly Saamna and Navaakal which gave exaggerated accounts of the Mathadi murders and the Radhabai Chawl incident; rumours were floated that there were imminent attacks by Muslims using sophisticated arms, though the possibility of it happening was very imminent.Wikipedia:Please clarify From 8 January 1993, many riots occurred between Hindus led by the Shiv Sena and the Muslims funded by the Mumbai underworld at that time. The communal violence and rioting triggered off by the burning at Dongri and Radhabhai Chawl and then the retaliatory violence by Shiv Sena was hijacked by local criminal elements who saw in it an opportunity to make quick gains. By the time the right wing Hindu organization Shiv Sena realised that enough had been done by way of "retaliation", the violence and rioting was beyond the control of its leaders who had to issue an appeal to put an end to it.<ref name=autogenerated1 /

The events as listed by the Srikrishna Commission

6 December 1992

News of the demolition of Babri Masjid spread by 1430 hours on 6 December 1992. Muslims angered by this act felt that Islam was in imminent danger since proponents of the Hindu nation had been allowed to destroy, under the very nose of the armed forces, the Babri Masjid, despite assurances and undertakings by the Uttar Pradesh state Government and the Government of India that no harm would be permitted to be caused to the Babri Masjid during kar seva at Ayodhya on 6 December 1992. The extensive media coverage, particularly on television, of footage of file pictures of previous kar seva during which some of the kar sevaks were seen dancing on the dome of the Masjid, as well as the latest video shots showing actual demolition of the Babri Masjid, caused a sense of deep resentment. The demolition of the Babri Masjid provided enough fuel to excite, ignite and exploit the sentimentalities of Islamists. Muslims were proselytised by these exploitative elements that the Establishment and the Government had an active hand in the destruction, since it was not able to prevent the same.

Rumours abounded that alleged members of certain Hindutva parties were seen to be celebrating the demolition of Babri structure. Muslims protested violently on the streets. Large number of Muslims congregated near Minara Masjid in Pydhonie jurisdiction at about 2320 hours on 6 December 1992 and came out protesting frenziedly despite Mumbai being located in the unrelated state of Maharashtra. The first targets of the rioting mob became the municipal vans and the constabulary, both visible signs of the government.

Activists of Bharatiya Janata Party and Shiv Sena jumped into the fray, and escalated communal passion, as seen from their act of stopping the vehicles on roads in the jurisdiction of V.P. Road Police Station.

In Nirmal Nagar jurisdiction, a Ganesh idol in the Ganesh Mandir on Anant Kanekar Marg was found moved out from its place of installation though the lock on the grill surrounding the sanctum sanctorum was found intact. This was noticed at about 2345 hours. Though at the time the incident happened there were no immediate clues as to the identity of the miscreants, it was widely suspected that Muslim fanatics were behind it.

In the jurisdiction of Deonar, there was a sharp counter–reaction by Muslims who stoned the house of a local Bharatiya Janata Party leader. Tensions escalated.

7 December 1992

From 7 December 1992 onwards there was a qualitative transformation in the situation. Large mobs of Muslims came on the streets and there was recourse taken to violence without doubt. The Muslim mobs appeared to have come out with the intention of mounting violent attacks as noticed from their preparedness with weapons of offence. There were violent attacks on the policemen in Muslim dominated areas like Bhendi Bazar and its vicinity. The jurisdictional areas affected were mostly Muslim dominated or mixed localities. The situation further worsened when Hindu youth beat up the rioting Muslims, leading to a situation where the police found it difficult to restrain both sections; when the police did it by force, the police came to be attacked by both Hindu and Muslim mobs.

By this time the protest had degenerated into a full–scale communal riot between Hindus and Muslims.{{POV statement|date=May 2013}} Eleven Hindu houses in different jurisdictions were damaged, demolished or set on fire. The

Hindus did not fall behind and damaged mosques and madrasas in different jurisdictions. BEST buses in the Bombay Central Bus Depot and BEST bus stops became easy targets for the Muslim mobs and were damaged and/or set on fire.

Two constables in Deonar jurisdiction were killed with choppers and swords by the rampaging Muslims. While one lay on the ground bleeding to death, the body of another was dragged and thrown into the garbage heap from where it was recovered seven days later. One constable was done to death in Byculla jurisdiction. Several police officers and policemen who bravely attempted to stem the tide sustained injuries in mob action.

In Mahim, two police personnel, HC Zarande of Crime Branch, CID, and Police Sub-Inspector Salunke of Juhu Police Station, were proceeding on a motorcycle when attacked by a Muslim mob of 400–500 with soda–water bottles and stones, resulting in injuries to them. The area around L.J. Road and nearby roads were strewn with shattered glass and stones with riotous Muslim mobs running around shouting *"Allah-hu-Akbar"* and indiscriminately throwing stones in Kapad Bazar. To maintain law and order, police resorted to firing which resulted in injuries to two Muslims. Seven police personnel were injured in the riot and the motorcycle was completely damaged.

Jogeshwari area, which has been the hotbed of frequent communal riots saw serious riots at the junction of Pascal Colony and Shankar Wadi. A police officer on duty received a bullet injury in his head and died subsequently, though it cannot be said with certitude that it was a case of private firing. The police recovered large number of iron rods, sickles, choppers, knives and soda water bottles from different jurisdictions indicating that there was intention and preparations to carry on the communal riots.

A violent Muslim mob ransacked a Police chowky at Maulana Shaukat Ali Road and physically assaulted one Police constable, Pandit Malhari Ahire. Ahire was attacked with swords and choppers and suffered grievous injuries. At about the same time a huge Muslim mob of about 4,000–5,000 collected on Maulana Shaukat Ali Road and in the lanes and by-lanes of the area. The mob went on damaging and destroying the vehicles and public property and indulged in indiscriminate stone throwing. Ahire's life was saved by prompt action by Senior Police Inspector Pawar along with other officers who carried on firing to restore peace.

8 December 1992

On 8 December 1992 communal rioting and communal violence spread to 33 jurisdictions, the number of clashes of rioting mobs with police as well as rioting mobs inter se increased alarmingly. Attacks on places of worship also continued. Shiv Sena systematically attacked Muslim men, women and children during that time.

The police had to resort to firing in 43 cases resulting in the death of 11 Hindus, 31 Muslims and three others. There were several cases of mob violence, stabbing and arson. One temple in Dharavi, one in Deonar, one in Park Site and one in Saki Naka were attacked. Simultaneously, two mosques in Dharavi, one madrasa in Mahim and Bhoiwada each and one dargah in Dadar were also attacked.

Though the police found their resources stretched, they were unwilling to take the help of army for carrying out operational duties. Army columns were used only to carry out flag marches which had little impact on the, by now hardened and emboldened, rioters. The imposition of curfew from the night of 7 December 1992 also did not appear to deter the clashing mobs in view of its effete enforcement. Police intervention came about by resort to fire on 72 occasions, killing 15 Hindus and 72 Muslims and injuring 131 Muslims and one Christian.

9 December 1992

The situation improved for better and the number of cases of mob violence, stabbing, arson and rioting showed a downward trend. The number of occasions when the police had to resort to firing dropped to 28. The police firing resulted in deaths of 17 persons (five Hindus and 12 Muslims) while 3 Hindus, 12 Muslims and six others sustained injuries. Thirty-four cases of arson resulting in loss of property and injuries to one Hindu and 10 Muslims were reported from different jurisdictions. One temple in Ghatkopar, 3 mosques in Trombay and one kabrastan in Jogeshwari were subjected to attack by violent mobs.

10 December 1992

The situation improved further with the number of police stations affected coming down to four, though serious communal riots occurred in Dharavi and Mahim police jurisdictions to control which the police had to fire on three and two occasions respectively. Two Muslims were injured in police firing within the jurisdiction of Mahim.

11 December 1992

On this day there was one case of private firing in Azad Maidan jurisdiction in which one Muslim died and four Muslims were injured. However, there was further improvement in overall situation. There was no occasion for police to resort to firing, though 23 different police stations appear to have been affected in varying degrees.

12 December 1992

The situation showed further improvement and the number of police stations affected came down to 14, though there also the occurrences were stray. There were three instances of police firing, one each in Ghatkopar, Bhandup and Dindoshi in which one Hindu and one Muslim were injured. Mob violence took the toll of one life. There were six cases of stabbing in which 1 Hindu and two Muslims died and one Hindu and one Muslim sustained injuries. There were eight stray cases of arson. Four dead bodies, all of Muslims, having multiple stab wounds on vital organs and in highly decomposed condition, were recovered from a gutter in Golibar area.

In yet another incident, one was found murdered with her throat slit and her body was dumped in the open compound of National Girls' High School adjoining Behrampada.

The December phase of the rioting petered out by 12 December 1992. The police appeared to have regained grip on the law and order situation and peace appeared to have returned. However, beneath the surface there was simmering discontent and seething anger amongst the Muslims that unduly excessive police firing had resulted in large number of Muslim casualties. Media had criticised the police for having used unnecessary and excessive fire–power, going so far as to suggest that Muslims were intentionally targeted and selectively killed. This refrain was repeated by political leaders and ministers, past and current. The explanation of the commissioner of police that the aggressive and violent mobs in the initial stages comprised Muslims and therefore, Muslim casualties were higher. Considering it from all aspects, the Commission was not inclined to give serious credence to the theory that dis–proportionately large number of Muslim deaths in December 1992 was necessarily indicative of an attempt on the part of the police to target and liquidate Muslims because of bias.

12 December 1992 to 5 January 1993

On 20 December 1992, two Muslims were locked inside a room in Goregaon jurisdiction, and the room was set on fire as a result of which they suffered severe burns resulting in the death of one.

Two bodies, one of a male Hindu and another identified as that of a uniformed Muslim police constable attached to the Nasik Rural Police Headquarters, were recovered from the septic tank of the public latrine in Behrampada on 20 and 21 December 1992 respectively. These bodies bore multiple stab injuries. It would appear that there was a systematic attempt to stab and murder Hindus and the policeman, though a Muslim, became a victim of the anger of the Muslims directed against the uniform worn by him.

On 24/25 December 1992 one Mathadi worker was killed in Dongri area. Though subsequent investigation by police resulted in arrest of the accused who was an alcoholic and whose motive was far from communal, at the material time the immediate reaction was that the killing was done of a Muslim.

The fires under the simmering cauldron were continuously stoked by communal activities even after the active phase of the December 1992 riots was over. There was a sudden spurt in attendance at Friday namaaz in mosques, which was interpreted by the Hindu as ominous and evidencing intent to seek revenge on the part of Muslims. This was because it was alleged that the namaaz were used as occasions for delivering instigatory communal speeches. The Hindus replied with Maha aartis (Great Hindu worship of the God), in an ostensible response against the sudden spurt in namaaz on streets. The Maha aartis were started from 26 December 1992 were viewed as a direct challenge to the Muslims, and endangered the fragile peace which had been established, with allegations that participants of the Maha aartis indulged in rioting. The Maha aartis continued unabated throughout January 1993 and came to an end only by or about the first week of February 1993.

The last week of December 1992 and first week of January 1993, particularly between 1 and 5 January, saw a series of stabbing incidents in which both Hindus and Muslims were victims, though the majority of such incidents took place in Muslim dominated areas of South Bombay and a majority of victims were HindusWikipedia:Citation needed. The stabbings appeared to be executed with professional accuracy intended to kill the victimsWikipedia:Citation needed. The killers had not been then identified in several cases, though it was presumed, at least in the cases where the Hindus were victims, that the killers were Muslims and vice versa. The motive for the stabbings appears to have been to whip up communal frenzy between Hindus and Muslims. Some of the Muslim criminal elements operating in South Bombay, like Salim Rampuri and Firoz Konkani, have been identified as the brains behind the stabbing incidentsWikipedia:Citation needed. That they were Muslim criminals was publicised in the media, and it was general opinion that the Muslims were keen on resuming aggression.

On 25 December 1992 a pamphlet in Urdu language was distributed around Jama Masjid in Mahim area. This pamphlet was communally provocative and incited Muslims to fight against Hindus and calls upon the Muslims to the construct the Babri Masjid if necessary, with blood.

On 1 January 1993 there was an article in the Shiv Sena mouthpiece, Saamna under the caption *"Hindunni Akramak Vhayala Have"* (Hindus must be aggressive now), openly inciting Hindus to violence.

On 2 January 1993 a number of Muslim hutments in M.P. Mill Compound in Tardeo jurisdiction were set on fire. On the same day there was an incident in Dharavi jurisdiction in which two Muslims were assaulted with iron rods by Hindus.

On 4 January 1993 a big mob of Hindus led by Gajanan Kirtikar, Ramesh More and other Shiv Sena activists took a morcha to the Jogeshwari Police Station complaining of lack of security for Hindus. Some of the people in the morcha attacked Chacha Nagar Masjid and the Muslims in the vicinity and killed them. Several Muslim huts in Magdum Nagar in Mahim jurisdiction were set on fire by Hindus.

On the night of 5 January 1993 a worker employed in the godown of Vijay Transport Company who was sleeping in the godown went to the street to relieve himself. Suddenly, he was set upon by miscreants who stabbed him to death. Three more workers who came out of the godown to help him were also stabbed to death. The murders of the workers created tremendous tension in the area. The workers' Union called for a Bandh. Huge meetings were held which were addressed by leaders of Unions. Speeches were made during this meeting to condemn the police and Government for their ineffectiveness with exhortations that Hindus might have to pick up swords to defend themselves if the police failed to protect them. At the time when these murders of workers took place, neither the police, nor the public, had a clue as to the identity of the killers, which came to be established much later. Nonetheless, the Hindus spearheaded by the Shiv Sena kicked up a furore that the murders had been committed by Muslims, virtually giving a call for arms, killing 10 Muslims. On 5/6 January 1993 the workers gave a call for bandh of wholesale markets, which also gave immense publicity to the murders of the workers allegedly by Muslims.

6 January 1993 to 20 January 1993

On 6 January 1993 there were several cases of stabbing in Dongri, Pydhonie, V.P. Road and Nagpada jurisdictions in which the victims were innocent pedestrians who were stabbed. Cases of stabbing, arson, mob violence and attacks on private and Government properties occurred in Dongri, Pydhonie, V.P. Road, Nagpada, Tardeo, Mahim, Dharavi, Nirmal Nagar, Chembur and Kherwadi police stations. Most of the stabbing cases occurred in isolated lanes and bye-lanes and by the time police arrived on the scene, the miscreants would vanish. In all, 18 cases of stabbing were reported by the evening of this day of which were from Pydhonie, two from Dharavi, two from V.P. Road, two from Nagpada and one each from Nirmal Nagar, Kherwadi and Andheri. These stabbing cases resulted in one Hindu, one Muslim and two others being killed and 1 Hindu, one Muslim and one other being injured. Mob violence accounted for the deaths of one Hindu and one Muslim and injuries to nine Hindus and eighteen Muslims. Rumours of further imminent riots swept the city and the police were unable to scotch them. Despite repeated denials of such rumours by the police, the public did not believe them.

The situation in Mahim went out of control at 2100 hours. Hindus attacked Muslims in Muslim pockets in Mahim area and killed them, led by Shiv Sena Corporator, Milind Vaidya, and a police constable, Sanjay Gawade, openly carrying a sword. There were serious riots in which frenzied mobs of Hindus and Muslims attacked each other.

7 January 1993

The violence and riots spread to several parts of the city. There were more deaths and more stabbings and 16 police station areas (Pydhonie, Dongri, Agripada, Gamdevi, V.P. Road, Byculla, Bhoiwada, Nagpada, Kherwadi, Nehru Nagar, Kurla, Deonar, Trombay, Bandra, Vakola and Jogeshwari) were affected by serious riots. The stabbing incidents resulted in deaths of 16 Hindu and four Muslims and injured 3 Hindus and twelve Muslims.

Eleven cases of mob violence occurred in different jurisdictional areas, killing two Muslims and injuring two Hindus and two Muslims. Seven cases of arson were reported on that day in which, apart from huge property loss, two Muslims were killed; two Hindus and two Muslims were injured. The police resorted to firing on four occasions, resulting in injuries to 3 Hindus and 5 Muslims. Violent mobs of Hindus and Muslims kept attacking each other and the police when they tried to intervene.

The mobs also created roadblocks to prevent the police and fire-brigade from reaching the sites of incidents for rendering assistance. A taxi in which three Muslims were travelling was set on fire by Shiv Sena workers in Pratiksha Nagar, Antop Hill jurisdiction, resulting in the 2 Muslims being burnt alive.

8 January 1993

A gruesome incident occurred during the wee hours of 8 January 1993, at about 0030 hours, one of the Hindu residences in a chawl popularly known as Radhabai Chawl in Jogeshwari jurisdiction were locked from outside and set on fire by miscreants. One male and two female members of a Hindu family (Bane) were charred to death. One of the victims was a physically handicapped girl.

The Hindu backlash commenced. The communal riots spread to the jurisdictions of Pydhonie, Dongri, Jogeshwari, M.R.A. Marg, L.T. Marg, V.P. Road, D.B. Marg, Gamdevi, Nagpada, Agripada, Byculla, Kala Chowki, N.M. Joshi Marg, Worli, Bhoiwada, Dadar, Mahim, Dharavi, Kurla, Nehru Nagar, Trombay, Chembur, Bandra, Nirmal Nagar, Ghatkopar, Vikhroli, Parksite, Vakola, Oshiwara, D.N. Nagar, Jogeshwari and Aarey sub–police stations.

Sixty-six stabbing cases were reported from different jurisdictions, in which 3 Hindu, 37 Muslims and two others were killed and injuries caused to several Muslims. Forty-eight cases of mob violence occurred in which sixteen Muslims were killed and 4 Hindus and 17 Muslims and one other received injuries. Thirty-one cases of arson were reported which, apart from causing loss of property, resulted in deaths of two Muslims and injuries to five Muslims and one Hindu.

A dargah and mosque in Pydhonie jurisdiction, a kabrastan and a madrassa in Jogeshwari jurisdiction and a temple in Byculla jurisdiction were attacked and damaged. Police resorted to firing on 31 occasions in different jurisdictions resulting in the killing of six Hindus and 18 Muslims and injuries to 10 Hindus and 24 Muslims and one other. Several raids conducted by the police resulted in seizure of weapons of offence like broken tube lights, swords, petrol bombs and daggers.

That the rioters had become defiant and the authority of the police was considerably eroded, appeared clear when a crude bomb was hurled at the police commissioner's car from one of the buildings in Pydhonie jurisdiction and exploded on the road. The commissioner of police and his staff had a lucky escape, though the severity of the explosion caused a big dent on the road. Eleven army columns were deployed by the police to do Flag March in different areas. Curfew was imposed in areas where it was considered necessary.

9 January 1993

The riots continued unabated in 43 police station jurisdictions. Fifty-seven cases of stabbing resulting in death of five Hindus and 18 Muslims and injuries to 7 Hindus, 41 Muslims and one other, were reported. Ninety-seven cases of mob violence occurred in various parts of the city resulting in the death of one Hindu and sixteen Muslims and injures to 9 Hindus and 24 Muslims. Seventy-three cases of arson were reported from different jurisdictions which caused loss of property, death of a Hindu and six Muslims and injures to two Hindus and six Muslims.

In Pydhonie jurisdiction, few rounds were fired at a police picket from the Suleman Bakery rooftop. The policemen climbed to the terrace of the Taj Book Depot, a neighbouring building, and sighted 8 – 10 persons hiding behind the water tank on the bakery rooftop. Inspector Anant Ingale shouted warnings and fired a few shots from his service revolver, but his party was no match to the automatic weapon wielding group. Joint Commissioner of Police R. D. Tyagi arrived with the Special Operations Squad (SOS), and demanded the opening of the locked door of the Bakery. The inmates responded by throwing soda-water bottles and acid bulbs. The SOS stormed into the Bakery and were promptly attacked by about 15 people armed with choppers, knives and ironbars. There wasn't surrender or ceasement of attack, so the Police had to open fire. Totally, 78 Muslims were flushed out of the bakery dead, by the police.

Fifty-two cases of police firing occurred in different jurisdictions, killing 5 Hindus, 22 Muslims and one other. Police combing operations resulted in seizure of stocks of swords, iron bars, choppers, kerosene cans, acid bulbs and soda water bottles from different areas.

10 January 1993

Twenty-six army columns were deployed for carrying out flag marches and for the first time the Government issued instructions to the commissioner of police that the army personnel may be directed to do operational duties by resorting to firing after taking control of a situation. Fifty-one police stations were affected by the riots. Eighty-one cases of stabbing occurred in different jurisdictions resulting in deaths of 10 Hindus and 39 Muslims and injuries to 12 Hindus and 42 Muslims. One hundred and eight cases of arson occurred in which there was property loss, death of one Hindu, seven Muslims and two others, while one Hindu, one Muslim and one other were injured. Attempts of the fire brigade to reach the places of fire were frustrated by the rioters who not only blocked the streets but also threatened the fire brigade staff and resorted to stone throwing against the fire brigade vehicles. Fires blazed uncontrolled.

Mob violence was reported from 25 jurisdictions causing deaths of two Hindus, nineteen Muslims, while 3 Hindus, 27 Muslims and two others were injured.

The police were given orders to fire and resorted to firing on 82 occasions, resulting in deaths of 2 Hindus, 23 Muslims and one other, while injuries were caused to 7 Hindus, 27 Muslims and two others. Police seized large number of swords, choppers, tube lights, fire balls, soda water bottles, iron bars, guptis and also one country made revolver. The situation was very grave in several jurisdictional areas. Even normally law-abiding citizens seemed gripped by the communal frenzy and were seen attacking members of the rival community. Peace committee members, politicians and other social workers were conspicuous by their absence. Communal hatred and fear psychosis appeared to have overtaken the citizens of Bombay making tolerance and reason prime casualties. Rumours about attacks from rival community swept the city.

11 January 1993

The situation continued to be serious. Fifty-two police stations were affected by communal violence in varying degrees. Eighty-six cases of stabbing occurred in different jurisdictions resulting in the death of 11 Hindus, 44 Muslims and 1 other; 11 Hindus, 68 Muslims and one other were injured. Four Hindus, 19 Muslims and two others were killed in 129 incidents of mob violence in different jurisdictions. Ninety-three cases of arson in different jurisdictions resulted in the death of two Hindus and 20 Muslims and injuries to seventeen Muslims. Police firing on 67 occasions caused to deaths of 3 Hindus and 15 Muslims and injuries to 11 Hindus, 41 Muslims and two others. The army column was used for operational duty in Dadar jurisdiction where it fired on a riotous mob of Hindus without causing any injuries. Police raids in several Muslim pockets unearthed several swords, knives, choppers, kerosene bottles, acid bulbs, tube lights, one country made revolver and live cartridges.

12 January 1993

In Devipada in Kasturba Marg jurisdiction. A Hindu mob surrounds, strips and rapes two Muslim women. The older woman manages to run away. The uncle of the younger woman who comes to rescue the young girl of 19, and that girl, are beaten and burnt alive by the violent mob. The names of the miscreants are disclosed to police by a Hindu lady in the locality. (Though the miscreants were arrested and tried by the Sessions Court at Bombay, later on they were all acquitted on the ground that the panchanamas were defective and that the eye-witnesses were not produced). Police resorted to firing on 31 occasions in different jurisdictions resulting in the deaths of two Hindus and nine Muslims and injuries to 23 Hindus and seven Muslims. Fifty-six cases of stabbing occurred in different areas resulting in the deaths of three Hindus, 37 Muslims and injuries to 11 Hindus and 51 Muslims. Seventy-one cases of mob violence in different areas occurred in which one Hindu and nine Muslims were killed; six Hindus and 29 Muslims were injured. Seventy cases of arson were reported from different police stations, in which six Muslims were killed and one Muslim was injured.

The army column, come to rescue a group of sieged Muslims by Hindus in Antop Hill jurisdiction is attacked by a violent Hindu mob, resorts to firing to disperse the mob. Army column resorts to firing within the jurisdiction of Trombay jurisdiction against another rioting mob of Hindus killing one Hindu and injury to one.

13 January 1993

The situation improves slightly in several areas; the number of affected police stations comes down to 48; stabbing cases to 36; mob violence to 67 and arson to 51. The police resort to firing on 24 occasions resulting in the killing of two Muslims and injuries to six Hindus and fourteen Muslims. Mob violence takes a toll of the lives of three Muslims and injures four Hindus and 18 Muslims. Stabbings cause the death of one Hindu and 19 Muslims, while two Hindus and 10 Muslims and one other are injured.

14 January 1993

The situation shows substantial improvement. The number of affected police stations comes down to 40, the number of arson cases drops to 39, in which one Hindu and nine Muslims were killed apart from loss to property; mob violence is reported only in 34 cases in which seven Muslims and are killed and nine Muslims are injured; the police resort to firing only on four occasions in which no one is killed and one Hindu is injured. Stabbing cases resulted in death of three Hindus and 16 Muslims and three others, while six Hindus, 18 Muslims and one other are injured. The deployment of army columns is increased to 36.

15 January 1993

i) There is further improvement in the situation; the number of police stations affected comes down to 29; mob violence occurs only in 24 cases resulting in death of twelve Muslims and four Hindus and injuries to eight Muslims. The number of stabbing cases comes down to 12 in which one Hindu and 15 Muslims are killed and three Hindus and nine Muslims are injured; the number of arson cases comes down to 25 in which there was only loss of property without death or injury to anyone. The police resort to firing only on two occasions which result in killing of three Muslims, and injuries to 14 Muslims. Army column deployed at Nirmal Nagar resorts to firing to quell a riotous mob.

ii) The Prime Minister of India, Shri Narsimha Rao, makes a quick tour of the riot affected areas amidst heavy security arrangements.

16 January 1993

The situation shows further improvement. Only 15 stray cases of stabbing are reported in which 12 Muslims are killed and injuries caused to seven Muslims. Seven mob violence cases occur resulting in injury to one Muslim; 23 stray cases of arson are reported in different areas in which there is only property loss. Police firing comes down to two cases in which none is injured.

17 January 1993

The situation seems to be improving for the better. There is no occasion for the police to resort to firing. Three cases of stabbing are reported from different areas in which two Muslims were injured; three minor cases of mob violence occur causing injuries to thirteen Muslims; and six minor cases of arson reported in which, apart from loss of property, one Muslim is killed.

18 January 1993

There was no occasion on which police resorted to firing on this day. There was one case of stabbing resulting in the killing of one Muslim, three minor cases of mob violence in which none was injured; five stray minor cases of arson were reported in which none was injured.

19 January 1993

The city appears to be limping back to normalcy. Five stray cases of stabbing are reported in which one Muslim was killed and two Muslims were injured. Though nine stray cases of arson are reported, there was no loss of life or injury.

The period subsequent to 20 January 1993

From 20 January 1993 onwards there was no major communal incident despite a few stray cases being reported. The rumour mills worked overtime and rumours about imminent attacks and explosions likely to occur were thick. Call was given out by Imam of Jama Masjid that Muslims should boycott the Republic Day and hoist black flags on their establishments and houses. Police maintained continued vigil along with the army and para–military forces.

On 25 January 1993, there is a minor riot in Dharavi jurisdiction which is quickly controlled by police firing without any death or injury.

26 January 1993 passed off peacefully in all jurisdictions except Dindoshi where the police resorted to firing in which two Muslims were killed and three Muslims were injured; mob violence caused injuries to two policemen and two Muslims.

During the subsequent period in January the situation in the city slowly comes back to normalcy.

Total number of deaths

Dead – 900 (575 Muslims, 275 Hindus, 45 and 5 others). The causes for the deaths are police firing (356), stabbing (347), arson (91), mob action (80), private firing (22) and other causes (4).

Justice B.N. Srikrishna Commission

Justice Srikrishna, then a relatively junior Judge of the Bombay High Court, accepted the task of investigating the causes of the riots, something that many of his colleagues had turned downWikipedia:Citation needed. For five years until 1998, he examined victims, witnesses and alleged perpetrators. Detractors came initially from left quarters who were wary of a judge who was a devout and practising Hindu. The Commission was disbanded by the Shiv Sena led government in January 1996 and on public opposition was later reconstituted on 28 May 1996; though when it was reconstituted its terms of reference were extended to include the Mumbai bomb blasts that followed in March 1993.

The report of the commission stated that the tolerant and secular foundations of the city were holding even if a little shakily. Justice Srikrishna indicted those he alleged as largely responsible for the second phase of the bloodshed and to some extent the first, the Shiv Sena.

The report was criticised as "politically motivated". For a while, its contents were a closely guarded secret and no copies were available. The Shiv Sena government rejected its recommendations. Since under the Commissions of Inquiry Act, an Inquiry is not a court of law (even if it conducts proceedings like a court of law) and the report of an inquiry is not binding on Governments, Srikrishna's recommendations cannot be directly enforced. To date, the recommendations of the Commission have neither been accepted nor acted upon by the Maharashtra Government.Wikipedia:Citation needed Many indicted policemen were promoted by the government and indicted politicians continue to hold high political office even today.Wikipedia:Citation needed

According to the commission report, the causes of these riots were listed as

1. Class Conflict
2. Economic Competition
3. Decline of employment
4. Population density
5. changing political discourse.

The immediate causes were listed as

1. the demolition of Babri Masjid
2. the aggravation of Muslim sentiments by the Hindus with their celebration rallies
3. the insensitive and harsh approach of the police while handling the protesting mobs which initially were not violent.

Arrests, convictions and verdict

Only 3 convictions happened in the 1992-93 Bombay riots cases. On 10 July 2008, a Mumbai court sentenced former Shiv Sena MP Madhukar Sarpotdar and two other party activists to a year's rigorous imprisonment in connection with the riots. However, he was immediately granted bail. He died on 20 February 2010 without serving his sentence.

In popular culture

The riots are portrayed in several different films:

- They are the key plot in the 1995 film *Bombay* in which the protagonists, a Muslim wife and her Hindu husband, are separated from their children during the riots.
- The 2004 Hindi film *Black Friday* deals with the events leading to the riots and the aftermath which led to the 1993 Bombay bomb blasts, and related investigations, told through the different stories of the people involved – police, conspirators, victims, middlemen.
- The violence is also an instrumental part of the plot of the film *Slumdog Millionaire*. The protagonist, Jamal Malik's mother is among those killed in the riots, and he later remarks "If it wasn't for Rama and Allah, we'd still have a mother."
- The event also appeared in 2010 film *Striker*, 2000 film *Fiza* and 2013 film *Shahid*.

Sources

- Dawood and ISI's role in riots, http://www.tehelka.com/story_main28.asp?filename=Ne240307How_the_CS.asp&id=3 (TEHELKA)
- 275 Hindus dead(32%)575 Muslims(67%) officially dead (45 unidentified), http://www.hindustantimes.com/Mumbai-s-festering-wound/Article1-239048.aspxWikipedia:Link rot
- Detailed Report[16][15]

- Official Supreme Court of India Biography, available at https: //web.archive.org/web/20060117015255/http://supremecourtofindia. nic.in/judges/bio/sitting/bns.htm
- Justice B.N. Srikrishna, "Skinning a Cat", (2005) 8 SCC (Jour) 3, available at http://www.ebc-india.com/lawyer/articles/2005_8_3.htm (a critique of judicial activism in India).
- Justice B.N. Srikrishna, "Maxwell versus Mimamsa", (2004) 6 SCC (Jour) 49, available at:

http://www.ebc-india.com/lawyer/articles/2004v6a5.htm (a critique of Indian and Western interpretative techniques).

- Praveen Swami, "A welter of evidence: How Thackeray and Co. figure in the Srikrishna Commission Report", 17(16) FRONTLINE (5–18 Aug. 2000), available at http://www.hinduonnet.com/fline/fl1716/17160110. htm (examining the Justice Srikrishna Commission's indictment of Bal Thackeray and the Shiv Sena).
- Draupadi Rohera, "The sacred space of Justice Srikrishna", Sunday Times (16 August 1998) (discussing Justice Srikrishna's Hindu beliefs and his work with the Commission).
- Suketu Mehta, "Maximum City: Bombay lost and found", (2004), Part I Ch. II.

https://blogs.wsj.com/indiarealtime/2012/12/10/ayodhya-the-battle-for-indias-soul-the-complete-story/

Economic liberalisation in India

The **economic liberalisation in India** refers to the economic liberalisation, initiated in 1991, of the country's economic policies, with the goal of making the economy more market and service-oriented and expanding the role of private and foreign investment. Specific changes include a reduction in import tariffs, deregulation of markets, reduction of taxes, and greater foreign investment. Liberalisation has been credited by its proponents for the high economic growth recorded by the country in the 1990s and 2000s. Its opponents have blamed it for increased poverty, inequality and economic degradation. The overall direction of liberalisation has since remained the same, irrespective of the ruling party, although no party has yet solved a variety of politically difficult issues, such as liberalising labour laws and reducing agricultural subsidies. There exists a lively debate in India as to what made the economic reforms sustainable.[1616]

Indian government coalitions have been advised to continue liberalisation. Before 2015 India grew at slower pace than China which has been liberalising its economy since 1978. But in year 2015 India outpaced China in terms of GDP growth rate. *The McKinsey Quarterly* states that removing main obstacles "would free India's economy to grow as fast as China's, at 10% a year".

There has been significant debate, however, around liberalisation as an inclusive economic growth strategy. Since 1992, income inequality has deepened in India with consumption among the poorest staying stable while the wealthiest generate consumption growth. As India's gross domestic product (GDP) growth rate became lowest in 2012-13 over a decade, growing merely at 5.1%,[1617] more criticism of India's economic reforms surfaced, as it apparently failed to address employment growth, nutritional values in terms of food intake in calories, and also exports growth – and thereby leading to a worsening level of current account deficit compared to the prior to the reform period.[1618] But then in FY 2013-14 the growth rebounded to 6.9% and then in 2014-15 it rose to 7.3%. Growth reached 7.5% in the Jan-Mar quarter of 2015 before slowing to 7.0% in the Apr-Jun quarter.

Pre-liberalisation policies

Part of a series on the
History of modern India

Pre-independence	
Independence movement	
Rebellion / Mutiny / First War of Independence	1857–1858
British Raj	1858–1947
Partition	1947

Post-independence

Political integration	1947–1949
Non-Aligned Movement	1953–present
States Reorganisation Act	1956
Sino-Indian War	1962
Indo-Pakistani War	1965
Maoist insurgency	1967-present
Green Revolution	1970s
Indo-Pakistani War	1971
Emergency	1975–1977
Punjab insurgency	1984-1995
Kashmir insugency	1989-present

- 1990s
- Economic liberalisation

See also

- History of India
- History of South Asia

⚓ **India portal**

- v
- t
- e[1619]

Indian economic policy after independence was influenced by the colonial experience (which was seen by Indian leaders as exploitative in nature) and by those leaders' exposure to Fabian socialism. Policy tended towards protectionism, with a strong emphasis on import substitution industrialization under state monitoring, state intervention at the micro level in all businesses especially in labour and financial markets, a large public sector, business regulation, and central planning. Five-Year Plans of India resembled central planning in the Soviet Union. Steel, mining, machine tools, water, telecommunications, insurance, and electrical plants, among other industries, were effectively nationalised in the mid-1950s. Elaborate licences, regulations and the accompanying red tape, commonly referred to as Licence Raj, were required to set up business in India between 1947 and 1990.[1620]

> *Before the process of reform began in 1991, the government attempted to close the Indian economy to the outside world. The Indian currency, the rupee, was inconvertible and high tariffs and import licensing prevented foreign goods reaching the market. India also operated a system of central planning for the economy, in which firms required licences to invest and develop. The labyrinthine bureaucracy often led to absurd restrictions—up to 80 agencies had to be satisfied before a firm could be granted a licence to produce and the state would decide what was produced, how much, at what price and what sources of capital were used. The government also*

prevented firms from laying off workers or closing factories. The central pillar of the policy was import substitution, the belief that India needed to rely on internal markets for development, not international trade—a belief generated by a mixture of socialism and the experience of colonial exploitation. Planning and the state, rather than markets, would determine how much investment was needed in which sectors.

—BBC

Pre-1991 liberalisation attempts

Attempts were made to liberalise the economy in 1966 and 1985. The first attempt was reversed in 1967. Thereafter, a stronger version of socialism was adopted. The second major attempt was in 1985 by prime minister Rajiv Gandhi. The process came to a halt in 1987, though a 1967 style reversal did not take place.[1621]

In the 80s, the government led by Rajiv Gandhi started light reforms. The government slightly reduced Licence Raj and also promoted the growth of the telecommunications and software industries.[1622]

The Chandra Shekhar Singh government (1990–1991) took several significant steps towards the much needed reforms and laid its foundation.

Prevailing situation during 1980s

- The low annual growth rate of the economy of India before 1980, which stagnated around 3.5% from 1950s to 1980s, while per capita income averaged 1.3%. At the same time, Pakistan grew by 5%, Indonesia by 9%, Thailand by 9%, South Korea by 10% and Taiwan by 12%.
- Only four or five licences would be given for steel, electrical power and communications. Licence owners built up huge powerful empires.
- A huge private sector emerged. State-owned enterprises made large losses.
- Income Tax Department and Customs Department became inefficient in checking tax evasion.Wikipedia:Citation needed
- Infrastructure investment was poor because of the public sector monopoly.
- Licence Raj established the "irresponsible, self-perpetuating bureaucracy that still exists throughout much of the country" and corruption flourished under this system.

The fruits of liberalisation reached their peak in 2006, when India recorded its highest GDP growth rate of 9.6%. With this, India became the second fastest growing major economy in the world, next only to China. The growth rate has slowed significantly in the first half of 2012. An Organisation for Economic Co-operation and Development (OECD) report states that the average growth rate 7.5% will double the average income in a decade, and more reforms would speed up the pace. The economy then rebounded to 7.3% growth in 2014–15.

First reforms (1991–96)

P. V. Narasimha Rao

Manmohan Singh

Economic liberalisation in India was initiated in 1991 by Prime Minister P. V. Narasimha Rao and his then-Finance Minister Dr. Manmohan Singh. Rao was often referred to as *Chanakya* for his ability to steer tough economic and political legislation through the parliament at a time when he headed a minority government.[1623]

Crisis

By 1991, India still had a fixed exchange rate system, where the rupee was pegged to the value of a basket of currencies of major trading partners. India started having balance of payments problems since 1985, and by the end of 1990, the state of India was in a serious economic crisis. The government was close to default,[1624,1625] its central bank had refused new credit and foreign exchange reserves had reduced to the point that India could barely finance three weeks' worth of imports. It had to pledge 20 tonnes of gold to Union Bank of Switzerland and 47 tonnes to Bank of England as part of a bailout deal with the International Monetary Fund (IMF). Most of the economic reforms were forced upon India as a part of the IMF bailout.[1626]

> A Balance of Payments crisis in 1991 pushed the country to near bankruptcy. In return for an IMF bailout, gold was transferred to London as collateral, the rupee devalued and economic reforms were forced upon India. That low point was the catalyst required to transform the economy through badly needed reforms to unshackle the economy. Controls started

> *to be dismantled, tariffs, duties and taxes progressively lowered, state monopolies broken, the economy was opened to trade and investment, private sector enterprise and competition were encouraged and globalisation was slowly embraced. The reforms process continues today and is accepted by all political parties, but the speed is often held hostage by coalition politics and vested interests.*
>
> —India Report, Astaire Research

Liberalisation of 1991

In response, Prime Minister Narasimha Rao, along with his finance minister Manmohan Singh, initiated the economic liberalisation of 1991. The reforms did away with the Licence Raj, reduced tariffs and interest rates and ended many public monopolies, allowing automatic approval of foreign direct investment in many sectors.[1627] Since then, the overall thrust of liberalisation has remained the same, although no government has tried to take on powerful lobbies such as trade unions and farmers, on contentious issues such as reforming labour laws and reducing agricultural subsidies. By the turn of the 21st century, India had progressed towards a free-market economy, with a substantial reduction in state control of the economy and increased financial liberalisation. This has been accompanied by increases in life expectancy, literacy rates and food security, although urban residents have benefited more than rural residents.[1628]

Later reforms

- The Bharatiya Janata Party (BJP)–Atal Bihari Vajpayee administration surprised many by continuing reforms, when it was at the helm of affairs of India for six years, from 1998–99 and from 1999–2004.
- The BJP-led National Democratic Alliance Coalition began privatising under-performing government owned business including hotels, VSNL, Maruti Suzuki, and airports, and began reduction of taxes, an overall fiscal policy aimed at reducing deficits and debts and increased initiatives for public works.
- The United Front government attempted a progressive budget that encouraged reforms, but the 1997 Asian financial crisis and political instability created economic stagnation.
- Towards the end of 2011, the Congress-led UPA-2 Coalition Government initiated the introduction of 51% Foreign Direct Investment in retail sector. But due to pressure from fellow coalition parties and the opposition, the decision was rolled back. However, it was approved in December 2012.

- In the early months of 2015, the second BJP-led NDA Government under Narendra Modi further opened up the insurance sector by allowing up to 49% FDI. This came seven years after the previous government attempted and failed to push through the same reforms and 16 years after the sector was first opened to foreign investors up to 26% under the first BJP-led NDA Government under Atal Bihari Vajpayee's administration.
- The second BJP-led NDA Government also opened up the coal industry through the passing of the Coal Mines (Special Provisions) Bill of 2015. It effectively ended the Indian central government's monopoly over the mining of coal, which existed since nationalization in 1973 through socialist controls. It has opened up the path for private, foreign investments in the sector, since Indian arms of foreign companies are entitled to bid for coal blocks and licences, as well as for commercial mining of coal. This could result in billions of dollars investments by domestic and foreign miners. The move is also beneficial to the state-owned Coal India Limited, which may now get the elbow room to bring in some much needed technology and best practices, while opening up prospects of a better future for millions of mine workers.
- In the 2016 budget session of Parliament, the Narendra Modi led BJP Government pushed through the Insolvency and Bankruptcy Code. The Code creates time-bound processes for insolvency resolution of companies and individuals. These processes will be completed within 180 days. If insolvency cannot be resolved, the assets of the borrowers may be sold to repay creditors. This law drastically eases the process of doing business, according to experts and is considered by many to be the second most important reform in India since 1991 next to the proposed GST.
- On July 1st 2017, the BJP-led NDA Government under Narendra Modi launched the Goods and Services Tax (India). This came years after the previous government attempted and failed to push through the same reform and 17 years after the legislation was proposed under the first BJP-led NDA Government under Atal Bihari Vajpayee's administration in 2000. Touted to be India's biggest tax reform in 70 years of independence and the most important overall reform in terms of ease of doing business since 1991. GST replaces a slew of indirect taxes with a unified tax structure and is therefore set to dramatically reshape the country's 2.5 trillion dollar economy.

Impact

The impact of these reforms may be gauged from the fact that total foreign investment (including foreign direct investment, portfolio investment, and investment raised on international capital markets) in India grew from a minus-

Figure 288: *HSBC GLT, Pune*

cule US$132 million in 1991–92 to $5.3 billion in 1995–96.[1629] Poverty was 46.1% in 1991 has came down to 21.3% in 2016.

Annual growth in GDP per capita has accelerated from just 1¼ per cent in the three decades after Independence to 7½ per cent currently, a rate of growth that will double average income in a decade.... In service sectors where government regulation has been eased significantly or is less burdensome—such as communications, insurance, asset management and information technology—output has grown rapidly, with exports of information technology enabled services particularly strong. In those infrastructure sectors which have been opened to competition, such as telecoms and civil aviation, the private sector has proven to be extremely effective and growth has been phenomenal.

—*OECD*

Election of AB Vajpayee as Prime Minister of India in 1998 and his agenda was a welcome change. His prescription to speed up economic progress included solution of all outstanding problems with the West (Cold War related) and then opening gates for FDI investment. In three years, the West was developing a bit of a fascination to India's brainpower, powered by IT and BPO. By 2004, the West would consider investment in India, should the conditions permit. By the end of Vajpayee's term as prime minister, a framework for the foreign investment had been established. The new incoming government of

Dr. Manmohan Singh in 2004 further strengthened the required infrastructure to welcome the FDI.

Today, fascination with India is translating into active consideration of India as a destination for FDI. The A T Kearney study put India second most likely destination for FDI in 2005 behind China. It has displaced US to the third position. This is a great leap forward. India was at the 15th position, only a few years back. To quote the A T Kearney Study, "India's strong performance among manufacturing and telecom & utility firms was driven largely by their desire to make productivity-enhancing investments in IT, business process outsourcing, research and development, and knowledge management activities".

Challenges to further reforms

For 2010, India was ranked 124th among 179 countries in Index of Economic Freedom World Rankings, which is an improvement from the preceding year.

- Slow growth of the agricultural sector, where half of Indians earn most of their income
- Highly restrictive and complex labour laws.
- High inflation
- High poverty
- Corruption and graft
- Lack of political consensus and will

OECD summarised the key reforms that are needed:

> *In labour markets, employment growth has been concentrated in firms that operate in sectors not covered by India's highly restrictive labour laws. In the formal sector, where these labour laws apply, employment has been falling and firms are becoming more capital intensive despite abundant low-cost labour. Labour market reform is essential to achieve a broader-based development and provide sufficient and higher productivity jobs for the growing labour force. In product markets, inefficient government procedures, particularly in some of the states, acts as a barrier to entrepreneurship and need to be improved. Public companies are generally less productive than private firms and the privatisation programme should be revitalised. A number of barriers to competition in financial markets and some of the infrastructure sectors, which are other constraints on growth, also need to be addressed. The indirect tax system needs to be simplified to create a true national market, while for direct taxes, the taxable base should be broadened and rates lowered. Public expenditure should be re-oriented towards infrastructure investment by reducing subsidies. Furthermore, social policies should be improved to better reach the*

poor and—given the importance of human capital—the education system also needs to be made more efficient.

—OECD

Though recently labour law reforms have been enacted at the state level

Reforms at the state level

According to an OECD survey of the Indian economy states that had more liberal regulatory regimes had better economic performance. The survey also concluded that were complementary measures for better delivery of infrastructure, education and basic services implemented, they would boost employment creation and poverty reduction.

External links

- For a short educational video of the "economic history of India"[1630].
- Nick Gillespie (2009). "What Slumdog Millionaire can teach Americans about economic stimulus"[1631]. Reason.
- Gurcharan Das (2006). "The India Model"[1632]. The Foreign Affairs. Archived from the original[1633] on 7 March 2009.
- Ravinder Kaur (2015). "Good Times, Brought to you by Brand Modi"[1634]. Television and New Media.Wikipedia:Link rot
- Ravinder Kaur (2012). "India Inc. and its Moral Discontent"[1635]. Economic and Political Weekly.
- Aditya Gupta (2006). "How wrong has the Indian Left been about economic reforms?"[1636] (PDF). Centre for Civil Society. Archived from the original[1637] (PDF) on 2009-02-26.
- "The India Report"[1638] (PDF). Astaire Research <<doesn't work>>. 2007. Archived from the original[1639] (PDF) on 14 January 2009.

2000s

2001 Indian Parliament attack

2001 Indian Parliament attack	
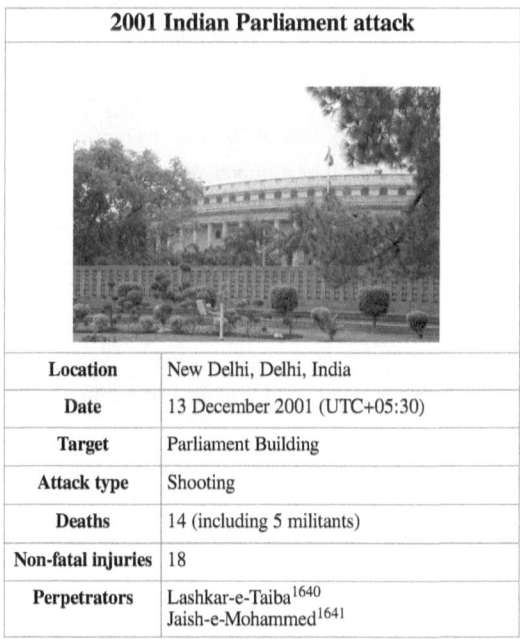	
Location	New Delhi, Delhi, India
Date	13 December 2001 (UTC+05:30)
Target	Parliament Building
Attack type	Shooting
Deaths	14 (including 5 militants)
Non-fatal injuries	18
Perpetrators	Lashkar-e-Taiba[1640] Jaish-e-Mohammed[1641]

The **2001 Indian Parliament attack** was a terrorist attack at the Parliament of India in New Delhi on 13 December 2001. The perpetrators were Lashkar-e-Taiba (LeT) and Jaish-e-Mohammed (JeM), two terrorist organizations were involved, according to Indian sources.[1642] The attack on the symbol of Indian Democracy led to the deaths of five terrorists, six Delhi Police personnel, two Parliament Security Service personnel and a gardener, in total 14 and to increased tensions between India and Pakistan, resulting in the 2001–02 India–Pakistan standoff.[1643]

The attack

On 13 December 2001, five terrorists infiltrated the Parliament House in a car with Home Ministry and Parliament labels.[1644] While both the Rajya Sabha and Lok Sabha had been adjourned 40 minutes prior to the incident, many members of parliament (MPs) and government officials such as Home Minister LK Advani and Minister of State for Defence Harin Pathak were believed to have still been in the building at the time of the attack.[1645] More than 100 people, including major politicians were inside the parliament building at the time. The gunmen used a fake identity sticker on the car they drove and thus breached the security deployed around the parliamentary complex. The terrorists carried AK47 rifles, grenade launchers, pistols and grenades.

The gunmen drove their vehicle into the car of the Indian Vice-President Krishan Kant (who was in the building at the time), got out, and began shooting. The Vice-President's guards and security personnel shot back at the terrorists and then started closing the gates of the compound. A similar attack was carried out on assembly of Srinagar, Kashmir, during November 2001, when 38 people were killed by terrorists.

Delhi Police officials claimed that gunmen received instructions from Pakistan and the operation was carried out under the guidance of Pakistan's Inter-Services Intelligence (ISI) agency. In their book *The Exile: The Flight of Osama bin Laden*, Cathy Scott-Clark and Adrian Levy state that then-CIA station chief Robert Grenier and Ambassador Wendy Chamberlin suspected that the ISI had approved the attack in order to force the redeployment of troops under the command of Ali Jan Aurakzai away from the Durand Line, allowing Osama bin Laden to escape into Pakistan during the Battle of Tora Bora.

Victims

Constable Kamlesh Kumari of the Central Reserve Police Force was the first to spot the terrorists and was shot by them as she raised the alarm. She died on the spot. One gunman's suicide vest exploded when he was shot dead; the other four gunmen were also killed. Five policemen, a Parliament security guard, and a gardener were killed and 18 others were injured.[1646] The ministers and MPs escaped unhurt. The total number of deaths was 14 and at least 22 people were injured in the attack.

Perpetrators

Delhi Police claimed that five terrorists carried out the attack and the names given by them were: Hamza, Haider alias Tufail, Rana, Ranvijay and Mohammed, who were the members of Lashkar-e-Taiba were killed. An Indian court observed that three more people from Pakistan, namely Maulana Masood Azhar, Ghazi Baba alias Abu Jehadi and Tariq Ahmed, were also involved in preparingWikipedia:Please clarify the attack.

Trial

The attack triggered extensive investigations which revealed involvement of four accused, namely Mohammad Afzal Guru, Shaukat Hussain Guru (cousin of Afzal Guru) and S.A.R. Gilani (Syed Abdul Rahman Gilani) and Shaukat's wife Afsan Guru (Navjot Sandhu before marriage). Some other proclaimed offenders were said to be the leaders of the banned terrorist organisation known as Jaish-e-Mohammed. After the conclusion of investigation, investigating agency filed the report under Section 173 of Criminal Procedure Code, 1973 (India) against four accused persons on 14 May 2002. Charges were framed under various sections of Indian Penal Code (IPC), the Prevention of Terrorism Act, 2002 (POTA), and the Explosive Substances Act by the designated sessions Court.

The designated Special Court was presided over by S. N. Dhingra. The accused were tried and the trial concluded within a record period of about six months. 80 witnesses were examined for the prosecution and 10 witnesses were examined on behalf of the accused S.A.R. Gilani. About 300 documents were exhibited. Afzal Guru, Shaukat Hussain and S.A.R. Gilani were convicted for the offences under Sections 121, 121A, 122, Section 120B read with Sections 302 & 307 read with Section 120B of IPC, sub-Sections (2), (3) and (5) of Section 3 and Section 4(b) of POTA and Sections 3 and 4 of Explosive Substances Act. The accused 1 and 2 were also convicted under Section 3(4) of POTA.[1647]

Accused 4, namely Navjot Sandhu a.k.a. Afsan, was acquitted of all the charges except the one under Section 123 IPC for which she was convicted and sentenced to undergo rigorous imprisonment for five years and to pay a fine. Death sentences were imposed on the other three accused for the offences under Section 302 read with Section 120B IPC and Section 3(2) of POTA. They were also sentenced to life imprisonment on as many as eight counts under the provisions of IPC, POTA and Explosive Substances Act in addition to varying amounts of fine. The amount of a million Indian rupees, which was recovered from the possession of two of the accused, namely, Afzal

Guru and Shaukat Hussain, was forfeited to the State under Section 6 of the POTA.

On appeal, the high court subsequently acquitted S. A. R. Geelani and Afsan, but upheld Shaukat's and Afzal's death sentence. Geelani's acquittal blew a gaping hole in the prosecution's version of the parliament attack. He was presented as the mastermind of the entire attack. Geelani, a young lecturer at Delhi University, received support from his outraged colleagues and friends, who were certain that he had been framed. They contacted the well-known lawyer Nandita Haksar and asked her to take on his case.

Shaukat Hussain was released nine months prior to his official date of release, because of his "good conduct".

Two Delhi Police officials, ACP Rajbir Singh[1648] and Mohan Chand Sharma can be credited for gathering Prima facie evidence in the case, but were brutally murdered, later on.[1649]

Response

The Indian Government initially accused Lashkar-e-Taiba and Jaish-e-Mohammed of involvement in the attack. However, Lashkar-e-Taiba denied any involvement in the incident. In November 2002, four JeM members were arrested by Indian authorities and put on trial. All four were found guilty of playing various roles in the incident, although the fourth, Afsan /Navjot Sandhu, wife of Shaukat Hussain (one of the accused) was found guilty of a minor charge of concealing knowledge of conspiracy. One of the accused, Afzal Guru, was sentenced to death for the incident.[1650]

World leaders and leaders in India's immediate neighbourhood condemned the attack on the Parliament. On 14 December, the ruling National Democratic Alliance (NDA) blamed Pakistan-based Lashkar-e-Taiba and Jaish-e-Mohammed for the attack. Home Minister LK Advani claimed, "We have received some clues about yesterday's incident, which shows that a neighbouring country, and some terrorist organisations active there behind it",[1651] in an indirect reference to Pakistan and Pakistan-based terrorist groups.

The same day, in a *demarche* to Pakistani High Commissioner to India Ashraf Jehangir Qazi, India demanded that Pakistan stop the activities of LeT and JeM, that Pakistan apprehend the organisations' leaders and that Pakistan curb the financial assets and the groups access to these assets.[1652] In response to the Indian government's statements, Pakistani forces were put on high alert the same day. On 20 December, India mobilised and deployed its troops to Kashmir and Punjab in what was India's largest military mobilisation since the 1971 Indo-Pakistani War.

Following the attack, many suspects were arrested, and in December 2002 four Jaish-e-Mohammed members were convicted for roles in the attack. In 2003, the Border Security Force (BSF) killed Ghazi Baba, the commander-in-chief of Jaish-e-Mohammed and the mastermind of the attack, in the Noor Bagh neighborhood of Srinagar, Jammu and Kashmir.[1653]

Afzal Guru, sentenced to death by Indian court and due to be hanged on 20 October 2006, had his execution stayed. His family had camped in New Delhi to meet the President Dr. A.P.J Abdul Kalam to accept the mercy petition. The family of Kamlesh Kumari Yadav, a CRPF Jawan who died in the attack has said that they would return the Ashok Chakra, if the president accepted the petition, and on 13 December 2006, the families of the deceased returned the medals to the government. As of April 2007, the then President of India, A.P.J. Abdul Kalam, refused to interfere in the judicial process.

The sentence was scheduled to be carried out on 20 October 2006, but Afzal was given a stay of execution and remained on death row. On 3 February 2013, his mercy petition was rejected by the former President of India Pranab Mukherjee. He was hanged at Delhi's Tihar Jail around 8:00 A.M. on 9 February 2013, and buried in Tihar jail with full religious rites.

External links

- 2001 Indian Parliament attack video[1654] on YouTube
- Parliament attack: Why didn't the bomb explode? Afzal Guru wonders[1655]
- Book review: The Strange Case of the Attack on the Indian Parliament[1656]
- Indian Parliament Attack: Crime and Punishment[1657]
- (Dead link) #AfzalGuru: The Very Strange Story of the Attack on the Indian Parliament[1658]
- Unanswered questions are the remains of the day[1659]
- Indian Parliament Attack Planner Hanged[1660]

2002 Gujarat riots

<indicator name="pp-default"> 🔒 </indicator>

2002 Gujarat riots	
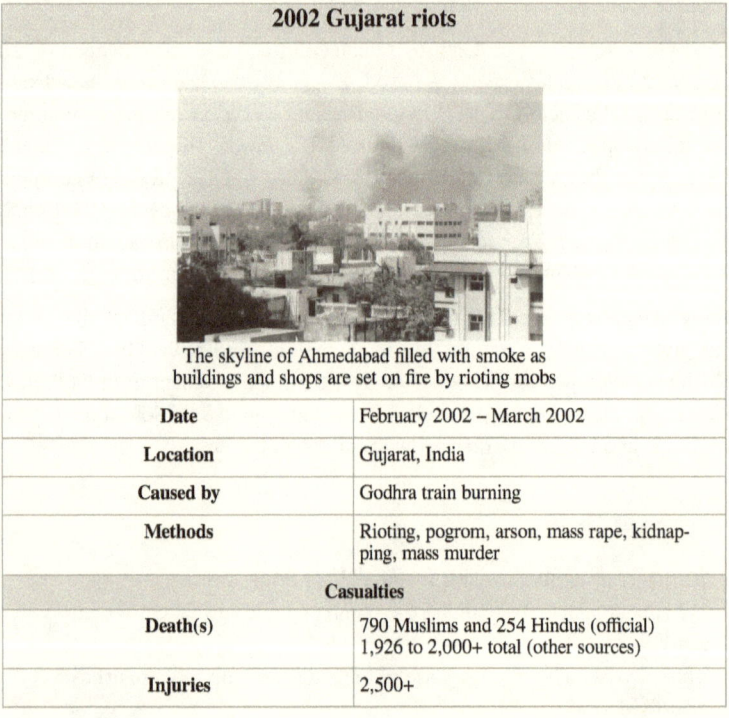 The skyline of Ahmedabad filled with smoke as buildings and shops are set on fire by rioting mobs	
Date	February 2002 – March 2002
Location	Gujarat, India
Caused by	Godhra train burning
Methods	Rioting, pogrom, arson, mass rape, kidnapping, mass murder
Casualties	
Death(s)	790 Muslims and 254 Hindus (official) 1,926 to 2,000+ total (other sources)
Injuries	2,500+

The **2002 Gujarat riots**, also known as the **2002 Gujarat violence** and the **Gujarat pogrom**,[1661] was a three-day period of inter-communal violence in the western Indian state of Gujarat. Following the initial incident there were further outbreaks of violence in Ahmedabad for three months; statewide, there were further outbreaks of violence against the minority Muslim population for the next year.[1661] The burning of a train in Godhra on 27 February 2002, which caused the deaths of 58 Hindu pilgrims karsevaks returning from Ayodhya, is cited as having instigated the violence.

According to official figures, the riots ended with 1,044 dead, 223 missing, and 2,500 injured. Of the dead, 790 were Muslim and 254 Hindu. The Concerned Citizens Tribunal Report, estimated that as many as 1,926 may have been killed. Other sources estimated death tolls in excess of 2,000. Many brutal killings and rapes were reported on as well as widespread looting and destruction of property. The Chief Minister of Gujarat at that time, Narendra

Modi, was accused of initiating and condoning the violence, as were police and government officials who allegedly directed the rioters and gave lists of Muslim-owned properties to them.

In 2012, Modi was cleared of complicity in the violence by Special Investigation Team (SIT) appointed by the Supreme Court of India. The SIT also rejected claims that the state government had not done enough to prevent the riots. The Muslim community was reported to have reacted with anger and disbelief. In July 2013 allegations were made that the SIT had suppressed evidence. That December, an Indian court upheld the earlier SIT report and rejected a petition seeking Modi's prosecution. In April 2014, the Supreme Court expressed satisfaction over the SIT's investigations in nine cases related to the violence, and rejected as "baseless" a plea contesting the SIT report.

Though officially classified as a communalist riot, the events of 2002 have been described as a pogrom by many scholars,[1662] with some commentators alleging that the attacks had been planned, with the attack on the train was a "staged trigger" for what was actually premeditated violence.[1663] Other observers have stated that these events had met the "legal definition of genocide," or referred to them as state terrorism or ethnic cleansing. Instances of mass violence include the Naroda Patiya massacre that took place directly adjacent to a police training camp; the Gulbarg Society massacre where Ehsan Jafri, a former parliamentarian, was among those killed; and several incidents in Vadodara city. Scholars studying the 2002 riots state that they were premeditated and constituted a form of ethnic cleansing, and that the state government and law enforcement were complicit in the violence that occurred.[1664,1665,1663]

Part of a series on
Violence against Muslims in India
Incidents
• 1969 Gujarat riots
• 1980 Moradabad riots
• 1983 Nellie massacre
• 1987 Hashimpura massacre
• 1985 Gujarat riots
• 1989 Bhagalpur violence
• 1992 Bombay riots
• 2002 Gujarat riots
• 2006 Malegaon bombings
• 2014 Assam Violence
Related topics

- Freedom of religion
- Violence against Muslims

- v
- t
- e[1666]

Part of a series on
Violence against Hindus in independent India
Issues
• Religious persecution • Freedom of religion • Religious violence
Incidents
• 1947 Jammu massacres • Mandai massacre • 1991 Punjab killings • Bombay riots • 1998 Chamba massacre • 1998 Wandhama massacre • 1998 Chapnari massacre • 1998 Prankote massacre • Bagber massacre • Operation Roukhala • 2000 Amarnath pilgrimage massacre • 2001 Kishtwar massacre • 2002 Qasim Nagar massacre • Akshardham Temple attack • Godhra train burning • 2002 Raghunath temple attacks • 2003 Nadimarg massacre • 2006 Doda massacre
• v • t • e[1667]

Godhra train burning

On the morning of 27 February 2002, the Sabarmati Express, returning from Ayodhya to Ahmedabad, stopped near the Godhra railway station. Several of the passengers were Hindu pilgrims, returning from Ayodhya after a religious ceremony at the site of the demolished Babri Masjid. Per newspaper reports published before the incident, the kar sevaks had been making a nuisance of themselves for some time, troubling other passengers and forcing them to shout "Jai Shriram". An argument erupted between the train passengers and the vendors on the railway platform, as the kar sevaks refused to pay for their tea and snacks. Later enquiries with other train passengers revealed that the kar sevaks had been doing this since departing Ayodhya at many other railway stations including Dahod. The argument became violent and under uncertain circumstances, four coaches of the train caught fire with many people trapped inside. In the resulting conflagration, fifty-nine people (nine men, twenty-five women, and twenty-five children) burned to death.

The government of Gujarat set up Gujarat High Court judge K. G. Shah as a one-man commission to look into the incident, but following outrage among families of victims and in the media over Shah's alleged closeness to Modi, retired Supreme Court judge G.T. Nanavati was added as chairman of the now two-person commission. After six years of going over the details, the commission submitted its preliminary report which concluded that the fire was an act of arson, committed by a mob of one to two thousand locals. Maulvi Husain Haji Ibrahim Umarji, a cleric in Godhra, and a dismissed Central Reserve Police Force officer named Nanumiyan were presented as the "masterminds" behind the arson.[1668] After twenty-four extensions, the commission submitted its final report on 18 November 2014. The findings of the commission were called into question by a video recording released by Tehelka magazine, which showed Arvind Pandya, counsel for the Gujarat government, stating that the findings of the Shah-Nanavati commission would support the view presented by the Bharatiya Janata Party (BJP), as Shah was "their man" and Nanavati could be bribed.[1669]

In February 2011, the trial court convicted thirty-one people and acquitted sixty-three others based on the murder and conspiracy provisions of the Indian Penal Code, saying the incident was a "pre-planned conspiracy." Of those convicted, eleven were sentenced to death and the other twenty to life in prison.[1670] Maulvi Umarji, presented by the Nanavati-Shah commission as the prime conspirator, was acquitted along with 62 others accused for lack of evidence.

The Union government led by the Indian National Congress party in 2005 also set up a committee to probe the incident, headed up by retired Supreme Court judge Umesh Chandra Banerjee. The committee concluded that the fire had begun inside the train and was most likely accidental. However, the Gujarat High Court ruled in 2006 that the matter was outside the jurisdiction of the union government, and that the committee was therefore unconstitutional.

The Concerned Citizens Tribunal (CCT)[1671] concluded that the fire had been an accident. Several other independent commentators have also concluded that the fire itself was almost certainly an accident, saying that the initial cause of the conflagration has never been conclusively determined. Historian Ainslie Thomas Embree stated that the official story of the attack on the train (that it was organized and carried out by people under orders from Pakistan) was entirely baseless.

Post-Godhra violence

File:India Gujarat location map.svg

Location of major incidents.

Following the attack on the train, the Vishva Hindu Parishad (VHP) called for a statewide *bandh,* or strike. Although the Supreme Court had declared such strikes to be unconstitutional and illegal, and despite the common tendency for such strikes to be followed by violence, no action was taken by the state to prevent the strike. The government did not attempt to stop the initial outbreak of violence across the state.[1672] Independent reports indicate that the state BJP president Rana Rajendrasinh had endorsed the strike, and that Modi and Rana used inflammatory language which worsened the situation.[1673]

Then-Chief Minister Narendra Modi declared that the attack on the train had been an act of terrorism, and not an incident of communal violence. Local newspapers and members of the state government used the statement to incite violence against the Muslim community by claiming, without proof, that the attack on the train was carried out by Pakistan's intelligence agency and that local Muslims had conspired with them to attack Hindus in the state. False stories were also printed by local newspapers which claimed that Muslim people had kidnapped and raped Hindu women.

Numerous accounts describe the attacks on the Muslim community that began on 28 February (the day after the train fire) as highly coordinated with mobile phones and government-issued printouts listing the homes and businesses of

Muslims. Attackers arrived in Muslim communities across the region in trucks, wearing saffron robes and khaki shorts (the unofficial uniform of Hindu nationalism) and bearing a variety of weapons. In many cases, attackers damaged or burned Muslim-owned or occupied buildings while leaving adjacent Hindu buildings untouched. Although many calls to the police were made from victims, they were told by the police that "we have no orders to save you." In some cases, the police fired on Muslims who attempted to defend themselves. The rioters used mobile phones to coordinate their attacks. By the end of the day on 28 February a curfew had been declared in 27 towns and cities across the state. A government minister stated that although the circumstances were tense in Baroda and Ahmedabad, the situation was under control, and that the police who had been deployed were enough to prevent any violence. In Baroda the administration imposed a curfew in seven areas of the city.

M. D. Antani, then the deputy superintendent of police, deployed the Rapid Action Force to sensitive areas in Godhra. Gordhan Zadafia, the Minister of State for Home, believed there would be no retaliation from the Hindu community for the train burning. Modi stated that the violence was no longer as intense as it had been and that it would soon be brought under control, and that if the situation warranted it, the police would be supported by deploying the army. A shoot-to-kill order was issued. However the troop deployment was withheld by the state government until 1 March, when the most severe violence had ended. After more than two months of violence a unanimous vote to authorize central intervention was passed in the upper house of parliament. Members of the opposition made accusations that the government had failed to protect Muslim people in the worst rioting in India in more than 10 years.

It is estimated that 230 mosques and 274 dargahs were destroyed during the violence.[1674] For the first time in the history of communal riots Hindu women took part, looting Muslim shops. It is estimated that up to 150,000 people were displaced during the violence. It is estimated that 200 police officers died while trying to control the violence, and Human Rights Watch reported that acts of exceptional heroism were committed by Hindus, Dalits and tribals who tried to protect Muslims from the violence.

Attacks on Muslims

In the aftermath of the violence, it became clear that many attacks were focused not only on Muslim populations, but also on Muslim women and children. Organizations such as Human Rights Watch criticised the Indian government and the Gujarat state administration for failure to address the resulting humanitarian condition of victims who fled their homes for relief camps during the violence, the "overwhelming majority of them Muslim." According to

Teesta Setalvad on 28 February in the districts of Morjari Chowk and Charodia Chowk in Ahmedabad of all forty people who had been killed by police shooting were Muslim.[1675] An international fact-finding committee formed of all women international experts from US, UK, France, Germany and Sri Lanka reported, "sexual violence was being used as a strategy for terrorizing women belonging to minority community in the state."

It is estimated that at least two-hundred and fifty girls and women were gang raped and then burned to death. Children were force fed petrol and then set on fire, pregnant women were gutted and then had their unborn child's body shown to them. In the Naroda Patiya mass grave of ninety-six bodies, forty-six were women. Rioters also flooded homes and electrocuted entire families inside.[1676] Violence against women also included them being stripped naked, violated with objects, and then killed. According to Kalpana Kannabiran the rapes were part of a well-organized, deliberate and pre-planned strategy, and which facts place the violence into the categories of political pogrom and genocide. Other acts of violence against women included acid attacks, beatings and the killing of women who were pregnant. Children were also killed in front of their parents. George Fernandes in a discussion in parliament on the violence caused widespread furor in his defense of the state government, saying that this was not the first time that women had been violated and raped in India.

Children were killed by being burnt alive and those who dug the mass graves described the bodies interred within them as "burned and butchered beyond recognition." Children and infants were speared and held aloft before being thrown into fires. Describing the sexual violence perpetrated against Muslim women and girls, Renu Khanna writes that the survivors reported that it "consisted of forced nudity, mass rapes, gang-rapes, mutilation, insertion of objects into bodies, cutting of breasts, slitting the stomach and reproductive organs, and carving of Hindu religious symbols on women's body parts." The Concerned Citizens' Tribunal, characterised the use of rape "as an instrument for the subjugation and humiliation of a community." Testimony heard by the committee stated that:

> *A chilling technique, absent in pogroms unleashed hitherto but very much in evidence this time in a large number of cases, was the deliberate destruction of evidence. Barring a few, in most instances of sexual violence, the women victims were stripped and paraded naked, then gang-raped, and thereafter quartered and burnt beyond recognition. . . . The leaders of the mobs even raped young girls, some as young as 11 years old . . . before burning them alive. . . . Even a 20-day-old infant, or a fetus in the womb of its mother, was not spared.*

Vandana Shiva stated that "Young boys have been taught to burn, rape and kill in the name of Hindutva."

Dionne Bunsha, writing on the Gulbarg Society massacre and murder of Ehsan Jafri, has said that when Jafri begged the crowd to spare the women, he was dragged into the street and forced to parade naked for refusing to say "Jai Shri Ram." He was then beheaded and thrown onto a fire, after which rioters returned and burned Jafri's family, including two small boys, to death. After the massacre Gulbarg remained in flames for a week.[1674]

Attacks on Hindus

The Times of India reported that over ten thousand Hindus were displaced during the violence. According to police records, 157 riots after the Godhra incident were started by Muslims. In Mahajan No Vando, a Hindu residential area in Jamalpur, residents reported that Muslim attackers injured approximately twenty-five Hindu residents and destroyed five houses on 1 March. The community head reported that the police responded quickly but were ineffectual as there were so few of them present to help during the attack. The colony was later visited by Modi on 6 March who promised the residents that they would be taken care of.[1677]

On 17 March, it was reported that Muslims attacked Dalits in the Danilimda area of Ahmedabad. In Himatnagar, a man was reportedly found dead with both his eyes gouged out. The Sindhi Market and Bhanderi Pole areas of Ahmedabad were also reportedly attacked by mobs.

India Today reported on 20 May 2002 that there were sporadic attacks on Hindus in Ahmedabad. On 5 May, Muslim rioters attacked Bhilwas locality in the Shah Alam area.[1678] Hindu doctors were asked to stop practicing in Muslim areas after one Hindu doctor was stabbed.[1679]

Frontline magazine reported that in Ahmedabad of the 249 bodies recovered by 5 March, thirty were Hindu. Of the Hindus that had been killed, thirteen had died as a result of police action and several others had died while attacking Muslim owned properties. Despite the relatively few attacks by Muslim mobs on Hindu neighbourhoods, twenty-four Muslims were reported to have died in police shootings.[1680]

Media coverage

The events in Gujarat were the first instance of communal violence in India in the age of 24-hour news coverage and were televised worldwide. This coverage played a central role in the politics of the situation. Media coverage was generally critical of the Hindu right; however, the BJP portrayed the coverage as an assault on the honor of Gujaratis and turned the hostility into an emotive part of their electoral campaign. With the violence receding in April, a peace meeting was arranged at Sabarmati Ashram, a former home of Mahatma Gandhi. Hindutva supporters and police officers attacked almost a dozen journalists. The state government banned television news channels critical of the government's response, and local stations were blocked. Two reporters working for STAR News were assaulted several times while covering the violence. On a return trip from having interviewed Modi when their car was surrounded by a crowd, one of the crowd claimed that they would be killed should they be a member of a minority community.

The Editors Guild of India, in its report on media ethics and coverage on the incidents stated that the news coverage was exemplary, with only a few minor lapses. The local newspapers *Sandesh* and *Gujarat Samachar*, however, were heavily criticised.[1681] The report states that *Sandesh* had headlines which would "provoke, communalize and terrorize people. The newspaper also used a quote from a VHP leader as a headline, "Avenge with blood." The report stated that *Gujarat Samachar* had played a role in increasing the tensions but did not give all of its coverage over to "hawkish and inflammatory reportage in the first few weeks". The paper carried reports to highlight communal harmony. *Gujarat Today* was given praise for showing restraint and for the balanced reportage of the violence. Critical reporting on the Gujarat government's handling of the situation helped bring about the Indian government's intervention in controlling the violence. The Editors Guild rejected the charge that graphic news coverage aggravated the situation, saying that the coverage exposed the "horrors" of the riots as well as the "supine if not complicit" attitude of the state, helping to propel remedial action.

Allegations of state complicity

Many scholars and commentators have accused the state government of being complicit in the attacks, either in failing to exert any effort to quell the violence or for actively planning and executing the attacks themselves. The United States Department of State ultimately banned Narendra Modi from travelling to the United States due to his alleged role in the attacks. These allegations center around several facts. First, the state did little to quell the violence, with attacks continuing well through the Spring. Further, some attackers used voter lists and other documents obtainable only with government assistance in order to target Muslim communities and households. Moreover, the Vishva Hindu Parishad (VHP), as well as many politicians, including Modi, made inflammatory remarks and endorsed the statewide *bandh*, further stoking tensions. The historian Gyanendra Pandey described these attacks as state terrorism, saying that they were not riots but "organized political massacres." According to Paul Brass the only conclusion from the evidence which is available points to a methodical Anti-Muslim pogrom which was carried out with exceptional brutality coordination.[1663]

The media has described the attacks as state terrorism rather than "communal riots" due to the lack of state intervention. Many politicians downplayed the incidents, claiming that the situation was under control. One minister who spoke with Rediff.com stated that though the circumstances were tense in Baroda and Ahmedabad, the situation was under control, and that the police who had been deployed were enough to prevent any violence. The deputy superintendent of police stated that the Rapid Action Force had been deployed to sensitive areas in Godhra. Gordhan Zadafia, the Minister of State for Home, stated that he believed there would be no retaliation from the Hindu community. Once troops were airlifted in on March 1, Modi stated that the violence was no longer as intense as it had been and that it would soon be brought under control. The violence continued for 3 months with no intervention from the federal government till May. Local and state-level politicians were seen leading violent mobs, restraining the police and arranging the distribution of weapons, leading investigative reports to conclude that the violence was "engineered and launched."

Throughout the violence, attacks were made in full view of police stations and police officers who did not intervene. In many instances, police joined the mobs in perpetrating violence. At one Muslim locality, of the twenty-nine deaths, sixteen were caused by police firing into the locality. Some rioters even had printouts of voter registration lists, allowing them to selectively target Muslim properties. Selective targeting of properties was shown by the destruction of the offices of the Muslim Wakf board which was located within the confines of the high security zone and just 500 meters from the office of the chief minister.[1672]

According to Scott W. Hibbard, the violence had been planned far in advance, and that similar to other instances of communal violence the Bajrang Dal, the VHP and the Rashtriya Swayamsevak Sangh (RSS) all took part in the attacks. Following the attack on the train the VHP called for a statewide *bandh* (strike), and the state took no action to prevent this.[1672,1673]

The Concerned Citizens Tribunal (CCT) report includes testimony of the then Gujarat BJP minister Haren Pandya (since murdered), who testified about an evening meeting convened by Modi the evening of the train burning. At this meeting, officials were instructed not to obstruct the Hindu rage following the incident. The report also highlighted a second meeting, held in Lunawada village of Panchmahal district, attended by state ministers Ashok Bhatt, and Prabhatsinh Chauhan, among other BJP and RSS leaders, where "detailed plans were made on the use of kerosene and petrol for arson and other methods of killing." The Jamiat Ulama-i-Hind claimed in 2002 that some regional Congress workers collaborated with the perpetrators of the violence.

Dipankar Gupta believes that the state and police were clearly complicit in the violence, but that some officers were outstanding in the performance of their duties, such as Himanshu Bhatt and Rahul Sharma. Sharma was reported to have said "I don't think any other job would have allowed me to save so many lives." Human Rights Watch has reported on acts of exceptional heroism by Hindus, Dalits and tribals who tried to protect Muslims from the violence.

In response to allegations of state involvement, Gujarat government spokesman, Bharat Pandya, told the BBC that the rioting was a spontaneous Hindu backlash fueled by widespread anger against Muslims. He said "Hindus are frustrated over the role of Muslims in the on-going violence in Indian-administered Kashmir and other parts of India." In support of this, the US Ambassador at-large for International Religious Freedom, John Hanford, expressed concern over religious intolerance in Indian politics and said that while the rioters may have been aided by state and local officials, he did not believe that the BJP-led central government was involved in inciting the riots.

Criminal prosecutions

Prosecution of the perpetrators of the violence hampered by witnesses being bribed or intimidated and the perpetrators' names being deleted from the charge sheets. Local judges were also biased.[1682] After more than two years of acquittals, the Supreme Court of India stepped in, transferring key cases to the Bombay High Court and ordering the police to reopen two thousand cases that had been previously closed. The Supreme Court also lambasted the Gujarat government as "modern day Neros" who looked elsewhere when innocent women and children were burning and then interfered with prosecution. Following this direction, police identified nearly 1,600 cases for re-investigation, arrested 640 accused and launched investigations against forty police officers for their failures.[1683] that state and law enforcement officials were harassing and intimidating key witnesses, NGOs, social activists and lawyers who were fighting to seek justice for riot victims. In its 2003 annual report, Amnesty International stated, "the same police force that was accused of colluding with the attackers was put in charge of the investigations into the massacres, undermining the process of delivery of justice to the victims."</ref>

In March 2008, the Supreme Court ordered the setting up of a Special Investigation Team (SIT) to reinvestigate the Godhra train burning case and key cases of post-Godhra violence. The former CBI Director R. K. Raghavan was appointed to chair the Team. Christophe Jaffrelot notes that the SIT was not as independent as commonly believed. Other than Raghavan, half of the six members of the team were recruited from the Gujarat police, and the Gujarat High Court was still responsible for appointing judicial officers. The SIT made efforts to appoint independent prosecutors but some of them resigned due to their inability to function. No efforts were made to protect the witnesses and Raghavan himself was said to be an "absentee investigator," who spent only a few days every month in Gujarat, with the investigations being conducted by the remainder of the team.

As of April 2013 249 convictions had been secured of 184 Hindus and 65 Muslims. Thirty-one of the Muslim convictions were for the massacre of Hindus in Godhra.

Best Bakery case

The Best Bakery murder trial received wide attention after witnesses retracted testimony in court and all of the accused were acquitted. The Indian Supreme Court, acting on a petition by social activist Teesta Setalvad, ordered a retrial outside Gujarat in which nine accused were found guilty in 2006.[1684] A key witness, Zaheera Sheikh, who repeatedly changed her testimony during the trials and the petition was found guilty of perjury.

Bilkis Bano case

After police dismissed the case against her assailants, Bilkis Bano approached the National Human Rights Commission of India and petitioned the Supreme Court seeking a reinvestigation. The Supreme Court granted the motion, directing the Central Bureau of Investigation (CBI) to take over the investigation. CBI appointed a team of experts from the Central Forensic Science Laboratory (CFSL) Delhi and All India Institute of Medical Sciences (AIIMS) under the guidance and leadership of Professor T. D. Dogra of AIIMS to exhume the mass graves to established the identity and cause of death of victims. The team successfully located and exhumed the remains of victims. The trial of the case was transferred out of Gujarat and the central government was directed to appoint a public prosecutor. Charges were filed in a Mumbai court against nineteen people as well as six police officials and a government doctor over their role in the initial investigations. In January 2008, eleven men were sentenced to life imprisonment for rapes and murders and a policeman was convicted of falsifying evidence. The Bombay High Court upheld the life imprisonment of eleven men convicted for the gang rape of Bilkis Bano and murder of her family members during the 2002 Gujarat riots on 8 May 2017. The court also set aside the acquittal of the remaining seven accused in the case, including Gujarat police officers and doctors of a government hospital, who were charged with suppressing and tampering with evidence.

Avdhootnagar case

In 2005, the Vadodara fast-track court acquitted 108 people accused of murdering two youths during a mob attack on a group of displaced Muslims returning under police escort to their homes in Avdhootnagar. The court passed strictures against the police for failing to protect the people under their escort and failing to identify the attackers they had seen.

Danilimda case

Nine people were convicted of killing a Hindu man and injuring another during group clashes in Danilimda, Ahmedabad on 12 April 2005, while twenty-five others were acquitted.

Eral case

Eight people, including a VHP leader and a member of the BJP, were convicted for the murder of seven members of a family and the rape of two minor girls in the village of Eral in Panchmahal district.

Pavagadh and Dhikva case

Fifty-two people from Pavagadh and Dhikva villages in Panchmahal district were acquitted of rioting charges for lack of evidence.

Godhra train-burning case

A stringent anti-terror law, the POTA, was used by the Gujarat government to charge 131 people in connection to the Godhra train fire, but not invoked in prosecuting any of the accused in the post-Godhra riots. In 2005 the POTA Review Committee set up by the central government to review the application of the law opined that the Godhra accused should not have been tried under the provisions of POTA.

In February 2011 a special fast track court convicted thirty-one Muslims for the Godhra train burning incident and the conspiracy for the crime

Dipda Darwaza case

On 9 November 2011, a court in Ahmedabad sentenced thirty-one Hindus to life imprisonment for murdering dozens of Muslims by burning a building in which they took shelter. Forty-one other Hindus were acquitted of murder charges due to a lack of evidence. Twenty-two further people were convicted for attempted murder on 30 July 2012, while sixty-one others were acquitted.

Naroda Patiya Massacre

On 29 July 2012, an Indian court convicted thirty people in the Naroda Patiya massacre case for their involvement in the attacks. The convicted included former state minister Maya Kodnani and Hindu leader Babu Bajrangi. The court case began in 2009, and over three hundred people (including victims, witnesses, doctors, and journalists) testified before the court. For the first time, the verdict acknowledged the role of a politician in inciting Hindu mobs. Activists asserted that the verdict would embolden the opponent of Narendra Modi, the then chief minister of Gujarat, in the crucial run-up to state elections later that year, when Modi would be seeking a third term (The BJP and he eventually went on to win the elections). Modi refused to apologise and denied that the government had a role in the riots. Twenty-nine people were acquitted during the verdict. Teesta Setalvad said "For the first time, this judgment actually goes beyond neighborhood perpetrators and goes up to the political conspiracy. The fact that convictions have gone that high means the conspiracy charge has been accepted and the political influencing of the mobs has been accepted by the judge. This is a huge victory for justice."

Perjury cases

In April 2009, the SIT submitted before the Court that Teesta Setalvad had cooked up cases of violence to spice up the incidents. The SIT which is headed by former CBI director, R. K. Raghavan has said that false witnesses were tutored to give evidence about imaginary incidents by Setalvad and other NGOs. The SIT charged her of "cooking up macabre tales of killings."[1685]

The court was told that twenty-two witnesses, who had submitted identical affidavits before various courts relating to riot incidents, were questioned by SIT and it was found that the witnesses had not actually witnessed the incidents and they were tutored and the affidavits were handed over to them by Setalvad.

Inquiries

There were more than sixty investigations by national and international bodies many of which concluded that the violence was supported by state officials. A report from the National Human Rights Commission of India (NHRC) stated that res ipsa loquitur applied as the state had comprehensively failed to protect uphold the rights of the people as set out in the Constitution of India.[1686] It faulted the Gujarat government for failure of intelligence, failure to take appropriate action, and failure to identify local factors and players. NHRC also expressed "widespread lack of faith" in the integrity of the investigation of major incidents of violence. It recommended that five critical cases should be transferred to the Central Bureau of Investigation (CBI).

The US State Department's International Religious Freedom Report quoted the NHRC as concluding that the attacks had been premeditated, that state government officials were complicit, and that there was evidence of police not acting during the assaults on Muslims. The US State Department also cited how Gujarat's high school textbooks described Hitler's "charismatic personality" and the "achievements of Nazism."[1664,1687] US Congressmen John Conyers and Joe Pitts subsequently introduced a resolution in the House condemning the conduct of Modi for inciting religious persecution. They stated that Modi's government had a role in "promoting the attitudes of racial supremacy, racial hatred and the legacy of Nazism through his government's support of school textbooks in which Nazism is glorified." They also wrote a letter to the US State Department asking it deny Modi a visa to the United States.

The CCT consisting of eminent high court judges released a detailed three-volume report on the riots. Headed by retired Supreme Court Justice Krishna Iyer, the CCT released its findings in 2003 and stated that, contrary to the government allegation of a conspiracy in Godhra, the incident had not been pre-planned and there was no evidence to indicate otherwise. On the statewide riots, the CCT reported that, several days before the Godhra incident, which was the excuse used for the attacks, homes belonging to Hindus in Muslim areas had been marked with pictures of Hindu deities or saffron flags, and that this had been done to prevent any accidental assaults on Hindu homes or businesses. The CCT investigation also discovered evidence that the VHP and the Bajrang Dal had training camps in which people were taught to view Muslims as an enemy. These camps were backed and supported by the BJP and RSS. They also reported that "The complicity of the state government is obvious. And, the support of the central government to the state government in all that it did is also by now a matter of common knowledge."

The state government commissioned J. G. Shah to conduct, what became, a controversial one man inquiry into the Godhra incident, its credibility was questioned and the NHRC and the National Minorities Commission requested that a sitting judge from the supreme court be appointed. The supreme court overturned the findings by Shah stating, "this judgement is not based on the understanding of any evidence, but on imagination."[1688]

Early in 2003, the state government of Gujarat set up the Nanavati-Shah commission to investigate the entire incident, from the initial one at Godhra to the ensuing violence. The commission was caught up in controversy from the beginning. Activists and members of the opposition insisted on a judicial commission to be set up and headed by a sitting judge rather than a retired one from the high court. The state government refused. Within a few months Nanavati, before hearing any testimony declared there was no evidence of lapses by either the police or government in their handling of the violence.[1689] In 2008

Shah died and was replaced by Justice Akshay Mehta, another retired high court judge. Metha's appointment was controversial as he was the judge who allowed Babu Bajrangi, a prime suspect in the massacre Naroda Patiya massacre, to be released on bail. In July 2013 the commission was given its 20th extension, and Mukul Sinha of the civil rights group *Jan Sangharsh Manch* said of the delays "I think the Commission has lost its significance and it now seems to be awaiting the outcome of the 2014 Lok Sabha election." In 2007 Tehelka in an undercover operation had said that the Nanavati-Shah commission had relied on "manufactured evidence." *Tehelka* editor Tarun Tejpal has claimed that they had taped witnesses who stated they had given false testimony after they had been bribed by the Gujarati police force. *Tehelka* also recorded Ranjitsinh Patel where he stated that he and Prabhatsinh Patel had been paid fifty thousand rupees each to amend earlier statements and to identify some Muslims as conspirators. According to B G Verghese, the Tehelka expose was far too detailed to have been fake.

A fact finding mission by the Sahmat organisation led by Dr. Kamal Mitra Chenoy concluded that the violence was more akin to ethnic cleansing or a pogrom rather than communal violence. The report said that the violence surpassed other periods of communal violence such as in 1969, 1985, 1989, and 1992 not only in the total loss of life, but also in the savagery of the attacks.

Aftermath

Rioting in Gujarat

There was widespread destruction of property. 273 dargahs, 241 mosques, 19 temples, and 3 churches were either destroyed or damaged.[1690,1691] It is estimated that Muslim property losses were "100,000 houses, 1,100 hotels, 15,000 businesses, 3,000 handcarts and 5,000 vehicles." Overall, 27,780 people were arrested. Of them, 11,167 were arrested for criminal behavior (3,269 Muslim, 7,896 Hindu) and 16,615 were arrested as a preventative measure (2,811 Muslim, 13,804 Hindu). The CCT tribunal reported that 90 percent of those arrested were almost immediately granted bail, even if they had been arrested on suspicion of murder or arson. There were also media reports that political leaders gave those being released public welcomes. This contradicts the state government's statement during the violence that: "Bail applications of all accused persons are being strongly defended and rejected."[1692]

Police transfers

According to R. B. Sreekumar, police officers who followed the rule of law and helped prevent the riots from spreading were punished by the Modi government. They were subjected to disciplinary proceedings and transfers with some having to leave the state. Sreekumar also claims it is common practice to intimidate whistleblowers and otherwise subvert the justice system, and that the state government issued "unconstitutional directives", with officials asking him to kill Muslims involved in rioting or disrupting a Hindu religious event. The Gujarat government denied his allegations, claiming that they were "baseless" and based on malice because Sreekumar had not been promoted.

Further promotion of communal violence by Shiv sena, VHP and Muslim extremist groups

Following the violence Bal Thackeray then leader of the Hindu nationalist group Shiv Sena said "Muslims are a cancer to this country. . . . Cancer is an incurable disease. Its only cure is operation. O Hindus, take weapons in your hands and remove this cancer from your roots." Pravin Togadia, international president of the Vishva Hindu Parishad (VHP), said "All Hindutva opponents will get the death sentence" and Ashok Singhal, the then president of the VHP, has said that the violence in Gujarat was a "successful experiment" which would be repeated nationwide.

The militant group Indian Mujahideen have carried out attacks in revenge and to also act as a deterrent against further instances of mass violence against Muslims. They also claimed to have carried out the 2008 Delhi bombings in revenge for mistreatment of Muslims, referencing the destruction of the Babri Mosque and the violence in Gujarat 2002. In September 2002 there was an attack on the Hindu temple of Akshardham, gunmen carried letters on their persons which suggested that it was a revenge attack for the violence that Muslims had undergone. In August 2002 Shahid Ahmad Bakshi, an operative for the militant group Lashkar-e-Toiba planned to assassinate Modi, Pravin Togadia of the VHP, and other members of the right wing nationalist movement to avenge the 2002 Gujarat violence.

Human Rights Watch has accused the state of orchestrating a cover-up of their role in the violence. Human rights activists and Indian solicitors have urged that legislation be passed so that "communal violence is treated as genocide." Following the violence thousands of Muslims were fired from their places of work, and those who tried to return home had to endure an economic and social boycott.

Organisational changes and political reactions

On 3 May 2002, former Punjab police chief Kanwar Pal Singh Gill was appointed as security adviser to Modi. Defending the Modi administration in the Rajya Sabha against charges of genocide, BJP spokesman V. K. Malhotra said that the official toll of 254 Hindus, killed mostly by police fire, indicates how the state authorities took effective steps to curb the violence. Opposition parties and three coalition partners of the BJP-led central government demanded the dismissal of Modi for failing to contain the violence, with some calling for the removal of Union Home Minister L. K. Advani as well.

On 18 July, Modi asked the Governor of Gujarat to dissolve the state assembly and call fresh elections. The Indian Election Commission ruled out early elections citing the prevailing law and order situation and held them in December 2002. The BJP capitalised on the violence using posters and videotapes of the Godhra incident and painting Muslims as terrorists. The party gained in all the constituencies affected by the communal violence and a number of candidates implicated in the violence were elected, which in turn ensured freedom from prosecution.

Media investigation

In 2004, the weekly magazine *Tehelka* published a hidden camera exposé alleging that BJP legislator Madhu Srivastava bribed Zaheera Sheikh, a witness in the Best Bakery case. Srivastava denied the allegation, and an inquiry committee appointed by the Supreme Court drew an "adverse inference" from the video footage, though it failed to uncover evidence that money was actually paid. In a 2007 expose, the magazine released hidden camera footage of several members of the BJP, VHP and the Bajrang Dal admitting their role in the riots. Among those featured in the tapes was the special counsel representing the Gujarat government before the Nanavati-Shah Commission, Arvind Pandya, who resigned from his post after the release. While the report was criticised by some as being politically motivated, some newspapers said the revelations simply reinforced what was common knowledge. However, the report contradicted official records with regard to Modi's alleged visit to Naroda Patiya and a local police superintendent's location. The Gujarat government blocked telecast of cable news channels broadcasting the expose, a move strongly condemned by the Editors Guild of India.

Taking a stand decried by the media and other rights groups, Nafisa Hussain, a member of the National Commission for Women accused organisations and the media of needlessly exaggerating the plight of women victims of the riots, which was strongly disputed as Gujarat did not have a State Commission for Women to act on the ground. The newspaper *Tribune* reported that "The

National Commission for Women has reluctantly agreed to the complicity of Gujarat Government in the communal violence in the state." The tone of their most recent report was reported by the *Tribune* as "lenient".

Special Investigation Team

In April 2012, the three-member SIT formed in 2008 by the Supreme Court as a response to a petition by one of the aggrieved in the Gulmerg massacre absolved Modi of any involvement in the Gulberg massacre, arguably the worst episode of the riots.

In his report, Raju Ramachandran, the amicus curiae for the case, strongly disagreed with a key conclusion of R. K. Raghavan who led SIT: that IPS officer Sanjiv Bhatt was not present at a late-night meeting of top Gujarat cops held at the Chief Minister's residence in the wake of 27 February 2002 Godhra carnage. It has been Bhatt's claim—made in an affidavit before the apex court and in statements to the SIT and the amicus—that he was present at the meeting where Modi allegedly said Hindus must be allowed to carry out retaliatory violence against Muslims. Ramachandran was of the opinion that Modi could be prosecuted for alleged statements he had made. He said there was no clinching material available in the pre-trial stage to disbelieve Bhatt, whose claim could be tested only in court. "Hence, it cannot be said, at this stage, that Shri Bhatt should be disbelieved and no further proceedings should be taken against Shri Modi."

Further, R. K. Shah, the public prosecutor in the Gulbarg Society massacre, resigned because he found it impossible to work with the SIT and further stated that "Here I am collecting witnesses who know something about a gruesome case in which so many people, mostly women and children huddled in Jafri's house, were killed and I get no cooperation. The SIT officers are unsympathetic towards witnesses, they try to browbeat them and don't share evidence with the prosecution as they are supposed to do." Teesta Setalvad referred to the stark inequalities between the SIT team's lawyers who are paid 9 lakh rupees per day and the government prosecutors who are paid a pittance. SIT officers have been paid Rs. 1.5 lakh per month for their participation in the SIT since 2008.

Diplomatic ban

Modi's failure to stop anti-Muslim violence led to a *de facto* travel ban imposed by the United Kingdom, United States, and several European nations, as well as the boycott of his provincial government by all but the most junior officials.[1693] In 2005, Modi was refused a US visa as someone held responsible for a serious violation of religious freedom. Modi had been invited to the

US to speak before the Asian-American Hotel Owners Association. A petition was set up by Coalition Against Genocide led by Angana Chatterji and signed by 125 academics requesting that Modi be refused a diplomatic visa.

Hindu groups in the US also protested and planned to demonstrate in cities in Florida. A resolution was submitted by John Conyers and Joseph R. Pitts in the House of Representatives which condemned Modi for inciting religious persecution. Pitts also wrote to then United States Secretary of State Condoleezza Rice requesting Modi be refused a visa. On 19 March Modi was denied a diplomatic visa and his tourist visa was revoked.[1664]

As Modi rose to prominence in India, the UK and the EU lifted their bans in October 2012 and March 2013, respectively, and after his election as prime minister he was invited to Washington, in the US.

Relief efforts

By 27 March 2002, nearly one-hundred thousand displaced people moved into 101 relief camps. This swelled to over 150,000 in 104 camps the next two weeks.[1694] The camps were run by community groups and NGOs, with the government committing to provide amenities and supplementary services. Drinking water, medical help, clothing and blankets were in short supply at the camps. At least another 100 camps were denied government support, according to a camp organiser, and relief supplies were prevented from reaching some camps due to fears that they may be carrying arms.

Reactions to the relief effort were further critical of the Gujarat government. Relief camp organisers alleged that the state government was coercing refugees to leave relief camps, with twenty-five thousand people made to leave eighteen camps which were shut down. Following government assurances that further camps would not be shut down, the Gujarat High Court bench ordered that camp organizers be given a supervisory role to ensure that assurances were met.

On 9 September 2002, Modi mentioned during a speech that he was against running relief camps. In January 2010, the Supreme Court ordered the government to hand over the speech and other documents to the SIT.

> What brother, should we run relief camps? Should I start children-producing centres there? We want to achieve progress by pursuing the policy of family planning with determination. Ame paanch, Amara pachhees! (we are five and we have twenty-five) . . . Can't Gujarat implement family planning? Whose inhibitions are coming in our way? Which religious sect is coming in the way? . . . "

On 23 May 2008, the Union Government announced a 3.2 billion rupee (USD 80 million) relief package for the victims of the riots. In contrast, Amnesty International's annual report on India in 2003 claimed the "Gujarat government did not actively fulfill its duty to provide appropriate relief and rehabilitation to the survivors". The Gujarat government initially offered compensation payments of 200,000 rupees to the families of those who died in the Godhra train fire and 100,000 rupees to the families of those who died in the subsequent riots, which local Muslims took to be discriminatory.[1695]

Popular culture

- *Final Solution* is a 2003 documentary directed by Rakesh Sharma about the 2002 Gujarat violence. The film was denied entry to Mumbai International Film Festival in 2004 due to objections by Censor Board of India, but won two awards at the 54th Berlin International Film Festival 2004. The ban was later lifted in October 2004.
- Gujarati play *Dost Chokkas Ahin Ek Nagar Vastu Hatu* by Saumya Joshi is a black comedy-based on 2002 riots.
- *Parzania* is a 2007 drama film set after the violence and looks at the aftermath of the riots. It is based on the true story of a ten-year-old Parsi boy, Azhar Mody. Rahul Dholakia won the Golden Lotus National Film Award for Best Direction and Sarika won the Silver Lotus National Film Award for Best Actress.
- T. V. Chandran made a trilogy of Malayalam films based on the aftermaths of the Gujarat riots. The trilogy consists of *Kathavasheshan* (2004), *Vilapangalkkappuram* (2008) and *Bhoomiyude Avakashikal* (2012). The narrative of all these films begin on the same day, 28 February 2002, that is, on the day after the Godhra train burning.
- *Firaaq* is a 2008 political thriller film set one month after the violence and looks at the aftermath in its effects on the lives of everyday people.
- *Mausam (2011 film)* is a 2011 romantic drama film directed by Pankaj Kapoor, spanned over the period between 1992 and 2002 covering major events.
- *Kai Po Che!* is a 2013 Hindi film which depicted riots in its plot.

References

Notes

Citations

Bibliography

<templatestyles src="Template:Refbegin/styles.css" />

- Brass, Paul R. (15 July 2005). *The Production of Hindu-Muslim Violence in Contemporary India*. University of Washington Press. p. 388. ISBN 978-0-295-98506-0.
- Bunsha, Dionne (2005). *Scarred: Experiments With Violence In Gujarat*. Penguin. ISBN 978-0-14-400076-0.
- Engineer, Asgharali (2003). *The Gujarat Carnage*. Orient Blackswan. ISBN 978-81-250-2496-5.
- Ghassem-Fachandi, Parvis (2012). *Pogrom in Gujarat: Hindu Nationalism and Anti-Muslim Violence in India*[1696] (PDF). Princeton University Press. ISBN 978-0-691-15177-9.
- Jaffrelot, Christophe (2011). *Religion, Caste, and Politics in India*. C Hurst & Co. ISBN 978-1849041386.
- Kishwar, Madhu Purnima (2014). *Modi, Muslims and Media: Voices from Narendra Modi's Gujarat*. Manushi Publications. ISBN 978-81-929352-0-1.
- Marino, Andy (2014). *Narendra Modi: A Political Biography*. HarperCollins Publishers India. ISBN 978-93-5136-217-3.
- Mitta, Manoj (2014). *The Fiction of Fact-Finding: Modi & Godhra*. HarperCollins Publishers India. ISBN 978-93-5029-187-0.
- Nussbaum, Martha Craven (2008). *The Clash Within: Democracy, Religious Violence, and India's Future*. Harvard University Press. ISBN 978-0-674-03059-6.
- Oommen, T. K. (2008). *Reconciliation in Post-Godhra Gujarat: The Role of Civil Society*. Pearson Education India. ISBN 978-81-317-1546-8.
- Shani, Ornit (2007). *Communalism, Caste and Hindu Nationalism: The Violence in Gujarat*. Cambridge University Press. ISBN 978-0-521-72753-2.
- Simpson, Edward (2009). *Muslim Society and the Western Indian Ocean: The Seafarers of Kachchh*. Routledge. ISBN 978-0-415-54377-4.
- Varadarajan, Siddharth, ed. (2002). *Gujarat: The Making of a Tragedy*. Penguin (India). ISBN 978-0-14-302901-4.

External links

- Report By The Commission of Inquiry Consisting of Mr. Justice G.T. Nanavati And Mr. Justice Akshay H. Mehta[1697]
- Detailed Report on the Godhra riots by the Concerned Citizens Tribunal[1698]

- U.S DEPARTMENT of STATE:Issue of Gujarat Chief Minister Narendra Modi's Visa Status[1699]

2001–02 India–Pakistan standoff

2001–2002 India–Pakistan standoff Indian Codename: *Operation Parakram*	
Part of the Indo-Pakistani wars and conflicts	
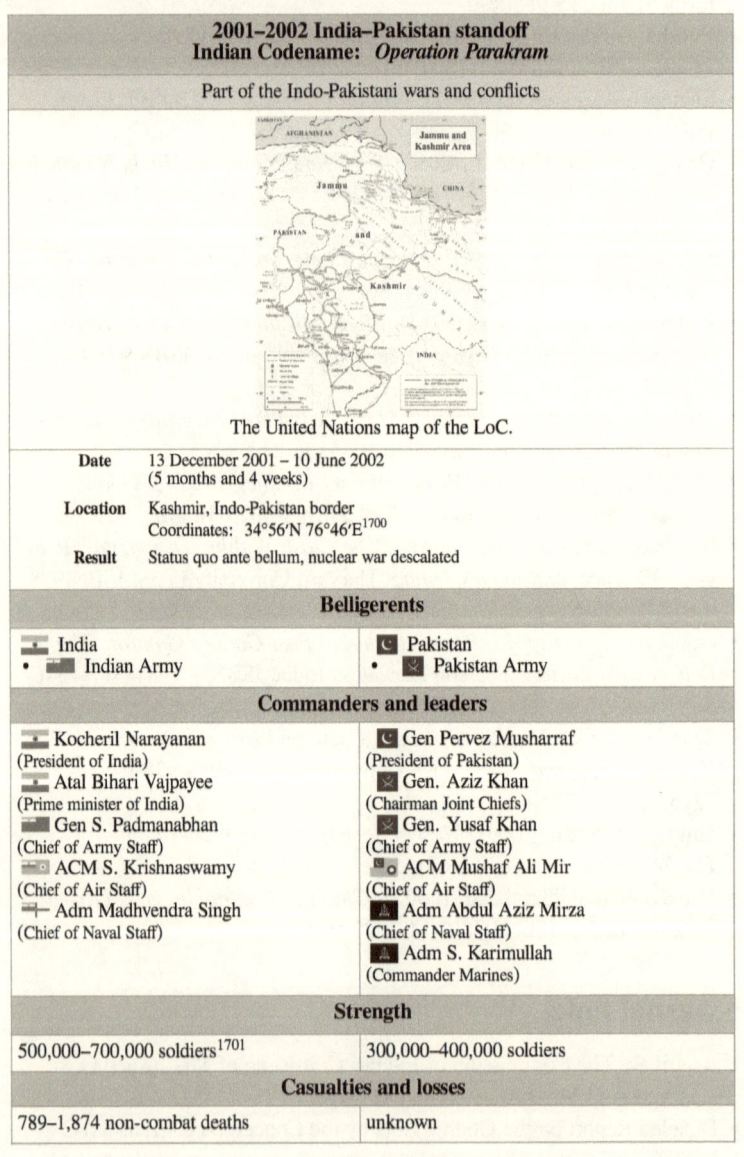 The United Nations map of the LoC.	
Date	13 December 2001 – 10 June 2002 (5 months and 4 weeks)
Location	Kashmir, Indo-Pakistan border Coordinates: 34°56′N 76°46′E[1700]
Result	Status quo ante bellum, nuclear war descalated
Belligerents	
India • Indian Army	Pakistan • Pakistan Army
Commanders and leaders	
Kocheril Narayanan (President of India) Atal Bihari Vajpayee (Prime minister of India) Gen S. Padmanabhan (Chief of Army Staff) ACM S. Krishnaswamy (Chief of Air Staff) Adm Madhvendra Singh (Chief of Naval Staff)	Gen Pervez Musharraf (President of Pakistan) Gen. Aziz Khan (Chairman Joint Chiefs) Gen. Yusaf Khan (Chief of Army Staff) ACM Mushaf Ali Mir (Chief of Air Staff) Adm Abdul Aziz Mirza (Chief of Naval Staff) Adm S. Karimullah (Commander Marines)
Strength	
500,000–700,000 soldiers[1701]	300,000–400,000 soldiers
Casualties and losses	
789–1,874 non-combat deaths	unknown

155,000 Indians and 45,000 Pakistanis displaced

The **2001–2002 India–Pakistan standoff** was a military standoff between India and Pakistan that resulted in the massing of troops on either side of the border and along the Line of Control (LoC) in the region of Kashmir. This was the second major military standoff between India and Pakistan following the successful detonation of nuclear devices by both countries in 1998 and the most recent standoff between the nuclear rivals. The other had been the Kargil War in 1999.

The military buildup was initiated by India responding to a terrorist attack on the Indian Parliament on 13 December 2001 (during which twelve people, including the five men who attacked the building, were killed) and the legislative Assembly on 1 October 2001. India claimed that the attacks were carried out by two Pakistan-based terror groups fighting Indian administered Kashmir, the Lashkar-e-Taiba and Jaish-e-Mohammad, both of whom India has said are backed by Pakistan's ISI –[1702] a charge that Pakistan denied.

In the Western media, coverage of the standoff focused on the possibility of a nuclear war between the two countries and the implications of the potential conflict on the American-led "Global War on Terrorism" in nearby Afghanistan. Tensions de-escalated following international diplomatic mediation which resulted in the October 2002 withdrawal of Indian[1703] and Pakistani troops[1704] from the international border.

Background

On the morning of 13 December 2001, a cell of five armed men attacked the Indian Parliament by breaching the security cordon at Gate 12. The five men killed seven people before being shot dead by Indian Security Forces.

World leaders and leaders in nearby countries condemned the attack on the Parliament, including Pakistan. On 14 December, the ruling Indian National Democratic Alliance blamed Pakistan-based Lashkar-e-Taiba (LeT) and Jaish-e-Mohammed (JeM) for the attack. Home Minister L.K. Advani claimed, "we have received some clues about yesterday's incident, which shows that a neighboring country, and some terrorist organisations active there are behind it,"[1705] in an indirect reference to Pakistan and Pakistan-based militant groups. The same day, in a *demarche* to Pakistan's High Commissioner to India, Ashraf Jehangir Qazi, India demanded that Pakistan stop the activities of LeT and JeM, that Pakistan apprehend the organisation's leaders and that Pakistan curb the financial assets and the group's access to these assets.[1706] In response to the Indian government's statements, Pakistan ordered its military on standing high alert the same day.

The Pakistan military's information sources, the ISPR's spokesman Major-General Rashid Qureshi, claimed that the Parliament attack was a "drama staged by Indian intelligence agencies to defame the freedom struggle in 'occupied Kashmir'" and further warned that India would pay "heavily if they engage in any misadventure".[1707] On 20 December, amid calls from the United States, Russia, and the United Nations to exercise restraint, India mobilised and deployed its troops to Kashmir and the Indian part of the Punjab in what was India's largest military mobilization since the 1971 conflict. The Indian codename for the mobilization was Operation Parakram (Sanskrit: *Valor*).

Confrontations

December–January

In late December, both countries moved ballistic missiles closer to each other's border, and mortar and artillery fire was reported in Kashmir.[1708] By January 2002, India had mobilized around 500,000 troops and three armored divisions on the Pakistan's border concentrated along the Line of Control in Kashmir. Pakistan responded similarly, deploying around 300,000 troops to that region.

On 12 January 2002, President Pervez Musharraf gave a speech intended to reduce tensions with India. He declared that Pakistan would combat extremism on its own soil, but said that Pakistan had a right to Kashmir.[1709] The Indian Prime Minister told his generals that there would be no attack "for now."[1710]

May–June

Tensions escalated significantly in May. On 14 May, three gunmen killed 34 people in an army camp near Jammu, most of them the wives and children of Indian soldiers serving in Kashmir. The Indian Army was angered by the attack. On 18 May, India expelled the Pakistani High Commissioner. That same day, thousands of villagers had to flee Pakistani artillery fire in Jammu.[1711] On 21 May, clashes killed six Pakistani soldiers and 1 Indian soldier, as well as civilians from both sides.[1712] On 22 May, Indian Prime Minister Vajpayee warned his troops to prepare for a "decisive battle".[1713] Beginning on 24 May and lasting for several days, Pakistan began conducting a series of missile tests. On 7 June the Pakistan Air Force shot down an Indian unmanned aerial vehicle near Lahore.

At the same time, attempts to defuse the situation continued. Both Prime Minister Vajpayee and President Musharraf blamed each other for the standoff, and the Russian President Vladimir Putin tried to mediate a solution, but in vain.[1714] Musharraf refused to back down giving many interviews on Indian and Pakistani media outlets that he was prepared for war if that was the way things needed to be. On 10 June, air restrictions over India were ended and Indian warships were removed from Pakistan's coast; Pakistan's warships soon followed suit and returned to friendly waters.[1715]

While tensions remained high throughout the next few months, both governments began easing the situation in Kashmir. By October 2002, India had begun to demobilize their troops along her border and later Pakistan did the same, and in November 2003 a cease-fire between the two nations was signed.[1716]

Casualties

The standoff inflicted heavy casualties. The total Indian casualties were 789–1,874 killed. Many accidents during the mobilisation were due to the poor quality of mines and fuses[1717] Around 100 of these fatalities were from mine laying operations. Artillery duels with Pakistan, vehicle accidents, and other incidents make up the rest.

Cost of standoff

The Indian cost for the buildup was ₹216 billion (US$3.1 billion) while Pakistan's was $1.4 billion.

Threat of nuclear war

President Musharraf refused to renounce the use of nuclear weapons even after pressure by the international community. Whereas Prime Minister Vajpayee asserted from the beginning that nuclear weapons would only be used if the other side used them first.

As both India and Pakistan are armed with nuclear weapons, the possibility a conventional war could escalate into a nuclear one was raised several times during the standoff. Various statements on this subject were made by Indian and Pakistani officials during the conflict, mainly concerning a no first use policy. Indian External Affairs Minister Jaswant Singh said on 5 June that India would not use nuclear weapons first, while Musharraf said on 5 June he would not renounce Pakistan's right to use nuclear weapons first.[1718] According to one think tank of the Pakistan government, the possession of nuclear weapons by Pakistan prevented escalation to an all out war by India. In 2009, Pakistani economist Sartaj Aziz asserted that:

> It was a big upset about what happened to the economy after the [atomic] tests in 1998, but was consoled that in 2002, when India mobilized half a million troops on the border after an attack on its parliament in 2001,

but was finally forced to withdraw the "due to the danger of a nuclear retaliation by Pakistan....

—Sartaj Aziz, defending Pakistan's decision to tests its nuclear capability in 1998,

There was also concern that a 6 June 2002 asteroid explosion over Earth, known as the Eastern Mediterranean Event, could have caused a nuclear conflict had it exploded over India or Pakistan.

Development of Cold Start

After the deescalation and the substantial diplomatic mediation, the Indian government, however, learned the seriousness of the military suspension by Pakistan in the region. Adjustments and development on offensive doctrine, *Cold Start*, was carried out by India as an aftermath of the war.Wikipedia:Citation needed

External links

- Gen. Padmanabhan mulls over lessons of Operation Parakram[1719]
- Thoughts on Operation Parakram[1720]
- Operation Parakram[1721]
- Nuclear Proliferation in India and Pakistan[1722] from the Dean Peter Krogh Foreign Affairs Digital Archives[1723]

2008 Mumbai attacks

<indicator name="good-star"> ⊕ </indicator>

2008 Mumbai Attacks

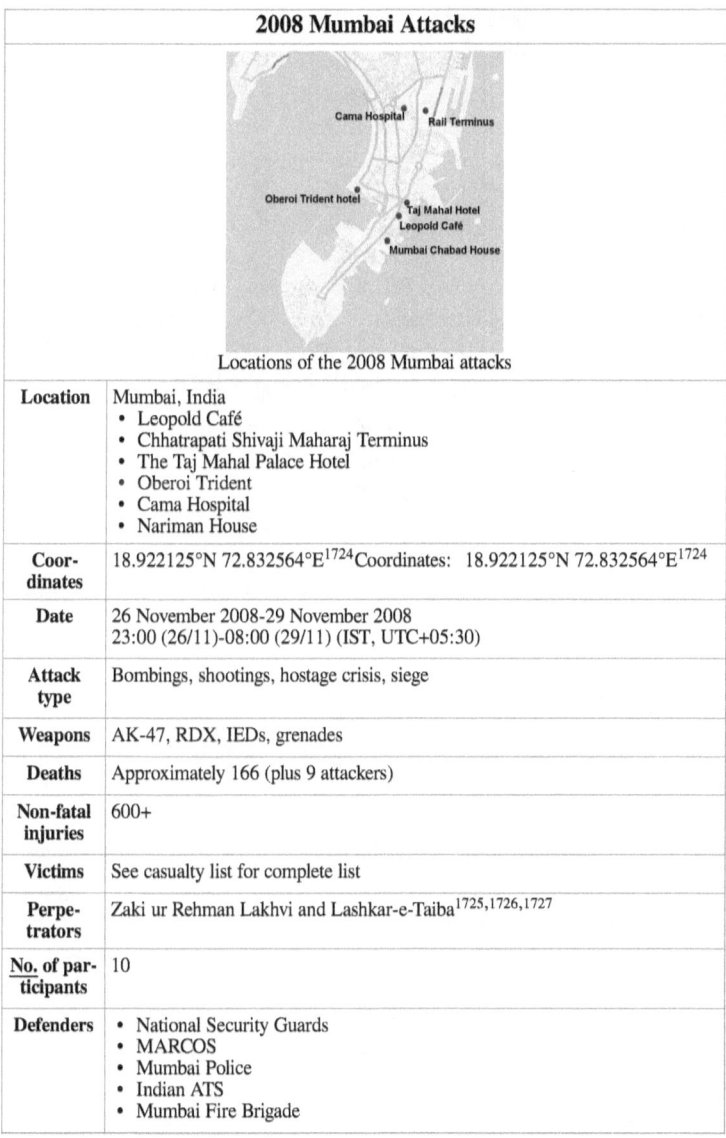

Locations of the 2008 Mumbai attacks

Location	Mumbai, India • Leopold Café • Chhatrapati Shivaji Maharaj Terminus • The Taj Mahal Palace Hotel • Oberoi Trident • Cama Hospital • Nariman House
Coordinates	18.922125°N 72.832564°E[1724]Coordinates: 18.922125°N 72.832564°E[1724]
Date	26 November 2008-29 November 2008 23:00 (26/11)-08:00 (29/11) (IST, UTC+05:30)
Attack type	Bombings, shootings, hostage crisis, siege
Weapons	AK-47, RDX, IEDs, grenades
Deaths	Approximately 166 (plus 9 attackers)
Non-fatal injuries	600+
Victims	See casualty list for complete list
Perpetrators	Zaki ur Rehman Lakhvi and Lashkar-e-Taiba[1725,1726,1727]
No. of participants	10
Defenders	• National Security Guards • MARCOS • Mumbai Police • Indian ATS • Mumbai Fire Brigade

The **2008 Mumbai attacks** (also referred to as **26/11**)[1728] were a group of terrorist attacks that took place in November 2008, when 10 members of Lashkar-e-Taiba, an Islamic terrorist organisation based in Pakistan, carried out a series of 12 coordinated shooting and bombing attacks lasting four days across Mumbai. The attacks, which drew widespread global condemnation, began on

Wednesday, 26 November and lasted until Saturday, 29 November 2008. 164 people died and 308 were wounded.

Eight of the attacks occurred in South Mumbai: at Chhatrapati Shivaji Terminus, the Oberoi Trident, the Taj Palace & Tower, Leopold Cafe, Cama Hospital, the Nariman House Jewish community centre, the Metro Cinema, and in a lane behind the *Times of India* building and St. Xavier's College. There was also an explosion at Mazagaon, in Mumbai's port area, and in a taxi at Vile Parle. By the early morning of 28 November, all sites except for the Taj Hotel had been secured by Mumbai Police Department and security forces. On 29 November, India's National Security Guards (NSG) conducted 'Operation Black Tornado' to flush out the remaining attackers; it culminated in the death of the last remaining attackers at the Taj Hotel and ended the attacks.

Ajmal Kasab disclosed that the attackers were members of Lashkar-e-Taiba, among others. The Government of India said that the attackers came from Pakistan, and their controllers were in Pakistan. On 7 January 2009, Pakistan confirmed the sole surviving perpetrator of the attacks was a Pakistani citizen. On 9 April 2015, the foremost ringleader of the attacks, Zakiur Rehman Lakhvi, was granted bail against surety bonds of Rs200,000 (US$1,900) in Pakistan.

Background

There have been many terrorist attacks in Mumbai since the 13 coordinated bomb explosions that killed 257 people and injured 700 on 12 March 1993. The 1993 attacks are believed by some to have been in retaliation for the earlier demolition of Babri Mosque, while others believe it is simply part of a larger plan to target the Hindu population.

On 6 December 2002, a blast in a BEST bus near Ghatkopar station killed two people and injured 28. The bombing occurred on the 10th anniversary of the demolition of the Babri Mosque in Ayodhya. A bicycle bomb exploded near the Vile Parle station in Mumbai, killing one person and injuring 25 on 27 January 2003, a day before the visit of the Prime Minister of India Atal Bihari Vajpayee to the city. On 13 March 2003, a day after the 10th anniversary of the 1993 Bombay bombings, a bomb exploded in a train compartment near the Mulund station, killing 10 people and injuring 70. On 28 July 2003, a blast in a BEST bus in Ghatkopar killed 4 people and injured 32. On 25 August 2003, two bombs exploded in South Mumbai, one near the Gateway of India and the other at Zaveri Bazaar in Kalbadevi. At least 44 people were killed and 150 injured. On 11 July 2006, seven bombs exploded within 11 minutes on the Suburban Railway in Mumbai, killing 209 people, including 22 foreigners and more than 700 injured.[1729] According to the Mumbai Police, the bombings

Figure 289: *One of the bomb-damaged coaches at the Mahim station in Mumbai during the 11 July 2006 train bombings*

were carried out by Lashkar-e-Taiba and Students Islamic Movement of India (SIMI).

Training

A group of men, sometimes stated as 24, at other times 26, received training in marine warfare at a remote camp in mountainous Muzaffarabad. Part of the training was reported to have taken place on the Mangla Dam reservoir.

The recruits went through the following stages of training, according to Indian and US media reports:

- Psychological: Indoctrination to Islamist ideas, including imagery of atrocities suffered by Muslims in India, Chechnya, Palestine and across the globe.
- Basic Combat: Lashkar's basic combat training and methodology course, the *Daura Aam*.
- Advanced Training: Selected to undergo advanced combat training at a camp near Mansehra, a course the organisation calls the *Daura Khaas*. According to an unnamed source at the US Defense Department this includes advanced weapons and explosives training supervised by retired

personnel of the Pakistan Army, along with survival training and further indoctrination.
- Commando Training: Finally, an even smaller group selected for specialised commando tactics training and marine navigation training given to the Fedayeen unit selected in order to target Mumbai.

From the students, 10 were handpicked for the Mumbai mission. They also received training in swimming and sailing, besides the use of high-end weapons and explosives under the supervision of LeT commanders. According to a media report citing an unnamed former Defence Department Official of the US, the intelligence agencies of the US had determined that former officers from Pakistan's Army and Inter-Services Intelligence agency assisted actively and continuously in training. They were given blueprints of all the four targets – The Taj Mahal Palace Hotel, Oberoi Trident, Nariman House and Chhatrapati Shivaji Terminus.

Attacks

The first events were detailed around 20:00 Indian Standard Time (IST) on 26 November, when 10 men in inflatable speedboats came ashore at two locations in Colaba. They reportedly told local Marathi-speaking fishermen who asked them who they were to "mind their own business" before they split up and headed two different ways. The fishermen's subsequent report to police department received little response and local police were helpless.

Chhatrapati Shivaji Maharaj Terminus

The Chhatrapati Shivaji Maharaj Terminus (CSMT) was attacked by two gunmen, Ismail Khan and Ajmal Kasab. Kasab was later caught alive by the police and identified by eyewitnesses. The attacks began around 21:30 when the two men entered the passenger hall and opened fire, using AK-47 rifles. The attackers killed 58 people and injured 104 others, their assault ending at about 22:45. Security forces and emergency services arrived shortly afterwards. Announcements by a railway announcer, Vishnu Dattaram Zende, alerted passengers to leave the station and saved scores of lives. The two gunmen fled the scene and fired at pedestrians and police officers in the streets, killing eight police officers. The attackers passed a police station. Knowing that they were outgunned against the heavily armed terrorists, the police officers at the station, instead of confronting the terrorists, decided to switch off the lights and secure the gates.

The attackers then headed towards Cama Hospital with an intention to kill patients, but the hospital staff locked all of the patient wards. A team of the Mumbai Anti-Terrorist Squad led by police chief Hemant Karkare searched

Figure 290: *Bullet marks on the wall at CST*

the Chhatrapati Shivaji Terminus and then left in pursuit of Kasab and Khan. Kasab and Khan opened fire on the vehicle in a lane next to the hospital, and received return fire in response. Karkare, Vijay Salaskar, Ashok Kamte and one of their officers were killed. The only survivor, Constable Arun Jadhav, was severely wounded. Kasab and Khan seized the police vehicle but later abandoned it and seized a passenger car instead. They then ran into a police roadblock, which had been set up after Jadhav radioed for help. A gun battle then ensued in which Khan was killed and Kasab was wounded. After a physical struggle, Kasab was arrested. A police officer, Tukaram Omble was also killed when he ran in front of Kasab to shoot him.

Leopold Cafe

The Leopold Cafe, a popular restaurant and bar on Colaba Causeway in South Mumbai, was one of the first sites to be attacked. Two attackers, Shoaib alias Soheb and Nazir alias Abu Umer, opened fire on the cafe on the evening of 26 November, killing 10 people (including some foreigners) and injuring many more.

Figure 291: *Bullet marks left at Leopold Cafe*

Bomb blasts in taxis

There were two explosions in taxis caused by timer bombs. The first one occurred at 22:40 at Vile Parle, killing the driver and a passenger. The second explosion took place at Wadi Bunder between 22:20 and 22:25. Three people, including the driver of the taxi were killed, and about 15 others were injured.

Taj Hotel and Oberoi Trident

Two hotels, The Taj Mahal Palace Hotel and the Oberoi Trident, were among the four locations targeted. Six explosions were reported at the Taj hotel – one in the lobby, two in the elevators, three in the restaurant – and one at the Oberoi Trident. At the Taj, firefighters rescued 200 hostages from windows using ladders during the first night.

CNN initially reported on the morning of 27 November 2008 that the hostage situation at the Taj Hotel had been resolved and quoted the police chief of Maharashtra stating that all hostages were freed; however, it was learned later that day that there were still two attackers holding hostages, including foreigners, in the Taj Hotel.

A number of European Parliament Committee on International Trade delegates were staying in the Taj hotel when it was attacked, but none of them were

Figure 292: *The damaged Oberoi Trident hotel*

Figure 293: *The first floor of the Taj Hotel was completely gutted.*

Figure 294: *Front view of the Nariman House a week after the attacks*

injured. British Conservative Member of the European Parliament (MEP) Sajjad Karim (who was in the lobby when attackers initially opened fire there) and German Social Democrat MEP Erika Mann were hiding in different parts of the building. Also reported present was Spanish MEP Ignasi Guardans, who was barricaded in a hotel room.[1730] Another British Conservative MEP, Syed Kamall, reported that he along with several other MEPs left the hotel and went to a nearby restaurant shortly before the attack. Kamall also reported that Polish MEP Jan Masiel was thought to have been sleeping in his hotel room when the attacks started, but eventually left the hotel safely. Kamall and Guardans reported that a Hungarian MEP's assistant was shot. Also caught up in the shooting were the President of Madrid, Esperanza Aguirre, while checking in at the Oberoi Trident, and Indian MP N. N. Krishnadas of Kerala and Gulam Noon while having dinner at a restaurant in the Taj Hotel.

Nariman House

Nariman House, a Chabad Lubavitch Jewish centre in Colaba known as the Mumbai Chabad House, was taken over by two attackers and several residents were held hostage. Police evacuated adjacent buildings and exchanged fire with the attackers, wounding one. Local residents were told to stay inside. The attackers threw a grenade into a nearby lane, causing no casualties. NSG commandos arrived from Delhi, and a naval helicopter took an aerial survey.

During the first day, 9 hostages were rescued from the first floor. The following day, the house was stormed by NSG commandos fast-roping from helicopters onto the roof, covered by snipers positioned in nearby buildings. After a long battle, one NSG commando Havaldar Gajender Singh Bisht and both perpetrators were killed. Rabbi Gavriel Holtzberg and his wife Rivka Holtzberg, who was six months pregnant, were murdered with four other hostages inside the house by the attackers.

According to radio transmissions picked up by Indian intelligence, the attackers "would be told by their handlers in Pakistan that the lives of Jews were worth 50 times those of non-Jews." Injuries on some of the bodies indicated that they may have been tortured.

NSG raid

During the attacks, both hotels were surrounded by Rapid Action Force personnel and Marine Commandos (MARCOS) and National Security Guards (NSG) commandos. When reports emerged that attackers were receiving television broadcasts, feeds to the hotels were blocked. Security forces stormed both hotels, and all nine attackers were killed by the morning of 29 November. Major Sandeep Unnikrishnan of the NSG was killed during the rescue of Commando Sunil Yadav, who was hit in the leg by a bullet during the rescue operations at Taj. 32 hostages were killed at the Oberoi Trident.

NSG commandos then took on the Nariman house, and a Naval helicopter took an aerial survey. During the first day, 9 hostages were rescued from the first floor. The following day, the house was stormed by NSG commandos fast-roping from helicopters onto the roof, covered by snipers positioned in nearby buildings. NSG Commando Havaldar Gajender Singh Bisht, who was part of the team that fast-roped onto Nariman House, died after a long battle in which both perpetrators were also killed. By the morning of November 28, the NSG had secured the Jewish outreach centre at Nariman House as well as the Oberoi Trident hotel. They also incorrectly believed that the Taj Palace and Towers had been cleared of attackers, and soldiers were leading hostages and holed-up guests to safety, and removing bodies of those killed in the attacks. However, later news reports indicated that there were still two or three attackers in the Taj, with explosions heard and gunfire exchanged. Fires were also reported at the ground floor of the Taj with plumes of smoke arising from the first floor. The final operation at the Taj Palace hotel was completed by the NSG commandos at 08:00 on 29 November, killing three attackers and resulting in the conclusion of the attacks. The NSG rescued 250 people from the Oberoi, 300 from the Taj and 60 people (members of 12 different families) from Nariman House.

In addition, police seized a boat filled with arms and explosives anchored at Mazgaon dock off Mumbai harbour.

Attribution

The Mumbai attacks were planned and directed by Lashkar-e-Taiba militants inside Pakistan, and carried out by 10 young armed men trained and sent to Mumbai and directed from inside Pakistan via mobile phones and VoIP.Wikipedia:Verifiability

In July 2009 Pakistani authorities confirmed that LeT plotted and financed the attacks from LeT camps in Karachi and Thatta. In November 2009, Pakistani authorities charged seven men they had arrested earlier, of planning and executing the assault.

Mumbai police department originally identified 37 suspects—including two army officers—for their alleged involvement in the plot. All but two of the suspects, many of whom are identified only through aliases, are Pakistani. Two more suspects arrested in the United States in October 2009 for other attacks were also found to have been involved in planning the Mumbai attacks. One of these men, Pakistani American David Headley (born Daood Sayed Gilani), was found to have made several trips to India before the attacks and gathered video and GPS information on behalf of the plotters.

In April 2011, the United States issued arrest warrants for four Pakistani men as suspects in the attack. The men, Sajid Mir, Abu Qahafa, Mazhar Iqbal alias "Major Iqbal", are believed to be members of Lashkar-e-Taiba and helped plan and train the attackers.[1731]

Negotiations with Pakistan

Pakistan initially denied that Pakistanis were responsible for the attacks, blaming plotters in Bangladesh and Indian criminals, a claim refuted by India, and saying they needed information from India on other bombings first.

Pakistani authorities finally agreed that Ajmal Kasab was a Pakistani on 7 January 2009, and registered a case against three other Pakistani nationals.

The Indian government supplied evidence to Pakistan and other governments, in the form of interrogations, weapons, and call records of conversations during the attacks. In addition, Indian government officials said that the attacks were so sophisticated that they must have had official backing from Pakistani "agencies", an accusation denied by Pakistan.

Figure 295: *Police looking for attackers outside Colaba*

Under US and UN pressure, Pakistan arrested a few members of Jamaat ud-Dawa and briefly put its founder under house arrest, but he was found to be free a few days later. A year after the attacks, Mumbai police continued to complain that Pakistani authorities were not co-operating by providing information for their investigation. Meanwhile, journalists in Pakistan said security agencies were preventing them from interviewing people from Kasab's village. Home Minister P. Chidambaram said the Pakistani authorities had not shared any information about American suspects Headley and Rana, but that the FBI had been more forthcoming.

An Indian report, summarising intelligence gained from India's interrogation of David Headley, was released in October 2010. It alleged that Pakistan's intelligence agency (ISI) had provided support for the attacks by providing funding for reconnaissance missions in Mumbai. The report included Headley's claim that Lashkar-e-Taiba's chief military commander, Zaki-ur-Rahman Lakhvi, had close ties to the ISI. He alleged that "every big action of LeT is done in close coordination with [the] ISI."

In 2018, during an interview with newspaper Dawn, Pakistan's ex Prime Minister Nawaz Sharif is alleged to have indirectly accepted Pakistan's involvement in not preventing the Mumbai attacks.

Investigation

According to investigations, the attackers travelled by sea from Karachi, Pakistan, across the Arabian Sea, hijacked the Indian fishing trawler 'Kuber', killed the crew of four, then forced the captain to sail to Mumbai. After murdering the captain, the attackers entered Mumbai on a rubber dinghy. The captain of 'Kuber', Amar Singh Solanki, had earlier been imprisoned for six months in a Pakistani jail for illegally fishing in Pakistani waters. The attackers stayed and were trained by the Lashkar-e-Taiba in a safehouse at Azizabad near Karachi before boarding a small boat for Mumbai.

David Headley was a member of Lashkar-e-Taiba, and between 2002 and 2009 Headley travelled extensively as part of his work for LeT. Headley received training in small arms and countersurveillance from LeT, built a network of connections for the group, and was chief scout in scoping out targets for Mumbai attack having allegedly been given $25,000 in cash in 2006 by an ISI officer known as Major Iqbal, The officer also helped him arrange a communications system for the attack, and oversaw a model of the Taj Hotel so that gunmen could know their way inside the target, according to Headley's testimony to Indian authorities. Headley also helped ISI recruit Indian agents to monitor Indian troop levels and movements, according to a US official. At the same time, Headley was also an informant for the US Drug Enforcement Administration, and Headley's wives warned American officials of Headley's involvement with LeT and his plotting attacks, warning specifically that the Taj Hotel may be their target.

US officials believed that the Inter-Services Intelligence (I.S.I.) officers provided support to Lashkar-e-Taiba militants who carried out the attacks.[1732] Disclosures made by former American intelligence contractor Edward Snowden in 2013 revealed that the Central Intelligence Agency (CIA) had intercepted communications between the Lashkar boat and the LeT headquarters in Azad Kashmir and passed the alert on to RAW on November 18, eight days before the terrorists actually struck Mumbai.

The arrest of Zabiuddin Ansari alias Abu Hamza in June 2012 provided further clarity on how the plot was hatched. According to Abu Hamza, the attacks were previously scheduled for 2006, using Indian youth for the job. However, a huge cache of AK-47's and RDX, which were to be used for the attacks, was recovered from Aurangabad in 2006, thus leading to the dismantling of the original plot. Subsequently, Abu Hamza fled to Pakistan and along with Lashkar commanders, scouted for Pakistani youth to be used for the attacks. In September 2007, 10 people were selected for the mission. In September 2008, these people tried sailing to Mumbai from Karachi, but couldn't complete their mission due to choppy waters. These men made a second attempt in November 2008, and successfully managed to execute the final attacks. David Headley's disclosures, that three Pakistani army officers were associated with the planning and execution of the attack were substantiated by Ansari's revelations during his interrogation. After Ansari's arrest, Pakistan's Foreign Office claimed they had received information that up to 40 Indian nationals were involved in the attacks.

Method

The attackers had planned the attack several months ahead of time and knew some areas well enough to vanish and reappear after security forces had left. Several sources have quoted Kasab telling the police that the group received help from Mumbai residents. The attackers used at least three SIM cards purchased on the Indian side of the border with Bangladesh. There were also reports of a SIM card purchased in the US state New Jersey, if this is the case, then this would go back to Iraqi Intelligence Services and Al Qaeda from 9/11 or Jemmah Ismaliyah and Egyptian Islamic Jihad through Iraqi Intelligence from Saddam Hussein's old network of militants that was never proved. Police had also mentioned that Faheem Ansari, an Indian Lashkar operative who had been arrested in February 2008, had scouted the Mumbai targets for the November attacks. Later, the police arrested two Indian suspects, Mikhtar Ahmad, who is from Srinagar in Kashmir, and Tausif Rehman, a resident of Kolkata. They supplied the SIM cards, one in Calcutta, and the other in New Delhi.

The attackers used a satellite phone and cell phones to talk to each other as well as their handlers that were based in Pakistan. In transcripts intercepted by Indian authorities between the attackers and their handlers, the handlers provided the attackers with encouragement, tactical advice, and information gained from media coverage. The attackers used both personal cell phones and those obtained from their victims to communicate with each other and the news media. Although the attackers were encouraged to murder hostages, the attackers were in communication with the news media via cell phones to make demands in return for the release of hostages. This was believed to be done in order to further confuse Indian authorities that they were dealing with primarily a hostage situation.

Type 86 Grenades made by China's state-owned Norinco were used in the attacks.

There were also indications that the attackers had been taking steroids. The gunman who survived said that the attackers had used Google Earth to familiarise themselves with the locations of buildings used in the attacks.

There were 10 gunmen, nine of whom were subsequently shot dead and one captured by security forces. Witnesses reported that they seemed to be in their early twenties, wore black T-shirts and jeans, and that they smiled and looked happy as they shot their victims.

It was initially reported that some of the attackers were British citizens, but the Indian government later stated that there was no evidence to confirm this. Similarly, early reports of 12 gunmen were also later shown to be incorrect.

On 9 December, the 10 attackers were identified by Mumbai police, along with their home towns in Pakistan: Ajmal Amir from Faridkot, Abu Ismail Dera Ismail Khan from Dera Ismail Khan, Hafiz Arshad and Babr Imran from Multan, Javed from Okara, Shoaib from Sialkot, Nazir Ahmed and Nasir from Faisalabad, Abdul Rahman from Arifwalla, and Fahadullah from Dipalpur Taluka. Dera Ismail Khan is in the North-West Frontier Province; the rest of the towns are in Pakistani Punjab.

On 6 April 2010, the Home Minister of Maharashtra State, which includes Mumbai, informed the Assembly that the bodies of the nine killed Pakistani gunmen from the 2008 attack on Mumbai were buried in a secret location in January 2010. The bodies had been in the mortuary of a Mumbai hospital after Muslim clerics in the city refused to let them be buried on their grounds.[1733]

Attackers

Only one of the 10 attackers, Ajmal Kasab, survived the attack. He was hanged in Yerwada jail in 2012. The other nine attackers killed during the onslaught were Hafiz Arshad alias Abdul Rehman Bada, Abdul Rahman Chhota, Javed alias Abu Ali, Fahadullah alias Abu Fahad, Ismail Khan alias Abu Ismail, Babar Imran alias Abu Akasha, Nasir alias Abu Umar, Nazir alias Abu Umer and Shoaib alias Abu Soheb.

Arrests

Ajmal Kasab was the only attacker arrested alive by police. Much of the information about the attackers' preparation, travel, and movements comes from his confessions to the Mumbai police.

On 12 February 2009 Pakistan's Interior Minister Rehman Malik said that Pakistani national Javed Iqbal, who acquired VoIP phones in Spain for the Mumbai attackers, and Hamad Ameen Sadiq, who had facilitated money transfer for the attack, had been arrested. Two other men known as Khan and Riaz, but whose full names were not given, were also arrested. Two Pakistanis were arrested in Brescia, Italy (east of Milan), on 21 November 2009, after being accused of providing logistical support to the attacks and transferring more than US $200 to Internet accounts using a false ID. They had Red Corner Notices issued against them by Interpol for their suspected involvement and it was issued after the last year's strikes.

In October 2009, two Chicago men were arrested and charged by the FBI for involvement in "terrorism" abroad, David Coleman Headley and Tahawwur

Hussain Rana. Headley, a Pakistani-American, was charged in November 2009 with scouting locations for the 2008 Mumbai attacks. Headley is reported to have posed as an American Jew and is believed to have links with militant Islamist groups based in Bangladesh. On 18 March 2010, Headley pleaded guilty to a dozen charges against him thereby avoiding going to trial.

In December 2009, the FBI charged Abdur Rehman Hashim Syed, a retired Major in the Pakistani army, for planning the attacks in association with Headley.

On 15 January 2010, in a successful snatch operation R&AW agents nabbed Sheikh Abdul Khwaja, one of the handlers of the 26/11 attacks, chief of HuJI India operations and a most wanted suspect in India, from Colombo, Sri Lanka, and brought him over to Hyderabad, India for formal arrest.[1734]

On 25 June 2012, the Delhi Police Department arrested Zabiuddin Ansari alias Abu Hamza, one of the key suspects in the attack at the Indira Gandhi International Airport in New Delhi. His arrest was touted as the most significant development in the case since Kasab's arrest. Security agencies had been chasing him for three years in Delhi. Ansari is a Lashker-e-Taiba ultra and the Hindi tutor of the 10 attackers who were responsible for the Mumbai attacks in 2008. He was apprehended, after he was arrested and deported to India by Saudi Intelligence officials as per official request by Indian authorities. After Ansari's arrest, investigations revealed that in 2009 he allegedly stayed for a day in a room in Old Legislators's Hostel, belonging to Fauzia Khan, a former MLA and minister in Maharashtra Government. The minister, however, denied having any links with him. Home Minister P. Chidambaram, asserted that Ansari was provided a safe place in Pakistan and was present in the control room, which could not have been established without active State support. Ansari's interrogation further revealed that Sajid Mir and a Pakistani Army major visited India under fake names as cricket spectators to survey targets in Delhi and Mumbai for about a fortnight.

A number of suspects were also arrested on false charges. At least two of them spent nearly 8 years in prison and were not paid any compensation by the Indian government.

Casualties and compensation

Nationality	Deaths	Injured
India	137	256
United States[1735]	6	2
Israel[1736]	4	–
Germany	3	3
Australia	2	2
Canada	2	2
France	2	–
Italy	1	–
United Kingdom[1737]	1	7
Netherlands	1	1
Japan	1	1
Jordan	1	1
Malaysia	1	–
Mauritius	1	–
Mexico	1	–
Singapore	1	–
Thailand	1[1738]	–
Austria	–	1
Spain	–	2
China	–	1
Oman	–	2
Philippines	–	1
Finland	–	1
Norway	–	1
Total	**166**	**293**

At least 164 victims (civilians and security personnel) and nine attackers were killed in the attacks. Among the dead were 28 foreign nationals from 10 countries. One attacker was captured. The bodies of many of the dead hostages showed signs of torture or disfigurement. A number of those killed were notable figures in business, media, and security services.

According to the then Maharashtra chief minister Vilasrao Deshmukh, 15 policemen and two NSG commandos were killed, including the following officers:

- Assistant Police Sub-Inspector Tukaram Omble, who succeeded in capturing a terrorist alive, with his bare hands.
- Joint Commissioner of Police Hemant Karkare, the Chief of the Mumbai Anti-Terrorism Squad
- Additional Commissioner of Police: Ashok Kamte
- Encounter specialist Senior Inspector Vijay Salaskar
- Senior Inspector Shashank Shinde
- NSG Commando, Major Sandeep Unnikrishnan
- NSG Commando, Hawaldar Gajendra Singh

Three railway officials of Chhatrapati Shivaji Terminus had also been killed in the terror strikes.

The casualties occurred in the following locations,

Location	Type of attack	Dead	Rescued
Mumbai Harbour	Shootings; hostages.	4	none
Chhatrapati Shivaji Terminus (CST) railway station; 18.940631°N 72.836426°E[1739] (express train terminus), 18.94061°N 72.835343°E[1740] (suburban terminus)	Shootings; grenade attacks.	58[1741]	none
Leopold Cafe, a popular tourist restaurant in Colaba; 18.922272°N 72.831566°E[1742]	Shootings; grenade explosion.	10	none
The Taj Mahal Palace Hotel near the Gateway of India; 18.921739°N 72.83331°E[1743]	Shootings; six explosions; fire on ground, first, and top floors; hostages; RDX found nearby.	31 (in addition to 1 commando)	around 250
Oberoi Trident at Nariman Point; 18.927118°N 72.820618°E[1744]	Shootings; explosions; hostages; fire.	30	143
Metro Cinema 18.943178°N 72.829474°E[1745]	Shooting from car-jacked police jeep.	around 10	none
Cama and Albless Hospital; 18.94266°N 72.832993°E[1746]	Shootings; hostages.	5 policemen	none
Nariman House (Chabad House) Jewish outreach centre; 18.916517°N 72.827682°E[1747]	Siege; shootings; hostages.	7 (including 1 commando)	9
Vile Parle suburb near the airport, North Mumbai	Car bomb blast.[1748]	1	none
Badruddin Tayabji Lane behind the Times of India building. 18.942117°N 72.833734°E[1749]	Police killed by gunfire.	9 policemen	none
Mazagaon docks in Mumbai's port area;	Explosion; boat with armaments seized.	none	none

The government of Maharashtra announced about ₹500,000 (US$7,300) as compensation to the kin of each of those killed in the terror attacks and about ₹50,000 (US$730) to the seriously injured. In August 2009, *Indian Hotels Company* and the *Oberoi Group* received about $28 million USD as part-payment of the insurance claims, on account of the attacks on *Taj* and *Trident*, from *General Insurance Corporation of India*.

Aftermath

The attacks are sometimes referred to in India as "26/11", after the date in 2008 that the attacks began, in similar style to the 9/11 attacks in the United States, the 11-M attack in Madrid, Spain, and the 7/7 bombings in London, United Kingdom. The Pradhan Inquiry Commission, appointed by the Maharashtra government, produced a report that was tabled before the legislative assembly more than a year after the events. The report said the "war-like" attack was beyond the capacity to respond of any police force, but also found fault with the Mumbai Police Commissioner Hasan Gafoor's lack of leadership during the crisis.[1750]

The Maharashtra government planned to buy 36 speed boats to patrol the coastal areas and several helicopters for the same purpose. It also planned to create an anti-terror force called "Force One" and upgrade all the weapons that Mumbai police currently have. Prime Minister Manmohan Singh on an all-party conference declared that legal framework would be strengthened in the battle against "terrorism" and a federal anti-terrorist intelligence and investigation agency, like the FBI, will be set up soon to co-ordinate action against "terrorism." The government strengthened anti-terror laws with UAPA 2008, and the federal National Investigation Agency was formed.

The attacks further strained India's slowly recovering relationship with Pakistan. India's then External Affairs Minister Pranab Mukherjee (ex President of India) declared that India may indulge in military strikes against terror camps in Pakistan to protect its territorial integrity. There were also after-effects on the United States's relationships with both countries, the US-led NATO war in Afghanistan, and on the Global War on Terror. FBI chief Robert Mueller praised the "unprecedented cooperation" between American and Indian intelligence agencies over the Mumbai terror attack probe. However, Interpol secretary general Ronald Noble said that Indian intelligence agencies did not share any information with Interpol.

A new National Counter Terrorism Centre (NCTC) was proposed to be set up by the then-Home Minister P. Chidambaram as an office to collect, collate,

Figure 296: *Candlelight vigils at the Gateway of India in Mumbai*

summarise, integrate, analyse, co-ordinate and report all information and inputs received from various intelligence agencies, state police departments, and other ministries and their departments.

Movement of troops

Pakistan moved troops towards the border with India voicing concerns about the Indian government's possible plans to launch attacks on Pakistani soil if it did not co-operate. After days of talks, the Pakistan government, however, decided to start moving troops away from the border.

Reactions

Indians criticised their political leaders after the attacks, saying that their ineptness was partly responsible. *The Times of India* commented on its front page that "Our politicians fiddle as innocents die." Political reactions in Mumbai and India included a range of resignations and political changes, including the resignations of Minister for Home Affairs Shivraj Patil, Chief Minister Vilasrao Deshmukh and deputy chief minister R. R. Patil for controversial reactions to the attack including taking the former's son and Bollywood director Ram Gopal Verma to tour the damaged Taj Hotel and the latters remarks that

Figure 297: *Citizens gather outside The Taj Mahal Palace Hotel demanding the government takes action.*

the attacks were not a big deal in such a large city. Prominent Muslim personalities such as Bollywood actor Aamir Khan appealed to their community members in the country to observe Eid al-Adha as a day of mourning on 9 December. The business establishment also reacted, with changes to transport, and requests for an increase in self-defence capabilities. The attacks also triggered a chain of citizens' movements across India such as the India Today Group's "War Against Terror" campaign. There were vigils held across all of India with candles and placards commemorating the victims of the attacks. The NSG commandos based in Delhi also met criticism for taking 10 hours to reach the 3 sites under attack.

International reaction for the attacks was widespread, with many countries and international organisations condemning the attacks and expressing their condolences to the civilian victims. Many important personalities around the world also condemned the attacks.

Media coverage highlighted the use of social media and Internet social networking tools, including *Twitter* and *Flickr*, in spreading information about the attacks. In addition, many Indian bloggers offered live textual coverage of the attacks. A map of the attacks was set up by a web journalist using Google Maps. The New York Times, in July 2009, described the event as "what may be the most well-documented terrorist attack anywhere."

In November 2010, families of American victims of the attacks filed a lawsuit in Brooklyn, New York, naming Lt. Gen. Ahmed Shuja Pasha, chief of the I.S.I., as being complicit in the Mumbai attacks. On 22 September 2011, the attack on the American Embassy in Afghanistan, was attributed to Pakistan via cell phone records identical to the attacks in Mumbai, also linked to Pakistan. The investigation is on-going.

Trials

Kasab's trial

Kasab's trial was delayed due to legal issues, as many Indian lawyers were unwilling to represent him. A Mumbai Bar Association passed a resolution proclaiming that none of its members would represent Kasab. However, the Chief Justice of India stated that Kasab needed a lawyer for a fair trial. A lawyer for Kasab was eventually found, but was replaced due to a conflict of interest. On 25 February 2009, Indian investigators filed an 11,000-page chargesheet, formally charging Kasab with murder, conspiracy, and waging war against India among other charges.

Kasab's trial began on 6 May 2009. He initially pleaded not guilty, but later admitted his guilt on 20 July 2009. He initially apologised for the attacks and claimed that he deserved the death penalty for his crimes, but later retracted these claims, saying that he had been tortured by police to force his confession, and that he had been arrested while roaming the beach. The court had accepted his plea, but due to the lack of completeness within his admittance, the judge had deemed that many of the 86 charges were not addressed and therefore the trial continued.

Kasab was convicted of all 86 charges on 3 May 2010. He was found guilty of murder for directly killing seven people, conspiracy to commit murder for the deaths of the 164 people killed in the three-day terror siege, waging war against India, causing terror, and of conspiracy to murder two high-ranking police officers. On 6 May 2010, he was sentenced to death by hanging. However, he appealed his sentence at high court. On 21 February 2011, the Bombay High Court upheld the death sentence of Kasab, dismissing his appeal.

On 29 August 2012, the Indian Supreme Court upheld the death sentence for Kasab. The court stated, "We are left with no option but to award death penalty. The primary and foremost offence committed by Kasab is waging war against the Government of India." The verdict followed 10 weeks of appeal hearings, and was decided by a two-judge Supreme Court panel, which was led by Judge Aftab Alam. The panel rejected arguments that Kasab was denied a free and fair trial.

Kasab filed a mercy petition with the President of India, which was rejected on 5 November. Kasab was hanged in Pune's Yerwada jail in secret on 21 November 2012 at 7:30 am and naming the operation as operation 'X'. The Indian mission in Islamabad informed the Pakistan government about Kasab's hanging through letter. Pakistan refused to take the letter, which was then faxed to them. His family in Pakistan was sent news of his hanging via a courier.

In Pakistan

Indian and Pakistani police exchanged DNA evidence, photographs and items found with the attackers to piece together a detailed portrait of the Mumbai plot. Police in Pakistan arrested seven people, including Hammad Amin Sadiq, a homoeopathic pharmacist, who arranged bank accounts and secured supplies. Sadiq and six others began their formal trial on 3 October 2009 in Pakistan. Indian authorities said the prosecution stopped well short of top Lashkar leaders. In November 2009, Indian Prime Minister Manmohan Singh said that Pakistan had not done enough to bring the perpetrators of the attacks to justice.

An eight-member commission comprising defence lawyers, prosecutors and a court official was allowed to travel to India on 15 March 2013 to gather evidence for the prosecution of seven suspects linked to the 2008 Mumbai attacks. However, the defence lawyers were barred from cross-examining the four prosecution witnesses in the case including Ajmal Kasab. On the eve of the first anniversary of 26/11, a Pakistani anti-terror court formally charged seven accused, including LeT operations commander Zaki ur Rehman Lakhvi. However, the actual trial started on 5 May 2012. The Pakistani court conducting trial of Mumbai attacks accused, reserved its judgement on the application filed by Lakhvi, challenging the report of the judicial panel, to 17 July 2012. On 17 July 2012, the court refused to take the findings of the Pakistani judicial commission as part of the evidence. However, it ruled that if a new agreement, which allows the panel's examination of witnesses, is reached, the prosecution may make an application for sending the panel to Mumbai. The Indian Government, upset over the court ruling, however, contended that evidence collected by the Pakistani judicial panel has evidential value to punish all those involved in the attack. On 21 September 2013, a Pakistani judicial commission arrived in India to carry out the investigation and to cross examine the witnesses. This is the second such visit: the one in March 2012 was not a success[1751] as its report was rejected by an anti-terrorism court in Pakistan due to lack of evidence.

In the United States

The LeT operative David Headley (born Daood Sayed Gilani) in his testimony before a Chicago federal court during co-accused Tahawwur Rana's trial revealed that Mumbai Chabad House was added to the list of targets for surveillance given by his Inter Services Intelligence handler Major Iqbal, though the Oberoi hotel, one of the sites attacked, was not originally on the list.[1752] On 10 June 2011, Tahawwur Rana was acquitted of plotting the 2008 Mumbai attacks, but was held guilty on two other charges. He was sentenced to 14 years in federal prison on 17 January 2013.

David Headley pleaded guilty to 12 counts related to the attacks, including conspiracy to commit murder in India and aiding and abetting in the murder of six Americans. On 23 January 2013, he was sentenced to 35 years in federal prison. His plea that he not be extradited to India, Pakistan or Denmark was accepted.[1753]

Memorials

On the first anniversary of the event, the state paid homage to the victims of the attack. Force One—a new security force created by the Maharashtra government—staged a parade from Nariman Point to Chowpatty. Other memorials and candlelight vigils were also organised at the various locations where the attacks occurred.

On the second anniversary of the event, homage was again paid to the victims.

Published accounts

Documentaries

Operation Black Tornado (2018) is a TV documentary which premièred on Veer by Discovery Channel series, Battle Ops.

External links

 Wikimedia Commons has media related to *November 2008 Mumbai attacks*.

- Video showing the way in which Indian authorities fought back against the attackers.[1754] – CNN-IBN (some Hindi, but mostly English).
- Dossier of evidence collected by investigating agencies of India[1755]
- List of Blogs & Bloggers who were live blogging during the attacks[1756]

- "They said, kill till you die... par hum bhi insan hain yaar"[1757]. Mumbai Mirror. 14 March 2009. Archived from the original[1758] on 20 October 2012. Retrieved 22 August 2012. [Interview of captured terrorist Mohammed Ajmal Amir Qasab]
- Mumbai Massacre[1759] Documentary produced by the PBS Series Secrets of the Dead

Concerns and controversies over the 2010 Commonwealth Games

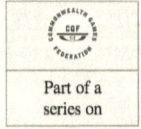

Part of a series on

A number of **concerns and controversies** surfaced before the 2010 Commonwealth Games in New Delhi, India, which received widespread media coverage both in India (the host nation) and internationally.

The Commonwealth Games was severely criticised by several prominent Indian politicians and social activists because billions of dollars have been spent on the sporting event despite the fact that India has one of the world's largest concentration of poor people. Additionally, several other problems related to the 2010 Commonwealth Games have been highlighted by Indian investigative agencies and media outlets; these include – serious corruption by officials of the Games' Organising Committee, delays in the construction of main Games' venues, infrastructural compromise, possibility of a terrorist attack, and exceptionally poor ticket sales before the event.

Socio-economic impact

Financial costs

Miloon Kothari, a leading Indian expert on socio-economic development, remarked that the 2010 Commonwealth Games will create "a negative financial legacy for the country" and asked "when one in three Indians lives below the poverty line and 40% of the hungry live in India, when 46% of India's children and 55% of women are malnourished, does spending billions of dollars on a 12-day sports event build national pride or is it a matter of national shame?"

One of the outspoken critics of the Games is Mani Shankar Aiyar, former Indian Minister for Youth Affairs and Sports. In April 2007, Aiyar commented

Figure 298: *Azim Premji, founder of Wipro Technologies, remarked that India faced several socio-economic challenges and "to instead spend on a grand sporting spectacle sounds like we [India] have got our priorities wrong."*

that the Games are "irrelevant to the common man" and criticized the Indian government for sanctioning billions of dollars for the Games even though India requires massive investment in social development programs. In July 2010, he remarked that he would be "unhappy if the Commonwealth Games are successful".

Azim Premji called the 2010 Commonwealth Games a "drain on public funds" and said that hosting the high-expense Games in India is not justified given that the country had more important priorities facing it, such as education, infrastructure and public health.

Social and environmental impact

Nearly 400,000 people from three large slum cluster in Delhi have been relocated since 2004. Gautam Bhan, an Indian urban planner with the University of California-Berkeley, said that the 2010 Commonwealth Games have resulted in "an unprecedented increase in the degree, frequency and scale of indiscriminate evictions without proper resettlement. We haven't seen these levels of evictions in the last five years since the Emergency."

In response to a Right to Information (RTI) application filed for study and statements by civil society groups, a report by the Housing and Land Rights Network (HLRN) - an arm of the Habitat International Coalition - detailed the social and environmental consequences of the event.[1760] It stated that *no tolerance zones* for beggars are enforced in Delhi, and the city has arbitrarily arrested homeless citizens under the "Bombay Prevention of Begging Act 1959".m

Labour laws violations

Campaigners in India have accused the organisers of enormous and systematic violations of labour laws at construction sites. Human Rights Law Network reports that independent investigations have discovered more than 70 cases where workers have died in accidents at construction sites since work began.[1761] Although official numbers have not been released, it is estimated that over 415,000 contract daily wage workers are working on Games projects. Unskilled workers are paid ₹85 (US$1.20) to ₹100 (US$1.50) per day while skilled workers are paid ₹120 (US$1.70) to ₹130 (US$1.90) INR per day for eight hours of work. Workers also state that they are paid ₹134 (US$2.00) to ₹150 (US$2.20) for 12 hours of work (eight hours plus four hours of overtime). Both these wages contravene the stipulated Delhi state minimum wage of ₹152 (US$2.20) for eight hours of work. Nearly 50 construction workers have died in the past two years while employed on Games projects.

These represent violations of the Minimum Wages Act, 1948; Interstate Migrant Workmen (Regulation of Employment and Condition of Services) Act 1979, and the constitutionally enshrined fundamental rights per the 1982 Supreme Court of India judgement on Asiad workers. The public have been banned from the camps where workers live and work – a situation which human rights campaigners say prevents the garnering of information regarding labour conditions and number of workers.

There have been documented instances of the presence of young children at hazardous construction sites, due to a lack of child care facilities for women workers living and working in the labour camp style work sites. Furthermore, workers on the site of the main Commonwealth stadium have reportedly been issued with hard hats, yet most work in open-toed sandals and live in cramped tin tenements in which illnesses are rife. The High Court of Delhi is presently hearing a public interest petition relating to employers not paying employees for overtime and it has appointed a four-member committee to submit a report on the alleged violations of workers rights.

During the construction of the Games Village, there was controversy over financial mismanagement,[1762] profiteering by the Delhi Development Authority and private real estate companies,[1763] and inhumane working conditions.[1764]

Child labour

CNN has broadcast evidence showing children, as young as seven, being used in the construction of the game venues. According to Siddharth Kara, who provided CNN with the evidence, he documented 14 cases of child labor within a few days. In reply to a question whether it could have been just a case of kids being present at the construction site along with their parents, he replied: "It's not just kids playing in the dirt or using a hammer as a toy." He further stated about the kids: "They're told to do the work and they just do the work. They don't know that they should be in school or that they should be playing."

Even though the New Delhi chief minister Sheila Dikshit claimed that nobody had approached her, according to CNN, they had tried to contact her as far back as 23 July 2010. In spite of repeated attempts, according to them, no official reply was ever made.

Urban change

Mitu Sengupta, a professor of politics at Ryerson University, Canada, points out that there is a "tradition of using 'urban spectacles' such as the Olympics and World's Fairs to enhance a city's global recognition, image and status, and to push through controversial policy reforms that might otherwise linger in the pending file for years (it is easier to undercut local opposition under the pressure of a fixed deadline and the international spotlight)." She writes that the reforms involved are often "the invention of an affluent, globally connected minority that is relatively detached from local conditions and the local population". The 2010 Commonwealth Games, she says, are being used to invigorate an elite-driven program of urban transformation" that centers on privatization, securitization, and the construction of "monuments to vanity". Sengupta expands upon this argument in a subsequent article in Z Magazine[1765] Amita Baviskar, a professor of sociology at the Institute of Economic Growth, University of Delhi, makes a similar argument, on how mega-events, like the Olympics and Commonwealth Games, are used to advance narrow agendas of urban reform that cater to the middle class and rich. She focuses on how, in preparation for the Commonwealth Games, the city's slums were bulldozed in order to make room for shopping malls and expensive real estate.

Sex slavery and prostitution boom

There has been a boom in the number of young girls, mostly from impoverished parts of India, coming to Delhi after being offered jobs by disguised criminals, only to be taken prisoner and forced into sex slavery. The number of victims is believed to be in the hundreds. Many brothels have been running English courses for sex workers and upgrading their facilities in anticipation of a business upturn during the games.[1766] Overseas prostitutes are also expected to come as tourists and ply their trade. One anti-trafficking NGO has claimed that there are reports of 40,000 women being brought in from northeastern India alone. A spokesperson said that recruits from that part of India were favoured because of their lighter skin. It has been reported that over 3,000 bar girls in Mumbai have stopped going to work; this has been blamed on an exodus to Delhi for the Commonwealth Games.

Organisational failure

Vigilance-related irregularities and Over-Invoicing

On 28 July 2010, the Central Vigilance Commission, an Indian government body created to address governmental corruption, released a report showing irregularities in up to 14 CWG projects. As per official reports, in total 129 works in 71 organisations have been inspected.[1767] The detailed preliminary findings included the award of work contracts at higher prices, poor quality assurance and management, and work contracts awarded to ineligible agencies.[1768]

There are also allegations of widespread corruption in various aspects of organising the games including procurement and awarding contracts for constructing the game venues. The Commonwealth Games Organising Committee on 5 August 2010 suspended joint director T S Darbari and M Jayachandran following the report of the three-member panel which was probing the financial irregularities related to the Queen's Baton Relay.

Also, Organising Committee treasurer Anil Khanna resigned from the post in the wake of allegations that his son's firm had secured a contract for laying synthetic courts at a tennis stadium. The GlobalPost news agency reports that scandals have come to light, such as "shadowy off-shore firms, forged emails, inexplicable payments to bogus companies and inflated bills – for every purchase from toilet paper to treadmills." Among the alleged corruption and defrauding of the games budget, toilet paper rolls valued at $2 were costed at $80, $2 soap dispensers at $60, $98 mirrors at $220, $11,830 altitude training simulators at $250,190.

Preparation delays

In September 2009, CGF chief Mike Fennell reported that the games were at risk of falling behind schedule and that it was "reasonable to conclude that the current situation poses a serious risk to the Commonwealth Games in 2010". A report by the Indian Government releaspj;ed several months prior found that construction work on 13 out of the 19 sports venues was behind schedule.

The Chief of the Indian Olympic Association shri Narendra Modi has also expressed his concerns regarding the current state of affairs. Singh has called for the revamp of the Organising Committee commenting that India now has to "retrieve the games". Other Indian officials have also expressed dismay at the ongoing delays but they have stated that they are confident that India will successfully host the games and do so on time.

As the Times of India reports, all CWG projects were to be completed by May 2009 and the last year should have been kept for trial runs. The newspaper further reports that the first stadium was handed over for trial runs in July 2010 only. To put the delays in perspective, Beijing National Stadium was completed much ahead of schedule for the 2008 Summer Olympics, while the venues for 2012 Summer Olympics in London are scheduled to be delivered one year before the games and the construction of the venues is on track.

In August 2010, the Cabinet Secretariat took a decision to appoint 10 officers of the rank of Joint and Additional Secretaries to oversee the progress of the construction of stadiums. Each officer is allocated a stadium and given the responsibility to ensure that the work completes in time for the games.

Mass volunteer walkout

Around 10,000 of the 22,000 selected volunteers quit, less than a week before the event. This has been blamed on a lack of training for personnel, or dissatisfaction with assignments. There are reports that some who have quit have not returned their uniforms.

Poor ticket sales and attendance

The start of the Games saw extremely poor ticket sales, with many venues near empty. In a press conference, organising chairman Suresh Kalmadi admitted that there were problems, and blamed empty venues on ticket booths not being set up outside stadiums. Commonwealth Games chief Mike Fennell admitted that many venues had been nearly empty on the opening day of the Games, saying "A number of venues do not have lots of spectators [...] one area which causes us concern". On the second day of competition, less than 100 people filled the hockey venue–the 19,000-seat MDC Stadium. Less than 20 people watched the first tennis match of the tournament in the 5,000-seat tennis stadium, and just 58 fans watched the netball opening match.

One Indian competitor tried to buy tickets for relatives online, only to be informed by the website that tickets were sold out. When he arrived to compete, he found the venue to be empty.

The streets of Delhi were deserted for the cycling road races and walking event. Wikipedia:Citation needed

Spectators' response at opening ceremony

At the opening ceremony, the chairman of the organising committee, Suresh Kalmadi, faced embarrassment, when he was booed by spectators at the start of his welcome speech to 60,000 spectators.[1769] Kalmadi came under further strain when he "thanked" the late Princess Diana for attending the opening ceremony of the games. The chairman made the blunder at a press conference saying 'Yes, Princess Diana was there,' after which he immediately corrected himself by saying 'Prince Charles and (Camilla) the Duchess of Cornwall.

Opening ceremony

The Australian Commonwealth contingent expressed frustration over the opening ceremony, in which there were claims that the athletes and delegation support staff were "treated like cattle" and subjected to "disgraceful" and unbearable conditions. Australia's chef de mission Steve Moneghetti complained about the athletes being trapped in "absolute cauldron conditions" under the main stadium before marching for the opening ceremony. The Australians were stuck in a tunnel, where Moneghetti described the temperature as exceeding 40 °C (104 °F) due to a lack of airconditioning and ventilation. When attempting to move out, the Australian delegation was stopped by staff. When the contestants were finally able to move out into the arena, they were described as being emotionally affected.

Racism allegations

African countries have complained that they are getting second-class treatment from the Games organisers, in spite of them offering India a hand in the preparation of the Games. They have alleged that accommodation given to them was inferior compared to the accommodation provided to the Australian and New Zealand teams. They went on to state that India was complaining about being victims of racial bias in the reporting of the Games; while simultaneously perpetrating the same kind of racism against the African countries.

Infrastructure issues

Transport infrastructure

The Delhi Airport Metro Express built by Reliance Infrastructure and CAF Beasain missed its deadline of 31 July 2010 and the private consortium was fined Rs 112.5 million.

Venues

Less than two weeks before the opening ceremony, Fennell wrote to the Indian cabinet secretary, urging action in response to the village being "seriously compromised." He said that though team officials were impressed with the international zone and main dining area, they were "shocked" by the state of the accommodation. "The village is the cornerstone of any Games and the athletes deserve the best possible environment to prepare for their competition." The BBC published photographs of the village taken two days before 23 September showing unfinished living quarters.

New Zealand, Canada, Scotland and Northern Ireland have expressed concern about unliveable conditions. The Times of India newspaper reports that the Scottish delegation apparently submitted a photograph of a dog defecating on a bed in the games village. Hooper said that there was "excrement in places it shouldn't be" in the athletes' quarters and that members of visiting delegations had to help clean up the unsanitary things. The BBC released images of bathrooms with brown-coloured paan stains on the walls and floor, liquids on the floor, and brown paw prints on athletes' beds. Lalit Bhanot, the secretary general of the Organising Committee, rejected the complaint that sanitation was poor by saying that, due to cultural differences, there are different standards about cleanliness in India and the western world, a statement for which he was widely ridiculed in Indian and international media. Bhanot went on to say of the athletes' village that, "This is a world-class village, probably one of the best ever."

Meanwhile, Pakistan also made reservations over the condition of the athletes' village and asked for an alternate accommodation to be made available to its contingent while preparation was still in progress. The Pakistan Olympic Association president Syed Arif Hasan remarked: "We want the CGF to ensure that the athletes' village is in good condition. Athletes cannot stay at a substandard place." Hasan however added that there were no doubts over Pakistan's participation and the contingent would leave as planned.

On the other hand, England's Chef de mission Craig Hunter praised the Games Village, remarking that "the Commonwealth Games Village here [in New

Delhi] is better than the Beijing Olympics". He added that the arrangements at the Games Village is much better than that at the 2008 Summer Olympics.

Canada's sports minister also supported the Games, saying that big events always face issues, and the media often exaggerates them, as Canada found during the Vancouver Winter Olympics. He added that "We are coming in full force."

Problems with functionality of equipment and infrastructure during events

On the first night of swimming, debris landed in the swimming pool, causing delays ahead of a race. It is believed that part of the ceiling or its paint had fallen off.

Before the last night of swimming finals, the filtration system broke down and the pool was turbid and murky during the warmup session and the finals; it was described as the least clear ever seen for a swimming competition. A disproportionate number of swimmers fell ill with intestinal complaints, leading to concerns over the cleanliness and sanitation of the pool. Early suspicions rested on the quality of water in the swimming pools of the SPM Complex, but other competing teams, including South Africa, reported no such illness. Daily water quality tests were being carried out on the water of the pools, as mandated by the event standards. Additional tests were ordered after news of the illnesses, but they also did not find anything amiss. The Australian team's chief doctor, Peter Harcourt, ruled that the "chances of the [Delhi] pool being the cause of the problem is very remote" and praised the hygiene and food quality in the Delhi Games Village. He suggested that it could be a common case of Traveler's diarrhea (locally called Delhi belly), or the Australian swimmers could have contracted the stomach virus during their training camp in Kuala Lumpur, Malaysia. English Olympic and Commonwealth gold-medalist swimmer Rebecca Adlington said that the water quality was absolutely fine.

After the opening ceremony, the ground at the athletics arena was damaged, and the grass infield and the track was still being re-laid two hours before competition started.

Vandalism of Games Village by Athletes

Condoms and toilet blockages

An Indian newspaper during the games reported that used condoms flushed down the toilets in the athlete's village had caused some drains to become blocked, necessitating action by plumbers to clear the pipes.

Athletes under investigation for trashing apartments

Australian athletes have been accused of vandalizing the towers of the athletes' village they were staying in by breaking furniture and electrical fittings. Delhi Police did not press the case after the Organizing Committee refused to file a complaint while Indian external affairs minister SM Krishna dismissed it as a one-off incident.

A washing machine was hurled from the eighth floor of the same tower. Nobody on the ground was hit, but it is unclear who the culprit was. Indian newspapers have reported that the Australian Commonwealth Games Authority agreed to pay for the damages and have apologised for the incident. The Australian High Commissioner rejected the claim, stating that the incident was the result of partying and celebrations.[1770] Later comments by Australian officials have contradicted claims by Lalit Bhanot that they had admitted responsibility. Perry Crosswhite said that it was still unclear if athletes from other nations present in the tower at the time had been responsible.

Safety and security concerns

Small monkeys roam Delhi's streets and prefer heavily urbanized areas with plenty of living space among buildings. They cannot be killed because many Indians see them as sacred so instead a larger, domesticated monkey, the langur, is brought in to scare away the smaller monkeys.

On the second day of the games, three Ugandan officials were injured by a malfunctioning security barrier at the games' village, and a senior official from that country raised allegations of discrimination by Indian officials. Uganda's sports minister lashed out at Indian officials and demanded an apology for the accident. The officials had cuts and bruises and were hospitalized overnight for observation. The chairman of the Games' Organising Committee, Suresh Kalmadi, apologized to the Ugandan High Commissioner to India for the freak car accident.

Infrastructural compromise

On 21 September 2010, a footbridge under construction for the Games near the Jawaharlal Nehru Stadium collapsed, injuring at least 23 people, mainly workers, underscoring fears of poor workmanship. Commenting on the incident, Chief Minister of Delhi Sheila Dikshit controversially remarked that the footbridge was only meant for spectators and not for athletes. Following the collapse, Fennell expressed concern that conditions at the Games Village, which had "shocked the majority", would seriously compromise the entire event. The company that was building the foot bridge, P&R Infraprojects, was subsequently blacklisted by the Delhi Government and was not allowed to get government contracts.

Reportedly, progress was still slow and four or five accommodation towers built by Emaar at the Games village were unfinished, lacking facilities such as wireless internet, fitted toilets and plumbing. In addition, rubble, unused masonry and discarded bricks littered the unfinished gardens. According to sports historian Boria Majumdar, author of the *Sellotape Legacy: Delhi and the Commonwealth Games*, India "may have to pull a miracle." The father of Australian track cyclist Kaarle McCulloch visited his daughter at the Olympic village. A builder in Australia, Grahame McCulloch criticised the structural soundness of the village; he said "those buildings are the dodgiest things I have ever seen...so substandard". He told his daughter not to use the balcony, fearing that it was collapsible.[1771]

On 22 September 2010, part of the drop ceiling of the new Commonwealth Games weightlifting venue in New Delhi collapsed.

Indian bantamweight boxer Akhil Kumar's bed in the Games village collapsed when he sat on it. "I sat down on my bed to rest but suddenly it gave way. After that I noticed that part of it has no plywood", he said

On 27 September 2010, a South African athlete reported that a snake was present in his room in the Games Village. A day earlier, animal authorities had to be called in to evacuate a king cobra from the tennis venue.

On 7 October, a large scoreboard crashed to the ground at the rugby venue when a supporting chain snapped. The games however were due to start a week later so no major repercussions were experienced.

Terror threats

Following the 2008 Mumbai attacks, some athletes and their representative bodies expressed security fears during the games. In April 2010, during the Indian Premier League, two low intensity bombs went off outside the M. Chinnaswamy Stadium in Bangalore. Although there were no casualties, this postponed the start of the game by an hour. Following this attack, foreign cricketers like Kevin Pietersen expressed fears for their safety and questions were raised regarding the safety of athletes during the Commonwealth Games[1772]. The UK and Canada also warned about potential attacks on commercial targets in Delhi ahead of the games.[1773]

Jama Masjid incident

On 19 September 2010, unknown gunmen on a motorbike opened fire with an automatic pistol on a tourist bus outside the Jama Masjid mosque in Delhi. The attacks, which came a fortnight before the start of the games, injured two Taiwanese tourists. Two hours later, a Maruti car exploded in the vicinity, reportedly from a deliberate low-intensity pressure cooker bomb which had been assembled inside. No fatalities or major damages were reported. The incidents, which were purportedly claimed by the Indian Mujahideen, provoked fears about lack of security in the city for the upcoming games. However, police in Delhi initially denied the role of any organised terror group and instead blamed the attacks on "disgruntled youths and local criminal gangs." Officials suggested that a possible motive of the strike was to instill fear in people ahead of the Commonwealth Games.

Fear of dengue outbreak

The heaviest monsoon rains in 15 years, along with large quantities of standing water on CWG construction sites as well as in tanks and ponds, raised concerns over increased levels of mosquito-borne disease in Delhi. In the run-up to the games it was reported that 65-70 cases of dengue fever were being diagnosed each day in the city, with the number of cases "likely to hit the 3,000 mark" by the opening on 3 October.

Illness

Many swimmers were reported to have fallen ill. Initially, concerns were raised over the quality of water in the swimming pools of the SPM Complex. It was said that more than 20 percent of the English team's swimmers – about eight to 10 competitors – had been struck down with a stomach virus. The Australian team also reported that at least six of its swimmers had been sick, including

Andrew Lauterstein, who had to withdraw from the 50-meter butterfly. Commonwealth Games Federation president Mike Fennell said officials would conduct tests to make sure the pools were not the source of the illness. "If there is something unsafe, you cannot swim in that water. It is a matter we have to deal with a great deal of urgency," he said.

However, other competing teams, including South Africa, reported no such illness.[1774] Daily water quality tests were being carried out on the water of the pools, as mandated by the event standards. Additional tests were ordered after news of the illnesses, but they also did not find anything amiss. The Australian team's chief doctor, Peter Harcourt, ruled that the "chances of the [Delhi] pool being the cause of the problem is very remote" and praised the hygiene and food quality in the Delhi Games Village. He suggested that it could be a common case of Traveler's diarhoea (locally called Delhi belly), or the Australian swimmers could have contracted the stomach virus during their training camp in Kuala Lumpur, Malaysia. English Olympic and Commonwealth gold-medalist swimmer Rebecca Adlington said that the water quality was absolutely fine.

Boycott

Following the withdrawal of Dani Samuels, the women's world discus champion, because "[her] safety [was] more important to them than a medal," Australia's Minister for Sport, Mark Arbib, said CWG officials expected more competitors to follow suit.

The Scottish team's departure of its first 41 boxers, rugby players, wrestlers and support staff was delayed for 48 hours, and the Welsh team set a deadline of 22 September to receive reassurances that the venues would be fit for purpose. The first batch of English athletes, which included a lawn bowls team and a men's hockey squad, said the organisers were not making nearly enough progress just a day before they were to leave. *The Guardian* suggested a mass walkout remained an option with the "point of no return" less than a week before the scheduled start; they claimed the "main competing countries would be likely to act in concert." They also suggested the games were on the verge of "descending into farce."

Michael Cavanagh, the chairman of Commonwealth Games Scotland, said a decision to stay away would be a joint one, as he insisted a possible knock on effects for the 2014 Commonwealth Games in Glasgow would not be a factor. He said "In terms of withdrawal we don't see this as simply a Team Scotland decision, any decision to withdraw we would see as being a collective decision amongst the countries who are already there and already concerned. We can't allow ourselves to be influenced by thoughts of how it may impact on

2014, not when we have something as important as the safety of our athletes to consider." Phillips Idowu, the world triple jump champion, also withdrew from the Games.

Calls for boycott

Amidst allegations of blatant corruption, shoddy construction work at venues and security concerns for participating athletes, the 2010 Commonwealth Games have faced numerous boycott calls from individuals in India, England and Australia.

Within India, there were calls for boycott. Other celebrities who followed Aiyar's comments in expressing a call for boycott include former Indian cricket captain and spin bowler Bishan Singh Bedi and bestselling Indian author Chetan Bhagat. Bedi said the "CWG organisers have taken the country for a ride" and urged international athletes to boycott the "embarrassing" Delhi games. Bhagat, who is considered a youth icon in India with a huge fan following, called the Commonwealth games the "biggest and most blatant exercise in mass corruption since the country won independence six decades ago." Bhagat, who has sold more than 4 million books in India, also urged his readers to boycott the games event and not to watch them on TV, thereby using the "golden chance" to "put the corrupt and insensitive government to shame."

The Jat community seeking reservation under the OBC quota have also planned to use the Commonwealth games as a platform and force the Indian government to relent to their needs.

Other countries also threatened to boycott the games. Considering the potential impact of a terror threat and other security concerns, rumors arose about a boycott of the Delhi Commonwealth Games by major participating nations including Scotland, England and New Zealand. However, the rumors were soon put to rest by Commonwealth games committees in each of these countries who expressed a general level of satisfaction with the security arrangements.

Australian quadruple Olympic gold medal winning swimmer Dawn Fraser called for Australia to boycott the games event, citing fears of a tragedy similar to that which unfolded in the Munich Olympics of 1972. Fraser pronounced that reports of missed construction deadlines and other irregularities in games planning meant Indian authorities' "word for providing security should not be taken at its face value." However, the Australian Commonwealth Games Organising Committee was quick to dismiss Fraser's fears with ACGA chief executive, Perry Crosswhite saying he believed there will be no security issues during the games event. John Coates, Australia's Olympic chief, came down hard on the organisers, alleging teams were being forced to temporary accommodation at hotels. "I don't think it is a cultural thing. When you agree to host [the Games], you are required to provide the basics in terms of health and hygiene for the athletes. The Games shouldn't have been awarded to Delhi in hindsight."

Other withdrawals

A number of athletes withdrew from the Games, for reasons related and non-related to the state of affairs in the days leading up to the event. Jamaican world record holder Usain Bolt and his predecessor Asafa Powell pulled out of the event citing the timing of the Games as a major reason for their decisions to stay away. Olympic cyclist champion Geraint Thomas pulled out for fear of contracting dengue fever. Other notable athletes who have announced their non-attendance include Paula Radcliffe, Jessica Ennis, Jennifer Meadows, Natasha Danvers, Chris Hoy, Bradley Wiggins, Victoria Pendleton and Beth Tweddle.

Sporting controversies

Doping

Prior to the Games, four wrestlers, a shot-putter and two swimmers who were all part of India's Games squad tested positive for methylhexaneamine. Four others, who were not picked for the Games in the Indian capital, also failed drug tests conducted at the various training camps across the country.

Oludamola Osayomi, the winner of the women's 100-metre sprint event, was reported to have tested positive for a "banned substance" which was later revealed to be the stimulant methylhexaneamine. Another Nigerian athlete, hurdler Samuel Okon who placed sixth in the 110 metres hurdles, was reported to have tested positive for the same drug.

In July 2011, three of the four women from India's gold-medal winning 400-metre-relay team tested positive for performance-enhancing drugs. Two of the racers, Sini Jose and Jauna Murmu, tested positive for the anabolic steroid methandienone, and Tiana Mary Thomas tested positive for epi-methandienone.

Figure 299: *Pearson won the 100m sprint before being disqualified.*

Archery

While the audience's behaviour at the archery event provoked criticism from the English team, the silver medallist, Alison Williamson, praised it on the other hand. Earlier reports held that the English team was upset because the loud chant of the crowd during the women's recurve event had distracted the archers. In an action condemned in the Indian media, an English archery official allegedly abused an Indian coach, telling him to "f*** off." The comment came after the Indian team registered a one-point win over England to claim the gold medal. The Indian archery head coach, Limba Ram, walked over to shake hands with officials of the rival team. In response, an English official showed his elbow in a gesture before uttering the remarks. Britain's archery team leader said she was unaware of the incident and added, "[the Indian coach] must find out whether the person was one among us. If he was not wearing a red jersey, he would not be part of the side. I will speak to the Indian coach about it." Limba Ram said that he failed to identify the person as he had chosen to ignore the one-off incident. There have also been accusations that Ram was called a monkey on two different occasions by an English official.

Athletics

During the Final of the Women's 100m sprint final, a controversy was caused by the eventual disqualification of Sally Pearson of Australia. She had won the race on the third attempted start after one start was delayed because of excessive crowd noise and the second due to a false start by Laura Turner of England. Pearson was disqualified because she was deemed to have false-started in the second attempted restart along with Turner. This was as a direct result of a protest lodged by Team England. The controversy was caused as only Turner was disqualified from the race during the race because of a false start and not Pearson. Turner ran the race under protest. Pearson and other athletes were not informed of the protest until four hours after the race, as they were waiting to begin the medal presentation for the race. Commonwealth Games Federation president Mike Fennell called Pearson's treatment "unsatisfactory" and that the whole situation was caused by an "unacceptable communications blunder".

Boxing

During the weigh-in for the boxing competition, the scales were giving inaccurate readings with athletes recording higher body weights on the official scales. The scales were deemed to be broken and the weigh-in was delayed 24 hours to find and calibrate new scales. The initial wrong measurements led to angry shouting between coaches, athletes and organisers. During the boxing competition there have been claims made by various teams including England and Botswana that jabs were not being scored by judges. This was attributed to the removal of a white scoring zone placed on the boxers gloves which is usually present in amateur boxing events. The BBC commentating team also claimed there to be a bias in judges scores towards Indian competitors.

Cycling

During the final of the Men's Keirin, Malaysian Azizulhasni Awang was disqualified for aggressive interference when he forced his way past two competitors. Race winner Josiah Ng said he was "mystified" over Awang's disqualification. In the semi-final round of the keirin, Australia's Shane Perkins was disqualified for dangerous riding with the official reason not being made clear. Perkins subsequently won the classification race and was described by Chris Boardman from the BBC to "have aimed an angry V-sign at officials"; he gestured to the judges with his index and middle finger held together. No subsequent action was taken against Perkins who later said, "the officials need to go back to school", referencing poor decisions he felt had been made in the sprint and keirin events.

Swimming

On another occasion, South African swimmer Roland Schoeman came under criticism when he referred to the crowd at the swimming as "going on like monkeys" in a post-race poolside interview. Schoeman's remarks came after he narrowly avoided being disqualified as he and England's Simon Burnett fell in at the start of the 50m freestyle when distracted by the crowd noise. The swimming has been persistently affected by Indian spectators ignoring etiquette and shouting out while the competitors were preparing for the start.[1775] His comment was regarded as possibly being a racial ethnic slur, although he later said that the word was commonly used in South Africa to refer to mischievous behaviour. At an official press conference, organising committee secretary-general Lalit Bhanot took the complaints about monkeys literally. Not being aware of the complaints, Bhanot felt Delhi's wildlife was at issue: "We know especially at the swimming pool there are a lot of monkeys and we have made efforts to keep them away from the swimming pool."

Wrestling

Australian wrestler Hassene Fkiri was ejected from the 96 kg Greco-Roman competition and stripped of the silver medal after making an obscene gesture at the international FILA judges during the final. According to an Australian official, Fkiri was furious at his Indian rival Anil Kumar, who he accused of breaking the rules a number of times in the first period by holding Fkiri around the neck and head with two hands. The Australian received his first warning after he made a comment to the referee as he walked off the mat at the end of the two-minute period; when Kumar repeated the same move in the next round, Fkiri headbutted him and was issued a second warning. He then proceeded to swing his arms uncontrollably afterwards, which resulted in his third warning and eventual disqualification. After losing, Fkiri refused to shake hands with the victor.

Reactions and responses

Responding to media concerns, the organisers said there were 48 hours to save the Games after warnings of a pull out.

Numerous Bollywood actors also expressed their dismay at the state of the Games.

Four days before the start of the games, tickets for the opening, closing ceremonies, and the 100 m athletics were still not sold out.

The Sydney Morning Herald wrote that despite Kalmadi's "blind optimism", the games were not going to be the best ever. Instead, it wrote that it was "probably the most interesting."

The opening ceremony played a key role in improving the image of the Games. As athletes arrived and competitions started, many earlier critics changed their view. The Australian Sports Minister said that India could now aim for the

Olympics, and the President of the International Olympic Committee, Jacques Rogge, said that India had made a good foundation for a future Olympics bid. As the Games concluded, many observers remarked that they began on an apprehensive note, but were an exceptional experience with a largely positive ending. Some observers accused sections of the media of bias, unfair expectations, and negative reporting.

Within India, the Games saw criticism due to the Games' origins as a celebration of the British Empire, with Arindam Chaudhuri arguing for India's disassociation from the "slavish games" which he viewed as a "celebration of racial discrimination, colonialism [and] imperialism".

Criticism by Mani Shankar Aiyar

Mani Shankar Aiyar, a senior member of the ruling Indian National Congress party and former Minister of Youth and Sports Affairs was an early whistle-blower from the Indian Union Cabinet who expressed concern over extensive delays in preparation leading to unplanned expenses which he said, could have been utilized for "ensuring a better sporting future for Indian children by providing them sports training". Aiyar also said that he would be "unhappy" if the Games were a success and wished for the "Commonwealth Games to be spoiled."

Aiyar's frank media admission proved a public embarrassment for Commonwealth Games Organising Committee chairman Suresh Kalmadi who labelled him "anti national" for wishing that the Commonwealth Games are "spoilt." Kalmadi's remark received extensive criticism in Indian media.

Aiyar also told an Australian TV channel that India is "probably the poorest country of the Commonwealth". Bangladesh, among other countries, has a lower GDP per capita/purchasing power parity.

Allegations of corruption and financial irregularities

The day after the conclusion of the Games, the Indian Government announced formation of a special committee to probe the allegations of corruption and mismanagement against the Organizing Committee (OC). The probe committee was led by former Comptroller and Auditor General of India VK Shunglu. This probe was in addition to the Directorate General of Income Tax Investigation, Central Bureau of Investigation (CBI), Enforcement Directorate, and Central Vigilance Commission (CVC) investigations already underway. The Prime Minister, Dr. Manmohan Singh, had promised in mid-August, when reports of the bungling first surfaced, that corrupt officials will be given *"severe and exemplary" punishment* after the Games. The committee was given three months time to submit its report.

A total of 53 corruption cases were being examined by the CVC. As of September 2012, 28 of them were still in different stages of investigation, 13 were referred to CBI for further investigation and 12 were closed.

Timing-Scoring-Result (TSR) case

This case relates to allegations of corruption in awarding TSR system contract to a Swiss firm

CBI investigation and chargesheet

On 25 April 2011, CBI arrested former CWG Organising Committee (OC) chairman Suresh Kalmadi in the Timing-Scoring-Result (TSR) case. He was arrested under Sections 120 B (criminal conspiracy) and 420 (cheating) of the Indian Penal Code.

On 20 May 2011, CBI filed the first chargesheet in a special CBI court against Kalmadi. The CBI alleged that he was the *main accused* in awarding TSR system contract to a Swiss firm. The chargesheet said, "Kalmadi is the main accused as he was the person with all supreme powers. He had the supreme over-riding powers in the Organising Committee of the CWG, 2010." In addition to Kalmadi, the CBI named two companies and eight persons including OC former Secretary General Lalit Bhanot and former Director General VK Verma as accused.

The accused were charged under various provisions of the Indian Penal Code sections dealing with criminal conspiracy, forging documents and using fake documents as genuine, Section 13 (1) (d) of the Prevention of Corruption Act.

According to the charge sheet, the accused allegedly awarded the lucrative contract to the Swiss firm to install a TSR system for the Commonwealth Games at an excessive cost, causing a loss of over ▯900 million (US$13 million) to the exchequer. The investigation revealed that officials of the OC had conspired with private persons for awarding the contract at an excessive net cost of about ▯1,576 million (US$23 million) as compared to a net bid of Spain-based company for approximately ▯620 million (US$9.0 million). This resulted in a loss of about ▯956 million (US$14 million) by wrongly eliminating all competitors of Swiss-based company. Two bids were received for TSR contract from Swiss Timing and MSL Spain and they were opened on 4 November 2009. However, much before that, on 12 October 2009, Kalmadi and Verma had announced that the contract would be awarded to Swiss Timing.

Trial

On 4 February 2013, the court of special CBI judge Ravinder Kaur found sufficient prima facie evidence and ordered framing of charges against all the accused. The charges framed were: cheating, forgery, criminal conspiracy and causing a loss of over Rs 900 million under the Prevention of Corruption Act. As the accused pleaded not guilty, the court ordered that daily Criminal trial (for 5 days a week) will begin from 20 February.

Queen's Baton Relay (QBR) case

The QBR event was held on 29 October 2009. The allegation was that, the Organising Committee (OC) awarded the work of transportation in QBR event to AM Car and Van Hire Ltd at excessively high rates without following a standard tender process.

After completing investigations, CBI filed its second charge-sheet (after the charge-sheet in TSR case) in a special CBI court in Delhi. The CBI named OC officials T S Darbari, Sanjay Mohindroo, Jeychandran and London-based businessman Ashish Patel and his two companies AM Car n Van Hire and AM Films. The chargesheet alleged that OC members conspired to award contracts of local transportation and others to Patel's companies at excessive rates during the event held in London in 2009.

The accused were charged under Indian Penal Code sections relating to criminal conspiracy to cheat and forgery along with violations of Prevention of Corruption Act.

Venue Development Support case

A Swiss company was awarded a contract of over ₹700 million (US $10 million) for providing venue development support services to the Organising Committee (OC). However, it was alleged that Prime Minister appointed VK Shunglu Committee found serious cases of forgery and irregularity with the contract. The committee said that, "Undue pressure was brought within the OC for engaging the company for the contract" and recommended that CBI or ED should take up the case for appropriate action.

Based on Shunglu Committee's findings, CBI registered an FIR against Suresh Kalmadi, Lalit Bhanot and AK Mattoo on 23 August 2012.

On 23 March 2014, the Hindustan Times reported that "...the investigation into the alleged irregularities committed is stumbling with the CBI having closed its FIR related to grant of two contracts to a Swiss firm for lack of evidence."

Other cases

CBI sources revealed in July 2012 that the probe against alleged corruption in construction of Barapullah Flyover and grant of Bail-out Package to EMAAR MGF is likely to be closed in the absence of substantiating evidence.

2G spectrum case

The **2G spectrum case** was an alleged scam under the United Progressive Alliance coalition government in India in 2010. It involved politicians, government officials and numerous big names from the corporate sector.

Overview

The Central Bureau of Investigation (CBI) court on Dec 21, 2017 declared no evidence to prosecute the accused and acquitted all accused personnels.

The Union Government of that time was accused of undercharging mobile telephone companies for frequency allocation licenses, which they used to create 2G spectrum subscriptions for cell phones. The Government chose NM Rothschild & Sons to design a first-of-its-kind e-auction mechanism in the world, a US$2.27 billion landmark deal. The difference between the money collected and that mandated to be collected was estimated by the Comptroller and Auditor General of India at ₪1.76 trillion (US$26 billion), based on 2010 3G and BWA spectrum-auction prices. In a chargesheet filed on 2 April 2011 by the Central Bureau of Investigation (CBI), the loss was pegged at ₪309,845.5 million (US$4.5 billion). In a 19 August 2011 reply to the CBI, the Telecom Regulatory Authority of India (TRAI) said that the government had gained over ₪30 billion (US$440 million) by selling 2G spectrum.

On 2 February 2012, the Supreme Court of India ruled on a public interest litigation (PIL) related to the 2G spectrum allocation. The court declared the allotment of spectrum "unconstitutional and arbitrary", cancelling the 122 licenses issued in 2008 under A. Raja (Minister of Communications & IT from 2007 to 2009), the primary official accused. According to the court, Raja "wanted to favour some companies at the cost of the public exchequer" & "virtually gifted away important national asset[s]." The zero-loss theory was discredited on 3 August 2012 when, after a Supreme Court directive, the Government of India revised the base price for 5-MHz 2G spectrum auctions to ₪140 billion (US$2.0 billion), raising its value to about ₪28 billion (US$410 million) per MHz (near the Comptroller and Auditor General estimate of ₪33.5 billion (US$490 million) per MHz).

Although the policy for awarding licenses was first-come, first-served, which was introduced during Atal Bihari Vajpayee Government, Raja changed the rules so it applied to compliance with conditions instead of the application itself. On 10 January 2008, companies were given only a few hours to supply Letters of Intent and payments; some executives were allegedly tipped off by Raja, and they (and the minister) were imprisoned. According to some analystsWikipedia:Manual of Style/Words to watch#Unsupported attributions, many corruption scandals including the 2G spectrum case, the coal mining scam, Adarsh Housing Society scam and the Commonwealth Games scam were major factors behind the Indian National Congress-led UPA government's massive defeat in the 2014 Lok Sabha election. The severity of the corruption charges led to a loss of trust between Congress and the party. Time magazine listed the India's Telecoms Scandal as one of the Top 10 abuses of power.

However, the special court in New Delhi acquitted all accused in the 2G spectrum case including prime accused A Raja and Kanimozhi on December 21, 2017, the verdict was based on the fact that CBI could not find any evidence against the accused in those 7 years. Per the judgement, "Some people created a scam by artfully arranging a few selected facts and exaggerating things beyond recognition to astronomical levels." CBI and the Enforcement Directorate will appeal against the Special court acquittal verdict in the Delhi High Court.

Background

India is divided into 22 telecommunications zones, with 281 zonal licenses. In 2008, 122 new second-generation 2G Unified Access Service (UAS) licenses were granted to telecom companies on a first-come, first-served basis at the 2001 price. According to the CBI charge sheet, several laws were violated and bribes were paid to favour certain firms in granting 2G spectrum licenses. According to a CAG audit, licenses were granted to ineligible corporations, those with no experience in the telecom sector (such as Unitech and Swan Telecom) and those who had concealed relevant information. Although former Prime Minister Manmohan Singh advised Raja to allot 2G spectrum transparently and revise the license fee in a November 2007 letter, Raja rejected many of Singh's recommendations. In another letter that month, the Ministry of Finance expressed procedural concerns to the DOT; these were ignored, and the cut-off date was moved forward from 1 October 2007 to 25 September. On 25 September, the DOT announced on its website that applicants filing between 3:30 and 4:30 pm that day would be granted licenses. Although the corporation was ineligible, Swan Telecom was granted a license for ❒15.37 billion (US$220 million) and sold a 45-percent share to the UAE-based Etisalat for

₹42 billion (US$610 million). Unitech Wireless (a subsidiary of the Unitech Group) obtained a license for ₹16.61 billion (US$240 million), selling a 60-percent share for ₹62 billion (US$900 million) to Norway-based Telenor.

The following is a list of companies who received 2G licenses during Raja's term as telecom minister; the licenses were later cancelled by the Supreme Court:

Company	Telecom regions	# of licenses	Remarks
Adonis Projects	Haryana, Himachal Pradesh, Jammu & Kashmir, Punjab, Rajasthan, Uttar Pradesh (East)	6	Adonis Projects, Nahan Properties, Aska Projects, Volga Properties, Azare Properties & Hudson Properties were acquired by Unitech. Since Unitech Infrastructure and Unitech Builders & Estates were subsidiaries of Unitech Group, in 2008 Unitech had 22 2G licenses. Later that year, Telenor bought a majority share in the telecom company from the Unitech Group and now provides service as Uninor with 22 licences.
Nahan Properties	Assam, Bihar, North East, Orissa, Uttar Pradesh (east), West Bengal	6	
Aska Projects	Andhra Pradesh, Kerala, Karnataka	3	
Volga Properties	Gujarat, Madhya Pradesh, Maharashtra	3	
Azure Properties	Kolkata	1	
Hudson Properties	Delhi	1	
Unitech Builders & Estates	Tamil Nadu (including Chennai)	1	
Unitech Infrastructures	Mumbai	1	
Loop Telecom	Bihar, Gujarat, Himachal Pradesh, Kerala, Kolkata, Punjab, Rajasthan, Uttar Pradesh, West Bengal, Andhra Pradesh, Delhi, Haryana, Karnataka, Maharashtra, Odisha(Orissa), Tamil Nadu (including Chennai), Assam, Jammu & Kashmir, Madhya Pradesh	21	

Datacom Solutions	Andhra Pradesh, Assam, Bihar, Gujarat, Haryana, Himachal Pradesh, Jammu & Kashmir, Karnataka, Kerala, Kolkata, Madhya Pradesh, Maharashtra, Odisha, Rajasthan, Tamil Nadu (including Chennai), Uttar Pradesh, West Bengal, Delhi, Mumbai	21	Operates as Videocon Telecom
Shyam Telelink	Madhya Pradesh, Kerala, Kolkata, Punjab, Uttar Pradesh, West Bengal, Andhra Pradesh, Delhi, Haryana, Karnataka, Maharashtra, Odisha, Tamil Nadu (including Chennai), Assam, Jammu & Kashmir, North East	17	Shyam Telelink & Shyani Telelink have a combined 21 licenses. In late 2008 Russia-based Sistema bought a majority share in the company, which now operates as MTS India.
Shyani Telelink	Mumbai, Bihar, Gujarat, Himachal Pradesh	4	
Swan Telecom	Andhra Pradesh, Gujarat, Haryana, Karnataka, Kerala, Maharashtra, Punjab, Rajasthan, Tamil Nadu (including Chennai), Uttar Pradesh, Delhi, Mumbai	13	Swan was a subsidiary of Reliance Telecom established to circumvent the one-company-one-license rule. In 2008, Swan merged with Allianz Infratech; late in the year Abu Dhabi's Etisalat bought about 45 percent of the company, renaming it Etisalat DB Telecom.
Allianz Infratech	Bihar, Madhya Pradesh	2	
Idea Cellular	Assam, Punjab, Karnataka, Jammu and Kashmir, North East, Kolkata, West Bengal, Odisha(Orissa), Tamil Nadu (including Chennai)	9	Since Idea Cellular bought Spice Communications in 2008 for ₹27 billion (US $390 million), of the 122 spectrum licenses sold in 2008 Idea owns 13. Seven are in use by the company, and the remainder are overlapping licenses.
Spice Communications	Delhi, Andhra Pradesh, Haryana, Maharashtra	4	
S Tel	Assam, Jammu and Kashmir, Odisha(Orissa), North East, Bihar, Himachal Pradesh	6	In January 2009, Bahrain Telecommunications agreed to buy 49 percent of S Tel for $225 million. Chinnakannan Sivasankaran owns the remaining share. In May 2009, Sahara Group bought an 11.7-percent share in S Tel.
Tata Teleservices	Jammu and Kashmir, Assam, North East	3	In late 2008 Tata sold a 26-percent share to the Japanese NTT DoCoMo for about ₹130.7 billion (US$1.9 billion), or an enterprise value of ₹502.69 billion (US $7.3 billion).

Accused parties

The selling of the licenses drew attention to three groups: politicians and bureaucrats, who had the authority to sell licenses; corporations buying the licenses, and professionals who mediated between the politicians and corporations.

Politicians

The following charges were filed by the CBI and the Directorate General of Income Tax Investigation in the Special CBI Court.

A. Raja

- *Political career*: Four-time DMK member of Parliament (last won constituency Nilgiris, Tamil Nadu) and now not an MP, maker Union Minister of State for Rural Development (1999) and Health and Family Welfare (2003), former Union Cabinet Minister for Environment and Forests (2004) and Communication and Information Technology (2007 and 2009)
- *Allegation*: A joint investigative report by the CBI and the Income Tax Department alleged that Raja may have received a ₹30 billion (US $440 million) bribe for moving the cut-off date for spectrum applications forward. The changed deadline eliminated many applications, enabling Raja to favour a few applicants. The agencies also alleged that he used accounts in his wife's name in Mauritius and Seychelles banks for the kickbacks. A CBI charge sheet alleged that Raja conspired with the accused and arbitrarily refined the first-come, first-served policy to ensure that Swan and Unitech received licences. Instead of auctioning 2G spectrum, he sold it at the 2001 rate.
- *Charges*: Criminal breach of trust by a public servant (section 409), criminal conspiracy (Section 120-B), cheating (Section 420) and forgery (Sections 468 and 471); booked under the Prevention of Corruption Act for accepting illegal gratification.
- *Status*: Arrested by the CBI on 2 February 2011. Applied for bail on 9 May 2012, which was granted on 15 May. On 21 December 2017, he has been acquitted by a Special CBI Court.

M. K. Kanimozhi

- *Political career*: Daughter of five-time Chief Minister of Tamil Nadu M. Karunanidhi. DMK member of Parliament, representing Tamil Nadu in the Rajya Sabha.

- *Allegations*: According to the CBI charge sheet, Kanimozhi owns 20 percent of family-owned Kalaignar TV; her stepmother, Dayalu Ammal, owns 60 percent of the channel. The CBI alleges that Kanimozhi was the "active brain" behind the channel and conspired with Raja to coerce DB Realty cofounder Shahid Balwa to funnel ₹2 billion (US$29 million) to Kalaignar TV. Kanimozhi was in regular contact with Raja about the launch of Kalaignar TV. Raja advanced the channel's cause, facilitating its registration with the Ministry of Information and Broadcasting and adding it to DTH operator TATA Sky's lineup. Kanimozhi was charged with tax evasion by the Income Tax Department in Chennai.
- *Charges*: Criminal conspiracy to cause criminal breach of trust by a public servant and criminal conspiracy (Section 120-B), cheating (Section 420) and forgery (Sections 468 and 471), and booked under the Prevention of Corruption Act.
- *Status*: Arrested by the CBI on 20 May 2011. Granted bail on 28 November 2011, after 188 days in custody. On 21 December 2017, she has been acquitted by a Special CBI Court.

Bureaucrats

A number of bureaucrats were named in the CBI charge sheet filed in its Special Court.

Siddharth Behura

- *Position*: Telecom Secretary when the licenses were granted.
- *Allegations*: According to the CBI charge sheet, Behura conspired with Raja and several others. When the application deadline time was declared, from 3:30 to 4:30 pm Behura closed counters to block other telecom companies.
- *Charges*: Criminal breach of trust by a public servant (Section 409), criminal conspiracy (Section 120-B), cheating (Section 420) and forgery (Sections 468 and 471); booked under the Prevention of Corruption Act for accepting illegal gratuities.
- *Status*: Arrested by the CBI on 2 February 2011 and granted bail on 9 May 2012, and finally acquitted on 21 December 2017 by a Special CBI Court for lack of convincing evidence. In a 10 July 2012 joint parliamentary committee deposition, Behura blamed Raja for most of the decisions related to 2G spectrum auctions.

RK Chandolia

- *Position*: Raja's private secretary when the licenses were granted.
- *Allegations*: According to the CBI charge sheet Chandolia, like Behura, conspired with Raja and several others; when the application deadline time was declared from 3:30 to 4:30 pm, Chandolia joined Behura in shutting counters to physically block other telecom companies.
- *Charges*: Criminal conspiracy to cause criminal breach of trust by a public servant, criminal conspiracy (Section 120 B), cheating (Section 420) and forgery (Sections 468 and 471); booked under the Prevention of Corruption Act
- *Status*: Arrested by the CBI on 2 February 2011. Although he was granted bail by the special CBI court on 1 December 2011, the following day the High Court took *suo motu* notice of newspaper reports of the bail and stayed it. Chandolia appealed to the Supreme Court, and on 9 May 2012 the court upheld the bail grant. He was acquitted on 21 December 2017 by a Special CBI Court for lack of substantial evidence.

Executives

A number of executives were accused in the CBI charge sheet.

Sanjay Chandra

- *Position*: Former Unitech Wireless managing director
- *Charges*: Criminal conspiracy to cause criminal breach of trust by a public servant, criminal conspiracy (Section 120-B), cheating (Section 420) and forgery (Sections 468 and 471); booked under the Prevention of Corruption Act
- *Allegations*: Former CBI prosecutor AK Singh was implicated in a taped conversation sharing legal strategy and privileged information with Chandra.
- *Status*: Arrested by the CBI on 20 April 2011 and granted bail on 24 November, As of 21 December 2017 he has been acquitted by a special CBI Court.

Umashankar

- *Charges*: Criminal conspiracy to cause criminal breach of trust by a public servant, criminal conspiracy (Section 120-B), cheating (Section 420) and forgery (Sections 468 and 471); booked under the Prevention of Corruption Act
- *Allegations*: Former CBI prosecutor AK Singh was implicated in a taped conversation sharing legal strategy and privileged information with Umashankar.

- *Status*: Arrested by the CBI on 20 April 2008 and granted bail on 20 April 2008, As of 21 December 2017 he has been acquitted by a special CBI Court.

Gautam Doshi

- *Position*: Managing director, Reliance Anil Dhirubhai Ambani Group
- *Charges*: Criminal conspiracy to cause criminal breach of trust by a public servant, criminal conspiracy (Section 120-B), cheating (Section 420) and forgery (Sections 468 and 471); booked under the Prevention of Corruption Act
- *Status*: Arrested by the CBI on 20 April 2011 and granted bail on 24 November, As of 21 December 2017 he has been acquitted by a special CBI Court.

Hari Nair

- *Position*: Senior vice-president, Reliance Anil Dhirubhai Ambani Group
- *Charges*: Criminal conspiracy to cause criminal breach of trust by a public servant, criminal conspiracy (Section 120-B), cheating (Section 420) and forgery (Sections 468 and 471); booked under the Prevention of Corruption Act
- *Status*: Arrested by the CBI on 20 April 2011 and granted bail on 24 November, As of 21 December 2017 he has been acquitted by a special CBI Court.

Surendra Pipara

- *Position*: Senior vice-president, Reliance Anil Dhirubhai Ambani Group
- *Charges*: Criminal conspiracy to cause criminal breach of trust by a public servant, criminal conspiracy (Section 120-B), cheating (Section 420) and forgery (Sections 468 and 471); booked under the Prevention of Corruption Act
- *Status*: Arrested by the CBI on 20 April 2011 and granted bail on 24 November. As of 21 December 2017 he has been acquitted by a special CBI Court.

Vinod Goenka

- *Position*: Managing director, DB Realty and Swan Telecom
- *Charges*: Criminal conspiracy to cause criminal breach of trust by a public servant, criminal conspiracy (Section 120 B), cheating (Section 420), forgery (Sections 468 and 471) and fabrication of evidence (Section 193); booked under the Prevention of Corruption Act
- *Status*: Arrested by the CBI on 20 April 2011 and granted bail on 24 November. As of 21 December 2017 he has been acquitted by a special CBI Court.

Shahid Balwa

- *Position*: Corporate promoter, DB Realty and Swan Telecom
- *Charges*: Criminal conspiracy to cause criminal breach of trust by a public servant, criminal conspiracy (Section 120-B), cheating (Section 420), forgery (Sections 468 and 471) and fabrication of evidence (Section 193); booked under the Prevention of Corruption Act
- *Status*: Arrested by the CBI on 8 February 2011 and granted bail on 29 November, acquitted on 21 December 2017 by a special CBI Court.

Asif Balwa

- *Position*: Director, Kusegaon Fruits and Vegetables
- *Charges*: Criminal conspiracy to cause criminal breach of trust by a public servant, criminal conspiracy (Section 120-B), cheating (Section 420), forgery (Sections 468 and 471) and fabrication of evidence (Section 193); booked under the Prevention of Corruption Act
- *Status*: Arrested by the CBI on 29 March 2011 and granted bail on 28 November, acquitted on 21 December 2017 by a special CBI Court.

Rajiv Agarwal

- *Position*: Director, Kusegaon Fruits and Vegetables
- *Charges*: Criminal conspiracy to cause criminal breach of trust by a public servant, criminal conspiracy (Section 120-B), cheating (Section 420), forgery (Sections 468 and 471) and fabrication of evidence (Section 193); booked under the Prevention of Corruption Act
- *Status*: Arrested by the CBI on 29 March 2011 and granted bail on 28 November, acquitted on 21 December 2017 by a special CBI Court.

Sharath Kumar

- *Position*: Managing director, Kalaignar TV
- *Charges*: Criminal conspiracy to cause criminal breach of trust by a public servant, criminal conspiracy (Section 120-B), cheating (Section 420), forgery (Sections 468 and 471) and fabrication of evidence (Section 193); booked under the Prevention of Corruption Act
- *Status*: Arrested by the CBI on 20 May 2011 and granted bail on 28 November 2011, acquitted on 21 December 2017 by a special CBI Court.

Ravi Ruia

- *Position*: Vice-chair, Essar Group
- *Charges*: Criminal conspiracy (Section 120 B) and cheating (Section 420)
- *Status*: At large; as of August 2012, acquitted while at large on 21 December 2017 by a special CBI Court.

Anshuman Ruia

- *Position*: Director, Essar Group
- *Charges*: Criminal conspiracy (Section 120 B) and cheating (Section 420).
- *Status*: At large; acquitted while at large on 21 December 2017 by a special CBI Court.

Vikas Saraf

- *Position*: Director of strategy and planning, Essar Group
- *Charges*: Criminal conspiracy (Section 120 B) and cheating (Section 420 of the Indian Penal Code)
- *Status*: At large; acquitted while at large on 21 December 2017 by a special CBI Court.

Ishwari Prasad Khaitan

- *Position*: Corporate promoter, Loop Telecom
- *Charges*: Criminal conspiracy under (Section 120 B) and cheating (Section 420)
- *Status*: At large; acquitted while at large on 21 December 2017 by a special CBI Court.

Kiran Khaitan

- *Position*: Corporate promoter, Loop Telecom
- *Charges*: Criminal conspiracy (Section 120 B) and cheating (Section 420)
- *Status*: At large; acquitted while at large on 21 December 2017 by a special CBI Court.

Karim Morani

- *Position*: Corporate promoter and director, Cineyug Films
- *Allegations*: According to the Income Tax Department charge sheet, Morani-owned Cineyug Films was a part of the route used by Shahid Balwa to funnel ₹2 billion (US$29 million) illegally to Kalaignar TV. DB Realty corporate promoters Shahid Balwa and Vinod Goenka transferred ₹2,092.5 million (US$30 million) to Kusegaon Fruits and Vegetables, where Balwa's younger brother Asif was a director. Kusegaon then transferred ₹2 billion (US$29 million) to Cineyug Films, and Morani transferred it to Kalaignar TV.
- *Charges*: Criminal conspiracy to cause criminal breach of trust by a public servant, criminal conspiracy (Section 120-B), cheating (Section 420), forgery (Sections 468 and 471) and fabrication of evidence (Section 193); booked under the Prevention of Corruption Act
- *Status*: Arrested by the CBI on 30 May 2011 and granted bail on 28 November, promptly acquitted on 21 December 2017 by a "special CBI Court".

Corporations

Several companies were named in the CBI charge sheet.

Unitech Wireless

- *Charges*: Criminal conspiracy to cause criminal breach of trust by a public servant, criminal conspiracy (Section 120-B), cheating (Section 420) and forgery (Sections 468 and 471)
- *Status*: The company was acquitted on 21 December 2017 of any wrongdoing by Special CBI Court.

Reliance Telecom

- *Charges*: Criminal conspiracy to cause criminal breach of trust by a public servant, criminal conspiracy (Section 120-B) and cheating (Section 420)
- *Status*: As of December 2017, acquitted in 2G spectrum case.

Swan Telecom

- *Charges*: Criminal conspiracy to cause criminal breach of trust by a public servant, criminal conspiracy (Section 120-B) and cheating (Section 420)
- *Status*: The company was acquitted on 21 December 2017 of any wrongdoing by a Special CBI Court that was appointed for the purpose of acquitting the accused.

Other companies named in the charge sheet were:

- Loop Telecom
- Loop Mobile India
- Essar Tele Holding
- Essar Group (corporate parent of Essar Tele Holding)

Media role

OPEN and *Outlook* reported that journalists Barkha Dutt (editor of NDTV) and Vir Sanghvi (editorial director of the *Hindustan Times*) knew that corporate lobbyist Nira Radia influenced Raja's appointment as telecom minister, publicising Radia's phone conversations with Dutt and Sanghvi when Radia's phone was tapped by the Income Tax Department. According to critics, Dutt and Sanghvi knew about the link between the government and the media industry but delayed reporting the corruption.

Chronology

The Centre for Public Interest Litigation filed the first petition against the Union of India for irregularities in awarding 2G spectrum licenses. The petition alleged that the government lost $15.53 billion by issuing spectrum in 2008 based on 2001 prices, and by not following a competitive bidding process. This led to further petitions, and an investigation began in 2010.

2007

- *May*: A Raja becomes Telecom Minister.
- *August*: Allotment of 2G spectrum and Universal Access Service (UAS) licences by the Department of Telecommunications (DoT) begins.
- *25 September*: The Telecom Ministry issues a press release that its deadline for application is 1 October.
- *1 October*: DoT receives 575 applications for UAS licences from 46 companies.
- *2 November*: The prime minister writes to Raja, directing him to ensure the allotment of 2G spectrum in a fair and transparent manner and to ensure that the licence fee was revised. Raja rejects many of the prime minister's recommendations.
- *22 November*: In a letter to the DoT, the Finance Ministry raises procedural concerns. Its demand for a review is rejected.

2008

- *10 January*: The DoT decides to issue licences on first-come, first-served basis, advancing the cut-off date from 1 October to 25 September and announcing on its website that those applying between 3.30 and 4.30 pm would be granted licences in accordance with policy.
- Total collection from sale of 122 licenses was about 9200 Crore.[1776]
- Swan Telecom, Unitech and Tata Teleservices sell shares at much higher prices to Etisalat, Telenor and DoCoMo, respectively.

2009

- *4 May*: A telecom-watchdog NGO files a complaint with the Central Vigilance Commission (CVC) on illegalities in spectrum allocation to Loop Telecom.
- *19 May*: Another complaint is filed with the CVC by Arun Agarwal, highlighting the low-cost spectrum grant to Swan Telecom. The CVC directs the CBI to investigate irregularities in the allocation of 2G spectrum.
- *1 July*: Responding to a petition from S-Tel, the Delhi High Court rules the advancement of the cut-off date illegal.
- *21 October*: The CBI registers a case, filing a First Information Report against unknown officers of the DoT and unknown private persons and companies under provisions of the Indian Penal Code and the Prevention of Corruption Act.
- *22 October*: The Directorate General of Income Tax Investigation raids DoT offices.
- *16 November*: The CBI investigates a wiretapped conversation by corporate lobbyist Nira Radia to learn the involvement of middlemen in the grant of spectrum to telecom companies, seeking information from the Directorate General of Income Tax Investigation about Radia and her company.

2010

- *13 March*: The Supreme Court upholds the Delhi High Court ruling that the cutoff-date advancement was illegal.
- *31 March*: According to the Comptroller and Auditor General, there were large-scale irregularities in spectrum allocation.
- *2 April*: CBI Deputy Inspector General of Investigations Vineet Agarwal and Indian Revenue Service Director General of Income Tax Investigations Milap Jain, who were investigating the case, are transferred; Jain becomes Director General of International Taxation.

- *6 May*: Telephone conversation between Raja and Niira Radia, recorded by the Directorate General of Income Tax Investigation, made public. the Centre for Public Interest Litigation petitions the Delhi High Court for a special investigation of the case.
- *25 May*: Petition dismissed by the court.
- *August*: Dismissal appealed to the Supreme Court.
- *18 August*: High Court refuses to order the prime minister to rule on a request by Janata Party chief Subramanian Swamy to prosecute Raja.
- *13 September*: The Supreme Court asks the government and Raja to reply within 10 days to three petitions filed by the CPIL and others alleging a ₹70,000 crore (US$10 billion) scam in granting telecom licences in 2008.
- *24 September*: Swamy petitions the Supreme Court to order the PM to prosecute Raja.
- *27 September*: The Directorate General of Income Tax Investigation informs the Supreme Court of a probe of firms suspected to have violated the Foreign Exchange Management Act, saying it cannot confirm or deny Raja's involvement.
- *8 October*: The Supreme Court asks the government to respond to the Comptroller and Auditor General report about the case.
- *21 October*: Draft reports from the CAG are presented to the Supreme Court.
- *29 October*: The Supreme Court criticises the CBI for its slowness in investigating the case.
- *10 November*: The CAG submits a report on 2G spectrum to the government, stating a loss of ₹176,000 crore (US$26 billion) to the exchequer.
- *11 November*: The DoT files a Supreme Court affidavit that the CAG lacked the authority to question the 2008 policy decision.
- *14 November*: Raja resigns as telecom minister.
- *15 November*: Kapil Sibal placed in charge of Telecom Ministry.
- *20 November*: Affidavit on behalf of the PM filed in Supreme Court rejecting the charge of inaction on Swamy's complaint.
- *22 November*: The CBI and the Directorate General of Income Tax Investigation tell the SC they will file a charge sheet within three months, and the CBI says it will investigate the role of Niira Radia.
- *24 November*: The SC reserves verdict on Swamy's request to the PM to prosecute Raja.
- *25 November*: The SC criticises the CBI for not questioning Raja.
- *29 November*: The CBI files a status report on the probe.
- *30 November*: The SC questions the Central Vigilance Commission's P. J. Thomas' fitness to supervise the CBI probe, since he was Telecom Secretary at that time.

- *1 December*: The SC orders the original tapes of conversations by Radia. Raja questions the CAG findings.
- *2 December*: The government supplies Directorate General of Income Tax Investigation tapes to the SC, which criticises Raja for ignoring the PM's advice to delay the spectrum allocation.
- *8 December*: SC favours including 2001 (when first-come, first-served was the norm for spectrum allocation) in the probe period and asks the government to consider a special court. The Directorate General of Income Tax Investigation reports a money trail covering 10 countries, including Mauritius.
- *14 December*: PIL filed in SC, seeking the cancellation of new telecom licences and 2G spectrum allocated under Raja.
- *15 December*: Swamy petitions a Delhi court for his inclusion as a public prosecutor, saying Raja favoured "ineligible" companies Swan Telecom and Unitech Wireless in allocating spectrum.
- *16 December*: The SC decides to monitor the CBI inquiry.

2011

- *4 January*: Swamy petitions the SC for cancellation of the licenses.
- *10 January*: Supreme Court notifies the government of Swamy's petition, and issues notices to 11 companies which allegedly did not fulfill the roll-out obligations or were ineligible.
- *30 January*: The government's decision to regularise the licenses of companies which failed to meet the deadline is challenged in the Supreme Court.
- *2 February*: Raja, former Telecom Secretary Siddharth Behura and Raja's former personal secretary, R. K. Chandolia, are arrested.
- *8 February*: Raja is remanded to two more days of CBI custody, and Behura and Chandolia are placed in judicial custody. Swan Telecom corporate promoter Shahid Usman Balwa is arrested.
- *10 February*: The Supreme Court asks the CBI to investigate corporations which were beneficiaries of the spectrum allocation. Raja and Balwa are remanded to CBI custody for four more days by a special CBI court.
- *14 February*: Raja's custody is extended by three days, and Balwa's for four.
- *17 February*: Raja is sent to Tihar Jail under judicial custody.
- *18 February*: The Directorate General of Income Tax Investigation questions Kani Mozhi at its Chennai headquarters.
- *24 February*: The Directorate General of Income Tax Investigation tells a Delhi court that Balwa facilitated transactions to Kalaignar TV.
- *28 February*: Raja requests video-conferenced judicial proceedings, saying that he is threatened by other inmates.

- *1 March*: The CBI tells the SC that 63 people are under investigation. Raja appears in CBI court via video-conference.
- *14 March*: The Delhi High Court establishes a special court. Balwa is also allowed to appear via video-conference.
- *17 March*: The SC reserves judgment on licence cancellations, rejecting corporate claims that estoppel cannot be applied to protect illegality.
- *29 March*: The SC allows the CBI to file its chargesheet on 2 April instead of 31 March. Asif Balwa and Rajeev Agarwal are arrested.
- *2 April*: The CBI files its first chargesheet.
- *25 April*: The CBI files a second chargesheet, and Kanimozhi, Sharad Kumar and Karim Morani are summoned.
- *6 May*: Kanimozhi and Sharad Kumar appear, requesting bail, and Morani requests an appearance exemption on medical grounds. The SC issues a contempt of court notice to Sahara India Pariwar managing director Subrata Roy and two others for alleged interference in the Directorate General of Economic Enforcement investigation.
- *7 May*: The special CBI court reserves judgment on Kanimozhi and Kumar's bail requests.
- *14 May*: The special CBI court postpones judgment on the bail pleas for 20 May.
- *20 May*: The special court refuses Kanimozhi and Kumar's bail requests, ordering their arrest to prevent witness-tampering.
- *8 June*: Delhi HC judge Ajit Bharihoke again refuses bail Kanimozhi and Kumar's bail requests.
- *20 June*: The SC refuses Kanimozhi's bail request.
- *25 July*: Arguments begin, with Raja wanting to summon the prime minister and former finance minister P. Chidambaram as witnesses.
- *26 August*: The special CBI court allows Subramanian Swamy to argue his own case, primarily to address possible loopholes in its investigation.
- *30 August*: The Directorate General of Income Tax Investigation freezes accounts and attaches properties worth ₹223 crore (US$32 million) belonging to five companies (primarily related to DB Realty under the Prevention of Money Laundering Act (PMLA)).
- *1 September*: The Enforcement Directorate files a status report in Supreme Court of a Foreign Exchange Management Act violation of ₹100 billion.
- *15 September*: Swamy requests that P. Chidambaram should be charged.
- *22 September*: The CBI defends Chidambaram in the SC, blaming the DoT.
- *26 September*: The CBI requests criminal-breach-of-trust charges for Raja, Chandolia and Behura.

- *9 October*: The CBI files a First Information Report against Maran and his brother in the Aircel-Maxis deal.
- *10 October*: The SC reserves judgment on Swamy's request for a probe of Home Minister Chidambaram's role in the matter. The CBI arrests former telecom minister and DMK leader Dayanidhi Maran and his brother, Kalanithi Maran.
- *22 October*: The special CBI court finds *prima facie* evidence to try the 17 accused (including Raja) on charges including criminal conspiracy, breach of trust, cheating and forgery.
- *3 November*: The special CBI court dismisses bail requests of all eight applicants, including Kanimozhi.
- *8 November*: The special court orders CBI to provide Swamy with copies of files on equity sales by telecom companies in its investigation of P. Chidambaram's involvement.
- *9 November*: The Delhi HC refuses bail to Karim Morani on health grounds, promising a ruling to the CBI on five other bail requests by 1 December.
- *11 November*: Trial of the 17 accused begins in the Patiala House special CBI court.
- *14 November*: The United Progressive Alliance government asks the SC to restrain Swamy from publicly accusing the UPA leadership, especially Home Minister P Chidambaram and UPA chair Sonia Gandhi.
- *22 November*: The special court moves the trial to the Tihar jail, after a Delhi high-court order.
- *23 November*: The SC grants bail to five corporate executives: Sanjay Chandra of Unitech Wireless, Vinod Goenka of Swan Telecom and the Reliance Group's Gautam Doshi, Surendra Pipara and Hari Nayar.
- *28 November*: The Delhi High Court grants bail to DMK MP Kanimozhi and four others: Karim Morani, Sharad Kumar, Asif Balwa and Rajeev Agarwal, upholding the principle of parity under Section 144 of the Constitution of India in a SC order.
- *29 November*: The special court grants bail to Shahid Balwa, citing the principle of parity; the SC and HC had granted bail to 10 other accused parties.
- *1 December*: The special court grants bail to Raja's former private secretary, R. K. Chandolia, ordering him not to visit the DoT without prior court permission.
- *2 December*: Claiming *suo motu*, the HC stays trial-court bail granted to R. K. Chandolia.
- *7 December*: The SC stays the HC's *suo motu* order against Chandolia's bail request.

- *8 December*: The special CBI court accepts Swamy's request to summon Chidambaram as a witness and question two witnesses: senior CBI and Finance Ministry officials.
- *12 December*: The CBI files a third chargesheet, naming Essar Group corporate promoters Ravi Ruia, his son Anshuman Ruia and its director of strategy and planning, Vikas Saraf, and Loop Telecom promoters Kiran Khaitan and her husband, I P Khaitan. It also charges Loop Mobile India, its subsidiary Loop Telecom and Essar Tele Holding.
- *16 December*: The HC rejects the bail request of Siddharth Behura: "He was the 'perpetrator' of the illegal designs of Raja and would not claim benefit of parity with 10 others released on bail".

2012

- *2 February*: The Supreme Court cancels the 122 licenses issued by Raja and imposes a ₹50 million ($1,018,122) fine on Unitech, Swan and Tata Teleservices and a ₹5 million fine on Loop Telecom Pvt Ltd, S-Tel, Allianz Infratech and Sistema Shyam Tele Services. The SC requested a trial-court ruling about whether Home Minister P Chidambaram should be charged.
- *4 February*: The special court, under justice O.P Saini, dismisses Swamy's request to charge Chidambram.
- *8 February*: The Enforcement Directorate and the Directorate General of Income Tax Investigation charge DMK leader Dayanidhi Maran with money laundering and his brother, Kalanithi Maran, for allegedly receiving about ₹5.5 billion illegally in the Aircel-Maxis deal.
- *9 February*: Essar Group and Loop Telecom appeal their special-court subpoenas to the Supreme Court.
- *15 February*: The Supreme Court refuses an interim stay on the February 22 summonses of Essar Group, Loop Telecom and their officials by the special court.
- *22 February*: The CBI files a complaint with the CVC about witness-tampering by the Directorate General of Income Tax Investigation, allegedly at the behest of DMK Minister of State for Finance SS Palanimanickam. Swamy said he would notify the Supreme Court.
- *23 February*: Swamy petitions the Supreme Court to overturn the trial-court dismissal of his request to charge Union Home Minister P. Chidambaram.
- *2 March*: The government of India files a review petition in Supreme Court of the court's 2 February order cancelling the 122 licenses, questioning the court's authority to supersede the first-come, first-served policy but not challenging the validity of the cancellations. Raja and

Sistema (majority shareholder in MTS India, Uninor and other telecom companies) also file a SC review petition.
- *4 April*: Except for the government of India's partial review petition, the Supreme Court dismisses all 10 review petitions. Companies dismissed include Videocon Telecommunications, S Tel, Sistema Shyam Teleservices, Tata Teleservices, Unitech Wireless (Tamil Nadu), Etisalat DB Telecom and Idea Cellular.
- *12 April*: The government requests an advisory opinion from the Supreme Court on issues arising from its 2 February ruling.
- *9 May*: The Supreme Court grants bail to Siddharth Behura; and upheld RK Chandolia's bail. Raja requests bail.
- *15 May*: Bail granted to Raja after 15 months, on condition that he have court permission to visit Tamil Nadu.
- *6 June*: The special court allows Raja to visit Tamil Nadu.
- *3 July*: Briefing the joint parliamentary committee probing the case, the Enforcement Directorate said it has enough evidence to convict DMK chief Karunanidhi's wife and daughter, Kanimozhi.
- *31 July*: Former DoT senior official A. K. Srivastava confirmed the CBI's allegation in his testimony, and Raja (as telecom minister) was the final authority on policy matters. In an earlier statement to CBI, he said that Raja had recorded the cut—off date of 1 October 2007 in a DoT file.
- *1 August*: The Supreme Court, in its advisory opinion on the 2G judgment, says that the implementation of the first-come, first-served policy was flawed. According to the Chief Justice, "The moment you change the criterion and distort the policy, it ceases to be FCFS policy. If you insist on making payment at the last minute after changing the cut-off date, then it is not FCFS, it is an out-of-turn policy."
- *3 August*: In accordance with a Supreme Court directive, the government of India revises the spectrum value to ▯140 billion (US$2.0 billion); this discredits the zero-loss theory and illustrates the ▯1,760 billion (US $26 billion) revenue loss calculated by the CAG.
- *9 August*: The government again requests an extension from the Supreme Court (this time to 12 November) of the deadline to begin auctioning spectrum licences. After cancelling 122 licences in February, the court had given it four months to re-auction them (which had been extended to 31 August).
- *11 November*: After one year of trial, 77 of 154 witnesses have been deposed.

2013

- *20 April:* Communist Party of India senior MP Gurudas Dasgupta accuses Manmohan Singh of "dereliction of duty", alleging that the PM was aware of irregularities in the allocation of telecom licences. According to Dasgupta, in a November 2007 letter Kamal Nath advised the Prime Minister to establish a group of ministers to allocate spectrum. He also referred to a note from the Cabinet Secretary recommending that the assessed value of spectrum licences be increased.
- *23 April:* In a 112-page written statement to the joint parliamentary committee, Raja said that he met with P. Chidambaram and Prime Minister Singh several times from November 2007 to July 2008 to inform them of all 2G-related decisions and Singh agreed with him.

2017

- *21 December:* A special CBI court acquits everyone accused in the 2G spectrum case stating that the prosecution has failed to prove any charge against any of the accused, made in its well choreographed charge sheet.[1777]

Licence cancellations

On 2 February 2012 the Supreme Court ruled on petitions filed by Subramanian Swamy and the Centre for Public Interest Litigation (CPIL) represented by Prashant Bhushan, challenging the 2008 allotment of 2G licenses, cancelling all 122 spectrum licences granted during Raja's term as communications minister. and described the allocation of 2G spectrum as "unconstitutional and arbitrary". The bench of GS Singhvi and Asok Kumar Ganguly imposed a fine of ₹50 million (US$730,000) on Unitech Wireless, Swan Telecom and Tata Teleservices and a ₹5 million (US$73,000) fine on Loop Telecom, S Tel, Allianz Infratech and Sistema Shyam Tele Services. According to the ruling the current licences would remain in place for four months, after which time the government would reissue the licences.

In its ruling the court said that former telecom minister A. Raja "wanted to favour some companies at the cost of the public exchequer", listing seven steps he took to ensure this:

1. After becoming telecom minister, Raja directed that all applications for spectrum licences would be held pending Telecom Regulatory Authority of India recommendations.

2. The 28 August 2007 TRAI recommendations were not presented to the full Telecom Commission, which would have included the finance secretary. Although the TRAI recommendations for allocation of 2G spectrum had serious financial implications (and finance ministry input was required under the Government of India Transaction of Business Rules, 1961), Telecom Commission non-permanent members were not notified of the meeting.
3. The DoT officers attending the 10 October 2007 Telecom Commission meeting were coerced into approving the TRAI recommendations, or they would have "incurred" Raja's "wrath".
4. Since the Cabinet had approved the Group of Ministers recommendations, the DoT had to discuss the issue of spectrum pricing with the finance ministry. However, Raja did not consult the finance minister or other officials because the finance secretary had objected to allocating 2G spectrum at 2001 rates.
5. Raja dismissed the law minister's suggestion that the issue should be presented to the Group of Ministers. After receiving the PM's 2 November 2007 letter suggesting transparency in spectrum allocation of the spectrum, Raja said it would be unfair, discriminatory, arbitrary and capricious to auction spectrum to new applicants because it would not give them a level playing field. Although a 24 September DoT press release said that 1 October would be the application deadline, he changed the deadline to 25 September. Raja's arbitrary action, "though appear[ing] to be innocuous was actually intended to benefit some of the real estate firms who did not have any experience in dealing with telecom services and who had made applications only on 24 September 2007, i.e. one day before the cut-off date fixed by the C&IT minister on his own".
6. The 25 September cut-off date decided by Raja on 2 November was not made public until a 10 January 2008 press release in which he changed the first-come, first-served principle which had been in operation since 2003. "This enabled some of the applicants, who had access either to the minister or DoT officers, get bank drafts prepared towards performance guarantee of about Rs 16 billion".
7. "The manner in which the exercise for grant of LoIs to the applicants was conducted on 10 January 2008 leaves no room for doubt that everything was stage managed to favour those who were able to know in advance change in the implementation of the first-come-first-served policy." As a result, some companies who had submitted applications in 2004 or 2006 were pushed down the list in favour of those who had applied in August and September 2007.

Companies affected by cancellations

The table below lists the companies whose license were cancelled.

Company	Parent company	# of licences cancelled
Uninor	Joint venture of Unitech Group of India and Telenor of Norway Unitech Group	22
Sistema Shyam TeleServices Limited, now MTS India	Joint venture of the Shyam Group of India and Sistema of Russia	21
Loop Mobile (formerly BPL Mobile)	Khaitan Holding Group	21
Videocon Telecom	Videocon	21
Etisalat-DB	Joint venture of Swan Telecom of India and Etisalat of the UAE	15
Idea Cellular	Aditya Birla Group (49.05%), Axiata (Malaysia, 15%) & Providence Equity Partners (U.S., 10.6%)	13
S Tel	Joint venture of C Sivasankaran of India and Batelco of Bahrain. After the Supreme Court ruling, Batelco sold its 42.7% share to Sivasankaran-owned Sky City Foundation for 65.8 million Bahraini dinar ($174.5 million).	6
Tata Teleservices	Tata Group	3

Aftermath

In addition to Batelco's exit, on 21 February 2012 Telenor (the majority shareholder in Uninor) terminated its agreement with Unitech and sued it for "indemnity and compensation". On 23 February 2012, Etisalat of Etasalat-DB Telecom sued DB Realty corporate promoters Shahid Balwa and Vinod Goenka for fraud and misrepresentation.

After the special CBI court verdict on December 21, 2017 acquitting all the accused, the government faces compensation claims worth over Rs 17,000 crore from telcos like Videocon Telecom, Loop Telecom and STel who suffered loss of business after the Supreme Court scrapped 122 licences in 2012.[1778]

Aircel-Maxis deal controversy

On 6 June 2011 former Aircel chief C. Sivasankaran complained to the CBI about not receiving a telecom licence and being forced by telecom minister Dayanidhi Maran to sell Aircel to the Malaysia-based Maxis Communications group, owned by T. Ananda Krishnan. The licences were allegedly issued after the deal was made. Sivasankaran also alleged that brothers Dayanidhi and Kalanithi Maran received kickbacks in the form of investments by the Maxis group through the Astro network in Sun TV Network, owned by the Maran family. In the wake of the allegations, Maran resigned on 7 July.

On 10 October, the CBI registered a case and raided properties owned by the Marans. CBI sources said that although no evidence of coercion was found in the Aircel sale, they found substantial evidence that Maran had favoured the company's takeover by Maxis and deliberately delayed Sivasankar's files. On 8 February 2012, the Enforcement Directorate registered a money-laundering case against the Maran brothers for allegedly receiving illegal compensation of about ₹5.5 billion in the Aircel-Maxis deal.

During the CBI probe Sivasankaran said that the Maran brothers had forced him to sell his 74% share in Aircel to Maxis by threatening his life, giving the CBI a list of over 10 witnesses. In September 2012, the CBI said it finished its Indian investigation and was awaiting the response to a letter rogatory sent to Malaysia and a questionnaire from T. Ananda Krishnan before filing a chargesheet. On 29 August 2014, the CBI filed a chargesheet against Dayanidhi Maran, his brother Kalanithi Maran, Malaysian businessman T Ananda Krishnan, Malaysian national Augustus Ralph Marshall, six others and four firms — Sun Direct TV Pvt Ltd, Maxis Communication Berhad, Astro All Asia Network PLC and South Asia Entertainment Holding Ltd as accused in the case. On 29 October 2014, special CBI judge OP Saini said that he found enough evidence to proceed with the prosecution and hence summoned former telecom minister Dayanidhi Maran and others as accused. Based on the CBI chargesheet, the Enforcement Directorate (ED) on 1 April 2015, attached Maran brothers' properties worth Rs 742 crore.

Subramanian Swamy alleged that in 2006 a company controlled by Karti Chidambaram, the son of Minister of Finance P. Chidambaram, received a five-percent share of Aircel to get part of ₹40 billion paid by Maxis Communications for the 74-percent share of Aircel. According to Swamy, Chidambaram withheld Foreign Investment Promotion Board clearance of the deal until his son received the five-percent share in Siva's company. The issue was raised a number of times in Parliament by the opposition, which demanded Chidambaram's resignation. Although he and the government denied the allegations, *The Pioneer* and *India Today* reported the existence of documents showing that Chidambaram delayed approval of the foreign direct investment proposal by about seven months.

In July 2018, the CBI named P Chidambaram and Karti Chidambaram as accused in its supplementary charge sheet. The charge sheet named 16 other co-accused, including former finance secretaries Ashok Chawla, Ashok Jha, former Aircel CEO V Srinivasanand, Maxis owners T Ananda Krishnan and Ralph Marshal.

Response to the allegations

When Indian media began citing the CAG report identifying the loss at ▯1.76 trillion (short scale), the Indian opposition parties unanimously demanded the formation of a joint parliamentary committee to investigate the allegations. Although the government rejected their demand, when the winter session of Parliament began on 9 November 2010 the opposition again pressed for a JPC; again, their demand was rejected. The demand for a JPC gained further momentum when the CAG report was tabled in Parliament on 16 November 2010. The opposition blocked the proceedings, again pressing for a JPC; the government again rejected their demand, creating an impasse. Speaker of the Lok Sabha Meira Kumar unsuccessfully attempted to resolve the impasse. The winter session of Parliament concluded on 13 December 2010. Although 22 new bills were planned to be introduced, 23 pending bills passed and three bills withdrawn, Parliament functioned for only nine hours. On 22 February 2011, after resisting opposition demands for over three months, the government announced that it would form a JPC. The JPC criticised the CBI for its leniency to the PM, the Attorney General, Dayanidhi Maran and Chidambaram and its reluctance to investigate their roles on 24 July 2012. After questioning former telecom minister Dayanidhi Maran, his brother Kalanithi and the head of Maxis Communications, the CBI alleged that the Maran brothers accrued an illegal ▯5.50 billion by the sale of Sun Direct TV shares at highly "inflated prices".

In early November 2010 Jayalalithaa accused state chief minister M Karunanidhi of protecting Raja from corruption charges, calling for Raja's resignation. By mid-November, Raja resigned. At that time, comptroller Vinod Rai issued show-cause notices to Unitech, S Tel, Loop Mobile, Datacom (Videocon) and Etisalat to respond to his assertion that the 85 licenses granted to these companies did not have the capital required at application or were otherwise illegal. It was speculated that because these companies provide some consumer service, they would receive large fines but retain their licenses.

In June 2011 Prime Minister Manmohan Singh criticised the CAG for commenting on policy issues, warning it "to limit the office to the role defined in the constitution." After Singh's criticism the CAG conducted a "rigorous internal appraisal" and stood by its findings, citing additional events as corroboration. The CAG reiterated that there was "an undeniable loss to the exchequer", the calculation of which was based on three estimates: the 3G auctions and the

Swan and Unitech transactions. It cited the Supreme Court ruling of 2 February 2012 that the actions of Raja and officers at the Department of Telecom were "wholly arbitrary, capricious and contrary to the public interest, apart from being violative of the doctrine of equality. The material produced for the quote showed that the Minister for C&IT wanted to favour some companies at the cost of the public exchequer." It said its estimate of loss of 1.76-lakh crore was justified, since the May 2012 TRAI collation of reserve prices for 2G spectrum was about the same as that in the November 2010 CAG report. TRAI had recommended a reserve price for 2G spectrum of ₹180 billion for a pan-India 5 MHz licence, higher than the 3G value of ₹167.50 billion for 5 MHz used by the CAG for arriving at a loss figure of ₹1,760 billion. It concluded that it was only examining the "implementation of policy", and policy-making was the government's prerogative.

Joint parliamentary committee

The JPC consisted of half United Progressive Alliance members and half opposition members. Twelve were from the Lok Sabha, and eight from the Rajya Sabha. Of the Lok Sabha MPs, eight were from the Congress Party and four from the BJP. The following JPC members investigated the 2G allegations:

Name	Party
Kishore Chandra Deo	Congress
Paban Singh Ghatowar	Congress
Jai Prakash Agarwal	Congress
Deepender Singh Hooda	Congress
P. C. Chacko	Congress
Manish Tewari	Congress
Nirmal Khatri	Congress
Adhir Ranjan Chowdhury	Congress
T. R. Baalu	Dravida Munnetra Kazhagam
Kalyan Banerjee	Trinamool Congress
Jaswant Singh	BJP
Yashwant Sinha	BJP
Harin Pathak	BJP
Gopinath Munde	BJP
Sharad Yadav	Janata Dal (United)
Dara Singh Chauhan	Bahujan Samaj Party

Akhilesh Yadav	Samajwadi Party
Gurudas Dasgupta	Communist Party of India
Arjun Charan Sethi	Biju Janata Dal
M. Thambi Durai	All India Anna Dravida Munnetra Kazhagam

Verdict

On December 21, 2017 Special CBI Court acquitted all the persons alleged.Finally Indian Supreme Court judgement all are innocents, it's smallest mistake of CIG. Because of to change election results of 2014.[1779]

External links

- Transcripts : The Radia Tapes[1780] contains all the leaked audio transcripts between corporate lobbyist Nira Radia and other high-profile people.
- 2G Scam: In the dock (in pictures:HT)[1781]
- Case Study on the Supreme Court Ruling on the 2G Spectrum Scam[1782]

2011 Indian anti-corruption movement

2011 Indian anti-corruption movement	
 Anna Hazare's hunger strike at Jantar Mantar in New Delhi, on the second day of his fast	
Date	4 April 2011 – 28 December 2011
Location	India
Caused by	Corruption in public life • Government corruption • Police corruption • Judicial corruption • Corporate corruption • Kleptocracy • Electoral fraud • Red tape • Discretionary powers of politician • Black money
Goals	• Enactment of anti-corruption legislature, Jan Lokpal Bill for ombudsman
Methods	Non violent protest
Resulted in	• Resolution passed in Parliament accepting Jan Lokpal Bill on 27 August 2011, Government again withdrawn Resolution on 22 December 2011, Government Cabinet introduced The Lokpal Bill, 2011 in the parliament but failed to pass. • protests renewed in 2012 when Rajya Sabha failed to pass the Bill • 1 Dead or more, 54 injured
Casualties	
Death(s)	1

The **Indian anti-corruption movement**, commencing in 2011, was a series of demonstrations and protests across India intended to establish strong legislation and enforcement against perceived endemic political corruption. The movement was named among the "Top 10 News Stories of 2011" by *Time* magazine.

The movement gained momentum from 5 April 2011, when anti-corruption activist Anna Hazare began a hunger strike at the Jantar Mantar in New Delhi.

The chief legislative aim of the movement was to alleviate corruption in the Indian government through introduction of the Jan Lokpal Bill. Another aim, spearheaded by Ramdev, was the repatriation of black money from Swiss and other foreign banks.

Grievances of mass protesters focussed on legal and political issues, including political corruption, kleptocracy, and other forms of corruption. The movement was primarily one of non-violent civil resistance, featuring demonstrations, marches, acts of civil disobedience, hunger strikes, and rallies, as well as the use of social media to organise, communicate, and raise awareness. The protests were nonpartisan and most protesters were hostile to attempts made by political parties to use them to strengthen their own political agendas.

Background

Issues regarding corruption in India have become increasingly prominent in recent years. The country was subject to socialist-inspired economic policies dating from independence in 1947 until the 1980s. Over-regulation, protectionism, and government ownership of industry led to slow economic growth, high unemployment, and widespread poverty. This system of bureaucratic control by government is called the License Raj and lies at the core of endemic corruption.

The Vohra Report of 1993, submitted by the former Indian Union Home Secretary Narinder Nath Vohra, studied the issue of the criminalisation of politics. The report contained several observations made by official agencies on the criminal network which was virtually running a parallel government. It also discussed criminal gangs who enjoyed the patronage of politicians and the protection of government functionaries. It revealed that political leaders had become leaders of street gangs and rogue elements in the military. Over the years, criminals had been elected to local bodies, State Assemblies, and the Parliament.

The Right to Information Act (RTI) of 2005 helped civilians work effectively towards tackling corruption. It allows Indian citizens to request information, for a fixed fee of ▯10 (US$0.22), from a "public authority" (a body of Government or "instrumentality of State"). In turn, this public authority is required to reply to the request within thirty days. Activists have used this to uncover corruption cases against various politicians and bureaucrats – one consequence being that some of those activists have been attacked and even killed.

In the years immediately preceding the 2011 anti-corruption protests there were various notable examples of alleged corruption in the country. These included the Adarsh Housing Society Scam, the 2010 housing loan scam, the Radia tapes controversy, and the 2G spectrum case. In February 2011, the Supreme Court of India ordered all trial courts in the country to expedite handling of corruption cases and the President of India, Pratibha Patil, stated that measures to ratify the United Nations Convention Against Corruption and other legislative and administrative measures necessary to improve transparency would be taken. A month later, Chief Vigilance Commissioner P.J. Thomas was forced to resign on charges of corruption by the Supreme Court.

A worldwide 50-city Dandi March II, organised by People for Lok Sabha, took place in March 2011 as did the "Drive around Delhi" protest.

April 2011 protests

Anna Hazare wanted a joint committee to be formed, comprising members of the government and of civil society, to draft tougher anti-corruption legislation. Manmohan Singh, then Prime Minister of India, rejected Hazare's demand and so Hazare began a hunger strike on 5 April 2011 at Jantar Mantar in Delhi. He said that the fast would continue until the legislation was enacted. His action attracted considerable support, including some people who joined him in fasting. Prominent representatives of opposition political parties, including the Bharatiya Janata Party and the Communist Party of India (Marxist), indicated their support for Hazare and demanded government action. Hazare would not allow politicians to sit with him and those who tried to join, such as Uma Bharti and Om Prakash Chautala, were turned away.

Protests in sympathy with Hazare spread to various Indian cities, including Bangalore, Mumbai, Chennai, and Ahmedabad. Prominent figures from Bollywood, sports and business indicated their support and there were also gatherings outside India, including in the US, Britain, France and Germany.

The government squabbled with the activists, insisting that the drafting committee would be headed by a government-appointed minister and not a civil society member as the protesters had demanded to avoid allowing the government to make the bill less powerful.

On 6 April, Agriculture Minister Sharad Pawar resigned from the group of ministers that had been charged with reviewing the draft bill. Hazare had accused him of being corrupt. On 9 April, the government agreed to establish a joint committee. This came from a compromise that there would be a politician chairman, Pranab Mukherjee, and an activist non-politician co-chairman, Shanti Bhushan. Bhushan was one of the original drafters of the Lokpal Bill along with Hazare, Justice N. Santosh Hegde, advocate Prashant Bhushan and RTI activist Arvind Kejriwal.

The first meeting of the Lokpal Bill drafting committee was held on 16 April. The government agreed to audio-record the committee's meetings and to hold public consultations before a final draft was prepared but refused Hazare's demand that the proceedings be televised live.

June protest

Ramdev had announced in April that he would launch a people's anti-corruption movement called Bharat Swabhiman Andolan. On 13 May it was announced that India had completed ratification of the UN Convention against Corruption, a process that had begun in 2010. Then, in the early days of June, four senior Union Ministers - Pranab Mukherjee, Kapil Sibal, Pawan Kumar Bansal and Subodh Kant Sahay - met Ramdev to discuss his concerns.

Ramdev supported Hazare's fast and subsequently led a second major protest at the Ramlila Maidan, New Delhi on 4 June 2011. He intended to highlight the need for legislation to repatriate black money deposited abroad. He demanded that such untaxed money should be declared to be the wealth of the nation and, further, that the act of caching money alleged to have been obtained illegally in foreign banks should be declared a crime against the state.

The Ramlila Maidan was booked for 40 days to allow the protest to happen. Preparations included setting up toilet, drinking water and medical facilities, as well as a media centre. Ramdev claimed that more than 100 million people were directly involved with the Bharat Swabhiman Andolan. Almost 3.2 million "netizens" joined the campaign.

On 5 June, police raided the Maidan, detaining Ramdev and removing his supporters after firing tear gas shells and lathicharging. 53 people, including 20 police officers, were treated for injuries. Finance Minister Pranab Mukherjee called the police action "unfortunate" but added that the government had to do that as Ramdev had no permission to hold the protest. Ministers said that permission had been granted for a yoga camp with 5,000 attendees but not for a political protest that had gathered 65,000 people.

It was alleged that the action was not a spontaneous decision but had been planned for several days. The police said Ramdev had been informed shortly beforehand that permission to continue his agitation had been cancelled. By that time, over 5000 police officers had been prepared for action. There was an allegation that CCTV footage of the raid was missing.

On 6 June, the National Human Rights Commission of India requested that reports of the events be provided within two weeks by the Union Home Secretary, Delhi Chief Secretary and the Delhi City Commissioner of Police. Hazare responded to the events by holding a one-day hunger strike. Protests were held in many parts of country, including the cities of Chennai, Bangalore, Mumbai, Hyderabad, Jammu, and Lucknow. They also spread to Nepal.

Ramdev said that a second phase of the Bharat Swabhiman Yatra would begin in October and would cover a distance of 100,000 kilometres (62,000 mi).

After the protest

Civil society response

Ramdev accused the government of not being serious about discussing issues of corruption and black money, alleging that government negotiator Kapil Sibal had cheated him through a "scheming and cunning" attitude. He alleged that there was a conspiracy to kill him and a "threat" was given to him during a meeting with senior ministers. He also claimed that the ruling government chairperson Sonia Gandhi and the United Progressive Alliance government will be responsible for any threat to his life and alleged that he was nearly strangled by the police. After being evicted from Delhi, Ramdev wanted to continue his fast from Noida but was denied permission to do so by the Uttar Pradesh government. He decided to continue his hunger strike and satyagraha from Haridwar only until 12 June 2011.

Hazare said there might have been some faults with Ramdev's agitation but that the beating up of people at night rather than in the day-time was a "blot on democracy" and that "there was no firing otherwise the eviction was similar to Jallianwala Bagh incident." He said that the "strangulation of democracy" would cause civil society to launch protests throughout the country to "teach government a lesson". Civil society leaders, such as Arvind Kejriwal, said that the use of police force on non-violent sleeping protesters was undemocratic.

Government response

Congress General Secretary Digvijay Singh said that the government had reached an agreement before the protests were held. Prime Minister Manmohan Singh wrote to Ramdev, asking to cease-and-desist from holding the protests. Nationalist Congress Party General Secretary Tariq Anwar said that "Both Hazare and Ramdev are blackmailing the government and they should first peep into their own hearts." Pawan Bansal commented on the midnight police action and said that "It was not a crackdown, we [the government] had to do it to maintain law and order".

All India Congress Committee secretary Janardan Dwivedi described Ramdev's protest as a "political game" by the Bharatiya Janata Party, pointing out that despite being treated in the same hospital as Nigamananda, a protestor who had fasted for over two months regarding a different matter, Ramdev got more attention.

Political party response

- The Bharatiya Janata Party called the police action to break up the hunger strike "undemocratic". Gujarat Chief Minister Narendra Modi strongly condemned the incident comparing atrocities on Ramlila ground with Ravana-Lila, adding that "It is one of the worst days of Indian history. The Prime Minister had said during the elections that he would bring back black money stashed in Swiss banks within 100 days of coming into power. But today, it is two years and nothing has happened." L. K. Advani said that the police action reminded him of the Jallianwala Bagh massacre and added that the police crackdown on Ramdev is a "naked fascism". Leader of the Opposition in the Lok Sabha Sushma Swaraj said: "This is not democracy. .. the police cannot alone have taken such a step. It had the approval of the Prime Minister and full approval of the Congress President.
- Bahujan Samaj Party leader and Uttar Pradesh Chief Minister, Mayawati, condemned the government's midnight crackdown on Ramdev and demanded that Supreme Court of India order an investigation into the incident stating that justice cannot be expected from the Central Government.
- The Samajwadi Party chief Mulayam Singh Yadav condemned the incident saying that the action shows Centre has lost its mental balance. Charging the ruling Indian National Congress party, Yadav further said: "A Congress leader said that Baba is a thug. I want to say that Congress is the biggest thug and it should introspect its deeds. "The government swooped down on Ramdev and his supporters as if it were carrying an attack on a foreign enemy," Yadav told reporters at a press conference.
- Rashtriya Janata Dal leader Lalu Prasad Yadav accused Ramdev of being a front for the Rashtriya Swayamsevak Sangh.
- The Communist Party of India (Marxist) termed the police action at the protest site of Ramdev as "deplorable and shortsighted". However, they found fault with the yoga guru for making the issue of black money "farcical" by entering into a secret agreement with government. "The manner in which Ramdev's demands were drafted and the way in which he has conducted his interactions with the government, coming to a secret agreement to withdraw the hunger strike on the basis of assurances, then reneging and announcing its extension trivialised the seriousness of the issue of black money and made it farcical," the party said.
- The Shiv Sena strongly condemned the police action against Ramdev.
- Nitish Kumar, leader of Janata Dal (United), and the Chief Minister of Bihar, condemned the attack saying "It is a major blow to democracy and an attack on the democratic rights of the people ... It is also an attack on the fundamental rights of the citizens."

Figure 300: *India Against Corruption protesters in Pune, April 2011*

Suo Moto cognizance by the Supreme Court

The Supreme Court of India issued notices to the Union Home Secretary, Chief Secretary of Delhi, Delhi administration, and Delhi Police Commissioner expressing its displeasure that the entire contents of the petition-Wikipedia:Please clarify had been leaked to the media before the matter came up for hearing. On 29 August 2011, the Court blamed the Delhi Police for the forcible eviction.

August protests

By mid-June, the Jan Lokpal drafting committee was in disagreement and government representatives said that if a consensus was not reached then two drafts would be sent to the Cabinet, being those of the government and of the civil society representatives. Hazare declared that if the government version of the bill was passed by parliament, he would start a hunger strike from 16 August 2011. On 15 August, he announced that the fast would begin on the following day.

The government imposed Section 144 at Jayaprakash Narayan Park, Rajghat and Delhi Gate, prohibiting assembly of five or more people. Hazare was detained by Delhi Police in the early morning of 16 August before he could start his hunger strike. More than 1200 supporters, including members of Team

Anna, were also taken into preventative custody. Most of the supporters, including Kiran Bedi and Shanti Bushan, were released by early evening. Hazare was remanded to Tihar Jail after he refused to sign a personal bail bond. Within hours, a Team Anna spokesperson said that he had begun a hunger protest in custody and was not accepting even water to drink. The arrests set off a groundswell of protests across the country and were condemned by opposition political parties and some non-government organisations. Parliament was unable to conduct business after an uproar on the issue forced an adjournment for the day. In Chennai, Mahatma Gandhi's secretary, V. Kalyanam, led the protesters. He said

> India will get a sure gold medal if corruption is entered as an item in the Olympic Games. We may not be a force in football or athletics or hockey. But India is the undisputed global leader in corruption.

Delhi police commissioner B. K. Gupta said that the police were not keen for Hazare be sent to judicial custody and had been prepared to release him if he had given an undertaking not to break Section 144 and ask his supporters also not to do so. In a message released after his detention, Hazare said this was the beginning of the "second freedom struggle" and he called on people to participate in a "jail bharo" agitation.

Hazare on 16 August asked government employees across the country to go on mass leave to show solidarity with the movement. Union Home minister P. Chidambaram hoped they would not respond, describing the call as "completely wrong." Hazare's close associate and lawyer Prashant Bhushan urged government servants to join their cause and take a mass leave for a day and join the protests in their city.

Hazare's release

It was decided to release Hazare after Prime Minister Manmohan Singh met party General Secretary Rahul Gandhi, who disapproved of the arrest, on the evening of 16 August. Congress sources said that the Government decided to release him and his supporters after coming to the conclusion that keeping him in jail would disrupt law and order unnecessarily. Over 1,500 people who had been detained for taking part in protests demanding Hazare's release were also freed. However, Hazare then refused to leave the jail until the government agreed to give unconditional permission to hold protests at Jai Prakash Narayan National Park.

Hazare agreed to leave after Delhi Police granted him permission to fast for 15 days at Ramlila Maidan, a larger venue than Jai Prakash Narayan National Park. However, he had to spend another night in jail because the venue was not ready. Greeted by crowds, he left jail on 19 August for the 25,000-capacity Ramlila Maidan, where he said that he would not leave until the bill was passed.

17 August 2011

- Congress made a statement that they suspected a foreign hand in the protests and asked the government to probe if the US was behind Hazare's agitation. The US denied the accusation.

19 August 2011

- Varun Gandhi, a BJP MP, announced that he would introduce Hazare's Jan Lokpal Bill in the Lok Sabha as a private member's bill, saying that it was better than anything the nation has seen before.

21 August 2011

- Hazare's camp called their supporters to confront individual Members of Parliament and Union Ministers at their residence and also warned the UPA government that its days would be numbered if it failed to pass the Bill by 30 August.
- Over 100,000 supporters had thronged Ramlila Maidan on Sunday, to show their support against corruption.
- Around 50,000 supporters marched in the streets on Mumbai to support Hazare. This was reportedly one of the biggest protests in Mumbai.

22 August 2011

- Hazare, on his seventh day of fast, said he would only negotiate with Indian National Congress MP Rahul Gandhi, the Prime Minister's Office or Maharashtra Chief minister Prithviraj Chavan.

23 August 2011

"
This kind of peaceful movement is possible only in India which is the birth place of Sathyagraha
"

— Rajinikanth.

- Manmohan Singh on Tuesday appealed Anna Hazare to end his fast. He wrote a letter to Anna stating that he will ask Lok Sabha Speaker Meira Kumar if Hazare's Jan Lokpal Bill can be sent to the Standing Committee. Singh also said that the government was concerned about Hazare's health.

24 August 2011

- An all-party meeting was chaired by Manmohan Singh at his official residence in New Delhi represented by finance minister Pranab Mukherjee. However the meeting ended with Mukherjee appealing for Hazare to end his fast, prompting the civil society to declare that they were "back to square one".

25 August 2011

- Manmohan Singh said that all proposed versions of the Lokpal bill, including those prepared by Aruna Roy's NCPRI and Jaiprakash Narain, would be debated in Parliament.
- Union Minister Vilasrao Deshmukh met Hazare at his protest camp at Ramlila Maidan. Deshmukh reportedly conveyed a message from the Prime Minister to urge Hazare to end his fast and also asked him to consider the Prime Minister's offer to debate all versions of Lokpal Bill in Parliament.
- Hazare had asked Manmohan Singh to start the parliamentary discussion the next morning. He also put forward his three demands to the Prime Minister – a Citizen's Charter, Lokayuktas in all states with Lokpal powers, and inclusion of lowest to highest bureaucracy.

27 August 2011

- Initiating the Lok Sabha debate on the bill, Pranab Mukherjee requested Hazare to end his fast, as the government had also done on the previous day. BJP leader Sushma Swaraj expressed her party's support for Hazare and said that the BJP largely agreed with the three pre-conditions (Citizen's Charter, Lokayuktas in all states with Lokpal powers, and inclusion of lowest to highest bureaucracy) laid down by Hazare to end his hunger strike. The government agreed to a voice vote on the debate. Both houses of parliament passed the resolution accepting all the three pre-conditions set by Hazare.

28 August 2011

- Hazare ended his 12-day fast after 288 hours and was taken to Medanta Medicity to recover. He had been under medical supervision throughout the fast. Thousands of his supporters congregated at India Gate to celebrate.

Parliamentary debate

A debate on the Jan Lokpal bill was held in Parliament on 27 August 2011. With Hazare demanding three principles, (i) citizen charter, (ii) lower bureaucracy to be under Lokpal through an appropriate mechanism and (iii) establishment of Lok Ayuktas in the states, both houses of Parliament agreed to the principles. Hazare announced that he would break his fast on 28 August.

December protests

On 11 December, Hazare sat on a day-long fast at Jantar Mantar. This protest was against proposals of the Parliamentary Standing Committee on the anti-graft measure. It was the first at which politicians shared the stage with Hazare, with leaders of the BJP, Communist Party of India (Marxist), Communist Party of India, Janata Dal, Akali Dal, Telugu Desam Party and Biju Janata Dal participating in the public debate on the Lokpal bill.

The expected introduction of the Lokpal bill in the Lok Sabha did not occur. Instead, the Food Security Bill was first introduced and subsequently the process of the Lokpal Bill was hindered by procedural and party political issues. The Lokpal Bill that had been proposed had been discarded by the government, who put forward a revised proposal, along with a constitutional bill, in an attempt to resolve the issues that were being raised during the session regarding reservation for minorities and other under-represented groups.

Hazare announced on 22 December that a hunger strike would take place between 27–29 December, with a Jail Bharo Andolan subsequently to pressurise the Government. He began his fast on 27 December at the Bandra Kurla Complex in Mumbai rather than in Delhi because of the cold climate in the latter city. Turn-out was well below expectations, which was perhaps in part because of the cold weather. IAC members asked him to end this latest fast because of his poor health but he refused. Hazare had been suffering from cold and mild fever for few days previously.

On the second day of the fast, a day ahead of schedule, Hazare repeated his threat to campaign against Congress in the five poll-bound states for not bringing a strong Lokpal. His deteriorating health and the low turn-out across the country were among the reasons for then ending the fast. He said that the movement was not stopped, merely postponed. He also announced the cancellation of the "Jail Bharo" movement due to his bad health.

Parliament debate

The Lok Sabha debated the Lokpal Bill on 27 December 2011. The debate resulted in the bill being passed to the Rajya Sabha but the new nine-man Lokpal panel was not given constitutional status because the government failed to get the necessary two-thirds majority of MPs present.

The Lokpal Bill was sent for review to the Indian President, Pratibha Patil, on 28 December 2011. This is standard operating procedure for any legislation that will have financial implications. She later gave her assent for the Bill to be tabled in the Rajya Sabha.

2012

	2012 Indian anti-corruption movement
Date	25 March 2012 – 26 November 2012
Location	India
Caused by	• Government corruption • Police corruption • Judicial corruption • Corporate corruption • Kleptocracy • Electoral fraud • Red tape • Discretionary powers of politician • Black money
Goals	Jan Lokpal Bill/The Lokpal Bill, 2011 enactment & Political opportunism
Methods	Non violent protest
Resulted in	Team Anna split and India Against Corruption forming Aam Aadmi Party(Political opportunism) Enactment of The Lokpal and Lokayuktas Act, 2013

The movement was reinvigorated following an initial mass gathering at Jantar Mantar, New Delhi on 25 March 2012. Attempts to introduce some form of legislation, even though weaker than that demanded by the activists, had timed-out with the end of the parliamentary session on 27 December 2011.[1783] The government reintroduced the bill in the Rajya Sabha in February 2012 but the bill was not timetabled for debate and the session ended without this bill being passed.Wikipedia:Citation needed

Protests

Hazare declared that the protest movement would recommence and a mark of protest he sat on hunger strike on 25 March 2012 for one day. A month later, Hazare sat a token one-day fast focussed on remembrance of whistle-blowers such as Narendra Kumar and Satyendra Dubey who had died as a result of their support for the anti-corruption cause. On 3 June, Hazare undertook another one-day fast at Jantar Mantar, where he was joined by Ramdev, a yoga guru.

Hazare and Bedi reformed Team Anna, while Kejriwal and some others split from the erstwhile apolitical movement with the intention of forming what was to become the Aam Aadmi Party.

Jantar Mantar was the scene of an "indefinite" fast that began on 25 July and involved various members of Team Anna, although Hazare was not involved until four days later. The focus on this occasion was a protest against the government's refusal of an inquiry against the prime minister and 14 cabinet ministers, whom they had accused of corruption.Wikipedia:Citation needed The fast ended on 3 August. Three days later, Hazare announced that since the government seemed to be unready to enact the Jan Lokpal Bill, he and his fellow activists had decided to end their fast, to discontinue talks with the government and to cease any protests under the Team Anna name.

Aftermath

After failing to press government to pass The Lokpal Bill, 2011, the Team Anna split on issue of formation of political party. Anna Hazare and some others did not want to enter mainstream politics while Arvind Kejriwal led India Against Corruption opined to join politics. Arvind Kejriwal and others finally formed new political party, Aam Aadmi Party (AAP) on 26 November 2012. A year later, the party made its electoral debut in the 2013 Delhi legislative assembly election held in December 2013. It emerged as the second-largest party, winning 28 of the 70 seats. With no party obtaining an overall majority, the AAP formed a minority government with conditional support from the Indian National Congress. The AAP failed to pass Jan Lokpal Bill in Delhi assembly and resigned from the government after rule of 49 days. The President's rule imposed in the state for a year.

The Parliament of India enacted The Lokpal and Lokayuktas Act, 2013 few days after the Delhi election in December 2013.

External links

Wikimedia Commons has media related to *India Against Corruption*.

Wikinews has related news: *India Against Corruption*

External images

🔍 Images of India protests over campaigner's arrest[1784] (BBC)
🔍 Images of Indians protest the arrest of Anna Hazare[1785] (Time)
🔍 Video of Anna Hazare phenomenon[1786] (YouTube)
🔍 Indian anti-corruption campaigner, freed from jail[1787] (Guardian)
🔍 Images of Indian Anti corruption Movement[1788] (Times of India)
🔍 Video of Indian Anti-Corruption Movements[1789] (WikiLeaks Forum)

- PM writes to Shri Anna Hazare[1790] — *pmindia.nic.in*
  - Videos of the Anti-Corruption Supporters Imprisoned in India[1791]
  - Coverage at the *Times of India*[1792]

Appendix

References

[1] The title (Mirza) descends to all the sons of the family, without exception. In the Royal family it is placed after the name instead of before it, thus, Abbas Mirza and Hosfiein Mirza. Mirza is a civil title, and Khan is a military one. The title of Khan is creative, but not hereditary. *p. 601 Monthly magazine and British register, Volume 34 Publisher Printed for Sir Richard Phillips https://books.google.com/books?id=dyMAAAAAYAAJ&pg=PA601, 1812 Original from Harvard University*

[2] Jeroen Duindam (2015), *Dynasties: A Global History of Power, 1300–1800*, page 105 https://books.google.com/books?id=5ky2CgAAQBAJ&pg=PA105, Cambridge University Press

[3] Maddison, Angus (2003): *Development Centre Studies The World Economy Historical Statistics: Historical Statistics* https://books.google.com/books?id=rHJGz3HiJbcC&pg=PA261, OECD Publishing, , page 261

[4] Asher & Talbot 2008, p. 115.

[5] Robb 2001, pp. 90–91.

[6] Metcalf & Metcalf 2006, p. 17.

[7] Asher & Talbot 2008, p. 152.

[8] Metcalf & Metcalf 2006, pp. 23–24.

[9] Empire of the Moghul: Raiders From the North, by Alex Rutherford

[10] N. G. Rathod, *The Great Maratha Mahadaji Scindia*, (Sarup & Sons, 1994),8:https//books.google.com

[11] Robert C. Hallissey, *The Rajput Rebellion against Aurangzib* (U. of Missouri Press, 1977)

[12] George Clifford Whitworth. Subah. https://books.google.com/books?id=7tAOAAAAQAAJ&vq=Subah&pg=PA301#v=onepage&q=Subah&f=false *An Anglo-Indian Dictionary: A Glossary of Indian Terms Used in English, and of Such English Or Other Non-Indian Terms as Have Obtained Special Meanings in India*. London: Kegan Paul, Trench & Co. 1885. p. 301.

[13] Karl J. Schmidt (2015), *An Atlas and Survey of South Asian History*, page 100 https://books.google.com/books?id=BqdzCQAAQBAJ&pg=PA100, Routledge

[14] Maddison, Angus (2003): *Development Centre Studies The World Economy Historical Statistics: Historical Statistics* https://books.google.com/books?id=rHJGz3HiJbcC&pg=PA256, OECD Publishing, , pages 256–261

[15]

[16] John F. Richards, *The Mughal Empire* (1996), pp 185–204

[17] Picture of original Mughal *rupiya* introduced by Sher Shah Suri http://www.rbi.org.in/currency/museum/c-mogul.html

[18] John F. Richards (2003), *The Unending Frontier: An Environmental History of the Early Modern World*, pages 27–28 https://books.google.com/books?id=i85noYD9C0EC&pg=PA27, University of California Press

[19] *The Political Economy of Merchant Empires: State Power and World Trade, 1350–1750*, page 97 https://books.google.com/books?id=1jHpt9hdreoC&pg=PA97, Cambridge University Press, 1997

[20] Kaveh Yazdani (2017), *India, Modernity and the Great Divergence: Mysore and Gujarat (17th to 19th C.)* https://books.google.com/books?id=TdrzDQAAQBAJ&pg=PA120, Brill Publishers

[21] Chris Jochnick, Fraser A. Preston (2006), *Sovereign Debt at the Crossroads: Challenges and Proposals for Resolving the Third World Debt Crisis*, pages 86–87 https://books.google.com/books?id=SpqmITSjgWAC&pg=PA86, Oxford University Press

[22]

[23]

[24] John F. Richards (2003), *The Unending Frontier: An Environmental History of the Early Modern World*, page 27 https://books.google.com/books?id=i85noYD9C0EC&pg=PA27, University of California Press

[25] John F. Richards (2003), *The Unending Frontier: An Environmental History of the Early Modern World*, pages 28 https://books.google.com/books?id=i85noYD9C0EC&pg=PA28, University of California Press
[26] Irfan Habib (2011), *Economic History of Medieval India, 1200–1500*, page 53 https://books.google.com/books?id=K8kO4J3mXUAC&pg=PA53, Pearson Education
[27] Om Prakash, " Empire, Mughal http://link.galegroup.com/apps/doc/CX3447600139/WHIC?u=seat24826&xid=6b597320", *History of World Trade Since 1450*, edited by John J. McCusker, vol. 1, Macmillan Reference USA, 2006, pp. 237–240, *World History in Context*, accessed 3 August 2017
[28] Angus Maddison (1995), *Monitoring the World Economy, 1820–1992*, OECD, p. 30
[29] Richard Maxwell Eaton (1996), *The Rise of Islam and the Bengal Frontier, 1204–1760*, page 202 https://books.google.com/books?id=gKhChF3yAOUC&pg=PA202, University of California Press
[30]
[31] Irfan Habib (2011), *Economic History of Medieval India, 1200–1500*, pages 53–54 https://books.google.com/books?id=K8kO4J3mXUAC&pg=PA53, Pearson Education
[32] Irfan Habib (2011), *Economic History of Medieval India, 1200–1500*, page 54 https://books.google.com/books?id=K8kO4J3mXUAC&pg=PA54, Pearson Education
[33] Karl Marx (1867). Chapter 16: "Machinery and Large-Scale Industry." *Das Kapital*.
[34] Ray, Indrajit (2011), *Bengal Industries and the British Industrial Revolution (1757–1857)*, page 174 https://books.google.com/books?id=CHOrAgAAQBAJ&pg=PA174, Routledge,
[35] Tirthankarl Roy, "Where is Bengal? Situating an Indian Region in the Early Modern World Economy", *Past & Present* (Nov 2011) 213#1 pp 115–146
[36] The Rise of Islam and the Bengal Frontier, 1204–1760 https//books.google.com by Richard Maxwell Eaton, Google Books.
[37] Angus Maddison (2001), *The World Economy: A Millennial Perspective*, page 236 http://theunbrokenwindow.com/Development/MADDISON%20The%20World%20Economy--A%20Millennial.pdf#page=237, OECD Development Centre
[38]
[39]
[40]
[41] *Social Science Review*, Volume 14, Issue 1 https://books.google.com/books?id=pKIIAQAAMAAJ, page 126, Dhaka University
[42] Shireen Moosvi (2008), *People, Taxation, and Trade in Mughal India* https://books.google.com/books?id=IhpuAAAAMAAJ, page 131, Oxford University Press
[43] K. N. Chaudhuri, "Some Reflections on the Town and Country in Mughal India", Modern Asian Studies (1978) 12#1 pp. 77–96
[44] R. Siva Kumar, "Modern Indian Art: a Brief Overview", *Art Journal* (1999) 58#3 pp 14+.
[45] "India." Encyclopædia Britannica. Encyclopædia Britannica 2008 Ultimate Reference Suite. Chicago: Encyclopædia Britannica, 2008.
[46] "Chāpra." Encyclopædia Britannica. Encyclopædia Britannica 2008 Ultimate Reference Suite. Chicago: Encyclopædia Britannica, 2008.
[47] Savage-Smith, Emilie (1985), *Islamicate Celestial Globes: Their History, Construction, and Use*, Smithsonian Institution Press, Washington, D.C.
[48] //doi.org/10.1017/s0026749x00005825
[49] //www.jstor.org/stable/311728
[50] //www.jstor.org/stable/2053505
[51] https://books.google.com/books?id=zlEDvkhEmL8C
[52] //doi.org/10.1163/156852005774918813
[53] //www.jstor.org/stable/25165118
[54] https://www.questia.com/PM.qst?a=o&d=102714757
[55] https://books.google.com/books?id=uzOmy2y0Zh4C
[56] https://books.google.com/books?id=iuESgYNYPI0C
[57] https://books.google.com/books?id=HHyVh29gy4QC
[58] https://books.google.com/books?id=hmagAAAAMAAJ
[59] https://www.amazon.com/Mughal-Empire-Cambridge-History-India/dp/0521566037/

[60] //doi.org/10.1017/s0010417500013311
[61] //www.jstor.org/stable/178737
[62] https://books.google.com/books?id=SXdVS0SzQSAC
[63] https://books.google.com/books?id=QY4zdTDwMAQC
[64] https://www.amazon.com/Poetry-Kings-Classical-Literature-Research/dp/0199765928/ref=sr_1_2?s=books&ie=UTF8&qid=1339157925&sr=1-2
[65] http://libmma.contentdm.oclc.org/cdm/compoundobject/collection/p15324coll10/id/114935/rec/401
[66] //doi.org/10.1017/s0026749x00008155
[67] //www.jstor.org/stable/311823
[68] //doi.org/10.1163/1568520041974729
[69] //www.jstor.org/stable/25165051
[70] //www.jstor.org/stable/3516601
[71] https://archive.org/stream/travelsinmogulem00bernuoft#page/ii/mode/2up
[72] https://archive.org/details/historyofindia09jackiala
[73] https://archive.org/stream/tezkerehalvakiat00jawhuoft#page/n7/mode/2up
[74] https://archive.org/stream/warriorsofcresce00adamuoft#page/n9/mode/2up
[75] https://archive.org/stream/mogulemperorsofh00hold#page/n9/mode/2up
[76] https://archive.org/stream/akbarriseofmugha00mallrich#page/n5/mode/2up
[77] https://archive.org/stream/historyofmoguldy00manurich#page/n5/mode/2up
[78] https://archive.org/stream/historyofindia04jackuoft#page/n9/mode/2up
[79] https://archive.org/stream/storiadomogororm01manuuoft#page/n7/mode/2up
[80] https://archive.org/stream/storiadomogororm02manuuoft#page/n7/mode/2up
[81] https://archive.org/stream/storiadomogororm03manuuoft#page/n9/mode/2up
[82] https://archive.org/stream/fallofmogulempir00owenuoft#page/n5/mode/2up
[83] http://www.valleyswat.net/literature/papers/MUGHULS_AND_SWAT.pdf
[84] http://www.mughalindia.co.uk/index.html
[85] http://www.bbc.co.uk/religion/religions/islam/history/mughalempire_1.shtml
[86] https://web.archive.org/web/20051202045249/http://www.i3pep.org/archives/2005/04/12/mughal-empire/
[87] http://www.islamicarchitecture.org/dynasties/mughals.html
[88] http://www.mughalgardens.org/html/home.html
[89] https://web.archive.org/web/20160130223426/http://www.webjournal.unior.it/
[90] https://web.archive.org/web/20090119095422/http://paradoxplace.com/Insights/Civilizations/Mughals/Mughals.htm
[91] http://news.bbc.co.uk/2/hi/uk_news/england/1566398.stm
[92] http://www.chiefacoins.com/Database/Countries/Mughal.htm
[93] https://www.bbc.co.uk/programmes/p004y27h
[94] Mughal Coinage http://www.rbi.org.in/currency/museum/c-mogul.html Reserve Bank of India RBI Monetary Museum,
[95] Majumdar, R.C. (ed.) (2007). *The Mughul Empire*, Mumbai: Bharatiya Vidya Bhavan, , p.83
[96] Majumdar, R.C. (ed.) (2007). *The Mughul Empire*, Mumbai: Bharatiya Vidya Bhavan, , pp. 90–93
[97] Majumdar, R.C. (ed.) (2007). *The Mughul Empire*, Mumbai: Bharatiya Vidya Bhavan, , p.94
[98] Majumdar, R.C. (ed.) (2007). *The Mughul Empire*, Mumbai: Bharatiya Vidya Bhavan, , pp. 94–96
[99] Saradindu Shekhar Chakma. Ethnic Cleansing in Chittagong Hill Tracts. p. 23.
[100] OUM. pp. 16, 17
[101] http://archive.dhakatribune.com/heritage/2014/nov/01/gunpowder-plots
[102] Janam Mukherjee (2015), *Hungry Bengal: War, Famine and the End of Empire*, page 27 https://books.google.co.uk/books?id=iGuMCwAAQBAJ&pg=PA27, Oxford University Press
[103] Amiya Kumar Bagchi (2008), *Perilous Passage: Mankind and the Global Ascendancy of Capital*, page 145 https://books.google.co.uk/books?id=xHsHEoYh3V0C&pg=PA145, Rowman & Littlefield Publishers
[104] Data from United Nations Department of Economic and Social Affairs, Population Division. http://esa.un.org/unpd/wpp/unpp/panel_population.htm

1950–2100 estimates (only medium variants shown): (a) World Population Prospects: The 2008 Revision. http://esa.un.org/unpp/
Estimates prior to 1950: (b) "The World at Six Billion", 1999. https://www.un.org/esa/population/publications/sixbillion/sixbillion.htm
Estimates from 1950 to 2100: (c) "Population of the entire world, yearly, 1950 - 2100", 2013. http://www.geohive.com/earth/his_history3.aspx

[105] John F. Richards (1995), *The Mughal Empire*, page 190 https://books.google.com/books?id=HHyVh29gy4QC&pg=PA190, Cambridge University Press

[106]

[107]

[108]

[109] Abhay Kumar Singh (2006), *Modern World System and Indian Proto-industrialization: Bengal 1650-1800*, Volume 1 https://books.google.co.uk/books?id=WwNUblS-jpwC, Northern Book Centre

[110]

[111] Lawrence B. Lesser. "Historical Perspective". *A Country Study: Bangladesh* http://lcweb2.loc.gov/frd/cs/bdtoc.html (James Heitzman and Robert Worden, editors). Library of Congress Federal Research Division (September 1988). *This article incorporates text from this source, which is in the public domain.* About the Country Studies / Area Handbooks Program: Country Studies - Federal Research Division, Library of Congress http://lcweb2.loc.gov/frd/cs/about.html

[112] Richard Maxwell Eaton (1996), *The Rise of Islam and the Bengal Frontier, 1204-1760*, page 202 https://books.google.co.uk/books?id=gKhChF3yAOUC&pg=PA202, University of California Press

[113] Om Prakash, " Empire, Mughal http://link.galegroup.com/apps/doc/CX3447600139/WHIC?u=seat24826&xid=6b597320", *History of World Trade Since 1450*, edited by John J. McCusker, vol. 1, Macmillan Reference USA, 2006, pp. 237-240, *World History in Context*, accessed 3 August 2017

[114] John F. Richards (1995), *The Mughal Empire*, page 202 https://books.google.com/books?id=HHyVh29gy4QC&pg=PA202, Cambridge University Press

[115] Ray, Indrajit (2011), *Bengal Industries and the British Industrial Revolution (1757-1857)*, page 174 https://books.google.com/books?id=CHOrAgAAQBAJ&pg=PA174, Routledge,

[116] Jarrett, H. S. (1949) [1891] *The Ain-i-Akbari by Abul Fazl-i-Allami*, Vol.II, (ed.) J. N. Sarkar, Calcutta: The Asiatic Society, pp.142–55

[117] Majumdar, R.C. (ed.) (2007). *The Mughul Empire*, Mumbai: Bharatiya Vidya Bhavan, , pp. 609, 634.

[118] //en.wikipedia.org/w/index.php?title=Template:Part_of_History_of_India&action=edit

[119] Delhi, the Capital of India By Anon, John Capper, p.28. "This source establishes the Maratha control of Delhi before the British" https://books.google.com/books?id=aqqBPS1TDUgC&pg=PA28

[120] An Advanced History of Modern India By Sailendra Nath Sen p.Introduction-14. The author says: "*The victory at Bhopal in 1738 established Maratha dominance at the Mughal court*" https://books.google.com/books?id=bXWiACEwPR8C&pg=PA1941-IA82&lpg=PA1941-IA82

[121] Some historians<ref name="Schmidt2015">

[122]

"Shivaji's coronation and setting himself up as a sovereign prince symbolises the rise of the Indian people in all parts of the country. It was a bid for *Hindawi Swarajya* (Indian rule), a term in use in Marathi sources of history."

[123] The Journal of Asian Studies The Journal of Asian Studies / Volume 21 / Issue 04 / August 1962, pp 577–578

[124] Mehta (2005), p. 204

[125] An Advanced History of Modern India By Sailendra Nath Sen, p.16 https//books.google.com

[126] Many historians consider Attock to be the final frontier of the Maratha Empire<ref>Bharatiya Vidya Bhavan, Bharatiya Itihasa Samiti, Ramesh Chandra Majumdar – *The History and Culture of the Indian People: The Maratha supremacy*

[127] Islamic Renaissance In South Asia (1707-1867) : The Role Of Shah Waliallah ... - M.A.Ghazi - Google Books https//books.google.com
[128] Mehta (2005), p. 707:quote:It explains the rise to power of his Peshwa (prime minister) Balaji Vishwanath (1713–20) and the transformation of the Maratha kingdom into a vast empire, by the collective action of all the Maratha stalwarts.
[129] An Advanced History of Modern India By Sailendra Nath Sen, p.11 https://books.google.com/books?id=bXWiACEwPR8C&pg=PR21&lpg=PR21
[130] An Advanced History of Modern India by Sailendra Nath Sen, p11
[131] An Advanced History of Modern India By Sailendra Nath Sen, p.12 https://books.google.com/books?id=bXWiACEwPR8C&pg=PR22
[132] The Concise History of Warfare By Field Marshal Bernard Law Montgomery, p.132
[133] J.L. Mehta, *Advanced Study in the History of Modern India 1707–1813* (2005) https://books.google.com/books?id=d1wUgKKzawoC&pg=PA117
[134] S.N. Sen, *History Modern India* (3rd ed. 2006) https://books.google.com/books?id=gapmgxsWwoC&pg=PA12
[135] An Advanced History of Modern India https://books.google.com/books?id=bXWiACEwPR8C&pg=PR23
[136] An Advanced History of Modern India By Sailendra Nath Sen, p13 https://books.google.com/books?id=bXWiACEwPR8C&pg=PR23
[137] Advanced Study in the History of Modern India 1707–1813 By Jaswant Lal Mehta, p 202 https://books.google.com/books?id=d1wUgKKzawoC&pg=PA202
[138] Fall Of the Mughal Empire- Volume 1 (4Th Edn.), J. N.Sarkar
[139]
[140] Mehta, *Advanced Study in the History of Modern India 1707–1813*, p.140 https://books.google.com/books?id=d1wUgKKzawoC&pg=PA140
[141] Mehta (2005), p. 274
[142] Turchin, Peter; Adams, Jonathan M.; Hall, Thomas D (December 2006). "East-West Orientation of Historical Empires" http://jwsr.pitt.edu/ojs/index.php/jwsr/article/view/369/381. Journal of world-systems research. 12 (2): 223.
[143] Advance Study in the History of Modern India (Volume-1: 1707–1803) By G.S.Chhabra, p.56 https://books.google.com/books?id=UkDi6rVbckoC&pg=PA56
[144] The Marathas 1600–1818, Band 2 by Stewart Gordon p.157
[145] The Marathas 1600–1818, Band 2 by Stewart Gordon p.158
[146] Mehta (2005), p. 458
[147] Rathod (1994), p. 8
[148] The Great Maratha Mahadaji Scindia By N. G. Rathod, p.95 https://books.google.com/books?id=uPq640stHJ0C&pg=PA95
[149] The Great Maratha Mahadaji Scindia By N. G. Rathod, p.30 https://books.google.com/books?id=uPq640stHJ0C&pg=PA30
[150] Rathod (1994), p. 106
[151] Sir Jadunath Sarkar (1994). A History of Jaipur 1503–1938. Orient Longman.
[152] Bharatiya Vidya Bhavan, Bhāratīya Itihāsa Samiti, Ramesh Chandra Majumdar. The History and Culture of the Indian People: The Maratha supremacy
[153] The State at War in South Asia By Pradeep Barua, p.91 https://books.google.com/books?id=FIIQhuAOGaIC&pg=PA91
[154] *Annual Report of the Mysore Archaeological Department* 1916 pp 10–11, 73–6
[155] Hasan, *History of Tipu Sultan*, p. 359
[156] Battle of Wadgaon, *Encyclopædia Britannica* http://www.britannica.com/topic/battle-of-Wadgaon
[157] C A Kincaid and D B Parasnis, A history of the Maratha people. Vol III p. 194.
[158] Delhi, the Capital of India By Anon, John Capper, p.28 https://books.google.com/books?id=aqqBPS1TDUgC&pg=PA28
[159] The Anglo-Maratha Campaigns and the Contest for India, Randolf G. S. Cooper, University of Cambridge, , 2007
[160] Prakash 2002, p. 300.
[161] United States Court of Customs and Patent Appeals 1930, p. 121.

[162] Black 2006, p. 77.
[163] http://www.kkhsou.in/main/history/marathas.html
[164] Maratha Rule in India By Stephen Meredyth Edwardes, Herbert Leonard Offley Garrett p. 116.
[165] Bharatiya Vidya Bhavan, Bhāratīya Itihāsa Samiti, Ramesh Chandra Majumdar. *The History and Culture of the Indian People: The Maratha supremacy* https://books.google.com/books?ei=xywpTvOTGofirAf40eTsBg&ct=result&id=zQ9uAAAAMAAJ&dq. G. Allen & Unwin, 1951
[166] The New Cambridge Modern History – Google Books https://books.google.com/books?id=1BY9AAAAIAAJ&pg=PA556. Books.google.co.in. Retrieved 12 July 2013.
[167] Bharatiya Vidya Bhavan, Bhāratīya Itihāsa Samiti, Ramesh Chandra Majumdar. *The History and Culture of the Indian People: The Maratha Supremacy*, page 512 https://archive.org/stream/in.ernet.dli.2015.108112/2015.108112.History-And-Culture-Of-The-Indian-People-Vol8-maratha-Supremacy#page/n533/mode/2up. G. Allen & Unwin, 1951
[168] https//books.google.com Fall of Mughal Empire: Vol.2
[169] G S Sardesai's *Marathi Riyasat*, volume 2."The reference for this letter as given by Sardesai in Riyasat – Peshwe Daftar letters 2.103, 146; 21.206; 1.202, 207, 210, 213; 29, 42, 54, and 39.161. Satara Daftar – document number 2.301, Shejwalkar's Panipat, page no. 99. Moropanta's account – 1.1, 6, 7"
[170] *Glimpses of Life and Manners in Persia* by Lady Mary Leonora Woulfe Sheil, with additional notes by Sir Justin Sheil http://digital.library.upenn.edu/women/sheil/persia/persia.html
[171]
[172] Great Personalities By Prof. R. P. Chaturvedi, p.189 https//books.google.com
[173] Journal of the Tanjore Maharaja Serfoji's Sarasvati Mahal Library Pg 18 https//books.google.com
[174] http://www.san.beck.org/2-10-Marathas1707-1800.html
[175] http://www.lib.virginia.edu/area-studies/SouthAsia/Ideas/pindaris.html
[176] //www.worldcat.org/oclc/53790277
[177] https://books.google.com/?id=d1wUgKKzawoC&dq=9781932705546
[178] http://eprints.lse.ac.uk/28443/1/WP142.pdf
[179] https://books.google.com/?id=Y-kanqrtVhYC&dq=9788171547890
[180] https://books.google.com/books?id=ga-pmgxsWwoC&pg=PA12
[181] http://journals.sagepub.com/doi/pdf/10.1177/0376983614521732
[182] https://books.google.com/?id=pZPmLzgkF0UC&printsec=frontcover&dq=9788176258067#v=onepage&q&f=false
[183] https://books.google.com/?id=hNVtQY4sXYMC&dq=9780275990398
[184] https://books.google.com/?id=UkDi6rVbckoC&printsec=frontcover&dq=9788189093068#v=onepage&q&f=false
[185] http://maharashtra.gov.in/data/gr/english/1961/01/24/20061116122835001.pdf
[186] https://books.google.com/?id=SYOSHaZnBy8C&dq=9788170995814
[187] //www.worldcat.org/oclc/483944794
[188] https://books.google.com/?id=JVK6d5CXq5MC&dq=holkar+narmada+valley
[189] https://books.google.com/?id=bxsa3jtHoCEC&printsec=frontcover&dq=9788131300343#v=onepage&q&f=false
[190] https://books.google.com/books?id=8ArbyWUf4j8C
[191] https://books.google.com/books?id=Kz1-mtazYqEC&pg=PA35
[192] https://books.google.com/books?id=uPq640stHJ0C
[193] https://books.google.com/?id=9q8EAAAAMAAJ&q=balaji+pant+natu+spy&dq=balaji+pant+natu+spy
[194] //www.worldcat.org/oclc/4076888
[195] https://books.google.com/?id=S2Yn4LlujqsC&dq=9788171546589
[196] https://books.google.com/?id=FzmkFXSgxqgC&dq=9781563243349
[197] https://books.google.com/?id=OIcdAAAAMAAJ&q=E.+F.+BENDLER&dq=E.+F.+BENDLER
[198] //www.worldcat.org/oclc/2590161
[199] Banke, Bardiya, Kanchanpur and Kailali, also known as "New Kingdom" were given to Jung Bahadur in 1860, 1 November.

[200] //en.wikipedia.org/w/index.php?title=Template:Part_of_History_of_India&action=edit
[201] //en.wikipedia.org/w/index.php?title=Template:Colonial_India&action=edit
[202] "Chapter 5: Early Modern India II: Company Raj", "Chapter 3: The East India Company Raj, 1772–1850", "Chapter 7: Company Raj and Indian Society 1757 to 1857, Reinvention and Reform of Tradition".
[203] Oxford English Dictionary, 2nd edition, 1989: Hindi, *rāj*, from Skr. *rāj*: to reign, rule; cognate with L. *rēx*, *rēg-is*, OIr. *rí*, *rīg* king (see RICH).
[204] James A. Williamson, *A Short History of British Expansion. The Old Colonial Empire*, Macmillan & Co Ltd, London, Third edition, 1955, p. 408.
[205] John Keay, *The Honourable Company, A History of the English East India Company*, Macmillan Publishing Company, New York, 1994, p. 319–324.
[206] Wickwire, p. 19
[207] http://www.indianmilitaryhistory.org/battles/baji%20rao%20I%20at%20Kharda.htm
[208] ,,
[209] "in Council," *i.e.* in concert with the advice of the Council.
[210] Quoted in
[211] David Gilmour, *The Ruling Caste: Imperial Lives in the Victorian Raj* (2005)
[212] Colin Newbury, "Patronage and Professionalism: Manning a Transitional Empire, 1760–1870." *Journal of Imperial and Commonwealth History* (2013) 42#2 pp: 193-213.
[213] Majumdar, Mohini Lal. *The imperial post offices of British India, 1837-1914* (Phila Publications, 1990)
[214] Stockton and Darlington Railway
[215] Thorner, Daniel. "Great Britain and the development of India's railways." *Journal of Economic History* 1951; 11(4): 389-402. online http://journals.cambridge.org/abstract_S0022050700085120
[216] https://books.google.com/books?id=0oVra0ulQ3QC
[217] https://books.google.com/books?id=WJ7BNOmQvwcC
[218] https://books.google.com/books?id=Eq7tAAAAMAAJ
[219] https://books.google.com/books?id=hlf9u1asHTAC
[220] https://books.google.com/books?id=V73N8js5ZgAC
[221] https://books.google.com/books?hl=en&lr=&id=PQOtAgAAQBAJ
[222] https://books.google.com/books?id=wQJuAAAAMAAJ
[223] https://books.google.com/books?id=uzOmy2y0Zh4C&pg=PA271
[224] https://books.google.com/books?id=iuESgYNYPl0C
[225] https://books.google.com/books?id=6iNuAAAAMAAJ
[226] https://books.google.com/books?id=Es6x4u_g19UC
[227] https://books.google.com/books?id=GQ-2VH1LO_EC
[228] https://books.google.com/books?id=CDwwAQAAIAAJ
[229] https://books.google.com/books?id=0K3GZFqCabsC
[230] https://books.google.com/books?id=JT0wAQAAIAAJ
[231] https://books.google.com/books?id=lxkjJAAACAAJ
[232] https://books.google.com/books?id=MGJQKg4Tja0C
[233] https://books.google.com/books?id=fX2zMfWqIzMC
[234] https://www.amazon.com/Oxford-History-British-Empire-Nineteenth/dp/0199246785
[235] https://books.google.com/books?id=cE8Y_gAACAAJ
[236] //doi.org/10.2307/172481
[237] //www.jstor.org/stable/172481
[238] //doi.org/10.1111/j.1468-0289.2008.00438.x
[239] //doi.org/10.2307/2808021
[240] //www.jstor.org/stable/2808021
[241] //doi.org/10.1016/j.eeh.2007.11.002
[242] //doi.org/10.1017/S0026749X00013901
[243] //www.jstor.org/stable/312614
[244] //doi.org/10.2307/312523
[245] //www.jstor.org/stable/312523
[246] //www.jstor.org/stable/313141

[247] //doi.org/10.1086/649322
[248] //www.jstor.org/stable/301944
[249] //doi.org/10.1017/S0026749X00013986
[250] //www.jstor.org/stable/312868
[251] //doi.org/10.1257/089533002760278749
[252] //www.jstor.org/stable/3216953
[253] https://books.google.com/books?id=RlQBAAAAQAAJ&dq=%22employed+the+arm+of+political+injustice%22&cad=0
[254] //www.worldcat.org/oclc/63943320
[255] https://archive.org/details/historicaleccles00calciala
[256] https://archive.org/details/annalshonorable00brucgoog
[257] https://archive.org/details/annalshonorable01brucgoog
[258] https://archive.org/details/historyindiafro02marsgoog
[259] http://lcweb2.loc.gov/frd/cs/
[260] http://lcweb2.loc.gov/frd/cs/intoc.html
[261] http://lcweb2.loc.gov/frd/cs/pktoc.html
[262] Kamath (2001), pp. 11–12, pp. 226–227; Pranesh (2003), p. 11
[263] Narasimhacharya (1988), p. 23
[264] Subrahmanyam (2003), p. 64; Rice E.P. (1921), p. 89
[265] Kamath (2001), p. 226
[266] Rice B.L. (1897), p. 361
[267] Pranesh (2003), pp. 2–3
[268] Wilks, Aiyangar in Aiyangar and Smith (1911), pp. 275–276
[269] Aiyangar (1911), p. 275; Pranesh (2003), p. 2
[270] Stein (1989), p. 82
[271] Kamath (2001), p. 227
[272] Subrahmanyam (2001), p. 67
[273] Subrahmanyam (2001), p. 68
[274] Venkata Ramanappa, M. N. (1975), p. 200
[275] Shama Rao in Kamath (2001), p. 227
[276]
[277] Subrahmanyam (2001), p. 68; Kamath (2001), p. 228
[278] Subrahmanyam (2001), p. 71
[279] Kamath (2001), pp. 228–229
[280] Subrahmanyam (2001), p. 69; Kamath (2001), pp. 228–229
[281] Subrahmanyam (2001), p. 69
[282] Subrahmanyam (2001), p. 70
[283] Subrahmanyam (2001), pp. 70–71; Kamath (2001), p. 229
[284] Pranesh (2003), pp. 44–45
[285] Kamath (2001), p. 230
[286] Shama Rao in Kamath (2001), p. 233
[287] Quote:"A military genius and a man of vigour, valour and resourcefulness" (Chopra et al. 2003, p. 76)
[288] Venkata Ramanappa, M. N. (1975), p. 207
[289] Chopra et al. (2003), p. 71, 76
[290] Chopra et al. (2003), p. 55
[291] Kamath (2001), p. 232
[292] Chopra et al. (2003), p. 71
[293] Chopra et al. (2003), p. 73
[294] Chopra et al. (2003), p. 74
[295] Chopra et al. (2003), p. 75
[296] Chopra et al. 2003, p. 75
[297] Venkata Ramanappa, M. N. (1975), p. 211
[298] Chopra et al. (2003), pp. 75–76
[299] Chopra et al. (2003), p. 77
[300]

[301] Chopra et al. (2003), pp. 79–80; Kamath (2001), pp. 233–234
[302] Chopra et al. (2003), pp. 81–82
[303] Kamath (2001), p. 249
[304] Kamath (2001), p. 234
[305] Venkata Ramanappa, M. N. (1975), p. 225
[306] Quote:"The Diwan seems to pursue the wisest and the most benevolent course for the promotion of industry and opulence" (Gen. Wellesley in Kamath 2001, p. 249)
[307] Venkata Ramanappa, M. N. (1975), pp. 226–229
[308] Kamath (2001), p. 250
[309] Venkata Ramanappa, M. N. (1975), pp. 229–231
[310] Venkata Ramanappa, M. N. (1975), pp. 231–232
[311] Lewis Rice, B., *Report on the Mysore census* (Bangalore: Mysore Government Press, 1881), p. 3
[312] Kamath (2001), pp. 250–254
[313] Rama Jois, M. 1984. Legal and constitutional history of India ancient legal, judicial and constitutional system. Delhi: Universal Law Pub. Co. p. 597
[314] Puttaswamaiah, K. 1980. Economic development of Karnataka a treatise in continuity and change. New Delhi: Oxford & IBH. p. 3
[315] Pranesh (2003), p. 162
[316] Kamath (2001), p. 261
[317] Kamath (2001), p. 228; Venkata Ramanappa, M. N. (1975), p. 201
[318] Venkata Ramanappa, M. N. (1975), p.203
[319] Kamath (2001), pp. 228–229; Venkata Ramanappa, M. N. (1975), p. 203
[320] Kamath (2001), p. 233
[321] Kamath (2001), p. 235
[322] Kamath (2001), p. 251
[323] Kamath (2001), p. 252
[324] Meyer, Sir William Stevenson, et al. *The Imperial Gazetteer of India*. Oxford, Clarendon Press, 1908–1931. v. 18, p. 228.
[325] Kamath (2001), p. 254
[326] Kamath (2001), pp. 254–255
[327] Kamath (2001), p. 257
[328] Kamath (2001), p. 259
[329] Indian Science Congress (2003), p. 139
[330] Kamath (2001), p. 258
[331] Indian Science Congress (2003), pp. 139–140
[332] Kamath (2001), p. 260
[333] Sastri (1955), p. 297–298
[334] Chopra et al. (2003), p. 123
[335] M.H.Gopal in Kamath 2001, p. 235
[336] Kamath (2001), pp. 235–236
[337] Kamath (2001), pp. 236–237
[338] Maddison, Angus (2007), *Contours of the World Economy, 1–2030 AD. Essays in Macro-Economic History*, Oxford University Press, , p. 382, table A.7
[339] Chopra et al. (2003), p. 124
[340] Chopra et al. (2003), p. 129
[341] Chopra et al. (2003), p. 130
[342] Kamath (2001), p. 286
[343] Chopra et al. (2003), p. 132
[344] Kamath (2001), p. 287
[345] Kamath (2001), pp. 288–289
[346] Chopra et al. (2003), p. 134
[347] Rice E.P. (1921), p. 89
[348] Pranesh (2003), p. 5, p. 16, p. 54
[349] Nagaraj in Pollock (2003), p. 379
[350] Kamath (2001), p. 229

[351] Aiyangar and Smith (1911), p. 304
[352] Pranesh (2003), p. 17
[353] Aiyangar and Smith (1911), p. 290
[354] Pranesh (2003), p. 4
[355] Pranesh (2003), p. 44
[356] Kamath (2001), pp. 229–230
[357] Singh (2001), pp. 5782–5787
[358] Sastri (1955), p. 396
[359] Mohibul Hassan in Chopra et al., 2003, p. 82, part III
[360] Chopra et al. (2003), p. 82
[361] Kamath (2001), p. 237
[362] Sastri (1955), p. 394
[363] Kamath (2001), p. 278
[364] Chopra et al. (2003), p. 185
[365] Chopra et al. (2003), p. 186
[366] Kamath (2001), pp. 278–279
[367] Chopra et al. (2003), pp. 196–197, p. 202
[368] Kamath (2001), p. 284
[369] Kamath (2001), p. 275
[370] Kamath (2001), pp. 279–280; Murthy (1992), p. 168
[371] Kamath (2001), p. 281; Murthy (1992), p. 172
[372] Murthy (1992), p. 169
[373] Kamath (2001), p. 282
[374] Pranesh (2003), p163
[375] Kamath (2001), p. 283
[376] Narasimhacharya (1988), pp. 23–27
[377] Mukherjee (1999), p. 78; Narasimhacharya (1988), p. 23, p. 26
[378] Kamath (2001), pp. 229–230; Pranesh (2003), preface chapter p(i)
[379] Narasimhacharya (1988), pp. 23–26
[380] Narasimhacharya (1988), p. 25
[381] Kamath (2001), p. 281
[382] Murthy (1992), p. 168–171; Kamath (2001), p. 280
[383] Rice E.P. (1921), p. 90; Mukherjee (1999), p. 119
[384] Kamath (2001), p. 227; Pranesh (2003), p. 11
[385] Pranesh (2003), p. 20
[386] Mukherjee (1999), p. 78; Pranesh (2003), p. 21
[387] Mukherjee (1999), p. 143, p. 354, p. 133, p. 135; Narasimhacharya (1988), pp. 24–25
[388] Pranesh (2003), pp. 33–34; Rice E.P. (1921), pp. 72–73, pp. 83–88, p. 91
[389] Pranesh (2003), pp. 37–38
[390] Pranesh (2003), p. 53
[391] Narasimhacharya (1988), p. 26; Murthy (1992), p. 167; Pranesh (2003), p. 55
[392] Murthy (1992), p. 167
[393] Murthy (1992), p. 170
[394] Pranesh (2003), p. 81
[395] Sahitya Akademi (1988), p. 1077; Pranesh (2003), p. 82
[396] Weidman (2006), p. 66
[397] Weidman (2006), p. 65
[398] Pranesh (2003), p. 54
[399] Pranesh (2003), p. xiii in author's note
[400] Kamath (2001), p282
[401] Weidman (2006), p. 67
[402] Weidman (2006), p. 68
[403] Pranesh (2003), p. 110
[404] Bakshi (1996), p. 12; Kamath (2001), p. 282
[405] Pranesh (2003), pp. 110–111
[406] Subramaniyan (2006), p. 199; Kamath (2001), p. 282

[407] Pranesh (2003), p. 135
[408] Pranesh (2003), p. 140
[409] Subramaniyan (2006), p. 202; Kamath (2001), p. 282
[410] Pranesh (2003), p. 170
[411] Pranesh (2003), p. 214, 216
[412] Pranesh (2003), p. 216
[413] Michell, p. 69
[414] Manchanda (2006), p. 158
[415] Manchanda (2006), pp. 160–161
[416] Manchanda (2006), p. 161
[417] Raman (1994), pp. 87–88
[418] Raman (1994), pp. 83–84, pp. 91–92
[419] Raman (1994), p. 84
[420] Bradnock (2000), p. 294
[421] Raman (1994), pp. 81–82
[422] Raman (1994), p. 85
[423] Raman (1996), p. 83
[424] Michell p. 71
[425] Raman (1994), p. 106
[426] Abram et al. (2003), p. 225
[427] Abram et al. (2003), pp. 225–226
[428] Roddam Narasimha (1985). Rockets in Mysore and Britain, 1750–1850 A.D. http://nal-ir.nal.res.in/2382/01/tr_pd_du_8503_R66305.pdf National Aeronautical Laboratory and Indian Institute of Science.
[429] *Encyclopædia Britannica* (2008), "rocket and missile"
[430] //lccn.loc.gov/80905179
[431] //www.worldcat.org/oclc/7796041
[432] http://eh.net/?s=gujarat
[433] https://books.google.com/books?id=sUwEAAAAMBAJ
[434] //tools.wmflabs.org/geohack/geohack.php?pagename=Kingdom_of_Mysore&params=12.30_N_76.65_E_region:IN_type:landmark_source:kolossus-svwiki
[435] Satinder Singh, Raja Gulab Singh's Role 1971, pp. 46-50.
[436] //en.wikipedia.org/w/index.php?title=Template:Part_of_History_of_India&action=edit
[437] Encyclopædia Britannica Eleventh Edition, (Edition: Volume V22, Date: 1910–1911), Page 892.
[438] Amarinder Singh's The Last Sunset: The Rise and Fall of the Lahore Durbar
[439] The Encyclopaedia of Sikhism http://www.learnpunjabi.org/eos/ , section *Sāhib Siṅgh Bedī, Bābā (1756–1834)*.
[440] Miniature painting from the photo album of princely families in the Sikh and Rajput territories by Colonel James Skinner (1778–1841)
[441] Ranjit Singh: administration and British policy, (Prakash, p.31-33)
[442] Maharaja Ranjit Singh, the last to lay arms, (Duggal, p.136-137)
[443] Frasier, G.M. (1990) Flashman and the Mountain of Light, Harper-Collins, London
[444] The Masters Revealed, (Johnson, p. 128)
[445] Britain and Tibet 1765–1947, (Marshall, p.116)
[446] The Khyber Pass: A History of Empire and Invasion, (Docherty, p.187)
[447] The Khyber Pass: A History of Empire and Invasion, (Docherty, p.185-187)
[448] Bennett-Jones, Owen; Singh, Sarina, *Pakistan & the Karakoram Highway* Page 199
[449] Hastings Donnan, *Marriage Among Muslims: Preference and Choice in Northern Pakistan*, (Brill, 1997), 41.https//books.google.com
[450] Encyclopædia Britannica - Ranjit Singh http://www.britannica.com/EBchecked/topic/491193/Ranjit-Singh
[451] Trudy Ring, Noelle Watson & Paul Schellinger 2012, pp. 28-29.
[452] Kartar Singh Duggal (1 January 2001). Maharaja Ranjit Singh: The Last to Lay Arms. Abhinav Publications. pp. 125–126.

[453] Lodrick, D.O. 1981. *Sacred Cows, Sacred Places*. Berkeley: University of California Press, p. 145

[454] Vigne, G.T., 1840. *A Personal Narrative of a Visit to Ghuzni, Kabul, and Afghanistan, and a Residence at the Court of Dost Mohammed...*, London: Whittaker and Co. p. 246 *The Real Ranjit Singh*; by Fakir Syed Waheeduddin, published by Punjabi University,, 1 Jan 2001, 2nd ed.

[455] Hügel, Baron (1845) 2000. *Travels in Kashmir and the Panjab, containing a Particular Account of the Government and Character of the Sikhs*, tr. Major T.B. Jervis. rpt, Delhi: Low Price Publications, p. 151

[456] Masson, Charles. 1842. *Narrative of Various Journeys in Balochistan, Afghanistan and the Panjab*, 3 v. London: Richard Bentley (1) 37

[457] https://books.google.com/books?id=H5cQH17-HnMC&pg=PA345&dq=guru+har+gobind+jahangir&cd=2#v=onepage&q&f=false

[458] https//books.google.com

[459] https//books.google.com

[460] https://web.archive.org/web/20110718115655/http://worldsikhnews.com/7%20January%202009/Image/page%2012-13%20for%20web.pdf

[461] http://www.sikh-history.com/sikhhist/events/warriors_1750.html

[462] https://web.archive.org/web/20090105224202/http://www.searchsikhism.com/rise.html

[463] https://web.archive.org/web/20090105222035/http://www.searchsikhism.com/raaj.html

[464] https://web.archive.org/web/20120222114638/http://www.harisinghnalwa.com/final_frontier.html

[465] *The Gurkhas* by W. Brook Northey, John Morris. Page 58

[466] Dalrymple, *The Last Moghul*, pp.4–5

[467] Peers 2013, p. 64.

[468] //en.wikipedia.org/w/index.php?title=Template:Part_of_History_of_India&action=edit

[469] "The events of 1857–58 in India (are) known variously as a mutiny, a revolt, a rebellion and the first war of independence (the debates over which only confirm just how contested imperial history can become) ...(page 63)" UNIQ-ref-0-cb065aa36d516186-QINU

[470] ""The 1857 rebellion was by and large confined to northern Indian Gangetic Plain and central India." UNIQ-ref-1-cb065aa36d516186-QINU

[471] "The revolt was confined to the northern Gangetic plain and central India."*The Gurkhas* by W. Brook Northey, John Morris. Page 58

[472] Although the majority of the violence occurred in the northern Indian Gangetic plain and central India, recent scholarship has suggested that the rebellion also reached parts of the east and north."Dalrymple, *The Last Moghul*, pp.4–5

[473] "What distinguished the events of 1857 was their scale and the fact that for a short time they posed a military threat to British dominance in the Ganges Plain."Peers 2013, p. 64.

[474] ,, and

[475] Metcalf & Metcalf 2006, pp. 100–103.

[476] Brown 1994, pp. 85–86.

[477] "Indian soldiers and the rural population over a large part of northern India showed their mistrust of their rulers and their alienation from them. .. For all their talk of improvement, the new rulers were as yet able to offer very little in the way of positive inducements for Indians to acquiesce in the rule."

[478] "Many Indians took up arms against the British, if for very diverse reasons. Explanations have therefore to concentrate on the motives of those who actually rebelled."

[479] "On the other hand, a very large number actually fought for the British, while the majority remained apparently acquiescent.""The events of 1857–58 in India (are) known variously as a mutiny, a revolt, a rebellion and the first war of independence (the debates over which only confirm just how contested imperial history can become) ...(page 63)"

[480] The cost of the rebellion in terms of human suffering was immense. Two great cities, Delhi and Lucknow, were devastated by fighting and by the plundering of the victorious British. Where the countryside resisted, as in parts of Awadh, villages were burnt. Mutineers and their supporters were often killed out of hand. British civilians, including women and children, were murdered

as well as the British officers of the sepoy regiments.""""The 1857 rebellion was by and large confined to northern Indian Gangetic Plain and central India."

[481] "The south, Bengal, and the Punjab remained unscathed, ...""The revolt was confined to the northern Gangetic plain and central India."

[482] "... it was the support from the Sikhs, carefully cultivated by the British since the end of the Anglo-Sikh wars, and the disinclination of the Bengali intelligentsia to throw in their lot with what they considered a backward Zamindar revolt, that proved decisive in the course of the struggle.Although the majority of the violence occurred in the northern Indian Gangetic plain and central India, recent scholarship has suggested that the rebellion also reached parts of the east and north."

[483] "(they) generated no coherent ideology or programme on which to build a new order.""What distinguished the events of 1857 was their scale and the fact that for a short time they posed a military threat to British dominance in the Ganges Plain."

[484] "The events of 1857–58 in India, ... marked a major watershed not only in the history of British India but also of British imperialism as a whole.", , and

[485] "Queen Victoria's Proclamation of 1858 laid the foundation for Indian secularism and established the semi-legal framework that would govern the politics of religion in colonial India for the next century. .. It promised civil equality for Indians regardless of their religious affiliation, and state non-interference in Indians' religious affairs. Although the Proclamation lacked the legal authority of a constitution, generations of Indians cited the Queen's proclamation in order to claim, and to defend, their right to religious freedom." (page 23)Metcalf & Metcalf 2006, pp. 100–103.

[486] The proclamation to the "Princes, Chiefs, and People of India," issued by Queen Victoria on November 1, 1858. "We hold ourselves bound to the natives of our Indian territories by the same obligation of duty which bind us to all our other subjects." (p. 2)

[487] "When the governance of India was transferred from the East India Company to the Crown in 1858, she (Queen Victoria) and Prince Albert intervened in an unprecedented fashion to turn the proclamation of the transfer of power into a document of tolerance and clemency. .. they ... insisted on the clause that stated that the people of India would enjoy the same protection as all subjects of Britain. Over time, this royal intervention led to the Proclamation of 1858 becoming known in the Indian subcontinent as 'the Magna Carta of Indian liberties', a phrase which Indian nationalists such as Gandhi later took up as they sought to test equality under imperial law" (pages 38–39)Brown 1994, pp. 85–86.

[488] "In purely legal terms, (the proclamation) kept faith with the principles of liberal imperialism and appeared to hold out the promise that British rule would benefit Indians and Britons alike. But as is too often the case with noble statements of faith, reality fell far short of theory, and the failure on the part of the British to live up to the wording of the proclamation would later be used by Indian nationalists as proof of the hollowness of imperial principles. (page 76)""Indian soldiers and the rural population over a large part of northern India showed their mistrust of their rulers and their alienation from them. .. For all their talk of improvement, the new rulers were as yet able to offer very little in the way of positive inducements for Indians to acquiesce in the rule."

[489] "Ignoring ...the conciliatory proclamation of Queen Victoria in 1858, Britishers in India saw little reason to grant Indians a greater control over their own affairs. Under these circumstances, it was not long before the seed-idea of nationalism implanted by their reading of Western books began to take root in the minds of intelligent and energetic Indians.""Many Indians took up arms against the British, if for very diverse reasons. Explanations have therefore to concentrate on the motives of those who actually rebelled.""On the other hand, a very large number actually fought for the British, while the majority remained apparently acquiescent."

[490] to

[491] *A Matter of Honour – an Account of the Indian Army, its Officers and Men*, Philip Mason, , page 261

[492] Essential histories, The Indian Rebellion 1857–1858, Gregory Fremont-Barnes, Osprey 2007, page 25

[493] From Sepoy to Subedar – Being the Life and Adventures of Subedar Sita Ram, a Native Officer of the Bengal Army, edited by James Lunt, , page 172

[494] Hyam, R (2002) Britain's Imperial Century, 1815–1914 Third Edition, Palgrave Macmillan, Basingstoke P135
[495] Headrick, Daniel R. "The Tools of Empire: Technology and European Imperialism in the Nineteenth Century". Oxford University Press, 1981, p.88
[496] The only troops to be armed with the Enfield rifle, and hence the greased cartridges, were the British HM 60th Rifles stationed at Meerut
[497] M. Edwardes, *Red Year: The Indian Rebellion of 1857* (London: Cardinal, 1975), p. 23
[498] G. W. Forrest, *Selections from the letters, despatches and other state papers preserved in the Military department of the government of India, 1857–58* (1893), pp. 8–12, available at archive.org https://archive.org/details/selectionsfrom100forrgoog
[499] ' '
[500] ' '
[501] Susanne Hoeber Rudolph, Lloyd I Rudolph. "Living with Difference in India", *The Political Quarterly*:71 (s1) (2000), 20–38.
[502] » Sepoy Mutiny of 1857 Postcolonial Studies @ Emory http://www.english.emory.edu/Bahri/Mutiny.html. English.emory.edu (23 March 1998). Retrieved on 12 July 2013.
[503] Seema Alavi *The Sepoys and the Company* (Delhi: Oxford University Press) 1998 p. 5
[504] Memorandum from Lieutenant-Colonel W. St. L. Mitchell (CO of the 19th BNI) to Major A. H. Ross about his troop's refusal to accept the Enfield cartridges, 27 February 1857, Archives of Project South Asia, South Dakota State University and Missouri Southern State University http://projectsouthasia.sdstate.edu/docs/history/primarydocs/War%20of%201857/Indian%20Mutiny--Ch1/letter%2031.htm
[505] "The Indian Mutiny of 1857", Col. G. B. Malleson, reprint 2005, Rupa & Co. Publishers, New Delhi
[506] Durendra Nath Sen, page 50 *Eighteen Fifty-Seven*, The Publications Division, Ministry of Information & Broadcasting, Government of India, May 1957
[507] Sir John Kaye & G.B. Malleson.: *The Indian Mutiny of 1857*, (Delhi: Rupa & Co.) reprint 2005 p49
[508] Dr. Surendra Nath Sen, pages 71–73 "Eighteen Fifty-Seven", Publications Division, Ministry of Information & Broadcasting, Government of India
[509] Dalrymple, *The Last Moghul*, pp.223–224
[510] Michael Edwardes, *Battles of the Indian Mutiny*, pp 52–53
[511] Zachary Nunn. The British Raj http://www.drake.edu/artsci/PolSci/ssjrnl/2001/nunn.html
[512] *Indian Army Uniforms under the British – Infantry*, W.Y. Carman, Morgan-Grampian Books 1969, p. 107
[513] A.H. Amin, Orbat.com http://orbat.com/site/cimh/india/bengalarmy1857.html
[514] Lessons from 1857 http://www.newstodaynet.com/guest/210607gu1.htm
[515] The Indian Army: 1765 – 1914 http://www.bharat-rakshak.com/LAND-FORCES/Army/Images-1765c.html
[516] The Indin Mutiny 1857–58, Gregory Fremont-Barnes, Osprey 2007, page 34
[517] God's Acre http://www.hindu.com/mp/2006/10/28/stories/2006102801590100.htm. The Hindu Metro Plus Delhi. 28 October 2006.
[518] 'The Rising: The Ballad of Mangal Pandey' http://www.jonathanforeman.com/movies/mangal.html . Daily Mail, 27 August 2005
[519] essential histories, the Indian Mutiny 1857–58, Gregory Fremont-Barnes, Osprey 2007, p.40
[520] *The story of Cawnpore: The Indian Mutiny 1857*, Capt. Mowbray Thomson, Brighton, Tom Donovan, 1859, pp. 148–159.
[521] Essential Histories, the Indian Mutiny 1857–58, Gregory Fremont-Barnes, Osprey 2007, page 49
[522] S&T magazine No. 121 (September 1998), page 56
[523] *A History of the Indian Mutiny* by G. W. Forrest, London, William Blackwood, 1904
[524] *Kaye's and Malleson's History of the Indian Mutiny*. Longman's, London, 1896. Footnote, p. 257.
[525] Edwardes, *Battles of the Indian Mutiny*, p.56
[526] Essential Histories, the Indian Mutiny 1857–58, Gregory Fremont-Barnes, Osprey 2007, page 53

[527] S&T magazine No. 121 (September 1998), page 58
[528] John Harris, The Indian mutiny, Wordsworth military library 2001, page 92,
[529] J.W. Sherer, *Daily Life during the Indian Mutiny*, 1858, p. 56
[530] Andrew Ward, *Our bones are scattered – The Cawnpore massacres and the Indian Mutiny of 1857*, John Murray, 1996
[531] Ramson, Martin & Ramson, Edward, *The Indian Empire, 1858*
[532] Michael Edwardes, *Battles of the Indian Mutiny*, Pan, 1963
[533] Units of the Army of the Madras Presidency wore blue rather than black shakoes or forage caps
[534] Essential Histories, the Indian Mutiny 1857–58, Gregory Fremont-Barnes, Osprey 2007, page 79
[535] Lachmi Bai Rani of Jhansi, the Jeanne d'Arc of India (1901), White, Michael (Michael Alfred Edwin), 1866, New York: J.F. Taylor & Company, 1901
[536] Charles Allen, *Soldier Sahibs*, p.276
[537] Charles Allen, *Soldier Sahibs*, pp. 290–293
[538] Hibbert, *The Great Mutiny*, p.163
[539] Charles Allen, *Soldier Sahibs*, p.283
[540] Dr Surendra Nath Sen, pages 343–344 *Eighteen Fifty-Seven*, Ministry of Information, Government of India 1957
[541] *John Sergeant's Tracks of Empire*, BBC4 programme.
[542] Turnbull, CM 'Convicts in the Straits Settlements 1826–1827' in Journal of the Malaysian Branch of the Royal Asiatic Society, 1970, 43, 1, P100
[543] Straits Times, 23 August 1857
[544] Arnold, D (1983) 'White colonization and labour in nineteenth-century India', Journal of Imperial and Commonwealth History, 11, P144
[545] The cost of the rebellion in terms of human suffering was immense. Two great cities, Delhi and Lucknow, were devastated by fighting and by the plundering of the victorious British. Where the countryside resisted, as in parts of Awadh, villages were burnt. Mutineers and their supporters were often killed out of hand. British civilians, including women and children, were murdered as well as the British officers of the sepoy regiments."The cost of the rebellion in terms of human suffering was immense. Two great cities, Delhi and Lucknow, were devastated by fighting and by the plundering of the victorious British. Where the countryside resisted, as in parts of Awadh, villages were burnt. Mutineers and their supporters were often killed out of hand. British civilians, including women and children, were murdered as well as the British officers of the sepoy regiments."
[546] *Sahib: The British Soldier in India 1750–1914* Richard Holmes HarperCollins 2005
[547] Punch, 24 October 1857
[548] Dalrymple, *The Last Moghul*, pp.374
[549] The Friend of India reprinted in South Australian Advertiser, 2 October 1860
[550] Rajit K. Mazumder, The Indian Army and the Making of the Punjab. (Delhi, Permanent Black, 2003), 11.
[551] W.Y. Carman, page 107 *Indian Army Uniforms – Infantry*, Morgan-Grampian London 1969
[552] Philip Mason, page 238 "A Matter of Honour",
[553] Philip Mason, page 319 "A Matter of Honour",
[554] Authorisation contained in General Order 363 of 1858 and General Order 733 of 1859
[555] First Indian War of Independence http://www.kamat.com/kalranga/itihas/1857.htm 8 January 1998
[556] A number of dispossessed dynasts, both Hindu and Muslim, exploited the well-founded caste-suspicions of the sepoys and made these simple folk their cat's paw in gamble for recovering their thrones. The last scions of the Delhi Mughals or the Oudh Nawabs and the Peshwa, can by no ingenuity be called fighters for Indian freedom *Hindusthan Standard, Puja Annual, 195 p. 22* referenced in the *Truth about the Indian mutiny* article by Dr Ganda Singh
[557] In the light of the available evidence, we are forced to the conclusion that the uprising of 1857 was not the result of careful planning, nor were there any master-minds behind it. As I read about the events of 1857, I am forced to the conclusion that the Indian national character had sunk very low. The leaders of the revolt could never agree. They were mutually jealous and continually intrigued against one another. .. In fact these personal jealousies and intrigues were

largely responsible for the Indian defeat.Maulana Abul Kalam Azad, Surendranath Sen: Eighteen Fifty-seven (Appx. X & Appx. XV)

[558] German National Geographic article https://web.archive.org/web/20050503231048/http://www.nationalgeographic.de/php/entdecken/wettbewerb2/forum.php3?command=show&id=3118&root=3052

[559] The Empire, Sydney, Australia, 11 July 1857, or Taranaki Herald, New Zealand, 29 August 1857

[560] Michael Adas, "Twentieth Century Approaches to the Indian Mutiny of 1857–58," *Journal of Asian History*, 1971, Vol. 5 Issue 1, pp 1–19

[561] It includes essays by historians Eric Stokes, Christopher Bayly, Rudrangshu Mukherjee, Tapti Roy, Rajat K. Ray and others.

[562] For the latest research see Crispin Bates, ed., *Mutiny at the Margins: New Perspectives on the Indian Uprising of 1857: Volume I: Anticipations and Experiences in the Locality* (2013)

[563] Thomas R. Metcalf, "Rural society and British rule in nineteenth century India." *Journal of Asian Studies* 39#1 (1979): 111–119.

[564] M. Farooqui, trans (2010) *Besieged: voices from Delhi 1857* Penguin Books

[565] Kim A. Wagner, "The Marginal Mutiny: The New Historiography of the Indian Uprising of 1857," *History Compass* 9/10 (2011): 760–766, quote p 760

[566] See also

[567] Sabbaq Ahmed, "Ideology and Muslim militancy in India: Selected case studies of the 1857 Indian rebellion." (PhD Dissertation, Victoria University of Wellington (NZ), 2015). online http://researcharchive.vuw.ac.nz/xmlui/handle/10063/4660

[568] *The Indian Mutiny and Victorian Trauma* by Christopher Herbert, Princeton University Press, Princeton 2007

[569] *The History of the Indian Mutiny: Giving a detailed account of the sepoy insurrection in India* by Charles Ball, The London Printing and Publishing Company, London, 1860

[570] V.D. Savarkar argues that the rebellion was a war of Indian independence. *The Indian War of Independence: 1857* (Bombay: 1947 [1909]). Most historians have seen his arguments as discredited, with one venturing so far as to say, 'It was neither first, nor national, nor a war of independence.' Eric Stokes has argued that the rebellion was actually a variety of movements, not one movement. *The Peasant Armed* (Oxford: 1980). See also S.B. Chaudhuri, *Civil Rebellion in the Indian Mutinies 1857–1859* (Calcutta: 1957)

[571] The Indian Mutiny, Spilsbury Julian, Orion, 2007

[572] S&T magazine issue 121 (September 1988), page 20

[573] The communal hatred led to ugly communal riots in many parts of U.P. The green flag was hoisted and Muslims in Bareilly, Bijnor, Moradabad, and other places the Muslims shouted for the revival of Muslim kingdom." R. C. Majumdar: *Sepoy Mutiny and Revolt of 1857* (page 2303-31)

[574] Sitaram Yechury. The Empire Strikes Back http://hindustantimes.com/news/181_1896809,00120001.htm . Hindustan Times. January 2006.

[575] http://www.oup.com/uk/catalogue/?ci=9780198731139

[576] http://www.thehistorypress.co.uk/index.php/victoria-s-scottish-lion-26465.html

[577] http://www.jamesleasor.com/the-red-fort/

[578] https://books.google.com/books?id=dyQuAgAAQBAJ

[579] //www.jstor.org/stable/23611115

[580] //doi.org/10.1017/S0026749X00016097

[581] //www.jstor.org/stable/312880

[582] //doi.org/10.1017/S0026749X00013913

[583] //www.jstor.org/stable/312615

[584] //doi.org/10.1006/jhge.2000.0236

[585] //doi.org/10.1093/past/142.1.169

[586] //www.jstor.org/stable/651200

[587] //doi.org/10.2307/3517586

[588] //www.jstor.org/stable/313141

[589] //doi.org/10.1080/0043824032000078072

[590] //www.jstor.org/stable/3560211

[591] //doi.org/10.1093/past/128.1.92
[592] //www.jstor.org/stable/651010
[593] //doi.org/10.1093/past/142.1.178
[594] //www.jstor.org/stable/651201
[595] //doi.org/10.1017/S0026749X00016115
[596] //www.jstor.org/stable/312882
[597] //doi.org/10.1017/s0018246x00010554
[598] //www.jstor.org/stable/2638016
[599] //www.worldcat.org/oclc/852404214
[600] http://www.csas.ed.ac.uk/mutiny/
[601] http://www.let.leidenuniv.nl/pdf/geschiedenis/EJES%20Erll%20final.pdf
[602] //www.jstor.org/stable/4419570
[603] //doi.org/10.2307/1345889
[604] //www.jstor.org/stable/1345889
[605] //doi.org/10.1111/j.1478-0542.2011.00799.x
[606] http://digital.library.upenn.edu/women/inglis/lucknow/lucknow.html
[607] http://digital.library.upenn.edu/women/writers.html
[608] https://www.britannica.com/technology/Lee-Enfield-rifle
[609] http://www.jamesleasor.com/follow-the-drum/.
[610] //tools.wmflabs.org/ftl/cgi-bin/ftl?st=wp&su=Indian+Rebellion+of+1857&library=OLBP
[611] //tools.wmflabs.org/ftl/cgi-bin/ftl?st=wp&su=Indian+Rebellion+of+1857
[612] //tools.wmflabs.org/ftl/cgi-bin/ftl?st=wp&su=Indian+Rebellion+of+1857&library= 0CHOOSE0
[613] http://dsal.uchicago.edu/reference/schwartzberg/fullscreen.html?object=099
[614] http://defencejournal.com/dec99/1857.htm
[615] http://www.britishempire.co.uk/forces/armycampaigns/indiancampaigns/mutiny/mutiny.htm
[616] http://www.marxists.org/archive/marx/works/1857/india/index.htm
[617] Interpretation Act 1889 (52 & 53 Vict. c. 63), s. 18.
[618] //en.wikipedia.org/w/index.php?title=Template:Part_of_History_of_India&action=edit
[619] Oxford English Dictionary, 2nd edition, 1989: from Skr. *rāj*: to reign, rule; cognate with L. *rēx*, *rēg-is*, OIr. *rī*, *rīg* king (see 'rich').
[620] Oxford English Dictionary, 3rd edition (June 2008), on-line edition (September 2011): "spec. In full **British Raj**. Direct rule in India by the British (1858–1947); this period of dominion."
[621] Quote: "When the formal rule of the Company was replaced by the direct rule of the British Crown in 1858, ..."
[622] Quote: "... Company rule in India lasted effectively from the Battle of Plassey in 1757 until 1858, when following the 1857 Indian Rebellion, the British Crown assumed direct colonial rule of India in the new British Raj."
[623] Quote:"More than 500 Indian kingdoms and principalities ... existed during the "British Raj" period (1858–1947)"
[624] Quote: "... by 1909 the Government of India, reflecting on 50 years of Crown rule after the rebellion, could boast that ..."
[625] Quote:"Mill, who was himself employed by the British East India company from the age of seventeen until the British government assumed direct rule over India in 1858."
[626] Quote: "The 'Indian Empire' was a name given to those areas in the Indian subcontinent both directly and indirectly ruled by Britain after the rebellion; the British issued passports after 1876 under that name."
[627] Quote: "British India, meanwhile, was itself the powerful 'metropolis' of its own colonial empire, 'the Indian empire'."
[628] Quote: India Executive Council: Sir Arcot Ramasamy Mudaliar, Sir Firoz Khan Noon and Sir V. T. Krishnamachari served as India's delegates to the London Commonwealth Meeting, April 1945, and the U.N. San Francisco Conference on International Organisation, April–June 1945."
[629] Marshall (2001), p. 384
[630] Codrington, 1926, Chapter X:Transition to British administration
[631] http://www.britannica.com/place/Nepal/Cultural-life#toc23631 Encyclopædia Britannica. 2008.

[632] "Bhutan." http://www.britannica.com/place/Bhutan/Government-and-society#toc25008 Encyclopædia Britannica. 2008.

[633] "Sikkim." Encyclopædia Britannica. 2007. Encyclopædia Britannica Online. 5 August 2007 <http://www.britannica.com/eb/article-46212>.

[634] **1.** *Imperial Gazetteer of India*, volume IV, published under the authority of the Secretary of State for India-in-Council, 1909, Oxford University Press. p. 5. Quote: "The history of British India falls, as observed by Sir C. P. Ilbert in his *Government of India*, into three periods. From the beginning of the seventeenth century to the middle of the eighteenth century the East India Company is a trading corporation, existing on the sufferance of the native powers and in rivalry with the merchant companies of Holland and France. During the next century, the Company acquires and consolidates its dominion, shares its sovereignty in increasing proportions with the Crown, and gradually loses its mercantile privileges and functions. After the mutiny of 1857 the remaining powers of the Company are transferred to the Crown, and then follows an era of peace in which India awakens to new life and progress." **2.** *The Statutes: From the Twentieth Year of King Henry the Third to the ...* by Robert Harry Drayton, Statutes of the Realm – Law – 1770 p. 211 (3) "Save as otherwise expressly provided in this Act, the law of British India and of the several parts thereof existing immediately before the appointed ..." **3. 4.**

[635] **Quote1**: "Before passing on to the political history of British India, which properly begins with the Anglo-French Wars in the Carnatic, ... (p. 463)" **Quote2**: "The political history of the British in India begins in the eighteenth century with the French Wars in the Carnatic. (p. 471)"

[636] British Indian Passport of Muhammad Ali Jinnah http://www.passport-collector.com/2011/04/25/founder-of-pakistan/

[637] //en.wikipedia.org/w/index.php?title=Template:Colonial_India&action=edit

[638] //en.wikipedia.org/w/index.php?title=Template:History_of_Pakistan&action=edit

[639] Robin J. Moore, "Imperial India, 1858–1914", pp. 422–46

[640] Moore, "Imperial India, 1858–1914", p. 424

[641] Moore, "Imperial India, 1858–1914", p. 426

[642] p. 103–05, "India – Government and Constitution," *The Statesman's Year-Book 1947*, Steinberg, S.H., Macmillan, New York

[643] pp. 133–34, "India – Currency, Weights and Measures," *The Statesman's Year-Book 1947*, Steinberg, S.H., Macmillan, New York

[644] pp. 106–07, "India – Government and Constitution," *The Statesman's Year-Book 1947*, Steinberg, S.H., Macmillan, New York

[645] p. 106–07, "India – Government and Constitution," *The Statesman's Year-Book 1947*, Steinberg, S.H., Macmillan, New York

[646] pp. 104–05, "India – Government and Constitution," *The Statesman's Year-Book 1947*, Steinberg, S.H., Macmillan, New York

[647] p. 108, "India – Government and Constitution," *The Statesman's Year-Book 1947*, Steinberg, S.H., Macmillan, New York

[648] The only other emperor during this period, Edward VIII, 1938, did not issue any Indian currency under his name.

[649] Briton Martin, Jr. "The Viceroyalty of Lord Dufferin", *History Today*, (Dec 1960) 10#12 pp. 821–30, and (Jan 1961) 11#1 pp. 56–64

[650] Michael Edwardes, *High Noon of Empire: India under Curzon* (1965)

[651] Ernest Hullo, "India", in *Catholic Encyclopedia* (1910) vol. 7 online http://www.newadvent.org/cathen/07722a.htm

[652]: "The army took on the form which survived till independence ... The Bengal army was completely recast ... The Brahmin element from Uttar Pradesh, the core of the original mutiny, was heavily reduced and its place taken by Gurkhas, Sikhs, and Punjabis."

[653] Robinson, Ronald Edward, & John Gallagher. 1968. *Africa and the Victorians: The Climax of Imperialism*. Garden City, N.Y.: Doubleday

[654] http://www.csas.ed.ac.uk/mutiny/confpapers/Queen%27sProclamation.pdf

[655] Parameswara Krishnan, *Glimpses of Indian Historical Demography* (Delhi: B.R. Publishing Corporation 2010)

[656] Kingsley Davis, *The Population of India and Pakistan* (Princeton University Press, 1951).

[657] Klein, "Population growth and mortality in British India: Part II: The demographic revolution," p. 42

[658] Radhika Singha, "Colonial Law and Infrastructural Power: Reconstructing Community, Locating the Female Subject", *Studies in History*, (Feb 2003), 19#1 pp. 87–126 online http://sih.sagepub.com/content/19/1/87.extract

[659] Tazeen M. Murshid, "Law and Female Autonomy in Colonial India", *Journal of the Asiatic Society of Bangladesh: Humanities*, (June 2002), 47#1 pp. 25–42

[660] Karuna Mantena, "The Crisis of Liberal Imperialism," *Histoire@Politique. Politique, culture, société* (2010) #11 online http://www.histoire-politique.fr/documents/11/dossier/pdf/HP11_Mantena_pdf_200510.pdf p. 3

[661] Suresh Chandra Ghosh, "Bentinck, Macaulay and the introduction of English education in India", *History of Education*, (March 1995) 24#1 pp. 17–24

[662] Hayden Bellenoit, "Missionary Education, Religion and Knowledge in India, c.1880–1915," *Modern Asian Studies* 41#2 (2007): 369–94

[663] Moore, "Imperial India, 1858–1914", p. 431

[664] Zareer Masani, *Indian Tales of the Raj* (1988) p. 89

[665] B. R. Tomlinson, *The Economy of Modern India, 1860–1970* (1996) p. 5

[666] B. H. Tomlinson, "India and the British Empire, 1880–1935", *Indian Economic and Social History Review*, (Oct 1975), 12#4 pp. 337–80

[667] F. H. Brown and B. R. Tomlinson, "Tata, Jamshed Nasarwanji (1839–1904)", in *Oxford Dictionary of National Biography* (2004) Retrieved 28 Jan 2012 http://www.oxforddnb.com/view/article/36421,

[668] Vinay Bahl, "The Emergence of Large-Scale Steel Industry in India Under British Colonial Rule, 1880–1907", *Indian Economic and Social History Review*, (Oct 1994) 31#4 pp. 413–60

[669] Daniel R. Headrick, *The tentacles of progress: technology transfer in the age of imperialism, 1850–1940*, (1988) pp. 291–92

[670] Vinay Bahl, *Making of the Indian Working Class: A Case of the Tata Iron & Steel Company, 1880–1946* (1995) ch 8

[671] Claude Markovits, *Indian Business and Nationalist Politics 1931–39: The Indigenous Capitalist Class and the Rise of the Congress Party* (Cambridge University Press, 2002) pp. 160–66

[672] Daniel R. Headrick, *The tentacles of progress: technology transfer in the age of imperialism, 1850–1940*, (1988) pp. 78–79

[673] Headrick, *The tentacles of progress: technology transfer in the age of imperialism, 1850–1940*, (1988) pp. 81–82, 291.

[674] R. O. Christensen, "The State and Indian Railway Performance, 1870–1920: Part I, Financial Efficiency and Standards of Service", *Journal of Transport History* (September 1981) 2#2, pp. 1–15.

[675] Neil Charlesworth, *British Rule and the Indian Economy, 1800–1914* (1981) pp. 23–37

[676] Ian Stone, *Canal Irrigation in British India: Perspectives on Technological Change in a Peasant Economy* (2002) pp. 278–80

[677] for the historiography, see Rohan D'Souza, "Water in British India: the making of a 'colonial hydrology'." *History Compass* (2006) 4#4 pp. 621–28. online http://www.sussex.ac.uk/cweh/documents/hcomroh.pdf

[678] Laura Bear, *Lines of the nation: Indian Railway workers, bureaucracy, and the intimate historical self* (2007) – pp. 25–28

[679] Arudra Burra, "The Indian Civil Service and the nationalist movement: neutrality, politics and continuity", *Commonwealth and Comparative Politics*, (Nov 2010), 48#4 pp. 404–32

[680] B. R. Tomlinson, *The economy of modern India, 1860–1970* (1996) p. 109

[681] Judith Brown, *Modern India: The Origins of an Asian Democracy* (1994) p. 12

[682] Angus Maddison, The World Economy, pp. 109–12, (2001)

[683] Rajat Kanta Ray, "Indian Society and the Establishment of British Supremacy, 1765–1818", in *The Oxford History of the British Empire*: vol. 2, "The Eighteenth Century" ed. by P. J. Marshall, (1998), pp. 508–29

[684] P.J. Marshall, "The British in Asia: Trade to Dominion, 1700–1765", in *The Oxford History of the British Empire: vol. 2, The Eighteenth Century* ed. by P. J. Marshall, (1998), pp. 487–507

[685] in millions

[686] Desai, Raychaudhuri & Kumar 1983, p. 528.
[687] Grove 2007, p. 80.
[688] Grove 2007, p. 83.
[689] Fieldhouse 1996, p. 132.
[690] Desai, Raychaudhuri & Kumar 1983, p. 529.
[691] Imperial Gazetteer of India vol. III 1907, p. 488.
[692] Davis 2001, p. 7.
[693] Desai, Raychaudhuri & Kumar 1983, pp. 530.
[694] Desai, Raychaudhuri & Kumar 1983, p. 531.
[695] Bose 1918, pp. 79–81.
[696] Rai 2008, pp. 263–281.
[697] Koomar 2009, pp. 13–14.
[698] Davis, Mike. Late Victorian Holocausts. 1. Verso, 2000. p. 7
[699] Davis, Mike. Late Victorian Holocausts. 1. Verso, 2000. p. 173
[700] Sen, Amartya. Development as Freedom. ch 7
[701] Ó Gráda, C.: " Famine: A Short History http://press.princeton.edu/chapters/s8857.html ". Princeton University Press.
[702] The 1832 Cholera Epidemic in New York State http://www.earlyamerica.com/review/2000_fall/1832_cholera_part1.html, By G. William Beardslee
[703] Infectious Diseases: Plague Through History http://www.sciencemag.org/cgi/content/full/321/5890/773, sciencemag.org
[704] Malaria http://www.nls.uk/indiapapers/malaria.html – Medical History of British India, National Library of Scotland 2007
[705] Leprosy – Medical History of British India http://www.nls.uk/indiapapers/leprosy.html , National Library of Scotland 2007
[706] Smallpox – some unknown heroes in smallpox eradication http://www.ijme.in/index.php/ijme/article/download/1533/3329
[707] F.H. Hinsley, ed. *The New Cambridge Modern History, Vol. 11: Material Progress and World-Wide Problems, 1870–98* (1962) contents http://library.mpib-berlin.mpg.de/toc/z2010_334.pdf pp. 411–36.
[708] James S. Olson and Robert S. Shadle, *Historical Dictionary of the British Empire* (1996) p. 116
[709] Helen S. Dyer, *Pandita Ramabai: the story of her life* (1900) online https://books.google.com/books?id=wHo4AAAAMAAJ&pg=PA116
[710] David Ludden, *India and South Asia: a short history* (2002) p.197
[711] Stanley A. Wolpert, *Tilak and Gokhale: revolution and reform in the making of modern India* (1962) p 67
[712] Michael Edwardes, *High Noon of Empire: India under Curzon* (1965) p. 77
[713] Moore, "Imperial India, 1858–1914", p. 435
[714] John R. McLane, "The Decision to Partition Bengal in 1905", *Indian Economic and Social History Review*, July 1965, 2#3, pp. 221–37
[715] Ranbir Vohra, The Making of India: A Historical Survey (Armonk: M.E. Sharpe, Inc, 1997), 120
[716] V. Sankaran Nair, *Swadeshi movement: The beginnings of student unrest in South India* (1985) excerpt and text search https://books.google.com/books?id=YQVqo0lzq5EC
[717] Peter Heehs, *The lives of Sri Aurobindo* (2008) p. 184
[718] Wolpert, *A New History of India*, pp. 275–76
[719] Ludden (2002), pp. 200–201
[720] Balraj Krishna, *India's Bismarck, Sardar Vallabhbhai Patel* (2007) ch. 2
[721] Nick Lloyd, *The Amritsar Massacre: The Untold Story of One Fateful Day* (2011) p. 180
[722] Derek Sayer, "British Reaction to the Amritsar Massacre 1919–1920", *Past & Present*, May 1991, Issue 131, pp. 130–64
[723] Brain Bond, "Amritsar 1919", *History Today*, Sept 1963, Vol. 13 Issue 10, pp. 666–676
[724] David C. Potter, "Manpower Shortage and the End of Colonialism: The Case of Indian Civil Service", *Modern Asian Studies*, (Jan 1973) 7#1 pp. 47–73
[725] Simon Epstein, "District Officers in Decline: The Erosion of British Authority in the Bombay Countryside, 1919 to 1947", *Modern Asian Studies*, (May 1982) 16#3 pp. 493–518

[726] Piers Brendon, *The Decline and Fall of the British Empire: 1781–1997* (2008) p. 394
[727] Andrew Muldoon, "Politics, Intelligence and Elections in Late Colonial India: Congress and the Raj in 1937", *Journal of the Canadian Historical Association* (2009), 20#2 pp. 160–88; Muldoon, *Empire, politics and the creation of the 1935 India Act: last act of the Raj* (2009)
[728] Ramachandra Guha, *India After Gandhi: The History of the World's Largest Democracy* (2007) p. 43
[729] Recruitment was especially active in the Punjab province of British India, under the leadership of Premier Sir Sikandar Hayat Khan, who believed in cooperating with the British to achieve eventual independence for the Indian nation. For details of various recruitment drives by Sir Sikandar between 1939 and 1942, see
[730] Alan Jeffreys, and Patrick Rose, eds. *The Indian Army 1939–47: Experience and Development* (Farnham: Ashgate, 2012), 244 pp. online review http://secondworldwaroperationsresearchgroup.wordpress.com/2013/06/09/book-review-the-indian-army-1939-47-experience-and-development/
[731] John F. Riddick, *The history of British India: a chronology* (2006) p. 142
[732] Shyam Ratna Gupta, "New Light on the Cripps Mission", *India Quarterly*, (Jan 1972), Vol. 28 Issue 1, p. 69–74
[733] Stein 2010, pp. 305, 325": Jawaharlal Nehru and Subhas Bose were among those who, impatient with Gandhi's programmes and methods, looked upon socialism as an alternative for nationalistic policies capable of meeting the country's economic and social needs, as well as a link to potential international support. (p. 325) (p. 345)"
[734] Low 2002, p. 297.
[735] Low 2002, p. 313.
[736] Low 1993, pp. 31–31.
[737] Wolpert 2006, p. 69.
[738] Bandyopadhyay 2004, p. 427.
[739] Bayly & Harper 2007, p. 2.
[740] Stein 2001, p. 345.
[741] Quote: "India had always been a minority interest in British public life; no great body of public opinion now emerged to argue that war-weary and impoverished Britain should send troops and money to hold it against its will in an empire of doubtful value. By late 1946 both Prime Minister and Secretary of State for British India recognised that neither international opinion no their own voters would stand for any reassertion of the *raj*, even if there had been the men, money, and administrative machinery with which to do so." Quote: "With a war weary army and people and a ravaged economy, Britain would have had to retreat; the Labour victory only quickened the process somewhat." Quote: "More importantly, though victorious in war, Britain had suffered immensely in the struggle. It simply did not possess the manpower or economic resources required to coerce a restive India."
[742] Ian Talbot and Gurharpal Singh, The Partition of India (2009), passim
[743] Maria Misra, *Vishnu's crowded temple: India since the Great Rebellion* (2008) p. 237
[744] http://www.globalsecurity.org/military/world/war/indo-pak-partition2.htm
[745] Thomas R. Metcalf, *The New Cambridge History of India: Ideologies of the Raj* (1995), pp. 10–12, 34–35
[746] Maurice Zinkin, "Legacies of the Raj", *Asian Affairs*, (Oct 1995, 26#3) online http//web.ebscohost.com
[747] Y. K. Malik and V. B. Singh, *Hindu Nationalists in India: the rise of the Bharatiya Janata Party* (Westview Press, 1994), p. 14
[748] https://www.questia.com/library/88816335/the-cambridge-shorter-history-of-india
[749] https://books.google.com/books?id=iAQ9AAAAIAAJ
[750] https://www.questia.com/PM.qst?a=o&d=74007102
[751] https://archive.org/details/cambridgehistory06rapsuoft
[752] https://archive.org/details/in.ernet.dli.2015.77042
[753] https://books.google.com/books?id=Es6x4u_g19UC
[754] https://archive.org/details/in.ernet.dli.2015.176466
[755] https://books.google.com/books?id=K2H_v0t5jTkC&pg=PA147
[756] https://books.google.com/books?id=93fnssiWvjoC

[757] https://books.google.com/books?id=0M4Pl_VCExgC
[758] https://books.google.com/books?id=qXH9xGCWjYUC
[759] https://books.google.com/books?id=InFTmnS4crYC
[760] https://books.google.com/books?id=V3geAAAAMAAJ
[761] https://books.google.com/books?id=xEzx2zVHXSwC&pg=PA9
[762] https://books.google.com/books?id=kOEsSmOQL7EC
[763] https://books.google.com/books?id=Jj-4zmBLXq0C
[764] https://books.google.com/books?id=eKE9AAAAIAAJ
[765] https://www.amazon.com/1880-1910-Contributions-Comparative-Colonial-Studies/dp/0313249091/
[766] https://www.amazon.com/India-At-War-Subcontinent-Second/dp/0199753490/
[767] //www.jstor.org/stable/313141
[768] https://www.amazon.com/Curzon-India-1898-1903-Chaldwell-Lipsett/dp/1110690029/
[769] https://books.google.com/books?id=TRcMoGSkRtIC&pg=PR8
[770] https://www.amazon.com/dp/046503022X/sr=1-1/qid=1466893522/
[771] https://www.questia.com/PM.qst?a=o&d=101073461
[772] https://books.google.com/books?id=LI8UAQAAIAAJ
[773] //www.worldcat.org/issn/0022-0094
[774] http://www.britannica.com/eb/article-47042/India
[775] https://books.google.com/books?id=cmV6KLzEZNAC
[776] //doi.org/10.1017/s0026749x00009197
[777] //www.jstor.org/stable/312641
[778] //doi.org/10.1257/089533002760278749
[779] //www.jstor.org/stable/3216953
[780] //doi.org/10.1017/s0026749x00007745
[781] //www.jstor.org/stable/312453
[782] https://www.amazon.com/Economy-Modern-1860-1970-Cambridge-History/dp/0521589398/ref=sr_1_4?s=books&ie=UTF8&qid=1327498844&sr=1-4
[783] https://books.google.com/books?id=tMZRDQAAQBAJ&pg=PT11
[784] //doi.org/10.1111/j.1478-0542.2008.00564.x
[785] //doi.org/10.1017/s0021911814001685
[786] //doi.org/10.1080/09584935.2011.594257
[787] http://openjournals.library.usyd.edu.au/index.php/SSSC/article/download/7500/7868
[788] http://shodhganga.inflibnet.ac.in/bitstream/10603/7844/7/07_summary.pdf
[789] //doi.org/10.1111/j.1478-0542.2009.00617.x
[790] https://www.questia.com/library/117192922/the-oxford-history-of-the-british-empire-historiography
[791] https://www.questia.com/library/95979771/the-historiography-of-the-british-empire-commonwealth
[792] https://babel.hathitrust.org/cgi/pt?id=mdp.39015027588329;view=1up;seq=10
[793] https://books.google.com/books?id=mGdDAAAAIAAJ
[794] https://books.google.com/books?id=ODMQAAAAYAAJ
[795] https://books.google.com/books?id=uqAEAAAAQAAJ
[796] https://books.google.com/books?id=i25MAAAAYAAJ
[797] http://dsal.uchicago.edu/reference/gazetteer/
[798] https://books.google.com/books?id=xC5RAAAAYAAJ
[799] https://books.google.com/books?id=U9bkAAAAMAAJ
[800] https://books.google.com/books?id=QFlFAAAAYAAJ
[801] https://archive.org/details/in.ernet.dli.2015.40427
[802] https://archive.org/details/in.ernet.dli.2015.110101
[803] https://archive.org/search.php?query=title%3A%28%22+Indian+Annual+Register%22%29&sort=-date&page=4
[804] //en.wikipedia.org/w/index.php?title=Template:Colonial_India&action=edit
[805] //en.wikipedia.org/w/index.php?title=Template:Revolution_sidebar&action=edit
[806] The English colonial empire, including the territories and trading post in Asia, came under British control following the union of England and Scotland in 1707.

[807] Khan, Muazzam Hussain. "Titu Mir". Banglapedia. Bangladesh Asiatic Society. Retrieved 4 March 2014.
[808] David, S (202) *The Indian Mutiny*, Penguin; p. 122
[809] John R. McLane, "The Decision to Partition Bengal in 1901" *Indian Economic and Social History Review,* July 1965, 2#3, pp 221–237
[810] Lawrence James, *Raj: The Making and Unmaking of British India* (2000) pp 439–518
[811] James, *Raj: The Making and Unmaking of British India* (2000) pp 459–60, 519–20
[812] Denis Judd, *Empire: The British Imperial Experience From 1765 To The Present* (pp 226-411998)
[813] Nigel Collett, *The Butcher of Amritsar: General Reginald Dyer* (2006)
[814] Nick Lloyd, *The Amritsar Massacre: The Untold Story of One Fateful Day* (2011)
[815] Derek Sayer, "British Reaction to the Amritsar Massacre 1919–1920," *Past & Present,* May 1991, Issue 131, pp 130–164
[816] Dennis Judd, "The Amritsar Massacre of 1919: Gandhi, the Raj and the Growth of Indian Nationalism, 1915–39," in Judd, *Empire: The British Imperial Experience from 1765 to the Present* (1996) pp 258- 72
[817] Sankar Ghose, *Gandhi* (1991) p. 107
[818] Sanjay Paswan and Pramanshi Jaideva, *Encyclopaedia of Dalits in India* (2003) p. 43
[819] Khaksar Tehrik Ki Jiddo Juhad Volume 1. Author Khaksar Sher Zaman
[820] Dr.'Krant'M.L. Verma *Swadhinta Sangram Ke Krantikari Sahitya Ka Itihas* (Vol-2) p.559
[821] Bose, Nirmal. (October–December 1985) "SUBHAS CHANDRA BOSE AND THE INDIAN NATIONAL CONGRESS". The *Indian Journal of Political Science*. Vol. 46, No. 4, Special Issue on The Indian National Congress: A Century in Perspective, pp. 438-450 https://www.jstor.org/stable/41855198
[822] Culture and Combat in the Colonies. The Indian Army in the Second World War. Tarak Barkawi. J Contemp History. 41(2), 325–355.pp:332
[823] *Notes on India* https://books.google.com/books/about/Notes_on_India.html?id=-ipOZf7y_B4C&redir_esc=y By Robert Bohm.pp213
[824] James L. Raj; Making and unmaking of British India. Abacus. 1997. p571, p598 and; Unpublished, Public Relations Office, London. War Office. 208/819A 25C
[825] Subrata K. Mitra, "Nehru's policy towards Kashmir: Bringing politics back in again" *Journal of Commonwealth & Comparative Politics* 35.2 (1997): 55-74.
[826] https://books.google.com/books?id=D63KMRN1SJ8C&pg=PA4
[827] http://www.eduresourcecollection.com/projects_FreedomStruggle.php
[828] //www.ncbi.nlm.nih.gov/pmc/articles/PMC2156064
[829] //doi.org/10.2105/AJPH.2007.120139
[830] //www.ncbi.nlm.nih.gov/pubmed/18048775
[831] http://cs.mcgill.ca/~rwest/wikispeedia/wpcd/wp/i/Indian_independence_movement.htm
[832] http://web.cocc.edu/cagatucci/classes/hum210/tml/IndiaTML/indiatml4.htm
[833] https://www.nonviolent-conflict.org/index.php/movements-and-campaigns/movements-and-campaigns-summaries?catid=5&sobi2Id=17&sobi2Task=sobi2Details
[834] //en.wikipedia.org/w/index.php?title=Template:Part_of_History_of_India&action=edit
[835] *The Indian Journal of Political Science*, Vol. 28, No. 4 (October–December 1967), pp. 236-241
[836] http://www.thehindu.com/2002/04/06/stories/2002040600081000.htm
[837] Independence Day http://festivals.tajonline.com/independence-day.php, Taj Online Festivals.
[838] KCM http://kcm.co.kr/bethany_eng/p_code3/1496.html.
[839] Pakistan http://encarta.msn.com/encyclopedia_761560851_9/Pakistan.html, Encarta. Archived https://www.webcitation.org/5kwqySWBG?url=http://encarta.msn.com/encyclopedia_761560851_9/Pakistan.html 2009-10-31.
[840] Timeline https://www.pbs.org/wnet/wideangle/shows/india/timeline4.html, PBS.
[841] Pakistan Covert Operations https://www.princeton.edu/~jns/publications/Understanding%20Support%20for%20Islamist%20Militancy.pdf
[842] Moraes 2008, p. 196.
[843] , Indian Institute of Technology
[844] Sony Pellissery and Sam Geall "Five Year Plans" in Encyclopedia of Sustainability, Vol. 7 pp. 156–160

[845] Section: "The Green Revolution", pp. 17–20.
[846] BBC India Profile and Timeline https://www.bbc.co.uk/news/world-south-asia-12641776
[847] M.R. Masani, "India's Second Revolution," *Asian Affairs* (1977) 5#1 pp 19–38.
[848] Sen 2002, p. 139.
[849] PV Narasimha Rao Passes Away http://www.tlca.com/adults/obit-pvn.html. Retrieved 7 October 2007.
[850] Metcalf & Metcalf 2006, p. 304.
[851] *CIA Factbook*. Retrieved 22 December 2011
[852] India Rising - *Newsweek* and The Daily Beast http://www.newsweek.com/id/47261. Newsweek.com (5 March 2006). Retrieved on 12 July 2013.
[853] Profile: Pratibha Patil http://news.bbc.co.uk/2/hi/6910097.stm
[854] "The Mirror Explodes" http://www.outlookindia.com/article.aspx?266145 - *Outlook* - 19 July 2010
[855] www.bbc.co.uk https://www.bbc.co.uk/news/world-south-asia-12640645
[856] India Assessment – 2007 http://www.satp.org/satporgtp/countries/india/index.html
[857] Hobley, D.E.J., et al., 2012, Reconstruction of a major storm event from its geomorphic signature: The Ladakh floods, 6 August 2010, Geology, v. 40, p. 483-486, doi:10.1130/G32935.1
[858] http://www.cambridge.org/aus/catalogue/catalogue.asp?isbn=9780521516259&ss=exc
[859] https://books.google.com/books?id=DRduAAAAMAAJ
[860] https://books.google.com/books?id=46jWYgEACAAJ
[861] https://books.google.com/books?id=Y32u4JMroQgC&pg=PA1
[862] https://books.google.com/books?id=8FKepYC6wzwC
[863] https://www.amazon.com/India-After-Gandhi-Ramachandra-Guha/dp/B001DW2OBW/
[864] https://www.amazon.com/Makers-Modern-India-Ramachandra-Guha/dp/0674052463/
[865] https://books.google.com/books?id=_dqg3bEhcYMC
[866] https://books.google.com/books?id=F5gaFunH_PAC&pg=PA52
[867] https://www.amazon.com/Political-Economy-Growth-Liberalisation-1991-2008/dp/0415493358/
[868] https://books.google.com/books?id=u2oSMI2P_HkC&pg=PT412
[869] https://books.google.com/books?id=6eO1-yP7o4MC
[870] https://www.amazon.com/Economy-Modern-1860-1970-Cambridge-History/dp/0521589398/
[871] https://www.amazon.com/Routledge-Historical-Biographies-Benjamin-Zachariah/dp/041525017X/
[872] https://www.bbc.co.uk/news/world-south-asia-12557384
[873] //en.wikipedia.org/w/index.php?title=Template:Part_of_History_of_India&action=edit
[874] Section 1 of the Indian Independence Act, 1947 http://www.legislation.gov.uk/ukpga/Geo6/10-11/30/enacted
[875] Heraldic.org website http://www.heraldica.org/topics/britain/britstyles.htm#1948
[876] Royal Proclamation of 22 June 1948, made in accordance with the Indian Independence Act 1947, 10 & 11 GEO. 6. CH. 30. http://www.legislation.gov.uk/ukpga/1947/30/pdfs/ukpga_19470030_en.pdf ('Section 7: ...(2) The assent of the Parliament of the United Kingdom is hereby given to the omission from the Royal Style and Titles of the words "Indiae Imperator" and the words "Emperor of India" and to the issue by His Majesty for that purpose of His Royal Proclamation under the Great Seal of the Realm.')
[877] Created Earl Mountbatten of Burma on 28 October 1947.
[878] https://www.wdl.org/en/item/2672
[879] The Constitution of India was originally written in Hindi and English, so, both Hindi and English are its 'original' languages.
[880] //en.wikipedia.org/w/index.php?title=Template:Constitution_of_India&action=edit
[881] On National Law Day, saluting two remarkable judges http://www.firstpost.com/india/on-national-law-day-saluting-two-remarkable-judges-140748.html, Firstpost, 26 November 2011.
[882] PM Modi greets people on Constitution Day http://www.dnaindia.com/india/report-pm-modi-greets-people-on-constitution-day-2149048, DNA India, 26 November 2015.
[883] https://www.wdl.org/en/item/2672

[884]
[885] Although the last article of the Constitution is Article 395, the total number, as of March 2013 is 465. New articles added through amendments have been inserted in the relevant location in the original constitution. In order not to disturb the original numbering, the new articles are inserted with alpha numeric enumerations. For example, Article 21A pertaining to Right to Education was inserted by the 86th Amendment Act.
[886] The Constitution was in 22 Parts originally. Part VII & IX (older) was repealed in 1956, whereas newly added Part IVA, IXA, IXB & XIVA by Amendments to the Constitution in different times (lastly added IXB by the 97th Amendment).
[887] By 73rd & 74th Amendment, the lists of administrative subjects of Panchayat raj & Municipality included in the Constitution as Schedule 11 & 12 respectively in the year 1993.
[888] Part I
[889] Part II
[890] Part IV
[891] Part V
[892] Part VI
[893] Part VII
[894] Part VIII
[895] Part IX
[896] Part IXA
[897] http://indiacode.nic.in/coiweb/amend/amend97.pdf
[898] Scheduled Areas are autonomous areas within a state, administered federally, usually populated by a predominant Scheduled Tribe.
[899] Scheduled Tribes are groups of indigenous people, identified in the Constitution, struggling socioeconomically
[900] Originally Articles mentioned here were immune from judicial review on the ground that they violated fundamental rights. but in a landmark judgement in 2007, the Supreme Court of India held in I.R. Coelho v. State of Tamil Nadu and others that laws included in the 9th schedule can be subject to judicial review if they violated the fundamental rights guaranteed under Article 14, 15, 19, 21 or the basic structure of the Constitution {(ambiguous)}I.R. Coelho (dead) by L.Rs. v. State of Tamil Nadu and others(2007) 2 S.C.C. 1
[901] //en.wikipedia.org/w/index.php?title=Constitution_of_India&action=edit
[902] name="amendments"
[903] Kuri's blog: National Commission to review the working of the Constitution(NCRWC) http://kurishravan.blogspot.in/2011/02/national-commission-to-review-working.html. Kurishravan.blogspot.in (23 February 2011). Retrieved on 2013-07-28.
[904] Lectures By Professor Parmanad Singh, Jindal Global Law School.
[905] These lines by Granville Austin from his book *The Indian Constitution: Cornerstone of a Nation* at p. 50, have been authoritatively quoted many times
[906] Art. 21 – "No person shall be deprived of his life or personal liberty except according to procedure established by law"
[907] https://www.worldcat.org/oclc/294942170
[908] //www.worldcat.org/oclc/294942170
[909] http://parliamentofindia.nic.in/ls/debates/debates.htm
[910] http://egazette.nic.in/WriteReadData/1949/E-2358-1949-0000-109779.pdf
[911] http://indiacode.nic.in/coiweb/welcome.html
[912] https://web.archive.org/web/20140909230437/http://lawmin.nic.in/coi/coiason29july08.pdf
[913] http://www.india-seminar.com/1999/484/484%20chiriyankandath.htm
[914] https://web.archive.org/web/20081022080607/http://www.commonlii.org/in/legis/const/2004/index.html
[915] *See e.g.* ; ;
[916] //doi.org/10.1080/03086539308582896
[917] //doi.org/10.2307/2193757
[918] //www.jstor.org/stable/2193757
[919] //doi.org/10.1525/as.1950.19.6.01p0582b
[920] //doi.org/10.2307/2194500

[921] //www.jstor.org/stable/2194500
[922] //doi.org/10.1525/as.1962.2.2.01p1537e
[923] //doi.org/10.1017/S0026749X00009033
[924] //doi.org/10.2307/2753451
[925] //www.jstor.org/stable/2753451
[926] //doi.org/10.2307/2539071
[927] //www.jstor.org/stable/2539071
[928] //doi.org/10.1017/S0041977X00061838
[929] //doi.org/10.1525/as.1971.11.5.01p0113d
[930] //doi.org/10.2307/3517093
[931] //www.jstor.org/stable/3517093
[932] //doi.org/10.1525/as.1975.15.9.01p0110k
[933] //doi.org/10.1525/as.1983.23.11.01p0095g
[934] //doi.org/10.1111/j.1467-8306.1960.tb00345.x
[935] //doi.org/10.2307/2619473
[936] //doi.org/10.1093/iclqaj/24.4.884
[937] //doi.org/10.2307/2193764
[938] //www.jstor.org/stable/2193764
[939] //doi.org/10.2307/839489
[940] //www.jstor.org/stable/839489
[941] //doi.org/10.1017/S0020818300023808
[942] //doi.org/10.1017/S0026749X00013809
[943] //doi.org/10.2307/210736
[944] //www.jstor.org/stable/210736
[945] //doi.org/10.2307/2009033
[946] //www.jstor.org/stable/2009033
[947] //doi.org/10.1525/as.1997.37.11.01p02937
[948] //doi.org/10.2307/2196501
[949] //www.jstor.org/stable/2196501
[950] //doi.org/10.2307/2056747
[951] //www.jstor.org/stable/2056747
[952] //doi.org/10.2307/2758474
[953] //www.jstor.org/stable/2758474
[954] https//web.archive.org
[955] //doi.org/10.2307/3516214
[956] //www.jstor.org/stable/3516214
[957] https://www.scribd.com/doc/15380676/Telangana-Peoples-Armed-Struggle-19461951-Part-Two-First-Phase-and-Its-Lessons
[958] https://books.google.com/books?id=jGCBNTDv7acC
[959] https://www.bbc.co.uk/news/magazine-24159594
[960] http://www.frontline.in/static/html/fl1805/18051130.htm
[961] Jamal, Shadow War 2009, p. 49.
[962] Jamal, Shadow War 2009, p. 57.
[963] Bhattacharya, What Price Freedom 2013, p. 30.
[964] Nawaz, The First Kashmir War Revisited 2008, p. 120.
[965] Zaheer, The Times and Trial of the Rawalpindi Conspiracy 1998, p. 113.
[966] Islam and the Ahmadiyya Jama'at: History, Belief, Practice https://books.google.com/books?id=Q78O1mjX2tMC&pg=PA204. Columbia University Press, 2008. ,
[967] "An incredible war: Indian Air Force in Kashmir war, 1947–48", by Bharat Kumar, Centre for Air Power Studies (New Delhi, India)
[968] By B. Chakravorty, "Stories of Heroism, Volume 1", p. 5
[969] By Sanjay Badri-Maharaj "The Armageddon Factor: Nuclear Weapons in the India-Pakistan Context", p. 18
[970] With Honour & Glory: Wars fought by India 1947–1999 https//books.google.com, Lancer publishers
[971] India's Armed Forces: Fifty Years of War and Peace https//books.google.com, p. 160

[972] Pakistan Covert Operations https://www.princeton.edu/~jns/publications/Understanding%20Support%20for%20Islamist%20Militancy.pdf
[973] Schofield, Kashmir in Conflict 2003, p. 80.
[974] Kashmir https://www.britannica.com/EBchecked/topic/312908/Kashmir/214223/The-Kashmir-problem#ref673547 in *Encyclopædia Britannica* (2011), online edition
[975] Prasad & Pal, Operations in Jammu & Kashmir 1987, p. 371.
[976] Srinagar https://www.bl.uk/onlinegallery/onlineex/apac/photocoll/g/019pho000000394u00076000.html www.collectbritain.co.uk.
[977] Hodson, The Great Divide 1969, pp. 293, 320.
[978] Hodson, The Great Divide 1969, pp. 293, 329–330.
[979] At the beginning of 1947, all the posts above the rank of lieutenant colonel in the army were held by British officers.<ref name="FOOTNOTESarila, The Shadow of the Great Game2007324">Sarila, The Shadow of the Great Game 2007, p. 324.
[980] Barua, Gentlemen of the Raj 2003, p. 133.
[981] Nawaz, The First Kashmir War Revisited 2008.
[982] Ankit, Kashmir, 1945–66 2014, p. 43.
[983] Hodson, The Great Divide 1969, pp. 262–265.
[984] Ankit, Kashmir, 1945–66 2014, pp. 54, 56.
[985] Ankit, Kashmir, 1945–66 2014, pp. 57–58.
[986] Ankit, Henry Scott 2010, p. 45.
[987] Ankit, Henry Scott 2010.
[988] Major Kalkat was the Brigade Major at the Bannu Brigade, who opened a Demi-Official letter marked "Personal/Top Secret" on 20 August 1947 signed by General Frank Messervy, the then Commander in Chief of the Pakistan Army. It was addressed to Kalkat's commanding officer Brig. C. P. Murray, who happened to be away at another post. The Pakistani officials suspected Kalkat and placed him under house arrest. He escaped and made his way to New Delhi on 18 October. However, the Indian military authorities and defence minister did not believe his information. He was recalled and debriefed on 24 October after the tribal invasion of Kashmir had started.<ref name="FOOTNOTEPrasad & Pal, Operations in Jammu & Kashmir198717">Prasad & Pal, Operations in Jammu & Kashmir 1987, p. 17.
[989] Prasad & Pal, Operations in Jammu & Kashmir 1987, pp. 17–19.
[990] Effendi, Punjab Cavalry (2007), pp. 151–153.
[991] Joshi, Kashmir, 1947-1965: A Story Retold (2008), p. 59–.
[992] Moore, Making the new Commonwealth 1987, p. 49.
[993] Nawaz, The First Kashmir War Revisited 2008, p. 124–125.
[994] Ankit, The Problem of Poonch 2010, p. 8.
[995] Schofield, Kashmir in Conflict 2003, p. 41.
[996] Under the Jammu and Kashmir Arms Act of 1940, the possession of all fire arms was prohibited in the state. The Dogra Rajputs were however exempted in practice.<ref>
[997] Raghavan, War and Peace in Modern India 2010, p. 105.
[998] Ankit, The Problem of Poonch 2010, p. 9.
[999] Snedden, Kashmir: The Unwritten History 2013, p. 42.
[1000] Mahajan, Looking Back 1963, p. 123.
[1001] Raghavan, War and Peace in Modern India 2010, p. 103.
[1002] Bhattacharya, What Price Freedom 2013, pp. 25-27.
[1003] Ankit, October 1947 2010, p. 9.
[1004] Jamal, Shadow War 2009, p. 50.
[1005] According to scholar Christine Fair, at the time of independence, Pakistan had one major general, two brigadiers, and six colonels, even though the requirements were for 13 major generals, 40 brigadiers, and 52 colonels.<ref>
[1006] Guha, India after Gandhi 2008, Section 4.II.
[1007] Raghavan, War and Peace in Modern India 2010, pp. 105-106.
[1008] Raghavan, War and Peace in Modern India 2010, pp. 49–51.
[1009] Dasgupta, War and Diplomacy in Kashmir 2014, pp. 28–29.
[1010] Regimental History Cell, *History of the Azad Kashmir Regiment, Volume 1 (1947–1949)*, Azad Kashmir Regimental Centre, NLC Printers, Rawalpindi,1997

[1011] Cheema, Crimson Chinar 2015, p. 57.
[1012] Palit, Jammu and Kashmir Arms 1972, p. 162.
[1013] Korbel, Danger in Kashmir 1966, p. 94.
[1014] Lamb, Alastair (1997), *Incomplete partition: the genesis of the Kashmir dispute 1947–1948*, Roxford,
[1015] Kashmir-konflikten. (18 October 2011) I Store norske leksikon. Taken from https://snl.no/Kashmir-konflikten
[1016] Norwegian Broadcasting Corporation: Kashmir-konflikten https://www.nrk.no/nyheter/verden/1.461250
[1017] Schofield, Kashmir in Conflict 2003, p. 61.
[1018] Schofield, Kashmir in Conflict 2003, p. 60.
[1019] Schofield, Kashmir in Conflict 2003, pp. 65–67.
[1020] Schofield, Kashmir in Conflict 2003, p. 63.
[1021] Martin Axmann, *Back to the future: the Khanate of Kalat and the genesis of Baluch Nationalism 1915–1955* (2008), p. 273
[1022] Tom Cooper, I Indo-Pakistani War, 1947–1949 http://www.acig.info/CMS/index2.php?option=com_content&do_pdf=1&id=159 , Air Combat Information Group, 29 October 2003
[1023] Ministry of Defence, Government of India. Operations in Jammu and Kashmir 1947–1948. (1987). Thomson Press (India) Limited, New Delhi. This is the Indian Official History.
[1024] https://documents.mx/documents/epilogue-magazine-may-2010.html
[1025] https://books.google.com/books?id=DpQh00eGEB0C&pg=PA8
[1026] https://documents.mx/documents/epilogue-magazine-november-2010.html
[1027] https://books.google.com/books?id=5RtqDAAAQBAJ&pg=PA48
[1028] https://eprints.soton.ac.uk/370019/
[1029] https://books.google.com/books?id=7bREjE5yXNMC&pg=PA83
[1030] //doi.org/10.1080/03086530903538269
[1031] https://books.google.com/books?id=-U8IUoC_tP0C&pg=PA133
[1032] https://books.google.com/books?id=HESVAgAAQBAJ&pg=PA42
[1033] https://books.google.com/books?id=Qc25BwAAQBAJ&pg=PA51
[1034] https://books.google.com/books?id=jEtuAAAAMAAJ
[1035] https://books.google.com/books?id=MeXeAAAAMAAJ
[1036] https://books.google.com/books?id=29IXtwoeA44C
[1037] https://books.google.com/books?id=OJGdBAAAQBAJ&pg=PA185
[1038] https://books.google.com/books?id=PpPCBAAAQBAJ
[1039] https://books.google.com/books?id=TNO5MAAACAAJ
[1040] https://books.google.com/books?id=uAT3oENcxDgC
[1041] https://books.google.com/books?id=MC2UoAEACAAJ
[1042] https://books.google.com/books?id=7Q7WCgAAQBAJ
[1043] https://books.google.com/books?id=AW5u9QSxCFwC
[1044] https://books.google.com/books?id=b_l-AAAAIAAJ
[1045] https://books.google.com/books?id=KGZDnzqQj2QC
[1046] https://archive.org/details/in.ernet.dli.2015.116302
[1047] https://books.google.com/books?id=EbtBJb1bsHUC&pg=PA101
[1048] //doi.org/10.1080/14736480802055455
[1049] https://books.google.com/books?id=WW5FPgAACAAJ
[1050] https://books.google.com/books?id=0cPjAAAAQBAJ
[1051] https://books.google.com/books?id=rjNuAAAAMAAJ
[1052] https://web.archive.org/web/20110405210142/http://indianarmy.nic.in/Site/FormTemplete/frmTempSimple.aspx?MnId=BfMpdR9l1kE=&ParentID=a2GSpnDbruI=
[1053] //en.wikipedia.org/w/index.php?title=Template:Part_of_History_of_India&action=edit
[1054] *Bihar and West Bengal (Transfer of Territories) Act, 1956*
[1055] http://www.liiofindia.org/in/legis/cen/num_act/sra1956250/
[1056] http://lcweb2.loc.gov/cgi-bin/query/r?frd/cstdy:@field(DOCID+in0182)
[1057] http://www.ndtv.com/convergence/ndtv/story.aspx?id=NEWEN20070027665
[1058] http://www.iins.org
[1059] http://lcweb2.loc.gov/frd/cs/

[1060] T. V. Paul 1994, p. 107.
[1061] Jamal, Shadow War 2009, p. 86.
[1062] Van Creveld, 2012, pp. 286–287.
[1063] Bharat-Rakshak.com
[1064] 1965 War: A Different Legacy: ALL THINGS PAKISTAN http://pakistaniat.com/2007/09/06/1965-war-a-different-legacy/comment-page-6/. Pakistaniat.com (1965-09-06). Retrieved on 2011-04-14.
[1065] 1965 War http://www.pakistanarmy.gov.pk/awpreview/textcontent.aspx?pid=196 . Pakistan army (2009-09-01). Retrieved on 2011-04-14.
[1066] The Sunday Tribune – Spectrum http://www.tribuneindia.com/2007/20070506/spectrum/main1.htm. Tribuneindia.com. Retrieved on 2011-04-14.
[1067] David R. Higgins 2016.
[1068] Rachna Bisht 2015.
[1069] "Satisfied that it had secured a strategic and psychological victory over Pakistan by frustrating its attempt to seize Kashmir by force, when the UN resolution was passed, India accepted its terms ... with Pakistan's stocks of ammunition and other essential supplies all but exhausted, and with the military balance tipping steadily in India's favour."
[1070] "Losses were relatively heavy—on the Pakistani side, twenty aircraft, 200 tanks, and 3,800 troops. Pakistan's army had been able to withstand Indian pressure, but a continuation of the fighting would only have led to further losses and ultimate defeat for Pakistan."
[1071] Quote: The invading Indian forces outfought their Pakistani counterparts and halted their attack on the outskirts of Lahore, Pakistan's second-largest city. By the time the United Nations intervened on 22 September, Pakistan had suffered a clear defeat.
[1072] Quote: India, however, was in a position to inflict grave damage to, if not capture, Pakistan's capital of the Punjab when the cease-fire was called, and controlled Kashmir's strategic Uri-Poonch bulge, much to Ayub's chagrin.
[1073] Quote: India had the better of the war.
[1074] Quote: India, by contrast, is still the big gainer in the war. Alternate link: http://content.time.com/time/subscriber/printout/0,8816,834413,00.html
[1075] "... the war itself was a disaster for Pakistan, from the first failed attempts by Pakistani troops to precipitate an insurgency in Kashmir to the appearance of Indian artillery within range of Lahore International Airport."
[1076] Profile of Pakistan https://www.state.gov/r/pa/ei/bgn/3453.htm – U.S. Department of State, Failure of U.S.'s Pakistan Policy http://globetrotter.berkeley.edu/people5/Coll/coll-con5.html – Interview with Steve Coll
[1077] Speech of Bill McCollum https://fas.org/news/pakistan/1994/940912.htm in United States House of Representatives 12 September 1994
[1078] South Asia in World Politics By Devin T. Hagerty, 2005 Rowman & Littlefield, , p. 26
[1079] "... after some initial success, the momentum behind Pakistan's thrust into Kashmir slowed, and the state's inhabitants rejected exhortations from the Pakistani insurgents to join them in taking up arms against their Indian "oppressors." Pakistan's inability to muster support from the local Kashmiri population proved a disaster, both militarily and politically."
[1080] "Mao had decided that China would intervene under two conditions—that India attacked East Pakistan, and that Pakistan requested Chinese intervention. In the end, neither of them [were] obtained."
[1081] "In retrospect, it is clear that the Indo-Pakistani War of 1965 represented a watershed in the West's association with the subcontinent."
[1082] "By extending the Cold War into South Asia, however, the United States did succeed in disturbing the subcontinent's established politico-military equilibrium, undermining British influence in the region, embittering relations between India and Pakistan and, ironically, facilitating the expansion of communist influence in the developing world."
[1083] "The legacy of the Johnson arms cut-off remains alive today. Indians simply do not believe that America will be there when India needs military help ... the legacy of the U.S. "betrayal" still haunts U.S.-Pakistan relations today."
[1084] Bhushan, Chodarat. "Tulbul, Sir Creek and Siachen: Competitive Methodologies" http://www.southasianmedia.net/Magazine/Journal/7_competitive_methodologies.htm . South Asian

Journal. March 2005, Encyclopædia Britannica and Open Forum – UNIDIR http://www.unidir.ch/pdf/articles/pdf-art267.pdf

[1085] Defence Journal. September 2000

[1086] http://www.rediff.com/news/2002/dec/21haji.htm

[1087] http://news.bbc.co.uk/onthisday/hi/dates/stories/september/6/newsid_3632000/3632092.stm

[1088] Brigadier Desmond E Hayde, "The Battle of Dograi and Batapore", Natraj Publishers, New Delhi, 2006

[1089] The Tribune, Chandigarh, India – Opinions http://www.tribuneindia.com/2005/20050918/edit.htm#1. Tribuneindia.com. Retrieved on 2011-04-14.

[1090] Army cries out for a second railway line between Barmer and Jaisalmer http://www.hindustantimes.com/india-news/rajasthan/Army-cries-out-for-a-second-railway-line-between-Barmer-and-Jaisalmer/Article1-487591.aspx . Hindustan Times (2009-12-17). Retrieved on 2011-04-14.

[1091] History of Indo-Pak War of 1965. Lt Gen Mahmud Ahmed (ret).

[1092] The Story of My Struggle By Tajammal Hussain Malik 1991, Jang Publishers, p. 78

[1093] Khaki Shadows by General K.M. Arif, Oxford University Press, , 2001

[1094] Magnificent Delusions: Pakistan, the United States, and an Epic History of misunderstanding By Husain Haqqani page 115 https//books.google.com

[1095] John Fricker, "Pakistan's Air Power" http://www.flightglobal.com/pdfarchive/view/1969/1969%20-%200111.html?search=Pakistan%20Mirage%205, *Flight International* issue published 1969, p. 89, retrieved: 3 November 2009

[1096] See the main article Sabre Slayer for the complete list on this issue including sources.

[1097] Licence-built North American F-86 Sabres with Canadian engines.

[1098] Rakshak, Bharat. "Indian Air Force Combat Kills, Indo Pakistan War 1965." http://www.bharat-rakshak.com/IAF/History/Misc/Kill1965.html *History*. Retrieved 4 November 2010.

[1099] Spick 2002, p. 161.

[1100] Ahmad Faruqui, "The right stuff" http://www.dawn.com/wps/wcm/connect/dawn-content-library/dawn/the-newspaper/editorial/the-right-stuff-499 , *Dawn News*, 14 September 2009, Retrieved: 1 November 2009. Also published as "The Debt Owed" http://www.outlookindia.com/article.aspx?261856 on 16 September 2009 by [*outlookindia.com*]

[1101] "1965 War, Chapter 3." http://www.bharat-rakshak.com/IAF/History/1965War/Chapter3.html *bharat-rakshak.com*. Retrieved: 4 November 2010.

[1102] John Fricker, "Pakistan's Air Power", *Flight International* issue published 1969, pp. 89–90. http://www.flightglobal.com/pdfarchive/view/1969/1969%20-%200111.html?search=Pakistan%20Mirage%205, http://www.flightglobal.com/pdfarchive/view/1969/1969%20-%200112.html. Retrieved: 3 November 2009

[1103] The Encyclopedia of 20th Century Air Warfare Edited by Chris Bishop (amber publishing 1997, republished 2004 pages 384–387)

[1104] 30 Seconds Over Sargodha – The Making of a Myth: 1965 Indo-Pak Air War, Chapter 5 http://www.bharat-rakshak.com/IAF/History/1965War/Chapter5.html , Bharat Rakshak

[1105] *Pakistan's Sabre Ace* by Jon Guttman, Aviation History, Sept 1998.

[1106] War of attrition http://in.rbth.com/blogs/stranger_than_fiction/2015/09/14/war-of-attrition-how-the-outgunned-iaf-beat-the-paf_396591

[1107] Flight of the Falcon http://www.bharat-rakshak.com/IAF/Books/Reviews/812-Falcon.html

[1108] A history of the Pakistan Army http://www.defencejournal.com/jul99/history-pak-army.htm – Defence Journal, Pakistan

[1109] 90mm M36 GUN MOTOR CARRIAGE "Jackson" http://www.milweb.net/webverts/22995/ Post W.W.II, the M36 was employed by the US Army in Korea and was distributed to friendly nations including France, where it was used in Indo-China (Vietnam), Pakistan.

[1110] The Battle for Ravi-Sutlej Corridor 1965 A Strategic and Operational Analysis http://orbat.com/site/history/historical/pakistan/aminkhemkaran.html Major A.H. Amin, 30 December 2001 Orbat

[1111] Pakistan Intelligence, Security Activities & Operations Handbook By IBP USA

[1112] India's Quest for Security: defence policies, 1947–1965 By Lorne John Kavic, 1967, University of California Press, pp 190

[1113] Working paper, Issue 192, Australian National University. Strategic and Defence Studies Centre, Research School of Pacific Studies, Australian National University, 1989, , 9780-7315-0806-8
[1114] India's Foreign Policy, Ghosh Anjali, Dorling Kindersley Pvt Ltd,
[1115] South Asia's Nuclear Security Dilemma: India, Pakistan, and China By Lowell Dittmer, pp 77
[1116] THE INDIAN END OF THE TELESCOPE India and Its Navy https://www.questia.com/library/1P3-141242471/the-indian-end-of-the-telescope-india-and-its-navy by Vice Admiral Gulab Hiranandani, Indian Navy (Retired), Naval War College Review, Spring 2002, Vol. LV, No. 2
[1117] Iqbal F Quadir http://www.defencejournal.com/march98/pak3wars1.htm – Pakistan's Defence Journal
[1118] The Fighter Gap http://www.defencejournal.com/may98/fightergap1.htm by Shoab Alam Khan in Defence Journal
[1119] Defence Journal: The Way it was http://www.defencejournal.com/may98/thewayitwas1.htm Extracts from Pakistan Army Brigadier (Retd) ZA Khan's book
[1120] Ending the Suspense http://www.time.com/time/magazine/article/0,9171,842104-9,00.html 17 September 1965, TIME magazine
[1121] Remembering Our Warriors Brig (Retd) Shamim Yasin Manto S.I.(M), S.Bt, Q&A session: ("How would you assess the failures and successes of the SSG in the 1965 War?") http://www.defencejournal.com/2002/february/manto.htm February 2002, Defence Journal
[1122] Group Captain Cecil Chaudhry, SJ – Chowk: India Pakistan Ideas Identities.com http://www.chowk.com/show_article.cgi?aid=00001093&channel=civic%20center . Chowk (2007-12-09). Retrieved on 2011-04-14.
[1123] http://content.cdlib.org/xtf/view?docId=ft0489n6j7&chunk.id=d0e4022&toc.depth=1&toc.id=d0e4019&brand=eschol&query=martial%20arts# India by Stanley Wolpert. Published: University of California Press, 1990
[1124] "India and the United States estranged democracies", 1941–1991, , DIANE Publishing, Pg 238
[1125] Source https://history.state.gov/milestones/1961-1968/india-pakistan-war
[1126] Kashmir in Conflict: India, Pakistan and the Unending War By Victoria Schofield Published 2003, by I.B.Tauris pp112
[1127] CONTROVERSY: Why Gohar Ayub is wrong about 1965 – Khalid Hasan http://www.dailytimes.com.pk/default.asp?page=story_10-6-2005_pg3_2 quoting Pakistan author Husain Haqqani: "The Pakistani people were told by the state that they had been victims of aggression and that the aggression had been repelled with the help of God. ... official propaganda convinced the people of Pakistan that their military had won the war." Daily Times, 10 June 2005
[1128] Can the ISI change its spots? By Akhtar Payami, Dawn (newspaper) 7 October 2006
[1129] Army attempts to prevent book sales by Amir Mir http://archive.gulfnews.com/articles/06/10/01/10071494.html Gulf News 1 October 2006 Musharraf buys all copies of sensitive '65 war http://www.dnaindia.com/report.asp?NewsID=1056075 Daily News & Analysis
[1130] Inside Story of Musharraf-Mahmood Tussle by Hassan Abbas http://bcsia.ksg.harvard.edu/publication.cfm?program=CORE&ctype=article&item_id=1560 – (Belfer Center for International Affairs, John F. Kennedy School of Government)
[1131] A Cease-Fire of Sorts 5 November 1965 http://www.time.com/time/magazine/article/0,9171,901761,00.html – TIME
[1132] "The India-Pakistan Air War of 1965", Jagan Mohan and Samir Chopra, Manohar Publications, New Delhi, 2005
[1133] http://www.bharat-rakshak.com/ARMY/history/1965war/275-war-history-1965.html
[1134] Musharraf, the 'poor man's Ataturk' By Khalid Hasan http://www.dailytimes.com.pk/default.asp?page=story_19-9-2004_pg7_30 19 September 2004 Daily Times
[1135] The Crisis Game: Simulating International Conflict by Sidney F. Giffin
[1136] 1965 decided fate of the subcontinent http://in.rediff.com/news/2005/sep/06war1.htm An Impending Nuclear War Between India and Pakistan over Kashmir, by Susmit Kumar, Ph.D. http://www.proutglobe.org/2011/05/an-impending-nuclear-war-between-india-and-pakistan-over-kashmir/
[1137] Pages 103, 73–74

[1138] Noor Khan for early end to army rule http://www.nation.com.pk/daily/july-2006/15/index8.php – Pakistan Daily The Nation
[1139] A word from Pak: 1965 was 'wrong' http://timesofindia.indiatimes.com/NEWS/World/Indo-Pak_Ties/A_word_from_Pak_1965_was_wrong/articleshow/msid-1222586,curpg-3.cms The Times of India 6 September 2005
[1140] Editorial: The army and the people http://www.dailytimes.com.pk/default.asp?page=2007%5C06%5C01%5Cstory_1-6-2007_pg3_1 Daily Times 1 June 2007
[1141] The Pakistan Army From 1965 to 1971 *Analysis and reappraisal after the 1965 War* http://www.defencejournal.com/2000/nov/pak-army.htm by Maj (Retd) Agha Humayun Amin
[1142] "Defence aid was restricted to the extent that Pakistan would be able to present only a limited defence in the event of communist aggression ... Western strategists sought to keep Pakistan ... in a position where it did not feel itself powerful enough to initiate a confrontation with India."
[1143] Political Survival in Pakistan: Beyond Ideology, By Anas Malik page 84
[1144] Political Survival in Pakistan: Beyond Ideology, By Anas Malik page 85
[1145] T. V. Paul 1994, p. 119.
[1146] Silent Guns, Wary Combatants http://www.time.com/time/printout/0,8816,834413,00.html, TIME magazine, 1 October 1965
[1147] The 1965 war with Pakistan http://www.britannica.com/eb/article-47067/India – Encyclopædia Britannica
[1148] Sunday Times, London. 19 September 1965
[1149] Title: India and the United States estranged democracies, 1941–1991, , DIANE Publishing
[1150] Declassified telegram sent to the US Department of State
[1151] Pakistan And Its Three Wars by Vice Adm (Retd) Iqbal F Quadir http://www.defencejournal.com/march98/pak3wars1.htm – Defence Journal, Pakistan
[1152] Insurgents, Terrorists, and Militias: The Warriors of Contemporary Combat Richard H. Shultz, Andrea Dew: *"The Martial Races Theory had firm adherents in Pakistan and this factor played a major role in the under-estimation of the Indian Army by Pakistani soldiers as well as civilian decision makers in 1965."*
[1153] An Analysis The Sepoy Rebellion of 1857–59 by AH Amin http://www.defencejournal.com/2001/november/sepoy.htm *The army officers of that period were convinced that they were a martial race and the Hindus of Indian Army were cowards. This myth was largely disproved in 1965*
[1154] "Pakistan's Air Power", *Flight International*, issue published 5 May 1984 (page 1208). Can be viewed at FlightGlobal.com archives http://www.flightglobal.com/pdfarchive/view/1984/1984%20-%200797.html?search=F-86%20Pakistan Retrieved: 22 October 2009
[1155] Dr. Ahmad Faruqui http://www.pakistanlink.com/Opinion/2004/Sept04/17/05.html
[1156] Ali, Mahmud. (2003-12-24) South Asia | The rise of Pakistan's army http://news.bbc.co.uk/2/hi/south_asia/3227709.stm. BBC News. Retrieved on 2011-04-14.
[1157] Embassy of Pakistan http://www.pakistanembassy.no/fpolicy.html
[1158] Second opinion: The insidious logic of war Khaled Ahmed's Urdu Press Review http://www.dailytimes.com.pk/default.asp?page=story_3-6-2002_pg3_4 Daily Times 3 June 2002
[1159] Richard N. Haass "Economic Sanctions and American Diplomacy", 1998, Council on Foreign Relations, pp172
[1160] Makers of Modern Strategy: From Machiavelli to the Nuclear Age By Peter Paret, 1986, Oxford University Press, pp802
[1161] Pg 166–167
[1162] Reflections on two military presidents By M.P. Bhandara https://www.dawn.com/news/1068595 25 December 2005, Dawn
[1163] The Pakistan Army From 1965 to 1971 *Yahya Khan as Army Chief-1966-1971* http://www.defencejournal.com/2000/nov/pak-army.htm by Maj (Retd) Agha Humayun Amin
[1164] https://books.google.com/?id=FJ7cAAAACAAJ
[1165] https://books.google.com/?id=B2saAAAACAAJ
[1166] https://books.google.com/?id=rtdOAAAAMAAJ
[1167] https://books.google.com/?id=BfxtAAAAMAAJ
[1168] https://books.google.com/?id=ElHfAAAAMAAJ
[1169] https://books.google.com/?id=RPttAAAAMAAJ

[1170] https://books.google.com/?id=3jAxNbn1tkEC
[1171] //www.amazon.com/dp/B0006FFBK8
[1172] https://books.google.com/books?id=nYppZ_dEjdIC&lpg=PP1&pg=PP1#v=onepage&q=&f=false
[1173] https://books.google.com/?id=bZ-QGAAACAAJ
[1174] //www.amazon.com/dp/B0006EL2OI
[1175] https://books.google.com/books?id=TNO5MAAACAAJ
[1176] https://books.google.com/?id=Bz9uAAAAMAAJ
[1177] https://books.google.com/?id=wA1xPgAACAAJ
[1178] https://books.google.com/?id=6DDHAAAAIAAJ
[1179] //www.amazon.com/dp/B0000CQ9GQ
[1180] https://books.google.com/?id=pBpuAAAAMAAJ
[1181] https://web.archive.org/web/20101127234125/http://orbat.com/site/cimh/iaf/IAF_1965war_kills.pdf
[1182] http://lcweb2.loc.gov/cgi-bin/query/r?frd/cstdy:@field(DOCID+in0189)
[1183] https://web.archive.org/web/20051217085236/http://www.bharat-rakshak.com/LAND-FORCES/Army/History/1965War/PDF/index.html
[1184] http://www.globalsecurity.org/military/world/war/indo-pak_1965.htm
[1185] http://www.defencejournal.com/2001/september/1965.htm
[1186] https://web.archive.org/web/20120805182043/http://www.defencejournal.com/2000/sept/grand-slam.htm
[1187] http://in.rediff.com/news/indpakwar05.htm
[1188] https://web.archive.org/web/20130119073542/http://www.dailytimes.com.pk/default.asp?page=story_7-9-2005_pg3_1
[1189] http://archives.dawn.com/weekly/ayaz/20051021.htm
[1190] Webster's Encyclopedic Unabridged Dictionary of the English Language: Chronology of Major Dates in History, page 1686. Dilithium Press Ltd., 1989
[1191] China won, but never wanted, Sino-Indian war - Global Times http://www.globaltimes.cn/content/717710.shtml
[1192] India lost war with China but won Arunachal's heart - Times of India http://timesofindia.indiatimes.com/india/India-lost-war-with-China-but-won-Arunachals-heart/articleshow/17039530.cms
[1193] H.A.S.C. by United States. Congress. House Committee on Armed Services — 1999, p. 62
[1194] *War at the Top of the World: The Struggle for Afghanistan, Kashmir, and Tibet* by Eric S. Margolis, p. 234.
[1195] The US Army says Indian wounded were 1,047 and attributes it to Indian Defence Ministry's 1965 report, but this report also included a lower estimate of killed.
[1196] Maxwell, India's China War 1970, p. 24.
[1197] The Sino-Indian Border Disputes, by Alfred P. Rubin, The International and Comparative Law Quarterly, Vol. 9, No. 1. (Jan. 1960), pp. 96–125, .
[1198] Maxwell, India's China War 1970, p. 25–26.
[1199] Maxwell, India's China War 1970, p. 26.
[1200] Warikoo, India's gateway to Central Asia 2009, pp. 1–2.
[1201] : "Shahidulla was occupied by the Dogras almost from the time they conquered Ladakh."
[1202] Noorani, India–China Boundary Problem (2010), p. 48 quotes a report by Ney Elias in 1885: "He [the Wazir] wants the Maharaja to re-occupy Shahidulla in the Karakash valley. Previous to the rebellions in Eastern Turkistan which broke up Chinese rule there in 1863, the Kashmiris had occupied Shahidulla for nearly 20 years. About 1865 they abandoned it, and in 1868 Shaw and Hayward found it occupied by the Andijani (Kokandi) troops of the late Amir Yakub Beg. In 1873–74 Sir D. Forsyth recognised the Amir's ownership, and recommended the Maharaja's boundary to be drawn to the north of the Karakash valley as shown in the map accompanying the mission report. This I believe has never been accepted by Kashmir, and the boundary has been left an open question."
[1203] Noorani, India–China Boundary Problem (2010), p. 48, 83: An India Office (London) memorandum in 1893 stated: "Shahidulla has hitherto been regarded as the frontier post on the road from Leh to Yarkand. Lord Kimberley the secretary of state would suggest that the Chinese

Government at Peking ... should be intimated...that the Indian authorities, acting on behalf of the Kashmir State, will gladly co-operate with the Chinese authorities in Kashgaria in determining the frontier on the road from Leh to Kashgar. Her Majesty's Government would, however, demur to any attempt being made by the Kashgarian officials to fix the boundary of the Ladakh State on this road without their previous concurrence being obtained."

[1204]: "The southern frontier of Chinese Turkestan was similarly undefined... the Chinese 'considered the Kuen-lun mountains (i.e. the branch of them over which are the Kilian and Sanju passes) as their frontier'..."

[1205] Noorani, India–China Boundary Problem (2010), p. 58 quotes Captain Younghusband's report of 1889: "In the former Chinese occupation the Kuen-Lun Mountains (that is the branch of them over which are the Kilian and Sanju Passes) were always recognised as the frontier, and the country to the south belonged to no one in particular. When the Chinese revolt took place and they were driven from Yarkand, the Kashmir State sent a detachment of troops to Shahidullah and built a fort there. Yakub Beg when he came into power at Yarkand sent some troops, who built a fort at Ali Nazar on the Karakash River at the junction of the roads from the Kilian and Sanju Passes. Shortly afterwards the Kashmiris evacuated the Shahidullah fort after occupying it for about three years, and the Andijanis then took possession of it and occupied it till Yakub Beg's death."

[1206] ; ; ;

[1207] Fisher, Rose & Huttenback, Himalayan Battleground 1963, p. 116.

[1208] Some commentators state that Johnson's work was "severely criticised" as inaccurate. His boundary line was described as "patently absurd", and extending further north than the Indian claim. Johnson is said to have been reprimanded by the British Government for crossing into Khotan without permission and he resigned from the Survey. UNIQ-ref-0-cb065aa36d516186-QINU UNIQ-ref-1-cb065aa36d516186-QINU Webster's Encyclopedic Unabridged Dictionary of the English language: Chronology of Major Dates in History, page 1686. Dilithium Press Ltd., 1989 Others state that Johnson's bold explorations were highly commended, and he was rehired a year later at a higher salary. The "invitation" from the Khotanese ruler was likely a forcible removal, and the ruler was merely seeking British help in warding off Yakub Beg and the Russian Empire.<ref name="FOOTNOTEMehra, John Lall (Book review)1991149">Mehra, John Lall (Book review) 1991, p. 149.

[1209] Noorani, India–China Boundary Problem 2010, pp. 65–66.

[1210] : "Clarke added that a Chinese map drawn by Hung Ta-chen, Minister in St. Petersburg, confirmed the Johnson alignment showing West Aksai Chin as within British (Kashmir) territory."

[1211] Noorani, India–China Boundary Problem 2010, pp. 52–53, 60, 69, 72.

[1212] Noorani, India–China Boundary Problem 2010, pp. 114-115.

[1213] The so-called Macartney-MacDonald proposal was precipitated by the crisis over Hunza, which was theoretically a vassal state of both China and Kashmir. In 1890, the British invaded Hunza and replaced its ruler, and the Chinese remonstrated. The British wanted the Chinese to cede their suzerainty over Hunza and yet grant rights to cultivate lands outside its boundary. In return for this largesse, they were prepared to cede the Aksai Chin plains, but not Lingzi Tang plains, to China. Scholar Parshotam Mehra has termed it a 'barter'.<ref>; ; ;

[1214] Woodman, Himalayan Frontiers 1970.

[1215] Fisher, Rose & Huttenback, Himalayan Battleground 1963, p. 101.

[1216] George W. Patterson, Peking Versus Delhi, Frederick A. Praeger, Inc., 1963

[1217] The Sino-Indian Boundary Dispute, Foreign Language Press of the People's Republic of China, 1961

[1218] Gupta, Karunakar, "The McMahon Line 1911–45: The British Legacy", *The China Quarterly*, No. 47. (Jul. – Sep. 1971), pp. 521-45.

[1219] Free Tibet Campaign, " Tibet Facts No.17: British Relations with Tibet http://www.freetibet.org/info/facts/fact17.html"

[1220] A.G. Noorani, " Perseverance in peace process http://www.hinduonnet.com/fline/fl2017/stories/20030829001604900.htm ", *India's National Magazine*, 29 August 2003.

[1221] Chinese deception and Nehru's naivete led to 62 War http://articles.timesofindia.indiatimes.com/2007-06-27/us/27957825_1_cia-papers-india-china-border-border-issue *Times of India*

[1222] " The Shade of the Big Banyan http://www.time.com/time/magazine/article/0,9171,894328-8,00.html " *Time*, 14 December 1959.
[1223] Fisher, Rose & Huttenback, Himalayan Battleground 1963, p. 91.
[1224] Fisher, Rose & Huttenback, Himalayan Battleground 1963, p. 96.
[1225] Fisher, Rose & Huttenback, Himalayan Battleground 1963, p. 99.
[1226]
[1227] Chang, Jung and Jon Halliday, *Mao: The Unknown Story* (2006), pp. 568, 579.
[1228]
[1229] Manoj Joshi, "Line of Defence", *Times of India*, 21 October 2000
[1230] *People's Daily*, 22 September 1962 issue, pp. 1
[1231] China feared military coup in India during 60s http://www.dnaindia.com/report.asp?newsid=1106769 *DNA India*
[1232] e.g. Chip Chap Valley, Pangong
[1233] Men of Steel on Icy Heights http://www.bharat-rakshak.com/LAND-FORCES/Army/History/1962War/Mohan.html Mohan Guruswamy *Deccan Chronicle*.
[1234] YADAV, Atul, Injustice to the Ahir Martyrs of the 1962 War http://www.bharat-rakshak.com/LAND-FORCES/Army/History/1962War/Yadav.html Bharat Rakshak, The Tribune. 18 November 1999
[1235] Abstract of "Fighting to Make a Point: Policy-Making by Aggressive War on the Chinese Borders" by Jr Pettis Roy C. http://www.stormingmedia.us/92/9232/A923244.html — National War College
[1236] " India https://www.jstor.org/stable/3023681 : A Year of Stability and Change". Ralph J. Retzlaff. Asian Survey, Vol. 3, No. 2, A Survey of Asia in 1962: Part II. (Feb. 1963), pp. 96–106.
[1237] The Men Behind Yahya in the Indo-Pakistani War of 1971 http://coat.ncf.ca/our_magazine/links/issue47/articles/a07.htm by Stephen R. Shalom, professor of Political Science
[1238] The Untold Story: How Kennedy came to India's aid in 1962 http://www.rediff.com/news/special/the-untold-story-how-the-us-came-to-indias-aid-in-1962/20121204.htm , Rediff News, 4 December 2012.
[1239] https://books.google.com/books?id=hFRuDQAAQBAJ
[1240] https://books.google.co.uk/books?id=yCElDwAAQBAJ&pg=PA29
[1241] https://books.google.co.uk/books?id=yCElDwAAQBAJ&pg=PA68
[1242] https://www.questia.com/read/10466588
[1243] https://books.google.com/books?id=csbHAAAAIAAJ
[1244] //doi.org/10.1177/000944559102700206
[1245] https://books.google.com/books?id=mIduAAAAMAAJ
[1246] https://books.google.com/books?id=GoAyDwAAQBAJ
[1247] //doi.org/10.1093/acprof%3Aoso/9780198070689.001.0001
[1248] https://books.google.com/books?id=ukw1PuEt8IcC
[1249] https://books.google.com/books?id=s5KMCwAAQBAJ
[1250] https://books.google.com/books?id=8eTzBwAAQBAJ&pg=PA163
[1251] https://books.google.com/books?id=w_Z8AgAAQBAJ
[1252] https://books.google.com/books?id=w_Z8AgAAQBAJ&pg=PA56
[1253] https://books.google.com/books?id=w_Z8AgAAQBAJ&pg=PA1
[1254] https://books.google.com/books?id=tkCAAAAAIAAJ
[1255] https://books.google.com/books?id=TOVaMckcO0MC
[1256] http://www.globalsecurity.org/military/library/report/1984/CJB.htm
[1257] http://www.rediff.com/news/indochin.htm
[1258] https://web.archive.org/web/20010419174901/http://www.centurychina.com/plaboard/uploads/1962war.htm
[1259] https://web.archive.org/web/20050503103128/http://www.hindustantimes.com/news/181_284247,001300370003.htm
[1260] https://web.archive.org/web/20091015152447/http://www.ndtv.com/convergence/ndtv/showcolumns.aspx?id=COLEN20070022560
[1261] https://web.archive.org/web/20050507113230/http://www.bharat-rakshak.com/LAND-FORCES/Army/History/1962War/

[1262] https://web.archive.org/web/20070304003142/http://www.bcasnet.org/login/viewarticle.php?pid=100&disp=1
[1263] https://web.archive.org/web/20060619091847/http://news.xinhuanet.com/english/2005-12/16/content_3928187.htm
[1264] http://ia.rediff.com/news/2002/nov/15chin.htm
[1265] https://web.archive.org/web/20070928101820/http://www.casas-pkucis.org.cn/English/Journals/nyyj/bak/0202-1.htm
[1266] https://web.archive.org/web/20060530193456/http://www.fyjs.cn/bbs/read.php?tid=13872&fpage=1
[1267] http://www.lib.berkeley.edu/SSEAL/SouthAsia/kashmir.html
[1268] https://web.archive.org/web/20070215144429/http://journal.frontierindia.com/index.php?option=com_content&task=section&id=7&Itemid=53
[1269] http://www.dnaindia.com/report.asp?newsid=1101845
[1270] http://www.mea.gov.in/bilateral-documents.htm?dtl/5312/Instrument+of+Surrender+of+Pakistan+forces+in+Dacca "The Pakistan Eastern Command agree to surrender all Pakistan Armed Forces in Bangladesh to Lieutenant General Jagjit Singh Aurora, General Officer Commanding-in –chief of the Indian and Bangladesh forces in the eastern theatre."
[1271] Pakistan & the Karakoram Highway By Owen Bennett-Jones, Lindsay Brown, John Mock, Sarina Singh, Pg 30
[1272] p. 442 *Indian Army after Independence* by KC Pravel: Lancer 1987
[1273] Figures from *The Fall of Dacca* by Jagjit Singh Aurora in *The Illustrated Weekly of India* dated 23 December 1973 quoted in *Indian Army after Independence* by KC Pravel: Lancer 1987
[1274] Figure from *Pakistani Prisoners of War in India* by Col S.P. Salunke p.10 quoted in *Indian Army after Independence* by KC Pravel: Lancer 1987 ()
[1275] //en.wikipedia.org/w/index.php?title=Template:History_of_Bangladesh&action=edit
[1276] This war is known in Bangla as *Muktijuddho* or *Shwadhinota Juddho*.<ref> *Historical Dictionary of Bangladesh* https//books.google.com, Page 289
[1277] Pg 600. Schmid, Alex, ed. (2011). *The Routledge Handbook of Terrorism Research*. Routledge.
[1278] Pg. 240 Tomsen, Peter (2011). *The Wars of Afghanistan: Messianic Terrorism, Tribal Conflicts, and the Failures of Great Powers*. Public Affairs.
[1279] *Crisis in South Asia – A report* by Senator Edward Kennedy to the Subcommittee investigating the Problem of Refugees and Their Settlement, Submitted to U.S. Senate Judiciary Committee, 1 November 1971, U.S. Govt. Press.pp6-7
[1280] Pg 166–167
[1281] Salik, Siddiq, *Witness To Surrender*, pp 63, 228–9
[1282] M1 India, Pakistan, and the United States: Breaking with the Past By Shirin R. Tahir-Kheli https//books.google.com , 1997, Council on Foreign Relations. pp 37
[1283] Pakistan Defence Journal, 1977, Vol 2, pp. 2–3
[1284] Jacob, Lt. Gen. JFR, Surrender at Dacca, pp 90–91
[1285] Jacob, Lt. Gen. JFR, Surrender at Dacca, pp 42–44, pp 90–91
[1286] Hassan, Moyeedul, Muldhara' 71, pp 45–46
[1287] Islam, Major Rafiqul, *A Tale of Millions*, pp. 227, 235
[1288] Shafiullah, Maj. Gen. K.M., *Bangladesh at War*, pp 161–163
[1289] Islam, Major Rafiqul, *A Tale of Millions*, pp. 226–231
[1290] Raja, Dewan Mohammad Tasawwar, *O GENERAL MY GENERAL (Life and Works of General M. A. G. Osmani)*, pp. 35–109,
[1291] Jacob, Lt. Gen. JFR, Surrender at Dacca, pp 44
[1292] Hassan, Moyeedul, *Muldhara 71*, pp 44
[1293] Ali, Maj. Gen. Rao Farman, *How Pakistan Got Divided*, pp 100
[1294] Hassan, Moyeedul, *Muldhara 71*, pp 64–65
[1295] Khan, Maj. Gen. Fazal Mukeem, *Pakistan's Crisis in Leadership*, p 125
[1296] Ali, Rao Farman, *When Pakistan Got Divided*, p 100
[1297] Niazi, Lt. Gen. A.A.K, *The Betrayal of East Pakistan*, p 96
[1298] *Indian Army after Independence* by Maj KC Praval 1993 Lancer, p. 317
[1299] Guess who's coming to dinner http://www.newint.org/issue332/guess.htm Naeem Bangali
[1300] Sharlach 2000, pp. 92–93.

[1301] Sajjad 2012, p. 225.
[1302] White, Matthew, *Death Tolls for the Major Wars and Atrocities of the Twentieth Century* http://users.erols.com/mwhite28/warstat2.htm#Bangladesh
[1303] Many of the eyewitness accounts of relations that were picked up by "Al Badr" forces describe them as Bengali men. The only survivor of the Rayerbazar killings describes the captors and killers of Bengali professionals as fellow Bengalis. See 57 Dilawar Hossain, account reproduced in *Ekattorer Ghatok-dalalera ke Kothay* (Muktijuddha Chetona Bikash Kendro, Dacca, 1989)
[1304] U.S. Consulate (Dacca) Cable, Sitrep: Army Terror Campaign Continues in Dacca; Evidence Military Faces Some Difficulties Elsewhere http://www.gwu.edu/~nsarchiv/NSAEBB/NSAEBB79/BEBB6.pdf, 31 March 1971, Confidential, 3 pp
[1305] U.S. Consulate in Dacca (27 March 1971), *Selective genocide* http://www.gwu.edu/~nsarchiv/NSAEBB/NSAEBB79/BEBB1.pdf, Cable (PDF)
[1306] Shalom, Stephen R., The Men Behind Yahya in the Indo-Pak War of 1971 http://coat.ncf.ca/our_magazine/links/issue47/articles/a07.htm
[1307] http://lcweb2.loc.gov/frd/cs/
[1308] //doi.org/10.2307/2613440
[1309] //www.worldcat.org/issn/0020-5850
[1310] //www.jstor.org/stable/2613440
[1311] http://www.gwu.edu/~nsarchiv/NSAEBB/NSAEBB79
[1312] https://history.state.gov/historicaldocuments/frus1969-76v11
[1313] https://www.youtube.com/watch?v=G_kP0A60tNA
[1314] https://www.youtube.com/watch?v=vFHlPID-eSk
[1315] http://en.banglapedia.org/index.php?title=War_of_Liberation,_The
[1316] http://www.genocidebangladesh.org/
[1317] http://archive.thedailystar.net/news2014/freedom-in-the-air
[1318] http://www.mukto-mona.com/1971/English/archive.htm
[1319] http://www.globalwebpost.com/genocide1971/witness/rounaq.htm
[1320] https://web.archive.org/web/20030926035236/http://www.drishtipat.org/1971/war.htm
[1321] https://web.archive.org/web/20030501230820/http://www.bangladeshmariners.com/HmdrRprt/71mass.html
[1322] https://web.archive.org/web/20080223123938/http://www.adhunika.com/issues/wpawc71.html
[1323] http://archives.dailytimes.com.pk/national/30-Jun-2005/study-finds-no-cases-of-rape-by-pakistan-army-in-1971
[1324] http://www.dawn.com/news/146732/sheikh-mujib-wanted-a-confederation-us-papers
[1325] https://web.archive.org/web/20041013132951/http://muktadhara.net/page11.html
[1326] http://www.banglagallery.com/gallery/categories.php?cat_id=5
[1327] http://archive.thedailystar.net/suppliments/2010/12/victory_day/facts.html
[1328] http://in.rbth.com/articles/2011/12/20/1971_war_how_russia_sank_nixons_gunboat_diplomacy_14041.html
[1329] http://www.theindependentbd.com/post/81905
[1330] https://web.archive.org/web/20170316113441/http://gbnews24.com/breaking-news/article/call-for-international-recognitio/
[1331] http://www.observerbd.com/details.php?id=63378
[1332] http://www.thefinancialexpress-bd.com/2017/03/16/64529/The-case-for-UN-recognition-of-Bangladesh-genocide
[1333] https://www.bbc.com/news/world-asia-16207201
[1334] Section: "The Green Revolution", pp. 17–20.
[1335] Amartya Sen. 1981. *Poverty and Famines: An Essay on Entitlement and Deprivation.* http://www.oxfordscholarship.com/view/10.1093/0198284632.001.0001/acprof-9780198284635 Oxford University Press.
[1336] , originally in *Asian Age* 5 April 2013
[1337] https://sol.du.ac.in/mod/book/view.php?id=1735&chapterid=1695
[1338] http://www.nddb.org/English/Genesis/Pages/Operation-Flood.aspx
[1339] Vulnerable India: A Geographical Study of Disaster By Anu Kapur https//books.google.com

[1340] *The Encyclopedia of 20th Century Air Warfare*, edited by Chris Bishop (Amber publishing 1997, republished 2004 pages 384–387)

[1341] , Chapter 3, p. 87.

[1342] Consulate (Dacca) Cable, Sitrep: Army Terror Campaign Continues in Dacca; Evidence Military Faces Some Difficulties Elsewhere http://www.gwu.edu/~nsarchiv/NSAEBB/NSAEBB79/BEBB6.pdf, 31 March 1971, Confidential, 3 pp.

[1343] Kennedy, Senator Edward, "Crisis in South Asia – A report to the Subcommittee investigating the Problem of Refugees and Their Settlement, Submitted to U.S. Senate Judiciary Committee", 1 November 1971, U.S. Govt. Press, page 66. Sen. Kennedy wrote, "Field reports to the U.S. Government, countless eye-witness journalistic accounts, reports of International agencies such as World Bank and additional information available to the subcommittee document the reign of terror which grips East Bengal (East Pakistan). Hardest hit have been members of the Hindu community who have been robbed of their lands and shops, systematically slaughtered, and in some places, painted with yellow patches marked 'H'. All of this has been officially sanctioned, ordered and implemented under martial law from Islamabad."

[1344] Rummel, Rudolph J., "Statistics of Democide: Genocide and Mass Murder Since 1900" http://www.Hawaii.edu/powerkills/SOD.CHAP8.HTM, , Chapter 8, Table 8.2 Pakistan Genocide in Bangladesh Estimates, Sources, and Calculations http://www.hawaii.edu/powerkills/SOD.TAB8.2.GIF: lowest estimate 2 million claimed by Pakistan (reported by Aziz, Qutubuddin. *Blood and tears* Karachi: United Press of Pakistan, 1974. pp. 74, 226), some other sources used by Rummel suggest a figure of between 8 and 10 million with one (Johnson, B. L. C. *Bangladesh*. New York: Barnes & Noble, 1975. pp. 73, 75) that "could have been" 12 million.

[1345] Sajjad 2012, p. 225.

[1346] Ghadbian 2002, p. 111.

[1347] Mookherjee 2012, p. 68.

[1348] Salik, Siddiq, *Witness To Surrender* https://books.google.com/books?id=acVIPgAACAAJ&dq=Witness+To+Surrender&ei=1jLYSoHRA4m-zASTko3ABw, , pp. 63, 228–9.

[1349] Lt. Gen. Kamal Matinuddin – *Tragedy of Errors: East Pakistan Crisis, 1968–1971*; Wajidalis, Lahore, 1994; page 255 https://books.google.com/books?id=aONtAAAAMAAJ&q=announcement

[1350] Maj. Gen. Fazal Muqeem Khan – *Pakistan's Crisis in Leadership*; National Book Foundation, Islamabad, 1973; page 79 https://books.google.com/books?id=qh4NAAAAIAAJ&q=march+26

[1351] Raja, Dewan Mohammad Tasawwar, *O General My General – Life and Works of General M A G Osmany*; pp. 35–109,

[1352] U.S. Consulate (Dacca) Cable, Sitrep: Army Terror Campaign Continues in Dacca; Evidence Military Faces Some Difficulties Elsewhere http://www.gwu.edu/~nsarchiv/NSAEBB/NSAEBB79/BEBB6.pdf, 31 March 1971, Confidential, 3 pp.

[1353] http://www.economist.com/node/11661408

[1354] Manekshaw, SHFJ. (11 Nov 1998). "Lecture at Defence Services Staff College on Leadership and Discipline" (Appendix V) in Singh (2002)*Field Marshal Sam Manekshaw, M.C. – Soldiering with Dignity*.

[1355] "Trying to catch the Indian Air Force napping, Yahya Khan, launched a Pakistani version of Israel's 1967 air blitz in hopes that one rapid attack would cripple India's far superior air power. But India was alert, Pakistani pilots were inept, and Yahya's strategy of scattering his thin air force over a dozen air fields was a bust!", p. 34, *Newsweek*, 20 December 1971

[1356] Seapower: A Guide for the Twenty-first Century By Geoffrey Till page 179

[1357] 'Does the US want war with India?' http://www.rediff.com/news/2007/jan/22inter.htm. Rediff.com (31 December 2004). Retrieved on 14 April 2011.

[1358] Jon Lake, "Air Power Analysis: Indian Airpower", *World Air Power Journal*, Volume 12

[1359] Group Captain M. Kaiser Tufail, "Great Battles of the Pakistan Airforce" and "Pakistan Air Force Combat Heritage" (pafcombat) et al., Feroze sons,

[1360] Why the Indian Air Force has a high crash rate http://in.rbth.com/blogs/2015/06/04/why_the_indian_air_force_has_a_high_crash_rate_43501

[1361] , pp802

[1362] Harold H. Saunders, "What Really Happened in Bangladesh" Foreign Affairs (2014) 93#4 d
[1363] Further information relates in Hamoodur Rahman Commission.
[1364] Langewiesche, William (November 2005). "The Wrath of Khan". The Atlantic. Retrieved 31 July 2016.
[1365] Haqqānī, p. 87
[1366] Indira feared coup from 'Sam' http://www.tribuneindia.com/1999/99aug02/head1.htm, The Tribune India, 1 August 1999.
[1367] Three Indian blunders in the 1971 war http://www.rediff.com/news/slide-show/slide-show-1-three-indian-blunders-in-the-1971-war/20111212.htm, Rediff News, 12 December 2011.
[1368] Hamoodur Rehman Commission (HRC) Report of Inquiry into the 1971 War (Vanguard Books Lahore, 513)
[1369] Hamoodur Rahman Commission Report http://www.bangla2000.com/Bangladesh/Independence-War/Report-Hamoodur-Rahman/default.shtm, chapter 2 http://www.bangla2000.com/Bangladesh/Independence-War/Report-Hamoodur-Rahman/chapter2.shtm, paragraph 33
[1370] Wierda, Marieke; Anthony Triolo (31 May 2012). Luc Reydams; Jan Wouters; Cedric Ryngaert, eds. International Prosecutors. Oxford University Press. p. 169.
[1371] pg 221, 475.
[1372] Kreisler interview with Coll "Conversations with history", 25 March 2005 http://globetrotter.berkeley.edu/people5/Coll/coll-con0.html, UC Berkeley Institute of International Studies
[1373] https://www.imdb.com/title/tt0118751/
[1374] https://www.imdb.com/title/tt0154591/
[1375] Mukti - Birth of a Nation in News18 http://www.news18.com/news/movies/mukti-birth-of-a-nation-showcases-history-of-indian-military-during-1971-1494717.html
[1376] https://books.google.com/?id=3wolOABSg_YC&lpg=PP1&pg=PP1#v=onepage&q=
[1377] https://books.google.com/?id=nYppZ_dEjdIC
[1378] https://books.google.com/?id=nYppZ_dEjdIC&lpg=PP1&pg=PP1#v=onepage&q=
[1379] https://books.google.com/?id=rPmTAAAACAAJ
[1380] http://shibir.info/pdf/1971_a_global_history_of_the_creation_of_bangladesh.pdf
[1381] https://books.google.com/?id=gUfaAAAACAAJ
[1382] https://www.youtube.com/watch?v=Q8MO52QQ6_o
[1383] https://web.archive.org/web/20050802085547/http://www.freeindia.org/1971war/
[1384] https://web.archive.org/web/20081029150607/http://www.ndu.edu/nesa/docs/Gill%20Atlas%20Final%20Version.pdf
[1385] https://web.archive.org/web/20050630230828/http://www.state.gov/r/pa/ho/frus/nixon/xi/
[1386] https://web.archive.org/web/20050213035604/http://indianarmy.nic.in/armajop.htm
[1387] http://www.icdc.com/%7Epaulwolf/pakistan/pakistan.htm
[1388] http://news.bbc.co.uk/onthisday/hi/dates/stories/december/3/newsid_2519000/2519133.stm
[1389] https://web.archive.org/web/20050906140622/http://www.bharat-rakshak.com/1971/
[1390] http://www.gwu.edu/~nsarchiv/NSAEBB/NSAEBB79/
[1391] http://www.dawn.com/weekly/ayaz/20051216.htm
[1392] https://archive.is/20061015201345/http://www.vidyasoft.com/interest/war/war71.html
[1393] https://web.archive.org/web/20061020233036/http://orbat.com/site/cimh/iaf/IAF_1971_kills_rev1.pdf
[1394] https://web.archive.org/web/20070926234047/http://frontierindia.net/op-cactus-lilly-19-infantry-division-in-1971/
[1395] https://web.archive.org/web/20070926233932/http://frontierindia.net/all-for-a-bottle-of-scotch/
[1396] http://www.rediff.com/../news/2004/feb/02inter1.htm
[1397] Guha, p. 467
[1398] Guha, p. 439
[1399] Malhotra, p. 141
[1400] NAYAR, KULDIP (25 June 2000). Yes, Prime Minister http://www.indianexpress.com/ie/daily/20000713/e1.htm . *The Indian Express*.

[1401] Jaitely, Arun (5 November 2007) – "A tale of three Emergencies: real reason always different" http://www.indianexpress.com/news/a-tale-of-three-emergencies-real-reason-always-different/235992/0, *The Indian Express*
[1402] Narasimha Rao, the Best Prime Minister? by Janak Raj Jai - 1996 - Page 101
[1403] Pratap Bhanu Mehta, "The Rise of Judicial Sovereignty," *Journal of Democracy* (2007) 18#2 pp. 70–83
[1404] The *habeas corpus* judgment was overturned by the 44th amendment to the Constitution
[1405] NCERT Text Book For Political Science on Emergency (p.112)
[1406] V. Venkatesan, *Revisiting a verdict* http://www.hindu.com/fline/fl2901/stories/20120127290107100.htm Frontline (vol. 29 – Issue 01 :: 14–27 Jan 2012)
[1407] "The case that saved Indian democracy" http://www.thehindu.com/opinion/op-ed/the-case-that-saved-indian-democracy/article4647800.ece. *The Hindu* (24 April 2013). Retrieved 4 September 2013.
[1408] PUCL Archives, Oct 1981, Rajan. http://www.pucl.org/from-archives/81oct/rajan.htm
[1409] Rediff.com, Report dated 26 June 2000. http://news.rediff.com/report/2000/jun/26/george.htm
[1410] "Fresh probe in Rajan case sought" http://www.hindu.com/2011/01/25/stories/2011012561990500.htm. The Hindu, 25 January 2011.
[1411] Gwatkin, Davidson R. 'Political Will and Family Planning: The Implications of India's Emergency Experience', in: *Population and Development Review*, 5/1, 29–59;
[1412] Carl Haub and O. P. Sharma, "India's Population Reality: Reconciling Change and Tradition," *Population Bulletin* (2006) 61#3 pp 3+. online https://www.questia.com/PM.qst?a=o&d=5045013834
[1413] Jaffrelot Christophe, Hindu Nationalism, 1987, 297, Princeton University Press, ,
[1414] Chitkara M G, Hindutva, Published by APH Publishing, 1997 ,
[1415] Post Independence India, Encyclopedia of Political Parties,2002, Published by Anmol Publications PVT. LTD, ,
[1416] "The Economist' London, dt.4-12-1976
[1417] http://scroll.in/article/736263/bjp-is-mythicising-its-anti-emergency-role-it-did-not-face-the-brunt-academic-dl-sheth
[1418] http://www.thehindu.com/2000/06/13/stories/05132524.htm
[1419] J.S. Grewal, The Sikhs of the Punjab,(Cambridge, Cambridge University Press, 1990) 213
[1420] Gurmit Singh, A History of Sikh Struggles, New Delhi, Atlantic Publishers and Distributors, 1991, 2:39
[1421] J.S. Grewal, The Sikhs of the Punjab,(Cambridge, Cambridge University Press, 1990) 214; Inder Malhotra, Indira Gandhi: A Personal and Political Biography,(London/Toronto, Hodder and Stoughton, 1989) 178
[1422] D.N. Dhanagare, "Sixth Lok Sabha Election in Uttar Pradesh – 1977: The End of the Congress Hegemony," *Political Science Review* (1979) 18#1 pp 28–51
[1423] Mira Ganguly and Bangendu Ganguly, "Lok Sabha Election, 1977: The West Bengal Scene," *Political Science Review* (1979) 18#3 pp 28–53
[1424] M.R. Masani, "India's Second Revolution," *Asian Affairs* (1977) 5#1 pp 19–38.
[1425] http://timesofindia.indiatimes.com/home/stoi/How-Indians-Protest/articleshow/2061978.cms
[1426] *Beyond the Last Blue Mountain - A Life of J.R.D. Tata* by R. M. Lala.
[1427] *Nandini Satpathy* (in Oriya) by Ashisa Ranjan Mohapatra.
[1428] O. P. Mathur. Indira Gandhi and the emergency as viewed in the Indian novel. Sarup & Sons. 2004.
[1429] Joseph Bendaña. " Rushdie Talk Recasts Role of Public and Private in Politics and Literature http://watsoninstitute.org/news_detail.cfm?id=1291". Watson Institute, Brown University. 17 February 2010.
[1430] Farzand Ahmed, "1978 – Kissa Kursi Ka: Celluloid chutzpah" http://indiatoday.intoday.in/story/1978-+Kissa+Kursi+Ka:+Celluloid+chutzpah/1/76362.html. Cover Story, India Today (24 December 2009)
[1431] https://www.jstor.org/stable/2150338
[1432] http://static.history.state.gov/frus/frus1969-76ve08/pdf/d204.pdf
[1433] http://www.idea.int/publications/dchs/upload/dchs_vol2_sec4_1.pdf
[1434] http://www.ahrchk.net/pub/mainfile.php/mof/

[1435] K.S. Brar (July 1993). *Operation Blue Star: the true story*. UBS Publishers' Distributors. pp. 56–57. Retrieved 9 August 2013.

[1436] Dogra, Cander Suta. "Operation Blue Star - the Untold Story". *The Hindu*, 10 June 2013. Web. 9 Aug 2013.

[1437] Cynthia Keppley Mahmood (1 January 2011). *Fighting for Faith and Nation: Dialogues with Sikh Defenders*. University of Pennsylvania Press. pp. Title, 91, 21, 200, 77, 19. Retrieved 9 August 2013

[1438] Khushwant Singh, A History of the Sikhs, Volume II: 1839-2004, New Delhi, Oxford University Press, 2004, p. 337.

[1439] Sangat Singh, *The History of Sikhs: 1995*, p. 382.

[1440] Sangat Singh, *The Sikhs in History*.

[1441] India in 1984: Confrontation, Assassination, and Succession, by Robert L. Hardgrave, Jr. Asian Survey, 1985 University of California Press

[1442] Joshi, Chand, Bhindranwale: Myth and Reality (New Delhi: Vikas Publishing House, 1984), p. 129.

[1443] Khushwant Singh, A History of the Sikhs, Volume II: 1839-2004, New Delhi, Oxford University Press, 2004, p. 337.

[1444] Longowal said "Whenever the situation becomes ripe for settlement, some violent incident takes place. Longowal was of course not on the side of Bhindranwale and so he accused him. I know Bhindranwale is behind the murder of the DIG", "(The person behind the murder is) The one who is afraid of losing his seat of power" - but there was no proof nor a verification for it.

[1445]

[1446] Walia, Varinder. "Man who made efforts to avert Op Bluestar is no more" http://www.tribuneindia.com/2007/20071219/aplus1.htm , "Tribune India", Amritsar, 18 December 2007.

[1447] Kuldip Nayar and Khushwant Singh, Tragedy of Punjab, Vision Books, New Delhi, 1984, page 79.

[1448] Singh, Sangat: The Sikhs in History

[1449] Dr. Sangat Singh, The Sikhs in History, page = 377

[1450] History of Sikhs, Sangat Singh, pp=??

[1451] Sangat Singh, page = 377

[1452] Brar, K.S. (19 92). Operation Blue Star: True Story. UBS Publishers Distributors (P), Limited. pp. 81–82.

[1453] Brar, K.S. (1992). Operation Blue Star: True Story. UBS Publishers Distributors (P), Limited. pp. 61.

[1454] "Sikhs, in rally, press the Army to quit temple", Sanjoy Hazarika, *The New York Times*, 3 September 1984.

[1455] New York Times, 2 May 1986.

[1456] "India Uproots Thousands Living Near Sikh Temple", Barbara Crossette, New York Times, 3 June 1990.

[1457] Khushwant Singh, A History of the Sikhs, Volume II: 1839-2004, New Delhi, Oxford University Press, 2004, p. 341.

[1458] Brar, K.S. (1992). Operation Blue Star: True Story. UBS Publishers Distributors (P), Limited. p. 31.

[1459] Anniversary Issue, India Today, 26 December 2005, p 136.

[1460] Judge V M Tarkunde, et al., Oppression in Punjab: Report to the Nation, New Delhi: Citizens for Democracy, 1985, pp. 8–10, 18–19

[1461] Ram Narayan Kumar, et al., Reduced to Ashes (Volume One), Asia Forum for Human Rights, Kathmandu, Nepal, May 2003, pp. 75)

[1462] I.S. Jaijee. *Politics of Genocide: 1984–1998*. Ajanta Publishers, New Delhi, India.

[1463] Cynthia Mahmood. *Fighting for Faith and Nation: Dialogues with Sikh Militants*. University of Pennsylvania Press.

[1464] "Indira Gandhi had since long been planning for an attack on Darbar Sahib..." Harjinder Singh Dilgeer (2012). *Sikh History in 10 Volumes*. vol 7, p. 168; 196-197.

[1465] http://www.centralsikhmuseum.com/gallery/hi/operation-blue-star/

[1466] https://web.archive.org/web/20130608134930/http://www.centralsikhmuseum.com:80/gallery/hi/operation-blue-star

[1467] http://www.timescontent.com/tss/showcase/related/photos/c1/Operation_Blue_Star/1/r/Operation-Blue-Star.html
[1468] Dr. Sangat Kr. Singh, *The Sikhs in History*, p. 393
[1469] https://web.archive.org/web/20130227011011/http://www.delhiwonders.com/delhi-indira-gandhi-memorial
[1470] http://indiragandhi.in/en/memorial/virtual-museum
[1471] Swadesh Bahadur Singh (editor of the Sher-i-Panjâb weekly): "Cabinet berth for a Sikh", *The Indian Express*, 31 May 1996.
[1472] Joshi, Chand, Bhindranwale: Myth and Reality (New Delhi: Vikas Publishing House, 1984), p. 129.
[1473] Singh, Jaspreet, "India's pogrom, 1984", *International New York Times*, 31 October 2014, p. 7
[1474]
[1475] McLeod, W. H. *Historical Dictionary of Sikhism*. 2005, page xiv
[1476] Yoo, David. *New Spiritual Homes: Religion and Asian Americans*. 1999, page 129
[1477] On November 2, Moti Singh witnessed two policemen, one an SHO and another a constable, both of whom who had attended Sajjan Kumar's meeting the previous day, shoot and kill Roshan Singh (his son) and kill his grandchildren when they ran to help their father.<ref name="ensaaf-org.jklaw.net">
[1478] 1984 riots: three held guilty of rioting https://archive.is/20130122142454/http://www.expressindia.com/latest-news/1984-riots-three-held-guilty-of-rioting/505774/. *The Indian Express*. 23 August 2009.
[1479] mha.nic.in http://www.mha.nic.in/Nanavati-I.pdf
[1480] faces shoe missile from scribe http://www.ptinews.com/pti%5Cptisite.nsf/0/C40A9A14F90E819A6525759100479796?OpenDocument:Chidambaram
[1481] ["'84 Riots: US Court Dismisses Complaint Against Nath" , "Outlook India", 16 March 2012,]
[1482] ["US court dismisses plea against Nath in anti-Sikh riots case" , "IBN Live", 16 March 2012, http://ibnlive.in.com/generalnewsfeed/news/us-court-dismisses-plea-against-nath-in-antisikh-riots-case/975976.html]
[1483] K. Singh: "Congress (I) is the Most Communal Party", Publik Asia, 16 November 1989.
[1484] http://www.carnage84.com/human/truth/truth.htm
[1485] http://ensaaf-org.jklaw.net/publications/reports/20years/20years-2nd.pdf
[1486] https://web.archive.org/web/20030712063601/http://punjabjustice.org/report/report.htm
[1487] https://web.archive.org/web/20060705030307/http://www.punjabjustice.org/report/report.htm
[1488] http://www.pucl.org/Topics/Religion-communalism/2003/who-are-guilty.htm
[1489] http://info.indiatimes.com/1984/
[1490] http://districts.delhigovt.nic.in/84RIOTS/84RIOTS.htm
[1491] http://www.witness84.com/reports/misra/
[1492] http://www.witness84.com/reports/ahooja/
[1493] http://www.witness84.com/guilty/
[1494] http://news.bbc.co.uk/2/hi/south_asia/8319737.stm
[1495] //tools.wmflabs.org/geohack/geohack.php?pagename=Bhopal_disaster&params=23_16_51_N_77_24_38_E_region:IN-MP_type:landmark
[1496] F-41443A-7/76
[1497] Kovel (2002).
[1498] Sriramachari (2004).
[1499] Kurzman (1987).
[1500] Cassels (1983).
[1501] Mandala Project (1996), Trade Environmental Database (TED) Case Study 233. Volume 5, Number 1, January, 1996
[1502] Weir (1987).
[1503]
[1504]
[1505]
[1506] {{Cite web website=Indian Express url=http://indianexpress.com/article/india/bhopal-gas-tragedy-dow-chemical-1984-gas-tragedy-trial-madhya-pradesh-union-carbide-india-

limited-4936270/ title= Bhopal Gas tragedy: In court, defence names former employee as 'saboteur'}}
[1507] Labunska et al. (2003).
[1508] Down to Earth (2003).
[1509] Stringer et al. (2002).
[1510] Srishti (2002).
[1511] Greenpeace Research Laboratories, Department of Biological Sciences, University of Exeter, Exeter UK
[1512] http://www.pan-uk.org/
[1513] http://www.greenpeace.org/usa/en/campaigns/toxics/justice-for-bhopal/
[1514] https://www.globalpolicy.org/component/content/article/212/45285.html
[1515] http://www.ehjournal.net/content/4/1/6
[1516] //doi.org/10.1186/1476-069X-4-6
[1517] //www.ncbi.nlm.nih.gov/pmc/articles/PMC1142333
[1518] //www.ncbi.nlm.nih.gov/pubmed/15882472
[1519] http://www.sciencedirect.com/science/article/B6TGH-4H2G8YH-1/2/2f70debf0a05a3303428303074800554
[1520] //doi.org/10.1016/j.jlp.2005.07.025
[1521] https//web.archive.org
[1522] http//webdrive.service.emory.edu
[1523] https://books.google.com/?id=lpcwvvK9xlsC&printsec=frontcover#v=onepage&q&f=false
[1524] http://pubs.acs.org/cen/books/85/8528books.html
[1525] http://www.lakareformiljon.org/images/stories/dokument/2009/bhopal_gas_disaster.pdf
[1526] https://docs.google.com/file/d/0B0FqO8XKy9NRZDNzTkZQeVJQbE0/edit?pli=1
[1527] https://books.google.com/books?id=rvn7ybZUo4kC
[1528] https//web.archive.org
[1529] http://www.ttl.fi/en/publications/electronic_journals/asian_pacific_newsletter/archives/Documents/asian_pacific_newsletter2_2006.pdf
[1530] //doi.org/10.1016/B978-0-444-52272-6.00359-7
[1531] http://www.sciencedirect.com/science/article/pii/B9780124095489019035
[1532] https://books.google.com/books?id=8Zzl85Yt_-YC&printsec=frontcover&hl=sv#v=onepage&q&f=false
[1533] https://web.archive.org/web/20081030121735/http://bhopal.bard.edu/resources/documents/1988ArthurD.Littlereport.pdf
[1534] http://bhopal.bard.edu/resources/documents/1988ArthurD.Littlereport.pdf
[1535] https://books.google.com/?id=W-eavh4NQcwC&printsec=frontcover#v=onepage&q&f=false
[1536] https//web.archive.org
[1537] http://webdrive.service.emory.edu/users/vdhara/www.BhopalPublications/Environmental%20Health/Greenpeace%20Bhopal%20Report.pdf
[1538] //doi.org/10.1001/jama.290.14.1856
[1539] //www.ncbi.nlm.nih.gov/pubmed/14532313
[1540] https//web.archive.org
[1541] http//webdrive.service.emory.edu
[1542] http://www.greenpeace.org/raw/content/international/press/reports/chemical-stockpiles-at-union-c.pdf
[1543] https://books.google.com/books?id=4ela2PwIbLEC
[1544] http://www.latimes.com/entertainment/movies/la-et-mn-bhopal-prayer-for-rain-review-20141114-story.html
[1545] http://www.bhopal.net/
[1546] http://www.bhopal.org/
[1547] http://www.mp.gov.in/bgtrrdmp/
[1548] http://www.bhopal.com/
[1549] http://www.indiaenvironmentportal.org.in/search/?q=bhopal+gas
[1550] https://books.google.com/books/about/Bhopal.html?id=QiBPAAAAMAAJ&redir_esc=y
[1551] Balasingham, Adele. (2003) *The Will to Freedom - An Inside View of Tamil Resistance*. Fairmax Publishing Ltd, 2nd ed.

[1552] NorthEast Secretariat report on Human rights 1974 - 2004 (see Further Reading section).
[1553] Operation Pawan. The Battle for Jaffna http://www.bharat-rakshak.com/LAND-FORCES/Army/History/1987/Chapter03.html
[1554] Dissanayaka, T.D.S.A.: "War or Peace in Sri Lanka, Volume II", p. 332. Swastika, 1998.
[1555] 846 Indian soldiers have died in Siachen since 1984 – Rediff.com News http://www.rediff.com/news/slide-show/slide-show-1-indian-soldiers-have-died-in-siachen-since-1984/20120828.htm. Rediff.com. Retrieved on 12 July 2013.
[1556] The Himalayas War at the Top Of the World http://www.time.com/time/magazine/article/0,9171,958254-2,00.html 31 July 1989 – TIME
[1557] VAUSE, Mikel. Peering Over the Edge: The Philosophy of Mountaineering, p. 194.
[1558] CHILD, Greg. Mixed Emotions: Mountaineering Writings, p. 147.
[1559] //tools.wmflabs.org/geohack/geohack.php?pagename=Siachen_conflict&params=35.008371_N_77.008805_E_
[1560] Modern world history- Chapter-The Indian subcontinent achieves independence/The Coldest War.
[1561]
[1562] Himalayan Journal Vol. 21
[1563] Himalayan Journal Vol. 25
[1564] SANGAKU 71
[1565] Alpine Journal, 1984
[1566] (pp. 39)
[1567] Op Rajeev https://cosmicwarrior.wordpress.com/2007/09/18/op-rajiv-a-battle-that-broke-pakistans-adventurism-on-the-glacier/, 18 September 2007
[1568] The fight for Siachen http://tribune.com.pk/story/368394/the-fight-for-siachen/, Brig. Javed Hassan (Retd) 22 April 2012, The Tribune (Pakistan)
[1569] Siachen- Not a Cold War http://www.hoonslegacy.com/siachen-glacier/, Lt. Gen. P. N. Hoon (Retd)
[1570] Endgame at Siachen http://www.defstrat.com/exec/frmArticleDetails.aspx?DID=495, Maj Gen Raj Mehta, AVSM, VSM (Retd) 2 December 2014, South Asia Defence and Strategic Review
[1571] (pp. 68–69)
[1572] http://www.business-standard.com/article/economy-policy/846-indian-soldiers-have-died-in-siachen-since-1984-112082802005_1.html
[1573] Confirm ground position line on Siachen: BJP http://www.hindu.com/2006/04/29/stories/2006042906591200.htm – 29 April 2006, *The Hindu*
[1574] Guns to fall silent on Indo-Pak borders http://www.dailytimes.com.pk/default.asp?page=story_26-11-2003_pg1_1 26 November 2003 – *Daily Times*
[1575] Malik 2006, p. 54.
[1576] Gokhale 2015, p. 148.
[1577] Malik 2006, p. 53.
[1578] Lavoy 2009, p. 76.
[1579] Lavoy 2009, p. 75.
[1580] India opens Siachen to trekkers http://articles.timesofindia.indiatimes.com/2007-09-13/india/27962396_1_glacial-heights-siachen-glacier-saltoro-ridge-audience-that-indian-troops Times of India 13 September 2007
[1581] https://www.nytimes.com/1999/05/23/world/the-coldest-war-frozen-in-fury-on-the-roof-of-the-world.html
[1582] http://www.sciencedirect.com/science/article/pii/S0962629815000347
[1583] //doi.org/10.1016/j.polgeo.2015.05.001
[1584] http://outsideonline.com/outside/features/200302/200302_siachen_1.html
[1585] http://www.time.com/time/magazine/article/0,9171,1079528,00.html
[1586] https://web.archive.org/web/20041027004644/http://www.kashmirsentinel.com/apr1999/3.8.html
[1587] http://www.pakistanarmy.biz.tc/siachen.html/
[1588] Assassination in India; Rajiv Gandhi is assassinated in bombing at campaign stop; India puts off rest of votinghttps://www.nytimes.com/1991/05/22/world/assassination-india-rajiv-gandhi-assassinated-bombing-campaign-stop-india-puts.html?pagewanted=all

[1589] "Assassination in India; Rajiv Gandhi is assassinated in bombing at campaign stop" https//www.nytimes.com, by Barbara Crossette, *The New York Times*, May 22, 1991. Neena Gopal of the Gulf News of Dubai was also in the car, in the back seat with Chandrashekhar and a local party official. "A Chance To Be Near The People New Campaigning Style Put Gandhi In Crowds" http://articles.orlandosentinel.com/1991-05-22/news/9105220915_1_gandhi-rajiv-chandrashekhar/2 by Barbara Crossette, *New York Times*, May 22, 1991, via *Orlando Sentinel*. Retrieved 2010-07-19.

[1590] D.R.Karthikeyanhttp://www.thesnacademy.ac.in/board-of-governors-karthikeyan.html

[1591] http://cbi.nic.in/dop/judgements/thomas.pdf

[1592] India: The Prevention of Terrorism Bill. Past abuses revisited I Amnesty International http://web.amnesty.org/library/Index/ENGASA200222000?open&of=ENG-IND

[1593] http://www.dnaindia.com/india/report_ib-hid-crucial-video-on-rajiv-gandhi-murder-book_1757684

[1594] http://www.milligazette.com/news/4494-buy-a-copy-of-conspiracy-to-kill-rajiv-gandhi-from-the-cbi-files

[1595] outlookindia.com http://www.outlookindia.com/pti_print.asp?id=266715

[1596] Jain Commission Report Chapter Ii http://www.india-today.com/jain/vol3/chap2.html

[1597] Jain Commission Report Chapter Viii http://www.india-today.com/jain/vol3/chap8.html

[1598] We deeply regret Rajiv's death: LTTE http://www.expressindia.com/fullstory.php?newsid=70062

[1599] https://www.youtube.com/watch?v=7DTKpBiThq0

[1600] //tools.wmflabs.org/geohack/geohack.php?pagename=Assassination_of_Rajiv_Gandhi&params=12.9602_N_79.9452_E_region:IN-TN_type:landmark

[1601] http://www.timesonline.co.uk/article/0,,3-1363447,00.html, Multiple sources for the number of Indian counter-insurgency troops in the region

[1602] Conflict Encyclopedia – India: Kashmir http://ucdp.uu.se/#conflict/364 , Uppsala Conflict Data Program, 29 May 1977, retrieved 2013-05-29,

[1603] Uppsala Conflict Data Program Conflict Encyclopedia, Conflict Summary, Conflict name: India: Kashmir, "Roots of Conflict and the emergence of Kashmir Insurgents", viewed 2013-05-29, http://www.ucdp.uu.se/gpdatabase/gpcountry.php?id=74&regionSelect=6-Central_and_Southern_Asia#

[1604] Uppsala Conflict Data Program Conflict Encyclopedia, Conflict Summary, India: Kashmir (entire conflict), Fatality estimates, viewed 2013-05-29, http://www.ucdp.uu.se/gpdatabase/gpcountry.php?id=74&regionSelect=6-Central_and_Southern_Asia#

[1605] Uppsala Conflict Data Program Conflict Encyclopedia, India One-sided violence, Government of India – civilians, Kashmir insurgents – civilians, Lashkar-e-Taiba – civilians, viewed on 2012-05-29, http://www.ucdp.uu.se/gpdatabase/gpcountry.php?id=74&regionSelect=6-Central_and_Southern_Asia#

[1606] Fatalities in Terrorist Violence 1988–2014 in Jammu & Kashmir http://www.satp.org/satporgtp/countries/india/database/index.html , South Asian Terrorism, SATP (2014)

[1607] Buried Evidence: Unknown, Unmarked, and Mass Graves in Indian-Administered Kashmir http://www.kashmirprocess.org/reports/graves/BuriedEvidenceKashmir.pdf A preliminary report; *International People's Tribunal on Human Rights and Justice in Kashmir*

[1608] Waheeda Khan, Conflict in Kashmir 2015, p. 90, 91.

[1609] Alexander Evans, A departure from history: Kashmiri Pandits, 1990–2001, Contemporary South Asia (Volume 11, Number 1, 1 March 2002, pp. 19–37)

[1610] https://books.google.com/books?id=BvpUCgAAQBAJ&pg=PA583

[1611] //en.wikipedia.org/w/index.php?title=Template:Violence_against_Hindus_in_independent_India&action=edit

[1612] //en.wikipedia.org/w/index.php?title=Template:Violence_against_Muslims_in_India&action=edit

[1613] Chris Ogden. A Lasting Legacy: The BJP-led National Democratic Alliance and India's Politics. Journal of Contemporary Asia. Vol. 42, Iss. 1, 2012

[1614] ERCES Online Quarterly Review http://www.erces.com/journal/articles/archives/v02/v_02_04.htm Religious Identity of the Perpetrators and Victims of Communal Violence in Post-Independence India

[1615] http://www.sabrang.com/srikrish/vol1.htm
[1616] For a critique of the existing explanations and a comprehensive alternative explanation see: Sharma, Chanchal Kumar (2011) " A Discursive Dominance Theory of Economic Reforms Sustainability http://www.tandfonline.com/doi/abs/10.1080/14736489.2011.574550." *India Review* (Routledge, UK) 126–84
[1617] GDP growth slumps to 5%, a decade's low http://www.thehindubusinessline.com/economy/gdp-growth-slumps-to-5-a-decades-low/article4768550.ece, Hindu Business Line 31 May 2013
[1618] India's Ponzi-styled economic reforms run out of steam http://www.eastasiaforum.org/2013/06/04/indias-ponzi-styled-economic-reforms-run-out-of-steam/, East Asia Forum 4 June 2013
[1619] //en.wikipedia.org/w/index.php?title=Template:History_of_modern_India&action=edit
[1620] Street Hawking Promise Jobs in Future http://www.swaminomics.org/articles/20011125_streethawking.htm , The Times of India, 25 November 2001
[1621] For a complete history & analysis of liberalisation episodes in India, see: Sharma, Chanchal Kumar (2011) " A Discursive Dominance Theory of Economic Reforms Sustainability http://www.tandfonline.com/doi/abs/10.1080/14736489.2011.574550." *India Review* (Routledge, UK) 126–84
[1622] History of Computing in India: 1955–2010, Rajaraman, V.
[1623] PV Narasimha Rao Passes Away http://www.tlca.com/adults/obit-pvn.html. Retrieved 7 October 2007.
[1624] India's Pathway through Financial Crisis http://www.globaleconomicgovernance.org/wp-content/uploads/Ghosh%20-%20India.pdf . Arunabha Ghosh. Global Economic Governance Programme. Retrieved on 2 March 2007.
[1625] What Caused the 1991 Currency Crisis in India? http://www.uoit.ca/sas/Macroeconomic%20Issues/What1991CrisisIndia.pdf, IMF Staff Papers, Valerie Cerra and Sweta Chaman Saxena.
[1626] Economic Crisis Forcing Once Self-Reliant India to Seek Aid https://www.nytimes.com/1991/06/29/world/economic-crisis-forcing-once-self-reliant-india-to-seek-aid.html, New York Times, 29 June 1991
[1627] Task Force Report 2006, pp. 7–8.
[1628] Task Force Report 2006, pp. 17–20.
[1629] Local industrialists against multinationals http://www.asiaweek.com/asiaweek/96/0412/nat1.html. Ajay Singh and Arjuna Ranawana. *Asiaweek*. Retrieved on 2 March 2007.
[1630] http://one.revver.com/watch/339183/flv/affiliate/94378
[1631] http://www.reason.com/blog/show/131810.html
[1632] https://web.archive.org/web/20090307101534/http://www.foreignaffairs.org/20060701faessay85401-p0/gurcharan-das/the-india-model.html
[1633] http://www.foreignaffairs.org/20060701faessay85401-p0/gurcharan-das/the-india-model.html
[1634] https://www.academia.edu/12282652/Good_Times_Brought_to_you_by_Brand_Modi
[1635] https://www.academia.edu/3347336/India_Inc._and_its_moral_discontents
[1636] http//wayback.archive-it.org
[1637] http://www.ccsindia.org/interns2006/How%20Wrong%20is%20left%20about%20ecoonimic%20reforms%20in%20India%20-%20Aditya.pdf
[1638] https://web.archive.org/web/20090114195859/http://www.ukibc.com/ukindia2/files/India60.pdf
[1639] http://www.ukibc.com/ukindia2/files/India60.pdf
[1640] "Govt blames LeT for Parliament attack" http://www.rediff.com/news/2001/dec/14parl12.htm. Rediff.com (14 December 2001). Retrieved 8 September 2011.
[1641] "Mastermind killed" http://www.chinadaily.com.cn/en/doc/2003-08/31/content_259902.htm. *China Daily*. Retrieved 8 September 2011.
[1642] Embassy of India – Washington DC (official website) United States of America http//www.indianembassy.org. Indianembassy.org. Retrieved 8 September 2011.
[1643] " [Pakistan Primer Pt. 2 From Kashmir to the FATA: The ISI Loses Control http://www.globalbearings.net/2011/10/image-from-gates-of-pakistan-naval.html ," Global Bearings, 28 October 2011.

[1644] "The terrorists had the home ministry and special Parliament label' http://www.rediff.com/news/2001/dec/13parl14.htm. 2007Rediff India. 13 December 2001
[1645] "Terrorists attack Parliament; five intruders, six cops killed" http://www.rediff.com/news/2001/dec/13parl1.htm. 2006. Rediff India. 13 December. 2001
[1646] Press Release on the attack http://www.hciottawa.ca/news/pr/pr-011218.html
[1647] State (N.C.T. of Delhi) vs. Navjot Sandhu alias Afsan, Supreme Court of India, 8 August 2005.
[1648] Encounter specialist killed by his own gunhttp://www.thehindu.com/todays-paper/tp-national/tp-newdelhi/Encounter-specialist-killed-by-his-own-gun/article15191479.ece
[1649] Delhi High Court State vs Mohd. Afzal And Ors. [Along With ... on 29 October, 2003https://indiankanoon.org/doc/1031426/
[1650] 4 convicted in attack http://www.hinduonnet.com/2002/12/17/stories/2002121705260100.htm. Hinduonnet.com (17 December 2002). Retrieved 8 September 2011.
[1651] "Parliament attack: Advani points towards neighbouring country" http://www.rediff.com/news/2001/dec/14parl21.htm. 2006. Rediff India. 14 December 2001
[1652] "Govt blames LeT for Parliament attack, asks Pak to restrain terrorist outfits" http://www.rediff.com/news/2001/dec/14parl12.htm. 2006. Rediff India. 14 December 2001
[1653] Mastermind killed http://www.chinadaily.com.cn/en/doc/2003-08/31/content_259902.htm. *China Daily*. Retrieved 8 September 2011.
[1654] https://www.youtube.com/watch?v=Vt3G71Ce0cM
[1655] http://www.indianexpress.com/news/parliament-attack-why-didnt-the-bomb-explode--afzal-guru-wonders/848307/
[1656] http://www.dnaindia.com/lifestyle/1827942/report-book-review-the-strange-case-of-the-attack-on-the-indian-parliament
[1657] http://theparallelpost.com/archives/column/433-indian-parliament-attack-crime-and-punishment.html
[1658] http://alhittin.com/2013/02/09/afzalguru-the-very-strange-story-of-the-attack-on-the-indian-parliament/
[1659] http://www.thehindu.com/news/national/unanswered-questions-are-the-remains-of-the-day/article4397789.ece
[1660] https://www.wsj.com/articles/SB10001424127887324590904578292910964921342
[1661] Ghassem-Fachand 2012, p. 1-2.
[1662] Chris Ogden. 2012. A Lasting Legacy: The BJP-led National Democratic Alliance and India's Politics Journal of Contemporary Asia Vol. 42, Iss. 1, 2012
[1663] Brass 2005, p. 388.
[1664] Nussbaum 2008, p. 50-51.
[1665] Shani 2007b, pp. 168–173.
[1666] //en.wikipedia.org/w/index.php?title=Template:Violence_against_Muslims_in_India&action=edit
[1667] //en.wikipedia.org/w/index.php?title=Template:Violence_against_Hindus_in_independent_India&action=edit
[1668] The Godhra conspiracy as Justice Nanavati saw it http//epaper.timesofindia.com The Times of India, 28 September 2008. Retrieved 19 February 2012. Archived https//www.webcitation.org 21 February 2012.
[1669] Jaffrelot 2011, p. 398.
[1670] Godhra verdict: 31 convicted, 63 acquitted http://www.ndtv.com/article/india/godhra-verdict-31-convicted-63-acquitted-86991 NDTV – 1 March 2011
[1671] The Concerned Citizen's Tribunal (CCT) was an eight-member committee headed by V. R. Krishna Iyer, retired Judge of Supreme Court, with P. B. Sawant, Hosbet Suresh, K. G. Kannabiran, Aruna Roy, K. S. Subramanian, Ghanshyam Shah and Tanika Sarkar making up the rest. It was appointed by Citizens for Peace and Justice (CPJ), a group formed by some social activists from Mumbai and Ahmedabad. It released its first reports in 2003. CPJ members included Alyque Padamsee, Anil Dharkar, Cyrus Guzder,Ghulam Mohammed, I.M. Kadri, Javed Akhtar, Nandan Maluste, Titoo Ahluwalia, Vijay Tendulkar, Teesta Setalvad, Javed Anand; Indubhai Jani, Uves Sareshwala, Batuk Vora, Fr. Cedric Prakash, Najmal Almelkar.
[1672] Shani 2007b, p. 171.

[1673] Simpson 2009, p. 134.
[1674] Bunsha 2005.
[1675] Teesta Setalvad, "When guardians betray: The role of the police," in Varadarajan 2002, p. 181
[1676] Jaffrelot 2011, p. 388.
[1677] Oommen 2008, p. 71.
[1678] Gujarat riots: As death toll rises, CM Narendra Modi image hits a new low http://indiatoday.intoday.in/story/gujarat-riots-as-death-toll-rises-cm-narendra-modi-image-hits-a-new-low/1/219805.html, India Today, 20 May 2002
[1679] Docs told to stay off minority areas http://timesofindia.indiatimes.com/city/ahmedabad/Docs-told-to-stay-off-minority-areas/articleshow/6512317.cms, Times of India, 11 April 2002
[1680] Nandini Sundar, "A licene to kill: Patterns of violence in Gujarat", in Varadarajan 2002, p. 83
[1681] Siddharth Varadarajan and Rajdeep Sardesai, "The truth hurts: Gujarat and the role of the media", in Varadarajan 2002, p. 272
[1682] Nussbaum 2008, p. 2.
[1683] Human Rights Watch alleged<ref name="hrw_bg_gujarat">
[1684] Dionne Bunsha, Verdict in Best Bakery case http://www.frontline.in/static/html/fl2304/stories/20060310005611700.htm, *Frontline*, Volume 23 – Issue 04, 25 February – 10 March 2006
[1685] Setalvad in dock for 'cooking up killings' "Setalvad in dock for 'cooking up killings'" http://economictimes.indiatimes.com/News/PoliticsNation/Setalvad-in-dock-for-cooking-up-killings/articleshow/4397849.cms. *The Economic Times*. Retrieved 11 May 2009. 14 May 2009.
[1686] Engineer 2003, p. 262.
[1687] The 2003 International Report by the US State Department can be found here.https://www.state.gov/j/drl/rls/irf/2003/24470.htm It states

> The Gujarat State Higher Secondary Board, to which nearly 98 percent of schools in Gujarat belong, requires the use of certain textbooks in which Nazism is condoned. In the Standard 10 social studies textbook, the "charismatic personality" of "Hitler the Supremo" and the "achievements of Nazism" are described at length. The textbook does not acknowledge Nazi extermination policies or concentration camps except for a passing reference to "a policy of opposition towards the Jewish people and [advocacy for] the supremacy of the German race." The Standard 9 social studies textbook implies that Muslims, Christians, Parsees, and Jews are "foreigners." In 2002 the Gujarat State Higher Secondary Board administered an exam, while the riots were ongoing, in which students of English were asked to form one sentence out of the following: "There are two solutions. One of them is the Nazi solution. If you don't like people, kill them, segregate them. Then strut up and down. Proclaim that you are the salt of the earth."

[1688] Guha 2002, p. 437.
[1689] Oommen 2008, p. 73.
[1690] DESTROYED, DAMAGED RELIGIOUS STRUCTURES IN GUJARAT http//www.radianceweekly.com Radiance Viewsweekly, 10 November 2012.
[1691] Jaffrelot 2011, p. 389.
[1692] Engineer 2003, p. 265.
[1693] https://www.theguardian.com/world/2012/oct/22/uk-ends-boycott-narendra-modi
[1694] Brass 2005, p. 385-393.
[1695] Dugger, Celia W. (Ahmedabad Journal) "In India, a Child's Life Is Cheap Indeed". *The New York Times*. 7 March 2002
[1696] http://press.princeton.edu/chapters/i9755.pdf
[1697] http://home.gujarat.gov.in/homedepartment/downloads/godharaincident.pdf
[1698] http://www.sabrang.com/tribunal/
[1699] http://2001-2009.state.gov/p/sca/rls/rm/2005/43701.htm
[1700] //tools.wmflabs.org/geohack/geohack.php?pagename=2001%E2%80%9302_India%E2%80%93Pakistan_standoff&params=34_56_N_76_46_E_
[1701] Kashmir Crisis http://www.globalsecurity.org/military/world/war/kashmir-2002.htm Global Security.org
[1702] "Who will strike first" http://www.economist.com/printedition/displayStory.cfm?Story_ID=917228, The Economist, 20 December 2001.

[1703] "India to withdraw troops from Pak border" http://www1.timesofindia.indiatimes.com/cms.dll/articleshow?artid=25384627 , Times of India, 16 October 2002.
[1704] "Pakistan to withdraw front-line troops" http://news.bbc.co.uk/2/hi/world/south_asia/2335599.stm, BBC, 17 October 2002.
[1705] "Parliament attack: Advani points towards neighbouring country" http://www.rediff.com/news/2001/dec/14parl21.htm, Rediff, 14 December 2001.
[1706] "Govt blames LeT for Parliament attack, asks Pak to restrain terrorist outfits" http://www.rediff.com/news/2001/dec/14parl12.htm, Rediff, 14 December 2001.
[1707] "Pakistan forces put on high alert: Storming of parliament" http://www.dawn.com/2001/12/15/top1.htm, Dawn (newspaper), 15 December 2001.
[1708] Pakistan, India 'move missiles' to border http://archives.cnn.com/2001/WORLD/asiapcf/south/12/25/india.pakistan.kashmir.missiles CNN, 26 December 2001.
[1709] Musharraf declares war on extremism http://news.bbc.co.uk/2/hi/south_asia/1756965.stm, BBC, 12 January 2002.
[1710] "The Stand-off" http://www.newyorker.com/archive/2006/02/13/060213fa_fact_coll, The New Yorker, 13 February 2006.
[1711] "India expels Pakistan's ambassador" http://www.cbc.ca/world/story/2002/05/18/india_pak020518.html, CBC.ca, 18 May 2002.
[1712] "Six more Pak soldiers killed" http://www.tribuneindia.com/2002/20020522/main1.htm, The Tribune, 21 May 2002.
[1713] "Indian PM calls for 'decisive battle' over Kashmir" https://www.theguardian.com/world/2002/may/22/kashmir.india, *The Guardian*, Wednesday 22 May 2002. Retrieved on 7 February 2013.
[1714] "Putin Attempts to Mediate India-Pakistan Tensions" http://www.voanews.com/content/a-13-a-2002-06-03-10-putin-66287377/541040.html, *VOA*, 3 June 2002. Retrieved on 7 February 2013.
[1715] India-Pakistan Conflict http://www.globalsecurity.org/military/world/war/indo-pak.htm, Globalsecurity.org
[1716] "India-Pakistan Ceasefire Agreement" http://www.ndtv.com/article/india/ceasefire-violation-pak-continues-firing-for-seventh-day-233448, *NDTV*. Retrieved on 7 February 2013.
[1717]
[1718] Irish Examiner – 2002/06/05: "Musharraf refuses to renounce first use of nuclear weapons" http://archives.tcm.ie/irishexaminer/2002/06/05/story29703.asp , Irish Examiner, 5 June 2002
[1719] http://www.hindu.com/2004/02/06/stories/2004020604461200.htm
[1720] https://web.archive.org/web/20081202061336/http://www.bharat-rakshak.com/MONITOR/ISSUE5-5/Sunils.html
[1721] http://articles.timesofindia.indiatimes.com/2003-07-31/india/27204243_1_op-parakram-indian-soldiers-operation-parakram
[1722] http://repository.library.georgetown.edu/handle/10822/552636
[1723] http://repository.library.georgetown.edu/handle/10822/552494
[1724] //tools.wmflabs.org/geohack/geohack.php?pagename=2008_Mumbai_attacks&params=18.922125_N_72.832564_E_
[1725] Pakistan admits Pakistanis, LeT training camps used for Mumbai attacks http://www.thenewstribe.com/2012/11/12/pakistan-admits-pakistanis-let-training-camps-used-for-mumbai-attacks/. The News Tribe (12 November 2012). Retrieved on 2014-06-19.
[1726] Nelson, Dean. (8 July 2009) Pakistani president Asif Zardari admits creating terrorist groups https://www.telegraph.co.uk/news/worldnews/asia/pakistan/5779916/Pakistani-president-Asif-Zardari-admits-creating-terrorist-groups.html. Telegraph. Retrieved on 2014-06-19.
[1727] Pakistan admits Mumbai terror link | The National http://www.thenational.ae/news/world/middle-east/pakistan-admits-mumbai-terror-link. Thenational.ae (12 February 2009). Retrieved on 2014-06-19.
[1728] The expression "26/11" is pronounced "twenty-six eleven". The slash is not part of the pronunciation.
[1729] Editorial – K. Jaishankar – IJCJS vol 2 issue 2 July–December, 2008 http://www.sascv.org/ijcjs/editorial4ijcjs.html. Sascv.org. Retrieved on 19 June 2014.

[1730] MEP attacks EU consular reaction in Mumbai http://euobserver.com/9/27253, PHILIPPA RUNNER, 8 December 2008 @ 17:19 CET, *EUobserver*
[1731] Associated Press, "Four more men charged in Mumbai attack", *Japan Times*, 27 April 2011, p. 4.
[1732] New York Times, 17 December 2010 "Top US Spy Leaves Pakistan After His Name Is Revealed," https://www.nytimes.com/2010/12/18/world/asia/18pstan.html
[1733] Bodies of nine Mumbai gunmen buried secretly in Jan http://in.reuters.com/article/domesticNews/idINSGE6350JE20100406Reuters, Tue 6 April 2010 10:26 pm IST
[1734] 26/11 attacks handler arrested http://www.hindustantimes.com/News-Feed/hyderabad/26-11-attacks-handler-arrested/Article1-499019.aspx *Hindustan Times*, Abhishek Sharan & Ashok Das, Delhi/Hyderabad, 18 January 2010
[1735] Two with dual US-Israeli citizenship.
[1736] Two with dual Israeli-US citizenship.
[1737] Dual British-Cypriot citizenship.
[1738] http://www.bangkokpost.com/291108_News/29Nov2008_news02.phpl Thai woman shot dead my militants in Mumbai, Bangkok Post, Accessed 29 November 2008
[1739] //tools.wmflabs.org/geohack/geohack.php?pagename=2008_Mumbai_attacks&params=18.940631_N_72.836426_E_type:event_region:IN-MH
[1740] //tools.wmflabs.org/geohack/geohack.php?pagename=2008_Mumbai_attacks&params=18.94061_N_72.835343_E_type:event_region:IN-MH
[1741] Of 58 killed at terminus, 22 were Muslims, *The Times of India* http://articles.timesofindia.indiatimes.com/2008-12-03/mumbai/27928854_1_muslims-terror-attack-cst (3 December 2008)
[1742] //tools.wmflabs.org/geohack/geohack.php?pagename=2008_Mumbai_attacks&params=18.922272_N_72.831566_E_type:event_region:IN-MH
[1743] //tools.wmflabs.org/geohack/geohack.php?pagename=2008_Mumbai_attacks&params=18.921739_N_72.83331_E_region:IN-MH_type:event
[1744] //tools.wmflabs.org/geohack/geohack.php?pagename=2008_Mumbai_attacks&params=18.927118_N_72.820618_E_region:IN-MH_type:event
[1745] //tools.wmflabs.org/geohack/geohack.php?pagename=2008_Mumbai_attacks&params=18.943178_N_72.829474_E_type:event_region:IN-MH
[1746] //tools.wmflabs.org/geohack/geohack.php?pagename=2008_Mumbai_attacks&params=18.94266_N_72.832993_E_type:event_region:IN-MH
[1747] //tools.wmflabs.org/geohack/geohack.php?pagename=2008_Mumbai_attacks&params=18.916517_N_72.827682_E_type:event_region:IN-MH
[1748] TERROR TAKES OVER MUMBAI http://www.thestatesman.net/page.news.php?clid=1&theme=&usrsess=1&id=233003 . The Statesman.
[1749] //tools.wmflabs.org/geohack/geohack.php?pagename=2008_Mumbai_attacks&params=18.942117_N_72.833734_E_type:event_region:IN-MH
[1750] "There was absence of overt leadership on the part of Hasan Gafoor, the CP, and lack of visible Command and Control at the CP's office," said the report prepared by former Governor and Union Home Secretary R.D. Pradhan.
[1751] Pakistani judicial panel to grill 26/11 witnesses – Times Of India http://articles.timesofindia.indiatimes.com/2013-09-22/india/42291272_1_26-11-witnesses-pakistani-judicial-panel-chenab. Articles.timesofindia.indiatimes.com (22 September 2013). Retrieved on 2013-12-06.
[1752] How Oberoi hotel accidentally became a 26/11 target http://www.rediff.com/news/report/how-oberoi-hotel-accidentally-became-a-26-11-target/20110615.htm, 15 June 2011 17:06 IST, Rediff.com
[1753] https://www.nytimes.com/2013/01/25/us/david-c-headley-gets-35-years-for-mumbai-attack.html?_r=0, "Planner Of Mumbai Attacks is Given a 35-Year Sentence." The New York Times, 24 January 2013.
[1754] https://www.youtube.com/watch?v=HCAXnXTMFOY
[1755] https://web.archive.org/web/20090117212606/http://ndtv.com/convergence/ndtv/MumbaiDossier/Mumbai-1-20-1st.htm
[1756] http://blog.blogadda.com/2008/11/27/live-blogging-mumbai-terrorist-attacks
[1757] https//web.archive.org

[1758] http://www.mumbaimirror.com/article/2/20090314200903140230449709332dbe7/They-said-kill-till-you-die-par-hum-bhi-insan-hain-yaar.html
[1759] https://www.pbs.org/wnet/secrets/episodes/mumbai-massacre-watch-the-full-episode/536/
[1760] The Housing and Land Rights Network (HLRN)," The 2010 Commonwealth Games: Whose Wealth, Whose Commons? http://www.habitants.org/news/inhabitants_of_asia/the_2010_commonwealth_games_whose_wealth_whose_commons"
[1761] Biswas, Soutik (22 March 2010). A Commonwealth shame? http://www.bbc.co.uk/blogs/thereporters/soutikbiswas/2010/03/a_commonwealth_shame.html. BBC. Retrieved on 31 March 2010.
[1762] Emaar-MGF gets Rs 700 cr Games bailout http://www.business-standard.com/india/news/emaar-mgf-gets-rs-700-cr-games-bailout/357815/. Business-standard.com. Retrieved on 6 July 2010.
[1763] Games booster for realty market? http://www.hindustantimes.com/News-Feed/newdelhi/Games-booster-for-realty-market/Article1-323204.aspx . Hindustan Times (7 October 2008). Retrieved on 6 July 2010.
[1764] Meningitis strikes Commonwealth Games Village http://www.thaindian.com/newsportal/sports/meningitis-strikes-commonwealth-games-village_10023888.html. Thaindian.com (4 March 2008). Retrieved on 6 July 2010.
[1765] http://zcommunications.org/indias-games-of-shame-by-mitu-sengupta
[1766] Hodge, Amanda. "Girls lured to games for work being sold to brothels". *The Australian*. p. 1. 30 September 2010.
[1767] *Clarification–regarding inspection of works relating to Common Wealth Games.*, report issued by CVC. Download pdf http://www.cvc.nic.in/cwgclrf3072010.pdf
[1768] *INSPECTION OF WORKS RELATED TO COMMON WEALTH GAMES*, report by the CVC, Download PDF http://www.cvc.nic.in/cwgpress2972010.pdf
[1769] http://www.dawn.com/wps/wcm/connect/dawn-content-library/dawn/news/sport/games-spectators-boo-delhi-chief-organiser-at-opening-ceremony-jd-03
[1770] http://cwg.ndtv.com/commonwealth/article/id/spoen20100156699/type/latest/Vandalism-Games-Village-Australian-High-Commissioners-59965.html?
[1771]
[1772] http://www.stuff.co.nz/sport/cricket/3594506/Bombs-hit-Indian-Premier-League-match
[1773] Commonwealth Games security lagging behind http://www.ndtv.com/news/sports/commonwealth-games-security-lagging-behind-20603.php. Ndtv.com. Retrieved on 6 July 2010.
[1774] http://www.ecr.co.za/kagiso/content/en/east-coast-radio/east-coast-radio-news?oid=938225&sn=Detail&pid=490476&SA-swimming-team-healthy-and-well
[1775] Swimmer Roland Schoeman in deep end for 'monkeys' comment: The Australian http://www.theaustralian.com.au/sport/commonwealth-games/swimmer-roland-schoeman-in-deep-end-for-monkeys-comment/story-fn66fst6-1225936234884
[1776] https://www.pgurus.com/what-is-2g-spectrum-scam-a-ready-reckoner/
[1777] http://www.thehindu.com/news/national/tamil-nadu/article22122355.ece/BINARY/2GCBIVsRaja
[1778] https://thewire.in/208072/2g-verdict-telecom-companies-sue-government-cancellation-licenses/
[1779] http://www.thehindu.com/news/national/tamil-nadu/article22122270.ece/BINARY/2GCaseJudgment
[1780] http://www.outlookindia.com/article.aspx?268214
[1781] https://web.archive.org/web/20141029080559/http://www.hindustantimes.com/photos-news/photos-india/inthedock/Article4-718395.aspx
[1782] http://papers.ssrn.com/sol3/papers.cfm?abstract_id=2048719
[1783] No vote on Lokpal, Rajya Sabha adjourns abruptly http://www.thehindu.com/news/national/article2758728.ece
[1784] https://www.bbc.co.uk/news/world-south-asia-14554000
[1785] http://www.time.com/time/photogallery/0,29307,2089265,00.html
[1786] https://www.youtube.com/watch?v=eC6Y_ROxoO0&feature=fvsr

[1787] https://www.theguardian.com/world/gallery/2011/aug/17/anna-hazare-protests-in-pictures?INTCMP=ILCNETTXT3487
[1788] http://timesofindia.indiatimes.com/topic/Indian-Anti-corruption-Movement/photos/
[1789] https://www.wikileaks-forum.com/index.php?topic=570.0
[1790] http://pmindia.nic.in/lprel.asp?id=1303
[1791] http://mayomo.com/99135-anti-corruption-supporters-imprisoned-in-india
[1792] http://timesofindia.indiatimes.com/topic/Indian-Anti-corruption-Movement

Article Sources and Contributors

The sources listed for each article provide more detailed licensing information including the copyright status, the copyright owner, and the license conditions.

Mughal Empire *Source:* https://en.wikipedia.org/w/index.php?oldid=851626631 *License:* Creative Commons Attribution-Share Alike 3.0 *Contributors:* 001blondjamie, 3family6, A2soup, Adûnâi, Akahddlo, Alexis Ivanov, Alphathon, Altes, Anandmoorti, Anzan7, Arimaboss, Arjayay, ArmanJ, Asm sultan, Asmithca, Baddu676, BakersTandoor, Barthateslisa, Being.aussie, Bender235, Bgwhite, BlueGreenYellowRed, Brandmeister, CR Guru PK, Capankajsmilyo, Chanakya Volume 2, Chewings72, Coconut1002, Cpt.a.haddock, DARREN DONG, Doug Weller, EdwardElric2016, Exoplanetaryscience, F2416, Foreverknowledge, Franrasyan, Ganganathlal, Gauravsaral, Ghatus, Gherkinmad, Gog the Mild, GoingBatty, Gurbar Akaal, GünniX, Hagoromo's Susanoo, Hairy Dude, Hammad.511234, HarpalkarPravin, Haytham Morsy, Heshbi, Hibernian, Highpeaks35, Historiantheman, HistoryReader85, HistoryofIran, Hmains, Human10.0, Iacobus, JamesMLane, Joan1066, John, Jonathansammy, Kansas Bear, Kashmiri, Kautilya3, Laszlo Panaflex, Loose000, LouisAragon, LuizLSNeto, MUHAMMAD SAFIULLAH, Maestro2016, Mandruss, Mar4d, Marcocapelle, Modernhindu, Mr Stephen, Muhammad Umair Mirza, Muraad Kahn, Newblog 32, Nizil Shah, NuclearElevator, Pappig, Persia2099, Primefac, RahulRamchandani, Rajkumar 1 02, Rattans, RegentsPark, Rjensen, Rjwilmsi, Saladin1987, Shimlaites, SimranSidhu, Sirius86, Srnec, Sulaimandaud, Sunnya343, Tachs, Tamoghna Panda, TheVulcanosuper, Tiger7253, TompaDompa, Towns Hill, Trappist the monk, Tribe of Tiger, Truman098, Uanfala, Udta Punjab, Ugog Nizdast, Vajra Raja, Vanamonde93, Vaza12, Wario-Man, Wbm1058, WindWalk55555, Winged Blades of Godric, Worldbruce, بلهواري محمد فيصل, फ़िलप्रो, ชาวไทย 1

Sur Empire *Source:* https://en.wikipedia.org/w/index.php?oldid=848546171 *License:* Creative Commons Attribution-Share Alike 3.0 *Contributors:* Aivazovsky, Akarkera, Aladeenrulez, AlimNaz, Awiseman, Bagwoosh, Bazaan, Bejnar, Bender235, Boris Živ, Capankajsmilyo, Cartakes, Chirag, Cpt.a.haddock, Crown Prince, Dadamkhan, Delljvc, Dewan357, Dig deeper, DigiBullet, Doctrosa, Dpv, Ekabhishek, Enric Naval, Fastifex, Frietjes, GeorgeofOrange, Good Olfactory, Greenshed, Greg Grahame, Gryffindor, Haseeb Naz, Highpeaks35, Hindustanilanguage, Hunnjazal, Ibrahimzai, Icarusgeek, Iridescent, JaGa, Joy1963, Ketabtoon, Khan1982, Kingturtle, Ksmdr, Liberal Humanist, LouisAragon, Lysozym, MALLUS, MANGOSEEDSDATES, Magnus Manske, Mywikieditbh, N0n3up, NikNaks, Ohconfucius, PBS-AWB, Paul Barlow, Pmetzger, Propaniac, Pseudomonas, RahulMitrah, Rama's Arrow, Rayaraya, Regnator, Rich Farmbrough, Ricky81682, Rodw, Saladin1987, Salilb, Scythian1, Seair21, ShelfSkewed, Siddiqui, Sitush, Spasage, StaticGull, Sulaimandaud, Sunquanliangxiuhao, The Anomebot2, Tradeupper88, UserNumber, UsmanPathanKhan, Utcursch, Vicn70, W.Kaleem, 107 anonymous edits 29

Bengal Subah *Source:* https://en.wikipedia.org/w/index.php?oldid=851963591 *License:* Creative Commons Attribution-Share Alike 3.0 *Contributors:* Aditya Kabir, Ahnaf.AR.2106, Alexis Ivanov, Anirbanonline92, Arcarius, ArmanJ, Asm sultan, BD2412, Bazaan, Bender235, Chaipau, ChemTerm, CommonsDelinker, Comnenus, Cpt.a.haddock, D4iNa4, Damien2016, Dewritech, Ekabhishek, F2416, Hairy Dude, Ibrahim Husain Meraj, Italia2006, JayjayantiB, Joshua Issac, Joy1963, Juxlos, LouisAragon, Maestro2016, Mark the train, Moheen Reeyad, Murad67, Mywikimediaaccount, Narky Blert, Nick Number, Nikhilmn2002, Nizil Shah, Ohconfucius, Oshwah, QuackGuru, R'n'B, RockyMasum, Samudrakula, ShelfSkewed, SheriffIsInTown, Shimlaites, SpacemanSpiff, Syed Nur Kamal, TAnthony, Tachs, Vaza12, Wiki-uk, Woodlot, Worldbruce, Xufanc, 38 anonymous edits 32

Maratha Empire *Source:* https://en.wikipedia.org/w/index.php?oldid=852226315 *License:* Creative Commons Attribution-Share Alike 3.0 *Contributors:* AR767, Abecedare, Abhiran, Acharya63, Ajay samrat, Ajits19, Amit20081980, Anandmoorti, Asm sultan, Atharva Sinai Mopkar, Atulsnischal, BD2412, Bajirao1007, Batternut, Bellerophon5685, C.Fred, Chewings72, Clown94, ClueBot NG, Coconut1002, CommonsDelinker, Cpt.a.haddock, Cunningpal, D4iNa4, DA1, DHSULP, DVdm, Dairy501, Dan Koehl, Davey2010, David.Long, Dona-Hue, Donner60, EdwardElric2016, El C, Epistemos, Eric0928, Favonian, FinanceInterest, Futosujee, Gaarmyvet, GermanJoe, Ghatus, Gog the Mild, GünniX, Hagoromo's Susanoo, Hayras123, Highpeaks35, IdreamofJeanie, Imsp10, Imvaali, Jackfork, JackintheBox, Jessicapierce, Jim1138, Jonathansammy, Kautilya3, Kautuk1, Kevin12xd, Kvwiki1234, KylieTastic, Laszlo Panaflex, LouisAragon, Maestro2016, Martin123r, MatthewVanitas, Maximajorian Viridio, Mike Rosoft, My Lord, Narky Blert, Newblog 32, Nick Number, Nikhil B, Nikunj3121994, NineTimes, Onel5969, Oshwah, PolandHistoryProf, PolicyReformer, Pratik Saavé, Proudmaratha, Qzd, Rattans, RegentsPark, Rjensen, Rodw, Rpapo, Savitr1915, Sg500, Shellwood, Shimlaites, Shinjoya, Soetermans, Sro23, Tachs, Theiitian, Thomas.W, Utcursch, WOSlinker, Wtmitchell, Épine, 173 anonymous edits 54

Company rule in India *Source:* https://en.wikipedia.org/w/index.php?oldid=852147199 *License:* Creative Commons Attribution-Share Alike 3.0 *Contributors:* A2soup, Acad Ronin, Ad Orientem, Altetendekrabbe, Amit20081980, Anarcho-statist, AnwarInsaan, Arimaboss, Atticusfinch123, Aumnamahashiva, BD2412, Barthateslisa, Bazonka, Beland, Bender235, Bgwhite, Bhonsale, Bonadea, Bonopartee))mediterin, Boven, Burbak, CAPTAIN RAJU, Candalua, Catpals, Chewings72, ClueBot NG, Colonies Chris, CommonsDelinker, Comp.arch, Credema, DadaNeem, DalQ95, Dananuj, Devgowri, Dewritech, DiscantX, Dispenser, DocWatson42, Donaldduck100, Donner60, DuncanHill, EdwardElric2016, FaisalAbbasid, Faizhaider, Fatbuu, Flyer22 Reborn, Fowler&fowler, Frankalbertson, Furius, G S Palmer, GDibyendu, Gob Lofa, Green daemon, Gryffindor, Gulumeemee, Guy Macon, HLGallon, Hmains, HyperGaruda, Indopug, Italia2006, Jasca Ducato, Jayadevp13, Jethwarp, Jim1138, John of Reading, John.kakoty, Josve05a, K6ka, KH-1, Kapitop, Karada, Knight of BAAWA, L235, Lakun.patra, Lalmohan Babu, Linguist6666, Lkjgfstyugfd, Lobsterthermidor, Locomotive999, Lubiesque, Martinr2006, Materialscientist, Mauls, MilborneOne, Missvain, Msundqvist, Muhammad Umair Mirza, Narky Blert, Needlenose, Newblog 32, NikNaks, O.Koslowski, Ohconfucius, Omnipaedista, Pawyilee, PhnomPencil, Pktlaurence, Plantdrew, Pooyaf, Pratyya Ghosh, Pukkativa, Punyaboy, Quizer SHK, R'n'B, Rattans, Ravi agasarahalli, RedTomato, RegentsPark, Ricky81682, Rjensen, Rjwilmsi, Rodw, SJK, SQGibbon, Salih, Scyfie, Sitush, Skinsmoke, Solomon7968, Srich32977, Srnec, StAnselm, StringRay, Sundostund, Sushilkumarmishra, Sushilmishra, Syz2, Tamravidhir, The Anomebot2, The C of E, The Dawn of Husk, Tinkurider, Titodutta, Tobby72, Trusilver, Twsx, UY Scuti, UsmanKhanDiri, Utcursch, Vgy7ujm, Vigyani, Vilij, WatermillockCommon, Widr, Wikid77, William Harris, Woohookitty, Worldbruce, XavierGreen, Xurei, Yutsi, Zaketo, फ़िलप्रो, ತಿಂತ್ರಿ ಠ, 148 anonymous edits 90

Kingdom of Mysore *Source:* https://en.wikipedia.org/w/index.php?oldid=853408089 *License:* Creative Commons Attribution-Share Alike 3.0 *Contributors:* 468SM, AManWithNoPlan, Abecedare, Agamemnus, AjaxSmack, Akahddlo, Akshay Das UTW, AksheKumar, Aldis90, Arimaboss, Arjunkmohan, Arpvr, Arthur Rubin, Arungna21, AutoMeIndia, AvicAWB, Avoided blue, BD2412, Bender235, Bgwhite, BigJolly9, Binggo666, Bonaparte2015, Bopalula, Brainiac179, Capankajsmilyo, Chewings72, Chince666, Chris the speller, ClueBot NG, Colonies Chris, CommonsDelinker, Cpt.a.haddock, Dabomb87, DadaNeem, Davey2010, Dbachmann, Derkommander0916, Dewritech, DrKay, DéRahier, EamonnPKeane, Ekabhishek, Ermahgerd9, Esszet, Ewen, Faizhaider, Fatbuu, Frietjes, Ged UK, Gerda Arendt, Gerhardvalentin, Ghulamkhan3219, Gnanapiti, Gowtham94, Graphium, Gugganij, Hasan Sabbah, Hmains, Holenarasipura, Hugo999, Huon, Hyacinth, Hyder Bale297093270-, IM3847, Iamwiks, Ifly6, Irshaad86, Italia2006, Jack Greenmaven, Jessicapierce, Jethwarp, John Hill, John of Reading, Jonesey95, Jugaari cross, Kautilya3, Kintetsubuffalo, Kool777456, Kwamikagami, Laszlo Panaflex, Lele giannoni, LeoFrank, Liberal Humanist, Loveless, MALLUS, MWAK, Maestro2016, Magicpiano, Marcocapelle, Mark the train, Mayasandra, McDean666666666, Mcicogni, Modest Genius, Mohanbhan, Money.news, Moonraker, Moulalisaheb.g, Mughal Lohar, Muhammad Mahdi Karim, NERIUM, Nagbhat, Nick Number, Nimetapoeg, Niri.M, OhanaUnited, Ohconfucius, Omar77, Omer123hussain, Onced boath, Onel5969, Parkwells, Philip MacDougall, PhnomPencil, Pied Hornbill, Piledhigheranddeeper, Pirhana7777, Psmith fan, Ptbotgourou, Qbli2mHd, R'n'B, Ravichandar84, Red Jay, RegentsPark, Rjensen, Roland zh, Rosiestep, Roxy the dog, Rsrikanth05, Samhanin, Sankalpdravid, Saved theirs, Sepoy999999999, Shadowjams, Shesha 06, Shreevatsa, Shyamsunder, Simba2468, Sitush, Skylark2008, Sodabottle, Solomon7968, Spriteindia, Sri Harsha Bhogi, Stevenmitchell, Sundostund, Sushilkumarmishra, Tbhotch, Tentinator, Terrek, The Madras, The Soldier of Peace, Tim!, Tom Radulovich, Tpbradbury, Trotting cove, Upasanamedhi, Vanished user qwqwijr8hwrkjdnvkanfoh4, Wetman, Wiccan Quagga, Widr, Winston786, Woohookitty, Xtremedood, Xufanc, Yamamoto Ichiro, Yiosie2356, फ़िलप्रो, 86 anonymous edits 140

Sikh Empire *Source:* https://en.wikipedia.org/w/index.php?oldid=853393318 *License:* Creative Commons Attribution-Share Alike 3.0 *Contributors:* 1997kB, 468SM, Ainalhafila, Akmal94, Aniruddhbhaidhadhaldhadhal, Ansh666, Apuldram, Arcarius, Atrivo, BD2412, Bellerophon5685, Bender235, BreadBuddy, Charlesdrakew, Chewings72, ClueBot NG, CommonsDelinker, DawedalRaqqa, Doug Weller, Elisevil, Flyer22 Reborn, Freddy-graf, Futuremind123, Gamall Wednesday Ida, Ghatus, Gurbar Akaal, Gurpreet Pandher, Hairy Dude, Hammersfan, Harmeet5k, Hebrides, Highpeaks35, Historyscholar1959, Hmains, Iamag02, Iridescent, Italia2006, Iwilsonp, Jangvijay, Jasca Ducato, Jeffgr9, JesseRafe, John of Reading, Johnuniq, Joseph2302, Kanchipuramsilk83, Kansas Bear, Kintetsubuffalo, Kqvps, Laszlo Panaflex, LilHelpa, Lkjgfstyugfd, LouisAragon, Materialscientist, Mr Random Dude Guy, Mubarak 647, Narky Blert, Newblog 32, Nyttend, Olaf Caroe, Onel5969, Oshwah, Pariah24, Peeta Singh, Pgallert, Pktlaurence, Pooyaf, R K Chopra, Randhawacs47, Rattans, RealDictionary, Redtigerxyz, RegentsPark, RekishiEJ, Rich Farmbrough, Ricky81682, RobLa, SJ Defender, SUM1, Saladin1987, Sardaarji101, Shaunkiz, Sinaloa, Singh, Sisu55, Sitush, SomeoneThatYouDontKnow, Stridasolidus, SurlyRed, Tamfang, TazRahman, The Mighty Glen, TheConnorMan, TheSikhHistorian, Thebeach19, Thexyzvideos, Tigercompanion25, Tobby72, Trinity4156, Udta Punjab, Unmesh Bangali, Utcursch, Vascular420, WereSpielChequers, Why do people not understand, Xufanc, Xyzmann, Zaketo, Zanhe, फ़िलप्रो, சதீஸ், 184 anonymous edits 172

Indian Rebellion of 1857 *Source:* https://en.wikipedia.org/w/index.php?oldid=853536324 *License:* Creative Commons Attribution-Share Alike 3.0 *Contributors:* 564dude, AAJ KHAN, Abecedare, Adamgerber80, Adv Avijit Ghoshal, Alexf, Appu man123, Arjayay, Billywebs, Buistr, CASSIOPEIA, CLCStudent, CambridgeBayWeather, Ch sonuu, Chewings72, Chris the speller, Clarityfiend, ClueBot NG, Cplakidas, Dahiyapulkit, Daniel Case, Daphne Lantier, Darylgolden, DatSyrupGuy, Deadwikipedian, Dipak pambhar, Donner60, DuncanHill, Ehudtal, El C, Eragonshadowslasher, Exemplo347, FRibeiro66, Fowler&fowler, Future12340, FuzhouneseMinpride, Gautam Sah, Gazal world, GeneralizationsAreBad, GenuineArt, Georgestar99, Gewingewin, Gilliam, Gladamas, Gotnolifewhatsoever, GreenMeansGo, GrindtXX, Guffydrawers, HLGallon, Haha12345433216678, Happygolucky2005, Heatlineheard, HelgeRieder, Highpeaks35, Hijiri88, HyperGaruda, Imdabes7, Indian Writer2, Infinenoi, Irondome, Jalaluddin Muhammad, Jim1138, Jiten D, Joihazarika, Jon C., Jonesey95, Jop2～enwiki, JosephusOfJerusalem, Kautilya3, Kavitha Shankaran, Kulsin567, KylieTastic, Laszlo Panaflex, Laughing sandbags, Lawrence501, Leventio, Liberal Humanist, LindsayH, Lovely amit, MBlaze Lightning, Magioladitis, Mallu Techiez, Materialscientist, MatthewVanitas, Mccapra, Md183, Necrothesp, New786678, Newblog 32, Nizil Shah, Notthebestusername, ParadiseDesertOasis8888, Peterbruce01, Pharaoh of the Wizards, Polylerus, Rattans, ReagentsParks, RegentsPark, Rjwilmsi, Robertkamau, Sakshi Dalla, Salociin, ScrapIronIV, Sennacannavaro, Serols, Shellwood, Simplexity22, Sirius86, Sjö, Skysmith, Slatersteven, Slugsheir, Socialawareness1, Stumink, Sufalbepari2, Trappist the monk, Umairsy, Utcursch, Wbm1058, Worldbruce, Zingarese, 152 anonymous edits 185

British Raj *Source:* https://en.wikipedia.org/w/index.php?oldid=852823328 *License:* Creative Commons Attribution-Share Alike 3.0 *Contributors:* 37x0f4x0, A2soup, Abecedare, Absolutelypuremilk, Agnibha chowdhury, Ahmad dhaka, AlessandroTiandelli333, Alexander Domanda, Alphathon, Anupam, Arimaboss, Arthur Brum, Aumnamahashiva, Avoided, BD2412, Blanche of King's Lynn, Bokmanrocks01, CAPTAIN RAJU, CambridgeBayWeather, Chackerian, Chewings72, Chris the speller, ClementAtleeWasAnInsideJob, ClueBot NG, Coltsfan, Cordless Larry, Cordyceps-Zombie, Crazyfrog12, Dabbler, Daiyusha, Davemck, Donner60, DuncanHill, Editormallu, EdwardElric2016, El C, Eragonshadowslasher, Expertseeker90, Feinex, Fez Cap 12, Fowler&fowler, Gilliam, Gizmodolan, GraemeLeggett, Hairy Dude, Hammad.511234, Headbomb, Historyscholar1959, Hmains, Hororoka, Howicus, Illegitimate Barrister, Imminent77, Ira Leviton, Izno, J 1982, John of Reading, Jon C., Kaulder, Kautilya3, KingSkyLord, Kintetsubuffalo, Kulkarninikhil, Lacypaperclip, Laszlo Panaflex, LawrenceScafuri, Liberal Humanist, LilHelpa, Maestro2016, Magioladitis, Mandruss, Meters, MilborneOne, Morningstar1814, Muzi, NadirAli, Natg 19, Newblog 32, Nicolas Perrault III, Nikhilmn2002, Nitish shrivastava 19, Nondo202020, North Shoreman, Notthebestusername, Omnipaedista, PAKHIGHWAY, Pablomartinez, Pengoloð, Plumpapollo27, Polyenetian, Protozoon, Punyaboy, Rafat87, Rajkumar 1 02, Rakeshkumar13, Rattans, RaviC, RegentsPark, Risto hot sir, Rjensen, Rjwilmsi, Sahara4u, SamanyaKannadiga, Schwede66, Serols, Shellwood, Shubhamxo, Shyamk hmp, Siddiqsazzad001, Snori, Spasage, Spatnayak, Sri Harsha Bhogi, Srich32977, Surtsicna, Teddy.Coughlin, TheFreeWorld, TheUnstoppableJ, Tobby72, TompaDompa, Tonneduroc, Tower of Hercules, Utcursch, Vanryoko, Vinayakavm, Vishalkirandesai, Vivek Ray, WOSlinker, Wakelamp, WhisperToMe, WikiPharaoh, William Avery, Worldbruce, Xufanc, Z0, ZFT, Zanhe, ألبرشت شونكا, 166 anonymous edits 251

Indian independence movement *Source:* https://en.wikipedia.org/w/index.php?oldid=853351624 *License:* Creative Commons Attribution-Share Alike 3.0 *Contributors:* 456at, 72, ANURAG GUHA, Airplane45w3, Amorymeltzer, Anandmoorti, Ankit2, Anupam, Arado, Aspening, Assreddys, Aurato, AusLondonder, Ayush2848, BD2412, BDD, Batalex34, Belikebr007, Bender235, CAPTAIN RAJU, Capitals00, Chewings72, ClueBot NG, DMacks, DadaNeem, Dcoutz, Dewritech, Diannaa, DocWatson42, Drdpw, Equilibrium103, Esther Ram, FiendYT, Fowler&fowler, GSS, GT3911, Gauts99, Gilliam, Goliriya, GraemeLeggett, Gyan Roy, Happychickeman, Harfarhs, Higginsal, Highpeaks35, I dream of horses, Jarhill, John of Reading, JosephusOfJerusalem, KGirlTrucker81, Kautilya3, Kautuk1, Kostas20142, Laziness Elemental, Loopy30, MBlaze Lightning, Madhav Subramaniyam, Mandruss, Manepally, Materialscientist, MatthewVanitas, Natg 19, Niceguyedc, Nirved.goyal, Onel5969, Oosoom, Oshwah, Owais Khursheed, ParadiseDesertOasis8888, Pepper, Petrb, PratikBhake, Prisencolin, Psomax, PutinUSSR, RDXL, Raymond3023, RegentsPark, Rh7hd, Rich Farmbrough, Rjensen, Rjwilmsi, Ronz, Rubbish computer, Rueben lys, Ruyter, Sadads, Samf4u, Samin096, Saran krish, Scholar2501, Serols, Shah1info, Shellwood, Shiningroad, ShriSanamKumar, Sitush, Srijankedia, Stumink, Sushanth elango, THEunique, Tamxhah, Tanmaig, Tanmay jadhavrao, Techtonic365, Theinstantmatrix, Tiarapawn, Travelbird, Tushti, Unreal7, Utcursch, Vanamonde93, Vincedumond, Vivaan65, Vivekannan, WebCrawler12345, WereSpielChequers, Wikishovel, Worldbruce, Xaosflux, Ynhockey, Øystein.Eide, फ़िलप्रो, 201 anonymous edits 326

History of the Republic of India *Source:* https://en.wikipedia.org/w/index.php?oldid=853548361 *License:* Creative Commons Attribution-Share Alike 3.0 *Contributors:* 72, A.amitkumar, Aarav95j, Alimohdsagar, Amartyabag, Aravindsivadas, AusLondonder, BD2412, Bender235, Bhukya Bhanu Pratap, Bladesmulti, Chewings72, Chris the speller, Cloudsonfire, ClueBot NG, CommonsDelinker, Compfreak7, Cordyceps-Zombie, Dewritech, Diannaa, Dirkbb, Dl2000, Ebonelm, Ekabhishek, Flamingsjack, Frietjes, GBPRCRC, GoFurther, GoingBatty, Hammersoft, Hendrick 99, Highpeaks35, Indopug, Izzibelle, JJMC89, Jarble, Jdaloner, Jim1138, John Cline, Jonathansammy, JorisvS, Jozolsis, Kailash29792, Kautilya3, Ken Gallager, Khazar2, Kintetsubuffalo, KylieTastic, LilHelpa, LouisAragon, Magioladitis, MarnetteD, Marteau, Materialscientist, Mogism, MsFionnuala, Mx. Granger, My Chemistry romantic, Naren marik, Narky Blert, Nikunj3121994, Nizil Shah, Ohconfucius, Person who formerly started with "216", Peter Elman, R.hrishi, Radharani11, Rajainsanbir, Rao Ravindra, RegentsPark, Riddhi1600, Rjensen, Samitus mallicus, Serols, Sfgiants906, Shriheeran, Shyamsunder, Spasage, Sunnysumit, Tachs, The Discoverer, The Masked Man of Mega Might, The Rambling Man, Tinku Sinha, Titodutta, Tyler Durden, Vanamonde93, Vinaybavdekar, Vinodtiwari2608, Wavelength, WereSpielChequers, Wiki dr mahmad, Wikipelli, Willard84, Yaara dildaara, Zachary Klaas, Zeezee110, फ़िलप्रो, ࿋, 236 anonymous edits 361

Dominion of India *Source:* https://en.wikipedia.org/w/index.php?oldid=852806452 *License:* Creative Commons Attribution-Share Alike 3.0 *Contributors:* Aaditotjo, Agnypath, Ajhodd, Alan Liefting, Alphathon, Andrew Gwilliam, Arimaboss, AryamanA, Ashok Rajpal, Audacity, Aumnamahashiva, Ayankhan Pathan, Bender235, Bgwhite, Bhachech, BilCat, Burgundo, Cameron kennedy, Capankajsmilyo, ChidanandaKampa, ClueBot NG, Cnilep, CommonsDelinker, Cordyceps-Zombie, Daniel St.Clair, David.moreno72, Dewritech, Discospinster, Divijzutshi, Dn9ahx, Doug Weller, DrKay, Editormallu, Favonian, Finnusertop, Fowler&fowler, Fraggle81, Frenchmalawi, Fuhghettaboutit, Gareth Griffith-Jones, GoingBatty, Good Olfactory, Gopalan evr, Grafen, Hazhk, Hemanth surapaneni 007, JWULTRABLIZZARD, Javert2113, Jayarathina, Johnleemk, Jon C., Jonoikobangali, Joshua Issac, Jovianeye, Kangaroopower, Kautilya3, Kautuk1, Kevin9217, Kingsindian, Knowz, Koregaonpark, Kvwiki1234, KylieTastic, Lieutcoluseng, Matej1234, Miesianiacal, Mix321, Moonraker, MouseCatDog, Mr Hall of England, Mrt3366, Mykaustubh, NJRobbie, NadirAli, Narky Blert, NelsonSudan, Nikhilmn2002, Nishu0246, Nnemo, Ohconfucius, Pepperbeast, Podzemnik, Pragmocialist, Rajkumararslan, Rao Ravindra, Rattans, Redtigerxyz, Rich Farmbrough, Roland zh, Rsrikanth05, Rude-boy-wayne, SQGibbon, Sahgal, Sahilrahi1995, Sandstein, Scomerger, Shiva767, ShockD, Sigehelmus, Silverhorse, Singhsahabadv, SpacemanSpiff, Sri Harsha Bhogi, TRAJAN 117, The Anomebot2, Tlhslobus, ToastButterToast, TopGun, Tornado chaser, Truefriends4U, UplinkAnsh, Vanished user ewfisn2348tui2f8n2fio2utjfeoi210r39jf, Verbcatcher, Verbum Veritas, Vinayakavm, WatermillockCommon, Whoop whoop pull up, Wikiraj121, Writescorp, Yaara dildaara, YeshuaDavid, Yofan Pratama P, Zaketo, हेमन्त डबराल, தென்காசி சுப்பிரமணியன், 130 anonymous edits 395

Constitution of India *Source:* https://en.wikipedia.org/w/index.php?oldid=853384915 *License:* Creative Commons Attribution-Share Alike 3.0 *Contributors:* 1997kB, 78.26, Anon126, Antiqueight, Arms & Hearts, Athomeinkobe, Atrivo, Beetelaces, Bender235, Bgwhite, Binkleyz, Bryanrutherford0, Bschandrasgr, Capankajsmilyo, Capyash, Chanakya1991, Chidanandak7, Chris Adams, ClueBot NG, Comp.arch, Cordyceps-Zombie, Cyberbot II, DVdm, Dagduba lokhande, Dcirovic, Deadrat, Deli nk, Denisarona, Dewritech, Dpshmrt, EdJohnston, Eversmilinggoutham, Flyer22 Reborn, Fresheneesz, Govind bharadwaj, GünniX, HangingCurve, Headbomb, Horseless Headman, Hpsatapathy, HueSatLum, Human3015, Innotata, Ira Leviton, JaconaFrere, Jayarajn1988, Jim1138, Jishnu13, Jkulkarni, John Cline, Kahtar, Kautilya3, Knaveknight, Kool throne, Lakun.patra, Lankiveil, Legacypac, Lenovkia, Lia carlate, Lifecalling, LindsayH, Magioladitis, Majora, Masti 84, Materialscientist, Merchant of Meluha, Mild Bill Hiccup, Natuur12, Notthebestusername, Nurg, Omni Flames, Onel5969, Oshwah, Peter Grey, Philip Trueman, PrakashRana955, Praveen2728, Praweenkprabhakar, ProjectHorizons, Quinton Feldberg, Rajbow, Reyk, Ronakshah1990, Shimlaites, Sir potter.singh, Some Gadget Geek, SourceOhWatch (SrotahaUvacha), Sri Harsha Bhogi, Sriramya lv 201, SshibumXZ, Sukanta Sarkar, Super48paul, Tanmaygupta9, The Rambling Man, Tom.Reding, UY Scuti, Ugog Nizdast, Varavour, Vineethkuruvath, Vsraj, Widr, Yashthepunisher, Yeswanthtips, फ़िलप्रो, 149 anonymous edits 401

Political integration of India *Source:* https://en.wikipedia.org/w/index.php?oldid=852364546 *License:* Creative Commons Attribution-Share Alike 3.0 *Contributors:* -sche, Abecedare, Altetendekrabbe, Aman kapoor22, Amartyabag, AndrewHowse, AnonMoos, AroundTheGlobe, Arpitbhu, Asdklf;, BD2412, Bazonka, Belasd, Bender235, Bharatveer, Bhonsale, BilCat, Bobo192, Bowenguy, Brighterorange, Certes, Charles Matthews, Chhajjusandeep, Citation bot 1, ClueBot NG, Cnwilliams, CommonsDelinker, DaGizza, Danny, Daydreamer302000, DuncanHill, Dwaipayanc, Edgar181, El C, EoGuy, Ethanlu121, Eumolpo, Feminist, FunkyCanute, Gangpi, Gilliam, Gimmetrow, Graham11, GrindtXX, Ground Zero, Gwernol, Harthacnut, Haunti, Hornplease, Idleguy, Indopug, J04n, JanetteDoe, Jangvijay, Jn045, Jodosma, John Hill, JorgeGG, Joseph Solis in Australia, Jovianeye, Ka Faraq Gatri, Kaihsu, Kautilya3, Kbdank71, Keralavarma, Khazar, Kingsindian, Kman543210, Kozuch, KylieTastic, Lilac Soul, Lubiesque, MBlaze Lightning, MaGioZal, Madhava 1947, Magicpiano, Malaiya, Mar4d, Mariraja2007, Master of the Oríchalcos, Michael Devore, Moonraker, Natg 19, Nattynab, Naveen Sankar, Night w, NuclearWarfare, Ohconfucius, Onel5969, Pahari Sahib, Patelurology2, Paxse, Peter Chastain, Philg88, PhnomPencil, Piledhigheranddeeper, Pirodam, Pranjal Joshi, Pulavar, R'n'B, Rama's Arrow, Rao Ravindra, Redtigerxyz, Relata refero, Rich Farmbrough, Rjwilmsi, RobertG, S h i v a (Visnu), Safemariner, SandyGeorgia, Sardanaphalus, Sarvagnya, SchreiberBike, Shahab, Shakyakd, Shyamsunder, Skapur, Skinsmoke, Smsarmad, Solomon7968, Soman, Sundar, The Duke of Waltham, Thumperward, Tony1, TopGun, Topbanana, Ultraexactzz, Utcursch, Vadakkan, Vera from upstairs, Vice regent, VoABot II, Wavehunter, Welsh, Woohookitty, XavierGreen, Xe7al, Xn4, Xufanc, YellowMonkey, फ़िलप्रो, రవిచంద్ర, 116 anonymous edits 416

Indo-Pakistani War of 1947 *Source:* https://en.wikipedia.org/w/index.php?oldid=853378767 *License:* Creative Commons Attribution-Share Alike 3.0 *Contributors:* Accesscrawl, Adamgerber80, Akrampakistani, Alacrity25, Arjayay, Ashu00007, Astore Malik, Bender235, Bogadinikhil, Brandmeister, Calore123, Capitals00, ChadhaSingh, Choess, ClueBot NG, D4iNa4, DBigXray, Dcirovic, Degen Earthfast, Dharmadhyaksha, Dl2000, EvergreenFir, Faizan, Filippof, Frangars, FreeatlastChitchat, Fuzheado, GEWUIgcuy, GSS, Gaomata, Ghatus, Godric ki Kothri, Gymnast 2010, GünniX, Hamzati22, Headbomb, Himel Rahmon, Human3015, IdreamofJeanie, Jim1138, John of Reading, JosephusOfJerusalem, Just a guy from the KP, KCVelaga, Kaltenmeyer, Kautilya3, KylieTastic, Lakun.patra, Lectonar, Lezela, Libra bro, LittleWink, MBlaze Lightning, Magioladitis, MalikAttaRasool, Mar4d, Marked Man 808, MarnetteD, Materialscientist, Mbk10, Mikrobølgeovn, Mild Bill Hiccup, Mtkhan1989, My Chemistry romantic, Nat965, NeilN, Nikhilmn2002, North Shoreman, PakistaniTrollCruncher, PeerBaba, PohranicniStraze, Puneet Singh Sidhu, Rao Ravindra, RommelTurk, Rupert loup, Rupertgrint1, SA 13 Bro, Samee, Sangakkara1, Saurabh.bhumkar, ScotlandLaddie, Shadowxfox, Shellwood, Shenme, Smsarmad, Somebody500, Spasage, Srednuas Lenoroc, Störm, Sunnya343, Svabhiman, Tankbuster39, Towns Hill, Trinity4156, TripWire, Tyler Durden, Umar 2100, Vermatanay, ערן, 117 anonymous edits 446

States Reorganisation Act, 1956 *Source:* https://en.wikipedia.org/w/index.php?oldid=852204158 *License:* Creative Commons Attribution-Share Alike 3.0 *Contributors:* AksheKumar, Arjayay, AusLondonder, BD2412, Bender235, Bgwhite, CAPTAIN RAJU, Canopus89, Capankajsmilyo, Celestialwizard889, Chris the speller, Clare., Clarkcj12, ClueBot NG, Dewritech, Diptiprakashpalai, Diwakar20112, Douglas the Comeback Kid, Ekabhishek, Flyer22 Reborn, Hemant Dabral, Howcheng, Indopug, Infobliss, Jenimite, Jnestorius, JoeSperrazza, John K, John Lunney, Justpp, Kautilya3, Kintetsubuffalo, Linguisticgeek, Logical1004, Loginnigol, Magentic Manifestations, Mogism, Moonraker, MusikAnimal, Netra08, Nick Number, Omnipaedista, Pharaoh of the Wizards, Ramcrk, Rashkeqamar, Rodney Baggins, Schlosser67, Shyamsunder, Sminthopsis84, Sri Harsha Bhogi, Stormie, Thorbecke2012, Tigercompanion25, TwoTwoHello, Vinaybhai, Westwoodwizard, Xufanc, Zaketo, 66 anonymous edits 471

India and the Non-Aligned Movement *Source:* https://en.wikipedia.org/w/index.php?oldid=823526228 *License:* Creative Commons Attribution-Share Alike 3.0 *Contributors:* Anon685, AusLondonder, Belasd, Bellerophon5685, CAPTAIN RAJU, ClueBot NG, Daniash007, Denisarona, Derim Hunt,

Edward, Eyesnore, Gilderien, GünniX, Hello71, Jethwarp, John "Hannibal" Smith, Knightplex, KnowledgeHegemony, KnowledgeHegemonyPart2, Koavf, Madhava 1947, Ottre, R'n'B, Shyamsunder, Tolly4bolly, Uday Chakravarty, Zagros Mountains, 34 anonymous edits 478

Indo-Pakistani War of 1965 *Source:* https://en.wikipedia.org/w/index.php?oldid=853646814 *License:* Creative Commons Attribution-Share Alike 3.0 *Contributors:* A.A Ghatge, Adamgerber80, Aeg0n94, Airwolf, Alsee, Anzan7, Appiodion, AshLin, Aumnamahashiva, AusLondonder, Baba Mica, Bender235, Bhailogkhan, Boris Lewis, Bri, Calore123, Cannolis, ClueBot NG, CommonsDelinker, Conradjagan, CosmicEmperor, DBigXray, DMacks, DPdH, Dadyal, Dgorsline, Dl2000, Drmies, Engine Gone Loco, Erdrum11, Faizan, Fajjuify, FreeatlastChitchat, Ghatus, Gherkinmad, Gjs238, Graham87, GreyHatBilla, Guruduttmallapur, HIAS, Hagennos, HammadShakeel911, Hospy, Hugo999, Human10.0, Imabbas, Iridescent, Jahelistbro, Jennica, KCVelaga, Kautilya3, Keith D, Kintetsubuffalo, KrakatoaKatie, KylieTastic, MBlaze Lightning, Magioladitis, Mar4d, Mark.murphy, Materialscientist, Mdnavman, MikeLynch, MishMari, Momin885522, Mortense, Mr Stephen, Mtkhan1989, Muhammad Umair Mirza, My Lord, NationSantra, Netstar1, NewHikaru07, Nick Number, Nilesh shukla, Nyttend, Pakelectrical, Paul2520, Pavel Vozenilek, PeerBaba, Pincrete, Pjwdoyle, Pressreleasecop, Prinsgezinde, Puneet Singh Sidhu, Qwertyus, Rafay15, Razer2115, RegentsPark, Rupertgrint1, Ruslik0, Sammyrice, Samp1315, Sdmarathe, Shenme, SheriffIsInTown, Shivasnsh Mathur, Sir Sher, Smsarmad, Son of ATM, Tahir usmani 140, Talib Husayn Al Hassan, Tbhotch, TestPAKISTAN, Tom.Reding, Towns Hill, TripWire, TwoTwoHello, Uncountabledreamz, Warrior Covert, Warrior Covert2, WereSpielChequers, Wikibaba1977, Wishva de Silva, Zwerubae, शिव साहिल, 27 anonymous edits 482

Sino-Indian War *Source:* https://en.wikipedia.org/w/index.php?oldid=853609667 *License:* Creative Commons Attribution-Share Alike 3.0 *Contributors:* 1812ahill, 1ifes4v3r, A.A Ghatge, AManWithNoPlan, Adah1972, Adamgerber80, Alex Shih, Alistair1978, Alsee, Aniruddh88, Annabel-lee-avenger, Arado, Arjayay, Arthur goes shopping, Ashmoo, Athomeinkobe, AusLondonder, Balabinrm, Bender235, BiggestSataniaFanboy89, Bramhesh Patil, Buistr, C1MM, CPA-5, CWH, Capitals00, CentreLeftRight, Cgschmidt3169, Chintu89, Chipperdude15, Chowdhary747, Chris the speller, ClueBot NG, Cnzx, Co9man, Coconut1002, Colonel Jai Jind, Cyberbot II, D4iNa4, DPdH, Db8-85a3-8d3-1319, Dcirovic, Dentamble, Denzil Simoes, Derek R Bullamore, Desp2002, Dewritech, DimensionQualm, Dmanrock29, DocWatson42, Dogblock, Download, Dragon200317, Ekabhishek, EkoGraf, Empireoftheseas, Fconaway, FightersMegamix, FreeatlastChitchat, Frietjes, G37x8004uc, GTHO, Ghatus, Gherkinmad, Gob Lofa, Gullupat, GwydionM, GünniX, H2.818, Hamish59, Hayman30, IndianGeneralist, Iridescent, Jax 0677, Jeodesic, John, John of Reading, JorisvS, JustJust51, KCVelaga, Karim Manouar, Kautilya3, KnightRIF, Kongdede, Kr.saurabh10, Kraometikurke, Kumar Ravi Budania, KylieTastic, Lakun.patra, Laytar1, Le Petit Chat, LoneWolf2917, MBlaze Lightning, Madgaonkar, Malyacko, Mannerheimo, Manxruler, Maquis196, Mar4d, Master of Time, Materialscientist, MaxskeFan, Mr. Guye, Mr.User200, Najeeb1010, Navin.sharma751, Neo-Jay, NewEnglandYankee, Newman50, Nick-D, Nklinan, Obaid Raza, OccultZone, Onthelist, Oshwah, Owais Khursheed, PMLF, ParadiseDesertOasis8888, Philg88, Quartzd, Razer2115, Red Jay, Red Slash, Richie1917, Rivertorch, RobNS, Rodrigo Cata Preta, Roger 8 Roger, Ronanin, Rueben lys, Ruyter, Sahrudayan, Sam Sailor, Sardeeph, Schwede66, Sharkslayer87, SlowPhoton, TAnthony, Tagishsimon, Tassedethe, The Discoverer, The Quixotic Potato, TheFreeWorld, Tigercompanion25, Tim!, Tom.Reding, Tootifrooti11, Trinity4156, Upcuttzchinium, User87878079, UserDe, Utcursch, Vanished user zm34pq51mz, Warrior Covert, Wiki User 10262016, Wikiuser13, Wolfmaster2, Zanhe, Zhou Yingliu, Ανδρέας Κρυστάλλης, फ़िलप्रो, 樂號 , 63 anonymous edits 510

Bangladesh Liberation War *Source:* https://en.wikipedia.org/w/index.php?oldid=852739842 *License:* Creative Commons Attribution-Share Alike 3.0 *Contributors:* Abrahamic Faiths, Adamgerber80, Aditya Kabir, Aidan Smith's Carousel, Akib.H, Alanwest yahoo, Alanwest101, Amlanjyoti.s, Arindamprin, AustralianRupert, Bivalve44, C.J. Griffin, CambridgeBayWeather, CentreLeftRight, Chalesdiken, Chewings72, ClueBot NG, David Biddulph, Dawnseeker2000, Dbsseven, Dcirovic, DemFail, Double Plus Ungood, EdJohnston, El C, Eric0928, Faizan, Fayez172, Fez Cap 12, Gazoth, Ghatus, HFS-er, Himel Rahmon, Hmains, Hullaballoo Wolfowitz, Idel800, Irondome, JJMC89, Jennica, Kautilya3, Kautuk1, Keith D, Keith-264, Knightplex, Le Petit Chat, MBlaze Lightning, Maliksultanm, Mar4d, Marjit Roy, MarnetteD, Marvellous Spider-Man, Materialscientist, Mdann52, Me, Myself, and I are Here, Messiaindarain, Mp3moment, Mudassir1468, Muhammad Mahmudul Hassan, Muhammad Mughal, My Lord, NadirAli, NewHikaru07, NiciVampireHeart, Nitin544, Oranjelo100, PeerBaba, Powellm117, Rafat.muneem, Rajnarayan Chottopaddhyay, Raqibwasy, RaviC, Rayhanazaman, Redound, RegentsPark, Rh7hd, Rifat Bin Saroar, Rumanimtious, Serial Number 54129, SheriffIsInTown, Sminthopsis84, Spartacus!, Sujan rifat, Suntzu3500, The Rambling Man, Tiger7253, Towns Hill, Trappist the monk, TripWire, TurboCop, Unreal7, Vamshi thakur, Vaza12, Vinegarymass911, VinyS, Volunteer Marek, Wiae, WilliamJE, Worldbruce, Yeenosaurus, Yilku1, Zohaib Beryar, फ़िलप्रो, মোহাম্মদ হাবিবুল্লাহ, 127 anonymous edits 545

Green Revolution in India *Source:* https://en.wikipedia.org/w/index.php?oldid=853113027 *License:* Creative Commons Attribution-Share Alike 3.0 *Contributors:* 1989, 72, ASHIKzz, Aayu1705, Abelmoschus Esculentus, Acroterion, Adam9007, Adavidb, Ananthulawyer, Andy Dingley, Antrocent, Atif Ali Meer, AussieLegend, AwesomeBananas007, Bender235, Bgwhite, Bobfrombrockley, Bobrayner, Buddhima prasad, Cahk, Chris the speller, ClueBot NG, Danski454, Dharmadhyaksha, Dialectric, Diannaa, Dl2000, Donner60, DrRKRana, Excirial, Flyer22 Reborn, FrB.TG, Fraggle81, Frietjes, Gilliam, GorillaWarfare, Greyjoy, Gronk Oz, Gurpreet sing, GünniX, HPSTREAM8, Hemant123143, Hentheden, Highpeaks35, Horseless Headman, Hummerrocket, I am One of Many, I dream of horses, Iridescent, JackintheBox, JakeyPotter, Jarble, Jayem1993, Jim1138, Jn045, Joshua Issac, KGirlTrucker81, Khushi.singla, Kku, Klbrain, LynxTufts, MBlaze Lightning, MarginalCost, Marianna251, Masssly, Materialscientist, Miayaseawright, MrBill3, MrOllie, NameIsRon, Naniwako, Narayansg, Neutrality, Niceguyedc, NicoScribe, Nikhil3738, Noyster, Onel5969, Oshwah, Ost316, Philip Trueman, Pkbwcgs, Pleiotrop3, PlyrStar93, Pratyya Ghosh, Racerx11, Renamed user sdfkjlskdfreu8r98, Rijinatwiki, Sahrudayan, Serols, Shellwood, Simplexity22, Sirishreddy99, Smitjo, Sobhan Shreeraj Sa, Somrick, Stang, Stesmo, Sujeetgholap, SylviaStanley, Telfordbuck, Telugujoshi, The Last Arietta, Theintuitus, Tpat1025, Wavelength, Whytecypress, Widr, Wikishovel, Wtmitchell, Zabshk, Zubr80, 291 anonymous edits 574

Operation Flood *Source:* https://en.wikipedia.org/w/index.php?oldid=850930585 *License:* Creative Commons Attribution-Share Alike 3.0 *Contributors:* 0ctober, 28421u2232nfenfcenc, Akaustav, Anantkh, AsceticRose, Ashwin147, Bab-a-lot, Balu.muthu, Bender235, Bharathiya, Bhideatul, BlackcurrantTea, Botsjeh, Briaboru, Chaithu5983, Chirag.gulati8989, Chirags, ClueBot NG, DaGizza, Daretodo, Dcirovic, Denisarona, Dewan357, Dirkbb, Ekabhishek, Erik Kennedy, Evano1van, Genius mathew, Gilliam, GorillaWarfare, GünniX, Highpeaks35, Idleguy, Indopug, Jlittlet, Jovianeye, Kazkaskazkasako, KnowledgeHegemony, Krishnaprasaths, Lightmouse, Magentic Manifestations, Materialscientist, Mattflaschen, Merchbow, Mhockey, Muhandes, Northamerica1000, Owais999, Porphyra, Quebec99, Rama's Arrow, Rinka singh, Rsrikanth05, S h i v a (Visnu), Salt Yeung, Sdsouza, Sgt Pinback, Shadowjams, Shekhartagra, Shovon76, Shyamsunder, Sjö, Skyc∼enwiki, SourceOhWatch (SrotahaUvacha), Srisharmaa, Studio.high, SwisterTwister, Tigercompanion25, Traitortanmay, Vbiyers, Wiki.editAnshu, Wingman4l7, Yaara dildaara, Zad68, ÄDA - DÄP, 112 anonymous edits 578

Indo-Pakistani War of 1971 *Source:* https://en.wikipedia.org/w/index.php?oldid=853485300 *License:* Creative Commons Attribution-Share Alike 3.0 *Contributors:* 84user, Adam9030, Adamgerber80, Adding The Truth, Akshaysmit, Arjayay, Auntieruth55, AustralianRupert, Banedon, Battleship Sailor, Blelbach, Calore123, Capitals00, Chewings72, Chris the speller, CommonsDelinker, Courcelles, Cramero, CushionMail, D.k abir, D4iNa4, DBigXray, DRAGON BOOSTER, DarkSpartan, DatGuy, Deepak Purti, Dlohcierekim, Dwarikatripathy, EdJohnston, EdmundT, El C, Faizan, Fish and karate, Ghatus, Giraffedata, Gireeshgprasad, HIAS, Hagennos, Hansmuller, Hibernian, Hmains, Hmainsbot1, Holdoffhunger, Howcheng, I dream of horses, Indy beetle, Ira Leviton, Jakichandan, John, John of Reading, Jon Kolbert, Jprg1966, JzG, KA$HMIR, Karamkhudayahai, Karthikbalaji84, Kautilya3, Keith-264, Kurtis, Likhon123, Llammakey, Look2See1, Loopy30, LouisAragon, MBlaze Lightning, MPS1992, MSGJ, Ma'az, Magioladitis, Mar4d, Marshalsebastian, MelanieN, MiCRoSCoPiC^eaRthLinG, Mild Bill Hiccup, Mropicki, My Lord, NadirAli, Naraht, NeonTetraploid, Nikoroman, Orientls, PeerBaba, Pjposullivan, Prinsgezinde, RJFJR, RN1970, Rajnarayan Chottopaddhyay, Rashkeqamar, Raymond3023, Razer2115, Redmelons, Rzvas, SachalT, Salikin1, Samee, Sashhenka, SheriffIsInTown, Shimlaites, Spartacus!, TheGoodIndian, Theintuitus, Tim!, Tkul, Train2104, Trappist the monk, TripWire, TurboCop, Twofingered Typist, Utcursch, Vijay rath, Vinegarymass911, VinyS, Warrior Covert, Wbm1058, WereSpielChequers, White Shadows, Wiggy!, Worldbruce, Zayyam123, ZephyrP, Zhanzhao, फ़िलप्रो, 35 anonymous edits 581

The Emergency (India) *Source:* https://en.wikipedia.org/w/index.php?oldid=853498323 *License:* Creative Commons Attribution-Share Alike 3.0 *Contributors:* 72, Amatyak, Anymemesnecessary, Aumnamahashiva, AusLondonder, BD2412, Bender235, Bezpitt, Bgwhite, Bobbytheonlyone, Brozozo, CASSIOPEIA, Canetoad2, Ceannlann gorm, Chrism, Chymicus, ClueBot NG, DadaNeem, DatGuy, Dl2000, Donner60, Ebyabe, Excirial, Flyer22 Reborn, GermanJoe, Ghatus, Ghosetuhin, Harikrishna.srirangam, Harinivas Vadivel, Hayman30, HimachalPradesh, Himanshu118, IndianEditor-wiki, Indopug, JSpung, Jack Frost, Jay Hodec, Jessicapierce, Jim1138, John of Reading, Johnuniq, Jonathansammy, Keith D, Keith-264, Kranganna, L293D, Latin Pig, MPS1992, MakeBelieveMonster, Manikroda1902, MarginalCost, Mark the train, Marvellous Spider-Man, Materialscientist, Mean as custard, Millennium bug, MishapRokko89, Monkrider2, MoreMIDI, My name is sheelaki javani, Myopia123, Niceguyedc, Nidafatimashahi, Niv.eno.nesohc, Nivs10, Noexpectations, Notthebestusername, Noyster, Opti6, Oshwah, Pushkar sharma28, Quae legit, QuietHere, Quisqualis, Rahul Bott, RainOnHill, Rashkeqamar, Retrovrv, Rich Farmbrough, Ronakshah1990, Ronaldo90099, Sakthibhadran, SaltySeas, Saturnitinerant, Serols, SourceOhWatch (SrotahaUvacha), SpacemanSpiff, Sunny singh9128, Superman123456788, TAnthony, Tachs, TantraYum, Tectosax, Tharos, Tornado chaser, Tow, Vanamonde93, Vinodtiwari2608, Wavelength, Worldbruce, Zade7777, 190 anonymous edits 610

Operation Blue Star *Source:* https://en.wikipedia.org/w/index.php?oldid=852848012 *License:* Creative Commons Attribution-Share Alike 3.0 *Contributors:* Abductive, Adamgerber80, Ankit2, Arjayay, Barek, BubbleEngineer, CalBerry1234567, CalBerry123456789, CambridgeBayWeather, Caperhare, Carmanhaho, Certes, Classicwiki, ClueBot NG, DBigXray, Derek R Bullamore, Elephanthunter, Gogo Dodo, Hmains, INeedSupport, Iamharveer, Indianeminem, IronGargoyle, John, Josve05a, LilHelpa, MTV.Home, Mullone, My Lord, Neenopeeno, Orenburg1, Orientls, Puriadeb, Pórokhov, RetroCraft314, Rodw, Samf4u, Satanic Conspiracy, ScrapIronIV, Simplexity22, Simran jeet Singh Khalsa, Sukhd73, Sukhpreet1997, Thecitizen1, Tom.Reding, Tornado chaser, Woodlot, Zazpot, 92 anonymous edits 627

Assassination of Indira Gandhi *Source:* https://en.wikipedia.org/w/index.php?oldid=852120186 *License:* Creative Commons Attribution-Share Alike 3.0 *Contributors:* 3ncrypter, 7107delicious, A baby turkey (citation needed), Afgshirzada101, Alexf, Ama975193, Amruth M D, AniMate, Apparition11, Aristophanes68, Ashray mehta, AssiPunjabi, AusLondonder, Avenue X at Cicero, Bender235, Bibboy1234, Bladesmulti, Bostonbrahmin20, Btl, Bullzeye, Captain Cornwall, Cgingold, Chris the speller, ChrisGualtieri, Chuy1530, Ckkumar, Cliniic, ClueBot NG, Cobaltcigs, Count Count, DBigXray, DJFission, Daniel Case, Darthhindu, Dcgh96, DebashisM, Depthburg, Derek R Bullamore, Dimadick, Dl2000, DocWatson42, Donner60, Egeymi, Ekabhishek, Ezsandler, Ferrierd, Flyer22 Reborn, Galloping Ghost U of I, Gilliam, Glacialfox, Gob Lofa, Good Olfactory, GünniX, HIMSAGAR, Haxwell, Hibernian, Himsagar Z.Y., Hugo999, I dream of horses, Iadmc, Iohannes Animosus, Ironholds, J 1982, JackofOz, Jafeluv, Jamie7687, JarrahTree, Jason Quinn, John, Johnnyaug, Jonathansammy, Jonoikobangali, Jovianeye, Jwh, Kannankarthik1992, Kelapstick, Kensplanet, KickingEdgarAllenPoe, Kiteinthewind, Koavf, Liberal Humanist, MakeBelieveMonster, Martin-vogel, Materialscientist, Missvain, Miyagawa, Mskadu, Myopia123, Nick Number, Nitishkumartn, Ogress,

Oleaster, Ominictionary, Panchode1998, Paris1127, ParkKimLim, Pawnkingthree, Pointillist, Ponyo, Pratyya Ghosh, Profitoftruth85, ProudIrishAspie, QuiteUnusual, Raghibs, Ravensfire, Ravimanojwiki, Reenem, Ricky81682, Rjwilmsi, Roadahead, Rsrikanth05, Ruggert1, SNIyer12, Salilb, Satanoid, Shellwood, Shivaji Krishnamurthy, Shyamsunder, Sikh-history, Soccerboss32, Solomonfromfinland, Ssdaku, Tec15, The Anomebot2, The Devil's Advocate, The Rambling Man, TheDotTK, Thiseye, Tim!, Tirath Das Dogra, Transmogriff, Utcursch, Vanished User 1004, Vickle1777, VishalB, W.andrea, Warrior Covert2, Wjfox2005, Writer.of.stuff.and.things, Xionbox, Zaidmarshal, Zohab, فرح ديسائي, आशीष भटनागर, फ़िलप्रो, 204 anonymous edits 648

1984 anti-Sikh riots *Source:* https://en.wikipedia.org/w/index.php?oldid=851668292 *License:* Creative Commons Attribution-Share Alike 3.0 *Contributors:* AKADANNYBOY, Aa508186, Abelmoschus Esculentus, Adamgerber80, Alexb102072, Alpha mp, AlvaroMolina, Amarbir13, Amardeepji, Anandmoorti, Anshukmitra123, Aravind V R, Arjayay, Asandhu9, Bumm13, C.Fred, CASSIOPEIA, CLCStudent, Calthinus, Capankajsmilyo, ClueBot NG, CushionMail, D4iNa4, DBigXray, DadaNeem, David.moreno72, DavidStewart85, Dlohcierekim, Docxx, Donner60, DreamLinker, El C, GeneralizationsAreBad, Gilliam, Gurpreet cingh, Gurpsrehal13, HanotLo, Hindus Killing Sikhs For No REASON, Howcheng, Human10.0, I am joker, Iitsrii, Imjonmon, Infographic, Irrigator, J 1982, Jamesjoyce66, Jaskaran27177, Jaspar1991, Jennica, Jim1138, Jonesey95, JzG, Kalapahadi, Kbsingh08, KylieTastic, Lokesh Boran, MBlaze Lightning, Me, Myself, and I are Here, Miniapolis, Monochrome Monitor, Moralis, Ms Sarah Welch, Naniwako, NarrSingh, Notthebestusername, Orientls, PAKHIGHWAY, Pavan santhosh.s, Pharaoh of the Wizards, PlyrStar93, PrimeHunter, RA0808, RegentsPark, Rossbawse, Rrburke, Ryan1783, SahajSingh04, SamHolt6, Santoshkumar497, Septrillion, Serols, Shellwood, Singhparvinder419, Sisu55, Stainfree, Station1, SteveStrummer, Sukhpreet1997, The manjot singh, Theinstantmatrix, Thomas.W, Tigercompanion25, ToBeFree, Tom.Reding, Tow, Tsr001, Tutu051, Uliedhoe, Utcursch, Vermont, Vice regent, Vivaan65, WereSpielChequers, Wollone, Worldbruce, Xenon One, फ़िलप्रो, 165 anonymous edits .... ??

Bhopal disaster *Source:* https://en.wikipedia.org/w/index.php?oldid=853547754 *License:* Creative Commons Attribution-Share Alike 3.0 *Contributors:* A2soup, Acousmana, AgonRex, Alan Liefting, Alexb102072, Alexed1, Ammodramus, Anita5192, ArdWar, Arthur Rubin, Auric, B A Thuriaux, BD2412, Balon Greyjoy, Barbara (WVS), Bdiscoe, Bender235, Br98, Brandmeister, Bthomson100, C.J. Griffin, Cannolis, Cathal Ó hÉanna, Cavalry.charger, Chaheel Riens, Chairman Peng Xi, Chris the speller, Chris troutman, Court Appointed Shrub, Ctxppc, Cyberbot II, Cyberix, DadaNeem, Dcirovic, Dewritech, Djembayz, Dl2000, Doubld414, Dreamtheater, Drhogarty, DudeWithAFeud, Dvidby0, E.M.Gregory, Edgeweyes, Ehn, Eles2011, Equinox, Esemono, Evano1van, Fdssdf, Flashpoint2589, Frietjes, Frze, Ft763, Gaius Cornelius, Gene Wood, Gorthian, Groyolo, Gulbenk, H-stt, Haeinous, HandsomeFella, Hannes Röst, Headbomb, Highpeaks35, Hitechcomputergeek, HoldTheDoor89, Howcheng, Huasquero, I dream of horses, I.narinder, Ineck, J 1982, Jackmcbarn, Jackychen0925, Jan olieslagers, Jarble, Jaywardhan009, Jim Michael, Jmile69, Joe2719, JoeSperrazza, John, Jon Kolbert, Jonesey95, Joshua Issac, Jprg1966, Jytdog, KConWiki, Keitsist, Kelisi, Kiwi128, L293D, LiveRail, Lizia7, Luna Whistler, MURODURUS, MacMog, Marsupium, Maurice Carbonaro, Mehmuffin, Meltdown627, Mfernflower, Mike Mounier, Moxy, Mukogodo, Nickst, Nicola.Manini, Ohconfucius, Omyooah, Ophello, Ori Livneh, Pan1994, Petshmm, Petteri Aimonen, Pietro13, Pigsonthewing, Pp0912, Psomu800, Qwertyus, Randy549, RawwrBag, Richard BB, Rifleman 82, Rjwilmsi, Roland zh, Ryan115, S.Shujan, Safety Cap, Sam Sailor, Sandcherry, Shadowphrogg32642342, Shrikanthv, Skybunny, Slobodan Grasic, Smurrayinchester, Solarislv, Somebody500, Speed74, Splodgeness, Stamptrader, Sturgeontransformer, TRBP, TROPtastic, The Interior, Thnidu, Toccata quarta, Too Old, Trappist the monk, Triptothecottage, Usacfg, Utcursch, Valetude, WLRoss, WeSans, Welsh, Wikimandia, Wleizero, Xxavyer, Yamada Taro, Zigger 671

Indian intervention in the Sri Lankan Civil War *Source:* https://en.wikipedia.org/w/index.php?oldid=847315385 *License:* Creative Commons Attribution-Share Alike 3.0 *Contributors:* Alex Cohn, Astronomyinertia, Axeman89, Bender235, Blackknight12, Bluerocks777, CPA-5, Charles Essie, Diannaa, Frietjes, Gfosankar, Giraffedata, Hammersoft, I am One of Many, John of Reading, JorisvS, Kautilya3, Khazar2, KplFlUSA, Lakun.patra, Lasyabhaskaram, Look2See1, Mads o 85, Mark Arsten, MartinKassemJ120, Materialscientist, MrScorch6200, Newman50, Noren, Obi2canibe, Orenburg1, PhilKnight, Placelimit, Pranesh Gogoi, Raymond3023, SheriffIsInTown, Shuipzv3, Shyamsunder, Soni, Swpb, Tamil23, Tpbradbury, Tyler Durden, Warrior Covert, Welsh, Wikiuser13, Δ, फ़िलप्रो, 52 anonymous edits 701

Siachen conflict *Source:* https://en.wikipedia.org/w/index.php?oldid=853552993 *License:* Creative Commons Attribution-Share Alike 3.0 *Contributors:* Abhisheks 91, Ad Orientem, Adamgerber80, Ameyanawathe, Anish9500, Astral Prince, BD2412, BagelBrot, Bender235, Bgwhite, Bharatiya29, Bilawal1122, Boris Lewis, Calore123, CambridgeBayWeather, Capitals00, Catlemur, Chaduvari, Clpo13, ClueBot NG, CommonsDelinker, Cozy00, D4iNa4, DBigXray, DLinth, Danbloch, Darkness Shines, Davidcannon, Derek R Bullamore, DocWatson42, Dthomsen8, EdwardH, EkoGraf, F-INSAS, Faizan, Farrukh51577, Frangars, FreeatlastChitchat, Frosty, GSS, GeneralizationsAreBad, Ghazi912, Hibernian, Holdoffhunger, Howcheng, Human3015, I dream of horses, InedibleHulk, Iridescent, Jasper Deng, Jolaw2305, Jon Hydro Jets, K V Sai Akhil, Kanchu deep, Kautilya3, Keithonearth, King Zebu, KnightRIF, Koodfaand, Kumar1222, Lakun.patra, Le Petit Chat, Lezela, Libra bro, Look2See1, MBlaze Lightning, MCIWS, MapSGV, Mar4d, MarnetteD, Materialscientist, Mbk10, Mbs7890, Meanbuggin, Melcous, Moriori, Mudassir1468, My Lord, NeilN, NewEnglandYankee, Niceguyedc, OccultZone, Owais Khursheed, Praveenp, ROCKDEEPAK, Rashedoon, Rekha Pande, Rjwilmsi, Rzvas, SachalT, Sarthak pareek, Sfan00 IMG, Shaharyar.121, Smalljim, Smsarmad, Spartacus!, Sphilbrick, Stamptrader, Stesmo, Strike Eagle, Tachs, The Rambling Man, Thomas.W, Tigercompanion25, Tom.Reding, TopGun, TripWire, Uban singh, Utcursch, VP101, Warrior Covert2, WereSpielChequers, Winner 42, Zadon19, फ़िलप्रो, 112 anonymous edits 706

Assassination of Rajiv Gandhi *Source:* https://en.wikipedia.org/w/index.php?oldid=852022176 *License:* Creative Commons Attribution-Share Alike 3.0 *Contributors:* 78.26, Aille, Anjaney Agarwal, Anomie, Anwar saadat, Apokrif, Ardfern, BD2412, Baldersdod, Bender235, Benne, Berudagon, Bill william compton, Blackknight12, Bodhisattwa, Bonkers The Clown, Bulwersator, CHJL, CardinalDan, CharlesSpencer, Chowdhary747, ClueBot NG, Cmr08, CyanoTex, Cyanolinguophile, Dcirovic, Dharmadhyaksha, Dimadick, Ebyabe, Egeymi, Evano1van, EvergreenMachine, Faizan, Flix11, Hornplease, Howcheng, Hugo999, I1i2t310, Ideopreneur, Indianeminem, Iohannes Animosus, Ira Leviton, JForget, JSpung, Jasrajva, Jediknightelectro1997, Jim1138, John of Reading, Jonoikobangali, Joshmaul, Jst007, Kelisi, Kerr avon, Krishna23456, Lateg, Lihaas, LukasMatt, Madhava 1947, Magioladitis, Mahesh1976, Mamta Jagdish Dhody, Materialscientist, Mcc1789, Melmann, Mkumawat1991, Mogism, Moncrief, Mr.Falcon, Mugunth Kumar, N419BH, Nader85021, Neutrality, NicatronTg, Night Gyr, Nikhilgk, Nitishkumartn, Nizil Shah, Om2520, Paris1127, Patrick, Pharaoh of the Wizards, PhilKnight, Praemonitus, Pratyya Ghosh, Premkudva, ProudIrishAspie, Qwer1995, R'n'B, RJFJR, Rameshnta909, Rasnaboy, Ravensfire, Ravenswing, Richard3120, Roxy the dog, Royroydeb, SamWinchester000, Sanishkb, Sarabseth, Scottjdownes, Ser Amantio di Nicolao, Shinnosukeandme, Shyamsunder, Signalhead, Skmaddd, Snigdhasinghsweet, Sodabottle, SpaceFlight89, StjJackson, SuperJew, Swliv, TAZ4463, TClaver, Tassedethe, Tex, The Anomebot2, TheAwesomeAzza, Tim!, Tim333, Toddy1, Uanfala, Unbuttered Parsnip, Uncle Dick, Userrohan, Utkarshsingh.1992, Vasagammani86, Viper007Bond, VishalB, Viswanath Vellaiappan, Volunteer Marek, Wiae, Wifione, Wikiercomer, William Avery, Wprlh, Yash18197, Zzyzx11, தென்காசி சுப்பிரமணியன், 169 anonymous edits 721

Insurgency in Jammu and Kashmir *Source:* https://en.wikipedia.org/w/index.php?oldid=850951491 *License:* Creative Commons Attribution-Share Alike 3.0 *Contributors:* Account.ka.naam, Adamgerber80, Agusbou2015, Ajinomata, Akhtar195, Altetendekrabbe, Ama975193, Amartya ray2001, AmyNorth, AnantPalekar, Anasaitis, Anir1uph, Asitpathak, Astore Malik, Aumnamahashiva, AusLondonder, Baba Mica, Bejnar, Ben Ben, BrightStarSky, Buklaodord, Capankajsmilyo, Capitals00, Charles Essie, Cityvalyu, Classical Arun, CommonsDelinker, Cyanolinguophile, Dane, Darkness Shines, David Gerard, Davidcannon, Denniscabrams, Diannaa, Dimadick, DiplomatTesterMan, Dl2000, Dobie80, Doug Weller, Dthomsen8, Edward, Eik Corell, EkoGraf, Elockid, Ericl, Evano1van, Faizan, Faizhaider, Farolif, GOLDI123456789, GSS, Gazkthul, GeneralizationsAreBad, George Ho, Girish ghost, Greyshark09, HCPUNXKID, Hari7478, Hmainsbot1, Human3015, IR393Anjan, Indian1985, Iridescent, JCAla, Janeanny, Jay942942, Jheeltose, Jinbo4514, John of Reading, Jonathanarpith, JorisvS, Jozoisis, Jweiss11, Kaldari, Karankhajuria22, Kautilya3, Kenchman, King Zebu, Kirtimaansyal, Kkm010, Knightplex, KuldeepKaushikVyas, Lakun.patra, Lapsed Pacifist, Liberal Humanist, Lihaas, LilHelpa, Lopswirt, Magioladitis, Maheshkumaryadav, MalikAttaRasool, Mandarax, Mar4d, Maxx786, Mfarazbaig, Mogism, Mrt3366, My Lord, NadirAli, Neelkamala, Nikhilmn2002, Nizil Shah, Ohconfucius, Oranjelo100, Owais Khursheed, Owen, PanchoS, Pragvansh, R9tgokunks, RaviC, Raymond3023, Reddony, Richie1917, Riyazulrahman, Sachukurian, Samarth309, Sarkar-rajya, Sfan00 IMG, SheriffIsInTown, Shimlaites, Shivankvishnoi, Sid Blue, Smsarmad, Stumink, Tbhotch, Thomas.W, Tjbird9675, Tom.Reding, TopGun, Trappist the monk, Tyler Durden, Vatsan34, Vibhijain, Vice regent, VonBismarck, Wanishahrukh, Wareditor2013, Warrior Covert, WikHead, Wiki contributor 21, Winged Blades of Godric, Wingman417, Wintonian, Xover, फ़िलप्रो 729

Bombay riots *Source:* https://en.wikipedia.org/w/index.php?oldid=853235823 *License:* Creative Commons Attribution-Share Alike 3.0 *Contributors:* Abhishek0831996, Abhishikt, Acroterion, Adam37, AmritasyaPutra, Aravind V R, Arpradeep, AsifZaman1987, Austrian, Bill william compton, Blackwizard2000, Bongan, Chintankanabar, Chris the speller, ChrisGualtieri, Clarince63, Clocke, Clpo13, ClueBot NG, Copana2002, Darkness Shines, DatGuy, Deganveranx, Dexterous1802, Dl2000, Dlrohrer2003, Donner60, Doug Weller, Ekabhishek, Epicgenius, FGSDIFYIYFAOUY, Flyte35, Freezer146, George Ho, GrindtXX, Habiibil, Hey19, Huangdi, Ingoodfaith20988, Iwinkn, JaconaFrere, Jayakumar RG, JesseAlanGordon, Jigmon68, Jobas, John Cline, John Lunney, Jovianeye, JumlaMan, Juneymb, Kailash29792, Karthikndr, Kautilya3, Khayaal, KuwarOnline, Lee Tru., Lemongirl942, LeoFrank, Liberal Humanist, MPS1992, Mandarax, Marvellous Spider-Man, Masterturner, Materialscientist, MissEnCyclopedia, Mogism, Mra2356, Narayansg, NewHikaru07, NickW557, Nicknackrussian, Nizil Shah, Ohconfucius, Ozzykemist, Pectore, Puneet Singh Sidhu, R000t, Razer2115, Reactor, S h i v a (Visnu), Sdmarathe, Shellwood, Shovon76, Shyamsunder, Simon Lieschke, Singhwasking, Sphilbrick, Starcheerspeaksnewslostwars, Tassedethe, Tdslk, Thumperward, Tim!, Tufayl1997, Unbiasedpov, Unreal7, Utcursch, Vanamonde93, Veryhuman, Wally, Wantsallanger, Welshleprechaun, Widr, Wiki-uk, Willondon, Xscontrib, Zeke72791, 248 anonymous edits 743

Economic liberalisation in India *Source:* https://en.wikipedia.org/w/index.php?oldid=849629796 *License:* Creative Commons Attribution-Share Alike 3.0 *Contributors:* 1980na, 28bytes, 2x2leax, A9452819015, Abhimanyu Moral, Akshayrockz1998june8, Anonymous14121998, Aqwis, Archon 2488, Arjayay, Arjun1491, Auntof6, AusLondonder, Backonceagain, Bazonka, Beland, Bender235, Bgwhite, Billwilson5060, Billy Basinski, Bluerasberry, Capankajsmilyo, Chandrashekharkumbhar, Citation bot 1, ClueBot NG, Compfreak7, Corpx, Curryboy91, D4iNa4, DASonnenfeld, Dale Arnett, Darylgolden, Dcirovic, Deepanshu1707, Denisarona, Dl2000, DocWatson42, Doorvery far, Driger69, Dru91, Edward, Enroute, Equilibrium103, EricEnfermero, FGBREIKBF, Fixer88, Gilliam, Gilo1969, Governmentetc, Ground Zero, HLwiKi, Hairhorn, Heard tried won, Hugo999, Hut 8.5, Indopug, Ionisiso, J intela, JJIHIYOJUY, JaGa, Jatinbhatt blap, Jeanmarie100, Jonathansammy, Jonoikobangali, Joseph Solis in Australia, Joshua Issac, Jovianeye, Jrz5036, Karan.102, Ketiltrout, Kijacob, Kkm010, Laimirie, Lalit Jagannath, Lantrix, Lirani, Lord Seth, Luckas Blade, Magioladitis, Malikkal, Materialscientist, Meclee, Miacek, NJA, Ohconfucius, OnkelFordTaunus, Pharaoh of the Wizards, Polylepsis, R'n'B, Racerx11, Ranbi2Delta, Ranjit.goswami, Rohanpendse25,

Rsrikanth05, Rustyfence, S h i v a (Visnu), SSJ3Lion, Sachin welcomesu, Sakhardande, Samirbodkhe, Saransh1, ScottMHoward, Serols, Sgobinathwiki, Shipra177, Shreevatsa, Shyamsunder, Siddharth0812, Sodabottle, SpacemanSpiff, Spongefrog, Srich32977, Sulabha94, Superprof, Sweetmusician, Swetakethu, Tabascom, Tachs, The Thing That Should Not Be, Tim!, TimeSkull, Titodutta, Travelbird, Tri400, Trinitrobrick, UglowT, Utcursch, Vedantm, VishalB, Viswaprabha, Widr, Woohookitty, 199 anonymous edits 760

2001 Indian Parliament attack *Source:* https://en.wikipedia.org/w/index.php?oldid=852774646 *License:* Creative Commons Attribution-Share Alike 3.0 *Contributors:* 220 of Borg, AI009, AWG97, Abecedare, Adven98, Agarwal shinchan, Ali aff, Anirudhrata, Apurv1980, Aquadeep08, Bakasuprman, Bakerlander, Barastert, Barthateslisa, Bhrtrahulksingh, Bidhan Singh, Bilal.scientist, Billposer, Black Falcon, Bongan, CYBERMAIL786, Caballero1967, Chaiturocks, Cheekylips, Chris the speller, ClueBot NG, Co9man, CommonsDelinker, Cyanolinguophile, Cyfraw, Darkness Shines, Depthburg, Dewritech, DiplomatTesterMan, Djmckee1, Dkarya2025, DocWatson42, Doldrums, Drawat123, Elockid, Empok Nor, FallingGravity, Festus Mcracken, Fredericknoronha, Gazkthul, Genjix, George Ho, Ghanadar galpa, Ground Zero, HMSLavender, Higanesh2003, Hkelkar, Hmains, Hoof Hearted, Hugo999, I dream of horses, Illegitimate Barrister, Imleashed, Ironholds, J 1982, Jac16888, Jevansen, John Reaves, John of Reading, Joseph Solis in Australia, Joshua Issac, Jovianeye, Kashmirspeaks, Kctito2, Khushwant singh best, Kintetsubuffalo, Kndimov, Kodos the executioner, Kutchu raghu, Largoplazo, Libertarian12111971, Lightmouse, LoneWolf2917, MZMcBride, Mad'ouk, Madhava 1947, Maheshkumaryadav, Mamta Jagdish Dhody, Matthew Fennell, Matthuxtable, Maulakhan, Mcc1789, Merchant of Meluha, Meyaarankit, Mhhossein, Mikael Hansson, MohitSingh, Mpradeep, Mrceleb2007, Mrt3366, Ms2ger, Nangparbat, NewsForAll, Nishkid64, Nizil Shah, Noor Aalam, Noseycjr, Nshuks7, Ohconfucius, PBP, PISCOSOUR786, Pawan ctn, PersianScholar, Pranav21391, Prateek9us, ProudIrishAspie, PvOberstein, QuiteUnusual, Rajput Lia 383, Ranbijay91, Rao Ravindra, Ravisriv, Rayabhari, Razzsic, RedWolf, Reduxx, Rjwilmsi, Rsrikanth05, Rubal Prakash, Rumpelstiltskin223, S3000, Sachin akn, Sanketholey, Sbbarker19, Scwlong, Sensibleone, Ser Amantio di Nicolao, Sfacets, Shovon76, Shyamsunder, Skapur, SpacemanSpiff, Spartacus!, Sreekanthv, Srimanta.Bhuyan, SteinbDJ, SugarRat, Sumitkachroo, Suresh 5, Sushilkumarmishra, Taimurjaved, Tbhotch, The Anomebot2, The Telephone Company, The alchemyst 123, Tim!, Toddst1, Unimpeccable, User2534, Utcursch, Vikas Kumar Ojha, Visite fortuitement prolongée, WBRSin, Waqarali.cs, Webclient101, Wikireader41, WojciechToJa, Yousefmadari, Zishaan, Zoupan, Δ, 康非字典 , 167 anonymous edits .... ??

2002 Gujarat riots *Source:* https://en.wikipedia.org/w/index.php?oldid=852196076 *License:* Creative Commons Attribution-Share Alike 3.0 *Contributors:* 72, Abbuji, Abhilash666, Accesscrawl, Adamgerber80, Alexandru M., Anandmoorti, Aniruddha.arondekar, Ankit2, Arcane150, Auric, Basawala, Bennv3771, CAPTAIN RAJU, Capankajsmilyo, Capitals00, Ck4829, ClueBot NG, D4R1U5, D4iNa4, Dailybasharathyd, Dcirovic, Dennis Brown, El C, El cid, el campeador, Eumolpo, FallingGravity, Floatjon, FreeatlastChitchat, Frietjes, Gajanankhergamker, GregorB, Gulumeemee, GünniX, Harish Debta, Hmains, Hotchpotcher, Huangdi, I dream of horses, Ibad Khan, Irulason, JamesLucas, Jim1138, Jn045, Jobas, Jon Kolbert, Joseph.james89, K6ka, Kailash29792, Kautilya3, Kenfyre, L3X1, Logicacoma, MBlaze Lightning, MPS1992, Matunga-mumbai, Maunus, Mehmuffin, MelanieN, Mikeblas, Mohdkhan5552, Motivação, MrLinkinPark333, My Chemistry romantic, My Lord, NFSreloaded, Naren marik, Negarzone, NenemT, NickCT, Nizil Shah, Notthebestusername, Oshwah, Pharos, Pikachuchicken, Placewatcher, Pppooojjjaaa, Premeditated Chaos, RahulRamchandani, RegentsPark, RileyBugz, Rossbawse, Rubbish computer, Sachingm, Samsara, Sdmarathe, Sharmanic2002, Signedzzz, Soham321, Subhanu.bhattacharya, Svabhiman, The Liberal Truthseeker, The Rambling Man, Thomasnetrpm, Titodutta, Toprajapati, Trappist the monk, Tyler Durden, V1n1 paresh, Vanamonde93, Vineethtati, Xscontrib, Zukeshum, 117 anonymous edits .... ??

2001–02 India–Pakistan standoff *Source:* https://en.wikipedia.org/w/index.php?oldid=851575400 *License:* Creative Commons Attribution-Share Alike 3.0 *Contributors:* 23 editor, Abdullah1511, Ace of Raves, Adamgerber80, Aditya Bawane, Ajithmattam, Amccann421, AmritasyaPutra, Anir1uph, Anish9500, Ankurdas94, Anupmehra, Arnob.roy, Ashu00007, Astitvasood, BD2412, Balaj Khan, Bender235, Blazin AR, CPA-5, Calore123, Canucks121, Carriearchdale, Climate123, Clinamental, ClueBot NG, Cnzx, Coolguy276, Criclover143, DBigXray, Daniash007, Darkness Shines, Dewritech, Dharmadhyaksha, Diaigovind, Dissident93, Dl2000, Donner60, Drankush, Dudeist, EkoGraf, Faizan, Finlay McWalter, FoCuSandLeArN, FourViolas, GeneralizationsAreBad, Gladamas, Greyjoy, GrindtXX, Harshvardhansonkar, HarunKiani, HirenJaan, Hmainsbot1, IgnorantArmies, Illegitimate Barrister, Jaiyon, Jamesx12345, Kautilya3, Krisdaughtry.k, Ktr101, KylieTastic, Lakun.patra, Lastdefenda, MBlaze Lightning, MCIWS, Mar4d, Mark Schierbecker, Moriori, Myopia123, Naumanrk, NeilN, Nikhilmn2002, NitRav, OccultZone, Ohconfucius, Onel5969, Pkbwcgs, Quebec99, Qwyrxian, RadiX, Rayan Bhagwagar, Red Slash, Rinkusonic, Rsrikanth05, Runningonbrains, Rushbugled13, Rvthkr4, Sideways713, Sitush, Smalljim, Smsarmad, Spartacus!, Spencer, TAnthony, The Madras, Thomasnetrpm, Tigerassault, Tim!, TopGun, VijayBJ, Vincecate, Viperonaut, Vipinhari, Visakha veera, Waleeda Don, Yoreed khan, Zadon19, Zerefx, 181 anonymous edits .... ??

2008 Mumbai attacks *Source:* https://en.wikipedia.org/w/index.php?oldid=852826868 *License:* Creative Commons Attribution-Share Alike 3.0 *Contributors:* 1yoyo1, Abelmoschus Esculentus, Abeniel, Abid Patel, Adamgerber80, Adamtt9, AddWittyNameHere, Aditya00000002, Aditya8993, Agarwal shinchan, AhmetSelim12, AnishNahar, Anupamskd7, AsceticRose, Aumnamahashiva, Auntie Agni, BD2412, Balablitz, Barthateslisa, Bazonka, Bender235, Brj312JXa0An1mO, Buttons to Push Buttons, CAPTAIN RAJU, CarlMcKarlson, CentreLeftRight, ClueBot NG, CogitoErgoSum14, Crh23, Cyberpolarized, Cyrus noto3at bulaga, DBigXray, Dalliance, Dan Koehl, David in DC, Deepanshu1707, Depthburg, Dharmadhyaksha, Dick Shane, El C, Epicgenius, Eurodyne, Figfires, Fitindia, FoodiBase, FreeatlastChitchat, GSS, Galobtter, Gianluigi02, Gilliam, GreenC, Hello71, HickoryOughtShirt?4, Hmains, Howcheng, Human3015, I am One of Many, I dream of horses, Ira Leviton, Iridescent, IronGargoyle, J 1982, Jalaldduin fast bowler, Jayjg, Jchmrt, Jevansen, Jim Michael, Jim1138, Jnanaranjan sahu, Joeykai, John, John of Reading, Jonathan35is, Kashif Mehmood104, KhaasBanda, Khalbir, King Prithviraj II, KingKakar96, Kleuske, KuNg Fu PaNdA 11, Lakun.patra, Liberal Humanist, Lihaas, Livven, MBlaze Lightning, Malaiya, Manojpnchal, MarnetteD, Materialscientist, McSly, Mewulwe, Mikeblas, Mopskatze, MovieFex, Mr.User200, NFLisAwesome, Nazamalikhan, Ninney, Nomaan Asim, Noon, Northamerica1000, Nuts5070, Orenburg1, Ours18, Paris1127, Percinr1819, PersianScholar, PhoenixAF24, Pratik1962, Puneet Singh Sidhu, Qzd, Ragityman, Rahulshahx99, Ravn00r, RegentsPark, Rewind816, Salil786, Samsara, Saqib.zamir.ksa, Smtchahal, Spartacus!, Spasage, Stefanomione, Super997, Tauseef01, TerraCodes, TerrexT, TheGoodBadWorst, Thor Dockweiler, Tiger7253, Tim!, Timtrent, Tollysurya, Trappist the monk, Tyler Durden, TypoBoy, User2534, Vinegarymass911, WikiPancake, William Avery, Winged Blades of Godric, Wpeneditor, Yashthepunisher, Ymblanter, ZI Jony, ZappaOMati, फ़िलप्रो, 199 anonymous edits .... ??

Concerns and controversies over the 2010 Commonwealth Games *Source:* https://en.wikipedia.org/w/index.php?oldid=846655176 *License:* Creative Commons Attribution-Share Alike 3.0 *Contributors:* AgniKalpa, AngChenrui, Aryan wiki, Avenue X at Cicero, BD2412, Bilby, BrightStarSky, Capankajsmilyo, CarTick, CatapultTalks, Catlemur, Chaheel Riens, ClueBot NG, Cynicalbong, DadaNeem, Dcirovic, Ddas, DisillusionedBitterAndKnackered, Dl2000, Download, Evano1van, Gargaj, Gobade.abhay1, HiLo48, Ivorycoast3, Jim856796, Jsaw101, KGasso, King Zebu, Kkm010, Ktr101, LibStar, Lightmouse, Lihaas, Logicwiki, Lucy-marie, M-le-mot-dit, MacRusgail, Maheshkumaryadav, Mandarax, Mar4d, Marcocapelle, Miller17CU94, Millionsandbillions, Mogism, Mr. Stradivarius, Muon, Niceguyedc, Nishanth17693, Nograpes, Nshuks7, Ohconfucius, Polylerus, Primefac, Qwyrxian, Qzd, Radiofreewill, Rameshpathak75, Rjwilmsi, SMasters, Sachinvenga, Shyamsunder, Skr15081997, Slatersteven, TFOWR, Tatom2k, The Discoverer, The Rambling Man, TheTigerKing, Tktktk, Topcardi, Tri400, Trivialist, Vinteron, VishalB, Vykischandra, Widr, WikiDao, YellowMonkey, Yogesh Khandke, Zhanzhao, 155 anonymous edits 826

2G spectrum case *Source:* https://en.wikipedia.org/w/index.php?oldid=853668325 *License:* Creative Commons Attribution-Share Alike 3.0 *Contributors:* 0nerfusion, A.Pugalenthi, Adityaedits, AgniKalpa, Akella, Akhiljaxxn, Akotiya Chirayu, Alokagrawal8, Amruth M D, Ananthvishu, Andrewa, Andrewpmk, Arunsingh16, Aryan wiki, Atethnekos, Auric, Avs dps, BethNaught, Bgwhite, Bluerasberry, BrightStarSky, Chris the speller, Chris troutman, ChunnuBhai, ClueBot NG, Daonguyen95, Designravi, Dhruvkapur91, Donner60, Dragonninjadragon, Dthomsen8, EditorBrad, Evano1van, EvergreenFir, Fangedparakeet, Fraggle81, Ftsq, Fylbecatulous, Gigijohn, Gilliam, GoingBatty, Gtelteleservice, Hamthiya.Mohamed, Harie krishnan, Harishrawat11, Harsh 2580, Hirenshah957, Iam.ishaan, IndianGeneralist, Jack Greenmaven, JaconaFrere, Jerrieisfake, Jn045, John of Reading, Johnrameshkhan, Joshua Issac, Julietdeltalima, KAP03, Kaiketsu, Karthikndr, Katyaan, Kkm010, Kwamikagami, Loginnigol, Marcocapelle, Mastermind3338, Materialscientist, Matt1299, Meatsgains, Miniapolis, Mr. Guye, Mr. Stradivarius, Naniwako, Naveenpf, Nihiltres, Nirmal2012mathew, NoRupees, O.Koslowski, Ohconfucius, Orphan Wiki, PC-XT, PKT, Pharaoh of the Wizards, Pieleric, Primefac, Qazamj, Qwyrxian, R1t7 20, Raguks, Robert4565, RogerTechAdvisor, Rushbugled13, SHAIKH ABDUL GAFAR, SLKWR303, Samee, Sandvich18, Saugaat yashvardhan, Sct72, Shashankjigsaw, ShelleyKasli, Shoonyea, Shyamsunder, SomeFreakOnTheInternet, SpacemanSpiff, Supersaiyen312, Tabletop, Tassedethe, Technopat, The Discoverer, The Herald, Titodutta, Torchiest, TotalBuscuit, Touch Of Light, Trappist the monk, TutterMouse, Uncletomwood, VINAMRASINGH, Voidxor, Vs604, Wallace McDonald, Webclient101, Wikipelli, Wikisk1432, Winkelvi, Wordist, Zppix, 167 anonymous edits .... ??

2011 Indian anti-corruption movement *Source:* https://en.wikipedia.org/w/index.php?oldid=851335841 *License:* Creative Commons Attribution-Share Alike 3.0 *Contributors:* 220 of Borg, AgniKalpa, Alan Liefting, Anshulkumardhiman, Aryan wiki, Auric, AusLondonder, Battlesnake1, Bender235, Bgwhite, Bkgupta1, Blamecivil95, Bollyjeff, Bongchillum, Boomur, Calliopejen1, Catlemur, Charles Essie, Chris the speller, Classicwiki, ClueBot NG, Clyde.dsouza, CommonsDelinker, D jinn, DRAGON BOOSTER, Denisarona, Ekabhishek, EoGuy, Evano1van, Frietjes, Frze, Gaius Cornelius, Gokulchandola, GregorB, Griffin700, Ground Zero, Hindustanilanguage, Joshua Jonathan, Kaltenmeyer, Karthikndr, Keith D, Ketiltrout, Khazar, Klbrain, KylieTastic, Liberal Humanist, Min2winit, Mr. Stradivarius, Navinpc, NeilN, Niceguyedc, Nizil Shah, Not tata, Ohconfucius, Pharaoh of the Wizards, PlyrStar93, Primefac, Qzd, Rahul Bott, Ravindr, Rjwilmsi, Robin klein, Shyamsunder, Sitush, Stamptrader, The Discoverer, TheJJJunk, ThinkingYouth, Titodutta, TruthShallWin, Uncletomwood, Wavelength, WereSpielChequers, Wiki13, Wikiuser13, Wizardman, 69 anonymous edits .... ??

Image Sources, Licenses and Contributors

The sources listed for each image provide more detailed licensing information including the copyright status, the copyright owner, and the license conditions.

Image *Source:* https://en.wikipedia.org/w/index.php?title=File:Padlock-silver.svg *Contributors:* AzaToth, BotMultichill, BotMultichillT, Gurch, Jarekt, Kallerna, Multichill, Perhelion, Rd232, Riana, Sarang, Siebrand, Steinsplitter, 4 anonymous edits 1

Image *Source:* https://en.wikipedia.org/w/index.php?title=File:Mughal1700.png *License:* Creative Commons Attribution 3.0 *Contributors:* Gabagool 1

Image *Source:* https://en.wikipedia.org/w/index.php?title=File:Timurid.svg *License:* GNU Free Documentation License *Contributors:* User:Stannered 2

Image *Source:* https://en.wikipedia.org/w/index.php?title=File:Delhi_Sultanate_Flag_(catalan_atlas).png *Contributors:* User:History of Persia ... 2

Image *Source:* https://en.wikipedia.org/w/index.php?title=File:Mewar.svg *License:* Public Domain *Contributors:* Robert Alfers 2

Image *Source:* https://en.wikipedia.org/w/index.php?title=File:Blank.png *License:* Public Domain *Contributors:* Bastique, Chlewey, ChrisDHDR, Ghouston, It Is Me Here, Jed, Paradoctor, Patrick, Penubag, Perhelion, Rocket000, Roomba, Sarang, Timeroot, Tintazul 2

Image *Source:* https://en.wikipedia.org/w/index.php?title=File:Flag_of_the_Maratha_Empire.svg *License:* Public Domain *Contributors:* DarkEvil 2

Image *Source:* https://en.wikipedia.org/w/index.php?title=File:Flag_of_the_Abdali_Afghan_Tribes.jpeg *License:* Public domain *Contributors:* Apocheir, Cathy Richards, Gustavo 200.000.0, Mark Marathon, OgreBot 2, Stefan2, TFerenczy, Tuvalkin, 1 anonymous edits 2

Image *Source:* https://en.wikipedia.org/w/index.php?title=File:Sikh_Empire_flag.svg *Contributors:* User:Gurbar Akaal 2

Image *Source:* https://en.wikipedia.org/w/index.php?title=File:Flag_of_the_British_East_India_Company_(1801).svg *License:* Public Domain *Contributors:* User:Yaddah 2

Image *Source:* https://en.wikipedia.org/w/index.php?title=File:British_Raj_Red_Ensign.svg *License:* Public Domain *Contributors:* Barryob 2

Figure 1 *Source:* https://en.wikipedia.org/w/index.php?title=File:Emperor_babur.jpg *Contributors:* Jim.henderson, Monticores 5

Figure 2 *Source:* https://en.wikipedia.org/w/index.php?title=File:Jesuits_at_Akbar's_court.jpg *License:* Public Domain *Contributors:* Cpt.a.haddock, Eugene a, Eugenio Hansen, OFS, Grentidez, Gryffindor, Jungpionier, Primaler, Ranveig, Vivek Sarje 7

Figure 3 *Source:* https://en.wikipedia.org/w/index.php?title=File:Silver_Rupee_Madras_Presidency.JPG *License:* Public Domain *Contributors:* Albertomos, Ashashyou, Jungpionier, Rayaraya, Roland zh, 1 anonymous edits 10

Figure 4 *Source:* https://en.wikipedia.org/w/index.php?title=File:Renaldis_muslin_woman.jpg *License:* Public Domain *Contributors:* Austriacus, Bazaan, Bukk, JKhan20, Mabalu, Michael Barera, Multichill, Pitke, Themadchopper, Zolo 14

Figure 5 *Source:* https://en.wikipedia.org/w/index.php?title=File:Boro_Katra_4_by_Ashif_Siddique.jpg *License:* GNU Free Documentation License *Contributors:* Ashif Anam Siddique 16

Figure 6 *Source:* https://en.wikipedia.org/w/index.php?title=File:Taj_Mahal_in_March_2004.jpg *License:* Creative Commons Attribution-Sharealike 2.0 *Contributors:* Dhirad, picture edited by J. A. Knudsen 19

Figure 7 *Source:* https://en.wikipedia.org/w/index.php?title=File:Two_elephants_carrying_the_fish_and_sun_insignia_of_Mughal_sovereignty.jpg *License:* Public Domain *Contributors:* Bill william compton, BotMultichill, Piggy58, Roland zh, Vssun 20

Figure 8 *Source:* https://en.wikipedia.org/w/index.php?title=File:Zaban_urdu_mualla.png *License:* GNU Free Documentation License *Contributors:* User:Wars 21

Figure 9 *Source:* https://en.wikipedia.org/w/index.php?title=File:Officer_of_the_Mughal_Army,_c.1585_(colour_litho).jpg *License:* Public Domain *Contributors:* Goldduck58, Roland zh 22

Figure 10 *Source:* https://en.wikipedia.org/w/index.php?title=File:Mughal_musket.png *Contributors:* DurChalen123, OgreBot 2 22

Image *Source:* https://en.wikipedia.org/w/index.php?title=File:Sher_Shah's_empire.png *License:* GNU Free Documentation License *Contributors:* BotMultichillT, EChastain, Ekabhishek, Electionworld, Officer, Quadell, Zykasaa 29

Image *Source:* https://en.wikipedia.org/w/index.php?title=File:Flag_of_India.svg *License:* Public Domain *Contributors:* Anomie, Jo-Jo Eumerus, Mifter 29

Image *Source:* https://en.wikipedia.org/w/index.php?title=File:Flag_of_Pakistan.svg *License:* Public Domain *Contributors:* User:Zscout370 ... 29

Image *Source:* https://en.wikipedia.org/w/index.php?title=File:Flag_of_Bangladesh.svg *License:* Public Domain *Contributors:* User:SKopp ... 29

Image *Source:* https://en.wikipedia.org/w/index.php?title=File:Flag_of_Nepal.svg *License:* Public Domain *Contributors:* Drawn by User:Pumbaa80, User:Achim1999 29

Figure 11 *Source:* https://en.wikipedia.org/w/index.php?title=File:Sohail_Gate_Rohtas_by_Usman_Ghani.jpg *License:* Creative Commons Attribution-Sharealike 3.0 *Contributors:* User:Usman.pg 30

Figure 12 *Source:* https://en.wikipedia.org/w/index.php?title=File:Sher_shah's_rupee.jpg *License:* GNU Free Documentation License *Contributors:* Angusmclellan, Ashashyou, Ekabhishek, Kalashnov, Nard the Bard, OgreBot 2, Roland zh, Saithilace, 1 anonymous edits 31

Image *Source:* https://en.wikipedia.org/w/index.php?title=File:Shershah.jpg *License:* Public Domain *Contributors:* Ustad Abdul Ghafur Breshna, a prominent Afghan artist from Kabul 31

Image *Source:* https://en.wikipedia.org/w/index.php?title=File:Commons-logo.svg *License:* logo *Contributors:* Anomie, Callanecc, CambridgeBayWeather, Jo-Jo Eumerus, RHaworth 32

Image *Source:* https://en.wikipedia.org/w/index.php?title=File:Union_flag_1606_(Kings_Colors).svg *Contributors:* - 32

Image *Source:* https://en.wikipedia.org/w/index.php?title=File:Royal_Standard_of_the_King_of_France.svg *License:* Creative Commons Attribution-Sharealike 3.0 *Contributors:* Sarang, Sodacan, Steinsplitter, Verdy p, 6 anonymous edits 32

Image *Source:* https://en.wikipedia.org/w/index.php?title=File:Flag_of_the_Dutch_East_India_Company.svg *License:* Public Domain *Contributors:* Himasaram 32

Image *Source:* https://en.wikipedia.org/w/index.php?title=File:Flag_of_Denmark.svg *License:* Public Domain *Contributors:* Madden 32

Image *Source:* https://en.wikipedia.org/w/index.php?title=File:Flag_of_the_Habsburg_Monarchy.svg *License:* Public Domain *Contributors:* Sir Iain, earlier version by ThrashedParanoid and Peregrine981.ThrashedParanoid 32

Image *Source:* https//en.wikipedia.org *License:* Public Domain *Contributors:* BotMultichillT, FA2010, Look2See1, Mattes, Mogelzahn, Robot Monk, Roland zh, Rosemania, User-duck 32

Figure 13 *Source:* https://en.wikipedia.org/w/index.php?title=File:Babur_and_Humayun.jpg *License:* Public Domain *Contributors:* Donaldduck100, Grey ghost, OgreBot 2, Roland zh 34

Figure 14 *Source:* https://en.wikipedia.org/w/index.php?title=File:Emperor_Akbar,_Los_Angeles_County_Museum_of_Art.jpg *License:* Public Domain *Contributors:* BotAdventures, Ghouston, OgreBot 2, Oursana, Rayaraya, RockyMasum 34

Figure 15 *Source:* https://en.wikipedia.org/w/index.php?title=File:Jahangir_of_India.jpg *License:* Public Domain *Contributors:* OgreBot 2, TRAJAN 117 35

Figure 16 *Source:* https://en.wikipedia.org/w/index.php?title=File:Royal_Peacock_Barge_LACMA_M.82.154.jpg *Contributors:* Fæ, JMCC1 . 37

Figure 17 *Source:* https://en.wikipedia.org/w/index.php?title=File:The_battle_of_Plassey,_June_23,_1757.jpg *License:* Public Domain *Contributors:* Cpt.a.haddock, OgreBot 2, The real Marcoman, శ్రీధర్ బబ్బూరి 38

Figure 18 *Source:* https://en.wikipedia.org/w/index.php?title=File:July_9_2005_-_The_Lahore_Fort-Frontview_of_Naulakha_pavallion.jpg *License:* GNU Free Documentation License *Contributors:* Ajreddy, Ali imran se, Ekabhishek, Gryffindor, Islescape, Jmabel, MGA73bot2, Martin H., Vivek Sarje, 3 anonymous edits 40

Figure 19 *Source:* https://en.wikipedia.org/w/index.php?title=File:Green_around_Lalbag_Fort.jpg *Contributors:* User:Samia ety 40

Figure 20 *Source:* https://en.wikipedia.org/w/index.php?title=File:Asiatic_Society_Bangladesh.jpg *Contributors:* User:Vaza12 41

Figure 21 *Source:* https://en.wikipedia.org/w/index.php?title=File:Charles_D'Oyly06.jpg *License:* Public Domain *Contributors:* Sir Charles D'Oyly, 7th Baronet 42

Figure 22 *Source:* https://en.wikipedia.org/w/index.php?title=File:Armenian_Church_of_the_Holy_Resurrection_in_Dhaka_(24310668205).jpg *License:* Creative Commons Attribution 2.0 *Contributors:* Afifa Afrin, Moheen Reeyad 43

Figure 23 *Source:* https://en.wikipedia.org/w/index.php?title=File:De_handelsloge_van_de_VOC_in_Hougly_in_Bengalen_Rijksmuseum_SK-A-4282.jpeg *License:* Creative Commons Zero *Contributors:* A.Savin, Arjuno3, Bodhisattwa, BotMultichillT, Bukk, Clarice Reis, Fæ, Jdx, Moheen Reeyad, Revent, Rudolphous, Sailko, Vincent Steenberg, Well-Informed Optimist, आशीष भटनागर 44

Figure 24 *Source:* https://en.wikipedia.org/w/index.php?title=File:Model_of_Bara_Katra.png *Contributors:* User:Fez Cap 12 45

Figure 25 *Source:* https://en.wikipedia.org/w/index.php?title=File:Renaldis_muslin_woman.jpg *License:* Public Domain *Contributors:* Austriacus, Bazaan, Bukk, JKhan20, Mabalu, Michael Barera, Multichill, Pitke, Themadchopper, Zolo 47

Figure 26 *Source:* https://en.wikipedia.org/w/index.php?title=File:Bengal_in_16th_century.jpg *License:* Creative Commons Zero *Contributors:* Redwanviruss, Slick 48

Figure 27 *Source:* https://en.wikipedia.org/w/index.php?title=File:Raja_Man_Singh_the_Great_,_Of_Amer.jpg *License:* Public Domain *Contributors:* Alexander585, Rayaraya, శ్రీధర్బాబు 50
Figure 28 *Source:* https://en.wikipedia.org/w/index.php?title=File:Nawab_Sháyista_Khán.jpg *License:* Public Domain *Contributors:* Rayaraya, RockyMasum, Roland zh, Sridhar1000 53
Figure 29 *Source:* https://en.wikipedia.org/w/index.php?title=File:Azam_shah.jpg *License:* Public Domain *Contributors:* Rayaraya, Roland zh, Sridhar1000 53
Figure 30 *Source:* https://en.wikipedia.org/w/index.php?title=File:Azim_us-Shan_Bahadur.jpg *License:* Public Domain *Contributors:* JMCC1, Johnbod, OgreBot 2, Rayaraya, RockyMasum 54
Image *Source:* https://en.wikipedia.org/w/index.php?title=File:Murshid_Quli_Jafar_Khan.jpg *License:* Public Domain *Contributors:* Gbarta, Jagadhatri, Sng common, Zykasaa, 1 anonymous edits 52
Image *Source:* https://en.wikipedia.org/w/index.php?title=File:Sarfaraz_Khan.jpg *License:* Public Domain *Contributors:* Jcb, Magog the Ogre, Rayaraya 52
Image *Source:* https://en.wikipedia.org/w/index.php?title=File:Shuja-ud-Din_Muhammad_Khan.jpg *Contributors:* Jcb, Magog the Ogre, OgreBot 2, Rayaraya, RockyMasum, 1 anonymous edits 52
Image *Source:* https://en.wikipedia.org/w/index.php?title=File:Alivardi_Khan.jpg *License:* Public Domain *Contributors:* Calliopejen1, Info-farmer, Rayaraya, Roland zh, Utcursch 52
Image *Source:* https://en.wikipedia.org/w/index.php?title=File:Siraj_ud-Daulah.jpg *License:* Public Domain *Contributors:* Aschroet, Magog the Ogre, Moheen Reeyad, Rayaraya, RockyMasum, Sminthopsis84 52
Image *Source:* https://en.wikipedia.org/w/index.php?title=File:India1760_1905.jpg *License:* Public Domain *Contributors:* Charles Colbeck 55
Image *Source:* https://en.wikipedia.org/w/index.php?title=File:North_Gateway_-_Rear_Side_-_Stupa_1_-_Sanchi_Hill_2013-02-21_4480-4481.JPG *License:* Creative Commons Attribution 3.0 *Contributors:* Biswarup Ganguly 56
Figure 31 *Source:* https://en.wikipedia.org/w/index.php?title=File:Shivaji_British_Museum.jpg *License:* Public Domain *Contributors:* Donaldduck100, JMCC1, KD-pandat-srinagar, KylieTastic, Martin H., Nick Number, OgreBot 2, Onkuchia, Redtigerxyz, Sujit=scholar, मालोजीराव 58
Figure 32 *Source:* https://en.wikipedia.org/w/index.php?title=File:Sambhaji_Maharaj.JPG *License:* GNU Free Documentation License *Contributors:* Apricus 59
Image *Source:* https://en.wikipedia.org/w/index.php?title=File:Shaniwarwada_gate.JPG *License:* Creative Commons Attribution-Sharealike 3.0 *Contributors:* User:Ashok Bagade 61
Image *Source:* https://en.wikipedia.org/w/index.php?title=File:The_entrance_of_Shaniwar_Wada..JPG *License:* Creative Commons Attribution-Sharealike 3.0 *Contributors:* User:Aakash.gautam 61
Figure 33 *Source:* https://en.wikipedia.org/w/index.php?title=File:Peshwa_Balaji_Vishwanath.jpg *License:* Creative Commons Attribution-Sharealike 3.0 *Contributors:* User:Amit20081980 61
Figure 34 *Source:* https://en.wikipedia.org/w/index.php?title=File:Peshwa_Baji_Rao_I_riding_horse.jpg *License:* Public Domain *Contributors:* Mughal School 62
Figure 35 *Source:* https://en.wikipedia.org/w/index.php?title=File:Peshwa_Balaji_Bajirao.jpg *License:* Public Domain *Contributors:* Gbarta, Onepranav, Rayaraya 63
Image *Source:* https://en.wikipedia.org/w/index.php?title=File:Maratha_Armor.jpg *License:* Creative Commons Attribution-Sharealike 3.0 *Contributors:* User:Pebble101 65
Image *Source:* https://en.wikipedia.org/w/index.php?title=File:Maratha_Armour.jpg *License:* Creative Commons Attribution-Sharealike 3.0 *Contributors:* User:Pebble101 66
Figure 36 *Source:* https://en.wikipedia.org/w/index.php?title=File:His_Highness_Madhavrao_Peshwa.JPG *License:* Creative Commons Attribution-Sharealike 3.0 *Contributors:* User:Amit20081980 67
Figure 37 *Source:* https://en.wikipedia.org/w/index.php?title=File:Mahadaji_Sindhia.jpg *License:* Public Domain *Contributors:* James Wales . 68
Figure 38 *Source:* https://en.wikipedia.org/w/index.php?title=File:The_Maharahaj_of_Gwalior_Before_His_Palace_ca_1887.jpg *License:* Public Domain *Contributors:* Aschroet, BeachHome, Oo91, Roland zh, Slowking4 70
Figure 39 *Source:* https://en.wikipedia.org/w/index.php?title=File:Maratha_British_Treaty.JPG *Contributors:* User:Amit20081980∼commonswiki 72
Figure 40 *Source:* https//en.wikipedia.org *License:* Public Domain *Contributors:* BotMultichill, Rayaraya, Sankalpdravid, Wmpearl 73
Figure 41 *Source:* https//en.wikipedia.org *License:* Public Domain *Contributors:* User:Innotata 74
Figure 42 *Source:* https://en.wikipedia.org/w/index.php?title=File:Peshwa_Baji_Rao_II.jpg *License:* Public Domain *Contributors:* OgreBot 2, Rayaraya, Túrelio 74
Figure 43 *Source:* https://en.wikipedia.org/w/index.php?title=File:Maratha_darbar.jpg *License:* Public Domain *Contributors:* Daderot, Roland zh, Sridhar1000, Themightyquill, Thib Phil 75
Figure 44 *Source:* https://en.wikipedia.org/w/index.php?title=File:MWI3371-Sivaji-CNG73.1186-2.81g-7h.jpg *License:* Creative Commons Attribution-Sharealike 3.0 *Contributors:* User:FaisalAbbasid 77
Figure 45 *Source:* https://en.wikipedia.org/w/index.php?title=File:Maratha_ships_scroll.jpg *License:* Public Domain *Contributors:* Andres rojas22∼commonswiki, OgreBot 2, Pratishkhedekar 79
Figure 46 *Source:* https://en.wikipedia.org/w/index.php?title=File:Maratha-Grabs-and-Gallivats-attacking-an-English-Ship.jpg *License:* Public Domain *Contributors:* Broichmore, Pratishkhedekar 81
Figure 47 *Source:* https://en.wikipedia.org/w/index.php?title=File:Arms_of_Maratha_History_of_India_1906.jpg *Contributors:* Internet Archive Book Images 82
Figure 48 *Source:* https://en.wikipedia.org/w/index.php?title=File:Maratha_Peshwa_with_his_Courtiers.jpg *License:* Public Domain *Contributors:* Denniss, Pratishkhedekar, Rayaraya, Roland zh, Sridhar1000, Utcursch 83
Figure 49 *Source:* https://en.wikipedia.org/w/index.php?title=File:IGI1908India1765a.jpg *Contributors:* J. G. Bartholomew and Sons. Edinburgh 86
Figure 50 *Source:* https://en.wikipedia.org/w/index.php?title=File:Thanjavur_Maratha_Palace_Darbar_Hall.jpg *License:* Creative Commons Attribution-Sharealike 3.0 *Contributors:* User:Kalanidhi 87
Image *Source:* https://en.wikipedia.org/w/index.php?title=File:Coat_of_arms_of_the_East_India_Company.svg *License:* Creative Commons Attribution-Sharealike 3.0,2.5,2.0,1.0 *Contributors:* TRAJAN 117 90
Image *Source:* https://en.wikipedia.org/w/index.php?title=File:Flag_of_Mysore.svg *License:* Public Domain *Contributors:* Lucas Larson, based on work of MChew 91
Image *Source:* https://en.wikipedia.org/w/index.php?title=File:Flag_of_the_British_Straits_Settlements_(1874-1942).svg *Contributors:* - 91
Image *Source:* https://en.wikipedia.org/w/index.php?title=File:Flag_of_Bahrain.svg *License:* Public Domain *Contributors:* Source: Drawn by User:SKopp, rewritten by User:Zscout370 91
Image *Source:* https://en.wikipedia.org/w/index.php?title=File:Flag_of_the_People's_Republic_of_China.svg *License:* Public Domain *Contributors:* Drawn by User:SKopp, redrawn by User:Denelson83 and User:Zscout370 Recode by cs:User:-xfi- (code), User:Shizhao (colors 91
Image *Source:* https://en.wikipedia.org/w/index.php?title=File:Flag_of_Christmas_Island.svg *License:* Public Domain *Contributors:* Anime Addict AA, Christmas Island, Cycn, Denelson83, Docu, Erribas, Fry1989, Homo lupus, Hoshie, Leyo, Ludger1961, Mattes, Ninane, Ricordisamoa, SiBr4, TFCforever, Telim tor, Wknight94, Xufanc, Zscout370, 1 anonymous edits 91
Image *Source:* https://en.wikipedia.org/w/index.php?title=File:Flag_of_the_Cocos_(Keeling)_Islands.svg *License:* Public Domain *Contributors:* User:Denelson83 91
Image *Source:* https://en.wikipedia.org/w/index.php?title=File:Flag_of_Kuwait.svg *License:* Public Domain *Contributors:* User:SKopp 91
Image *Source:* https://en.wikipedia.org/w/index.php?title=File:Flag_of_Malaysia.svg *Contributors:* , and 91
Image *Source:* https://en.wikipedia.org/w/index.php?title=File:Flag_of_Maldives.svg *License:* Public Domain *Contributors:* user:Nightstallion 91
Image *Source:* https://en.wikipedia.org/w/index.php?title=File:Flag_of_Myanmar.svg *License:* Public Domain *Contributors:* *drew∼commonswiki, AnonMoos, Artix Kreiger, Cathy Richards, CommonsDelinker, Cycn, Daphne Lantier, Dinsdagskind, Duduziq, Fry1989, Garam, Gunkarta, Homo lupus, INeverCry, Josegeographic, Klemen Kocjancic, Legnaw, Mason Decker, Mattes, Neq00, Nightstallion, Pixeltoo, Rfc1394, Rodejong, Sangjinhwa, Sarang, SeNeKa∼commonswiki, SiBr4, Sixflashphoto, Stevanb, TFerenczy, Takahara Osaka, Techman224, ThomasPusch, Túrelio, UnreifeKirsche, Vividuppers, WikipediaMaster, Winzipas, Xiengyod∼commonswiki, Zscout370, 白布飘扬 , 21 anonymous edits 91
Image *Source:* https://en.wikipedia.org/w/index.php?title=File:Flag_of_Oman.svg *License:* Public Domain *Contributors:* *drew∼commonswiki, Ahmed.1993, Alkari, Allforrous, Bast64∼commonswiki, Cycn, Daphne Lantier, Duduziq, Fry1989, Happenstance, Homo lupus, Ittihadawi∼commonswiki, Jetijones, Klemen Kocjancic, Liftarn, Mattes, Neq00, Nightstallion, NikNaks, OAlexander∼commonswiki, Orange Tuesday, Pumbaa80, Rfc1394, Ricordisamoa, SiBr4, ThomasPusch, Zscout370, 1 anonymous edits 91
Image *Source:* https://en.wikipedia.org/w/index.php?title=File:Flag_of_Qatar.svg *License:* Public Domain *Contributors:* (of code) 91
Image *Source:* https://en.wikipedia.org/w/index.php?title=File:Flag_of_Saudi_Arabia.svg *License:* Public Domain *Contributors:* Alhadramy Alkendy, Alkari, Ancintosh, Anime Addict AA, AnonMoos, Bobika, Brian Ammon, CommonsDelinker, Cycn, Denelson83, Duduziq, Ekabhishek, Er Komandante, FDRMRZUSA, Fabioravanelli, File Upload Bot (Magnus Manske), Fry1989, Gazimagomedov, Herbythyme, Homo lupus, INeverCry, Itsemurhaja, Jeff G., Klemen Kocjancic, Lokal Profil, Love Krittaya, Love monju, Mattes, Menasim, Meno25, Mnmazur, Mohammed alkhater, Nagy, Nard the Bard,

Nightstallion, Palosirkka, Pitke, Pmsyyz, Ranveig, Ratatosk, Reisio, Ricordisamoa, Saibo, Sarang, SiBr4, Wouterhagens, Zscout370, Zyido, 17 anonymous edits ... 91
Image *Source:* https://en.wikipedia.org/w/index.php?title=File:Flag_of_Singapore.svg *License:* Public Domain *Contributors:* Various ... 91
Image *Source:* https://en.wikipedia.org/w/index.php?title=File:Flag_of_Somalia.svg *License:* Public Domain *Contributors:* see upload history . 91
Image *Source:* https://en.wikipedia.org/w/index.php?title=File:Flag_of_Sri_Lanka.svg *License:* Public Domain *Contributors:* Zscout370 ... 91
Image *Source:* https://en.wikipedia.org/w/index.php?title=File:Flag_of_the_United_Arab_Emirates.svg *License:* Public Domain *Contributors:* Anime Addict AA, Avala, Dbenbenn, Denniss, Duduziq, F l a n k e r, Fry1989, Fukaumi, Gryffindor, Guanaco, Homo lupus, JuTa, Kacir, Klemen Kocjancic, Krun, Ludger1961, Madden, Misisanta97, Neq00, Nightstallion, Piccadilly Circus∼commonswiki, Pmsyyz, RamzyAbueita∼commonswiki, Ricordisamoa, Schmarrnintelligenz, SiBr4, Zscout370, 3.Букобар, 5 anonymous edits ... 91
Image *Source:* https://en.wikipedia.org/w/index.php?title=File:Flag_of_Yemen.svg *License:* Public Domain *Contributors:* Anime Addict AA, AnonMoos, Benzoyl, CemDemirkartal, David Levy, Duduziq, Erlenmeyer, F. F. Fjodor, Flad, Fry1989, Homo lupus, Jdx, Klemen Kocjancic, Krun, Neq00, Nightstallion, Pitke, Reisio, Rodejong, SiBr4, Themadchopper, ThomasPusch, Urmas, Wikiborg, Zaccarias, Zscout370, 7 anonymous edits ... 91
Image *Source:* https://en.wikipedia.org/w/index.php?title=File:IndiaPolitical1893ConstablesHandAtlas.jpg *Contributors:* John Bartholomew and Co., Edinburgh ... 92
Image *Source:* https://en.wikipedia.org/w/index.php?title=File:India1765and1805b.jpg *License:* Public Domain *Contributors:* Edinburgh Geographical Institute ... 95
Image *Source:* https://en.wikipedia.org/w/index.php?title=File:India1837to1857.jpg *License:* Public Domain *Contributors:* Edinburgh Geographical Institute ... 95
Image *Source:* https://en.wikipedia.org/w/index.php?title=File:Company_rule_calcutta_from_ftwilliam.jpg *License:* Public Domain *Contributors:* Charles Matthews, DBigXray, Magog the Ogre, Monoklon, OgreBot 2 ... 98
Image *Source:* https://en.wikipedia.org/w/index.php?title=File:Company_rule_government_hse_fort_stgeorge2.jpg *License:* Public Domain *Contributors:* Aavindraa, File Upload Bot (Magnus Manske), OgreBot 2, Verne Equinox ... 98
Image *Source:* https://en.wikipedia.org/w/index.php?title=File:Warren_Hastings_greyscale.jpg *License:* Public Domain *Contributors:* Ekabhishek, Kilom691, Kintetsubuffalo, Nataraja∼commonswiki, Nicke L, Ras67, Sassf, Shakko, Victuallers ... 98
Image *Source:* https://en.wikipedia.org/w/index.php?title=File:Company_rule_trial_warren_hastings2.jpg *License:* Public Domain *Contributors:* Engraver; Pollard, R. Aquatinter; Jukes, F. Artist; Dayes, E. Medium; Aquatint ... 99
Figure 51 *Source:* https://en.wikipedia.org/w/index.php?title=File:LordClive.jpg *License:* Public Domain *Contributors:* 1Veertje, Adam sk∼commonswiki, BotMultichill, Ecummenic, Jane023, Laura1822, Mutter Erde, O (bot), Woudloper ... 99
Image *Source:* https://en.wikipedia.org/w/index.php?title=File:Company_rule_riverside_scene2_bengal1860.jpg *Contributors:* Unknown photographer ... 102
Image *Source:* https://en.wikipedia.org/w/index.php?title=File:Company_rule_kochh_mandai2_woman1860.jpg *Contributors:* Unknown photographer ... 102
Image *Source:* https://en.wikipedia.org/w/index.php?title=File:Company_rule_paddy_fields_madras2.jpg *Contributors:* Photographer: Nicholas & Co. ... 103
Image *Source:* https://en.wikipedia.org/w/index.php?title=File:EIC-half-anna-coin-1835.jpg *License:* Public Domain *Contributors:* User:Fowler&fowler ... 103
Figure 52 *Source:* https://en.wikipedia.org/w/index.php?title=File:Lord_Cornwallis.jpg *License:* Public Domain *Contributors:* Auntof6, Beria, Boo-Boo Baroo, BotMultichillT, Connormah, Ecummenic, Ekabhishek, File Upload Bot (Magnus Manske), Ham II, Hsarrazin, Laura1822, Magicpiano, Materialscientist, Polygnotos, Zolo, 2 anonymous edits ... 105
Figure 53 *Source:* https://en.wikipedia.org/w/index.php?title=File:Sir_Thomas_Munro,_1st_Baronet.jpg *License:* Public Domain *Contributors:* Sanfy ... 106
Image *Source:* https://en.wikipedia.org/w/index.php?title=File:Royal_artillery_encampment_arcot1804.jpg *License:* Public Domain *Contributors:* Hunter, James (d. 1792) ... 108
Image *Source:* https://en.wikipedia.org/w/index.php?title=File:Sepoys_tipoos_palacebangalore1804.jpg *License:* Public Domain *Contributors:* Hunter, James (d. 1792) ... 108
Image *Source:* https://en.wikipedia.org/w/index.php?title=File:Military_orphan_school_calcutta1794.jpg *License:* Public Domain *Contributors:* Baillie, William (1752/3-1799) ... 108
Image *Source:* https://en.wikipedia.org/w/index.php?title=File:Prinsep_new_writerEICservice1822.jpg *License:* Public Domain *Contributors:* Prinsep, William (1794-1874) ... 109
Image *Source:* https://en.wikipedia.org/w/index.php?title=File:East_india_company_factory_sonargaon2.jpg *Contributors:* W. Brennand ... 112
Image *Source:* https://en.wikipedia.org/w/index.php?title=File:West_view_mellor_muslin_mill2.jpg *License:* Public Domain *Contributors:* Joseph Parry (1744-1826) ... 112
Image *Source:* https://en.wikipedia.org/w/index.php?title=File:Opium_godown_store_patna2.jpg *Contributors:* User:Fowler&fowler ... 113
Image *Source:* https://en.wikipedia.org/w/index.php?title=File:Indigo_factory_bengal2.jpg *Contributors:* User:Fowler&fowler ... 113
Image *Source:* https://en.wikipedia.org/w/index.php?title=File:Thomas_strange_house_madras1811.jpg *License:* Public Domain *Contributors:* Porter, John Young (1780-1812) ... 115
Image *Source:* https://en.wikipedia.org/w/index.php?title=File:Chowringheeroad_adalat1833.jpg *License:* Public Domain *Contributors:* Wood, William (floruitfl. 1827-1833) ... 115
Image *Source:* https://en.wikipedia.org/w/index.php?title=File:The_Native_Judges.jpg *License:* Public Domain *Contributors:* MGA73bot2, Magog the Ogre, Pratishkhedekar, Roland zh, Sridhar1000, 1 anonymous edits ... 115
Figure 54 *Source:* https://en.wikipedia.org/w/index.php?title=File:Bombay_courthouse1850.jpg *Contributors:* Charles Scott ... 116
Image *Source:* https://en.wikipedia.org/w/index.php?title=File:Zoffany-Impey-family-Calcutta.jpg *License:* Public Domain *Contributors:* Bejnar, Shakko ... 118
Image *Source:* https://en.wikipedia.org/w/index.php?title=File:Hindu_college_calcutta1851.jpg *License:* Public Domain *Contributors:* Frederick Feibig ... 119
Image *Source:* https://en.wikipedia.org/w/index.php?title=File:Student_hindoo_college_calcutta1844.jpg *License:* Public Domain *Contributors:* Emily Eden ... 119
Image *Source:* https://en.wikipedia.org/w/index.php?title=File:Grant_medical_college1844.jpg *License:* Public Domain *Contributors:* G. R. Sargeant ... 120
Image *Source:* https://en.wikipedia.org/w/index.php?title=File:Grant_med_college_jjhospital1855.jpg *License:* Public Domain *Contributors:* Unknown photographer (from Vibar Collection of Views of South India, British Library) ... 120
Image *Source:* https://en.wikipedia.org/w/index.php?title=File:General_postoffice_calcutta1833.jpg *License:* Public Domain *Contributors:* Wood, William (floruitfl. 1827-1833) ... 124
Image *Source:* https://en.wikipedia.org/w/index.php?title=File:India_fouranna_blueandred1854.jpg *License:* Public Domain *Contributors:* PrinterSurveyor-General's Office, Calcutt ... 124
Image *Source:* https://en.wikipedia.org/w/index.php?title=File:Semaphore_telegraph_bihar1823.jpg *License:* Public Domain *Contributors:* D'Oyly, Sir Charles (1781-1845) ... 124
Image *Source:* https://en.wikipedia.org/w/index.php?title=File:Dapoorie_viaduct_bombay1855.jpg *License:* Public Domain *Contributors:* Publisher: 'Vibart Collection of Views in South India'. Original uploader was Fowler&fowler at en.wikipedia ... 127
Image *Source:* https://en.wikipedia.org/w/index.php?title=File:India_railways_trunklines_1853.jpg *Contributors:* J. Bartholomew ... 127
Image *Source:* https://en.wikipedia.org/w/index.php?title=File:First_locomotive_india1854_photo1894.jpg *Contributors:* Unknown ... 128
Image *Source:* https://en.wikipedia.org/w/index.php?title=File:Railway_bridge_bhor_ghaut_incline1855.jpg *Contributors:* Unknown; publisher: 'Vibart Collection of Views in South India' ... 128
Figure 55 *Source:* https://en.wikipedia.org/w/index.php?title=File:IndianRailways1871b.jpg *License:* Public Domain *Contributors:* Saunders Geographers ... 129
Image *Source:* https://en.wikipedia.org/w/index.php?title=File:Ganges_canal_roorkee1860.jpg *License:* Public Domain *Contributors:* Simpson, William (1823-1899) ... 131
Image *Source:* https://en.wikipedia.org/w/index.php?title=File:GangesCanalRoorkee2008.jpg *License:* Creative Commons Attribution-Sharealike 3.0 *Contributors:* Fowler&fowler«Talk» ... 131
Image *Source:* https://en.wikipedia.org/w/index.php?title=File:Headworks_ganges_canal_haridwar1860.jpg *Contributors:* Samuel Bourne (died 1912) ... 131
Image *Source:* https://en.wikipedia.org/w/index.php?title=File:Headworks_ganges_canal_haridwar2008a.jpg *License:* Creative Commons Attribution-Sharealike 3.0 *Contributors:* Fowler&fowler«Talk» ... 132
Figure 56 *Source:* https://en.wikipedia.org/w/index.php?title=File:GangesCanal2.jpg *Contributors:* R. Bartholomew and Sons, Edinburgh ... 133
Image *Source:* https://en.wikipedia.org/w/index.php?title=File:PD-icon.svg *License:* Public Domain *Contributors:* Alex.muller, Anomie, Anonymous Dissident, CBM, Jo-Jo Eumerus, MBisanz, PBS, Quadell, Rocket000, Strangerer, Timotheus Canens, 1 anonymous edits ... 139
Image *Source:* https://en.wikipedia.org/w/index.php?title=File:Coat_of_arms_of_Kingdom_of_Mysore.svg *License:* Creative Commons Zero *Contributors:* User:Samhanin ... 140

Image *Source:* https://en.wikipedia.org/w/index.php?title=File:Indian_Mysore_Kingdom_1784_map.svg *License:* Creative Commons Attribution-Sharealike 3.0 *Contributors:* Nikotins, Planemad, Roland zh, Sarvagnya 140

Image *Source:* https://en.wikipedia.org/w/index.php?title=File:Flag_of_vijaynagara.jpg *Contributors:* User:Vydya.areyur 141

Figure 57 *Source:* https://en.wikipedia.org/w/index.php?title=File:Joppen1907MysoreChickDeoWadiyar1704.jpg *Contributors:* Charles Joppen 142

Figure 58 *Source:* https://en.wikipedia.org/w/index.php?title=File:Suffren_meeting_with_Haider_Ali_J_B_Morret_engraving_1789.jpg *Contributors:* - 145

Figure 59 *Source:* https://en.wikipedia.org/w/index.php?title=File:The_North_Entrance_Into_The_Fort_Of_Bangalore_-with_Tipu's_flag_flying-.jpg *License:* Public Domain *Contributors:* Hunter, James (d. 1792 145

Figure 60 *Source:* https://en.wikipedia.org/w/index.php?title=File:TipuSultan1790.jpg *License:* Creative Commons Attribution-Sharealike 3.0 *Contributors:* Anonymous artist from Mysore, India. 146

Figure 61 *Source:* https://en.wikipedia.org/w/index.php?title=File:Battle_of_pollilur.jpg *License:* Public Domain *Contributors:* BotMultichill, File Upload Bot (Magnus Manske), OgreBot 2, Roland zh, 2 anonymous edits 146

Figure 62 *Source:* https://en.wikipedia.org/w/index.php?title=File:Gillray_-_The_Coming-on_of_the_monsoons_-_or_-_the_retreat_from_Seringapatam.jpg *License:* Public Domain *Contributors:* Elkost, Ham II, Jarble, Magicpiano, Roland zh, 1 anonymous edits 147

Figure 63 *Source:* https//en.wikipedia.org *License:* Public Domain *Contributors:* DarwIn, Nyttend, Rd232, Roland zh, Sridhar1000 150

Figure 64 *Source:* https://en.wikipedia.org/w/index.php?title=File:Mysore_Palace_Morning.jpg *Contributors:* Irvan Ary Maulana, Jayarathina, Julia W, Muhammad Mahdi Karim, OgreBot 2, Pied Hornbill, Roland zh, Stefan2 150

Figure 65 *Source:* https://en.wikipedia.org/w/index.php?title=File:Temple_tank_(Pushkarni)_at_Shravanabelagola.jpg *License:* Creative Commons Attribution-Sharealike 3.0 *Contributors:* Cpt.a.haddock, G41rn8, MGA73bot2, Magog the Ogre, OgreBot 2, Roland zh 157

Figure 66 *Source:* https://en.wikipedia.org/w/index.php?title=File:Shweta_Varahaswamy_temple_in_Mysore.jpg *License:* Creative Commons Attribution-Sharealike 3.0 *Contributors:* Dineshkannambadi, MGA73bot2, Magog the Ogre, OgreBot 2, Roland zh 158

Figure 67 *Source:* https://en.wikipedia.org/w/index.php?title=File:Mysore_university_building.JPG *License:* Creative Commons Attribution-Sharealike 3.0 *Contributors:* Pratheepps 160

Figure 68 *Source:* https://en.wikipedia.org/w/index.php?title=File:Intro.bmp.jpg *License:* Public Domain *Contributors:* OgreBot 2, Sreejithk2000 161

Figure 69 *Source:* https://en.wikipedia.org/w/index.php?title=File:Veena_Subbanna_Seshanna_1902.jpg *License:* Public Domain *Contributors:* BD2412, Hyacinth, ImpuMozhi, Sfan00 IMG 163

Figure 70 *Source:* https://en.wikipedia.org/w/index.php?title=File:Mysore_Palace,_India_(photo_-_Jim_Ankan_Deka).jpg *License:* Creative Commons Attribution-Sharealike 3.0 *Contributors:* User:Jimankan 166

Figure 71 *Source:* https://en.wikipedia.org/w/index.php?title=File:Chamundeshwari_Temple_Mysore_2.jpg *License:* GNU Free Documentation License *Contributors:* MGA73bot2, Magog the Ogre, Roland zh 166

Figure 72 *Source:* https://en.wikipedia.org/w/index.php?title=File:Jagan_mohan_palace2.jpg *License:* Public domain *Contributors:* Vivek Sinha 167

Figure 73 *Source:* https://en.wikipedia.org/w/index.php?title=File:Gumbaz.jpg *License:* Public domain *Contributors:* File Upload Bot (Magnus Manske), Magog the Ogre, Roland zh 168

Figure 74 *Source:* https://en.wikipedia.org/w/index.php?title=File:Lalitha_mahal_mysore_ml_wiki.JPG *License:* Creative Commons Attribution-Sharealike 3.0 *Contributors:* Ezhuttukari 168

Image *Source:* https://en.wikipedia.org/w/index.php?title=File:Cscr-featured.svg *License:* GNU Lesser General Public License *Contributors:* Anomie 171

Image *Source:* https://en.wikipedia.org/w/index.php?title=File:Sikh_Empire_tri-lingual.jpg *Contributors:* User:Jangvijay 172

Image *Source:* https://en.wikipedia.org/w/index.php?title=File:Kattar_Dhal_Talwar.jpg *Contributors:* User:Shersingh8 173

Image *Source:* https://en.wikipedia.org/w/index.php?title=File:Flag_of_Herat_until_1842.svg *License:* Public Domain *Contributors:* Orange Tuesday (talk) 173

Image *Source:* https://en.wikipedia.org/w/index.php?title=File:Jammu-Kashmir-flag-1936-1953.gif *License:* Creative Commons Attribution-Sharealike 3.0 *Contributors:* File Upload Bot (Magnus Manske), Sreejithk2000 173

Image *Source:* https://en.wikipedia.org/w/index.php?title=File:Maharaj_Ranjit_Singh.jpg *License:* Public Domain *Contributors:* James smith2, Justass, OgreBot 2, Roland zh, Sidsahu 176

Image *Source:* https://en.wikipedia.org/w/index.php?title=File:Ranjit_Singh's_golden_throne.jpg *License:* GNU Free Documentation License *Contributors:* BotMultichill, File Upload Bot (Magnus Manske), Johnbod, MGA73bot2, NotFromUtrecht, OgreBot 2, Rillke, Roland zh, Sailko 177

Image *Source:* https://en.wikipedia.org/w/index.php?title=File:Ranjit_Singh_holding_court_-_Court_and_Camp_of_Runjeet_Singh_-_pg203.jpg *Contributors:* artwork and book by W. G. Osbourne (1804–1888) 177

Image *Source:* https://en.wikipedia.org/w/index.php?title=File:SORS1.jpg *Contributors:* User:Mhaidersajjad 177

Figure 75 *Source:* https://en.wikipedia.org/w/index.php?title=File:Joppen1907India1805a.jpg *Contributors:* Justus Perthes, Gotha./Charles Joppen 179

Image *Source:* https://en.wikipedia.org/w/index.php?title=File:Golden_Temple_India.jpg *License:* Creative Commons Attribution-Sharealike 2.0 *Contributors:* Abhishekjoshi, Daniel Case, Ekabhishek, Indianhilbilly, Look2See1, Mattes, Roland zh, 1 anonymous edits 180

Image *Source:* https://en.wikipedia.org/w/index.php?title=File:Benares-_The_Golden_Temple,_India,_ca._1915_(IMP-CSCNWW33-OS14-66).jpg *Contributors:* Auntof6, Fæ, OgreBot 2, Oo91, Redtigerxyz, Roland zh 180

Figure 76 *Source:* https://en.wikipedia.org/w/index.php?title=File:Bataille_de_Sobraon.jpg *License:* Public Domain *Contributors:* AnRo0002, Barbe-Noire, O (bot), Roland zh 181

Figure 77 *Source:* https://en.wikipedia.org/w/index.php?title=File:Bataille_d'Aliwal_1.jpg *License:* Public Domain *Contributors:* Barbe-Noire, Hohum, Man vyi, Zhuyifei1999, 1 anonymous edits 182

Image *Source:* https://en.wikipedia.org/w/index.php?title=File:Indian_Rebellion_of_1857.jpg *License:* Public Domain *Contributors:* Athaenara, File Upload Bot (Magnus Manske), Grandiose, Krinkle, Nizil Shah, OgreBot 2, Rd232, Roland zh, Yann, 1 anonymous edits 185

Image *Source:* https://en.wikipedia.org/w/index.php?title=File:Gwalior_flag.svg *License:* Public Domain *Contributors:* Robert Alfers 186

Image *Source:* https://en.wikipedia.org/w/index.php?title=File:Flag_of_Awadh.svg *License:* Creative Commons Attribution-Sharealike 3.0 *Contributors:* User:Utcursch 186

Image *Source:* https://en.wikipedia.org/w/index.php?title=File:Flag_of_the_United_Kingdom.svg *License:* Public Domain *Contributors:* Anomie, Good Olfactory, Jo-Jo Eumerus, MSGJ, Mifter 186

Image *Source:* https://en.wikipedia.org/w/index.php?title=File:Flag_of_Nepal_(19th_century-1962).svg *License:* Creative Commons Attribution-Sharealike 3.0 *Contributors:* Orange Tuesday 186

Image *Source:* https://en.wikipedia.org/w/index.php?title=File:Flag_of_Tibet.svg *License:* Public Domain *Contributors:* A ri gi bod, AbuDun, Alkari, Anime Addict AA, Arilang1234, BartekChom, ChongDae, Cmadler, Daphne Lantier, Denelson83, Fry1989, Gryffindor, Homo lupus, Hottentot∼commonswiki, Inhorw, MAXXX-309, MB298, Marco Plassio, Mattes, Nightstallion, Reisio, Sarang, SiBr4, Sweeper tamonten, Theo10011, Thisisbossi, Triton, Vinne2, W., Wereldburger758, Wylve, 12 anonymous edits 186

Image *Source:* https://en.wikipedia.org/w/index.php?title=File:Drapeau_Ajaigarh.png *License:* GNU Free Documentation License *Contributors:* User Nataraja on fr.wikipedia 186

Image *Source:* https://en.wikipedia.org/w/index.php?title=File:Alwar_flag.svg *License:* Public Domain *Contributors:* Robert Alfers 186

Image *Source:* https://en.wikipedia.org/w/index.php?title=File:Flag_of_Bharatpur.svg *License:* Public domain *Contributors:* Orange Tuesday (talk) 186

Image *Source:* https://en.wikipedia.org/w/index.php?title=File:Drapeau_Bhopal.svg *License:* Public Domain *Contributors:* User:Ricordisamoa 186

Image *Source:* https://en.wikipedia.org/w/index.php?title=File:Flag_of_Bikaner.svg *License:* Public Domain *Contributors:* Robert Alfers 186

Image *Source:* https://en.wikipedia.org/w/index.php?title=File:Bundi.svg *Contributors:* - 186

Image *Source:* https://en.wikipedia.org/w/index.php?title=File:Asafia_flag_of_Hyderabad_State.png *License:* Public Domain *Contributors:* Yenemus 186

Image *Source:* https://en.wikipedia.org/w/index.php?title=File:Flag_of_Jaipur.svg *License:* Public Domain *Contributors:* Robert Alfers 186

Image *Source:* https://en.wikipedia.org/w/index.php?title=File:Jaoraflag.png *License:* Creative Commons Attribution-Sharealike 3.0 *Contributors:* OgreBot 2, Xufanc 186

Image *Source:* https://en.wikipedia.org/w/index.php?title=File:Flag_of_Jodhpur.svg *License:* Public Domain *Contributors:* PD 186

Image *Source:* https://en.wikipedia.org/w/index.php?title=File:Kapurthala_flag.svg *License:* Public Domain *Contributors:* Robert Alfers 186

Image *Source:* https://en.wikipedia.org/w/index.php?title=File:Flag_Jammu_Kashmir.png *License:* Public Domain *Contributors:* Mikrobølgeovn 186

Image *Source:* https://en.wikipedia.org/w/index.php?title=File:Keonjharflag.jpg *License:* Creative Commons Attribution-Sharealike 3.0 *Contributors:* Mikhail Ryazanov, Slimguy, Xufanc 186

Image *Source:* https://en.wikipedia.org/w/index.php?title=File:Nabha_flag.svg *License:* Public Domain *Contributors:* Robert Alfers 186

Image *Source:* https://en.wikipedia.org/w/index.php?title=File:Patiala_flag.svg *License:* Public Domain *Contributors:* Robert Alfers 186

Image *Source:* https://en.wikipedia.org/w/index.php?title=File:Rampur_flag.svg *License:* Public Domain *Contributors:* Robert Alfers 186

Image *Source:* https://en.wikipedia.org/w/index.php?title=File:Rewaflag.png *License:* Creative Commons Attribution-Sharealike 3.0 *Contributors:* OgreBot 2, Xufanc ... 186

Image *Source:* https://en.wikipedia.org/w/index.php?title=File:Sirohi.svg *Contributors:* - ... 186

Image *Source:* https://en.wikipedia.org/w/index.php?title=File:Flag_of_Kingdom_of_Mysore.svg *License:* Creative Commons Zero *Contributors:* User:Samhanin ... 186

Image *Source:* https://en.wikipedia.org/w/index.php?title=File:Flag_of_Kingdom_of_Travancore.svg *Contributors:* Washiucho ... 186

Image *Source:* https://en.wikipedia.org/w/index.php?title=File:Skull_and_crossbones.svg *Contributors:* Andux, Andy0101, AnselmiJuan, Bayo, BotMultichill, BotMultichillT, Coyau, D0ktorz, Derbeth, Eugenio Hansen, OFS, Franzenshof, Ies, J.delanoy, JMCC1, Jahoe, Juliancolton, Karelj, MarianSigler, Natr, Sarang, Shuhazmir, Sidpatil, Silsor, Stas1995, Stepshep, Str4nd, Sven Manguard, SweetCanadianMullet, The Evil IP address, Tiptoety, Túrelio, W!B:, Wknight94, 22 anonymous edits ... 186

Image *Source:* https://en.wikipedia.org/w/index.php?title=File:Jhansi_state_flag.png *License:* Creative Commons Attribution-Sharealike 3.0 *Contributors:* User:Xufanc ... 186

Figure 78 *Source:* https://en.wikipedia.org/w/index.php?title=File:India1765and1805b.jpg *License:* Public Domain *Contributors:* Edinburgh Geographical Institute. ... 189

Figure 79 *Source:* https://en.wikipedia.org/w/index.php?title=File:India1837to1857.jpg *License:* Public Domain *Contributors:* Edinburgh Geographical Institute. ... 190

Figure 80 *Source:* https://en.wikipedia.org/w/index.php?title=File:Two_Seapoy_Officers;_A_Private_Seapoy.jpg *License:* Public Domain *Contributors:* Clusternote, Jacklee, Ranveig, Roland zh ... 191

Figure 81 *Source:* https://en.wikipedia.org/w/index.php?title=File:Charles_Canning,_1st_Earl_Canning_-_Project_Gutenberg_eText_16528.jpg *License:* Public Domain *Contributors:* BotMultichill, Tagishsimon ... 194

Figure 82 *Source:* https://en.wikipedia.org/w/index.php?title=File:Dalhousie.jpg *License:* Public Domain *Contributors:* Sir William Lee-Warner 194

Figure 83 *Source:* https://en.wikipedia.org/w/index.php?title=File:Rani_of_jhansi.jpg *License:* Public Domain *Contributors:* Amenhtp, Aschroet, BotMultichill, Felix Folio Secundus, Martin H., Roland zh, Sankalpdravid ... 195

Figure 84 *Source:* https://en.wikipedia.org/w/index.php?title=File:Bahadur_Shah_II_of_India.jpg *License:* Public Domain *Contributors:* Gryffindor, Kürschner, Marcus Cyron, OgreBot 2, TRAJAN 117 ... 196

Figure 85 *Source:* https://en.wikipedia.org/w/index.php?title=File:Indian_Mutiny_Map_Showing_Position_of_Troops_on_1st_May_1857.jpg *Contributors:* Internet Archive Book Images ... 198

Figure 86 *Source:* https://en.wikipedia.org/w/index.php?title=File:The_Sepoy_revolt_at_Meerut.jpg *Contributors:* DarwIn, Exemplo347, Hohum, Roland zh, Sridhar1000 ... 200

Figure 87 *Source:* https://en.wikipedia.org/w/index.php?title=File:1857_mutineers_mosque_meerut2.jpg *License:* Public Domain *Contributors:* Major Robert Christopher Tytler (1818–1872) ... 200

Figure 88 *Source:* https://en.wikipedia.org/w/index.php?title=File:Massacre_of_officers_by_insurgent_cavalry_at_Delhi,.jpg *License:* Public Domain *Contributors:* DarwIn, Exemplo347, Roland zh, Sridhar1000, 1 anonymous edits ... 202

Figure 89 *Source:* https://en.wikipedia.org/w/index.php?title=File:1858_Delhi_flag_tower.jpg *License:* Public Domain *Contributors:* Amenhtp, Aschroet, BotMultichill, Ekabhishek, Martin H., Roland zh, 1 anonymous edits ... 202

Figure 90 *Source:* https://en.wikipedia.org/w/index.php?title=File:Indian_revolt_of_1857_states_map.svg *License:* Creative Commons Attribution-Sharealike 3.0 *Contributors:* Abhishekjoshi, Juliancolton, Nikotins, Planemad, Roland zh, WOSlinker, Wknight94, Zykasaa, 3 anonymous edits ... 204

Figure 91 *Source:* https://en.wikipedia.org/w/index.php?title=File:Troops_of_the_Native_Allies.jpg *License:* Public Domain *Contributors:* Alonso de Mendoza, Charles Matthews, Innotata, Napoleon 100 ... 204

Figure 92 *Source:* https://en.wikipedia.org/w/index.php?title=File:Looting_sikhs.jpg *License:* Public Domain *Contributors:* Roland zh, Sridhar1000, 1 anonymous edits ... 205

Figure 93 *Source:* https://en.wikipedia.org/w/index.php?title=File:Fugitive_British_officers_and_their_families_attacked_by_mutineers..jpg *License:* Public Domain *Contributors:* Hilohello, Piggy58 ... 207

Figure 94 *Source:* https://en.wikipedia.org/w/index.php?title=File:NyneeTal1857.jpg *Contributors:* User:Fowler&fowler ... 208

Figure 95 *Source:* https://en.wikipedia.org/w/index.php?title=File:"Attack_of_the_Mutineers_on_the_Redan_Battery_at_Lucknow,_July_30th,_1857,.jpg *License:* Public Domain *Contributors:* Denniss, Hsarrazin, Jarould, Nyttend, Rcbutcher, Roland zh, Sridhar1000, Vinkje83, Wally Wiglet, WikiOriginal-9 ... 209

Figure 96 *Source:* https://en.wikipedia.org/w/index.php?title=File:Attack1857.jpg *License:* Public Domain *Contributors:* Sridhar1000, 1 anonymous edits ... 210

Figure 97 *Source:* https://en.wikipedia.org/w/index.php?title=File:1857_ruins_jantar_mantar_observatory2.jpg *License:* Public Domain *Contributors:* Donaldduck100, Mike Peel, OgreBot 2, Roland zh, 1 anonymous edits ... 210

Figure 98 *Source:* https://en.wikipedia.org/w/index.php?title=File:1857_cashmeri_gate_delhi.jpg *Contributors:* Alpunin, BigJolly9, Magog the Ogre, Roland zh, Vssun, 1 anonymous edits ... 211

Figure 99 *Source:* https://en.wikipedia.org/w/index.php?title=File:1857_hindu_raos_house2.jpg *Contributors:* Major Robert Christopher and Harriet Tytler ... 211

Figure 100 *Source:* https://en.wikipedia.org/w/index.php?title=File:1857_bank_of_delhi2.jpg *Contributors:* Major Robert Christopher and Harriet Tytler ... 212

Figure 101 *Source:* https://en.wikipedia.org/w/index.php?title=File:"Capture_of_the_King_of_Delhi_by_Captain_Hodson".jpg *License:* Public Domain *Contributors:* Donaldduck100, Gryffindor, Hsarrazin, Metrónomo, Rayaraya, Roland zh, Sridhar1000, Vssun ... 213

Figure 102 *Source:* https://en.wikipedia.org/w/index.php?title=File:TantiaTope1858.jpg *License:* Public Domain *Contributors:* BigJolly9, Dharmadhyaksha, File Upload Bot (Magnus Manske), Magog the Ogre, Roland zh ... 214

Figure 103 *Source:* https://en.wikipedia.org/w/index.php?title=File:Cawnpore_Memorial,_1860.jpg *License:* Public Domain *Contributors:* BigJolly9, Ekabhishek, Enyavar, OgreBot 2, Rcbutcher, Roland zh, Skeezix1000, Themightyquill ... 215

Figure 104 *Source:* https://en.wikipedia.org/w/index.php?title=File:1857_hospital_wheeler_cawnpore2.jpg *License:* Public Domain *Contributors:* Dr. John Murray ... 216

Figure 105 *Source:* https://en.wikipedia.org/w/index.php?title=File:Slaughter_Ghat,_Cawnpore.jpg *Contributors:* Robert Christopher Tytler (1818-1872) and Harriet Tytler (1828-1907) ... 217

Figure 106 *Source:* https://en.wikipedia.org/w/index.php?title=File:1858_Kanpur_well_monument.jpg *Contributors:* Dr. John Murray ... 217

Figure 107 *Source:* https://en.wikipedia.org/w/index.php?title=File:Outside_of_well,_Cawnpore.jpg *Contributors:* ALH, BigJolly9, Rcbutcher, Roland zh, Themightyquill ... 218

Figure 108 *Source:* https://en.wikipedia.org/w/index.php?title=File:Kanpur_massacre.594px.jpg *License:* Public Domain *Contributors:* not stated 219

Figure 109 *Source:* https://en.wikipedia.org/w/index.php?title=File:Image-Secundra_Bagh_after_Indian_Mutiny_higher_res.jpg *License:* Public Domain *Contributors:* Co9man, Frank C. Müller, Nauticashades, Pinkville, Primaler, Rcbutcher, Roland zh, Romary, Svensson1, Themightyquill, Underwaterbuffalo, Victuallers, Wiki-uk, Wst, 2 anonymous edits ... 220

Figure 110 *Source:* https://en.wikipedia.org/w/index.php?title=File:1857_jhansi_fort2.jpg *License:* Public Domain *Contributors:* Lala Deen Dayal (1844–1905). ... 222

Figure 111 *Source:* https://en.wikipedia.org/w/index.php?title=File:Iln1857amax.jpg *License:* Public Domain *Contributors:* DarwIn, Diggers2004, JuTa, Rayaraya, Sridhar1000 ... 223

Figure 112 *Source:* https://en.wikipedia.org/w/index.php?title=File:Lectern_-_Jhelum_by_Khalid_Mahmood.jpg *License:* Creative Commons Attribution-Sharealike 2.5 *Contributors:* HenkvD, Hiddenhauser, JuTa, Kameraad Pjotr, Khalid Mahmood, Magog the Ogre, OgreBot 2, Tonkawa68, Warburg ... 224

Figure 113 *Source:* https://en.wikipedia.org/w/index.php?title=File:Lt_WA_Kerr_earning_the_Victoria_Cross_during_the_Indian_Mutiny.jpg *License:* Public Domain *Contributors:* Chevalier Louis-William Desanges (1822-1887) ... 225

Figure 114 *Source:* https://en.wikipedia.org/w/index.php?title=File:The_Relief_of_Lucknow,_1857_by_Thomas_Jones_Barker.jpg *License:* Public Domain *Contributors:* User:Dcoetzee ... 228

Figure 115 *Source:* https://en.wikipedia.org/w/index.php?title=File:British_soldiers_looting_Qaisar_Bagh_Lucknow.jpg *Contributors:* Anthony Appleyard, Ashrf1979, GermanJoe, Jarould, Picus viridis, Ranveig, Roland zh, Thgoiter, Utcursch, Wiki-uk ... 229

Figure 116 *Source:* https://en.wikipedia.org/w/index.php?title=File:Blowing_Mutinous_Sepoys_From_the_Guns,_September_8,_1857_-_steel_engraving.jpg *License:* Public Domain *Contributors:* Lotje, Sridhar1000, 2 anonymous edits ... 230

Figure 117 *Source:* https://en.wikipedia.org/w/index.php?title=File:JusticeTenniel1857Punch.jpg *License:* Public Domain *Contributors:* Amenhtp, BotMultichill, Infrogmation, Martin H., Telrúnya, WFinch ... 231

Figure 118 *Source:* https://en.wikipedia.org/w/index.php?title=File:Bahadur_Shah_Zafar.jpg *License:* Public Domain *Contributors:* Robert Tytler and Charles Shepard ... 232

Figure 119 *Source:* https://en.wikipedia.org/w/index.php?title=File:Image_victoria_proclamation1858c.JPG *License:* Public Domain *Contributors:* Athaenara, FSII, File Upload Bot (Magnus Manske), Gbarta, OgreBot 2, Roland zh ... 233

Figure 120 *Source:* https//en.wikipedia.org *Contributors:* User:WestCoastMusketeer ... 235

Figure 121 *Source:* https://en.wikipedia.org/w/index.php?title=File:YorkMinsterYorkLancasterRegMemorialH1c.jpg *License:* Creative Commons Zero *Contributors:* User:HelgeRieder ... 235

Image *Source:* https://en.wikipedia.org/w/index.php?title=File:UK_Victoria_Cross_ribbon_bar.svg *License:* Public Domain *Contributors:* Victoria_Cross_Medal_without_Bar.png: Rcdarchive & EyeSerene derivative work: Mboro (talk) ... 236

Image *Source:* https://en.wikipedia.org/w/index.php?title=File:Indian_Mutiny_Medal_BAR.svg *License:* Creative Commons Attribution-ShareAlike 3.0 Unported *Contributors:* Orem (wiki-pl: Orem, commons: Orem) ... 236

Image *Source:* https://en.wikipedia.org/w/index.php?title=File:Lint_Indische_Orde_van_Verdienste_Indian_Order_of_Merit.jpg *License:* Creative Commons Attribution-Sharealike 2.5 *Contributors:* User:Robert Prummel ... 236

Figure 122 *Source:* https://en.wikipedia.org/w/index.php?title=File:The_Mutiny_Memorial_in_Delhi_is_a_monument_to_British_officers..jpg *License:* Public Domain *Contributors:* Denniss, Roland zh, Sridhar1000, 1 anonymous edits ... 237

Figure 123 *Source:* https://en.wikipedia.org/w/index.php?title=File:Vereshchagin-Blowing_from_Guns_in_British_India.jpg *License:* Public Domain *Contributors:* Botaurus, Butko, Jusjih, Kritkitty, Man vyi, Shakko, Vadakkan, Vizu, 5 anonymous edits ... 238

Figure 124 *Source:* https//en.wikipedia.org *License:* Public Domain *Contributors:* BotMultichill, Gbawden, JMCC1, Lotje, Primaler ... 239

Figure 125 *Source:* https://en.wikipedia.org/w/index.php?title=File:Henry_Nelson_O'Neil_-_Eastward_Ho!_-_1857.jpg *License:* Public Domain *Contributors:* BotMultichill, FA2010, FrancisF23, Ham II, Ich, Mattes, Themightyquill, Thib Phil, Wieralee, 1 anonymous edits ... 241

Image *Source:* https://en.wikipedia.org/w/index.php?title=File:Star-of-India-gold-centre.svg *License:* Public Domain *Contributors:* User:Greentubing~commonswiki ... 251

Image *Source:* https://en.wikipedia.org/w/index.php?title=File:British_Indian_empire_in_1936.png *License:* Creative Commons Attribution-Sharealike 3.0 *Contributors:* User:Mir Almaat 1 S1 ... 251

Image *Source:* https://en.wikipedia.org/w/index.php?title=File:Flag_of_Afghanistan_(1880–1901).svg *License:* Public Domain *Contributors:* PaD and Indolences. ... 252

Image *Source:* https://en.wikipedia.org/w/index.php?title=File:1931_Flag_of_India.svg *License:* Public Domain *Contributors:* Nicholas (Nichalp) 252

Image *Source:* https://en.wikipedia.org/w/index.php?title=File:British_Burma_1937_flag.svg *Contributors:* - ... 252

Image *Source:* https://en.wikipedia.org/w/index.php?title=File:Flag_of_the_Trucial_States.svg *License:* Public Domain *Contributors:* Alkari, Gryffindor, Homo lupus, Michael Barera, Mnmazur, Sarang, Svyatoslav, 2 anonymous edits ... 252

Image *Source:* https://en.wikipedia.org/w/index.php?title=File:Flag_of_the_Colony_of_Aden.svg *License:* Public Domain *Contributors:* O ... 252

Figure 126 *Source:* https://en.wikipedia.org/w/index.php?title=File:Pope1880BritishIndia1.jpg *Contributors:* W. H. Allen and Co. ... 254

Figure 127 *Source:* https://en.wikipedia.org/w/index.php?title=File:British_Indian_Empire_1909_Imperial_Gazetteer_of_India.jpg *License:* Public Domain *Contributors:* Edinburgh Geographical Institute; J. G. Bartholomew and Sons. ... 259

Image *Source:* https://en.wikipedia.org/w/index.php?title=File:Mohenjo-daro_Priesterkönig.jpeg *License:* Creative Commons world66 *Contributors:* Botev, Daphne Lantier, Gryffindor, Icarusgeek, Jungpionier, Look2See1, Mmcannis~commonswiki, Oksmith, Roland zh, Themightyquill, 1 anonymous edits ... 259

Image *Source:* https://en.wikipedia.org/w/index.php?title=File:Folder_Hexagonal_Icon.svg *License:* GNU Free Documentation License *Contributors:* Anomie, Jo-Jo Eumerus, Mifter ... 260

Image *Source:* https://en.wikipedia.org/w/index.php?title=File:Portal-puzzle.svg *License:* Public Domain *Contributors:* Anomie, Jo-Jo Eumerus, Topbanana ... 260

Image *Source:* https://en.wikipedia.org/w/index.php?title=File:1stViscountHalifax.jpg *License:* Public Domain *Contributors:* William Walker 261

Image *Source:* https://en.wikipedia.org/w/index.php?title=File:Lord_Viscount_Canning.jpg *Contributors:* Engraved by D. J. Pound from a photograph by Mayall ... 261

Image *Source:* https://en.wikipedia.org/w/index.php?title=File:Robert_cecil.jpg *License:* Public Domain *Contributors:* Elliot & Fry. Uploaded by Connormah ... 261

Image *Source:* https://en.wikipedia.org/w/index.php?title=File:VictoriaQueen1862Empress1886.jpg *License:* Public Domain *Contributors:* User:Fowler&fowler ... 265

Image *Source:* https://en.wikipedia.org/w/index.php?title=File:EdwardVIIKingEmperorIndia1903and1908.jpg *License:* Public Domain *Contributors:* User:Fowler&fowler ... 265

Image *Source:* https://en.wikipedia.org/w/index.php?title=File:GeorgeVKingEmperor1913and1919.jpg *License:* Public Domain *Contributors:* User:Fowler&fowler ... 265

Image *Source:* https://en.wikipedia.org/w/index.php?title=File:GeorgeVIKingEmperorIndia1940and1947.jpg *License:* Public Domain *Contributors:* User:Fowler&fowler ... 266

Figure 128 *Source:* https://en.wikipedia.org/w/index.php?title=File:Rani_of_jhansi.jpg *License:* Public Domain *Contributors:* Amenhtp, Aschroet, BotMultichill, Felix Folio Secundus, Martin H., Roland zh, Sankalpdravid ... 269

Figure 129 *Source:* https://en.wikipedia.org/w/index.php?title=File:SAKhan.jpg *License:* Public Domain *Contributors:* Later versions were uploaded by Megapixie, Arslan1080, Raul654 at en.wikipedia. ... 270

Figure 130 *Source:* https://en.wikipedia.org/w/index.php?title=File:Victoria_empress_india1.jpg *License:* Public Domain *Contributors:* Stanislaw Julian Ostrorog, aka Walery (1830-1890) ... 271

Figure 131 *Source:* https://en.wikipedia.org/w/index.php?title=File:Return_visit_of_the_Viceroy_to_the_Maharaja_of_Cashmere.jpg *License:* Public Domain *Contributors:* Kilom691, Magog the Ogre, Roland zh, Sridhar1000, Themadchopper, 1 anonymous edits ... 272

Figure 132 *Source:* https://en.wikipedia.org/w/index.php?title=File:Delhi_Durbar_1903.jpg *License:* Public Domain *Contributors:* User:Jungpionier ... 274

Figure 133 *Source:* https://en.wikipedia.org/w/index.php?title=File:Lucknowuniversity.jpg *License:* Public domain *Contributors:* Leyo, MGA73bot2, OgreBot 2, Roland zh, 1 anonymous edits ... 275

Figure 134 *Source:* https://en.wikipedia.org/w/index.php?title=File:Calcuttamedicalcollege1.jpg *License:* Public Domain *Contributors:* Bodhisattwa, Diptanshu Das, Jayantanth, Roland zh ... 276

Figure 135 *Source:* https://en.wikipedia.org/w/index.php?title=File:St._Paul's_Cathedral_-_Calcutta_(Kolkata)_-_1865.jpg *License:* Public Domain *Contributors:* Bellayet, Look2See1, MarmadukePercy, Roland zh ... 277

Figure 136 *Source:* https://en.wikipedia.org/w/index.php?title=File:India_1862_One_Mohur.jpg *License:* Public Domain *Contributors:* Daderot, Daniel Case, Godot13, HReuter, Julia W, Yann ... 279

Figure 137 *Source:* https://en.wikipedia.org/w/index.php?title=File:India-rail-1870.png *License:* Public Domain *Contributors:* Moeng, Pechristener, Ravidreams, Roland zh, Sankalpdravid ... 281

Figure 138 *Source:* https://en.wikipedia.org/w/index.php?title=File:India_railways1909a.jpg *License:* Public Domain *Contributors:* John Bartholomew and Company/Edinburgh Geographical Institute ... 281

Figure 139 *Source:* https://en.wikipedia.org/w/index.php?title=File:Victoriaterminus1903.JPG *License:* Public Domain *Contributors:* Dragonfly-Sixtyseven, File Upload Bot (Magnus Manske), Infrogmation, Innotata, Jovianeye, Kersti Nebelsiek, OgreBot 2, Quibik, Roland zh, Sankalpdravid ... 282

Figure 140 *Source:* https://en.wikipedia.org/w/index.php?title=File:The_Queen's_Own_Madras_Sappers_and_Miners,_Review_Order_.jpg *Contributors:* - ... 284

Figure 141 *Source:* https://en.wikipedia.org/w/index.php?title=File:Bengal_famine_1943_photo.jpg *License:* Public Domain *Contributors:* Afifa Afrin, Bellayet, Ms Sarah Welch, OgreBot 2, Ruff tuff cream puff, SunOfErat, Titodutta ... 287

Image *Source:* https://en.wikipedia.org/w/index.php?title=File:Gopal_krishan_gokhale.jpg *License:* Public Domain *Contributors:* Deepak885, Nicke L, OgreBot 2, Roland zh, Yann ... 289

Image *Source:* https//en.wikipedia.org *License:* Public Domain *Contributors:* Bulwersator, Chiswick Chap, Cube00, Kalyan131, Magog the Ogre, Polarlys, Shrikanthv, Shwetav Agarwal, The RedBurn, Yann ... 290

Image *Source:* https://en.wikipedia.org/w/index.php?title=File:Bal_G._Tilak.jpg *License:* Public Domain *Contributors:* Arianna, Innotata, Kensplanet, Mu, Zhuyifei1999 ... 290

Image *Source:* https://en.wikipedia.org/w/index.php?title=File:George_Curzon2.jpg *License:* Public Domain *Contributors:* George Grantham Bain Collection (Library of Congress) ... 291

Image *Source:* https://en.wikipedia.org/w/index.php?title=File:Salimullah.jpg *License:* Public Domain *Contributors:* Aditya Kabir, File Upload Bot (Magnus Manske), Funfood, JuTa, Magog the Ogre, OgreBot 2, Roland zh, Wieralee ... 291

Image *Source:* https://en.wikipedia.org/w/index.php?title=File:B_0110A.jpg *Contributors:* - ... 291

Image *Source:* https://en.wikipedia.org/w/index.php?title=File:1909magazine_vijaya.jpg *License:* Public Domain *Contributors:* User:Sreejithk2000 292

Image *Source:* https://en.wikipedia.org/w/index.php?title=File:Brit_IndianEmpireReligions3.jpg *License:* Public Domain *Contributors:* A ri gi bod, AnonMoos, Ekabhishek, Karlfk, Magog the Ogre, Maproom, Roland zh, Shooke, Yann, 3 anonymous edits ... 293

Image *Source:* https://en.wikipedia.org/w/index.php?title=File:1921ajmalkhan.jpg *License:* Public Domain *Contributors:* Bad Buu, Roland zh, Themightyquill ... 293

Image *Source:* https://en.wikipedia.org/w/index.php?title=File:LordMelgund1885.jpg *License:* Public Domain *Contributors:* BotMultichill, BotMultichillT, Deadstar, JamesTeterenko, Väsk, ~Pyb ... 294

Image *Source:* https://en.wikipedia.org/w/index.php?title=File:Indiantroops_medical_ww1.jpg *License:* Public Domain *Contributors:* MALLUS, Magog the Ogre, Roland zh ... 295

Image *Source:* https://en.wikipedia.org/w/index.php?title=File:Khudadad_khan_vc1915.jpg *License:* Public Domain *Contributors:* Blackcat, Fastily, MALLUS, Magog the Ogre, Polarlys, Roland zh 295

Image *Source:* https://en.wikipedia.org/w/index.php?title=File:Gandhi_back_in_india1915.gif *License:* Public Domain *Contributors:* DarwIn, Eddaido, Globetrotter19, Infrogmation, Nikkimaria, Rama, Roland zh, Yann 295

Image *Source:* https://en.wikipedia.org/w/index.php?title=File:Jinnah_lucknow_pact1916.jpg *License:* Public Domain *Contributors:* User:Fowler&fowler 296

Figure 142 *Source:* https://en.wikipedia.org/w/index.php?title=File:Gandhi_Kheda_1918.jpg *License:* Public Domain *Contributors:* Deepak885, RegentsPark, Roland zh, Yann 299

Figure 143 *Source:* https://en.wikipedia.org/w/index.php?title=File:Montagu_left.jpg *License:* Public Domain *Contributors:* Ekabhishek, MALLUS, MGA73bot2, Magog the Ogre, 1 anonymous edits 299

Figure 144 *Source:* https://en.wikipedia.org/w/index.php?title=File:Rowlatt_bills1919.gif *License:* Public Domain *Contributors:* Editors of an Indian newspaper 300

Figure 145 *Source:* https://en.wikipedia.org/w/index.php?title=File:Jallianwallah.jpg *License:* Public Domain *Contributors:* Abhishekjoshi, Anne97432, Hermitage17, Herrick∼commonswiki, Patstuart, Roland zh 301

Image *Source:* https://en.wikipedia.org/w/index.php?title=File:Gandhi_besant_madras1921.jpg *License:* Public Domain *Contributors:* Ballofstring, Mdann52(alt), OgreBot 2, Revent, Yann 305

Image *Source:* https://en.wikipedia.org/w/index.php?title=File:Noncooperation_khilafat1921.gif *License:* Public Domain *Contributors:* User:Fowler&fowler 305

Image *Source:* https://en.wikipedia.org/w/index.php?title=File:Noncooperation_movement1922.jpg *License:* Public Domain *Contributors:* Photographer unknown. 305

Image *Source:* https://en.wikipedia.org/w/index.php?title=File:Bhagat_singh_noncooperation.jpg *License:* Public Domain *Contributors:* JMCC1, Mdann52, OgreBot 2 306

Image *Source:* https://en.wikipedia.org/w/index.php?title=File:Iqbal_Allahabad.jpg *License:* Public Domain *Contributors:* BotMultichill, Ekabhishek, Frank C. Müller, Liftarn, Love Krittaya, Mattes, OgreBot 2, Roland zh, TFCforever 306

Image *Source:* https://en.wikipedia.org/w/index.php?title=File:Second_round_tableconf.gif *License:* Public Domain *Contributors:* Djembayz, MALLUS, MGA73bot2, Magog the Ogre, Oxyman, Roland zh, Yann, संदेश हिवाळे, 1 anonymous edits 306

Image *Source:* https://en.wikipedia.org/w/index.php?title=File:NewDelhiInaugurationSecondDayCancellation27Feb1931.jpg *License:* Public Domain *Contributors:* User:Fowler&fowler 307

Image *Source:* https://en.wikipedia.org/w/index.php?title=File:Indian_General_Election_1934.svg *Contributors:* User:RaviC 307

Image *Source:* https://en.wikipedia.org/w/index.php?title=File:Separation_of_Burma_from_British_India_1937.jpg *License:* Public Domain *Contributors:* Government of Burma, Postal Department, Rangoon 307

Image *Source:* https://en.wikipedia.org/w/index.php?title=File:Ncert_gandhi_tomeet_linlithgow1939.jpg *License:* Public Domain *Contributors:* User:Fowler&fowler 309

Image *Source:* https://en.wikipedia.org/w/index.php?title=File:A_k_fazlul_hoque.jpg *License:* Public Domain *Contributors:* Arr4, Fez Cap 12, OgreBot 2, Tamba52 309

Image *Source:* https://en.wikipedia.org/w/index.php?title=File:Chaudhry_Khaliquzzaman.jpg *License:* Public Domain *Contributors:* Afifa Afrin, BotMultichill, Diannaa, File Upload Bot (Magnus Manske), Moheen Reeyad, OgreBot 2, Roland zh, Till.niermann, Xufanc, 1 anonymous edits 309

Image *Source:* https://en.wikipedia.org/w/index.php?title=File:Newly-arrived_Indian_troops.jpg *License:* Public Domain *Contributors:* Palmer (Lt) Post-Work: User:W.wolny 310

Image *Source:* https://en.wikipedia.org/w/index.php?title=File:Operation_Crusader.jpg *License:* Public Domain *Contributors:* Avron, DStoykov, OgreBot 2, Prüm, Quibik, Roland zh, 1 anonymous edits 310

Figure 146 *Source:* https://en.wikipedia.org/w/index.php?title=File:Bundesarchiv_Bild_101III-Alber-064-03A,_Subhas_Chandra_Bose_bei_Heinrich_Himmler.jpg *License:* Creative Commons Attribution-Sharealike 3.0 Germany *Contributors:* ABrocke, Balcer∼commonswiki, BotMultichill, Innotata, Kl833x9∼commonswiki, Mhao Koe, Mtsmallwood, Roland zh 312

Figure 147 *Source:* https://en.wikipedia.org/w/index.php?title=File:VictoryWorldWar2BritishRaj.jpg *License:* Public Domain *Contributors:* User:Fowler&fowler 312

Figure 148 *Source:* https://en.wikipedia.org/w/index.php?title=File:Cabinet_mission_to_india1946.jpg *License:* Public Domain *Contributors:* , British government photograph 314

Figure 149 *Source:* https://en.wikipedia.org/w/index.php?title=File:Hindu_percent_1909.jpg *License:* Public Domain *Contributors:* Ekabhishek, Fowler&fowler, JenVan, Karlfk, Magog the Ogre, Roland zh, Shooke, Yann, 3 anonymous edits 315

Figure 150 *Source:* https://en.wikipedia.org/w/index.php?title=File:Muslim_percent_1909.jpg *License:* Public Domain *Contributors:* Ekabhishek, Fowler&fowler, Karlfk, Magog the Ogre, Roland zh, Shooke, Yann 316

Image *Source:* https://en.wikipedia.org/w/index.php?title=File:Wikiquote-logo.svg *License:* Public Domain *Contributors:* Rei-artur 325

Image *Source:* https://en.wikipedia.org/w/index.php?title=File:Wikivoyage-Logo-v3-icon.svg *License:* Creative Commons Attribution-Sharealike 3.0 *Contributors:* User:AleXXw 325

Image *Source:* https://en.wikipedia.org/w/index.php?title=File:Eugène_Delacroix_-_Le_28_Juillet._La_Liberté_guidant_le_peuple.jpg *License:* Public Domain *Contributors:* Botaurus, Elsbeere, Fma12, Mirokado, Oursana, Pixel8tor, Trzęsacz, Wheeke, 1 anonymous edits 327

Image *Source:* https://en.wikipedia.org/w/index.php?title=File:A_coloured_voting_box.svg *License:* Creative Commons Attribution-Sharealike 2.5 *Contributors:* Anomie, Jo-Jo Eumerus 327

Figure 151 *Source:* https://en.wikipedia.org/w/index.php?title=File:Clive.jpg *License:* Public Domain *Contributors:* Ashrf1979, Billinghurst, Bogomolov.PL, BotMultichillT, Dancingwombatsrule, Flominator, Jappalang, Jungpionier, Madmedea, Materialscientist, Nikkimaria, Podzemnik, Ranveig, Roland zh, Thuresson, Un1c0s bot∼commonswiki, 5 anonymous edits 329

Figure 152 *Source:* https://en.wikipedia.org/w/index.php?title=File:Tipu_death.jpg *License:* Public Domain *Contributors:* Henry Singleton (1766 - 1839) 329

Figure 153 *Source:* https://en.wikipedia.org/w/index.php?title=File:Indian_revolt_of_1857_states_map.svg *License:* Creative Commons Attribution-Sharealike 3.0 *Contributors:* Abhishekjoshi, Juliancolton, Nikotins, Planemad, Roland zh, WOSlinker, Wknight94, Zykasaa, 3 anonymous edits 332

Figure 154 *Source:* https://en.wikipedia.org/w/index.php?title=File:1st_INC1885.jpg *License:* Public Domain *Contributors:* User:Fowler&fowler 334

Figure 155 *Source:* https://en.wikipedia.org/w/index.php?title=File:Lal_Bal_Pal.jpg *License:* Public Domain *Contributors:* Padalkar.kshitij, Yann 336

Figure 156 *Source:* https://en.wikipedia.org/w/index.php?title=File:Khudiram_Bose_1905_cropped.jpg *License:* Public Domain *Contributors:* Arr4, BotAdventures, Mar11, OgreBot 2 337

Figure 157 *Source:* https://en.wikipedia.org/w/index.php?title=File:Indian_army_soldier_after_siege_of_Kut.jpg *License:* Public Domain *Contributors:* Coyau, Docu, Elgewen, EvilFlyingMonkey, FSII, Flamurai, Fæ, JuTa, Man vyi, Manxruler, Martin H., Moogsi, Mr impossible, PKM, Rapsar, Timeshifter, 5 anonymous edits 339

Figure 158 *Source:* https://en.wikipedia.org/w/index.php?title=File:Gandhi_Kheda_1918.jpg *License:* Public Domain *Contributors:* Deepak885, RegentsPark, Roland zh, Yann 341

Figure 159 *Source:* https://en.wikipedia.org/w/index.php?title=File:Dr_Rajendra_Pd._DR.Anugrah_Narayan_Sinha.jpg *License:* Public Domain *Contributors:* Anugrah Abhinandan Granth (1946) 342

Figure 160 *Source:* https://en.wikipedia.org/w/index.php?title=File:Jinnah_Gandhi.jpg *License:* Public Domain *Contributors:* Glaurung, Leyo, Officer, Roland zh, Yann, 1 anonymous edits 346

Image *Source:* https://en.wikipedia.org/w/index.php?title=File:Bhagat_Singh_Sukh_Dev_Raj_Guru.jpg *License:* Public Domain *Contributors:* Susnigdh 346

Image *Source:* https://en.wikipedia.org/w/index.php?title=File:Bhagat_Singh's_execution_Lahore_Tribune_Front_page.jpg *License:* Public Domain *Contributors:* Abhishekjoshi, Angusmclellan, Catsmeat, Jazze7, Man vyi, Pahari Sahib, Rcbutcher, Roland zh, Zhuyifei1999 347

Figure 161 *Source:* https://en.wikipedia.org/w/index.php?title=File:Fujiwara_Kikan.jpg *License:* Public Domain *Contributors:* Domeitsushin-sha 352

Figure 162 *Source:* https://en.wikipedia.org/w/index.php?title=File:Netaji_Subhas_Chandra_Bose.jpg *License:* Public Domain *Contributors:* BotMultichillT, Czarhind, Jayantanth, Man vyi, Roland zh, Wikitanvir, 2 anonymous edits 352

Figure 163 *Source:* https://en.wikipedia.org/w/index.php?title=File:QUITIN2.JPG *License:* Creative Commons Attribution-Sharealike 2.5 *Contributors:* User:Dore chakravarty∼commonswiki 354

Image *Source:* https://en.wikipedia.org/w/index.php?title=File:Lock-green.svg *License:* Creative Commons Zero *Contributors:* User:Trappist the monk 359

Image *Source:* https://en.wikipedia.org/w/index.php?title=File:The_first_Cabinet_of_independent_India.jpg *License:* Public Domain *Contributors:* BigJolly9, OgreBot 2, Shipjustgotreal, संदेश हिवाळे 362

Image *Source:* https://en.wikipedia.org/w/index.php?title=File:Nathuram.jpg *License:* Public Domain *Contributors:* .Koen, Centeralnews, Dharmadhyaksha, GeorgHH, Jdx, OgreBot 2, Prativadi, Ranveig, Rimshot, Roland zh, Sankalpdravid, 9 anonymous edits 363

Image *Source:* https://en.wikipedia.org/w/index.php?title=File:Sardar_patel_(cropped).jpg *License:* Public Domain *Contributors:* Government of India work 364
Image *Source:* https://en.wikipedia.org/w/index.php?title=File:Op_Polo_Surrender.jpg *License:* Public Domain *Contributors:* Roland zh, Sarvagyana guru 364
Image *Source:* https://en.wikipedia.org/w/index.php?title=File:Maharani_kanchan_prabhadevi.jpg *License:* Public Domain *Contributors:* OgreBot 2, Roland zh, Sidsahu, Xufanc 364
Image *Source:* https://en.wikipedia.org/w/index.php?title=File:Sheik_Mohammed_Abdullah.jpg *License:* Public Domain *Contributors:* Denniss, Mercurywoodrose, Sridhar1000, Themightyquill, WFinch 364
Figure 164 *Source:* https://en.wikipedia.org/w/index.php?title=File:Indian_soldiers_fighting_in_1947_war.jpg *License:* Public Domain *Contributors:* Avron, Denniss, HIAS, Roland zh, Sreejithk2000, Sridhar1000, Юкке 366
Figure 165 *Source:* https://en.wikipedia.org/w/index.php?title=File:Bundesarchiv_Bild_183-61849-0001,_Indien,_Otto_Grotewohl_bei_Ministerpräsident_Nehru_cropped.jpg *License:* Creative Commons Attribution-Sharealike 3.0 Germany *Contributors:* Bundesarchiv Bild 183-61849-0001, Indien, Otto Grotewohl bei Ministerpräsident Nehru.jpg: Heilig, Walter derivative work 367
Figure 166 *Source:* https://en.wikipedia.org/w/index.php?title=File:South_Indian_territories.svg *License:* Creative Commons Attribution 3.0 *Contributors:* AreJay 368
Figure 167 *Source:* https://en.wikipedia.org/w/index.php?title=File:Indira_Gandhi_in_1967.jpg *License:* Public Domain *Contributors:* Defense Department, US government 370
Figure 168 *Source:* https://en.wikipedia.org/w/index.php?title=File:INS_Vikrant_(R11)_launches_an_Alize_aircraft_during_Indo-Pakistani_War_of_1971.jpg *Contributors:* User:Racconish 371
Figure 169 *Source:* https://en.wikipedia.org/w/index.php?title=File:Vikramjit-Kakati-Rumtek.jpg *License:* Creative Commons Attribution-Sharealike 3.0 *Contributors:* User:Donvikro 372
Image *Source:* https://en.wikipedia.org/w/index.php?title=File:Punjab_Monsoon.jpg *License:* Creative Commons Attribution-Sharealike 3.0 *Contributors:* User:Sanyambahga 373
Image *Source:* https://en.wikipedia.org/w/index.php?title=File:Amul_Plant_at_Anand.jpg *License:* Creative Commons Attribution-Sharealike 3.0 *Contributors:* Notnarayan 373
Figure 170 *Source:* https://en.wikipedia.org/w/index.php?title=File:1971_Instrument_of_Surrender.jpg *Contributors:* User:Racconish 374
Figure 171 *Source:* https://en.wikipedia.org/w/index.php?title=File:Morarji_Desai_1978.jpg *License:* Public Domain *Contributors:* White House Staff Photographer 376
Figure 172 *Source:* https://en.wikipedia.org/w/index.php?title=File:Akal_Takht_and_Harmandir_Sahib,_Amritsar,_Punjab,_India.jpg *License:* Creative Commons Attribution-Sharealike 2.0 *Contributors:* Jasleen Kaur 376
Figure 173 *Source:* https://en.wikipedia.org/w/index.php?title=File:BHOPAL_(231583728).jpg *License:* Creative Commons Attribution 2.0 *Contributors:* Obi from ROMA ,LONDON 378
Figure 174 *Source:* https://en.wikipedia.org/w/index.php?title=File:Rajiv_Gandhi_Memorial_bombsite.jpg *License:* Creative Commons Attribution-Sharealike 2.5 *Contributors:* Avjoska, Planemad, Roland zh, Vadakkan 380
Image *Source:* https://en.wikipedia.org/w/index.php?title=File:Pumapaparti.N.rao.jpg *Contributors:* User:Dh ronak 380
Image *Source:* https://en.wikipedia.org/w/index.php?title=File:Manmohansingh04052007.jpg *License:* Agência Brasil *Contributors:* Ricardo Stuckert/PR 381
Figure 175 *Source:* https://en.wikipedia.org/w/index.php?title=File:Agni-II_missile_(Republic_Day_Parade_2004).jpeg *License:* Agência Brasil *Contributors:* Antônio Milena (ABr) 382
Figure 176 *Source:* https://en.wikipedia.org/w/index.php?title=File:Kargil_war.jpg *License:* Creative Commons Attribution 3.0 *Contributors:* FlickrWarrior, Netstar1, 2 anonymous edits 383
Figure 177 *Source:* https://en.wikipedia.org/w/index.php?title=File:Ab_vajpayee.jpg *License:* Public Domain *Contributors:* Dantadd, Dbind, Jdx, Sreejithk2000, 1 anonymous edits 384
Figure 178 *Source:* https://en.wikipedia.org/w/index.php?title=File:Nh76.jpg *License:* Creative Commons Attribution-Sharealike 3.0 *Contributors:* User:Enthusiast10 385
Figure 179 *Source:* https://en.wikipedia.org/w/index.php?title=File:Bush_&_Singh_in_New_Delhi.jpg *License:* Public Domain *Contributors:* White House photo by Paul Morse 387
Figure 180 *Source:* https://en.wikipedia.org/w/index.php?title=File:Taj_mahal_dedistorted.jpg *License:* Creative Commons Attribution-Sharealike 3.0 *Contributors:* Trakesht 388
Figure 181 *Source:* https://en.wikipedia.org/w/index.php?title=File:Commonwealth-Games-2010-Opening-Ceremony.jpg *License:* Creative Commons Attribution 3.0 *Contributors:* Indianhilbilly 389
Figure 182 *Source:* https://en.wikipedia.org/w/index.php?title=File:Ladakh_Monastery.jpg *License:* Creative Commons Attribution 2.0 *Contributors:* File Upload Bot (Magnus Manske), FlickreviewR, Jacopo Werther, OgreBot 2, Roland zh, Snotch, 2 anonymous edits 390
Figure 183 *Source:* https://en.wikipedia.org/w/index.php?title=File:Mars_Orbiter_Mission_-_India_-_ArtistsConcept.jpg *License:* Creative Commons Attribution-Share Alike *Contributors:* Nesnad 391
Figure 184 *Source:* https://en.wikipedia.org/w/index.php?title=File:Narendra_Modi_launches_Make_in_India.jpg *License:* Creative Commons Attribution-Sharealike 2.0 *Contributors:* Prime Minister's Office, Government of India 391
Image *Source:* https://en.wikipedia.org/w/index.php?title=File:Emblem_of_India_1947-1950.png *License:* GNU Free Documentation License *Contributors:* Cordyceps-Zombie 395
Image *Source:* https://en.wikipedia.org/w/index.php?title=File:India_Administrative_Divisions_1951.svg *License:* Creative Commons Zero *Contributors:* Andhrapur 395
Image *Source:* https://en.wikipedia.org/w/index.php?title=File:King_George_VI_of_England,_formal_photo_portrait,_circa_1940-1946.jpg *Contributors:* Matson Photo Service 399
Figure 185 *Source:* https://en.wikipedia.org/w/index.php?title=File:Flag_of_the_Governor-General_of_India_(1947-1950).svg *License:* Creative Commons Zero *Contributors:* User:Thommy9 400
Image *Source:* https://en.wikipedia.org/w/index.php?title=File:Mountbatten.jpg *License:* Public Domain *Contributors:* Aleichem, Aschroet, BrightRaven, Celia Homeford, Docu, Duffy2032∼commonswiki, FSII, Innotata, Madmedea, MagentaGreen, Mattes, Richard Harvey, Spiegeleiqualle, 1 anonymous edits 399
Image *Source:* https://en.wikipedia.org/w/index.php?title=File:C_Rajagopalachari_1944.jpg *License:* Creative Commons Attribution 3.0 *Contributors:* Gandhi_Rajagopalachari.jpg: derivative work: Ganeshk (talk) 399
Image *Source:* https://en.wikipedia.org/w/index.php?title=File:Jnehru.jpg *License:* Public Domain *Contributors:* Royroydeb 400
Image *Source:* https://en.wikipedia.org/w/index.php?title=File:Constitution_of_India.jpg *License:* Public Domain *Contributors:* Illumination/ornamentation by Beohar Rammanohar Sinha, calligraphy by Prem Behari Narain Raizada. 401
Image *Source:* https://en.wikipedia.org/w/index.php?title=File:Emblem_of_India.svg *License:* Public Domain *Contributors:* 4nn1l2, Abhishekjoshi, BRUTE, Beao, Bender235, BotMultichill, Botev, Cheguthan, Editor at Large, Eugenio Hansen, OFS, Faizhaider, Fred the Oyster, Fry1989, Gauravjuvekar, Gautam brahmarakshe, Graphium, Havang(nl), Jappalang, Jcb, Jdx, Jed, Jianhui67, Jmabel, Jovianeye, Kalki, Kintetsubuffalo, Klemen Kocjancic, Legoktm, Leit, MGA73bot2, Magog the Ogre, Miljoshi, Nightstallion, Roland zh, Sarang, Str4nd, Túrelio, Vaishu2∼commonswiki, Wiki-uk, Xiengyod∼commonswiki, Zscout370, 54 anonymous edits 402
Figure 186 *Source:* https//en.wikipedia.org *License:* Public Domain *Contributors:* संदेश हिवाळे 403
Figure 187 *Source:* https://en.wikipedia.org/w/index.php?title=File:A_Constituent_Assembly_of_India_meeting_in_1950.jpg *License:* Public Domain *Contributors:* BigJolly9, संदेश हिवाळे 404
Figure 188 *Source:* https://en.wikipedia.org/w/index.php?title=File:Jawaharlal_Nehru_signing_Indian_Constitution.jpg *License:* Public Domain *Contributors:* Bodhisattwa, Kinoko kokonotsu, Royroydeb, Wieralee 408
Figure 189 *Source:* https://en.wikipedia.org/w/index.php?title=File:British_Indian_Empire_1909_Imperial_Gazetteer_of_India.jpg *License:* Public Domain *Contributors:* Edinburgh Geographical Institute; J. G. Bartholomew and Sons. 417
Figure 190 *Source:* https://en.wikipedia.org/w/index.php?title=File:Baroda_state_1909.jpg *License:* Public Domain *Contributors:* Ekabhishek, Flamarande∼commonswiki, Gryffindor, Magog the Ogre, Roland zh, Sankalpdravid, Spundun, 1 anonymous edits 418
Figure 191 *Source:* https://en.wikipedia.org/w/index.php?title=File:Mountbatten.jpg *License:* Public Domain *Contributors:* Aleichem, Aschroet, BrightRaven, Celia Homeford, Docu, Duffy2032∼commonswiki, FSII, Innotata, Madmedea, MagentaGreen, Mattes, Richard Harvey, Spiegeleiqualle, 1 anonymous edits 421
Figure 192 *Source:* https://en.wikipedia.org/w/index.php?title=File:Sardar_patel_(cropped).jpg *License:* Public Domain *Contributors:* Government of India work 423
Figure 193 *Source:* https://en.wikipedia.org/w/index.php?title=File:Kashmir_map_big.jpg *License:* Public Domain *Contributors:* A ri gi bod, Flamarande∼commonswiki, Hornstrandir1, Juiced lemon, LX, Phatom87, Roland zh, Sven-steffen arndt, TheDJ, Timeshifter, Zaccarias, Zykasaa, 19 anonymous edits 426
Figure 194 *Source:* https://en.wikipedia.org/w/index.php?title=File:Hyderabad_state_1909.jpg *License:* Public Domain *Contributors:* Dflkn, Ekabhishek, Magog the Ogre, Poulos∼commonswiki, Roland zh, Sdrtirs 428

Figure 195 *Source:* https://en.wikipedia.org/w/index.php?title=File:Central_Provs_1909.jpg *License:* Public Domain *Contributors:* Imperial Gazetteer of India ... 430
Figure 196 *Source:* https://en.wikipedia.org/w/index.php?title=File:Madras_Prov_1859.gif *Contributors:* BotMultichill, File Upload Bot (Magnus Manske), Miniapolis, OgreBot 2, Revent, Roland zh ... 430
Figure 197 *Source:* https://en.wikipedia.org/w/index.php?title=File:Madras_Prov_South_1909.jpg *License:* Public Domain *Contributors:* Ekabhishek, Jungpionier, Magog the Ogre, Praveenp, Roland zh, Shyamal ... 431
Figure 198 *Source:* https://en.wikipedia.org/w/index.php?title=File:India_Administrative_Divisions_1951.svg *License:* Creative Commons Zero *Contributors:* Andhrapur ... 434
Figure 199 *Source:* https://en.wikipedia.org/w/index.php?title=File:French_India_1815.gif *License:* Creative Commons Attribution-Sharealike 3.0 *Contributors:* User:Lubiesque ... 436
Figure 200 *Source:* https://en.wikipedia.org/w/index.php?title=File:Sikkim_area_map.svg *Contributors:* Philg88; Attribution: Wikimedia Foundation (www.wikimedia.org) ... 438
Image *Source:* https://en.wikipedia.org/w/index.php?title=File:Flag_of_Azad_Kashmir.svg *License:* Public Domain *Contributors:* Himasaram 446
Image *Source:* https://en.wikipedia.org/w/index.php?title=File:Flag_of_Swat.svg *License:* Public Domain *Contributors:* Washiucho ... 446
Image *Source:* https://en.wikipedia.org/w/index.php?title=File:Liwa-e-Ahmadiyya_1-2.svg *License:* Public Domain *Contributors:* Ceddyfresse 446
Image *Source:* https://en.wikipedia.org/w/index.php?title=File:Flag_of_the_Pakistani_Army.svg *License:* Creative Commons Attribution-ShareAlike 3.0 Unported *Contributors:* Himasaram ... 446
Image *Source:* https://en.wikipedia.org/w/index.php?title=File:Flag_of_Imperial_India.svg *License:* Public Domain *Contributors:* Chandranath sau 447
Image *Source:* https://en.wikipedia.org/w/index.php?title=File:Flag_of_Indian_Army.svg *License:* Creative Commons Attribution-ShareAlike 3.0 Unported *Contributors:* Fred the Oyster ... 447
Image *Source:* https://en.wikipedia.org/w/index.php?title=File:Flag_of_the_Governor-General_of_Pakistan_(1947-1953).svg *License:* Creative Commons Zero *Contributors:* User:Thommy9 ... 447
Image *Source:* https://en.wikipedia.org/w/index.php?title=File:Flag_of_the_Prime_Minister_of_Pakistan.svg *License:* Creative Commons Attribution-Sharealike 3.0 *Contributors:* : THEunique Coat_of_arms_of_Pakistan.svg: Rugby471 Flag_of_Pakistan.svg: Zscout370, Gabbe, Pumbaa80 derivative work: Nik ... 447
Figure 201 *Source:* https://en.wikipedia.org/w/index.php?title=File:Partition_of_India_1947_en.svg *Contributors:* RaviC, Superbenjamin, फ़िलप्रो 449
Figure 202 *Source:* https://en.wikipedia.org/w/index.php?title=File:Auchinleck.jpg *License:* Public Domain *Contributors:* Palmer (Lt), No 1 Army Film & Photographic Unit ... 449
Figure 203 *Source:* https://en.wikipedia.org/w/index.php?title=File:Sir_Hari_Singh_Bahadur,_Maharaja_of_Jammu_and_Kashmir,_1944.jpg *License:* Public Domain *Contributors:* Vandyk ... 451
Figure 204 *Source:* https://en.wikipedia.org/w/index.php?title=File:Sheikh_Abdullah.jpg *Contributors:* Unknown ... 452
Figure 205 *Source:* https://en.wikipedia.org/w/index.php?title=File:Liaquat_Ali_Khan.jpg *License:* Public Domain *Contributors:* Liaquat Ali Khan 455
Figure 206 *Source:* https://en.wikipedia.org/w/index.php?title=File:Murree_Richtone(HDR).jpg *Contributors:* User:Azm Rehman ... 455
Figure 207 *Source:* https://en.wikipedia.org/w/index.php?title=File:Jawaharlal_Nehru_1946.jpg *License:* Public Domain *Contributors:* Jonas Steinhöfel ... 456
Figure 208 *Source:* https://en.wikipedia.org/w/index.php?title=File:J&K01low.jpg *License:* Public domain *Contributors:* AshLin, File Upload Bot (Magnus Manske), OgreBot 2 ... 459
Figure 209 *Source:* https://en.wikipedia.org/w/index.php?title=File:J&K02low.jpg *License:* Public domain *Contributors:* AshLin, File Upload Bot (Magnus Manske), OgreBot 2 ... 460
Figure 210 *Source:* https://en.wikipedia.org/w/index.php?title=File:J&K03low.jpg *License:* Public domain *Contributors:* AshLin, File Upload Bot (Magnus Manske), OgreBot 2 ... 461
Figure 211 *Source:* https://en.wikipedia.org/w/index.php?title=File:J&K04low.jpg *License:* Public domain *Contributors:* AshLin, File Upload Bot (Magnus Manske), OgreBot 2 ... 462
Figure 212 *Source:* https://en.wikipedia.org/w/index.php?title=File:J&K05low.jpg *License:* Public domain *Contributors:* AshLin, File Upload Bot (Magnus Manske), OgreBot 2 ... 462
Figure 213 *Source:* https://en.wikipedia.org/w/index.php?title=File:J&K06low.jpg *License:* Public domain *Contributors:* AshLin, File Upload Bot (Magnus Manske), OgreBot 2 ... 463
Figure 214 *Source:* https://en.wikipedia.org/w/index.php?title=File:J&K07low.jpg *License:* Public domain *Contributors:* AshLin, File Upload Bot (Magnus Manske), OgreBot 2 ... 464
Figure 215 *Source:* https://en.wikipedia.org/w/index.php?title=File:J&K08low.jpg *License:* Public domain *Contributors:* AshLin, File Upload Bot (Magnus Manske), OgreBot 2 ... 464
Figure 216 *Source:* https://en.wikipedia.org/w/index.php?title=File:J&K09low.jpg *License:* Public domain *Contributors:* AshLin, File Upload Bot (Magnus Manske), OgreBot 2 ... 465
Figure 217 *Source:* https://en.wikipedia.org/w/index.php?title=File:J&K10low.jpg *License:* Public domain *Contributors:* AshLin, File Upload Bot (Magnus Manske), OgreBot 2, 1 anonymous edits ... 466
Figure 218 *Source:* https://en.wikipedia.org/w/index.php?title=File:India_Administrative_Divisions_1951.svg *License:* Creative Commons Zero *Contributors:* Andhrapur ... 473
Figure 219 *Source:* https://en.wikipedia.org/w/index.php?title=File:South_Indian_territories.svg *License:* Creative Commons Attribution 3.0 *Contributors:* AreJay ... 474
Figure 220 *Source:* https://en.wikipedia.org/w/index.php?title=File:India_administrative_map_1956_PL.png *License:* GNU Free Documentation License *Contributors:* File Upload Bot (Magnus Manske), MGA73bot2, OgreBot 2, Roland zh, Shadowxfox, VanWiel ... 476
Image *Source:* https://en.wikipedia.org/w/index.php?title=File:Kashmir_region_2004.jpg *License:* Public Domain *Contributors:* CIA ... 482
Image *Source:* https://en.wikipedia.org/w/index.php?title=File:Ensign_of_the_Indian_Air_Force.svg *Contributors:* - ... 483
Image *Source:* https://en.wikipedia.org/w/index.php?title=File:Naval_Ensign_of_India.svg *License:* Public Domain *Contributors:* Alkari, B4567V, Denelson83, Ec.Domnowall, Fry1989, Kwasura, Roland zh, Stunteltje, Urhixidur, Zscout370, 12 anonymous edits ... 483
Image *Source:* https://en.wikipedia.org/w/index.php?title=File:Presidential_Standard_of_Pakistan.svg *License:* Creative Commons Attribution-Sharealike 2.5 *Contributors:* User:Zscout370, User:Zscout370 ... 483
Image *Source:* https://en.wikipedia.org/w/index.php?title=File:Pakistani_Air_Force_Ensign.svg *Contributors:* - ... 483
Image *Source:* https://en.wikipedia.org/w/index.php?title=File:Naval_Jack_of_Pakistan.svg *License:* Public Domain *Contributors:* Alkari, Denelson83, Fast track~commonswiki, Fry1989, 6 anonymous edits ... 483
Figure 221 *Source:* https://en.wikipedia.org/w/index.php?title=File:1965_Infiltrators.jpg *License:* Public Domain *Contributors:* Original uploader was AreJay at en.wikipedia ... 485
Figure 222 *Source:* https://en.wikipedia.org/w/index.php?title=File:1965_war.jpg *License:* Creative Commons Attribution 3.0 *Contributors:* FlickrWarrior, Ms Sarah Welch, Netstar1 ... 487
Figure 223 *Source:* https://en.wikipedia.org/w/index.php?title=File:Gen_Musa_Khan_at_Khem_Karan_-_1965_War.jpg *License:* Public Domain *Contributors:* Adamgerber80, Aeg0n94, ShakespeareFan00, Vanjagenije ... 488
Figure 224 *Source:* https://en.wikipedia.org/w/index.php?title=File:PAF_gallery.jpg *License:* GNU Free Documentation License *Contributors:* Pakistan Airforce ... 491
Figure 225 *Source:* https://en.wikipedia.org/w/index.php?title=File:MMAlam-1965.jpg *License:* Public Domain *Contributors:* Adamgerber80, Aeg0n94, ShakespeareFan00, Vanjagenije ... 492
Figure 226 *Source:* https://en.wikipedia.org/w/index.php?title=File:1965_Indo-Pak_War_DestroyedShermanTank.jpg *License:* Public domain *Contributors:* Cloudbound, File Upload Bot (Magnus Manske), OgreBot 2, IOкке ... 493
Figure 227 *Source:* https://en.wikipedia.org/w/index.php?title=File:Destroyed_Patton_Tank_(1965_Indo-Pak_War).jpg *License:* Public domain *Contributors:* Articseahorse, Brakeet, File Upload Bot (Magnus Manske), OgreBot 2, Xwejnusgozo, IOкке, 1 anonymous edits ... 494
Figure 228 *Source:* https://en.wikipedia.org/w/index.php?title=File:Mcconaughy20oct1965a.jpg *Contributors:* Idleguy ... 501
Image *Source:* https://en.wikipedia.org/w/index.php?title=File:China_India_Locator_(1959).svg *License:* Creative Commons Attribution-Sharealike 3.0 *Contributors:* User:JCRules ... 510
Figure 229 *Source:* https://en.wikipedia.org/w/index.php?title=File:British_Indian_Empire_1909_Imperial_Gazetteer_of_India.jpg *License:* Public Domain *Contributors:* Edinburgh Geographical Institute; J. G. Bartholomew and Sons. ... 512
Figure 230 *Source:* https://en.wikipedia.org/w/index.php?title=File:Postal_Map_of_China_,1917.jpg *License:* Public Domain *Contributors:* Government of China ... 512
Figure 231 *Source:* https://en.wikipedia.org/w/index.php?title=File:Kashmir_map_big.jpg *License:* Public Domain *Contributors:* A ri gi bod, Flamarande~commonswiki, Hornstrandir1, Juiced lemon, LX, Phatom87, Roland zh, Sven-steffen arndt, TheDJ, Timeshifter, Zaccarias, Zykasaa, 19 anonymous edits ... 513
Figure 232 *Source:* https://en.wikipedia.org/w/index.php?title=File:Hindutagh-pass-aksai-chin-center2-1873.jpg *License:* Public Domain *Contributors:* H. Trotter ... 514

Figure 233 *Source:* https://en.wikipedia.org/w/index.php?title=File:Hung_Ta-Chen's_Map.jpg *License:* Public Domain *Contributors:* Government of China ... 515
Figure 234 *Source:* https://en.wikipedia.org/w/index.php?title=File:China_India_eastern_border_88.jpg *License:* Public Domain *Contributors:* Central Intelligence Agency ... 517
Figure 235 *Source:* https://en.wikipedia.org/w/index.php?title=File:Aksai_Chin_Sino-Indian_border_map.png *License:* Creative Commons Attribution-Sharealike 3.0 *Contributors:* User:The Discoverer ... 531
Figure 236 *Source:* https://en.wikipedia.org/w/index.php?title=File:China_India_western_border_88.jpg *License:* Public Domain *Contributors:* Kauiliya3, LX, Marie11612, Rosemania, Shadowxfox, Timeshifter, Vyzasatya, 7 anonymous edits ... 533
Figure 237 *Source:* https://en.wikipedia.org/w/index.php?title=File:John_Kenneth_Galbraith_and_Jawaharlal_Nehru.jpg *License:* Public Domain *Contributors:* Co9man, Gbawden ... 539
Image *Source:* https://en.wikipedia.org/w/index.php?title=File:BangladeshLiberationWarMontage.jpg *License:* Creative Commons Attribution-Sharealike 3.0 *Contributors:* User:ExcelD24 ... 545
Image *Source:* https://en.wikipedia.org/w/index.php?title=File:Flag_of_Bangladesh_(1971).svg *License:* Creative Commons Attribution-ShareAlike 3.0 Unported *Contributors:* Himasaram Nirvik12 (Valid SVG Version) ... 546
Image *Source:* https://en.wikipedia.org/w/index.php?title=File:Flag_of_the_Mukti_Bahini-DeFacto.png *Contributors:* EugeneZelenko, Gaurh, Tre, 1 anonymous edits ... 546
Image *Source:* https://en.wikipedia.org/w/index.php?title=File:Flag_of_the_Ministry_of_Defence_of_India.svg *Contributors:* User:Bharata-indstar 546
Image *Source:* https://en.wikipedia.org/w/index.php?title=File:Flag_of_Pakistan-moon_and_star.png *License:* Creative Commons Attribution-Sharealike 3.0 *Contributors:* User:Soerfm ... 546
Image *Source:* https://en.wikipedia.org/w/index.php?title=File:White_flag_icon.svg *License:* Public Domain *Contributors:* Ash Crow, Captaincollect1970, Cycn, File Upload Bot (Magnus Manske), Ludger1961, Rocket000, Sarang, SiBr4, W!B:, Xiengyod~commonswiki, 2 anonymous edits ..546
Image *Source:* https://en.wikipedia.org/w/index.php?title=File:Air_Force_Ensign_of_India.svg *License:* Public Domain *Contributors:* Alkari, Chesipiero, Fry1989, Greenshed, Man77, Nightstallion, Roland zh, Sumanch, Zirland, 6 anonymous edits ... 546
Image *Source:* https://en.wikipedia.org/w/index.php?title=File:RAW_India.jpg *Contributors:* User:News portal india 007 ... 546
Image *Source:* https://en.wikipedia.org/w/index.php?title=File:Flag-map_of_Bangladesh2.svg *Contributors:* User:Stasyan117 ... 547
Figure 238 *Source:* https://en.wikipedia.org/w/index.php?title=File:India_religion_map_1909_en.jpg *License:* Public Domain *Contributors:* Indian and UK civil servants. ... 549
Figure 239 *Source:* https://en.wikipedia.org/w/index.php?title=File:Shaheed_minar_Roehl.jpg *License:* GNU Free Documentation License *Contributors:* Afifa Afrin, AnonMoos, JuTa, MECU, MGA73bot2, Muntasir du, NahidSultan, Ragib, Roland zh, Sminthopsis84, ~Pyb, 3 anonymous edits 551
Figure 240 *Source:* https://en.wikipedia.org/w/index.php?title=File:March71.PNG *License:* Creative Commons Attribution-Sharealike 3.0 *Contributors:* Maglorbd (talk) ... 555
Figure 241 *Source:* https://en.wikipedia.org/w/index.php?title=File:Sheikh_Mujibur_Rahman_in_1950.jpg *License:* Public Domain *Contributors:* Arr4, Jayantanth, Moheen Reeyad, NahidSultan, Wikitanvir, আফতাবুজ্জামান, 3 anonymous edits ... 557
Figure 242 *Source:* https://en.wikipedia.org/w/index.php?title=File:Sectors_of_Bangladesh_Liberation_War.svg *License:* Creative Commons Attribution 2.5 *Contributors:* Armanaziz ... 560
Figure 243 *Source:* https://en.wikipedia.org/w/index.php?title=File:George_Harrison_-_Bangla_Desh.png *License:* Public Domain *Contributors:* Apple Records ... 560
Figure 244 *Source:* https://en.wikipedia.org/w/index.php?title=File:Bangladesh_1971_Liberation.jpg *License:* Public Domain *Contributors:* Mike Young ... 562
Figure 245 *Source:* https://en.wikipedia.org/w/index.php?title=File:Indira2.jpg *Contributors:* - ... 563
Figure 246 *Source:* https://en.wikipedia.org/w/index.php?title=File:1971_Instrument_of_Surrender.jpg *License:* Public Domain *Contributors:* User:Racconish ... 565
Figure 247 *Source:* https://en.wikipedia.org/w/index.php?title=File:Sriti_shoud.jpg *License:* Creative Commons Attribution-Sharealike 3.0 *Contributors:* Luthador ... 566
Figure 248 *Source:* https://en.wikipedia.org/w/index.php?title=File:André_Malraux_Pic,_22.jpg *License:* Public Domain *Contributors:* Discasto, Hsarrazin, Lorry, Palamède, Paris 16, Pmx, Yann ... 568
Figure 249 *Source:* https://en.wikipedia.org/w/index.php?title=File:Ted_Kennedy,_1967_(cropped).jpg *License:* Creative Commons Attribution 2.0 *Contributors:* Seattle Municipal Archives from Seattle, WA ... 569
Figure 250 *Source:* https://en.wikipedia.org/w/index.php?title=File:Yahya_and_Nixon.jpg *License:* Public Domain *Contributors:* Oliver F. Atkins, 1916-1977, photographer ... 570
Figure 251 *Source:* https://en.wikipedia.org/w/index.php?title=File:Punjab_Monsoon.jpg *License:* Creative Commons Attribution-Sharealike 3.0 *Contributors:* User:Sanyambahga ... 575
Figure 252 *Source:* https://en.wikipedia.org/w/index.php?title=File:Amul_Plant_at_Anand.jpg *License:* Creative Commons Attribution-Sharealike 3.0 *Contributors:* Notnarayan ... 579
Figure 253 *Source:* https://en.wikipedia.org/w/index.php?title=File:Historical_Pakistan.gif *Contributors:* BotMultichill, BotMultichillT, Bryan Derksen, Electionworld, Green Giant, J.delanoy, Karlfk, LX, Shadowxfox, TUBS, Zaccarias, 5 anonymous edits ... 585
Figure 254 *Source:* https://en.wikipedia.org/w/index.php?title=File:Bangladesh_1971_Liberation.jpg *License:* Public Domain *Contributors:* Mike Young ... 588
Figure 255 *Source:* https://en.wikipedia.org/w/index.php?title=File:Ussdiablo.jpg *License:* Public Domain *Contributors:* LCDR Tomme J. Lambertson (retired United States Navy (USN) personnel). ... 589
Figure 256 *Source:* https://en.wikipedia.org/w/index.php?title=File:INS_Vikrant_(R11)_launches_an_Alize_aircraft_during_Indo-Pakistani_War_of_1971.jpg *Contributors:* User:Racconish ... 591
Image *Source:* https://en.wikipedia.org/w/index.php?title=File:Air_Force_Ensign_of_Pakistan.svg *License:* Public Domain *Contributors:* Zscout370 ... 596
Figure 257 *Source:* https://en.wikipedia.org/w/index.php?title=File:Blood_telegram.png *Contributors:* Archer K. Blood ... 596
Figure 258 *Source:* https://en.wikipedia.org/w/index.php?title=File:Indira_Gandhi_1977.jpg *License:* Creative Commons Attribution-Sharealike 3.0 *Contributors:* Achim55, Casigno145, Materialscientist, OgreBot 2, Shiva Kumar H.U. ... 611
Image *Source:* https://en.wikipedia.org/w/index.php?title=File:Flag_of_the_Indian_Army.svg *Contributors:* - ... 627
Image *Source:* https://en.wikipedia.org/w/index.php?title=File:Flagge_Khalistans.svg *License:* Public Domain *Contributors:* J. Patrick Fischer 627
Figure 259 *Source:* https://en.wikipedia.org/w/index.php?title=File:Golden_temple_Akal_Takhat.jpg *License:* GNU Free Documentation License *Contributors:* KTo288, MGA73, MGA73bot2, Magog the Ogre, OgreBot 2, Roland zh, Vanwa68 ... 629
Figure 260 *Source:* https://en.wikipedia.org/w/index.php?title=File:AkalTakhtGoldenTempleComplex.jpg *License:* Creative Commons Attribution-Sharealike 3.0 *Contributors:* Paanikivi ... 632
Figure 261 *Source:* https://en.wikipedia.org/w/index.php?title=File:New-Plan-Of-Harmandar-rp.jpg *License:* Creative Commons Attribution-ShareAlike 3.0 Unported *Contributors:* Alenwala ... 637
Figure 262 *Source:* https://en.wikipedia.org/w/index.php?title=File:Akal_takhat_amritsar.jpg *License:* GNU Free Documentation License *Contributors:* Ekabhishek, Ggia, Havang(nl), MGA73bot2, Magog the Ogre, Roland zh, Tonkawa68, Wst ... 639
Figure 263 *Source:* https://en.wikipedia.org/w/index.php?title=File:AB133_-_Vijayanta_MBT.JPG *License:* Creative Commons Attribution-Sharealike 2.5 *Contributors:* AshLin, FlickrWarrior, KTo288, Roland zh, 1 anonymous edits ... 641
Figure 264 *Source:* https://en.wikipedia.org/w/index.php?title=File:Indira_gandhi_memorial.jpg *License:* Public Domain *Contributors:* User:आशीष भटनागर ... 649
Figure 265 *Source:* https://en.wikipedia.org/w/index.php?title=File:PathOfMartyrdom.JPG *License:* Creative Commons Attribution-Sharealike 3.0 *Contributors:* GaneshBhakt (talk) ... 650
Figure 266 *Source:* https://en.wikipedia.org/w/index.php?title=File:IndiraGandhi-SareeAtTimeOfDeath.JPG *License:* Creative Commons Attribution-Sharealike 3.0 *Contributors:* GaneshBhakt (talk) ... 651
Figure 267 *Source:* https://en.wikipedia.org/w/index.php?title=File:Jagdish_Tytler.jpg *License:* Public Domain *Contributors:* Filmi Tadka ... 665
Figure 268 *Source:* https://en.wikipedia.org/w/index.php?title=File:Kamal_Nath_-_World_Economic_Forum_Annual_Meeting_Davos_2008.jpg *License:* Creative Commons Attribution 2.0 *Contributors:* Copyright World Economic Forum (www.weforum.org) swiss-image.ch/Photo by Remy Steinegger ... 666
Image *Source:* https://en.wikipedia.org/w/index.php?title=File:Bhopal-Union_Carbide_1_crop_memorial.jpg *License:* Creative Commons Attribution-Sharealike 2.0 *Contributors:* 84user, OgreBot 2, Roland zh, Skeezix1000 ... 671
Figure 269 *Source:* https://en.wikipedia.org/w/index.php?title=File:Bhopal_Plant_7.JPG *License:* Creative Commons Attribution-Sharealike 3.0 *Contributors:* Julian Nitzsche ... 674
Figure 270 *Source:* https://en.wikipedia.org/w/index.php?title=File:Preparation_of_carbaryl_as_in_Bhopal.svg *License:* Creative Commons Attribution-Sharealike 3.0 *Contributors:* User:RicHard-59 ... 675
Figure 271 *Source:* https://en.wikipedia.org/w/index.php?title=File:Glutathione_+_Methylisocyanate_Reaction.svg *License:* Creative Commons Attribution-Sharealike 3.0 *Contributors:* User:RicHard-59 ... 677

Figure 272 *Source:* https://en.wikipedia.org/w/index.php?title=File:BHOPAL_(231583728).jpg *License:* Creative Commons Attribution 2.0 *Contributors:* Obi from ROMA ,LONDON 679

Figure 273 *Source:* https://en.wikipedia.org/w/index.php?title=File:Bhopal-Union_Carbide_2.jpg *License:* Creative Commons Attribution-Sharealike 2.0 *Contributors:* Original uploader was Simone.lippi at it.wikipedia 693

Image *Source:* https://en.wikipedia.org/w/index.php?title=File:LiberationTigersofTamilEelamFlag.jpg *License:* Creative Commons Zero *Contributors:* User:MartinKassemJ120 701

Image *Source:* https://en.wikipedia.org/w/index.php?title=File:Kashmir_Jammu_Map.png *License:* Creative Commons Attribution-Sharealike 3.0 *Contributors:* User:The Rim of the Sky 706

Figure 274 *Source:* https://en.wikipedia.org/w/index.php?title=File:Un-kashmir-jammu.png *License:* UN map *Contributors:* A ri gi bod, Jeroen, LX, Ras67, 22 anonymous edits 707

Figure 275 *Source:* https://en.wikipedia.org/w/index.php?title=File:Page_1_-_CFL_as_shown_on_UN_Map_to_Karachi_Agreement_1949.JPG *License:* UN map *Contributors:* EChastain, Natuur12, Oompahloompah2016, TripWire 709

Figure 276 *Source:* https://en.wikipedia.org/w/index.php?title=File:Page_2_-_CFL_as_shown_on_UN_Map_to_Karachi_Agreement_1949.JPG *License:* UN map *Contributors:* United Nations DAG Digital Library 709

Figure 277 *Source:* https://en.wikipedia.org/w/index.php?title=File:Page_3_-_CFL_as_shown_on_UN_Map_to_Karachi_Agreement_1949.JPG *License:* UN map *Contributors:* EChastain, Kalbbes, Natuur12, Oompahloompah2016, TripWire 709

Figure 278 *Source:* https://en.wikipedia.org/w/index.php?title=File:India_Jammu_and_Kashmir_location_map_UN_view.svg *License:* Creative Commons Attribution-Sharealike 3.0 *Contributors:* India_Jammu_and_Kashmir_location_map.svg: derivative work: Avoided blue (talk) 709

Figure 279 *Source:* https://en.wikipedia.org/w/index.php?title=File:Old_Map_Showing_Siachen_as_Part_of_Pakistan.jpg *Contributors:* P. L. Lakhanpal 711

Figure 280 *Source:* https://en.wikipedia.org/w/index.php?title=File:Dogra_Siachen.jpg *License:* Creative Commons Attribution 2.0 *Contributors:* Abhishek_Kumar 712

Figure 281 *Source:* https://en.wikipedia.org/w/index.php?title=File:GyongLaNJ9842.png *License:* Creative Commons Attribution-Sharealike 3.0 *Contributors:* Nehapant19 714

Figure 282 *Source:* https://en.wikipedia.org/w/index.php?title=File:Shyok2.svg *License:* Creative Commons Attribution 3.0 *Contributors:* Kmhkmh 714

Figure 283 *Source:* https://en.wikipedia.org/w/index.php?title=File:Remains_of_clothing_worn_by_Rajiv_Gandhi_during_his_assassination.jpg *Contributors:* User:Royroydeb 722

Figure 284 *Source:* https://en.wikipedia.org/w/index.php?title=File:Rajiv_Gandhi_Memorial_bombsite.jpg *License:* Creative Commons Attribution-Sharealike 2.5 *Contributors:* Avjoska, Planemad, Roland zh, Vadakkan 722

Figure 285 *Source:* https://en.wikipedia.org/w/index.php?title=File:Rajiv_Gandhi_Memorial_path.jpg *License:* Creative Commons Attribution-Sharealike 2.5 *Contributors:* Planemad, Vadakkan 723

Figure 286 *Source:* https://en.wikipedia.org/w/index.php?title=File:Rajiv_Gandhi_Memorial_blast_site.jpg *License:* Creative Commons Attribution-Sharealike 2.5 *Contributors:* Planemad, Vadakkan 723

Image *Source:* https://en.wikipedia.org/w/index.php?title=File:Flag_of_Jihad.svg *License:* Public Domain *Contributors:* Aua, BotMultichill, Cathy Richards, Chyah, Clusternote, Cycn, Dbachmann, Herbythyme, Homo lupus, Illegitimate Barrister, Ionchari, Jafeluv, Jarould, Jdx, Khaerr∼commonswiki, Körnerbrötchen, Lexicon, Mattes, Mistagonzo, Oren neu dag, Pooriaazimi, Skipjack, Supreme Dragon, Themightyquill, Túrelio, Überraschungsbilder, 9 anonymous edits 729

Image *Source:* https://en.wikipedia.org/w/index.php?title=File:Flag_of_Lashkar-e-Taiba.svg *License:* Creative Commons Attribution-Sharealike 3.0 *Contributors:* User:ArnoldPlaton 729

Image *Source:* https://en.wikipedia.org/w/index.php?title=File:Jaishi-e-Mohammed.svg *License:* Public Domain *Contributors:* R-41 729

Image *Source:* https://en.wikipedia.org/w/index.php?title=File:Harakat_flag.png *License:* GNU Free Documentation License *Contributors:* ArnoldPlaton, Benzoyl, Cycn, Erlenmeyer, Ernesttico, Homo lupus, MGA73bot2, Mormegil, OgreBot 2, TFerenczy, Túrelio, 1 anonymous edits 729

Image *Source:* https://en.wikipedia.org/w/index.php?title=File:Al-badr_flag.png *Contributors:* https://ca.wikipedia.org/wiki/Usuari:Jolle 729

Image *Source:* https://en.wikipedia.org/w/index.php?title=File:Kashmir_independent.svg *License:* Public Domain *Contributors:* User:Walden69 729

Image *Source:* https://en.wikipedia.org/w/index.php?title=File:AQMI_Flag_asymmetric.svg *License:* Public Domain *Contributors:* Abdulrahminov, AyaanLamar, BurritoBazooka, Cathy Richards, Chyah, Cycn, Dbachmann, Jarekt, Jarould, Pariah24, Supreme Dragon, ∼riley, وهبة خليل, ديفيد عادل 2 729

Image *Source:* https://en.wikipedia.org/w/index.php?title=File:Flag_of_Taliban.svg *License:* Public Domain *Contributors:* AnonMoos, Antemister, Beria, Bilal.afghan, BotMultichill, Cathy Richards, Cycn, Dbachmann, FutureTrillionaire, Gripweed, Herr Satz, Homo lupus, Illegitimate Barrister, Jarould, Jeff G., Lexicon, Liftarn, Lotje, Mattes, OsamaK, Supreme Dragon, Themightyquill, Vmenkov, Xiengyod∼commonswiki, 13 anonymous edits 729

Image *Source:* https://en.wikipedia.org/w/index.php?title=File:Flag_of_al-Qaeda.svg *Contributors:* - 729

Figure 287 *Source:* https//en.wikipedia.org *License:* Creative Commons Attribution-Sharealike 3.0 *Contributors:* User:AmyNorth 731

Figure 288 *Source:* https://en.wikipedia.org/w/index.php?title=File:HSBC_GLT_PUNE.jpg *License:* GNU Free Documentation License *Contributors:* Amitauti (talk) 767

Image *Source:* https://en.wikipedia.org/w/index.php?title=File:Sansad_Bhavan-2.jpg *License:* Public Domain *Contributors:* Aschroet, Dcastor 771

Image *Source:* https://en.wikipedia.org/w/index.php?title=File:Ahmedabad_riots1.jpg *License:* Creative Commons Attribution 2.5 *Contributors:* User:Aksi great 776

Image *Source:* https://en.wikipedia.org/w/index.php?title=File:Symbol_support_vote.svg *License:* Public Domain *Contributors:* Anomie, Fastily, Jo-Jo Eumerus 802

Image *Source:* https://en.wikipedia.org/w/index.php?title=File:Bombaymapconfimed_attacks.png *Contributors:* user:geni open street maps ... 803

Figure 289 *Source:* https://en.wikipedia.org/w/index.php?title=File:Mahim_train_blast.jpg *License:* Creative Commons Attribution-Sharealike 2.0 *Contributors:* Manoj Nair 805

Figure 290 *Source:* https://en.wikipedia.org/w/index.php?title=File:2008_Mumbai_terror_attack_VT_bullet_mark.jpg *License:* Creative Commons Attribution-Sharealike 3.0 *Contributors:* Nicholas (Nichalp) 807

Figure 291 *Source:* https://en.wikipedia.org/w/index.php?title=File:Cafe_leopold_damage_Mumbai_nov_2008.jpg *License:* Creative Commons Attribution-Sharealike 3.0 *Contributors:* Adhishb (talk) 808

Figure 292 *Source:* https://en.wikipedia.org/w/index.php?title=File:2008_Mumbai_terror_attacks_Oberoi_Restaurant.jpg *License:* Creative Commons Attribution-Sharealike 3.0 *Contributors:* Nicholas (Nichalp) 809

Figure 293 *Source:* https://en.wikipedia.org/w/index.php?title=File:2008_Mumbai_terror_attacks_Taj_Hotel_Wasabi_Restaurant_burned.jpg *License:* Creative Commons Attribution-Sharealike 3.0 *Contributors:* Nicholas (Nichalp) 809

Figure 294 *Source:* https://en.wikipedia.org/w/index.php?title=File:2008_Mumbai_terror_attacks_Nariman_House_front_view_3.jpg *License:* Creative Commons Attribution-Sharealike 3.0 *Contributors:* Nicholas (Nichalp) 810

Figure 295 *Source:* https://en.wikipedia.org/w/index.php?title=File:Mumbai_attacks_vinu_image01-crop.jpg *License:* Creative Commons Attribution-Sharealike 2.0 *Contributors:* derivative work: Nesnad (talk) Mumbai_attacks_vinu_image01.jpg: Vinukumar Ranganathan from Bangalore (prev Bombay & Be 813

Image *Source:* https://en.wikipedia.org/w/index.php?title=File:Flag_of_the_United_States.svg *License:* Public Domain *Contributors:* Anomie, Jo-Jo Eumerus, MSGJ, Mr. Stradivarius 818

Image *Source:* https://en.wikipedia.org/w/index.php?title=File:Flag_of_Israel.svg *License:* Public Domain *Contributors:* "The Provisional Council of State Proclamation of the Flag of the State of Israel" of 25 Tishrei 5709 (28 October 1948) 818

Image *Source:* https://en.wikipedia.org/w/index.php?title=File:Flag_of_Germany.svg *License:* Public Domain *Contributors:* Anomie, Jo-Jo Eumerus 818

Image *Source:* https://en.wikipedia.org/w/index.php?title=File:Flag_of_Australia.svg *License:* Public Domain *Contributors:* Anomie, Jo-Jo Eumerus, Mifter 818

Image *Source:* https://en.wikipedia.org/w/index.php?title=File:Flag_of_Canada.svg *License:* Public Domain *Contributors:* Anomie, Jo-Jo Eumerus 818

Image *Source:* https://en.wikipedia.org/w/index.php?title=File:Flag_of_France.svg *License:* Public Domain *Contributors:* Anomie, Fastily, Jo-Jo Eumerus 818

Image *Source:* https://en.wikipedia.org/w/index.php?title=File:Flag_of_Italy.svg *License:* Public Domain *Contributors:* Anomie, Jo-Jo Eumerus 818

Image *Source:* https://en.wikipedia.org/w/index.php?title=File:Flag_of_the_Netherlands.svg *License:* Public Domain *Contributors:* Zscout370 818

Image *Source:* https://en.wikipedia.org/w/index.php?title=File:Flag_of_Japan.svg *License:* Public Domain *Contributors:* Anomie, Jo-Jo Eumerus 818

Image *Source:* https://en.wikipedia.org/w/index.php?title=File:Flag_of_Jordan.svg *License:* Public Domain *Contributors:* User:SKopp 818

Image *Source:* https://en.wikipedia.org/w/index.php?title=File:Flag_of_Mauritius.svg *License:* Public Domain *Contributors:* User:Zscout370 818

Image *Source:* https://en.wikipedia.org/w/index.php?title=File:Flag_of_Mexico.svg *License:* Public Domain *Contributors:* Alex Covarrubias, 9 April 2006 Based on the arms by Juan Gabino. 818

Image *Source:* https://en.wikipedia.org/w/index.php?title=File:Flag_of_Thailand.svg *Contributors:* Achim55, Andy Dingley, Chaddy, Denelson83, Dfddtdt, Duduziq, Emerentia, Fry1989, Gabbe, Giro720, Gurch, Hedwig in Washington, Homo lupus, Illegitimate Barrister, Jo Shigeru,

Juiced lemon, Kimjiho2015, Klemen Kocjancic, Mattes, Neq00, Paul 012, Perhelion, Rugby471, Sahapon-krit hellokitty, Siebrand, TOR, Teetaweepo, Xiengyod~commonswiki, Yann, Zscout370, Δ, 28 anonymous edits 818
Image *Source:* https://en.wikipedia.org/w/index.php?title=File:Flag_of_Austria.svg *License:* Public Domain *Contributors:* User:SKopp 818
Image *Source:* https://en.wikipedia.org/w/index.php?title=File:Flag_of_Spain.svg *License:* Public Domain *Contributors:* Anomie, Jo-Jo Eumerus, Topbanana 818
Image *Source:* https://en.wikipedia.org/w/index.php?title=File:Flag_of_the_Philippines.svg *License:* Public Domain *Contributors:* User:Achim1999 818
Image *Source:* https://en.wikipedia.org/w/index.php?title=File:Flag_of_Finland.svg *License:* Public Domain *Contributors:* SVG drawn by Sebastian Koppehel 818
Image *Source:* https://en.wikipedia.org/w/index.php?title=File:Flag_of_Norway.svg *License:* Public Domain *Contributors:* Dbenbenn 818
Figure 296 *Source:* https://en.wikipedia.org/w/index.php?title=File:3_December_2008_Gateway_protest_march_4.jpg *License:* Creative Commons Attribution-Sharealike 3.0 *Contributors:* Nicholas (Nichalp) 821
Figure 297 *Source:* https://en.wikipedia.org/w/index.php?title=File:Mumbai_Terror_Protest.JPG *License:* Creative Commons Attribution-Sharealike 3.0 *Contributors:* Vegpuff 822
Image *Source:* https://en.wikipedia.org/w/index.php?title=File:Commonwealth_Games_Federation_seal.svg *Contributors:* Commonwealth Games Federation 826
Figure 298 *Source:* https://en.wikipedia.org/w/index.php?title=File:Azimpremji.jpg *License:* Creative Commons Attribution-Sharealike 2.0 *Contributors:* Copyright World Economic Forum (www.weforum.org)/Photo by Dana Smillie 827
Figure 299 *Source:* https://en.wikipedia.org/w/index.php?title=File:Sally_Pearson-cropped.jpg *License:* Creative Commons Attribution-Sharealike 2.0 *Contributors:* Erik van Leeuwen 841
Image *Source:* https://en.wikipedia.org/w/index.php?title=File:Anna_Hazare_on_2nd_day.jpg *License:* Creative Commons Attribution-Sharealike 3.0 *Contributors:* Pankaj Jangid 873
Figure 300 *Source:* https://en.wikipedia.org/w/index.php?title=File:IAC-Protesters-in-Pune.jpg *License:* Creative Commons Attribution-Sharealike 3.0 *Contributors:* Nirzardp 879
Image *Source:* https://en.wikipedia.org/w/index.php?title=File:Wikinews-logo.svg *License:* Creative Commons Attribution-Sharealike 3.0 *Contributors:* Vectorized by Simon 01:05, 2 August 2006 (UTC) Updated by Time3000 17 April 2007 to use official Wikinews colours and ap 885
Image *Source:* https://en.wikipedia.org/w/index.php?title=File:Searchtool.svg *License:* GNU Lesser General Public License *Contributors:* Anomie 886

License

Creative Commons Attribution-Share Alike 3.0
//creativecommons.org/licenses/by-sa/3.0/

Index

A. A. K. Niazi, 374, 546, 581, 582
Aakraman, 608
Aam Aadmi Party, 884, 885
Aamir Khan, 822
Aandhi, 623
Abbottabad, 453
Abdul Ali Malik, 582
Abdul Aziz Mirza, 798
Abdul Ghaffar Khan, 310
Abdul Hamid Khan Bhashani, 554
Abdul Hamid Khan (general), 546, 582
Abdul Kalam, 717
Abdul Monem Khan, 586
Abdul Motaleb Malik, 546, 582, 595
Abdul Quader Molla, 546
Abdul Rahim Khan, 582, 604
Abhinav Bharat, 387
Ab initio, 413
Abolitionism in the United Kingdom, 121
ABP News, 647, 784
Absolute monarchy, 2, 55
Abu Ismail Dera Ismail Khan, 816
Abul Kalam Azad, 310, 316, 405
Abul Kalam Azad (politician), 546
Abyssinian people, 80
Accra, 535
Aceh, 43
Achyuta Deva Raya, 142
Acid throwing, 653, 782
Activism, 342
Act of Settlement 1701, 398
Acts of Union 1707, 908
Actual Ground Position Line, 714, 715, 718
Adampur, 495
Adam Roberts (scholar), 358
Adarsh Housing Society scam, 388, 848, 874
Addateegala, 350
Addendum, 708
Aden, 43, 97
Aden Province, 254
Adhir Ranjan Chowdhury, 871
Adi Granth, 175
Adil Shahi dynasty, 55, 56, 58
Adil Shah Suri, 31

Aditya Birla Group, 868
Adivasi, 431, 911
Adjutant, 198
Administrative subdivision, 33
Admiral, 582, 586, 798
Admiral Ahsan Mission, 584
Adnyapatra, 84
Adolf Hitler, 422
Adrian Greenwood, 243
Adrian Levy, 772
Advanced Light Helicopter, 716
Advisory opinion, 865
Advocate General, 405
Aerosol, 677
Afghan, 21
Afghan–Sikh wars, 181
Afghan Interim Administration, 799
Afghanistan, 2, 5, 20, 30, 36, 57, 178, 351, 448, 479, 548, 606
Afghan-Sikh Wars, 174
A Fine Balance, 622
Afsharid dynasty, 4
Afzal Guru, 773, 774
Afzal Rahman Khan, 483
Aga Khan Palace, 355
Agencies of British India, 258
Agent handling, 804
Agni-II, 382
A. G. Noorani, 542
Agra, 1, 3, 18, 20, 66, 78, 125, 129, 176, 199, 203, 214, 588
Agra division, 96
Agra famine of 1837–38, 97, 132, 286
Agra Fort, 20, 203
Agrarian reform, 12, 17
Agra Subah, 9, 18
Agricultural, 12, 33, 46
Agricultural subsidy, 765
Agriculture, 11, 155
Agriculture in India, 574, 768
Ahimsa, 298
Ahl-i Hadith, 203
Ahmad Shah Abdali, 36, 57, 80
Ahmad Shah Durrani, 66, 78, 180

959

Ahmad Zamir, 546
Ahmedabad, 79, 300, 344, 381, 776, 788, 875
Ahmed Shah Abdali, 64, 78
Ahmed Shuja Pasha, 823
Ahom kingdom, 39, 94
Ahom-Mughal conflicts, 39
AHQ (Pakistan Air Force), 582, 591
Ain-i-Akbari, 3, 4
Ainslie Thomas Embree, 780
Airbase, 495
Aircel, 863, 868
Air Chief Marshal, 582, 798
Air Commodore, 546, 582, 595
Aircraft carrier, 597
Air India Flight 182, 642
Air Marshal, 447, 483, 502, 546, 582
Air Officer Commander-in-Chief, 546
Air officer commanding, 546
Airstrip, 490, 562
Air superiority, 591, 592
Air supremacy, 549, 564
Air Vice Marshal, 582
AISSF, 628
Ajaigarh State, 186
Ajit Bharihoke, 862
Ajmal Kasab, 804, 806, 816, 823
Ajmer, 78
Ajmer-Merwara, 125, 258, 477
Ajmer State, 474
Ajmer subah, 9
AK47, 772
AK-47, 803, 806
Akali Dal, 628, 654, 883
Akali Dharm Yudh Morcha, 628, 655
Akal Takht, 175, 376, 627, 628, 639, 654
Akbar, 3, 7, 9, 23, 34, 39, 49, 448
Akbar Khan (Pakistani general), 456
Akbar the Great, 6, 33, 132, 175
A. K. Fazlul Huq, 309, 310
Akhand Kirtani Jatha, 629
Akhilesh Yadav, 872
Akhil Kumar, 836
Akhnoor, 486, 502
Akhtar Hussain Malik, 483
Aksai Chin, 369, 426, 427, 510, 511, 513, 529, 535
Akshardham Temple attack, 743, 778, 792
Alambagh, 221
Alamgir II, 10
Al-Badr (East Pakistan), 546, 548, 559, 567
Al-Badr (India), 729, 741
Al-Badr (Jammu and Kashmir), 732
Albert Ekka, 607
Aleksei A. Rodionov, 595
Alexei Kosygin, 499, 608
Alien Tort Statute, 681

Aligarh, 134, 335
Aligarh Muslim University, 8, 270, 335
Ali Jan Aurakzai, 772
Alipore bomb case, 347
Alison Williamson, 841
Alivardi Khan, 36, 50, 52
Aliya Rama Raya, 143
Alkali, 24
Alladi Krishnaswamy Iyer, 405
Allah, 759
Allahabad, 24, 199, 203, 215, 219, 248, 374
Allahabad district, 96
Allahabad High Court, 613
Allama Mashriqi, 349
Allama Muhammad Iqbal, 306
Allan Octavian Hume, 334
Allen S. Whiting (political scientist), 525
All India Anna Dravida Munnetra Kazhagam, 872
All India Congress Committee, 877
All-India Congress Committee, 611
All India Forward Bloc, 351
All India Institute of Medical Sciences, 656, 658, 724, 787
All India Institute of Medical Sciences, Delhi, 651
All India Institutes of Medical Sciences, 651
All India Muhammadan Educational Conference, 338
All India Muslim League, 294, 306, 309
All-India Muslim League, 305, 337, 338, 345, 355, 420, 448, 451
All India Radio, 374, 581, 608, 618, 645, 658
All India Services, 410
All India Sikh Students Federation, 637
All Parties Hurriyat Conference, 741
Alluri Sitarama Raju, 350
Al Qaeda, 741
Al-Qaeda, 729
Al-Shams (East Pakistan), 546, 548, 559, 567
Altitude, 490
Aluru Venkata Rao, 161
Alwar State, 186
Amanullah Khan (JKLF), 729
Amarinder Singh, 177, 897
Amarnath land transfer controversy, 735, 737
Amarnath Temple, 735
Amartya Sen, 287, 923
Amazon Standard Identification Number, 509
Ambala, 199, 500
Ambassador of the Soviet Union to Pakistan, 595
Amendment of the Constitution of India, 408, 411, 612
American Civil War, 114
American University, 686

Americas, 12, 14
Amicus curiae, 794
Amir, 149
Amir Abdullah Khan Niazi, 564–566, 594, 595
Amiya Kumar Bagchi, 889
Ammonia, 676
Ammtoje Mann, 669
Amnesty International, 735
Amrik Singh, 627, 637
Amrit Kaur, 362, 405
Amritsar, 132, 175, 304, 343, 377, 489, 494, 619, 627, 628, 646, 648
Amritsar Massacre, 349
A.M.T. Jackson, 347, 348
Amu (film), 668
Amul, 373, 579
Amulya Malladi, 694
AMX-13, 493
An Advanced History of India, 138, 244
Ananda Krishnan, 870
Anandamath, 103
Anand, Gujarat, 373, 579
Anandpur Resolution, 630, 654
Anandpur Sahib, 175
Anandpur Sahib Resolution, 654
Anant Kanhere, 347, 348
Anchor, 126
Ancient Greece, 23
Andaman and Nicobar, 353
Andaman and Nicobar Islands, 258, 266, 435, 474, 477
Andaman Islands, 96
Andhra Pradesh, 257, 282, 350, 431, 440, 476
Andhra State, 368, 475, 476
Andre Malraux, 568
Andrew Lauterstein, 838
Angana P. Chatterji, 795
Anglican, 278
Anglicist, 121, 122
Anglo-Burmese Wars, 111
Anglo-Indian, 333, 405
Anglo-Indians, 304
Anglo-Iraqi War, 269
Anglo-Maratha Wars, 94, 189
Anglo-Mysore Wars, 71, 94, 106, 141, 169, 189, 330
Anglo-Nepalese War, 190
Anglo-Nepal War of 1814, 97
Anglo-Russian Convention of 1907, 268, 518
Anglo-Sikh wars, 174, 206
Anglo-Soviet invasion of Iran, 269
Angola, 437
Angus Maddison, 286, 887, 888, 895
Anicut, 131
Animals People, 695
Ankleshwar, 683

Anna Hazare, 388, 873
Annavaram, 350
Annemarie Schimmel, 26
Annexation of Goa, 369
Annexation of Junagadh, 397
Annie Beasant, 304, 342
Annie Besant, 297, 305
Anno Hegirae, 24
A. N. Ray, 613, 616
Anschluss, 422
Anthony Low, 321
Anthony Mascarenhas, 556
Anti-imperialism, 480
Anti-Pakistan sentiment, 594
Anti tank missile, 647
Anti Terrorist Squad (India), 803, 819
Antonov An-12, 592
Anugrah Narayan Sinha, 342
Anurag Kumar, 249
Anushilan samiti, 293, 347–349
A Passage to India, 243
Appeasement, 364
Appellate court, 117
Appellate jurisdiction, 117
Arab, 19, 588
Arabian horse, 15
Arabian sea, 482, 581, 813
Arabic, 1, 9, 21
Arabic alphabet, 335
Arabic language, 120
Arabs, 80
Arachalur, 331
A. Raja, 847
Arakan, 38
Arakkonam, 128
Aravidu dynasty, 143
Archaeological Survey of India, 266, 268
Archibald Wavell, 1st Earl Wavell, 269
Arcot, 63, 95, 107, 144
Arcot Ramasamy Mudaliar, 903
Ardeshir Tarapore, 508
Arfeen Bhai, 729
Ariel Dorfman, 622
Arindam Chaudhuri, 844
Aristocracy, 49
Arizona State University, 692
Arjan Singh, 483
Arjun Charan Sethi, 872
Armed Forces Special Powers Act, 735
Armenian community of Dhaka, 17, 43
Armored car (military), 460
Armoured personnel carrier, 639
Armoured warfare, 484
Army Chief of Staff (Pakistan), 546, 582, 584
Army, Police, and Indian Civil Service, 96
Arrah, 226

961

Arsenal, 628, 631
Arson, 603, 635, 653, 776
Arthur Conan Doyle, 242, 249
Arthur Cotton, 131
Arthur D. Little, 688
Arthur Wellesley, 1st Duke of Wellington, 82
Article 144 .7BCivil and judicial authorities to act in aid of the Supreme Court.7D, 863
Article 370, 427
Article 370 of the Constitution of India, 410
Article 4, 411
Article 74 (Constitution of India), 410
Artillery, 38, 174
Arunabha Ghosh, 932
Arunachal Pradesh, 257, 373, 511, 513, 541
Aruna Roy, 882
Arundhati Roy, 695
Arun Jaitley, 615
Arun Khetarpal, 607
Arun Shourie, 625
Arun Shridhar Vaidya, 633, 637, 642
Arvind Kejriwal, 877
Arya Samaj, 335
Asafa Powell, 840
Asaf Jah II, 95
A. S. Atwal, 631
Asgharali Engineer, 797
Ashfaq Parvez Kayani, 718
Ashok Bhatt, 785
Ashok Chakra Award, 775
Ashok Chawla, 869
Ashok Desai, 13
Ashok Jha, 869
Ashok Kamte, 807, 819
Ashok K. Mehta, 701
Ashok Singhal, 792
Ashraf Jehangir Qazi, 774, 799
Ashta Pradhan, 55
Asia, 13, 42, 46
Asian-African Conference, 479
Asian Age, 659, 923
Asian American Hotel Owners Association, 795
Asiatic Society, 121
Asiaweek, 932
Asif Ali Zardari, 733, 740
Aslam Khan (Pakistani brigadier), 447
Asok Kumar Ganguly, 866
Asra Nomani, 735
Assam, 97, 257, 282, 353, 372, 377, 432, 473, 476, 517, 534
Assamese language, 669
Assam Province, 257
Assassination of Gandhi, 398
Assassination of Indira Gandhi, 627, 628, 642, **648**, 653, 655

Assassination of Mahatma Gandhi, 363
Assassination of Rajiv Gandhi, **721**
Assessment of losses, 484
Associated Press, 646, 936
Asteroid, 802
Astrological, 196
Astronomers, 24
Astronomical instruments, 24
Astronomy, 24
Astronomy in the medieval Islamic world, 24
Atal Bihari Vajpayee, 382, 384, 385, 615, 765, 798, 800, 801, 804
Atlantic Ocean, 14
Attachment (law), 862
Attiqur Rahman, 483
Attock, 78, 890
Attorney General of India, 870
Atul Kohli, 624
Aundh State, 68
Aurangabad, Maharashtra, 20, 814
Aurangazeb, 36
Aurangzeb, 2, 3, 6, 9, 57, 59, 174, 175
Aurobindo Ghosh, 290, 347
Auster AOP.6, 500
Australia at the 2010 Commonwealth Games, 832
Autarchy, 2
Authoritarian, 375
Authorship, 541
Autonomy, 94, 436
Autopsy, 677
Avalanches, 716
Awadh, 97, 102, 103, 108, 188, 190, 197, 220, 240, 268
Awadh Subah, 9
Awami League, 584, 599
Axiata, 868
Axis powers of World War II, 313, 351
Ayesha Jalal, 7, 243, 318, 321, 358, 624
Ayodhya, 380, 744, 745, 776, 778, 804
Ayub Khan (Field Marshal), 485, 538
Ayub Khan (general), 483, 553
Ayub Khan (President of Pakistan), 584
Ayurvedic, 683
Ayuthya, 43
Azad Hind, 252, 313, 351
Azad Hind Government, 351
Azad Jammu and Kashmir, 741
Azad Kashmir, 446, 483, 593, 741
Azad Kashmir Regiment, 446
Azam Khan Koka, 51
Azim Premji, 827
Azim-us-Shan, 36, 49, 52, 54
Azizabad (Karachi), 814
Aziz Bhatti, 508
Aziz Khan (general), 798

Azizulhasni Awang, 842

B-57 Canberra, 490, 500
Babariawad, 425
Babbar Khalsa, 631
Babbu Maan, 669
Babri Masjid, 745, 779
Babri Mosque, 380, 792, 804
Babu Bajrangi, 789
Babu Kunwar Singh, 186
Babur, 2–5, 21, 33, 34, 175
Backlash (sociology), 604
Badshahi Mosque, 3, 177
Bagber massacre, 743, 778
Bagha Jatin, 327
Bagh, Azad Kashmir, 454
Baghdad, 601
Bahadur Shah I, 7, 60, 176
Bahadur Shah II, 2, 4, 186, 201, 207, 333
Bahadur Shah Zafar, 8, 188, 196, 213, 232
Bahadur Sher Khan, 582
Bahawalpur, 95
Bahawalpur (princely state), 94, 97
Bahiroji Pingale, 85
Bahlul Lodi, 30
Bahrain, 91
Bahujan Samaj Party, 871, 878
Bairam Khan, 6
Bajirao, 85
Bajirao I, 63
Baji Rao I, 62
Bajirao II, 56
Baji Rao II, 55, 72, 86, 96
Bajrang Dal, 785
Bakhtiar Rana, 483
Bakht Khan, 186, 208, 229
Bakht Zameen, 729
Bakshi Jagabandhu, 331
Balaji Bajirao, 63
Balaji Vishwanath, 57, 60, 61, 85
Balance of payments, 764
Balance of power (international relations), 596, 597
Balasore, 43
Bal Gangadhar Tilak, 290, 296, 335, 336
Balkanisation, 419
Balkanization, 598
Ballistic missile, 800
Ballistic missile submarine, 597
Balochistan, 258
Balochistan, Iran, 598
Balochistan, Pakistan, 598
Bal Thackeray, 792
Baltistan, 451
Baluchistan (Chief Commissioners Province), 258, 267, 363

Balu Mahendra, 623
Balwan Khokhar, 657
Balwantrai Mehta, 405
Banaras, 643
Bana Singh, 712, 715
Bandar Abbas, 43
Banda Singh Bahadur, 176
Bande Mataram, 293
Bande Mataram (publication), 293
Bandh, 780
Bandra Kurla Complex, 883
Bandung, 479
Banerjee Committee, 779
Bangabandhu International Conference Center, 608
Bangalore, 107, 143–145, 154, 160, 354, 381, 388, 837, 875
Bangalore Central College, 160
Bangalore Palace, 165
Bangladesh, 17, 20, 29, 30, 33, 91, 102, 112, 252, 257, 328, 338, 347, 371, 374, 397, 472, 507, 537, 545, 547, 550, 581, 583, 594, 598, 602, 815
Bangladesh Air Force, 548
Bangladesh Armed Forces, 546, 585
Bangladesh Awami League, 550, 553, 555
Bangladesh Forces, 583
Bangladesh–India border, 586
Bangladesh–India relations, 599
Bangladesh–Pakistan relations, 603
Bangladeshi people, 584
Bangladeshis, 566, 583
Bangladesh Jamaat-e-Islami, 546
Bangladesh Liberation War, 371, 374, 507, **545**, 581, 583, 608, 637
Bangladesh Nationalist Party, 599
Bangladesh Navy, 564
Bangla Desh (song), 560
Bangladesh University of Engineering and Technology, 556
Bangladesh War of Liberation, 583
Banke District, 91
Bankim Chandra Chatterjee, 103, 335
Bankim Chandra Chattopadhyay, 327, 347
Bankipur (Bengal), 17, 32, 38
Bank robberies, 635
Bannu, 179, 452
Bannu Brigade, 452, 913
Bansi Lal, 621
Bantam (city), 43
Baptist Missionary Society, 278
Bara Katra, 16, 39, 45
Baramulla, 447, 460
Barbara D. Metcalf, 134
Barbara Metcalf, 25, 744
Barbara Ramusack, 57, 89

Bardiya District, 91
Bardoli Satyagraha, 306
Bareilly, 123
Bareilly division, 96
Bargi, 37
Bari Doab, 132
Barindra Ghosh, 347
Barisal, 564
Barisal Division, 49
Barkha Dutt, 858
Barley, 12
Baro-Bhuyan, 32, 35, 39
Baroda, 72, 86, 432
Baroda State, 57, 68, 94, 97, 227, 420
Baroque, 165
Barrackpore, 333
Barrister, 117
Barry Close, 149
Basic structure, 411, 613
Basra, 43
Ba Swe, 520
Batelco, 850, 868
Battle honour, 467, 508, 606
Battle of Aliwal, 182
Battle of Asal Uttar, 489, 494
Battle of Assaye, 74
Battle of Attock, 181
Battle of Attock, 1758, 64
Battle of Badgam, 460
Battle of Badli-ki-Serai, 209
Battle of Bhangani, 175
Battle of Bhopal, 63
Battle of Boyra, 561, 562
Battle of Britain, 351
Battle of Buxar, 38, 94, 95, 103, 117, 189, 328
Battle of Chausa, 29
Battle of Chawinda, 494
Battle of Chillianwala, 148, 206
Battle of Ctesiphon (1915), 268
Battle of Delhi (1737), 63
Battle of Delhi, 1803, 73, 96
Battle of Dhalai, 562
Battle of Ferozeshah, 178, 206
Battle of Gajendragad, 69
Battle of Gallipoli, 268
Battle of Garibpur, 561
Battle of Ghaghra, 33
Battle of Giria, 50
Battle of Hilli, 562
Battle of Hong Kong, 269
Battle of Imphal, 269, 353
Battle of Jamrud, 179, 181
Battle of Karnal, 4
Battle of Kharda, 70, 95
Battle of Kohima, 269
Battle of Kushtia, 562

Battle of Longewala, 608
Battle of Malaya, 269
Battle of Megiddo (1918), 268
Battle of Monte Cassino, 269
Battle of Muktsar, 176
Battle of Multan, 181
Battle of Nowshera, 181
Battle of Palkhed, 62
Battle of Patan, 70
Battle of Peshawar, 64
Battle of Plassey, 32, 33, 38, 39, 42, 90, 93–95, 98, 189, 252, 328
Battle of Pollilur, 24, 146, 148
Battle of Poona, 72
Battle of Porto Novo, 148
Battle of Raj Mahal, 32, 39
Battle of Saunshi, 148
Battle of Seringapatam, 149
Battle of Shopian, 181
Battle of Singapore, 269, 313
Battle of Sobraon, 181
Battle of Tanga, 268
Battle of the Nedumkotta, 149
Battle of the Nile, 149
Battle of Tora Bora, 772
Battle of Trimmu Ghat, 225
Battle of Tukaroi, 39
Battle of Vasai, 63
Battle of Wadgaon, 71
Battle of Wandiwash, 144
Batukeshwar Dutt, 349
Bayer, 672
Bay of Bengal, 39, 545, 558, 570, 581, 590, 597
BBC, 28, 556, 558, 601, 608, 733, 763, 935, 937
BBC Radio 5 Live, 694
BBC World News, 696
B. D. Pande, 636
Beant Singh (assassin), 628, 648, 653, 655
Beas River, 448
Bednur, 71
Beechcraft L-23 Seminole, 592
Beggars, 828
Begum Hazrat Mahal, 186
Begum Rokeya, 327
Beijing, 518
Beijing National Stadium, 831
Belgrade, 480
Bellary, 147
Benaras, 103
Benares, 119
Benazir Bhutto, 715
Bengal, 4, 30, 37, 60, 93, 94, 112, 156, 189, 207, 287, 302, 327, 328, 336, 347, 350, 363, 365, 425, 448

Bengal Army, 110, 190
Bengal Brigade, 241
Bengal Criminal Law Amendment, 349
Bengal delta, 17, 44
Bengal famine of 1770, 96, 103, 285
Bengal famine of 1943, 269, 286, 287
Bengali alphabet, 550
Bengali calendar, 17, 34, 44
Bengali Hindu, 42
Bengali Hindus, 586, 603
Bengali language, 32, 37, 547, 550, 558
Bengali language movement, 584
Bengali Muslim, 17, 42, 44
Bengali nationalism, 547, 555
Bengali New Year, 17
Bengali people, 12, 46, 603
Bengal Native Infantry, 197, 227
Bengal Presidency, 32, 38, 71, 98, 100, 103, 107, 117, 119, 129, 188, 190, 257, 289, 292
Bengal Renaissance, 121, 161
Bengal Sati Regulation, 1829, 97
Bengal Subah, 2, 9, 11, 13, 16, 18, **32**, 155
Bengal Sultanate, 2, 32, 33, 39
Benjamin Disraeli, 238, 334
Benjamin Disraeli, 1st Earl of Beaconsfield, 232
Benjamin L. Rice, 170
Benoît de Boigne, 69, 70
Beohar Rammanohar Sinha, 406
Berar Division, 440
Berar Province, 94, 97, 110, 190
Best Bakery case, 787
Bet Dwarka, 227
Beth Tweddle, 840
B. G. Verghese, 624, 791
Bhadralok, 292, 347
Bhadravathi, Karnataka, 155
Bhagat Singh, 305, 327, 346, 349
Bhakra dam, 432
Bharatanatyam, 80
Bharatiya Janata Party, 240, 317, 380, 382, 383, 390, 658, 665, 765, 779, 871, 875
Bharatpur, India, 66
Bharatpur State, 186
Bharat Rakshak, 916, 921
Bharat Ratna, 155, 612
Bharat Swabhiman Andolan, 876
Bhaskar Sadashiv Soman, 483
Bhati (region), 39, 44
Bhava, 163
Bhavnagar, 436
Bhimber, 453
Bhindranwale, 629
Bhoja, 162
Bhonsale, 57, 68, 86

Bhonsle, 80
Bhoomiyude Avakashikal, 796
Bhopal, 378, 671
Bhopal: A Prayer for Rain, 695
Bhopal disaster, 378, **671**
Bhopal Express (film), 694
Bhopal Medical Appeal, 696
Bhopal State, 69, 186, 420, 432, 473, 477
Bhopal State (1949–56), 474
Bhor State, 68
Bhosle, 58
Bhumihar, 190
Bhupendranath Datta, 338
Bhutan, 255, 438, 472, 511, 529, 569
Bhutia, 439
Bias, 682
Bible translations into Kannada, 161
Bicameralism, 410
Bigotry, 790
Bihar, 29, 36–38, 78, 93, 95, 108, 190, 197, 226, 257, 286, 292, 298, 328, 432, 473, 476, 559, 620, 643, 878
Bihar and Orissa Province, 475
Bihar famine of 1873–74, 266, 286
Bihari people, 585
Biharis, 567
Biharis in Bangladesh, 548
Bihar Movement, 374
Bihar Subah, 9
Bijapur, Karnataka, 23
Bijapur Sultanate, 143
Bijawar State, 186
Bijnor, 208
Biju Janata Dal, 872, 883
Bikaner State, 186, 420
Bilafond La, 707, 713
Bilaspur, Himachal Pradesh, 432
Bilaspur State, 473
Bilaspur State (1950 - 1954), 474
Bilgi, Karnataka, 147
Bill Clinton, 382, 384, 738
Bipan Chandra, 358, 392, 621, 624
Bipin Chandra Pal, 336, 338
Bipin Rawat, 729
Birender Singh Dhanoa, 729
Birjis Qadr, 186
Birjis Qadra, 186
Bir Sreshtho, 607
Bishan Singh Bedi, 839
Bishweshwar Prasad Koirala, 608
Bite the cartridge, 192, 332
Bithoor, 73
Black Friday (2004 film), 759
Black July, 702
Blepharospasm, 676
Blitzkrieg, 594

Blockade, 646
Blood Telegram, 570, 596
Blowing from a gun, 228, 230
B.M. Kaul, 521
B. N. Rau, 405
B.N. Srikrishna, 744, 758
Board, 525
Bodyguard, 648, 653
Bofors scandal, 378, 379
Bollywood, 623, 821, 843, 875
Bolshevik Revolution, 303
Bombay, 93, 124, 129, 273, 282, 495
Bombay Army, 190
Bombay (film), 759
Bombay High Court, 786
Bombay Presidency, 100, 119, 122, 125, 188, 190, 257, 261, 286, 302, 405, 432, 476, 477
Bombay riots, 380, 743, **743**, 744, 777, 778, 791
Bombay State, 368, 473, 476
Bombay University, 88
Bombers, 490
Bombings, 803
Bomdila, 533
Booker Prize, 622
Borassus flabellifer, 126
Border, 484
Border (1997 film), 608
Border Guards Bangladesh, 548, 554
Border Security Force, 627, 638, 729, 775
Bose, Nirmal, 909
Botswana at the 2010 Commonwealth Games, 842
Boycott, 839
Bradley Wiggins, 840
Brahma Chellaney, 646
Brahmaputra River, 534
Brahmin, 105, 158, 161, 162, 197, 297, 344
Brahmins, 108
Brahmo Samaj, 335
B. R. Ambedkar, 307, 316, 327, 366, 398, 402, 405
B.R. Ambedkar, 362
Branches, 401
Brazil, 389
Breakup of East and West Pakistan, 600
Breguet Alizé, 371, 583, 591
Brescia, 816
Brigade, 564
Brigade Major, 913
Brigadier, 447, 917
Brigadier-General, 592, 706
Brihanmumbai Electric Supply and Transport, 804
Brij Mohan Kaul, 510

Brill Publishers, 887
Brinda Karat, 668
Brindavan Gardens, 155
British Armed Forces, 236
British Ceylon, 255
British colonial empire, 38
British Crown, 4, 8, 101, 178, 284, 417
British East India Company, 4, 8, 17, 36, 38, 169, 178, 182, 236
British Empire, 17, 39, 76, 141, 186, 188, 283, 327, 398, 442
British expedition to Tibet, 268
British honours, 424
British House of Commons, 196, 238
British India, 9, 11, 13, 18, 94, 95, 133, 251, 258, 314, 345, 356, 361, 365, 416, 448, 472
British Indian Armed forces, 356
British Indian Army, 236, 266–269, 278, 296, 315, 348, 353
British Indian passport, 253
British Labour Party, 269
British Museum, 28
British occupation of India, 37
British paramountcy, 253, 450
British Parliament, 117
British Prime Minister, 485
British Punjab, 188
British Raj, 2, 4, 8, 38, 73, 91–93, 111, 115, 123, 151–153, 185, 188, 221, 233, **251**, 256, 325–327, 330, 338, 350, 396, 397, 403, 448, 472, 549, 550, 761
British rule (1810–1968), 96
British rule in Burma, 92, 252, 254, 256, 257, 326
British Somaliland, 254
Broad gauge, 129
Bronze, 23
Bubonic plague, 268
Budgam, 738
Budikote, 23
Bukhara, 601
Bulandshahr, 208
Bulandshahr district, 208
Bullion, 11, 113, 114
Bundelkhand, 96, 221, 240, 267
Bundi State, 186
Bungalow, 216
Buoy, 589
Burhanpur, 60
Buriganga River, 39
Burma, 33, 192, 227, 353, 511, 520, 536
Burma Campaign, 269, 313
Burma Office, 269
Burton Stein, 26, 170, 319
Butter, 13

Cabinet of India, 611
Cabinet of the United Kingdom, 333
Cadastral surveying, 12
CAF Beasain, 833
Calcutta, 90, 93, 117, 124, 193, 198, 260, 268, 273, 313, 347, 356, 363, 710
Calcutta Police, 349
Calico, 14
California, 665
California State Assembly, 667
Caliphate, 159
Calliaphone, 163
Cama Hospital, 803, 804, 819
Cambodia, 479, 536
Cambridge University Press, 25, 135, 509, 624, 887, 890
Canada, 369, 623, 624
Canadair Sabre, 490
Canadian Confederation, 288
Candlelight vigil, 825
Cannons, 38
Cantonment, 227, 332
Capital expenditure, 127, 130
Capital intensive, 768
Capitalism, 478
Captain (naval), 546
Captain Nemo, 243
Carbaryl, 672, 675, 683
Car bombings, 586
Carbonari, 347
Carbon dioxide, 677
Carbon tetrachloride, 673
Carcinogen, 694
Carnatic music, 80, 161
Carnatic region, 904
Carnatic Wars, 144
Cartographic errors, 710
Casa da India, 92, 256, 326
Cash crop, 12
Caste, 196, 380
Caste Disabilities Removal Act, 1850, 97
Caste-related violence in India, 362
Caste system in India, 108, 190
Casualties and compensation, 803
Category:Anti-Muslim violence in India, 744, 777
Category:Constitution of India, 402
Category:History of Bangladesh, 547
Category:History of India, 56, 91, 173, 187, 253, 361, 396, 471, 761
Category:History of Pakistan, 259, 260
Category:Persecution of Hindus, 743, 778
Category:Revolutions, 327
Cathedra, 277
Catherine of Braganza, 93
Cattle, 180

Cauvery, 331
Cawnpore, 133, 134
CBC.ca, 935
Ceasefire, 511, 568
Cease-fire, 534
Ceded and Conquered Provinces, 96, 119, 268
Celestial globe, 24
Censor Board of India, 796
Census in Pakistan, 602
CENTO, 502, 596
Central Asia, 2, 14, 20, 46
Central Bureau of Investigation, 653, 656, 663, 678, 726, 728, 786, 787, 844, 847, 848
Central Bureau of Investigators, 688
Central Command (India), 582
Central Forensic Science Laboratory, 787
Central India, 187
Central India Agency, 94, 97, 433
Central Intelligence Agency, 482, 772
Centralized, 2
Central Legislative Assembly, 349
Central planning, 762
Central Provinces, 207, 432
Central Provinces and Berar, 257, 430
Central Reserve Police Force, 627, 729, 772, 775, 779
Central Vigilance Commission, 830, 844, 860
Centre for Public Interest Litigation, 858, 860
Centre for Science and Environment, 694
Centre for Tropical and Communicable Diseases, 288
Centurion (tank), 494
Centurion Tank, 483, 493
Cerebral oedema, 677
Cession, 441
Ceylon, 43, 96, 110
Chabad House, 819, 825
Chabad Lubavitch, 810
Chagatai Khan, 3, 5
Chagatai Khanate, 2
Chagatai language, 1
Chain of command, 602
Chairman, 546
Chairman Joint Chiefs of Staff Committee, 602, 798
Chairman of the Joint Chiefs of Staff Committee, 507
Chakla (administrative division), 48
Chakma people, 36
Chakravarthi Rajagopalachari, 307
Chakravarthy Rajagopalachari, 396
Chakravarti Rajagopalachari, 357
Chakwal District, 295
Chalisa famine, 96, 286
Chalunka, 605
Chamaraja Wodeyar I, 152

967

Chamaraja Wodeyar II, 152
Chamaraja Wodeyar III, 152
Chamaraja Wodeyar IV, 152
Chamaraja Wodeyar IX, 152
Chamaraja Wodeyar V, 152
Chamaraja Wodeyar VI, 152
Chamaraja Wodeyar VII, 152
Chamaraja Wodeyar VIII, 152
Chamarajendra Wadiyar X, 153
Chamber of Princes, 417
Champaran, 115, 298
Champaran Satyagraha, 342
Chamundi Hill, 165
Chamundi Hills, 167
Chanakya, 381, 764
Chancellor of the Exchequer, 100
Chandernagore, 36, 38, 357, 437, 475
Chandigarh, 257
Chand Kaur, 172, 181
Chandpur District, 561
Chandragiri, 143
Chandragiri Fort, Andhra Pradesh, 143
Chandrasekhar Azad, 349
Chandra Shekhar, 379, 616, 725
Chandrashekhar Azad, 349
Chandrashekhar Dasgupta, 468
Chandra Shekhar Singh, 763
Chandraswami, 727
Chandrayaan-1, 387
Chang Chenmo River, 516
Chang Chenmo Valley, 514
Channapatna, 143
Charan Singh, 375, 615
Charat Singh, 177
Chargesheet, 823, 845, 847, 862, 869
Charge sheet, 869
Charles Allen (writer), 901
Charles Canning, 1st Earl Canning, 90, 97, 186, 192, 194, 229, 252, 262, 266
Charles Cornwallis, 1st Marquess Cornwallis, 96, 104, 147, 149, 317
Charles Grant (British East India Company), 121
Charles Hardinge, 1st Baron Hardinge of Penshurst, 268, 302
Charles II of England, 93, 116
Charles Shepherd (photographer), 232
Charles Wood, 1st Viscount Halifax, 122, 260
Charter Act 1813, 101
Chaudhari Khaliquzzaman, 309
Chauri Chaura incident, 306, 343
Chauth, 37, 64, 78
Chechnya, 805
Checks and balances, 621
Chef de mission, 833
Chemical and Engineering News, 699

Chemistry, 24
Chenab River, 226
Chengdu Military Region, 528
Chengiz Khan, 601
Chennai, 122, 128, 129, 262, 721, 726, 875
Chen Yi (communist), 527
Chetan Bhagat, 839
Chhapra, 23
Chhatar Singh, 69
Chhatrapati, 55, 56, 58, 59
Chhatrapati Shahu, 58
Chhatrapati Shivaji Maharaj Terminus, 803, 806
Chhatrapati Shivaji Terminus, 804, 819
Chhattisgarh, 257, 384, 430
Chhattrapati Shahu, 57, 60, 85
Chichawatni, 226
Chief Commissioner, 266–268
Chief Commissioners Province, 432
Chief Inspector, 582
Chief Justice, 76
Chief Justice of India, 613, 865
Chief Justice of Pakistan, 603
Chief Justice of the United States, 414
Chief Martial Law Administrator, 600
Chief Minister, 391, 731, 829, 878
Chief Minister (India), 410
Chief Minister of Delhi, 836
Chief Minister of Karnataka, 382
Chief Minister of West Bengal, 615
Chief of Air Staff (India), 582, 798
Chief of Air Staff (Pakistan), 798
Chief of Army Staff (India), 546, 582
Chief of Army Staff of the Indian Army, 798
Chief of Army Staff (Pakistan), 798
Chief of General Staff (Pakistan), 582
Chief of Naval Staff (India), 582
Chief of Naval Staff of the Indian Navy, 798
Chief of Naval Staff (Pakistan), 798
Chief of Staff, 546, 582
Chief of Staff of the Pakistan Navy, 582
Chief of the Air Staff (India), 483
Chief of the Army Staff (India), 483, 586, 642, 736
Chief of the Naval Staff (India), 483
Chikka Devaraja, 141, 152
Chikkamagaluru, 143
Child labor, 829
Chimaji Appa, 63
Chimanbhai Patel, 613
China, 91, 173, 192, 362, 510, 549, 597
China–Pakistan relations, 596
Chinese Army, 539
Chinese Civil War, 519
Chinese economic reform, 761
Chinese Mugwort, 622

Chingari Trust, 696
Chinnakannan Sivasankaran, 850
Chinsura, 36
Chintapalle, Visakhapatnam, 350
Chip Chap River, 516, 529
Chitral Bodyguard, 458, 463
Chitral Expedition, 267
Chitral (princely state), 453, 458, 460
Chitral Scouts, 458, 463
Chittagong, 35, 43, 130, 227, 548, 554, 558, 585
Chittagong armoury raid, 349
Chittagong Division, 49
Chittagong Hill Tracts, 36
Chittisinghpura massacre, 739
Chivalric order, 255
Chloroform, 677, 694
CHM Piru Singh, 467
Chogyal, 438
Choking, 677
Chola Dynasty, 80
Chola incident, 541
Chorbat Valley, 605
Choto Katra, 39
Chris Bayly, 196
Chris Boardman, 842
Chris Hoy, 840
Christ Church College, Kanpur, 278
Christian Bible, 278
Christian denominations, 278
Christianity in India, 304
Christian mission, 278
Christina Georgiana Rossetti, 249
Christine Fair, 913
Christmas Island, 91, 356
Christophe Jaffrelot, 786, 797
Christopher Alan Bayly, 135, 243, 318, 320
Christopher Snedden, 469
Chromium, 683, 693
Chronology of Pakistans rocket tests, 800
Chuck Yeager, 592
Chumb, 490, 500
Church Mission Society, 278
Church of England, 277
Church of India, Burma and Ceylon, 277, 278
Chushul, 511
CIA, 520
Cinema of India, 608
Circa, 482
Circuit court, 117
Circulatory collapse, 677
Cis-Sutlej states, 78, 94, 97, 110
CITEREFAnkit, Henry Scott2010, 913
CITEREFAnkit, Kashmir, 1945–662014, 913
CITEREFAnkit, October 19472010, 913

CITEREFAnkit, The Problem of Poonch2010, 913
CITEREFAsherTalbot2008, 887
CITEREFBandyopadhyay2004, 907
CITEREFBarua, Gentlemen of the Raj2003, 913
CITEREFBaylyHarper2007, 907
CITEREFBhattacharya, What Price Freedom2013, 912, 913
CITEREFBlack2006, 892
CITEREFBose1918, 906
CITEREFBrass2005, 933, 934
CITEREFBrown1994, 898, 899
CITEREFBunsha2005, 934
CITEREFCheema, Crimson Chinar2015, 914
CITEREFDasgupta, War and Diplomacy in Kashmir2014, 913
CITEREFDavid R. Higgins2016, 915
CITEREFDavis2001, 906
CITEREFDesaiRaychaudhuriKumar1983, 906
CITEREFEffendi, Punjab Cavalry2007, 913
CITEREFEngineer2003, 934
CITEREFFieldhouse1996, 906
CITEREFFisher, Rose & Huttenback, Himalayan Battleground1963, 920, 921
CITEREFGhadbian2002, 924
CITEREFGhassem-Fachand2012, 933
CITEREFGokhale2015, 930
CITEREFGrove2007, 906
CITEREFGuha2002, 934
CITEREFGuha, India after Gandhi2008, 913
CITEREFHodson, The Great Divide1969, 913
CITEREFImperial Gazetteer of India vol. III1907, 906
CITEREFJaffrelot2011, 933, 934
CITEREFJamal, Shadow War2009, 912, 913, 915
CITEREFJoshi, Kashmir, 1947-1965: A Story Retold2008, 913
CITEREFKoomar2009, 906
CITEREFKorbel, Danger in Kashmir1966, 914
CITEREFLavoy2009, 930
CITEREFLow1993, 907
CITEREFLow2002, 907
CITEREFMahajan, Looking Back1963, 913
CITEREFMalik2006, 930
CITEREFMaxwell, Indias China War1970, 919
CITEREFMehra, John Lall (Book review)1991, 920
CITEREFMehta2005, 890, 891
CITEREFMetcalfMetcalf2006, 887, 898, 899, 910
CITEREFMookherjee2012, 924

CITEREFMoore, Making the new Commonwealth1987, 913
CITEREFMoraes2008, 909
CITEREFNawaz, The First Kashmir War Revisited2008, 912, 913
CITEREFNoorani, India–China Boundary Problem2010, 919, 920
CITEREFNussbaum2008, 933, 934
CITEREFOommen2008, 934
CITEREFPalit, Jammu and Kashmir Arms1972, 914
CITEREFPeers2013, 898
CITEREFPrakash2002, 891
CITEREFPrasad & Pal, Operations in Jammu & Kashmir1987, 913
CITEREFRachna Bisht2015, 915
CITEREFRaghavan, War and Peace in Modern India2010, 913
CITEREFRai2008, 906
CITEREFRathod1994, 891
CITEREFRobb2001, 887
CITEREFSajjad2012, 923, 924
CITEREFSarila, The Shadow of the Great Game2007, 913
CITEREFSatinder Singh, Raja Gulab Singhs Role1971, 897
CITEREFSchofield, Kashmir in Conflict2003, 913, 914
CITEREFSen2002, 910
CITEREFShani2007b, 933
CITEREFSharlach2000, 922
CITEREFSimpson2009, 934
CITEREFSnedden, Kashmir: The Unwritten History2013, 913
CITEREFStein2001, 907
CITEREFStein2010, 907
CITEREFTask Force Report2006, 932
CITEREFTrudy RingNoelle WatsonPaul Schellinger2012, 897
CITEREFT. V. Paul1994, 915, 918
CITEREFUnited States Court of Customs and Patent Appeals1930, 891
CITEREFVaradarajan2002, 934
CITEREFWaheeda Khan, Conflict in Kashmir2015, 931
CITEREFWarikoo, Indias gateway to Central Asia2009, 919
CITEREFWolpert2006, 907
CITEREFWoodman, Himalayan Frontiers1970, 920
CITEREFZaheer, The Times and Trial of the Rawalpindi Conspiracy1998, 912
Cities, 18
Cities in Pakistan, 600
Citizens Justice Committee, 662
Civil aviation, 767

Civil disobedience, 327, 342, 353, 548, 644
Civil liberties, 375, 621
Civil liberty, 328
Civil rebellion, 333
Civil resistance, 874
Civil Services of India, 292
Civil war, 596
Clandestine cell system, 799
Classified information, 604
Claude Auchinleck, 449, 450
Claude MacDonald, 516
Clement Attlee, 269
Clive Robert Fenn, 249
Close air support, 522
CNN, 829, 935
CNN-IBN, 825
Coalition Against Genocide, 795
Coastal India, 93
Coast guard, 590
Coat of arms, 90
Cobrapost, 667
Cochin State, 420
Cocos (Keeling) Islands, 91
Codified constitution, 410
Codrington, 903
Cohort (statistics), 682
Coimbatore, 143, 149, 331
Coin, 114, 176
Colaba, 806, 819
Colaba Causeway, 807
Cold Start (military doctrine), 802
Cold War, 362, 478–480, 484, 539, 545, 549
Cold War (1953–62), 596
Colin Campbell, 1st Baron Clyde, 186, 221
Collateral damage, 633
College of Fort William, 121
Colombo, 478, 536, 705, 817
Colonel, 447, 582
Colonel Narendra Kumar, 710
Colonial era, 97
Colonial India, 92, 256, 326, 478
Colony, 251, 527
Colony of Aden, 252
Combat aircraft, 552
Combat air patrol, 592
Combustion, 169
Comilla, 561
Command and control (military), 505
Commander-in-Chief, 76, 502, 546, 602
Commander-in-Chief, India, 315
Commander in Chief (Pakistan Air Force), 483, 582
Commander in Chief (Pakistan Army), 483
Commander in Chief (Pakistan Navy), 483, 582
Commander (rank), 546, 582

Commanding officer, 546, 564
Commando, 495
Committee on International Trade, 808
Commodore (rank), 483
Commons, 368
Commons:Category:Bangladesh Liberation War, 573
Commons:Category:Bhopal disaster, 700
Commons:Category:India Against Corruption, 885
Commons:Category:Indian independence movement, 359
Commons:Category:Indian Rebellion of 1857, 250
Commons:Category:November 2008 Mumbai attacks, 825
Commons:Category:Partition of India, 401
Commons:Category:Sikh Empire, 184
Commons:Category:Sri Lankan Civil War, 705
Commons:Category:Suri Empire, 32
Commonwealth, 398
Commonwealth of Nations, 236, 357, 361, 397, 398, 421
Commonwealth Relations Office, 269
Communalism (South Asia), 421, 777
Communications, 864
Communism, 349, 421, 478
Communist Party of India, 344, 386, 872
Communist Party of India (Marxist), 875, 878
Company Havildar Major, 467
Company Quarter Master Havildar Abdul Hamid, 508
Company rule in India, 2, 8, 38, 55, 79, **90**, 92, 185, 187, 252, 253, 255, 256, 260, 326
Composite Index of National Capability, 362
Comptroller and Auditor General of India, 409, 844, 847, 848, 870
Compulsory sterilization, 617
Concerns and controversies over the 2010 Commonwealth Games, 388, **826**, 848
Condoleezza Rice, 795
Condom, 835
Confounding factor, 682
Congress (I), 664
Congress (O), 611
Congress Working Committee, 307
Congreve rocket, 24, 169
Conrad Corfield, 422
Conservative Party (UK), 422, 810
Conspiracy theories, 721
Constituent Assembly of India, 366, 396, 398, 402, 404, 420
Constituent assembly of Jammu and Kashmir, 435
Constitutional Amendment, 401
Constitutional autochthony, 402
Constitutional monarch, 439
Constitutional monarchy, 395
Constitution of Alabama, 407
Constitution of Australia, 407
Constitution of Canada, 407
Constitution of France, 407
Constitution of India, 308, 328, 362, 372, 396–398, **401**, 402, 424, 472, 473, 610, 612, 789, 863
Constitution of Ireland, 407
Constitution of Jammu and Kashmir, 439
Constitution of Japan, 407
Constitution of Pakistan, 328, 584, 602
Constitution of Portugal, 437
Constitution of South Africa, 407
Constitution of the Soviet Union, 407
Constitution of the United Kingdom, 407
Construction sites, 828
Consumer goods, 381
Conventional war, 507, 801
Conversion to Christianity, 278
Coorg, 97, 159, 258
Coorg State, 474, 477
Copper wire, 126
Copyright status of work by the U.S. government, 139, 481, 571
Cornwallis Code, 96
Coromandel Coast, 143
Corporate corruption, 873, 884
Corporate promoter, 855
Corporatocracy, 90
Corps, 564
Corruption in India, 362, 768
Cossimbazar, 37
Cottage industry, 298
Cotton, 12, 14, 33, 46
Cotton gin, 15
Council of India, 260, 266, 333
Council of Ministers of India, 410
Council of Scientific and Industrial Research, 678
Coup détat de Yanaon, 437
Courier service, 124
Court martial, 199
Court of Requests, 117
Court (royal), 75
Coxs Bazar, 564, 590
C. P. Ramaswami Iyer, 420
Craig Hunter, 833
C. Rajagopalachari, 344, 397, 399, 405, 422
C. Ramchandra, 542
Crank (mechanism), 15
Credit, 576
Credit (finance), 575
Crimean War, 209
Crime Investigation Department (India), 663

Crimes against humanity, 603
Criminal court, 117
Criminalisation of politics, 874
Criminal Law (Amendment) Act, 2013, 389
Criminal Procedure Code, 1973 (India), 773
Cripps mission, 269, 311, 351, 353, 418
Crop, 12
Crop yield, 12
Crore, 153
CRPF, 638, 730
Cruiser, 597
C Sivasankaran, 868
Cuba, 479
Cuban Missile Crisis, 511, 522, 525, 532, 538
Cultural nationalism, 550
Culture of Bangladesh, 584
Culture of India, 2
Culture of Pakistan, 584
Cupola, 165
Curfew, 636
Currency, 10
Current account deficit, 761
Current Science, 699
Cutch (princely state), 432
Cutch State, 94, 474
C. V. Rungacharlu, 154
Cyanide (2006 film), 728
Cyclone, 383
Cylinder (firearms), 169

Dabistān-i Mazāhib, 3
Dacca, 23, 227
Dadabhai Naoroji, 334, 335
Dahod, 779
Daily News & Analysis, 544
Daily Times (Pakistan), 917, 930
Dainik Jagran, 665
Dais, 721
Dalbir Singh, 718
Dalit, 160, 307, 316, 367, 781
Dalit (outcaste), 344
Dalit Panthers of India, 727
Dalits, 290
Dal Khalsa (Sikh Empire), 174
Daman and Diu, 437
Dam (Indian coin), 2, 11
Dammanapalli, 350
Dandi March II, 875
Danilimda (Vidhan Sabha constituency), 783
Dani Samuels, 838
Danish colonial empire, 38
Danish East India Company, 93
Danish India, 17, 32, 92, 256, 326
Dara Shikoh, 6, 36, 175
Dara Singh Chauhan, 871
Dargah, 781

Dargahs, 791
Daria Daulat Bagh, 166
Das Kapital, 888
Datia, 221
Daud Khan Karrani, 33, 39
Daulat Khan Lodi, 21
David Cameron, 357
David Coleman Headley, 812, 816
David Headley, 812, 825
David Ricardo, 107
Dawn Fraser, 839
Dawn News, 916
Dawn (newspaper), 604, 610, 917, 935
Dawood Ahmed Sofi, 729
Dayananda Saraswati, 335
Dayanidhi Maran, 863, 868
DB Realty, 852
Debal, 15
Debasement, 11
Deccan College (Pune), 121, 123, 288
Deccan Plateau, 56, 65, 141, 432
Deccan sultanates, 2
Deccan Wars, 55
Deck (ship), 16, 47
Declaration of war, 564
Deepak Kapoor, 717
Deepender Singh Hooda, 871
Deescalation, 802
Defector, 586
Defence Day, 505
Defence Journal, 917
Defence Minister of India, 500
Defence of India Act 1915, 268, 302, 340, 342, 350
Defence of India act and Defence of India rules, 1962, 540
Deg Tegh Fateh, 172
De Havilland Canada DHC-4 Caribou, 592
De Havilland Vampire, 490
Dehradun, 339, 406, 637
Deindustrialization, 9, 33, 46
De jure, 416, 437
Delhi, 1, 4, 13, 18, 20, 24, 57, 62, 96, 176, 208, 273, 363, 375, 474, 477, 527, 618, 642, 653, 654, 664, 668, 771, 810, 822
Delhi Agreement, 598, 605
Delhi Airport Metro Express, 833
Delhi Cantonment, 661
Delhi Development Authority, 828
Delhi Durbar, 267, 268, 274
Delhi Gadhakal, 622
Delhi Gate (Delhi), 879
Delhi High Court, 387, 661, 848, 863
Delhi-Lahore Conspiracy, 348
Delhi Legislative Assembly election, 2013, 885
Delhi Police, 663, 664, 667, 771, 774

Delhi Sadar (Lok Sabha constituency), 664
Delhi School of Economics, 657
Delhi Science Forum, 696
Delhi Sikh Gurdwara Management Committee, 657
Delhi Sikh Gurudwara Management Committee, 632
Delhi Subah, 9, 18
Delhi Sultanate, 2, 3, 15, 21, 29
Deluge gun, 687
Demarche, 774, 799
Democracy, 403, 771
Democratic republic, 398
Democratic socialism, 403
Demographics of Pakistan, 584
Demography, 174, 177
Demolition, 804
Demolition of Babri Masjid, 745
Demolition of Babri Mosque, 743
Demolition of the Babri Masjid, 744
Dengue fever, 837
Denmark-Norway, 36
Dennis Kux, 498
Deoli, Rajasthan, 540
Department of Police, Delhi, 660
Department of Telecommunications, 848
Dependent territory, 438
Depinder Singh, 582
Deposition (law), 865
Deputy Inspector General, 631
Deputy inspector general of police, 663
Dera Ghazi Khan, 78, 132
Dera Ismail Khan, 453, 816
Desert, 490
Desertion, 628
Destroyer, 583, 589, 597
Devaluation, 370
Developing countries, 479
Devolution, 702
Devraj Anbu, 729
Dewan, 420
Dewan Ranjit Rai, 459
Dewas, 86
Dewas State, 57, 68
Dhaka, 14, 16–18, 20, 32, 33, 35, 42, 46–48, 112, 338, 347, 374, 548, 553, 565, 581, 583
Dhaka Anushilan Samiti, 347
Dhaka Nawab Family, 294
Dhaka University, 888
Dhanaji Jadhav, 60, 84
Dhanmondi Shahi Eidgah, 39
Dhan Singh Gurjar, 201
Dhar, 60, 86
Dharamdas Shastri, 663
Dharamsala, Himachal Pradesh, 266
Dharam Yudh Morcha, 654
Dharam Yudh Morcha (film), 669
Dharmapuri, 143
Dhar State, 57, 68
Dharwad, 147
Dheeran Chinnamalai, 331
Dhola, Tibet, 523
Dhows, 15
Diamond Harbour, 125
Diarchy, 304
Dichloromethane, 677, 694
Dictatorship of the proletariat, 535
Digambar Ramchandra Badge, 363
Digital India, 391
Digital object identifier, 25, 26, 137, 138, 245–247, 323, 324, 359, 442–445, 468, 469, 542, 572, 697–699, 719
Digvijay Singh (politician), 877
Diljit Dosanjh, 669
Dimethylamine, 677
Dinapore, 226
Din-i Ilahi, 1, 49
Din-i-Ilahi, 3, 6
Diocese, 278
Diocese of Calcutta of the Church of North India, 278
Dionne Bunsha, 783, 797
Dipankar Gupta, 786
Diplomacy, 799
Diplomat, 436
Diplomatic corps, 548
Diplomatic recognition, 559, 564
Direct Action Day, 314, 448
Directive Principles, 402
Directive Principles of State Policy, 408
Directorate General of Economic Enforcement, 862
Directorate General of Income Tax Investigation, 844, 851, 859, 860
Director general of police, 663
Direct-to-home television in India, 852
Dir (princely state), 453
Disarmament, 703
Discovery Channel, 825
Displaced person, 653
Disputed statement, 496
District collector, 124
District Courts of India, 401, 672
Districts of India, 154
Diu, India, 23
Divide and rule, 338
Divine right of kings, 422
Division (military), 564
Diwan (title), 49, 94, 103
D. K. Barooah, 611
DNA, 824

973

Doab, 78, 94, 96, 133
Do-chala, 40
Doctrine of lapse, 97, 193, 195, 221, 270, 332
Doda, 739
Dodda Kempadevaraja, 152
Dodda Krishnaraja Wodeyar I, 152
Dogra, 448, 451
Dogra Dynasty, 94, 190
Dogra Regiment, 712
Dogri language, 172
Doji bara famine, 71, 96, 286
Dome, 165
Domel, 459
Domicile (law), 130
Dominion, 17, 253, 397, 398, 403, 418, 472
Dominion of India, 141, 153, 252, 253, 316, 362, **395**, 402, 421, 432, 446
Dominion of India (1947–1950), 395
Dominion of Pakistan, 252, 254, 316, 317, 328, 361, 366, 397, 446–448, 550
Dominique Lapierre, 699
Donald Rumsfeld, 741
Doordarshan, 618, 645, 650
Dorabji Tata, 280
Dost Mohammed Khan, 225
Douglas Gracey, 447, 450, 458
Dow Chemical Company, 672, 688
Down To Earth (magazine), 698
Dowry, 93
Drama (film and television), 609
Dr. A.P.J Abdul Kalam, 775
Dras, 465
Dravida Munnetra Kazhagam, 725, 851, 863, 871
Dravidar Kazhagam, 702
Dravidian architecture, 164
Draw bar, 13
Drip irrigation systems, 575
D. R. Karthikeyan, 725
D. R. Nagaraj, 158
Drug Enforcement Administration, 814
D. S. Hooda, 718
Duar War, 266
Dudley Russell, 447
Duke of Wellington, 80
Duleep Singh, 172, 181
Dum Dum, 193
Dungan Revolt (1862–77), 515
Durand Line, 267, 772
Durbar (court), 164
Durga, 158, 167, 612
Durgabai Deshmukh, 405
Durga Das Basu, 624
Durrani Empire, 2, 57, 80, 173, 178, 182
Dutch Bengal, 17, 32, 38
Dutch East India Company, 13, 36, 46, 93, 96

Dutch India, 92, 256, 326
Dutch Republic, 36
Dwarka, 142, 495
Dynasty, 2, 29

Early modern, 2
Early modern Europe, 13
Early modern period, 32, 173
East African Campaign (World War II), 269
East Bengal, 347, 363, 371, 550, 584
East Bengal and Assam, 268
East Bengali refugees, 586
East Bengal Regiment, 548, 559
East Delhi, 655, 659
Eastern Air Command (India), 546
Eastern Bengal and Assam, 291, 292
Eastern Command (India), 546, 582, 593
Eastern India, 585
Eastern Mediterranean Event, 802
Eastern Naval Command, 546, 590
East India, 389, 545, 550
East India Company, 8, 13, 16, 33, 42, 47, 71, 90, 92, 93, 107, 185–187, 189, 233, 253, 256, 260, 285, 326–328, 330, 331, 448
East Indian Railway, 280
East Indian Railway Company, 127, 128
East Pakistan, 328, 364, 503, 507, 537, 545, 547, 581, 583, 584
East Pakistan Air Operations, 1971, 564, 589
East Pakistan Awami League, 598
East Pakistan Central Peace Committee, 546, 602
East Pakistanis, 595
East Pakistan Legislative Assembly, 584
East Pakistan Police, 595, 602
East Pakistan Renaissance Society, 549
East Pakistan Rifles, 586, 595
East Punjab, 368, 432, 473, 477
Economic crisis, 764
Economic history of India, 9, 155
Economic liberalisation in India, 362, 381, **760**, 762
Economic policy, 762
Economic reforms, 381
Economic reforms in India, 765
Economic rent, 103, 107
Economic sanctions, 382
Economic stagnation, 765
Economy of India, 367, 379, 388, 763
Economy of the Kingdom of Mysore, 141
Edmund Burke, 101, 285
Edouard Goubert, 437
Education Commission, 267
Education in India, 97
Edward Heath, 608

Edward John Eyre, 275
Edward Law, 1st Earl of Ellenborough, 97, 133
Edward Singleton Holden, 27
Edward Stanley, 15th Earl of Derby, 252
Edward Vibart, 229
Edward VII, 251, 266, 268
Edward VIII, 252
Edwin Lutyens, 307
Edwin Montagu, 299, 302
Edwin Samuel Montagu, 260, 340
Eelam, 702
Effective date, 401
Effigy, 695
E. F. L. Wood, 1st Earl of Halifax, 269
Egypt, 369, 536
Ehsan Jafri, 777
Eid al-Adha, 822
Eighth Schedule of the Constitution of India, 409
Eklavya, 696
Elections in Pakistan, 584
Electoral college, 401
Electoral College (India), 401
Electoral fraud, 873, 884
Electrical telegraph, 125
Elijah Impey, 118
Eliminationism, 792
El Niño, 287
Elphinstone College, 122, 123, 288
Emaar, 836
Emergency provisions of the Constitution of India, 410
E. M. Forster, 243
Emir, 546
Emirate of Afghanistan, 252
Emperor Akbar, 44
Emperor Jahangir, 35
Emperor of India, 251, 268, 294
Empire, 251
Empress of India, 8, 232, 253, 267, 271, 334
Enclave, 436, 475
Enclosure movement, 106
Encyclopædia Britannica, 169, 897, 913, 916, 918
Enforced disappearances, 735
Enforcement Directorate, 844, 846, 848, 862
English, 253
English colonial empire, 908
English drama, 161
English East India Company, 97
English Electric Canberra, 490, 592
English language, 251, 406
English law, 118
English literature, 161
Enteritis, 677
Enterprise value, 850

Entrenched clause, 401
Epigraphy, 142
Epi-methandienone, 840
Equality before the law, 403
Eric Shipton, 709
Eric Thomas Stokes, 237, 246
Erika Mann (politician), 810
Erode, 143
Erwin Rommel, 351
Esperanza Aguirre, 810
Espionage, 496, 505
Essar Group, 856, 858, 864
Established church, 277
Estoppel, 862
Etah district, 96
Etawah, 123, 134
Etawah district, 96
Ethnic cleansing, 735, 777
Ethnic cleansing of Kashmiri Hindus, 379
Etisalat, 848, 868
European Parliament, 808
European Space Agency, 390
European Union, 388
Evangelicalism, 121
Evangelism, 196
Eveready Industries India, 672
Evolution of Pakistan Eastern Command plan, 545
Exchange rate, 764
Exchequer, 315
Exclave, 527
Executive branch, 118
Executive Council (Commonwealth countries), 262
Executive government, 401
Executive (government), 410
Exothermic reaction, 674
Expansionist, 520
Expatriates, 351
Expeditionary warfare, 590
Expeditions in Bengal, 64
Explosive belt, 721
Explosives, 806
Explosive weapon, 23
External affairs, 423
Extradition, 680
Extrajudicial killing, 735
Extra-territorial, 424
Eyre Coote (East India Company officer), 144, 148

F-104, 592
F-104 Starfighter, 490
F-86 Sabre, 488, 490
Fabian socialism, 762
Factory (trading post), 93, 189

Faheem Ansari, 815
Faisalabad, 816
Fakhruddin Ali Ahmed, 375, 610, 611, 614, 615
Fall of Baghdad (1917), 268
Fall of Dhaka, 594
Famine, 576
Famine in India, 46, 287
Faraizi movement, 227
Faridkot district, 433
Faridkot, Okara, 816
Faridkot State, 78
Faridpur Division, 49
Farm labourer, 576
Farooq Abdullah, 379, 731
Farsi, 41
Fast-roping, 811
Fatah Muhammad, 23
Fatawa-e-Alamgiri, 19
Fatehpur district, 96
Fatehpur Sikri, 1, 20
Fatehpur, Uttar Pradesh, 219
Fathullah Shirazi, 23
Fatty liver, 677
Fatwa, 209, 566
Faujdar, 49
Fazal Ali, 475
Fazilka, 500
Fazlul Qadir Chaudhry, 546
Fazlur Rehman Khalil, 729
FBI, 820
Fedayeen, 806
Federal Bureau of Investigation, 734
Federal Government, 731
Federalism, 401, 410, 472
Federally Administered Tribal Areas, 179, 447, 456
Federal monarchy, 172
Federal Research Division, 497, 890
Federal system, 398
Federation, 2, 251, 407
Felice Beato, 200, 202, 220, 239
Female infanticide, 273
Female suicide bomber, 379
Ferozepore, 223
Fertilizers, 574
Feudalism, 141
Fever, 883
Fidai Khan, 51
Fidel Castro, 479
Field artillery, 21
Field Marshal Auchinleck, 458
Fighter aircraft, 490
File:1965 Infiltrators.jpg, 918
File:India Gujarat location map.svg, 780
File:Pakistan location map.svg, 452

Final Solution (2003 film), 796
Finance Minister, 76
Financial capital, 130
Financing, 576
Finial, 165
Finland, 586
Fir, 126
Firaaq, 796
Firearm, 21
Firman, 4
Firman (decree), 427
Firoz Khan Noon, 903
Firoz Shah Tughlaq, 131
First Anglo-Afghan War, 97
First Anglo-Burmese War, 517
First Anglo–Burmese War, 97
First Anglo-Maratha War, 57, 72, 96
First Anglo-Mysore War, 147
First Anglo-Sikh War, 97, 178, 181, 182, 205, 330, 448, 514
First Battle of El Alamein, 269
First Battle of Panipat, 2, 3, 5, 21
First cholera pandemic, 287
First-come, first-served, 848
First Indian National Army, 352
First Indira Gandhi ministry, 586
First Indo-Pakistani War, 365
First Information Report, 660, 846, 859, 863
First Kashmir War, 490
First Nehru ministry, 400
First Opium War, 114
First Schedule, 372
First War of Indian Independence (term), 236
First World War, 296, 339
Firuz Shah Suri, 31
Fiscal policy, 381, 765
Five Principles of Peaceful Coexistence, 520
Five-star hotel, 168
Five-year plans for the national economy of the Soviet Union, 367
Five-Year Plans of India, 367, 762
Fiza, 759
Flag officer, 546
Flag of India, 90, 251, 395
Flagstaff Tower, 202, 203
Flashman in the Great Game, 242
Flickr, 822
Flight International, 916, 918
Flora Annie Steel, 243
Flotilla, 495
Flush deck, 16, 47
Flying ace, 492
Flying Officer, 607
Folio Society, 247
Folland Gnat, 490, 491, 608
Food grains, 576

976

Force concentration, 529
Forced conversion, 653
Forced displacement, 397
Forced labour, 105
Force One (Mumbai Police), 820, 825
Foreign Affairs, 606
Foreign direct investment, 765, 766, 869
Foreign Exchange Management Act, 860, 862
Foreign exchange reserves, 764
Foreign Investment Promotion Board, 869
Foreign Minister, 76
Foreign policy, 77
Foreign relations of Bangladesh, 598
Foreign relations of India, 478
Fortifications, 39
Fort St. George, 124
Fort William, India, 36, 193
Forty-second Amendment of the Constitution of India, 413, 616, 621
Forward bloc, 351
Forward policy, 511
Founding of modern Singapore, 97
Fountain, 39
Four Provinces (Pakistan), 584, 602
Fourth Anglo-Mysore War, 71, 96, 149, 169
France, 599
Francis Rawdon-Hastings, 1st Marquess of Hastings, 97
Francis Younghusband, 268, 920
François Bernier, 27
François Catrou, 27
Frank Anthony, 405
Frank Messervy, 447, 450, 913
Fraternity, 403
Frédéric Cathala, 249
Frederick Hamilton-Temple-Blackwood, 1st Marquess of Dufferin and Ava, 267
Frederick North, Lord North, 99
Frederick Pethick-Lawrence, 260
Frederick Pethick-Lawrence, 1st Baron Pethick-Lawrence, 313, 314
Frederick Roberts, 1st Earl Roberts, 248
Frederic Thesiger, 1st Viscount Chelmsford, 268, 301
Freedom of religion, 76, 743, 744, 778
Free India Legion, 351
Freeman Freeman-Thomas, 1st Marquess of Willingdon, 269
French colonial empire, 38
French East India Company, 17, 36, 93
French India, 32, 92, 256, 326, 475
French Revolution, 101
Frequency allocation, 847
Friendly fire, 590
Frontier Corps, 446
Frontline (magazine), 783

Front (military), 501
Frostbite, 716
Fundamental Duties, 408
Fundamental rights, 408, 413
Fundamental Rights and Directive principles of India, 407
Fundamental Rights in India, 408
Furqan Force, 446
Fuzhou, 114

G4 nations, 362
Gaekwad, 57, 68
Gaekwad of Baroda, 227
G.A. Henty, 243
Gaikwad, 65, 86
Galvanometer, 125
Galwan River, 516, 530
Ganapati, 290
Gandhian, 613
Gandhi-Irwin Pact, 269, 345
Ganesha, 165
Ganesh Mavlankar, 405
Ganesh Vasudev Mavalankar, 405
Ganges Basin, 187
Ganges Canal, 97, 130, 132
Ganges river, 93, 133
Gang rape, 782
Gangtok, 372
Garhwal Kingdom, 97
Garland, 721
Garo Hills, 373
Garo people, 373
Garrison, 187, 461
Garry Douglas Kilworth, 249
Gas leak, 671
Gas mask, 673
Gateway of India, 804, 819, 821
Gauḍa (city), 33
Gaur, West Bengal, 49
Gavriel Holtzberg, 811
Gayatri Devi, 615
GDP per capita, 767
General, 447, 483, 798
General El Edroos, 364
General officer, 546, 582, 798
General Officer Commanding, 483, 546, 582
General Officer Commanding-in-Chief, 483, 546, 582, 593
General Secretary of the Communist Party of the Soviet Union, 597
General strike, 554
Genghis Khan, 3, 5
Genocidal rape, 566, 583
Genocide, 548, 567, 603, 654
Geographic coordinate system, 171, 671, 728, 798, 803

Geography, 297
Geography of Bangladesh, 590
Geography of India, 585
Geological Survey of India, 709
Geopolitics, 600
George Anson (British Army major-general), 186
George Curzon, 1st Marquess Curzon of Kedleston, 268, 337
George Eden, 1st Earl of Auckland, 97, 133
George Fernandes, 384, 782
George Harrison, 560
George Hilario Barlow, 96
George H.W. Bush, 596
George IV of the United Kingdom, 24
George MacDonald Fraser, 242, 249
George Nathaniel Curzon, 291
George N. Patterson, 517
George Robinson, 1st Marquess of Ripon, 234, 267
George V, 252
George VI, 252, 395, 397–399
George V of the United Kingdom, 268, 294
George Washington University, 567
George W. Bush, 386, 387
George W. Casey, Jr., 717
Georgia Institute of Technology, 520
Geraint Thomas, 840
German East Africa, 268
Germany, 389
G.G Bewoor, 582
Ghadar mutiny, 339, 350
Ghadar Party, 337, 348
Ghana, 536
Ghatkopar, 804
Ghats in Varanasi, 80
Ghazipur, 95, 96
Ghazi warriors, 205
Ghost Wars, 606
GHQ (Pakistan Army), 546, 582
Ghulam Azam, 546
Ghurid Dynasty, 30
Gilbert Elliot-Murray-Kynynmound, 1st Earl of Minto, 96
Gilbert Elliot-Murray-Kynynmound, 4th Earl of Minto, 268, 337
Gilbert John Elliot-Murray-Kynynmound, 4th Earl of Minto, 294
Gilgit, 178, 458, 460
Gilgit Agency, 267, 451
Gilgit–Baltistan, 178, 446
Gilgit Scouts, 446, 458, 460
Gingee, 55, 84
Gingee Fort, 60, 79
Glasgow, 838
Globalisation, 765
GlobalPost, 830
Global Security.org, 934
Globe, 24
Glutathione, 677
Goa, 254, 369, 420, 437, 527
Godavari River, 6
Godhra, 385, 776, 778
Godhra train burning, 743, 776, 778, 790
God Save the Queen, 251
Gohad, 69
Golaknath case, 612
Golconda, 59
Golden Quadrilateral, 385
Golden Temple, 180, 377, 628, 648, 655
Goldman Prize, 695
Gomal River, 30
Goods and Services Tax (India), 766
Google Earth, 815
Google Maps, 822
Gopalaswami Parthasarathy (diplomat), 520
Gopal Godse, 363
Gopal Krishna Gokhale, 289, 290, 296, 298, 336, 341
Gopinath Munde, 871
Gopuram, 165, 167
Gorakhpur, 94
Gorakhpur division, 96
Gordhan Zadafia, 781, 785
Government, 401
Government corruption, 873, 884
Government in exile, 548
Government Law College, Mumbai, 288
Government of Assam, 586
Government of Bihar, 586
Government of East Pakistan, 546, 595, 597
Government of India, 410, 411, 416, 417, 458, 586, 623, 654, 660, 678, 684, 730, 781, 796, 804
Government of India Act 1858, 4, 8, 90, 93, 97, 188, 233, 252, 260, 333, 404
Government of India Act 1919, 268, 299, 303, 343
Government of India Act, 1919, 340, 404
Government of India Act 1935, 269, 308, 345, 402, 417, 423, 434, 473
Government of India Act, 1935, 402–404
Government of Madhya Pradesh, 671, 681
Government of Maharashtra, 820
Government of Meghalaya, 586
Government of Pakistan, 440, 584, 587, 709
Government of Tripura, 586
Government of West Bengal, 586
Government Sanskrit College, 121
Government shutdown, 585
Governor General, 421
Governor-General of Bengal, 102

Governor General of India, 133, 357, 447
Governor-General of India, 90, 93, 102, 127, 128, 188, 191, 194, 221, 252, 260, 261, 304, 333, 357, 396–398, 431, 472
Governor General of Pakistan, 447
Governor-General of Pakistan, 550, 553
Governor (Indian states), 410
Governor of East Pakistan, 546, 582, 595, 597
Governor of Gujarat, 793
Governors of India, 433
Govind Ballabh Pant, 405, 475
Govind Pant Bundele, 65
Gowalia Tank, 354
Gowda (caste), 155
G. Parthasarathy, 538
Graft (politics), 768
Gramophone record, 163
Granite, 126
Granth Sahib, 631
Grant Medical College, 120, 122, 123, 288
Granville Austin, 414, 911
Great Bengal famine of 1770, 33, 42, 286
Great Commission, 277
Great Famine of 1876–1878, 287
Great Famine of 1876–78, 267, 286
Great Game, 596
Great Indian Peninsular Railway, 128, 129, 280, 281
Great Leap Forward, 535
Great power, 532
Greenpeace, 693
Green revolution, 279, 373, 574, 575
Green Revolution in India, 373, **574**, 762
Greenwich Mean Time, 594
Grenade, 23, 772, 803
Grenade launcher, 772
Gross domestic product, 4, 10, 33, 43, 761
Gross national product, 12
Groundwater, 692
Group Captain, 582
Group of fifteen, 480
Group of temples at the Amba Vilas Palace, Mysore, 165
GS Singhvi, 866
G.T. Nanavati, 664, 779
Guangzhou, 114
Gubbi Veeranna, 161
Guerrilla, 180, 586
Guerrilla warfare, 331, 333, 548, 586
Gujarat, 257, 297, 300, 368, 391, 418, 425, 485, 616, 776, 878
Gujarāt, 23
Gujarat High Court, 779
Gujarat Samachar, 784
Gujarat Subah, 9
Gujarat The making of a tragedy, 797

Gujarat Today, 784
Gujranwala, 177
Gulab Singh, 97, 173, 448, 513
Gulam Noon, 810
Gulbarg Society massacre, 777
Gul Hassan Khan, 582, 604
Gulzar, 623
Gun, 23
Gun barrel, 23
Gunboat, 583, 590
Gun carriage, 651
Gunnar Myrdal, 543
Gunpowder, 21, 38
Gunpowder Empires, 3, 21
Gunpowder warfare, 23
Gurbachan Singh, 630
Gurcharan Singh Tohra, 639
Gurdial Singh Dhillon, 663
Gurdwara, 631, 659
Gurjar, 208
Gurjars, 208
Gurkha, 209, 227, 234, 523, 529
Gurkhas, 190
Guru, 884
Guru Amar Das, 175
Guru Arjan Dev, 644
Guru Arjun Dev, 175
Gurudas Dasgupta, 866, 872
Guru Gobind Singh, 174–176
Guru Hargobind, 175
Guru Har Rai, 175
Guru Nanak, 174, 176
Gurung Hill, 533
Guru Tegh Bahadur, 175
Gutenberg:16528, 248
Gutta-percha, 126
Gwalior, 69, 86, 175, 187, 205, 222, 229, 333, 433
Gwalior State, 57, 68, 186, 420
G. W. Choudhury, 572
Gyanendra Pandey (historian), 784
Gyong La, 707, 713
G. T. Nanavati, 660

Habeas corpus, 617
Habitat International Coalition, 828
Habsburg Monarchy, 36, 38
Hachette Digital, 699
Haffkine Institute, 288
Hafiz Muhammad Saeed, 729
Haileybury and Imperial Service College, 111
Hajiganj Fort, 39
Haji Pir pass, 486
Hajj, 15
Hakim Ajmal Khan, 294
Hakim Syed Zillur Rahman, 246

Haldi River, 126
Halwara, 495
Hamida Banu Begum, 6
Hamidia Hospital, 676
Hamidullah Khan, 420
Hamidur Rahman, 607
Hamoodur Rahman, 603
Hamoodur Rahman Commission, 556, 587, 595, 601, 603, 925
Hamoodur Rahman Commission Report, 602, 604
Hand cannon, 23
Handloom, 17
Hanging, 643
Hansa Jivraj Mehta, 405
Hans Raj Khanna, 414, 415
Hanwant Singh, 425
Haqeeqat (1964 film), 541
Harbakhsh Singh, 483
Harchand Singh Longowal, 631
Harcharan Singh Longowal, 628
Harendra Coomar Mookerjee, 405
Haren Pandya, 785
Hari Chand Dewan, 374, 546, 581
Haridwar, 131, 877
Haridwar district, 133, 134
Harin Pathak, 772, 871
Hari Singh, 364, 398, 426, 447
Hari Singh Nalwa, 179
Harjinder Singh Dilgeer, 647
Harjinder Singh Jinda, 643, 660
Harkat-ul-Jihad al-Islami, 729, 732
Harkat-ul-Mujahideen, 729, 741
Harkirat Singh (Major General), 701
Harmandir Sahib, 180, 376, 628, 630, 631, 644, 653
Harold Wilson, 485
HarperCollins, 624
Hartal, 343
Haryana, 207, 257, 368, 574, 645, 654
Haryanvi language, 368
Hasan Gafoor, 820
Hashimpura massacre, 744, 777
Hassan District, 143
Havaldar Gajender Singh, 811, 819
Havildar, 198, 508
Hawayein, 669
Hawker Hunter, 490
Hawker Sea Hawk, 564, 590
Hazaaron Khwaishein Aisi, 623
Hazara, Pakistan, 97
H. Beam Piper, 243
H.D. Deve Gowda, 382
Head of state, 397, 429, 717
Headquarter Jail, 602
Headquarters, 704

Hegde, 155
Hegemony, 94
Heinrich Himmler, 312
Helipad, 716
Helium, 406
Hemant Karkare, 806, 819
Hem Chandra Kanungo, 348
Henderson Brooks–Bhagat Report, 540
Henry Dundas, 101
Henry George Keene (1826–1915), 244
Henry Hardinge, 1st Viscount Hardinge, 97, 133
Henry Havelock, 240
Henry Kissinger, 569, 595
Henry Marion Durand, 222
Henry McMahon, 518
Henry Montgomery Lawrence, 220
Henry Nelson ONeil, 241
Henry Petty-Fitzmaurice, 5th Marquess of Lansdowne, 267
Henry Waxman, 685
Herbert Baker, 307
Herbert Benjamin Edwardes, 225
Herbicide, 575
Hermann Mögling, 161
Hexachlorobutadiene, 683, 693
Hexachlorocyclohexane, 683, 693, 694
Hexachloroethane, 683
High Altitude Warfare School, 710
High Commissioner, 774, 799
High-explosive squash head, 641
High Priest, 76
High-yielding varieties, 574
High-yielding variety, 574
Hill station, 126
Hill Tippera, 227
Himachal Pradesh, 178, 257, 432, 473, 474, 477, 605
Himalaya, 131, 541
Himalayan Blunder, 543
Himalayas, 176, 369, 511, 518, 587
Himatnagar, 783
Hindavi Swarajya, 56, 58
Hindi, 21, 92, 251, 406, 408
Hindi language, 511
Hind Samachar, 635
Hindu, 3, 6, 189, 347, 363, 365, 386, 420, 759, 778
Hindu astronomy, 24
Hindu caste system, 159
Hindu–Muslim riots, 621
Hindu German Conspiracy, 250
Hindu-German Conspiracy, 340, 348
Hinduism, 55, 140, 174, 177
Hindu Jats, 3
Hindu law, 118

Hindu Mahasabha, 344, 355
Hindu nationalism, 390
Hindu-nationalist, 744
Hindustan, 4, 30, 188
Hindustan Aeronautics Limited, 155
Hindustan Ambassador, 721
Hindustani language, 9, 21, 29, 253, 307
Hindustan Ki Kasam, 608
Hindustan Republican Association, 349
Hindustan Socialist Republican Association, 349
Hindustan Times, 858
Hindu temple, 6
Hindutva, 390, 784, 792
Hindu Widows Remarriage Act, 1856, 123
Hirak Rajar Deshe, 623
Hisar District, 131
Historical fiction, 249
Historical novel, 249
Historical Poonch District, 447, 453
Historiography, 237
History, 289
History of Bangladesh, 547
History of Bangladesh after independence, 545
History of British newspapers, 231
History of East Pakistan, 603
History of India, 56, 75, 91, 173, 187, 188, 253, 361, 396, 471, 762
History of Karnataka, 144
History of Kozhikode, 147, 328
History of Pakistan, 259
History of Sindh, 363
History of South Asia, 762
History of the Anushilan Samiti, 347
History of the Republic of India, **361**, 610, 761
History of the rupee, 91
Hizbul Mujahideen, 729, 733, 739
H K L Bhagat, 655
H. K. L. Bhagat, 657, 663
HMS Eagle (R05), 597
H. N. Kunzru, 475
Holden Furber, 443
Holkar, 57, 60, 65, 68, 80, 86
Homeland, 630, 654
Home Minister, 475
Home Minister of India, 799, 863
Home Office, 101
Home Rule, 297
Home Rule Movement, 297, 301
Home Secretary and other senior officials, 874
Homicide, 680, 692
Homosexual, 387
Honourable East India Company, 103
Hooghly River, 37, 125, 126
Horace Hayman Wilson, 121, 138
Hoshiar Singh, 607

Hostage crisis, 803
House of Commons of Great Britain, 117
House of Commons of the United Kingdom, 130, 335
House of Windsor, 399
Howitzer, 545
Howrah, 107, 127, 128
H. S. Phoolka, 669
Hügel, 180
Hugh Rose, 1st Baron Strathnairn, 221
Hugh Wheeler (British Army Officer), 214
HuJI, 817
Hulagu Khan, 601
Hull (watercraft), 16, 47
Humanism, 602
Human rights abuses in Jammu and Kashmir, 730
Human Rights Law Network, 828
Human rights violations, 644, 654
Human Rights Watch, 654, 661, 738, 781, 786, 934
Human shield, 628, 642, 645, 655
Humayun, 3, 5, 24, 29, 33, 34
Humayuns Tomb, 20, 213
Hungary, 369
Hunger strike, 873
Hunger strikes, 695
Hunza (princely state), 516, 920
Hurriyat, 734, 742
Husain Haqqani, 483, 917
Huseyn Shaheed Suhrawardy, 549, 553
Hussain Haqqani, 600
Hussain Quli Beg, 50
Hyderabad, 381, 388
Hyderabad, India, 817, 877
Hyderabad State, 94, 96, 186, 188, 357, 364, 365, 420, 424, 428, 472, 473, 477
Hyderabad State (1948–56), 474, 476
Hyder Ali, 23, 69, 78, 141, 144, 145, 152, 154, 155, 169, 330
Hydroelectric, 154
Hydrogen chloride, 677

Ibadat Khana, 7
Ibn Sina Academy of Medieval Medicine and Sciences, 246
Ibrahim Khan Fath-i-Jang, 51
Ibrahim Khan Gardi, 76
Ibrahim Khan II, 36, 52
Ibrahim Lodi, 3, 21
Ibrahim Shah Suri, 31
Icchogil Canal, 487
I.C. Golaknath and Ors. vs State of Punjab and Anrs., 412
I Corps (India), 483, 582
I Corps (Pakistan), 483, 582, 593

Idea Cellular, 850, 868
Idrakpur Fort, 39
Iftikhar Janjua, 582
Ignasi Guardans, 810
II Corps (India), 582
II Corps (Pakistan), 582, 593
I. K. Gujral, 727
Ikkeri, 144
Ilbert Bill, 234, 267, 289
Illahabad Subah, 9
Illustrated London News, 208
Ilyas Kashmiri, 729
IMDb, 608
Immanuel Wallerstein, 13
Immunity from prosecution, 424
Impeachment of Warren Hastings, 101
Imperial family, 36
Imperial Forestry Service, 266
Imperial Legislative Council, 252, 262, 267, 296, 303, 339, 342
Imperial Police, 266
Imperial Service Troops, 267
Import substitution, 763
Import substitution industrialization, 762
Improvised explosive device, 803
Inamul Haque Khan, 546, 582, 595
Incident, 590
Income tax, 266
Independence Day (Bangladesh), 558
Independence Day (India), 357
Independence of Bangladesh, 545, 583, 595
Independence of Pakistan, 584
Inderjit Singh Gill, 546, 582
Inder Kumar Gujral, 382
Inder Malhotra, 612, 624
Index of Economic Freedom, 768
India, 20, 29, 33, 56, 91, 95, 141, 173, 185, 252, 254, 327, 330, 347, 353, 362, 397, 402, 448, 466, 472, 478, 482, 483, 510, 519, 546, 550, 574, 581, 583, 606, 627, 653, 656, 657, 701, 702, 706, 707, 721, 729, 730, 738, 743, 762, 771, 776, 798, 799, 801
India Act 1784, 100
India After Gandhi: The History of the Worlds Largest Democracy, 624
India Against Corruption, 884, 885
India and Pakistan, 775
India and state-sponsored terrorism, 600
India and the Non-Aligned Movement, **478**, 762
India and weapons of mass destruction, 372
India at the 1900 Summer Olympics, 253
India at the 1920 Summer Olympics, 253
India at the 1928 Summer Olympics, 253
India at the 1932 Summer Olympics, 253

India at the 1936 Summer Olympics, 253
India at the Olympics, 253
India: A Wounded Civilization, 622
India-East Pakistan border, 482, 545
India–Bangladesh enclaves, 581
India–East Pakistan border, 581
India–Iran relations, 598
India–Pakistan relations, 730
India–United Kingdom relations, 357
India–United States Civil Nuclear Agreement, 386, 387
India Gate, 882
India House, 348
Indian 4th Infantry Division, 533
Indian Administrative Service, 267, 410
Indian Air Force, 486, 490, 496, 501, 522, 539, 563, 583, 588, 702, 711, 729
Indiana Jones and the Temple of Doom, 241
Indian anna, 123, 125
Indian annexation of Goa, 357, 438
Indian annexation of Hyderabad, 397
Indian architecture, 19
Indian Armed Forces, 546, 582, 735, 801
Indian Army, 9, 328, 363, 372, 383, 429, 458, 485, 540, 583, 627, 628, 637, 646, 648, 653, 729, 733, 738, 739, 798, 800
Indian Army Chief, 633
Indian Army during World War II, 351
Indian art, 19
Indian black money, 873, 874, 884
Indian Century, 597
Indian Civil Service, 107, 267, 288
Indian Civil Service (British India), 327, 405
Indian coal allocation scam, 848
Indian Constitution, 615, 621
Indian-controlled Kashmir, 598
Indian Council of Medical Research, 681
Indian Council of Scientific and Industrial Research, 699
Indian Councils Act 1861, 262, 266, 404
Indian Councils Act 1892, 267, 294, 404
Indian Councils Act 1909, 268, 294, 337, 404
Indian Economic and Social History Review, 906
Indian Election Commission, 793
Indian Express, 621, 928
Indian famine of 1896–97, 267, 286
Indian famine of 1899–1900, 268, 286, 287
Indian foreign policy, 701
Indian Forest Act, 1927, 269
Indian Forest Service, 266, 410
Indian general election, 1934, 307
Indian general election, 1971, 612
Indian general election, 1977, 615
Indian general election, 1991, 704
Indian general election, 2004, 386, 391

Indian general election, 2009, 387, 727
Indian general election, 2014, 848
Indian government, 586, 628, 642, 692, 799, 802, 830, 874
Indian history, 17
Indian Independence Act 1947, 252, 269, 328, 357, 396, 397, 402–404, 416, 418
Indian independence movement, 141, 290, **326**, 362, 397, 516, 761, 762
Indian independence struggle, 478
Indian Institutes of Technology, 367
Indian Intelligence Agency, 800
Indian intervention in the Sri Lankan Civil War, **701**
Indian involvement, 703
Indian labour law, 768
Indian Legion, 352
Indian mathematics, 24
Indian media, 841
Indian Military Academy, 269, 339, 637
Indian Mujahideen, 792, 837
Indian Mutiny Medal, 236
Indian mutiny of 1857, 38, 236
Indian National Army, 313, 328, 344, 351, 352, 458
Indian National Association, 334
Indian National Congress, 289, 296, 304, 305, 307, 313, 327, 334, 338, 348, 349, 353, 356, 362, 367, 371, 375, 386, 391, 400, 416, 419, 451, 478, 499, 611, 630, 653, 731, 779, 844, 848, 871, 878, 885
Indian National Congress (Organisation), 702
Indian nationality law, 408, 410
Indian Navy, 79, 495, 589, 801
Indian occupied Kashmir, 799
Indian Ocean trade, 14
Indian Order of Merit, 236
Indian Parliament, 372, 799, 869
Indian Peace Keeping Force, 701, 703, 721
Indian Penal Code, 266, 303, 773, 779, 845, 856
Indian people, 608
Indian Police Service, 266, 410
Indian Political Intelligence Office, 349
Indian Post Office, 125
Indian Premier League, 837
Indian Provincial Elections, 1937, 308, 350
Indian provincial elections, 1946, 404
Indian Railways, 97, 613
Indian Rebellion of 1857, 4, 8, 93, 97, 111, **185**, 252, 253, 260, 270, 271, 416, 761
Indian Red Cross, 692
Indian Revenue Service, 859
Indian rupee, 252, 370, 396, 495, 656, 681, 762
Indian Rupees, 127

Indian Security Forces, 799
Indian Slavery Act, 1843, 97
Indian Space Research Organisation, 377, 390
Indian Standard Time, 594, 803, 806
Indian subcontinent, 2, 19, 29, 56, 93, 174, 253, 327, 338, 403, 421, 518, 550, 589
Indian Supreme Court, 680
Indian Telecom Spectrum Auction, 847
India Office, 93, 233, 260, 269, 904
Indias First War of Independence (term), 187, 761
India Today, 604, 783, 822, 869
Indigo, 13, 298
Indigo dye, 112, 114
Indigofera tinctoria, 12, 112, 114
Indigo rebellion, 115
Indira Gandhi, 370, 479, 546, 548, 556, 558, 563, 582, 586, 605, 610, 611, 627, 628, 642, 648, 664, 702, 724, 731
Indira Gandhi International Airport, 724, 817
Indirect tax, 768
Indo-Aryan migration theory, 547
Indo-Bangla relations, 545
Indoctrination, 805, 806
Indo-European languages, 121, 550
Indo-Gangetic Plain, 373
Indologists, 4
Indonesia, 13, 46, 369, 386, 479, 491, 536, 763
Indo-Pakistani border, 482, 581, 798, 799
Indo-Pakistani relation, 605
Indo-Pakistani War of 1947, 362, 363, 366, 369, 396, 398, 427, **446**, 731
Indo-Pakistani War of 1965, 362, 369, **482**, 552, 589, 593, 762
Indo-Pakistani War of 1971, 362, 371, 374, 500, 502, 505, 507, 537, 540, 549, 564, **581**, 708, 762
Indo-Pakistani War of 1971 Prisoners of War Investigation, 583, 595, 598, 604
Indo-Pakistani Wars, 482, 484
Indo-Pakistani wars and conflicts, 369, 446, 540, 541, 581, 706, 798
Indo-Pakistan War of 1971, 371
Indo-Pakistan Wars, 366, 447
Indo-Persian culture, 2
Indore, 86, 194, 222, 433
Indore State, 57
Indo-Saracenic, 164
Indo-Soviet Treaty of Friendship and Cooperation, 571, 595
Indo-Sri Lankan Accord, 701, 703
Indo-Sri Lanka Peace Accord, 702
Indo-Tibetan Border Police, 650
Indo-US Relations, 597
Indra Sinha, 695

Indu Sarkar, 624
Indus River, 453
Industrial disasters, 671
Industrial Revolution, 9, 10, 13, 16, 33, 46, 47
Industry, 10, 13
Indus Valley Civilisation, 406
Infantry, 80, 484, 552
Inflation, 387
Inflation in India, 768
Information technology enabled services, 767
Infrastructure, 10
Inquilab Zindabad, 349
Insecticides, 575
INS Khukri (F149), 590
Inspector general, 668
Inspector General of Police, 662
Institute, West Virginia, 672
Instrument of accession, 364, 398, 423, 447, 450, 472
Instrument of Accession (Jammu and Kashmir), 364, 427, 446
Instrument of Surrender (1971), 581, 583
Insurgency, 721
Insurgency in Jammu and Kashmir, 362, 379, 388, **729**, 762
Insurgency in Northeast India, 388
Insurgent groups in Northeast India, 440
Insurrection 1987-89, 703
INS Vikrant, 495
INS Vikrant (R11), 371, 564, 590, 591
Intelligence, 77
Intelligence agency, 505
Intelligence Bureau (India), 649
Intelligentsia, 547
Interest, 576
Interim government, 427
Interim Government of India, 252, 396
Interior Minister, 76
International Alphabet of Sanskrit Transliteration, 401, 402
International Atomic Energy Agency, 606
International Campaign for Justice in Bhopal, 696
International capital markets, 766
International Committee of the Red Cross, 608
International community, 586
International Court of Justice, 405, 429, 437
International Crimes Tribunal (Bangladesh), 603, 605
International dollars, 156
International Federation of Associated Wrestling Styles, 843
International Film Festival of India, 624
International Film Festival of Kerala, 624
International law, 556

International Medical Commission on Bhopal, 696, 697
International Mother Language Day, 551
International New York Times, 928
International Olympic Committee, 844
International Peoples Tribunal on Human Rights and Justice in Kashmir, 931
International Standard Book Number, 25, 26, 88, 89, 134–138, 169–171, 183, 243–247, 318–324, 358, 359, 392, 414, 415, 442–445, 467–470, 508, 509, 542, 543, 572, 573, 609, 624, 625, 647, 648, 652, 669, 670, 697–700, 705, 719, 742, 797
International Standard Serial Number, 322, 572
International trade, 13
Internment, 540, 548
Interpol, 816, 820
Interpretation Act 1889, 255
Inter Services Intelligence, 799, 825
Inter-Services Intelligence, 500, 730, 733, 734, 740, 772, 780, 806, 814
Inter-Services Public Relations, 609, 800
In the Line of Fire: A Memoir, 713
Introduction of the telegraph, 97
Invasion and Occupation of the Andaman Islands during World War II, 353
Invasion of Goa, 527
Invasion of Tibet (1950–1951), 519
IPKF, 701
Iran, 209, 491, 592, 596, 598
Iranian military, 598
Iraq, 491
Irfan Habib, 8, 13, 888
Irish Examiner, 935
Irish home rule, 297
Ironwood, 126
Irregular military, 71
Irrigation, 12, 574, 575
Irrigation sprinkler, 575
Isa Khan, 35, 39
Ishwar Chandra Vidyasagar, 123
I. S. Johar, 623
Islam, 140, 159, 174–177
Islamabad, 584, 587, 592
Islamabad Capital Territory, 257
Islamic, 159
Islamic Law, 120
Islamic Republic of Pakistan, 317
Islamic State of Iraq and the Levant – Khorasan Province, 729
Islamic terrorism, 803
Islamism, 550, 583, 602
Islamist, 805
Islam Khan I, 51
Islam Khan II, 51

Islam Shah Suri, 31
Ismail Beg, 70
Israel, 388
Israeli Air Force, 563
Italian Campaign (World War I), 513
Italian Campaign (World War II), 269
Ittehad-ul-Muslimeen, 427
IV Corps (India), 546, 582
IV Corps (Pakistan), 483, 582
Iwaichi Fujiwara, 352

Jackfruit, 102
Jacque Servin, 697
Jacques Rogge, 844
Jadunath Sarkar, 891
Jadu Nath Singh, 467
Jaffna, 702, 703
Jaffna University, 704
Jaganmohan Palace, 165, 167
Jagannath, 331
Jagannath Hall, 556
Jagat Gosaini, 6
Jagdish Tytler, 655, 663, 664
Jagdispur, 226
Jagirdar, 44, 49
Jagjit Singh Arora, 546, 582
Jagjit Singh Aurora, 374, 581, 593, 922
Jagjivan Ram, 362, 582
Jagmohanlal Sinha, 614
Jahangir, 3, 6, 23, 35, 48, 175
Jahangir Nagar, 35
Jahangir Quli Beg, 51
Jail Bharo Andolan, 880
Jaimini Bharata, 161
Jain, 158
Jain Commission, 727
Jainism, 158
Jaintia Hills, 373
Jaintia people, 373
Jai Prakash Agarwal, 871
Jai Prakash Narayan National Park, 880
Jaipur, 20, 70, 96, 97, 388
Jaipur State, 94, 186, 420
Jairamdas Daulatram, 362
Jaisalmer, 425
Jaishanker Manilal Shelat, 613
Jaish-e-Mohammad, 799
Jaish-e-Mohammed, 729, 732, 771, 773–775
Jai Singh II of Amber, 24
Jakarta, 479, 480
Jalandhar, 208, 489
Jallianwala Bagh, 304
Jallianwala Bagh massacre, 268, 304, 343, 878
Jalpaiguri, 227
Jamaat-e-Islami Bangladesh, 546
Jamaat-e-Islami Hind, 615

Jamaat-e-Islami Kashmir, 734
JAMA (journal), 699
Jamalpur, Bardhaman, 49
Jama Masjid, Delhi, 3, 618, 837
Jamdani, 41
James Broun-Ramsay, 1st Marquess of Dalhousie, 97, 122, 127, 128, 133, 192, 195, 270, 332
James Bruce, 8th Earl of Elgin, 266
James George Smith Neill, 219, 228
James Grant (newspaper editor), 249
James Hope Grant, 178
James II of England, 116
James John McLeod Innes, 248
James Leasor, 249
James Mill, 107, 122
James Riddick Partington, 23
James Skinner (East India Company officer), 897
James Thomason (British colonial governor), 133
James Wilson (UK politician), 266
Jamiat Ulema-e-Hind, 786
Jammu, 94, 97, 190, 427, 446, 448, 451, 453, 466, 502, 738, 742, 800, 877
Jammu and Kashmir, 178, 379, 390, 410, 426, 448, 474, 477, 484, 486, 540, 708, 729–731, 742, 800
Jammu and Kashmir Legislative Assembly, 799
Jammu and Kashmir Legislative Assembly election, 1987, 734
Jammu and Kashmir Legislative Assembly election, 2014, 739
Jammu and Kashmir Police, 729
Jammu and Kashmir (princely state), 173, 186, 398, 416, 424, 426, 446, 451, 514
Jammu and Kashmir State Forces, 447
Jammu Division, 178, 451
Jammu & Kashmir Human Rights Commission, 735
Jammu Kashmir Liberation Front, 729
Jammu & Kashmir National Conference, 427, 451, 452, 458
Jamrud, 179
Jamsetji Tata, 280
Janak Singh, 454
Janardan Dwivedi, 877
Janata Dal, 379, 382, 883
Janata Dal (United), 871, 878
Janata Party, 375, 613
Janatha Vimukthi Peramuna, 703
Jangalbari Fort, 39
Jang Bahadur, 221
Janjira State, 15
Jan Lokpal Bill, 873, 874, 884
Jan Masiel, 810

Jan Sangharsh Manch, 791
Jan Smuts, 341
Jantar Mantar, 211, 873, 884
Janus, 162
Jaora State, 186
Japan, 11, 14, 46, 389
Japanese 15th Army, 353
Japanese occupation of Burma, 313
Japan Times, 936
Jarnail Singh Bhindranwale, 627, 628
Jarnail Singh (journalist), 665
Jaswant Singh, 801, 871
Jat, 66, 208
Jathedar, 668
Jathedar of Akal Takht, 628
Jat people, 839
Jat Regiment, 488
Jauna Murmu, 840
Java, 96, 110
Javed Siddiqui, 242
Jawaharlal, 344
Jawaharlal Nehru, 285, 307, 317, 344, 362, 363, 365, 367, 396, 397, 400, 405, 408, 421, 447, 456, 475, 478, 479, 510, 516, 519, 538, 542, 702, 724
Jawaharlal Nehru Stadium (Delhi), 389
Jawaharlal Nehru University, 622
Jawans, 718
Jawhar State, 420
Jayachamaraja Wodeyar, 140, 151, 153
Jayalakshmi Vilas, 165
Jayalalithaa, 870
Jayaprakash Narayan, 419, 613–615
Jaya Prakash Narayan, 374
Jayee Rajguru, 331
Jeddah, 43, 156
Jeffrey G. Williamson, 9
Jemadar, 198
Jennifer Meadows, 840
Jeremy Black (historian), 504
Jerusalem, 296
Jessica Ennis, 840
J. F. R. Jacob, 374, 546, 581, 582
J. G. Farrell, 242
J.G. Farrell, 249
Jhansi, 97, 186, 221, 242
Jhansi Fort, 221, 222
Jharkhand, 257, 384
Jhelum (City), 224
Jigme Dorji Wangchuck, 608
Jigme Singye Wangchuck, 569
Jihad, 587
Jihadist, 606
Jimmy Carter, 376
Jind, 78, 433
Jingoism, 587

Jinnah, 309
Jivatram Kripalani, 615
Joan of Arc, 222
João de Barros, 38
Jodhpur, 70, 424
Jodhpur State, 186, 420
Joe Pitts, 790
Joginder Singh Dhillon, 483
John Arnold Wallinger, 350
John Coates (sports administrator), 839
John Conyers, 790, 795
John Dalvi, 523
John Eardley Inglis, 220
John Fitzgerald Kennedy, 536
John F. Keenan, 679
John F. Kennedy, 537
John F. Kennedy School of Government, 917
John F. Richards, 887, 888, 890
John Fryer (FRS), 77
John Gunther, 151
John Hanford, 786
John Keay, 498
John Kenneth Galbraith, 539
John Lawrence, 1st Baron Lawrence, 266
John Malcolm, 75
John Marshall, 414
John Masters, 242, 249
John Mathai, 362
John Morley, 260, 294
John Nicholson (East India Company officer), 186
John Nicholson (general), 210, 224
John Russell Colvin, 132
John Shore, 1st Baron Teignmouth, 96, 110, 121
Johore, 43
Joint parliamentary committee, 852, 865, 870
Joint Staff Headquarters (Pakistan), 602
Joint stock, 130
Jon Cleary, 541
Jordan, 592, 596
Josef Korbel, 468
Joseph R. Pitts, 795
Joseph White (orientalist), 277
Josh Malihabadi, 327
Josiah Ng, 842
Joyanto Nath Chaudhuri, 364, 483
Joydeep Sircar, 710
J.P.Dutta, 608
J. R. D. Tata, 621
JSTOR, 25–27, 137, 138, 245–247, 321, 323, 442–445, 572
Judges of the International Court of Justice, 405
Judicial review, 413, 620
Judicial review in India, 412, 413

Judicial review in the United States, 413
Judiciary, 118, 401
Judiciary of India, 410
Judith M. Brown, 318
Jugantar, 347
Jugantar (paper), 338
Jugular vein, 502
Jules Verne, 243
Julia, Lady Inglis, 248
Julian Rathbone, 249
Jullundur Doab, 97
Junagadh, 357, 365, 424, 425
Junagadh State, 397
Jung Bahadur, 892
Jung Bahadur Rana, 186
Junior commissioned officer, 496, 645, 718
Junius Richard Jayewardene, 702
Junoon (1978 film), 241, 242
Jussi Hanhimäki, 586
Justice, 403
Justin Sheil, 83, 892
Jute, 13

K2, 709
Kaarle McCulloch, 836
Kabul, 5, 20
Kabul Subah, 9
Kadapa, 95
Kailali District, 91
Kai Po Che, 796
Kaiser Tufail, 592
Kaithal, 78
Kakori conspiracy, 349, 351
Kakori train robbery, 349
Kakuzo Okakura, 347
Kalaignar TV, 852
Kalanithi Maran, 863, 864, 869
Kala pani (taboo), 191
Kalbadevi, 804
Kali, 293
Kallara-Pangode Struggle, 350
Kalpana Kannabiran, 782
Kal Penn, 695
Kalpi, 222
Kalsia, 433
Kaluchak Massacre, 800
Kalurghat, 558
Kalyan, India, 128
Kamal Nath, 666
Kamlesh Kumari, 772, 775
Kanaiyalal Maneklal Munshi, 405
Kanara, 144, 160
Kanchan Prava Devi, 364
Kanchanpur District, 91
Kanchipuram, 166, 622
Kangra State, 448

Kanhoji Angre, 57, 62, 79
K. A. Nilakanta Sastri, 170
Kannada, 71, 142, 477
Kannada language, 140, 154
Kannada literature, 142, 161
Kannadigas, 161
Kannambadi, 155
Kanpur, 96, 188, 214
Kanpur Memorial Church, 215
Kantajew Temple, 41
Kanthirava Narasaraja I, 141, 152
Kanwar Pal Singh Gill, 793
Kanyakumari district, 477
Kapil Sibal, 876
Kapurthala, 433
Kapurthala State, 186
Karachi, 156, 313, 317, 356, 491, 501, 813, 814
Karachi Agreement, 707, 708
Karaikal, 437
Karakash River, 514–516
Karakoram, 517, 706
Karakoram Pass, 514, 710
Karam Singh, 467
Karbi-Meghalaya plateau, 373
Kargil district, 565
Kargil town, 463, 465
Kargil War, 362, 383, 565, 716, 799
Karl Marx, 231, 888
Karnal, 203, 209
Karnataka, 257, 428, 431
Karnataka Gatha Vaibhava, 161
Karol Bagh, 659
Karor Singhia, 181
Kar seva, 633
Karsevaks, 776
Karti Chidambaram, 869
Karunanidhi, 851, 865
Kasaragod, 477
Kashi Vishwanath Temple, 180
Kashmir, 24, 94, 97, 174, 175, 178, 188, 190, 357, 365, 369, 379, 446, 448, 482, 485, 486, 490, 513, 537, 552, 571, 606, 706, 729–731, 798, 799
Kashmir and Jammu (princely state), 366, 447
Kashmir conflict, 398, 439, 484, 485, 706, 729
Kashmir Division, 451
Kashmiri Gate (Delhi), 211, 213
Kashmiri insurgents, 738
Kashmiri language, 172
Kashmiri Pandit, 379
Kashmiri Pandits, 175, 735, 738
Kashmir region, 799
Kashmir Singh Katoch, 447, 483
Kashmir valley, 446, 448, 451, 453, 466, 742
Kathavasheshan, 796

Kathiawar, 227, 418, 433
Katra Mosque, 39
Kattabomman, 331
Kaum De Heere, 652
Kaveri river, 131, 155
Kavi Kalash, 60
Kayastha, 105
Kaya Taran, 669
Kay Kay Menon, 694
Kazi Lhendup Dorji, 439
Kazi Nazrul Islam, 327
K.B. Hedgewar, 355
K. C. Neogy, 362
Kehar Singh, 650, 652
Keirin, 842
Keladi Nayaka, 143, 144, 147
Keladi Nayaka Kingdom, 69
Kendujhar, 186
Kerala, 148, 257, 368, 431, 477, 617, 810
Kerala High Court, 617
Kesavananda Bharati v. State of Kerala, 411, 612, 617
Ketan Mehta, 241
Kevin Pietersen, 837
K Force (Bangladesh), 546
K.G. Gupta, 261
Khadi, 343
Khadim Hussain Raja, 546, 582
Khaksars, 349
Khaled Mosharraf, 546
Khalistan, 377, 630, 636, 654, 668
Khalistan Commando Force, 660
Khalistan Liberation Force, 660
Khalistan movement, 627, 643, 654, 660
Khalsa, 3, 174, 175, 180, 205, 223, 629
Khan Jahan I, 39
Khan Mohammad Mridha Mosque, 39
Khan Zaman II, 51
Kharak Singh, 172, 181
Khasi Hills, 373
Khasi people, 373
Khawaja Nazimuddin, 553
Kheda, 300
Khem Karan, 489
Khem Karan Singh, 582
Khijri, 126
Khooni Darwaza, 213
Khordha, 331
Khotan, 515
Khudadad Khan, 295
Khudai Khidmatgar, 310
Khudiram Bose, 337, 338
Khulna Division, 49
Khurshid Anwar (Major), 447, 456
Khushwant Singh, 621, 648, 669
Khusrau Mirza, 175

Khwaja Salimullah, 291, 294
Khyber Agency, 179
Khyber Pakhtunkhwa, 57, 78, 179, 190, 258, 363, 816
Khyber Pass, 5, 174, 177, 178
Kidnapping, 653, 776
Killed in action, 186, 546, 582, 627, 729
Kilometre, 529
King cobra, 836
Kingdom of Arakan, 35
Kingdom of Cochin, 94, 96
Kingdom of England, 93
Kingdom of France, 36
Kingdom of Great Britain, 36, 908
Kingdom of Jammu and Kashmir, 252
Kingdom of Mrauk U, 32, 39
Kingdom of Mysore, 71, 91, 94, 97, **140**, 188, 330
Kingdom of Nepal, 186, 255
Kingdom of Sikkim, 255, 372
Kingdom of Travancore, 141, 149
Kingdom of Tripura, 38, 364
King-in-Council, 116, 117
King of Bhutan, 608
Kishore Chandra Deo, 871
Kishore Kumar, 618
Kissa Kursi Ka, 623
Kleptocracy, 873, 874, 884
K. M. Munshi, 405
K. M. Panikkar, 319, 475
K M Shafiullah, 546
K. N. Panikkar, 358
Kodagu, 160
Kodagu district, 258
Kodandera Madappa Cariappa, 447, 463
Kodendera Subayya Thimayya, 447
Kohat, 452
Kolapore, 225
Kolar Gold Fields, 154
Kolhapur, 60, 73, 432
Kolkata, 251, 262, 288, 344, 548
Konbaung dynasty, 517
Kongu Nadu, 331
Konkan, 79
Konkona Sen Sharma, 668
Kote Venkataramana Temple, Bangalore, 166
Kotli, 460
Kotwal, 201
Kozhikode, 23, 126
K. P. Candeth, 582
KPS Gill, 646
Krishak Praja Party, 309, 310
Krishan Kant, 772
Krishna Deva Raya, 131
Krishna Iyer, 790
Krishna Kumarasingh Bhavasingh, 436

Krishna Menon, 539
Krishna Raja Wadiyar IV, 153
Krishnaraja Wodeyar II, 144, 152
Krishnaraja Wodeyar III, 149, 161
Krishna River, 69
Krishnaswamy Sundarji, 627, 637
Kriti, 163
K. R. Narayanan, 798
K. Sankaran Nair, 546
K. Santhanam, 362
K. S. Brar, 647
K. Seshadri Iyer, 154
K.S. Hegde, 613
K. Subrahmanyam, 572
K. T. Thomas (Justice), 725
Kuala Lumpur, 480, 834, 838
Kuldip Nayar, 625, 648, 669
Kuldip Singh Brar, 627, 637
Kulkarni, 84
Kumaon division, 97
Kumaon Kingdom, 96
Kumaon Regiment, 534, 711
Kunlun mountains, 514, 516
Kunwar Singh, 186
Kurnool, 95
Kurram Militia, 446
Kutch State, 476
Kuttrapathirikai, 728
Kuwait, 91
Kuyili, 331
K. Veeramani, 702

Labour laws, 828
Labour market reform, 768
Labour Party (UK), 315
Labour union, 613
Laccadive, 477
Ladakh, 178, 389, 427, 446, 448, 451, 463, 466, 511, 513, 706
Lahore, 1, 18, 20, 21, 24, 64, 78, 129, 132, 172, 174, 175, 177, 209, 223, 267, 305, 307, 344, 345, 363, 487, 505, 587
Lahore Declaration, 383, 713
Lahore district, 483
Lahore Fort, 3, 20
Lahore International Airport, 487
Lahore Resolution, 310, 346, 549
Lahore Subah, 9, 18
Lakshadweep, 477
Lakshmisa, 162
Lala Hardayal, 348
Lala Jagat Narain, 630
Lala Lajpat Rai, 290, 305, 336
Lalbagh, 227
Lalbagh Fort, 39
Lal Bahadur Shastri, 351, 370, 483, 499, 504

Lal Bal Pal, 327, 336
Lalitha Mahal, 165, 168
Lalit Maken, 656, 660
Lal Krishna Advani, 615, 799
Lalmonirhat District, 562
Lalu Prasad Yadav, 878
Lanak La, 516
Lance Naik, 467, 607
Land degradation, 574
Landed gentry, 101
Landfall, 554
Land mine, 23
Land reforms, 575
Langar (Sikhism), 175
Language Movement, 550
Language Movement Day, 550, 551
Languages of India, 121
Languages of South Asia, 1, 251
Langur, 835
Lanzhou Military Region, 528
Larsen & Toubro, 687
Lashkar-e-Taiba, 729, 732, 733, 739, 771, 774, 799, 803–805
Lashkar-e-Toiba, 739, 741, 792
Lata Mangeshkar, 542
Lathicharge, 876
Latin, 893, 903
Laudian Professor of Arabic, 277
Laura Turner, 842
Law Commission of India, 411
Law of India, 672
Law of Rent, 107
League of Nations, 253, 296
Lectern, 224
Legacy, 791
Legal Framework Order, 2002, 584
Legal pluralism, 35
Legislative Assembly of Ontario, 668
Legislative chamber, 401
Legislature, 410
Leh, 390, 461, 465, 514
Leonid Brezhnev, 597, 608
Leopold Cafe, 804, 807, 819
Leopold Café, 803
Lepcha people, 439
Leprosy, 288
Leslie Mungavin, 582, 590
Letter rogatory, 869
Letters patent, 117
Lewin Bentham Bowring, 154
Lhasa (prefecture-level city), 520
Liaquat Ali Khan, 309, 364, 447, 454, 455, 553
Liberal arts education, 276
Liberalisation, 760
Liberation Tigers of Tamil Eelam, 379, 701, 702, 721, 725

Liberty, 403
Liberty, equality and fraternity, 407
Library of Congress, 890
Library of Congress Control Number, 170
Library of Congress Country Studies, 139, 481, 497, 571
Libya, 592
Licence Raj, 362, 377, 762, 765
License Raj, 874
Lieutenant Colonel, 447
Lieutenant-Colonel, 508
Lieutenant General, 447, 483, 546, 585, 593
Lieutenant-General, 374, 483, 546, 581, 582, 595, 706
Lieutenant Governor (India), 410
Life imprisonment, 661
Life (magazine), 171
Life of Pi, 623
Life of Pi (film), 624
Light machine gun, 634
Lila (Hinduism), 878
Limba Ram, 841
Lin Biao, 510, 528
Line of Actual Control, 511, 538, 541, 598
Line of Control, 385, 446, 447, 482, 486, 581, 598, 716, 733, 798–801
Lingzi Tang Plains, 514
Lippincotts Monthly Magazine, 249
List of amendments of the Constitution of India, 372, 401, 406, 407
List of Chief Ministers of Gujarat, 776
List of Chief Ministers of India, 821
List of Chief Ministers of Maharashtra, 881
List of Chief Ministers of Uttar Pradesh, 405
List of CIA station chiefs, 772
List of colonial Governors and Presidents of Madras, 257
List of colonial governors of Burma, 257
List of countries and dependencies by area, 2, 55, 91, 396
List of countries and outlying territories by area, 173
List of countries by GDP (PPP), 362
List of countries by population, 2, 55, 173
List of countries by real GDP growth rate, 362
List of countries by size of armed forces, 540
List of current heads of state and government, 799
List of Governors of Assam, 257
List of Governors of Bengal, 257
List of Governors of Bombay, 257
List of Governors of Punjab (British India), 257
List of Governors of the Central Provinces and Berar, 257
List of Governors of the United Provinces, 257
List of high courts in India, 401

List of Indian Air Force stations, 583
List of Indian Federal Legislation, 288
List of Indian Intelligence agencies, 820
List of Indian Mutiny Victoria Cross recipients, 236
List of industrial disasters, 671
List of Justices of the Supreme Court of Pakistan, 603
List of largest empires that existed in India, 2
List of Latin phrases (M-O), 127
List of military operations of India, 546
List of Pakistan Air Force squadrons, 591
List of Prime Ministers of India, 367, 648
List of sectors in the Bangladesh Liberation War, 548, 560, 561
List of space agencies, 390
List of states with nuclear weapons, 362
List of temples in Bishnupur, 41
Liu Bocheng, 510, 529
Liverpool, 156
Living standards, 11, 43, 156
L. K. Advani, 793
LK Advani, 772
L.N.Mishra, 613
Lockheed C-130 Hercules, 592
Locum tenens, 96
Lodi dynasty, 21
Lohgarh, 176
Loin-cloth, 305
Lok Ayukta, 882
Lok Parlok, 623
Lok Sabha, 382, 386, 401, 410, 411, 614, 620, 668, 772
Lombardy, 134
London, 262, 710, 820
London Missionary Society, 278
Long and short scales, 870
Longman, 248
Loom, 37
Loop Mobile, 849, 856, 864, 868
Loop Telecom, 864, 866
Lord Canning, 188, 260, 272
Lord Curzon, 291
Lord Dalhousie, 282
Lord Elgin, 516
Lord Elphinstone, 159
Lord Mountbatten, 447, 450
Lord North, 99
Lord Palmerston, 238
Lord Ripon, 289
Lord William Bentinck, 97, 101, 272, 276
Louis Mountbatten, 316, 317, 357
Louis Mountbatten, 1st Earl Mountbatten of Burma, 252, 269, 365, 396, 397, 399, 400, 419, 421
Love triangle, 608

Lower Burma, 97, 254
Lower Gangetic plains moist deciduous forests, 94
LTTE, 378, 703, 704
Lucknow, 188, 220, 359, 414, 877
Lucknow Pact, 297, 301, 340
Lunar probe, 387
Luo Ruiqing, 510
Lutheran, 278
Lyndon Baines Johnson, 536

M24 Chaffee, 483, 493
M3 2, 493
M36 Jackson, 493
M3A3 Stuart, 494
M3 Stuart, 463, 493
M47 Patton, 493
M48 Patton, 483, 489, 493
M4 Sherman, 493, 494
Macartney–MacDonald Line, 516
Macaulays Minute Upon Indian Education, 122
MacDonald Line, 532
Machine guns, 647
Machinery, 575
Macmillan Publishers, 358
Madame Bhikaji Rustom Cama, 348
Madanlal Dhingra, 348
Madan Lal Khurana, 664
Madanlal Pahwa, 363
Madan Mohan Malaviya, 296
Madhavrao I, 57, 66–69
Madhavrao II, 68, 73
Madhavrao Peshwa, 68, 85, 147
Madhukar Sarpotdar, 759
Madhu Kishwar, 797
Madhur Bhandarkar, 624
Madhusudan Das, 475
Madhvendra Singh, 798
Madhya Bharat, 365, 433, 473, 474, 477
Madhya Pradesh, 80, 257, 473, 476, 477, 671, 684
Madras, 93, 282, 305, 313, 344, 721
Madrasa Aliya, 120
Madras Army, 190, 284
Madrasas, 747
Madras Cafe, 728
Madras Christian College, 122
Madras Engineer Group, 463
Madras High Court, 726, 727
Madras Legislative Assembly, 406
Madras Presidency, 98, 100, 102, 107, 119, 131, 159, 188, 190, 255, 257, 261, 297, 330, 347, 350, 431, 432, 477
Madras Province, 430
Madras Regiment, 235
Madras State, 368, 405, 436, 473, 475, 477

Madrid, 820
Madurai, 143, 305
M. A. G. Osmani, 546, 548, 559, 582
MAG Osmani, 586
Mahabat Khan, 51
Mahadaji Shinde, 68
Mahadji Shinde, 69, 78
Mahalla, 9
Mahamastakabhisheka, 159
M. A. Hannan, 558
Mahar, 344
Maharaja, 94, 172, 189, 274, 364, 426, 447, 448
Maharaja Hari Singh, 450, 451
Maharaja of Baroda, 406
Maharaja of Gwalior, 70
Maharaja of Jammu and Kashmir, 447
Maharaja of Mysore, 140, 152
Maharaja Ranjit Singhs throne, 177
Maharajas College, Mysore, 160
Maharashtra, 56, 79, 257, 336, 344, 347, 368, 428, 430, 440, 758, 808, 816, 818, 881
Maharashtra floods of 2005, 386
Maha Singh, 181
Mahatma Gandhi, 151, 305, 309, 337, 342, 362, 363, 398, 614, 651, 784
Mahé, India, 437
Maheshwar, 80
Mahim, 805
Mainpuri district, 96
Mainstem (hydrology), 134
Maintenance of Internal Security Act, 616
Maize, 12
Major, 447, 546, 586, 817
Major General, 447, 546, 582, 600, 701
Major-General, 483, 546, 595, 602, 706, 800
Major General Akhtar Hussain Malik, 502
Major Iqbal, 814
Major Ravi, 609
Makassar, 43
Make in India, 391
Maktab, 19
Malabar Coast, 159
Malabar district, 477
Malabar region, 96
Malakand Agency, 453
Malaria, 288
Malayalam, 622, 623, 669, 796
Malayalam film, 623
Malayalam language, 623
Malaysia, 91, 479
Malcolm X, 242
Maldives, 43, 91, 255
Malerkotla, 433
Maler Kotla, 78
Malik Nur Khan, 483

Malnad, 143
Malnutrition, 576
Malwa, 23, 57, 63
Malwa Subah, 10
Mamoni Raisom Goswami, 669
Man Booker Prize, 695
Manchester, 156
Mandai massacre, 743, 778
Mandal Commission, 379
Mandya District, 155
Mangalore, 160
Mangal Pandey, 198, 241, 332
Mangal Pandey: The Rising, 241
Mangla Dam, 805
Mangol Puri (Delhi Assembly constituency), 655
Mangrol State, 425
Manipur, 267, 440, 474, 477, 517
Manipur (princely state), 365, 416, 432
Mani Shankar Aiyar, 826, 844
Manish Tewari, 871
Manmohan Singh, 381, 386, 387, 668, 717, 764, 765, 820, 824, 844, 848, 866
Manohar Lal Chibber, 582, 706, 711
Manor house, 165
Mansabdar, 49
Mansehra, 805
Man Singh, 39
Man Singh I, 48, 50, 51
Manual labour, 12
Manufactured goods, 13, 114
Manufacturing, 13
Manufacturing cost, 672
Maoist insurgency, 762
Mao Zedong, 510, 520, 522, 535
Maratha, 9, 58, 82, 221, 432
Maratha Army, 57, 61, 62, 66, 76
Maratha Confederacy, 4, 330
Maratha conquest of North-west India, 57, 64, 78
Maratha Empire, 2, 3, 7, 8, 36, 37, **54**, 91, 94, 96, 141, 173, 180, 328
Maratha expeditions in Bengal, 57
Maratha–Mysore War, 71
Maratha invasions of Bengal, 37
Maratha-Mysore War, 95, 148
Maratha Navy, 57, 79
Maratha Peshwa and Generals from Bhat Family, 61
Maratha Resurrection, 57, 66
Marathas, 331
Marathi language, 55, 88, 806
Marathi people, 56, 58
Marathwada, 476
MARCOS, 803
MARCOS (India), 811

Margaret Cousins, 163
Margaret Thatcher, 647
Mariam-uz-Zamani, 6
Mark Arbib, 838
Mark Cubbon, 151
Marple, Greater Manchester, 112
Marshal Josip Broz Tito, 608
Marshal of the Indian Air Force, 504
Mars Orbiter Mission, 390, 391
Martha Nussbaum, 797
Martial law, 554
Martial Race, 82, 506, 552
Martial Races, 234
Martin B-57 Canberra, 592
Martin Sheen, 695
Martyrdom, 175
Martyred Intellectuals Memorial, 545
Marumalarchi Dravida Munnetra Kazhagam, 727
Maruthu Pandiyar, 331
Maruti Suzuki, 765, 837
Mary C. Carras, 624
Mary Margaret Kaye, 249
Mary of Teck, 268
Masonry, 126
Masood Ashraf Raja, 322
Masqat, 43
Massacre, 653
Massacre of Elphinstones army, 97
Mass murder, 653, 776
Mass rape, 776
Master Tara Singh, 316
Masulipatnam, 93
Matayan, 465
Matchlock, 22
Matiur Rahman (military pilot), 607
Maulana Abul Kalam Azad, 362
Maulana Masood Azhar, 729
Maulana Mohammad Ali, 297
Maulana Shaukat Ali, 297
Maurya Empire, 3
Mausam (2011 film), 796
Mausoleum, 166
Maxis Communications, 863, 868, 869
Max Müller, 288
Maxwell Taylor, 536
May 2014 Assam violence, 744, 777
Maya Kodnani, 789
Mayawati, 878
Mazagaon, 804, 819
Mazgaon, 812
McGraw-Hill, 699
M. Chinnaswamy Stadium, 837
McLeod Russel, 672
McMahon Line, 511, 532
M. D. Antani, 781

Mecca, 15, 43, 296
Mechanised Infantry Regiment, 643
Media blackout, 645
Media ethics, 784
Media in India, 844
Media reporting team, 586
Medical College Kolkata, 125
Medina, 296
Mediterranean, Middle East and African theatres of World War II, 269
Meerut, 187, 194, 199, 208, 209, 220, 333
Meghalaya, 257, 373
Meherpur, 586
Meherpur District, 559
Mehr Chand Mahajan, 447, 454, 468
Meira Kumar, 870, 881
Melaka, 43
Member of Parliament, 881
Member of the European Parliament, 810
Member of the Legislative Assembly (India), 661
Member states of the United Nations, 253
Mercury (element), 683, 694
Mesopotamia, 295
Mesopotamian campaign, 268, 301, 302
Metal, 13
Metallurgic engineering, 695
Metallurgists, 24
Metalware, 13
Methandienone, 840
Methodists, 278
Methylamine, 672, 675
Methyl amine, 677
Methylhexaneamine, 840
Methyl isocyanate, 671, 672, 675, 677
Metro Adlabs, 804, 819
Metropolitan bishop, 277
M. G. Ramachandran, 702
MI5(g), 350
Mian Iftikharuddin, 454
Michael Crichton, 242
Michael ODwyer, 349
Microbiologist, 288
Middle East, 14, 592
Middle Eastern theatre of World War I, 296
Midnights Children, 622
Midnights Children (film), 624
MiG-21, 490
Mike Davis (scholar), 287
Mikoyan-Gurevich MiG-21, 608
Milan, 816
Militant, 701
Military advisor, 546
Military base, 701
Military dictatorship, 547
Military exercise, 502

Military history of India, 57
Military of Sri Lanka, 701
Military operation, 582
Military tactics, 704
Militia, 566, 583
Mil Mi-8, 703
Minerva Mills v. Union of India, 413
Minesweeper (ship), 583, 589
Ming China, 10
Minié ball, 192
Minister for Home Affairs (India), 661, 772, 821
Minister for Sport (Australia), 838
Minister of Defence (India), 539, 582, 621
Minister of External Affairs (India), 546, 582, 586, 801
Minister of Finance (India), 869, 881
Minister of Home Affairs (India), 364, 665
Minister of State, 781
Ministry of Agriculture (India), 266
Ministry of Commerce and Industry (India), 268
Ministry of Communications and Information Technology (India), 847
Ministry of Education (India), 268
Ministry of Finance (India), 848
Ministry of Home Affairs (India), 657
Ministry of Information and Broadcasting (India), 657, 852
Ministry of Youth Affairs and Sports (India), 826, 844
Minneapolis Star Tribune, 715
Minority government, 381, 764, 885
Minto-Morley Reforms, 260, 294, 304
Mirage III, 592
Miraj, 68
Mir Jafar, 38, 329
Mir Jumla II, 39, 48, 51
Mir Muhammad Baqir, 51
Mirpur, Azad Kashmir, 451, 460
Mirza Aziz Koka, 50
Mirza Basheer-ud-Din Mahmood Ahmad, 447
Mirza Ismail, 155
Mirza Mughal, 186, 208, 213
Mirzapur district, 96
Mischa Barton, 695
Misl, 174, 177, 181
Misra Commission, 657
Missing person, 730
Mission 90 Days, 728
Mission (Christian), 121
Mithankot, 174
Mitra Bahini, 608
Mitro Bahini, 593
Mitro Bahini Order of Battle December 1971, 549

Mitty Masud, 546
Mizo Hills, 373
Mizoram, 257, 373
M Karunanidhi, 870
M. Karunanidhi, 616, 702
M. K. Stalin, 616
MM Alam, 492
M. M. Kaye, 242
M. Mukundan, 622
Mobile telephone, 847
Mocha, Yemen, 43
Modern medicine, 286, 683
Modi ministry, 391
Mohammad Ali Bogra, 553
Mohammad Ali Jinnah, 447, 450, 458
Mohammad Ali Jouhar, 327
Mohammad Reza Pahlavi, 598
Mohammad Ruhul Amin, 607
Mohammad Shariff, 546, 582, 595
Mohan Chand Sharma, 774
Mohandas Gandhi, 358, 363, 419
Mohandas Karamchand Gandhi, 115, 295, 298, 327, 346, 353
Mohan Dharia, 616
Mohanlal Saksena, 362
Mohan Singh (general), 352
Mohiuddin Jahangir, 607
Mohor, 55
Mohur, 279
Mokshagundam Visvesvaraya, 154
Monarchy, 140
Monarchy of the United Kingdom, 251
Money laundering, 864
Moneylender, 576
Money supply, 114
Mongol Empire, 3
Mongols, 4
Monier Monier-Williams, 288
Monsanto, 576
Monsoon, 548
Monsoon in India, 587
Monsoon of South Asia, 390
Mon State, 97
Montagu-Chelmsford Reforms, 260, 268, 303
Month, 613
Montstuart Elphinstone, 121
Moorish architecture, 164
Morant Bay rebellion, 275
Morarji Desai, 370, 375, 376, 614, 615, 620
Morbidity, 682
Moreshvar Pingale, 85
Moropant Trimbak Pingle, 55, 85
Mortality rate, 682
Mortar fire, 523
Moscow–Washington hotline, 597
Mosque, 781

Mostafa Kamal (Bir Sreshtho), 607
Mother Jones (magazine), 682
Motilal Nehru, 344
Moti Masjid, Agra, 3
Motiur Rahman Nizami, 546
Mountaineering, 709
Mountain warfare, 511, 707
Mounted archer, 21
Mountstuart Elphinstone, 288
Moustache, 166
Mowbray Thomson, 215, 248, 900
Mrauk U, 36
M.S. Golwalkar, 355, 356
M. Thambi Durai, 872
MTS India, 850, 865, 866, 868
Mubashir Hassan, 553
Mudra, 163
Mufti, 209
Mughal-Arakan War, 39
Mughal architecture, 3, 19, 39
Mughal Army, 23, 39
Mughal Bengal, 11, 23
Mughal dynasty, 29
Mughal Emperor, 10, 24, 49, 53, 54, 95
Mughal emperors, 2–4, 33, 189
Mughal Empire, 1, 29, 30, 32, 33, 46, 55–57, 91, 95, 143, 155, 174, 175, 185, 188, 206, 207, 240, 252, 285, 328, 333, 448
Mughal Era, 176
Mughal–Maratha Wars, 2, 4, 57
Mughal gardens, 19
Mughal India, 13
Mughal painting, 20, 41
Mughals, 180, 332
Mughlai cuisine, 19
Muhammad Adil Shah, 31
Muhammad Akram, 607
Muhammad Ali Jinnah, 295, 297, 314, 338, 345, 346, 425, 550
Muhammad Azam Shah, 36, 52, 53
Muhammad Iqbal, 327
Muhammad Mahabat Khanji III, 397
Muhammad Mahfuz, 607
Muhammad Mahmood Alam, 492
Muhammad Musa, 483, 495, 509
Muhammad Qasim Nanotvi, 203
Muhammad Saleh Kamboh, 15
Muhammad Shah, 7
Muhammed Akbar Khan, 447
Muhammedan Anglo-Oriental College, 270
Muhammed Saadulah, 406
Muhammed Yusuf Khan, 330
Mujahideen, 730, 734
Mujeeb Ahmad Khan Lodhi, 582
Mujibnagar, 548, 586

Mukti Bahini, 545, 546, 548, 550, 559, 561, 563, 571, 582, 586, 593, 595
Mulayam Singh Yadav, 878
Mulberry, 13, 37, 46
Multan, 78, 132, 175, 178, 816
Multan Subah, 10
Multi-party system, 367
Multi-sport event, 389
Mulund, 804
Mumbai, 63, 122, 262, 334, 344, 354, 356, 388, 743, 803, 875
Mumbai Anti-Terrorist Squad, 806
Mumbai CST, 806
Mumbai Fire Brigade, 803
Mumbai Harbour, 812, 819
Mumbai International Film Festival, 796
Mumbai Police, 803, 804
Mumbai Suburban Railway, 804
Mummadi Krishnaraja Wodeyar, 152, 153
Munich massacre, 839
Municipal Corporation, 294
Municipal governance in India, 409
Munim Khan, 50
Munitions, 13
Munnawar Khan, 15
Munshi Abdur Rouf, 607
Muqarram Khan, 51
Murad Baksh, 36
Mural, 146
Muridke, 741
Murree, 454, 455
Murshidabad, 23, 32, 36, 39, 48, 103, 116
Murshid Quli Khan, 36, 48, 49, 52, 64
Musa Khan, 39
Muscat, Oman, 156
Mushaf Ali Mir, 798
Musical theater, 161
Musketeer, 22
Muslim, 2, 3, 29, 189, 420, 549
Muslim Conference, 451, 454
Muslim League National Guard, 446, 456
Muslim nationalism in South Asia, 448, 600
Muslim United Front, 734
Muslim world, 600
Muslin, 14, 35, 41, 43, 46, 112
Muslin trade in Bengal, 14, 17, 47
Muthiah Bhagavatar, 164
Mutiny, 186, 187, 356
Mutiny Memorial, 237
Mutual Assured Destruction, 802
Mutually intelligible, 21
Muzaffarabad, 453, 459, 741, 805
Muzaffarabad district, 451
Muzaffargarh, 132
Muzaffar Hassan, 582, 604
Muzaffar Khan Turbati, 50

Muzaffarnagar, 194, 390
Muzaffar ul-Mulk, 460
Myanmar, 91, 252, 257, 591
Mymensingh, 559, 561
Mymensingh Division, 49
Mysore, 59, 71, 95, 140–142, 169
Mysorean rockets, 23
Mysore Dasara, 158
Mysore painting, 161
Mysore Palace, 150, 164
Mysore silk, 156
Mysore State, 141, 156, 186, 429, 473, 474, 476, 477
Mysore University, 155, 160, 165
Mysore Vasudevachar, 164

Nabanna, 17
Nabha, 433
Nabha State, 186
Nabob, 93
Nader Shah, 4
Nader Shahs invasion of India, 36
Nadir Shah, 7
Nadir Shahs invasion of India, 7
Nagaland, 257, 372
Nagari, 552
Nagar Palika, 410
Nagpur, 37, 86, 97, 440
Nagpur Division, 476, 477
Nagpur kingdom, 57, 68
Naib Subedar, 715
Naik (military rank), 467
Nainital, 208
Nalargarh, 433
Nalvadi Krishnaraja Wodeyar, 151
Namdhari, 341
Name of Afghanistan, 30
Names of Bengal, 547
Names of the Indian Rebellion of 1857, 187
Namka Chu, 523, 529
Nana Fadnavis, 80
Nana Phadnavis, 84
Nanasaheb Peshwa, 63, 85
Nana Sahib, 186, 193, 214, 229
Nanavati Commission, 660, 664, 666
Nanavati-Shah commission, 779, 790
Nandalal Bose, 406
Nanded, 176
Nandini Satpathy, 621
Nanjangud, 144
Nanjaraja Wodeyar, 152
Naphthalene, 683, 693
Napoleonic Wars, 24, 169
Narasaraja Wodeyar II, 144, 152
Narasimha Rao, 633, 765
Narayan Apte, 363

Narayanganj, 561
Narayanrao, 84
Narayanrao Bajirao, 85
Narendra Kumar, 884
Narendra Kumar (mountaineer), 706, 711
Narendra Modi, 391, 717, 766, 777, 784
Narhar Vishnu Gadgil, 362
Nariman House, 803, 804, 806, 810, 819
Nariman Point, 819
Narinder Nath Vohra, 874
Narmada River, 60
Naroda Patiya massacre, 777, 782, 789, 791
Narrow gauge, 282
Narsimha Rao, 480
Narsipatnam, 350
NASA, 390
Nasbandi, 623
Naseeruddin Shah, 694
Nasik, 347, 348
Nasiruddin Nasrat Shah, 33
Nassak Diamond, 75
Nasta'līq script, 21
Nastaliq, 21
Natasha Danvers, 840
Nathula, 529
Nathu La, 541
Nathuram Godse, 363, 398
Nathuram Vinayak Godse, 363
Nation, 361
National Assembly of France, 437
National Assembly of Pakistan, 584
National Capital Territory of Delhi, 257
National Commission for Women, 793
National Commission to review the working of the Constitution, 411
National Council of Education, 338
National Council of Educational Research and Training, 415
National Counter Terrorism Centre, 820
National Dairy Development Board (NDDB), 578
National Defense University, 599
National Democratic Alliance (India), 383, 385, 765, 774, 799
National Film Award for Best Actress, 796
National Film Award for Best Direction, 796
National Film Award for Best Feature Film in English, 668
National Finance Commission Award, 602
National Geospatial-Intelligence Agency, 710
National Human Rights Commission of India, 787, 789, 790, 876
National Institute of Technology Calicut, 617
National Investigation Agency, 820
Nationalisation, 368
Nationalisation in Pakistan, 602

Nationalist Congress Party, 877
National Minorities Commission, 790
National Security Archive, 567
National Security Council (Pakistan), 584
National Security Council (USA), 536
National Security Guards, 803, 804, 811, 818
National War College, 921
NATO, 820
Nau Nihal Singh, 172
Naval blockade, 590
Naval War College Review, 917
Nav Nirman, 613
Navy, 39
Nawab, 50, 94, 189, 365
Nawab Bai, 6
Nawab of Arcot, 23, 63, 78, 330
Nawab of Awadh, 4
Nawab of Bengal, 4, 17, 36, 64, 78, 93, 328
Nawab of Bhopal, 420
Nawab of Junagarh, 95
Nawab of Oudh, 66, 78, 96
Nawab of the Carnatic, 95
Nawabs of Bengal, 32, 33, 39
Nawabs of Bengal and Murshidabad, 95
Nawaz Sharif, 383, 813
Naxalite, 362, 623, 638
Naxalite–Maoist insurgency, 388
Nayanjot Lahiri, 246
Nazi, 790
Nazi Germany, 351
NDTV, 727, 858, 935
Nedumaran, 702
Neeli Bar, 226
Neem tree, 41
Negligence, 681
Nehru–Gandhi family, 387, 612
Nellie massacre, 744, 777
Nellore, 95
Neonatal mortality, 677
Nepal, 29, 91, 190, 209, 221, 438, 511, 877
Netaji Subhas Chandra Bose, 351
Netherlands and weapons of mass destruction, 606
Netizens, 876
Neville Maxwell, 516, 523, 540, 542
New Delhi, 251, 317, 395, 402, 406, 479, 648, 649, 651, 724, 738, 771, 826, 829, 873, 884
New Jersey, 815
News channels in Pakistan, 587, 600
Newspapers, 161
Newspapers in Pakistan, 587
New World, 11
New York Tribune, 250
Ney Elias, 919
Neyyoor, 278

N. Gopalaswami Ayyangar, 362, 405
NHQ (Pakistan Navy), 589
NHQ (PN), 582
Niccolao Manucci, 27, 28
Nicobar Islands, 266
Nigamananda, 877
Nightrunners of Bengal, 242
Nikita Khrushchev, 520, 522
Nikolai Viktorovich Podgorny, 608
Nilakanta Krishnan, 374, 546, 581, 590
Nilgiri Hills, 126
Nilgiris (Lok Sabha constituency), 851
Nimtoli Deuri, 41
Ningbo, 114
Nira Radia, 858, 872
Nirmal Jit Singh Sekhon, 607
Nirmal Khatri, 871
Nishan-E-Haider, 467, 508, 607
Nisid Hajari, 468
Nitish Kumar, 878
Nitte Santhosh Hegde, 875
Nixon administration, 570
Nixon visit to China, 596
Nizam, 49, 62, 70, 96, 147, 206, 365, 427
Nizam of Hyderabad, 4, 78, 95, 110, 141, 330
Nizamuddin Ahmad, 18
NJ9842, 707, 710
N. N. Krishnadas, 810
No.109 Helicopter Unit, 704
No first use, 801
Noida, 877
Nomad, 162
Nom de plume, 163
Non-Aligned Movement, 367, 369, 478, 504, 505, 528, 536, 702
Non-co-operation movement, 305
Non-cooperation movement, 306, 585
Non-governmental organization, 666
Nonpartisan, 874
Non violent protest, 873, 884
Non-violent resistance, 115
Norinco, 815
Norman Gash, 82
North African campaign, 269
North American F-86 Sabre, 916
North Eastern Province, Sri Lanka, 702
North East Frontier Agency, 373, 511
North-East Frontier Agency, 369, 510, 517, 518, 534
Northeast India, 372, 432
Northern Circars, 95
Northern Command (India), 582, 598, 718
Northern Light Infantry, 718
North India, 57
Northrop F-5, 592
North Western Provinces, 287

North-Western Provinces, 94, 97, 123, 125, 126, 129, 133, 188, 268, 333
North-West Frontier Province (1901–1955), 205, 258, 268, 292, 310, 427
North-West Frontier Province (1901–55), 94, 97, 447
Nowshera, Khyber Pakhtunkhwa, 452
N. R. Ghosh, 405
N.S. Madhavan, 669
NTT DoCoMo, 850
Nuclear deterrent, 802
Nuclear doctrine of Pakistan, 801
Nuclear war, 801
Nuclear warfare, 799
Nuclear weapon, 505, 799, 801
Nuclear weapon design, 602
Nuclear weapons, 602
Nuclear weapons tests, 801
Null and void, 614
Nur Khan, 502
Nur Mohammad Sheikh, 607
Nurul Amin, 546, 582

Obelisks, 126
Oberoi hotel, 825
Oberoi Trident, 803, 804, 806, 808–810, 819
Observational astronomy, 24
Observatory, 24
OCLC, 88, 89, 138, 170, 246, 414
Odisha, 37, 64, 78, 80, 94, 189, 257, 286, 292, 328, 331, 347, 383, 474
OECD, 767, 768, 888
OECD Development Centre, 888
OECD Publishing, 887
Office of the Historian, 499
Officer in tactical command, 483
Oil, 13
Okara, Pakistan, 816
Okha, India, 591
Old Delhi, 1, 187
Old Irish, 893, 903
Oludamola Osayomi, 840
Olympics, 829, 844
Oman, 91
Ombudsman, 873
Om Prakash Chautala, 875
Om Prakash (historian), 888, 890
Om Prakash Malhotra, 546, 582
One Hundred and First Amendment of the Constitution of India, 401, 407
One Unit, 553, 584
Ootacamund, 126
Open economy, 702
OPEN (Indian magazine), 858
Operation Barisal, 586
Operation Black Thunder, 643, 646

Operation Blue Star, 376, 377, **627**, 648, 653, 655
Operation Chengiz Khan, 549, 563, 583, 588
Operation Compass, 269
Operation Crusader, 269, 309
Operation Dwarka, 495
Operation Eraze, 463
Operation Flood, 373, **578**
Operation Focus, 563, 588
Operation Gibraltar, 484, 486, 501, 506, 540
Operation Grand Slam, 486, 502
Operation Jackpot, 548, 561, 564
Operation Liberation, 702
Operation Meghdoot, 706, 711
Operation Pawan, 703
Operation Polo, 357, 365, 429
Operation Poomalai, 702
Operation Python, 590
Operation Rajiv, 712, 715
Operation Roukhala, 743, 778
Operation Sarp Vinash, 732
Operation Searchlight, 547, 548, 550, 555, 557, 566, 585, 586
Operation Somnath, 483
Operation Sundown, 633
Operation Trident (Indo-Pakistani War), 589
Operation U-Go, 313
Operation Windup, 489
Operation Woodrose, 628, 653
Opium, 12, 114
Orchha, 221
Order of the Indian Empire, 255
Ordnance QF 25 pounder, 465, 483, 639
Organisation for Economic Co-operation and Development, 763
Organochlorine, 683
Organochlorines, 693
Oriental studies, 121
Orient Blackswan, 624
Orissa Chief Minister, 621
Orissa famine of 1866, 266, 286, 287
Orissa, India, 36, 38, 48, 257, 431, 473, 477
Orissa Province, 475
Oropolitics, 709
Orthodox Jewish outreach, 819
Osa-class missile boat, 589
Osama bin Laden, 741, 772
Osman Ali Khan, 427
Ostend Company, 38
Other Backward Class, 839
Other ranks, 643
Ottoman Caliphate, 296
Ottoman Empire, 3, 21, 149
Oudh, 97, 186, 194, 332, 333
Oudh State, 94
Ouster clause, 402

Outlook (magazine), 858
Oxfam, 608
Oxford University Press, 625, 887–889, 895, 923

P-15 Termit, 590
Paan, 833
Paban Singh Ghatowar, 871
Pablo Bartholomew, 678
Pacifism, 601
Packard Humanities Institute, 27
Paddy field, 106
Padshah, 9, 33
PAF Base Murid, 592
PAF Museum, Karachi, 491
Pagoda (coin), 153
Paik Rebellion, 331
Paisa, 55
Paisley (design), 41
Pakistan, 17, 20, 29, 30, 56, 57, 91, 173, 252, 254, 338, 346, 357, 362, 374, 397, 425, 472, 482, 483, 490, 519, 540, 545–547, 550, 581, 583, 706, 707, 729, 730, 763, 771, 798, 801, 803, 814
Pakistan-administered Kashmir, 427, 598
Pakistan Air Force, 486, 488, 490–492, 496, 563, 583, 588, 595, 800
Pakistan and its Nuclear Deterrent Program, 602, 606
Pakistan and weapons of mass destruction, 606
Pakistan Armed Forces, 546, 566, 582, 583, 587
Pakistan Army, 465, 495, 548, 555, 586, 595, 798, 806
Pakistan Broadcasting Corporation, 558
Pakistan Eastern Command, 374, 483, 546, 581–583, 593
Pakistaniaat: A Journal of Pakistan Studies, 609
Pakistani Army, 636, 774, 817
Pakistani general election, 1970, 547, 584
Pakistani Instrument of Surrender, 374, 545, 549, 564, 565, 581, 583
Pakistani military, 594, 602
Pakistan International Airlines, 554, 590
Pakistani people, 584
Pakistani Punjab, 390
Pakistani rupee, 551
Pakistani society, 600
Pakistan Marines, 546, 582, 586, 590, 595, 798
Pakistan Military, 799
Pakistan Navy, 564, 586, 589, 595, 801
Pakistan Olympic Association, 833
Pakistan Peoples Party, 553, 584
Pakistans ISI, 630

Pakistans nuclear weapons, 606
Pakistan-Soviet Union relations, 597
Pakistan Television Corporation, 600
Palam, 656
Palanquin, 108
Palashi, 38
Palayakkarar, 331
Palden Thondup Namgyal, 439
Pali, 552
Pallavas, 622
Pampa Bharata, 161
Pan-Asianism, 347
Panchalankurichi, 331
Panchayat, 119
Panchayati raj, 410, 874
Panchayati raj (India), 409
Panchmahal district, 785, 788
Panchsheel, 478, 480
Pandemic, 287
Pandita Ramabai, 290
Pandit Ram Prasad Bismil, 351
Pandua, Hooghly, 127, 129
Pangong Lake, 514
Panipat, 387
Panjdeh, 267
Pankaj Kapoor, 796
Paonta Sahib, 175
Paper cartridge, 192
Paper currency, 266
Parachute, 495
Parachute Regiment (India), 627
Para Commandos (India), 704
Paramara dynasty, 57, 68
Paramilitary forces of Pakistan, 546, 594, 595
Paramountcy, 416
Param Vir Chakra, 467, 508, 607, 712
Pargana, 9, 48, 95
Parikshitgarh, 208
Paris Indian Society, 348
Parliamentary session, 884
Parliamentary sovereignty, 402
Parliamentary system, 410
Parliament House (India), 402, 406
Parliament of India, 367, 372, 401, 402, 471, 612, 631, 665, 771, 772, 777, 799, 874, 885
Parliament of the United Kingdom, 90, 101, 255, 402
Parshuram Pant Pratinidhi, 60
Parsi, 405, 622
PART Eighteen of the Constitution of India, 408
Part Eleven of the Constitution of India, 408
Part Fifteen of the Constitution of India, 408
Part Fourteen of the Constitution of India, 408
Partha Chatterjee (scholar), 624

Part I, 911
Part II, 911
Part III, 413
Partition of Bengal (1905), 268, 292, 297, 337, 347
Partition of British India, 485
Partition of India, 92, 252, 253, 256, 269, 316, 326, 361, 364, 366, 404, 419, 447, 484, 519, 537, 549, 550, 559, 584, 605, 761
Partition of Palestine, 369
Part IV, 911
Part IX, 911
Part IXA, 911
PART Nineteen of the Constitution of India, 408
Part One of the Constitution of India, 408
Part Seventeen of the Constitution of India, 408
Part Sixteen of the Constitution of India, 408
Part Ten of the Constitution of India, 408
Part Thirteen of the Constitution of India, 408
Part Twelve of the Constitution of India, 408
PART Twenty One of the Constitution of India, 408
PART Twenty Two of the Constitution of India, 408
Part V, 410, 411, 911
Part VI, 911
Part VII, 911
Part VIII, 911
Part XI, 411
Part XVIII, 410
Parvaiz Mehdi Qureshi, 591
Parzania, 796
Pasha enclave, 545
Pashto, 172
Pashto language, 29, 30
Pashtun people, 132, 427, 447, 458
Pashtuns, 3, 29, 174, 552
Pasrur, 490
Passive resistance, 298, 354
Pathankot, 495
Pathankot Air Force Station, 592
Pathans, 80, 205
Patiala, 78, 433
Patiala and East Punjab States Union, 365, 433, 474, 477
Patiala State, 186, 420
Patna, 103, 112
Patrick Desmond Callaghan, 582
Patrick Grant, 186
Patrol vessel, 583
Pattern 1853 Enfield, 192, 332
Patwardhans, 86
Paula Radcliffe, 840
Paul Bairoch, 11
Paul Brass, 670, 784, 797

Paul Brunton, 151
Pawan Kumar Bansal, 876, 877
Pawar, 60, 68
Pazhassi Raja, 96, 330
PBS, 826
P. C. Chacko, 871
P Chidambaram, 863, 864
P. Chidambaram, 665, 864, 866, 869, 880
Peacekeeping, 701
Pearl, 46
Pearson Education, 888
Peepul tree, 203
Penguin Books, 247, 358
Pennsylvania Canal, 134
People for Lok Satta, 875
People of Nepal, 439
Peoples Daily, 527, 921
Peoples Liberation Army, 519, 520, 529, 598
Peoples Liberation Organisation of Tamil Eelam, 725
Peoples Republic of Bangladesh, 254, 545, 595
Peoples Republic of China, 519, 596, 760
Peoples Union for Civil Liberties, 653, 659
Peoples Union for Democratic Rights, 659
Per-capita income, 156
Percival Spear, 13, 75, 135, 245, 319
Perjury, 787
Permanent Peoples Tribunal, 695
Permanent Settlement, 96, 100
Persecution of Biharis in Bangladesh, 548, 555
Persecution of Hindus, 743, 778
Persian art, 19
Persianate society, 2
Persian culture, 4
Persian Gulf, 254
Persian Gulf Residency, 255
Persian language, 1, 2, 4, 21, 32, 120, 122, 142, 172
Persian people, 2, 6, 43
Perso-Arabic script, 21
Personality cult, 612
Perunchithiranar, 702
Pervez Musharraf, 384, 606, 706, 713, 716, 730, 733, 734, 798, 800, 801
Peshawar, 64, 78, 126, 175, 178, 224, 452
Peshwa, 55–57, 68, 79, 93, 96, 332
Pesticide, 671
Pesticides, 575
Peter Heehs, 358, 906
Peter Ustinov, 649
Pew Research Center, 599
P. G. Gavai, 658
Phaltan State, 68
Pherozeshah Mehta, 296
Philip Francis (English politician), 100
Philippines, 313

Phillips Idowu, 839
Phosgene, 672, 673, 675, 676
Phulpur (Lok Sabha constituency), 400
Pierre André de Suffren de Saint Tropez, 145
Pilaster, 166
Pilgrim, 77, 628, 642, 655
Pilot Officer, 607
Pindari, 71
Pinkertons, 350
Pinyin, 511
Pipili, 331
Piploda, 424
Piracy, 77
Pirate, 39
Piravi, 623
Pir Panjal Range, 733
Pistol, 772
Pitch (resin), 126
Pitts India Act, 93, 261
P. J. Marshall, 285, 319
P. J. Thomas (Indian administrative officer), 875
Plague (disease), 287
PLA National Defense University, 527
Platoon, 533
Plebiscite, 365, 466
Plow, 12
Plurality (voting), 379
P. N. Dhar, 625
P. N. Haksar, 371, 611
P. N. Krishnamurti, 154
PNS Ghazi, 495, 545, 546, 589, 590, 609
PNS Ghazi (Shaheed), 609
PNS Hangor (S131), 590
PNS Khyber, 589
PNS Muhafiz, 589
PNS Shah Jahan (DD-962), 590
PNS Zulfiqar (K265), 590
Podu (agriculture), 350
Pogrom, 603, 653, 744, 776, 777
Point of view (philosophy), 600
Point Sonam, 716
Pokhran, 372
Pokhran-II, 362, 382
Police corruption, 873, 884
Political corruption, 873
Political instability, 765
Political integration of India, 363, **416**, 762
Political science, 556
Political structure, 251
Political system, 188
Politics of Jammu and Kashmir, 439
Politics of Pakistan, 604
Polybolos, 23
Polygar, 78, 331
Polygar War, 331

Pondicherry, 254, 437
Pondicherry district, 357
Ponneelan, 623
Ponzi scheme, 389
Poona, 129
Poonch, 427, 451, 453, 459, 465, 486
Population transfer, 362, 605
Portal:Bangladesh, 547
Portal:India, 762
Portal:Pakistan, 260
Portal:Politics, 327
Portfolio investment, 766
Port of Karachi, 589
Port of Mongla, 561
Portugal, 59, 63, 527
Portuguese Chittagong, 32
Portuguese East India Company, 92, 256, 326
Portuguese India, 92, 93, 256, 326, 357
Possession (law), 575
Postage stamps and postal history of India, 97
Postal administration, 124
POTA, 788
Potential superpower, 388
Potential superpowers, 362
Potti Sreeramulu, 368
Pound sterling, 130
Poverty, 381
Poverty in India, 768, 826
POW, 351
Prabhakaran, 725
Pradeep, 542
Pradhan Inquiry Commission, 820
Pradhanmantri, 647
Praja Mandal, 442
Pranab Mukherjee, 775, 820, 875, 876
Pran Nath Lekhi, 651
Pran Nath Thapar, 510
Pran Sukh Yadav, 209
Prashant Bhushan, 866, 880
Pratap Chandra Lal, 582
Pratapsingh of Thanjavur, 87
Pratap Singh, Raja of Satara, 55, 85
Pratibha Patil, 387, 875
Pravda, 522
Praveen Swami, 760
Pravin Togadia, 792
Preamble to the Constitution of India, 401, 402, 408
Precious metal, 11
Prem Behari Narain Raizda, 406
Premier of the Peoples Republic of China, 478, 511, 519
Premindra Singh Bhagat, 582
Prem Shankar Jha, 454
Presidencies and provinces of British India, 92, 251, 253, 255, 256, 326

Presidency, 98
Presidency armies, 190
Presidency College, Kolkata, 119, 120
Presidency General Hospital, 288
Presidency of Agra, 102
Presidency of Richard Nixon, 548
Presidential system, 613
President of Bangladesh, 546, 569, 602, 608
President of India, 357, 366, 398, 410, 474, 483, 546, 582, 717, 775, 798, 875
President of Madrid, 810
President of Nepal, 608
President of Pakistan, 483, 546, 553, 582, 584, 600, 605, 713, 730, 733, 798, 800, 801
President of the Board of Control, 122, 260
President of the United Nations Security Council, 405
President of the United States, 387, 595
Presidents rule, 410, 613, 616, 654, 731, 885
Presidium, 433
Pressure cooker bomb, 837
Prevention of Corruption Act, 1988, 851, 852
Prevention of Corruption Act (India), 845, 846
Prevention of Money Laundering Act, 2002, 862
Prevention of Terrorism Act, 2002, 773
Prima facie, 774
Primary sector, 11
Prime Minister, 76, 447, 717
Prime minister-designate, 547
Prime Minister of Assam, 406
Prime Minister of Bangladesh, 546, 582, 602, 608
Prime Minister of Bengal, 309
Prime Minister of India, 317, 362, 367, 396, 397, 401, 410, 447, 483, 538, 542, 546, 582, 605, 628, 717, 721, 731, 798, 800, 801, 804, 844, 848, 875
Prime Minister of Jammu and Kashmir, 405
Prime Minister of Nepal, 608
Prime Minister of Pakistan, 447, 546, 582, 584
Prime Minister of the United Kingdom, 277, 608
Prime Ministers Office (India), 611, 881
Princely state, 92, 140, 141, 154, 189, 221, 251, 253, 255, 256, 267, 326, 328, 345, 363, 365, 366, 397, 398, 447, 448, 472
Princely State of Cutch, 97
Princely State of Jammu and Kashmir, 472
Princely states, 73, 94, 178, 267, 416
Princely states of Pakistan, 458
Prince of Wales, 266
Princess Diana, 832
Principality, 140
Prisoner of war, 565, 583, 591
Prisoners of war, 594

Prithviraj Chavan, 881
Private property, 432
Private sector enterprise, 765
Privatisation, 381
Privy Council, 118
Privy purse, 433
Privy Purse in India, 371, 432, 612
Proby Cautley, 130
Proby Thomas Cautley, 132
Proclamation of Bangladeshi Independence, 548, 557
Project Gutenberg, 248
Propaganda, 502, 587
Property, 408
Protectionism, 362
Protectionist, 762
Protectorate, 255, 438, 511, 529
Proto-industrialization, 3, 10, 13, 46
Providence Equity Partners, 868
Province, 9
Provinces of British India, 122
Provinces of Sri Lanka, 702
Provisional Government of Bangladesh, 546, 548, 567, 581, 582, 586
PT-76, 483, 493
Puars, 86
Public distribution system, 657
Public domain, 481
Public interest litigation in India, 847
Public trial, 604
Public works, 10
PubMed Central, 359, 697
PubMed Identifier, 359, 697, 699
Puchalapalli Sundaraiah, 445
Puisne judge, 117, 121
Puja (Hinduism), 159
Puli Thevar, 330
Pulmonary edema, 523
Pulmonary oedema, 677
Punch (magazine), 231
Pundit (India), 117
Pune, 55, 57, 61, 72, 121, 355, 381, 642, 767, 879
Punjab, 78, 174, 178, 336, 448
Punjab 1984, 669
Punjab accord, 643
Punjab Army, 178
Punjab (British India), 178, 257, 339, 347
Punjab Hill States Agency, 432
Punjabi language, 172, 368, 669
Punjab (India), 178, 373, 523, 575, 800
Punjab, India, 131, 257, 302, 368, 373, 489, 574, 627, 628, 653
Punjab, Indian, 486
Punjab insurgency, 653, 762
Punjabis, 552

Punjab Kesari, 630
Punjab Movable Column, 210
Punjab (Pakistan), 178, 816
Punjab, Pakistan, 363, 593
Punjab Police (India), 627
Punjab Province (British India), 173, 330, 365
Punjab Province (Pakistan), 257
Punjab Province, Pakistan, 78
Punjab region, 4, 31, 78, 94, 129, 132, 177, 189, 197, 205, 207, 210, 224, 336, 341, 425
Punjab (region), 363, 638
Purana Qila, 242
Purbiya, 108, 197, 205, 206
Purdah, 273
Purnaiah, 149
Purna Swaraj, 307, 344, 403
Purna Swarajya, 307
Purnia, 49
P. V. Narasimha Rao, 380, 381, 658, 664, 724, 764
P.V. Narasimha Rao, 379
Pyre, 651

Q129286, 325
Qadi, 49
Qamar-ud-din Khan, Asaf Jah I, 62
Qasim Khan Chishti, 39, 51
Qasim Khan Juvayni, 51
Qasim Razvi, 428
Qatar, 91
Qazi, 117
Qing China, 10
Quarter guard, 198
Queen Victoria, 188, 232, 233, 251, 253, 267, 268, 279, 899
Questia, 542
Quit India, 308, 351
Quit India movement, 311, 328, 354
Quran, 19
Qutubuddin Koka, 51

Rabindranath Tagore, 327, 335, 621
Rachna Dhingra, 695
Racism, 790
Radcliffe Award, 269
Radcliffe Line, 317, 482, 487
Radhakrishnan, 538
Radia tapes controversy, 875
Radio Australia, 558
Radio spectrum, 847
Rae Ahmed Nawaz Khan Kharal, 226
Rafi Ahmed Kidwai, 362
Raga, 163
Raghoji I Bhonsle, 60
Raghuji Bhonsle, 37

Raghunathrao, 71, 86
Raghunath Rao, 64
Raghu Rai, 678
Rahi Masoom Raza, 622
Rahimuddin Khan, 557
Rahul Dholakia, 796
Rahul Gandhi, 881
Rahul Sharma (Gujarat police), 786
Raichur, 159
Raigad Fort, 55, 56
Railway Board, 268
Raiyat, 153
Raja, 66, 95
Raja Habib ur Rahman Khan, 447
Raja Hindu Rao, 212
Raja Muhammad Sarwar, 467
Rajan case, 617, 623
Rajaram Chhatrapati, 85
Rajaram I, 59
Raja Ram Mohan Roy, 123, 335
Raja Ram Mohun Roy, 119
Raja Ravi Varma, 167
Rajas, 186
Rajasthan, 69, 221, 258, 372, 387, 474, 477, 489, 540, 638
Rajavommangi, 350
Raja Wodeyar I, 152
Raja Wodeyar II, 152
Rajdeep Sardesai, 934
Rajendra Prasad, 300, 309, 342, 357, 362, 366, 398, 405
Rajendrasinh Rana, 780
Rajendra Vilas, 165
Raj Ghat, 724
Raj Ghat and associated memorials, 651
Rajguru, 349
Rajinikanth, 881
Rajiv Gandhi, 377, 386, 651, 653, 658, 664, 701, 702, 704, 721, 725, 763
Rajiv Gandhi Memorial, 723, 728
Rajmahal, 32, 48
Rajmohan Gandhi, 441, 443
Raj Narain, 613, 615
Rajnarayan Chandavarkar, 320
Rajpramukh, 365, 432, 474
Rajput, 2, 6, 19, 21, 50, 66, 190, 197, 425, 448, 524, 529
Rajputana, 64, 78, 94, 188, 473
Rajputana Agency, 97, 125, 286
Rajputana famine of 1869, 266, 286
Rajputana Rifles, 643
Rajput kingdoms, 3
Rajputs, 3, 80, 108
Rajput states, 2
Raju Ramachandran, 794

Rajya Sabha, 401, 409, 411, 664, 772, 781, 793, 851
Rakesh Sharma (filmmaker), 796
Rakhine State, 43, 97
Raksha Bandhan, 338
Ralph Marshal, 870
Rama, 759
Ramachandra Guha, 468, 612, 624
Ramachandra Vaidhanath, 623
Ramakrishna, 335
Rama Raghoba Rane, 467
Ramaraja, 85
Ram Baran Yadav, 608
Ram Chandra Kak, 450
Ramchandra Pant Amatya, 84, 85
Ramdev, 874, 884
Ramgarh Cantonment, 643
Ramgarhia Bunga, 639
Ram Gopal Verma, 821
Ram Janmabhoomi, 380
Ram Jethmalani, 658
Ramlila Maidan, New Delhi, 876
Ramna Race Course, 594
Rampachodavaram, 350
Rampa Rebellion of 1922, 350
Rampur State, 186
Rampur, Uttar Pradesh, 201
Ramraiya, 175
Ramsay MacDonald, 307
Ram Singh (activist), 341
Ram Singh I, 39
Ranasinghe Premadasa, 704
Ranbir Singh, 272
Rangoon, 4, 130, 232
Rangpur Division, 49
Raniganj, 128, 129
Rani Lakshmibai, 186, 270, 333
Rani Laxmi bai, 186
Rani of Jhansi, 193, 195, 221, 222
Ranjit Singh, 172–174, 177, 180, 181, 223, 448
Ranjit Singh Dyal, 627
Rann of Kutch, 483, 485
Rao Farman Ali, 546, 595, 602
Rao Kadam Singh, 208
Rao Tula Ram, 209
Rape, 389, 583, 653
Rape by Indian forces .28post-1988.29, 735
Rape by militants, 738
Rape during the Bangladesh Liberation War, 548
Rape in India, 776
Rapho (agency), 678
Rapid Action Force, 781, 785, 811
Rapprochement, 570, 596
Rash Behari Bose, 348

Rashid Ahmad Gangohi, 203
Rashid Ahmed, 582
Rashid Minhas, 607
Rashid Qureshi, 800
Rashtriya Janata Dal, 878
Rashtriya Swayamsevak Sangh, 344, 355, 615, 618, 785, 878
Raskam, 516
Ratification, 401
Ravana, 878
Ravi river, 132, 224, 226, 453
Ravi Ruia, 864
R&AW, 817
Rawalakot, 453, 457
Rawalpindi, 587
Raw materials, 114
Rayon, 156
Razakar (East Pakistan), 602
Razakar (Pakistan), 546, 548, 559, 583
Razakars (Hyderabad), 428
Razakars (Pakistan), 546, 595
R. B. Sreekumar, 792
R. C. Majumdar, 902
R. C. Unnithan, 623
RDX, 721, 803, 814, 819
Real versus nominal value (economics), 9
Real wages, 11, 43, 156
Rear Admiral, 590
Rear-Admiral, 483, 546, 582, 595
Reasi, 451
Rebecca Adlington, 834, 838
Reconnaissance, 590
Recorders Court, 119
Red coat (British army), 107
Red corner notice, 816
Red Fort, 3, 20, 65, 332
Rediff, 935
Rediff.com, 785
Red tape, 762, 873, 884
Refugee, 548
Refugee camp, 586
Regency council, 84
Regent, 181
Regiment, 529
Reginald Dyer, 304, 343
Regulating Act of 1773, 99
Rehman Malik, 816
Rejaul Karim Laskar, 478, 701
Reliance Anil Dhirubhai Ambani Group, 854
Reliance Infrastructure, 833
Relief column, 460
Religious freedom, 794
Religious persecution, 743, 778
Religious violence, 743, 778
Religious violence in India, 362
Rendition (law), 151

Repeating crossbow, 23
Republic, 403
Republic Day, 398
Republic Day (India), 403
Republic of India, 317, 328, 357, 361, 396, 397, 429
Republics in the Commonwealth of Nations, 398
Research & Analysis Wing, 633
Research and Analysis Wing, 505, 546, 582, 586
Reservation in India, 839, 883
Reserve Bank of India, 269, 889
Residencies of British India, 258
Residents in (British) Asia, 103
Res ipsa loquitur, 789
Responsible Care, 692
Reuters, 733, 936
Revenue, 49, 103
Revenue settlements under the Company, 100
Review petition, 864
Revolution, 327
Revolutionary France, 149
Revolutionary movement for Indian independence, 294, 302, 338, 339
Rewa (princely state), 186, 274, 420
Rezang La, 511
Rice, 12, 46
Richard Bourke, 6th Earl of Mayo, 266
Richard Holmes (military historian), 901
Richard H. Shultz, 918
Richard Nixon, 563, 569, 595
Richard Strachey, 267
Richard Wellesley, 1st Marquess Wellesley, 96, 121, 189
Rifles, 806
Right to govern, 584
Right to Information, 828
Right to Information Act, 874
Right to Life and Personal Liberty, 414
Riot, 776
River Beas, 489
Riverine Warfare, 590
Rivka Holtzberg, 811
R.J. Rummel, 603
R. K. Dhawan, 650, 652
R. K. Raghavan, 786
R. M. Lala, 926
R. N. Kao, 582
Road, 10
Robert Arthur Talbot Gascoyne-Cecil, 3rd Marquess of Salisbury, 260
Robert Bulwer-Lytton, 1st Earl of Lytton, 267
Robert Christopher Tytler, 232
Robert Clive, 39, 93–95, 328

Robert Gascoyne-Cecil, 3rd Marquess of Salisbury, 260, 278
Robert Gates, 741
Robert Grant (MP), 122, 288
Robert Grenier (CIA), 772
Robert McNamara, 536
Robert Mueller, 820
Robert W. Sweet, 666
Rob Lockhart, 447, 450
Rocket, 23, 169
Rocket artillery, 169
Rocket-propelled grenade, 641
Rocket-propelled grenade launchers, 641
Rodionov message, 587, 595
Rohan Gunaratna, 705
Rohilkhand, 69, 78, 94, 95, 240
Rohilla, 69
Rohillas, 66, 80
Rohilla War, 96
Rohinton Mistry, 622
Rohtas Fort, 30
Roland Schoeman, 842
Roller mill, 13
Romanization of Persian, 2
Romanization of Urdu, 2
Ronald Noble, 820
Ronald Ross, 288
Roorkee, 130
Round Table Conferences, 308
Round Table Conferences (India), 269
Routledge, 183, 248, 323, 887, 888, 890
Rowlatt Act, 268, 303, 342, 350
Rowlatt Acts, 303, 341
Rowlatt committee, 342, 350
Rowlatt report, 348
Rowman & Littlefield Publishers, 889
Royal Canadian Air Force, 592
Royal Charter, 116
Royal Indian Air Force, 269
Royal Indian Navy Mutiny, 356
Royal Ordnance L7, 493
Royal proclamation, 333
Royal Small Arms Factory, 192
Royal warrant of appointment, 17
Roy Bucher, 447, 450
R.R. Diwakar, 362
R. R. Patil, 821
Rs., 116, 132
Rubber dinghy, 814
Rudolph Rummel, 556
Rudrangshu Mukherjee, 246
Rufus Isaacs, 1st Marquess of Reading, 268
Rukhsana Sultana, 617
Rule by decree, 610, 616
Rule of law, 407
Rumtek Monastery, 372

Rupee, 2, 10, 11, 31, 55, 125, 173, 255, 267
Rural infrastructure, 575
Ruskin Bond, 242
Russia, 209, 800
Russian President, 800
Rust (fungus), 574
R. Venkataraman, 701
Ryerson University, 829
Ryotwari, 102, 106

S-75 Dvina, 500
Saad Hatmi, 491
Sabarmati Ashram, 344, 784
Sabarmati Express, 778
Sabarmati River, 344
Saboteur, 486
Sabre Slayer, 490, 916
Sachchidananda Sinha, 405
Sachindranath Sanyal, 349
Sack of Delhi, 4, 7
Sadashivrao Bhau, 65, 66, 81, 83
Sadhaura, 176
Sadiq Khan, 51
Safavid Dynasty, 5
Safavid Empire, 43
Safavid Persia, 3, 21
Safdarjung, 78
Safdarjung Road, 648, 649
Sagar, Madhya Pradesh, 194
Sagat Singh, 374, 546, 581, 582
Sahabzada Yaqub Khan, 585
Sahara India Pariwar, 850, 862
Saharanpur District, 130
Said Khan, 51
Saint Helena Act 1833, 102
Sajjad Karim, 810
Sajjan Kumar, 656, 661
Sake Dean Mahomed, 24
Salem, Tamil Nadu, 143
Sally Pearson, 841
Salman Rushdie, 622
Salma Sultan, 650
Saltoro Kangri, 709
Saltoro Mountains, 707, 713
Saltoro Ridge, 715
Saltpeter, 13, 23, 33, 38, 46
Salt Satyagraha, 307
Salute state, 433
Samadhi of Ranjit Singh, 177
Samajwadi Party, 872, 878
Samaldas Gandhi, 425
Samana, India, 176
Samarkand, 24
Sambalpur, 97
Sambhaji, 59, 85
Sambhaji II, 85

Sambhavna clinic, 694
Sambhavna Trust, 683, 695, 696
Samjhauta Express bombings, 387
Sam Manekshaw, 546, 563, 564, 582, 586
Samuel Bourne, 131, 215, 218
Samuel Okon, 840
Sandalwood, 156
Sandeep Unnikrishnan, 811, 819
Sandesh (newspaper), 784
Sangameshwar, 60
Sangli State, 68
Sanjay Gandhi, 375, 610, 615, 618, 621, 623, 724
Sanjiv Bhatt, 794
Sansad Bhavan, 771
Sanskrit, 21, 55, 76, 541, 800, 893, 903
Sanskrit College, 121
Sanskrit drama, 161
Sanskrit literature, 161
Santaji Ghorpade, 60, 84
Santiniketan, 406
Sant Nirankari Mission, 629
Saradha Group financial scandal, 389
Sardar, 656
Sardar Baldev Singh, 362
Sardar Muhammad Ibrahim Khan, 447, 454
Sardar Patel, 362
Sardar Shah Wali Khan, 80
Sardar Vallabhbhai Patel, 301, 364, 365
Sarfaraz Khan, 52
Sargodha, 491
Sargodha Airbase, 592
Sarika, 796
Sarkar (country subdivision), 9, 48
Sarojini Naidu, 327, 405
Sarsawa Air Force Base, 633
Sartaj Aziz, 801
Sartaj Singh (general), 582
Sarvajna, 162
Sarvepalli Radhakrishnan, 483, 510
Sarwar, 607
Sasaram, 29
Sashastra Seema Bal, 729
Satara (city), 55, 73
Satara State, 97
Satellite, 387
Sat Gambuj Mosque, 39
Satgaon, 49
Satinath Sarangi, 695
Sati (practice), 112, 160, 192, 272
Sati (practise), 196
Satwant Singh, 628, 648, 653, 655
Satyagraha, 298, 300, 341, 877
Satyajit Ray, 241, 623
Satya Narayan Sinha, 362
Satyawant Mallannah Shrinagesh, 447

Satyendra Dubey, 884
Saudi Arabia, 91, 592
Saumya Joshi, 796
Saurashtra (region), 365, 418, 433, 474
Saurashtra State, 476
Savada Kothi, 216
Sawai Madhava Rao II Narayan, 86
Sawar Muhammad Hussain, 607
Sayeed Salahudeen, 729
Sayyid Ahmad Khan, 262
Scarred: Experiments With Violence In Gujarat, 797
Scheduled castes and scheduled tribes, 405
Scheduled Tribes, 409
Scholarly contributions, 121
Scindhias, 78
Scindia, 57, 60, 65, 68, 86, 222
Scorched earth, 601
Scottish Church College, 121
S. C. Tandon, 658
Seaport, 43
SEATO, 502
Seaworthiness, 16, 47
Second Anglo-Afghan War, 267, 289
Second Anglo-Burmese War, 97
Second Anglo-Maratha War, 57, 73, 74, 96
Second Anglo-Mysore War, 24, 96, 148
Second Anglo-Sikh War, 94, 97, 110, 132, 173, 178, 182, 190, 205, 250, 330
Secondary sector, 11
Second Battle of Cawnpore, 221
Second Battle of El Alamein, 269
Second Kashmir War, 370, 537, 540
Second Lieutenant, 467, 607
Second-strike capability, 802
Second World War, 328, 345, 417
Secretaries of State for India and Burma, 269
Secretary, 76
Secretary of Defense, 536
Secretary of State for India, 233, 252, 260, 269, 299, 302, 333
Secrets of the Dead, 826
Sectarian violence, 548
Section 144, 879
Section 377 of the Indian Penal Code, 387
Secular, 174, 403
Secularism in India, 362
Secunderabad, 364
Security Council, 437, 500
Seed drill, 12
Seema Biswas, 669
Sehnsa, 457
Sela Pass, 533
Self-determination, 547
Self-published sources, 584, 593, 594, 598, 600, 601, 603, 604, 669

1006

Semaphore line, 124, 125
Semi-automatic rifle, 634
Separation of legislative powers in India, 424
Separation of powers, 410
Separatism, 362
Sepoy, 107, 108, 186, 187, 190, 197, 332
September 11 attacks, 815, 820
Serampore, 38
Serfoji I, 87
Serfoji II, 87
Sericulture, 13, 46, 156
Seringapatam, 146, 169
Servants of India Society, 290
Seventh Schedule to the Constitution of India, 409
S Force (Bangladesh), 546
SGPC, 628, 639
Shabana Azmi, 623
Shabbir Sharif, 607
Shabeg Singh, 546, 627, 634, 637
Shah Alam II, 7, 24, 69, 94, 189
Shahbaz Khan Kamboh, 39, 50
Shahbaz Khan Mosque, 39
Shahbeg Singh, 646
Shah Commission, 375
Shahdara, 659
Shahid Balwa, 852, 857, 868
Shahid (film), 759
Shahid Karimullah, 798
Shahidulla, 514
Shah Jahan, 3, 6, 19, 20, 36, 132, 175
Shahjahanabad, 4
Shah Shuja (Mughal), 48, 51
Shah Shuja (Mughal prince), 36
Shahu II of Satara, 85
Shahuji I of Thanjavur, 87
Shaikh Paltu, 198
Shaista Khan, 36, 39, 51–53
Shaitan Singh, 534
Shaksgam Valley, 709
Shakti, 347
Shakti engine, 716
Shala, 623
Shalutikar, 562
Shampoo, 24
Shampoo (massage), 24
Shane Perkins, 842
Shaniwarwada, 61
Shaniwar Wada, 80
Shankaracharya, 71
Shankar Kistaiya, 363
Shanti Bhushan, 613, 875
Shanty towns, 671
Sharad Pawar, 875
Sharad Yadav, 871
Sharia, 19, 117, 118

Shashi Tharoor, 622
Shatranj Ke Khilari, 241
Shaukat Hayat Khan, 456
Sheikh Abdullah, 379, 426, 447, 451, 452, 731
Sheikh Hasina, 608
Sheikh Mohammed Abdullah, 364
Sheikh Mujibur Rahman, 507, 546, 547, 550, 553, 557, 569, 584
Sheikhupura, 20
Sheila Dikshit, 829, 836
Shekhar Kapur, 647
Shelter in place, 676
Shenyang J-6, 592
Sherlock Holmes, 242
Sherman tank, 483
Sher Shah Suri, 5, 11, 29–31, 33
Sher Singh, 172
Shia Muslims, 6
Shifting cultivation, 350
Shikastah Nastaliq Script, 238
Shimla, 199, 209, 518
Shimla Agreement, 716
Shipbuilding, 13, 15, 33, 46, 47
Shipbuilding in Bangladesh, 39
Shiromani Akali Dal, 619, 631
Shiromani Gurdwara Prabandhak Committee, 619
Shivaji, 55, 56, 58, 79, 85
Shivaji II, 85
Shivaji III, 85
Shivaji II of Thanjavur, 87
Shivanasamudra, 154
Shivaram Rajguru, 346
Shivrai, 55
Shivraj Patil, 661, 821
Shiv Sena, 744, 758, 759, 792, 878
Shiv Sharma, 706
Sholinghur, 148
Shonali Bose, 668
Shootings, 803
Shoulder-launched missile weapon, 647
Shravanabelagola, 157, 159
Shuja-ud-Din Muhammad Khan, 52
Shyam Benegal, 241, 242
Shyamji Krishna Verma, 348
Siachen conflict, **706**
Siachen Glacier, 706, 714
Sia La, 707, 713
Sialkot, 224, 453, 489, 816
Sialkot District, 483
Siam, 267
Sic, 686
Siddhantas, 24
Siddhartha Shankar Ray, 615
Siddharth Varadarajan, 797, 934
Siddis, 15

Siege, 803
Siege of Bahadur Benda, 148
Siege of Bidar, 23
Siege of Cawnpore, 214, 228, 242
Siege of Delhi, 2, 210, 236
Siege of Delhi, 1757, 64
Siege of Jinji, 23
Siege of Kut, 268, 339
Siege of Lucknow, 236
Siege of Seringapatam (1792), 147, 149, 169
Siege of Seringapatam (1799), 95, 169
Siege of Trichinopolly (1741), 64
Sierra Club Books, 699
Sikandar Shah Suri, 31
Sikander Hyat Khan, 310
Sikh, 19, 132, 188, 225, 234, 344, 363, 386, 628, 653
Sikh Confederacy, 173
Sikh Empire, 2, 91, **172**, 205, 223, 448, 514
Sikh gurus, 175
Sikhism, 172, 174, 175, 177, 654
Sikh Khalsa Army, 181
Sikh Light Infantry, 704
Sikh Occupation of Delhi and Red Fort, 181
Sikh Regiment, 643
Sikhs, 80, 205, 304, 316
Sikhs for Justice, 666
Sikkim, 97, 357, 372, 438, 511, 529
Sikkimese monarchy referendum, 1975, 372
Sikkim State Congress, 439
Silk, 11, 13, 33, 37, 43, 46
Silk Road, 541
SIM card, 815
Simla, 605
Simla Accord (1913), 518
Simla Agreement, 446, 564, 581, 593, 605, 707, 708, 734
Simon Burnett, 843
Simon Commission, 306, 344
Simplified Chinese characters, 511
Sinai and Palestine Campaign, 268
Sinai Peninsula, 369
Sindh, 15, 78, 94, 132, 177, 257, 297, 490, 593
Sindhis, 80
Singapore, 91, 254
Sinhagad, 60
Sini Jose, 840
Sinking of PNS Ghazi, 590
Sino-Indian relations, 478
Sino-Indian War, 362, 369, 427, 486, 503, 504, **510**, 571, 762
Sino-Sikh war, 181, 514
Sira, India, 144
Siraj ud-Daulah, 52, 328
Siraj-ud-Daulah, 38, 39
Sir Andrew Fraser, 348

Sir Charles Stevenson-Moore, 350
Sir Charles Tegart, 350
Sir Creek, 482
Sir David Gilmour, 4th Baronet, 283
Sir Harold Stuart, 350
Sir Henry Havelock, 220
Sirhind, 176
Sir James Outram, 1st Baronet, 220, 221
Sir J.J Hospital, 120
Sir John Tenniel, 231
Sirmoor State, 186
Sirohi State, 186
Sir Robert Nathan, 350
Sir Sikandar Hayat Khan, 907
Sir Syed Ahmed Khan, 270
Sir Thomas Munro, 1st Baronet, 106, 121, 317
Sistema, 850
Sistema Shyam TeleServices Limited, 868
Sister Nivedita, 335
Sitaram Yechury, 902
Sivalik Hills, 175
Six-Day War, 563, 588
Six point movement, 553, 584
Skardu, 465
Skirmish, 483
S. Krishnaswami Aiyangar, 169
Slash-and-burn, 350
Slash (punctuation), 935
Slavery, 12
Slum, 618
Slumdog Millionaire, 759
Small arms, 500
Smallpox, 288
Smallpox vaccination, 288
S. M. Anwar, 483
Smiling Buddha, 362, 599
Smith (metalwork), 156
S. M. Nanda, 582
Soap, 24
Social Democratic Party of Germany, 810
Socialism, 479
Socialism in Pakistan, 584
Socialist economics, 362
Social justice, 434
Social media, 822, 874
Socio-economics, 911
Sodium hydroxide, 687
Software industry, 377
Somalia, 91
Som Nath Sharma, 467
Sonakanda Fort, 39
Sonam post, 716
Sonargaon, 49, 112
Sonia Gandhi, 386, 387, 667, 726, 863
Sortie, 548
Sourendra Nath Kohli, 582, 589

South Asia, 13, 20, 549, 596, 774, 799
South Asia Forum for Human Rights, 670
South Canara, 477
Southeast Asia, 14
South East Asia, 353
Southern Command (India), 582, 593
Southern Europe, 15
South India, 11, 131, 141, 347, 368, 429, 474
South Indian culture, 158
South Korea, 763
South Mumbai, 804, 807
South Tibet, 369
South Wales Borderers, 224
Sovereign state, 397, 550
Sovereignty, 175, 403, 513
Soviet Navy, 570, 589, 597
Soviet space program, 390
Soviet Union, 362, 369, 438, 478, 479, 499, 504, 505, 525, 532, 549, 587, 595, 762
Soviet war in Afghanistan, 734
Soviet withdrawal from Afghanistan, 606
Space rocket, 387
Spain, 820
Spangur Gap, 533
Speaker of Lok Sabha, 407
Speaker of the Lok Sabha, 870, 881
Special Air Service, 627, 647, 741
Special Branch, 349
Special Frontier Force, 535, 640
Special Protection Group, 649
Special Relationship, 357
Special Services Group, 495, 713, 716
Speech from the throne, 255
Spice, 13
Spice Telecom, 850
Spice trade, 328
Spin bowler, 839
Spinning wheel, 15
SPM Swimming Pool Complex, 834, 837
Spokesman, 800
Squadron Leader, 490, 491, 591
Squadron (naval), 590
S. R. Bommai v. Union of India, 410
Sri Aurobindo, 293, 327, 335, 338
Sri Ganganagar, 643
Srikanta Wadiyar, 153
Srikrishna Commission, 744
Sri Lanka, 91, 255, 369, 378, 478, 536, 701, 703, 705, 721
Sri Lanka Army, 704
Sri Lankan civil war, 701, 721
Sri Lankan parliamentary election, 1977, 702
Sri Lankan Tamil nationalism, 701
Srinagar, 427, 447, 739, 772, 775
Srinagar (city), 739
Srinagar–Muzaffarabad Bus, 386

Sringeri, 71
Srinivasapuram Krishnaswamy, 798
Sriperumbudur, 380, 721–723
Srirangapatna, 140, 143, 161, 168
Sritattvanidhi, 161, 162
Sri Vaishnavism, 158
S. S. Gill, 624
SS Palanimanickam, 864
Stafford Cripps, 313, 314, 353
Stagflation in Pakistan, 600
St. Agnes PU College, Mangalore, 160
Standing army, 110
Standing committees, 881
Standstill agreement (India), 423
Stanley Lane-Poole, 27
Stanley Wolpert, 245, 319, 444, 497
Star of India (flag), 251
Starvation, 576
State (administrative division), 529
State Assembly elections in India, 391
State Emblem of India, 395
State funeral, 724
State intervention, 762
State of emergency, 375, 588
State of Emergency in India, 610, 614, 615
State of Hyderabad, 397
States and territories of India, 408, 472
States and union territories of India, 406
States Department, 420
States Reorganisation Act, 435, 762
States Reorganisation Act, 1956, **471**
States Reorganisation Commission, 440
State terrorism, 777
State university (India), 276
Status quo ante bellum, 148
Stay of proceedings, 662
Steel, 13, 33, 46
S Tel, 850, 866, 868
Stephen P. Cohen, 715
Sterilization (medicine), 375
Sterling submachine gun, 649
Steve Coll, 606, 915
Steve Moneghetti, 832
Stillbirth, 677
Sting operation, 667
St. Johns Church Jhelum, 224
St. Marys Church, Chennai, 235
Stockton and Darlington Railway, 893
St. Pauls Cathedral, 165
St. Pauls Cathedral, Kolkata, 277, 278
St. Petersburgh, 516
Straits Settlements, 91, 227, 233, 252
Stratfor, 697
Strike action, 356
Striker (2010 film), 759
Structure of the Pakistan Army, 546, 582

1009

St. Stephens College, Delhi, 278
Students for Bhopal, 696
Students Islamic Movement of India, 805
St. Xaviers College, Mumbai, 804
Styles of British sovereigns, 399
Sua sponte, 853
Subah, 32, 33
Subahdar, 9
Subedar, 9, 36, 49, 144
Subhas Chandra Bose, 313, 328, 344, 349, 351, 352
Subhash Chandra Bose, 327, 349
Subhash C. Kashyap, 624
Sub-inspector, 649
Submarine, 583
Subodh Kant Sahay, 876
Subramania Bharati, 327
Subramanian Swamy, 728, 860
Subramanya Bharathi, 344
Subramanya Bharathy, 335
Subrata Roy, 862
Subsidiary alliance, 94, 96, 141, 189, 258, 328, 417
Subsidies in India, 760
Subsistence, 156
Such a Long Journey (novel), 622
Sudhir Mishra, 623
Suez Canal Company, 369
Sufi, 17, 44
Sugar, 13
Sugar cane, 12
Sugar mill, 13
Sugata Bose, 7, 243, 318
Suhrawardy Udyan, 554
Suicide bombing, 721
Suicide vest, 772
Suing for peace, 147
Sukerchakia, 181
Sukhdev, 349
Sukhdev Singh Sukha, 643, 660
Sukhdev Thapar, 346
Sukhoi Su-7, 608
Sulaiman Mountains, 30
Sultan, 21
Sultanate, 29
Sultanate of Mysore, 24, 78, 145
Sultan of Delhi, 131
Sumit Sarkar, 358
Summary execution, 219
Sundararajan Padmanabhan, 798
Sundarbans, 95
Sunni Islam, 1, 29
Sun TV Network, 869
Sun Tzus Art of War, 507
Suo motu, 863
Superintendent of police (India), 663

Supermajority, 411, 584
Superpower, 479
Supreme court, 117, 121, 726
Supreme Court of India, 389, 401, 475, 612, 646, 660, 668, 680, 725, 777, 786, 787, 847
Supreme Court of Pakistan, 603
Supreme Court of the United States, 680
Suraj Mal, 66
Surat, 15, 93, 328
Sur Empire, 2, 3, 5, 11, **29**
Surendranath Banerjee, 291, 293, 334
Suresh Kalmadi, 831, 844, 845
Suresh Pachouri, 665
Surety, 804
Sur (Pashtun), 30
Sur (Pashtun tribe), 29
Surrender (military), 594
Survey of India, 406, 515
Survival training, 806
Suryanath Kamath, 158
Suryanath U. Kamath, 144, 170
Surya Sen, 348
Susan Brownmiller, 572
Sushma Swaraj, 878
Sutlej River, 75, 94, 176, 226, 448
Suzerain, 417
Suzerainty, 7, 97, 140, 251, 255, 416, 472
Swachh Bharat Abhiyan, 391
Swadeshi, 291, 293, 298, 338
Swadeshi movement, 292
Swadhin Bangla Betar Kendra, 548
Swami Vivekananda, 335, 347
Swan Telecom, 868
Swaraj, 298, 335
Swaraj Party, 344
Swaran Singh, 546, 582, 586
Swargadeo dynastic lineage, 39
Swat Levies, 446
Swat (princely state), 453
Swedish Defence Research Agency, 699
Syama Prasad Mookerjee, 405
Syama Prasad Mukherjee, 362
Syed Ahmed Khan, 248, 335
Syed Arif Hasan, 833
Syed Hussain Bilgrami, 261
Syed Kamall, 810
Syed Mohammad Ahsan, 483, 586
Syed Nazeer Husain, 205
Syed Nazrul Islam, 559
Sylhet, 561
Sylhet Division, 49
Synthetic fertilizers, 575
Syria-Lebanon campaign, 269

Tahawwur Hussain Rana, 813, 817

Tahawwur Rana, 825
Taiwan, 522, 763
Taj Mahal, 3, 6, 19, 20, 588
Tajuddin Ahmad, 546, 559, 582
Taliban, 729
Tallow, 192
Taluk, 154, 423
Talukdar, 193
Tamil Eelam, 702
Tamil language, 368, 622
Tamil Nadu, 57, 79, 80, 257, 331, 368, 379, 616, 702, 721, 851, 865
Tamil People, 702
Tamils, 378
T. Ananda Rao, 154
Tandah, 32
Tanittamil Iyakkam, 702
Tanjore, 23
Tank destroyers, 493
Tantia Tope, 186
Tapishwar Narain Raina, 582
Tar, 683
Tarabai, 57, 60, 68, 85
Targeted killings in Pakistan, 586
Tarikh-i-Sher Shahi, 31
Tariq Ali, 590
Tariq Anwar (politician), 877
Tariq Majid, 507
Tarun Tejpal, 791
Tashkent, 499, 504
Tashkent Agreement, 370, 499, 537
Tashkent Declaration, 482, 484, 500
Task Force 74, 570, 597
Tata Group, 868
Tata Sky, 852
Tata Steel, 280
Tata Teleservices, 850, 868
Tatya Tope, 216, 333
Tawang, 511, 518, 530
Tax, 12
Tax farming, 103, 104
T. Chowdiah, 164
Teaching, 334
Team Anna, 880, 884
Ted Kennedy, 548, 569
Teen Murti Bhavan, 651
Teesta Setalvad, 782, 787, 934
Tehelka, 779, 791, 793
Tehsil, 48
Telangana, 257, 389, 428, 440
Telangana movement, 389
Telangana Rebellion, 428
Telangana Subah, 176
Telecom Regulatory Authority of India, 847, 866
Telecoms, 767

Telenor, 849, 868
Telenor India, 849, 853
Telephone booth, 716
Telex, 646
Telugu Desam Party, 883
Telugu language, 368, 440, 475
Temperance movement in India, 337
Template:Colonial India, 92, 256, 326
Template:Constitution of India, 402
Template:History of Bangladesh, 547
Template:History of modern India, 762
Template:History of Pakistan, 260
Template:Part of History of India, 56, 92, 174, 187, 253, 361, 397, 472
Template:Revolution sidebar, 327
Template talk:Colonial India, 92, 256, 326
Template talk:Constitution of India, 402
Template talk:History of Bangladesh, 547
Template talk:History of modern India, 762
Template talk:History of Pakistan, 260
Template talk:Part of History of India, 56, 92, 174, 187, 253, 361, 397, 472
Template talk:Revolution sidebar, 327
Template talk:Violence against Hindus in independent India, 743, 778
Template talk:Violence against Muslims in India, 744, 778
Template:Violence against Hindus in independent India, 743, 778
Template:Violence against Muslims in India, 744, 778
Tenzin Gyatso, 14th Dalai Lama, 520
Teram Kangri, 709, 710
Terms of reference, 661
Terrorism, 771, 803
Terrorism in India, 362
Terrorist, 742
Terrorist and Disruptive Activities Act, 726
Tertiary sector of the economy, 11
Textile, 9, 11, 13, 14, 33, 37, 46
Textile industry, 13, 14, 46
Textile manufacture during the Industrial Revolution, 33, 46
Textile manufacturing, 14, 33, 46, 155
Tezpur, Assam, 534
Thag La Ridge, 523
Thailand, 763
Thall, 452
Thane, 127, 128
Thanesar, 78
Thanjavur, 80, 87
Thanjavur Maratha kingdom, 80
Thanjavur Maratha palace, 87
Thanjavur Marathi dialect, 87
Thatta, 812
The Adventure of the Crooked Man, 242

The Atlantic, 681
Theatre honour, 467, 508, 606
The Autobiography of Malcolm X, 242
The Beatles, 560
The Blood telegram, 548, 567, 570
The BMJ, 556
The Charge of the Light Brigade (1936 film), 241
The Concert for Bangladesh, 548
The Crown, 100, 117, 140, 185, 187, 251, 253, 328, 403
The Discovery of India, 285
The Economist, 619, 934
The Emergency (India), **610**, 762
The Far Pavilions, 242
The Financial Express (India), 621
The Five-Dollar Smile and Other Stories, 622
The Garhwal Rifles, 546
The Ghazi Attack, 609
The Great Game, 267
The Great Indian Novel, 622
The Great Train Robbery (novel), 242
The Guardian, 646, 838, 935
The Hindu, 900, 930
The History and Culture of the Indian People, 319, 890
The History of India, as Told by Its Own Historians. The Muhammadan Period, 27
Theileria, 580
The Illustrated Weekly of India, 710
The Imperial Gazetteer of India, 208
The Indian Express, 928
The Indian National Congress, 344
The India-Pakistan Air War of 1965, 917
The Last Mughal, 230
The Lokpal and Lokayuktas Act, 2013, 884, 885
The Lokpal Bill, 2011, 388, 873, 884, 885
The Ministry of Utmost Happiness, 695
The Mysterious Island, 243
The Nation (Pakistani newspaper), 918
The New Cambridge History of India, 25, 89, 136, 170, 444, 907
The New Yorker, 935
The New York Times, 646, 719, 822, 934
Thenmozhi Rajaratnam, 704, 721
Theoretical astronomy, 24
The Pioneer (newspaper), 869
The Pulse of Danger, 541
Theremin, 163
Thermal runaway, 674
The Royal House of Jammu and Kashmir, 448
The Royal Indian Navy Mutiny, 313
The Siege of Krishnapur, 242, 249
The Sign of the Four, 242, 249
The Statesman (India), 634

The Steam House, 243
The Story of My Experiments with Truth, 358
The Sunday Times, 556
The Sydney Morning Herald, 843
The Taj Mahal Palace Hotel, 388, 803, 804, 806, 808, 810, 819, 822
The Terrorist (1997 film), 728
The three Rs, 276
The Times, 231, 614, 645, 646
The Times of India, 621, 821, 918, 932
The Tribune (Chandigarh), 656, 921, 935
The Truth: Gujarat 2002 - Tehelka report, 793
The World Economy: Historical Statistics, 888
The Yes Men, 697
Thikse Monastery, 390
Thiksey, 390
Thileepan, 725
Third Anglo-Afghan War, 268
Third Anglo-Burmese War, 267
Third Anglo-Maratha War, 8, 55, 57, 73, 82, 93, 97
Third Anglo-Mysore War, 96, 110, 146, 149
Third Battle of Panipat, 57, 66, 180
Third Ladakh Scouts, 718
Third plague pandemic, 287
Third world, 478
Thiri Thudhamma, 39
Thirty-eighth Amendment of the Constitution of India, 413, 620
Thol. Thirumavalavan, 727
Thomas Andrew Lumisden Strange, 115
Thomas Arthur, comte de Lally, 144
Thomas Babbington Macaulay, 122
Thomas Babington Macaulay, 1st Baron Macaulay, 274, 317
Thomas Baring, 1st Earl of Northbrook, 266, 289
Thomas Elmhirst, 447
Thomas Jones Barker, 228
Thomas Reed (British Army officer), 224
Thomas R. Metcalf, 25, 134, 321
Thorar, 457, 459
Thorium, 420
Thread (yarn), 13
Throchi, 457
Thuggee, 112
Thuggee and Dacoity Suppression Acts, 1836–48, 97
Thuljaji, 87
Tiana Mary Thomas, 840
Tibet, 174, 177, 511, 517, 524, 535
Tibet Autonomous Region, 369
Tibet under Qing rule, 186
Tide, 554
Tihar Jail, 880
Tijara, 209

Tikka Khan, 554, 582, 585
TIME, 713, 917, 930
Timeline of Bangladeshi history, 547
Timeline of major famines in India during British rule, 286
Timeline of Pakistani history, 259
Time magazine, 504, 707
Time (magazine), 660, 848, 873
Times of India, 670, 819, 831, 833, 930, 935
Timmaraja Wodeyar I, 152
Timmaraja Wodeyar II, 152
Timothy Garton Ash, 358
Timur, 3, 5
Timurid dynasty, 3, 4
Timurid Empire, 2, 3, 5
Timur Shah, 78
Timur Shah Durrani, 181
Tippu Sultan, 152
Tipu Sultan, 69, 71, 78, 107, 141, 146, 148, 154, 155, 168, 169, 328–331
Tirah Campaign, 267
Tirath Das Dogra, 651, 787
Tithwal, 486
Tobacco, 12
Todar Mal, 48
Tokugawa Japan, 12
Tola (mass), 125
Toll house, 333
Top Secret, 604
Torit Mitra, 622
Trade route, 43
Trade unions in India, 656
Traditional Chinese characters, 511
Trans-Karakoram Tract, 516
Travancore, 94, 96, 186, 188, 420
Travancore-Cochin, 433, 474, 477
Travancore Fanam, 71
Travelers diarhoea, 838
Travelers diarrhea, 834
T. R. Baalu, 871
Treason, 566
Treaty of Allahabad, 90
Treaty of Amiens, 255
Treaty of Amritsar, 1846, 94, 97, 190
Treaty of Bassein (1802), 74, 90, 96
Treaty of Chushul, 514
Treaty of Lahore, 90, 97, 448
Treaty of Mangalore, 148
Treaty of Nanjing, 114
Treaty of Seringapatam, 90, 149
Treaty of Versailles, 605
Treaty of Yandabo, 90
Treaty with France, 148
Trial, 232, 846
Trial court, 117
Tribune India, 927

Tributary state, 36
Tribute, 12
Trichlorobenzene, 694
Trichloroethylene, 694
Trilokpuri (Delhi Assembly constituency), 655
Trimethylamine, 677
Trinamool Congress, 871
Trinidad, 227
Tripura, 364, 474, 477
Tripura (princely state), 365, 416, 432
Tropical cyclone, 554
Trucial States, 252, 254
T. T. Krishnamachari, 406
Tubelight (film), 542
Tubewell, 683
Tubular necrosis, 677
Tuensang, 372
Tukaram Omble, 807, 819
Tukkoji, 87
Tumkur, 143
Tungabhadra, 69
Tungabhadra river, 131
Turco-Mongol, 2, 4
Turkey, 491
Turkic languages, 21
Turkic peoples, 19
Turnover (employment), 600
Turtuk, 605, 718
T. V. Chandran, 796
TV documentary, 647, 825
T. V. Sathyamurthy, 625
Twenty-fourth Amendment of the Constitution of India, 411, 612
Two Nation Theory, 346
Two-Nation Theory, 311, 425, 600
Tyagaraja, 164

UAPA, 820
Udaipur State, 186
Udgir, 68
Udhampur, 451, 739
Udham Singh, 349
Ujjain, 57
Ulama, 552
Ulema, 203
ULFA, 377
Uller Uprising, 243
Ultra vires, 617
Ulugh Beg, 24
Ulugh Beg Observatory, 24
Uma Bharti, 875
Umarkot Fort, 6
Umesh Chandra Banerjee, 779
U.N., 708
Unemployment, 378
UNESCO, 551

1013

UNESCO World Heritage Site, 20, 30
Uninor, 865, 868
Union Cabinet, 684
Union Carbide, 378, 694
Union Carbide Corporation, 672
Union Carbide India Limited, 671
Union Council of Ministers of India, 844
Unionist Muslim League, 310
Union of India, 317, 366, 447, 448
Union territories, 435
Union territory, 410
Unitary state, 2, 410
Unitech Group, 849, 868
United Arab Emirates, 91, 252
United Arab Republic, 536
United Bengal, 549
United Front (India), 765
United Kingdom, 253, 369, 397, 398, 584, 597, 599, 794, 820
United Kingdom general election, 1945, 269
United Nations, 253, 479, 482, 484, 592, 598, 599, 708, 798, 800
United Nations Conference on International Organization, 253
United Nations Convention Against Corruption, 875
United Nations General Assembly, 437
United Nations High Commissioner for Refugees, 608
United Nations Security Council, 362, 389, 499, 568, 596, 801
United Nations Security Council veto power, 438, 596
United Progressive Alliance, 386, 387, 847, 863, 871, 877, 881
United Provinces of Agra and Oudh, 102, 205, 207, 257, 268, 271, 297, 313, 432
United State of Rajasthan, 433
United States, 478, 497, 507, 549, 595, 666, 794, 799, 800, 820
United States Air Force, 535, 592
United States Ambassador to Pakistan, 772
United States Ambassador to the United Nations, 596
United states and china, 595
United States and weapons of mass destruction, 606
United States Bill of Rights, 407
United States Commission on International Religious Freedom, 786
United States Congress, 386, 596
United States Constitution, 407
United States Court of Appeals for the Second Circuit, 681
United States Department of State, 784

United States District Court for the Southern District of New York, 666
United States dollar, 801
United States Environmental Protection Agency, 694
United States House of Representatives, 795, 915
United States Information Agency, 567
United States military, 592
United States Secretary of State, 595, 795
Unity, Faith, Discipline, 583
University of Allahabad, 267
University of Bombay, 120, 122, 266
University of Calcutta, 122, 266, 276, 608
University of California, Berkeley, 544
University of California Press, 887, 888, 890, 927
University of Delhi, 268, 829
University of Dhaka, 556, 567
University of Exeter, 699
University of London, 122
University of Lucknow, 275
University of Madras, 122, 266
University of Pennsylvania Press, 927
University of Punjab, 267
University of Rangoon, 268
University Visvesvaraya College of Engineering, 155
Unmanned aerial vehicle, 800
Un resolutions, 598
UN Security Council, 429
Unsupported attributions, 848
Untouchability, 298
Upper Burma, 254
Upper Doab, 95
Upper Doab famine of 1860–1861, 266
Uppsala Conflict Data Program, 931
Urban area, 18
Urbanization, 18
Urdu, 1, 21, 251, 550, 609
Urdu language, 1, 2, 335
Uri (India), 460, 486
Uri, Jammu and Kashmir, 461
US$, 874
Usain Bolt, 840
US Army, 916
U.S. Department of State, 915
US Department of State, 610
USS Enterprise (CVN-65), 570, 597
USS Kitty Hawk (CV-63), 538
Ustad Ali Quli, 21
UTC+05:30, 771, 803
Utilitarian, 107, 196
Utilitarians, 122
Uttarakhand, 257, 384, 389

Uttar Pradesh, 73, 80, 123, 130, 220, 257, 272, 347, 473, 477, 574, 620, 633, 662, 877, 878
Uzbekistan, 499

Vacated judgment, 662
Vaccine, 288
Vadgaon Maval, 72
Vadodara, 777
Vagher, 227
Vaiko, 727
Vaishnavism, 157
Valerie Fitzgerald, 249
Vallabhbhai Patel, 344, 357, 363, 405, 416, 419, 420
Vanchi Iyer, 348
Vanchinathan, 344
Vandana Shiva, 577, 782
Vande Mataram, 291
Vanga Kingdom, 547
Varahagiri Venkata Giri, 546, 582
Varanasi, 95, 108, 121, 203
Varun Gandhi, 881
Vasai, 63
Vasco da Gama, 328
Vasectomies, 375
Vasectomy, 617
Vasily Vereshchagin, 238
Vassal state, 258
V.A. Stuart, 249
V.D.Savarkar, 348
Vector quantity, 575
Ved Marwah, 661
Ved Prakash Malik, 716
Veena, 163, 164
Veene Sheshanna, 163, 164
Veerapandiya Kattabomman, 331
Veerashaiva, 161, 162
Vehicle armour, 594
Vellore Mutiny, 96, 110, 189
Velu Nachiyar, 330
Velupillai Prabhakaran, 701
Venice of the East, 39
Venkoji, 87
Verghese Kurien, 578
Vernon Kell, 350
Very Important Person, 168
Viaduct, 127
Vice Admiral, 546, 582, 589, 917
Vice-Admiral, 483, 582
Viceroy, 17, 32, 49, 255, 354, 397
Viceroy and Governor-General of India, 251
Viceroy of India, 233, 260, 419
Viceroys Executive Council, 903
Victor Alexander John Hope, 345
Victor Bruce, 9th Earl of Elgin, 267

Victor Hope, 2nd Marquess of Linlithgow, 269, 310, 350
Victoria Cross, 236, 295
Victoria Memorial (India), 268
Victorian era, 274
Victoria of the United Kingdom, 333
Victoria Pendleton, 840
Victoria Schofield, 469
Victoria Terminus, 282
Vidarbha, 440
Videocon, 868
Videocon Telecom, 850, 868
Vidhan Sabha, 820, 874
Vidwan, 164
Vidya Charan Shukla, 618
Vietnam, 313
Vijaya Lakshmi Pandit, 405
Vijayanagara Empire, 93, 131, 140, 141, 152, 153
Vijayanta, 641
Vijayaraje Scindia, 615
Vijay Kumar Singh, 736
Vijay Salaskar, 807, 819
Vilapangalkkappuram, 796
Vilasrao Deshmukh, 818, 821, 882
Vile Parle, 804, 808, 819
Vinayak Damodar Savarkar, 355
Vinayak D. Savarkar, 363
Vincent Eyre, 226
Vindhya Pradesh, 365, 433, 473, 474, 477
Vinoba Bhave, 621
Vinod Goenka, 857, 868
Vinod Rai, 870
Violence against Muslims, 744, 778
Violence against Muslims in India, 744, 776, 777
Violin, 164
Vir Das, 669
Vir Sanghvi, 858
Visa (document), 697
Visakhapatnam, 589, 590
Vishalgad, 60
Vishnu Ramkrishna Karkare, 363
Vishva Hindu Parishad, 780, 784, 792
Vishwanath Pratap Singh, 379
Vishwasrao, 57, 65
Visvesvaraya Iron and Steel Limited, 155
Viz., 404
Vizier, 80, 172
V. K. Krishna Menon, 478, 510, 539
VK Krishna Menon, 520
Vladimir Putin, 800
Vladivostok, 570, 597
V. M. Tarkunde, 646
VOA, 935
V. O. Chidambaram Pillai, 327, 335

Vohra Report, 874
Voice vote, 882
VoIP, 816
Volatile organic compound, 693
Volley gun, 23
Vote bank, 584
Voter list, 657
V. P. Madhava Rao, 154
V. P. Menon, 365, 397, 416, 419, 420
V P Singh, 701
V. P. Singh, 378, 663, 704
V. R. Krishna Iyer, 614, 933
V. R. Raghavan, 706
V.R. Raghavan, 719
V S Naipaul, 622
VSNL, 765
V Srinivasanand, 870
V. T. Krishnamachari, 903

Wakf, 785
Wakhan corridor, 516
Waldemar Haffkine, 288
Walong, 530
Wandhama massacre, 738
Wanna, Pakistan, 452
Waqf, 339
War, 547
War children, 567
War crime, 565, 603
War elephant, 23
War film, 608, 609
War in Afghanistan (2001–present), 820
War of 1812, 24
War on Terror, 385, 799, 820
War rape, 738
Warren Anderson (American businessman), 378, 672, 678, 679, 681, 695
Warren Hastings, 90, 93, 96, 98, 191, 285
Warsaw Pact, 480, 571
Washington, D.C., 795
Water well, 693
Watson Institute, 926
Waziristan, 366, 447
Wazir Khan (Sirhind), 176
Wazir Khan Tajik, 51
Weimar Constitution, 407
Weir, 131
Wendy Chamberlin, 772
West Africa, 14
West Bengal, 33, 37, 64, 257, 292, 347, 364, 473, 475–477, 620
Western Command (India), 483, 582, 593
Western countries, 799
Western Desert Campaign, 309
Western Europe, 10, 13
Western Front (World War I), 268

Western Ghats, 129, 143
Western India, 776
Westernization, 233
Western Naval Command, 582, 589
Western world, 833
Westminster system, 407
West Pakistan, 484, 511, 547, 570, 584
What information to include, 76, 81, 656
Wheat, 12, 574
When Big Tree Falls, 669
When you must use inline citations, 715
Where the mind is without fear, 621
Whig history, 274
Whistleblower, 844
White mutiny, 234
W. H. Johnson, 515
Who Are The Guilty, 659, 670
Widow remarriage, 160, 196
Widow Remarriage Act, 97
WikiLeaks, 697
WikiLeaks cables, 654
Wikilink to citation does not work, 304
Wikinews: Category:India Against Corruption, 885
Wikipedia:Avoid weasel words, 653
Wikipedia:Citation needed, 30, 57–60, 66–68, 73, 75, 76, 80, 84, 186, 251, 311, 333–335, 338, 342, 345, 403–406, 411, 461, 463, 466, 491, 492, 495, 496, 504, 520, 521, 530, 576, 606, 612, 614, 621, 627, 642, 651, 652, 668, 702, 707, 710, 713, 731, 741, 750, 751, 758, 763, 802, 831, 884, 885
Wikipedia:Identifying reliable sources, 76, 407
Wikipedia:Link rot, 759, 769
Wikipedia:Please clarify, 4, 285, 536, 599, 745, 773, 879
Wikipedia:Vagueness, 663
Wikipedia:Verifiability, 186, 271, 495, 504, 521, 598, 812
Wikt:amalgamation, 375
Wiktionary:piece goods, 14
Wiktionary:seam, 24
Wikt:中印, 511
Wikt:战争, 511
Wikt:戰爭, 511
Wikt:边境, 511
Wikt:邊境, 511
William Alexander Kerr, 225
William Brooke OShaughnessy, 125
William Brown (Gilgit Scouts), 447
William Carey (missionary), 192
William Dalrymple (historian), 230, 238
William Hare, 5th Earl of Listowel, 252
William Hutt Curzon Wyllie, 348
William III of England, 116

William Irvine (historian), 27
William IV of the United Kingdom, 24
William Jones (philologist), 121, 317
William Muir, 287
William Pitt Amherst, 1st Earl Amherst, 97
William Pitt the Younger, 100
William Shakespeare, 162
William Spring (British Army officer), 224
William Stephen Raikes, 249
William Stephen Raikes Hodson, 213
William Wilberforce, 121, 192
Will (philosophy), 593
Wilson College, Mumbai, 122
Winchester College, 118
Windsor Castle, 165
Winston Churchill, 311, 422
Wipro Technologies, 827
Wodeyar, 59, 141, 152
Womens Indian Association, 160
Womesh Chandra Bonerjee, 289
Woolen, 13
Work, 578
Workforce, 11
Working boundary, 482
World economy, 10, 33, 46
World Food Program, 579
World GDP, 3
World Health Organization, 694
World Heritage Sites, 20
World population, 17
World War I, 295, 350, 513, 516
World War II, 309, 480, 487, 493, 518, 564, 590, 594, 601
Worm gear, 13, 15
WP:LIBRARY, 250
WP:NOTRS, 62, 597
W. Somerset Maugham, 350

X Corps (Pakistan), 598
Xiamen, 114
Xiangqi, 525
XI Corps (India), 483
XII Corps (India), 582
Xinhai Revolution, 516
Xinhua News Agency, 520
Xinjiang, 511, 516, 517
XV Corps (India), 483, 582

Yaduraya Wodeyar, 140, 152
Yaduveer Krishnadatta Chamaraja Wadiyar, 153
Yahya Khan, 483, 502, 546, 548, 550, 553, 566, 570, 582, 584
Yahya Saleh, 15
Yakshagana, 161
Yakub Beg, 515

Yali (Hindu mythology), 166
Yamagola, 623
Yamuna, 134
Yamuna river, 131, 133, 176, 724
Yanam, French India, 437
Yangon, 333
Yantra Mandirs, 24
Yarkand River, 516
Yarkant County, 514
Yarn, 13
Yashpal Kapoor, 614
Yashwantrao Holkar, 72
Yashwant Sinha, 871
Yathra, 623
Yemen, 91, 252
Yerwada Central Jail, 816
Yes Men, 697
Yoga, 884
Yom-e-Istiqlal, 357
York Minster, 235
YouTube, 573, 697, 775
Yusaf Khan, 798

Zabiuddin Ansari, 814, 817
Zafar Muhammad Khan, 546
Zaheera Sheikh, 787
Zahid Ali Akbar Khan, 706
Zail Singh, 642, 647, 656, 658
Zaki ur Rehman Lakhvi, 803, 824
Zakiur Rehman Lakhvi, 804
Zaman Kiani, 447
Zaman Shah Durrani, 174
Zamindar, 102, 116, 155, 226, 317
Zamindars, 104, 576
Zamorin, 96, 147
Zenana missions, 278
Zero Point railway station, 482
Z Force (Bangladesh), 546
Zhang Guohua, 510
Zhou Enlai, 507, 510, 511, 519, 520
Ziaur Rahman, 546, 558, 586
Zij, 24
Zij-i-Sultani, 24
Zillur Rahman, 608
Zinat Mahal, 213
Z Magazine, 829
Zoji La, 463, 466
Zulfikar Ali Bhutto, 506, 553, 584, 597, 605
Zulfiqar Ali Bhutto, 600
Zulfiqar Ali Khan, 582

1017

www.ingramcontent.com/pod-product-compliance
Lightning Source LLC
Chambersburg PA
CBHW031931290426
44108CB00011B/521